MW01170000

WINDOWS NT WORKSTATION

PROFESSIONAL REFERENCE

KATHY IVENS

WITH

DAVID CHERNICOFF
BOB CHRONISTER
VINAY NADIG
JEFFREY R. SHAPIRO
BARRIE SOSINSKY
DAVID YARASHUS
SERDAR YEGULALP
CRAIG ZACKER

New Riders Publishing, Indianapolis, Indiana

Windows NT Workstation Professional Reference

By Kathy Ivens with David Chernicoff, Bob Chronister, Vinay Nadig, Jeffrey R. Shapiro, Barrie Sosinsky, David Yarashus, Serdar Yegulalp, and Craig Zacker

Published by:
New Riders Publishing
201 West 103rd Street
Indianapolis, IN 46290 USA

Printed in the United States of America 1 2 3 4 5 6 7 8 9 0

Library of Congress Cataloging-in-Publication Data

CIP data available upon request

Warning and Disclaimer

This book is designed to provide information about the Windows NT Workstation. Every effort has been made to make this book as complete and as accurate as possible, but no warranty or fitness is implied.

The information is provided on an "as is" basis. The authors and New Riders Publishing shall have neither liability nor responsibility to any person or entity with respect to any loss or damages arising from the information contained in this book or from the use of the disks or programs that may accompany it.

Publisher *Don Fowley*
Publishing Manager *Julie Fairweather*
Marketing Manager *Mary Foote*
Managing Editor *Carla Hall*

Acquisitions Editor
Jeff Durham
Software Specialist
Steve Flatt
Senior Editor
Sarah Kearns
Development Editor
Stacia Mellinger
Project Editor
Amy Bezek
Copy Editors
Geneil Breeze
Keith Cline
Sydney Jones
Technical Editors
Axel Larson
John Flynn Matthew
Robert Oliver
Michael E. Porter
Acquisitions Coordinator
Stephanie Layton
Administrative Coordinator
Karen Opal
Cover Designer
Sandra Schroeder
Cover Illustration
©Sandra Dionisi/SIS
Cover Production
Aren Howell
Book Designer
Sandra Schroeder
Production Manager
Kelly D. Dobbs
Production Team Supervisor
Laurie Casey
Graphics Image Specialists
Debra Bolhuis
Kevin Cliburn
Wil Cruz
Tammy Graham
Daniel Harris
Oliver Jackson
Production Analysts
Jason Hand
Erich J. Richter
Production Team
Angela Calvert
Elizabeth SanMiguel
Christy Wagner
Indexer
Craig Small

About the Author

Kathy Ivens writes books about a variety of computer subjects, specializing in operating systems. Her kids grew up and left before she was old enough to collect retirement benefits (she was a teenage mom), so she dabbles as a weenie to keep her brain in gear and the bills paid, waiting until her children accumulate enough money to support her in the style to which she would like to become accustomed.

Trademark Acknowledgments

Dedication

This book is dedicated to my girls: Deborah, Beverly, Judith, and Sarah.

—Kathy Ivens

Acknowledgments

A lot of people work hard to get a book into your hands. In this case, there are some very special people who deserve kudos for their contributions.

The names listed under mine as authors are a group of awesome propeller heads and weenies who contributed an incredible amount of knowledge, interrupting their own considerable workloads to meet deadlines. David Chernicoff and Bob Chronister are offered my special thanks for putting up with my brain-picking, nagging and use of their contacts whenever I could wheedle that stuff out of them.

At New Riders, Don Fowley is an author's dream of a publisher and should be cloned immediately throughout the entire industry. Stacia Mellinger undertook the job of developing this book and keeping it on track, and performed with her usual incredible level of care, intelligence, and common sense (which she does so often I tend to take it for granted). Jeff Durham conceived this book and managed to beat us all up about deadlines and goals without making any of us vindictive (not an easy task, congratulations Jeff). John Flynn Matthew, Michael E. Porter, Robert Oliver, and Axel Larson took on the burden of checking technical accuracy to make sure we all look good, and Keith Cline, Geneil Breeze, and Sydney Jones made sure we all seem literate with their copy editing skills. Amy Bezek had the unenviable job of coordinating everything and everyone in sight and did it with extraordinary proficiency.

—Kathy Ivens

Contents at a Glance

Table of Contents

Part III: Networking with Windows NT Workstation 357

10 The Ins and Outs of TCP/IP 359

11 NT Workstation Networking in Action 415

Introduction

This book is written for system administrators who are responsible for setting up and maintaining networks with Windows NT Workstation 4 clients. The topics range from basic introductions to concepts, from instructions for configuration and maintenance chores to more advanced explanations of the way the operating system works in a variety of circumstances. The goal is to provide a comprehensive look at this new operating system in an effort to make administration of it easier to understand.

You will find quite a bit of information about Windows NT Server 4 throughout this book. This is because many issues exist for which it is important to know what to do at the server in order to make workstation administration easier.

Also included is some information to help you plan your work with an eye toward the future. Windows NT 4 is a stopover on the road to Cairo (now called NT 5), and it's important to configure and administer it with that in mind.

A group of awesome experts have been gathered to help in this effort, and you'll find the information relevant and useful. The chapters are divided into broad categories, so when you need information about those issues you can find it easily.

We've taken for granted your knowledge of basic chores in setting up and maintaining operating systems (you won't find any explanations of how to put a NIC in a box or how to plug in the cable). In fact, we've taken for granted that you're at least a propeller head, if not a weenie.

We all use jargon that might seem inconsistent, and probably is. You'll find the words "directory" and "subdirectory" throughout this book. It's a weenie approach, some of us have never gotten past our comfort at dropping to the command line, writing some code, getting the job done quickly. There's something about being at the command line that invokes the word "directory" instead of folder. When we deal with the GUI, and we're staring at a picture of a folder, we all usually remember to use that term. I think it's safe to assume you know that the words can be used interchangeably.

This book is written to be a general reference for you. It is not a step-by-step guide to setting up a workstation as if you were an ordinary user.

Special Elements

Throughout this book you will find examples of special text. These passages have been given special treatment so that you can instantly recognize their significance and so that you can easily find them for future reference.

Notes, Tips, Cautions, and Sidebars

Windows NT Workstation Professional Reference features several special "asides" set apart from the normal text. These asides add extra meaning by illustrating graphically the *kind* of information being presented. This book offers four distinct asides:

- Notes
- Tips
- Cautions
- Sidebars

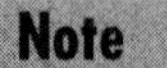

A Note includes "extra"—and useful—information that complements the discussion at hand rather than being a direct part of it. A Note might describe special situations that can arise when you use Windows NT Workstation 4 under certain circumstances, and it tells you what steps to take when such situations do arise. Notes also might tell you how to avoid problems with your software or hardware.

A Tip provides you with quick instructions for getting the most from your Windows NT 4 system as you follow the steps outlined in general discussion. A Tip might show you how to conserve memory in some setups, how to speed up a procedure, or how to perform one of many time-saving and system-enhancing techniques.

A Caution tells you when a procedure might be dangerous—that is, when you run the risk of losing data, locking your system, or even damaging your hardware. Cautions generally tell you how to avoid such losses, or describe the steps you can take to remedy them.

Sidebar

A Sidebar, conceptually, is much like a Note—the exception being its length. A Sidebar is by nature much longer than a Note but offers the same extra, complementary information. Sidebars offer in-depth insight into the topic under discussion.

New Riders Publishing

The staff of New Riders is committed to bringing you the very best in computer reference material. Each New Riders book is the result of months of work by authors and staff who research and refine the information contained within its covers.

As part of this commitment to you, our reader, New Riders invites your input. Please let us know if you enjoy this book, if you have trouble with the information and examples presented, or if you have a suggestion for the next edition.

Please note, though: New Riders staff cannot serve as a technical resource for Windows NT Workstation 4 or for questions about software- or hardware-related problems. Please refer to the documentation that accompanies NT 4 or to the applications' Help systems.

If you have a question or comment about any New Riders book, there are several ways to contact us. We will respond to as many readers as we can. Your name, address, or phone number will never become part of a mailing list or be used for any purpose other than to help us continue to bring you the best books possible. You can write us at the following address:

New Riders Publishing
Attn: Publisher
201 W. 103rd Street
Indianapolis, IN 46290

If you prefer, you can fax New Riders Publishing at (317) 817-7448.

You can also send electronic mail to New Riders at the following Internet address:

jfairweather@newriders.mcp.com

New Riders is an imprint of Macmillan Computer Publishing. To obtain a catalog or information, or to purchase any Macmillan Computer Publishing book, call (800) 428-5331.

Thank you for selecting *Windows NT Workstation Professional Reference*!

Part I

Windows NT Workstation —an Orientation

CHAPTER 1

The Windows NT Workstation Architecture

This chapter discusses the basics of Windows NT's architecture and design. Windows NT has its roots in other operating systems that go back for years, even decades, and has borrowed ideas from many of those operating systems. NT has also introduced innovations of its own that make it relatively unique in the field of desktop, server, and enterprise-wide operating environments.

The word "architecture," when it applies to an an operating system, refers to a number of things. First and foremost, it refers to the way the system functions internally—the way the kernel deals with itself, with the machine around it, with memory, and with device drivers. The various breeds of Unix, for example, have their kernel systems implemented entirely differently than the way Windows NT has its kernel implemented. Unix also deals with device drivers in an entirely different fashion than NT. Under Unix, device drivers are designed to be compiled directly into the kernel when they are installed. While this has the advantage of being efficient, it is also cumbersome and makes working with device drivers in Unix that much more difficult. In Windows NT, device drivers are stored as discrete files and are loaded at runtime, meaning that while more live RAM is required on the whole for Windows NT, the tradeoff of memory for ease of use and flexibility is usually more than worth it.

This chapter covers the following subjects:

- The history and development of Windows NT from DOS and OS/2
- The ways in which Windows NT can be compared to DOS, OS/2, 16-bit Windows, Windows 95, Unix, and NetWare
- The Windows NT file system and its power and flexibility
- The strengths of Windows NT:
    - Multiprocessor support
    - Scalability
    - Ring and kernel modes
    - System services
    - The WoW subsystem
    - Device handling
- A peek ahead to Cairo

Understanding the History of Windows NT

Windows NT and OS/2 share a great deal of common background. By studying the history of both operating systems, it is possible to understand the way in which Windows NT has evolved and become what it is today. The decisions of policy that shaped both operating systems—what to support, what directions to move the operating systems in, what kind of customer base and machine base to suppor—still live on and will continue to influence NT's evolution well into the next millennium.

IBM's First Try

In the early 1980s, IBM had expanded the definition of the personal computer explosively. It had introduced the original IBM PC, its technological successor, the PC/AT, and had tried (and failed) to appeal to the educational and *kid-puter* markets with the PCjr. With all the straining at the leash, IBM realized that they needed to do something about the rapidly approaching discrepancies between the existing systems software it had (DOS) and the hardware it would soon be exploiting (the Intel 286 and the then-prototypical 386).

The 386, for instance, had the ability to multitask in a unique way—not only as a single 386, but as multiple, virtual 8086s. A program could be run in its own virtual machine, complete with its own memory segment. The advantages to this were a little obscure to most users, but to a fairly advanced programmer, the advantages spoke for themselves. A program or an operating environment that took proper advantage of these features could do some truly remarkable things. Unfortunately, the 386 did not exist at the time except as a prospectus for Intel.

In 1985, IBM was ready to bank on the 286—it was readily available, and IBM could produce software for it and systems incorporating it with little delay. But the 286 had design limits that were to be eliminated by the arrival of the 386. One of the software companies that also saw the advantage to the 386 architecture was Microsoft.

The first attempts by Microsoft and IBM to work together, to exploit the power of the new processors, fizzled. Advanced DOS, as this first joint effort was called, was supposed to have taken advantage of the as-yet-unrealized 386's capabilities. IBM, however, was committed to building the AT around the 286; because conventional DOS was already a strong seller, IBM did not see any reason to complicate matters.

Something else happened in 1985, which would begin to shove Microsoft and IBM further apart—the release of the first versions of Windows from Microsoft. Originally called Interface Manager, Windows was designed to work as a standardized interface between MS-DOS and applications—a giant API, basically. By the time it hit the market, however, many in the industry were dubious about GUIs ever taking off; other companies' attempts at the same had died painful deaths: IBM's own TopView, VisiCorp's VisiOn, and even the Mac were all in trouble. (The Mac's popularity would come later, slowly and carefully.) Microsoft wanted to push Windows as being the all-purpose interface of choice, but IBM wasn't interested. The future didn't seem to lie with GUIs anyway, and if they wanted to work with one, IBM's own TopView was readily available, weak sales notwithstanding.

The Appearance of OS/2

In 1986, things changed radically for IBM. Strong competition from Macintosh and Compaq (who had just introduced the first 386-based PC) made IBM realize it was starting to fall behind. With that, the green light was given to accelerate the development of Microsoft's Advanced DOS, which now had the snazzier name of OS/2. IBM, however, demanded that the new operating system also work on extant 286-based PCs.

This formed another wedge, deeply driven, between both companies. Microsoft had been more interested in the greater potentials that lay in the 386, while IBM was simply trying to exploit the active installed base of 286 machines. The technical shortcomings in the 286 chip—its inability to do virtual machines, for instance—was less important to IBM than just getting a product created and sold.

The next big wedge was Windows itself. As mentioned before, Microsoft originally had plans for Windows to be the GUI for OS/2, in much the same fashion that it had been planned as the GUI for DOS. IBM fought Microsoft's plans and demanded instead that a custom version of Windows called the Presentation Manager be developed for OS/2. The prospect of two totally incompatible APIs in OS/2 didn't appeal to Microsoft, and Windows development continued on its own. By the time OS/2 1.0 finally came out, it required hardware and memory demands that few could satisfy, and applications and software development were slow in coming. OS/2 just didn't flesh out as the alternative to DOS that many hoped for, and it remained moribund.

Microsoft, meanwhile, developed and released Windows 2.0, which incorporated many attractive new features sophistications (such as overlapping windows), and—more importantly—had been slipped into software vendors' hands quite freely, stimulating the creation of Windows-specific applications and shareware. IBM and Microsoft slipped further and further away from each other in the meantime. OS/2 did find an active market in high-end server installations—as you'll learn later on in this chapter, many banks and financial institutions rely in it widely—but never became the "next step from DOS" that IBM had hoped it would be. That role was reserved for Windows.

With OS/2 no longer one of Microsoft's concerns, Microsoft decided to take the lessons learned from OS/2 and apply them to a new operating system it was planning as a replacement for its existing network OS, Microsoft LAN Manager. That new operating system was Windows NT, with the NT meaning "new technology." These lessons covered such things as the 386 virtual-machine technology and using hard-disk space as virtual memory. Such things had been already put to work in Windows 3.1 and Windows for Workgroups, but in a limited, 16-bit fashion that wasn't robust enough to be used as a network OS.

Windows NT Appears

The first versions of Windows NT products shipped in 1993, as a version 3.1 release, named Windows NT and Windows NT Advanced Server. Advanced Server migrated the features in LAN Manager and was intended to be used for centralized file, print, and application sharing. The more conventional NT 3.1 was designed to run on a workstation and could network freely with LAN Manager or the also newly introduced Windows for Workgroups.

The 3.1 iteration of Windows NT had problems that couldn't be ignored. Big problems. It required, at the very least, a then-excessive amount of memory (32 MB at *least*), and was therefore restricted to machines that at the time cost tens of thousands of dollars. It also suffered from performance problems that were also due to the lack of proper tuning and usage of memory. Seeing that these factors were some of the biggest obstacles keeping NT from really flowering, Microsoft went back to work and produced Windows NT 3.5 the following year.

NT 3.5 solved, or at least began to address, a great many of the problems that NT 3.1 had been plagued with. It also introduced a new distribution model for the program. The desktop product was renamed Windows NT Workstation, and Advanced Server was renamed, simply, Windows NT Server. Both were built around from the same kernel, but Server had modifications and performance tunings that enabled it to perform better as a network server. More live RAM in Windows NT Server was used to buffer network operations than in Workstation, and also included more robust network stack, which supported protocol routing.

Workstation, on the other hand, was tuned to provide the best possible emulation for 16-bit programs and locally executed binaries. Because of these improvements, and the increased efforts Microsoft made to make NT noticeable as a solution and not just a neat toy, attention (and sales) began to jump.

NT 3.5 in turn gave way to NT 3.51, which featured a number of other changes and fixes: the incorporation of PCMCIA support, which made Workstation more useful on laptops; support for far more hardware; and most importantly, significant changes in the amount of RAM NT needed to be workable. NT 3.51 made NT useful in as little as 16 MB, enabling a whole new realm of systems to run NT with greater performance and usability than before. During NT 3.51's lifespan, Windows also introduced the first pieces of what was to be NT 4, especially the Windows 95 shell, ported to NT.

NT 4 incorporates a number of important changes to its architecture that enhances its performance and makes it far more powerful for certain users, especially those using NT as a key component in building Ethernet-based networks.

Now you turn to the features that NT 4 sports and see how it stacks up against other operating systems of its type.

Understanding Where NT Shines

NT's biggest legacy, so far, has been enabling users to enter into the industrial-strength, server-class operating system game without laying out hundreds of thousands of dollars for both hardware and software. NT is designed to make the most use of existing hardware, all the way back to the Intel 486 platform, and will run well in as little as 16–24 MB. With that hardware, or better, users can enjoy many of the features formerly restricted only to top-of-the-line computers running equally top-of-the-line software:

- **True 32-bit Multitasking.** Windows NT enables users to run programs wholly independently of each other, in their own separate memory spaces. NT also uses cooperative multitasking to ensure that individual programs don't hog the system. Cooperative multitasking is meant here to be in contrast with *competitive* multitasking, in which applications run simultaneously but their timeslices are not governed by the operating system. (To paraphrase a common saying, it's every app for itself and the OS against all.)

- **Security.** Windows NT is designed to enable systems to be C2 (Controlled System Access) certifiable. This is a U.S. government-defined protocol for security and integrity that protects the system from being accessed illegitimately, protects memory from being read by anything except the program that should be reading it, and keeps rogue programs from bringing the rest of the system down.

Note Windows NT does not come C2-compliant out of the box. A good deal of work has to be done before a Windows NT system can be certified as being C2-compliant. To assist you in this regard, Microsoft has developed a number of products and programs that can assist you in creating and maintaining a C2-secure installation of Windows NT. (See Chapter 19, "Security in NT Workstation 4," for more information about C2.) You can also pay a contractor to have a C2 installation of Windows NT installed and checked against official DOD C-level specifications, but this is a fairly rigorous and involved process.

- **Graphical User Interface (GUI).** Windows NT's GUI is an integral part of the operating system. Writing applications that exploit the GUI is relatively straightforward and also highly standardized. In Unix environments, for instance, various interface standards such as Motif and OPEN LOOK coexist uneasily.

- **Fault Tolerance.** Windows NT is designed to absorb the bruises of demanding computing tasks, including ill-behaved programs and security violations. For this reason, Windows NT is a preferred development environment; a badly debugged program will be at far less risk to contaminate the system than in, say, Windows 95.

- **Networking.** Windows NT is designed to support a whole range of robust networking options—a variety of network hardware, as well as common network protocols, including Novell file and print services, generic IPX/SPX, NetBEUI, TCP/IP, Macintosh networks, and many others. NT is designed to fit into an existing heterogenous environment and work seamlessly with existing network resources.

Comparing NT to Other Operating Systems

Windows NT has and will continue to have strong competition from many other products in the marketplace—more than most other operating systems because NT is designed to cover many different areas of necessity, all previously mentioned. NT works as a file and print server, a desktop operating system, a protocol router, and an all-purpose NOS.

Because of this, NT meets challenges from many other products: the various breeds of Unix, NOS products like Novell NetWare and Banyan VINES, and the perennial DOS/Windows challenger OS/2.

Due to its robustness, NT does not exclusively fit into any one of these niches, but it can do so if need be. How it compares against each one of these competitors is worth a detailed look, and in this section, you will examine how Windows NT compares in features and in implementation (such as how it executes what it has been equipped to do) to many of the other popular server- and desktop-level operating systems, including OS/2, the various Unixes, Novell Netware, Banyan VINES, and even Windows 95.

NT Versus Unix

NT is considered to have its roots in Unix and many Unix-like operating systems. This is hardly surprising; NT borrowed a great many innovations from Unix—the way devices and paths are handled, file-naming conventions, internal memory models, and so on. NT was also designed, however, to enable users and programmers to break free from a great many of the restrictions and older elements that continue to make Unix dated.

Despite the similarities that Windows NT has to Unix, the two couldn't be more dissimilar when it comes to day-to-day operations. Also, many critical areas in the design of both operating systems set them further apart from each other. The biggest differences between the two operating systems also point up their respective strengths and weaknesses:

- How NT and Unix handle operating as graphical environments
- How they function as client/server operating systems, an area rapidly increasing in importance
- How they handle file and directory sharing
- How they deal with other platforms besides themselves, such as cross-platform issues

Graphic Environments

An operating system that does not use some form of GUI is considered hopelessly behind the times.

As for Unix...

Almost all the various versions of Unix boast a windowing subsystem, or *server*, called X Windows. X Windows has a very robust set of graphics commands that have been extended on in a variety of ways through third-party libraries—some of them open standards that anyone can write a version of if he has the standard description available, and some of them are marketed as commercial products.

Without X Windows, however, Unix works exclusively in character mode, and the majority of applications that exist for Unix machines are character-based. Also, X Windows, despite its name, is not exactly a windowing system; it is, instead, just a way of enabling Unix to work with graphics primitives in a systematized fashion. The actual construction and management of windows, icons, and other screen components is entirely the whim of the programmer and whatever graphics libraries he chooses to implement.

The result is that most Unix programs that do use X Windows do not have the consistency of look and feel that Windows NT—and even the other breeds of Windows—boast.

As for NT...

Windows NT works almost exclusively in a graphical environment. The graphics subsystem in Windows—referred to as the GDI—is not actually part of the kernel, but operates closely with it. Very few Windows programs work without some kind of GDI interaction.

It is entirely possible to write a 32-bit Windows program that uses nothing but the command-line interface. For instance, the ftp client packaged with Windows NT is such a program. Not exploiting the power of the GDI, however, is something of a waste.

Windows NT's graphics system is far more consistent, even across platforms, than Unix's. Some libraries enable you to create and use special controls, but no confusion exists as to what the core display elements are in Windows NT. Creating suites of programs with a uniform look and feel is far easier in Windows NT for this reason.

Client/Server

With client/server computing becoming more and more important with every passing month, system administrators are paying close attention to the way Windows NT and other operating systems work in this fashion.

Unix...

Unix stands very much at the pinnacle of client/server applications, both because of the number of applications that have been written to support it in its various implementations, and because of the number of existing implementations still in use today. Unix was originally designed to work in a multiuser environment, and carries that strength forward to this day.

NT...

Most of the abuse heaped on Microsoft regarding NT has to do with NT's apparent lowly origins as a desktop operating system, but this is a deceptive argument to get caught up in. The guts of NT owe more to Unix and OS/2 than to 16-bit Windows. The look and feel of Windows NT, however, is designed to keep the look and feel of 16- and 16/32-bit Windows (that is, Windows 95), as well as the ease of use and intuitiveness that both operating systems featured in their graphic design. Because of this, Windows NT stands ready to challenge Unix in the client/server department; Windows NT has similar products to Unix with similar feature sets, but provides the kind of convenience and ease of use that comes with an off-the-shelf product for more mainstream use. The gauntlet is down.

Microsoft's SQL Server, for instance (already in its sixth iteration), is not only a fast performer but is much easier to install and administer than comparable Unix-based SQL products. The vast realm of other well-supported and popular commercial and shareware products written for Windows, both 16- and 32-bit, are freely executable on NT.

NT Provides C/S Access in Unique Ways

Windows NT's architecture also enables it to provide client/server access in a number of unique ways. A company named Citrix has been providing a solution package called WinFrame for Windows NT 3.51 and soon for Windows NT 4. This package enables you to use an NT server to replicate NT desktop, complete with applications and user-configured settings, on just about any kind of thin client: Unix, DOS, OS/2, 16-bit Windows, what have you. Because all the applications are executed on the server side, the client end of Citrix consists of just providing the graphic front end for Windows NT in whatever environment one could desire. Also, this kind of thin client architecture is relatively bandwidth-friendly and can be implemented across a variety of network schemes.

File Sharing and Directory Trees

File sharing and directory management have never really been a strong point of Unix. The biggest slice of the file-server-management pie has been routinely eaten up by

Novell NetWare, but Windows NT poses a solid threat to NetWare's presence. Also, NT's file and print services are extremely straightforward and easy to configure and administer, compared to Unix and Novell NetWare.

Both NT and the various Unixes support remote procedure calls (RPCs). They also support standards for object-sharing—a high-level methodology for dealing with data as easily handled objects rather than just bunches of bytes. Windows NT's Distributed *Common Object Model* (DCOM)—a standard evolving into a very powerful and high-level way of using and programming objects both locally and across any kind of network—is shaping up as a far more powerful and versatile way of working with data objects than similar technologies in Unix, such as CORBA, the Unix object-model standard that is the closest thing to OLE/DCOM in Unix.

Cross-Platform Issues

Unix has the edge over Windows NT in that far more breeds of Unix for far more breeds of machine exist than there are versions of NT. But the platforms that NT does exist for are high-performance platforms that can outrun, say, a comparably equipped SPARC machine running any breed of Unix. Windows NT, however, is now supported on a variety of platforms: the Intel x86 chipset and its clones, the MIPS R4000 and R4400 chipsets, Digital Equipment Corporation's Alpha chipset, and Motorola's PowerPC series of processors.

The End of MIPS on NT?

After the release of Windows NT 4, Microsoft took a long, hard look at the Windows NT installed base and decided that their attempts to deploy NT on MIPS were not worth pursuing. Traditionally, Windows NT installation CD-ROMs have always included versions for both the Intel and MIPS chipsets (and more recently the DEC Alpha and the Motorola PowerPC), especially since MIPS was the platform that Windows NT was initially developed most aggressively for. The much vaster installed base of Intel-platform computers, however, allowed Windows NT to come into the limelight much faster.

To date, less than 10 percent of all Windows NT installations use MIPS machines. On top of that, the amount of application software developed for MIPS processors, despite the ready availability of code libraries for the chipset, is even smaller. The bleak future of the processor itself as well—NEC, the biggest supporter of MIPS, has decided to stop manufacturing and supporting their line of MIPS processors—has convinced Microsoft that NT's future lies primarily in Intel and, to a lesser extent, on the Alpha and PowerPC platforms.

Producing different versions of Windows NT for different processors is less of a chore than creating a new version of Unix. Most Unixes have to be rewritten from scratch—including device drivers—to accommodate a new processor. Windows NT, on the other hand, makes the job much simpler by splitting off all hardware-specific calls into the Hardware Abstraction Layer (HAL), a segment of the core code that deals with platform-specific hardware. Creating a new implementation of NT generally does not mean more than writing a HAL for the new hardware and making some local changes in the kernel. Recompiling drivers and programs to work with the new hardware, as previously described, is a lot easier because of this.

Because of the way NT is constructed, porting programs from one version of NT to another is a relatively painless exercise. A smart programmer puts extensions in his code to enable a compiler to automatically include needed statements for different processor versions. This way, porting to another platform involves little more than bringing over a copy of the source code and whatever other files are needed for compiling and linking, and feeding them to a compiler on the target platform. Windows NT's own kernel is written in this fashion, enabling a fair amount of platform independence in the source code. Obviously, a certain amount of hand-coding in assembler is required for the best possible performance. The amount of manual labor that has to be done in this regard, however, is significantly less than with other operating systems that do not use this abstraction technique.

NT Versus NetWare (and Other Network Operating Systems)

Before Windows NT, an operating system of the same class was not readily available for the Intel platform. The closest thing was Novell NetWare, which was not an operating system for running applications, but rather an operating system for hosting file volumes across a network—a *network operating system* (NOS).

Because NetWare is one of the most well-established and strongest-selling NOS products available, it stands as one of NT's largest challengers in the NOS realm. NetWare's strength is the fact that it's designed to do one thing well: work as a file and print server. NetWare was not designed as an application-development platform, nor as a desktop operating system. Nonetheless, what it does, it does very well and greatly satisfies many. NetWare has more than half the file/print-sharing server market, and might continue to hang on to that edge into the next century. The vast majority of NetWare installations are of the 3.x iteration. Novell has long offered a 4.0/4.x iteration of the product, but the adoption rate has been slower than expected.

Go NetWare!

One of the biggest advantages NetWare has long held over NT is that NT does not support *directory trees*—the capability to have collections of directories from various volumes appear as one volume. NetWare's newest features in its 4.x version include support for X.500-style directory services and enterprise-wide features, all designed to compete directly with NT.

Go NT!

A disadvantage that NetWare has in comparison to Windows NT is that writing software for the NOS, known as *NetWare loadable modules* (NLMs), is not an easy task. By contrast, writing services and drivers for NT is more straightforward.

A fair number of NetWare loadable modules are available, having been written and developed during the long and venerable life of NetWare in its many previous incarnations.

NT's list of additional services and drivers is also quite impressive, among the most recent being items as diverse as McAfee's antivirus software and web server programs offered by O'Reilly and Netscape.

As for the others...

Other NOSes being challenged strongly by NT include Banyan VINES and IBM's own LAN Server.

LAN Server is a direct-line descendent of the same project that produced OS/2, although the current version of OS/2 is itself descended from LAN Server. LAN Server is popular in the same environments where OS/2 is itself popular, obviously, since it is designed to integrate most effectively with OS/2.

VINES is one of the few NOSes that has excellent support for enterprise-wide/WAN-type networks through a symbolic resource-naming service called *StreetTalk.* VINES is also more Unix-like than other NOSes, making it a little easier for seasoned Unix hands to master the system.

NT has plans on the board, through third-party vendors and through its own labs, to make all these services available on NT—and make them seamlessly integrateable with heterogeneous networks so that an NT machine can assume the place of a similarly configured VINES or NetWare server.

Windows NT Versus Windows 95

Windows 95 and Windows NT have many things in common—more now in NT 4 than before—but they were developed to fulfill vastly different needs.

NT was developed as a server and a secure workstation environment. Windows 95 was developed to satisfy home- and small-office users who had vastly different needs: running existing 16-bit Windows software, including legacy hardware drivers, without difficulty; running DOS programs; and playing games. NT was not designed to satisfy these specific needs, and so the next version of Windows (after Windows 3.1) that would exploit more of the 32-bit power of the computer than Windows 3.x, while remaining as backward-compatible as possible, needed to be developed.

As a result of these differences in design philosophy, an issue that remains important today in the minds of many corporate IS managers is whether to use Windows 95 or Windows NT Workstation 4 when they perform the next massive upgrade of their Windows-centric hardware. A good many corporate desktop planners have looked at Windows NT Workstation 4 and decided that the security features, the resource demands, and the general compatibility with existing software makes Windows NT Workstation 4 a better choice to migrate to than Windows 95.

Exploring Windows 95...

Windows 95 was developed as an upgrade for users of Windows 3.x, not just as a wholesale replacement. Because of this, it had to be designed to accept legacy (such as 16-bit DOS and Windows) software and work with it gracefully, while at the same time enabling users to better exploit their systems without many of the inherent limitations of resources and processing power that the old DOS/Windows 3.x architecture placed on them.

Unlike Windows 3.x, Windows 95 has the capability to run true 32-bit multithreaded software. Because it also has to be capable of dealing with 16-bit drivers and 32-bit .VXDs—both of which might require direct access to hardware and cannot easily be emulated without performance being affected—a crucial decision about Windows 95 was made early on. The following two points help clarify this decision:

- **Protected memory model.** First, Windows 95 does not use the same protected memory model as Windows NT: 32-bit programs run in protected memory, but 16-bit programs all share space along with the operating system. This means that a rogue 16-bit program can bring everything down—operating system included! Windows 95 does not use a VDM, or virtual DOS machine, to run each 16-bit task. OS/2 is stronger than Windows 95 in this respect, since it uses VDMs to run 16-bit Windows and DOS programs.

- **Thunking.** Second, Windows 95 uses a technique called *thunking* to allow 16- and 32-bit programs to coexist. The system shuttles back and forth between 16- and 32-bit modes, enabling 16-bit programs to make calls to the 32-bit portion of the operating system. Thunking makes it possible to retain old 16-bit DOS-based hardware drivers, but also impacts performance.

Graphics and windowing environments...

What's the difference between Windows 95 and Windows NT's ways of dealing with graphics and their windowing environments? As of NT 4, the look and feel is identical to Windows 95, but the *under the hood* performance is very different. Windows 95's graphics subsystem makes a great many concessions to enable 16-bit programs and 16-bit code to exist without too much trouble, and the result is a performance decrease.

Although it does not make Windows 95 so slow that it might as well be Windows 3.x, the decrease is substantial when compared against a wholly 32-bit environment like Windows NT. Even Windows NT's internal security concessions are not as big a hindrance to performance as Windows 95's 16-bit concessions. Performance studies on Pentium Pro and 200 Mhz Pentium machines have revealed that Windows NT, despite its internal security model that impacts performance on slower machines, runs much faster than Windows 95—almost solely because no 16/32-bit thinking is taking place.

NT Versus OS/2

Another of Windows NT's major opponents is, of course, IBM's OS/2.

OS/2 has long been marketed on a number of different fronts—as a network operating system, as a desktop OS, and as a file server. The first and third areas are where OS/2 has the strongest showing, making OS/2 strategically important even if not as visible as conventional Windows or Windows NT.

OS/2 has been long vaunted as having many technical superiorities to Windows 3.x, and even in some respects to Windows NT. Although OS/2 does not enjoy the same breadth of support as Windows and Windows NT, it is very enthusiastically kept in active use by the core of users, user groups, and system administrators who have taken it to heart.

OS/2 2.0 and 2.1 make up the majority of OS/2 installations in the world today. The 2.x revision of OS/2 was designed to capitalize on the power of the 386 (and later the 486 processors), with many of the same features that Windows would later lay claim to: virtual DOS machines, protected memory for 32-bit programs, a graphical desktop, and so on. As Windows exploded in popularity and became a desktop-oriented operating system, however, OS/2 became a key figure in file and print servers, mail hubs, and database servers.

While Microsoft was readying Windows 95 (originally code named Chicago), IBM tried hard to push OS/2 as a substitute for Windows, repackaging it as "OS/2 Warp" and adding software that would give it Internet functionality and an Office-like suite of applications. Much of the promotion centered around OS/2 having the capability to run 16-bit Windows applications (including Windows itself in a separate VDM) and some single-threaded 32-bit Windows applications as well. The advantages to this scheme were quickly eclipsed when the big question on everyone's lips became, "When does OS/2 run Windows 95 applications?" Many felt that IBM had committed a strategic error by not enabling or even *forcing* development of more OS/2 applications, and that by making that many more concessions to the Windows community, it had not won its own battle.

IBM moved to acquire Lotus shortly thereafter in an attempt to drum up a couple of important application suites that would make OS/2 more of a choice for SOHO, consumer desktop, and wide-area workplaces or telecommuting environments. Lotus Notes was supposed to be to OS/2 what Microsoft Word and later MS Office had been to Windows. Unfortunately, Windows 95 was already out by then, and Lotus Notes for OS/2 received at best a lukewarm reception—especially because Notes had also been developed for Windows, in both 16- and 32-bit versions, and was selling strongly on that platform.

OS/2's Faithful Following

As mentioned before, OS/2, although not as popular as Windows, has a strongly devoted following of users, with the strongest being those who use it in a server environment. Most of OS/2's core server installations are not going anywhere because OS/2 has gained a number of strategic footholds in both the server market and the NOS market. Many banking and financial institutions rely heavily on OS/2, and database-server installations are primarily the domain of both OS/2 and Unix. Because of the "set-in-stone"-ness of these types of installations, little chance exists that a long-standing OS/2 installation would suddenly switch over to NT.

The most devoted of the OS/2 user groups, Team OS/2, remains to this day a font of tips, utilities, resources, and people who are more than willing to step in on a moment's notice with impromptu OS/2 technical support. Team OS/2 strongly proselytizes OS/2's vaunted technical superiority over Windows, especially when it comes to areas like OS/2's object-oriented shell model, and its system-wide scriptability through REXX.

Many of the Unix installations are being run on relatively old hardware, and are being prepared to be phased out by newer machines. On brand-new hardware, Windows NT makes a very attractive choice—especially for database-centric installations, because Windows NT's BackOffice products are designed to hook into existing legacy database systems and eventually replace them. OS/2's core devotees would be more difficult to woo away. Like OS/2, NT can communicate with existing IBM mainframes by using the Data Link Control (DLC) protocol.

Many of the differences between NT and OS/2 also point out how NT differs from many other products in the marketplace in its philosophy and strategy. In the next few sections, you'll explore how NT and OS/2 diverge in many key areas:

- NT and OS/2's implementation of objects in their system models and programming paradigms
- The windowing and graphics subsystems in OS/2

IBM's System Object Model

One significant difference in the architectures of NT and OS/2 revolves around IBM using an object-oriented method called the System Object Model (SOM). The SOM presents users and programmers with a standardized way to talk about and to the operating system and everything in it, making it easier to write code that can be transported across many different platforms.

Microsoft, in comparison, has its own object-oriented methodology specific to Windows NT—named DCOM, or Distributed Common Object Model—and is not really designed to be exported to other operating systems. (Microsoft plans to make up for this by having NT work across multiple platforms.)

Microsoft's Object-Oriented Methodology at Work

A good example of Microsoft's approach *qua* cross-platform issues would be what happened with Digital's Alpha AXP processor. Because Microsoft sees its biggest product for other platforms as being Windows NT itself, it wrote a version of NT specifically for the Alpha and provided developers with tools to bring their code over into the Alpha versions of NT. Usually the conversion does not take more than a day or two to compile the code and ensure that it works, and perhaps to add code to take advantage of processor-specific features. But the attitude is clear: Microsoft has worked to extend its presence to other platforms aggressively, by providing not only the paradigm but the OS and the libraries.

OLE/DCOM Versus OpenDoc

OLE/DCOM and OpenDoc, respectively, are Microsoft and IBM's data frameworks for creating open-ended, boundaryless information structures that not only exist within individual computers, but across networks. Both, however, were devised to fulfill different types of needs in different environments and implementations.

OpenDoc was, and still is, the result of planning on the part of a number of different companies: IBM (obviously), Novell, Oracle, SunSoft, Taligent, WordPerfect (absorbed at first into Novell and now part of Corel), and Xerox.

Hands Off OLE?

While OpenDoc is something of a public venture, which can be freely adapted by anyone who wants to invest the time and energy into doing so, OLE/DCOM, on the other hand, is very much the product of Microsoft and no other company. This gives ammunition to those who state that OLE/DCOM is not an open standard; if someone wanted to write, for example, a version of OLE/DCOM for a system that Microsoft did not support, he would have to license OLE/DCOM from Microsoft or risk a lawsuit. OpenDoc, on the other hand, does not require licensing to be produced for a specific platform.

The single biggest problem with OpenDoc is that although it is good on paper, almost no applications exist on the Windows platform that can make use of it, either as an object or as a container. Many facilitations that exist for OLE/DCOM don't exist yet as OpenDoc tools: authorware (such as Visual Basic or Visual C++), components (such as OCX controls), and lack of real cross-platform and network support. OLE, in contrast, is very richly implemented and supported in Windows. There are few applications that do not function as OLE containers or clients of some sort, or development tools that can't make use of custom controls.

What's so important about either of these technologies? OLE and OpenDoc are both examples of what is called a *component software architecture*—the idea that stand-alone applications, such as word processors or spreadsheets, can be replaced by bundles of little programs that, when hitched together, can do the same things, except with far more flexibility and open-endedness.

OpenDoc consists of a number of discrete components: the actual OpenDoc software architecture; the Bento multimeda-information interchange standard; the *Open Scripting Architecture* (OSA) standard, which enables multiple scripting languages to coexist; and IBM's System Object Model (SOM) architecture, a dynamic-object linking architecture. The last item on the list bears the closest resemblance to OLE/DCOM in functionality.

OLE/DCOM was developed as an adjunct to existing Microsoft programs, as a way of getting them to share information with something more sophisticated than the usual cut-and-paste technology. With OLE, it became possible to take a document or a piece of a document and paste it into another document without losing its original formatting or functionality. A graphic image, for instance, could be embedded into a text file, with both text and graphics being freely editable.

OLE 2.0 went further by enabling the functionality of applications to interpenetrate. In the original OLE, if a picture was embedded in a document, double-clicking on the picture would launch the application associated with that picture and enable you to edit it in a separate window. In OLE 2.0, it became possible to not only do that, but also to enable the program doing the graphics editing to run *inside* the text processor as it did its work, enabling both programs to communicate freely and closely.

OpenDoc has been vaunted by many to be technically superior to OLE (and by extension, DCOM), and in many ways this is true. OpenDoc is a general model for the design of objects system-wide; DCOM/OLE is more or less restricted to information transactions within the operating system. Although a Windows-based version of OpenDoc is currently available, almost no applications make use of it. The implementation of the standard exists; what's lacking are applications that make active and robust use of it. A possible compromise is Taligent's CommonPoint Application System, which works with both OpenDoc and OLE to enable programmers to write applications that can address both of these standards.

OS/2's Graphics System

Because OS/2 is being deployed at least partly as an alternative to Windows, it makes sense to examine how it shapes up against Windows (and especially Windows NT) in terms of its GUI.

OS/2 has a graphics system that works like a cross between the Unix model and the Windows model. Once again, in Windows, the graphics system is nearly indispensible—it is not part of the kernel, and you don't have to write Windows applications that exploit it. But so much of the strength of Windows lies in its tightly managed, unified, and well-developed graphics system that to not make use of it is something of a waste. In Unix, graphics and windowing are usually the domain of whatever X Window server is loaded into the system. Since there are several contrasting and conflicting windowing paradigms that can be used under Unix, writing an X Windows-enabled program in Unix usually requires having many libraries for rudimentary support, instead of just one bundled with the OS (as in the case of Windows).

OS/2 uses a subsystem called the Presentation Manager that handles windowing and graphics for the system, but because OS/2 started out as a character-mode–based operating system, the Presentation Manager is detached from the operating system. It's possible to boot a command-line–based session of OS/2 and work with it, so long as you don't need to run programs that deal with the Presentation Manager.

Exploring NT's File Systems

Back in the stone-age days of DOS, CP/M, and the first breeds of Unix, the file system *was* the operating system. DOS's own name—Disk Operating System—belied the fact that DOS was not much more than a command-line file manager. And back then, that was pretty much all that was demanded of an operating system of DOS's caliber.

Eventually, Unix (and OS/2 and later Windows NT) introduced the concept of an *installable file system.* Rather than have the file system an inseparable part of the OS, it was to be detached and handled through a device driver. This way, a single operating system could read many different varieties of media and different types of disk formats, and the way programs dealt with different kinds of media could be standardized by channeling all such operations through the OS.

For the sake of enabling users to upgrade gracefully from existing installations, Windows NT supports two major disk storage schemes—FAT and NTFS.

HPFS, the extended file system used in OS/2, has been supported in Windows NT up until release 3.51. With the release of NT 4, HPFS support is no longer included. It is possible to convert an HPFS volume to NTFS during installation or while formatting or mounting disks, but reading and writing to and from HPFS volumes is not supported.

FAT

The FAT file system, abbreviated from the File Allocation Table that formed a good part of its structure, was the file system DOS 1.0 and all its future successors used in various forms. Many of its inherent limits—including media size, file size, file name length, and problems with error-correction—have continued to this day.

The way the FAT system works is by keeping two discrete lists on the disk. The first list is the directory itself—a list of file names and locations at the head of the disk in a simple lookup table. Each of the entries in this table contains the file name and its attributes, with the attributes allocated as two bits per attribute:

- ◆ Archive file
- ◆ System file
- ◆ Hidden file
- ◆ Read-only file

Also included in the directory are the last time and date access of the file, and a pointer to an entry in the File Allocation Table.

The second part of the FAT system is the File Allocation Table itself—a list of pointers, each one telling you where to go next. Assume that you have a file named README.TXT, and its directory-table pointer points to block 0 in the FAT. When you look at block 0 in the FAT, you see the number 50, which indicates that you must go to block 50 in the FAT to keep reading the same file. If the next block in the chain is the hexadecimal FFFF, then you have reached the end of the file. By multiplying the block number with the size of the allocation units on the disk, you can find the exact address on the disk from which to read the data.

Cluster Number	Table Entry	Description
5800	[BAD]	Unuseable cluster (has been marked bad)
5801	[0]	Available cluster
5802	[Reserved]	Reserved by operating system
5803	[5805]	Identifies where the next cluster is for this file
5804	[EOF]	Last cluster of a file
5805	[5806]	Next cluster marker

At first, FAT was only designed to support drives no larger than a single floppy. The explosion of hard drives on personal computers forced DOS's designers to rethink the way FAT stored its data. With each successive version of DOS, all the way up to 6.2 and beyond, FAT became more and more adept at handling larger drives, but it was still a retrofit at best. The original version of FAT was not even written to support subdirectories.

FAT's upper limit of storage for any one drive is 2 GB, and even within that scope problems still exist with extremely long files, and the ever-present problem of disk fragmentation persists. As more files get written to and deleted from the disk, the files themselves become less and less physically sequential. This slows down file operations a great deal. Also, more file entries in the FAT table means the computer has to search further to find the needed entries (more time wasted). And if the FAT itself is ever damaged, there's very little way to reconstruct the resulting mess other than by painstakingly going through the disk sector by sector. Later versions of DOS tried to alleviate this problem by including two copies of the FAT on disk and using cyclic redundancy checks to make certain that if one of them fell out of sync, the other could be used to reconstruct the damage; but even this couldn't alleviate the problem entirely.

Other limits, such as the infamous 8.3 file name convention, have been worked around; but the core of FAT is still problematic for those who want to do serious computing: its instability under heavy use and its lack of inherent security features make it hard to stay with.

Windows NT has supported the FAT file system since its first release (version 3.1) and continues to do so to the current day. It seems likely that it will continue to support FAT for at least one to two more major releases, although FAT is itself ready to be eclipsed by FAT32 (which will soon be supported by NT) and NTFS.

Using FAT on NT is not a bad idea—depending on what you are using NT for. System administrators who are deploying NT in an environment where more than one user is accessing the system—in other words, a server environment—will be far happier with the security and integrity features that NTFS affords. If you are using Windows NT Workstation on the same machine as Windows 95, in a dual-boot arrangement, then using the FAT file system is almost a prerogative.

In general, FAT should only be used with a Windows NT installation when it is impossible to avoid doing so—to provide interoperability with other operating systems, for instance.

HPFS

HPFS is the file system that OS/2 introduced as a replacement for FAT. Up until NT 4, NT included an OS.2 subsystem that enabled continuing access to HPFS, although this is no longer the case. Windows NT 4 and beyond no longer support direct access to HPFS drives. The only real support for HPFS drives in Windows NT 4 and beyond is the capability to convert existing HPFS volumes to NTFS.

HPFS has several distinct advantages over FAT. First of all, it's possible to have file names of up to 255 characters, something which has only recently been addressed in FAT (and with something tantamount to a kludge). HPFS supports long file names inherently, and also reserves space for extended attributes, access-control lists, and pointers to where the rest of the file is stored if it's too big to fit in one block.

Also, HPFS uses a more logical and advanced scheme of organization than FAT. The data segment of a disk is divided up into chunks of 8 MB each, with a 2 KB bitmap that describes the data segment located alternately at the beginning and the end of each 8 MB block. This arrangement enables as much as 16 MB of data exist in a continuous stripe on the disk before it's interrupted by a bitmap zone. As new files are allocated and staked out on the disk, HPFS deliberately leaves room for new files to move in between existing ones. This way, the amount of fragmentation is kept down and data can be retrieved from the drive much faster.

Because of the way HPFS is organized, it keeps shortened versions of all long file names in DOS-compatible 8.3 format. In some cases, it's much easier to access files from the command line this way; it also enhances backward compatibility with older software that only sees 8.3 file names.

HPFS also supports two technologies that increase performance and reliability—lazy writing and hot-fixing.

- **Lazy writing.** Lazy writing is just a version of caching writes. *Disk caching* is the technique in which data that's to be read or written from a disk is held in a temporary area of memory before being committed. With lazy writing, all writes to the disk are held until a background process in HPFS decides that it is time to write all the data. The reason for this in HPFS is so that the program can write data as contiguously as possible.
- **Hot-fixing.** Write errors are a common problem with disk systems, and for that reason HPFS has a technique to handle this as well—*hot-fixing*. Somewhere on the disk, HPFS has a reserved section that handles write errors, called the *hot-fix pool*. If an error is detected, it uses a block from the hot-fix pool to write data there, and then updates the file maps to point away from the bad sector. The data then gets recommitted to a safe portion of the disk. If the pool gets dangerously close to being filled up, the system bugs you about it and recommends you run CHKDSK or some other disk-maintenance utility to do something about the problem.

Despite its sophistication, HPFS still has a number of drawbacks:

- It cannot handle drives larger than 2 GB, a limitation it shares with FAT. HPFS uses a 512-byte sector scheme not suited for volumes over 2 GB, and is therefore not suited to RAID arrays or other forms of ultra-high–volume storage.
- If the first sectors of the disk (boot information, pointers to the root directory) are damaged and not backed up, the rest of the drive is inaccessible.
- Every time the system is booted, HPFS runs CHKDSK to determine if there are allocation errors anywhere on the volume. On larger volumes with many extended attributes, this can take a long time (upward of 10 to 20 minutes).

When Windows NT supported HPFS in versions 3.5 and 3.51, it did not support a full implementation of the file system—the access controls and the hot-fixing schemes were *not* supported.

NTFS

NTFS, the file system that Windows NT introduced to replace FAT and HPFS, was designed from the ground up to augment and support NT in every possible way. FAT had not originally been designed with anything more than storing files on floppy disks in mind, and had certainly never been intended to embrace such things as security features and auditing—both of which are, among many other things, extremely important to users of NT and other server-level operating systems.

NTFS is designed to be used heavily and on large volumes. For that reason, it has many safety and security features, as well as enhancements to reduce fragmentation and increase overall performance. Sixteen *billion* gigabytes (no, that's not a misprint!) can be stored on a *single* NTFS volume, reliably. NTFS also does away with 8.3 character name-length limit that made FAT so stodgy.

NTFS is designed to be stable and secure—to enable problems such as fragmentation to be minimized, and to ensure that every single byte of space and every file can be properly access controlled.

Under NTFS, every file is considered an object that has both user- and system-assigned attributes. What's unique is that these attributes are stored in the file and not as separate tables. Because of this, a single lookup gets all the information on a small file, including the data. Under FAT, the system would first have to get the FAT info, and then go to the file itself to get the rest of the information. NTFS also supports the 8.3 abbreviation system, so older applications that only see 8.3 files will not have problems working under NTFS.

Another innovation in NTFS is that the descriptors for the various segments are stored redundantly, including the boot sector. FAT used a form of fault tolerance by keeping a second copy of the FAT itself, but not of its boot sector. With NT, the boot sector is kept mirrored in the logical middle of the disk, far from harm.

All of these innovations in NTFS make it far better suited to the kinds of tasks that Windows NT is made for, such as file sharing and controlling permissions to files, Unix-style.

Converting File Systems

Windows NT 4 can work with existing FAT file systems without trouble. Earlier versions of NT also worked, to a limited degree, with HPFS file systems, although NT did not make use of HPFS's security features. With NT 4, live support for HPFS has been removed and only FAT and NTFS are supported as live file systems.

If you load NT 4 into a system with an HPFS volume, you are given the option to convert the volume over to FAT or NTFS while installing NT. The only other option available for HPFS drives is to reformat them completely as FAT or NTFS.

To convert a file system after the fact, you can use the CONVERT program, which is usually executed through the command line. Following is an example of this command executed:

```
CONVERT drive: /FS:NTFS [/V]
```

The CONVERT program has the following options (as indicated in the preceding command-line code):

- **drive.** Specifies the drive to convert to NTFS. Note that you cannot convert the current drive. This means that if you have booted from the C drive, or have operations in progress that need the C drive, you cannot convert the drive at that time. If you attempt to do so, CONVERT will enable the drive to be converted the next time you reboot.
- **/FS:NTFS.** Specifies to convert the volume to NTFS. You cannot convert an NTFS volume back to FAT. This option has been left in to enable future support for FAT32 and other types of drive formatting schemes.
- **/V.** Specifies that Convert should be run in verbose mode. This provides you with explicit prompts during the entire process.

When a volume is formatted as an NTFS volume during installation, it is actually formatted as FAT and then converted to NTFS after the first successful reboot.

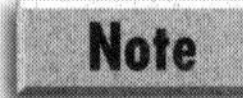

In the event that the Windows NT installation process is not successful, you will still have access to the drive, provided it hasn't been reformatted or repartitioned.

Exploring the Strengths of NT's Architecture

NT was designed to meet specific goals and perform specific tasks, and to that end, Microsoft's software engineers devised a robust and internally protected architecture for it. This section goes into detail about the various ways Windows NT's architecture exhibits robustness.

Multiprocessor Support

Another area in which Windows NT shines is multiprocessor support. Windows NT can support a system with up to four processors, right out of the box. It is also designed to enable 32-bit applications that use multithreading to take advantage of multiple processors without extra programming.

NT handles the dispatching of threads and applications to various processors in a multiprocessor system. It's also possible to write applications for NT that specifically address multiple processors through the HAL. The HAL is designed to operate as a virtual-processor interface, even if multiple processors are not present in the system. This way, a program written to take advantage of multiple processors still performs well on a uniprocessor machine.

Multiprocessor support in other operating systems is also usually handled through a programming interface in the operating system. OS/2, for example, also supports multiple processors. Doing this, however, requires the purchase of a version of OS/2 specifically for multiprocessor systems. NT works as a multiprocessor OS out of the box.

Machines that comes with more than four processors can still be used with NT. A HAL from the hardware manufacturer is needed to make proper use of more than four processors, however, because the default HAL for a given platform (Intel, for instance) is not designed to address more than four physical processors.

Scalability

A big buzzword with today's high-end operating systems is scalability. *Scalability* is basically the potential a given piece of hardware or software has to work better if used in more high-performance surroundings. A legacy ISA video card does not scale well, for example, because it was not designed to exploit more than a certain amount of power in the system it's installed in. A PCI video card would scale better because it would be better able to make the maximum use of any PCI-compliant system in which it was installed.

Likewise, Windows NT is able to exploit having more memory, much more so than Windows 95 or DOS.

If the OS in question is an older version of Windows or even DOS, such OSes are not designed to scale well, if at all. They do not know how to take advantage of the presence of more than a certain amount of memory; both Windows 3.x and DOS were hindered horribly by the 640 KB lower-memory limit.

Windows 95 obviated this problem to a great degree. Although when it's a question of the scalability of Windows 95 versus Windows NT on higher-end machines, Windows NT always has the advantage because it is not hindered by OS-level concessions to 16-bitness. NT can directly address up to 4 GB of system memory, and can store drivers, services, and programs in any memory segment it needs to. Also, because Windows NT is not limited by 16-bit concessions, it can better exploit the power of the processors on which it is designed to run. Windows NT is designed to scale from the desktop to the enterprise and every stage in between.

The Ring Model

Most operating systems designed with a certain amount of strength and fault tolerance in mind use a design that has come to be called the *ring* model. Windows NT is no exception to this rule.

In the ring model, the computer and its operating system are broken up into discrete layers, or rings. The centermost layer of the model is the computer's hardware itself. For something to go from an outer ring to the hardware—for instance, a call to memory—it must pass through all the intervening layers. This way, the more crucial parts of the computer and the operating system are protected from being casually accessed, overwritten, or damaged.

Immediately surrounding the hardware is the layer of the operating system that does all the dealing with hardware. This layer is referred to as Ring 0. In Windows NT, Ring 0 contains most of the kernel and the Hardware Abstraction Layer (HAL). Nothing else, save the HAL and the kernel, touches the hardware in Windows NT.

Outer rings contain the subsystems that deal more directly with the user. GDI and Win32 subsystems are examples of such subsystems. Whenever these layers want to communicate with the hardware, they must first go through the lower layers. Also, with this model, programs can be protected from each other and can be carefully regimented to access the hardware only in permissible ways.

One significant change from Windows NT 3.51 that is in Windows NT 4 is the rewriting of the graphics system. Graphics drivers now reside in Ring 0, although they are not considered part of the kernel.

Windows NT's ring design stands in sharp contrast to operating systems like DOS or Windows 95. In DOS, any program that knows where a piece of hardware is can make a call to it. Programs are not protected from each other, nor is the operating system protected from them. Total system crashes due to badly debugged programs are common.

One of the other strongest areas of contrast is in the way Windows NT has specific *modes* of operation.

Modes of Operation

Two discrete modes of operation exist in Windows NT—*user* and *kernel*. These general terms can apply to other operating systems and platforms as well. When a system component runs in kernel mode, it is considered to be capable of accessing all the available resources on that computer: all the memory, the full range of chipset instructions, all the hardware.

Windows NT places the kernel itself, the HAL, and the Executive Services—which manages objects, security, processes, virtual memory, drivers and local procedure calls—all in kernel mode. Obviously the HAL has to be a kernel-mode device; after all, most of the communications to the system's hardware are done through the HAL.

User mode consists of the subsystems that the user works with most of the time: the Win32 subsystem (which runs applications) and the security system (which controls logon procedures and passwords). The Win32 subsystem is also host to the DOS/Win16 subsystem, the OS/2 subsystem, and the POSIX subsystem, through which applications of those types are also executed. These subsystems can be changed with greater ease by their designers, without having to also make modifications to kernel-mode components.

System Services

An important area of difference between Windows NT, Windows 95, and Windows 3.x is system services, or drivers. When Windows was little more than a graphical extension to DOS, drivers for hardware were DOS's responsibility. Usually this meant a device driver statement in CONFIG.SYS or AUTOEXEC.BAT, with the device drivers eating into the crucial lower 640 KB block of memory and sharing space with programs.

These drivers worked through a DOS principle known as *terminate and stay resident*, or TSR for short. They remained resident in memory and only asserted control over things when a call was made to the hardware they were meant to govern. The idea of a program being *re-entrant*, as was the term commonly applied to such program behavior, in fact dated from one of DOS and Windows's predecessors, Unix. In Unix, re-entrant programs are called *daemons*, and unlike DOS can be loaded into any available segment of memory. OS/2 also borrowed this model and used it to its advantage over DOS.

Eventually, with the introduction of Windows 3.1 and 3.11, more of the drivers that had taken up lower DOS memory appeared in Windows versions—especially drivers for multimedia devices, which were notorious lower-memory hogs. After Windows NT (and later 95) appeared, *all* hardware was to be controlled through 32-bit drivers. In Windows 95's case, as much of it as possible was to be redirected in such a fashion, but there were still provisions to enable older 16-bit DOS-based lower-memory drivers to run in it. Windows NT, from the beginning, stuck with the idea of using wholly 32-bit drivers that abstracted programs completely from the task of dealing with hardware of any kind.

Unix daemons were not, however, principally hardware drivers. They were designed to govern higher-level system functions, such as packet communications or the receiving and transmission of mail. In Windows NT, daemons and drivers share a great many similarities of deployment and design and are called *services.* The EventLog service, for example, sits and waits for word from the operating system of something worth noting in the system operations log, such as the failure of a driver or a breach of security. When this happens, the EventLog service writes information about the event into the log. Other services govern directory replication, the browsing of the directories in the computer from across the network, logon and logoff operations, and so on.

NT adds flexibility to services by enabling them to be dynamically started, paused, and stopped as the need arises. Also, users can create hardware profiles in which certain sets of services are loaded or rendered inactive. The term *hardware profile* comes from the origination of the concept in Windows 95, where a user could define certain pieces of hardware as being present or absent in certain configurations, and specify which drivers were to be loaded. The mechanic has been brought over to Windows NT with great success.

Caution Starting and stopping Windows NT drivers manually can have highly adverse effects on the integrity of the system if you do so without knowing exactly what you're doing. Most of the time, Windows NT will be alert to attempts to stop a critical system driver (such as a video driver), and will prevent you from doing so.

WoW, or Windows on Win32

One of the biggest advantages NT has over its 16-bit predecessors is the capability to run VDMs or *virtual DOS machines.* This means that any 16-bit applications will be run in their own memory space, isolated and protected from each other. When this technology applies to Windows programs specifically, Windows NT uses a special VDM subsystem called *Windows on Win32* (WoW).

The Windows NT 3.1 version of WoW ran all 16-bit Windows applications in a single virtual machine. This had some of the same drawbacks of conventional Windows because all 16-bit applications would share the same address spaces. With NT 3.5 (and 4), users had the option of running each Windows application in its own VDM. This way, one bad apple (or application) would not bring all the rest down.

The drawback to this scheme is that approximately 2500 KB is required for each VDM; on machines with less than 24 MB of RAM, therefore, running several VDMs can impact performance. The best long-term solution to enhancing performance is to phase out the use of 16-bit applications wherever possible and introduce 32-bit equivalents—which run in less memory and do not require the overhead of a VDM. Also, 16-bit applications in VDMs cannot share information directly and have to work through 16- to 32-bit DCOM (formerly OLE), which slows things down even further.

Device Handling

Unix handles device drivers by having the driver compiled into the kernel. This is done mostly to keep the size of the operating system down. Instead of having a subsystem for dealing with device drivers, the support for the device rests directly with the kernel.

Unfortunately, this scheme has more than its fair share of drawbacks. Without a certain amount of expertise with the kernel, it is hard to add (and especially remove) device support. Also, it is not an intuitive process. Most of Unix's work is done from the command line with Unix's infamous cryptic command-set. Unless you know exactly what to type, you will probably not be able to puzzle your way through it. Also, you run the risk of trashing the kernel if something goes wrong. Under NT, a badly installed or debugged driver either generates a loggable error or forces a reboot with no permanent damage to the system.

NT handles drivers for hardware in something of the same fashion as OS/2, DOS, Windows 3.x, and Windows 95. Drivers are packaged as discrete files, which are loaded into memory when needed—usually at boot time—and called dynamically from the kernel, usually through some kind of intermediate driver manager layer in the OS.

NT's driver management scheme is far more intuitive than most Unixes. The Devices applet in the Control Panel lists all the available device drivers, and they can be stopped, started, and assigned startup parameters through this applet (see fig. 1.1).

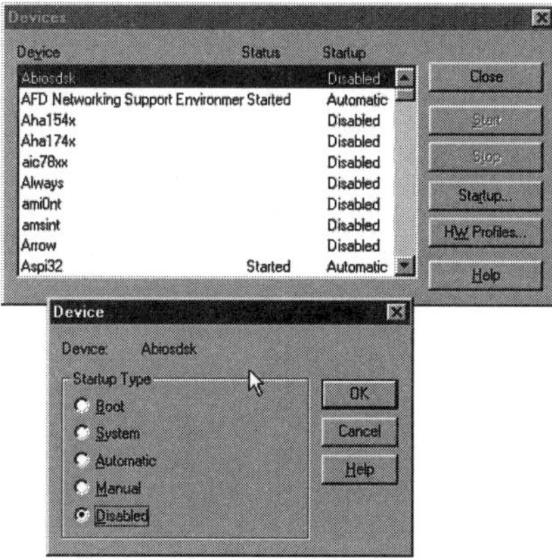

Figure 1.1

Device handling in Windows NT is dynamic and can be controlled very closely by the user.

Some devices, such as the video driver, cannot be stopped and started dynamically. Any device that hooks into the system at boot time, for instance, is not stoppable. If any changes are made to their configuration, the system has to be rebooted before those changes can take effect.

In the NT driver/kernel model, no driver ever speaks directly to the hardware. Drivers talk instead to the HAL—the piece of machine-specific code that lies between the kernel and the hardware itself. The kernel does talk directly to the hardware in a few circumstances, but the vast majority of the way the operating system deals with machine-level commands is through the HAL.

Each platform that NT runs on has its own specific HAL: one for the chips on the Intel platform, one for the Alpha chips, for PowerPC, for MIPS processors, and so on. Each HAL is written by the chip vendor itself. Because of this design, the NT kernel can be written in a machine-independent fashion, and thus ported from platform to platform with greater ease.

To increase I/O and throughput on certain hardware devices, including 100-megabit Ethernet and the video subsystem, the NT designers moved a great many of its service drivers from Ring 2 of the system architecture into Ring 0 for NT 4.

Many misinterpreted this by thinking that NT now had its video subsystem as part of the kernel. This isn't what happened. Ring 0 consists of more than just the kernel in the first place. The Ring 0 change-over only means that when the system uses certain devices, it does not have to make ring transitions (which are slow) every time it accesses them. Because of this, NT 4's video and Ethernet performance are noticeably faster.

Another concern that people had was for system integrity and security with the new model. Because the graphics system was located in the user processes in NT 3.x, a bug in the graphics hardware driver would cause the entire user subsystem to crash and the system would fail to restart because the kernel would not trap this as a BSOD fault. In NT 4, locating such drivers in Ring 0 enables the kernel to trap the problem, write a report, and reboot the machine, at least enabling proper debug information to be generated about the problem. The problem is only really significant for programmers designing such drivers and less so for end users.

Even with all the improvements and technical achievements that have been made in NT 4 so far, Microsoft is convinced that the surface hasn't even been scratched yet. What comes next will probably be doubly revolutionary, and its name is Cairo.

Heading for Cairo

Windows NT 4 is not the end of the line for NT as you know it. Quite the contrary: Microsoft has plans for NT to continue to grow and develop as a multifunctional operating system, well into the next millennium. The next stage in NT's evolution is code-named Cairo, which for all intents and purposes is slated to appear during 1997.

Cairo has been variously touted and lambasted as either the next quantum leap for the evolution of Windows, or the biggest piece of vaporware ever.

Part of the reason for this is that Cairo will most likely not come all at one time, but rather as a series of incremental changes to Windows NT, with one of the first big changes rumored to be the Object File System (the successor to NTFS). With this scenario in mind, it seems likely that the first waves of changes will not be kernel modifications per se, but rather the support structure of the software surrounding the kernel, such as the OLE-to-DCOM changeover.

What will Cairo be capable of doing, exactly? For starters, with the Object File System in place, users will be enabled to deal with files on their computers—and on computers anywhere in the network—in a far more object-oriented fashion. OFS is designed to have the entire network visible as one giant hard disk with as many virtual directories as needed. Microsoft is also laboring to provide an API set that enables programmers to write to OFS, and to create applications that can work across multiple directories and throughout an enterprise. Apparently, most of the guts of the system are being derived from the directory services technology in Microsoft's Exchange messaging server, a single core system that handles both Internet DNS (domain name services) and X.400/X.500 protocols. (Exchange's directory structure is already X.500 compliant, but it needs to be reworked to operate better as a system for exchanging DCOM/OLE objects.)

Another important feature, one that sharply distinguishes Windows 95 from the present versions of NT, will be the inclusion of Plug and Play support in Windows NT. As it stands, Windows NT does not support the Plug and Play standard, in which devices can be detected quickly and intelligently through hardware without having to forcefully probe for every possible device that might be installed. Plans are on the drawing board to include this feature in Cairo, which would make installing and configuring hardware far simpler. It would also make Windows NT far more useful on laptops, because the Plug and Play mechanisms written for Cairo would then be reverse-adopted and used in NT's PCMCIA subsystem. Right now the Plug and Play project is slowed by the need to have Plug and Play work without violating NT's internal security features.

Summary

Windows NT 4 is both a break from the past and a continuation of many existing traditions that exist in the NOS and desktop operating system worlds. NT takes inspirations from Unix, OS/2, and NetWare, and adds many of its own unique features to produce an operating system that grows more suited to a broad variety of powerful tasks with every successive revision.

The next chapter examines in depth the differences between Windows NT Workstation 4 and Windows NT Server 4—both of which are based on similar source code but are packaged, tuned, and refined for very different purposes.

CHAPTER 2

NT Workstation Versus NT Server

Windows NT is deployed in two different basic configurations—Windows NT Workstation and Windows NT Server. Windows 95 and Windows NT are designed to fulfill different kinds of computing needs, just as Workstation and Server are designed to fit into different places in the enterprise.

Workstation is designed to be the more commonly deployed version of Windows NT. Its feature set and included software reflect this purpose; it's neither coded nor performance-tuned to meet the demands of a server. It does a more than adequate job of small-scale serving from one desktop to another—sharing files and folders—but it's not designed or equipped with the proper support utilities to satisfy the demands of hundreds or thousands of users. Workstation is designed to be deployed on desktops, as a stable and powerful environment for a single user.

Server, on the other hand, is designed to satisfy the needs that hundreds of users will have—file- and resource-sharing, for the most part. Server is designed to host large volumes of data out to hundreds or thousands of users simultaneously, in environments that range from an office LAN to an enterprise-wide WAN.

This chapter explores the major differences between Workstation and Server. Before making a commitment to purchase one or the other, it is important to know what each one will afford the user and the system administrator. This chapter covers the features that exist in Server as opposed to Workstation, including packaged software.

New Features in Windows NT 4—Server Versus Workstation

Windows NT 4 stands in marked contrast to 3.51, both in its Workstation and Server implementations.

Windows 95 Interface

The first and most obvious change to Windows NT as a whole, in both Workstation and Server, is the addition of the Windows 95 user interface. The interface was available as a stand-alone patch for Windows NT 3.51, but it only added the raw look and feel without many of the underlying ways in which the operating system could exploit the new shell. Properties for system objects, for example, didn't work. The full release of Windows NT 4 made all the shell changes fully functional.

Another of the new software technologies which Microsoft developed first for Windows 95 came in the form of *wizards* (see fig. 2.1). Wizards are small programs that take the user step-by-step through a given task, describing each step of the task, providing options in plain English, and enabling the user to go back one or any number of steps and either fix mistakes or review settings. In Windows 95, for example, wizards were used to make adding new hardware easier, stepping the user through the process of deciding which type of hardware to install, the brand name and model of the hardware, and the hardware settings themselves.

In Windows NT Server 4, a number of wizards have been written and added to the operating system to make certain administrative tasks simpler and less daunting.

- **Add User Accounts wizard.** Manually creating a new user account for domains and networks can be a daunting process. The Add User Accounts wizard automates the process, enabling the systems administrator to easily and quickly specify the new user name, account permissions, password, account status, and so on.
- **Groups Management wizard.** As with individuals, so with user groups: The Group Management wizard enables you to quickly create new user groups or configure existing ones, enabling you to define permissions and rights for groups on-the-fly.

- **Managing File and Folder Access wizard.** This wizard simplifies the task of sharing out and controlling access to files and folders from a Windows NT Server machine to Macintosh, Microsoft, Novell, and other network clients. The wizard also enables you to control permissions and security for shared objects.
- **Network Client Administrator wizard.** This wizard enables the administrator of a server to install or update a network client workstation, either locally or remotely.
- **License wizard.** Windows NT Server includes a built-in software license tracker that makes it easy for an administrator to determine the status of any piece of software that's been installed across the network with a usage license. The License wizard makes the whole process of installing, maintaining, and evaluating software licensing even easier.
- **Add Printer wizard.** Another item imported directly from Windows 95, the Add Printer wizard takes you step-by-step through the process of adding and configuring either a newly installed printer or an existing one that hasn't been set up yet for use by Windows NT Workstation. The Add Printer wizard also installs printer drivers on the server that can be downloaded and installed by clients on Windows or Macintosh platforms, a feature unique to NT Server 4.
- **Add/Remove Programs wizard.** One of the most hotly demanded features in Windows 95, the capability to track and remove programs installed without leaving behind extraneous files or directories, now appears in Windows NT 4.

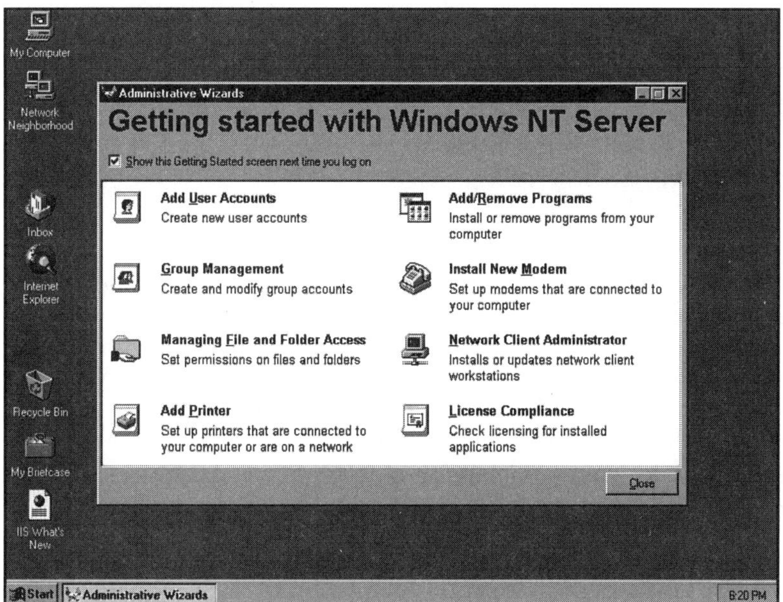

Figure 2.1

The administrative wizards in NT Server 4 enable you to easily jump to the programs that control the most important administrative functions for disks, for users, and so on.

Software Utilities

Wizards are not the only thing in Windows NT Server that have been included to make a difference. A number of software utilities that are not included with Windows NT Workstation are designed to help an administrator fine-tune, troubleshoot, maintain, and get maximum results out of any Windows NT Server installation.

- **Network Monitor.** The Network Monitor is a network-wide diagnostic tool that can examine network traffic to or from the server at the packet lever (see fig. 2.2). Network traffic can be captured, redirected to a file, and analyzed separately; the administrator can profile traffic on the network to produce statistics and performance reports on-the-fly.

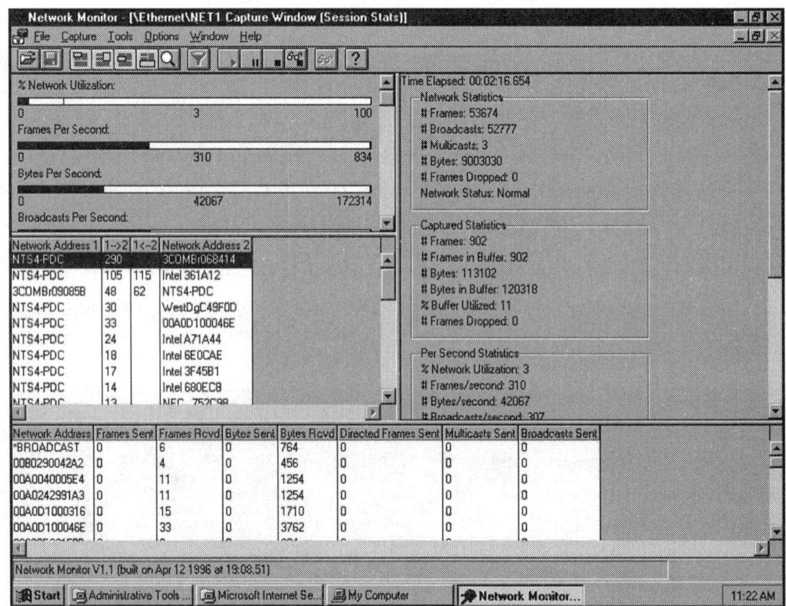

Figure 2.2

The Network Monitor in NT Server 4, rife with statistics, allows a knowledgeable network administrator to analyze network traffic, diagnose bottlenecks, and do generic troubleshooting of network problems.

- **System Policy Editor.** Because Windows NT Server is designed to work as a multiuser environment, it is important to have ways of governing the deployment and configuration of user's desktops and work environments. The System Policy Editor enables an administrator to configure what is and is not possible on network user's desktops, and to allow and disallow certain kinds of actions. The presence of the Control Panel icon in the Start button can be remotely governed through the System Policy Editor, for example, to prevent tampering at the console.

- **User Profiles.** Under Windows NT (both Workstation and Server), an individual user's user-definable settings—desktop colors, remote-drive connections, and so forth—are contained in a user profile. It is possible to have user profiles kept on a network server, enabling users to have a consistent work environment even if they log on at completely different physical terminals. The User Profile utility enables the administrator to examine and manage user profiles.

The Workstation/Server Kernel Controversy

One important difference that had been enforced by Microsoft in the original beta releases of Windows NT Server 4 and Workstation 4 was the number of inbound connections across the Internet that the operating system could support.

To reinforce the marketing roles that Microsoft had designed for Workstation and Server, Microsoft had included a provision in Windows NT Workstation that severely limited the number of simultaneous inbound TCP/IP connections to 15. On Windows NT Server, the limitations were not present. Many beta testers and users of the release-candidate editions of both Workstation and Server, however, complained vociferously about this limit.

Under this pressure, Microsoft removed the code limitations, but maintained that to use Workstation in a server-style implementation (that is, to use it to support more than 15 inbound Internet connections) was a violation of the Windows NT licensing agreement, and that Microsoft reserved the right to prosecute any violators. Many were and still are upset about the issue, contending that Microsoft does not have the right to charge several times as much for a server product which, in its inherent code design, is no different than its workstation product.

On the other hand, Microsoft makes it clear that Workstation and Server are not only tuned for different degrees of performance, but are deployed with different sets of utilities and network services. The price goes not only toward the licensing agreement but toward the additional software that enables a user to make that much more use of Windows NT Server.

Network Applications

Another area where difference in operation between Workstation and Server becomes important is the issue of network applications, such as Citrix WinFrame. In such setups, the Windows NT Server machine is used to remotely execute applications across the network. The remote terminal is used just for displaying output and fetching input for said programs; the actual executable runs on the server.

In the case of Citrix WinFrame, an entire Windows NT desktop, complete with remote logon that perfectly resembles the local version, is replicated from the Server out to almost any kind of client. The term *thin client* has been coined to describe this kind of behavior, where the terminal is used as little more than a graphical front end.

Citrix WinFrame comes as a kernel-customized installation of Windows NT Server. Similarly, other applications that run remotely require NT Server because of the way NT Server allocates memory and processes to network functions. On Workstation, a program like Citrix WinFrame would not run at the proper level of performance and might not even be compatible on a code level, no thanks to differences in the construction of the Workstation and Server network services. The kernel is not everything.

Managing Users

Windows NT Server requires that every person who uses the network on a regular basis shall have a user account in a domain (one of the NT machines) on the network. If you use the User Manager utility, in either Windows NT Workstation or Server, you can examine some of the contents of the user account: the user's logon name and real name, the user's password (which is kept invisible), various options that control how the passwords and logons are governed, and also which network connections are associated with the user's account.

Windows NT Workstation machines, and Windows NT Server machines that aren't themselves domain controllers, also keep databases of user accounts, security policies, and user groups that are discrete from the domain controller. This is done so that the built-in accounts that reside on these systems, such as the Administrator account, echo the rights to the built-in user groups on the domain level.

After a Windows NT system is configured, the built-in accounts grant the administrator a set of privileges, such as the ability to log on locally or stop and start services. The administrator figures out which users deserve to belong to the various groups—administrative, power-user, and so on, each with their own attendant levels of access and administrative rights—and can use the User Manager to assign users to these groups. If you are running NT Workstation, however, the way accounts are managed is different from the way NT Server accounts are managed.

With Windows NT Workstation, the administrator for that computer can only manage accounts on that individual machine, by using the User Manager program.

With Windows NT Server, the administrator manages accounts across the entire domain. Any server or workstation attached to that system that you have access to and control over can have its user database managed through NT Server, by using the User Manager for Domains program (a rewritten version of User Manager with some extra features for domain control).

User Manager for Domains can be run on NT Workstation or Windows 95, and can be installed on those systems by using client-based Administration Tools. The only reason it's not run by default on these operating systems is because it's not packaged with them, not because they are technically incapable of running it.

User Groups, Profiles, and the Policy Editor in NT Workstation and NT Server

In this section, you examine how NT Server deals with the problems of user and system permissions.

Windows NT manages users by enabling administrators to place them into user groups. A user can belong to more than one group at a time, which makes it possible to create extremely flexible and creative user management strategies.

You might, for example, want to enable different sets of users different degrees of access depending on whether they log on locally, use Dial-Up Networking, or log on from another machine on the LAN.

User groups define the permissions and rights that specific users can have, all of which are controlled through the User Manager program (in Windows NT Server, the User Manager for Domains program). The User Rights Policy window shows a list of rights and the user groups that they are assigned to. Full details on user rights and permissions can be found in Chapter 7, "Managing Users."

Domains and Trusts

In small networks, usually with less then 10 users, a peer-to-peer network will usually be sufficient. In such a case, Windows NT Workstation can run on all the systems in the network, and the network can be set up as a workgroup, much the same way that Windows 95 and the earlier Windows for Workgroups operated.

If more than 10 users are involved, however, it is better to switch over to a token ring or other centralized network system, in which a master server is running Windows NT Server, and the server uses a *domain* and *trust* system. This is also an almost indispensable model for working if you are using more than one group of networked computers in remote locations.

One of the most important concepts in Windows NT networking is the notion of *domains* and *trusts*. The whole way Windows NT Server administrates groups of computers is based around these concepts.

A *domain* is any collection of computers that feature a common policy of security and access control, and which share a user account database. Domains are designed to be centralized; the user accounts are kept in a central location, and the rights and privileges granted to those users is also administered centrally. Note that this model is not limited to a single server with a cluster of workstations attached to it—it can also mean a set of servers, with workstations, that cluster around a central *domain controller*. A domain controller is the master machine for the entire domain.

In this way, if a user has access to the domain through a user account in the domain, he can theoretically log on from any machine attached to the domain, as long as he has a local account on that machine that he can use. The local account gives him access to that machine, and the centrally controlled domain account gives him access to the rest of the domain.

No Windows NT computer can be used in a domain unless it is first *authenticated*. Authentication involves taking the computer's unique system ID number, generated when Windows NT is first installed on the machine, and entering it into the master domain controller's database.

Creating and Using Domains with NT Server and NT Workstation

Windows NT Server is the one indispensable element in creating a Windows NT domain. To start creating a domain, the administrator needs to install NT Server on a machine and designate the machine during installation as either a primary or backup domain controller.

A primary domain controller works as the main hub around which the domain is organized. A backup domain controller works as a standby, in case the main domain controller fails; copies of the system and user databases are maintained continuously on both machines.

If the primary domain controller fails for whatever reason, the backup domain controller takes over its functions. In effect, the two trade places; the primary becomes a backup and vice versa, a process known as *promotion*. This can also be done manually by an administrator using the Server Manager tool.

You can also promote a backup domain controller to become a primary through the Server Manager. This automatically makes the current primary into a backup, of course. You cannot, however, explicitly demote a primary controller to a backup controller; you can only do this indirectly.

A server in an NT domain must be a Windows NT Server computer, but the client to an NT domain can be any of a number of machines:

- **A Windows NT Workstation.** Only workstations in the domain that have been trusted to be part of the domain can be allowed, and a local account for a domain user must be set up on a given workstation for that user to be able to log on.
- **A Windows 95 machine.** The same local logon rules (previously explained) apply, although unless configured correctly, it is entirely possible for someone to use a Windows 95 machine (outside the network) without logging on.
- **A Windows 3.1 or Windows 3.11/Windows for Workgroups machine.** The same rules about domain trust apply, but individual user accounts on given workstations don't apply for Windows 3.x machines.
- **OS/2 workstations, MS-DOS workstations.** All of these machines, provided they have the proper client access software, can access a Windows NT domain.

Trust Relationships

You can't access a domain unless you are a valid user in that domain or unless you have been given a trust relationship of some kind.

A trust relationship is an adjunct to being a member of a domain. It is possible for any given Windows NT computer to be part of only one domain at a time; you can't have one computer be part of more than one domain. If you need to access resources only available on a computer in another domain, however, you can establish a trust relationship to gain access to those resources.

A trust relationship exists between the domain granting the trust and the domain being trusted. The trusting domain will allow access from all users in the domain being trusted, as long as access for such uses has been explicitly given in the trusting domain. In other words, a trust relationship is not the same thing as valid user access. Trust has to be accompanied by the creation of a user account in the trusting domain. Also, if necessary, the trusting domain has to grant access to specific resources such as files or peripherals. Because of this arrangement, a user working in a trusted domain might be able to access a totally different degree or kind of resource than he could in his home domain.

To make assigning privileges in trusted domains a little simpler, Windows NT enables you to have local groups in a trusting domain (such as the Administrators group) contain user accounts from the domain accounts in a trusted domain. This way, local groups in a trusting domain can be used to set access to a resource for trusted users.

Trusts make certain administrative tasks simpler. If you have a number of domains, each with their own security and accounts database, each of them have to be managed separately for specific resources. By allocating resources within domains and then assigning trusts appropriately, it becomes much easier to have the domain controllers be governors of given resources. This way, one user account can be used to access resources throughout several domains. You can also get access to a resource without having to have an explicit user account on the machine that controls the resource.

Another way trusts make administration simpler is that they enable the remote administration of multiple domains—a very useful tool if you have a network that consists of several domains that need to be administered regularly. A one-to-many relationship of trust can be established between the administrator's domain and the other domains that need to be worked on, enabling one user to govern several domains simultaneously.

Trusts can only be enforced between NT domains and not between heterogenous machines. You can't enforce trust between an NT domain and a NetWare domain.

NT Workstation does not let you create these kinds of complex relationships between machines. If you have a network consisting of NT Workstations, the only kinds of relationships that can be created are simple, workgroup-type arrangements in which certain folders can be shared out to given users. Actively replicating directories or pass-through permissions filtering is not possible with a network of NT Workstation-only machines.

Types of Trust

Trust relationships come in two basic varieties:

- **One-way.** A one-way trust can also be called a one-to-many trust. In this model, one domain trusts another, but not vice versa. Those with user accounts in the trusted domain can access trusting resources, but no reverse access is possible.
- **Two-way.** Two-way trusts have each domain acting as a trusting and a truster. Users in each domain can access the resources in the other. Note of course that this is the ideal way a two-way trust would work, and that it would be limited by whatever specific access permissions are granted in each domain to the other.

Trusts are not inherited. If you have a domain named WORK trusting a domain named PLAY, and PLAY trusting a third domain named SLEEP, SLEEP does not inherently trust WORK. The reverse is also true; WORK would not inherently trust SLEEP either. You must explicitly enable all trusts.

When you organize trusts, make certain that you know where everything is going to be located. If you are going to have a centralized domain with resources and users logging on from many other domains to access them, you need a different trust model than if you have all users in one domain and resources in many others.

Finally, if you've got a network setup that does not have the kind of complexity to merit setting up trust relationships, you might want to stick with the peer-to-peer networking that NT Workstation provides.

Pass-Through Validation in Trust Relationships

If you have a trust relationship established, and a trusting server does not have user account information for someone trying to log on locally to a trusted server, the trusting server passes the logon request to the trusted server for validation. This enables the user to use the intermediate domain as a bridge to the domain where they do have logon access. In this model, a user would not be getting access to the intermediate domain, but rather to the domain where he has his user account.

Pass-through validation only works in the following circumstances:

- The user is trying to log on to a domain that is not local.
- The domain in question is a trusted one.
- The computer where the physical logon is taking place is trusting the domain in question.

Pass-through validations are not inherited, either. You can't have pass-through validations work between domains that don't have explicit trusts enforced.

Again, keep in mind that Windows NT Workstation cannot support these kinds of transactions in a peer-to-peer network; only a Server-supported network will be able to do so.

Some Models for Domains

In smaller networks, where there may be only one or two domains, establishing trusts between domains usually is not a difficult task because the relationships between domains are often easy to determine. In larger, more complicated organizations, the issue is not as cut-and-dry, and several possible ways to organize domains and trusts may exist, each with its own inherent advantages and disadvantages. Microsoft has mapped out these scenarios in detail.

- **Single domain.** With this method, there is only one domain. This setup works best when there are few users or physical machines in the entire domain, and the user accounts and physical resources can all be managed from one server without problems. This particular setup is easy to create, maintain, and administer, because there is only one server. The downside is that if the model changes—that is, if there is an explosion in the number of resources or users—the system can slow down drastically. This model should really only be settled on if it's extremely unlikely that there will be any growth or change in the domain.

- **Master domain.** In this model, one domain works as the master for the rest of the network of domains, with each domain trusting the main domain for use of resources (such as the central accounts database). The subdomains don't have trust enforced between themselves. This sort of model is good when the resources are clustered into a single area and the users are spread out fairly wide. It is also a good model when there is a need for a certain amount of autonomy amongst each domain, with each domain having its own administrators that handle accounts and whatever resources may exist for that particular domain. The downside of this model is that it requires that the network connections to the master domain and the master domain itself be high speed and of quality—otherwise, there will be a significant degradation of performance as more and more users get added on. Also, it forces each local administrator to take responsibility for defining and keeping tight control over his group memberships.
- **Multiple master domain.** In this model, more than one master domain handles the workload that would previously have been concentrated in one master domain. As with the preceding example, each trusting domain establishes trust but not just with one master domain. This way resources and user account controls can be distributed more evenly among master domains, and the master domains themselves can be trusted to each other for additional flexibility. This model is excellent in an environment where a great deal of growth and change is foreseen, because it is very scalable and very easy to add additional master and trust domains as time goes by. Also, it works in organizations where multiple divisions need to be master-managed by more than one authority. The drawbacks are that network traffic in this model is drastically increased and will put a severe load on just about any network hub. Also, there is a marked decrease in the amount of centrality with more than one master domain, and the establishment of trust relationships can get very complicated if not managed by one central trust authority.
- **Complete trust.** This model is the most taxing on the network and also the most complicated to administer. In it, a two-way trust relationship runs from and to all master domains; every domain is both an accounts domain and a resource domain. The trusting domains are trusted to every single master domain. This model is best suited for an organization where it's not possible to support centralized administration—where there is a great degree of autonomy in departments or MIS strategies. It also works best in situations where there is a great degree of inherent security because the establishment of so many trust

relationships can easily give rise to abuse of privileges. This model is also very scalable because it can support a theoretically unlimited number of domains and users. The biggest downsides are the lack of central management authority inherent in this scheme, the difficulty in managing the trust relationships (which can grow to become extremely unwieldy in very large organizations), and the strain placed on the network by this scheme. The final caveat is that this model can wind up being the de facto model for *any* domain setup if the administrators are careless about the way they handle trusts or if they don't plan ahead, which can degenerate into a spaghetti-trust mess, in which no one is certain who should or does trust another.

Many of the problems that arise from trusts can be resolved through what Microsoft is planning to introduce with its own particular version of the Distributed Computing Environment (DCE). DCE implementation is planned to be part of the Cairo upgrades.

Domains Versus Workgroups

Earlier in the chapter, workgroups were mentioned, as well as how they could be useful in small-network (less then 10 nodes) setups, consisting of Windows NT Workstation machines.

A *workgroup* is not the same as a domain. Workgroups are less formal and structured and also are less easy to control security within.

Workgroups also do not have automatic synchronization of password or user account properties.

The difference between workgroups and domains is mostly a matter of cost and whether you have the resources to devote to a centralized scheme. If you are just looking for an informal way to get a set of computers that do not require exceptionally high security to communicate with each other, a workgroup is a good solution. If you are looking to enforce security between computers that, for instance, are not in the same physical location, the domain model makes more sense.

Remote Workstation Management: Editing the Registry Remotely

One of the more powerful functions that can be accomplished across a network, provided that the permissions have been set to allow it, is the remote editing of another computer's Registry.

In the Registry Editor, click on the Registry selection from the main program menu, and then select Connect Network Registry.

A dialog box appears that prompts you for the network name of the computer whose Registry you want to edit. If you know the name of the computer whose Registry you want to work with, type it in (using the \\computername naming convention), and click on OK.

If you don't know the name of the system you want to edit, click on Browse. A hierarchical list of computers in the network appears. Scroll down through the display until you find the computer you want, and then click on OK.

If you have permission to edit the Registry on that computer, the other computer's Registry opens up as though it were being examined locally.

Make certain that you understand thoroughly the implications of editing the Registry before attempting to do this. Editing the wrong Registry settings can damage your Windows NT installation.

Also, different network settings are stored for Workstation and Server. In Server, many of the settings pertain to networking options that are not supported in Workstation, such as protocol routing. Be aware that implementing or editing these settings in Workstation will have at best no effect, or a detrimental one at worst.

Users should be allowed to access the computer from the network if they are to be allowed remote Registry editing privileges.

Server Alerts

Every so often, conditions may arise on a server that require the attached users to be notified. These conditions could be one of a range of items:

- Storage space is low on the server.
- An access violation occurred.
- An application error on the server occurred.
- A server shutdown is imminent due to power loss or administrative control.
- A printer attached to the server is experiencing trouble.

Note that in this context, the word "server" does not necessarily refer to a machine exclusively running Windows NT Server. It can also refer to a Windows NT Workstation machine with shared resources, such as directories or printers.

Administrative alerts, by default, are not sent out to every computer on the network. The server has to be configured to send out administrative alerts to specific machines.

Configuring Administrative Alerts

For administrative alerts to be functional from a server and properly received on a workstation, two services need to be activated and configured:

- **The Alerter Service.** The Alerter Service is the service that does the actual broadcasting of administrative alerts. To enable the Alerter Service, go into the Services window (available from the Services icon in the Control Panel), scroll through the Services list, and highlight the Alerter service. If the Alerter is listed as Disabled, click on the Startup button and select Automatic or Manual in the Startup Type section. Automatic is useful if you know the Alerter service is going to be in constant use, and Manual ensures that the service is loaded when it is needed. Click on OK to back out of the Service Startup window, and then click on Close to close the main Services window.

- **The Messenger Service.** The Messenger Service is the service that receives and acknowledges administrative alerts on both workstations and servers. To enable the Messenger Service, go into the Services window (available from the Services icon in the Control Panel), scroll through the Services list, and highlight the Messenger service. If the Messenger service is listed as Disabled, click on the Startup button and select Automatic in the Startup Type section. Selecting Manual for the Messenger service may not enable you to receive alerts properly. Click on OK to back out of the Service Startup window, and then click on Close to close the main Services window.

Note that sending alerts from any computer requires that both Alerter and Messenger be running, or at the very least enabled. Receiving administrative alerts requires only that the Messenger service be running.

Adding Computers to the Alerts List

A computer running the Alerter service needs to have a list of machines to send alerts to. To administer this list, click on the Server icon from the Control Panel, and click on the Alerts button in the Server window.

Type the name of a computer you want to send administrative alerts to in the New Computer or Username text box, and then press Enter or click on OK. The name will be added to the Send Administrative Alerts To list on the right.

To remove a name from the list, highlight it and click on the Remove button.

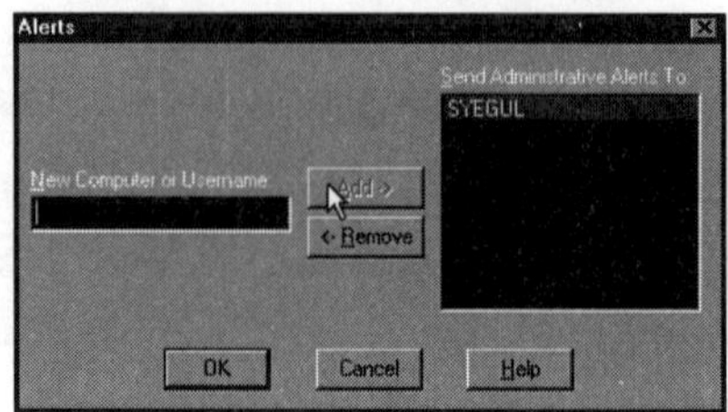

Figure 2.3

Controlling the Alerter service: To add names to the list, type the name of the computer in the New Computer or Username box and click on OK.

Note that no automatic validation of computer names is performed. This is important in the event that you want to add computer names that might not be visible at certain times. If a certain computer is switched off or not logged on, for instance, you cannot send an alert to that computer's name.

Directory Replication

Another powerful and useful feature that distinguishes Windows NT Server from Windows NT Workstation is directory replication. Directory replication involves directories on a server being exported to given workstations whenever changes are made to those directories on the server.

The Mechanics of Directory Replication

Directory replication can be of great value in many scenarios. In environments where much shared work takes place, automatic updates to files maintained centrally can be accomplished through directory replication without having to force users on workstations to take the time to manually update files.

Windows NT Server machines can function as both servers and recipients for replicated directories; Windows NT Workstation machines, however, can act only as recipients for exported directories.

By default, a Windows NT Workstation receives whichever replicated directories are being exported to it from its domain server, if it's attached to one.

Configuring Directory Replication on Workstations

To configure directory replication on a Windows NT Workstation, open the Control Panel and double-click on the Server icon. The Server window appears. Click on the Replication button. The Directory Replication window opens.

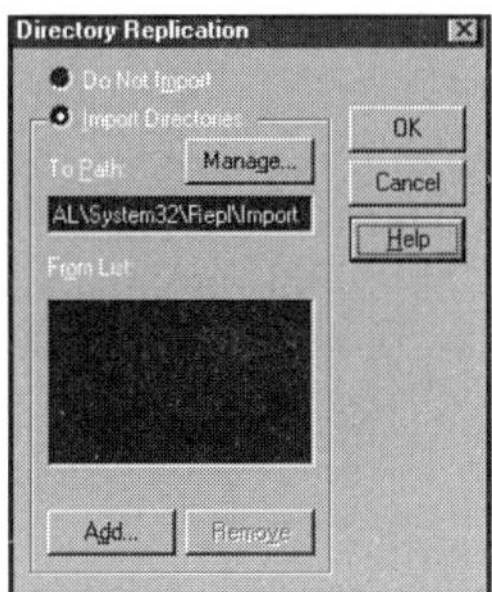

Figure 2.4

The Directory Replication control is kept as simple as possible in NT Workstation.

To completely disable directory replication on the current workstation, select the Do Not Import radio button. This prevents any and all directories from being exported to your workstation.

To configure the way directories are being replicated, select the Import Directories radio button.

Imported directories and files are replicated to the directory specified in the To Path dialog box. To change the name of the directory, click on an area within the text box and then type the name of a valid directory.

By clicking on the Manage button, you can bring up the Manage Imported Directories window, which enables you to edit specific properties of imported directories.

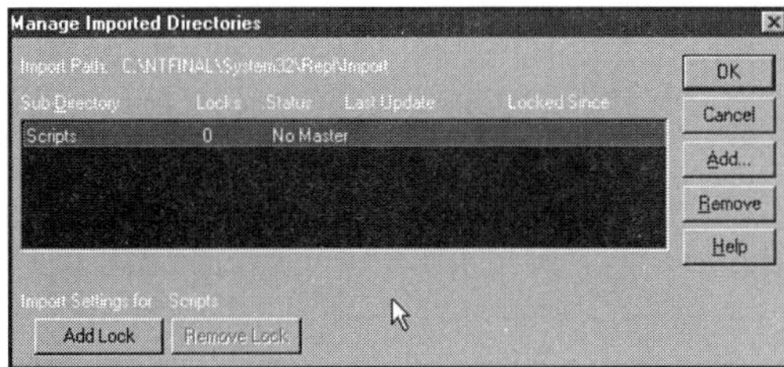

Figure 2.5

The Manage Imported Directories window gives more details about imported directories.

Each subdirectory being imported to the workstation is listed in the Sub-Directory window. The Last Update column in the list indicates the last time and date that this subdirectory received changes from the server.

To add a subdirectory, click on Add and type the name of the subdirectory to add to the list. You cannot add the names of directories not being actively exported from the server.

To remove a subdirectory from the list, highlight its name in the list by clicking on it, and then click on Remove.

The Add Lock/Remove Lock buttons add and remove locks, or prohibitions to import, to the highlighted directory. This can be useful if more than one user is trying to restrict access to a given directory. A directory can only receive imports if no locks are currently placed on it.

Summary

Windows NT Workstation and Windows NT Server are built to satisfy entirely different needs in a Windows NT environment. The Server product has a great many differences, most of them in the realm of added functionality, and exploring them in depth would take a book all its own. It is important to know the differences between the two, however, because they are not designed to perform the same jobs. NT Server does not function well as a desktop operating system, and Workstation is not an ideal server, for technical as well as licensing reasons. An administrator trying to devise a good network strategy that includes Windows NT should know the differences when they deploy Windows NT in a network environment.

NT Workstation is designed as a desktop operating system. Its memory consumption, network stacks, and tasking performance are optimized for that job. NT Server is designed to serve files, route network packets, and run applications remotely. The network stack uses more live RAM in NT Server than it does in Workstation, and while its performance is tunable, it is still designed to work under heavy loads, hence the heavier memory usage than in NT Workstation. NT Server is also better designed to handle web- and mail-serving tasks. Finally, many products are specifically engineered to *only* run on Windows NT Server and will not operate on Windows NT Workstation. Many HTTP servers, for instance, follow this operational model.

After a user comes to an understanding of Windows NT Workstation, however, he or she is equipped with the best beginning knowledge possible to also undertake learning about Windows NT Server, because there are plenty of similarities between the two products.

CHAPTER 3

NT Workstation Hardware Considerations

It is no secret that a key element to Windows NT lies in the computer-related hardware in a system. This hardware includes the motherboard, keyboard, video card, serial and parallel ports, storage devices, and the mouse, modem, and other input devices. It seems reasonable to ask why the hardware is so important to NT. This is a perfectly valid question and one that truly needs a realistic reply.

Windows NT (all versions) isolates users from the hardware. This isolation occurs via specific drivers for specific hardware compartments. All the drivers from Microsoft are written to exacting specifications. IDE CD-ROMs and hard drives (including EIDE), for example, are written to the ATAPI 1.2 specification. Please note that the driver is written to the specification, not the device. If the device that you have is not 1.2 compliant, it probably will not work in NT 4. Surprisingly, the same device that worked in NT 3.51 might not work in NT 4.

This chapter examines the major pieces of hardware and includes a look at what is coming and what is showing up now. In many places, the discussions might appear to be NT-non specific. In many instances, that is the case because NT uses industry standards for drivers.

Specifically, this chapter examines the following:

- Motherboard and its bus
- Hard drives and controllers
- Fault tolerance and RAID
- Scanners
- Notebook support
- High-speed ports
- Specialized input devices, such as tablets
- Video cards and monitors
- Pointing devices
- Hardware profiles

Introducing the Major Hardware Components

When you purchase a system to run Windows NT, numerous decisions have to made about the components of the system. What is important and why? Clearly the two most important parts of any system are the motherboard and hard drives. In fact, the major hardware components category includes the bus/CPU, hard drives, and tape devices. All these are critical to the performance of Windows NT. For this reason, a detailed discussion is given here of these crucial aspects of a computer system. The first topic dealt with is motherboards, their design, and the reasons for selecting one type over another.

Selecting a Bus Type

What is a bus? The *bus* is the communication standard used by the motherboard. It enables devices to be connected to the motherboard. This definition can be carried further to include the specifications for boards or controllers that attach to the motherboard. After examining the structure and design of the bus in detail, you reach the obvious conclusion that some things were done for design and others for complex pragmatic reasons that no longer make sense.

Certain aspects of the bus have great bearing on the performance of Windows NT. In particular, this chapter examines data handling, Direct Memory Access, arbitration, and dual-bus designs. Before dealing with the specific bus designs, a few points about Windows NT seem germane:

- Windows NT is a full 32-bit operating system. This means that the data path of the processor is a double 16-bit word. Ideally, the data path from the processor should be the same size as the data path on the bus. Why break the double word to a single word to pass the data? In such a case, the bus is a major bottleneck.
- Windows NT is a preemptive fully re-entrant operating system (OS). This means that there has to be a smooth transition between threads; otherwise, performance suffers.
- The bus and the expansion cards need to maintain reasonable arbitration; that is, the bus must be able to pass work to cards and thus release the CPU from unnecessary work.

In the discussion of the influence of the bus, two designs are left out—the XT and Micro Channel Architecture (MCA). The first is obsolete and does not run on Windows, let alone Windows NT. The second, although technically quite substantial, has been abandoned for all practical purposes. (IBM still sells MCA-based machines, but they are rapidly being replaced with PCI designs.)

With the emergence of the Pentium and Pentium Pro processors, communication on the bus is no longer limited to a 4-bit address to memory. This latter change is major and, even though not discussed very much anywhere, it has a significant impact on performance issues with Windows NT.

Almost all systems today come with various portions of buses sandwiched together. It is not uncommon to find systems that are combined PCI/ISA or PCI/EISA. In general, high-end servers are the latter while most workstations are the former. Seldom, however, is an explanation given of each design's advantages or disadvantages over any other design. The following sections deal with ISA, EISA, and PCI. Mention will also be given to the VL-Bus, but this bus has been somewhat superseded by the emergence of the Pentium processor.

Industry Standard Architecture (ISA)

After developing the 286 CPU, it became obvious to IBM that XT bus was obsolete. The 286 was a 16-bit CPU; the XT was an 8-bit CPU. You can imagine the issues flying around about backward compatibility and related topics. A compromise bus was designed that would accept both the old expansion cards as well as the new. Thus, the AT bus and its clone, the ISA bus, were born. For reasons of simplicity, the ISA bus will be discussed because it is really the one still in existence today.

The basic changes that occurred with the AT bus were:

- An increase of four address lines, making a total of 24. This increase enables 16 MB of motherboard RAM (2^{24}).
- Eight more data lines, making a 16-bit data path. This enables the system to function in standard 16-bit words.
- Four additional DMA channels, bringing the total to seven.
- Eight more IRQs (8–15), but only five are really available in many machines.

ISA was designed for the AT specification of the 286. It uses a bus synchronized to a 8.33 MHz clock signal. At zero wait state, two bus clock cycles are required to move data. Furthermore, because the architecture is 16 bits wide, the maximum transferred at any one time is two bytes. At best, the ISA bus is capable of only four million transfers per second. More importantly, the ISA bus has 24 address lines to memory. This means that the maximum memory that can be addressed directly (DMA) is 2^{24} or 16 MB.

Several bus changes transpired as a result of the development of the AT. First of all, IBM realized the problems with the XT bus and literally doubled the IRQs and DMA channels available on the AT; yet great dissatisfaction with the bus remained. In early 1987, Compaq introduced the dual bus; namely a bus with an 8.25 MHz to the expansion cards, but 16 MHz from CPU to memory. IBM also realized the deficiency of the AT bus and tried to replace it with Micro Channel Architecture (MCA), which is far superior to the ISA and EISA bus. Because of IBM's very high licensing fees, no one was willing to pay the price. For all practical reasons, therefore, the MCA bus has disappeared.

Although the originator of the ISA bus and one of the forthcoming PC powerhouses (Compaq) saw deficiencies in the ISA bus, it rapidly gained extreme popularity. Even with CPUs soon reaching 50 MHz, manufacturers stuck with the ISA bus. As a consequence, vendors kept making ISA expansion cards, and a vicious cycle started that still has yet to abate. The interesting attitude now prevalent is that ISA is fast enough for most cards. In the best situation, the ISA bus is far from optimal for Windows NT systems.

EISA (Extended Industry Standard Architecture)

Unlike ISA (with which it is backward-compatible), the EISA bus is a true 32-bit bus and can support DMA requests up to 4 GB. The so-called Gang of Nine (AST, Compaq, Epson, Hewlett-Packard, NEC, Olivetti, Tandy, Wyse, and Zenith) also realized that the ISA bus could not keep up with the newer CPUs, so they brought forth an add-on to the ISA bus that enabled it to be a full 32-bit CPU. Several features of backward compatibility have kept the EISA bus as non-optimal. EISA also uses the

8.33 bus clock, for example. At its best, it completes a data move in one cycle; because the data path is 32 bits, 4 bytes can be moved simultaneously. This translates to a maximum transfer of 33 MB per second in 32 bit DMA transfer mode (so-called EISA burst rate of 8.33Mhz bus on 32-bit data path). This speed is unfortunately the EISA burst rate. As long as the dominant CPU was in the x86 family (by name), the ISA and EISA buses were deemed adequate by many users and developers. After the Pentium's introduction, the ISA bus seriously compromised the performance of the system.

EISA and its big brother MCA did bring forth some great improvements. First of all, the number of lines that enabled direct access to memory was increased to 32. This means that a bus master card can access 4 GB of memory directly (2^{32}). Even more important, the bus address (data path) was increased to 32-bit. Data could travel twice as fast as on the ISA. In truth, the old EISA and MCA systems were remarkable for their stability and smoothness of use. Perhaps the area that EISA was really tweaked was DMA transfer rates. It is here that considerable work was done to extend the EISA specification.

A 32-bit burst DMA was added. In this case, the C mode compresses all the signal characteristics into a single bus cycle. The signal transitions occur at the leading and trailing edges of the clock. This is a surprisingly sophisticated design, but very few motherboards seem to support it adequately.

Another very ingenious feature was the design that enabled IRQs (EISA ones called level) to be shared. No matter what reference you seem to find, they all dogmatically state that IRQs cannot be shared. EISA IRQs, however, can be shared. If you only have IRQ 12 available (no PS2 mouse), you can in theory put a NIC and two SCSI cards on IRQ 12. It does work.

Significant effort was also taken to ensure arbitration worked well. Much of this design was taken directly from MCA. In all cases, after the microprocessor/bus master is selected, one or the other gains control and keeps control for a cycle. Whichever one that went unchosen during the prior cycle is now chosen. This design purposely refreshes memory every cycle. DMA is the next highest priority with the microprocessor/bus master last on the list.

VL (Video Electronic Standards Association Local Bus)

This bus was designed for the 486. It has a maximum burst rate of 133 MB per second and a sustained rate of 66 MB per second. It does not have the memory limitation of the ISA bus, is faster than the EISA bus, but has very poor arbitration characteristics. Thus, a single active device can totally hog the bus. By far, however, the worst aspect of the VL design is that it is tied to the 386/486 bus architecture. Because the processor of choice for Windows NT on the Intel platform is the Pentium or Pentium Pro processor, PCI is rapidly replacing the VL bus.

PCI (Peripheral Component Interconnect)

PCI was designed by Intel to provide support for the expanding Pentium and Pentium Pro markets. Several features set PCI above the rest:

- All transfers are burst transfers, and the length of the burst is negotiated on a device-by-device basis.
- The design is bus-related, not CPU-related.
- The maximum transfer rate is 132 MB per second on the 33 MHz bus, and 528 on the 66 MHz bus.
- Most current peripheral cards, such as video adapters, are designed for the PCI bus. This makes PCI the bus of choice today. To maximize system performance, you need the key elements to be PCI.
- Electrical signals of 5 volts originally, but 3.3 in later designs.
- Designs for notebook PCI bus (SPCI or small PCI).

Of significance to this discussion are several very important factors. First of all, there is a *bridge* or special chipset between the bus and the CPU. This bridge can buffer transfers and implement special handshaking protocols depending on the type of CPU. PCI, for example, can be implemented for RISC or Intel CPUs.

Although currently not a factor, the PCI bus can be a 64-bit bus in its latest specification. This enables PCI to grow into 64-bit operating systems. Likewise, the PCI bus is faster than ISA and EISA and runs at 33 MHz. The latest specification enables 66 MHz speeds, but many industry specialists insist that this high speed is a very serious problem and might not come into fruition soon. (As will soon be apparent, the PCI bus is not fast enough for the new drives that will soon show up.)

As previously stated, the theoretical transfer rate of the PCI bus is 132 MB/sec. Unfortunately, reality does not support the theory. The Intel chipsets that support PCI cannot attain such transfer rates. The neptune chipset will support 40 MB/sec. The triton and orion are better, but are still in the 70–100 MB per second range.

Given the fact that the PCI bus is the bus of choice, you must now decide on a CPU. The choice is far clearer in this regard than it was a year ago. For servers and very high-end workstations, there is a choice between Pentium Pros and Alphas. For workstations, the choice is between Alpha, Pentium and Pentium Pro, or the Power PC. It is safe to say that the bulk of Alphas are in servers, but there clearly are Alpha workstations. The Power PC is being touted by Motorola as a challenge to the Pentium systems. For now, the logical choice for a system is either the Pentium or Pentium Pro unless specific reasons encourage the RISC platforms (the use of floating point intensive processing, for example). For this reason, the current discussion focuses on the Pentium and Pentium Pro processors.

Selecting a CPU: Pentium Versus Pentium Pro

The Pentium processor was an impressive jump from the 386/486. For starters, the Pentium set an impressive performance standard with its pipelined, superscalar (capability to execute two instructions in one clock cycle) microarchitecture. The Pentium processor's pipelined implementation uses five stages to extract high throughput.

For the Pentium Pro, new processing algorithms remove the constraint of linear instruction sequencing between the traditional *fetch* and *execute* phases and enables the use of an instruction pool in an instruction window. This approach enables the execute phase of the Pentium Pro processor to have better scheduling in the running of a program. The optimized scheduling, for example, uses a decoupled dispatch/ execute phase and retire phase. Instructions can be started in any order, but are always be completed in the original program order.

Intel developed the Pentium to be easily designed to support one or two processors. The Pentium Pro, on the other hand, is easily scalable to up to four microprocessors in a multiprocessor system. The Pentium Pro processor uses a process that is the next step beyond superscalar architecture—namely, Dynamic Execution. This advance enables the advanced 3D visualization and interactive capabilities used in Windows NT. Dynamic Execution technology can be summarized as optimally adjusting instruction execution by predicting program flow, analyzing the program's dataflow graph to choose the best order to execute the instructions, and then having the capability to speculatively execute instructions in the preferred order. In other words, the Pentium Pro processor dynamically adjusts its work, as defined by the incoming instruction stream, to minimize overall execution time. The Pentium Pro processor also has advanced data integrity, reliability, and serviceability features. In short, the Pentium Pro is clearly designed for optimized use in Windows NT.

The following list identifies the key features of the Pentium Pro:

- Binary compatible with applications running on previous members of the Intel microprocessor family
- Optimized for 32-bit applications running on advanced 32-bit operating systems
- Dynamic Execution microarchitecture
- Scalable up to four processors and 4 GB memory
- Separate dedicated external system bus and dedicated internal full-speed cache bus
- 8K/8K separate data and instruction, non-blocking, level one cache

- Available with integrated 256 KB or 512 KB, non-blocking, level two cache on the processor
- Data integrity and reliability features include Error Checking and Correcting (ECC), Fault Analysis/Recovery, and Functional Redundancy Checking

Windows NT runs well on both the Pentium and Pentium Pro. The additional cost of the Pentium Pro is well worth the money on any serious workstation or server. In the case of photo editing and other intensive situations, the availability of well-threaded applications make dual processor systems a very viable option. If you are serious about using a system that runs NT, get a Pentium Pro.

Bus Setup Issues with Windows NT

Nothing specifically has to be set up in Windows NT to handle any of the buses or processors discussed. Certain features of system BIOS, however, need comment. With the Plug and Play hardware being used in Windows 95, most motherboard manufacturers use BIOS that supports Plug and Play. This is not always advantageous with NT; in fact, it can cause setup problems. The BIOS that causes the most trouble is Phoenix because it cannot be modified on an IRQ by IRQ basis. If you do use an ISA card that requires a specific IRQ, however, set the IRQ on the card, insert it into the bus, and boot into the BIOS setup. Have the system reset itself, and rescan the bus. The legacy IRQ should be reserved for that card and not for the PCI cards. With both AMI and Award, you can usually reserve specific IRQs for specific slots or just reserve an IRQ for ISA.

If you are using a system that has an EISA bus, you must run the EISA Configuration Utility (ECU). Any device on an EISA card that has not been configured will not be seen or usable. This is also true of memory setups. Note that no ECU will run in NT. You must have a DOS bootable floppy that you can use to gain access to the system, and then run the ECU. Many users seem to ignore this critical step.

For the faster Pentium and Pentium Pro systems, it is essential to use 60 ns SIMMs (or faster). In fact, on the Pentium Pro systems you need to use matched SIMMs. Do not mix 32 MB SIMMs with 16 MB SIMMs. Furthermore, do not mix memory types (regular with EDO). The speed of the systems requires specific attention to memory.

An Introduction to Drives and Terminology

Drives have gotten smaller in size, faster in transfer rate, and bigger in capacity. These changes have happened in a very limited time span. Drives have gone in a few years from full-height GB sizes to very small 3 1/2-inch, 4 GB drives. Standard copper cable will soon be replaced with fiber-optic connectors, and the bus as known today will soon disappear because PCI cannot keep up with the transfer rates of the new drives.

Storage devices are not well appreciated. They include, but are not limited to, the following:

- Hard drives
- Magneto-optical (MO) drives
- Tape drives
- CD-ROMs and drives that use jukebox libraries

Devices with jukebox libraries are usually MO drives or tape drives. Recently, RAID (Redundant Array of Independent Disks, or sometimes translated as Redundant Array of Inexpensive Disks) has become very popular.

A *hard drive* is just permanent storage for data; that is, after the computer is turned off, the files are still present. The drive itself consists of a platter or multiple platters that spin at various speeds. A read/write head travels across distinct concentric circles from the center to the periphery of the platter (which is rigid and accounts for the name hard drive). Information is conveyed by an electrical current sent to the read/write head. This current magnetizes particles on the platter tracts. During a read phase, the head passes over the magnetic fields, resulting in inductive currents in the head coils. Such currents are the actual binary stored bits of data. After the computer is turned off, the magnetic changes to the drive are maintained. A hard drive is dependent on several basic components:

- The rotation speed that controls the read/write speed of the device (a 7200 rpm drive, for example, will always be faster than a 5400 rpm drive).
- The electrical components dictate the type of drive.
- The number of platters dictate the size of the drive.

All the above relate to developments in many fields. To give you a comparison of some devices, a standard floppy drive rotates at 360 rpm. Fast Small Computer System Interface (SCSI) drives rotate at 7200 rpm (based on rotational speed only, this is 20 times faster than a floppy drive) and will probably soon get faster. Although the hard drive was first developed in 1973 by IBM, it was not until the development of the XT in 1983 that hard drives started becoming popular. In the 13 years, development has really skyrocketed.

Exploring Mass Storage Interfaces (a.k.a. Drives)

Only two drive types should be considered today—IDE/EIDE (Intelligent Drive Electronics or Enhanced IDE) and SCSI (Small Computer System Interface). Numerous discussions of SCSI versus IDE have always broken down into near-religious types of discussions. Many claim that SCSI gives better performance in preemptive multiprocessing while others point out that IDE is faster on a single task. In fact, Windows NT works very well with both drive forms.

IDE/EIDE Drives

With the great acceptance of EIDE drives in the past year, prices have fallen. In fact, all prices for EIDE components have fallen drastically in the last few years. This EIDE competition has enabled a large portion of the price drop seen recently even in SCSI pricing.

As implemented originally, the IDE drive was controlled by a PIO card (programmed I/O); that is, the CPU handles all data transfers. No handshaking or synchronization at all occurs in such transfers. Data is transferred in 512-byte sectors, and nothing can use the CPU until the transfer completes. In a multitasking design such as Windows NT, this design is far from optimal. Other limiting issues exist with IDE:

- Two devices are all that can be used.
- All drive activity is CPU dependent.

Systems were equipped with the original WD1003 controller that is controlled by the INT13 BIOS call. INT13 has a limitation of 1024 cylinders, 16 heads (although supposedly 255 of the task file registers are limited to 16), and 63 sectors. This yields a 528 MB hard drive. EIDE drives greater than 4 GB are now available; the original IDE controller, however, cannot support such a drive.

Western Digital introduced the Enhanced IDE specification in 1994. It fixes many of the problems in IDE. EIDE uses LBA (Logical Block Address) to translate the cylinder, head, and sector information into a 28-bit block address—much as is done in SCSI translation schemes. This LBA is used by BIOS to set up an Enhanced Drive Parameter Table, which the system reads. In other words, the drive parameters are translated so that the system can deal with the drive via standard BIOS calls (INT13).

The other major changes included faster transfer rates via mode changes developments in PIO—even faster with Mode 2 DMA transfers. To be practical, EIDE drives need to be connected to a fast bus. After Intel started supplying motherboards with on-board EIDE controllers last year, the drives quickly became the industry standard.

The EIDE standard also incorporates support for four devices. The primary channel is designated for hard drives, and the secondary is for slower devices. In each situation, a device is either slave or master. The primary channel uses IRQ14, and the secondary uses IRQ15. With this expansion and the use of the backward-compatible 40-pin ribbon connectors, the speed of the transfer limits the cable length to 18 inches.

As far as Windows NT is concerned, the most dramatic change in EIDE is the incorporation of the ATAPI (Advanced Technology Attachment Packet Interface) standard. In Windows NT 4, all EIDE is incorporated into the ATAPI driver; the ATDISK driver handled drives in NT 3.51. Currently, support is limited to hard drives and CD-ROMs. Interestingly, the major change seen in ATAPI is the incorporation of packet-based transport rather than computer register-based architecture. In other words, ATAPI runs SCSI-2 commands over an IDE interface. (No support for command queuing, multiple LUNs (logical units), or disconnect features is found in SCSI-2.)

It is apparent that IDE has come a long way. For most workstations, EIDE is more than adequate. If multiple drives and other devices are needed, however, EIDE just does not provide suitable resources.

SCSI

SCSI began in 1980 as the Shugart Associates System Interface (SASI) and was concerned with finding an inexpensive interface for drives. In 1982, the American National Standards Institute (ANSI) committee started working on the first SCSI specifications, but it was an industry adoption by Apple that made SCSI successful. Devices today are SCSI, SCSI-2, or SCSI-3. Only SCSI 2 and 3 are of current value.

SCSI is device independent. The computer to which the device is attached does not need to know anything about the device, so nothing needs to be entered in BIOS. In reality, the SCSI specification provides a specified language to communicate across the bus with all devices being treated as logical units.

SCSI is a peer-to-peer implementation enabling devices to communicate with all other devices. Unfortunately, special devices (CD recorders, for example) need special drivers to fully utilize device functions. These drivers, termed device drivers, are essential in Windows NT. They are finally starting to appear.

SCSI uses a defined set of signals over a defined set of lines. In the standard SCSI-2 bus, there are nine control lines and nine data lines. The rest of the lines (except 25) form ground lines. In such a configuration, all signals are 8-bit. With the advent of Wide SCSI, the number of data lines went from 8 to 16.

Modern SCSI controllers use an on-board RISC processor that assists in the transfer of information from devices to the parent system. If a file is needed, the system (the initiator) informs the controller and a request is sent over the bus to the appropriate responder. The device acknowledges the request and fulfills it. During this process, the device can go offline (disconnect) to find the file. It then informs the controller that the file is found. During the time of disconnection, a different request can go over the control lines. This design enables SCSI to function very well in a multiprocessing environment.

Certain issues in SCSI systems are critical for understanding SCSI. These include:

- **Single-ended SCSI.** In single-ended SCSI (by far the most popular), the signals are determined by voltage relative to a common ground. This signal can be 5 volts, but typically is considered present if it exceeds 2.5 volts relative to a ground of 0. A signal is considered negative if the voltage on the bus falls below 0.4–0.5 volts. As easily seen, the crucial step in setting up a SCSI bus is the control of proper voltages on the bus. Because the bus is voltage related, all cables must meet the SCSI specifications and length limits. The specification states 19 feet as the limit. In reality, however, fast SCSI and fast wide SCSI should be limited to about 10 feet. Although this type of SCSI is very popular, it is susceptible to noise.

- **Differential SCSI.** The major difference between differential and single-ended SCSI is the manner that signals are determined. Instead of a comparison to ground, all voltage is read by contrasting the voltage between 2 lines. This provides better control of the signal; as a consequence, cables can be longer (up to 80 feet or so). This version of SCSI is not very popular, and devices are hard to find. Unfortunately, you cannot mix differential and single-ended devices. Several vendors (Digital is one) now have translators that convert single-ended to differential SCSI.

- **Termination.** Termination refers to stopping the signal at a given point. Having proper termination on the bus is mandatory. Simple rules for termination apply. Always use active terminators because they are specified in SCSI-2 and they also provide the control of bus voltage. Most devices have on-board terminators; you can disable/enable them via jumpers or by removing the resister packs (basically in-line resisters). You can also have the bus or the device provide the power to the terminator. Wherever possible, have the bus and not the device provide termination power.

  A properly terminated bus has a termination at each end. If you use both internal and external devices, the last physical device both internal and external needs to be terminated, and termination removed from the controller card. With most newer controllers this is all set in firmware. The Adaptec controllers, for example, are all configured by using Ctrl+A as the card is initiated or by setting an EISA configuration utility.

- **SCSI ID.** Each SCSI device needs a unique identifier or ID. The higher the ID, the greater the priority given to the device. For this reason, most SCSI cards have an ID of 7. Drives are given the lowest priority in part because they are faster than other components on the bus. The boot drive is 0, and the next drive is usually 1. Tape drives are typically 3 or 4, and CD-ROMs are given the highest priorities. All these IDs are set with jumpers. The first jumper block (0) is 1, the second is 2, and the third is 4. Combinations are easily determined.

Given the previous considerations, SCSI functions very well. The internal SCSI language is well described and covers the basic mechanisms of device operation. On the other hand, it should be apparent that a lot of communication is necessary for the bus to function properly. This language is referred to as SCSI overhead, and many consider it to be a liability. This overhead, however, supplies many functions that make SCSI ideal for multiprocessing. On a single task, EIDE is faster. The last topics considered here are the SCSI specifications and where SCSI seems headed in the near future.

SCSI Specifications

SCSI-2 is really built on the SCSI specification. SCSI-2 actually evolved from the Common Command Set standard that defined much of the functions for hard drives. This was seen as an opportunity to add other command sets. Specifically, command sets were set for CD-ROMs, jukebox arms (media changers), scanners, and communications. In addition, the command sets were expanded. Several very important features were added:

- Terminator resistance was reduced from 132 ohms to 100 ohms, making it possible to easily make cables that matched the termination. This was done because most cables did not match the 132 ohm resistance. Unfortunately, manufacturers of cables continue to make cables that are not to SCSI-2 specification. One sure method of determining SCSI-2 compliance is finding an Adaptec certification on the cable.

- Bus arbitration is no longer optional, but is in fact mandatory.

- Parity checking is mandatory.

- Optional features added include command queuing, enabling up to 256 commands to be placed in a queue; this enables a device to complete many requests without asking the initiator. The capability to tag the commands enables priorities to be assigned to commands. All this was designed to enhance SCSI I/O.

- Fast SCSI was added, enabling the standard 50-pin connector to handle up to 10 MB/sec in synchronous mode.

- Wide SCSI was added. This kept the command set as 8 bits, but the data path was opened to 16 bits. A 68-pin connector was added to support wide SCSI.

SCSI-3 was started before SCSI-2 was finished. The basic justification for SCSI-3 was to improve functionality and transfer rates. This set of specifications are very exciting and offer great functionality and speed to servers. The important additions (not inclusive) include:

- Support for Fast 20 devices (UltraSCSI) that enable 20 MB/sec transfers over 8-pin devices and 40 MB/sec over wide SCSI.
- Support for SCSI commands over Fiber Channel. This addition adds transfer rates up to 100 MB/sec over nearly 100 feet of cable.
- Support was added for FireWire or the 1394 bus. Among other additions, FireWire adds the capability of data and commands to coexist on the bus.

All these additions are now being introduced to the market. In a few months, new types of drives and buses/adapters will appear. The new specifications will be discussed in more detail in the section "Examining the Future of the Bus and the Hard Drive," later in this chapter.

Drives in Windows NT

All hard drive information is maintained in the Registry. For EIDE drives, the information is stored in HKEY_LOCAL_MACHINE\HARDWARE\DEVICEMAP\Atdisk\Controller(n)\Disk(n) where n is the number of the controller or disk. Figure 3.1 shows a typical Registry entry for a Western Digital hard drive.

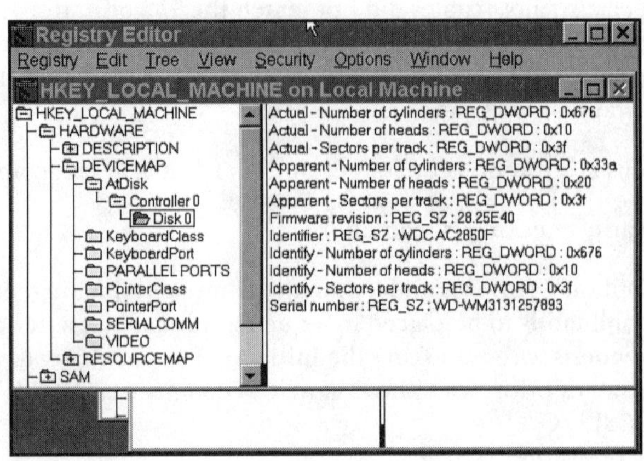

Figure 3.1
The actual description of the drive including its sectors, heads, and cylinders is shown in the Registry of a workstation.

SCSI hard drives and devices are also all maintained in the Registry in a similar place as the EIDE devices but under SCSI. Specifically, all SCSI information is maintained in HKEY_LOCAL_MACHINE\HARDWARE\DEVICEMAP\Scsi\SCSIPort(n)\ScsiBus(n)\Target ID (x). SCSIPort(n) is the number of the port, and ScsiBus(n) is the number of the Bus. Target ID (x) is the SCSI ID (see fig. 3.2).

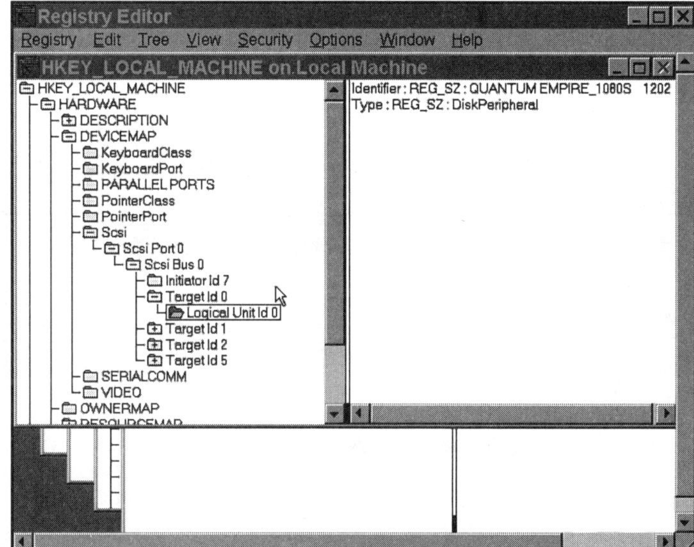

Figure 3.2

The description of a SCSI hard drive, a Quantum Empire drive, is shown in the Registry.

Formatting and Partitioning Drives in Windows NT

One of the most powerful of all the administrator tools is Disk Administrator (choose Start, Programs, Administrative Tools). This tool enables you to assign partitions, save configurations, assign drive letters, and format drives. It is very straightforward and easy to use, but you must have administrator privilege to gain access to it. Figure 3.3 shows the drive information in a typical Windows NT system. This system has three SCSI drives called Disks 0, 1, and 2. It is important to remember this information in case you have a drive failure. Event Viewer identifies a drive problem with a specific drive number.

In general, Disk Administrator is used for all partitioning and formatting in Windows NT with one notable exception. If you format at the command prompt, you have greater control over cluster sizes. In fact, the following list shows the sizes available:

format /A:size   This overrides default settings.

NTFS supports 512, 1024, 2048, 4096, 8192, 16K, 32K, 64K.

FAT supports 8192, 16K, 32K, 64K, 128K, 256K.

Note NTFS compression is not supported for allocation unit sizes above 4096.

Using large cluster size is not a good idea unless you have large files. With large photo editing files (10–30 MB files) or even professional file editing of very large files, the increased cluster size minimizes fragmentation. Unless specific reasons exist (as previously stated), use the default settings.

Disk Administrator is discussed in more detail in the sections of this chapter examining RAID and Windows NT. It is a very useful tool that everyone needs to be familiar with.

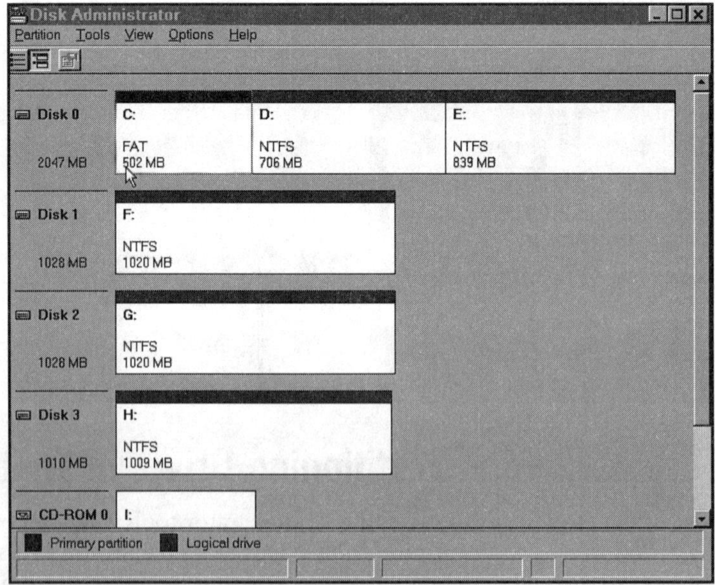

Figure 3.3
This is a view of Disk Administrator showing the drive configuration of a standard Windows NT system.

Nonstandard Storage Devices

As a rule, people always think of drives as being fixed drives—unless they are considering floppy drives. In reality, numerous drives are removable or otherwise different. The following list identifies examples of such drives:

Zip drives (Iomega)

Jazz drives (Iomega)

Syquest drives

Bernoulli drives

Magneto-optical drives

CD-ROM jukeboxes

CD-Recordable (CD-R) drives

These all work well in Windows NT. The best types are the SCSI-based ones, but the parallel Zip drives work well in NT. Of importance to these devices, use Disk Administrator to partition and to format the drive. Proprietary formats are not recognized by NT. If the device is removable, you cannot commit changes now, but you can exit Disk Administrator after assigning a partition. You are asked whether you wish to save the changes; do so. Re-open Disk Administrator, and you can format the removable drive. Unless security is important, it is best to format removables as FAT.

Examining the Future of the Bus and the Hard Drive

Within the next few months, new bus/device combinations will become available. It should be no surprise that the major issue addressed will be performance. In fact, shortly, bottlenecks will move away from drive I/O and to the next obvious bottleneck, the network. It is well known that the current bus design has very serious speed limitations. In fact, the about-to-be-released fiber-optic drives exceed the speed of the PCI bus. Unless some drastic change is made in fundamental design, only very serious RAID configurations will be able to supply needed I/O to such new systems as Pentium Pro 200s or Alpha 500s. Fortunately, such design is in the works. Of great interest is the fact that drives will be available for Windows NT.

FC-AL (Fiber Channel-Arbitrated Loop)

Fiber Channel is traditionally held to be an optical point-to-point communication method. Recent enhancements to the standard have changed the positioning of Fiber Channel. These advancements enable Fiber Channel to be used as a storage interface, bringing new levels of performance, functionality, and enough sheer speed to disk storage subsystems that disk I/O will no longer be the serious bottleneck that it is today. The technical definition of the new enhancement is Fiber Channel-Arbitrated Loop (FC-AL).

Fiber Channel is also much more than a disk interface. It will be widely used for networking and connecting to WAN links. Moreover, all its supported protocols can be used on the same facility at the same time. Thus, a workstation on a loop of Fiber Channel devices can talk to storage devices by using SCSI and to other systems by using TCP/IP, sharing a communication path as fast as most computer backplanes.

Fiber Channel is an interconnect method that links large numbers of data processing equipment throughout a company. It does so at a level of performance that rivals a mainframe's internal speeds.

Unlike the standard SCSI bus implementations, FC-AL is actually a loop connected to the backplane in two separate places. This enables rapid transfer of data from device to device. In a single-channel design, FC-AL can send information at 100 MB/sec. In a dual-channel design, the speed is 200 MB/sec. Such bandwidth eliminates most of the complaints dealing with SCSI overhead. In addition, FC-AL can support up to 126 devices per loop. Expect early implementations of FC-AL to be UltraSCSI drives (and other storage devices such as tape drives), maintained on the FC-AL architecture. This should prove to be very efficient and fast (and available toward the end of 1996).

As stated earlier, the speed of the FC-AL exceeds the PCI specification. This is actually causing great concern for the viability of Fiber Channel because it means an entirely new motherboard design with drives plugging directly into the motherboard. As you might expect, the initial incarnation of these systems will be exclusively oriented to very high-end workstations and servers. An interesting compromise, however, is being developed by Genroco—namely, a PCI controller that translates SCSI-3 drives into FC-AL devices.

This controller, the TURBOstor® FC-10632P PCI Fiber Channel disk controller, interfaces PCI-based DEC Alpha AXP computers and Intel computers to SCSI drives equipped with FC-AL connectors (Seagate Barracuda-4 [ST15150FC] Fiber Channel disk drive, for example). This intelligent controller has a very efficient, patented architecture designed for the highest possible throughput of data between the host computer and the storage subsystem; yet it employs a minimal amount of CPU overhead. Each FC-10632P is capable of sustaining aggregate transfer rates up to the sustainable data rate of the host PCI bus (100 MB/sec). Although truly a stopgap controller, this controller enables drives and other devices to maintain the highest possible transfer rates on the PCI bus.

FireWire or the 1394 Initiative

FireWire is proposed as a low-cost serial bus. Texas Instruments and Apple originally developed it, and it was approved as an IEEE standard at the end of 1995. FireWire can handle SCSI protocols and has several interesting features:

- It is Plug and Play-compliant (perhaps one reasons Microsoft supports it so fully).
- It allows hot plugging of devices.
- The implementation is isochronous, meaning slices of bandwidth can be assigned to each device.

Unlike other protocols discussed here, FireWire uses a memory model of interaction. As you should recall, SCSI supports channels. In FireWire, all devices are viewed as memory type transactions accessed directly by the CPU.

Sony's digital video (DV, formerly called DVC) camcorders, introduced in September 1995, were the first commercial products implementing the IEEE 1394 High Performance Serial Bus. The IEEE 1394 standard for the High Performance Serial Bus defines a serial data transfer protocol and interconnection system. Although 1394 incorporates quite advanced technology, the key selling feature is the incorporation of a lower-cost feature that ensures 1394's adoption. One of the earliest areas where FireWire will be adopted is a variety of high-end digital audio/video applications, such as PC-based linear A/B roll, nonlinear video editing, and digital audio mixing.

The 1394 standard consists of two bus designs—backplane and cable. The backplane bus is designed to supplement parallel bus structures by adding a serial communication path between devices plugged into the backplane. The cable bus is a noncyclic (you cannot create loops by plugging devices together) network with finite branches (up to 16 cable hops are allowed between nodes) consisting of bus bridges and nodes (cable devices). The 16-bit addressing in 1394 provides up to 64,000 nodes in a system.

A bus bridge serves to connect buses of similar or different types; a 1394-to-PCI interface within a PC constitutes a bus bridge with bus master capability. A bus bridge would also be used to interconnect a 1394 cable and a 1394 backplane bus. 6-bit Node_IDs enable up to 63 nodes to be connected to a single bus bridge; 10-bit Bus_IDs accommodate up to 1,023 bridges in a system. Each node usually has three connectors, although the standard provides for 1–27 connectors depending on a device's physical layer or PHY. Up to 16 nodes can be daisy-chained through the connectors with standard cables up to 4.5 m in length for a total standard cable length of 72 m. Additional devices can be connected in a leaf-node configuration. Physical addresses are assigned on bridge power up (bus reset) and whenever a node is added or removed from the system, either by physical connection/disconnection or power up/down. No device ID switches are required, and hot plugging of nodes is supported.

As you can imagine, there is great enthusiasm for the FireWire initiative. Microsoft is pushing the Universal Serial Bus on the low end and FireWire on faster devices. Fast devices are emerging presently as UltraSCSI or Fiberoptic devices. The first use of these drives in new technology will be SCSI over fiber-optic cable. FireWire is not currently a contender because it does not currently support fiber-optic. In the near future, new generations of motherboards and components will most probably be developed as FC-AL (or related). Such devices will be fast and will redefine system capabilities.

Each of the discussed designs has advantages. FireWire is by far the cheapest. FC-AL has the fastest physical layer but is the most expensive. In addition, FC-AL supports the longest cable length. Finally, Fiber Channel affords the greatest flexibility in mapping protocols to a common physical layer. The next year will prove to be very interesting.

USB or Universal Serial Bus

Although not in competition with FC-AL or FireWire, the Universal Serial Bus (USB) has gotten a lot of attention lately. The Universal Serial Bus is aimed at the low- and medium-speed devices. Although not related specifically to drives, USB is under serious development for other devices. This will obviously be related to bus performance. The following criteria were applied in defining the architecture for the Universal Serial Bus:

- Ease of use
- Low-cost solution that supports transfer rates up to 12 MB/sec
- Full support for the real-time data for voice, audio, and compressed video
- Protocol flexibility for mixed-mode, isochronous data transfers and asynchronous messaging
- Provide a standard interface capable of quick diffusion into product
- Enable new classes of devices that augment the PC's capability
- Support for up to 127 physical devices

Two basic classes of support exist in USB—low speed (10–100 KB/s) and medium speed (500 KB/s to 10 MB/s). Low-speed devices include mouse, other pointers, keyboard, and monitor configurations. Medium-speed devices include ISDN lines, PBX, and so on.

USB devices attach to the USB via a port on hubs. After a device is detected, the hub indicates the addition or removal of a USB device in its port status. Hosts periodically query the hub to determine the cause of the status message. After the hub receives the query string, it tells the host which port. The host then issues a control pipe command and addresses the device by using the USB Default Address. The host identifies the device attached to the port and notifies the software of the arrival or removal of the device (or function). In the USB 1.0 specification, the devices stipulated are slow devices rather than fast ones. The advantage of the USB specification is that it eliminates port setups and IRQ/IO contention.

Multiple connections to the host (root) connector require hubs. These hubs notify the host when nodes (called functions) attach or detach from the hub. This notification provides the dynamic reconfiguration and device identification required by the Windows 95 Plug and Play specification. Termination at each end of the cable provides attach/detach notification and identification of low-speed devices. Each hub can have up to seven connectors to nodes or other hubs. A USB keyboard can include both node and hub functionality so that a mouse and tablet could plug into the keyboard. High-end USB peripherals, such as CD-ROM drives and ISDN modems, would also be expected to include hub capability, eliminating the need to purchase stand-alone USB hubs. Another likely candidate for USB is the forthcoming cable modem. All in all, USB will do much to eliminate today's IRQ hassles.

Configuring Device Controllers and Devices

The safest way to set up EIDE drives is to put all the drives on the primary channel. Although this restricts the system to two hard drives, 4 GB drives have just been introduced, and LBA enables their use in NT. Save the secondary channel for CD-ROMs, being certain to obtain ATAPI 1.2 compliant drives.

Many users like booting off a small EIDE drive onto NT installed to a SCSI hard drive (for example, EIDE drive C with NT on a SCSI drive E). Although this does work, mixing buses can cause serious bus contention. Unless extremely compelling reasons exist, do not mix EIDE and SCSI hard drives.

New controllers and devices are very easy to set up. All the new fast controllers are PCI. Make certain that the controller has on-board BIOS control. The Adaptec 2940 and 3940 controllers, for example, can be configured by on-board SCSI utilities that can be used by pressing Ctrl+A at initiation time.

By convention, SCSI IDs need to follow standards. The controller needs the highest priority and is assigned an ID of 7. The boot drive is assigned the lowest priority (ID0), and subsequent drives start at 1. Dat drives are usually given intermediate IDs, with 3 or 4 being the most common. CD-ROMs typically receive IDs of 5 or 6.

Serious attention must be given to cables and termination. Currently, the best are from Granite, but they are expensive. On the other hand, cheaper cables that do not work are actually more expensive. Keep cable length to a minimum. If in doubt, use the diagnostic cables from Granite. You need to eliminate noise and echo on the bus or data corruption results.

Whenever possible, terminate the bus and not the device. On an external chain, for example, put a terminator on the second SCSI connector, not on the device. Remember, buy a good active terminator. Some internal cables are also terminated, although these are relatively difficult to find. Newer SCSI controllers actually automatically determine the best termination for the bus. If you use a combined wide/narrow controller, you can only use two of the ports simultaneously.

Understanding Fault Tolerance and RAID

Fault tolerance is a very complex issue involving everything from hard drives to power supplies. Most importantly, however, it involves planning for disaster recovery and prevention. For present purposes, this chapter examines the issue of hard drive redundancies and their value in Windows NT 4. Everyone will tell you that NT Workstation only supports striping and does not provide any fault tolerance. What is really being stated is that NT software drivers do not provide fault tolerance. There is every reason to think that a workstation can also use fault tolerant setups. In fact, all systems used for *work* need some type of data security and integrity. Hardware RAID supplies this data security/integrity.

Several independent sources have estimated that the amount of data storage is increasing 50–100 percent per year. These estimates cause alarm. Not that many years ago, everyone was using a 40 MB hard drive; that seemed massive. Today, worries about gigabyte or even terabyte data files are common. With this explosion in storage size, disk arrays have become more and more prominent. Quite simply, a disk array is a logical grouping of drives designed to be faster, fault tolerant, or both. The most common of disk arrays is Redundant Array of Independent Disks (RAID).

Fault tolerance, in the large sense, suggests the capability of a system to handle disasters in such a way that continuous operation is maintained. Considerable effort and money is required to provide such capability. Using specific RAID methods, you can assist in designing a data-based fault-tolerant system.

Almost every book that discusses RAID assumes that all you need to know are the levels of RAID; the discussion nearly always stops there. The major concern should be not what RAID is but how you use it. For completeness, this chapter does need to define various RAID levels.

RAID levels:

- **Just a bunch of drives.** This is nothing more than placing drives together for convenience. There is no implied fault tolerance in this level. In Windows NT, this is termed a volume.

- **Level 0.** In RAID 0, the data are striped across drives, enabling simultaneous I/Os to all the drives. As the number of drives increases, so does the speed of the array; the risk of data loss, however, increases.
- **Level 1.** RAID 1 is perhaps the best of all levels. All writes of data occur on at least two drives. In other words, drive A is duplicated on to drive B. If both drives are on the same controller, this process is termed mirroring. If the drives are on separate controllers, the process is called duplexing.

  Several important things about RAID 1 should be considered. It is generally an option in operating systems. In fact, you can accomplish both mirroring and duplexing in Windows NT Server 4. On the workstation, all such RAID must be done in hardware. Undeniably, RAID 0 provides the greatest redundancy in RAID.
- **RAID 2.** RAID 2 is very seldom used. Striping is accomplished at the bit level, bringing about serious overhead and expense.
- **RAID 3.** Like RAID 2, RAID 3 is seldom used. All correction data are maintained on a single drive, and information is striped across the remaining drives a byte at a time. For this level to function properly and at optimal speed, drive spindles need to be synchronized. There is no need to consider Level 3.
- **RAID 4.** Similar to RAID 3, with the exception of data being striped at the block level. Like 3, there is no compelling reason to use it.
- **RAID 5.** RAID 5 is actually a compromise level. Striping is at the block level, and error correction is distributed across all drives. This level uses the simultaneous writes seen in levels 0 and 1, but parity data are distributed across all drives resulting in increased overhead.
- **Combined RAID levels.** An additional level of RAID is sometimes discussed; RAID 0+1 (sometimes called RAID 10). In this configuration, you first establish RAID 0 arrays and then mirror them. Doing this enables redundancy and speed, but the cost increases dramatically. Another combined level is RAID 0+5 or 50. In this variant, multiple level 0 volumes are striped with parity, producing RAID 50.

Setting Up RAID in Windows NT

RAID can be set up in software in Windows NT, or the setup can be done directly in a hardware device. From a security issue, the hardware-based RAID is far superior to the software RAID in Windows NT. The primary reason for hardware- over software-based RAID is the decrease in system overhead when the control of RAID is being done in hardware.

Using Software-Based RAID in Windows NT

Windows NT Workstation only supports volumes and striping (RAID 0). As previously stated, these two sets are very similar. They provide no fault tolerance and are done only for ease of use and speed. This review start by examining volume sets made in Windows NT.

In this example, consider three SCSI drives on a single controller. With the mouse, click on one of the unpartitioned/unformatted drives. Holding down the Ctrl button on the keyboard, click on another drive. Both are now highlighted, and you can go to Partition, Create Volume Set and make a volume (see fig. 3.4).

Figure 3.4

Disk Administrator showing the generation of a two-drive volume set; the full size of both drives is used in this case.

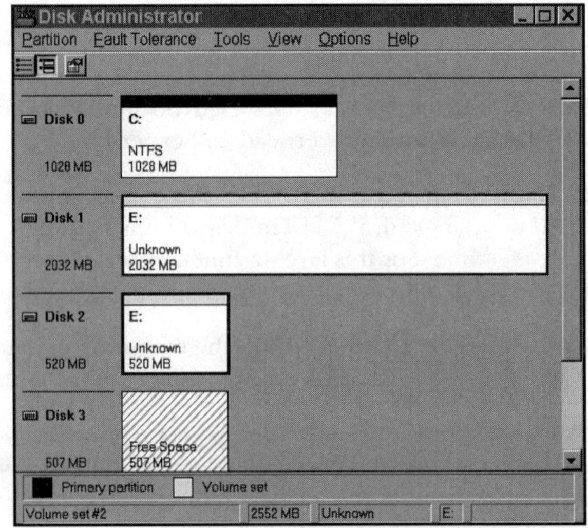

After the volume is set, you have to go to Partition, Commit Changes Now. Unless you are changing a volume set present, you will be asked to reboot. After doing so, you can format the volume. In this example, the volume is being formatted as NTFS (see fig. 3.5).

After the volume set is made, it is very easy to extend it. In this example, click on the volume set, hold down the Ctrl button, and then click on the third drive. Going to the Partition drop-down, choose Extend Volume Set. A drop-down window appears asking whether you want to extend the volume set (see fig. 3.6).

After you click on OK, the new drive is automatically placed in the volume set. In this example, the addition was immediate. You will not have to reboot the system. The primary reason to use a volume set is to reserve a single drive letter rather than three, as in this example (see fig. 3.7). There is no performance improvement at all since the data are written in single read/write operations.

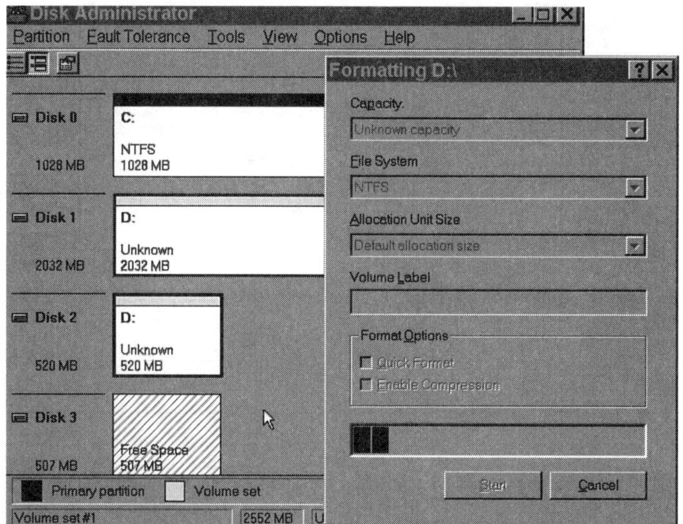

Figure 3.5

Formatting a volume set in Disk Administrator; the format drop-down page is found under the Tools menu.

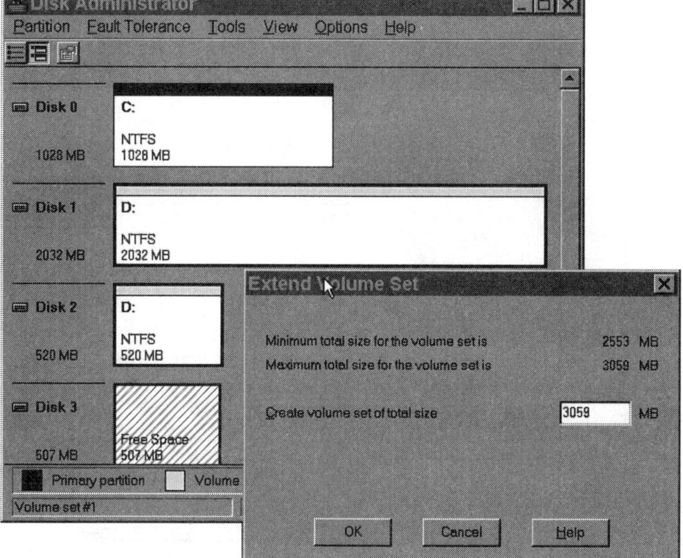

Figure 3.6

A drop-down window in Disk Administrator enables you to extend a volume set.

After the set is made, you can also use Disk Administrator to remove it easily. Click on the volume set and go to Partition, Delete. This removes the volume set (see fig. 3.8).

Figure 3.7

Disk Administrator showing the finished three-drive volume set; note the single drive letter for all three drives.

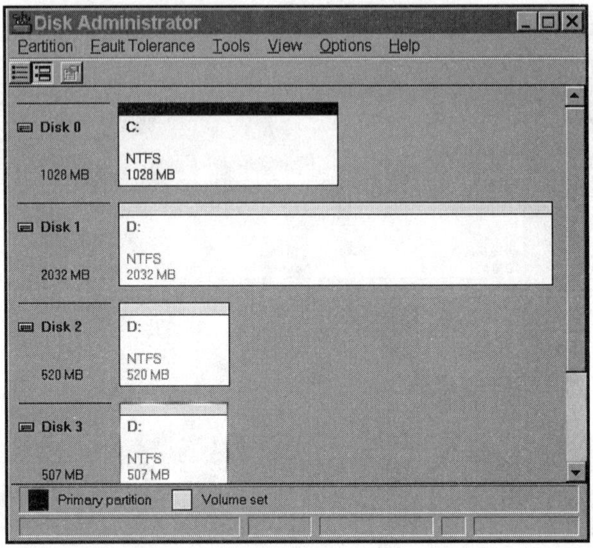

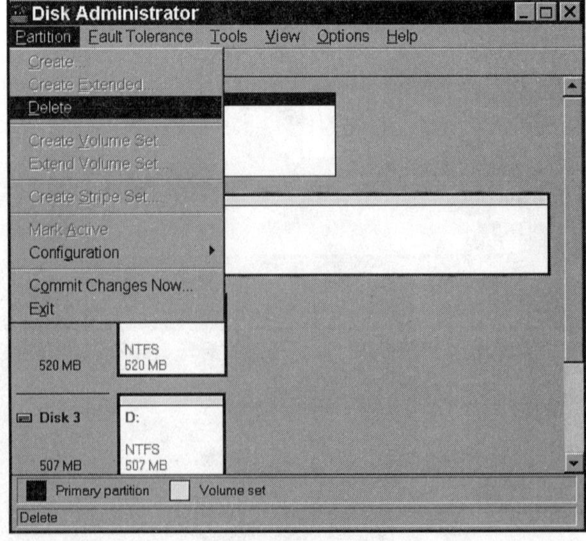

Figure 3.8

Using Disk Administrator, it is very easy to remove a volume set (or simple partition).

The creation of a stripe set is exactly the same as making a volume set. In this example, however, you cannot extend a stripe set so that all three drives are chosen. Selecting one drive, hold down Ctrl, and select the other two drives. With all three chosen, you go to Partition, Create Stripe Set (see fig. 3.9).

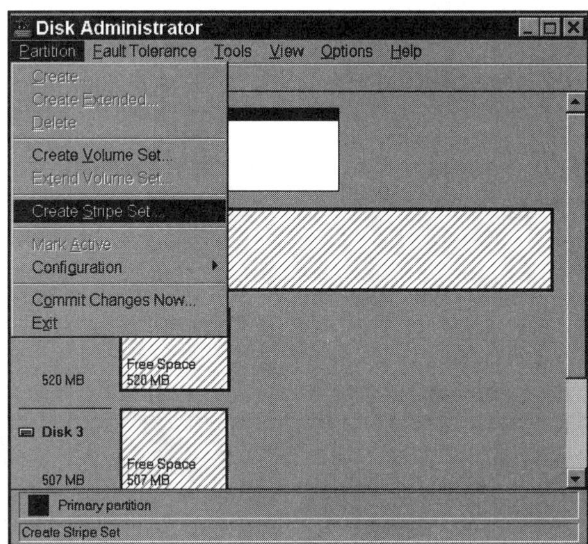

Figure 3.9
Disk Administrator shows the generation of a stripe set.

Unlike a volume set, all partitions on a stripe set must be the same size. For this reason, one of the drives used has a small unpartitioned section. Figure 3.10 shows the formatting of the stripe set.

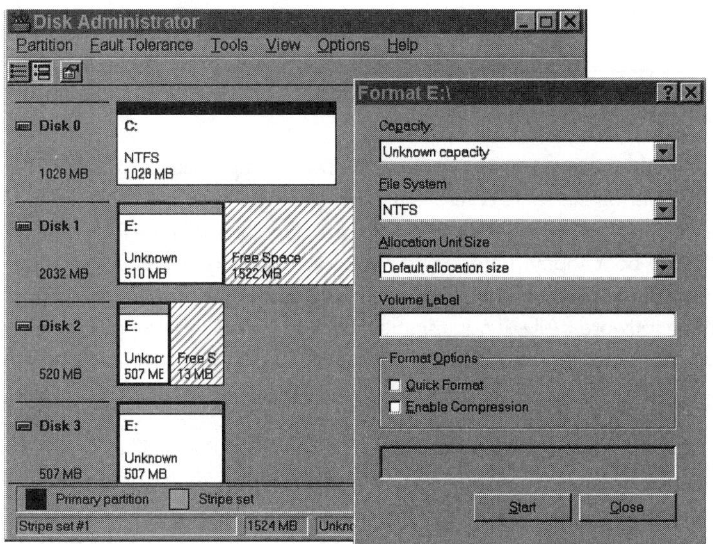

Figure 3.10
Disk Administrator shows here the Format drop-down window describing the Format options for the stripe set.

After the stripe set is made, it also has a single drive letter assigned by the system. In this case, the system assigned drive letter H. Because the system was not rebooted, E and F were still in use by the previous volume set. After the system was rebooted, the drive letter could be changed to E. Figure 3.11 shows the completed formatting of the stripe set.

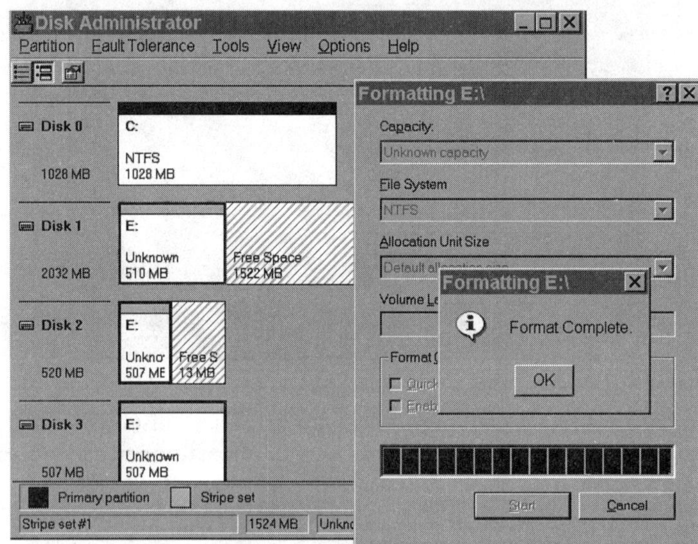

Figure 3.11

The finalized formatting of the stripe set.

> **RAID on the NT Server!**
>
> NT Server also enables the use of fault-tolerant RAID sets. In particular, you can create RAID 1 (either on the same controller or across controllers) or RAID 5. In this case, a moderate amount of fault tolerance is provided by the OS. If RAID 1 is made, it is essential that a boot floppy is made that will enable booting to the mirrored (termed shadow) or the primary drive (see the troubleshooting chapter). RAID 5 is powerful, but for software RAID, it adds significant overhead to the system.

Using Hardware-Based RAID in Windows NT

For all practical purposes, RAID is strictly a SCSI implementation. This of course brings us back to the system independence. If you create a hardware device that in turn creates and controls a disk array independent of NT, Windows NT accepts the configuration communicated to the system by the controller. Figure 3.12 shows a C drive that is 1.5 GB. In reality, the drive is a hardware array of three drives on a Mylex controller. The drives are made into a system volume and formatted on the controller or by a vendor-supplied utility. If any drive fails on a RAID 5 system volume, it can be replaced easily by running the utility one more time.

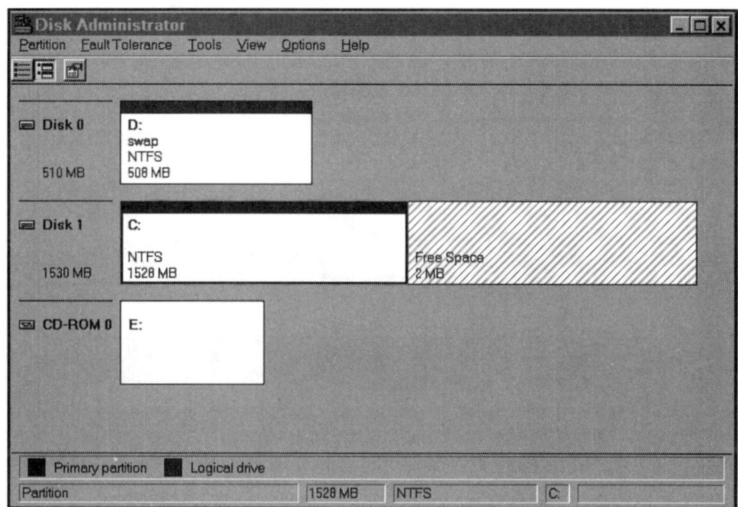

Figure 3.12

Disk Administrator showing two drives (C and D) on a Windows NT Workstation; the C drive is a hardware RAID set.

Hardware RAID exists in several configurations. You can obtain a RAID controller from Mylex, DPT, AMI, and a few other vendors. These enable you to attach drives and build your own RAID enclosure. You can also purchase preconfigured RAID enclosures that come in many different configurations. Of interest here is the emergence of Auto-RAID; this asks several questions and offers the best RAID configuration for your situation. In the next year or so, these PnP-like RAID setups will become more common.

For standard systems, a controller from AMI, Mylex, or DPT (among others) makes an excellent storage addition to a system. It is very important that any controller have applications that run in NT and enable you to keep track of and configure drives on the controller. For example, Mylex has the elegant GAM2 application that even enables you to examine the RAID set across the network. Figures 3.13 and 3.14 show the actual drive configuration used to make the RAID Drive C shown in the preceding figure.

Applications such as GAM2 are invaluable for the maintenance of any RAID volume. You can configure GAM2 to respond to any severe error occurrences. Typical responses include a number code sent to a pager, the delivery of a MAPI-compliant message, or even a fax if a fax server is available.

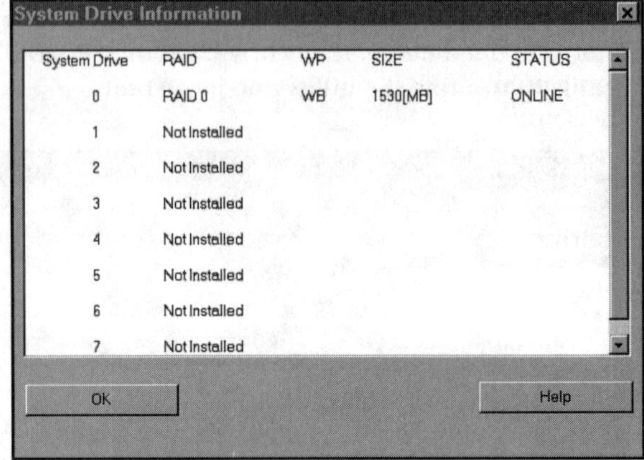

Figure 3.13

The Mylex Global Array Manager 2 (GAM2) application shows the RAID 0 volume (as shown in fig. 3.11).

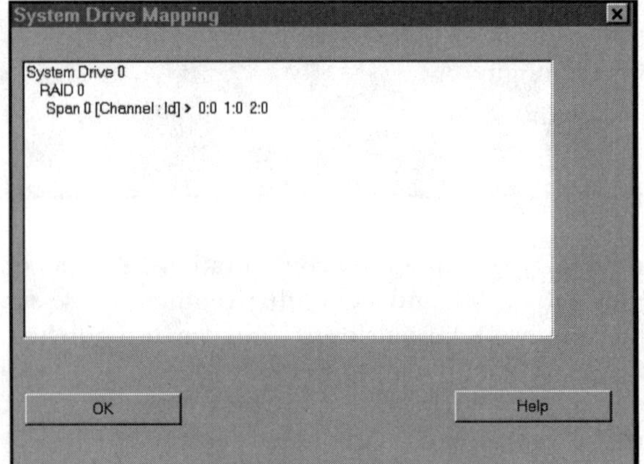

Figure 3.14

GAM2 shows that the system volume is made of three drives with SCSI IDs of 0, 1, and 2.

When considering RAID, it is important to keep specific uses of RAID in mind. RAID 0, for example, provides high performance without redundancy. The areas where 0 is of great value are in digital video editing and image processing. Any broadcast-quality compressed video requires 13 MB/sec transfer rate, which is currently only available with RAID 0 (or its bigger brother RAID 50).

On the other hand, RAID 5 is not suitable for photo editing. It is, however, clearly suitable for protective data storage. In all cases, writing is slow because of the reads necessary for maintaining parity information. Although it is easy to argue that RAID 5 is solely for server use, no reason precludes RAID 5's use on a high-end workstation not connected to any storage protection. In conjunction with RAID 0, RAID 5 is very powerful protective and fast.

Fault Tolerant Essentials

Here are some numbers that might be surprising. The highest probability of component failure is not a hard drive.

Mean times between failure values for common system components:

Hard drive	300,000–500,000 hours
Adapter	200,000–300,000 hours
Array Controller	300,000–1,000,000 hours
Power Supply	50,000–300,000 hours

As you might expect, any serious use of fault tolerance in NT demands that you pay attention to all aspects of the system. Auto-switchover power supplies are mandatory in any serious fault-tolerant design.

In hardware configurations, unlike software RAID, the RAID can actually fix itself if spare drives are present. The parity information is used to fix the missing drive. At such a time, only a system slowdown occurs.

The latest high-end RAID configurations actually enable real-time configuration and repair. Drives can be added and RAID levels switched, totally independent of the OS. One such example of this type of enclosure is the SuperFlex 3000/DRG system from Storage Dimensions. Obviously, you pay a premium for such a system. On the other hand, being able to dynamically expand and configure can be very important to a specific systems.

The interesting question is always raised about the use of caching controllers in Windows NT. Cache on a simple controller is not a very good idea. The memory supplied should be used as system cache instead. On the other hand, cache on a RAID controller can substantially lower system overhead and thereby dramatically improve performance of the RAID. Systems based on the new RAID controllers using cache always show better performance than noncached controllers. The controllers from AMI, Mylex, DPT, and Compaq are all superb in this regard.

Examining Tape Devices

Like hard drives, tape drives come in many styles and varieties. By far, the most cost-effective type of device is based on DAT or DDS (digital data storage). These drives range in price from $600–$1,000. Many think that the DAT drive is overpriced for a workstation. Such reasoning based on price alone is somewhat faulty.

When determining the type of drive to purchase for NT, several factors play a great role in the decision. First of all, how much data will be backed up? It is ideal to have all the data on one storage tape rather than spanning tapes. The bulk of the controller-based or EIDE drives do not support compression in NT. This means that compression must be enabled by the software package and is not supplied in NT backup. DAT drives, on the other hand, support compression very well.

The speed of the backup is also always a concern. A DAT drive such as the HP C1533a provides backup rates of 40–50 MB/min. If the amount of data that you have is large, a DAT drive might be the one for you. In general, get the best and most supported device that you can afford. As with everything else, no tape device ever has too large a capacity or too great a speed.

Unlike with servers, there is no need to include tape libraries in this discussion. They work on a workstation, but it is hard to justify their usage. On the other hand, you can have a tiered approach to backup. In such a setup, you copy files to a different hard drive such as a Jazz drive, and then over time migrate the files to tape. For typically small amounts of data seen on workstations, this proves an excellent idea.

Setting up tape devices in NT is very easy. Open the Tape Device applet in the Control Panel. This application is very Plug and Play-aware. The applet shows the devices and whether a driver is loaded. If the 4 CD-ROM is loaded, the system loads the necessary drivers. Unlike earlier version of Windows NT, you do not have to reboot to use the new tape devices. Figure 3.15 shows a standard, loaded 4 mm DAT drive.

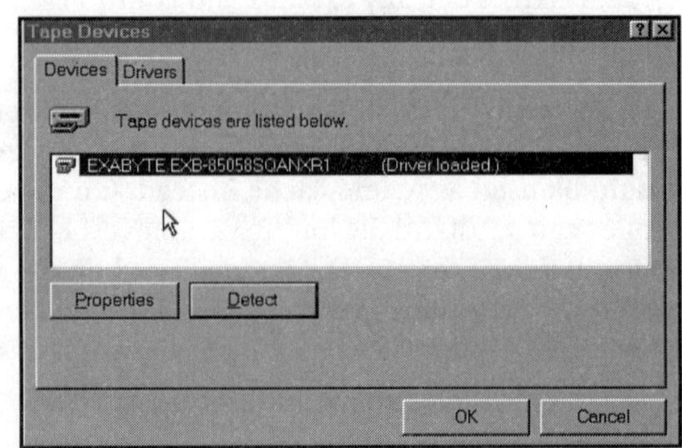

Figure 3.15

The Tape Devices applet of the Control Panel shows a loaded HP C1533A on a Windows NT Workstation.

Looking at Scanners

Until very recently, the HP scanners were the only ones supported in Windows NT. In fact, one of the first drivers written for NT was for the HP scanner. Unfortunately, the person who wrote the driver is no longer working for HP, but is now working for

Microsoft. As a consequence, the development of drivers for Windows NT 4 are somewhat problematic. The most recent version of deskscan (2.3.1) does in fact seem to work very well in NT 4.

Other scanners now install very easily into NT 4. Perhaps the easiest to install are those from MicroTek. The setup recognizes and installs all without any user alterations necessary. In all cases, the installation is based on 32-bit Twain installations. (Twain defines a standard software protocol and application programming interface (API) for communication between software applications and image acquisition devices.) Any software that can address this level of Twain works well in Windows NT (Photoshop 3.0.5 or higher, for example).

To install the MicroTek, place the scanner on any ASPI compliant controller. They ship with an ISA controller, but the scanner works well on controllers such as the 2940u or 3940u. Just run the setup (always use the Add/Remove applet in the Control Panel). The appropriate applications are loaded, and a slight addition is made to the Twain portion of WIN.INI (Default Source=C:\winnt\TWAIN_32\Scanwiz\SCANWZ32.DS). Reboot, and you can acquire scans very easily.

Examining Notebook Support

Many have argued that Windows NT does not belong on a notebook. There are no power management tools and hot swappable devices, although this is changing rapidly. Digital has developed power management tools for NT 4 and is working on full, swappable support. Several other vendors are working on the same applications.

Of great significance to notebooks and NT is the development of the PCI bus for the notebook. This enables hard drives and other peripherals to work very efficiently and fully support the Pentium processors now found in most notebooks.

Several important developments have occurred in the recent PC Card (PCMCIA) standard. One of these involves the socket services. Socket Services are the lowest layer in a multilayer architecture that manages resources on PC Cards. The services provide a software interface to the hardware that controls sockets for PC Cards. This masks the details of the hardware used to implement these sockets, enabling higher-level software to be developed independent of the hardware. Software layers above Socket Services provide additional capabilities. The sockets are in reality the receptacles for the PC Cards. Host systems can have more than one adapter, and each adapter can have one or more sockets. Socket Services reports the number of sockets and windows provided by each adapter installed. This standardization has enabled standard Socket Services to be supported in NT 4 (but not in earlier versions).

In addition, Card Services describes an API (Application Programming Interface), which enables PC Cards and sockets to be shared by multiple clients. These clients include device drivers, configuration utilities, or application programs. Again, the specification is independent of the hardware that actually manipulates PC Cards and sockets. This standardization provides two things. First is the capability to support PC Card-aware device drivers, configuration utilities, and application programs. Second is to provide a centralized resource for the common functionality required by these clients.

These two specifications enable standardized drivers to be written in Windows NT. In fact, the Card and Socket Services work very well in NT 4. Notebook drivers for SCSI adapters, ethernet cards, and modems are readily available. Figure 3.16 shows PC Card (PCMCIA) services and cards on a notebook running Windows NT 4.

Figure 3.16

The PC Card applet in the Control Panel shows the Card Services with a SCSI card and a modem.

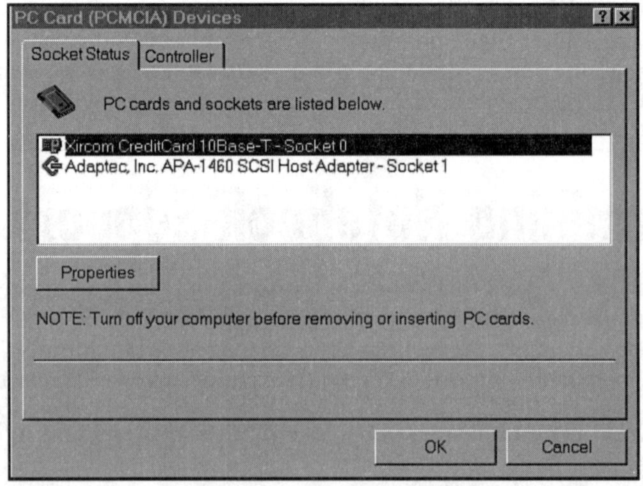

Although not ideal because most notebooks do not support hot swapping of PC Cards, Windows NT 4 is clearly better than previous versions. It will not be long until support for swapping PC Cards and power management will be built into Windows NT.

Understanding Hardware Profiles

Introduced in NT 4 is the capability to create hardware profiles. After doing so, the profiles are presented to you when you boot into NT. Although profiles can be set up on a server or a conventional workstation, they clearly make more sense on a notebook.

The concept of a hardware profile is very simple. All devices and services are enabled in a profile called normal. You just open the System applet in the Control Panel, go to the Hardware Profile page, and copy the normal profile. You then save it under a different name. Figure 3.17 shows five profiles for a notebook. In the case of multiple profiles, the one at the top is the default. You can move the profiles up and down by highlighting a profile and using the up and down arrows on the right-hand side of the profile window.

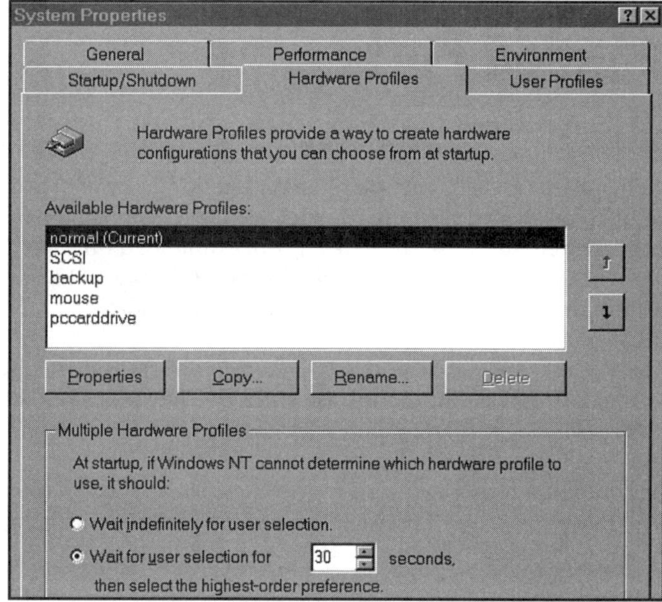

Figure 3.17

You can choose from five hardware profiles shown on this notebook at boot-up time.

After you have created the profiles, you can disable any device or service for that profile. In the hardware profiles created on the notebook, for example, the 4 mm driver is only enabled for the backup option (see fig. 3.18).

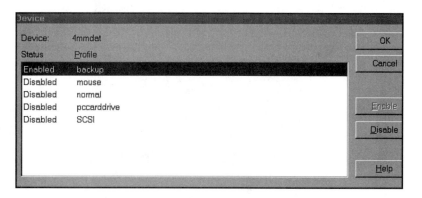

Figure 3.18

As is evident in this figure, the 4 mm driver is disabled for all but the backup profile.

Using hardware profiles can save you from having a faulty boot or numerous pop-up error messages. If you have the Adaptec SlimSCSI card enabled but no devices attached, for example, the system does not boot unless a profile is chosen that has the card disabled.

Using High-Speed Ports

Microsoft has seriously hampered the Workstation in several places. One of these is the inability to use the Workstation as a RAS server (you can only have one RAS port available for dial in). Nonetheless, any use of a Workstation in cyberspace benefits from the use of co-processed port boards such as those from Digiboard. These are well worth purchasing because they take a processing load off the CPU. The ports can also be used for other types of applications that simply make use of a COM port. The USR Pilot, for example, works well on Digiboard ports.

If you need to add more ports to the system, these high-speed ports are very useful. The Digiboards just use a I/O space, but do not use an IRQ. They work well, help the system by reducing overhead, and are seamless in use.

Figure 3.19 shows the setup of a Digiboard card in the Network applet, Adapters. In this case, a standard memory space and I/O were used successfully in setting up the card.

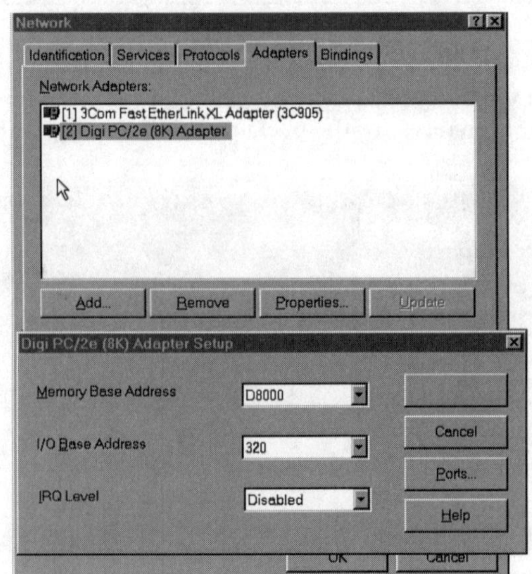

Figure 3.19

The network settings of a Digiboard card showing the memory base D8000 and 320 I/O chosen to avoid overlap with other cards.

Using Video Monitors and Cards

One of the most perplexing choices that you can make on a computer system running Windows NT is choice of monitor and video card. This choice can actually be narrowed down appreciably. First consider the monitor.

Monitors come in various sizes with even more varying prices. When searching for a monitor to buy, consider the following recommendations:

- Do not get a monitor with less than a 15-inch screen. In fact, preferably, get a minimum of a 17-inch monitor if you look at it all the time.
- Make certain that the monitor is a multisyncing monitor; that is, it can handle different screen resolutions automatically and you do not need to adjust the image on the screen.
- The horizontal frequency used in advertising is the number of times that a beam sweeps horizontally per second; the higher the number, the less irritating the screen flicker.
- For dot pitch, do not accept anything larger than .28 mm.

Currently, several of the better monitors come from NEC, Viewsonic, Nanao, and Hitachi. The larger Hitachi are probably among the best presently available (based on image clarity, control, and scanning speed) but carry a sizable cost (as do all 21-inch monitors).

The video card that you buy should be matched to the monitor. There is no reason to purchase a high-end video card to run a low-end monitor. For larger monitors, you need more memory on the video card to run higher screen resolutions. Finally, newer video cards enable the use of multiple cards and monitors on a system. The following recommendations are a beginning basis for choosing video cards:

- For a standard 15-inch monitor, get an S3-based (ATI is acceptable also) video card with 1 MB (2 is fine) of memory (Dram will be okay). These cards have well designed drivers for Windows NT.
- For high-resolution 17-inch monitors, get a card with 4 MB of RAM. Cards based on the S3 chipset (make certain that the card is using the current S3 chipsets with NT drivers), those from ATI, and higher-end cards such as the Matrox Millenium are excellent choices.

- For multiple monitors, use cards such as the Millenium or obtain dual-port cards such as those from STB.
- For 20- to 21-inch monitors, expect to obtain cards with greater than 4 MB of RAM. A good starting place is a Millenium with 8 MB of RAM. For rendering and related video editing, the cards from Intergraph are among the best and fastest available.

Follow simple guidelines in obtaining a monitor and video card. You will stare at it all the time, so make certain that the combination is easy to look at not irritating to your eyes.

Using Pointing Devices

When thinking of pointing devices, most people think of a mouse. Others exist, however. The Wacom tablets have been supported in Windows NT since 3.1 days. As this is being written, new drivers are being developed and are in open beta. They are available for download from the Wacom Web site (www.wacom.com). Drivers for the Alpha are also available for a small purchase price.

If you set up a tablet in NT, you do not have to disable your standard mouse. Both pointing devices can work on the same cursor. This makes tablet use in NT very easy and powerful. You can have fine control of the cursor when needed.

Using Network TCP/IP Print Servers

With the movement toward an Internet-based computer community, almost everyone is using TCP/IP in one form or another. It is fortunate that TCP/IP print servers are available for use in Windows NT. The following setup is for an Axis 560 print server. This device has one serial and two parallel ports on it. For system control and a controlled print spooler, the device can be placed on a BDC or, less optimally, a PDC. They can also be loaded on a workstation. In this latter case, only 10 clients can use the printer at any one time without violating the license agreement for Workstation.

To manage an Axis print server effectively, you need to load TCP/IP print services in the Network applet, Services window. For complete control, you also need ftp server. The server uses a standard Ethernet connection to the network. Connect it to a standard 10BASE-T hub or switch (always use Cat 5 cable), for example. Connect a printer to the server, and then print a test page. This provides you a list of the major parameters of the server.

To set up the server, go to the Printer applet in the Control Panel. You need to add a port. The port added will be a LPR (Line Printing utility). You then enter the IP address of the server (in this case 199.34.56.18) and the name of the port that the printer is connected to (pr2 which is equivalent to lpt2 in this case). Figure 3.20 shows this configuration.

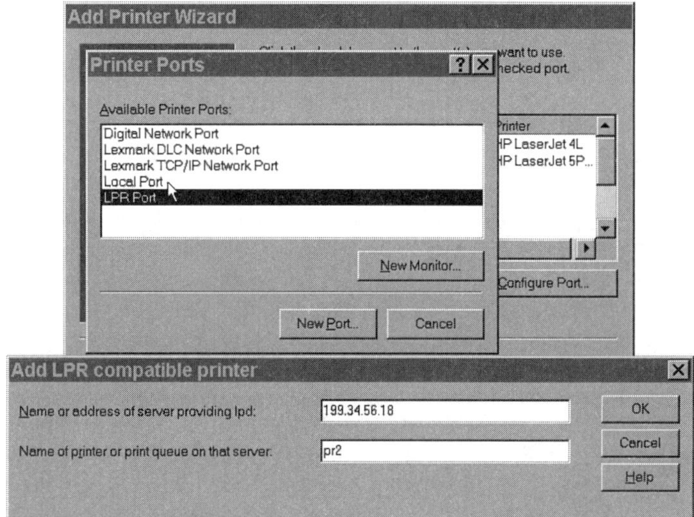

Figure 3.20

The addition of a LPR port and device is shown.

After the port is added on the system that will control the server, you choose a printer (in the preceding example, pr1 is an HP LaserJet 5MP, and pr2 is an HP LaserJet 4L), and then add the drivers. You can then share the printers as if they were any network printers.

The only problem in configuring the print server for TCP/IP is related to the IP address supplied. The Axis ships with 192.36.253.80 as the resident address. Without a router or other way of crossing subnets, you cannot ping the print server, and you will receive a message that the server is unreachable. This is actually very easy to overcome.

Change the IP address of the system loading the print server to 192.36.253.82 (or similar). This does not cause you to reboot. You can then Telnet into the server or ftp into it. This enables you to examine the various aspects of the server, to change the IP address, or to change any other variable in the configuration.

Figure 3.21 shows a Telnet session between the BDC (which is controlling the print server) and the print server. You start the session by typing Telnet, the IP address of the server; enter Telnet 199.34.56.18 at the command prompt. You then connect to the print server.

```
Telnet - 199.34.56.18
Connect  Edit  Terminal  Help

AXIS 560 TELNET Print server V5.20 Aug 02 1996

AXIS 560 network login: root
Password:

AXIS 560 TELNET Print server V5.20 Aug 02 1996

Root> account
Current account file:
  JOB  USER            PROT     LPR  S     BYTES  ETIME  OTIME

   91  bigclyde        LPD      PR2  C      4140      1      0
   92  bigclyde        LPD      PR2  C      4141      1      0
   93  bigclyde        LPD      PR2  C      4141     24      0
   94  bigclyde        LPD      PR2  C      4141     79      0
   95  bigclyde        LPD      PR2  C     32977      2      0
   96  bigclyde        LPD      PR1  C     12380      1      0
   97  bigclyde        LPD      PR2  C     30984      4      0
   98  bigclyde        LPD      PR2  C      4140      1      0
   99  bigclyde        LPD      PR1  C    234167      1      0
  100  bigclyde        LPD      PR1  C    209172      1      0
Root>
```

Figure 3.21
A Telnet session between a Windows NT system and an Axis 560 print server showing the print use information on the print server.

To change parameters in the unit, you have to ftp into the print server and obtain the configuration. Although very Unix-like in implementation, obtaining the information is very easy. Figure 3.22 shows the use of the ftp to establish a connection and obtain the configuration for the Axis unit.

```
Com Prompt - ftp 199.34.56.18

C:\>ftp 199.34.56.18
Connected to 199.34.56.18.
220 AXIS 560 FTP Printer Server V5.20 Aug 02 1996 ready.
User (199.34.56.18:(none)): root
331 User name ok, need password
Password:
230 User logged in
ftp> get config
200 PORT command successful.
150 Opening data connection for config (199.34.56.16.13.140)
226 Transfer complete.
8252 bytes received in 0.12 seconds (68.77 Kbytes/sec)
ftp>
```

Figure 3.22
After logging on to the printer with ftp, use "get config" (without quotation marks) to download the configuration.

After the config file is downloaded, you can easily edit it in Notepad. Figure 3.23 shows a typical config file being edited.

After you edit the file, you need to upload it to the print server. This is done by typing **put config CONFIG**, and pressing Enter. The new IP address is enabled (see fig. 3.24). You can change the IP address of the computer back to the original one.

config - Notepad

File Edit Search Help

```
(AXIS 560 Print server V5.20 Aug 02 1996. S/N: 00408C1A3331)

Parameter settings:

--- CONFIG MENU
NODE_ADDR.    : 00 40 8C 1A 33 31
ROOT_PWD.     : pass
USERS.        :

--- TCPIP MENU
TCP_ENB.      : YES
INT_ADDR.     : 199 34 56 18
DEF_ROUT.     : 0 0 0 0
NET_MASK.     : 0 0 0 0
PROS_PWD.     : netprinter
PROS_PRT.     : 35
LPD_BANN.     : NO
BOOTP_ENB.    : YES
RARP_ENB.     : YES
RTN_OPT.      : YES
RTEL_PR1.     : 0
RTEL_PR2.     : 0
RTEL_PR3.     : 0
RTEL_PR4.     : 0
```

Figure 3.23

The Axis configuration that has been edited to change the IP address from 192.36.253.80 to 199.34.56.18 (INT_ADDR.).

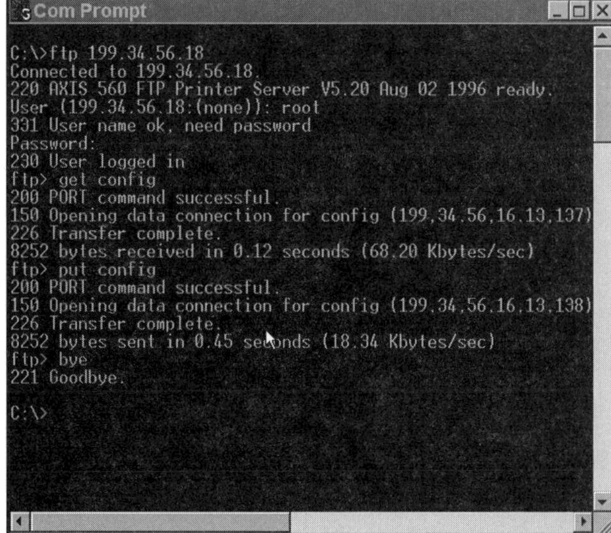

Com Prompt

```
C:\>ftp 199.34.56.18
Connected to 199.34.56.18.
220 AXIS 560 FTP Printer Server V5.20 Aug 02 1996 ready.
User (199.34.56.18:(none)): root
331 User name ok, need password
Password:
230 User logged in
ftp> get config
200 PORT command successful.
150 Opening data connection for config (199,34,56,16,13,137)
226 Transfer complete.
8252 bytes received in 0.12 seconds (68.20 Kbytes/sec)
ftp> put config
200 PORT command successful.
150 Opening data connection for config (199,34,56,16,13,138)
226 Transfer complete.
8252 bytes sent in 0.45 seconds (18.34 Kbytes/sec)
ftp> bye
221 Goodbye.

C:\>
```

Figure 3.24

The ftp session showing the uploading of the edited configuration successfully uploaded to the Axis print server.

The use of these print servers greatly improves the speed of printing. Assuming print access is given to users, all printing can be easily centralized on to a system that functions as the spooler for all printers.

Summary

Most of the common parts of a computer have been examined in some detail here. All the parts discussed have a great bearing on any system running Windows NT Workstation 4. Make certain to purchase the right type of system for your needs. In general, match the system requirement to your user needs. For new systems, buy Pentium or Pentium Pro computers with 16 MB or higher amounts of RAM (32 is better, and 64 is a decent amount for using applications like Photoshop). Match components. Do not get a very fast system and put a slow monitor on it.

In a few months, systems and devices will show up and new terms will appear in advertising. These terms will include USB, FireWire, FC-AL, and perhaps a few others. Controllers with NT drivers will appear also. New speeds on systems will be reached. These changes will appear on the high-end systems originally, but expect a new generation of nearly everything in a year or so.

CHAPTER 4

Startup and Shutdown

Windows NT is a state-of-the-art operating system; as such, it uses appropriately sophisticated startup and shutdown procedures to ensure its system integrity. Like other advanced operating systems, Windows NT has to manage virtual memory and maintain system integrity. Its startup procedures are designed to identify the current hardware configuration and initialize its various software subsystems. Its shutdown procedures are designed to make certain that open files and the Registry get updated and closed properly so they are not corrupted.

Understanding the details of the startup and shutdown processes can help a system administrator prevent problems. Understanding how the system is supposed to work can also help in troubleshooting when it isn't working as expected. After you have made a few configuration changes and added some hardware, for example, if Windows NT Workstation fails to initialize properly, what do you do? How can you isolate the problem and correct it? If you are able to determine at what point in the startup process the trouble occurs or are able to utilize some of the startup troubleshooting techniques, then you are more likely to be able to solve the problem.

This chapter covers each of the steps in the startup process for both x86 systems and RISC-based systems, then goes through troubleshooting the startup process. You will learn how to configure the workstation for multiple operating systems, as well as for different hardware profiles and the dial-up networking logon option. The final part of the chapter will cover the shutdown procedures.

From a high-level view, the Windows NT Workstation startup procedures are very similar to what other advanced operating systems such as Unix do. All operating systems that support multiple users and virtual memory have some requirements in common. The details of the startup and shutdown procedures differ between operating systems because the architectures and implementations of those operating systems differ. The main steps, or stages, of the startup process occur in the following order:

- The Power On Self Test (POST)
- Initial Startup
- The Boot Loader
- Windows NT Hardware Detection
- Loading the Windows NT Kernel
- Windows NT Initialization
- Logging On
- User Profile

Although the Windows NT Workstation startup process has many steps, it does not take a very long time (especially if you have a fast processor and enough system memory). Each step is significant to the overall functioning of the system. Several of the steps have options you can configure, such as the support for multiple operating systems or hardware types.

Exploring the Startup Process

Windows NT has slightly different startup procedures for x86-based systems, such as a typical PC, and for RISC-based systems, such as Power PC or Alpha-based computers. Both systems go through the same overall steps listed previously, but the details of how each executes the steps are unique to its system type—except for the last few. The startup details for x86- and RISC-based systems are covered separately in this chapter; however the last two stages, logging on and user profiles, are the same for both systems. These two stages are covered in the section, "The Final Stages..." which follows the startup details for the RISC-based systems.

The Startup Process for x86-Based Systems

The most popular computers running Windows NT Workstation are based on the Intel x86 system architecture. This means that Windows NT Workstation works on the same types of systems that MS-DOS and Windows 95 use—although it does have more substantial resource requirements than most other single-user systems. This section covers each of the startup steps through Windows NT initialization, in the order that they occur.

The Power On Self Test (POST) for x86-Based Systems

After an x86-based system is turned on, its Basic Input Output System (BIOS) performs a Power On Self Test (POST) that checks to see whether the system has at least a minimally valid configuration. The POST typically checks the amount of physical RAM installed, makes certain there is a working video card, checks for the existence of a working keyboard, and enables cards that use BIOS extensions to perform their own hardware tests. If a problem exists in this phase of the startup process, the system usually signals it with a pattern of beeps (that are different depending on the system manufacturer, but generally can be decoded to help you identify the problem). A problem in this phase of the startup process is hardware related, and usually makes the system unusable until the problem is resolved.

Initial Startup for x86-Based Systems

After the POST has completed, the BIOS attempts to read the Master Boot Record (MBR) from its startup disk. Most x86-based computers default to trying the A drive first and then using the C drive if a disk is not in drive A. Most recently made systems enable you to change the order in which the BIOS tries different drives. You can effect this change by editing the setup variables stored in CMOS, which is a type of nonvolatile memory. If you change your computers to try C before A, it reduces the chances of attack by boot sector viruses from disks accidentally left in the A drive.

After reading the MBR into memory, the BIOS steps out of the picture by turning over control to the MBR. The MBR contains a little program that takes over the next part of the boot process, reading the partition table. The MBR tries to find a partition marked as "active" in the partition table. If it does not find one, it displays an error such as `Missing Operating System` (it will also display this error if the Windows NT boot files are missing or corrupt). If it does find an active partition, the MBR attempts to read the logical sector 0 from that partition into memory.

Sector 0 in an active partition should contain a valid partition boot sector, which is a small program that loads the executable code to start an operating system. This code is operating system dependent and works differently for different operating systems. For Windows NT, it invokes the boot loader.

The Boot Loader for x86-Based Systems

The Windows NT 4 boot loader (NTLDR) supports multiple boot options, including support for other operating systems. The NTLDR file resides in the root directory or folder. Control is passed to NTLDR before the operating system to run is actually selected from the boot menu. NTLDR itself hands over control of the system to whichever operating system is selected to run from the boot menu.

You can see when control has been passed to the Windows NT boot loader because it clears the screen and displays the text

```
OS Loader V4.0
```

against a black background.

At this point, the Windows NT boot loader has shifted the processor into 32-bit mode. Next, it initializes a basic file system by using the standard INT 13 interface for non-SCSI computers, or by loading the SCSI host adapter driver from the NTBOOTDD.SYS file if it is needed. The NTBOOTDD.SYS file is just a copy of a SCSI host adapter driver file that has been renamed and placed in the root folder with its attributes changed so that it is marked as a hidden system file.

With the basic file system support loaded, NTLDR reads the hidden, read-only BOOT.INI file and displays a menu of operating system choices listed in the file. The syntax of the BOOT.INI file is covered later in this chapter in the section "Configuring NT to Support Multiple Operating Systems." Figure 4.1 shows a sample Select Operating System menu.

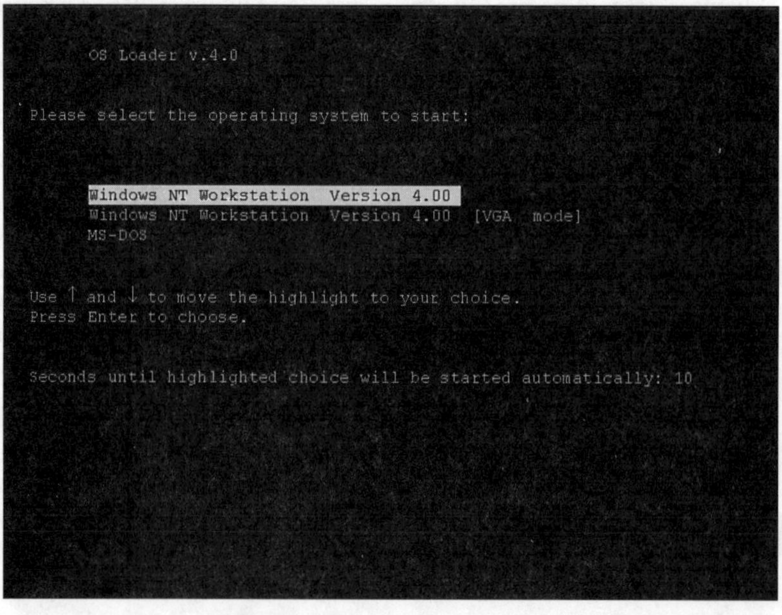

```
     OS Loader v.4.0

Please select the operating system to start:


     Windows NT Workstation  Version 4.00
     Windows NT Workstation  Version 4.00  [VGA mode]
     MS-DOS


Use ↑ and ↓ to move the highlight to your choice.
Press Enter to choose.


Seconds until highlighted choice will be started automatically: 10
```

Figure 4.1

The Windows NT startup can be configured to boot from multiple operating systems.

Windows NT defaults to using a 30-second countdown before invoking the default operating system, but the length of the countdown can be changed to just about any value you like, including:

1. Do not start any operating system automatically (a value of -1).
2. Select the default operating system immediately without prompting (a value of 0).
3. Wait between 1 and 999 seconds before starting the default operating system.

Configuring these options is covered in detail later in this chapter in the section about multiple operating systems. You can configure the latter two choices through the System Properties, but the first choice has to be done by editing the BOOT.INI file directly. You should beware of trusting the values shown in the System Properties if you have edited the BOOT.INI file directly. The System Properties program is just a graphical way of filling in boxes and enabling the system to edit its BOOT.INI behind the scenes, and it does not handle all possible valid values. If, for example, you enter a -1 by manually editing the BOOT.INI, the value shown in the Control Panel will be 429 seconds. When in doubt, check the BOOT.INI file yourself.

When the countdown reaches zero, the highlighted default operating system is invoked. You can select any operating system on the menu and press Enter to start it before the countdown finishes; but if you press an arrow key to highlight one of the other choices, you have all the time in the world to consider which one you want because the countdown stops as soon as you press an arrow key. If you want to watch the system boot up (perhaps while troubleshooting), you can press an arrow key at the boot menu to stop the countdown until it is convenient for you to make the operating system selection and watch it come up. You might do this, for example, if you were just getting ready to watch the initialization process on a system you are testing when your boss comes in to congratulate you on getting an unexpected raise.

The default operating system on the NTLDR menu is the most recent installation of Windows NT unless you have changed it manually. If you select an operating system other than Windows NT, the BOOTSEC.DOS is loaded and control is passed to it.

Windows NT Hardware Detection on x86-Based Systems

After the NT boot loader invokes a copy of Windows NT Workstation either by counting down and invoking the default OS or by the user selecting it manually, the NTLDR next executes NTDETECT.COM to check the system's hardware configuration. NTDETECT.COM searches for the following components in the following order:

1. **Computer ID.** Identifies systems that need things done in other than the usual ways. This is something like AT/AT Compatible for most systems.

2. **Bus/Adapter type.** Detects whether you have a PCI, an EISA, a Micro-Channel, or an ISA bus in the system. Additionally, it will note which types of adapters (PnP, for example) your system supports.

3. **Disk geometry.** Determines the physical layout of the system's boot drive.

4. **ROM blocks.** Identifies which blocks of upper memory are being used by system and adapter card ROM.

5. **Keyboard controller.** Identifies which low-level keyboard controller your system board uses.

6. **Serial controller and ports.** Identifies the type of UART(s) the system uses and the number of serial ports the system has.

7. **Parallel ports.** Identifies to Windows NT how many parallel ports are in the system and the type of each parallel port (EPP, IEEE 1284, and so on).

8. **Disk controller.** Identifies the type of hard disk controller on a system for Windows NT. Common types include IDE, EIDE, and SCSI.

9. **Floppy disks.** Checks for the existence and types of floppy drives.

10. **Disk peripherals.** Checks for devices on the disk controller and reports their types (CD-ROM, hard drive) back to Windows NT.

11. **Pointer peripheral.** Identifies the type of pointing device installed. It reports MICROSOFT SERIAL MOUSE, for example, if one is plugged in. It can also detect other pointing devices such as a bus mouse or a trackball.

12. **Keyboard peripheral.** Checks the type of keyboard installed. The most common one today is the PCAT_ENHANCED, but Windows NT detects and supports several others.

Whichever version you choose, after performing this hardware detection, NTDETECT.COM returns control to the NT boot loader. At this point, you are given the option to use the detected hardware profile or the "last known good" hardware profile. The last known good hardware profile is the one that was stored to the Registry the last time someone successfully logged on to the console.

Generally, you should only choose the last known good hardware profile after changing the device settings for the system to something so drastically incorrect that it will not boot successfully any more. Having the option to roll back changes this way can save you a lot of grief when a system fails to boot after you made some changes to its settings.

If you only have one hardware configuration profile defined, Windows NT loads it. If you have multiple hardware configurations defined—perhaps because you are running NT Workstation on a notebook computer that sometimes plugs in to a docking station—Windows NT pauses at a Hardware Profile/Configuration Recovery menu that lists the system's different hardware configurations and waits either until you select one of them or until the countdown completes before proceeding to load the kernel. You can configure multiple hardware profiles by using the System Properties Program; this is covered later in the chapter, in the section "Configuring Hardware Profiles."

After you either select the hardware configuration (the default hardware configuration is selected automatically if you do not choose the last known good hardware configuration), the Windows NT kernel starts loading.

Loading the Windows NT Kernel on x86-Based Systems

In this phase of the startup process, the boot loader loads the Windows NT kernel (NTOSKRNL.EXE) and the hardware abstraction layer (HAL.DLL) into memory. Next, the Windows NT boot loader uses the information NTDETECT.COM returned to create the HKEY_LOCAL_MACHINE\System\CurrentControlSet hive of the Registry. The boot loader's last job is to load the low-level device drivers specified in the CurrentControlSet by Start values of 0 into memory. After that is done, the boot loader turns program control over to the kernel files, and they begin execution.

Windows NT Initialization on x86-Based Systems

You can easily tell when the kernel begins running, because the first thing it does is turn the display background from black to blue and display a message that contains the operating system version, the build number, the number of processors found in the computer, and the amount of memory.

Now the kernel is in full control of the system. During this part of the Windows NT startup process, the operating system kernel:

1. Initializes the previously loaded low-level device drivers.
2. Loads and initializes additional device drivers.
3. Runs CHKDSK.EXE if scheduled.
4. Loads and initializes the configured services.
5. Creates the paging file(s).
6. Starts the various software subsystems Windows NT needs—including a Virtual DOS Machine (VDM) to run the WoW subsystem.

It is in this part of the startup process that the kernel loads KERNEL32.DLL, GDI32.DLL, and USER32.DLL. These three files provide the Win32 API to client programs.

If you have device configuration problems, this is a likely place for you to run into the "blue screen of death," in which Windows NT Workstation encounters a fatal STOP error. If you run into these, you might want to revert to your last known good configuration. If that does not help, see the section later in this chapter, "Troubleshooting the Startup Process."

In addition to the Client/Server Runtime (CSR) subsystem (see fig. 4.2), other subsystems will also load and initialize at this point if they have been configured to do so. WINLOGON.EXE, which is run by the CSR subsystem, finds which other subsystems to start from the Registry under:

HKEY_LOCAL_MACHINE\System\CurrentControlSet\Control\
Session Manager\Subsystems

Figure 4.2

The Client/Server Runtime system finds the information on other subsystems to start in the Registry.

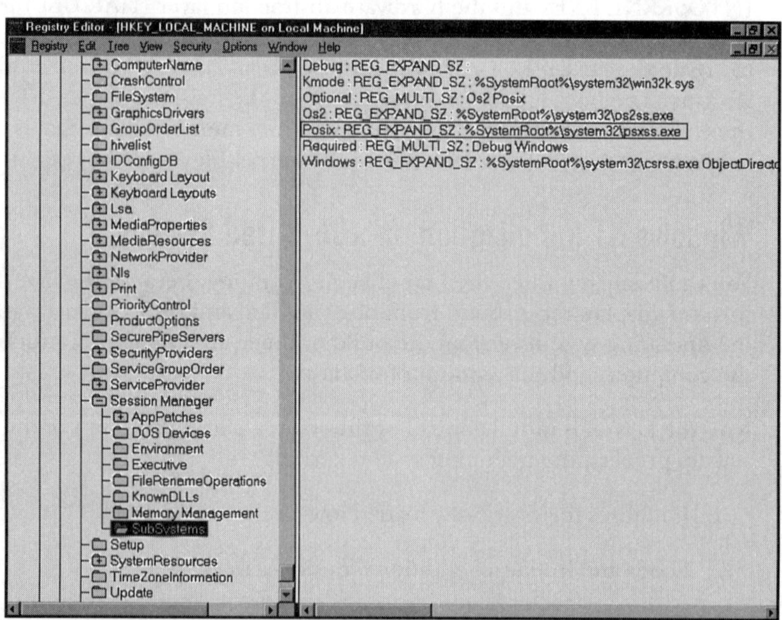

The preceding startup steps for the x86-based system bring you all the way from powering on the system through the initialization phases. RISC-based systems go through these same stages in a different way that is discussed next.

The Startup Process for RISC-Based Systems

Windows NT Workstation is built to support different hardware architectures; in addition to the common x86-based architecture, several other ones all fall under the broad category of RISC-based. These are the Alpha, MIPS, and PowerPC systems designed to be compatible with the Advanced RISC Computer (ARC) standard. None of the RISC-based systems are as popular as systems based on the x86 architecture. The primary reasons RISC-based systems do not have a larger market share are that they are newer than x86-based systems, less versatile than x-86 based systems in that they have vastly fewer operating system and native application choices, and that they tend to cost more. Their primary advantage is that they can be faster than x86-based systems when running applications compiled for their native architecture. This section covers the startup steps, from the Power On Self Test through the Windows NT initialization, for RISC-based systems in the order these steps occur. The final two steps, logging on and user profiles, are in the next section because these last two steps are the same for both x86- and RISC-based systems.

The Power On Self Test (POST) for RISC-Based Systems

When a RISC-based system is turned on, its Basic Input Output System (BIOS) performs a Power On Self Test (POST) that checks to see whether the system has at least a minimally valid configuration. The POST typically checks the amount of physical RAM installed, checks for the existence of a working keyboard, and enables cards that use BIOS extensions perform their own hardware tests (typically video and mass storage cards). If a problem exists in this phase of the startup process, the system usually signals it with a pattern of beeps (the patterns are different depending on the system manufacturer, but generally can be decoded to help you identify the problem). A problem in this phase of the startup process is hardware related, and it usually makes the system unusable until the problem is resolved.

Initial Startup for RISC-Based Systems

After the POST has completed, a RISC-based system begins to act differently from its x86-based counterparts. One of the most obvious differences is the extent to which Windows NT compatible RISC-based systems rely on configuration information stored in Non-Volatile RAM (NVRAM). At this point in the startup process, the BIOS in a RISC-based system reads a boot precedence table from its NVRAM. This is only roughly equivalent to the BIOS on an x86-based platform reading its CMOS settings to find the order in which to try its drives. The NVRAM on a RISC-based system contains a great deal more boot and configuration information, including the path to the operating system loader file, OSLOADER.EXE.

The OSLOADER.EXE performs similar functions to the NTLOADER for x86-based systems. A RISC version of NTDETECT.COM is not needed because Windows NT's OSLOADER.EXE can read all the hardware settings from the NVRAM of ARC compatible systems.

Among other things, the NVRAM holds the full path to the Windows NT boot partition and contains environment variables that ARC-compatible systems use to build their boot menus. The default boot choice on an ARC-compatible system is always the most recently installed operating system unless you select otherwise by using the system's boot configuration tool.

The ARC system's firmware is running the computer based on the information in its BIOS ROMs and its NVRAM until an operating system to boot is selected. The ARC Boot Menu supports multiple boot options, including support for other operating systems (most RISC-based systems can run some variety of Unix).

Here is a sample boot menu from an ARC-compatible computer:

```
ARC Multiboot MIPS R4000 Version 3.5-12
Copyright (c) 1993 Microsoft Corporation
Copyright (c) 1993 Digital Equipment Corporation
Boot Menu:
        Boot Windows NT Workstation Version 4.0
        Boot an alternate operating system
               Run a program
               Supplementary menu. . .
        Use the arrow keys to select, then press Enter.
        Seconds until auto-boot.  Select another option to override: 16
```

The first line of the boot menu (the one that reads `Boot Windows NT Workstation Version 4` in this example) will be highlighted, much as it would be in the x86-based boot menu NTLDR provides for x86-based platforms.

At this point, you can either let the boot menu count down to 0, or you can highlight one of the choices and press enter. Pressing an arrow key stops the timer if you ever want to stop the countdown without selecting an operating system. If Windows NT Workstation is selected, the ARC-compatible computer uses the environment variables stored in its NVRAM to load the correct Windows NT OSLOADER.EXE into memory and turn over program control to it.

RISC-based systems running Windows NT have one major restriction that their x86-based counterparts do not share. The system partition (the one that holds the %systemroot% folder) on a RISC-based system must be formatted with the FAT file system, not the NTFS file system. Remember that the FAT file system does not support any security controls.

Windows NT Hardware Detection on RISC-Based Systems

When the NT operating system loader (OSLOADER.EXE) begins running, the first thing it does is check the system's hardware configuration by reading NVRAM. The operating system loader reads variables for the following components in the following order:

1. **Computer ID.** Tells Windows NT which sort of computer it is running on. On a RISC-based system, it differentiates between DEC Alpha, MIPS R4000, and PowerPC types of systems (along with subtypes within each).

2. **Bus/Adapter type.** Tells Windows NT if you have a PCI, an EISA, or a MicroChannel bus in the system. ARC-compatible systems generally have a PCI bus, but they often have a dual-bus architecture that enables them to have more than one bus. The second bus is usually an EISA bus. They might also have more than one bus of the same type—this is usually done with PCI busses to increase the number of expansion cards a system can support.

3. **Disk geometry.** Determines the physical layout of the system's boot drive.

4. **ROM blocks.** Identifies which blocks of upper memory are being used by system and adapter card ROM.

5. **Keyboard controller.** Identifies which low-level keyboard controller your system board uses.

6. **Serial controller and ports.** Identifies the type of UART(s) the system uses and the number of serial ports the system has.

7. **Parallel ports.** Identifies to Windows NT how many parallel ports are in the system and the type of each parallel port (EPP, IEEE 1284, and so on).

8. **Disk controller.** Identifies the type of hard disk controller on the system for Windows NT. On RISC-based systems this is always some kind of SCSI.

9. **Floppy disks.** Checks for the existence and types of floppy drives.

10. **Disk peripherals.** Checks for devices on the disk controller and reports their types (CD-ROM, hard drive) back to Windows NT.

11. **Pointer peripheral.** Identifies the type of pointing device installed. It reports MICROSOFT SERIAL MOUSE, for example, if one is plugged in. It can also detect other pointing devices such as a bus mouse or a trackball.

12. **Keyboard peripheral.** Checks the type of keyboard installed to make certain that it can recognize which key scan codes correspond to which characters.

After performing this hardware detection, the OS loader gives you the option to use the detected hardware profile or the "last known good" hardware profile. The last known good hardware profile is the one that was stored to the Registry the last time someone successfully logged on to the console.

Generally, you should only select the last known good hardware profile after changing the device settings for the system to something so drastically incorrect that it will not boot successfully any more. Having the option to roll back changes this way can save you a lot of grief when a system fails to boot after you made some changes to its settings.

If you only have one hardware configuration profile defined, Windows NT loads it without prompting. If you have multiple hardware configurations defined—perhaps because you are in a test lab and you have to change peripherals frequently—Windows NT pauses at a Hardware Profile/Configuration Recovery menu that lists the system's different hardware configurations and waits either until you select one of them or until the countdown completes before proceeding to load the kernel. You can use the Hardware Profiles tab of the System dialog box in the Control Panel to set how long Windows NT waits before loading the default hardware profile or to tell it to wait indefinitely until you make a selection manually. If you use one hardware configuration significantly more than the other, you probably want to set it as your default with a relatively short countdown time.

After you either select the hardware configuration (the default hardware configuration is selected automatically if you do not choose the last known good hardware configuration), the Windows NT kernel starts loading.

Loading the Windows NT Kernel on RISC-Based Systems

In this phase of the startup process, the boot loader loads the Windows NT kernel (NTOSKRNL.EXE) and the hardware abstraction layer (HAL.DLL) into memory. Next, the Windows NT boot loader uses the information NTDETECT.COM returned to create the HKEY_LOCAL_MACHINE\System\CurrentControlSet hive of the Registry. The boot loader's last job is to load the low-level device drivers specified in the CurrentControlSet by StartS values of 0 into memory. After that is done, the boot loader turns program control over to the kernel files, and they begin execution.

Windows NT Initialization on RISC-Based Systems

You can easily tell when the kernel begins running, because the first things it does are turn the display background from black to blue and display a message that contains the operating system version, the build number, the number of processors found in the computer, and the amount of memory.

Now the kernel is in full control of the system. During this part of the Windows NT startup process, the operating system kernel:

1. Loads and initializes its device drivers.
2. Runs CHKDSK.EXE if scheduled.
3. Loads and initializes its services.
4. Creates the paging file(s).
5. Starts the various software subsystems Windows NT needs—including a Virtual DOS Machine (VDM) to run the WoW subsystem.

It is in this part of the startup process that the kernel loads KERNEL32.DLL, GDI32.DLL, and USER32.DLL. These three files provide the Win32 API to client programs.

If you have device configuration problems, this is a likely place for you to run into the "blue screen of death," in which Windows NT Workstation encounters a fatal STOP error. If you run into these, you might want to revert to your last known good configuration. If that does not help, see "Troubleshooting the Startup Process" later in this chapter.

In addition to the Client/Server Runtime (CSR) subsystem, which always starts now, other subsystems can also load and initialize at this point if they are configured to do so. WINLOGON.EXE, run by CSR, finds which subsystems to start now from the Registry key:

HKEY_LOCAL_MACHINE\System\CurrentControlSet\Control\
Session Manager\Subsystems

The startup process for x86-based systems and RISC-based systems has been different up to this point. The last few stages of the start-up process are the same for both types of systems.

The Final Stages of Startup—All Systems

The last two steps of the startup process for Windows NT Workstation include logging on and user profiles. These two steps occur in the exact same manner for both x86-based and RISC-based systems. The logon information provides NT with the information it needs to finish its startup process by using the appropriate user profile.

Logging On

You know the system is in its final stages of initialization when you see the Begin Logon window with its familiar `Press Ctrl+Alt+Del to log on` message (see fig. 4.3). This message is displayed by the local security administration subsystem (LSASS.EXE), which is invoked by WINLOGON.EXE. At the point in which Windows NT displays the login box, it might still be initializing some of its drivers, but the core operating system functions are running.

Once the Begin Logon window is displayed, you can enter your user name and password to log on to the system. If drivers are still loading after you have entered your user name and password, you might notice a few more seconds delay than usual while the system displays a message that it is logging you on.

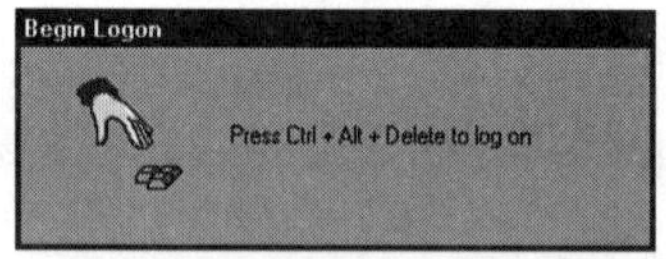

Figure 4.3
Press Ctrl+Alt+Del at the Begin Logon Window.

The Windows NT Workstation operating system has essentially finished its startup process by this time. The only thing left to do is to copy the CloneControlSet (a copy of the CurrentControlSet) to the Registry to be used as the last known good configuration in case you need it for the next startup. Updating the Registry of the Windows NT Workstation by copying the CloneControlSet into the last known good configuration does not happen until someone successfully logs on. This protects against situations where Windows NT thinks it has loaded successfully when it really has not.

After you have successfully logged on to the system the first time, Windows NT displays a Welcome screen (see fig. 4.4). You can choose to have the Welcome screen show each time you start up by leaving the box for Show this Welcome Screen checked. If you would rather not see the Welcome screen every time you start Windows NT, you can uncheck the Show this Welcome Screen box the next time you see it. Leaving it on until you know all the tips that it displays by heart is an easy way to learn more about using Windows NT in a fairly painless way.

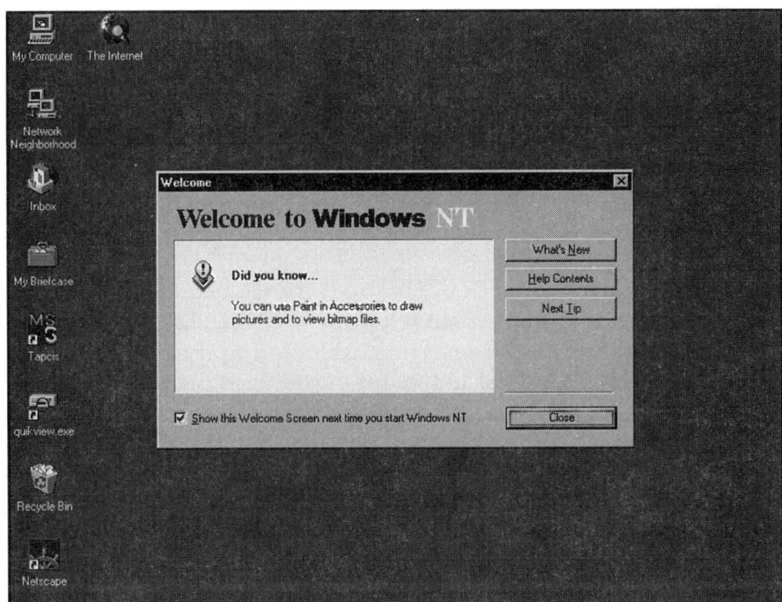

Figure 4.4
You can have the Windows NT Welcome screen display each time you start up.

After you know all the tips it offers, no compelling reason remains to continue viewing them. Some people like having their computer welcome them, but other people find it annoying. Windows NT Workstation enables you to click on one checkbox to have it whichever way you prefer. If you have turned off the Welcome screen and decide you would like to see it again, run Windows Help and search for "Welcome Screen, viewing" in the index.

If you try to log on with an invalid user name or password, the Windows NT security subsystem refuses to enable you to log on. One of the most common problems people have with logon passwords is remembering that the passwords are case sensitive. Entering MYPASSWORD is different than entering mypassword, and neither one is the same as entering MyPassWord. Security is covered later in this book, but remember that generally good practice suggests including some numbers or symbols in your password to make it harder to guess—you should never use passwords like your spouse's name, your favorite sports team, or a type of car you like. Pick the most complicated password you are confident you can remember without writing down.

User Profile

As the last step in the logon process, NT accesses the folders that contain your User Profile. Rather than storing user profile information in the Registry as the previous versions of Windows NT did, Windows NT 4 stores your user profile information in an NTUSER.DAT file that it loads into the Registry each time you log on.

Windows NT loads your NTUSER.DAT file into the Registry hive HKEY_USERS\<Logon Account's Security Identifier>. All the settings from that file and the folders within your Profile directory are visible to Windows NT through an examination of the Registry this way, and yet the data can be stored outside of the Registry. Storing the data outside the Registry makes the Registry much smaller because it does not have to hold information for every user defined in the system. Storing much of the information in folders also makes user management easier if you are administering the system.

Folders and subfolders are under %systemroot%\Profile for each user (see fig. 4.5). These folders contain the details of your system setup and the NTUSER.DAT file loaded into the Registry each time you log on. This enables you to personalize your workstation (desktop arrangement, colors, and so on) to your own tastes.

Figure 4.5

The user profiles are stored in folders under each user's name.

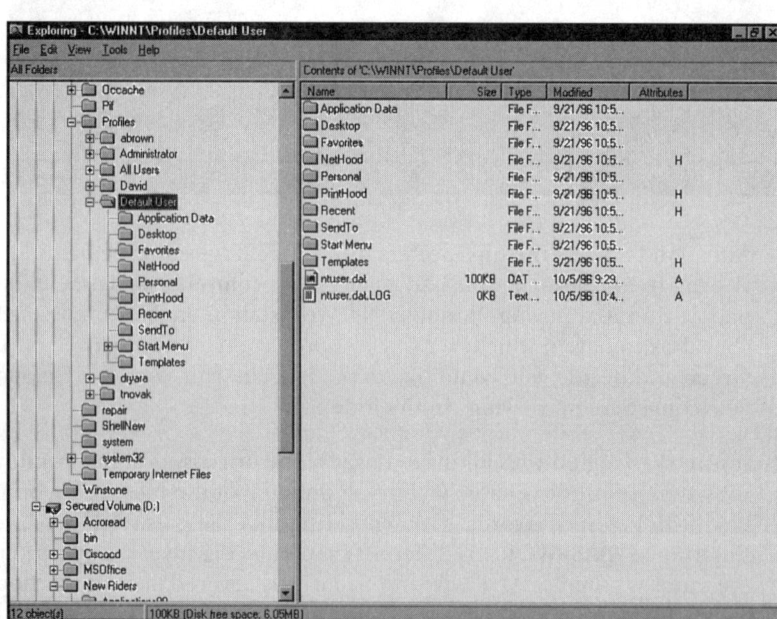

After another user logs on, that user can personalize the working environment to taste, and those personalizations won't affect your settings. In addition to the NTUSER.DAT file, your individual user profile information is stored in the following subfolders under your personal folder in the %systemroot%:\Profile folder:

- Application Data
- Desktop
- Favorites

- NetHood
- Personal
- PrintHood
- Recent
- SendTo
- Start Menu
- Templates

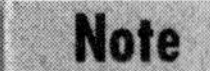

The details of working with user profiles are covered in Chapter 7, "Managing Users."

Now that you know the details on how Windows NT Workstation starts up, you need to know what to do if you encounter a problem during one of the startup steps.

Troubleshooting the Startup Process

Some of the most frequent problems encountered in the startup process are very simple to remedy, though determining the cause might be harder than determining the solution.

This section focuses on the following startup troubleshooting topics:

- Startup & boot loader trouble
- Creating a Windows NT boot floppy
- Creating an emergency repair disk (ERD)
- STOP errors
- Windows NT hardware trouble
- Using the last known good configuration
- Troubleshooting particulars for RISC-based systems
- Logon trouble
- Network trouble

For more information about troubleshooting in general, see Chapter 21, "Troubleshooting and Optimization."

Startup and Pre-Boot Loader Execution Trouble

A problem at the very first stage of the startup process, before the boot loader actually loads, can be indicative of several things, none of them good—but some are easily solved. Some of the possibilities are:

- Hardware problems
- Corrupt master boot record
- Corrupt partition tables or partition boot sector

If the Windows NT Workstation fails before displaying the OS Loader message, likely causes include a hardware failure, hardware misconfiguration, or a damaged disk. Although tracking down the exact cause might not be easy, at least the problem is straightforward to solve. You might have to replace a memory SIMM or a failed interface card of some sort, but it is very unlikely any data on the system was damaged (unless the hard drive or perhaps the disk controller failed—either of those two could imply corrupted data or the need to restore from backup).

If the system hangs without displaying any messages at all, you are likely to be experiencing a serious hardware failure in either the main system board or the video card. The easiest way to identify these for certain is by swapping in a known good part and seeing if the problem goes away. Before swapping parts in and out, however, you should check the connections on everything and reseat the interface cards. If that does not help, you might need to replace some hardware.

If the system gets through its POST and displays messages such as:

- Missing operating system
- A disk read error occurred
- Insert a system disk and restart the system
- Invalid partition table

The problem might be either hardware or software. The boot disk might have broken, but these problems are more commonly caused by some sort of corruption or misconfiguration.

If you have recently made some configuration changes to your system, you should check for some common mistakes. If you have added any sort of interface or peripheral support card to the system, try taking the card out of the system to see if the problem goes away. If it does, you might be experiencing an interrupt conflict, an I/O port conflict, or a shared memory conflict. To resolve these problems, you should document which interrupts, I/O ports, and shared memory areas are already used on your system—or, more to the point, which ones are not in use yet. After you know which interrupts, I/O ports, and shared memory address spaces are available for you to use, make certain that the interface card you are installing is configured to use resources nothing else will try to claim. Only change one thing at a time, or else you will have trouble figuring out what it was that actually resolved the problem.

Remember that systems reserve some interrupts, I/O ports, and shared memory address space for their own system board's use, so be certain to check for the system's reserved resources when you are documenting which ones are available.

If your system uses SCSI devices, you should check that the SCSI bus is terminated properly. An incorrectly terminated SCSI bus can evidence itself in many ways, but the most obvious of these is when nothing on the SCSI bus appears to be visible to the system. Some less obvious failure modes include devices only visible to the system some of the time or device errors when you are using them.

If you intend to boot from a SCSI device, your system needs to have the SCSI host adapter's BIOS enabled so that it can hook into the boot process. If everything else seems all right, but you do not see any messages from your SCSI host adapter at boot time, this might be the problem.

If you are concerned that some of the Windows NT startup files might have been corrupted, you can easily check that by booting from a Windows NT Startup disk.

If you suspect that your problem lies with a driver, you can add the /sos switch to the NT Workstation line in BOOT.INI as follows:

```
multi(0)disk(0)rdisk(0)partition(1)\winnt=Windows NT Workstation 4.0 /sos
```

Edit the BOOT.INI file to have NT display each driver as it is loaded. See the section later in the chapter for editing the BOOT.INI file for more details.

Creating a Windows NT Boot Floppy

In some circumstances, you might want to boot Windows NT from a floppy. If you suspect that the partition table on the drive might have become corrupted, or if one half of a mirror set has failed, you might choose to use a Windows NT boot floppy to work around the problem so that you can solve it.

To create a Windows NT boot floppy, you must format the floppy under Windows NT instead of using a floppy formatted on another system. This is because a Windows NT format copies the Windows NT partition's boot sector (which you need for the Windows NT boot loader to run) to the floppy.

The files that you need to copy have their Read Only, Hidden, and System attributes set. You can select View, Show All Files in the Windows Explorer and edit their properties there, or you can do it from the command line by using ATTRIB.EXE. You need to remove the Hidden and System properties before copying the files.

You need to change the properties of the following files:

- **NTLDR.** The Windows NT boot loader program.
- **BOOT.INI.** Describes the location of the boot partition for each operating system installed and configured. You might want to edit the one on the floppy if you are intending to use it for special purposes, like booting off the secondary drive in a mirror set.
- **NTDETECT.COM.** Detects the hardware installed on your system.
- **BOOTSECT.DOS.** Dual-boots another root-based operating system. You do not need it unless you are planning on using the dual-boot features from the disk when using the Windows NT startup floppy disk.
- **NTBOOTDD.SYS.** A copy of the boot SCSI host adapter's driver file, and required only if you are using the scsi() syntax in the BOOT.INI file. Note that sometimes the multi() syntax only works when the BOOT.INI is on the hard disk, and you might need to use the scsi() syntax here. Test it on your system to be certain.

After you have copied these files to the boot disk, it is ready to test. Make certain that your system's CMOS settings enable it to boot from drive A and restart your system. If it reads the A drive and starts successfully, the boot disk is valid. You should take the boot disk and store it in a safe place in case you ever need it.

Creating an Emergency Repair Disk

You can take some important precautions so that you are ready to recover from a startup problem. One of the most important is creating a Windows NT emergency repair disk (ERD). The emergency repair disk is used to check your current configuration against the configuration in use when the repair disk was made. The ERD contains a copy of your system's Registry and a list of the installed Windows NT files. Because this configuration information is specific to and different for each system's configuration, a single ERD is not sufficient for your workgroup. Each Windows NT computer needs its own ERD. If you did not make one at installation, make one now! In fact, make a spare copy and keep both of them well-labeled and in different safe places. Whenever you make significant hardware or configuration changes, make certain to update your ERDs.

The following steps illustrate how to create an emergency repair disk:

1. From the Start menu, select Run.

2. Type in **rdisk** (this runs the file %systemroot%\system32\rdisk.exe)

3. The Repair Disk Utility dialog box opens. Click on Update Repair Info (see fig. 4.6). This does not write anything to the disk drive. Instead, it builds a new copy of the required information for your Windows NT system. You should do this every time you make changes to your system's configuration. It is safest to do it every time you make a set of repair disks, even if you have not changed the system's configuration recently just to be certain that the information is up to date. The repair information compiled by this is stored in the %systemroot%\Repair folder.

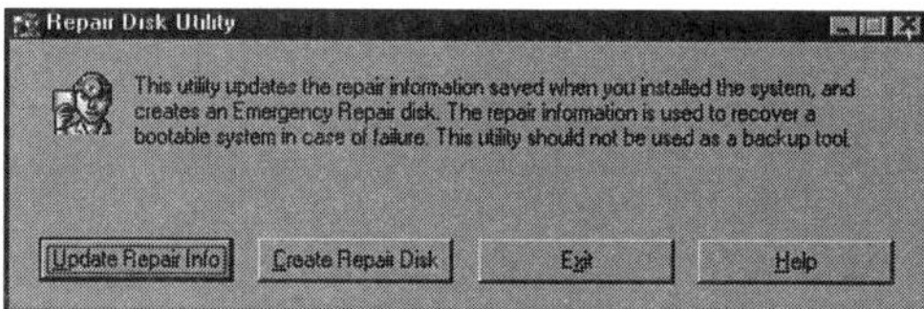

Figure 4.6

Update the repair information before creating your repair disk.

4. The next dialog box offers you the option of creating an emergency repair disk from the newly updated information (see fig. 4.7). This overwrites previous repair information. Click on the Yes button.

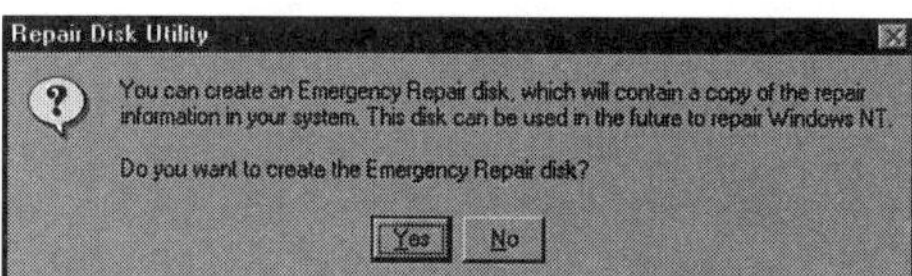

Figure 4.7

Create a repair disk before you need it!

5. Figure 4.8 shows the next dialog box, which prompts you to put a labeled, formatted disk in the A drive and then click on OK.

Figure 4.8
Insert a labeled floppy disk; all previous contents will be erased.

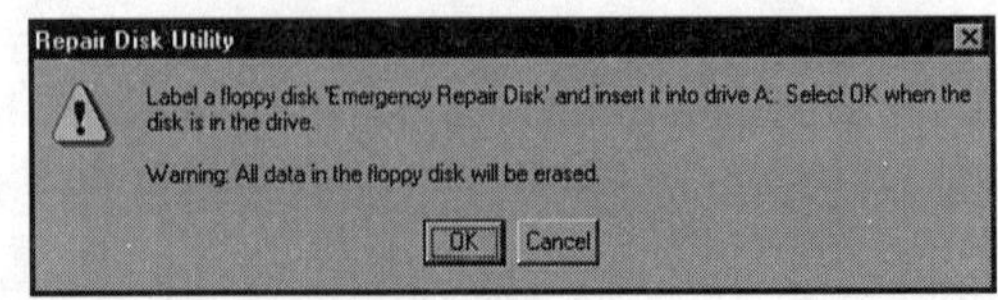

After it finishes, you have an emergency repair disk. Here is a sample directory of an emergency repair disk:

```
Directory of A:\

09/21/96  11:25a              47,066 setup.log
10/01/96  04:44p             160,582 system._
10/01/96  04:45p             369,478 software._
09/21/96  11:28a               4,591 security._
09/21/96  11:28a               3,649 sam._
09/21/96  11:28a              21,757 default._
10/01/96  04:45p              18,419 ntuser.da_
08/09/96  01:30a                 438 autoexec.nt
09/21/96  11:24a               2,510 config.nt
               9 File(s)      628,490 bytes
                              827,904 bytes free
```

You have probably noticed that this disk does not have any of the files you need to boot Windows NT on it. This is because the ERD is not a boot disk. All the files on the emergency repair disk, except for the SETUP.LOG, are backup copies of data from the system on which the emergency repair disk was created. The SETUP.LOG file is a record of the files Windows NT Setup copied to your system, including the path names where they were installed and checksums for all the files so that they can be verified.

The following is a section of the SETUP.LOG file:

```
 [Paths]
TargetDirectory = "\WINNT"
TargetDevice = "\Device\Harddisk0\partition1"
SystemPartitionDirectory = "\"
SystemPartition = "\Device\Harddisk0\partition1"
[Signature]
Version = "WinNt4.0"
[Files.SystemPartition]
ntldr = "ntldr","2a36b"
```

```
NTDETECT.COM = "NTDETECT.COM","b69e"
[Files.WinNt]
\WINNT\Help\31users.hlp = "31users.hlp","12bfc"
\WINNT\Help\acc_dis.cnt = "acc_dis.cnt","cc99"
\WINNT\Help\acc_dis.hlp = "acc_dis.hlp","b82c"
\WINNT\inf\accessor.inf = "accessor.inf","13070"
\WINNT\system32\acledit.dll = "acledit.dll","2be50"
\WINNT\system32\advapi32.dll = "advapi32.dll","408a5"
\WINNT\system32\drivers\afd.sys = "afd.sys","17142"
\WINNT\system32\alrsvc.dll = "alrsvc.dll","fa69"
\WINNT\system32\amddlg.dll = "amddlg.dll","4e1a"
\WINNT\system32\ansi.sys = "ansi.sys","2aa6"
\WINNT\Fonts\app850.fon = "app850.fon","14845"
\WINNT\system32\append.exe = "append.exe","448b"
\WINNT\inf\apps.inf = "apps.inf","11c5f"
\WINNT\system32\appwiz.cpl = "appwiz.cpl","1b943"
\WINNT\Fonts\arial.ttf = "arial.ttf","2d945"
\WINNT\Fonts\arialbd.ttf = "arialbd.ttf","2d595"
\WINNT\Fonts\arialbi.ttf = "arialbi.ttf","32fb1"
\WINNT\Fonts\ariali.ttf = "ariali.ttf","2e6e8"
\WINNT\system32\at.exe = "at.exe","99c1"
\WINNT\system32\drivers\atapi.sys = "atapi.sys","e3a9"
\WINNT\system32\drivers\atdisk.sys = "atdisk.sys","c769"
\WINNT\system32\atsvc.exe = "atsvc.exe","b4d5"
\WINNT\system32\attrib.exe = "attrib.exe","fe3e"
\WINNT\system32\audiocdc.hlp = "audiocdc.hlp","64b6"
\WINNT\system32\autochk.exe = "autochk.exe","5fee8"
\WINNT\system32\autoconv.exe = "autoconv.exe","6768c"
\WINNT\system32\autolfn.exe = "autolfn.exe","b3e0"
\WINNT\system32\avicap.dll = "avicap.dll","1fb6f"
\WINNT\system32\avicap32.dll = "avicap32.dll","1ac84"
\WINNT\system32\avifil32.dll = "avifil32.dll","1f886"
\WINNT\system32\avifile.dll = "avifile.dll","1db85"
\WINNT\system32\backup.cnt = "backup.cnt","112e"
\WINNT\system32\backup.exe = "backup.exe","8f18"
\WINNT\system32\backup.hlp = "backup.hlp","ec8b"
\WINNT\system32\basesrv.dll = "basesrv.dll","1014b"
\WINNT\system32\drivers\beep.sys = "beep.sys","f7fb"
\WINNT\system32\bios1.rom = "bios1.rom","14b82"
\WINNT\system32\bios4.rom = "bios4.rom","b29b"
\WINNT\black16.scr = "black16.scr","cbef"
\WINNT\system32\bootok.exe = "bootok.exe","b0fd"
```

```
\WINNT\system32\bootvrfy.exe = "bootvrfy.exe","11b7f"
\WINNT\system32\c_10000.nls = "c_10000.nls","1ab4a"
\WINNT\system32\chcp.com = "chcp.com","129f3"
\WINNT\system32\chkdsk.exe = "chkdsk.exe","1311d"
\WINNT\system32\dc21x4.hlp = "dc21x4.hlp","fb66"
...
etc.
```

When To Use the Emergency Repair Disk

Error messages that occur before or during the loading of NTLDR can indicate a problem with the root directory, and you generally resolve these messages by using the NT emergency repair disk. You should use the emergency repair disk any time the system files have been accidentally deleted or damaged, any time the Registry has been corrupted, or any time the partition boot sector has been damaged.

The most common cause of missing system files is operator error. It is easy to delete one too many files when cleaning up a system; if this happens, you might need to use the emergency repair disk to recover. If you are working on a FAT file system with a dual boot configuration, you might be able to boot up under some other operating system such as DOS and run a utility for recovering deleted files. If you were working on an NTFS partition, however, you need to go through the emergency repair process.

Damaged registries can be caused by many things, but user error is the most common cause of problems. Any time you need to look at the Registry, use %SYSTEMROOT%\REGEDIT.EXE in read-only mode unless you have a specific need to change the Registry. Always verify that you have a current backup of the Registry before you make any changes whenever you plan to edit it.

The partition boot sector of a hard drive is rarely damaged through normal system operation, but many computer viruses out there will damage it. The most common computer viruses are transmitted by people accidentally booting from infected disks. By the time you see the message telling you the disk was not a system disk, your system might have already been infected, and very few anti-virus systems can protect you before the system has booted.

If you have a problem booting, and using the last known good configuration does not help, it is time to try using the emergency repair process. Microsoft could have picked a less intimidating name for the process, but are probably trying to impress people that these things are not to be taken lightly. In any case, you need to know how to perform an emergency repair.

How To Use the Emergency Repair Disk

To perform an emergency repair of a system's Windows NT Workstation installation, follow this procedure:

1. Make certain that you have a current emergency repair disk made for the particular system that you need to repair.
2. Start Windows NT from the Windows NT Workstation Setup Disk 1. If you do not have copies of the Windows NT Workstation setup disks, you can make a new set from the Windows NT Workstation CD-ROM by running WINNT /OX from a workstation running DOS, 16-bit Windows, or Windows 95; or by running WINNT32 /OX from another Windows NT system.
3. Your system should be configured to boot from its A drive. Insert the Windows NT Workstation Setup Disk 1 and power on the system.
4. The system reads the A drive and begins loading Windows NT. After it finishes loading the first disk, it prompts you for the second disk.
5. After the system reads the second disk, the system prompts you to select whether you are performing a new installation or a repair. Press R to begin the repair process (see fig. 4.9).

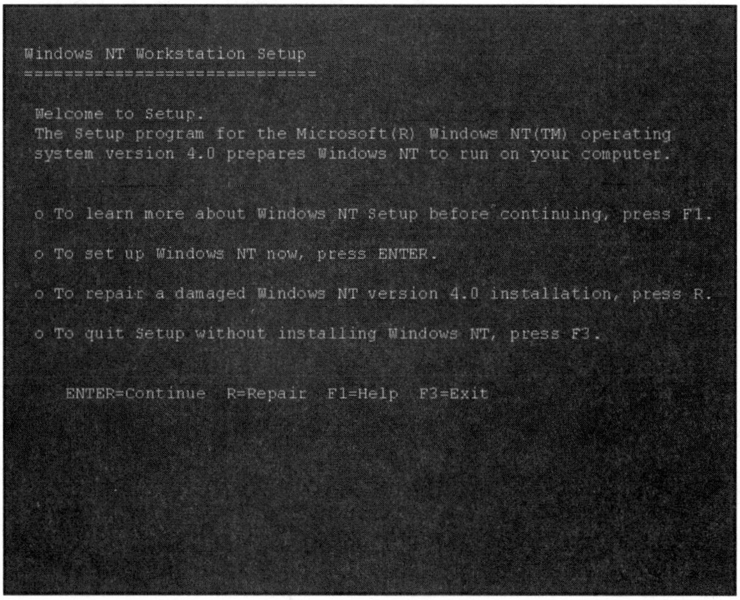

```
Windows NT Workstation Setup
=============================

 Welcome to Setup.
 The Setup program for the Microsoft(R) Windows NT(TM) operating
 system version 4.0 prepares Windows NT to run on your computer.

 o To learn more about Windows NT Setup before continuing, press F1.

 o To set up Windows NT now, press ENTER.

 o To repair a damaged Windows NT version 4.0 installation, press R.

 o To quit Setup without installing Windows NT, press F3.

    ENTER=Continue  R=Repair  F1=Help  F3=Exit
```

Figure 4.9

Use the Windows NT Workstation Setup disks to start a Windows NT emergency repair session.

6. Figure 4.10 shows several additional tasks associated with repairing Windows NT Workstation. By default, the Windows NT repair process tests for all of them. If you want Windows NT to skip testing one or more of them, highlight the choices you want to change and deselect them. You might do this if you already know what the problem is and you want to hurry the repair process along.

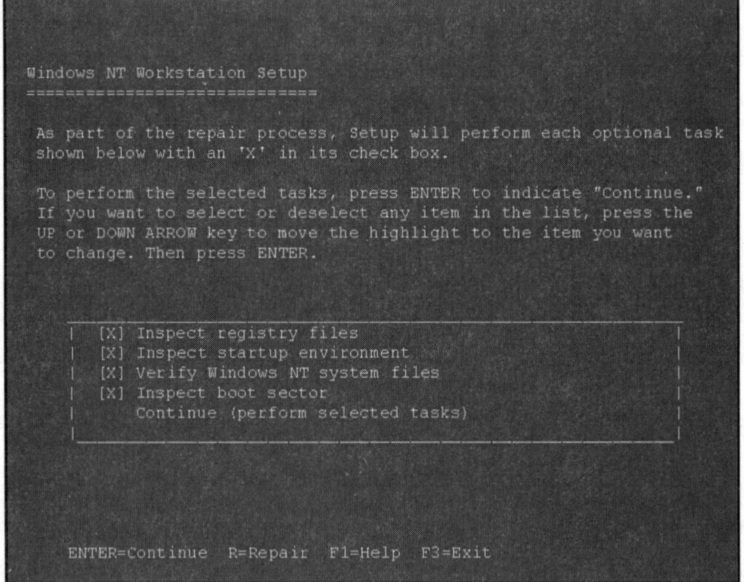

Windows NT Workstation Setup
As part of the repair process, Setup will perform each optional task shown below with an 'X' in its check box.
To perform the selected tasks, press ENTER to indicate "Continue." If you want to select or deselect any item in the list, press the UP or DOWN ARROW key to move the highlight to the item you want to change. Then press ENTER.
[X] Inspect registry files
[X] Inspect startup environment
[X] Verify Windows NT system files
[X] Inspect boot sector
Continue (perform selected tasks)
ENTER=Continue R=Repair F1=Help F3=Exit

Figure 4.10

Select which optional repair tasks you want performed.

7. Press Enter to Continue the repair process.
8. The setup program automatically detects standard hard and floppy drives. Some devices, such as certain types of CD-ROM drives or tape-backup devices, can cause the system to hang. You can select whether to have setup try to automatically detect these devices by pressing Enter. If you want to skip this step and identify the mass storage devices manually, press S (see fig. 4.11).
9. A prompt requests disk 3. Insert and press Enter. Windows NT now attempts to detect mass storage devices by loading the drivers for all the ones it supports and testing to see which ones load successfully.
10. The setup program displays its findings. To accept them, press Enter.
11. Setup now prompts you to insert the emergency repair disk. Do so, and press Enter (see fig. 4.12).

```
Windows NT Workstation Setup
============================

 Setup automatically detects floppy disk controllers and standard
 ESDI/IDE hard disks without user intervention. However, on some
 computers detection of certain other mass storage devices, such as
 SCSI adapters and CD-ROM drives, can cause the computer to become
 unresponsive or to malfunction temporarily.

 For this reason, you can bypass Setup's mass storage device detection
 and manually select SCSI adapters, CD-ROM drives, and special disk
 controllers (such as drive arrays) for installation.

    o To continue, Press ENTER.
      Setup will attempt to detect mass storage devices in your
      computer.

    o To skip mass storage device detection, press S.
      Setup will allow you to manually select SCSI adapters,
      CD-ROM drives, and special disk controllers for installation.

    ENTER=Continue  R=Repair  F1=Help  F3=Exit
```

Figure 4.11

The Windows NT Workstation can autodetect certain hardware.

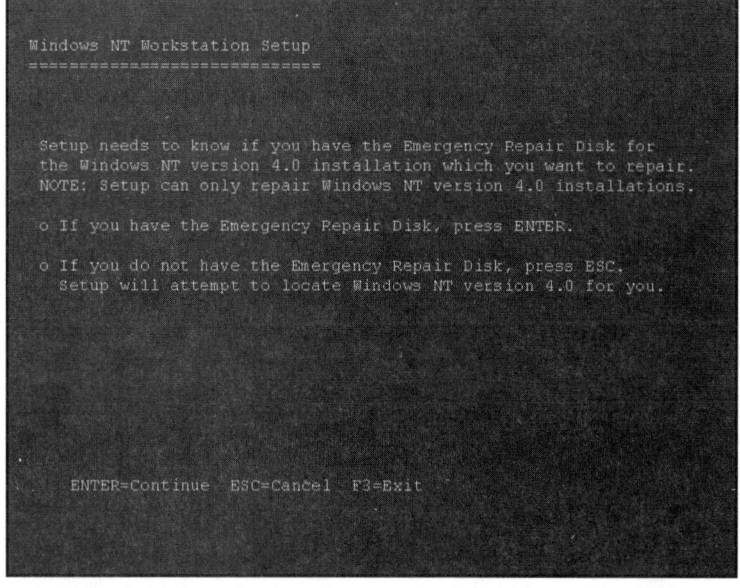

Windows NT Workstation Setup
============================
Setup needs to know if you have the Emergency Repair Disk for
the Windows NT version 4.0 installation which you want to repair.
NOTE: Setup can only repair Windows NT version 4.0 installations.
o If you have the Emergency Repair Disk, press ENTER.
o If you do not have the Emergency Repair Disk, press ESC.
Setup will attempt to locate Windows NT version 4.0 for you.
ENTER=Continue ESC=Cancel F3=Exit

Figure 4.12

Insert the emergency repair disk.

12. Windows NT selects each of the Registry files that it believes it needs based on its capability to access the Registry. If you want to replace a part of the Registry that Windows NT did not detect a problem with, you can select it here as part of the repair process. If you restore a Registry file, your current configuration will be overwritten and you will lose any changes made since creating the ERD files (see fig. 4.13).

Figure 4.13

You can choose to restore selected Registry files.

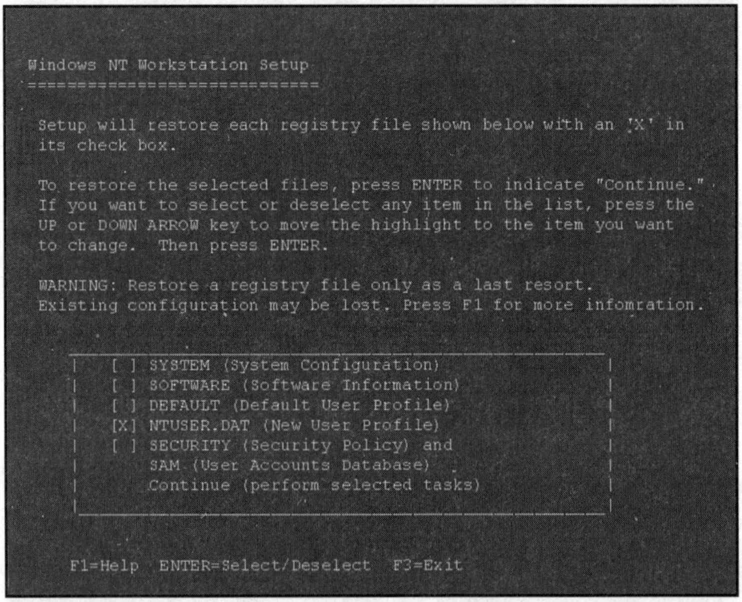

```
Windows NT Workstation Setup
============================

 Setup will restore each registry file shown below with an 'X' in
 its check box.

 To restore the selected files, press ENTER to indicate "Continue."
 If you want to select or deselect any item in the list, press the
 UP or DOWN ARROW key to move the highlight to the item you want
 to change.  Then press ENTER.

 WARNING: Restore a registry file only as a last resort.
 Existing configuration may be lost. Press F1 for more infomration.

    ________________________________________________
    |  [ ] SYSTEM (System Configuration)           |
    |  [ ] SOFTWARE (Software Information)         |
    |  [ ] DEFAULT (Default User Profile)          |
    |  [X] NTUSER.DAT (New User Profile)           |
    |  [ ] SECURITY (Security Policy) and          |
    |      SAM (User Accounts Database)            |
    |      Continue (perform selected tasks)       |
    |______________________________________________|

    F1=Help  ENTER=Select/Deselect  F3=Exit
```

13. The Setup program, now running the emergency repair disk, checks your system-critical files to determine if there are problems. In figure 4.14, the Setup found that the file NTDETECT.COM is different from the original NTDETECT.COM that was installed initially. Choose to repair the file by pressing Enter, otherwise skip the repair of the file by pressing Esc. Also, you can choose to repair all files by pressing A.

You might have some files that have been updated to newer versions either as known bug fixes or for application support. You might not want to update them, because doing so might introduce problems in your application environment.

14. Before you press Enter to restart the system, make certain that you have removed the disk from the floppy drive.

NT comes with Disk Administrator Tools that you can access if you can get to NT. If the system will not boot, try booting from the Windows NT floppy disk. The Disk Administrator is covered in more detail in Chapter 20, "Protecting Hardware and Files."

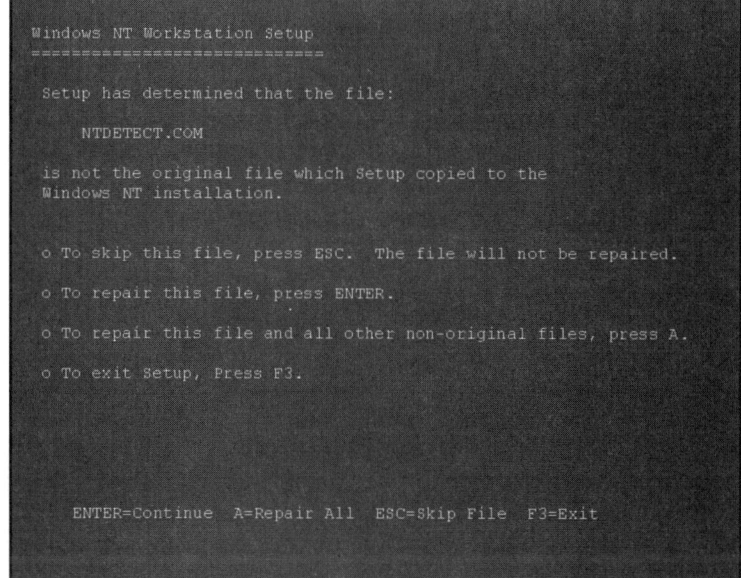
Windows NT Workstation Setup
============================

Setup has determined that the file:

NTDETECT.COM

is not the original file which Setup copied to the
Windows NT installation.

o To skip this file, press ESC. The file will not be repaired.

o To repair this file, press ENTER.

o To repair this file and all other non-original files, press A.

o To exit Setup, Press F3.

ENTER=Continue A=Repair All ESC=Skip File F3=Exit

Figure 4.14

Setup repairs non-original files if selected.

STOP Error

One of the more dreaded system problem indicators is a STOP error—the "blue screen of death." The computer gets to the blue screen in the start up process and then collapses. This type of system crash has many possible causes:

- Registry errors or corrupt Registry files
- Configuration or hardware problems with the system critical devices, such as the video adapter or hard drive
- Bad or missing partition boot sector
- Virus
- Incompatible logical block addressing (LBA) on a hard drive

What happens after a STOP error depends on what settings you have chosen in the system configuration.

If you have administrator privileges, you can select options for the system recovery. Some of the options are dependent on disk space and amount of memory.

1. From the Control Panel, double-click on the System icon.

2. Select the Startup/Shutdown tab (see fig. 4.15). Under the Recovery section, check the options you want under When a STOP error occurs do the following:

   - Write an event to the system log
   - Send an administrative alert
   - Write debugging information to:
   - Automatically reboot

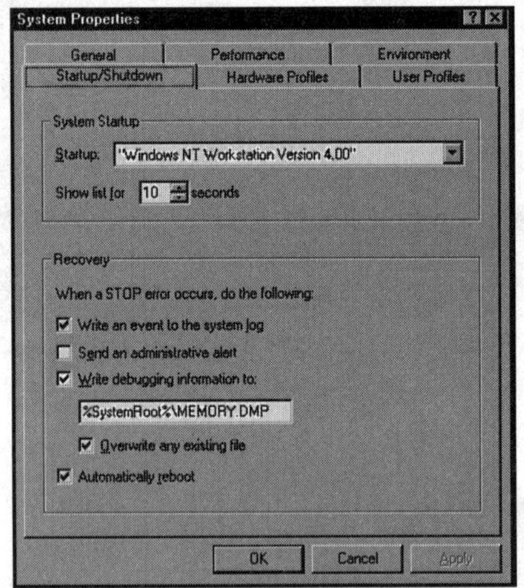

Figure 4.15

You can configure NT to respond to a STOP error with several options.

3. Select the options you want.

Selecting all three options necessitates the existence of a paging file of 2 MB or more. The memory dump, which contains the debugging information, requires a paging file 1 MB larger than the amount of RAM on your computer.

This memory dump file is always saved to the same file, which means that a previous dump is overwritten. If you want to keep track of these previous files you need to rename them. If you are continuing to try to solve the problem, it might be helpful to see the results of your changes. Also, product support might want the memory dump file to help determine the problem.

Windows NT Hardware Trouble

An error message or system crash during the NTDETECT phase might indicate a hardware configuration problem. You can see all the devices load in the level of detail an operating systems programmer would need while debugging (in other words, a *lot* of detail is here), by running a special version of the NTDETECT.COM included on the installation CD-ROM but not installed automatically. The file that does this is NTDETECT.CHK in the installation CD-ROM's \SUPPORT\DEBUG\I386 folder. To use it, follow this procedure:

1. Using the Windows NT Explorer, locate and right-click the NTDETECT.COM in the root folder of your boot drive. (You might need to select Hidden files, Show all files from the View tab of the options dialog box in order to see it listed. Also, if you want to see the COM file extension, you can enable this from the Options dialog box View tab if you haven't already. The default is to hide file extensions for known file types, of which COM is one.)

2. Choose Properties from the menu. The file properties of NTDETECT.COM appears (see fig. 4.16).

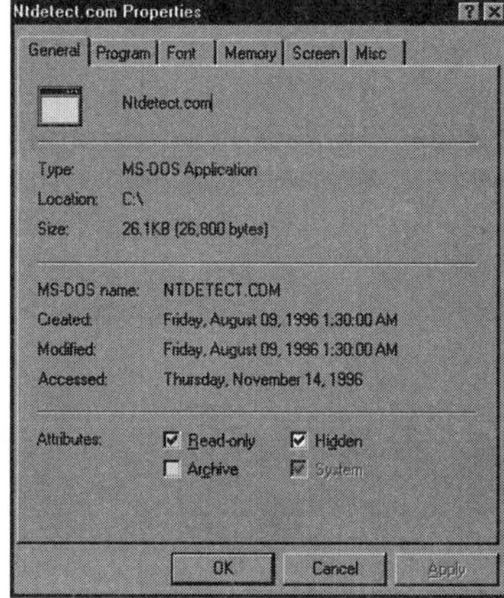

Figure 4.16

The NTDETECT.COM file properties must be changed in order to rename the file.

3. Uncheck the Hidden and Read-only boxes.

4. Click on the Apply button, and then click on the OK button to close the Property dialog box.

5. Back up the NTDETECT.COM by leaving it in place and renaming it to NTDETECT.BAK.

6. Copy the appropriate NTDETECT.CHK (there is a different one for each hardware architecture that Windows NT supports) to the root folder of your boot drive.

7. Rename the NTDETECT.CHK to NTDETECT.COM.

8. The next time you reboot, the details of what NTDETECT.COM discovers about the system appears.
9. When you want to go back to using an NTDETECT.COM that does not prompt you several times during the startup process, rename the NTDETECT.COM file to NTDETECT.CHK and put the original NTDETECT.COM back (by renaming it or copying it from the CD-ROM).

Here is the type of NTDETECT.COM information you will see during the startup process:

```
GetPnpBiosData:  PnpBios Get DeviceNode returns nodesize 0019 for node 0004
GetPnpBiosData:  PnpBios Get DeviceNode returns nodesize 0016 for node 0005
GetPnpBiosData:  PnpBios Get DeviceNode returns nodesize 0019 for node 0006
GetPnpBiosData:  PnpBios Get DeviceNode returns nodesize 0010 for node 0007
GetPnpBiosData:  PnpBios Get DeviceNode returns nodesize 0014 for node 0008
GetPnpBiosData:  PnpBios Get DeviceNode returns nodesize 007E for node 0009
GetPnpBiosData:  PnpBios Get DeviceNode returns nodesize 0016 for node 000A
GetPnpBiosData:  PnpBios Get DeviceNode returns nodesize 002F for node 000B
GetPnpBiosData:  PnpBios Get DeviceNode returns nodesize 0039 for node 000C
GetPnpBiosData:  PnpBios Get DeviceNode returns nodesize 0059 for node 000D
GetPnpBiosData:  PnpBios Get DeviceNode returns nodesize 0059 for node 000E
GetPnpBiosData:  PnpBios Get DeviceNode returns nodesize 003E for node 000F
GetPnpBiosData:  PnpBios Get DeviceNode returns nodesize 003E for node 0010
GetPnpBiosData:  PnpBios Get DeviceNode returns nodesize 0016 for node 00FF
GetPnpBiosData:  PnpBios total size of nodes 0005037D
Pnp Bios  Data collection complete. . .
Detecting Bus/Adapter Component . . .
Collecting Disk Geometry . . .
Detecting ROM Blocks . . .
Invalid heap deallocation . . .
Detecting Keyboard Component . . .
Detecting ComPort Component . . .
Detecting Parallel Component . . .
Detecting Mouse Component . . .
Detecting Floppy Component . . .
67f3704b-a7d26e90-A
b8a5585d-f00000fd-X
Detection done. Press a key to display hardware info . . .
```

```
Current Node: 00050000
     Type = MaximumType
            Child = 00050045
            Parent = 00000000
            Sibling = 00000000
            ConfigurationData = 0005048B
IdentifierLength = 00000011
Identifier = AT/AT COMPATIBLE
ConfigdataLength = 00000058
Version = 0000 Revision = 0000
Count = 0002
Type = Device Data
Size = 00000018
0080 0000 006B 0002 0000 0000 003F 0000 003F 0000 0001 0000 0081 0000 00FF 0003
0000 0000 0000 0000 00FF 0000 0001 0000


Current Node: 00050045
     Type = MultifunctionAapter
            Child = 00000000
            Parent = 00050000
            Sibling = 00050416
            ConfigurationData = 0005007D
IdentifierLength = 00000004
Identifier = PCI
ConfigdataLength = 0000001C
Version = 0000 Revision = 0000
Count = 0001
Type = Device Data
Size = 00000004
0002 0010 0001 0001


Current Node: 00050416
     Type = MultifunctionAapter
            Child = 00000000
            Parent = 00050000
            Sibling = 00050453
            ConfigurationData = 00050099
```

```
IdentifierLength = 00000009
Identifier = PNP BIOS
ConfigdataLength = 0000037D
Version = 0000 Revision = 0000
Count = 0001
Type = Device Data
Size = 00000365
0024 0050 006E 0050 0010 0021 0000 0000 0098 0000 0000 0000 0000 002A 00A2 0000
00F0 0054 00A2 0000 0000 000F 0000 0000 0000 0000 0000 0040 0000 0000 0004 0000
0000 001D 0000 0000 0041 00D0 0000 0000 0008 0000 0001 0003 0000 004B 0020 0000
0002 004B 00A0 0000 0002 0022 0004 0000 0079 0000 0079 0000 0079 0000 0055 0000
```

If you are having startup problems after you have added an additional hard drive, the problem might be an incorrect HAL.DLL and\or NTOSKRNL.EXE. With some hard drives, if you install NT and later add another drive you might get HAL errors. It is probably necessary to reinstall NT on the remaining drive. Otherwise, changing to the correct HAL.DLL and NTOSKRNL.EXE might solve any problems here.

If you suspect RAM problems (perhaps you just added more), you can restrict NT to use only a certain amount of the total memory available. Do not specify less than 12 MB. This can be helpful in pinpointing problems like parity errors that the memory subsystem is not able to report.

1. Right-click on the BOOT.INI file in the C:\ directory.
2. Choose Properties from the menu, and uncheck the read-only and hidden attributes if they are checked.
3. Click on the Apply button, and then click on OK.
4. Open the file with a text editor such as Notepad by double-clicking on it.
5. Edit the operating system(s) line by adding the /maxmem switch and specifying the amount of memory.

If you want to limit your computer to use only 16 MB of memory, for example, your Windows NT line in the BOOT.INI would look something like this:

```
multi(0)disk(0)rdisk(0)partition(1)\winnt=Windows NT Workstation 4.0 /maxmem=16
```

Using the Last Known Good Configuration

The last known good configuration is stored in the Registry (see fig. 4.17). Each time NT successfully initializes, it compares its current configuration with the last known good configuration. If they do not match, NT overwrites the old last known good configuration with the new one. If you changed something in the system's configuration, and it would not boot successfully, you can select to use the last known good configuration at startup. Sometimes NT detects a problem and automatically chooses to use the last known good configuration.

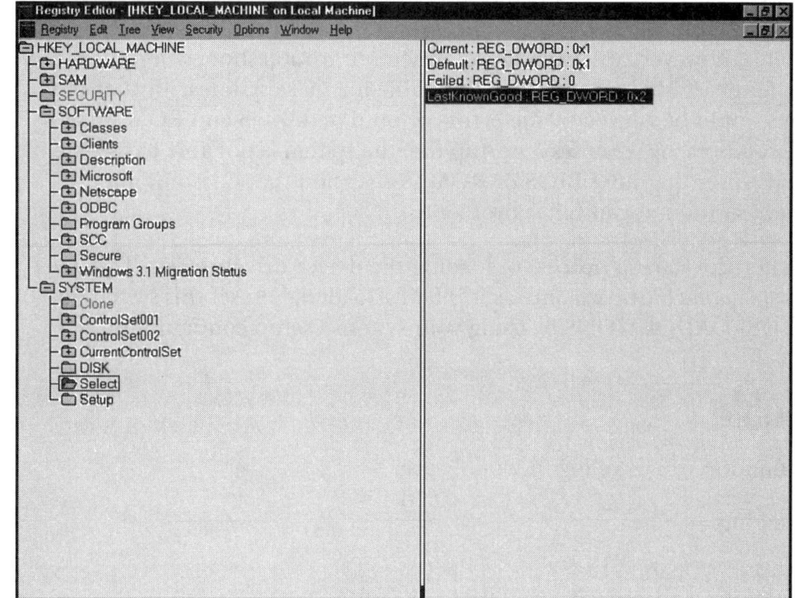

Figure 4.17

The Registry holds information about the last known good configuration.

The last known good controls are found in the Registry under:

HKEY_LOCAL_MACHINE\System\Select

If you press the spacebar when the boot screen appears that says `Press spacebar now to invoke last-known-good menu`, you start the system by using the previously successful configuration.

The last known good configuration provides a fall-back if the system does not boot under its current configuration. This is particularly helpful if you have just made some configuration or hardware changes. After you use the last known good configuration, this configuration becomes the Current Configuration and your previous changes are overwritten. It is important not to log on if the system seems to be having trouble. After you actually log on, NT considers your configuration to be acceptable and saves it as the last known good configuration.

Troubleshooting Particulars for RISC-Based Systems

Due to the booting differences between RISC-based computers and x86 computers, the RISC-based systems have a more trouble-resistant startup. Because the booting information is stored in the NVRAM, viruses cannot attack those elements critical for startup—the master boot record and the partition boot sector.

RISC-based systems, however, are often more difficult to troubleshoot when there is a problem due to fewer troubleshooting tools available for these systems. Most of the startup problems would be caused by file errors or outdated BIOS and ROM versions. If a user moves, removes, or renames a startup file, the system is not able to use the file for startup. If a user upgrades BIOS or ROM to a version that does not interact well with his configuration, it can cause problems.

A verbose mode for the startup process of loading the device drivers exists. This /sos switch option displays each driver name as it is being loaded. You set this switch on the variable for OSLOADOPTIONS by using your system's setup configuration.

Logon Trouble

The two most common causes of logon trouble are:

- Password matching
- Password Expiration

Because Windows NT passwords are case sensitive, it is important to type them in exactly, capitals and all. Using mixed-case words makes it more difficult for someone to guess your password, but it also might make it more difficult for you to remember.

NT does not come with a password recovery program; if you forget your password, your administrator will have to assign you a new logon. You will not lose your user profile, however, because the new user account can point to your old profile location.

After your password expires, your workstation will not permit you to logon. Unless you have administrative privileges under another account you know the password to, you need to get an administrator to correct this problem. The administrator can use the User Manager to set a new password for you. This is covered in more detail in Chapter 7, "Managing Users."

Network Trouble

If your workstation is on a network, and you see a network error message, but no device failure messages, the problem is likely the network and not your particular system. On the other hand, if you use the Event Viewer and see that some services or devices are failing to initialize properly, the problem is usually your NT Workstation. By double-clicking on the Network Neighborhood icon on the desktop, you can determine if the rest of the network is visible to your workstation.

Windows NT 4 comes with a Network Troubleshooter in the Help section. This helps to pin down the trouble by walking you through a series of questions (see fig. 4.18). Each question you answer clarifies the problem a bit more precisely, and your answers take you progressively closer to a solution.

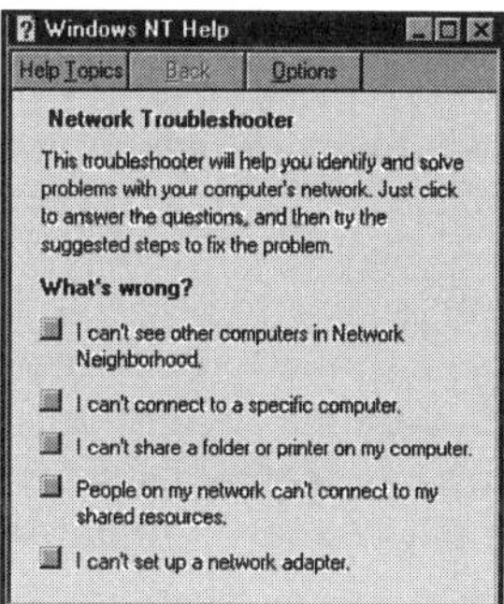

Figure 4.18

The Network Troubleshooter guides you in solving problems by interactive question/response windows.

You can think of the Network Troubleshooter as an interactive troubleshooting flow chart.

Knowing how to troubleshoot startup problems is important because you will encounter them sooner or later. Knowing where in the startup process the problem occurs can help you to isolate it and solve it faster. Once you can identify when the problem occurs, it is easier to identify the causes and to affect a remedy. Sometimes you might need to utilize troubleshooting methods, such as installing NETDETECT.CHK or even going back to the last known good configuration.

After the startup process executes without any trouble, you can customize some of the portions of the startup process to make your workstation more versatile and useful.

Configuring Options in the Startup Process

You can configure certain portions of the startup process to make your computer more useful. This is particularly important if you want the option of using a different operating system at times. The three main things you can configure in the startup process are:

- Multiple boot options for different operating systems
- Hardware profile options for portable computers
- Logon options for accessing the computer from a remote location

Configuring NT to Support Multiple Operating Systems

During the startup process, the Windows NT boot loader hands over control to an operating system. If you are only running NT, then you can skip this section. If you are running other operating systems on your computer or would like to be able to run other operating systems on it without removing Windows NT, then you'll want to configure the startup process to allow you to choose which operating system to use at boot time.

This section covers how to configure your system to give you the option at boot time to select another operating system, as well as how to customize some of the options related to supporting booting multiple operating systems. It is very common to configure Windows NT to dual boot with a version of DOS because some applications (especially games or undelete utilities) might not run under Windows NT.

Root-Based versus Non-Root-Based

The two general classes of operating systems (in terms of their installation requirements) are root-based and non-root-based operating systems. The difference between these two classes is where they require their boot files to be. To boot from certain operating systems, they must be set up in the root directory or folder. MS-DOS, Windows NT, and Windows 95 are some examples of these root-based operating systems. On the other hand, OS/2 and some types of Unix are not root-based, so they do not need to be located in the root directory.

Although you can have numerous operating systems available for booting, NT only works with one other root-based operating system on a given system in a normal installation. Therefore, you can dual-boot between NT and OS/2 or NT and MS-DOS, but cannot have all three of these options without a lot of work and a very non-standard installation. This is because the NT OS Loader only creates one boot sector image booting a non-Windows NT operating system.

Configuring System To Use Multiple Operating Systems

NT needs its boot files on the primary C partition. Other files can reside elsewhere. OS/2 will boot from an extended partition, but needs the Boot Manager to do so. The NT boot loader enables you to set up a system with multiple operating systems. The order for installing operating systems when you will be using more than one should be: DOS, Windows, Windows for Workgroups, Windows 95, Windows NT, and then Linux. Note that you can only reliably have two of these installed at the same time.

If you only have Windows 95 or Windows for Workgroups installed, when you add NT, the system automatically sets up a dual-boot between those programs or DOS. Although you can add Windows 95 or Windows for Workgroups after installing NT and setting up a dual-boot, you will have fewer problems (especially if you decide to have more than just two operating systems) if you install in the order specified. To add Windows 95 or Windows for Workgroups, first boot to MS-DOS and then do the installation.

The next sections cover how Windows NT boot device names are built, options you can set in the BOOT.INI file, some specific options for multibooting RISC workstations, and configuring default options in a multiboot environment.

ARC Naming

The BOOT.INI specifies a path to execute for each operating system option. This path is specified using Advanced RISC Computing (ARC) naming conventions so that it will work on both ARC-compatible computers and x86-based computers. Understanding how ARC path names are written enables you to control the boot process on your computer in the way you will need to if there are startup problems.

ARC paths have the following general forms:

```
multi(W)disk(X)rdisk(Y)partition(Z)\%systemroot%
```

or

```
scsi(W)disk(X)rdisk(Y)partition(Z)\%systemroot%
```

The first part of the name identifies the type of controller used to access the device. If you have a non-SCSI controller, or if your SCSI controller boots through its BIOS, your system defaults to using the multi() syntax. If your system does not boot Windows NT from a host adapter that uses its BIOS to hook INT13, it requires using the SCSI syntax. The part inside the () is just a numeric counter so that it can support systems with several adapters.

The next part of the name is the disk() parameter. This is the SCSI ID number of the disk on that particular adapter's channel if you are using a SCSI controller; otherwise, it is 0.

The rdisk() parameter is used to identify the SCSI Logical Unit Number (usually 0) if you are using SCSI drives. It is also used to identify the order of the disks in non-SCSI systems.

The partition() parameter identifies the logical partition number on a physical device from which to boot. The first partition is always 1.

The last part of the ARC name is the name of the %systemroot% folder in which Windows NT can find the startup files it needs.

You need to edit the BOOT.INI file directly to have the ARC names needed to do anything other than the default.

Editing the BOOT.INI

The BOOT.INI file holds the startup menu entries that you see when you turn on your computer. Whether you are working with setting up support for multiple operating systems, troubleshooting a startup problem, or just trying to change how long the system waits before it defaults to loading your operating system of choice, you need to know about the BOOT.INI.

To edit the BOOT.INI, perform the following steps:

1. Right-click on the file in the C:\ directory.
2. Choose Properties from the menu, and uncheck the read-only and hidden attributes if they are checked.
3. Click on the Apply button and then click on OK.
4. Open the file with a text editor such as Notepad by double-clicking on it.
5. Type in the path and descriptive label for each operating system in your boot setup.

Here is a sample BOOT.INI file that specifies a boot option of MS-DOS 6.22 and Windows NT Workstation.

```
[boot loader]
timeout=10
default=multi(0)disk(0)rdisk(0)partition(1)\WINNT
[operating systems]
multi(0)disk(0)rdisk(0)partition(1)\WINNT="Windows NT Workstation Version 4.00"
multi(0)disk(0)rdisk(0)partition(1)\WINNT="Windows NT Workstation Version 4.00
[VGA mode]" /basevideo /sos
C:\="MS-DOS"
```

Risc-Based Multiboot Configuration

For RISC-based computers, you need to run the ARC setup program in order to install alternate operating systems because the multiboot information is stored in

NVRAM instead of in a BOOT.INI file. If you are adding the other operating system to a system already running Windows NT, the boot loader automatically detects the additional operating system. Relatively few operating system choices exist for RISC-based systems; the choices are typically either some version of Windows NT or some version of Unix.

Changing Boot Preferences, Specifying Default

After you have installed alternate Operating systems, and edited the BOOT.INI, you can specify the default operating system. Although the startup process gives you a certain amount of time to choose your preferred operating system, at the end of the countdown, the default system launches.

1. From the Control Panel, double-click on the System icon.
2. Select the Startup/Shutdown tab.
3. Under System startup, select the operating system you want from the drop-down list by clicking on it. This operating system will then be the default system (see fig. 4.19).

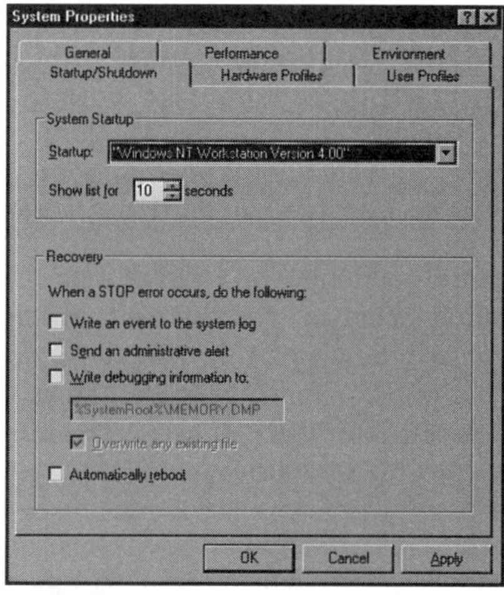

Figure 4.19

Change the default operating system by selecting an option from the System Properties Startup tab.

4. You can also edit the countdown time.
5. Click on the Apply button, and then click on OK.
6. These changes take effect the next time you start the computer.

Compatibility/File System Issues

Windows NT Workstation natively supports two types of file systems—FAT and NTFS. RISC-based systems must boot from a disk formatted with the FAT file system, but x86-based computers do not share this restriction.

Typical application programs do not care about the type of file system on which they store data or executable files. The only programs that typically care about the type of file system they are using are ones that take advantage of the strong security features built into NTFS.

NTFS

NTFS is an advanced file system that includes transaction journaling for data protection, access controls for security, and optimized indexes for speed. Do not, however, think that using a secure file system guarantees data security. It does not do you much good if someone can cart off your computer and pull off what he needs with a disk sector editor. NTFS's security features are only valuable while Windows NT is running on the system in a physically secure environment.

FAT

FAT is a much older file system that does not support any forms of journaling, security access controls, or indexing. The major advantage to using FAT is that you have easier access to your data if you choose to boot up with a different operating system. If your data is damaged somehow, you might need to boot up under an operating system that enables direct access to system hardware, for example.

If you intend to use multiple operating systems, you need to make certain that any information you want both operating systems to have access to is stored on a disk formatted with the FAT file system, as other operating systems do not generally support the NTFS file system. It is now possible to access data stored on an NTFS partition from DOS by loading a third-party device driver. NTFS is not widely supported, however, outside the Windows NT operating system.

Note Windows NT Workstation will not install on an OS/2 HPFS partition or access one directly, and this might be a limitation if you have character-mode OS/2 programs that access particular features of HPFS. Programs that do this, however, are very uncommon.

After you have configured your computer for multiboot options, you have the flexibility of easily selecting to use whichever operating system suits your needs at a specific time on a specific computer.

In addition to using different operating systems, you might also use different hardware configurations at different times. You can configure Windows NT Workstation to use one of several different hardware profiles that you specify at system startup time in order to support this. The most common reason to use hardware profiles is to support portable computers that have docking stations, which give them different hardware resources when they are plugged in than when they are not.

Configuring Hardware Profiles

An especially convenient feature of NT 4 for mobile users is the multiple hardware-profiles configuration. After you choose to load the Windows NT operating system, you can select a particular hardware profile if you have configured this startup option. Probably the most common application of this option is configuring a laptop for two hardware profiles, one startup for when the computer is connected to the network and another for when it is not. When you are at the office and connected to the LAN, your computer needs to load the drivers for the network card and so on. When you take the lap-top home or on the road, however, the network configuration is unnecessary. You can name your profiles whatever you want, but Windows NT refers to the computer as "undocked," when it is not connected to the network and "docked" when it is connected.

You can set how long Windows NT waits before loading the default hardware profile or tell it to wait indefinitely until you make a selection manually. If you use one hardware configuration significantly more than you use the other, you probably want to set it as your default with a relatively short countdown time.

1. From the Control Panel, double-click on the System icon.
2. Select the Hardware Profiles tab (see fig. 4.20).

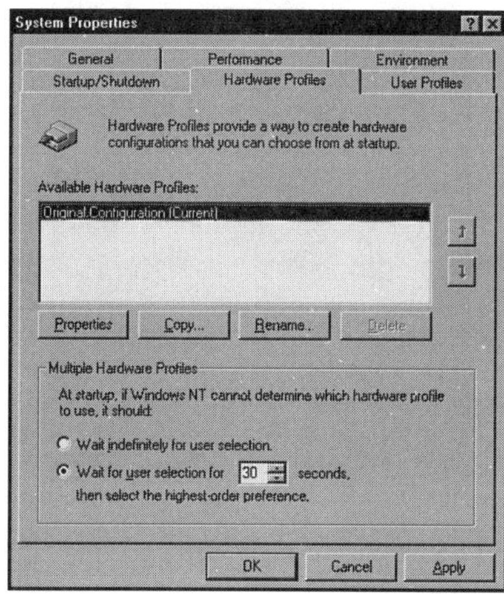

Figure 4.20

The Hardware Profiles tab of the System Properties program enables you to make multiple hardware configurations.

3. Highlight the Original Configuration (Current), and click on the Copy button. The Copy Profile Dialog box appears, and you can name your new configuration. Click on the OK button when finished.

4. Click on the Properties button. Figure 4.21 illustrates the Stand-Alone Configuration dialog box at the General tab. If the computer is a portable computer, check this box, and then indicate the docking state by choosing The docking state is unknown, or The computer is docked, or The computer is undocked.

Figure 4.21

Set the docking state of the new hardware profile on the General tab.

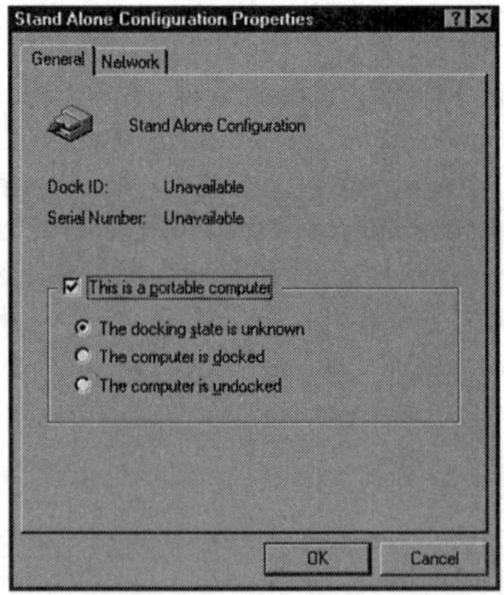

5. Select the Network tab.

6. Check the box if you want to disable network devices for this profile. Click on the OK button (see fig. 4.22).

Figure 4.22

You can disable all the network devices for a particular profile by using the Network tab.

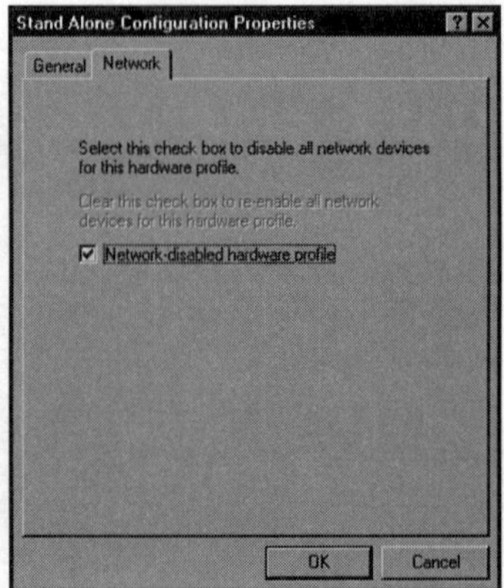

Use the Service settings to enable or disable a particular service in your hardware profile.

1. From the Control Panel, double-click on the Services icon.
2. Highlight the desired service from the list, and then click on the HW Profile button. The current status of the service appears on the left, and the Hardware Profile configuration label appears on the right.
3. Highlight the hardware profile that you want to modify. Click on the Enable or Disable button.
4. Click on the OK button.
5. Repeat this process for each service you wish to enable or disable.
6. After finishing, click on the Close button to close the Service dialog box.

If you have configured your computer for multiple hardware profiles, the startup process allows you to choose which hardware profile you would like to use. Another startup option you can configure concerns logging on from a remote location.

Configuring Logon Options

What do you do when you want access to your computer but you aren't in front of it? That important document you were working on at the office is still sitting there on your hard-drive, or maybe you would like to work at home but have access to the files on your computer at the office? Dial-Up Networking is a special feature in Windows NT Workstation that allows you the convenience of accessing your computer from a remote location without needing any other remote access software. When you reach the Logon Information dialog box during the startup procedure, you can select Logon using Dial-Up Networking once you install and configure this option.

Installing Dial-Up Networking

Dial-Up Networking gives you the flexibility of being in a remote location and yet still able to access both your workstation and its network. This feature is not available unless it has been enabled for you in the user manager program by someone with administrative privileges. Chapter 7, "Managing Users," covers enabling Dial-Up Networking in more detail.

If you need to access your workstation at the office from your home, or another workstation, you have rights to access. You can do so by using the Dial-Up Networking program. This must be installed in order to run. Each computer must have a modem or ISDN adapter installed.

1. Click on the Start button to display the Start menu. Choose Programs.
2. Choose Accessories.
3. From the Accessories, choose Dial-up Networking.

This starts the Dial-Up Networking wizard. See Chapter 13, "Remote Access Services (RAS) and Dial-Up Networking," for more details on setting up Dial-Up Networking.

Using Dial-Up Networking at Logon

Once you have dial-up networking installed, you can utilize this feature by checking the box next to Logon using Dial-Up Networking in the Logon Information dialog box.

1. At your initial logon screen, choose the domain you want to log on to.
2. Type your password and check the Use Dial-up logon.
3. Select your Phonebook entry from the list, then click on the Dial button (see fig. 4.23).

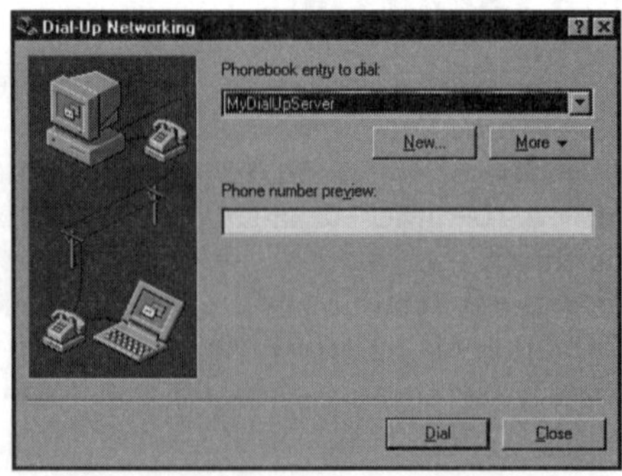

Figure 4.23

You can use the dial-up logon feature to connect to a remote computer.

4. The "Connect to…" window appears. Type in your User name, Password, and Domain. You have the option of letting the Dial-Up Networking program remember your password; check the Save password box if you want this option (see fig. 4.24).
5. Click on the OK button.

Now you know the details of what happens when you start Windows NT Workstation, how to troubleshoot the startup process, how to configure startup options such as multiple operating systems and hardware types, and how to use Dial-Up Networking to log on remotely. At this point, you're probably too exhausted to actually use the computer, so now you need to know how to turn it off!

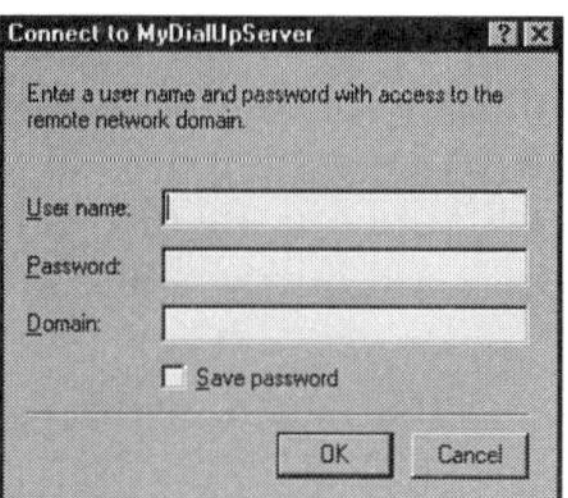

Figure 4.24

Type in your user information to enable the dial-up logon feature to connect to a remote computer.

Shutting Down

If you planned on just flipping the power switch to turn off your computer—wait! Windows NT Workstation utilizes a shutdown sequence to prevent your data and configuration information from being corrupted. It is important that you use the shutdown command to allow the workstation to go through the cleanup procedures it performs to ensure system integrity.

If a power loss shuts down the computer for you unexpectedly, Windows NT Workstation will be able to recover what you were working on. Even though the operating system itself seems to deal fairly well with this type of interruption, don't make a practice of turning off your computer without going through the shutdown process—especially while any applications are running.

This section covers what happens during the shutdown process as well as what to do when you experience common shutdown problems. Lastly, you will go through the shutdown options of restarting the computer and logging on as a different user.

The shutdown process takes three steps:

- Closing any open applications
- Logging off all users
- Clearing the cache

The shut down process closes any open programs it can. It displays a Shutdown window with the message `Please wait while system closes programs`. The desktop will be cleared of icons. The next message that appears on the screen is the Logging off window with the message `Please wait while system logs you off`. This logs off the user from both the workstation and the network if applicable. The next screen contains the message `Please wait while system writes any unsaved data to disk`. The system then clears the cache. This might take several seconds, or even close to a minute. It is important to wait until the computer displays `It is now safe to turn off the computer` before you power it off. After shutting it down, a dialog box will appear with a Restart button in the middle of it. If you decide that you want to restart the computer at this point, you can do so without having to power off.

Remember, if you have shared resources on your workstation, users who might be logged on to your computer will be forcibly logged off during the shutdown process. NT does not send a notice to users who are logged on to your workstation that the system is going to be shut down. They will find out the next time their workstation tries to access your shared resources; their computers will tell them that the current drive is invalid.

Shut Down

You can shut down the computer by Using the Start menu or by pressing Ctrl+Alt+Del and selecting Shutdown.

1. Close your applications.
2. Click on Shut Down from the Start menu.
3. The Shutdown Windows dialog box appears, and the desktop dims (see fig.4.25). Choose Shut Down from the menu.

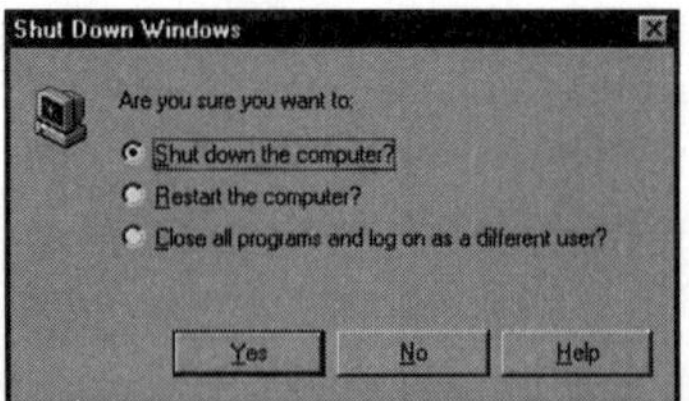

Figure 4.25

The Shutdown Window provides several options.

NT will not automatically close certain applications, such as DOS programs. If such a program is running when you select shutdown, NT displays an End Task request box (see fig. 4.26).

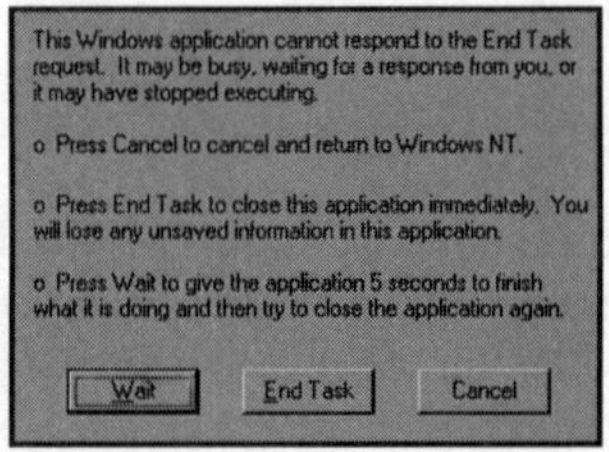

Figure 4.26

The End Task request displays when you have certain applications still running when you choose to shut down NT.

While shutting down the workstation is conceptually a very simple process, there are a few problems that can occur. Two of the most common problems are covered next along with steps for solving them.

An Application Won't Close

If one or more applications does not respond, you can use the Task Manager to help.

1. Right-click on the Taskbar, then select Task Manger from the menu.
2. Select the Applications tab. The list of programs and the status of each appears in the Task Manager window.
3. Highlight the program you wish to end, then click on the End Task button (see fig. 4.27).

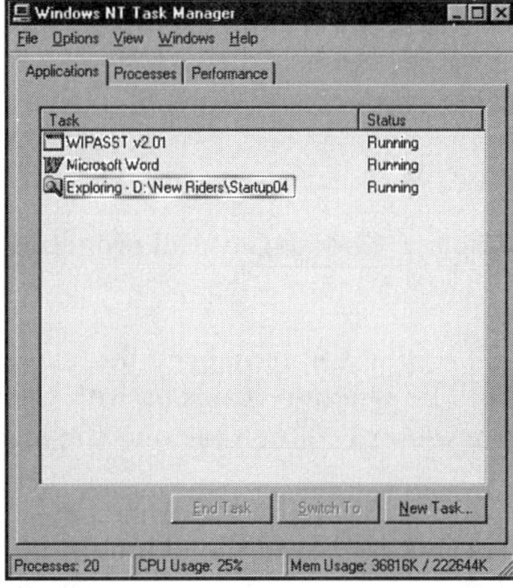

Figure 4.27
The Task Manager can forcibly terminate running applications.

System Has Hung

If your system refuses to respond, and you can't close your program even after trying to use the Task Manager, try shutting down the system by pressing Ctrl+Alt+Del or going to the Start menu and choosing Shut Down. If your system has hung, this might not work either. In that case, your only option is to turn the computer off. When you turn it back on and have logged on, it will attempt to recover those things you were working on to the best of its capability. If you are having this type of problem frequently, you might have encountered a defect in the operating system, your hardware, or even your application.

Restart

If you need to restart the computer, it is simpler to do so from the Shut Down options instead of turning the system completely off and then back on again. This feature is particularly helpful when you are changing configurations and need to restart the computer for the new configuration to take effect.

1. Go to the Start Menu by clicking on the Start button.
2. Choose Shut Down from the menu.
3. The Shut Down dialog box displays. Choose Restart the computer.

New User Logon

It is not necessary to completely shut down the computer to log on a different user. If another user needs to use your NT Workstation computer:

1. Go to the Start Menu by clicking on the Start button.
2. Choose Shut Down from the menu.
3. The Shut Down dialog box displays. Choose Close all programs and log on as a different user.

This procedure closes all the programs that you have been using and logs you off as a user, which closes your user profile. The system remains up with the previous boot choice and hardware profile. The new user can then log on. The logon process then opens this user's profile.

Logging on and off this way without shutting down the system is the network-friendly way of using your system. Remember, you do not know when someone on the network is accessing your shares.

Summary

This chapter discussed the startup process for Intel and RISC-based systems, how to troubleshoot the startup process, how to configure some startup options, the shutdown process, and how to troubleshoot the shutdown process. Understanding these topics will help you customize your Windows NT Workstation environment and understand what is going on when your system doesn't behave the way you expect it to.

CHAPTER 5

The NT Workstation Help System

Every Windows NT Administrator should be familiar with the Windows NT help system. It provides categorized and indexed searchable help for just about every part of NT Workstation, from how to change the desktop colors to how to recover failed disk partitions. Additionally, it is an extensible system that can be easily customized.

Wouldn't it be nice to have a personal instructor who would answer all your questions about Windows NT in a timely fashion, or that would never put you on hold and would never laugh at your questions? The Windows NT help system is set up in such a way to provide you with the information you need, and it is accessible no matter what program you are in. It might not be able to answer all your questions, but it definitely won't put you on hold.

The following major types of help are available for Windows NT Workstation:

- Main system help
- Dialog box help

- Context-sensitive help
- Setup wizards

This chapter covers each of the types of help and how to use each. You will spend less time searching for answers if you know where to look and how to use the different types of help available. You start out by covering the structure of the help system, including its files and how to use them. You then go on to cover all the different kinds of help available and the context each is used in. As you go along, you'll also look at how the help system is built.

Main System Help

The main system help is what appears when you select Help from the Start menu (see fig. 5.1). The Start, Help option launches WinHelp (using the file WINHLP32.EXE), which reads the WINDOWS.CNT file from the %SYSTEMROOT%\SYSTEM32 directory to find out what to display. This type of help consists of a topical and searchable database of linked help files that come organized with contents, index, and find tabs.

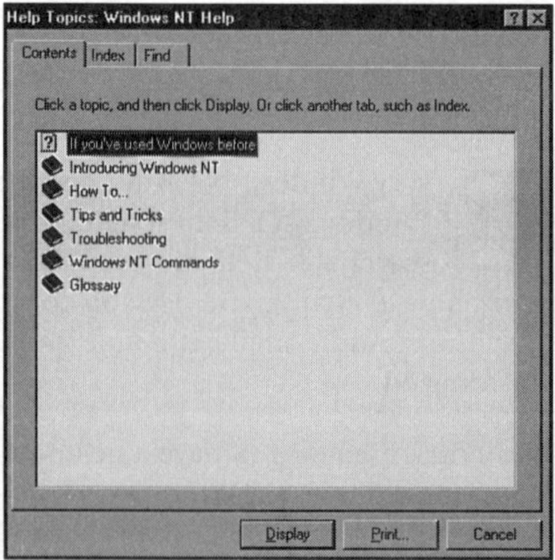

Figure 5.1
The Contents tab displays the Windows NT main help topics.

The main system help usually provides more comprehensive information than other forms of help, such as the context-sensitive help. Each Windows NT window can have a help button for invoking context-sensitive help as part of its title bar.

You have three options for closing help: clicking on the Cancel button at the bottom of the window, clicking the close X in the right side of the window title bar, or pressing the Escape key.

The Windows NT help system uses four types of files:

- ***.HLP files (help files).** Compiled binary files that contain the actual text of the help system.
- ***.CNT files (table of contents files).** Plain text files that contain hierarchical listings of topics as they will appear in WinHelp's Contents tab. They group specific other files and subheadings together on the Contents tab.
- ***.FTS files (full-text search files).** Binary files that hold index information used when searching for keywords or phrases from the Find tab.
- ***.GID files.** Automatically generated binary files that contain a compiled form of the CNT files and some other information, such as the size of help windows and dialog boxes.

Most HLP help files have associated FTS, GID, and CNT files after they have been used one time. The first time each help file is used, WinHelp prompts the user to build a text search database. This creates the GID and the FTS files. The CNT files do not change in the normal course of working with Windows NT, but they can be edited in any text editor.

Individual help files are interconnected with links and macros that run other help files. This makes help interactive to some degree, similar to hypertext. A help display might contain several links either to more information on the same topic or to a related topic, a definition, or a program executable.

The next three sections cover the types of help information found in the main system help. These types of help utilize the macros and linked files to provide information in an accessible and clear manner.

Training Cards

Training cards are an interactive part of the help system that guide you through common tasks using a cue card approach. A training card has a few questions or directions and a clickable button or two on it. A common task will have a set of training cards that prompt you for information that they can use to guide you down the right path to solve your question. You might think of Windows NT Workstation as having almost a little expert system built in. Microsoft sorted through its lists of common tasks and identified some that many people need help with. Training cards are just one more way of displaying help, but they default to always being on top of the current application while they are active because their reason for being is to guide you through complicated topics. As you work through the help they provide, you can click on a button on the training card help to show you the next step of each part of the task on which you're working.

Shortcut Executable Buttons

When the help topic contains information about a configuration process, the help text might contain a "Click here" button to access a program used in the configuration process (see fig. 5.2). Clicking on the arrow runs the executable program. By providing a convenient way to start the needed program, WinHelp makes it easy for you to go through the steps in the help text box as you read them.

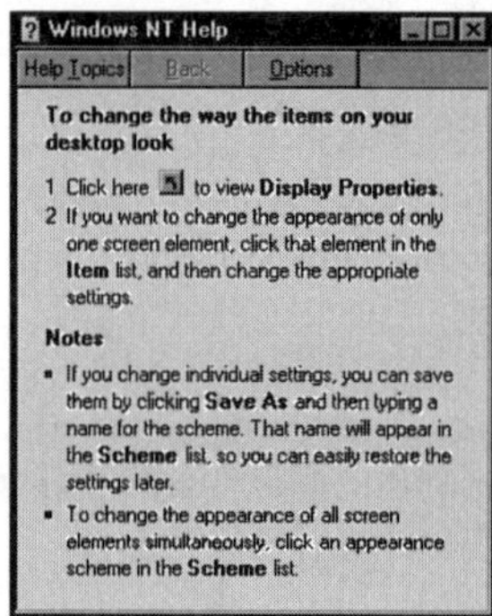

Figure 5.2

Some help windows contain shortcuts to an executable, such as this one to bring up the Display Properties dialog box.

Linked Text

Some help files have words within the help text that are underlined with a dotted line and in a contrasting color (usually green). This indicates that the word is linked to a pop-up definition. You can access the definition by moving your pointer to the underlined word (see fig. 5.3). When your pointer is over the underlined word, the arrow becomes a hand with a pointing finger. Click on the word and the pop-up definition appears.

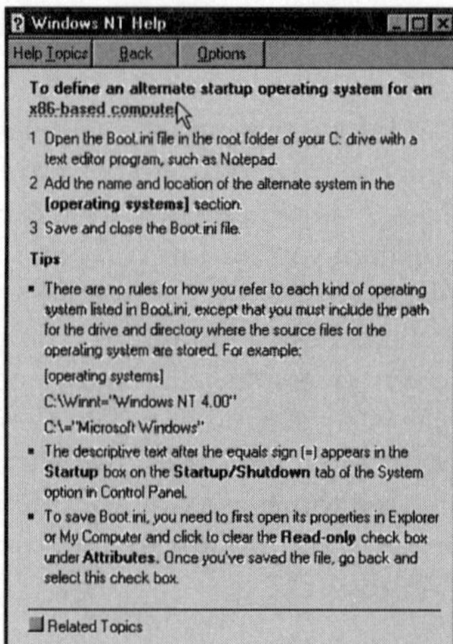

Figure 5.3

Defined term in the Help information window.

Most of the defined words have a unique ID. This ID is embedded into the display so that when you click on the word, its ID is passed to the help system where it is used to identify which help text should be displayed in a pop-up box containing the definition. By having a unique ID, multiple separate help files containing the same term can all access the same definition pop-up box. At the end of some of the help files, a "See also" list contains contrasting color words underscored with a solid line. These are linked to related help topics, usually in separate help files. By clicking on one of these, you can access the different help topics.

Related Topic Button

After selecting a topic from the index, sometimes you are presented with a sublist of related topics on your subject. Choose one of them to display the help text box. At the end of the help text box is a Related Topics button. Click on this button to display the sublist of related topics again (see fig. 5.4).

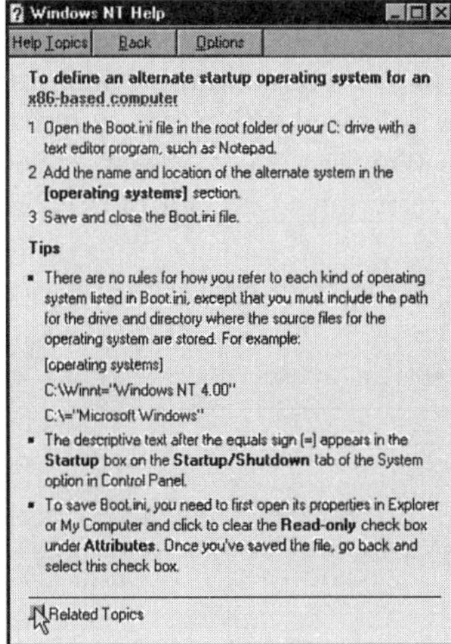

Figure 5.4

A Related Topics button is at the bottom of a Help information window.

Knowing what files comprise the help system and how they work together is useful in terms of understanding the system's design, but it is not nearly as useful as knowing how to use help effectively.

Using Help

Often the help system seems to be overflowing with information on things you already know everything about, while being almost void of those topics you really need help with. Depending on the build of your version of Windows NT Workstation, you might even come across various help files that are not finished, are not accurate, or even a few that have editorial or proofreaders' comments in them! More than a few of these made it into the final release.

The main system help has three tabs, each designed to aid you in finding information in a different way. You are more likely to use the main system help by selecting the Index tab and using the Find tab only when the Index tab fails to turn up anything. The Contents tab, however, has a lot of overview information that you will miss out on if you don't take the time to look through it. For instance, do you know how to configure NT to use sticky keys? Do you even know what sticky keys are? That topic is just one of many with its own subheading in the Contents tab.

The Contents Tab

The Contents tab, like the table of contents in a book, contains entries like chapter titles (refer to fig. 5.1). Each of these has subtitles beneath it that can be viewed by clicking on the book icon next to each main title; these subtitles might also have their own subtitles. The overall structure is that of an inverted tree—much like a file system. Titles with a book icon next to them contain more headings (like directories). Final entries (analogous to files) are indicated with a question mark superimposed over a document icon. In a standard Windows NT Workstation installation, the Contents tab contains the following selection of main topic headings:

- If you've used Windows before
- Introducing Windows NT
- How to...
- Tips and Tricks
- Troubleshooting
- Windows NT Commands
- Glossary

The following sections describe the organization and content of these. The hierarchical structure is significant, as is the less obvious way that the help files are linked together.

If You've Used Windows Before

The main Windows NT help has a quick reference section for those familiar with the older Windows 3.1 systems. You can access this information from the Contents tab of the Help window. Click the very first help heading "If you've used Windows before." The desktop of NT is significantly different from the old-style Program Manager window (see fig. 5.5). Many of the same programs, however, such as the Control Panel, still exist, but in different places.

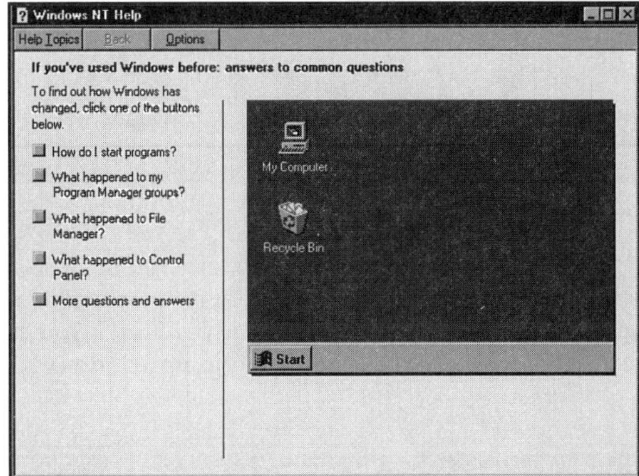

Figure 5.5
Help has a special section for those who are familiar with older versions of Windows.

Move the mouse to the various questions and the display to the right indicates with large red arrows how to accomplish the task. A description of the steps is written above the display. The following sections go through each of the questions step by step and include the information provided by the Help window.

How Do I Start Programs?

Unless you have installed a shortcut to a program on your desktop, the Programs are accessed through the Start menu or from a command line. Choose the Programs folder from the Start menu. The contents of the Programs folder will be displayed and you can run your program by clicking on it (see fig. 5.6).

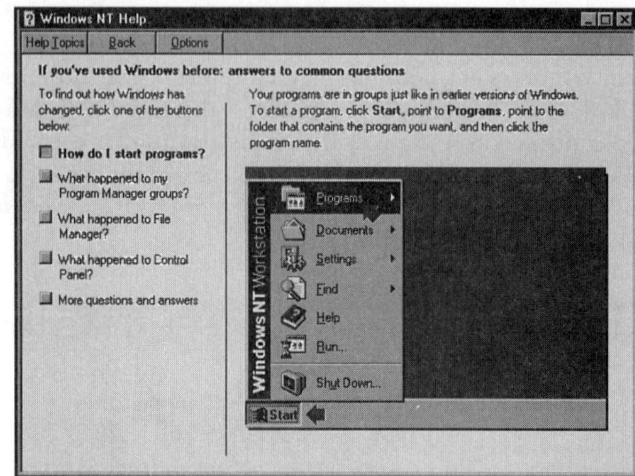

Figure 5.6
How do I start programs?

What Happened to My Program Manager Groups?

Windows NT has replaced the Program Manager with a different arrangement. The programs are in the Program folder on the Start menu (see fig. 5.7). If you can not find the program you are looking for, you can search for it using Windows NT Explorer.

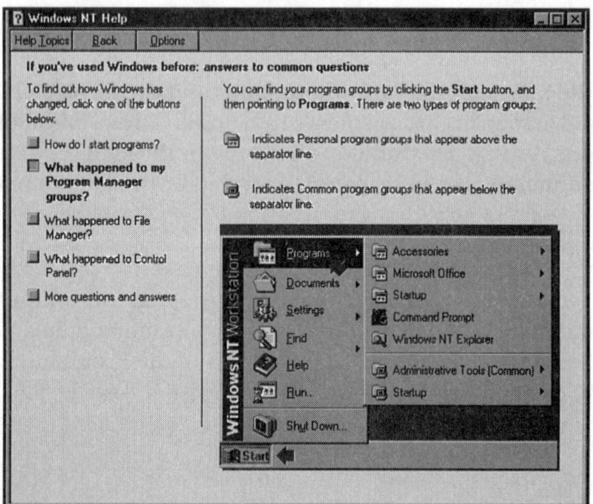

Figure 5.7
What happened to my Program Manager groups?

What Happened to File Manager?

File Manager has been replaced with Windows NT Explorer (see fig. 5.8). The Explorer works like File Manager, but displays a directory tree on the left and the contents to the right of its split window.

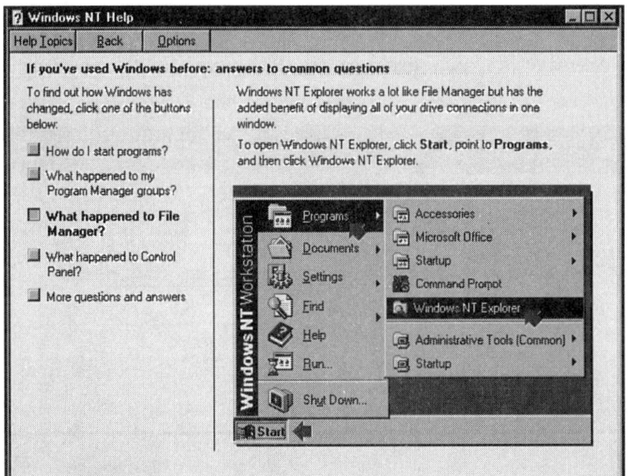

Figure 5.8

What happened to File Manager?

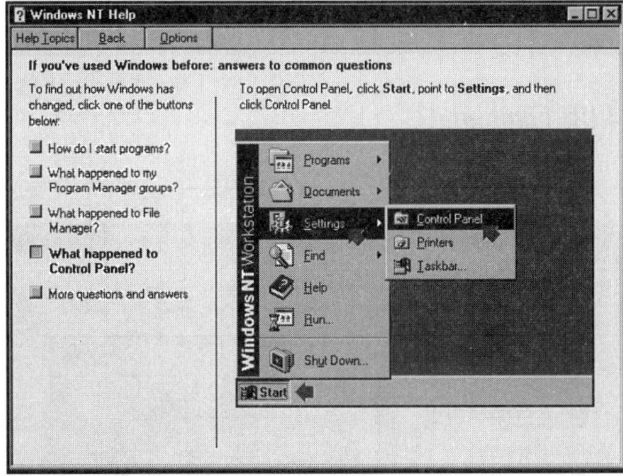

Figure 5.9

What happened to Control Panel?

What Happened to Control Panel?

The Control Panel, familiar to Windows users, still exists in Windows NT Workstation, but it has been moved. You can access it by clicking the Start button and selecting the Settings folder. The Control Panel is found in the Settings folder (see fig. 5.9).

Note You can also access the Control Panel by double-clicking on the My Computer icon.

To see more, select More questions and answers.

Where Did the MS-DOS Prompt Go?

The MS-DOS command prompt is now found in the Program folder (see fig. 5.10).

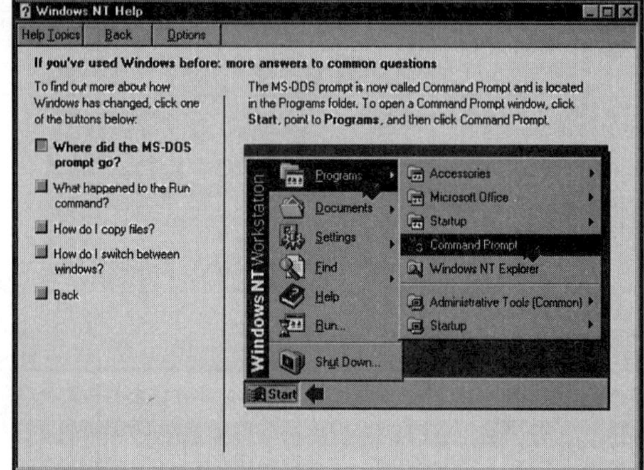

Figure 5.10
Where did the MS-DOS prompt go?

What Happened to the RUN Command?

The Run program is on the Start menu (see fig. 5.11).

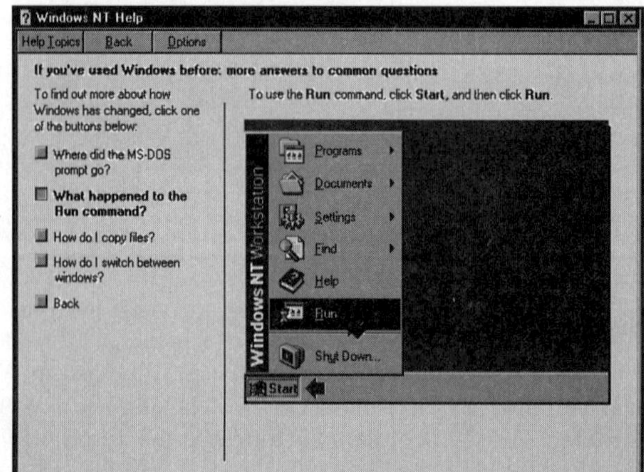

Figure 5.11
What happened to the Run command?

How Do I Copy Files?

When you want to copy files from one directory to another, or from your hard drive to a floppy, you can use Windows NT Explorer. Alternatively, you can double-click the My Computer icon on the desktop and use a similar procedure.

1. Using Windows NT Explorer, click on the file or folder you want.
2. Choose Copy from the Edit menu. (Or right-click, and choose Copy from the shortcut menu.)
3. Move your mouse pointer to the location you want the file copied to, and choose Paste from the Edit menu (see fig. 5.12). (Or right-click, and choose Paste from the shortcut menu.)

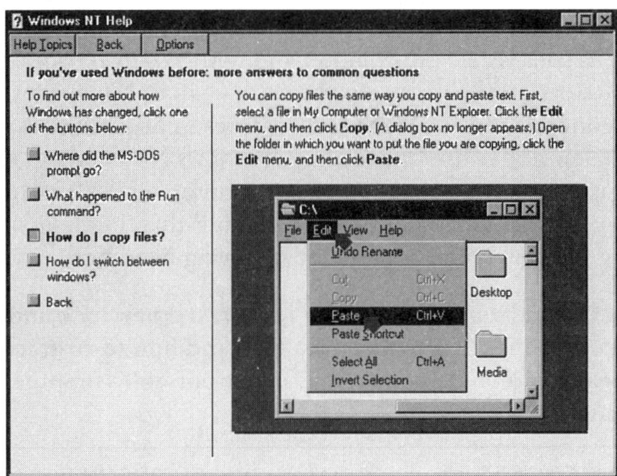

Figure 5.12

How do I copy files?

How Do I Switch Between Windows?

Windows NT Workstation can multitask to allow you to run multiple programs simultaneously. You can switch between programs that are running by clicking on the representative program button on the Taskbar at the bottom of the screen near the Start button (see fig. 5.13).

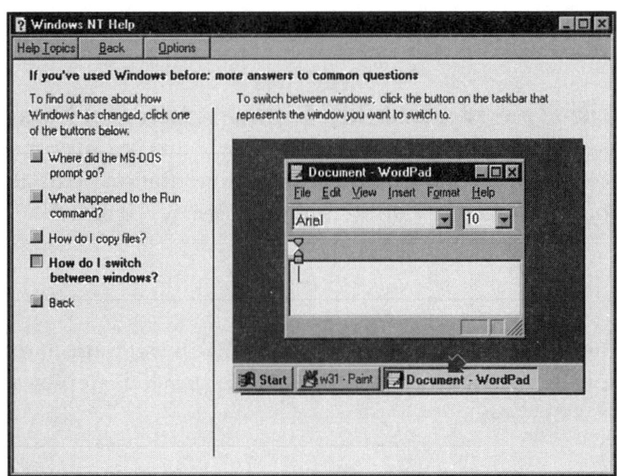

Figure 5.13

How do I switch between windows?

Most computer users have some experience with the old Windows interface. Because the desktop of the Windows NT Workstation looks so different due to the absence of the Program Manager window, using the new setup can be somewhat confusing. By providing a section for those familiar with Windows, this part of help makes it easier to learn the new NT system.

Introducing Windows NT

This introduction to Windows NT concentrates on the way NT is set up as well as which programs and services come with NT. If you want a general overview of the NT operating system, as well as some basic information about Microsoft services, this is the place to find it. If you were familiar with a previous version of NT, for instance, you might want to get a general idea about the new features in NT version 4. By clicking A List of What's New under the Introducing Windows NT heading, you are presented with a list of topics you can select for information on all the new features. The help here focuses on providing basic information rather than implementation information. Introducing Windows NT contains the following headings:

- **A List of What's New.** This section of help covers the new look and feel of Windows NT 4. It covers the programs and features and how to customize the workstation. New features include better support for portable computers and improved networking.
- **Using Windows Accessories.** These accessories are basic programs provided as part of the Windows NT Workstation 4. They include: Games, Calculator, Paint, WordPad, Notepad, Phone Dialer, Messaging, HyperTerminal, CD Player, Media Player, Sound Recorder, Volume control, and My Briefcase.
- **Network Services.** This section of help contains network related information for both Windows NT Workstation and Windows NT Server.
- **Microsoft Support & Education Services.** If you need information about product support or availability, or information on other Microsoft services, education, or certification, you'll find it here.
- **Microsoft Accessibility and Disability Services.** Microsoft has a variety of Services and products for the disabled, such as keyboard layouts for single-handed users and recorded Microsoft Software Documentation. This also provides information on third-party utilities to enhance accessibility.

How To...

The How To section of the Contents tab is very pragmatic. You will want to do various things with your computer; this section of the Contents tab provides step-by-step information about doing the most common tasks, such as running programs, using files and folders, and printing. Double-click the How To heading and you will see the following topics:

- **Run Programs.** Covers information on starting a program, switching between programs, installing and removing programs, starting a command prompt window, and optimizing MS-DOS programs, as well as shutting down the computer when you are finished.
- **Work with Files and Folders.** Focuses on utilizing the Windows NT Explorer to do things such as finding a file or folder; opening a document you used recently; and creating, copying, moving, deleting, and sharing files or folders. It also covers how to use the Recycle Bin to retrieve something that has been deleted.
- **Print.** Provides all the basic facts about printing from setting up a printer and printing a document to sharing a printer on a network. It even goes over troubleshooting printing problems.
- **Use a Network.** Focuses on the functions of Network Neighborhood and covers finding and connecting to a computer, opening a shared folder on another computer, and backing up files over a network.
- **Communicate with Others.** Explains how to use Windows Messaging and the Phone Dialer. It also covers how to set up a modem.
- **Safeguard Your Work.** Windows NT has various means of protecting your work built in to its features. This part of help covers how to use Backup to back up your files and how to select a screen saver and assign it a password. It also covers shutting down the computer—doing so correctly helps prevent file corruption.
- **Change Windows NT Settings.** Many of the programs and features in NT can be customized to suit your work needs. The changes can be merely cosmetic or can be functionally valuable.
- **Set Up Hardware.** Provides you with setup information and steps for a printer or a modem.
- **Maintain Your Computer.** Maintaining your computer correctly can save you a lot of headaches. This part of help covers everything from backing up, compressing, or fixing errors on your hard disk to emptying the recycling bin.
- **Use a Portable Computer with Windows NT.** Concentrates on keeping your files synchronized with the My Briefcase feature in Windows NT Workstation.

- **Set Up Windows Accessibility Features.** The accessibility features are designed to aid those who can not use the workstation in the normal manner. There are keyboard options to help single-handed users and those who can not use a mouse. You can change the way the screen looks to help those who might have trouble reading the small menu type. You can also set sound options to indicate certain events or actions.
- **Use Help.** By the time you have actually gotten to this section of the Windows NT help, you have probably figured out much of the contents of the Use Help section. It covers finding a topic, getting information on a dialog box setting, copying, and printing a help topic. A section on MS-DOS command help is also available.

Troubleshooting

The Troubleshooting section of the Contents tab is perhaps the most useful section of the system help because it helps you solve problems in addition to giving you information. It is geared toward system devices, but provides step-by-step help on how to diagnose what is causing the trouble as well as how to go about fixing it (see fig. 5.14).

In this section, you'll actually run through a sample situation that you might encounter while you are working with Windows NT to show you how the help system can really help you.

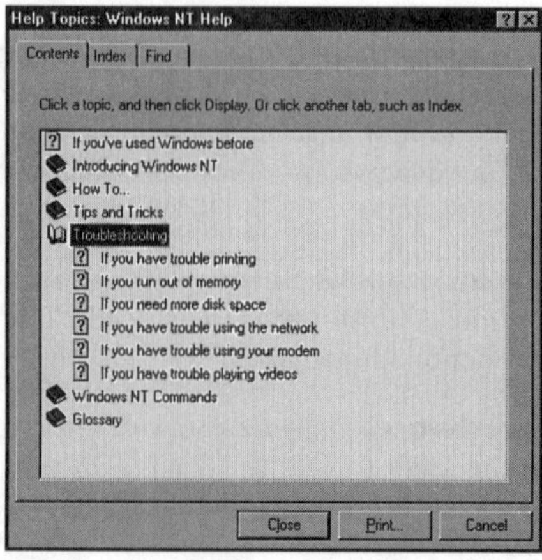

Figure 5.14
The Troubleshooting help topics are provided with NT.

The topics covered include:

- Printing
- Memory

- Disk space
- Using the network
- Using your modem
- Playing videos

Each topic is set up in a dialog format. Figure 5.15 shows, for example, under the general category of Modem Troubleshooter, certain problems under What's wrong?. Select the description that best fits your situation and click on the button next to it. This action displays another help window with a more specific question.

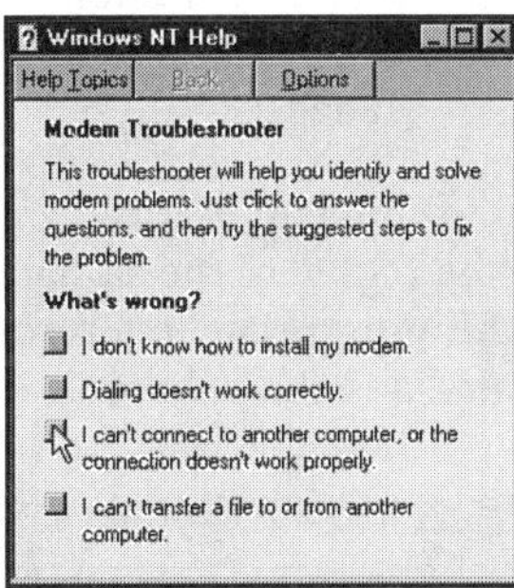

Figure 5.15

One of the Troubleshooting help topics is the Modem Troubleshooter.

If the trouble is that you can't connect to another computer, click on that button. Figure 5.16 shows the next step. The new question, What kind of connection problem is occurring?, helps focus the issue some more.

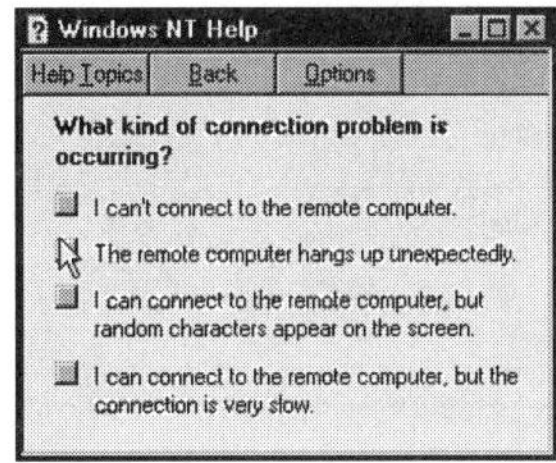

Figure 5.16

The Modem Troubleshooter asks, "What kind of connection problem is occurring?"

Assume, for example, that the connection dies after a short period, so you click on the button next to The remote computer hangs up unexpectedly. This displays the help seen in figure 5.17.

After trying the suggestion, select Yes if it solved your problem. This action closes the help window. Otherwise, select No for it to suggest alternative fixes. As with many of the help windows, you can click on the Back button from the toolbar to return to the previous help window.

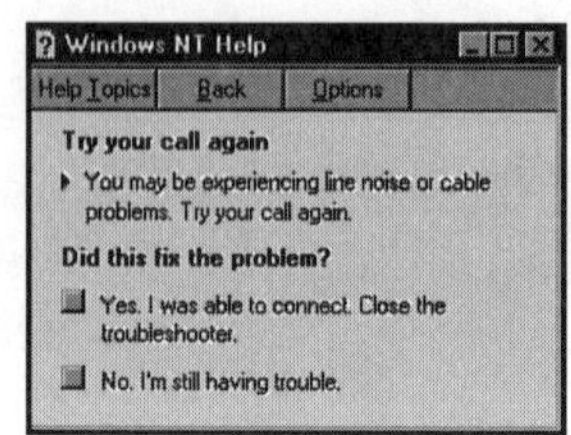

Figure 5.17 *The Modem Troubleshooter suggests a solution.*

Windows NT Commands

A whole section of the Windows NT Help system is devoted to defining and explaining each Windows NT Workstation command. It includes a comprehensive subsection giving an alphabetic listing of the commands and subsections explaining the differences between the Windows NT versions of the commands and the commands of the same name that are a part of DOS or LAN Manager.

- **Windows NT Commands.** These commands are arranged index-style in alphabetic groups. You can locate the region of the alphabet for the command you are interested in by selecting the appropriate letter from the key display above the entries. Double-click on the entry, and the help topic displays (see fig. 5.18).

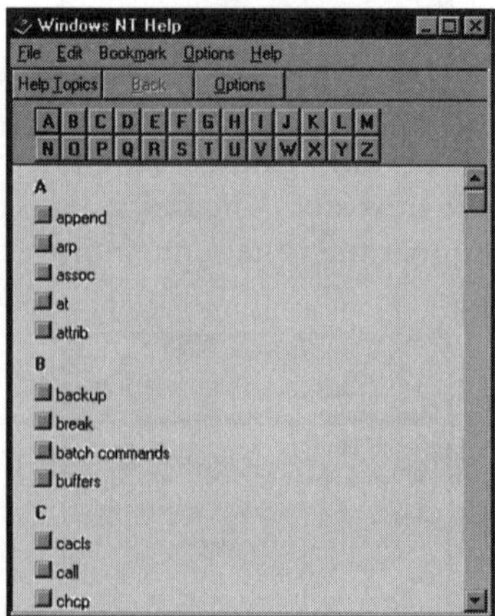

Figure 5.18 *Windows NT Commands are arranged in alphabetic groups.*

- **What's New or Different from MS-DOS.** This part of the main system help is composed of three sections: the new commands provided with NT, the MS-DOS commands that have changed, and the MS-DOS commands that are not available or do not function with NT. If you are looking for information about a particular command, you can select the letter it begins with from the letter keys at the beginning of the topic to display the alphabetic list. To get back to the three categories view, select the Back button from the toolbar.

- **What's New or Different from LAN Manager.** If you are looking for information about a particular command, you can select the letter it begins with from the letter keys at the beginning of the topic to display the alphabetic list. To get back to the three categories view, select the Back button from the toolbar.

Glossary

For those times when you just need the definition of a term, the Glossary can provide a quick and easy means of getting the definition. The Glossary contains an alphabetical listing of various terms. Click on a term to display the definition. The main difference between this and the alphabetic index of commands discussed a few paragraphs ago is that this section just gives definitions, whereas the other section gives command line syntax. The Glossary also has many general terms that are not commands, and so can serve as a handy reference.

The Index Tab

The Index is an alphabetical listing of all the help entries, comprised of indicated keywords in the HLP help files. By typing the topic you want in the space provided, the lower list scrolls to the alphabetic region of the first word you type (see fig. 5.19). From the lower list, you can select the items that most closely match what you want. Or, you can scroll down the list until you reach your topic. You can display the topic by double-clicking on it, or by clicking on the Display button. A help message box then appears on that subject.

Often the Index tab is the fastest means of finding information. If you can provide a keyword for the subject you need help with, the Index can usually supply the help topic.

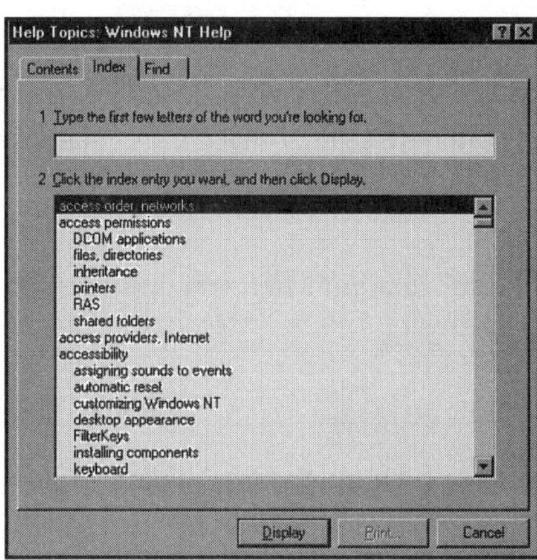

Figure 5.19

You can select topics from the Help Topics Index tab.

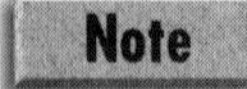

Every now and then, when you select a topic, the Topics Found window displays one or more titles that are untitled. If there is more than one, they are labeled sequentially, such as, *(untitled #0)*, *(untitled #1)*, and so on. You can minimize the number of these by minimizing your full-text search database.

The Find Tab

The Find tab provides another means of getting information about a topic. It finds help for the topic of choice by searching through the text of the help files utilizing FTS files, not just the keyword indices of topics. Type in the topic you are interested in, and in the center window an alphabetic list scrolls down to the topic (similar to the Index tab). In the lower window, you can check the subtopics you want, and then click on Display (see fig. 5.20).

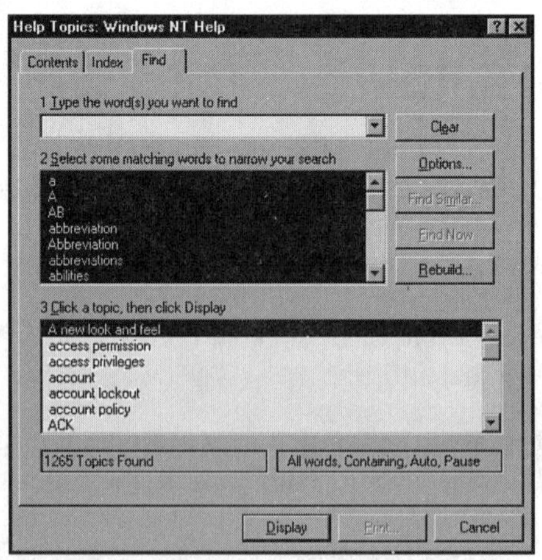

Figure 5.20

The Help Topics Find tab provides another means of getting information about a topic.

The subtopic you have highlighted in the lower window displays first. To view the other subtopics, close the current one and select one of the remaining subtopics from the Find tab. The Find tab remains in the background with all the subtopics you checked.

The Find tab is terrific for finding information when you don't remember quite exactly the heading you're looking for.

Configuring the Database

When you select the Find tab for the first time, the Find Setup wizard automatically walks you through building the Find word list (see fig. 5.21). The word list is not available for use until it is configured, so if you want to use the Find tab, you must go through the steps the Find Setup wizard presents.

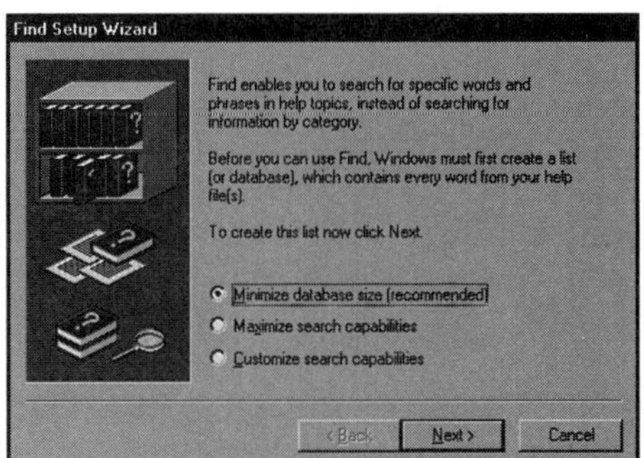

Figure 5.21

The Find Setup wizard will walk you through the Find word list configuration.

The options you select at this point will affect the Find functionality—although you can change the Find Setup by choosing the Rebuild button at any later point. The only reason you might do this is if the help file changes or if you need to reduce the disk space the Index files take on your computer.

In the Find Setup wizard, the first options are:

- Minimize database size
- Maximize search capabilities
- Customize search capabilities

The better search capabilities require more space. Minimizing the database size limits you to single word searches, whereas the other two options enable phrase searches. Microsoft recommends that you start off by minimizing the database size. If you are then unable to find the topics you need, go back and rebuild with one of the other two options.

Maximizing search capabilities generally doubles (at least) the size of your help files. (I prefer to maximize my searching ability even though it takes a little more disk space and turns up a few more false hits.)

Find utilizes the FTS files, which hold information used in full-text searches. The FTS are generated differently depending on how the word list was built. The FTS files contain more information when Maximize search capabilities is chosen.

If you choose to customize search capabilities, the Find Setup wizard presents you with several more options. Customizing generally creates a database that takes up as much space as the Maximize search capabilities options or more, depending on the options included.

The following steps are to help you configure the Find word list. Each of the steps from the Custom configuration of the Find Setup wizard is covered. If you choose either Minimize database size or Maximize search capabilities, you will not be presented with all of the following options.

1. Select the help files you want to include in the searches. You can select individual files, or click on the Select All button if you want to include all of them (see fig. 5.22). Click on the Next button.

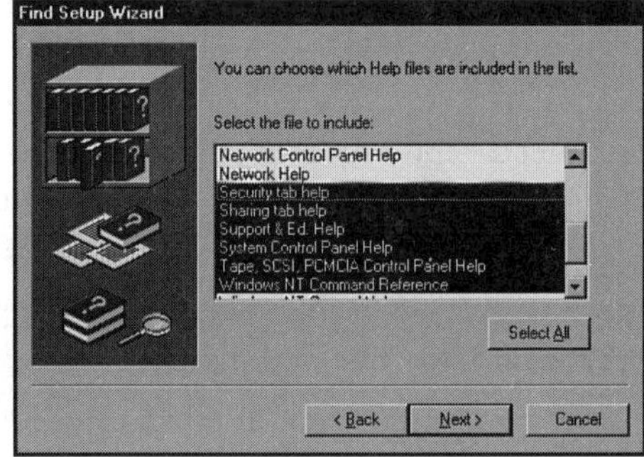

Figure 5.22

You can select which files you want Find to search for help topics.

2. Choose whether to include untitled help in the searches. Untitled help mostly consists of definition boxes rather than actual help topics. Including these makes the searches take longer. The default behavior is not to include untitled help. Select Include untitled topics or Ignore untitled topics (see fig. 5.23). Click on the Next button.

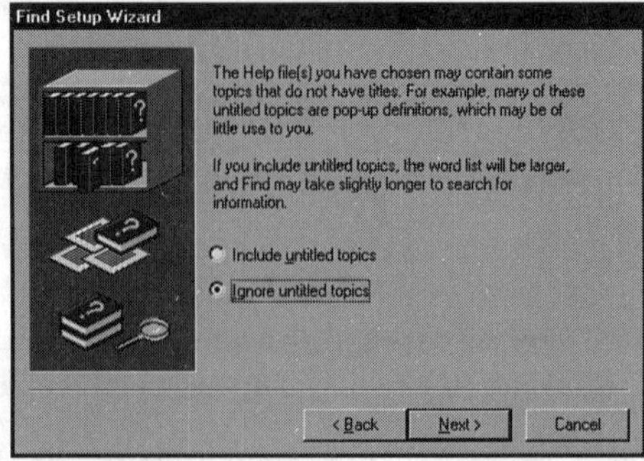

Figure 5.23

Select whether or not you want to include untitled help in the search.

3. Decide if you want the capability to search for phrases. Select Include phrase searching or Don't include phrase searching (see fig. 5.24). Including phrase search ability creates a longer word list, and thus makes the search take longer. Click on the Next button.

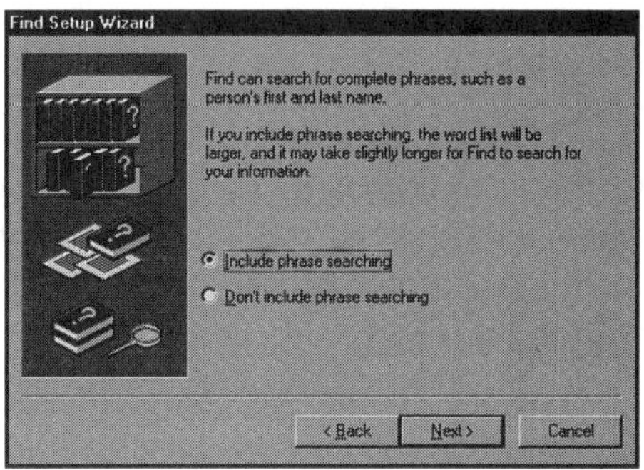

Figure 5.24

You can utilize phrase searching if you want.

4. If you choose, Find will display matching phrases as you are typing (similar to how it scrolls to matching words in the middle window as you are typing.) Select Display matching phrases or Don't display matching phrases (see fig. 5.25). Click on the Next button.

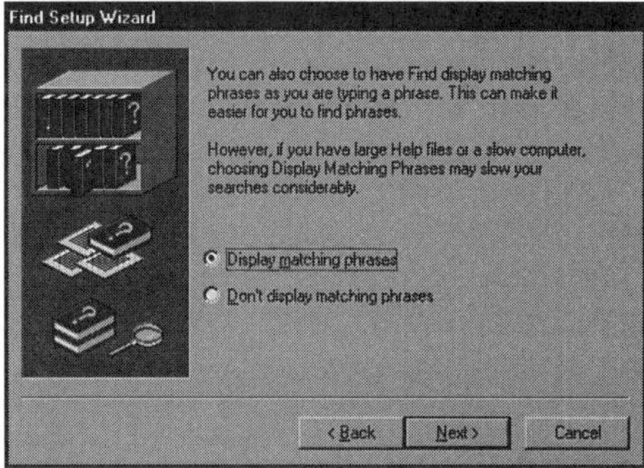

Figure 5.25

If you are using phrase searching, you can opt to have Find display matching phrases.

5. If you are going to go through many help files on a topic, being able to mark the files helps. You want to support similarity searches. Select Support similarity searches or Don't support similarity searches (see fig. 5.26). Click on the Next button.

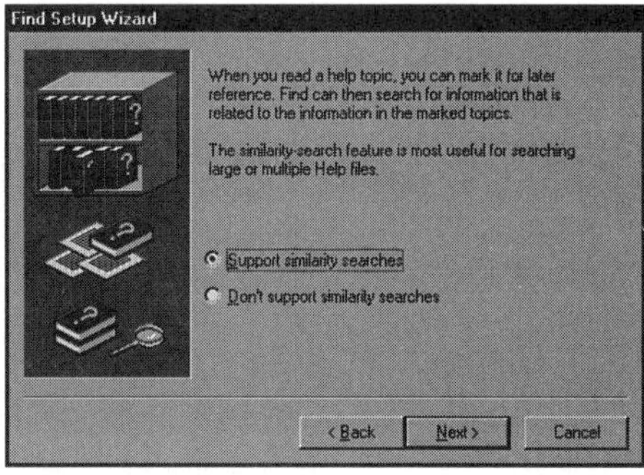

Figure 5.26

Select whether or not to support similarity searches.

6. Click on the Finish button to complete the customization process.

Now that you have configured the Find word list, or database, you can use the Find tab to help locate information.

In addition to generating an FTS help file associated with the HLP help file, the word list generates a binary GID index file. This is a hidden file and will not generally be visible in the contents of the Help folder when using Windows NT Explorer.

Determining Selection Options for Find

You want the search for a topic to provide you with the relevant information as efficiently as possible. If you have to wade through 50 help texts to see if they contain the information, you have probably included too much indexing.

To change the details of Find functions, select the Options button from the Find tab. The Find Options dialog box appears (see fig. 5.27).

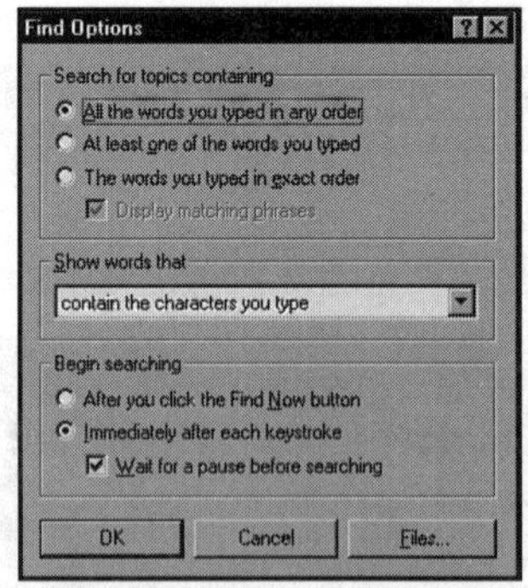

Figure 5.27
You can configure different options in the Find Options dialog box.

From the section Search for topics containing, choose one of three options:

- All the words you typed in any order
- At least one of the words you typed
- The words you typed in exact order

If you select the last item, you can also choose to check Display matching phrases.

Note These last options are not available if Find is configured to minimize database size.

The Show words that field offers the following options:

- Begin with the characters you type
- Contain with the characters you type

- End with the characters you type
- Match the characters you type
- Have the same root (This is not available if Find is configured to minimize database size.)

In the next section, Begin searching, you can select between:

- After you click on the Find Now button
- Immediately after each keystroke

For the latter option, you can choose to check Wait for a pause before searching.

Select the Files button to select which help files you want to utilize in your search. If you want to use all of them, just click on the Select All button (see fig. 5.28).

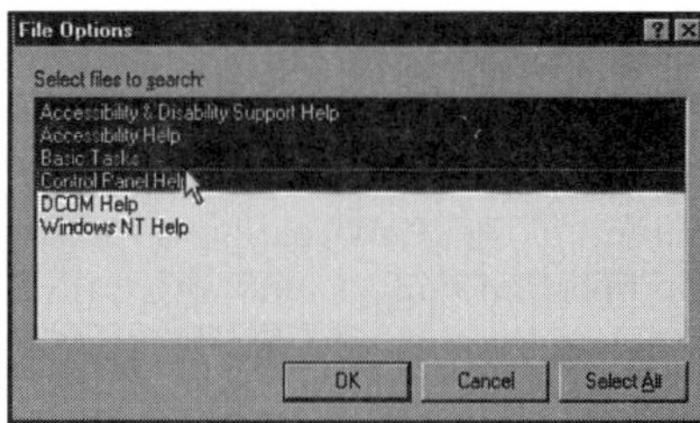

Figure 5.28

Select which files to search for help topics.

Figure 5.29 shows the options summarized on the Find tab.

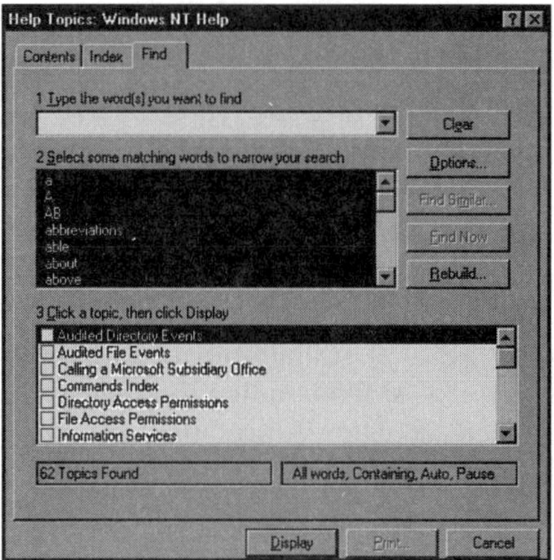

Figure 5.29

The file search options are summarized on the Find tab.

Now that you understand how to use each of the tabs of the main system help, you will be able to get the answers to your questions more easily. It is important to remember that help for specific applications is not part of the main system help. If you use help for a certain application a lot and would like it to be a part of the main system help, you can add it in. The next section shows you how.

Adding Help Files to the Basic Linked Files

Most users will not need or want to add help files to the main system help. However, understanding how to add help files can aid in understanding the details of how the main system help works. This section elaborates on the underlying control files of the main system help.

The main system help contents display is controlled by the WINDOWS.CNT file (see extended code listing that starts on the next page). This file is found in the \%SYSTEMROOT%\SYSTEM32 directory and can be viewed with a text editor. Each of the :Index lines tell the main help to include the contents of the indicated help file when creating its indices (in addition to the main help index file generated from the WINDOWS.HLP file). The :include line tells the main help which other CNT help files it is to include in the main help contents.

The :include UPDATE.CNT at the end of the :Link section is specifically designed to automatically incorporate any help files that might come with an NT update or new version. The other :include lines such as the :include RKDOCS.CNT and RKDOCW.CNT are for the Resource Kit help contents for the server and workstation respectively. After the Resource Kit is installed, its help is automatically included here. The help is included by reference. These CNT files exist separately with their own heading levels. The numbers indicate heading levels. Introducing Windows NT, for example, is a level 1 heading. It contains the subheadings A List of What's New and Using Windows Accessories, which are level 2 headings. These in turn are followed by level 3 subheadings. The final result (usually a level 3 or 4) is the actual information indicated by the title followed by an equal sign (=) and the information location.

The default location help file is WINDOWS.HLP, indicated by the very first line of the file:

```
:Base windows.hlp>proc4
```

Then the equal sign is followed by the label of that information in the WINDOWS.HLP file, such as the APP_GAMES heading for Windows games information or APP_CALCULATOR for the Calculator information.

```
4 Windows games=APP_GAMES
4 Calculator: for making calculations =APP_CALCULATOR
```

If the information is found elsewhere, the label is followed by an at symbol (@) and the name of the help file that contains the information—in the following case, the EXPO.HLP file.

```
4 Microsoft Exposition: a catalog of Microsoft products =expo@expo.hlp>proc4
```

```
:Base windows.hlp>proc4
:Title Windows NT Help
:Index Accessibility & Disability Support Help=acc_dis.hlp
:Index Accessibility Help=access.hlp
:Index Basic Tasks =common.hlp
:Index Control Panel Help=control.hlp
:Index DCOM Help=dcomcnfg.hlp              ; distributed com help
:Index Glossary=glossary.hlp
:Index Help on Help =winhlp32.hlp
:Index If you've used Windows before=31users.hlp
:Index Joystick Control Panel Help=joy.hlp
:Index Mouse Help=mouse.hlp
:Index Network Control Panel Help=netcfg.hlp
:Index Network Help =network.hlp
:Index Security tab help=ntsecui.hlp
:Index Sharing tab help=ntshrui.hlp
:Index Support & Ed. Help=supp_ed.hlp
:Index System Control Panel Help=sysdm.hlp
:Index Tape, SCSI, PCMCIA Control Panel Help=devapps.hlp
:Index Windows Help =windows.hlp
:Index Windows NT Command Reference=ntcmds.hlp
:Index Windows NT General Help=winnt.hlp
:Link 31users.hlp
:Link access.hlp
:Link common.hlp
:Link glossary.hlp
:Link mouse.hlp
:Link mspaint.hlp
:Link network.hlp
:Link notepad.hlp
:Link regedit.hlp
:Link tcpip.hlp
:Link winhlp32.hlp
:include update.cnt
1 If you've used Windows before=WIN31_TRANSITION_PIECE@..\..\..\genhelp\
➥usa\build\31users.hlp>big
1 Introducing Windows NT
```

```
2 A List of What's New
3 A new look and feel=NEW_WHATS_NEW>medium
3 Faster ways to get your work done=NEW_FASTER_WAYS>medium
3 More ways to customize Windows NT=NEW_CUSTOMIZING_WINDOWS>medium
3 New programs and features=NEW_PROGRAMS_ACCESSORIES>medium
3 New accessories in Windows NT=NEW_ACCESSORIES_ACCESSORIES>medium
3 Support for portable computers=NEW_PORTABLES>medium
3 Improved networking=NEW_NETWORKING>medium
2 Using Windows Accessories
3 For General Use
4 Windows games=APP_GAMES
4 Calculator: for making calculations =APP_CALCULATOR
4 Microsoft Exposition: a catalog of Microsoft products =expo@expo.hlp>proc4
3 For Writing and Drawing
4 Paint: for creating a picture =APP_PAINTBRUSH
4 WordPad: for writing and formatting documents =APP_WORDPAD
4 Notepad: for writing and editing text files=APP_NOTEPAD
3 For Communicating with Others
4 Phone Dialer: for dialing the telephone from your computer=APP_DIALER
4 Windows Messaging: for sending and receiving messages=APP_MAIL
4 HyperTerminal: for connecting to other computers=APP_TERMINAL@windows.hlp>
➥proc4
3 For Sound and Video
4 CD Player: for playing compact discs=APP_CDPLAYER
4 Media Player: for playing multimedia files=APP_MEDIAPLAYER
4 Sound Recorder: for creating and playing sound files=APP_SOUNDRECORDER
4 Volume Control: for adjusting sound level=APP_VOL_CTRL
3 For Using with Two Computers
4 My Briefcase: for synchronizing files=APP_BRIEFCASE
3 For Maintaining Your Computer
4 Backing up your files=APP_BACKUP
4 Increasing disk space=APP_DRIVESPACE
4 Detecting and repairing disk errors=IDH_DISK_LOGICAL
2 Network Services
3 For Windows NT Workstation=ADVANCED_SERVICES_W@winnt.hlp
3 For Windows NT Server=ADVANCED_SERVICES_S@winnt.hlp
3 Installing Network Services=Installing_network@winnt.hlp
:include supp_ed.cnt
:include acc_dis.cnt
1 How To...
2 Run Programs
3 Starting a program =WIN_TRAY_START_PROG
3 Switching between programs =WIN_TRAY_SWITCH_BETWEEN_APPS
```

```
3 Installing a program from a CD-ROM=WIN_ADDPROG_INSTALL_PROGRAM
3 Removing a program from your computer=WIN_ADDPROG_REMOVE_SOFTWARE
3 Starting a command prompt window=WINDOWS_DOS_START_DOS
3 Optimizing MS-DOS programs=WINDOWS_DOS_CONFIGURE
3 Shutting down your computer =WIN_TRAY_SHUTDOWN
2 Work with Files and Folders
3 Finding a file or folder=WIN_TRAY_FIND_FILE
3 Opening a document you've used recently=WIN_TRAY_OPEN_DOC
3 Seeing what's on your computer =WINDOWS_FCAB_LOOK_AT_FILES
3 Copying a file or folder =WINDOWS_FCAB_COPY_FILE
3 Moving a file or folder=WINDOWS_FCAB_MOVE_FILES
3 Deleting a file or folder =WINDOWS_FCAB_DELETE_FILES
3 Sharing a folder=NTSHRUI_SHARING_FOLDER@ntshrui.hlp>proc4
3 Retrieving deleted files or shortcuts=WINDOWS_WASTE_RETRIEVE_FILES
3 Copying a file to a floppy disk=WIN_COPY_FILE_TO_FLOPPY
3 Creating a folder =WINDOWS_FCAB_CREATE_FOLDER
3 Changing the name of a file or folder =WINDOWS_FCAB_RENAME_FILE
2 Print
3 Setting up a printer =WINDOWS_PRINT_SETUP_PRINTER
3 Printing a document=WINDOWS_PRINT_PRINT_DOC@common.hlp>proc4
3 Viewing documents waiting to be printed =WINDOWS_PRINT_VIEW_PRINT_QUEUE
3 Changing printer settings=WINDOWS_PRINT_CHANGING_SETTINGS
3 Using a shared printer=HOW_CONNECT_NET_PRINTER@network.hlp>proc4
3 Sharing your printer=WINDOWS_PRINT_SHARING
3 Troubleshooting printing problems =PTS_WHAT_WRONG
2 Use a Network
3 Finding a computer=WIN_TRAY_FIND_NETRES@network.HLP>proc4
3 Connecting to a computer=net_connect_lan@network.hlp>proc4
3 Browsing your workgroup=WINDOWS_NETWORK_BROWSEWORKGROUP@network.hlp>proc4
3 Opening a shared folder on another computer=NET_OPEN_NET_FOLDER@NETWORK.HLP>
➥proc4
3 Sharing a folder or printer=WINDOWS_FCAB_SHARING_FOLDER@server.hlp>proc4
3 Backing up files over a network=APP_BACKUP_AGENT@network.hlp>proc4
2 Communicate with Others
3 Exchanging mail messages =APP_MAIL
3 Dialing the telephone from your computer by using Phone Dialer=APP_DIALER
3 Setting up a modem =WIN_MODEM_SET_UP
2 Safeguard Your Work
3 Backing up your files =APP_BACKUP
3 Setting up a screen saver =WIN_DESKPR_SCRSAVERSETUP
3 Assigning a screen-saver password =WIN_DESKPR_SCRSAVERPASSWORD
3 Shutting down your computer =WIN_TRAY_SHUTDOWN
3 Controlling access to a folder or printer=SECUR_CONTROL_ACCESS@server.hlp>
➥proc4
```

```
2 Change Windows NT Settings
3 Change How Windows NT Looks
4 Changing the background of the desktop =WIN_DESKPR_CHANGEBACKGRND
4 Changing the way items on the desktop look=WIN_DESKPR_COLORS
4 Changing how much you can fit on your screen =WIN_DESKPR_MONITORRES
4 Changing the size of the fonts your computer displays =WIN_DESKPR_FONTSIZE
4 Setting up a screen saver =WIN_DESKPR_SCRSAVERSETUP
4 Adjusting the rate at which your cursor blinks=WIN_KBD_CURSOR_BLINK_RATE
3 Customize My Computer or Windows NT Explorer
4 Changing the appearance of items in a folder=WINDOWS_FCAB_APPEARANCE_FILES
4 Seeing all files and filename extensions=WIN_FCAB_SHOW_FILE_EXTENSIONS
3 Change Taskbar Settings
4 Customizing the Start menu =WIN_TRAY_PROGMENU
4 Moving the taskbar=WIN_TRAY_MOVEBAR
4 Hiding or displaying the taskbar=WIN_TRAY_PROPERTIES
3 Add or Remove Fonts
4 Adding a font to your computer=WINDOWS_FONTS_ADDNEW
4 Deleting a font from your computer=WINDOWS_FONTS_DELETE
4 Viewing a font on your computer=WINDOWS_FONTS_VIEW
4 Printing a font sample=WINDOWS_FONTS_PRINT
4 Finding a similar font=WINDOWS_FONTS_SIMILAR
3 Change Keyboard Settings
4 Changing the way your keyboard responds =WIN_KBD_REPEAT_RATE
:include keyboard.cnt
4 Changing the keyboard layout for an installed language=WIN_KBD_CHANGE_KEYB_
➥LAYOUT
:include mouse.cnt
3 Change Multimedia Settings
4 Assigning sounds to program events =WINDOWS_MMCPL_ASSIGNEVENT
4 Adjusting the volume for multimedia devices=WINDOWS_MMCPL_SETPLAYRECORD
4 Adding multimedia device drivers=WINDOWS_MMCPL_ADDNDDEV
4 Configuring multimedia devices=WINDOWS_MMCPL_CONFIGSNDDEV
4 Setting up a MIDI instrument=WIN_MMCPL_SETUP_MIDI_INST
3 Set Up Windows NT for Multiple Users
4 Logging off of your computer so others can use it=WIN_TRAY_LOGOFF
:include idevice.cnt
2 Set Up Hardware
3 Setting up a printer =WINDOWS_PRINT_SETUP_PRINTER
3 Setting up a modem =WIN_MODEM_SET_UP
2 Maintain Your Computer
3 Backing up your hard disk =APP_BACKUP
3 Compressing disks to create more free space=APP_DRIVESPACE
```

```
3 Detecting and repairing disk errors=IDH_DISK_LOGICAL
3 Formatting disks =WIN_FORMAT
3 Changing your computer's date=WINDOWS_DATE_CHANGE_DATE
3 Changing your computer's time=WINDOWS_DATE_CHANGE_TIME
3 Emptying the Recycle Bin=WINDOWS_WASTE_EMPTY_BSKT
2 Use a Portable Computer with Windows NT
3 Keeping files synchronized using a floppy disk=BFC_FLOPPY
3 Separating My Briefcase files from the originals=BFC_SPLIT_FILE
3 Checking the status of a file or folder in My Briefcase=BFC_UPDATE_STATUS
2 Set Up Windows Accessibility Features
3 Installing Accessibility components=ACCESSIBILITY_OPTIONS_INSTALLS
3 Change Keyboard Settings
4 Changing the way your keyboard responds=WIN_KBD_REPEAT_RATE
:include keyboard.cnt
4 Turning on MouseKeys=IDH_ACCESS_MOUSE_KEYS@access.hlp>proc4
4 Turning on StickyKeys=IDH_ACCESS_STICKY_KEYS@access.hlp>proc4
4 Turning on FilterKeys=IDH_ACCESS_FILTER_KEYS@access.hlp>proc4
4 Turning on ToggleKeys=ACCESS_TOGGLEKEYS_TURNON@access.hlp>proc4
:include mouse.cnt
3 Change How Windows NT Looks
4 Making text more readable=WIN_DESKPR_FONTSIZE
4 Changing the screen colors =WIN_DESKPR_COLORS
4 Changing how much you can fit on your screen =WIN_DESKPR_MONITORRES
4 Changing the appearance of items on the desktop =WIN_DESKPR_COLORS
4 Adjusting the rate at which your cursor blinks =WIN_KBD_CURSOR_BLINK_RATE
4 Displaying high-contrast colors and fonts for easy reading=ACCESS
➥HIGHCONTRAST_TURNON@access.hlp>proc4
3 Use Sound
4 Assigning sounds to program events =WINDOWS_MMCPL_ASSIGNEVENT
4 Turning on SoundSentry=ACCESS_SOUNDSENTRY_TURNON@access.hlp>proc4
4 Turning on ShowSounds=ACCESS_SHOWSOUNDS_ON@access.hlp>proc4
3 Set Up Windows for Multiple Users
4 Turning accessibility features off after a specified time=ACCESS_TIMEOUT
➥@access.hlp>proc4
2 Use Help
3 Finding a topic in Help=WINHELP_FINDING_TOPICS@winhlp32.hlp>proc4
3 Getting information on a dialog box setting=WINHELP_POPUP_HELP
➥@winhlp32.hlp>proc4
3 Copying information from a Help topic=WINHELP_COPY@winhlp32.hlp>proc4
3 Printing a Help topic=WINHELP_PRINT@winhlp32.hlp>proc4
3 Changing the font or color in a Help topic=WINHELP_FONTS@winhlp32.hlp>proc4
3 Displaying Help for an MS-DOS command=WINDOWS_DOS_GET_HELP
1 Tips and Tricks
```

```
2 For Setting Up the Desktop Efficiently
3 Customizing the Start menu=WIN_TRAY_PROGMENU>proc4
3 Grouping programs so they are easier to find=TRAY_GROUP_PROGRAMS>proc4
3 Putting shortcuts on the desktop=WINDOWS_FCAB_LINK>proc4
3 Minimizing all open windows=WIN_TRAY_MINWINDOWS>proc4
3 Viewing all open windows=WIN_TRAY_ARRANGEWIN>proc4
3 Customizing the taskbar=WIN_TRAY_PROPERTIES>proc4
2 For Maintaining Your Computer
3 Backing up your hard disk regularly=APP_BACKUP>proc4
3 Deleting old files to free up disk space=IDH_WASTE_FREEING_DISK_SPACE>proc4
3 Checking your hard disk for errors=IDH_DISK_LOGICAL>proc4
2 For Running Programs
3 Customizing the Start menu=WIN_TRAY_PROGMENU>proc4
3 Grouping programs so they are easier to find=TRAY_GROUP_PROGRAMS>proc4
3 Putting shortcuts on the desktop=WINDOWS_FCAB_LINK>proc4
3 Using the Run command to start programs=WIN_TRAY_RUNCOMMAND>proc4
3 Having a program start when you start Windows NT=WIN_TRAY_START_PROG_AUTO
2 For Working with Files and Folders
3 Dragging icons instead of using menus=OPT_DRAG
3 Using shortcut menus=OPT_RIGHT
3 Putting shortcuts on the desktop=WINDOWS_FCAB_LINK
3 Putting part of a document on the desktop=WIN_FCAB_SCRAPS
3 Creating a shortcut in a folder=WIN_FCAB_CREATE_NEW_SHORTCUT
3 Using the Run command to open files and folders=WIN_TRAY_RUNCOMMAND
3 Quickly sending files to another place=WIN_FCAB_SENDTO
3 Selecting more than one file or folder=WINDOWS_FCAB_SELECT_FILES
3 Previewing a document=IDH_FILEVIEWER_PREVIEW
3 Changing which program starts when you open a document=WIN_FCAB_EDIT_FILE_
➥TYPE
3 Having Windows Explorer start when you start Windows=WIN_TRAY_START_PROG_AUTO
2 For Printing
3 Putting a shortcut to a printer on the desktop=WINDOWS_FCAB_LINK>proc4
2 For Networking
3 Customizing your Network Neighborhood=NET_CUSTOMIZE_HOOD@network.hlp>proc4
3 Opening a shared folder on another computer=NET_OPEN_NET_FOLDER@network.hlp>
➥proc4
2 Tips of the Day
3 Using Help=TIPS_WELCOME_HELP>proc4
3 Getting your work done=TIPS_WELCOME_WORK>proc4
3 Personalizing Windows=TIPS_WELCOME_PERSONALIZE>proc4
3 Printing=TIPS_WELCOME_PRINTING>proc4
3 Exploring and maintaining your computer=TIPS_WELCOME_COMPUTER>proc4
3 Becoming an expert=TIPS_WELCOME_EXPERT>proc4
3 Viewing the Welcome screen=TIPS_WELCOME_WELCOME>proc4
```

```
:include oem.cnt
:include pws.cnt
:include iis.cnt
1 Troubleshooting
2 If you have trouble printing=PTS_WHAT_WRONG
2 If you run out of memory=MEMORY_WHAT_WRONG
2 If you need more disk space=IDH_WASTE_FREEING_DISK_SPACE
2 If you have trouble using the network=NET_WHAT_WRONG@network.hlp>proc4
2 If you have trouble using your modem=IDH_DIAL_WHAT_WRONG
2 If you have trouble playing videos=WIN_MMCPL_VIDEO_WINDOW_ADVANCED
1 Windows NT Commands
2 Windows NT Commands=index_commands@ntcmds.hlp>main
2 What's New or Different from MS-DOS?=DOS_diffs@ntcmds.hlp>main
2 What's New or Different from LAN Manager?=LAN_diffs@ntcmds.hlp>main
1 Glossary
2 Glossary Entries=idh_glossary_contents@glossary.hlp
:include rkdocs.cnt
:include rkdocw.cnt
```

The main system help does not display help for every application—not even those that are a part of Windows NT Workstation. If you want help on Open Database Connectivity (ODBC), for example, and type in "ODBC" in the Index tab of the main system help, you get a message telling you that ODBC is not part of the Index. If you want to see help on ODBC, you must go to the Control Panel, double-click the ODBC icon, and click Help from the menu bar once the application is open. What if you access this help frequently and would like it to be available in the main system help? It is not only possible to add the ODBC help, but it is also fairly simple to do so.

Adding Other Existing Help Files to the Main Help

To add help files to the main help, either from the other help files in NT or from a program you have installed, you can do so by editing the WINDOWS.CNT file.

1. Find the name of the help file you want to add and its location in Windows NT. If you want to include the dialog box help contents provided with Telnet, for example, check for the name of the help file, which in this case is TELNET.CNT. It is found in the \%SYSTEMROOT%\SYSTEM32 directory.

2. Open the WINDOWS.CNT file with a text editor such as WordPad.

3. Add the following line to the file:

   ```
   :include Telnet.cnt
   ```

   Provide the full path if the file you choose is not in the \%SYSTEMROOT%\SYSTEM32 directory.

4. Save and close the file.
5. Open the main help and select the Find tab. The Find Setup wizard rebuilds the database after you choose from the three options.
6. Click on the Options button to display the Find Options dialog box, and then click on the Files button.
7. Scroll down through the files. Figure 5.30 shows that Telnet help was included.

Figure 5.30

Telnet help is included in the main help files.

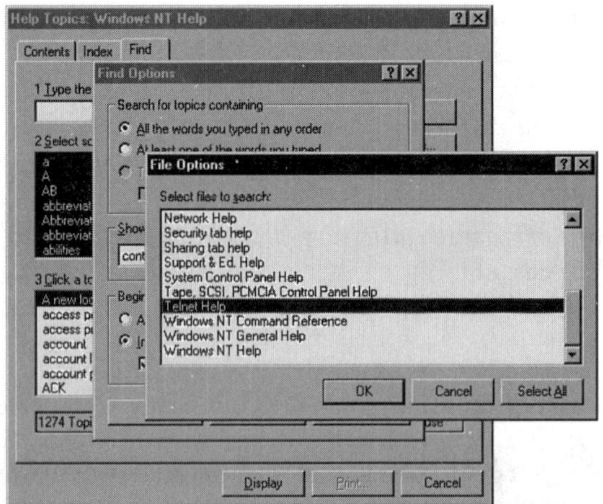

Creating and Adding New Help Files

In addition to adding existing help files to the main help, you can add your own help files to the main help. To actually create the help text display window containing the help, you need a help compiler. This is something that usually only software developers have. You can incorporate the files you generate, however, in the following way.

Assume, for example, that you want to add to the main help some company policy information for your employees. On the Contents tab of help, you want a category called Company Policies.

1. Open WINDOWS.CNT with a text editor, such as WordPad.
2. Decide where in the Contents you want the new category to appear. Make certain that it is after the end of a previous entry (that is, just before a level 1 heading). Type in the following line:

```
1 Company Policy Manual
```

3. If you want to include subheadings under this, type them in accordingly (using level 2 and level 3 headings). The following lines are an example:

```
2 Welcome for new employees
3 Company benefits
3 Company holidays
3 Vacation and leave policies
2 Time sheet information
3 Policies about overtime
```

4. Label the help information like the following example:

```
4 Health Benefits=Health_Ben@company.hlp
```

When you use a help compiler to create the help text, be certain to save it as COMPANY.HLP. Put the Health Benefits information under the section Health_Ben.

The following is an example of the whole new section completed:

```
1 Company Policy Manual
2 Welcome for new employees
3 Company benefits
4 Health Benefits=Health_Ben@company.hlp
4 Training and Eucational Benefits=Train_Ben@company.hlp
3 Company holidays=Holidays@company.hlp
3 Vacation and leave policies
4 Vacation and Time off=Vac@company.hlp
4 Sick leave=Sick@company.hlp
4 Leave without pay=Leave@company.hlp
2 Time sheet information
3 Policies about overtime=O_Time@company.hlp
```

Figure 5.31 shows what these headings and subheadings look like in the Contents tab of the main help. It is important to note that these new headings and subheadings will not appear on the Contents page until the referenced HLP file exists.

The capability of Windows NT to dynamically change what WinHelp displays based on the existence of certain files is a great step toward making documentation changes easier.

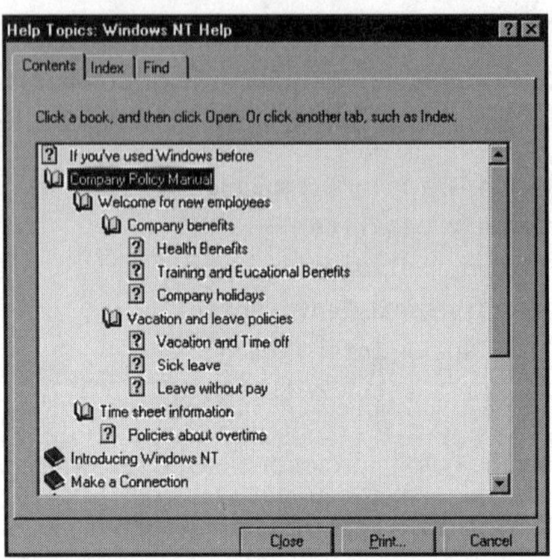

Figure 5.31

Customized Help files are included in the main help.

Now you've seen how to edit the help headings and links in Windows NT's help system. While you probably won't be doing it a lot, poking around with the guts of it like that is a good way to learn how the system works. Now other kinds of help will be discussed.

Using Other Help

The main system help is only a part of the help information included with Windows NT. In fact, most of the NT applications have help files associated with them and dialog boxes often have context-sensitive help available. Windows NT also uses a relatively new type of help, called wizards, which are a means of stepping you through various configuration processes.

Dialog Box Help

Many of the dialog boxes you encounter using NT have a help button on them. The dialog box help works like the main help, but limits its source files to just those few immediately relevant—ODBC in the Control Panel, for example. Figure 5.32 shows the help box with the title bar ODBC Help.

The help files used to provide help for the dialog box are found by clicking on the Index button from the toolbar, selecting the Find tab, and then clicking on the Options button. From the Find Options dialog box, you must then click on Files. Figure 5.33 shows the file for the ODBC help is the ODBC help file.

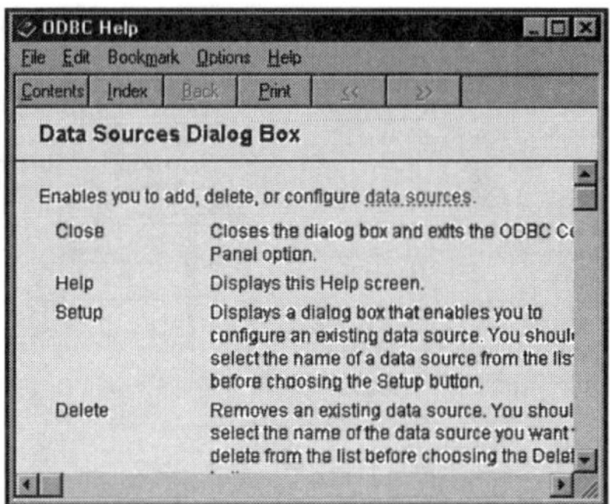

Figure 5.32

ODBC Help is an example of dialog box help.

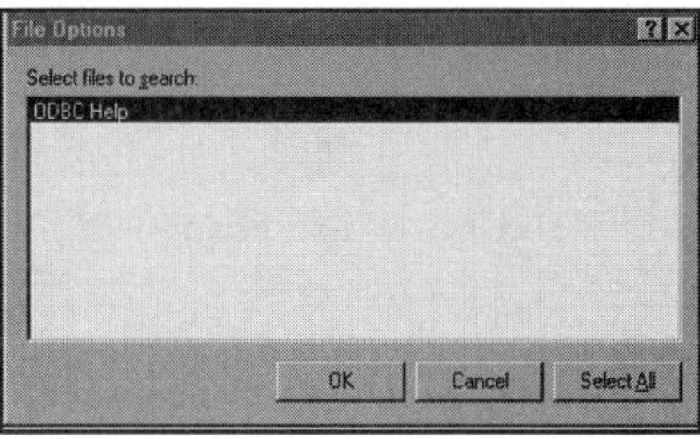

Figure 5.33

Clicking on Files in the Find Options dialog box displays the ODBC Help file.

Often, the help that is provided for the dialog boxes and for a number of applications is not available through the main system help. If you want information about a specific application or dialog box, the best source is the Help button or menu that is part of the application or dialog box.

Context-Sensitive Help

Many windows and some dialog boxes also provide a question mark pointer. The context-sensitive help files, accessed using the question mark pointer, each have a unique ID. This ID is embedded into the display so that clicking on the question mark pointer on a particular item calls the help with that specific ID, which is then displayed as a pop-up box. Context-sensitive help is particularly valuable if you need information about a particular part of a dialog box. If you are trying to fill out the information on the Connection tab of the Internet Properties dialog box, for instance, and you aren't sure what is meant by the Address of proxy to use, you can use the context-sensitive help to provide some assistance. Click on the question mark in the top right of the dialog box. Now, move your question mark pointer over and click the space provided for the Address of proxy to use. Figure 5.34 shows the context-sensitive help displayed for this part of the dialog box. This information is specific, to-the-point, and more useful in this case than some type of overview on proxies.

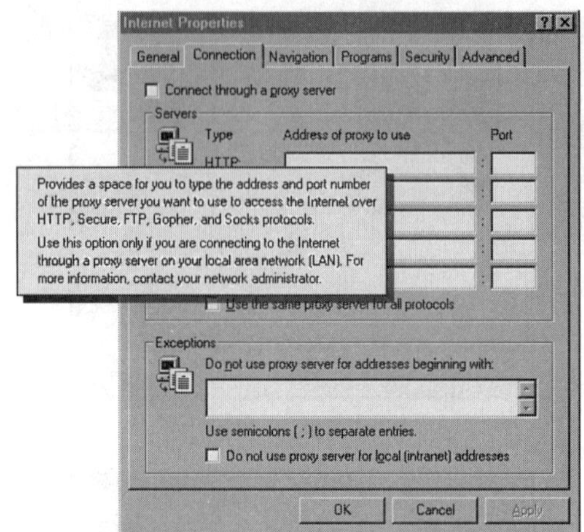

Figure 5.34

Pop-up box help information for a dialog box is context sensitive.

Note If no pop-up box appears after clicking on a particular item, no help is available for that item.

Many applications have small definition boxes for their various icons on toolbars, which are displayed when you pause your mouse pointer over the icon (see fig. 5.35).

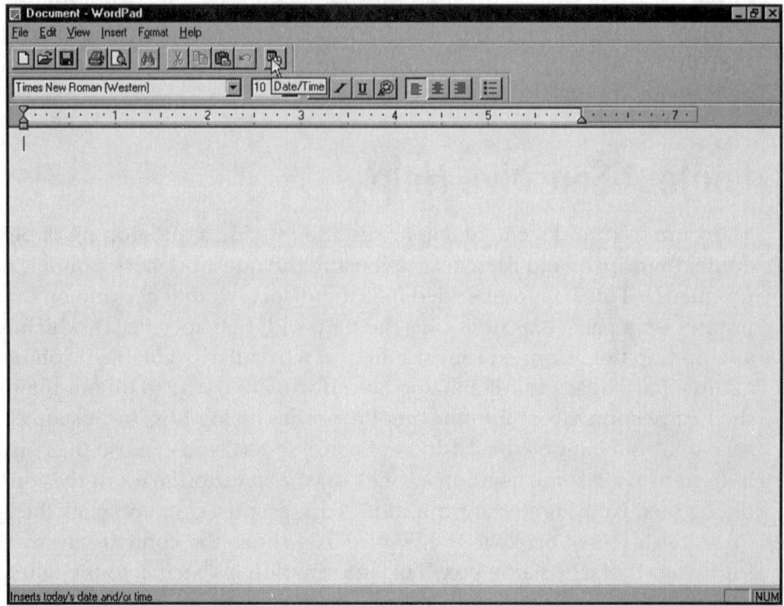

Figure 5.35

A pop-up identifier for toolbar icon is displayed when you pause your mouse pointer over the icon.

Wizards

Unlike the other types of help which you must choose to use, wizards are used in certain places whether you want help or not. Windows NT Workstation 4 incorporates a variety of wizards that provide a step-by-step walkthrough of certain procedures. Examples include an Add Printer wizard, a Find Setup wizard, and many others. The wizards prompt you to make certain configuration choices before enabling you to proceed to the next step of the configuration. Figure 5.36 shows the Add Printer wizard. Often, as in the Add Printer wizard, using the wizard is not an optional part of the configuration. In order to prevent misconfiguration due to a missing piece of information, NT has made the configuration "fool-proof" by utilizing wizards. Unfortunately there is no way to get around them if you don't want to use one.

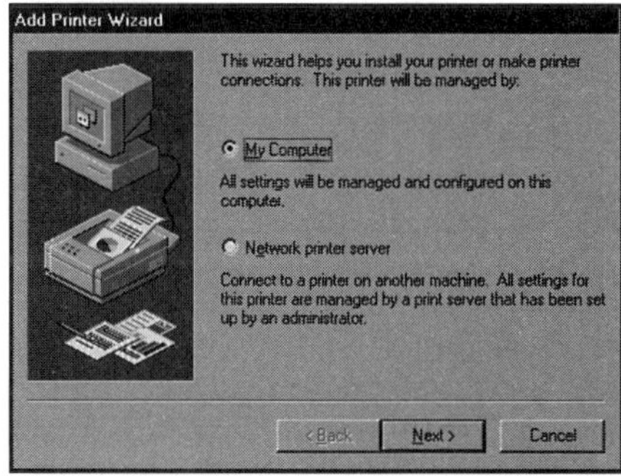

Figure 5.36
The Add Printer wizard walks you through adding and configuring a printer.

Exploring Help Features

Most of the help windows have features, such as annotating or printing. You can use these features to get more out of help. Each of the following help features can be accessed through the Option button on the toolbar, or by right-clicking on the topic itself:

- Annotating help topics
- Printing help topics
- Copying help topics
- Other options for help topics

Annotations

After a help topic is displayed, you can annotate the topic by selecting Options, Annotate from the toolbar. A text box appears for you to type in (see fig. 5.37).

Alternatively, you can right-click on the text box and select Annotate from the shortcut menu. This feature is useful if you encounter a particular problem or piece of information while dealing with a given help topic. You can save the information here as an annotation so that you can easily find it in the future.

Figure 5.37

You can annotate a help topic.

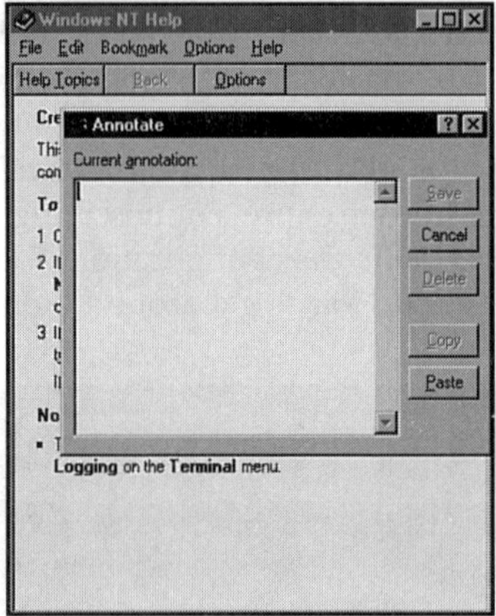

After you type in your notes or comments in the annotation window, you can save them. Annotations are saved in the Help folder with ANN extensions. After a topic is annotated, a paper clip appears on the topic. Clicking on the paper clip displays the annotation. The annotation can be edited or deleted at any point (see fig. 5.38). You might annotate topics that you find hard to understand, to clarify them later or to make sure that you won't forget the details.

Figure 5.38

An Annotated Help topic is indicated by a paper clip.

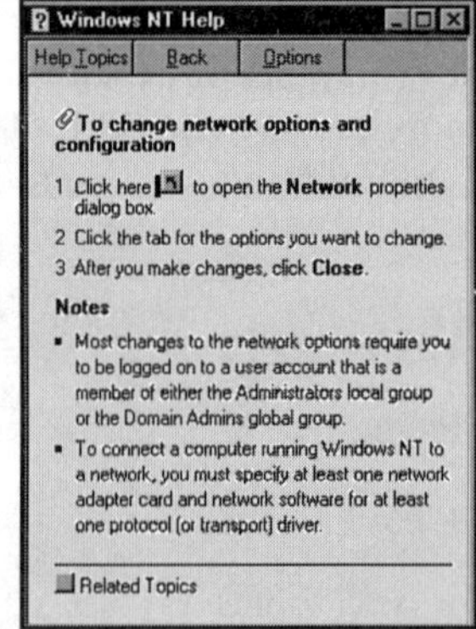

Printing

To print a help topic, select Print topic from the Options button on the toolbar or from the shortcut menu. The Print dialog box appears (see fig. 5.39). You can select the number of copies you want as well as change the printer properties, but you do not have the option to print only a portion of the topic. You can, however, choose to print the contents of a whole book from the Contents tab. Click on the book icon, and then select print.

Even though you have help online, you might find that you need to print some of it. If, for example, you were on a trans-Atlantic flight on your way to Paris and your laptop batteries couldn't last the whole trip, you might browse over some printouts if you had them.

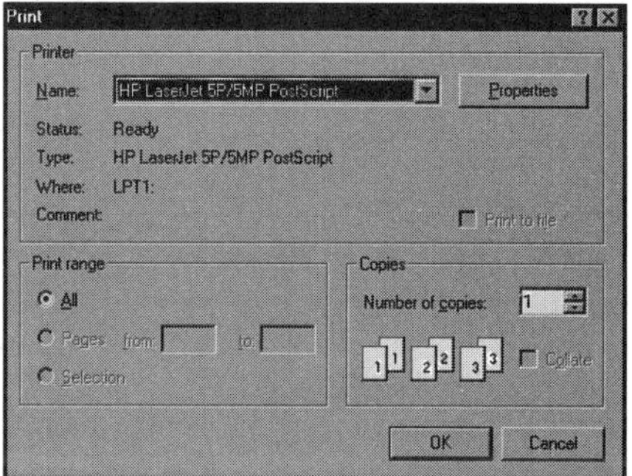

Figure 5.39

You can print a help topic.

Copying

To copy the help topic (presumably to paste later in a document or e-mail to someone), choose Copy from the Options menu or the shortcut menu. If you only want to copy a portion of the topic, highlight that portion, and then choose Copy.

Other Options

Some other options that can be manipulated include the following:

- Font
- Keep on top
- Use system colors
- Bookmarks
- Display history

Each of these options is discussed in the following sections.

Font

You have three options for the font size: small, normal, or large. A check mark indicates the current setting, normal being the default. The setting is not permanent, and the default setting will reappear after you reboot.

Keep on Top

This option enables you to specify if the help box is to remain in the forefront even if it is not active—meaning you are working on a different program. This enables you to read the help and follow it as you are working on something. The default usually keeps it on top. In figure 5.40, the help box has remained on top even though the active window is the Disk Administrator program.

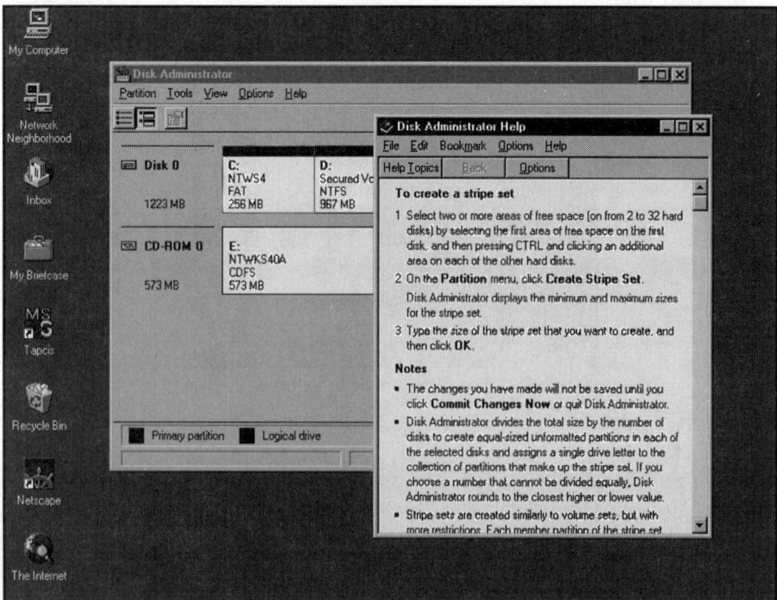

Figure 5.40
Help is usually on top by default.

Use System Colors

To have standardized color help files, you can choose Use System Colors from the Options menu. For this to take effect, you need to restart Help. Click on the Yes button when prompted.

Bookmarks

This feature is not found on all the help topics, only on help that displays a menu bar in addition to the toolbar. Choose Bookmark from the menu bar, and then Define. A text box appears suggesting a name for the bookmark (see fig. 5.41). You can change the name or accept the one provided. Bookmarks for 32-bit applications are saved in the WINHLP32.BMK file; bookmarks for 16-bit applications are saved in the WINHLP.BMK file. These are saved into the \%SYSTEMROOT%\ directory rather than the Help folder.

To use the bookmark feature, display a marked topic, go to the help topic, and select Bookmark from the menu bar. A list of bookmarks for that help file display. Click on the one in which you are interested.

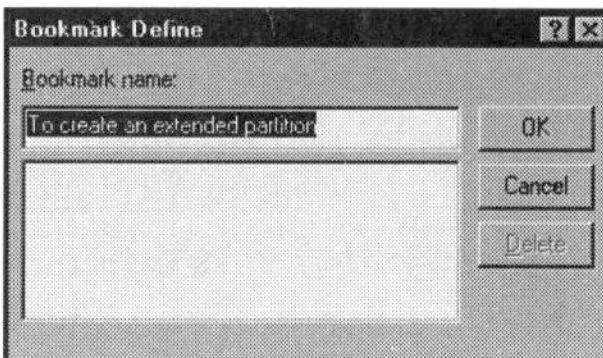

Figure 5.41

A help bookmark can be defined.

Display History

The display history feature is also only available with certain help boxes (usually the same ones with the bookmark feature). This feature enables you to keep track of which help topics you have read. Choose Options from the menu bar, and then select Display history window. If this option is not available for this particular help, Display history window does not appear on the Options menu.

The history window only picks up topics you can access using the arrow keys on the toolbar. After a topic is listed in the history window, you can click on the text in the history window to view that particular help topic again (see fig. 5.42).

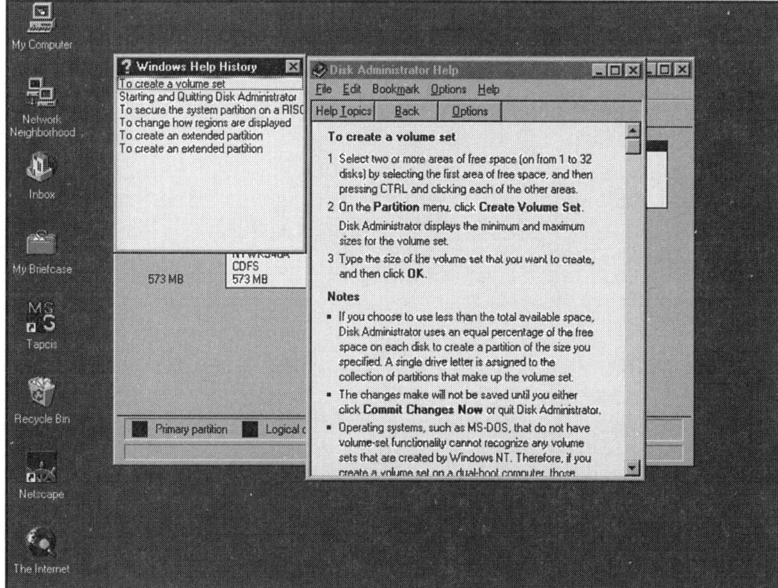

Figure 5.42

Windows Help history enables you to return to a particular help topic again.

Summary

The Windows NT Workstation help system is a set of files related by a linked and hierarchical table of contents. These files are also searchable by subject and by key words and phrases. This chapter offers an overview of the main help system and introduces the idea of linked help files. It walks you through each of the possible steps when actually using the help system in each of its different ways (using the Contents tab, using the Index tab, and so on). It covers other means of accessing help, including dialog box help, content-sensitive help, and wizards. Finally, it explores the various features available with the help system.

Part II

Managing Windows NT Workstation

CHAPTER 6

Configuring the Workspace

The window that appears when Windows NT 4 has booted is called the *desktop*, and it is the basic workspace for users.

To the operating system, the user interface (the desktop, the default icons placed on the desktop, and the management tools consisting of the Start menu and Taskbar) is called the *Explorer*. That is why you always see Explorer in the list of running processes when you open Task Manager.

To users, Explorer is an executable program that enables them to examine their systems.

This chapter discusses both definitions of Explorer and covers administrative tasks regarding the interface and the file management tools in Explorer. Some of these functions can be accomplished through the Registry.

Setting Interface Controls with the Registry

To the operating system, the interface that greets the users of Windows NT Workstation 4 is an entity called the Explorer interface. You can configure the interface for users, not just to alter or control its appearance but also its behavior.

You can control what users see and how they use what they see, through the Registry. You can make changes directly to the Registry to manipulate the interface. For your reference, the following section covers the Registry data types and controls that are usually of particular interest to administrators.

Registry Data Types

The values for Registry entries are entered according to the data type needed for that entry. The available data types are as follows:

- **REG_BINARY.** Raw binary data. The data displays in the Registry Editor as hex. This data type is used primarily for hardware information.
- **REG_DWORD.** Data consisting of a number that is 4 bytes long. It can be displayed in hex, decimal, or binary. This data type is used mostly for services and device drivers.
- **REG_EXPAND_SZ.** A data string. The string is text containing a variable that is replaced when an application calls it, looking for information. The most common example is the use of Systemroot, which is replaced by the name of the directory that holds the Windows NT system files.
- **REG_MULTI_SZ.** A data type made up of multiple strings. This is usually used for values that hold lists (each entry is separated by a NULL character).
- **REG_SZ.** A series of characters (text). It is mostly used to describe components, giving the display names of the components.
- **REG_FULL_RESOURCE_DESCRIPTOR.** A hierarchy of nested arrays. These are used to store resource lists for hardware or drivers. When you view them, they usually look like a table.

Set Policy Controls

You can set a number of controls in the Registry that control user behavior based on the protocols and policies you want to implement. You can make the changes directly to the Registry for any computer you want to control. For the most part, Registry changes do not take effect until the next startup of the operating system.

Note The Policy Editor, available with Windows NT Server, performs some of these tasks on a wholesale level across any number of workstations that you want to change at once. This chapter also discusses using the Policy Editor. (There's an inherent assumption here that you have the necessary rights on an NT Server to use the Policy Editor.)

The controls detailed in the upcoming list are found in the Registry path HKEY_CURRENT_USER\Software\Microsoft\Windows\CurrentVersion\Policies\Explorer. You can make these entries directly into the Registry to control the user's interface environment. All the values discussed in this section have a data type of REG_DWORD. The entries follow:

- **NoClose.** Has choices of 0 and 1. If the value is 1, the Start menu's Shut Down command is disabled for this user. The default value is 0, which enables Shut Down. Changing this value affects only the menu option on the Start menu. It does not change the ability to shut down via the Logon dialog box.
- **NoCommonGroups.** Has choices of 0 and 1. If the value is 1, common program groups do not display on this user's Start menu. The default value is 0. Because the administrative tools appear in the common groups section of the Start menu, this is an effective way of keeping this user out of those tools.
- **NoDesktop.** Has choices of 0 and 1. If the value is 1, the default desktop elements are hidden (Briefcase, Recycle Bin, My Computer, Network Neighborhood). The default value is 0.
- **NoDrives.** Has choices that encompass an extensive range of 32-bit words. The default value of 0 means that all drives are displayed in Network Neighborhood, My Computer, and Explorer. The lower 26 bits of the value represent all the possible drives in the system. The bit farthest to the right is drive A, and then, moving from right to left, each bit represents another possible drive letter, going through to drive Z. To hide a drive, set the bit for the particular drive you want to hide to 1. To hide all drives, use a decimal value of 67108863 (or 0x3FFFFFF hex).

  This feature is used frequently for hiding drive A from users, thereby preventing the introduction of disks brought from home (or obtained from other users) that might have viruses. You should also be forewarned that you cannot hide drives from File Manager. If you are hiding drives on user machines, also remove WINFILE.EXE, which is the executable for File Manager.

- **NoFind.** Has choices of 0 or 1. If the value is 1, the Find command will not be on the Start menu.
- **NoNetHood.** Has choices of 0 or 1. A value of 1 hides the Network Neighborhood icon on the desktop. This effectively prevents the user from accessing the network.

Note There are variations on the NoNetHood entry.

You can find NoEntireNetwork in HKEY_CURRENT_USER\Software\Microsoft\Windows. The choices are 0 or 1. If the value of this entry is 1, no network icons are displayed in Network Neighborhood, limiting the user's access to the local workgroup or domain. Users can, however, access computers outside the workgroup by typing the computer name on the Run command in the Start menu, or by using the Map Network Drive button in My Computer or Explorer.

NoWorkgroupContents is also found in HKEY_CURRENT_USER\Software\Microsoft\Windows. The choices are 0 and 1. If the value of the entry is 1, no icons representing computers in the local workgroup are displayed in Network Neighborhood.

- **NoRun.** Has choices of 0 or 1. A value of 1 hides the Run command on the Start menu.
- **NoSaveSettings.** Has choices of 0 or 1. A value of 1 prevents changes to the desktop settings. Actually, the user can move icons, change the position of the Taskbar, and make other changes to the desktop. Those changes, however, cannot be saved, and the next time the user logs on, the original desktop settings will be back.
- **NoSetFolders.** Has choices of 0 or 1. A value of 1 prevents the Control Panel and Printers choices from appearing on the Start menu. They will also be missing in My Computer and in Explorer.
- **NoSetTaskbar.** Has choices of 0 or 1. If the value is 1, the Taskbar settings menu choice does not appear on the Start menu. If the user attempts to configure the Taskbar by right-clicking on the Taskbar and selecting Properties from the shortcut menu, an error message appears. Because the Taskbar menu choice also controls configuration of the Start menu, this Registry entry prevents changes to the Start menu (except that users can continue to drag items to the Start button, which adds those items to the top of the Start menu).

- **RestrictRun.** Has choices of 0 or 1. If the value is 1, the Run command works only for a specific list of applications (set by the administrator). That list must exist in the Registry in the key HKEY_CURRENT_USER\Software\ Microsoft\ Windows\CurrentVersion\Policies\Explorer\RestrictRun.

  The system Policy Editor creates the RestrictRun key automatically. If you are making these additions and changes manually, you will have to create the key. To do so, move to the parent (which is the level we're working in here) and right-click on a blank spot in the right pane of the Registry Editor; choose New and then choose Key.

Note If you've administered earlier versions of NT and used the Registry to enable or disable fast task switching (Alt+Tab) with the CoolSwitch entry, the entry is still in the Registry, but Windows NT 4 ignores it. You cannot turn off fast task switching in Windows NT 4.

Other User Controls in the Registry

There are a variety of controls, many of which are established by the user during configuration processes, that you can restrict, amend, or add to in the Registry.

The following entries are found in the key HKEY_CURRENT_USER\Software\ Microsoft\Windows NT\CurrentVersion\Windows.

- **Documents.** Defines files that are to be considered document files by Windows NT. This entry is only for document file extensions not listed in the Extensions subkey because those extensions are automatically considered documents. (Adding a file type to the system through Explorer or My Computer places extensions in the Extensions subkey.) The extensions you put in this entry are not associated with any application. The data type is REG_SZ. When you enter the extensions, separate them with a space. Do not include the preceding periods before the extensions.

- **Load.** Names the applications that are to be run as icons when Windows NT is started. This entry is a list of application file names, or documents associated with an application, with each file name separated by a space. Make sure to specify the path if the file is not located in the SystemRoot directory. This entry can be changed by the user by adding the application to the Startup group in Program Manager and checking Minimize On Use in the application's Properties dialog box.

The following entries are found in HKEY_LOCAL_MACHINE\ Software\ Microsoft\Windows NT\CurrentVersion\Winlogon.

- **AutoAdminLogon.** If set to a value of 1, sets automatic logon, bypassing the Logon Information dialog box. The logon is for a specific user, and you must add the value entry of the user name for DefaultUserName and the user's password in DefaultPassword.
- **AutoRestartShell.** Determines whether the user interface (Explorer) is restarted automatically after an unexpected stop. This is set to a value of 1 (enabled) by default. Changing the value to 0 disables the automatic restart, and the user will have to restart the interface by logging off and logging on again. This value will apply to a third-party interface if Explorer is replaced with it.
- **DontDisplayLastUserName.** Eliminates the name of the last person to log on from the Logon Information dialog box. By default, the entry is 0. If you change it to 1, the Username space is always blank, and if the same user is logging on, the name will have to be entered manually.
- **ShutdownWithoutLogon.** Enables or disables the Shut Down button in the Logon Information dialog box. If the value is set to 1, users can click the button to stop the operating system before logging on. By default, Windows NT Workstations are set to 1 (Servers are set to 0).

AutoRun

Even though it's not directly connected to the workspace, there is one Registry change I rush to perform, so I thought I would mention it here. It's my personal favorite—the Registry entry that controls AutoRun. I don't like AutoRun. I find it annoying to have the presence of a CD announced on my screen before I'm ready to work with it. I almost always close the window and then open it again from My Computer when I'm ready to access the CD. On a laptop with a CD drive, AutoRun sucks up power like crazy. The only cogent reason to keep AutoRun is for game CDs that require it to run properly (I haven't seen any of those, but I'm told they exist).

To turn off AutoRun, go to the Registry key HKEY_LOCAL_MACHINE\System\ CurrentControlSet\Services\Cdrom. The AutoRun entry is set to 1 by default. Change it to 0. The next time you boot, it's gone.

Desktop Appearance Registry Entries

The changes users make to the desktop are written to the Registry. The desktop key controls are found in HKEY_CURRENT_USER\Control Panel\Desktop\WindowMetrics. The entries in this key reflect the settings for wallpaper, screen savers, icons, and WindowMetrics. WindowMetrics settings indicate the dimensions of the elements displayed. These settings are expressed in pixels, X-Y coordinates, and twips (a *twip* is 1/20th of a point; twips are listed in the Registry with a hyphen, which shouldn't be construed as a negative number).

You can use these keys to create the settings you want and then turn off the capability to save changes in settings to ensure consistent desktops.

Some controls you might want to change in this key are the following:

- **BorderWidth.** Available range is 1 (narrowest) to 49 (widest). The default is 15.
- **CaptionFont.** Available range is all available fonts. The default is MS Sans Serif.
- **CaptionHeight.** For caption buttons. Available range is any twip. The default is –270.
- **CaptionWidth.** Also for caption buttons. Available range is any twip. The default is –270.
- **IconFont.** For text associated with icons. Range is all available fonts. Default is MS Sans Serif.
- **IconTitleWrap.** Determines whether icon titles will wrap or truncate. 0 is disabled (the title will truncate); 1 is enabled (the title will wrap). Default is 1.
- **MenuFont.** For font used in menu bars. Range is all available fonts. Default is MS Sans Serif.

One of the useful entries in the key HKEY_CURRENT_USER\Control Panel\Desktop\WindowMetrics is

- **MenuShowDelay.** The determination of the length of time a mouse pointer sits on a menu item before a submenu appears. It is measured in milliseconds (the default is 400), and you can make it all move faster if you want by changing this entry.

If you are working with a few specific workstations and a few specific changes to the Registry, all these controls are easy to get to and change. For larger, system-wide changes, the Policy Editor provides a lot of administrative help.

Using the Policy Editor to Make Changes

Make your way to the NT Server that receives your workstation logons and launch the System Policy Editor (POLEDIT.EXE). This program enables you to make changes throughout an NT domain, and those changes can affect computer and user groups as your needs demand.

This is not a complete explanation of the System Policy Editor, it is only a roadmap to help you use it for the issues discussed in this chapter.

This section deals with the capability of the System Policy Editor to make changes to the Registry that have an effect on the user interface. You can modify settings for one computer or for an entire domain.

Manipulate One Computer

If you want to work on one computer, perform the following steps:

1. From the File menu, choose Connect.
2. When the Connect dialog box appears, enter the name of the computer to which you want to connect.
3. The Users on Remote Computer dialog box appears to show you the name of the user currently logged on. Click on OK.

When you work on a single computer, the need to display the current user is really in case there are multiple logons. That way, if you change Registry settings for the current user, you have a chance to decide which logged-on user you want to manipulate settings for. It would be highly unusual, however, to see multiple user names in the Users on Remote Computer dialog box. Therefore, just click OK to accept the single user displayed.

4. The Policy Editor window then displays icons for the local computer and the local user (see fig. 6.1).

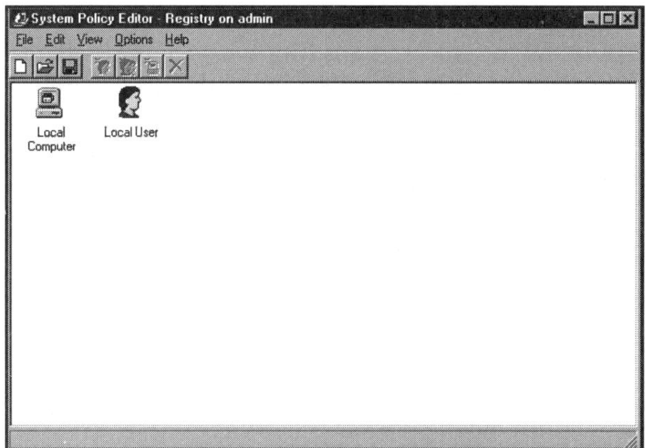

Figure 6.1

The Policy Editor is connected to the computer named admin and can begin to make policy changes to machine and user settings.

The icons represent the following Registry sections:

- ◆ The Local Computer icon represents HKEY_LOCAL_MACHINE Registry settings.
- ◆ The Local User icon represents HKEY_CURRENT_USER Registry settings.

You can make changes to either Registry section.

Manipulate All Workstations

To make changes for all the computers on a domain, choose New Policy from the File menu. The icons for Default Computer and Default User appear in the Policy Editor window (see fig. 6.2).

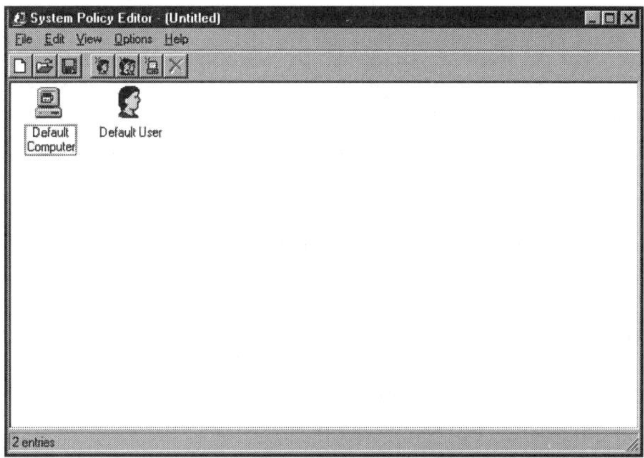

Figure 6.2

When you work with multiple computers, you can change the user settings or the machine settings for all the workstations.

Double-click the Default Computer icon to change settings for HKEY_LOCAL_MACHINE on all the workstations. Double-click the Default User icon to change settings for HKEY_CURRENT_USER on all the workstations.

Manipulate Specific Workstations

If you want to make changes to multiple workstations, but not the entire domain, you can make your Registry changes to the local or default entities and then choose the machines or users you want to target.

To select computers:

1. From the Edit menu, choose Add Computer.
2. The Add Computer dialog box appears, and you can enter the name of the computer you want to add. Or, you can choose Browse to see an Explorer-like display of all the available NT computers (servers and workstations).

No error-checking is performed when you choose computers if you opt to enter a name instead of browsing. You can enter "Zeke," and even if there's no computer on the system with that name, you'll see an icon. It's safer to browse. Also note that the only computers you'll see in the browse window are NT computers; you will not see Windows 95 or Word for Windows workstations.

3. Choose the computer you want to add to your target group.
4. Continue to add computers until you've created the group you need.

To select users, follow these steps:

1. From the Edit menu, choose Add User.
2. In the Add User dialog box, enter the name of the user, or choose Browse to see a user list (you can specify which list to use, choosing among the domains you're connected to). You must have the appropriate trust relationships to work on another domain.
3. Select the target users, choosing Add Names until you have completed your target user list.

Perform the following steps to select groups:

1. From the Edit menu, choose Add Group.

2. Enter the name of the target group in the Add Group dialog box, or choose Browse to use a list of groups (you can specify the source of the list, choosing from the domains available).

3. Select and add the groups you want to target.

As you select computers, users, or groups, icons for each selection appear in the software window.

Create Policies for the Interface

Because this chapter is concerned with the settings for the interface, you must look at the user policies, which is where most of those settings are.

Click on the appropriate user icon to see the Default User Properties dialog box (see fig. 6.3).

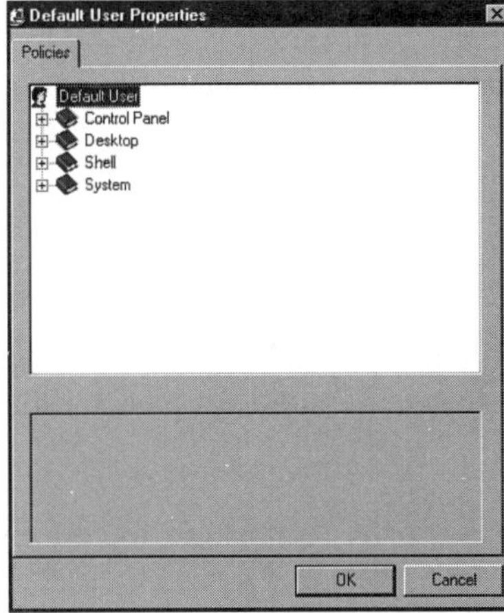

Figure 6.3

The various Registry entries are accessed by opening the appropriate books in the Policy Editor.

The Shell

Most of the controls of interest for this chapter are found by expanding the Shell book and then expanding the Restrictions book (see fig. 6.4).

To modify settings, use the checkbox next to the restriction you want to change. After you have finished making your changes, the state of the checkbox becomes part of the saved policy file. The next logon implements the changes, as Windows NT looks at the state of each checkbox to determine whether any changes have to be made during startup.

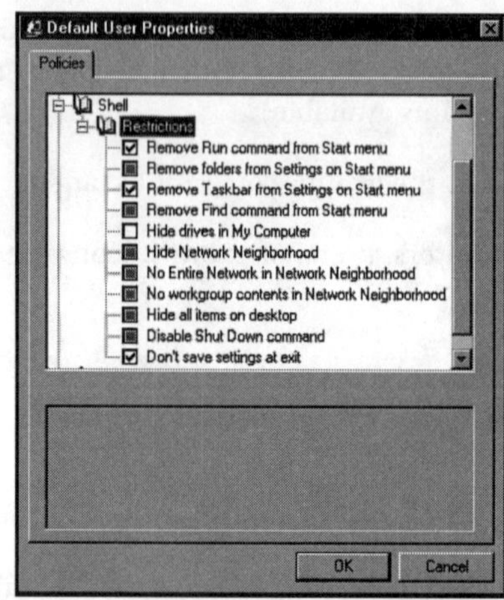

Figure 6.4
You can control a host of user interface settings through the Registry.

The checkboxes next to each option announce their current state by their appearance:

- Gray shading indicates that the setting hasn't changed since the user logged on last. Windows NT skips grayed options when it searches for policy changes that have to be implemented during a logon.
- A check mark means that the restriction will be implemented during the next logon. Because this is a user restriction, it doesn't matter which machine the user logs on from; the restriction will be implemented from the logon machine.
- A clear box indicates that a restriction has been lifted, and the next logon will implement those changes.

You can toggle through the three settings for a checkbox by continuing to click on it.

The System

The System book opens to its own Restrictions book. The available restrictions are as follows:

- Disable the local Registry editing tools, which is a very good idea, especially for users who know just enough to be dangerous.
- Run only allowed Windows applications, which requires that you enter a list of those applications.

If you choose the latter, you can either enter the list directly in the appropriate Registry key (see the earlier discussion) or take the easy way—use the dialog box. When you put a check mark in the box for this restriction, a Show button appears at the bottom of the dialog box.

Click the Show button to display the Show Contents dialog box. Choose Add, then enter the executable file name for the program you are permitting this user to run. Continue to add any additional programs you want allowed for this user (see fig. 6.5).

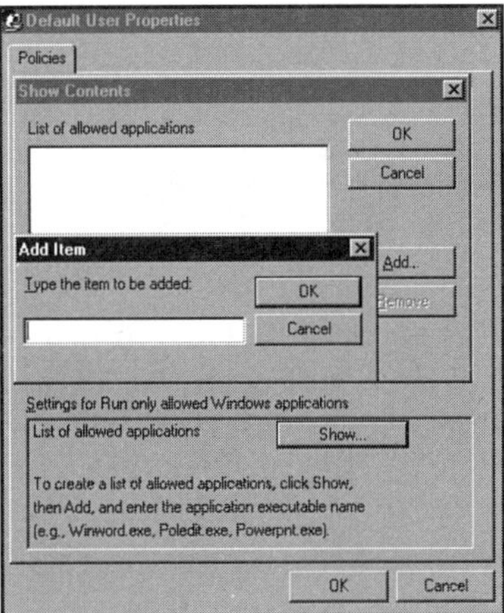

Figure 6.5

Provide a list of allowed applications for this user.

Allowed Applications

Creating a list of allowed applications is a powerful idea. Think about how much easier it is to omit the accounting package from all users except bookkeepers than to set up the directory security or security in the accounting application itself.

If you're considering using the allowed applications restriction, begin by establishing groups for users that are organized around their job descriptions or departments. The accounting department, the human resources department, the clerical workers, the sales department, and any other organizational group in your company should have its own user group. You can assign rights and permissions, of course, but you can also create allowed application lists that make sense for each group.

Control Panel

Expand the Control Panel book; then expand the Display book. The only entry under Display is Restrict display. This enables you to restrict user access to the Display Properties dialog box. If you can control a user's capability to change the display properties, you can make sure that all desktops look the same.

If you click the box next to Restrict display, the bottom of the dialog box offers specific restrictions that you can impose:

- Deny access to the Display icon in the Control Panel
- Hide the Background tab
- Hide the Screen Saver tab
- Hide the Appearance tab
- Hide the Settings tab

The first choice obviously also imposes all the other restrictions. Or, you can choose whichever specific restrictions match your goal for this policy.

Desktop

Expand the Desktop book to see the restrictions you can place on the configuration of the desktop. You can restrict users to one specific wallpaper and one specific color scheme.

Machine Settings

There is one interface item of interest in the policy options available through the default computer (or any individual computer or group of computers). Double-click on the appropriate computer icon in the Policy Editor window and expand the Run book.

The single available item under Run is the checkbox named Run, which determines items to run at startup on this workstation, regardless of which user logs on.

Like the allowed applications setting, Run has a Show dialog box where you can enter the name(s) of the applications you want to launch during startup.

Save Policy Changes

Although it is beyond the scope of this chapter to enter into a full discussion of the Policy Editor, it is probably a good idea to tell you how to save the changes you made.

If you connected to an individual workstation and made changes to its Registry, just use Save to save those changes.

When you make changes to workstations throughout the domain, to enforce them, you need a policy file with an extension of POL. From the File menu, choose Save As to save your new policy file. In the Save In box, enter the Netlogon directory for the domain controller (\\PDCServerName\netlogon); then name the file NTCONFIG.POL. The policy file is read by workstations that log on to that netlogon directory during their logon procedure.

Be sure to replicate the Netlogon folder from the PDC to any BDC's on the LAN during the next directory replication.

Send Policy Changes from Other Servers

You can configure individual workstations to receive updates to the policies from a computer other than the logon PDC. Any other server that can be accessed by a workstation can update that workstation's policies. (The fact is, you could do this using any computer the workstation can see, but because the Policy Editor runs on a server and because you can be pretty sure that all workstations will see a server, it seems more logical to use a server.)

To configure a workstation for an alternate site for policy updates, follow these steps:

1. At the workstation, open Policy Editor (located on the server).
2. From the File menu, choose Connect.
3. Double-click on the Local Computer icon.
4. Expand the Network book.
5. Expand the System Policies update book.
6. Click Remote Update, which opens a Settings section at the bottom of the dialog box (see fig. 6.6).

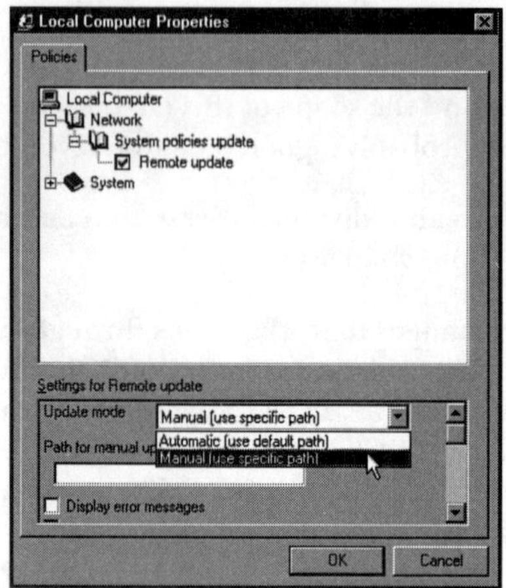

Figure 6.6
Change the settings for updating policies.

7. Change the Update mode from Automatic to Manual.
8. Enter the path for the manual update.
9. If you want this computer to see Registry process error messages, choose Display error messages.
10. When you finish making policy changes, choose Save As from the File menu and save the file to the path specified in step 8. Be sure that the file has a POL extension.

Specifying the Policy File Location in the Registry

This change can also be made from the Registry. If you save the policy file, you can specify the location of the file from which system policies are read.

The Registry key is HKEY_LOCAL_MACHINE\System\CurrentContrlSet\Control\Update.

The value can be 0, 1, or 2 (the data type is REG_DWORD).

0 disables system policies.

1 means that system policies are read from the netlogon share of the authenticating server.

2 means that the system policy file is specified in the NetworkPath value entry (in the same Registry location). In the NetworkPath key, set the full path and file name (use a logical drive letter for a mapped drive or enter the full UNC path).

Set Group Priorities

If you create policies by group, some of the users are likely to belong to more than one group, and those groups might provide different policies. To avoid any possible conflicts, you have to arrange the groups affected by your changes into a priority list.

From the Options menu, choose Group Priority (the choice is grayed out if you haven't created group policies). The Group Priority dialog box appears so that you can arrange the order in which you want the policies to affect users in the group (see fig. 6.7).

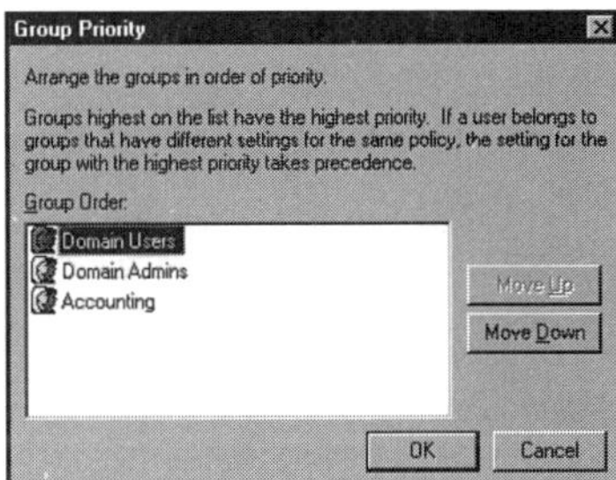

Figure 6.7

Setting group priorities straightens out conflicts for users with multiple group memberships.

After the priorities are made, a user who is a member of more than one group will have the policy settings belonging to the group with the higher priority. Any conflicting policies for groups with lower priorities for this user will be ignored.

Working with the Explorer Program

To users, Explorer is a program, EXPLORER.EXE, which is stored in the Windows NT directory. It's accessed through the Programs section of the Start menu (until you create a shortcut for it, which is almost a necessity because users access Explorer so often).

Explorer opens with a hierarchical view of your computer's directory structure (see fig. 6.8).

The left pane (called All Folders) shows the tree; the right pane (called Contents) shows the contents of the object selected in the left pane.

Figure 6.8

The Explorer view of a computer shows the directory structure in a hierarchical view.

Compare to File Manager

It impossible to avoid having users compare the functions and display of Explorer to the familiarity of File Manager. I've found that users who face Windows NT 4 for the first time almost always ask "How do I get to File Manager?" When they're shown Explorer, they can grasp the concept of the display quite easily. Explorer, like File Manager, displays an outline with each sublevel of the hierarchy indented. To make it easier to follow the way each level is connected, both Explorer and File Manager display vertical and horizontal lines in the left pane.

All the system administrators I've spoken with who rolled out NT 4 as a replacement to NT 3.x or Windows 3.x have had to deal with user questions (and comments) about translating File Manager tasks to Explorer.

To help you deal with the questions you'll surely hear, this section presents an overview of the differences and similarities between the two programs.

View Folders and Folder Contents

The Explorer display is a complete hierarchy, and all the drives and computers you can see are represented in the left pane. Computers do not have to be mapped to a drive letter to appear in the left pane.

In File Manager, the left pane shows only the currently selected drive, and you must map connected computers to drive letters to display their contents.

To view subfolders in Explorer, click on the plus sign next to the parent folder in the left pane. This does not select that folder, and the right pane does not display the folder's contents. Explorer lets you expand a folder without selecting it.

In File Manager, you expand a folder by double-clicking on it, which also selects it. The right pane displays the contents of the folder.

This difference makes moving and copying files quite a bit easier in Explorer. You can select a folder and view its contents in the right pane. Then, in the left pane, move to another folder (which can be on another drive or another computer). If you need to get to a subfolder, you just use the plus sign(s) to navigate downward until you've found the correct one. These independent views make it much easier to cut and paste.

Multiple Windows

In File Manager, to view the contents of two folders or two drives (including mapped drives), you open another window.

You cannot open multiple windows in Explorer. You can, however, have multiple instances of Explorer, and there are a couple of ways to accomplish this:

- With Explorer open, right-click on the My Computer icon and choose Explore.
- In Explorer, right-click a folder in the left pane and choose Open from the shortcut menu. Right-click the system icon of the folder window (it looks like a folder and is on the left end of the title bar) and choose Explore. (You can close the original folder window at this point.)

Open a New Explorer Window from the Shortcut Menu

You can, in fact, configure Explorer to open a new window quite easily. This is useful because it's often awkward to drag between panes in Explorer. Having a new Explorer window for either your source or target directory would make it easy to move objects between that directory and another directory in Explorer. After you find out how useful this is, you can make the process of opening a new window easier by having it as an item on the shortcut menu. Right-clicking on a directory object and choosing New Window is faster than any other method of performing this task.

This is done through the Registry, using Regedit:

1. In HKEY_CLASSES_ROOT, scroll through the first set of alphabetic entries to the second set of alphabetic entries. Find the folder icon named Directory and expand it.

continues

2. Select the folder icon named Shell and right-click on any blank spot in the right pane. Choose New, Key to create a new directory. Name it OpenWindow or OpenNew or some other name that indicates the purpose of this command. If you select the new object in the left pane, you'll see a single listing, a Default entry with no value set for the data.
3. Double-click on the Default entry to bring up the Edit String dialog box. Enter **Open New &Window** in the Value data entry box. (The ampersand means that the letter W will be the hot key for this menu choice and will be underlined when it appears on the shortcut menu.) Click on OK.
4. Right-click on a blank spot in this new directory entry and again choose New, Key. Another subdirectory is created, which you must name Command. A Default entry appears in the right pane for this Command subdirectory.
5. Double-click on the Command folder's Default entry and enter **Explorer %1**. Click on OK.

Hereafter, when you right-click on a directory in either pane of Explorer, the shortcut menu displays the command Open New Window. When you choose it, a new window opens that displays the contents of the current directory (the one you right-clicked). It's easy to drag files between the original Explorer window to this window.

In addition to these differences in how you view contents, there are also some differences in the way you accomplish tasks.

Move, Copy, Open, and Delete

The File menu in File Manager offers Move, Copy, Open, and Delete for any selected file(s).

Explorer carries out these tasks through the right-click shortcut menu, which includes Open, Delete, Cut, Copy, and Paste.

Note Actually, you can use the File menu on Explorer's menu bar, but the shortcut menu is certainly faster and easier.

File Manager supports drag-and-drop for moving and copying files, but you have to remember to hold down the Ctrl key to copy a file instead of moving it (unless you are copying across drives, which is always a copy and never a move).

Explorer offers the right-drag maneuver, which eliminates the chance of an accidental move rather than a copy. Of course, you can also left-drag files in Explorer to move them, holding down the Ctrl key to copy rather than move.

Rename

File Manager renames files and folders with a dialog box that supports wild cards, which makes renaming a group of files easy.

Explorer permits renaming of one file or folder at a time. There is no dialog box; you rename directly on the file or folder's listing in the right pane. (I drop to the command line to rename with wild cards.) By the way, there are several methods for renaming a file. In order of ease of use (easiest first) they are as follows:

- Select the file and press F2.
- Click twice on the file name slowly (not fast enough to qualify as a double-click).
- Right-click on the file and choose Rename from the shortcut menu.
- Select the file and choose Rename from the File menu.

Create a Directory/Folder

In File Manager, you create directories/folders by selecting the folder (or drive, if you are creating a folder in the root directory) in which you want to place this new subfolder and then choosing Create Directory from the File menu. A dialog box opens so that you can enter the name of the new directory.

In Explorer, you create new folders while you are in the contents pane of the parent folder by choosing New from the shortcut menu (right-click on a blank spot in the right pane). You name the folder directly in the right pane. (You could, of course, use the New command in the File menu.)

Use File Manager

In the end, if there are advantages to File Manager that seem to be important to users, it's still there. The executable name for it is WINFILE.EXE, and you can find it in the \system32 subdirectory under your Windows NT directory.

Configure File Manager

If you do have users who want to avail themselves of File Manager, you can control the way it is used through the Registry. Most of the controls in File Manager are set for safety, and the only reason to change any of them is to speed up the process of manipulating files (the keys are for determining whether confirmation dialog boxes will appear).

Changes to values in the key HKEY_CURRENT_USER\Software\Microsoft\File Manager\Settings can place controls on the way File Manager works. Some of the values you may want to change in the Registry are as follows:

- **ConfirmDelete.** Determines whether the user will be asked to confirm file deletions. The range is Boolean. The default is 1.
- **ConfirmFormat.** Determines whether the user will be asked to confirm formatting requests. The range is Boolean. The default is 1.
- **ConfirmMouse.** Determines whether the user will be asked to confirm drag-and-drop tasks. The range is Boolean. The default is 1.
- **ConfirmReplace.** Determines whether the user will be asked to confirm file replacements. The range is Boolean. The default is 1.
- **ConfirmSubDel.** Determines whether the user will be asked to confirm the deletion of subdirectories. The range is Boolean. The default is 1.
- **ConfirmSystemHiddenReadOnly.** Determines whether the user will be asked to confirm changes in attributes. The range is Boolean. The default is 1.

Working with File Types

You can see the list of registered file types in Explorer by choosing View, Options (see fig. 6.9). Select any file type to view information about it.

File Types in the Registry

The default file types established by Windows NT are defined in the Registry in HKEY_LOCAL_MACHINE\software\classes.

The user-configured extension information is found in HKEY_CLASSES_ROOT. Software that is installed will add extensions to the listing in this key, and extensions for file types invented by users will also be added here.

Note Registered file types are those that are placed in the Registry during the installation process. Most applications written for Windows NT (or for Windows 95) will insert the extension used for its software files into the Registry and link that extension to the executable file for the application.

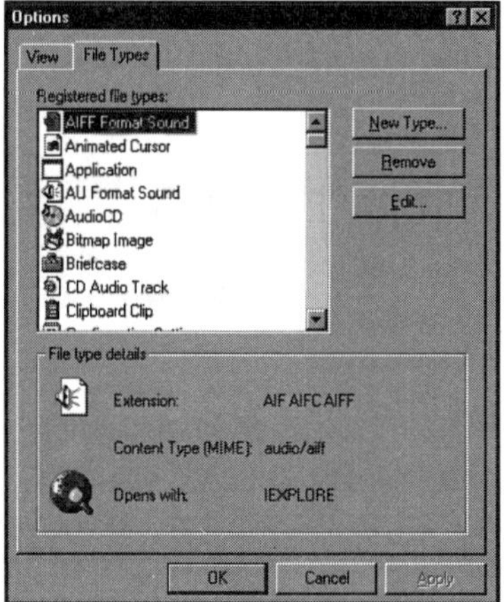

Figure 6.9

Registered file types are listed in the File Types tab of the Options dialog box.

You can add, remove, change, or manipulate file types from Explorer. You can perform all the same tasks in My Computer. The changes you make are written to the Registry. Document file types are the ones you'll be manipulating most of the time. (You generally do not want to mess around with program files.)

Create a File Type

Not all software applications register their file types during the installation process. Legacy software, DOS software, and software developed in-house are the common applications for which this is true.

Additionally, a common practice in many companies is to give specific extensions to database or spreadsheet reports that are written to disk. For instance, a report from a database could use an extension CUS if it's a customer list. These files are frequently used for mail-merge operations, or brought into word processors or desktop publishing applications for presentations. Telling Windows NT about that extension and associating it with the software of choice means that any such files will open in the appropriate software when a user accesses them.

Another frequent practice is the exchange of text files (with an extension of TXT) around the company, with the expectation that these files will be used in a word processor so that formatting and other features can be applied. You can tell Windows NT to use the word processor instead of Notepad (or to give a choice between the two).

Many companies have conventions about file extensions that override the default extensions of installed software. For example, a company that uses WordPerfect (which has registered the extension WPD as a file type), might choose to use LTR for letters, CTR for contracts, and so on. You do not need to register these file types because if the files were created in WordPerfect, they will open WordPerfect when they are double-clicked (the information about the software that created the file is read from the file's header).

To create a new file type, choose View, Options, and go to the File Types tab of the Options dialog box. Choose New Type to display the Add New File Type dialog box (see fig. 6.10).

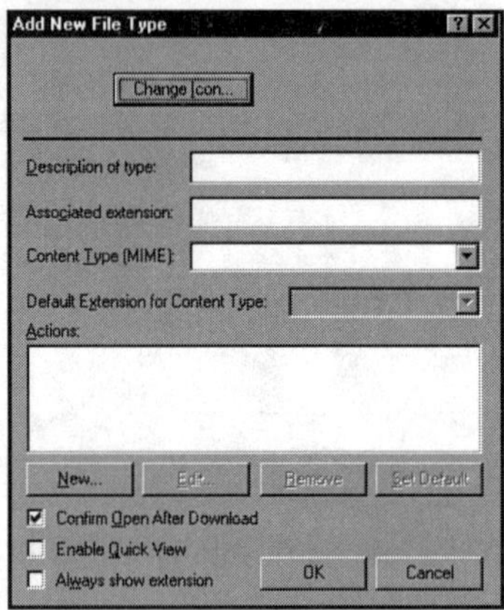

Figure 6.10

Add a new file type to your system and configure it for user action.

The options in the dialog box are for the following preferences:

- **Description of type.** The description that appears in Explorer and My Computer folder windows when you choose Details view.
- **Associated extension.** The three-letter file name extension for this file type. Any file with this extension will use the configuration options you establish.
- **Content Type (MIME).** The MIME type you want to associate with this file type. This permits Internet browsers to find an association when users open files over the Internet. Click the arrow to the right of the field to see the available choices. This field is optional.
- **Default Extension for Content Type.** For choosing a file name extension for the MIME association. Some MIME types permit more than one extension, and this field is for setting the default extension. This field is also optional.

At the bottom of the dialog box are three options you can select or deselect, as needed.

- **Confirm Open After Download.** This option indicates that you want a confirmation dialog box before this file type is opened automatically following a download (the dialog box asks whether you want to open the file).

- **Enable Quick View.** This option should be selected if the file type is supported for Quick View.
- **Always show extension.** This option forces the display of the file type's extension in folder windows.

Attach an Action to a File Type

The Actions box is where the power is. This is where you configure the commands you want to run when any file of this file type is opened. The program you specify becomes the file type's associated program. Choose New to open the New Action dialog box (see fig. 6.11).

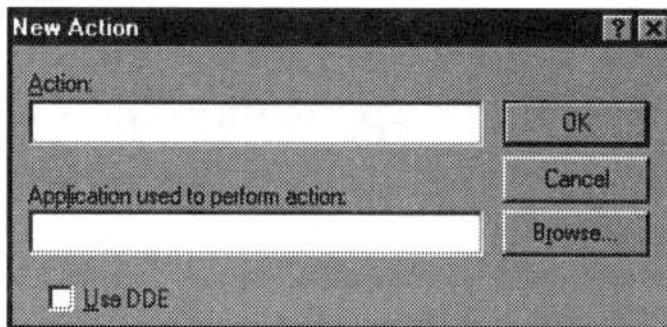

Figure 6.11

The action(s) you configure will be attached to any and every file of this type.

- In the Action box, enter the command you want to appear on the shortcut menu (usually Open). If you want the command to have a menu hotkey (an underlined letter the user can press instead of clicking on the item), precede that letter with an ampersand (&). Be careful not to use a letter that is already claimed by other items on the shortcut menu.
- In the Application used to perform action box, enter the path to the software that you want to associate with this file type.
- If the application can use DDE, select the Use DDE box.

Clicking on OK returns you to the Add New File Type dialog box.

If you want, you can perform the same steps again to add a different action. If it is another Open choice (for another software application so that users can have a choice), make sure that you change the text for Open to something else. You cannot duplicate the Action you already entered (the new configuration will replace the previous one), and you'll have to add text such as OpenWithWord.

If you do configure a file type for multiple actions, you can highlight one in the Add File Type dialog box and select Set Default. The default action will be invoked if the user double-clicks on the file.

If there are multiple associations with a file type, the shortcut menu that displays when a user right-clicks the file's object will show all of them. The default action will be listed first and will be bold.

> **Add Parameters to File Type Actions**
>
> You can add startup parameters to the executable file you insert in an action.
>
> In WordPerfect, for example, I developed a macro that launches the import delimited text feature. For the file type that represents a disk file report from a database that includes delimiters, I have an action named OpenInWP. When I configured the action, I added the switch that opens WordPerfect with the macro (/m-macroname).
>
> As you become familiar with the ways to open your software applications using switches and parameters, you'll think of inventive ways to use this Actions feature on file types.

Incidentally, at the top of the dialog box is a Change Icon button. Click on it and choose an icon to attach to this file type. Many applications automatically assign their own icons to data files, so you only need to do this if the associated application doesn't, or if you're creating a file type.

Edit File Associations

Most of the file types listed in the Options dialog box are already associated. You can see the association by selecting the file type and viewing the bottom of the dialog box, which indicates the associated program.

If a user double-clicks on any file type that is not associated, the Windows NT Open With dialog box appears so that a program can be chosen. If no appropriate application is listed, the user can specify any executable file that will work with this file type.

You can edit the associated program information for any file type. Select the file type and choose Edit; then select an action and choose Edit. Enter the appropriate command, add a parameter, or make any other necessary changes.

Manipulating the Send To Menu

The shortcut menu that appears when you right-click an object includes a menu item called Send To. The default Send To submenu usually includes Drive A, the Briefcase, and Mail Recipient.

Send To is a substitute for dragging an object to the Send To target. When a container such as the briefcase or a floppy drive is chosen, the object is copied. When the target is Mail Recipient, the Messaging application is launched.

You can change the options that display on the Send To menu, adding more options or removing any that you don't want users to have.

The items that display in the Send To list are a reflection of the items that have been placed in a user's Send To subdirectory. If a workstation has multiple user profiles, each user has an individual Send To subdirectory and therefore can have an individual submenu for Send To.

The Send To subdirectory is \Profiles\UserLogonName\Send To under the Windows NT directory. All the objects in the subdirectory are shortcuts.

Adding to the Send To Folder

You can add items to the Send To submenu for all users (or for specific users). I find it easiest to use Explorer and My Computer simultaneously to do this, especially if there are multiple profiles:

1. Open My Computer and move to the Profiles subdirectory.
2. For each profile you want to manipulate, open the user's subdirectory; then open the Send To subdirectory.
3. Close the user's subdirectory window as you open the Send To subdirectory. (You don't need the parent, and it clutters the desktop.)
4. Widen each Send To window to make sure that you can see the user name on each Send To window. (If you don't see the path in the title bar, you should change the options for My Computer to include it.)
5. When your desktop has all the appropriate user Send To subdirectories open, open Explorer (which is where you're going to find the objects you'll place in the various Send To windows). Figure 6.12 displays an example of this scenario.
6. Find and right-drag objects between Explorer and the Send To windows. Release the mouse and choose Create Shortcut(s) Here.

Actually, I've found it really quick to move an item into one Send To window and then right-click the object and choose Copy. I can then move through all the other Send To windows and continuously Paste.

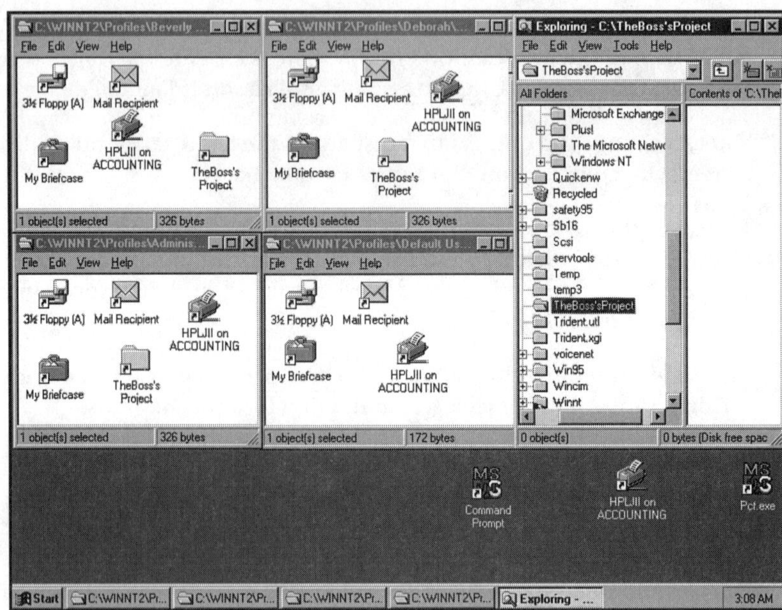

Figure 6.12
All the windows and objects needed are on the desktop.

This approach works with multiple users across computers, although in order to use My Computer you have to map the computers first. You can use Explorer to get to user profiles on connected drives without mapping.

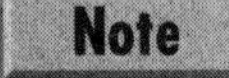

Note If you place a new object into the Send To directory of the Default User, any new users who log on to this workstation will have this choice on their Send To menu. The Default User profile configuration is automatically replicated for any new logon name.

The common additions to the Send To submenu are as follows:

- ◆ Shortcuts to printers
- ◆ Shortcuts to shares on connected mapped drives
- ◆ Shortcuts to directories that hold documents for special uses
- ◆ Shortcuts to the Recycle Bin (which sends the object directly to the Recycle Bin without a confirmation dialog box)

Using Send To with Directories Can Be Very Productive!

Creating shortcuts to directories is a productive decision. If users are working on a project using a variety of applications, for instance, create a project directory and then put a shortcut to it in Send To.

Applications written for Windows NT 4 (or written for Windows 95) provide right-click functions for document files in the Open and Save As dialog boxes. Sending data files to special directories right from the application makes it easy to keep data organized.

Use Send To to archive files that you don't need, but don't want to delete. Create a directory for this purpose and put a shortcut to it in the Send To folder. Then as you come across files you want to archive, send them to this directory. Eventually, you can move the directory to a floppy disk or to another drive (or computer) and store the files.

Most of the time, you won't want to place directories relating to projects on the Default User Send To menu. They tend to be temporary, and there's no point in having them on a new user's menu.

If you add a number of items to Send To, you might find it easier to manipulate the Send To menu if you group similar items into a submenu.

Although you can only perform a Send To operation to a shortcut, a subdirectory in a Send To directory will act as a menu item that points to shortcuts in a submenu. You can create subdirectories and name them, and the name appears on the Send To menu. Clicking on the listing doesn't send the selected object anywhere; it just leads to the submenu (an arrow will display to the right of the entry, indicating the submenu's existence).

A Real-Life Example for Using Cascading Send To Menus

The best way to illustrate this is to use a real-life example. I have a number of directories in my system that hold specific types of documents or act as a holding bin for documents that I need to work on. For example, I have a number of subdirectories under the directory that holds my file-zipping software. These subdirectories are divided by topic because as I unzip files that I've downloaded or zip files that I need to upload, I like to keep each project together. (For me a project is a book; for you it might be something else.)

continues

All the documents and messages I receive from online services and the Internet get downloaded to the same directory. I move through that directory, selecting files and sending them to the appropriate locations on my drive for later manipulation. Before I came up with this scheme, I would send files to a directory and then later have to cut and paste my way around my drive with Explorer until everything was where it should be.

Then I tried adding all those target directories to the Send To menu item, but it made the menu busy and hard to read.

Using a cascading menu from my Send To menu, I can send each file to the appropriate target without opening Explorer and cutting, pasting, or dragging.

Summary

Whether you're making changes to a single workstation or all the workstations on a domain, being able to manipulate the user's access within in the operating system interface is a powerful tool.

CHAPTER 7

Managing Users

The user logon process is a great deal more than just announcing a user name and gaining access to the workstation. Part of logon is the granting of rights, the determination of access to programs and utilities, and a customized interface for the user who is logging on. All of these elements can be controlled by an administrator.

The ability to control what the user sees, what the user can access, and what privileges the user has to the workstation and programs is a powerful tool. An administrator can use this power to ensure that every workstation in the system matches a desired design. In addition, specific users can be given rights that other users should be denied. The determination of which groups of users get advanced rights varies, depending upon company policies, level of user expertise, or any other criteria that has importance for a specific enterprise.

This chapter covers the issues that affect the interface and the rights of users who are logging on to an NT 4 workstation. Information about imposing controls and restrictions is covered so that you can apply controls to specific workstations or to a group of workstations in one fell swoop.

The Workstation Logon Process

Regardless of whether a user is logging on to Windows NT Workstation 4 to join a domain or working in a peer network environment, the user has to log on to the local computer.

The logon process is part of Windows NT startup; if there is no logon, the system is not considered to be started successfully. Logon occurs after the kernel is initialized and before drivers are loaded. The drivers actually begin loading as soon as the Begin Logon dialog box displays, so the logon process and the completion of startup process go on at the same time.

After users log on to a Windows NT workstation, the Registry is searched to see whether a profile exists for the user logon name. If there is, that user's configuration is loaded from the user's profile subdirectory on the hard drive. If there isn't, the Default User configuration is loaded and saved as a new profile for this user.

The profile list appears in HKEY_LOCAL_MACHINE\Software\Microsoft\Windows NT\CurrentVersion\ProfileList\SID_#. Every profile that has been installed has its own unique SID number. This is a binary number, displayed in hex, that is assigned by the operating system. The SID subkey contains the path for the profile hive for the user. In fact, the path, which has the profile folder name in it, is really the only way to figure out which SID subkey belongs to which user because you can't tell by the SID subkey name.

Utilizing User Manager

User management for workstations starts with User Manager, which creates user accounts and groups and manages the user security for the workstation (see fig. 7.1).

If you've been using Windows NT 3.x, the topics covered in this section should be pretty familiar. If you've just moved to NT with NT 4, this section is an overview of the basic user configuration options available at the workstation. Most of them are easy to understand and apply.

Creating and Modifying Users

Choosing New User from the User menu displays the New User dialog box, which contains all the elements for configuring the user (see fig. 7.2).

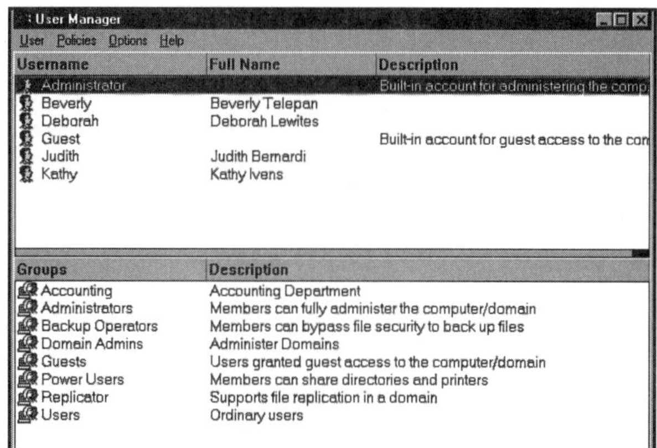

Figure 7.1

User Manager is your primary tool for basic user account tasks.

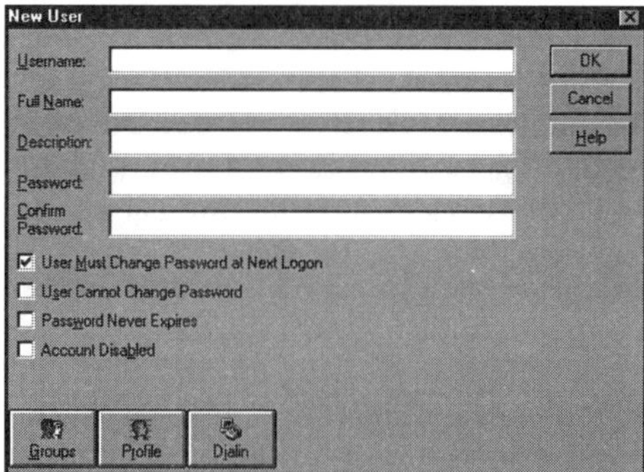

Figure 7.2

The New User dialog box opening screen is the first step in controlling user accounts.

Username is a unique identity and is the main NT identity for this user account. The uniqueness applies to both users and groups. It can contain up to 20 characters (upper-, lower-, and mixed case are acceptable). Spaces and periods are fine, but there must be at least one other character besides the spaces and periods. The following characters cannot be used:

" / \ : ; | = , + * ? < >

Full Name is the real name of the user.

Description is an optional entry, and most companies insert the user's title.

Password and **Confirm Password** (you must enter the identical characters in each of these fields) can be a combination of up to 14 characters. Passwords are case-sensitive.

User Must Change Password at Next Logon is a way to permit a user to select his or her own password when logging on. You can also use this selection to force a user to change the password if you think the current password has been compromised.

Note Some administrators find it's easier to bring new users on to the system by making this initial password a blank field. The user is forced to create a password during the first logon.

User Cannot Change Password is useful for guest accounts, either the built-in one or others you invent. If workstations are established for special tasks (perhaps the accounting department keeps checks in a printer attached to one workstation, and you want to restrict access), this is a useful tool. If the password is believed to have been compromised, an administrative change locks the new password in (don't forget to tell the authorized users).

Password Never Expires has more power than some of the other settings in the NT workstation. It outranks the maximum password age setting if you established one in Account Policy. It also overrides the User Must Change Password at Next Logon selection. It's usually a good idea to select this option for user accounts named when you are assigning services from the Services icon in the Control Panel.

Account Disabled is selected when you want to prevent the account from logging on. It's also useful for creating a template. In fact, it's a good idea to create several disabled template accounts, each with specific configurations. They can be copied to new user accounts that require the same configuration. Just display the account and press F8 to copy it, and then enter a new user's information (and don't forget to enable the new account). You cannot disable the built-in account for Administrator.

Groups is for setting up or changing the group memberships for the user.

Profile is used to enter the user's profile path, logon script, or home directory path. The manipulation of user profiles involves this dialog box (more information about that is found later in this chapter).

Dialin is for giving dial in permission to a remote user. You can establish the dial-in configuration so that the user is called back, and security is heightened if you call back to a fixed telephone number.

Creating and Modifying Groups

Groups created on Windows NT Workstation are local groups. Choose New Local Group from the User menu to display the New Local Group dialog box (see fig. 7.3).

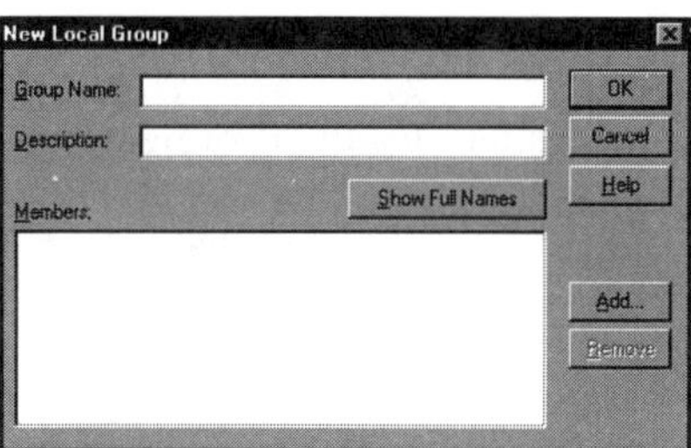

Figure 7.3
Add a new local group for any department or division that needs specific rights.

Group Name must be a unique name for the workstation. The maximum number of characters is 256 uppercase, lowercase, or mixed. The only illegal character is the backslash. If you are modifying a group's record, this field cannot be changed.

Description is used to explain or further describe a group.

Show Full Names is used if you don't want to select members for this group by user name, but prefer to use the full names.

Members is the list of members of the group. They can be users from the workstation or from the domain. You can nest groups. You can add or remove members easily:

- Choose Add to add members to a group (the members can be chosen from the list of local users or the domain).
- Remove members from the group by selecting them, then choosing Remove.

If a user (or multiple users) is selected when you begin to create a group, that user becomes a member of the group automatically and appears in the membership list as soon as the New Local Group dialog box opens.

If you are copying a local group, all the members of the source group become members of the new one.

To change any of the characteristics of a group (except the name), select the group and choose Properties from the File menu.

Setting User Policies

You can set workstation policy options from User Manager for specific users or for groups. Workstation policies include a wide variety of configuration options, covering logon procedures, rights, and security.

Configuring Rights

Defining the rights for groups is a far better idea than configuring every user individually, because after the groups are set up for rights, any users you add inherit those rights. Rights are determined in the User Rights Policy dialog box which you reach from the Policies menu (see fig. 7.4).

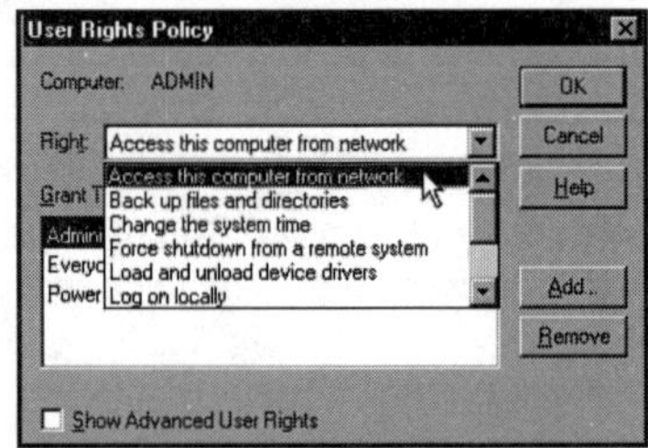

Figure 7.4

Pick rights and grant them to a group or multiple groups to set up the permissions for this workstation.

Available User Rights

The following rights can be given to groups and users:

- **Access this computer from network.** Enables the user to connect to this computer from any other computer on the network.
- **Back up files and directories.** Enables the user to use backup applications for files and directories, even if no file and directory permissions are given for other file manipulations.
- **Change the system time.** Enables the user to set the clock for this computer.
- **Load and unload device drivers.** Enables the user to manipulate device drivers dynamically.
- **Log on locally.** Enables the user to log on to the computer through the local logon dialog box.
- **Manage auditing and security log.** Gives the user permission to manage auditing. The right is limited to specifying audits of objects through their Properties (using the Security tab) and being able to view the results in the Event Viewer. The right does not extend to configuring the options for auditing on the Policies menu of the User Manager.
- **Restore files and directories.** Enables the user to restore files and directories from a backup.

- **Shut down the system.** Enables the user to perform a shutdown of the workstation.
- **Take ownership of files or other objects.** Enables the user to take ownership of any object on the workstation.

Account Policies

From the Policies menu, choose Account. You then use the Account Policy dialog box to set defaults for this workstation (see fig. 7.5). Account policies determine the control for the way passwords are used in order for the account to be recognized (and permitted access to the workstation). Policies you set in individual user accounts take priority over these defaults you establish for groups.

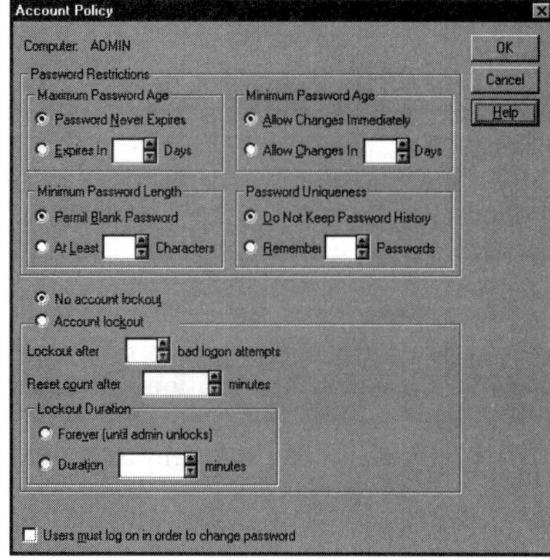

Figure 7.5

Set up default security policies for users on this workstation.

The fields are all straightforward and self-explanatory.

Audit Policies

To keep an eye on what the users on this workstation are up to, turn on auditing. Choose Audit from the Policies menu, and then select the events you want to audit from the Audit Policy dialog box (see fig. 7.6).

The audit log appears in the Security Log of the Event Viewer. Remember that the log is limited as to size, so don't fill it up so fast that events roll off before you see them. The way to avoid overrunning the log is to pick events to audit judiciously, and don't choose to audit successful events without a darn good reason.

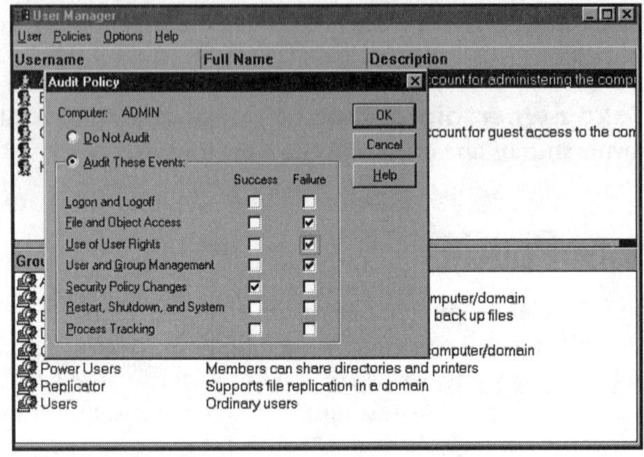

Figure 7.6

Track successful and unsuccessful events performed by users with the Audit Policy dialog box.

NT Server Logons

If a workstation user logs on to a Windows NT Server, the information about the user is maintained in the Server's User Manager for domains. Some additional polices are available for user management on a domain:

- Logon hours enables a domain administrator to determine the days and time periods in which a user can connect to a server.
- The Server maintains a global group for all users in its domain. Members of that group can be given permissions to access shares on any other trusted domain. They can also be given permissions for this workstation. On the other hand, if there are trusted domains in the organization, it's possible to assign a workstation user to an account called a local account and deny access to other domains.

A host of policies that control users connected to a server can be created with the Windows NT Server Policy Editor (covered in the next section).

Managing Local User Profiles

Every user of a Windows NT computer has a profile that contains the configuration information for that user on that workstation. The information about the configuration options they choose (or are chosen for them by an administrator) is recorded in profiles linked to their logon names. If multiple users access a Windows NT workstation, a separate user profile exists for each of them. During the logon process, the appropriate profile is loaded. The profile determines what the user sees, what the user can access, and the amount of manipulation the user can perform on those elements. An administrator can establish control over the workstation's appearance and the user's ability to access programs and utilities.

The Default User Profile

A default user profile is established during the installation of NT Workstation. As each workstation user logs on for the first time, that default profile is duplicated in the new user's name. As the user makes configuration changes (if changes are permitted), the profile expands to include all the additional options and settings.

After the installation of the operating system, the first logon name presented is Administrator, so there is also a profile for Administrator established on all NT workstations. After that, the number of profiles, and the names attached to them, depend on the number of users who log on to the workstation.

Viewing Profile Information

You can look at any user profile in Explorer or My Computer. To find the profiles, look in your Windows NT folder and click on the plus sign next to the Profiles folder (or open it if you are using My Computer). The Profiles folder expands to show all the profile folders on the computer (see fig. 7.7).

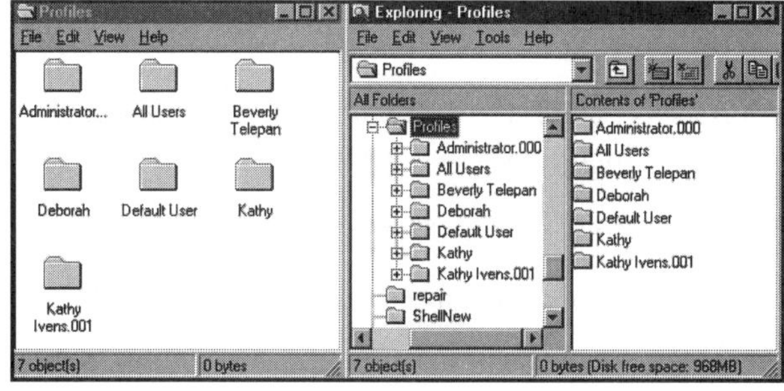

Figure 7.7

Profiles are stored on the workstation's hard drive under the operating system directory.

To examine an individual user profile, click on the plus sign next to the user's profile folder in Explorer, or open the folder in My Computer (see fig. 7.8).

The two profile subdirectories manipulated the most are the Desktop and Start Menu subdirectories.

Objects representing My Computer, Network Neighborhood, Inbox, Internet Explorer, and the Recycle Bin are not displayed in the user's desktop subdirectory. They are taken for granted as a result of installation defaults.

The Start Menu subdirectory contains objects for all the menu options available to that user. The accessories and programs selected from the Installation Options dialog box during the installation of the operating system (and are in the Start Menu subdirectory of the Default User) are automatically installed on every user's Start menu. As a user installs software, menu items for that software are added to the user's Start menu.

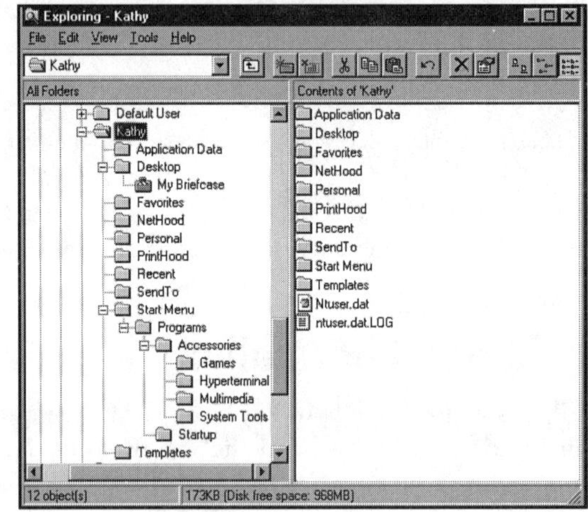

Figure 7.8

Multiple subdirectories under a user's profile directory hold all the configuration options for that user.

Start Menu Common Groups

You can add common menu items to the common groups portion of the Start menu. Common groups appear on every user's start menu and are listed below the separator line. A common group item has the following characteristics:

- ◆ It is automatically placed on the Start menu of every user.
- ◆ It is listed below the separator line that appears at the bottom of the Programs menu.
- ◆ It does not appear in the Programs subfolder of the Profiles folder for any user.

The notion of a common group is a powerful one because it's a way to make certain that every user of a workstation has access to a software application without having each user go through an installation program for the application.

The process of adding a common group application to every user's Start menu is simple:

1. Install the software. Expand your own profile directory in Explorer to find the \Start Menu\Programs subdirectory.

2. Right-click on the Start button, and then select Open All Users. The WindowsNTRoot\Profiles\All Users\Start Menu subdirectory opens on the desktop (you could also open that subdirectory in My Computer). The Programs subdirectory icon displays.

3. With the two folders on the desktop, right-drag the program's icon from your Programs subdirectory to the Programs icon (you don't have to open the Programs folder to copy items into it). Choose Copy Here from the menu that appears when you release the mouse button.

You can also add a Startup group to the Common section of the Program menu if you want every user to launch an application or utility during startup.

Copy Another Profile Folder

If you want multiple users to have access to certain applications, but don't want to place those programs on the Common section of the Programs menu, just copy program objects from one user's profile to another user's profile.

The fastest way to do this is to open My Computer, and then open the source Programs subdirectory and all the target Programs subdirectories you need. Right-drag items from the source folder to the target folder(s) and choose Copy Here when you release the mouse. You can move multiple items by holding down the Ctrl key while you select items from the source folder.

You can do the same thing with the source user's desktop folder, copying desktop items (folders and shortcuts) to the target user profiles. Open the target Desktop subfolder and use this process to add items to each user's desktop. Or, open Explorer and drag executable file objects from their directories to user desktop folders.

If you are adding objects to the desktops of multiple users, after you've placed the first shortcut in one user profile, right-click on it and choose Copy, and then Paste repeatedly until all users have the shortcut. This is faster than bringing the same object into each profile, one at a time, from Explorer or My Computer.

Registry Settings for Profile Information

User configuration options are stored in the Registry in a variety of keys. Although the settings can be established through the Control Panel or User Manager, knowing where to look in the Registry can be useful for troubleshooting. This section lists some of the important configuration entries with their Registry locations. (For complete and thorough coverage of the NT Registry, see Chapter 22, "The Registry.")

You should be aware that some Registry entries don't appear unless configuration options are changed from the defaults (for those subkeys, defaults are taken for granted and not written to the Registry).

Registry Data Types

The values for Registry entries are entered according to the data type needed for that entry. The data types are:

REG_BINARY. This is raw binary data displayed in the Registry Editor as hex. This data type is used primarily for hardware information.

REG_DWORD. This is data consisting of a number that is 4 bytes long. It can be displayed in hex, decimal, or binary. This data type is used mostly for services and device drivers.

REG_EXPAND_SZ. This is a data string. The string is text that contains a variable replaced when an application calls it, looking for information. The most common example is the use of Systemroot, which is replaced by the name of the directory that holds the Windows NT system files.

REG_MULTI_SZ. This is a data type made up of multiple strings. This is usually used for values that hold lists (each entry is separated by a NULL character).

REG_SZ. This is a series of characters (text). It's mostly used to describe components, giving the display names of the components.

REG_FULL_RESOURCE_DESCRIPTOR. This is a hierarchy of nested arrays. These are used to store resource lists for hardware or drivers. They usually look like a table.

Window Colors, found in HKEY_CURRENT_USER\Control Panel\Colors, specifies colors for windows. The data type is REG_SZ.

Color Schemes, found in HKEY_CURRENT_USER\Control Panel\Appearance\Schemes, lists the settings for the available predefined color schemes. The data type is REG_SZ.

Patterns, found in HKEY_CURRENT_USER\Control Panel\Patterns, lists the color values for system bitmap patterns. The data type is REG_SZ (the data consists of a set of eight numbers which correspond to the colors in the eight elements of the pattern.

Screen Savers, found in HKEY_CURRENT_USER\Control Panel\ScreenSaverName (each screen saver has its own folder), defines user preferences for screen savers. The data type is REG_SZ.

Active Screen Saver (if there is one), found in HKEY_CURRENT_USER\Control Panel\Desktop, specifies the path of the selected screen saver; whether or not it's active(Boolean data with 0 for no, and 1 for yes); whether it's password protected (Boolean data with 0 for no, and 1 for yes—the password is not registered); and the TimeOut (in seconds). The data type is REG_SZ.

Console Entries, found in HKEY_CURRENT_USER\Console, has font, cursor, and screen control values for the console. The data type varies depending on the element.

If you change console values for a particular console window, it creates a subkey with the name of that console window. After you open a console window, Windows NT searches the Registry for a subkey with the same name as the window title (for example, Command Prompt). If the subkey is found, any values in it take priority over the values stored in the \CONSOLE key.

Environment Variables, found in HKEY_CURRENT_USER\Environment, holds the user environment variables set on the Environment tab of the System icon in the Control Panel (temporary directory locations). The data in this key usually stays the same regardless of the logged on user and changes only if a user with administrator rights changes them.

File Manager Software Settings, found in HKEY_CURRENT_USER\Software\Microsoft\File Manager\Settings, are any user preferences that have been changed from the default for the appearance of objects in File Manager. The data type is REG_SZ. This is one of the keys that has no entries unless there have been changes made to the default. The options that might appear (due to user changes) include Confirm Settings, Typeface Settings, Other Settings for File Manager (toolbar, window size and placement, and so on). The Confirm settings (for tasks such as delete, format, replace, and so on), are Boolean.

Keyboard Entries, found in HKEY_CURRENT_USER\Control Panel\Keyboard, holds user preferences from configuration tasks performed in the Keyboard icon in Control Panel. The data type is REG_SZ. The NUMLOCK state is 0 for turned off after logon and 2 for turned on after logon. The reason for determining the state after logon is that the state of NUMLOCK is saved during shutdown. The KeyboardDelay entry is a range of 0 to 3 (0 is the shortest delay—about 250 milliseconds). The KeyboardSpeed entry is a range from 0 to 31, and indicates the number of repetitions of a character when a key is held down. The default is 31 (about 30 per second), and the repetitions per second get slower as the entry gets lower.

Keyboard Layout, found in HKEY_CURRENT_USER\Keyboard Layout\Preload, holds the user's preferred layout, which is loaded and activated during logon. The data type is REG_SZ. The standard keyboard is the default (00000409 for U.S. English).

Keyboard Layout Substitute, found in HKEY_CURRENT_USER\Keyboard Layout\Substitutes, holds the entry for a substitute keyboard if the user has configured one. The key is empty if no substitute option has been chosen by the user. Commonly, the substitute is Dvorak U.S. English (00010409). This key is checked to see whether there is an entry during the point in startup for keyboard checking.

Network Connection is found in HKEY_CURRENT_USER\Network\X where X is a subkey for each shared directory configured for reconnection at system startup (otherwise, the key does not exist). The subkey name is the drive letter designation for the connection. The data type is REG_DWORD for the ConnectionType, and REG_SZ for the ProviderName and UNC.

Note If Windows NT was installed on the workstation via a share point from a server or from installation disks in a connected computer, the Registry key HKEY_CURRENT_USER\SOFTWARE\Microsoft\WindowsNT\CurrentVersion\Network\NCAdmin exists to identify the source of installation. Actually, except for the subkey NCAdmin, the key always exists; it is the use of the NCAdmin program for installation that creates that key.

Administrative Tools Configuration is found in individual subkeys under HKEY_CURRENT_USER\SOFTWARE\Microsoft\Windows NT\CurrentVersion\Network. All the entries in these subkeys have a data type of REG_SZ. Each subkey holds settings specific to the configuration of its attendant tool. In addition to the tools, a subkey exists for all persistent connections. Figure 7.9 displays the specific subkeys.

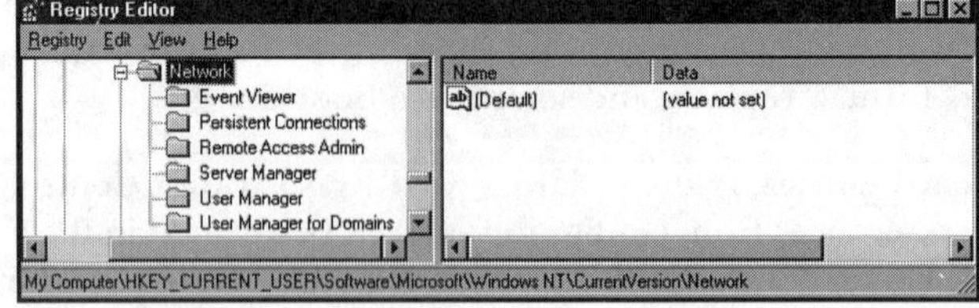

Figure 7.9

The subkeys hold user configuration information for the appearance and behavior of administative tools.

Default Printer, found in HKEY_CURRENT_USER\Printers, displays the currently selected default printer.

RAS Entries, found in HKEY_CURRENT_USER\Software\Microsoft\RAS Autodial and subkeys below it, contains the information about the user configuration for RAS and Dial-Up Networking. Each subkey exists as a result of a configuration process by the user. The RAS Phonebook and its subkeys are also in this section of the Registry (see fig. 7.10).

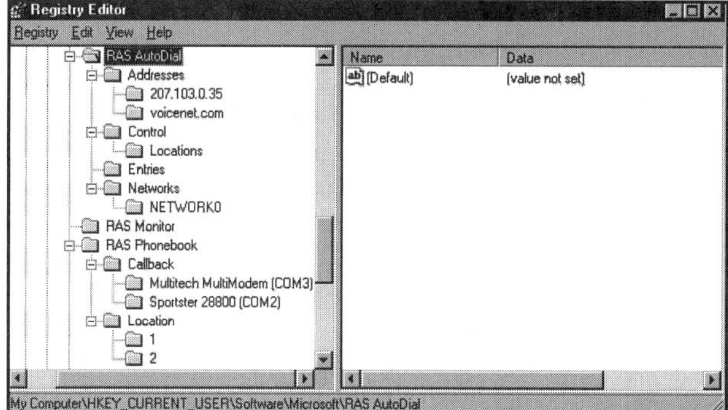

Figure 7.10

RAS and Dial-Up Networking subkeys are added to reflect user configuration options for each element in those applications.

If a problem occurs, the Registry entries can be reached and changed from a remote computer by using the Policy Editor. Although the Policy Editor is part of NT Server, it runs in NT Workstation so that you can access any workstation from another workstation for troubleshooting.

Managing System-Wide Profiles

Network administrators can configure user profiles throughout the network. Two of the important and commonly used powers available to an administrator include:

- Roaming profiles so that users can go to any NT 4 workstation and have their own desktop configuration appear at each one.
- Mandatory profiles to make desktops consistent.

Roaming Profiles

A *roaming profile* is a user profile stored on the server rather than the local drive. This means the user's configuration options can be brought up on any computer connected to the server. Actually, a copy of the profile is kept on the local drive so that if the network is unavailable, the user can still log on to the workstation.

This is particularly useful for those users who spend the work day at different computers. Some employees in accounting departments, for example, move between computers depending on the task at hand. Checkwriting might have to take place at a specific workstation because that workstation has the printer for checks attached to it, and the room in which it is located is kept locked until checkwriting is needed.

Help Desk personnel also work at various computers throughout the day, installing or repairing workstation configurations.

For these roaming users, logging on to any workstation produces the same desktop and other configuration options as they get when they log on to their normal workstation.

This all works by downloading the profile to the workstation after a roaming user logs on to that workstation. If changes to the configuration are made during that work session, those changes are saved back to the server-based profile. The next logon, from any computer connected to that server, results in the new configuration being loaded.

During logon for a user that has a roaming profile, the user is asked to choose between the local and server profile if the last saved date of the local profile is later than the server profile's last saved date.

Create Roaming Profiles

Creating a roaming profile starts with User Manager for Domains on the NT Server (the PDC). Select the user for whom you want to create the profile, and choose Properties from the User menu. When the User Properties dialog box appears, choose Profile and then enter the configuration data in the User Environment Profile dialog box (see fig. 7.11).

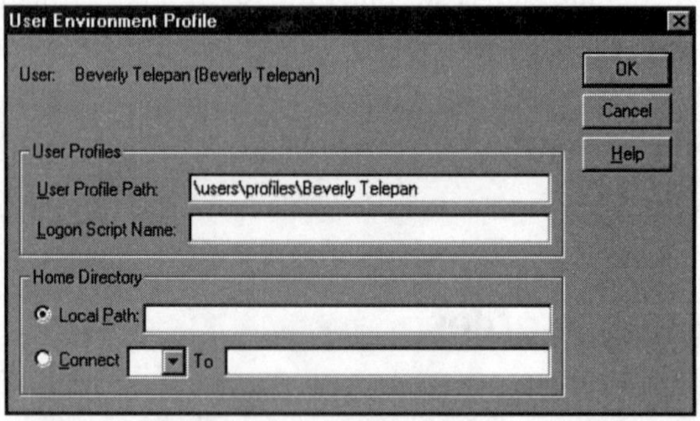

Figure 7.11

Start roaming profiles by placing the profile path on the server.

User Environment Profile
User: Beverly Telepan (Beverly Telepan)
OK
Cancel
Help
User Profiles
User Profile Path: \users\profiles\Beverly Telepan
Logon Script Name:
Home Directory
Local Path:
Connect To

In the User Profile Path, enter a network path in the form \\servername\sharename (for the profile directory). You do not have to use the PDC for storing workstation user profiles.

Be certain to create a specific share for the profile directory and give all users full permissions.

Back at the workstation, open User Manager and open the User Properties dialog box for the user for whom you want to establish the roaming profile. Choose Profile and enter the path you established on the server.

Most of the time, this user has already established some configuration options that are stored in the local profile. The local profile can be copied to the new roaming profile on the server. To do this, go to the System icon in the workstation Control Panel and click on the User Profile tab (or use the faster method for getting to the System Properties by right-clicking on My Computer and choosing Properties).

The User Profiles tab lists all the profiles stored on the workstation (see fig. 7.12).

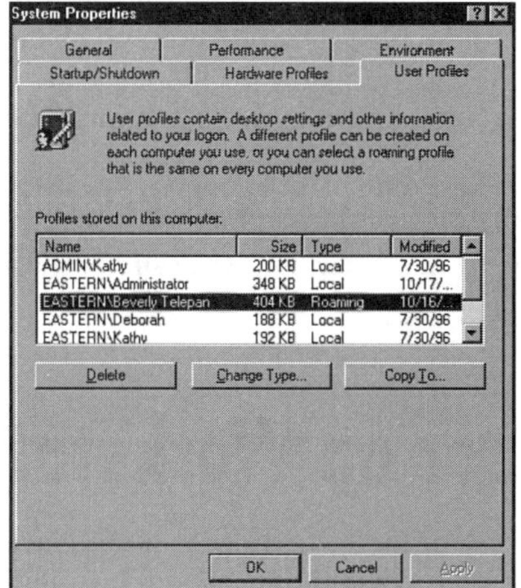

Figure 7.12

User profiles are listed, along with their types, in the System Properties dialog box.

The roaming user's existing profile can be copied to the server share by choosing Copy To. To make certain that the right profile is copied, change the profile type to local, make the copy, change the type back to roaming.

If the user has a roaming server path, but no profile is established because this user has not yet logged on, at the time of logon the default workstation profile is created on the network.

Mandatory Profiles

Mandatory profiles enable you to deny users the right to change configuration. Well, they can make changes to their profiles, but they aren't saved if the mandatory profile policy is in effect, so the next time the user logs on, the changes aren't there.

The power for the administrator is in the ability to design and install a profile configuration on a desktop and be assured it will never be changed, by configuring the profile as a mandatory one.

A number of reasons encourage using this feature, not the least of which is the obvious one—users can't mess up a configuration to the point that things don't work as they should. Some additional benefit accrues because when help desk personnel are called to troubleshoot problems, they know what to expect on each workstation. No time is wasted figuring out what's what in the environment, and the expert can move to the problem at hand immediately.

Mandatory profiles do not have to be global, you can select specific users as your target.

To make a profile mandatory, first create the profile and store it on the server. Then, in the user's profile directory, find the file NTUSER.DAT and change the extension to MAN. That's all there is to it. You can copy the profile to as many users as you want and can change the NTUSER file's extension to invoke the mandatory profile.

Incidentally, it's probably a good idea to explain mandatory profiles to the target users so that they don't think they're going crazy when changes aren't kept at the next logon. (There's no message from NT saying, "You can't really make changes," when they change their profiles.)

Using Policy Editor on Workstations

Earlier, this chapter discussed some of the restrictions you can place on a workstation by changing the Registry. It's easier to make those changes by using the Windows NT System Policy Editor. This program comes as part of Windows NT Server 4, but it runs just fine on NT Workstation 4. It's far more efficient, however, to use the application on the server so that you can make changes to multiple workstations.

The System Policy Editor is found in the Administrative Tools menu group on Windows NT Server. To begin designing a new policy, choose New Policy from the File menu. Two icons appear in the application window, one representing the default user and the other representing the default computer. Using these targets changes policies for all users and computers on the domain.

This section covers the basics of the System Policy Editor, with discussion of the different ways to select target workstations, as well as some of the specific changes you can make on a system-wide (or group-wide) basis.

Select the Targets for the New Policy

If the entire domain is not what you have in mind, you can choose your own targets. You make those choices from the Edit menu. As you specify them, icons appear in the window:

- Choose Add User to specify one or more individual users.
- Choose Add Group to specify all the users in a group, or multiple groups.
- Choose Add Computer to specify one or more computers.

For each type of target, a dialog box appears so that you can add the individual units you want to. If you don't know the exact names, there is a Browse button. After you have chosen target units, their icons appear in the window (see fig. 7.13).

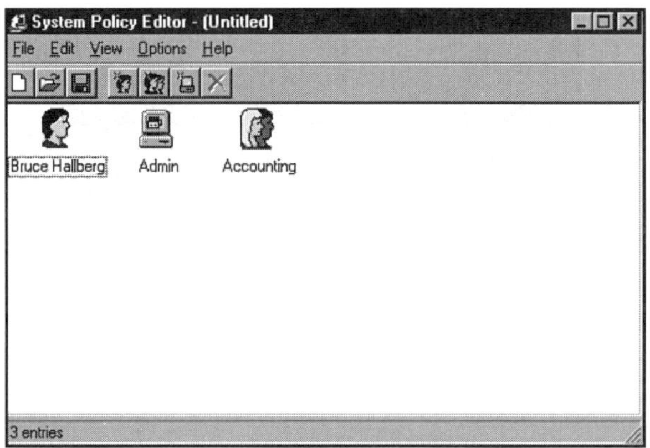

Figure 7.13

A user, computer, and group are the targets for the policies being added.

If you do target specific entities, delete the default icons from the window (select and press Del).

The policies available depend on the target. If you choose a user or group, the Registry settings in HKEY_CURRENT_USER and its subkeys are affected. If you choose a computer, the Registry settings in HKEY_LOCAL_MACHINE and its subkeys are affected.

Create User Policies

User and group policies are changed by double-clicking on the appropriate icon to see a hierarchical display of the properties (see fig. 7.14).

Although it is beyond the scope of this book to offer a full explanation of all the resources available in the System Policy Editor, it seems worthwhile to discuss the significant effects on workstations and the users who sit at those workstations.

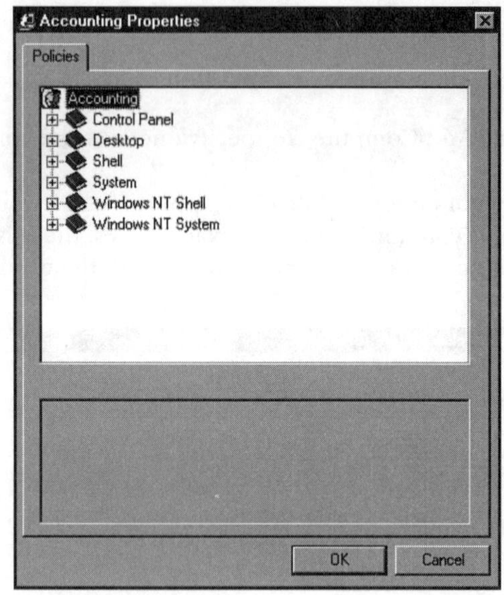

Figure 7.14
The user properties are organized into logical units and presented in a hierarchical display.

Restrict Shell Access

The most powerful restrictions in terms of limiting user access are found in the Shell heading, after you expand the Restrictions subheading (see fig. 7.15). These restrictions can be imposed to limit the amount of control a user has on a workstation. You can limit what the user can see, what the user can do (such as run software you don't want him or her to run), and whether the user can have access to other machines on the network.

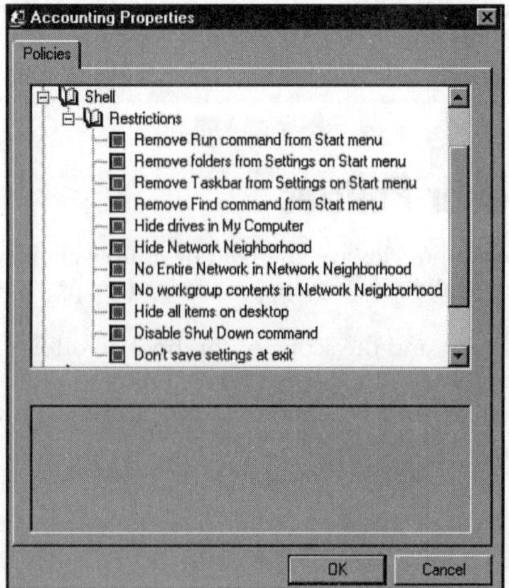

Figure 7.15
The available restrictions for users can be very limiting if you choose to invoke them.

The key to reading the Policy Editor listings is:

- Gray checkboxes are policies that have not been specified; there is no policy in effect.
- Selected checkboxes mean the policy is in effect.
- Deselected checkboxes mean the policy is not in effect.

The Restrictions you can place on the workstation user in this heading include the following:

- **Remove Run command from Start menu.** This prevents the workstation user from launching applications that do not have shortcuts on the Start menu.
- **Remove folders from Settings on Start menu.** This means that no folders appear as a submenu when the pointer is placed on Settings.
- **Remove Taskbar from Settings on Start menu.** This removes the Taskbar folder from the submenu of Settings.
- **Remove Find command from Start menu.** This prevents users from searching for files or computers via the Find command. This does not shut down other Find options (Explorer and F3 when the desktop has the focus).
- **Hide drives in My Computer.** This prevents drive icons from appearing in the My Computer window. This is useful for keeping viewers away from drive utilities and tools (some of which can be dangerous), and also stops them from browsing the drives in order to launch software or move files around.
- **Hide Network Neighborhood.** The Network Neighborhood object does not appear on the desktop. This prevents users from browsing network drives for applications or manipulating files and directories (the manipulations you might want to prevent can include moving, deleting, and so on).
- **No Entire Network in Network Neighborhood.** This limits the objects in Network Neighborhood to the workstation itself and the server.
- **No workgroup contents in Network Neighborhood.** This limits the objects in Network Neighborhood to the domain. Other connected computers (peer networking) are not available.
- **Hide all items on desktop.** Creates the ultimate clean desktop with only the Start menu options available.

- **Disable Shut Down command.** Restricts the user from shutting down the workstation.
- **Don't save settings at exit.** Whatever changes a user makes in the workstation environment are lost at shutdown.

Restrict System Access

In addition to the Shell restrictions, you might want to consider two restrictions under the System heading for workstation users. These restrictions provide a guarantee that a user with enough knowledge to be dangerous can't do any damage:

- **Disable Registry editing tools.** Keeping workstation users away from REGEDIT.EXE and REGEDT32.EXE is always a good idea.
- **Run only allowed Windows applications.** You can prevent users from running any Windows applications except those that you specifically allow. If you choose this option, a dialog box opens so that you can list the applications you will permit. Choose Add, and then enter an executable file name, such as WINWORD.EXE, repeating the process as often as needed.

Configure the NT Shell

The capability to add third-party utilities or customize the workspace is enhanced by the customization and restrictions you can invoke. Under the NT Shell heading are two subheadings:

- **Custom folders.** Enables you to redirect the functions of the standard Windows NT 4 objects.
- **Restrictions.** Enables you to enforce the customizations you enter in the System Policy Editor.

You can provide the following customizations with the Custom folders subheading:

- **Custom Programs Folder.** If selected, you must provide the path to its location.
- **Custom desktop icons.** If selected, provide the path to the location.
- **Hide Start menu subfolders.** Use this if menu access is controlled by the selections you have made in the two previous items.
- **Custom Startup folder.** Provide the path to its location.
- **Custom Network Neighborhood.** Provide the path to its location.
- **Custom Start menu.** Provide the path to its location.

These restrictions to the Windows NT Shell are available:

- **Only use approved shell extensions.** This forces the use of the extensions you have installed.
- **Remove common program groups from Start menu.** For your target users, this eliminates the capability to run any administrative tools or other programs you might have placed on the common section of the Start menu.

Configure the NT System

For selected users, you can invoke a couple of options that affect the way the system mounts:

- **Parse AUTOEXEC.BAT.** If you select this option, AUTOEXEC.BAT is checked for environment variables. If any are found, they are included in the environment for this user.
- **Run logon scripts synchronously.** Selecting this option forces a delay in the startup of the user's shell until any and all logon scripts have completed.

You can also restrict the user's capability to change the display values for the desktop by using the Control Panel and Desktop headings. See Chapter 6, "Configuring the Workspace," for detailed information about these settings.

Create Computer Policies

Open the computer icon in the System Policy Editor window to establish policies for the workstation (see fig. 7.16).

Again, this chapter does not go into a full discussion of all the settings available in the System Policy Editor, but some of the options you can invoke that affect workstations are of particular interest.

The Windows NT System heading contains two subheadings that control workstation behavior—Logon and File system.

The Logon subheading provides the following configuration options:

- **Logon banner.** This enables the addition of a banner for the logon process. You can specify a caption and text.
- **Enable shutdown from Authentication dialog box.** For a workstation, the shutdown option is enabled. Deselecting this option disables shutdown from the Logon dialog box.

- **Do not display last logged on user name.** Use this option to have this workstation force users to enter their logon names.
- **Run logon scripts synchronously.** This is the same option as available for user policies, discussed in the previous section. If the user policies and the computer policies are both configured, the computer policy takes priority.

The File system subhead provides these configuration options for a workstation:

- **Do not create 8.3 file names for long file names.** Use this option if you have some reason to prevent the automatic translation of long file names.
- **Allow extended characters in 8.3 file names.** Select or deselect this option depending on whether you have computers that do not use the standard code page that sees the extended characters.
- **Do not update last access time.** Selecting this option speeds up file access. It does not affect updates when a file is resaved.

You can browse through the other computer policy configuration options to determine whether any of them are important to you as you administer workstations.

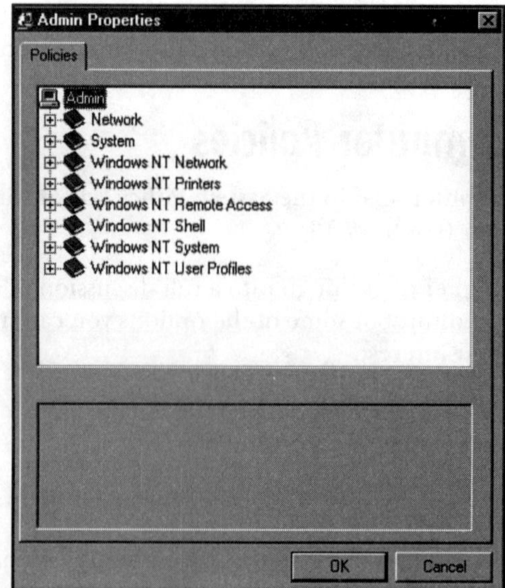

Figure 7.16

Policies for the entire workstation, regardless of the logged on user, can be set from the System Policy Editor.

Saving Policy Changes

After you have selected and deselected options for either user policies or computer policies, choose Save As from the System Policy Editor File menu. Save the file as

NTCONFIG.POL in the netlogon directory of the PDC. If you're working on the PDC, use drive C in the path; if you're working from another computer use the mapped drive letter for the PDC. Make certain that there is replication to any BDC on the system.

Troubleshooting Workstation Users

Users constantly need attention—they request additional rights and permissions, they forget their passwords, they get promoted and change groups and their rights change. Administrators frequently hear from users who complain that they can't do something they want to do, and, even more frequently hear "I forgot my password." This section covers your options (or lack of them) when you have to troubleshoot user problems.

User Password Problems

Users get into trouble with passwords in a number of ways:

- They forget them.
- A password expiration policy exists along with a policy of forcing users to be logged on before they can change passwords. That's a bad combination if the user does not pay attention to the warnings that the password is about to expire.
- Passwords are assigned by administrators, and a password was given to the user incorrectly (usually a typo).

Use your Administrator logon (or other logon that has administrative rights) to log yourself on and enter a new password for the user. You cannot read the existing password, you will have to define a new one. Unless you are operating under very stringent security protocols, it's a good idea to ask the user what the password should be (under the assumption that a user that invents it will remember it, but that's not always a safe assumption).

If you don't have an account on the workstation with administrative rights, but the workstation is connected to an NT domain, you can do a couple of things.

If the password-less user logs on to the domain, go to the server, open User Manager for Domains, and then assign a new password.

If the user logs on locally to the workstation, and the workstation is part of the domain (other users log on to the domain), open User Manager for Domains on the server. From the User menu, choose Select Domain. The Select Domain dialog box opens. Don't select any of the listed domains. Instead, enter the workstation name in the Domain text box, preceding the name with \\. You are connected to the workstation and, in effect, you are running that workstation's User Manager. Give the troubled user a new password. (While you're there, create a user for yourself with full administrator rights so that you can get into that workstation in the future. There is no excuse for not having an administrator logon for every workstation in your system).

I Love the Command Line

Sometimes I miss the speed of DOS and the command line; so whenever I get the opportunity, I use it (I'm a very fast typist and a slow mouser).

To create or modify a user, you can also use the command line. The command you use for this is Net User. This is a nifty net command with plenty of power. The syntax available is:

```
net user [username [password ¦ *] [options]] [/domain]

net user username {password ¦ *} /add [options] [/domain]

net user username [/delete] [/domain]
```

The parameters are:

- **none.** Lists all the user accounts on the workstation.
- **username.** The user account you want to add, delete, change, or view.
- **password.** Assigns that word as user account password; if there is an existing password the new entry replaces it.
- ***.** Produces the prompt `Type a password for the user:`. Nothing is displayed as you type the password. When you press enter, the prompt `Retype the password to confirm:` appears. After you retype the password and press Enter, `The command completed successfully` appears, and the cursor returns to the prompt.
- **/domain.** Performs the task on the PDC (assuming this is being performed on NT Workstation, because NT Server performs net user operations on the PDC by default).
- **/add.** Adds a user account to the database.
- **/delete.** Removes a user account from the database.

So, as an example, if you have a user named HowardR who has forgotten his password from a workstation that logs on to an NT domain, enter:

```
net user HowardR stupid
```

Press Enter, and then go tell HowardR about his new password (make certain that you explain it's nothing personal). He can change it after he logs on.

Bad News in the Password Department

Here's some very bad news about password problems. If you log on to your workstation as the administrator, and the workstation is not part of an NT Domain, and no user is established on the workstation who can access the computer remotely with administrator rights, and you forget your password, it's all over. That's a long sentence, so read it again to make certain that you got it. Because when those circumstances occur, you have to install NT 4 all over again. And you have to install it as a brand new installation into a different directory, which means that none of the configuration work you did will be there for you.

Right this moment, create at least one more user for this workstation with administrator rights. Use a different password. If you're the forgetful type, create several users and passwords in the hope that you will remember one of them. Or write down the name and password and take it home with you.

Be Prepared for Disaster

To safeguard against these potential calamities, follow these rules (and add any others you think of):

- Always have at least two administrator accounts on every workstation.
- Back up the Registry to another computer or a floppy disk (use Export from the Registry Editor). This is in addition to backing up the Registry during a tape backup because you have to get on to the computer to do a tape restore.
- Constantly update the emergency repair disk.

Utilities also exist for getting the pertinent parts of the Registry backed up to disk or connected computers. And, I hear tell there's a program you can launch on a computer that you can't get into that uses the dictionary algorithms that hackers use.

Summary

The care and feeding of users and their workstations is a major part of an administrator's job. It is also the part that can't be planned well. It involves putting out fires, applying band-aids, and doing other quick-fix work to keep your system going. With some understanding of the controls you can impose on users, workstations, or groups of users and workstations, you can plan intelligent policies and implement them. Hopefully, that will cut down on the number of times during the day you're called by a panic-stricken (or angry) user who is trying to perform a task that he or she either can't or shouldn't perform.

Planning and implementing user and workstation policies should not stop at imposing those policies through the Registry or the System Policy Editor. Be sure to explain the company philosophy to users about who can do what, and why they can or can't do other things. This will save you a lot of griping phone calls from users.

CHAPTER 8

Running Non-Windows NT Applications

Windows NT Workstation was designed so that it could support both native Windows NT applications and applications written for other popular operating systems. Windows NT 4 includes support for Windows 95, DOS, 16-bit Windows, OS/2, and Unix applications.

Windows NT uses software subsystems that allow it to provide different application programming interfaces to different types of applications. These different subsystems allow Windows NT to interact with applications written for different operating systems. For more details on the Windows NT system architecture, see Chapter 1, "The Windows NT Workstation Architecture." Understanding the Windows NT system architecture is fundamental to understanding how applications work with Windows NT.

Not all applications written for other platforms are NT compatible. Specifically, applications that directly access the hardware directly or through their own device drivers, including graphics device drivers, are unlikely to work. A utility, for example, that lets you edit a disk sector on your hard disk might start running, but NT will kill it when it tries to access your system's hardware directly. Though many of these "foreign" applications do run, they will not run as quickly as they would in their native environment due to the overhead associated with having Windows NT emulate their native operating environments. WordPerfect 5.1 for DOS is a 16-bit DOS program that runs under Windows NT 4 but is slower because of the overhead associated with emulating the DOS environment it expects.

Some of the benefits of being able to run diverse applications on one system include having to support fewer desktop workstations and increased user productivity from the capability to multitask and to cut and paste between applications. While earlier versions of Windows allowed people to have several applications running in different windows, the multitasking support was just not robust enough to be heavily used without loosing a lot of system stability—and user productivity. In organizations running Windows NT Workstation 4, it is much more common to see users relying on the ability to run whatever application they need in a Window on their desktop computer—even when those applications might have been written to run on another operating system. In places where people used to have two or even three terminals on their desk, Windows NT Workstation has enabled many companies to consolidate all of this functionality into a single desktop system for each user.

Exploring NT 4 Application Support

Windows NT Workstation supports the following major application types in addition to supporting applications written specifically for Windows NT:

- 16-bit (DOS and Windows 3.x)
- Windows 95
- OS/2
- POSIX

Each of these application types is discussed in its own section below. About the only applications that are not supported are non-POSIX Unix-based applications and Mac applications. Those can't be supported on non-native systems because they tend to be extremely platform sensitive.

This comprehensive application support allows you to install Windows NT Workstation and know that your users will not have to give up the applications they have already learned on their current systems. This can save you a lot of time and money by reducing the training costs that are typically incurred when changing computer platforms.

16-Bit Applications

Two big advantages Windows NT has over Windows 95 and other operating systems are that it can preemptively multitask 16-bit applications, which is something Windows 95 cannot do, and it can protect applications from having their memory space corrupted by misbehaving, poorly written, or hostile applications. This protection makes Windows NT a much more reliable system for running 16-bit applications—at the cost of not being able to run applications that don't follow the programming rules for polite multitasking.

The Virtual DOS Machine Subsystem

Windows NT was built using software modules called "subsystems" for its major components. This use of subsystems gives Windows NT a structured and flexible design that can be extended and modified easily.

The Windows 16-bit compatibility subsystem is built in a layered fashion. Each virtual DOS machine (VDM) is a single 32-bit multithreaded process that emulates the 16-bit DOS and the Windows 3.x environments.

Each application that runs inside a VDM is transparently allocated its own 32-bit thread by the VDM. Although the 32-bit threading is invisible to Win16 programs, this has architectural implications in terms of Windows NT's preemptive multitasking design.

The default method of running 16-bit applications is to run all of them within the same VDM so that they share the same memory space. This allows the 16-bit applications to corrupt each other if they contain programming errors, but uses less overhead than running each 16-bit application in its own memory space. Alternatively, you can force 16-bit applications to run in their own memory space, but doing so requires a new VDM instance for each one and correspondingly more overhead. You can use the Windows NT Task Manager to see how many resources each VDM takes. The amount of memory a VDM requires is almost entirely dependent on what it is doing. Starting a new VDM on an x86-based system uses more than 1.5 MB of memory, but if the VDM is inactive, it reduces its memory utilization considerably—down to as little as 200 KB or so.

The Windows NT kernel handles the multitasking by application, where it sees each 32-bit process such as a VDM as a single unit to multitask. When a VDM is running multiple 16-bit Windows 3.x applications (each runs as a separate thread), the VDM itself is responsible for allocating time slices among the 16-bit applications. This is called *cooperative multitasking* and means that the Windows NT kernel does the multitasking for the 32-bit processes, but each running copy of NTVDM.EXE is responsible for multitasking the 16-bit Windows applications running as threads inside it.

You can start each important 16-bit application in its own memory space if you want the multitasking for your 16-bit applications to be handled by the kernel (indirectly though it will be). Realistically, you will want to look into upgrading to 32-bit applications if you need better multitasking performance from them than you are getting.

Windows NT VDMs work on all hardware platforms for which Windows NT is available, including both RISC and x86-based systems. The major difference between a VDM on a RISC-based system and a VDM on an x86-based system is the requirement to emulate the x86 instruction set on the RISC-based systems. This is handled by a virtual *instruction execution unit* (IEU), which is essentially a software version of an x86 processor. On native x86 platforms, this layer of the VDM exists mostly as a pass-through layer that does not have to do any translation or emulation. Its real job on an x86-based system is to be a watchdog and to trap instructions that would violate system integrity. These would typically be instructions that try to access hardware directly. On RISC-based systems, the IEU has to work much harder to emulate an x86-based system when you are running 16-bit programs because it not only polices for illegal instructions, it also translates each and every instruction from x86-based machine code into equivalent RISC machine code.

A VDM includes a 32-bit MS-DOS emulator to allow the applications running inside it to use the standard DOS Protected Mode Interface (DPMI) to access more than one megabyte of memory. This takes requests for extended or expanded memory and maps them into the physical memory space Windows NT Workstation has available so that the physical memory looks like a normal block of directly accessible RAM.

Windows NT VDMs emulate BIOS functions, DOS functions, and Windows 3.x functions. This emulation is handled through what programmers call *thunking*, which is a way of translating between 16- and 32-bit functions. In a Windows NT VDM, the thunking is handled by the 32-bit layer of the Win16-on-Win32 (WoW) subsystem. When a 16-bit application makes an API call to the BIOS, an MS-DOS function, or part of the Win16 API, it actually contacts a *stub* function that takes that request and passes it onto the underlying 32-bit emulation program. After the request has been serviced by the 32-bit emulator, the reply is passed back through the same path so that the 16-bit application has no way of knowing its request was satisfied by a 32-bit process.

Stub functions have several different major uses in software. They are most often used during software development to allow programmers to call complicated processes that have not yet been programmed; but they are sometimes also used as *wrappers*, in which they take a request from one subsystem and hand it off to another subsystem. It is this latter type of use that Windows NT makes of them.

Thunking is necessary because a normal 16-bit application cannot interact directly with systems that require a 32-bit interface. Thunking can add a significant amount of overhead to applications, but it allows them to work in situations where they otherwise would not.

Running a Virtual DOS Machine

There are three major files used by the WoW subsystem:

- NTVDM.EXE
- WOWEXEC.EXE
- WOW32.DLL

The NTVDM.EXE is the primary file used. Windows NT invokes a copy of NTVDM.EXE for each separate VDM you run, and running that file creates the VDM. The first copy of NTVDM.EXE loads WOWEXEC.EXE into memory as soon as a 16-bit application starts running, and WOWEXEC.EXE loads WOW32.DLL. Together they provide the services that make up a VDM.

A Windows NT VDM will run the programs listed in the %systemroot%\system32\CONFIG.NT and the %systemroot%\system32\AUTOEXEC.NT when it initializes just as an MS-DOS system would run the programs listed in its CONFIG.SYS and AUTOEXEC.BAT. In fact, if you have installed Windows NT Workstation as an upgrade on a system that was running some form of DOS, the contents of your AUTOEXEC.NT file will have been modified to reflect what was in your AUTOEXEC.BAT. The contents of the CONFIG.NT are not automatically updated to reflect the contents of your CONFIG.SYS because very few programs that load from the CONFIG.SYS are directly compatible with Windows NT Workstation. A sample CONFIG.NT is as follows:

```
REM Windows NT MS-DOS Startup File
REM
REM CONFIG.SYS vs CONFIG.NT
REM CONFIG.SYS is not used to initialize the MS-DOS environment.
REM CONFIG.NT is used to initialize the MS-DOS environment unless a
REM different startup file is specified in an application's PIF.
REM
REM ECHOCONFIG
REM By default, no information is displayed when the MS-DOS environment
REM is initialized. To display CONFIG.NT/AUTOEXEC.NT information, add
REM the command echoconfig to CONFIG.NT or other startup file.
REM
REM NTCMDPROMPT
REM When you return to the command prompt from a TSR or while running an
REM MS-DOS-based application, Windows NT runs COMMAND.COM. This allows the
REM TSR to remain active. To run CMD.EXE, the Windows NT command prompt,
REM rather than COMMAND.COM, add the command ntcmdprompt to CONFIG.NT or
REM other startup file.
```

```
REM
REM DOSONLY
REM By default, you can start any type of application when running
REM COMMAND.COM. If you start an application other than an MS-DOS-based
REM application, any running TSR may be disrupted. To ensure that only
REM MS-DOS-based applications can be started, add the command dosonly to
REM CONFIG.NT or other startup file.
REM
REM EMM
REM You can use EMM command line to configure EMM(Expanded Memory Manager).
REM The syntax is:
REM
REM EMM = [A=AltRegSets] [B=BaseSegment] [RAM]
REM
REM  AltRegSets
REM     specifies the total Alternative Mapping Register Sets you
REM     want the system to support. 1 <= AltRegSets <= 255. The
REM     default value is 8.
REM  BaseSegment
REM     specifies the starting segment address in the DOS conventional
REM     memory you want the system to allocate for EMM page frames.
REM     The value must be given in Hexdecimal.
REM     0x1000 <= BaseSegment <= 0x4000. The value is rounded down to
REM     16KB boundary. The default value is 0x4000
REM  RAM
REM     specifies that the system should only allocate 64KB address
REM     space from the Upper Memory Block (UMB) area for EMM page frames
REM     and leave the rests (if available) to be used by DOS to support
REM     loadhigh and devicehigh commands. The system, by default, would
REM     allocate all possible and available UMB for page frames.
REM
REM  The EMM size is determined by pif file (either the one associated
REM  with your application or _default.pif). If the size from PIF file
REM  is zero, EMM will be disabled and the EMM line will be ignored.
REM
dos=high, umb
device=%SystemRoot%\system32\himem.sys
files=20
```

The various new commands that Windows NT supports in the CONFIG.NT file are documented through the comments in it. Notice that the memory manager loaded, %SystemRoot%\system32\himem.sys, is the one supplied with Windows NT. The older HIMEM.SYS supplied with DOS and Windows 3.x is not compatible with Windows NT because it requires direct access to the computer's memory. The HIMEM.SYS supplied with Windows NT is mostly a stub implementation that allows 16-bit programs to see the interface they are expecting while passing off the real memory management duties to the Windows NT kernel.

After the system finishes reading the CONFIG.NT, it reads the AUTOEXEC.NT and executes the commands in it. Here is a sample AUTOEXEC.NT:

```
@echo off

REM AUTOEXEC.BAT is not used to initialize the MS-DOS environment.
REM AUTOEXEC.NT is used to initialize the MS-DOS environment unless a
REM different startup file is specified in an application's PIF.

REM Install CD ROM extensions
lh %SystemRoot%\system32\mscdexnt.exe

REM Install network redirector (load before dosx.exe)
lh %SystemRoot%\system32\redir

REM Install DPMI support
lh %SystemRoot%\system32\dosx
```

The AUTOEXEC.NT provides different drivers than were used in the DOS environment for common applications that would otherwise require direct hardware access. These include the following:

- **MSCDEXNT.EXE.** Used to provide the standard Microsoft CD-ROM Extensions to 16-bit applications running under Windows NT
- **REDIR.EXE.** Used in place of a DOS compatible network redirector
- **DOSX.EXE.** Provides the extended DOS mode support to applications using a DPMI interface

You can see what programs a 16-bit application will have access to and display the memory available to WoW clients on your system by using the MEM /C | MORE command from a command prompt. If you try to run it from the Start, Run menu you might not be able to see the last screen of output. A sample follows:

```
D:\MEM /C | MORE

Conventional Memory :

  Name                Size in Decimal        Size in Hex
---------         -----------------------   -------------
  MSDOS                11424        ( 11.2K)         2CA0
  KBD                   3280        (  3.2K)          CD0
  HIMEM                 1248        (  1.2K)          4E0
  COMMAND               3136        (  3.1K)          C40
  FREE                   112        (  0.1K)           70
  FREE                635984        (621.1K)        9B450

Total  FREE :         636096        (621.2K)

Upper Memory :

  Name                Size in Decimal        Size in Hex
----------       -------------------------  --------------
  SYSTEM              167920        (164.0K)        28FF0
  MOUSE                12528        ( 12.2K)         30F0
  MSCDEXNT               464        (  0.5K)          1D0
  REDIR                 2672        (  2.6K)          A70
  DOSX                 38864        ( 38.0K)         97D0
  FREE                   576        (  0.6K)          240
  FREE                 96304        ( 94.0K)        17830
  FREE                  8176        (  8.0K)         1FF0

Total  FREE :         105056        (102.6K)

Total bytes available to programs (Conventional+Upper) :     741152    (723.8K)
Largest executable program size :                            635408    (620.5K)
Largest available upper memory block :                        96304    ( 94.0K)

   1048576 bytes total contiguous extended memory
         0 bytes available contiguous extended memory
    931840 bytes available XMS memory
           MS-DOS resident in High Memory Area
```

You can see that these programs use relatively little memory. Part of the reason for this is that they are all stub programs whose primary purpose is to help with the translation between 16-bit applications and the 32-bit services that actually do the work they request.

Limitations and Considerations for VDMs

There are a number of limitations on the 16-bit emulation capabilities of Windows NT. Most of these stem from the design requirement of needing to support secure and reliable operations, which means that direct access to the system's hardware cannot be allowed. Consequently, all functions that use direct hardware access will not work properly anymore. Applications that use standard Virtual Device Drivers (VDDs) to access standard character-mode hardware will still work. Windows NT VDMs use 32-bit VDDsto emulate standard DOS devices like COMx and LPTx that are available to 16-bit applications through thunking.

Windows NT uses an input queue for each 32-bit process it is executing. This is a wonderful improvement over other operating systems that only had a single input queue for all applications to share. Having multiple input queues means that a single hung application will not prevent other applications from getting the input they need. Each VDM uses only a single input queue. This is consistent with both the Windows NT model and the Windows 3.x models. The Windows NT model of one input queue per 32-bit application matches it because the VDM is a single 32-bit application regardless of how many 16-bit applications are running as separate threads inside it. Because there is only a single input queue that all the threads in a VDM share, however, a single misbehaving 16-bit program can block an entire VDM and all its 16-bit application threads from receiving input. This matches the Windows 3.x model, which only has one input queue for all applications to share. By adhering to both these models simultaneously, Windows NT provides the same interface to 16-bit applications that they were written to expect while maintaining its own optimized 32-bit design for native applications.

If you like the idea of each 16-bit application being protected from every other 16-bit application, having its own input queue, and being preemptively multitasked, you can configure your 16-bit applications to run in their own VDMs at the cost of using more system resources.

Windows 16-Bit (Windows 3.x)

Windows NT Workstation uses the Win16 on Win32 (WoW) subsystem, which emulates the 16-bit Windows interface for the 32-bit environment, to run old 16-bit Windows applications. The WoW subsystem runs within a VDM environment that has its own memory space. This DOS-like environment is similar to the enhanced mode of Windows 3.x. In addition to this VDM environment, supporting Windows applications requires emulating the Windows programming API. Windows NT utilizes a kind of translation system for these 16-bit Windows programs that accepts 16-bit function calls and performs their functions in 32-bit code. This is called thunking.

Migration

If you are upgrading from Windows 3.x or Windows for Workgroups, you can keep most of the customizations to your work environment. Install Windows NT Workstation into the same directory as your previous version to have it detect and migrate the customizations over to the NT environment. The first time a user logs on after the Windows NT installation, the system will prompt him to select the data he would like to migrate from the Windows 3.x installation.

The key to making this work is installing Windows NT Workstation into the same directory as an existing, earlier version of Windows 3.x. If you do this, then the first time someone new logs on to Windows NT Workstation after it has been installed, the system will read the Windows 3.x Registry file REG.DAT and parts of the various Windows INI files. These include all Object Linking and Embedding (OLE) information from the REG.DAT, some sections of the WIN.INI, CONTROL.INI, WINFILE.INI, and SYSTEM.INI. This information is stored in the Windows NT Registry under HKEY_CLASSES_ROOT.

If Windows NT is installed into the same directory as Windows 3.x and the user selected to perform a migration of the old information, Windows NT will read the WIN.INI and the SYSTEM.INI files each time the user logs on. The more surprising thing about this is that not only does Windows NT read these files to learn its own configuration each time someone logs on, but it also dynamically updates these files each time a user logs off to keep them synchronized with the Windows NT view of the system. This is useful if you are using dual boot because when you make a change inside Windows NT to a setting that has an analog in the Windows 3.x environment you do not have to make that change to Windows 3.x separately. There are, however, some parts of Windows 3.x that are be updated by Windows NT when changes are made. These would primarily consist of changes to the program groups and changes to the desktop environment.

Each user who logs on to the system locally (except for the Administrator and the Guest accounts) has the option to select the parts of the previous version of Windows she wants to migrate to her Windows NT environment. Tracking the migration status is done per user, and Windows tracks the status of whose environment has been migrated and whose environment has not been migrated by checking for the existence of two Registry keys:

```
HKEY_CURRENT_USER\Windows 3.1 Migration Status and
HKEY_LOCAL_MACHINE\SOFTWARE\Windows 3.1 Migration Status
```

If a user migrated the settings when she should not have, or if she failed to migrate the settings when she should have, it is possible to have Windows NT Workstation offer her the chance to do it again. All she must do is delete the HKEY_CURRENT_USER\Windows 3.1 Migration Status key from the Registry, log off, and log back on. Because that key is not there for her user account, Windows NT Workstation offers her the option of doing a migration again.

Because migration is a one-time occurrence for each user that happens at the user's first logon, it will not happen if you install some version of Windows 3.x after you install and begin using Windows NT Workstation.

You can use the Event Viewer to see exactly what was migrated and to see if there were problems with any part of the migration. Run the Event Viewer and select the Application Log to see each step of the migration.

Figure 8.1 is a sample of the sort of entries you should expect to see after a successful migration. It shows the Application Log of the Event Viewer, with the details of one of the events in the foreground. To display the details of an event, highlight it in the Application Log and press Enter or select detail from the menu.

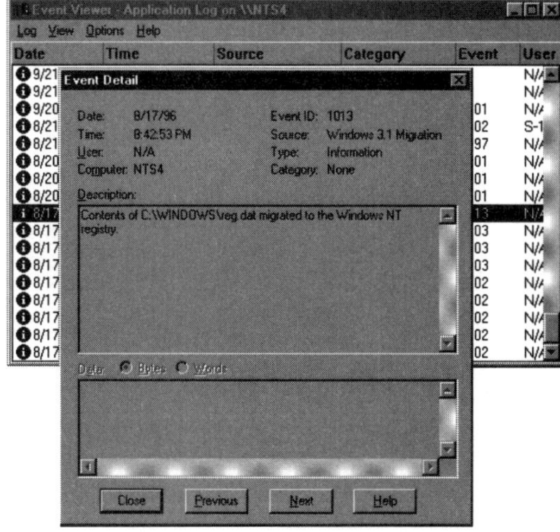

Figure 8.1

The Application Log has entries for the information migrated.

By clicking on Detail in the View menu while a migration-related entry is highlighted, you can see specifically what information was migrated into the Windows NT Workstation Registry (see fig. 8.2).

Settings Migrated Over

This section contains a complete list of the information normally migrated over to the Registry when upgrading from Windows 3.x or Windows for Workgroups to Windows NT Workstation.

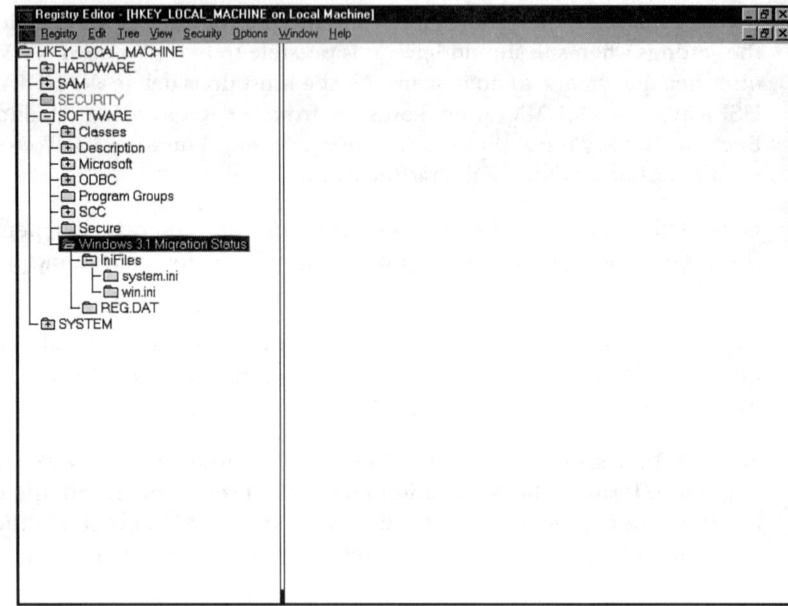

Figure 8.2
The Registry contains the information migrated from Windows 3.x.

The following section and entries from are WIN.INI:

```
[Windows]
CursorBlinkRate
BorderWidth
ScreenSaveTimeOut
ScreenSaveActive
KeyboardSpeed
KeyboardDelay
Beep
SwapMouseButtons
DoubleClickSpeed
DoubleClickHeight
DoubleClickWidth
MouseThreshold1
MouseThreshold2
MouseSpeed
SnapToDefaultButton
Spooler
DeviceNotSelectedTimeout
TransmissionRetryTimeout
```

The following section is from SYSTEM.INI:

```
[Drivers]
```

The following sections are from CONTROL.INI:

```
[Color Schemes]
[Current]
[Custom Colors]
[Patterns]
[Screen Saver.Marquee]
[Screen Saver.Mystify]
[Screen Saver.Stars]
```

The following section is from WINFILE.INI:

```
[Settings]
```

All OLE information from the Windows REG.DAT file is migrated over, and the following files are migrated in their entirety:

```
REG.DAT
VIEWER.INI
CLOCK.INI
SCHDPL32.INI
```

Additionally, all program groups that do not have names that conflict with Windows NT program groups and are listed in the PROGMAN.INI file are migrated in their entirety without checking each icon's properties for validity.

Settings Not Migrated Over

Although the preceding migrated information might seem like a lot (particularly if you are familiar with the contents of those files), there is also a fair bit not migrated into Windows NT Workstation. This includes program groups that have the same name as Windows NT Workstation groups. Because the contents of the Windows NT Workstation program groups of the same name are similar to the contents of the Windows 3.x program groups, you might not notice this except for the Startup group, which you will have to edit to suit your needs under Windows NT Workstation. Other program groups not migrated are the Games group, the Accessories group, and the Main group. If you have not added or changed many icons within those groups, you might not even notice the differences in their contents.

You might be surprised to see some drive letters change, but if you had multiple partitions with different file systems, then you might see Windows NT Workstation default to assigning them different drive letters than you expect. This is most likely to happen if you had some non-DOS partitions, perhaps an HPFS partition from an OS/2 installation or an NTFS partition you had forgotten about from an old test you did. You can use the Windows NT Disk Administrator to reassign drive letters if necessary.

Program Manager settings do not migrate over because there is no direct equivalent to Program Manager to migrate them to. These options include Auto Arrange, Minimize on Run, and Save Settings on Exit. You will also lose your default screen saver and any settings you have made to screen savers (such as a customized banner for the Marquee screen saver). The 16-bit screen savers that Windows 3.x and Windows for Workgroups use are incompatible with Windows NT because they access the system's video to directly.

The default font information for applications that run in text windows will be lost, and applications will use the default text font for your system unless you edit their settings after the migration.

Network user account and password information will not migrate to Windows NT Workstation from Windows for Workgroups or from existing LANMAN.INI files. Persistent shares from Windows for Workgroups will not migrate. If you were using an add-on product such as WINLOGIN to maintain user profiles under Windows for Workgroups, the profiles will not migrate.

Running 16-Bit Windows Applications

From a user perspective, there is no difference between running a 16-bit Windows application and a 32-bit Windows application. The real differences come behind the scenes, where the multitasking is handled differently and a translation layer connects the 16-bit application with the 32-bit operating system.

You should remember, however, that 16-bit Windows applications are not native applications to Windows NT, and as such they might not work correctly. The following is a comprehensive list of the functions that worked under Windows 3.x that do not work under Windows NT Workstation:

- MS-DOS task-switching APIs (application programming interface functions).
- Block mode device drivers. (Block devices are not supported, so MS-DOS IOCTL APIs that deal with block devices and SETDPB functions are not supported.)
- Interrupt 10 function 1A returns 0; all other functions are passed to read-only memory (ROM).
- Interrupt 13 calls that deal with prohibited disk access are not supported.
- Interrupt 18 (ROM BASIC) generates a message that says ROM BASIC is not supported.

- Interrupt 19 will not reboot the computer, but will cleanly terminate the current virtual DOS machine (VDM).
- Interrupt 2F dealing with the DOSKEY program call outs (AX = 4800) is not supported.
- Microsoft CD-ROM Extensions (MSCDEX) functions 2, 3, 4, 5, 8, E, and F are not supported.
- The 16-bit Windows subsystem on an x86 computer does not support 16-bit VDDs (virtual device drivers).

If you want to run a 16-bit Windows 3.x program, consider whether you would like it to run in its own memory space. This provides a safeguard for the system; if there is trouble running that particular application, it will not crash other Win16 applications that are in a different memory space. On the other hand, creating additional VDMs does take more resources. The right decision on this sort of matter is always dependent on the particulars of your situation. There are two primary ways that you can start a 16-bit Windows application in its own VDM. You can either use the command `line START /SEPARATE <application file>`, or you can use the graphical interface as described in the following steps:

1. Click on the Start button to access the Run command.
2. Type in the name of the program you want to run, with its path. You can use the Browse button to help locate the file, if necessary.
3. Check the box next to Run in Separate Memory Space (see fig. 8.3). If this box is grayed out, then the application is not a 16-bit Windows application. The box will stay grayed out for DOS applications even though Windows NT runs them in a separate VDM because you do not have the option of running multiple DOS applications inside a single VDM.

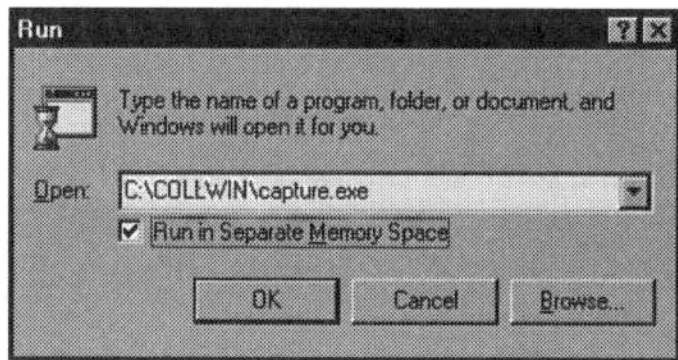

Figure 8.3

A 16-bit application can be set to run in a separate memory space.

4. Click on OK.

To set the Windows 3.x program properties, follow these steps:

1. Right-click on the icon for the shortcut to the Windows program. (You can edit the Properties for the program if you want, but the shortcut is more accessible and will apply the properties to the program when run from the shortcut.)
2. Select Properties from the menu. You see the Properties dialog box with the following tabs:
   - General
   - Version
   - Security

The Security tab does not show up if your shortcut exists on a non-NTFS partition. If, for instance, you have a FAT partition as well as an NTFS partition and your desktop information (which is stored in your user's profile folder) is on the FAT partition, you will only have two tabs. Also the Compressed option on the General tab only shows up for NTFS because it is only possible to compress files on NTFS partitions.

General

The General tab provides you with the information about the shortcut to the program:

- Type of program
- Location
- Size
- Compressed size (NTFS only)
- MS-DOS name
- Created
- Modified
- Accessed
- Attributes

The first three pieces of information refer to the shortcut, not to the actual program if you access the properties information from the shortcut. You can select attributes by checking the boxes next to those you want. Read-only allows access to the file or program, but does not allow any modifications to be made to it.

The following is a description of the attributes you can set from the General tab (see fig. 8.4):

- The Read-only attribute is fairly self-explanatory. If it is set (as indicated by a check in the box), you cannot save changes you make to the file in an editor or delete it without specifically overriding the read-only protection.
- Hidden files don't show up in the Windows NT Explorer unless you specifically select Show All Files from the Options dialog box found under the View menu. You can hide any file you want to hide.
- Archive marks the file as "Archive needed" so that the next time a differential or incremental backup is performed, the file will be included.
- System files are specially protected by the system. You cannot copy them or change their attributes unless you also remove the System attribute. This option is grayed out because Windows NT does not allow you to change it from the worksheet. If you want to set or remove the System attribute, you will need to use the command line ATTRIB.EXE program.
- Compressed only shows up as an option for files on an NTFS partition. If a file has been compressed, this box will be checked. Also, there will be a field above that listing the compressed size so that you can see the difference between that and the uncompressed size.

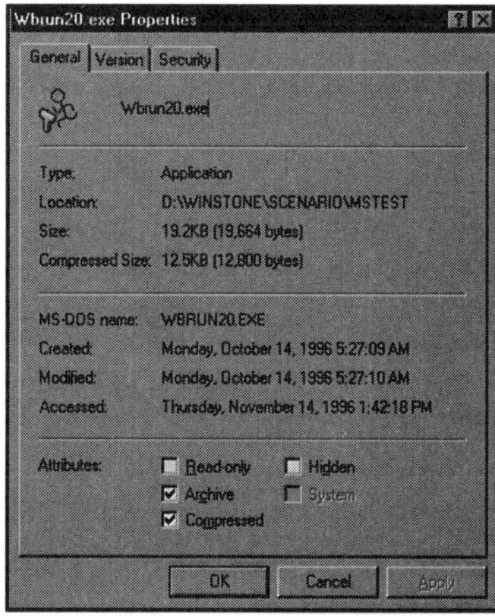

Figure 8.4

The General information tab on a Windows 3.x program displays basic information about the program such as the name and location.

Version

The Version tab lists the following information:

- File version
- Description

- Copyright
- Other version information

There will not always be a Version tab on all Windows executables. The Version tab provides the version information on the given program and the copyright holder. The other version information concerns relevant information about items within the given program (see fig. 8.5).

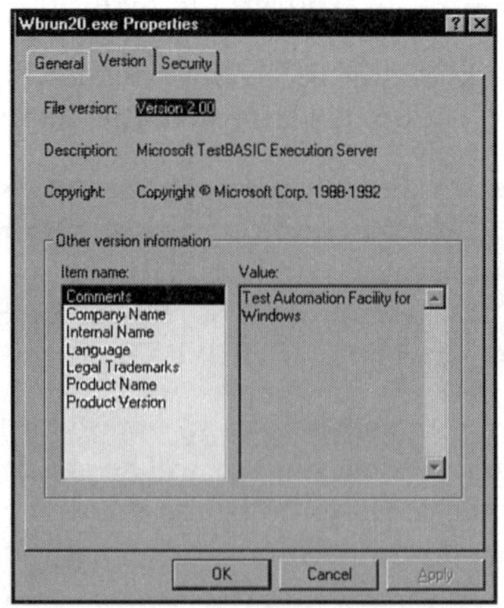

Figure 8.5
The Version information tab on a Windows 3.x program provides version information about the program.

Security

There are three security properties you can change (see fig. 8.6):

- Permissions
- Auditing
- Ownership

You can limit access to specific individuals or groups using the Permissions setting.

1. Click on the Permissions button and the File Permissions dialog box appears.
2. Click on Add to add users or groups to the access list. You can limit the types of access a given user or group has in the Type of Access dialog box. Click on OK to get back to the Security tab.
3. Click on the Auditing button. This displays the File Auditing dialog box. You can specify audits on users or on events.
4. To add users or groups, click the Add button. This displays the standard Add Users and Groups dialog box. When you have finished adding users, click on OK.

5. If you want to monitor events, add the group Everyone to the Name window. The events will then have active check boxes. Select those events you want audited.
6. Click on the Ownership button to display the current owner. If you want to take ownership, click the Take Ownership button. This enables an administrator to gain access to files he was blocked from, if necessary.

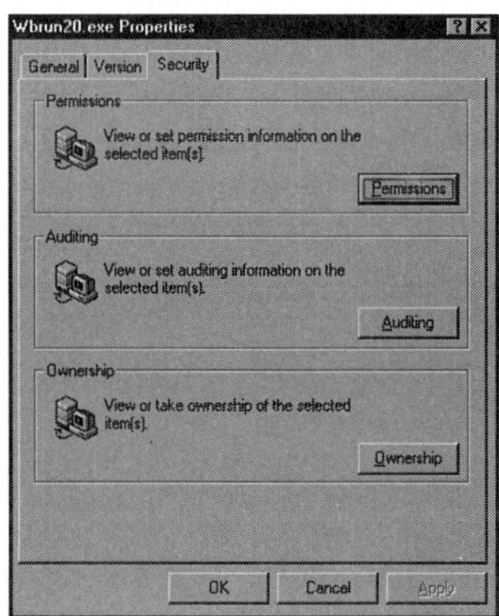

Figure 8.6
The Security information tab on a Windows 3.x program allows you to configure permissions, auditing, and ownership settings.

More security issues are covered in Chapter 19, "Security in Windows NT Workstation 4."

If a 16-bit Windows application hangs the WoW subsystem, you might have to terminate that application to free the rest of the applications running in the subsystem. To terminate the misbehaving application, follow these steps:

1. Press Ctrl+Shift+Esc to display the Windows NT Task Manager.
2. Click on the Applications tab.
3. Click on the application to select it.
4. Click on the End Task button.
5. If the application does not respond, an additional dialog box will appear and give you the options to wait, end the task, or cancel your attempt to close the task. Selecting End Task here forces the application to close even if it is doing something important, so be careful when forcing applications to close.

Because of the security and reliability requirements of Windows NT, programs and device drivers do not directly interact with the hardware of the system. Each hardware interface is through Virtual Device Drivers (VDDs). 16-bit Windows applications do not use the VDD setup, and NT cannot use Windows 3.x device drivers. To use 16-bit Windows applications, which access hardware, you will need both the Windows NT VDD as well as a 32-bit device driver written for Windows NT.

DOS

Unlike Windows 3.x applications, each DOS application requires its own separate VDM. If your system is low on memory, running many DOS applications will make that very apparent to you by using so much system memory.

In figure 8.7, you can see the Task Manager summary of processes. There are three copies of CAPTURE.EXE (a 16-bit Windows program) running; two are in their own memory space. Each of these has its own NTVDM and WoW. The third CAPTURE.EXE is not set to run in its own memory space. Under its NTVDM, you can see IMGMGR.EXE, another Windows program also not set to run in its own memory space. These are sharing a single WOWEXEC.EXE. There are also two DOS programs open, each running in its own NTVDM.

Windows NT Task Manager
File Options View Help
Applications Processes Performance

Image Name	PID	CPU	CPU Time	Mem Usage
lsass.exe	43	00	0:00:00	356 K
nddeagnt.exe	95	00	0:00:00	0 K
netdde.exe	137	00	0:00:00	44 K
ntvdm.exe	138	00	0:00:00	484 K
capture.exe		00	0:00:00	
wowexec.exe		00	0:00:00	
ntvdm.exe	150	00	0:00:00	1188 K
capture.exe		00	0:00:05	
imgmgr.exe		00	0:00:00	
wipasst.exe		00	0:00:07	
wowexec.exe		00	0:00:00	
ntvdm.exe	162	49	0:00:19	2388 K
ntvdm.exe	164	00	0:00:00	516 K
capture.exe		00	0:00:00	
wowexec.exe		00	0:00:00	
ntvdm.exe	165	49	0:00:24	2392 K
rasman.exe	84	00	0:00:00	60 K
RpcSs.exe	87	00	0:00:20	260 K
services.exe	40	00	0:00:04	600 K

End Process
Processes: 23 CPU Usage: 100% Mem Usage: 44036K / 222644K

Figure 8.7

Each DOS application gets its own VDM; Windows applications only get their own if they are set to run in a separate memory space.

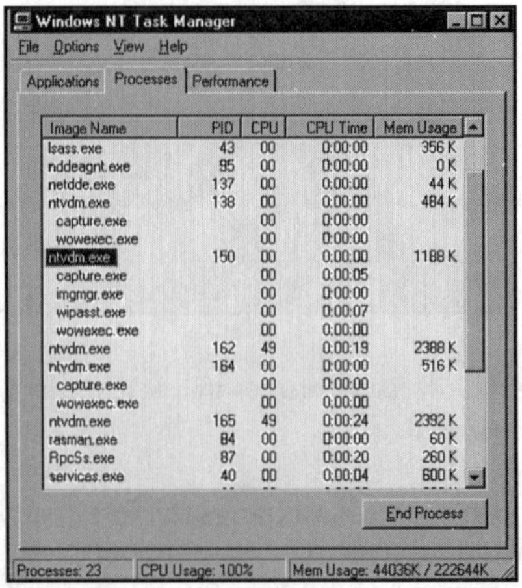

Because of the security features in NT, certain DOS commands and programs do not run under NT:

- UNDELETE.EXE
- MSCDEX.EXE
- Any applications that directly interact with hardware devices, such as DOS fax programs or backup software

There are several ways to access an MS-DOS command prompt:

- Select Command Prompt from the Programs menu.
- Type **command** in the Run window.

- Double-click either CMD or Command from Explorer when displaying the Windows NT files.
- Invoke a command shell from within an application program that supports that option.

You can invoke additional copies of the DOS command interpreter by repeating either of these steps, but it might be easier to type **START COMMAND** from a command window you already have open. Because each DOS box you open uses an entire VDM, you should minimize the number of DOS sessions you have running at a time to ensure optimum system performance.

To run a DOS application in full-screen mode, press Alt+Enter. This works like a toggle, so pressing it again switches you back to a window. Type **exit** at the command prompt to close your DOS VDM.

For DOS programs you will run frequently, it is easy to put a shortcut on your desktop. Perform the following steps:

1. Find the executable using Windows NT Explorer or My Computer.
2. Click the executable and drag the icon onto the desktop.
3. The icon will be labeled "Shortcut to..." (see fig. 8.8).

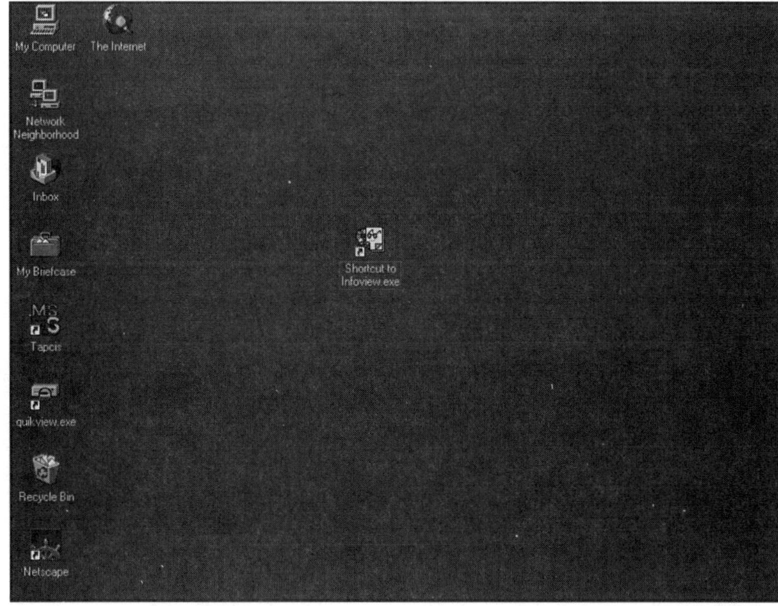

Figure 8.8

A desktop shortcut icon makes starting a program easier.

DOS Program Properties

Follow these steps to optimize a DOS program:

1. Right-click on the icon for the shortcut to the DOS program. (You can edit the properties for the program if you want, but the shortcut is more accessible and will apply the properties to the program when run from the shortcut.)

2. Select Properties from the menu. You will see a Properties window similar to figure 8.9.

Figure 8.9

The DOS program Properties information is saved in a PIF file.

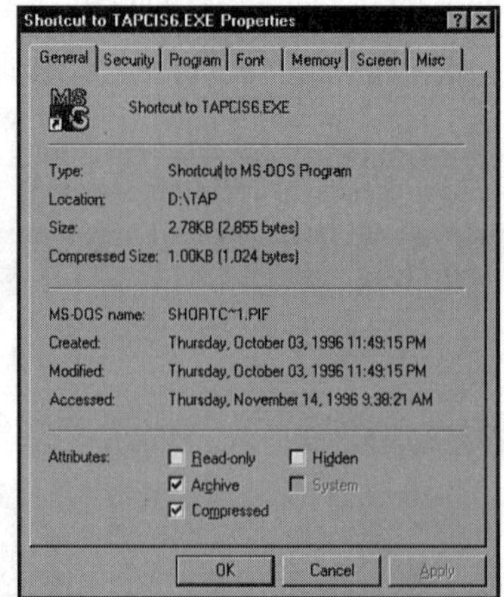

The information you generate from the Properties dialog box is saved in a PIF file (Program Information File). You can override these settings by running the DOS program from the command prompt.

The seven Properties tabs are as follows:

- ◆ General
- ◆ Security
- ◆ Program
- ◆ Font
- ◆ Memory
- ◆ Screen
- ◆ Misc

The Security tab does not appear if your shortcut exists on a non-NTFS partition. If, for instance, you have a FAT partition as well as an NTFS partition and your desktop information (which is stored in your user profile folder) is on the FAT partition, you will only have six tabs. Also the Compressed option on the General tab only appears for NTFS because it is only possible to compress files on NTFS partitions.

General

The General tab of the Properties dialog box provides you with the following information about the shortcut to the program:

- Type of program
- Location
- Size
- MS-DOS name
- Created
- Modified
- Accessed
- Attributes

The first three pieces of information refer to the shortcut, not to the actual program. You can select attributes by checking the boxes next to those you want. Read-only allows access to the file or program but does not allow any modifications to be made to it.

Following is a description of the attributes you can set from the General tab of the Properties dialog box:

- The Read-only attribute is fairly self-explanatory. If it is set (as indicated by a check in the box), you will not be able to save changes you make to the file in an editor or to delete it without specifically overriding the read-only protection.
- Hidden files don't show up in the Windows NT Explorer unless you specifically select Show All Files from the Options dialog box found under the View menu. You can hide any file you want to hide.
- Archive marks the file as "Archive needed" so that the next time a differential or incremental backup is performed, the file will be included.

- System files are specially protected by the system. You cannot copy them or change their attributes unless you also remove the System attribute. This option is grayed out because Windows NT does not allow you to change it from the worksheet. If you want to set or remove the System attribute, you will need to use the command line ATTRIB.EXE program.
- Compressed only appears as an option for files on an NTFS partition. If a file has been compressed, this box will be checked. Also, there will be a field above that listing the compressed size so that you can see the difference between that and the uncompressed size.

Security

In figure 8.10, you can see the three security properties you can change:

- Permissions
- Auditing
- Ownership

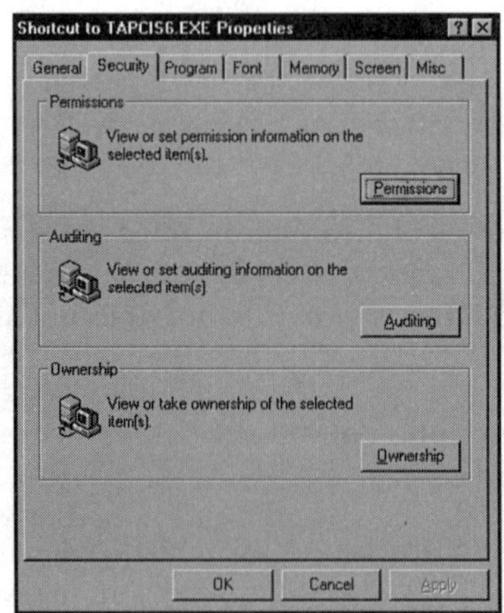

Figure 8.10
The Securities settings for a DOS application include auditing and ownership.

The security features allow you to set limitations on who can access files and to specify the types of access a user or group has. You can also audit specific users, groups of users, or events in order to get information such as how often a particular program is accessed or to verify that your security design is working as expected. Be careful about turning on auditing where you don't need it because it adds overhead to the system and slows it down. A little auditing here and there is no problem—just don't use it on everything at its most detailed level if you don't need to.

1. Click on the Permissions button, and the File Permissions dialog box appears (see fig. 8.11).

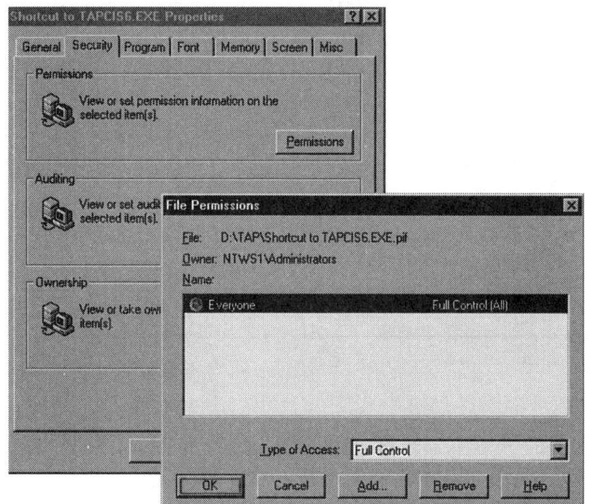

Figure 8.11

File Permissions lists the users and groups that currently have permission to access the specified file.

2. Click Add to add users or groups to the access list. You can limit the types of access a given user or group has in the Type of Access window (see fig. 8.12). Click on OK to get back to the Security tab.

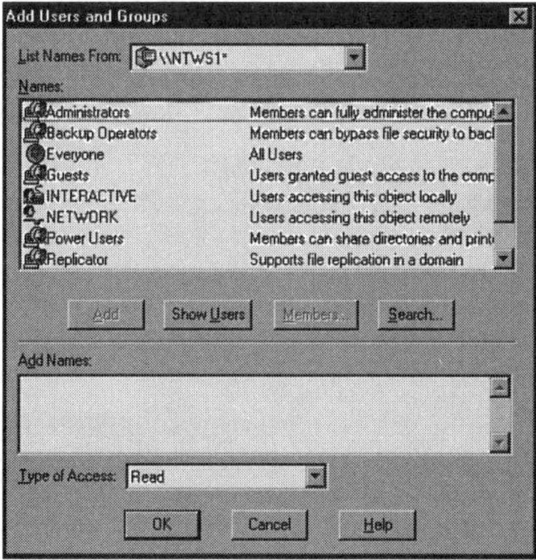

Figure 8.12

You can set which users or groups have access to a program as well as the type of access they have.

3. Click on the Auditing button. The File Auditing screen shown in figure 8.13 appears. You can specify audits on users or on events.

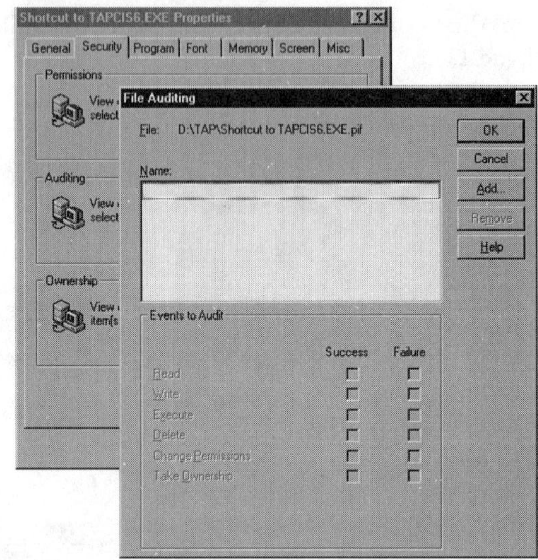

Figure 8.13

The File Auditing tab can set up auditing on individuals, groups, or events.

4. To add users or groups, click on the Add button. This displays the standard Add Users and Groups window. When you have finished adding users, click on OK.

5. If you want to monitor events, add the group Everyone to the Name window. The events will then have active check boxes. Select those events you want audited.

6. Click on the Ownership button to display the current owner. If you want to take ownership, click on the Take Ownership button. This enables an administrator to gain access to files he was blocked from, if necessary (see fig. 8.14).

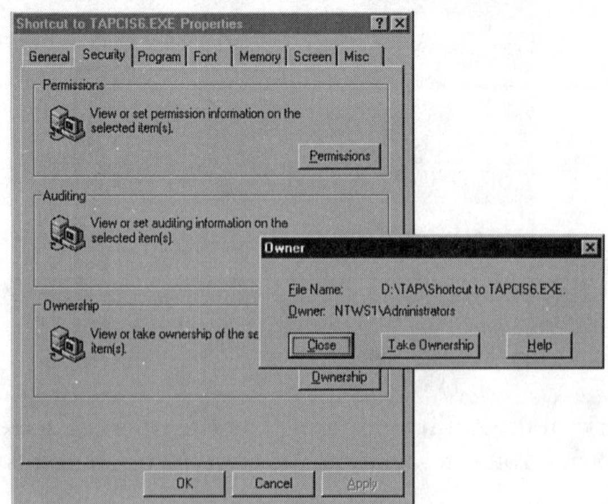

Figure 8.14

Ownership displays the owner of the file and the file location.

More security issues are covered in Chapter 19, "Security in NT Workstation 4."

Program

The Program tab displays the DOS program's icon and name or title at the top (see fig. 8.15). You need to fill in several of the command lines here when you are manually creating or editing a new file or a shortcut to a file.

1. Type in the command line you want this icon to invoke in the Command line text box.

2. Provide the working directory for the application in the Working text box.

3. Type the name (and location) of any batch file you want to run when you start this program. This item is not functional in Windows NT Workstation yet, but you might potentially use it if there were some TSRs that you needed when running a particular program, but you did not want to keep them loaded all the time.

4. If you have a shortcut key, type it in the Shortcut key window. Otherwise type **None**.

5. In the Run window you have the following three options:

    - Normal window
    - Maximized
    - Minimized

    Select which option you prefer.

6. Check the Close on exit box if you want to close the DOS window when you terminate the program.

7. If you want to change the icon associated with the program, click on the Change Icon button.

8. You see a selection of different icons in the Change Icon dialog box (see fig. 8.16). Click on one and click on OK. The default file used is the PIFMGR.DLL. If you have other icon images stored somewhere else, you can click on the Browse button to find the file. The images are displayed in the Current icon window.

9. After highlighting your choice, click on OK.

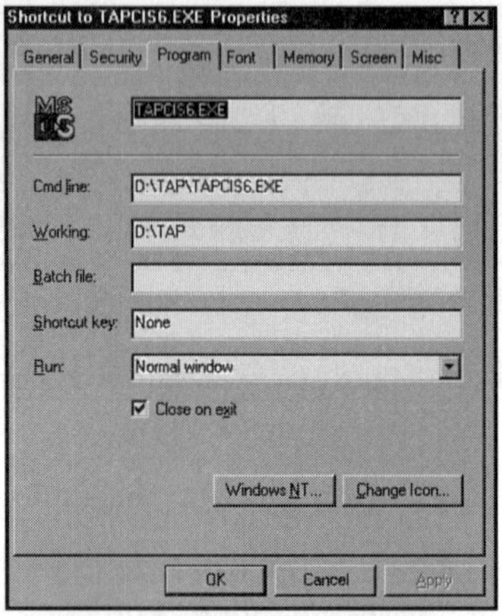

Figure 8.15

The DOS Program Properties tab can set such things as a shortcut key and a batch file.

Figure 8.16

Different icons are available for applications.

10. Click on the Windows NT button for the Windows NT PIF settings. This displays the Custom MS-DOS Initialization Files (see fig. 8.17).

    The default files are the %SYSTEMROOT%\AUTOEXEC.NT and the %SYSTEMROOT%\CONFIG.NT. If your DOS program relies on certain information to be in the AUTOEXEC.BAT or the CONFIG.SYS (or any other particular file), you can change these. You can provide the necessary settings by using a text editor to cut the relevant parts out of your old AUTOEXEC.BAT and CONFIG.SYS files and into the AUTOEXEC.NT files if you so choose. These files are not used by NT to boot up.

11. Check the box for Compatible Timer Hardware Emulation if you know your application can reduce the frequency with which it gets a timing signal from the system.

12. Click on OK when you are finished.

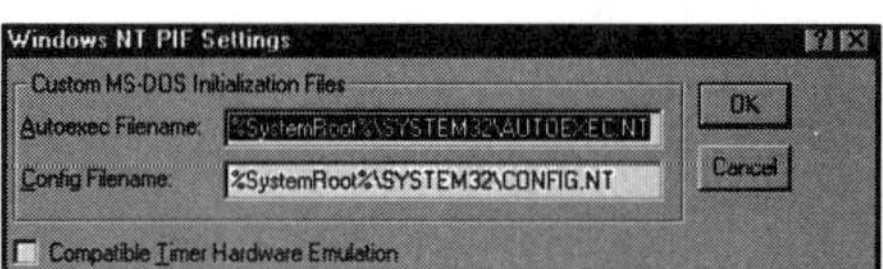

Figure 8.17

The NT initialization files take the place of the old DOS AUTOEXEC.BAT and CONFIG.SYS.

Font

The Font tab allows you to choose the type of font you will be able to use in your DOS application, as well as the font size. The preview screen enables you to test out your selection (see fig. 8.18). Here is how you configure the font size of your choice:

1. In the Available types area, choose one of the following:
   - Bitmap only
   - TrueType only
   - Both font types
2. In the Font size window, select the size you want by clicking on it. The range is from 2×4 to 16×12.
3. Click on OK when you are finished.

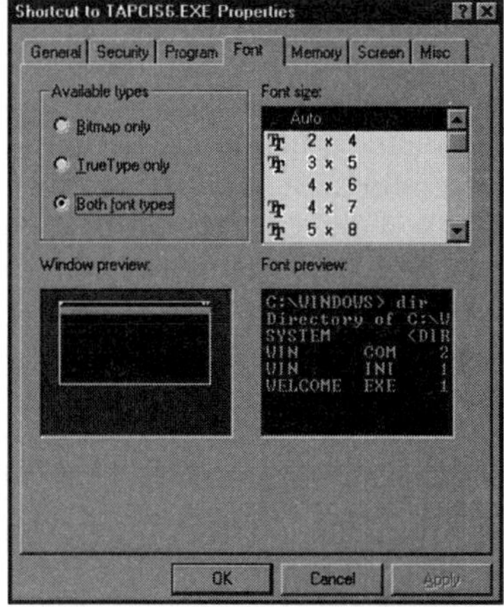

Figure 8.18

The font size and type can be changed for a DOS application.

Memory

You use the Memory tab to view and to change the configured memory options for a DOS application. The options you have from this tab are:

- **Conventional memory.** From the drop-down lists, you can select amounts for Total conventional memory and the Initial environment size, or select Auto. The default is Auto, which in Windows NT just means use the default amount. Under Windows 95, the value used by Auto for the environment size is taken from the SHELL= line of the CONFIG.SYS, but that feature is not available in Windows NT. Check the Protected box if the application should be kept from modifying memory inside the VDM that it has not been allocated to it.

- **Expanded (EMS) memory.** You can select Total maximum amount up to 16 MB in 1 MB increments from the drop-down list, or None. The default is None because most applications use either the preferred DPMI interface or the XMS interface for requesting more memory.

- **Extended (XMS) memory.** You can select an amount for Total or None. The default is 0 KB because it is recommended that applications needing more memory should use the DPMI interface. You can select between no XMS and 16 MB of XMS in 1 MB increments. Check Use HMA if the application you are configuring can use the High Memory Area to gain an extra 64 KB of conventional memory and would benefit from doing so.

- **MS-DOS protected-mode (DPMI) memory.** Select an amount or Auto for Total. Auto is the default setting, and it will generally work well because it simply allocates memory as the memory is requested.

Some programs do not function well without a specified EMS or XMS quantity. If that is the case, select the maximum amount the application will need rather than Auto for these settings (see fig. 8.19). If you have selected Auto and your DOS-based application claims to have run out of memory before exhausting your system's virtual memory, you have a program that might benefit from setting this.

The disadvantages of selecting Auto are that Windows NT has to guess for you how much memory of which type to provide, which adds some overhead and might not be an optimal use of your system's RAM. For most common applications, the benefits of not having to worry about knowing those details outweigh the benefits of tweaking your system's memory allocation so that it is perfectly optimal. How do you know how memory is being used? Use the Windows NT Performance Monitor as described in Chapter 11, "NT Workstation Networking in Action."

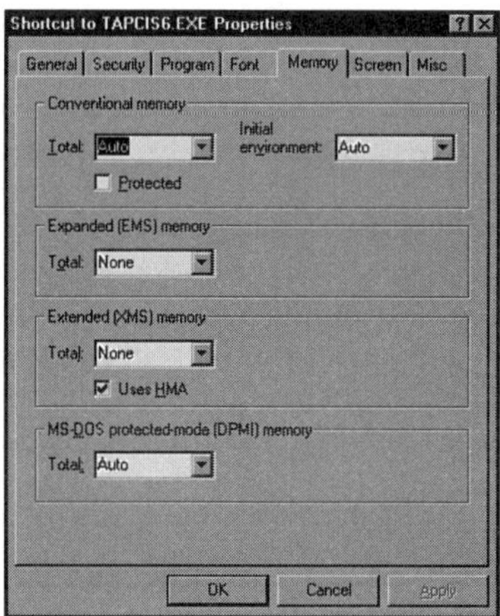

Figure 8.19

This is the Memory settings tab, where you can make changes to the way memory is allocated to DOS programs.

Screen

There are several options you can configure that are relevant to the way a DOS-based program displays on the screen. Here, the ones available from the Screen tab of the Properties dialog box are discussed (see fig. 8.20).

- **Usage.** Select Full-screen or Window.

  Some DOS programs will not run in a DOS window. You need to specify full-screen for these. Text mode programs generally run in a window without any difficulty, but programs that use a graphics mode need to run full-screen.

  For the Initial size option, select the initial size from the drop-down list or select Default. The choices are 25 lines, 43 lines, or 50 lines. These correspond to the historical text mode screen sizes under the DOS operating system for Hercules/MDA/CGA, EGA, and VGA text displays. The default is 25 lines unless the application you are running changes it. The default is usually a reasonable size unless you are running at a high graphics resolution or a smaller screen. You can customize the default window size by using the Console tool in the Control Panel to change the text size.

- **Window.** Check the options you want. The two options you have are as follows:

  - **Display toolbar.** Displays a DOS toolbar while the application is running.

  - **Restore settings on startup.** Remembers the window size and placement from the last time it was run.

- **Performance.** Check the options you want. You have the following two options:

- **Fast ROM emulation.** Specifies whether BIOS functions are emulated at the graphics device driver or at a higher layer. Unless your application has problems with the fast ROM emulation setting, leave it at the default of on because it will be able to update the display faster.
- **Dynamic memory allocation.** Specifies whether to return memory this application releases when it changes video modes to the main system pool or hold onto it in case the application needs it again. This is only used for applications that change between text and graphics modes and does not benefit most of them. Its real purpose is to help memory-starved systems by reclaiming all possible memory as quickly as possible.

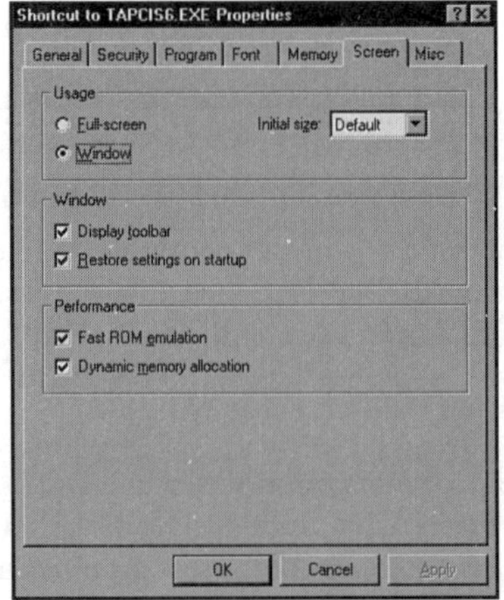

Figure 8.20

These are the DOS application display settings.

Misc

The Misc tab presents a collection of options (see fig. 8.21).

Figure 8.21

The Misc tab has a variety of DOS settings.

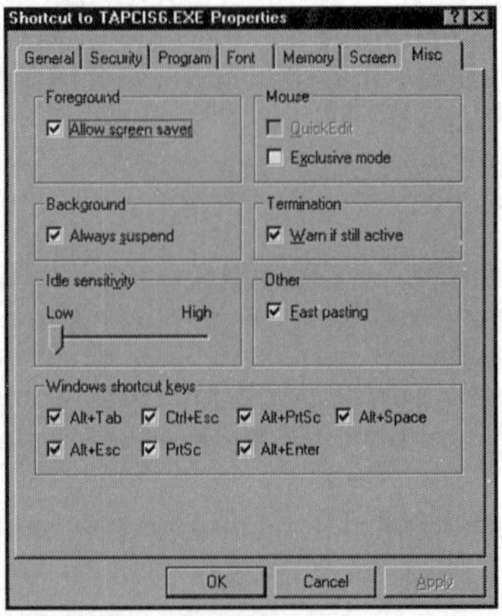

Many of these options are to improve compatibility between Windows NT and applications written for DOS environments. Because these properties can be set program by program, you can customize how the system treats each one:

- **Foreground.** Some DOS programs will fail if the screen saver kicks in, so you can disable the screen saver while that DOS program has the foreground. DOS-based communications programs are usually among the most sensitive.
- **Mouse.** QuickEdit mode allows you to use the primary mouse key to mark text. It is grayed out because the checkbox is only valid under Windows 95. Under Windows NT, you can always use QuickEdit to mark text. Exclusive mode captures the mouse pointer inside the DOS application window as long as the DOS application is running. You probably should not use Exclusive mode unless your applications require it.
- **Background.** Checking Always suspend keeps DOS applications from executing in the background and using CPU cycles unless they have the focus.
- **Termination.** Warn if still active prevents you from closing DOS applications by clicking the Close button on their window or by using the Task Manager. You can ignore the warning and close the application anyway, but the warning is there because there is no standard way to send a message to a DOS program asking it to perform a graceful shutdown the way there is with Windows programs. Terminating a DOS application that has not shut itself down might result in file corruption and is therefore discouraged.
- **Idle sensitivity.** This is used to identify applications that do not well tolerate running in the background. Pay attention to setting this one because many people find the slider counterintuitive. A Low idle sensitivity means that the application cannot tolerate long idle periods without being serviced. A DOS communications program running in the background is a good example of a program that might need the default setting modified so that it does not drop characters during background transfers. A High idle sensitivity means that the application can wait a relatively long while between times that Windows NT services it.
- **Other.** Fast pasting allows you to click the secondary mouse button to paste in text from the edit buffer.
- **Windows shortcut keys.** Shortcut keys are important. If your program requires any of these keys, make sure to uncheck their boxes here. Otherwise, Windows NT interprets the keys as a Windows command because Windows traps the keystrokes before your application sees them and never passes them to your application.

Windows 95

Windows 95 shares a user-friendly interface with Windows NT, but Windows NT's architectural improvements make it a more reliable, robust, secure, and scalable operating system. Windows 95 is a mostly 32-bit platform. Its native applications run in 32-bit mode just as they do on Windows NT. In fact, almost all programs that run under Windows 95 will run in native 32-bit mode under Windows NT. Microsoft even went so far as to require that programs carrying the Windows 95 logo must be able to run under Windows NT. In other words, a program must be tested on Windows NT before being approved as fully Windows 95 compatible. The key differences between the two platforms center on the mutually exclusive unique features of the different operating systems. One system cannot do it all. Windows NT offers security features and software crash protection, whereas Windows 95 offers applications direct hardware access and real-mode driver support.

Upgrading from Windows 95 to Windows NT

For all the application compatibility between Windows 95 and Windows NT, there is no automated upgrade procedure to step up from Windows 95 to Windows NT. Microsoft plans to incorporate that feature in the next Windows NT Workstation release after version 4. One of the main reasons that upgrading is not simple is that the two systems have vastly different Registries and styles of hardware interaction. If you want to upgrade from Windows 95 to Windows NT, you might find that some of your applications that rely on direct hardware access do not work anymore.

If you want to install both Windows 95 and Windows NT on the same system to dual boot between them, you can do it without much trouble. The big issue is that Windows NT will not migrate over any customizations from Windows NT and will not update the information in the Windows 95 Registry as changes are made from NT.

The recommended workaround for this is to install Windows 95 on the computer first. After that is working, install Windows NT Workstation on the computer next. Verify that it works correctly. After both operating systems are installed, you will have to install all your applications twice—once while running Windows NT and once while running Windows 95. Install all application files to the same directories whether you are installing under Windows 95 or Windows NT. If you know that before you start, then it is not as bad, compared to finding out after you have installed and tweaked the settings on the first installation. A word of advice is appropriate here—check the installation under both operating systems before you start customizing things.

Comparison of the Windows NT and Windows 95 Platforms

Table 8.1 provides a quick overview of some of the similarities and differences between the Windows 95 and Windows NT systems.

TABLE 8.1
Similarities and Differences Between NT and 95

Windows 95		Windows NT
	Similarities	
	32-bit processing	
	Long file names	
	System components in kernel	
	Windows 3.x applications	
	Windows 95 applications	
	Differences	
Non-preemptive multitasking of DOS applications		Preemptive multitasking of DOS applications
No NTFS		NTFS
Compression by drive letter only		NTFS compression (by file or directory)
Plug and Play		No Plug and Play

The main goal of Windows 95 was ease of use. Security and bulletproof reliability were less important than backward compatibility in Windows 95, whereas Windows NT focused more on such issues as security and reliability. The architecture of each system reflects these different goals. Windows NT protects its own code from applications, as well as protecting each application from every another application.

In Windows 95, applications have fewer restrictions on what parts of system memory they can access. Windows NT not only places severe restrictions on which application can use which memory, but it also carries that restriction into its backward compatibility subsystems, which support applications written for different operating systems. Each subsystem runs in its own memory space. This prevents the system from crashing in the event of a problem with an application written for a compatible operating system that did not have memory protection built in. In other words, supporting applications from notoriously unstable operating systems has no effect on the stability of Windows NT itself or applications running in other subsystems.

Windows 95 is not a completely 32-bit operating system in that it has to translate between Win16 and Win32 constantly for system kernel functions. Windows 95 runs only on standard x86 computers using a single processor at a time. Windows NT, on the other hand, can support multiple processors and run on Alpha, R4XOO, and PowerPC systems.

The Security Differences Between Windows 95 and NT

As already mentioned, Windows 95 was designed for ease of use, whereas Windows NT focuses more on security and reliability issues. The architecture of each system reflects these different goals in this and in other areas.

Windows NT Workstation uses a secure logon screen that cannot be bypassed, whereas a Windows 95 user can simply elect not to log on but still use all the local resources. Windows NT Workstations support secure file systems using NTFS, whereas Windows 95 systems can only access FAT file systems.

One of the most notable differences in security between Windows 95 and Windows NT Workstation is the way cumulative rights assignments are handled. In Windows 95, rights are cumulative, meaning that your user account has the maximum level of rights it was given for any object. In Windows NT, your rights are more restrictive. If any rights assignment explicitly blocks you from a resource, no other assignment can override it to give you access.

Migrating Programs to NT

Unlike Windows 3.x applications, you cannot migrate your Windows 95 applications to Windows NT. If you currently are running Windows 95, and would like to have some of the benefits of Windows NT Workstation, your options are setting up a dual boot between the two systems or starting from scratch, loading Windows NT Workstation, and reinstalling your applications. Microsoft does not recommend the dual boot option, but the manual upgrade is tedious. You can install Windows NT under a different directory on your computer. Because there is no automated migration tool, you must install each application into Windows NT. The reinstallation is necessary for Windows NT to make the appropriate Registry entries as far as application settings are concerned.

Like DOS and Windows 3.x, Windows 95 utilizes some device drivers that access the hardware. Because this is not supported by NT—the hardware is actually protected from any direct access except through the Hardware Abstraction Layer (HAL)—Windows 95 device drivers are not necessarily NT compatible.

Running Windows 95 Programs Under Windows NT Workstation

Because of the close relationship between Windows NT and Windows 95, running Windows 95 applications is exactly like running native Windows NT applications. You can start a Windows 95 program from anywhere inside Windows NT Workstation that you can start a native program. This could be from the Explorer, from the Start menu's Run option, from the Task Manager's New Task menu choice, from a shortcut, from a command line, or from a BAT or CMD file.

OS/2

OS/2 is another operating system that Windows NT has some level of support for and compatibility with. OS/2 is a 32-bit operating system available from IBM that has a special, almost parental, relationship with Windows NT. Microsoft and IBM worked on OS/2 together but had differing visions for the future. The current versions of OS/2 are no longer joint projects between Microsoft and IBM—instead they are competition for Microsoft from IBM. OS/2 supports 16-bit DOS and Windows applications and 32-bit applications written for either Win32s or a native OS/2 interface. It can use either the FAT file system or a different, proprietary file system called the High Performance File System (HPFS). OS/2 uses a graphical interface called the *Presentation Manager interface*, which is roughly equivalent to the Windows NT graphical interface.

The majority of the OS/2 applications are graphically based, and these are the very programs that you would want to run under NT. This makes NT's OS/2 support not very useful if you really need to support graphical OS/2 applications.

The Windows NT OS/2 Subsystem

Only Windows NT computers running on x86-based systems provide support for OS/2-specific applications, and then only fully for 16-bit character-based applications written for version 1.x of OS/2. Applications meeting these requirements can almost universally be called *legacy* applications because modern OS/2 applications (those developed in the last few years) tend to be graphical and use the 32-bit interface to take advantage of OS/2's features. Windows NT on supported RISC computers only supports those OS/2 applications that can run under emulated DOS as bound 16-bit executables.

Some specific types of OS/2 applications not supported include those that use the graphical Presentation Manager interface; applications that use features added in OS/2 versions 2.x, 3.x, or 4.x; Advanced Video I/O (AVIO) applications; and applications that access hardware directly or in a privileged processor mode. Microsoft does sell an add-on to Windows NT that expands the level of OS/2 support to cover some Presentation Manager programs and AVIO applications that meet the Windows NT criteria of being well-behaved.

The primary files that make up the OS/2 subsystem are the OS2SRV.EXE, OS2.EXE, DOSCALLS.DLL, and NETAPI.DLL.

When a supported OS/2 application launches an OS/2 thread, the Windows NT OS/2 subsystem launches a native Windows NT thread to support it.

The Windows NT Workstation 4 OS/2 subsystem does not support the HPFS file system, although it does support long file names and extended file attributes.

When the OS/2 subsystem loads, it reads the Registry for its configuration information. Updating the OS/2 information in the Registry, however, is done in an unusual way—by editing a special C:\CONFIG.SYS file.

The contents of the C:\CONFIG.SYS file are stored in the Windows NT Registry under the following:

```
HKEY_LOCAL_MACHINE\Software\Microsoft\OS/2 Subsystem for NT\1.0\config.sys
```

Here is a sample of the default settings for that Registry entry:

```
NTREM Here is a summary of what is allowed to appear in this registry entry:
NTREM   Comments starting with REM will be visible to the user when s/he opens
NTREM     c:\config.sys.
NTREM   Comments starting with NTREM are only visible by direct access to the
NTREM     Registry.
NTREM   The following OS/2 configuration commands are significant:
NTREM     COUNTRY=
NTREM     CODEPAGE=
NTREM     DEVINFO=KBD,
NTREM   Any other commands apart from the exceptions listed below will be
NTREM   visible to an OS/2 program that opens c:\config.sys, however they are
NTREM   not used internally by the NT OS/2 SubSystem.
NTREM   Exceptions:
NTREM     The following commands are completely ignored. Their true values
NTREM     appear in the system environment and should be modified using the
NTREM     Control Panel System applet. Note that LIBPATH is called Os2LibPath
NTREM     in the NT system environment.
SET PATH=<ignored>
LIBPATH=<ignored>
NTREM     In addition, any "SET=" commands (except COMSPEC) will be
NTREM     completely ignored. You should set OS/2 environment variables just
NTREM     like any other Windows NT environment variables by using the Control
NTREM     Panel System applet.
NTREM   If you have an OS/2 editor available, it is highly recommended that you
NTREM   modify NT OS/2 config.sys configuration by editing c:\config.sys with
NTREM   this editor. This is the documented way to make such modification, and
NTREM   is therefore less error-prone.
```

```
NTREM   Now comes the actual text.
REM
REM This is a fake OS/2 config.sys file used by the NT OS/2 SubSystem.
REM The following information resides in the Registry and NOT in a disk file.
REM OS/2 Apps that access c:\config.sys actually manipulate this information.
REM
PROTSHELL=c:\os2\pmshell.exe c:\os2\os2.ini c:\os2\os2sys.ini
C:\WINNT\System32\cmd.exe
SET COMSPEC=C:\WINNT\System32\cmd.exe
```

Running OS/2 Applications

The OS/2 subsystem starts the first time you launch an OS/2 program. It then continues running until the system is shut down or until you manually terminate the subsystem using the Windows NT Task Manager. Windows NT automatically knows whether it should use the OS/2 subsystem for an application program because of header information embedded in the program file. If you want to see the sort of header information that Windows NT reads, you can run the C:\WINNT\SYSTEM32\VIEWERS\QUIKVIEW.EXE. A sample of the sort of header information you might see for an OS/2 related file is shown in figure 8.22.

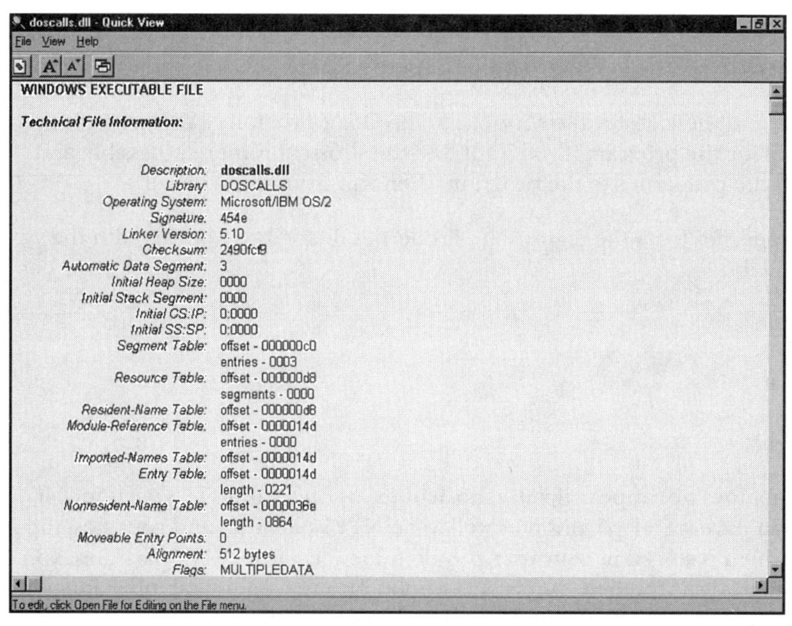

Figure 8.22

You can use Quik View to get header information from an OS/2 file.

Windows NT reads this information from every program before starting it to make sure that the program is handled by the correct subsystem.

After Windows NT has determined that the program about to run is an OS/2-based application, it invokes the OS2SRV.EXE file to start the OS/2 subsystem and load the program the user requested. After the application closes, the OS/2 subsystem stays active until the system is shut down or until it is manually closed through the Task Manager.

To start an OS/2 application, perform the following steps:

1. Click the Start button to access the Run command.
2. Type in the name of the program you want to run, with its path. You can use the Browse button to help locate the file if necessary.

Alternatively, you can double-click on the OS/2 program executable icon in the NT Explorer.

For OS/2 programs you will run frequently, it is easy to put a shortcut on your desktop. Follow these steps:

1. Find the executable using Windows NT Explorer or My Computer.
2. Click on the executable and drag the icon onto the desktop.
3. The icon will be labeled "Shortcut to…."

Follow these steps to set the OS/2 program properties:

1. Right-click on the icon for the shortcut to the OS/2 program. (You can edit the Properties for the program if you want, but the shortcut is more accessible and will apply the properties to the program when run from the shortcut.)
2. Select Properties from the menu. The Properties dialog box appears with the following tabs:
   - ◆ General
   - ◆ Shortcut
   - ◆ Security

The Security tab does not appear if your shortcut exists on a non-NTFS partition. If, for instance, you have a FAT partition as well as an NTFS partition and your desktop information (which is stored in your user profile folder) is on the FAT partition, you will only have two tabs. Also the Compressed option on the General tab only appears for NTFS because it is only possible to compress files on NTFS partitions.

General

The General tab provides you with the following information about the shortcut to the program:

- Type of program
- Location
- Size
- MS-DOS name
- Created
- Modified
- Accessed
- Attributes

The first three pieces of information refer to the shortcut, not to the actual program. You can select attributes by checking the boxes next to those you want. Read-only allows access to the file or program, but does not allow any modifications to be made to it.

Following is a description of the attributes you can set from the General tab:

- The Read-only attribute is fairly self-explanatory. If it is set (as indicated by a check in the box), you will not be able to save changes you make to the file in an editor or to delete it without specifically overriding the read-only protection.
- Hidden files don't show up in the Windows NT Explorer unless you specifically select Show All Files from the Options tab found in the Explorer's View dialog box. You can hide any file you want to hide by editing its attributes.
- Archive marks the file as "Archive needed" so that the next time a differential or incremental backup is performed the file will be included.
- System files are specially protected by the system. You cannot copy them or change their attributes unless you also remove the System attribute. This option is grayed out because Windows NT does not allow you to change it from the worksheet. If you want to set or remove the System attribute, you will need to use the command line ATTRIB.EXE program.
- Compressed only appears as an option for files on an NTFS partition. If a file has been compressed, this box will be checked. Also, there will be a field above that listing the compressed size so that you can see the difference between that and the uncompressed size.

Shortcut

The Shortcut tab provides a means of customizing the way a shortcut to a given program operates. You can select a special icon to represent the shortcut, choose a hotkey for it, or have the program run in a minimized mode from the shortcut tab.

1. Select the Shortcut tab to edit the information on the shortcut.
2. The Target specifies the location of the program executable. You can click the Find Target button to help locate the program executable. If you already have the folder specified in the window, the Find Target window displays the contents of that folder.
3. You can specify the folder you want to have as the default by typing its name in the Start In text box.
4. If you want to be able to access the program with a keystroke, type in the keystroke combination you want in the Shortcut Key text box.
5. In the Run window, select whether you want the program to run minimized, maximized, or in a normal window. After you launch the program, you can change this mode; the Run setting merely sets how the program starts.
6. To change the icon representing the program, click the Change Icon button.
7. You see a selection of different icons in the Change Icon window. Click on one and click on OK. The Default File used is the PIFMGR.DLL. If you have other icon images stored somewhere else, you can click the Browse button to find the file. The images are displayed in the Current Icon window.
8. After highlighting your choice, Click on the OK button.

Security

Using the Security tab, you can limit who has access to a given file and can specify the exact level of access individual users or groups have. Also you can specify auditing of certain events or users. There are three security properties you can change:

- Permissions
- Auditing
- Ownership

In order to turn on security protections for a file:

1. Click on the Permissions button, and the File Permissions window appears.
2. Click on Add to add users or groups to the access list. You can limit the types of access a given user or group has in the Type of Access window. Click on OK to get back to the Security tab.
3. Click on the Auditing button. This displays the File Auditing screen. You can specify audits on users or on events.
4. To add users or groups click on the Add button. This displays the standard Add Users and Groups window. When you have finished adding users, click on OK.
5. If you want to monitor events, add the group Everyone to the Name window. The events will then have active checkboxes. Check those events you want audited.
6. Click on the Ownership button to display the current owner. If you want to take ownership, click on the Take Ownership button. This enables an administrator to gain access to files he was blocked from, if necessary.

More Security issues are covered in Chapter 19, "Security in NT Workstation 4."

OS/2 HPFS Workaround

Although Windows NT 4 does not officially support HPFS as older versions of Windows NT did, there is a workaround—if you have a copy of Windows NT 3.51.

1. Copy the file PINBALL.SYS to the \%systemroot%\system32\drivers directory on your NT workstation. The PINBALL.SYS is an HPFS driver file.
2. Run the Registry Editor. (For more information on the Registry see Chapter 22, "The Registry.")
3. Go to the key HKEY_LOCAL_MACHINE\SYSTEM\CURRENTCONTROLSET\SERVICES\PINBALL
4. Type in the following lines:

   ```
   ErrorControl: REG_DWORD: 0x1
   Group: REG_SZ: Boot file system
   Start: REG_DWORD: 0x1
   Type: REG_DWORD: 0x2
   ```

5. Close the Registry Editor and reboot your system for the changes to take effect.

POSIX

Portable Operating System Interface (POSIX) applications are typically Unix-based applications that meet a particular set of programming standards. The POSIX standards are defined by the Institute of Electrical and Electronic Engineers (IEEE).

Most POSIX applications are character-based and would have to be so because the graphic POSIX standards have not yet been approved. There are 12 different POSIX standards, and NT supports POSIX.1 applications. These applications run inside the Windows NT POSIX subsystem.

Because POSIX describes a machine-independent standard for building applications, those applications have to be recompiled for each hardware platform they are to run on. POSIX compliant applications run on Windows NT in a *POSIX window,* which is similar to a DOS or OS/2 window.

The POSIX Registry entries are found in the following (see figure 8.23):

HKEY_LOCAL_MACHINE\SYSTEM\CurrentControlSet\Control\Session Manager\SubSystems

Figure 8.23

The POSIX subsystem information is found in the Registry.

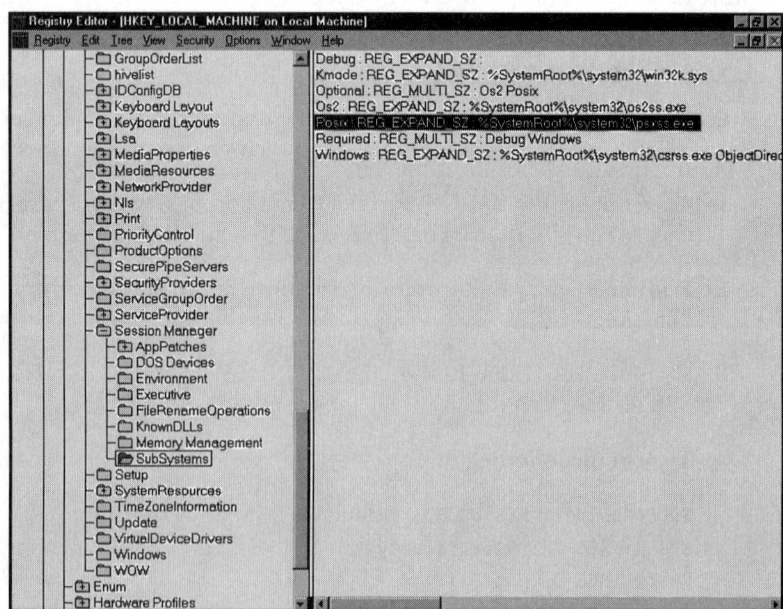

The POSIX Subsystem

The POSIX subsystem uses the PSXSS.EXE as the POSIX subsystem server, the POSIX.EXE as the POSIX console session manager, and the PSXDLL.DLL as the

POSIX dynamic link library. Together these make a working POSIX subsystem that you can use to run POSIX applications.

Like applications in other subsystems, the applications running within the POSIX subsystem can interact with all other applications in Windows NT.

Running POSIX Applications

You can start POSIX applications from a Windows NT command prompt, My Computer, Network Neighborhood, the Windows NT Explorer, or from a launch menu on another program such as the Windows NT Task Manager. The only special requirement that POSIX applications have is that they require some functions in the file system that only NTFS supports on an NT platform. Therefore, if you are running POSIX applications that need to access a file system, make sure that they are accessing an NTFS file system.

For POSIX programs you will run frequently, it is easy to put a shortcut on your desktop:

1. Find the executable using Windows NT Explorer or My Computer.
2. Click the executable and drag the icon onto the desktop.
3. The icon will be labeled "Shortcut to...."

To set the POSIX program properties, follow these steps:

1. Right-click on the icon for the shortcut to the POSIX program. (You can edit the Properties for the program if you want, but the shortcut is more accessible and will apply the properties to the program when run from the shortcut.)
2. Select Properties from the menu. You see the Properties dialog box. You will see the following tabs:
    - General
    - Shortcut
    - Security

The Security tab does not appear if your shortcut exists on a non-NTFS partition. If, for instance, you have a FAT partition as well as an NTFS partition and your desktop information (which is stored in your user profile folder) is on the FAT partition, you will only have two tabs. Also the Compressed option on the General tab appears only for NTFS because it is only possible to compress files on NTFS partitions.

General

The General tab provides you with the following information about the shortcut to the program:

- Type of program
- Location
- Size
- MS-DOS name
- Created
- Modified
- Accessed
- Attributes

The first three pieces of information refer to the shortcut, not to the actual program, if you have accessed the properties dialog box from the shortcut. You can select attributes by checking the boxes next to those you want. Read-only allows access to the file or program, but does not allow any modifications to be made to it.

Following is a description of the attributes you can set from the General sheet:

- The Read-only attribute is fairly self-explanatory. If it is set (as indicated by a check in the box), you will not be able to save changes you make to the file in an editor or to delete the file without specifically overriding the read-only protection.
- Hidden files don't show up in the Windows NT Explorer unless you specifically select Show All Files from the Options dialog box found under the View menu. You can hide any file you want to hide.
- Archive marks the file as "Archive needed" so that the next time a differential or incremental backup is performed, the file will be included.
- System files are specially protected by the system. You cannot copy them or change their attributes unless you also remove the System attribute. This option is grayed out because Windows NT does not allow you to change it from the worksheet. If you want to set or remove the System attribute, you will need to use the command line ATTRIB.EXE program.

- Compressed will only show up as an option for files on an NTFS partition. If a file has been compressed, this box will be checked. Also, there will be a field above that listing the compressed size so that you can see the difference between that and the uncompressed size.

Shortcut

The Shortcut tab lets you edit the configuration of the shortcut.

1. The Target specifies the location of the program executable. You can click the Find Target button to help locate the program executable. If you already have the folder specified in the window, the Find Target window will display the contents of that folder.
2. You can specify the default folder to start in by typing the folder's name in the Start In window.
3. If you want to be able to access the program with a keystroke, type in the keystroke combination you want in the Shortcut Key window.
4. In the Run window, select whether you want the program to run minimized, maximized, or in a normal window. After you launch the program, you can change this mode; the Run setting merely sets how the program starts.
5. To change the icon representing the program, click on the Change Icon button.
6. You see a selection of different icons in the Change Icon window. Click on one and click on OK. The Default File used is the PIFMGR.DLL. If you have other icon images stored somewhere else, you can click on the Browse button to find the file. The images are displayed in the Current Icon window.
7. After highlighting your choice, Click on the OK button.

Security

There are three security properties you can change:

- Permissions
- Auditing
- Ownership

To assign security rights, change the auditing levels, and change the ownership of files you could follow the steps below.

1. Click on the Permissions button, and the File Permissions window appears.
2. Click on Add to add users or groups to the access list. You can limit the types of access a given user or group has in the Type of Access window. Click on OK to get back to the Security tab.
3. Click on the Auditing button. This displays the File Auditing screen. You can specify audits on users or on events.
4. To add users or groups click on the Add button. This displays the standard Add Users and Groups window. When you have finished adding users, click on OK.
5. If you want to monitor events, add the group Everyone to the Name window. The events will then have active check boxes. Check those events you want audited.
6. Click on the Ownership button to display the current owner. If you want to take ownership, click on the Take Ownership button. This enables an administrator to gain access to files he was blocked from, if necessary.

More Security issues are covered in Chapter 21, "Troubleshooting and Optimization."

Now that you've covered what happens when you run applications and the different options Windows NT gives you for configuring them, you will cover how you actually get those applications installed.

Installing Applications

There are several different ways to install applications on Windows NT Workstation. The best way to install an application depends on the application and how its installation was designed to work. If the application is distributed on CD-ROM, it might automatically display a menu asking if you would like to install it when you put it into your CD-ROM drive. If the application was distributed with Windows NT or designed specifically for Windows NT, you can use the Control Panel Add/Remove tool. You can also use the Control Panel's Add/Remove tool for applications that require you to run a specific setup program that they provide such as SETUP.EXE.

If you want to add or remove a native Windows NT application, perform these steps:

1. Open the Control Panel and select the Add/Remove icon by double-clicking on it. The Add/Remove Programs Properties window appears (see fig. 8.24).
2. Click on the Install button on the Install/Uninstall tab.
3. The next window tells you to insert your installation disk in the floppy drive or your installation CD-ROM in the CD-ROM drive. Click on the Next button.

4. The Add/Remove Program application searches for the installation files. If it does not find them, you might need to specify the file name or command line in the Run Installation Program window (see fig. 8.25). You can click on the Browse button to help locate the correct file.

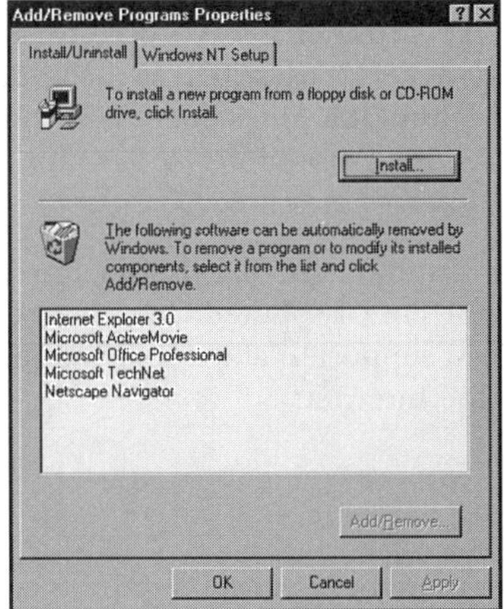

Figure 8.24

The Add/Remove Programs Properties application automates the installation process of new programs.

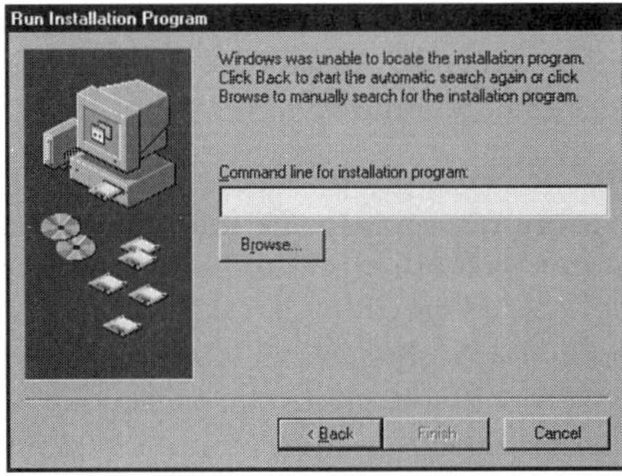

Figure 8.25

Type in the command line for the Run Installation Screen.

5. Click on the Finish button. If you are installing a program from floppy disks, the Run Installation Program prompts you for the next diskette, if needed.

Understanding Object Technologies

The idea behind object technology is that applications should be able to interact and to share data among themselves. Microsoft has developed several different component technologies. The first type of component or object programming Microsoft provided was Dynamic Data Exchange (DDE). It provided the capability for different

Windows programs to send messages to each other. DDE is typically used by two programs to give them a way to share information or for one to control the other, but it is usually considered difficult to use.

Next in Microsoft's offerings was OLE (Object Linking and Embedding). OLE is used to embed visual links between programs, such as embedding a spreadsheet into a financial report written in Word. OLE provided a less programmatic way for applications to share data and control each other. It uses DDE as the underlying mechanism for the communication and control, but OLE hides the details from the users. OLE2 was largely an extension of this that added more inter-application communication and control options.

OLE2 was later renamed COM, for Component Object Model programming. A network version is named DCOM, for the Distributed Component Object Model. Windows NT Workstation has DCOM support to allow applications to share components across a LAN or even across the Internet.

OLE

OLE is based on the concept of component integration. OLE is comprised of functional services, which themselves can be customized and extended. OLE is unique in that its services are not dependent on a particular program or application. One of the most familiar examples of using OLE is the Windows cut/copy and paste feature, which can be done between documents and applications. However, this is merely the simplest example. OLE encompasses much more.

Although OLE is fundamental to the NT application structure, it is not necessarily supported by all applications that can run on NT. The information that OLE-compatible applications need about each other is found in the Registry under HKEY_CLASSES_ROOT (see fig. 8.26). Everything in OLE format is considered an object. Each object has an object menu (right-click the object). The choices in the object menu are dependent on the object's native program. For instance, a bitmap object has certain art-relevant selections in its menu, whereas a text object has certain text-relevant selections instead.

For an illustration of OLE, you can try the following example. Perhaps you need to write a report documenting your company's employee training investment. Using Microsoft Word and Microsoft Excel, you have information in two formats. The Word document contains the description, summary, and analysis; the Excel spreadsheet contains the detailed data. You can incorporate these several ways:

- Embed the spreadsheet in the document with no remaining link to the original spreadsheet.
- Link the spreadsheet to the document so that it appears in the document.
- Link the spreadsheet to the document using an icon to represent the spreadsheet.

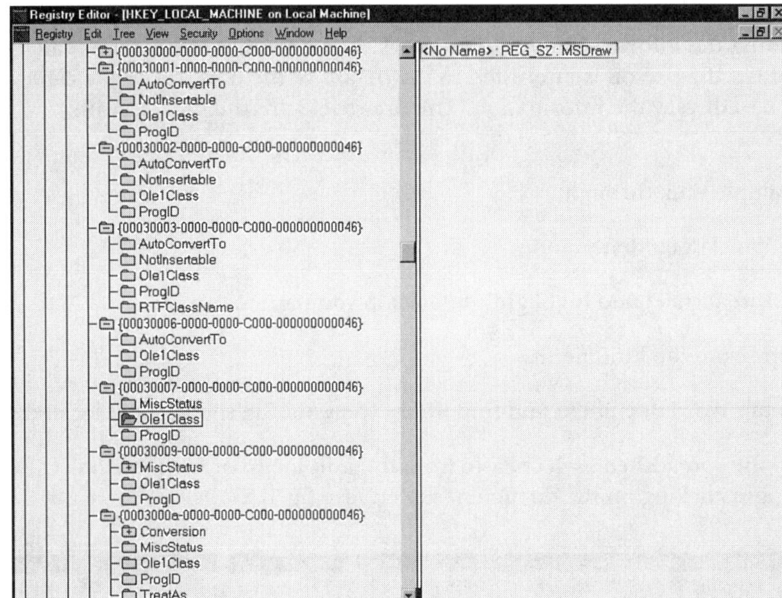

Figure 8.26

OLE information is stored in the Registry.

Linking and embedding are not supported by all applications. Applications that do not support linking do not have the Paste Special option on the Edit menu. Applications that do not support embedding generally allow the cut/paste feature. The difference between a simple cut-and-pasted item and an embedded item is the lack of the object identity. The cut item is merely a “photograph,” as it were. The embedded item is considered an object and has its identity in its native application. The object has an object menu associated with it, which can be seen by right-clicking on the object.

Embedding the spreadsheet has certain advantages. The embedded object is now a complete part of the document. If the actual Excel spreadsheet is deleted, moved, or altered, your information remains unscathed. If you want to edit the information, you can do so without affecting the original also. The disadvantages include the lack of full spreadsheet tools and functions with which to edit the embedded object. Also, if you want all updates made to the original spreadsheet to be reflected in your document, embedding is not the best choice.

Linking automatically incorporates all the updates made in the original spreadsheet because the object is linked to the original. Double-clicking on the object launches Excel with the spreadsheet information. Although the updated information is a wonderful plus, linking has several drawbacks. If the original file is deleted or renamed, your document no longer contains the information you need. Also, if you want to edit the spreadsheet, the native application (in this case, Excel) must be open.

Using an icon to represent the data in a different program can be particularly helpful if you are providing the information on the network. The document can contain all the descriptive text. If a person is interested in the details of the data, he or she can click on the icon to display the information. The drawbacks are the same as with generic linking.

Following is a sample walk-through:

1. Open the Word document.
2. Open the spreadsheet and highlight the portion you want to use.
3. Chose Copy from the Edit menu.
4. Return to the Word document and find where you want the spreadsheet located.
5. To embed the spreadsheet, select Paste from the Edit menu or from the object menu by right-clicking on the document screen (see fig. 8.27).

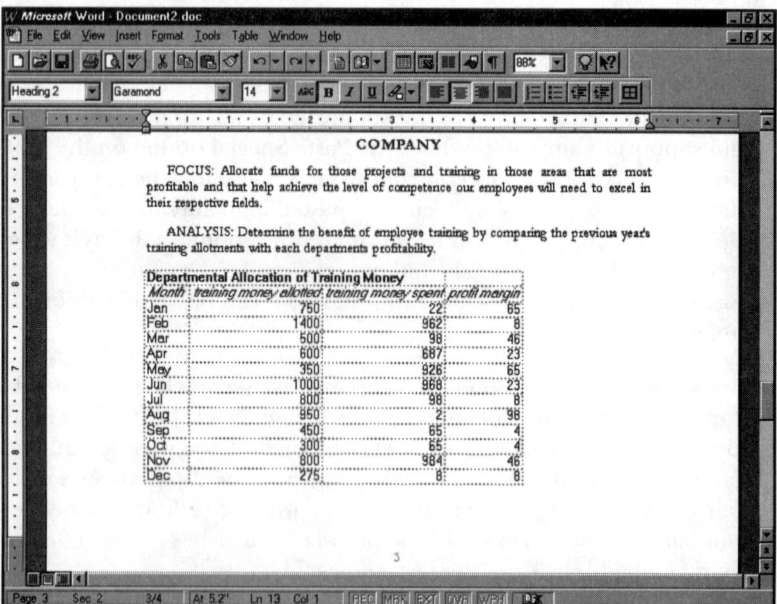

Figure 8.27

Here is an embedded Excel spreadsheet in a Word document.

6. To link the object, select Paste Special from the Edit menu. This displays the Paste Special dialog box (see fig. 8.28).

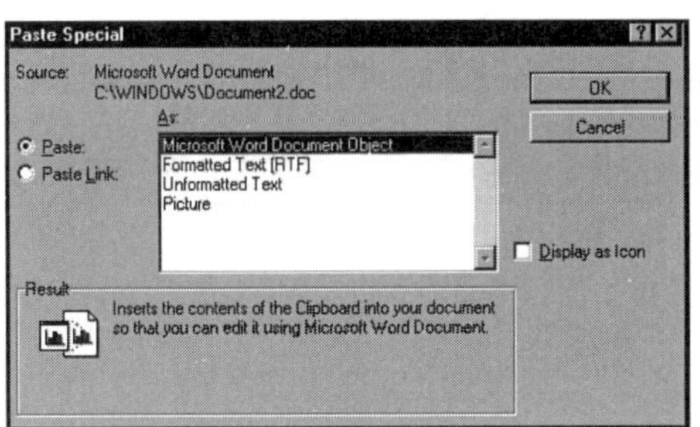

Figure 8.28

Here is the Paste Special dialog box.

7. Select Paste Link and choose the format you want the linked spreadsheet displayed in. The spreadsheet object then appears in your document, as shown in figure 8.29.

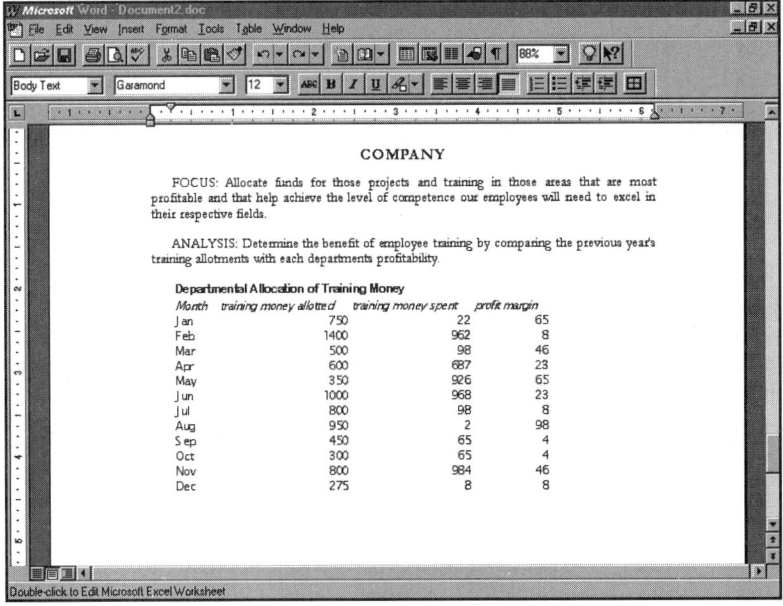

COMPANY

FOCUS: Allocate funds for those projects and training in those areas that are most profitable and that help achieve the level of competence our employees will need to excel in their respective fields.

ANALYSIS: Determine the benefit of employee training by comparing the previous year's training allotments with each departments profitability.

Departmental Allocation of Training Money

Month	*training money allotted*	*training money spent*	*profit margin*
Jan	750	22	65
Feb	1400	962	8
Mar	500	98	46
Apr	600	687	23
May	350	926	65
Jun	1000	968	23
Jul	800	98	8
Aug	950	2	98
Sep	450	65	4
Oct	300	65	4
Nov	800	984	46
Dec	275	8	8

Figure 8.29

Here is the linked Excel spreadsheet in the Word document.

8. To Link using an icon representative, select Paste Special. When the Paste Special dialog box appears, select Paste Link and then check the Display As Icon box (see fig. 8.30).

Manipulating or editing the linked or embedded information shows the versatility that OLE provides. If you want to change the information in the compound document, you can edit the original embedded document and have the updates made automatically.

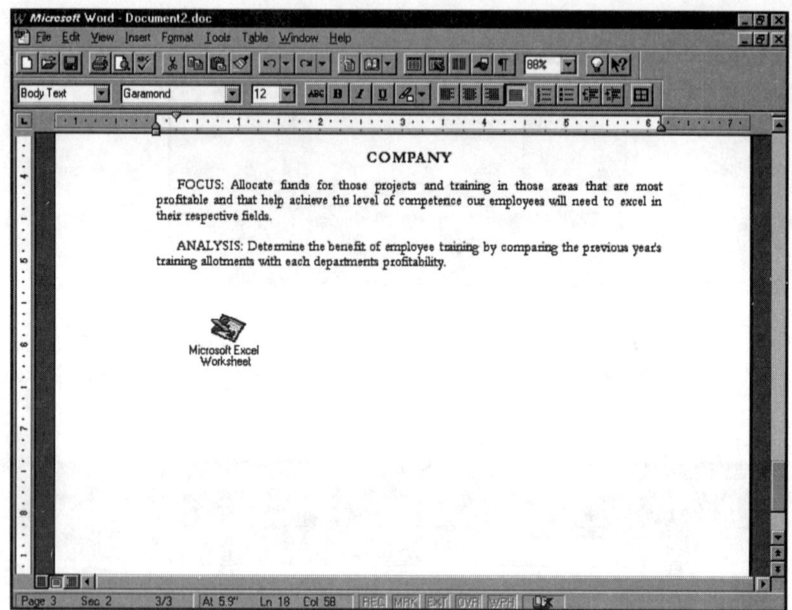

Figure 8.30
Here the Excel spreadsheet is represented by an icon.

DDE

Most users are familiar with the functionality of OLE, but are not familiar with the underlying technology. OLE depends on the Dynamic Data Exchange (DDE). You might not have many occasions to go through the steps enumerated below, but it will be helpful to understand the inner workings of the Windows operating environment, in this case, Windows NT Workstation. OLE does not support network functions, something that DDE does. To add or edit a DDE, share you must have administrator privileges.

To start the DDE, follow these steps:

1. At the RUN command type **DDESHARE**. This launches the DDESHARE.EXE program and its associated help.

2. The DDE Share window appears with two types of shares represented by a hand holding a program box. The trusted shares are represented by the check in the program box (see fig. 8.31).

3. To view the shares select DDE Shares or Trusted Shares from the Shares menu or double-click on the appropriate icon. In figure 8.32, you can see the list of shares automatically set up in Windows NT. The trusted shares list is a subset of the shares list.

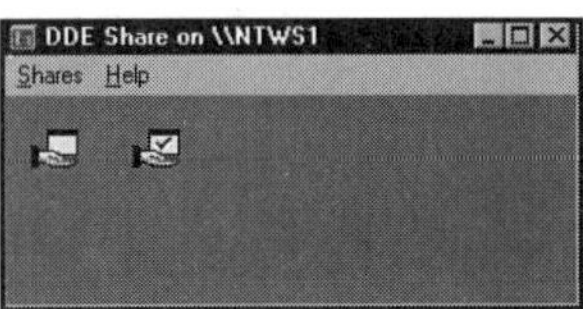

Figure 8.31

This is the DDE Share window.

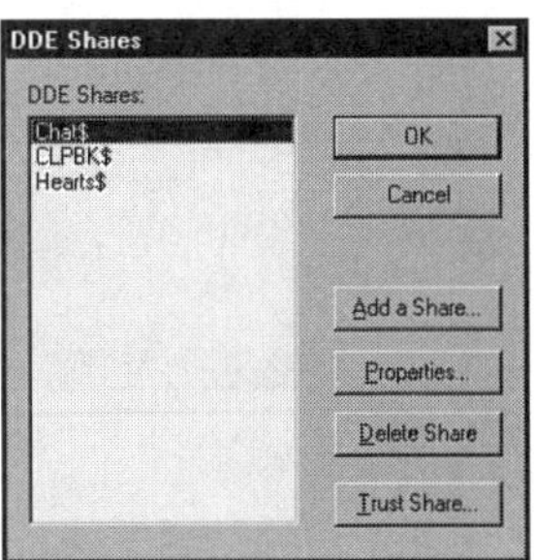

Figure 8.32

Here is a list of NT Workstation DDE shares.

4. Choose Select Computer from the Shares menu to view shares on a different computer. You see the Select Computer window displaying the computers in your domain (see fig. 8.33).

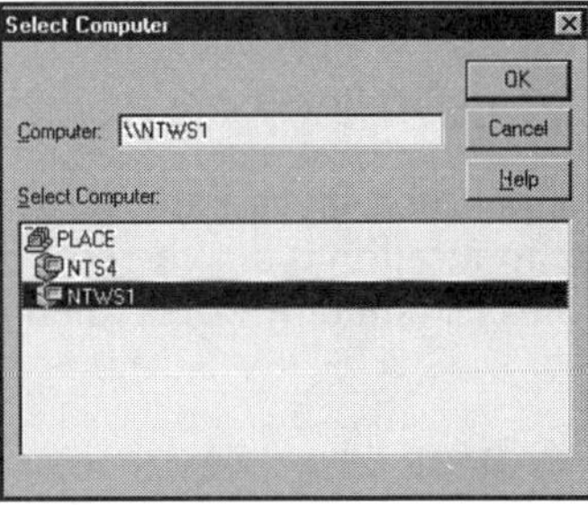

Figure 8.33

You can choose Select Computer to see shares on a remote computer.

5. Double-click on the computer you want. The DDE Shares window box title says what computer shares it is displaying.

Perform the following steps to add a share:

1. Select DDE Share from the Shares menu.

2. Click on the Add a Share button. The DDE Share Properties dialog box appears (see fig. 8.34).

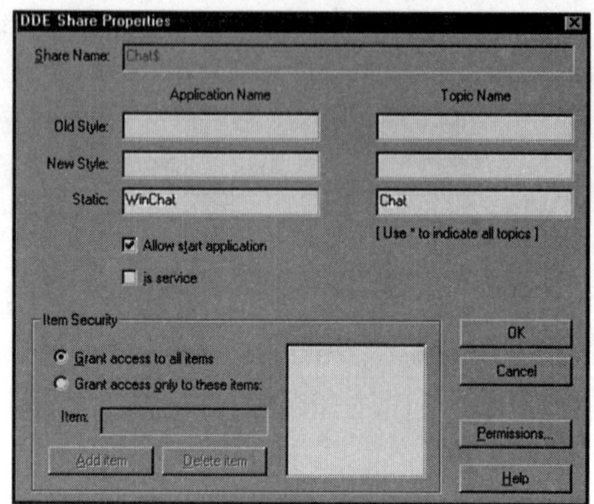

Figure 8.34

The DDE Share Properties dialog box appears when you click Add a Share.

3. Type in the name of the share.

   The three options for share naming differentiate applications or services that use static DDE links from those that use OLE. The old name style is for applications with topics having DDE extensions. The new name style is for applications with topics having OLE file extensions. Both the old and new style require that the application have NDDE_SHARE_TYPE_LINK permission. The Static name style is for applications that use static DDE links.

4. Type in the topic across from the application name.

5. Check the box for Allow start application if you want a DDE conversation to start the specified application if that application is not currently running. If you do not check this box, the DDE conversation only works when the application is already running.

6. You can specify two modes for the DDE server, service or application. Check the is service box if you want the DDE server to run as a service.

   The security of the DDE share is twofold. You can specify users or user groups who have access, and you can specify which items have access.

7. Select the Grant access only to these items if you want to limit the share access to certain components or items.

8. Click on the Permissions button to set user access limits.

9. The DDE Share Name Permissions window appears (see fig. 8.35).

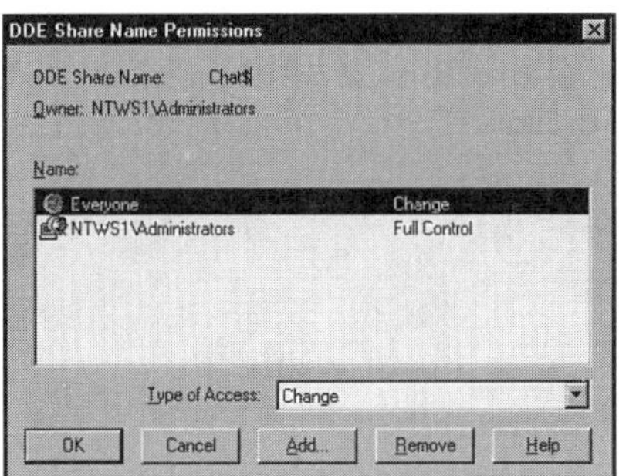

Figure 8.35

The DDE Share Name Permissions dialog box appears when you click on Permissions.

10. Click on Add to add users. The Add Users and Groups window appears (see fig. 8.36).

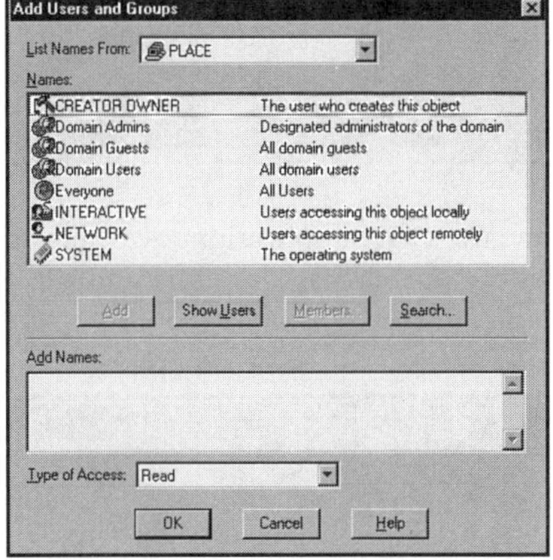

Figure 8.36

Use this dialog box to give users and groups permission to use specific DDE Shares.

11. Select Exit from the Shares menu when you have completed everything. All changes are saved automatically.

You must first create a share to make it a trusted share. If you want to see or edit the properties of any of the shares just click on the Properties button.

DCOM

To use an application or applications with DCOM, the applications must be configured. Configuring identifies such things as the application location and access permissions. You can configure 32-bit applications for DCOM. You must have an administrator equivalent account to change the DCOM settings; the settings are computer specific, not user specific. To start the DCOM configuration, perform the following steps:

1. In the RUN window type **dcomcnfg**. The program is found in the \%systemroot%\system32 directory. In figure 8.37, you see the Distributed COM Configuration Properties worksheet.

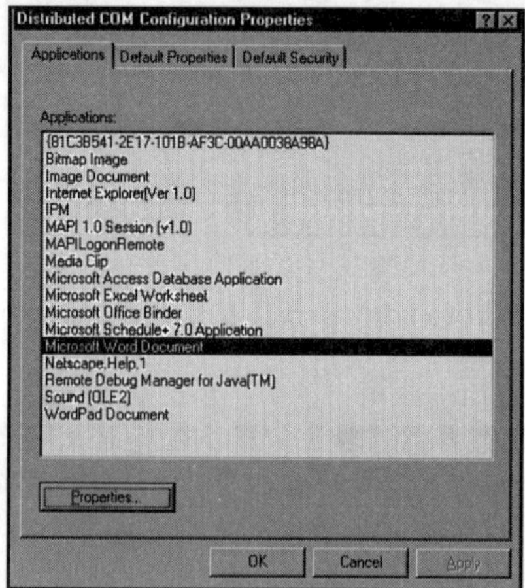

Figure 8.37

These are the applications that can be configured to use Distributed COM.

2. The Applications tab displays the COM applications available. The next tab, Default Properties, provides the property settings that apply to all the COM applications by default (see fig. 8.38).

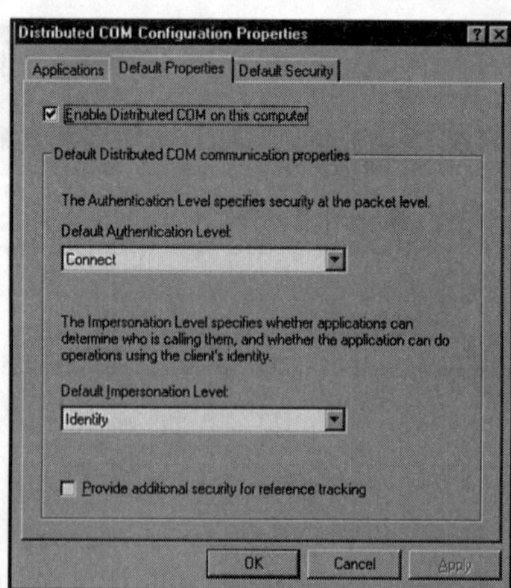

Figure 8.38

These are the default properties for COM applications.

3. If you want to disable DCOM on the particular computer you are on, clear the checkbox for Enable Distributed COM on this computer.

4. Select the Default Authentication Level from the drop-down list.

Your choices range from None to Packet Privacy. None means that there is no authentication, whereas Packet Privacy means that every single packet is verified as being from an authorized source.

5. Set the Default Impersonation Level from the drop-down list. Your choices are Anonymous, Delegate, Identity, or Impersonate.

6. If you want, check the box next to Provide additional security for reference Tracking.

7. The Default Security tab enables you to edit both the access permissions as well as the launch permissions (see fig. 8.39).

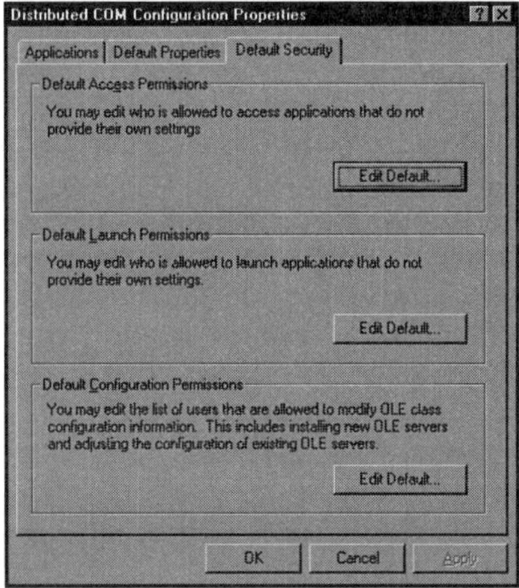

Figure 8.39

You use the Default Security dialog box for setting Access and Launch Permissions.

8. Select the Edit Default button. This launches the Registry Value Permissions window (see fig. 8.40). This is the standard permissions type form. To add users or groups, click on the Add button. Click on OK when you have finished adding users. Click on OK to close the Registry Value Permissions window.

The Registry Value Permissions window is the same as the User Manager interface. If you want to see all the users for a given computer or domain, click on the Show Users button. Only computers in your domain appear. To see who the users are in a particular group, click on the Members button. Remember that NT will not permit an individual access, even if she is a member of a group with access, if that individual is also a member of another group that is denied access. Windows NT does not override the restriction. You must do so manually if you want that individual to have permission for access or launching.

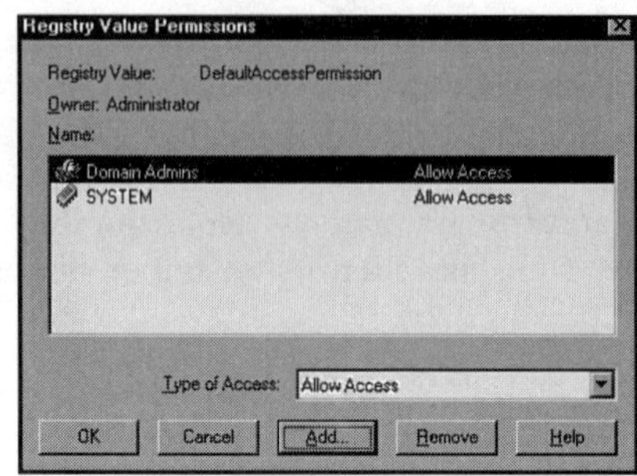

Figure 8.40

You can configure User and Access type settings.

Now that you have edited the default settings, you need to edit the settings for each DCOM application you will be using. Specifically, you need to provide the location of the server application or the user account(s) that has permission to access your server application.

1. Highlight the application you want to set its properties on the Applications tab and click on the Properties button.

2. The Properties worksheets are displayed for the particular application you highlighted. The General tab displays basic information about the application—the application type and path. If you have set the location to a remote computer, that too appears here (see fig. 8.41).

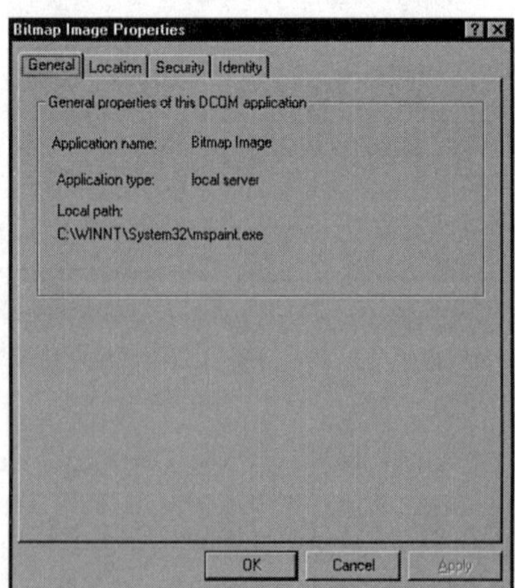

Figure 8.41

The General tab displays the name and current location of the DCOM application.

3. On the Location tab, specify where you want the application to run (see fig. 8.42).

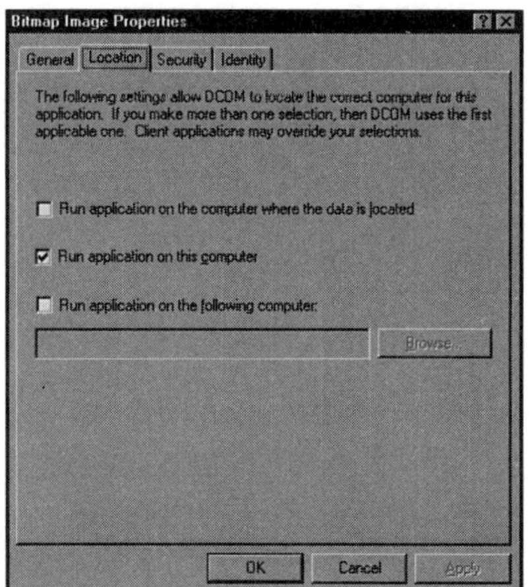

Figure 8.42

Set the DCOM application location settings.

4. You can elect to use the default security settings or set unique permissions for each application on the Security tab (see fig.4.43).

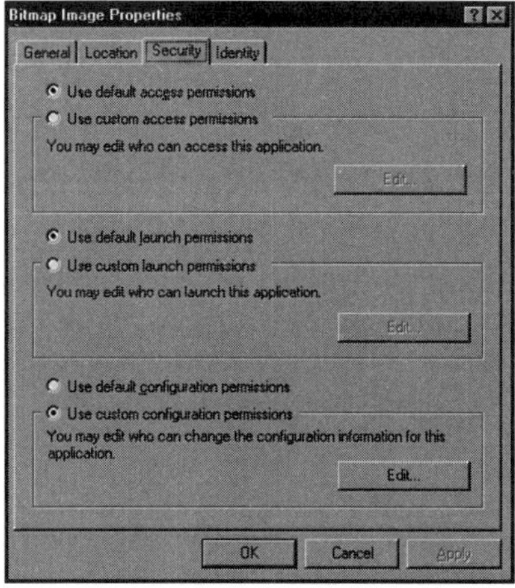

Figure 8.43

The security settings can be unique for each application.

5. Select Use custom access permissions and then select Edit to display the Registry Value Permissions window. This is the same interface as the Default Security settings.

6. Select a user account for this on the Identity tab. If the server application is a service, you can check the box for The System Account. This option allows the built-in system account to run the service (see fig. 8.44).

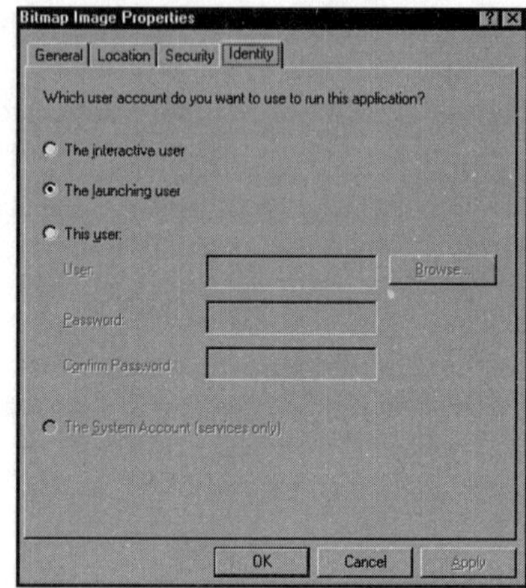

Figure 8.44

You can change the Identity settings for the application.

7. If you want to disable DCOM for a selected application, highlight the application and click the Properties button.
8. Select the Security tab and select the Use custom access permissions option.
9. Click on the Edit button. In the Registry Value Permissions, highlight the Administrator and select Deny Access in the Type of Access window.
10. Do the same thing for the System account.

Distributed COM is a powerful new model for running applications across a network, and it has many configuration options. When running applications across a network, you will often be using server-based applications, and you will find DCOM covered more thoroughly in the *Windows NT Server Professional Reference,* also published by New Riders.

Running Server-Based Applications

There are two types of server-based applications. One type is client/server applications like those in Microsoft's BackOffice. These applications have a workstation component and a server component. What really defines client/server technology is that parts of the application run on different computers to do different functions. A good example of this is Microsoft's SQL Server. The Server part of SQL Server runs on one system and takes requests from client computers anywhere on the network. The server specializes in data crunching and retrieval, whereas the clients concern themselves with ease of use and user interface issues.

The other kind of server-based applications is regular programs stored on a shared server. These make up the bulk of what is typical for file-and-print server networks. There are typically no differences between how a program works or executes when it is stored on a local drive versus when it is stored on a network drive. The program can still be run in all the same ways: from the Explorer, the Network Neighborhood, command lines, the Start menu, or applications such as the Task Manager that have a menu option to launch other programs.

Summary

Windows NT Workstation can run many different types of applications. Because Windows NT uses application support subsystems that run as native 32-bit Windows NT applications, all programs running on Windows NT can be protected from each other. The way Windows NT has implemented its application support makes it easy to run any compatible application. Indeed, it often succeeds in keeping the type of application you are running from getting in your way. You can run any type of supported application from anywhere inside Windows NT that has a launch point.

Understanding the system architecture and what happens when you run applications written for other operating systems is a fundamental part of mastering Windows NT Workstation. This chapter has given you the background you'll need to understand what is involved in installing and running applications of all kinds and has used DDE, OLE2, and DCOM to introduce you to object technologies, the basis of network-based applications.

CHAPTER 9

Printing in NT Workstation 4

The installation and configuration of printers and printing services in Windows NT seems amazingly easy, if you've installed and configured other NOS print services and print servers.

Once printers are installed and configured, and a Windows NT user wants to print a document, the steps aren't difficult. Click and print, point and print, or drag and print, and presto, there is a hard copy. Achieving that simplicity, however, takes a great deal of complicated processing by Windows NT, all performed behind the scenes.

Any Windows NT workstation that has a printer connected to it can be a print server for other connected users. The difference between using NT Workstation 4 as a print server, as opposed to using NT Server, is that you're limited to 10 connections. Otherwise, printing works the same way.

This chapter tackles printing services in Windows NT. The components and actions of the operating system's print services are explained. Once you understand what happens, when it happens, and which element of the operating system makes it happen, it is easier to know where to look in case of problems. The chapter also covers printer installation, configuration, and administration.

Understanding NT Printing

Windows NT is a protected-mode operating system with no direct access to hardware. The operating system, therefore, uses a virtual printer (sometimes called a logical printer) to control the printing features and to interact with the physical printing device.

This virtual printer is a software interface that uses Print Manager for the user interface. Sending a print job to the printer means sending it to the virtual device.

To comprehend NT printing, the following facts need to be understood:

- The icon in the Printers folder represents the virtual printer.
- Print jobs are sent to the virtual printer, not the physical printer.
- Installed printer drivers are loaded at print time and sent to the virtual printer.
- Configuration changes to the printer's properties (paper size, bins, memory, and so on) are made to the virtual printer (configuration options must match the capabilities of the physical printer).

Windows NT printing services provide quite a bit of flexibility. The operating system can support a variety of relationships between the virtual printer and the physical printer. In fact, much like a relational database, you can devise any of several relationships between a virtual printer and the physical printer:

- One-to-one
- One-to-many
- Many-to-one

In a one-to-one relationship, all print jobs are sent to a single virtual printer, which passes them to the physical printer (see fig. 9.1). Because the drivers are accessed through the virtual printer, all the correct codes are sent along with the print job.

In a one-to-many relationship, all print jobs are sent to a single virtual printer, which passes them to multiple physical printers that are attached to the computer (see fig. 9.2). This process is called *printer pooling*, and you can use it to ensure printing services in mission-critical operations, or to spread the printing load in situations where there is so much printing activity that users have to wait too long for documents to emerge from the printer.

To use printer pooling, all the physical printers have to be the same (or at least have an emulation mode that means the single printer driver loaded by the virtual printer will work). Information about installing and configuring pooled printers is found later in this chapter.

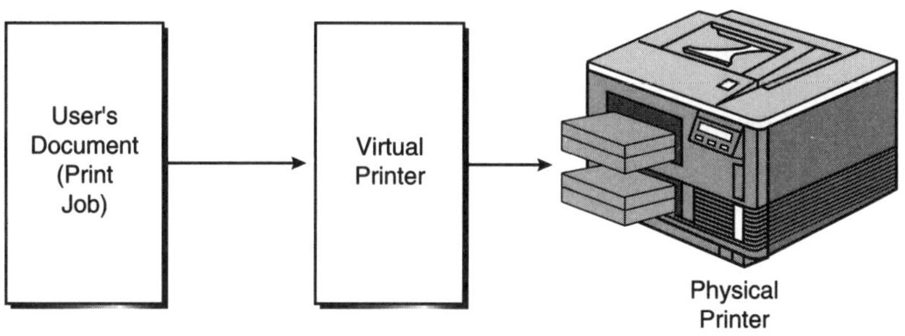

Figure 9.1

There is a one-to-one relationship between a virtual printer and the physical printer when no user configuration needs differ from the current setup of the physical printer.

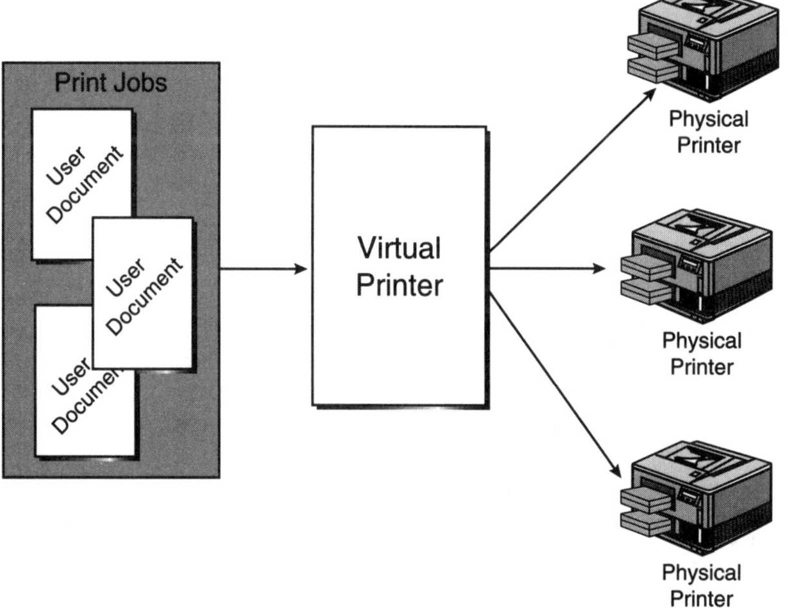

Figure 9.2

One virtual printer controls multiple physical printers.

In a many-to-one relationship, print jobs are sent to multiple virtual printers, all of which send the jobs on to the same single physical printer (see fig. 9.3). This type of relationship is useful when different users (or departments) want different features from printing services. One group of users, for example, might require banners and send their print jobs to the virtual printer configured to print them.

The user interaction with the virtual printer is easy to visualize, regardless of the relationship(s) between virtual and physical devices. When the user sends a command to print, there are a number of processes controlled by the operating system that result in the right document going to the right printer.

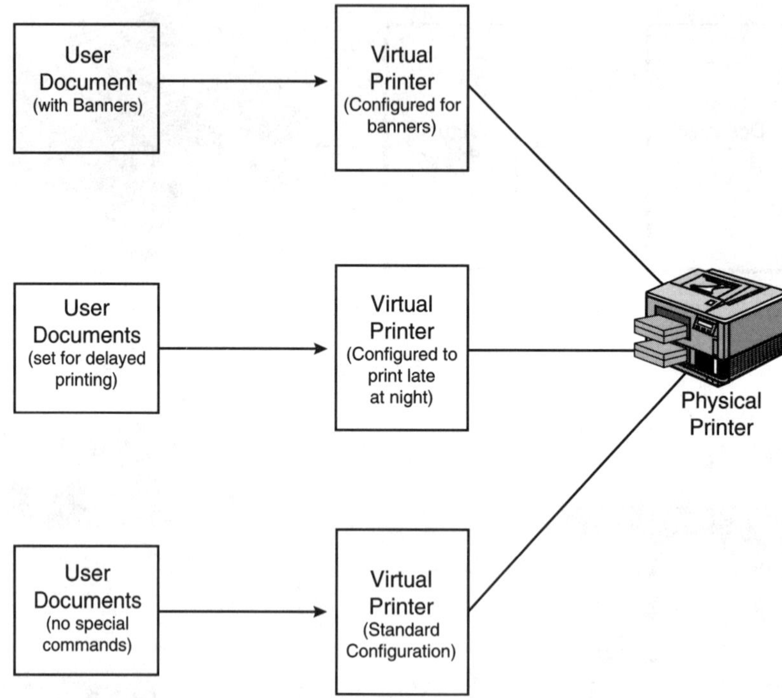

Figure 9.3
Printer jobs are sent to specific virtual printers, each of which pass the jobs to the same physical printer.

Printing Processes

Before a print job is actually sent to the printer, the NT operating system performs a number of processes. What follows is a brief overview of these processes.

Note The section following this overview defines and explores the specific terms and processes that are addressed in the overview.

Remember that what is happening is an application has sent a document to the printer. In fact, the application thinks it has sent the document to the printer port and the printer, but Windows NT has grabbed it and is now in control of the processes. The following sections outline the steps the operating system performs.

Load the Printer Driver

The printer driver is loaded into memory. This makes all of the printer-specific codes and instruction sets available to the processes that are performed.

Many Windows applications actually load the printer driver into memory upon launching. The information in the printer driver provides the WYSIWYG interface.

Create an Output File

The application that is sending the print job generates an output file. This file contains instructions (called Device Driver Interface calls) it sends to the printer driver. The output file is referred to as a DDI Journal File.

The application uses the Windows NT Graphics Device Interface (GDI) to generate the output file. The graphics engine (GDI32.DLL) translates the GDI commands into the DDI commands that can be read by the print processors and the printer drivers. The GDI also manages the screen output, giving the user a WYSIWYG interface.

Process the Output File

The output file is passed to the spooler, which examines the data type and then passes the print job to the print processor, along with information about the data type it found. The print processor creates the print data format that is expected by the physical printer.

The spooler that receives the output file is local, regardless of whether or not the client computer has a local printer or sends the job to a remote printer.

Route the Print Job

The operating system's router accepts the job from the client computer, checks the location of the physical printer, and sends the processed job to the spooler located on the server computer (which is the same as the client computer for workstations with attached printers).

Send the Print Job

The spooler on the print server hands the print job off to the operating system's print monitor. The monitor checks the destination port, and if it is free, sends the print job. (If the port is not free, the monitor holds the job in the queue on the spooler until the port is free.)

Understanding the Components

Windows NT provides all these printing services through a number of components and processes. This section discusses the components in the operating system that make everything previously described happen.

The Spooler

The spooler is software—a group of DLLs that take care of the chores needed when a document is sent to the printer. These chores include the following:

- Tracking the printer ports associated with each printer.
- Tracking the configuration of the physical printer, such as memory, trays, and other elements.
- Assigning priorities to the print jobs in the queue.
- Sending the print job through a series of software processes that depend upon the type of job, the type of data, and the location of the physical printer.
- Sending the job to the physical printer.

The spooler receives the print job, stores the job on disk, and then passes the job through the print processes and on to the printer. As soon as the print job is stored on disk, the user can go back to work in the sending application. All of the print processing is done in the background.

By default, the directory used for spooling is \winnt\system32\spool\printers (assuming the Windows NT directory is named winnt).

You can change the location of the print spooler if you have another drive. This is useful if the drive that contains the default spooler is short on free space; when there is a lot of printing activity, the queue can take up quite a bit of space.

To move the spooler, you have to change its path in the Registry. The Registry key is:

HKEY_LOCAL_MACHINE\SYSTEM\CurrentControlSet\Control\Print\Printers

Change the path of the DefaultSpoolDirectory data item. You must reboot in order to have the change take effect.

If the spooler resides on an NTFS partition, you have to make sure that everyone has write permissions for the spool directory.

You can also change the spooler location for one specific printer, leaving all other printers in the default location. Use the same Registry key, and find the key for the printer you want to change. Add a new SpoolDirectory setting and enter the value, using the new path to the spooler for this printer.

The spooler is implemented as a Windows NT 4 service and can be found in the Services icon of the Control Panel. It has a startup configuration of automatic (meaning the service is started during the operating system startup) and can be stopped and restarted from the Services icon. You can also stop and start the spooler from the command line using the commands net stop spooler and net start spooler.

Spool Files

The spooler directory holds the *spool* files. (The list of files is called the *queue*.) If the print server is shut down before all the spooled jobs are printed, when the print server is started again, the printing restarts.

For each spooled job, there are actually two files written to the spooler directory:

- **The spool file.** This file is actually the print job. It has an SPL extension.
- **The shadow file.** This file contains the administrative information needed to print the job (the target printer, the job's priority, the name of the sending user, and so on). This file has an extension of SHD.

The Queue

The list of print job files in the spool directory waiting to be sent to the physical printer is called the *queue*.

NT Queues are Different!

If you've been using OS/2 or NetWare 3.x, you're probably noticing a difference in the definition of the word "queue" when used in Windows NT. The queue used by these other network operating systems is the primary software interface between the application programs and the physical printer. The queue's relationship to the printer is a one-to-one concept. In OS/2, for instance, when a user sends a print job to a printer, the job is intercepted by the OS/2 spooler, which holds the job in a queue (which you can think of as an alias for a printer since the queue is linked to a single printer). In effect, the print job is submitted to the queue for handling. The spooler and the queue are a merged concept. The printer driver, the spooler, and the queue do not individually manipulate the print job, the job is grabbed, held, and shipped to the physical printer by one entity.

NetWare 3.x (and NetWare 4.x if you choose to use a queue instead of a virtual printer—you have your choice) operates in much the same manner as OS/2 (except setting up the queue and the print server requires more work).

The Printer Driver

Printer drivers translate the data and codes in the print job document to the form needed by the printer. The operating system uses the printer driver for three specific tasks, and in fact, breaks down the functions of the printer driver into three distinct parts. The three individual component parts, each of which is a set of files, are the following:

- Graphics Drivers
- Printer Interface Drivers
- Characterization Data Files

Each of these components plays a specific role in print processing.

Graphics Drivers

The imaging functions (rendering of graphic images) are implemented by Windows NT as a DLL. The Print Graphics Driver DLL provides the API calls that are used as a graphics device interface during the building of the DDI journal file. The graphics driver also converts the DDI commands into commands that printers can accept.

These files are stored in \system32\spool\drivers\w32x86 under your Windows NT directory. Specifically, they are the following:

- **RASDD.DLL.** Handles raster printers (including PCL) and dot matrix printers.
- **PSCRIPT.DLL.** Handles PostScript printers.

Printer Interface Drivers

The printer interface drivers are linked to the configuration options available to the user (the options that are configured through Print Manager). They are used to provide the options that a user can choose when configuring a printer.

Stored in \system32\spool\drivers\w32x86 under your Windows NT directory, the drivers are the following:

- **RASDUI.DLL.** For raster printers.
- **PSCRPTUI.DLL.** For PostScript printers.

Characterization Data Files

Characterization data files are really configuration files for the physical printer, and they contain the information provided by printer manufacturers for the development of Windows NT printer drivers.

For raster printers, these files are called minidrivers and are implemented as DLLs. They are source-code compatible across platforms and processors.

For PostScript printers, they are PPD (PostScript Printer Description) files, which are text files provided by the printer manufacturer. They are binary-compatible across platforms and processors.

There are other files in the \system32\spool\drivers\w32x86 subdirectory under your Windows NT directory that should be identified here.

A help file (RASDDUI.HLP or PSCRPTUI.HLP) provides the help information (the What's This? feature) for the device settings in the printer's Properties dialog box.

The subdirectory also contains the printer driver files for installed printers.

The Print Processor

The print processor (WINPRINT.DLL, which is in the system32\spool\prtprocs\w32x86 subdirectory under your Windows NT directory) does the rendering of the print job after it receives the file from the spooler. *Rendering* means translating all the data in the print job into data that is understood and accepted by the printer.

Actually, before passing the job, the spooler checks for the data type and if rendering is necessary, it passes that message on to the print processor along with the print job.

The question of whether or not the job needs processing is dependent upon the data type sent by the client application.

During the configuration of a printer, the default data type option is RAW and it would be unusual to change that. The default data type, however, is only used if the client application fails to specify a data type for the print job. Most applications that are written for Windows NT 4 send print jobs with NT EMF as the data type and the print processor can pass the job to the printer with full confidence that the printer can understand and handle the print job.

You can find the configuration for data type in the printer's Properties dialog box (right-click the printer icon and choose Properties). Choose Print Processor on the General tab of the dialog box to see the Print Processor selected for the printer (see fig. 9.4).

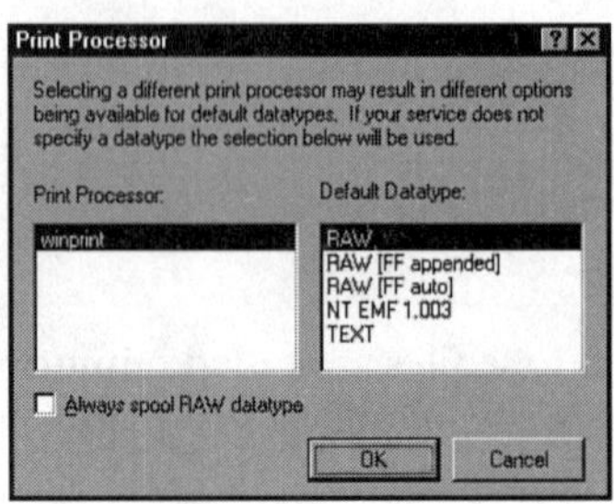

Figure 9.4

The print processor and the default data type are displayed in the configuration options for a printer.

These data types are handled by the print processor in the following manner:

- **RAW.** This data type indicates that the job has been rendered and is ready for the printer. The print processor takes no action.
- **RAW [FF appended].** Indicates that the client has sent a document with no graphics, but the print processor checks to see whether or not there is a form feed at the end of the job (so the last page ejects).
- **RAW [FF auto].** Indicates the same as RAW [FF appended], but there is definitely no form feed at the end of the job and the print processor adds the form feed command.
- **TEXT.** Indicates that the job is simple text and is usually applied to print jobs that are being sent to PostScript printers or plotters (which don't accept text as a valid data type). The print processor uses the printer driver to render the job into printer commands that are acceptable to the target printer.
- **NT EMF.** EMF (enhanced metafiles) is the default data type chosen by most applications written for Windows NT 4. EMF information is generated by the GDI before spooling, then the spooler delivers the print job to the queue in the background. EMF files are typically smaller than RAW data type files. More importantly, they are portable and can be translated to meet the expectations of any printer.

When the print processor completes its work, it passes the print job back to the spooler, which places the job into the queue.

Macintosh Print Processor

There are two print processors available with Windows NT 4—WINPRINT.DLL for Windows and SFMPSPRT.DLL for Macintosh. The latter is installed only if you installed Macintosh services on an NT Server (the Macintosh DLL and printing services are handled through NT Server).

> When a Mac sends the print job to the server, the DLL examines the target printer and then applies the appropriate services. If the printer is PostScript, the processor assigns RAW as the data type. If the target is not PostScript, PSCRIPT1 is assigned as the data type, and the processor turns the PostScript code into pages made up of bitmap images that imitate the way the job would look if it were printed by a PostScript printer. Those images are sent to the Windows NT graphics engine, which produces the bitmapped product for the printer.
>
> Incidentally, along the way, the Mac client spools the document to the NT Server computer, freeing up the client workstation for other tasks.
>
> There's a raster image processor (RIP) that's built into the Mac processor to make all of this happen when Mac clients send jobs to non-PostScript printers. However, there's a limitation in this scenario that makes Mac users (who tend to be extremely fussy about graphics and output—and some believe they have every right to be) a trifle annoyed. The impediment is a 300 dpi limit on resolution, regardless of the capabilities of the physical printer. Almost as annoying to Mac users, is the fact that the RIP output is limited to monochrome, even if the printer supports color. The best way to handle Mac clients is to have PostScript printers (color would be nice).

In addition to the print processor that is built into Windows NT 4, you can add third-party print processors to your Windows NT system. These processors are made available by software companies that ship applications which produce data requiring special handling in order to be understood by the printer.

The Print Router

The print router accepts requests from clients and determines the spooler component that should be used to fulfill the request. The print router works between the client and the print server (which might be on the same computer, of course).

The print router is implemented with WINSPOOL.DRV in the \system32\ subdirectory of the Windows NT directory.

The first task of the print router is to find the printer to which the print job wants to print. When the printer is found, the router looks at the printer driver attached to it and compares it to the printer driver on the client computer (if there is one). If there is no printer driver on the client, or if the date of the client's printer driver is earlier than the date of the driver on the server, the driver is sent to the client.

Once the client has the appropriate driver and has not received any error messages from the router (such as printer not found), the job can be processed on the client.

The processed print job is sent to the print router, which sends the print job to the spooler on the computer that has the printer. If the client has no printer, the print router copies the job from the client spooler to the server spooler.

The Print Monitors

A Print Monitor is the component that controls the port, as well as the communication between the port and the spooler. It sends the jobs to the ports.

The print monitor performs the following tasks:

- Accesses the port (sends the job to the port).
- Releases access to the port at the end of a job.
- Sends notification to the spooler when a job has finished printing (the spooler deletes the job from the queue).
- Monitors the printer for error messages.

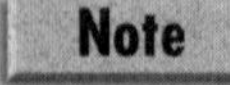

When the print monitor sees an error message from the printer, it notifies the spooler. Usually the spooler sends the job again. If the error is preventing printing, an error message is displayed at the client.

There are several print monitors supplied with Windows NT 4.

Local Print Monitor

The local print monitor (LOCALMON.DLL in the \system32 subdirectory of the Windows NT directory) controls the local ports. The following port assignments for printers are considered local (any printer can be configured to print to any port in this list):

- Parallel
- Serial
- File (the print monitor prompts for a file name when this port is used)
- Explicit file names (each job sent to a specific file name overwrites the last job sent to that file name)
- UNC designation for a shared printer
- NUL

The NUL port is generally used for testing network printing. Set a printer to use the NUL port and pause it. Then send a job to that printer from a connected client. You should be able to see the job in Print Manager (open the printer object). If you don't see the job, check the setup. If you do see the job, resume printing, which really does nothing because jobs sent to an NUL port just disappear. Instead of paper, documents print to thin air as they travel to lost document heaven.

In addition to the local monitor, several other ports can be used in Windows NT 4, and monitors can be installed for each of them. These are covered in the next sections.

Digital Print Monitor

The Digital print monitor (DECMON.DLL) controls any Digital Network Ports you select in order to use Digital Equipment Corporation PrintServer devices, or a DEC printer such as the DEColorwriter.

The port selection is available in the Windows NT 4 list of available printer ports, but you must get the DECnet protocol from Digital.

HP Print Monitor

The Hewlett Packard monitor (HPMON.DLL) controls HP devices such as printer-installed network adapters and JetDirect adapters. Many of HP's JetDirect devices are able to use various network protocols, but this monitor requires the DLC (Data Link Control) protocol. DLC only needs to be running on the print server. To load DLC, perform the following tasks:

1. Open the Network icon in Control Panel and go to the Protocols tab.
2. Choose DLC.
3. Enter the path to your NT 4 CD.
4. After the files are transferred, choose Close.
5. Reboot to put the settings into effect.

There are a couple of limitations in the way the HP monitor works, depending upon your configuration. You have two choices for configuring an HP monitor:

- **Job-based connection.** The print server connects, prints, and disconnects.
- **Continuous connection.** The print server connects permanently and sends jobs as they are received by the server.

Choosing the latter means that no other print server can get to that device, so if you are accessing an HP port from multiple print servers be sure to configure the port as job-based. If only one print server connects to the port, choosing continuous connection provides security and auditing.

DLC cannot be routed, although it can be bridged. If a Windows NT print server is on a physical subnet and the JetDirect device is on a different subnet, the server can talk to the device if there's a bridge. No jobs can be sent if the subnets are connected via a router.

DLC is nifty because it can be bound to more than one network adapter in the same computer (incidentally, DLC works with token ring and ethernet). The HP monitor software, however, doesn't match this capacity. Therefore, you have to make sure that multiple JetDirect printers are all on the same physical subnet.

Incidentally, DLC is also used for connecting to an IBM mainframe, and in fact is probably used more frequently for that than for attaching to printers that are directly attached to networks.

Lexmark Print Monitors

Windows NT has two Lexmark printer ports available for your configuration needs:

- **Lexmark DLC monitor (LEXMON.DLL).** Controls any Lexmark DLC network ports.
- **The Lexmark TCP/IP monitor (LEXLMPM.DLL).** Controls any Lexmark TCP/IP network port.

If you have Lexmark printing devices that can use the capabilities of the Lexmark ports, you should have received the print monitor software.

Macintosh Print Monitor

The Macintosh monitor (SFMMON.DLL) controls printing over AppleTalk protocols. You can install it in any NT Workstation in order to send print jobs, but only NT Server can receive the print jobs. The installation steps are quite simple:

1. Open the Network icon in Control Panel.
2. Click on the Protocol tab.
3. Choose Add.
4. Select AppleTalk and click on OK.
5. Enter the drive and path to your Windows NT 4 files on the original media.

6. After the files are copied to your drive, choose Close.

7. A dialog box asks you to select a default adapter and AppleTalk Zone (a simple decision for most because the norm is one NIC and one zone). Choose OK when you have selected the defaults.

8. The bindings are reviewed and stored. You must shut down in order to have the new protocol take effect.

LPR Print Monitors

LPR is a part of the protocols developed with and for TCP/IP. It began as a service for Unix printing (it actually started with Berkeley Unix, which only some of us who are aging remember). Today, LPR still works for many Unix clients. The biggest exception is System V Unix systems, unless they have been configured specifically to work with this protocol.

LPR protocols permit client applications to send print jobs directly to a print spooler on another computer. The client side of this is named LPR and the host side is named LPD.

Windows NT 4 supports LPR with an executable file named LPR.EXE, which is stored in the \system32 subdirectory of your windows directory after the service is installed. The service, when launched, supplies a print monitor (LPRMON.DLL).

On the server side, Windows NT 4 provides LPD services through LPDSVC.DLL. Lpdsvc can support any print format, but does not have any processing power. The client application must send the format expected by the printer.

A printer and port for LPR-compatible printing has to be installed and the LPR clients have to know the network address of the print server and the name of the print device. The Unix computer uses the Unix lpr utility to send the print job to the NT queue.

On the client side, the Lprmon service permits NT clients to print to a printer connected to a Unix computer.

While it is possible to use LPR/LPD for printing between computers running Windows NT, it's not the norm for a network environment.

To use these services and the client monitor, you must install Microsoft TCP/IP Printing. To do so, perform the following steps:

1. Open the Network icon in Control Panel and click on the Services tab.

2. Choose Add.

3. When the Select Network Service dialog box opens (see fig. 9.5), choose Microsoft TCP/IP printing.

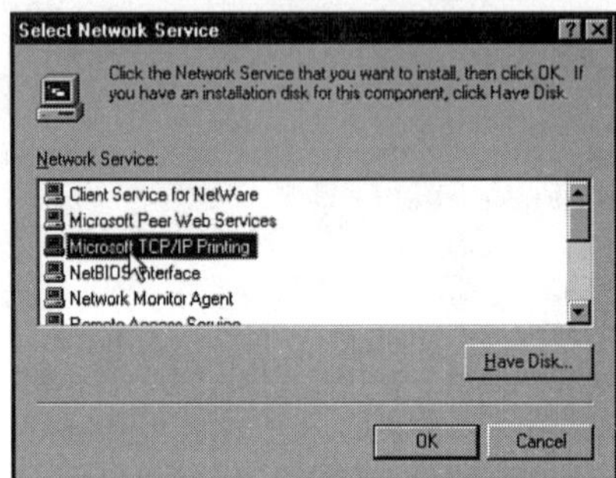

Figure 9.5

You have to add Microsoft TCP/IP Printing services to add LPR printing services.

4. Enter the path to the Windows NT 4 distribution media (usually D:\i386, where D is the drive letter for your CD-ROM).

When the files are copied, choose Close, then restart your computer so that the new service can take effect.

After the service is installed, you can install an LPR-compatible printer on the NT workstation that will be the designated print server for LPR services. This really means you're installing an LPR-compatible port.

1. Open the Printers folder and open Add Printer.
2. Choose My Computer and click Next.
3. When the Available ports list displays, choose Add Port.
4. Double-click LPR Port (if the choice isn't available, go back and install the TCP/IP printing service as described previously).
5. When the Add LPR compatible printer dialog box displays (see fig. 9.6), enter the required information:
    - ◆ In the top text box (Name or address of server providing lpd:), enter the DNS name or the IP address of the host for this printer.
    - ◆ In the bottom text box (Name of printer or print queue on that server:), enter the printer's name. Use the name used by the host (either the connected printer or the Unix computer).
6. Continue the installation following the instructions in the section "Installing Printers," found a little later in this chapter.

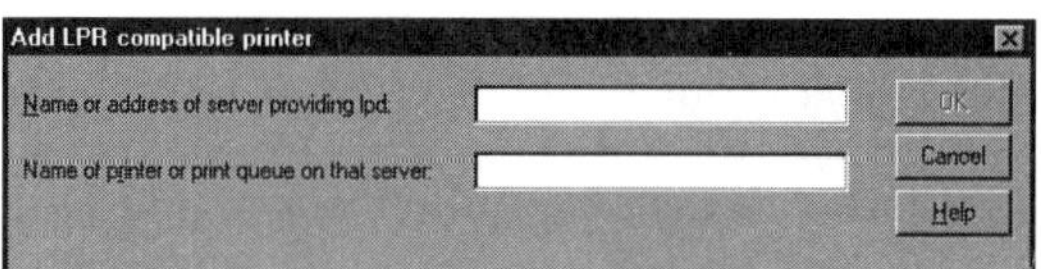

Figure 9.6

The host computer and the printer have to be named specifically for LPR printing.

The Print Providers

The print providers send the job to the print device, using the configuration options for that print device. In effect it implements the choices you make in the Properties dialog box for the printer. For example, if you've opted to print spooled jobs as soon as the spooling begins, it sends the job to the printer immediately, instead of waiting for the entire job to be received. The options available for configuring printers are discussed later in this chapter.

There are two print providers—local and remote.

Local Print Provider

The local print provider (LOCALSPL.DLL in the \system32 subdirectory of the Windows directory) sends print jobs to the locally attached printer. To do so, it performs the following tasks:

- When the job is received (from a local application or a remote user) it writes the job to disk as a spool file. It also writes the Shadow file.
- If there is a configuration option for separator pages, it processes them.
- It checks to see which print processor is needed for the job's data type and passes the job to that print processor. (When the print processor is finished doing its modifications, if any are needed, it passes the job back).
- It checks the port for the target printer and then passes the job to the print monitor for that port.

Remote Print Provider

Remote print providers are employed when a Windows NT 4 computer sends print jobs to another print server. This can be because the computer has no printers attached, or because the computer is a print server that is forwarding certain print jobs to another print server.

There are two remote print providers available in Windows NT Workstation 4 (both found in the \system32 subdirectory of your Windows NT directory):

- **WIN32SPL.DLL.** Moves jobs to Windows print servers.
- **NWPROVAU.DLL.** Moves jobs to Novell NetWare print servers.

Windows Remote Print Provider

If the target printer is on a print server running Windows NT, the Windows remote print provider makes remote procedure calls (RPCs) to the print router of the remote print server. When the route receives the print job it processes it.

If the target printer is on a print server running another Windows operating system, the Windows remote print provider contacts the Windows Network redirector, which sends the job across the network to the appropriate print server. That server takes over the responsibility of printing the job.

Note The Windows redirector is a component of the Windows Network APIs. It lets client computers have access to resources on other computers as if those accesses were local. Communication is accomplished with the protocol stack to which it is bound (usually NetBIOS or WINSOCK).

NetWare Remote Print Provider

The NetWare print provider takes control of a print job when the router polls print providers with a server name that is recognized as a NetWare print server. The NetWare print provider turns the job over to the NetWare redirector, which passes the job to the print server.

Installing Printers

The installation of printers (really printer drivers) in Windows NT 4 is a snap. You can install a local printer or a printer on another, connected computer through the Add Printer wizard. You must have the administrator rights to add a printer.

Installing a Local Printer

To add a printer that's connected to your computer, perform the following tasks:

1. Open the Add Printer icon in the Printers folder, and choose My Computer from the first wizard page. Then choose Next.

2. Select the port this printer is connected to and choose Next.

3. Choose a manufacturer from the list displayed in the Manufacturers list box, then choose the model from the choices in the Printers list box (see fig. 9.7).

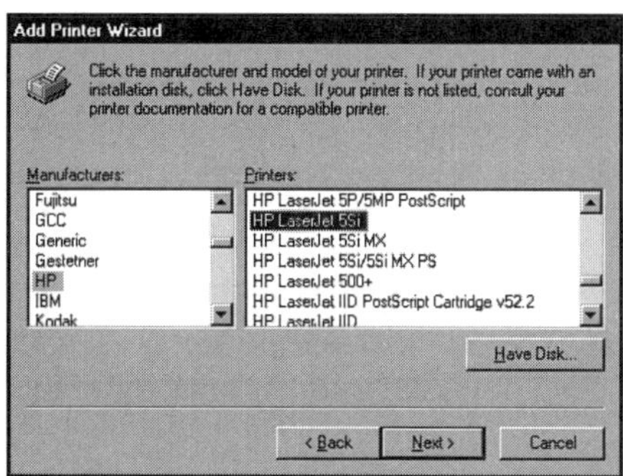

Figure 9.7

Choose the manufacturer and model of your printer.

Note If your printer is not listed you'll need a driver from the manufacturer. Make sure the driver you receive is written for Windows NT 4. Drivers written for previous versions of NT do not work in NT 4. Choose Have Disk in the Add Printer Wizard dialog box.

4. Choose Next to move to the next wizard page, where you name the printer and indicate whether or not you want this printer to be the default printer for Windows applications.

5. The next wizard page is where you indicate whether or not this printer is going to be shared with other computers on the network. If you choose Not shared, you're basically finished with the installation. For this exercise, we'll choose to share the printer by selecting Shared.

6. Enter a name for the Share. Then select the operating systems for all the computers that have access to this printer. Choose Next when you have finished.

7. The last page of the wizard asks if you want to print a test page to check the installation, once all the files have been copied to the drive. There's no reason not to, so select Yes and press Finish.

The drivers are copied to the computer (You'll probably have to enter the path for the Windows NT CD; for some reason NT 4 does not remember the source drive for the original media and always assumes drive A.)

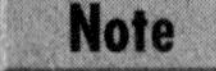

If you're sharing this printer, when you enter the Share name be sure the name is specific enough to identify it to all users who access it. I usually find it works to use a name that identifies both the location and the printer model, such as AcctHPII for the HP LaserJet Series II in the Accounting department or ExecutiveSI for the HP 5si in the executive offices.

The ability to install drivers for other Microsoft operating systems as you configure a printer for sharing is unique to Windows NT. It means that when other users install this printer on their client computers, they don't have to load drivers for the printer since they are copied to the client when needed.

One distinct advantage is that it makes it unnecessary for users on client computers to have a copy of the CD (or disks) of the original operating system files available. Finding original media is a constant problem in most companies.

Setting Up Permissions

When you establish a local printer as a shared resource, you also have to set up the permissions for users who access the printer.

From the printer's Properties dialog box (right-click on the printer object and choose Properties), choose the Security tab. Then choose Permissions. The Printer Permissions dialog box displays a list of current users with their respective permissions (see fig. 9.8).

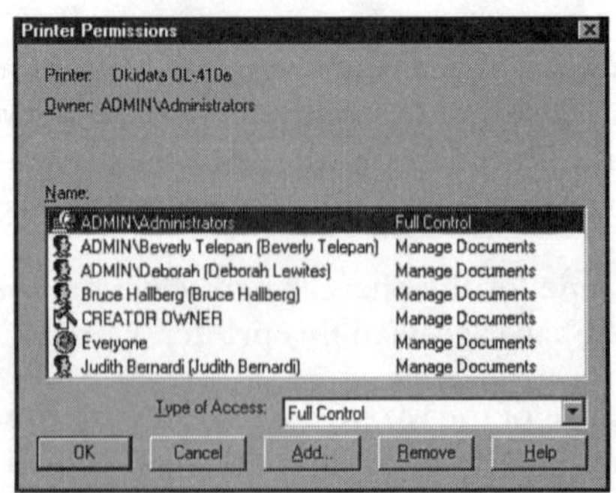

Figure 9.8
Permissions are manipulated through the Printer Permissions dialog box.

In figure 9.8, some of the names are preceded by \ADMIN. This indicates they are users on the local computer (which is named ADMIN). The other names have been added from the domain user list. This process is explained later in this section.

Granting permissions is a two-step process. First you must add the user (or group), then give the specific permissions. You can also select an existing user and change the permissions.

To add a user or group, choose Add from the dialog box. The Add Users and Groups dialog box appears, showing a list of groups (see fig. 9.9).

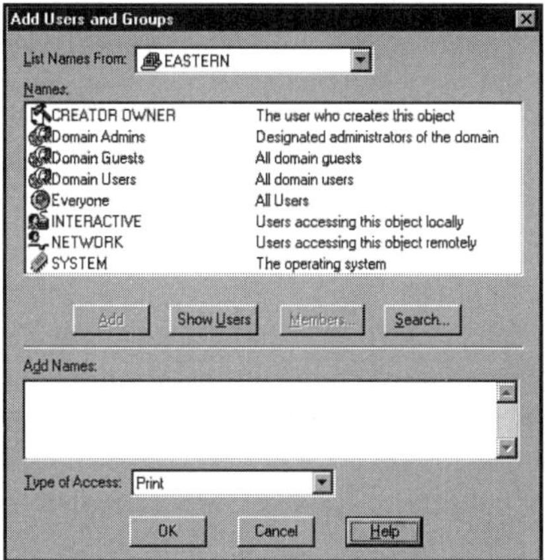

Figure 9.9

You can view groups or users from domains and computers.

The listing in the Names box changes, depending upon the way you want to view them. (For example, in figure 9.9, the groups that are listed are a reflection of the domain to which this computer logs on.) You can see a different listing by choosing another domain, the local computer, or an attached computer.

To see users as well as groups, choose Show Users. To see the users who are members of a group, select the group and choose Members. Remember that these lists change as you change their source in the List Names From box.

Move through the list and select the groups and users you want to give permission to use or manage this printer. The quickest way to select one is to double-click the name, which adds that name to the Add Names box. (Multiple names are separated by semicolons.)

There are two approaches to assigning permissions:

- You can select only those names (or only a single name) you want to give a specific permission level and assign that permission level by choosing a Type of Access. Then select the group of names for a different permission level and repeat the process.

- You can select all the names you want, for whom you plan varying permission levels, and add them all. Then, when you return to the Printer Permissions dialog box you can select each name and give it a permission level.

Either way, you can always change any permissions by selecting the name and changing the Type of Access in the Printer Permissions dialog box.

The permissions, which are referred to as Type of Access, are as follows:

- **Full Control.** All management permissions. Change priorities, pause and resume the printer, change printer properties, delete the printer, change the permissions.
- **Manage Documents.** Control document settings. Delete, pause, resume print jobs.
- **Print.** Print documents.
- **No Access.** Cannot use this printer.

The permissions are cumulative, of course. The Creator Owner by default has an access of Manage Documents. This means that when a user is the creator and owner of a document, for that print job the access level of Creator Owner is inherited. This is important, so don't delete or change the Creator Owner name in the Printer Permissions dialog box (and for obvious reasons, don't delete the administrator).

Installing a Remote Printer

To install a printer that's connected to a Windows print server, you have two options:

- Use the Add Printer wizard as described in the preceding section, "Installing a Local Printer," to indicate that the printer being installed is a network printer rather than a local printer.
- Find the printer share in Network Neighborhood or Explorer, right-click it and choose Install.

If the print server is running Windows NT 4, you won't have to install any drivers and the printer just shows up in your Printers folder.

If the print server is running another operating system, you have to install suitable drivers for it on the client computer. The operating system notifies you that the print server does not have a Windows NT 4 driver for this printer and offers to transfer one. Make sure the Windows NT 4 CD is in its drive and follow the instructions found therein to copy the driver.

At the conclusion of the installation, a test page is printed.

Troubleshooting When the Test Page Fails

The operating system displays a dialog box when the test document is sent to the printer. The dialog box asks if the test page printed correctly. If you respond Yes, all is well and you are finished with the installation of the printer.

If the test page fails to print, or prints garbage characters, you must troubleshoot the installation. Troubleshooting starts by selecting No on the dialog box that asks if the test page printed correctly.

The printer troubleshooter (see fig. 9.10) is part of the Windows NT 4 help system, and it's a step-by-step checklist for many of the problems that could cause the failure to print properly.

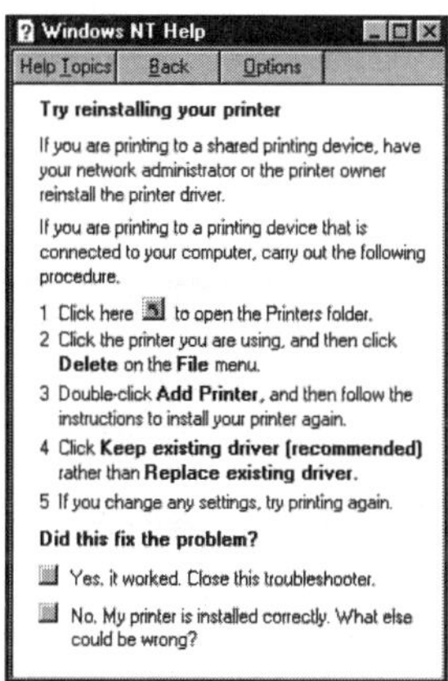

Figure 9.10

Windows help troubleshoots printer installations that failed by asking questions and making suggestions.

The troubleshooter makes a suggestion, then asks if the recommendation worked. Answering in the affirmative completes the troubleshooting process. Answering No brings up additional suggestions. Every time you tell the troubleshooter that the recommended action didn't work, another suggestion appears, sometimes several on the same page.

Many of the troubleshooter suggestions contain a Click here arrow that brings up the appropriate dialog box to implement the suggestion.

Eventually, if following every suggestion still results in failure, the troubleshooter admits defeat and advises you to get some expert help.

Note

The most common failure in printer installation is the lack of a third-party driver that is written correctly for Windows NT 4. Drivers from previous versions of NT don't work in NT 4. Nag your manufacturer for a properly written driver if you have a printer that's not listed in the NT 4 HCL (Hardware Compatibility List).

Configuring the Print Server

You can set properties for the print server by opening the Printers folder and choosing Server Properties from the File menu. The properties you set for the server are those that are not printer dependent and are the defaults for all printers on this server.

Server Forms

When you open the Print Server Properties dialog box, the Forms tab is in the foreground (see fig. 9.11).

Figure 9.11

Set or create the forms that can be used on this print server.

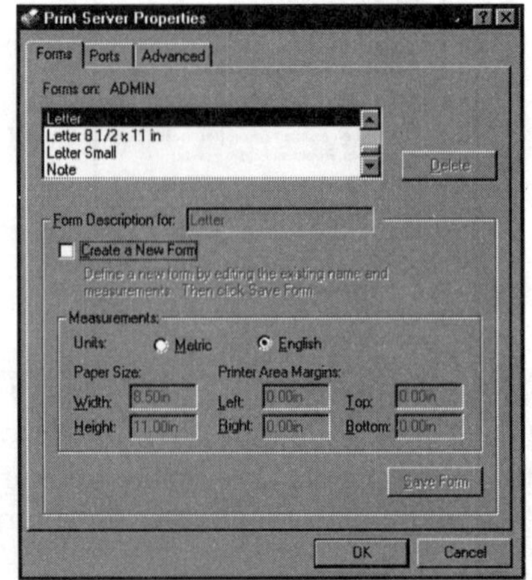

Windows NT has always dealt with paper sizes and formats a bit differently than Windows 3.x or even Windows 95, and NT 4 follows this pattern. The difference is that NT bases configuration for this item on forms rather than trays. A form is, by definition, a paper of a particular size.

Forms give administrators a way to let users choose a form without having to worry about which tray is holding which size form. Today, with most companies operating on networks with print servers, the printer is frequently not in sight and the user can't lean over and see that the top tray is holding letter-sized paper and the bottom tray is holding legal-sized paper. In fact, the user cannot see how many trays are in the printer.

When a user chooses to print to legal paper, he or she merely picks the form. The printer's configuration (covered in the next section) matches the form to the tray that holds it, which of course has to be set up by an administrator.

Windows applications are capable of presenting different forms to the user and when a selection is made that is other than the default, the spooler checks the printer's configuration options and includes the codes for the appropriate tray when the document is sent to the printer.

You can create a new form in this tab of the dialog box by selecting Create a New Form and then changing the measurements to match your creation. Give the form a name and it is available to all the printers on this print server (as long as they can physically handle the form).

Server Ports

Move to the Ports tab (see fig. 9.12) to view and manipulate the ports that are available on this print server.

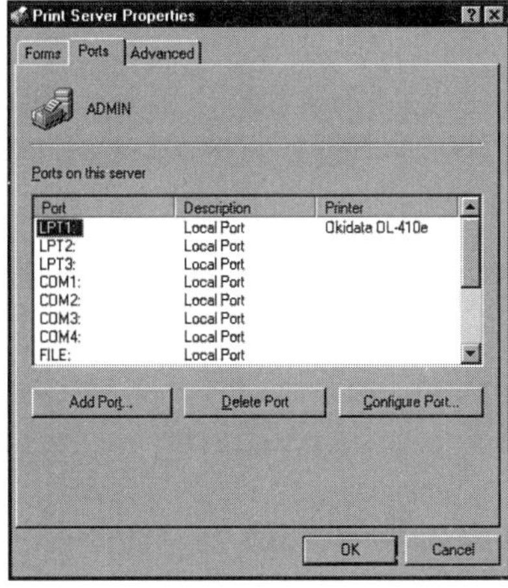

Figure 9.12

The ports to which printers can be connected are listed in the Ports list box.

You can take the following actions:

- Choose Add to add vendor-specific ports and port monitors.
- Choose Delete to remove a port you no longer are using.
- Choose Configure Port to change the time-out transmission retry period for a parallel port, or set serial port settings (the same settings available through the Port applet in Control Panel).

Server Spooler Options

Move to the Advanced tab (see fig. 9.13) to set options for the spooler on this print server.

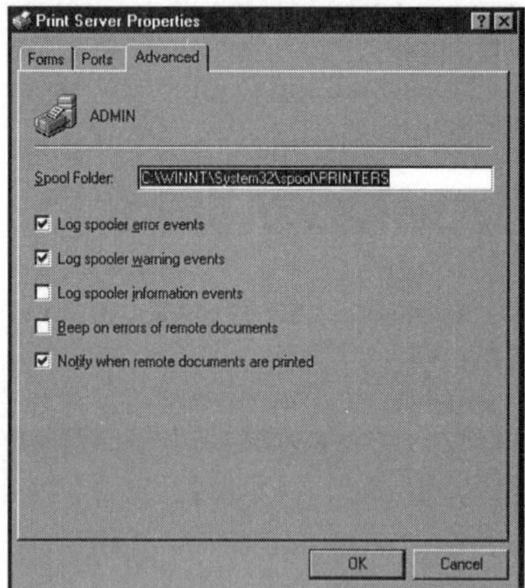

Figure 9.13

Configure the way the print server's spooler works with the Advanced tab.

The configurable items on this dialog box are self explanatory. I suggest, however, that you think about deselecting the default option of notifying users when remote documents are printed. I've found this to be an annoying pop-up, I always assume the print job went to the printer, and I don't like having to click on OK to clear the informational dialog box.

Configuring Printers

The configuration options available for printers vary from printer to printer. Dot matrix printers tend to have fewer options than lasers, color printers have more options than monochrome, PostScript printers have unique options, etc.

This section covers the configuration options available from two of the items in the printer's shortcut menu—Document Defaults and Properties. We'll go through the dialog boxes for both of these configuration options.

Document Defaults

To view or change the defaults for forms, right-click the printer object and choose Document Defaults. The Page Setup tab of the Default Document Properties dialog box appears (see fig. 9.14).

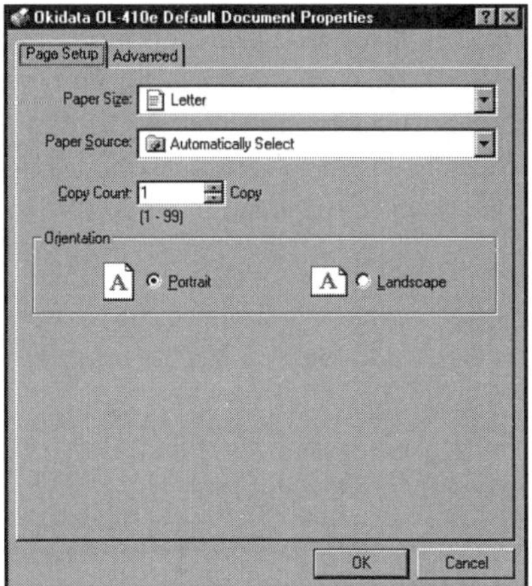

Figure 9.14

Set the form defaults for printing to this printer with the Page Setup options.

Most of the time it is letter forms that are the default. For Paper Source, you should leave the choice at Automatically Select and then match up the forms and trays in the printer's Properties (covered next).

If this printer is used for special forms, define them and make them the default. You can change the default form by clicking the arrow to the right of the Paper Size box and choosing a new form, or by moving to the Advanced tab of this dialog box (see fig. 9.15).

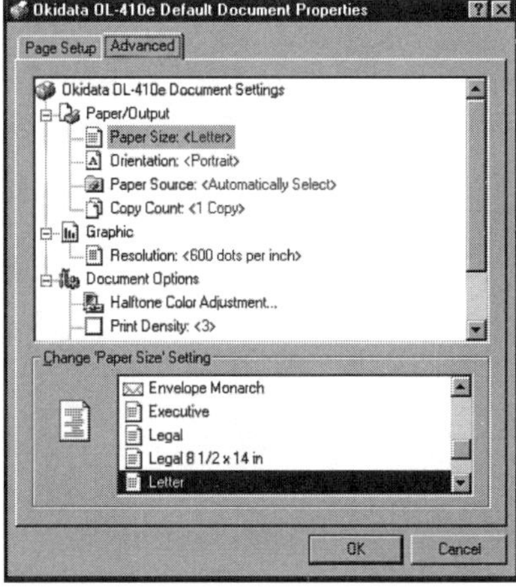

Figure 9.15

The Advanced tab offers more choices for default settings for a printer.

In the Advanced tab, you can configure the printer resolution and a variety of document options. These configuration choices vary from printer to printer. Select an option to see the choices for that option on the bottom of the dialog box.

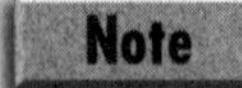

In many companies, especially if there are plenty of printers available, there are printers used for rough drafts of documents and internal correspondence. Other printers are used for finished documents and external correspondence. This evens out the printer traffic significantly. Printers that are established for internal printing can be set for lower resolution, which speeds printing up and saves toner. You can even use cheaper paper.

Printer Properties

The configuration of properties for a printer is accomplished through the printer's Properties dialog box which is accessed by right-clicking the printer object and choosing Properties.

The Properties dialog box for a printer has six tabs and the information for most of the tabs is identical. It is the Device Settings tab that varies from printer to printer.

The following sections discuss the Properties dialog box, exploring each tab.

General Tab

The General tab of a printer's Properties dialog box (see fig. 9.16) offers a number of options for configuration.

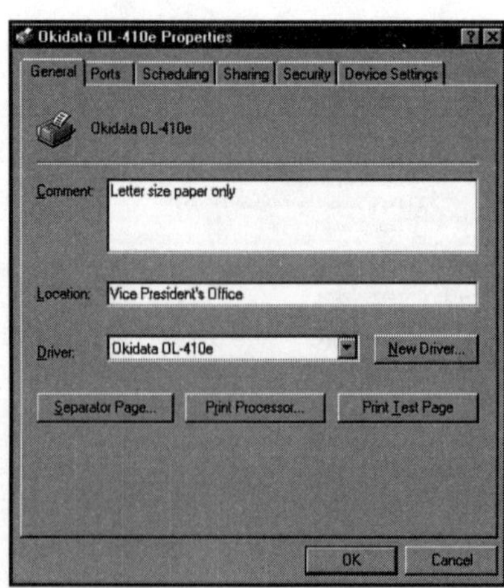

Figure 9.16

There are plenty of configuration options you can set from the General tab of the printer's Properties dialog box.

The following sections outline these options.

Descriptions

You can use the Comment and Location fields for internal information. The comment that displays about a shared resource when you view it in Explorer or Network Neighborhood is not taken from this comment field—it is from the comment field on the Sharing tab.

Drivers

Choose New Driver to install a new or updated driver for this printer. This driver could be a new one from the manufacturer, or an updated version for Windows NT 4 from Microsoft.

Separator Pages (a.k.a. Banners)

In Windows NT 4, enabling separator pages requires a bit of work, as opposed to other network operating systems, which have a boolean approach to them and just send pre-set pages.

Separator pages are sent to the printer at the beginning of each print job and they print in front of the first page. They do not have any effect on the numbering or pagination of the print job they precede.

They are also called *banners* (especially by those of us who spent many years with NetWare), header pages, or burst pages. They're used to identify the print job that is printing behind them—usually to name the user who sent the job.

When multiple users access the same printer, eventually they all mosey down the hall to get their printouts. Users have a habit of grabbing sheets of paper as they come out of the printer, glancing at them, and tossing them back into the printer tray if they belong to someone else. By that time, of course, the next page has ejected (or several more pages have ejected) and the print job is totally out of order, infuriating the print job owner who has to collate the pages.

In some companies, documents are removed from the printer's output tray and placed in a container near the printer. As users examine these pages, looking for their own print jobs, the papers in the container can become incredibly mixed up.

With separator pages enabled, users can find their print jobs easily, and they don't have to read each page to see when the job ends—they just look for the next separator page.

Note As handy as they are, there are circumstances under which separator pages are more annoying than they are useful. If a printer is accessed by users who send one page documents most of the time, the separator pages become a pain rather than a convenience. Every other page is tossed in the waste basket, which means we're cutting down forests for nothing and the cleaning staff has to work twice as hard.

To enable separator pages:

1. Choose Separator Page to display the Separator Page dialog box (see fig. 9.17).

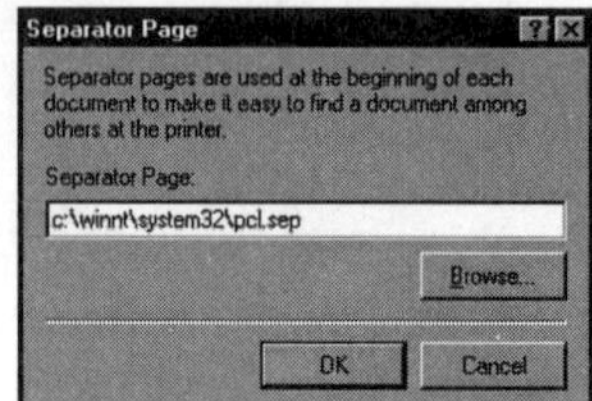

Figure 9.17

Choose a separator page to notify users about the owner of each print job.

2. Enter the name of the separator file you want to use, choosing one of the following files (which are found in the \system32 subdirectory under your Windows NT directory):

   - **PCL.SEP.** Switches a dual-language HP printer to PCL printing.
   - **SYSPRINT.SEP.** Used for Postscript printers.
   - **PSCRIPT.SEP.** Switches dual-language HP printer to PostScript printing.

3. Click on OK when you have selected the separator file. Then click on OK to close the Properties dialog box.

The separator file itself is not printed, it is a series of instructions that is printed by the local print provider, which has an interpreter for the codes contained in the separator file.

By default, the separator page prints the user name, the date, and the job number. You can edit the separator file or create one of your own and specify it in the dialog box. If you want to create one, it's best to copy an existing one and then modify it to suit your needs.

For example, here is PCL.SEP:

```
\
\H1B\L%-12345X@PJL ENTER LANGUAGE=PCL
\H1B\L&l1T\0
\H34
\B\S\N\4
\I\4
\U\D\4
\E
```

Each of the lines is an escape code. Table 9.1 shows the functions for each escape code you can use in a separator file.

TABLE 9.1
Escape Codes and Functions for Separator Files

Escape Code	Function
\N	The name of the user submitting the job
\I	The job number
\T	Time the job was printed (follows the format set by the user in the International applet in Control Panel)
\L*xxx*	Prints characters (*xxx*) following the escape code
\Fpath	Prints the contents of the file specified in the path
\H*nn*	Sets a printer-specific control sequence where *nn* is a hex code sent to the printer (and changes depending on the printer)
\Wnn	Sets the width of the separator page (characters beyond the width are truncated)
\B\S	Prints text in single-width block characters, continues to print until \U is encountered
\E	Ejects a page
\n	the number of lines to skip (a zero moves to the next line)
\B\M	Prints text in double-width block characters, continues to print until \U is encountered
\U	Turns off block character printing

Sometimes the escape codes are preceded by @ instead of the backslash.

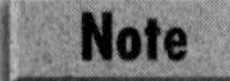

If the printer is located on a Windows 95 computer, the separator page configuration must be done at that computer. It doesn't matter what your permissions are for that printer, you cannot establish separator pages from a connected computer. What can fool you is that if you attempt to configure a separator page from a Windows NT 4 machine onto a Windows 95-connected printer, everything will go smoothly during the configuration, you will not see any error messages. Separator pages, however, will never print.

Ports Tab

The Ports tab (see fig. 9.18) is where you change, configure, and manipulate the use of the ports.

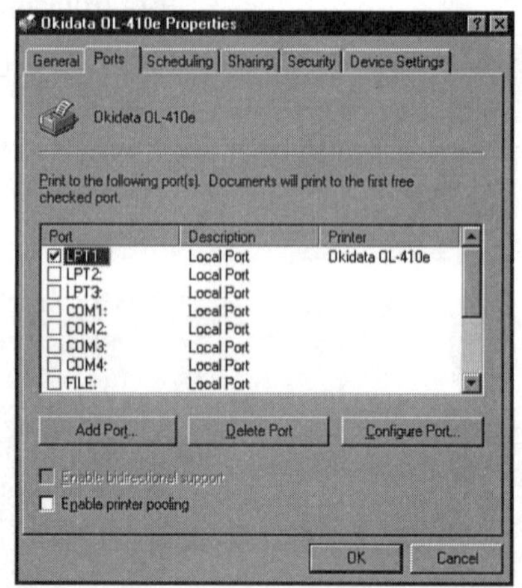

Figure 9.18

All the available ports are displayed (scroll through the list to see connected ports if they exist).

The port is established when you install the printer, and you would only want to change it if you moved the printer's connection to a different port. Notice that ports can be physical ports (for locally connected printers) or the Share of a connected computer (using the UNC).

Bidirectional Support

If the printer is connected to a port capable of bidirectional communication, you can enable bidirectional support. This means you can get detailed messages from the physical printer.

In order to have bidirectional communication, you need the following components:

- A port capable of, and configured for, bidirectional communication.
- A printer capable of bidirectional communication.
- A bidirectional cable (look for "1284" on the cable's packaging or directly on the cable). This means it matches IEEE 1284 specifications for bidirectional communication.

What bidirectional communication brings to your printing processes is the ability to receive messages from the printer without asking a question first. Without it, the operating system probes the printer (for example, to see if it is on or ready) and then awaits an answer. With bidirectional communication the printer spontaneously sends messages whenever an event seems to warrant it. For instance, the printer might let the operating system know it's out of paper, or there's a paper jam.

Printer Pooling

The other item of interest in the Ports tab is the ability to enable printer pooling.

This is a handy feature for high-volume or mission-critical printing. A *printing pool* is two (or more) printers connected to the same computer. The printers must be identical or be able to emulate the same printer (that is, they must accept the same codes, instructions, and so on). When you enable pooling, you select multiple ports, one for each of the physical printers. If a printer breaks, dies, eats the paper, spills its toner, or otherwise is incapable of completing a print job, you can restart the print job and another printer takes over.

To restart the job on the next available printer, right-click the original printer's icon and choose Properties. Then, on the Ports tab, change the port to the one that is occupied by the other printer.

Restarting, of course, means start again and is not the same as resume; the print job isn't picked up where the now-defunct printer left off.

Scheduling Tab

A shared printer can be scheduled for use through the Scheduling tab of the printer's Properties dialog box (see fig. 9.19). But there are other configuration options available on this tab besides scheduling the printer's time.

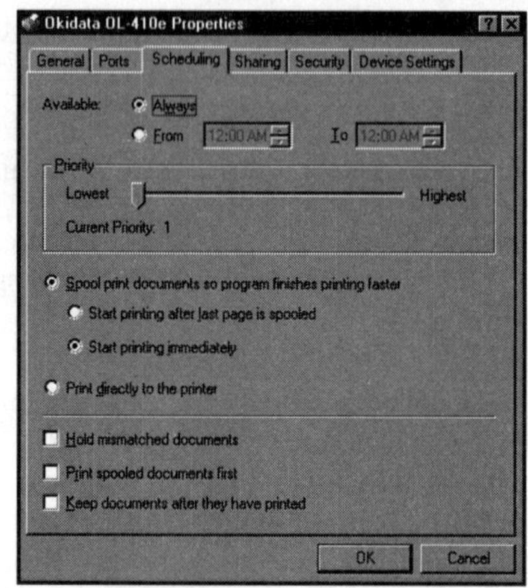

Figure 9.19

The Scheduling tab does more than schedule the printer's use, offering several other configuration options.

Set Available Times

The printer can be set as always available or it can be made available only for a specific period of time. For the latter, choose From and To times to create the period of availability. This is useful if a printer is part of a pooled printer setup and you want to use it during heavy periods of use.

Set Default Priorities for Documents

You can set a default priority level for each document that is sent to the printer. It's best to set the default priority to low, which makes it easier to move a document to a higher priority level if you need it in a rush. (As you move the slider arrow, you're really moving from 1 to 99).

Set Spooling Options

You can choose to start printing after last page is spooled, or you can print immediately after the document has begun to arrive at the spooler directory.

Opting for the former means the spooler does not begin processing the file until it has received the entire file (the application sends an end-of-file marker to indicate the entire file has been sent). The latter choice means the spooler begins sending pages through the printing process as they are received.

Waiting for the last page to spool before starting print processing means that there is a delay before the document emerges from the printer. It ensures, however, that the whole document prints, and that nothing is wrong with the document. This is actually a choice between speed and safety and you should pick the one that matches your needs.

Print Directly to the Printer

The option to Print directly to the printer means you bypass the spooler and move the file directly from the application software to the printer. This is not really a very good option, because the spooler keeps documents intact, separating multiple documents from each other. This option should only be used if there is some sort of problem with the spooler that you don't have time to fix because you need this document, or if you are sure there are no other print jobs for this printer and you need instant printing.

Hold Mismatched Documents

Selecting to hold mismatched documents forces the spooler to match the printer codes in the document against the printer setup. For instance, if the printer codes for your document call for an envelope and the printer setup shows no envelope tray, the spooler holds the job in the queue.

Other jobs that are not mismatched move ahead of the mismatched job and print normally. Eventually you can insert the tray in the printer, and change the setup to reflect the tray, and print the job. Or you can go back into the application and change the document to get rid of the mismatched setup.

Print Spooled Documents First

Selecting print spooled documents first tells the spooler to treat documents that have completed the spooling process with a higher priority than documents that are still in the process of spooling. While this generally makes the printing process more efficient, there is a small drawback when a document that is spooling is more important to you than the document that has finished the spooling process.

If all documents are in the process of spooling, the printing is performed by printing the largest document first, then the next largest, and so on.

If you don't enable the option, the spooler looks at document priority before sending print jobs to the printer.

Keep Documents after They Have Printed

Telling the spooler to keep documents after they have been printed means you can print the job again right from the queue instead of resending it from software. This is rarely useful, and it certainly uses disk space, so do not choose this option without good reason. If you enable this option, you'll have to remove print jobs from the spooler manually.

When you have configured the options you want to use on the Scheduling tab, click on OK to close the Properties dialog box.

Sharing Tab

The configuration for sharing the printer was set during installation. You can use this tab to install additional alternate drivers for computers that are not running Windows NT 4, if they were not included during installation.

Security Tab

You can limit the access to any printer, and keep an eye on the usage of a printer by setting options in the Security tab. The security tab has three sections:

- Permissions
- Auditing
- Ownership

Permissions

You established permissions during the installation of a shared printer, you can return here to add, remove, or modify the permissions of users.

Auditing

Windows NT 4 provides the ability to audit printing events on a printer-by-printer basis. You can track printing operations, and administrative events.

Doing this is a two-step process. First, you have to enable auditing in your Windows NT Workstation setup. Then you enable auditing of the printer(s). The printer's audit log becomes part of the Security log file of the computer's Event Viewer.

To enable auditing in Windows NT Workstation perform the following steps:

1. Go to the User Manager in Administrative Tools.
2. Choose Policies, Audit from the menu bar to see the Audit Policy dialog box. Select Audit These Events to make the event list available.
3. Select File and Object Access. Then choose whether you want to audit Success, Failure, or both.

Once system auditing is turned on, you can establish auditing for each printer you want to track:

1. On the Security Tab of the printer's Properties dialog box, choose Auditing to see the Printer Auditing dialog box (see fig. 9.20).

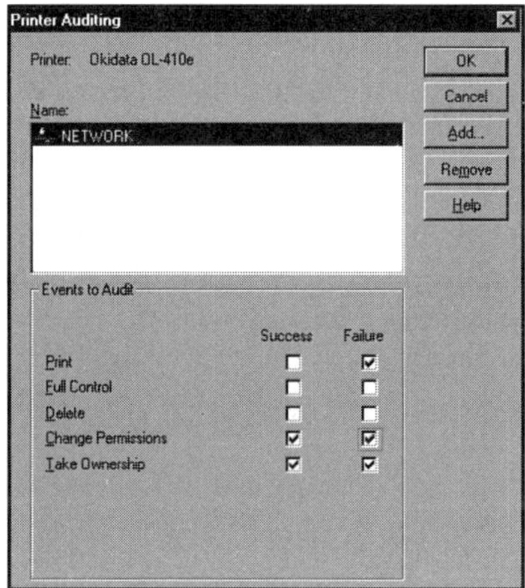

Figure 9.20

Choose the users and events you want to track.

2. Choose Add to specify the groups and users you want to audit. From the Add Users and Groups dialog box, select the users you want to audit by double-clicking the entry. As you select groups and users, they're added to the Add Names box. Click on OK when you finish.

3. In the Printer Auditing dialog box, select the events you want to audit, indicating whether you want to track Success, Failure, or both

4. Click on OK to close the Auditing dialog box. Then click on OK again to close the Properties dialog box.

Now the Security log lists the events you've chosen to track. To see the log, go to the Event Viewer and look at the Security log. Double-click an event to see the audit details.

There might be a reason you need to know about every successful access of a printer, but that is not the norm. Event Viewer logs have a maximum size (which you can set in the Event Viewer) and you should choose auditing configuration options with that in mind. When the maximum size is reached, older events are deleted to make room for the newest event.

Remember that every process described earlier in this chapter accesses the virtual printer during the printing task. If you choose to audit Everyone, you are including the system, and you are going to have a very large log.

Ownership

To change permissions on a printer, you have to take ownership. Choosing Ownership on the Security tab displays the Owner dialog box, which states the current owner and offers the option to Take Ownership.

Choose Take Ownership if you are not the current owner and you want to manipulate the printer's security options. Any user who has been given Full Control permissions can take ownership, as can an administrator. Keep in mind that ownership is a one-way street, you can take it but you can't give it away. The current owner remains the owner until another user takes ownership.

Device Settings Tab

The Device Settings tab shows the options available on this particular printer and indicates whether or not you've enabled them (see fig. 9.21). This page differs from printer to printer. In fact, it can differ radically.

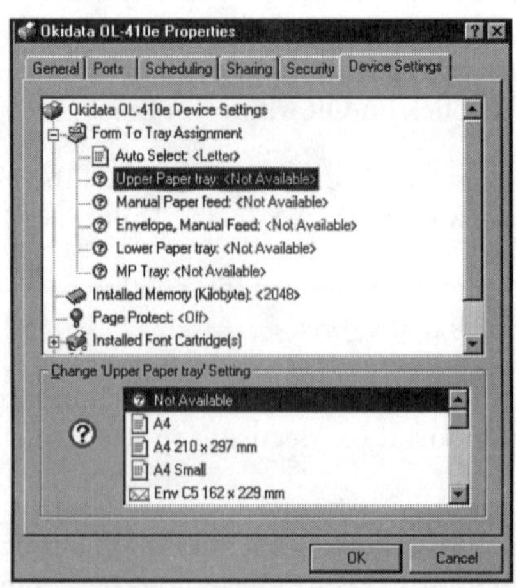

Figure 9.21

Choose a printer element for which you want to change the settings.

Select each available element for this printer and then select the way you want to use it (or choose Not Available if you don't want to use it). As each element is selected, the bottom of the dialog box displays its options.

Managing Print Jobs

Welcome to the world of operating system objects! Print Manager is dead! To manage print jobs, you go directly to the printer object in the Printers folder, double-click on it, and manage the print jobs from the printer's window (see fig. 9.22).

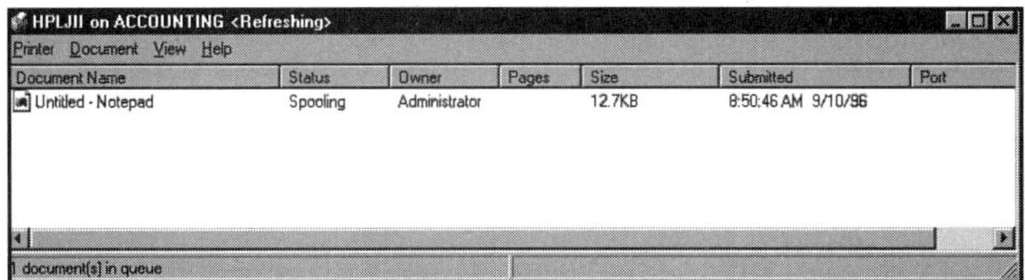

Figure 9.22

The printer's window replaces Print Manager, and you can configure the printer and manipulate the documents from it.

The Printer menu and the Document menu provide all the commands you need to manipulate the printer and the documents.

From the Printer menu you can do each of the following:

- Pause the printer, which stops all the jobs
- Set the printer to be the default printer
- Set the document defaults for the printer
- Configure sharing for the printer
- Purge all the documents in the printer window
- Go to the Properties dialog box

From the Document menu, you can do the following:

- Pause the currently printing job
- Resume a job that had been paused
- Restart a job
- Cancel a job
- See the properties of a job

When you open a printer window, the jobs that display depend on whether you are looking at the printer, at a client workstation, or at the print server.

The jobs that are shown at a client workstation are those jobs that were sent to the printer from this workstation.

The jobs that are shown at the print server are all the jobs currently in the queue for this printer, from all the client computers that use the printer.

Printing to Disk

Most Windows applications have an option to print to a disk file. In addition, you can establish a printer to print to a disk file. There are several reasons you might want to do this:

- You want to print the document from another location. To do so, you need to take the print file with you and then send the file to the printer.
- The printer is temporarily down.
- You want to give the file to another user.

When you take a print file to another location, the printer you use must be the same printer that was selected to print this document (or must emulate the original printer) because the printer codes are included in the print file.

Drag-and-Drop Printing

Users can drag a document to a printer object to print it. When they do, the software that prepared the document (or software that is able to load the document) opens, loads the document, issues the print command, and closes.

It's much easier to accomplish drag-and-drop printing if you place a shortcut to the printer on the user's desktop. Right-drag the printer object from the Printers folder to the desktop, then choose Create Shortcut(s) Here from the menu that appears when you release the right mouse button.

Printing from DOS

If your printer is connected to your computer you won't notice a problem when you print from DOS software or from the command line.

If you are using a printer that is located on a remote print server, however, printing from DOS is not simply a matter of selecting a printer.

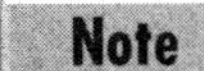

If you log on to a NetWare network system that is capturing and redirecting ports to a network printer (using NetWare programs or third party add-ons), your DOS software should print without any additional steps on your part.

During the installation of a remote printer on a client workstation (or, for that matter, during the installation of a local printer on a print server), there is no way to configure the printer for DOS printing. If you are familiar with installing printers for Windows 95, you know that there's an option for DOS printing in the setup process. No such option appears during the installation of a printer in Windows NT.

To print from DOS software or from the command line to a remote printer, you must manually redirect printing. The redirection command is:

```
net use lptx \\computername\printersharename
```

where x is the port you want to redirect (usually 1).

You can make this a permanent command by adding the parameter `/persistent:yes` to the command.

For example, on my Windows NT Workstation computer, in order to enable DOS printing to the HPLJII on the computer named Accounting, the command is:

```
net use lpt1 \\accounting\HPLJII /persistent:yes
```

There are a number of other parameters available for the `net use` command, and information on such is available in Appendix B, "NT Command Reference."

Once the redirection is in place, you can send files to the printer via the DOS command line in addition to printing from DOS applications. For example, the command `copy file name prn` sends a file to the remote printer to which you have redirected LPT1.

If you have several remote printers to choose from, you can redirect LPT2 to one of them, LPT3 to another, and so on. Then, establish the ability to print to those ports in your DOS software, or use the port in your command line parameters (for instance, **copy file name lpt2:**).

The persistent parameter is really persistent; it survives shutdown and startup. It is always there. However, it is always there only for the user who entered the command. The state of LPT redirection is a user profile issue.

Summary

This chapter discussed printing services in Windows NT, and the components and actions of the operating system's print services were explained. It also covered printer installation, configuration, and administration.

Part III

Networking with Windows NT Workstation

CHAPTER 10

The Ins and Outs of TCP/IP

The growth of Windows NT into an enterprise-class network operating system and the meteoric popularity of the Internet are two of the factors that have made the TCP/IP protocol suite into the de facto networking standard that it is today. Enterprise networks have become more heterogeneous in recent years, either through the addition of new technologies or the consolidation of existing ones, and one of the problems resulting from this phenomenon has been the general increase in network traffic congestion due to the different protocol types used by different platforms.

To relieve this congestion, many network administrators have sought to standardize on a single set of network protocols, in the hope of making their network traffic easier to manage. For a number of reasons, the obvious protocol suite of choice is TCP/IP. Among these reasons are:

- **Compatibility.** Most major network operating systems in use today are capable of using TCP/IP as a native protocol. Those that do not are now seen as being noticeably lacking in their support for industry standards.
- **Scalability.** TCP/IP was designed for use on what is now the world's largest internetwork, the Internet. It provides protocols to suit most any communications task, with varying degrees of speed, overhead, and reliability.

- **Heterogeneity.** TCP/IP is capable of supporting virtually any hardware or operating system platform in use today. Its modular architecture allows support for new platforms to be added without reengineering the core protocols.
- **Addressability.** Every machine on a TCP/IP network is assigned a unique identifier, making it directly addressable by any other machine on the network.
- **Availability.** The TCP/IP protocols are designed to be open standards, freely usable by all, and are developed through an "open forum" approach in which contributions from all interested parties are welcome.

TCP/IP is partially responsible for the growing popularity that Windows NT enjoys today. NT's original native protocol, NetBEUI, is suitable for use only on small networks because it has no network layer and is therefore not routable between network segments. The TCP/IP protocols contained most of the functionality required for use with Windows NT, and what it lacked, Microsoft helped to develop by working with other industry leaders to create new open standards.

Microsoft's TCP/IP Rollout

Development of the TCP/IP protocols for use on the fledgling ARPAnet (later called the Internet) began in the 1970s, but some of the innovations that have made it a practical choice for use on private enterprise networks were not conceived until much later. Microsoft's own adoption of TCP/IP for its 35,000-node global corporate internetwork was a telling case in point.

In the early 1990s, as Microsoft's Information Technology Group examined the various candidates that might replace the archaic XNS protocols they were then using, TCP/IP was a front-runner from the very beginning, but presented certain major obstacles to a worldwide rollout of this size. Primary among these obstacles were the administration and configuration of IP addresses, network name resolution, and the use of broadcasts to locate other computers.

On a small or medium-sized network, the task of assigning IP addresses to workstations is an onerous chore; but on a 35,000-node internetwork spread over 50 countries, it is a major administrative expense. Not only must the network address assignments be carefully planned and meticulous records be kept at a central location, but the task of actually configuring those thousands of nodes must be dealt with. Do you send trained personnel to every remote sale office? Do you train people that are already there? Do you develop documentation that will (hopefully) enable end-users to configure their own workstations?

Name resolution on this scale is another difficult problem. To use TCP/IP with Windows NT, you must have a means of equating NetBIOS names (the standard machine names used by NT) with IP addresses. On a local network segment, this was done using broadcasts (which could cause network traffic problems themselves). Connections to machines on other networks required entries in an LMHOSTS file on each workstation, which listed NetBIOS names and their equivalent IP addresses. The task of maintaining these files on so many computers dwarfed even that of assigning IP addresses.

Fortunately, Microsoft was in a unique position to help resolve these problems. It was clear to Microsoft that the difficulties it was facing would afflict any large corporate adoption of TCP/IP, to some extent. By devoting its internal resources to the development of TCP/IP solutions, Microsoft could not only resolve its own networking problems, but include its inventions as part of the Windows NT product, as well.

The results of Microsoft's efforts, in collaboration with other network engineers and product manufacturers, are the DHCP and WINS modules that provide IP address configuration and name resolution services, respectively, to network users. By using these services, you can greatly reduce the administrative overhead required by a large TCP/IP network and insulate your users from the need to know anything about protocols and IP addresses.

The term TCP/IP is, of course, a misnomer. As it is generally used, the name actually refers to a collection of more than a dozen protocols and is taken from the two that are used most often. The standards on which the protocols are based are published by the Internet Engineering Task Force (IETF) and are known as Requests for Comments (RFCs). These documents are much more accessible than many networking standards, both in their availability and their readability. They can be freely downloaded from many different FTP servers, such as:

- ds.internic.net
- nis.nsf.net
- nisc.jvnc.net
- ftp.isi.edu
- wuarchive.wustl.edu
- src.doc.ic.ac.uk
- ftp.ncren.net
- ftp.sesqui.net
- nis.garr.it

Most of the sites store the documents in a top-level directory called RFC. They are predominantly ASCII text files, with some that contain illustrations available in PostScript format.

As a stand-alone operating system, Windows NT Workstation is like an orphaned child. Much of its functionality is devoted to communications with other systems, and the TCP/IP protocols are the means by which this communication is possible on most Windows NT networks. Many of the functions covered in this chapter are invisible to the user after TCP/IP has been properly configured on the workstation, but you can not fully understand Windows NT until you examine the networking processes that run beneath the surface.

This chapter examines many of these processes, including:

- The use of TCP/IP within the Windows NT networking model
- The various TCP/IP protocols and their layered functionality
- The elements of a client TCP/IP configuration
- The automatic configuration of TCP/IP clients using DHCP
- The name registration and resolution processes
- The use of the Windows NT TCP/IP utilities

After you have achieved an understanding of these subjects, your conception of Windows NT networking—and of the Internet—will become clearer, and you will be more capable of dealing with problems when they arise.

Fitting TCP/IP into the Windows NT Networking Model

Windows NT's networking architecture is particularly well suited for use by different sets of protocols. With the Transport Device Interface (TDI) at the top of the OSI model's Transport layer, and the Network Device Interface Specification (NDIS) interface beneath the Network layer, the core transport protocols are largely isolated from the rest of the networking stack, as shown in figure 10.1. As long as they can address these two interfaces, any competent protocols can be used to send data over the network. Indeed, different transport protocols can function simultaneously in Windows NT, resulting in the double-edged sword of platform interoperability and network traffic congestion.

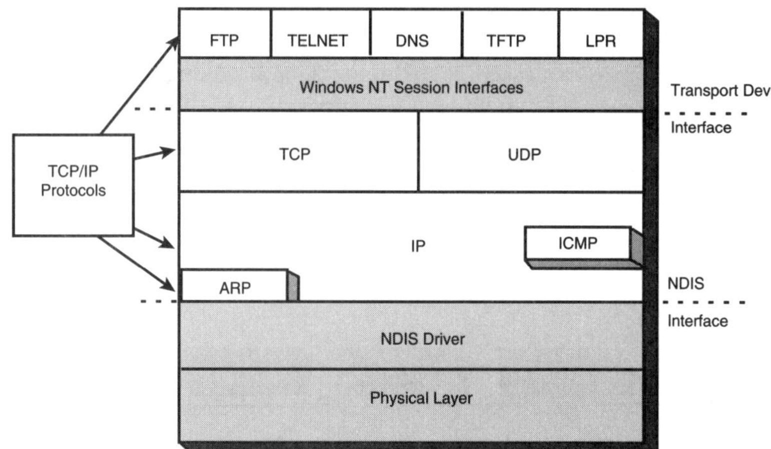

Figure 10.1

The TCP/IP protocol suite operates at various levels of the networking stack.

Above the TDI are the user-mode interfaces (also known as application programming interfaces, or APIs). These interfaces are addressed by applications when they require network services. Chief among these interfaces are the NetBIOS interface, which Windows NT uses for its core file services, and Windows Sockets, which is the standard interface for many TCP/IP and Internet utilities. Other supported APIs are:

- Remote Procedure Calls (RPCs)
- Server Message Blocks (SMBs)
- Named Pipes
- Mail Slots.

These APIs are not necessarily associated with a particular set of protocols. The original Windows NT release, for example, could only pass data from its APIs to the NetBEUI protocol and then to an NDIS driver. This simplified system lacked the functionality of TCP/IP but provided basic network services on a small scale.

The TDI provides a distributed interface that enables network requests from the different APIs to be directed to whichever protocol is needed to access the required resource. NetBIOS file requests, for example, can be directed to the TCP/IP protocols when accessing a Windows NT drive on the network, or to the NWLink protocol when the application needs a file from a NetWare server. Multiple applications running on a Windows NT workstation might be processing several network requests simultaneously, meaning that various function calls can be passing through the TDI to the TCP/IP protocol stack, or the NWLink stack, or both, at the same time.

All the protocol stacks operating on a Windows NT machine deliver their network service requests to the same place—the NDIS interface. NDIS is the standard used to create the device driver that provides access to the networking hardware. Thus the network architecture of Windows NT can be seen as a series of funneling procedures. Applications at the top of the model generate requests that can utilize any of a handful of APIs. The APIs then pass the requests on to a smaller number of protocols (usually one or two). Different kinds of requests might be intermingled in the individual protocol stacks, and at the NDIS interface, they are all funneled into a single stream and packaged into discrete packets that pass through the network adapter and out onto the network medium itself, as shown in figure 10.2.

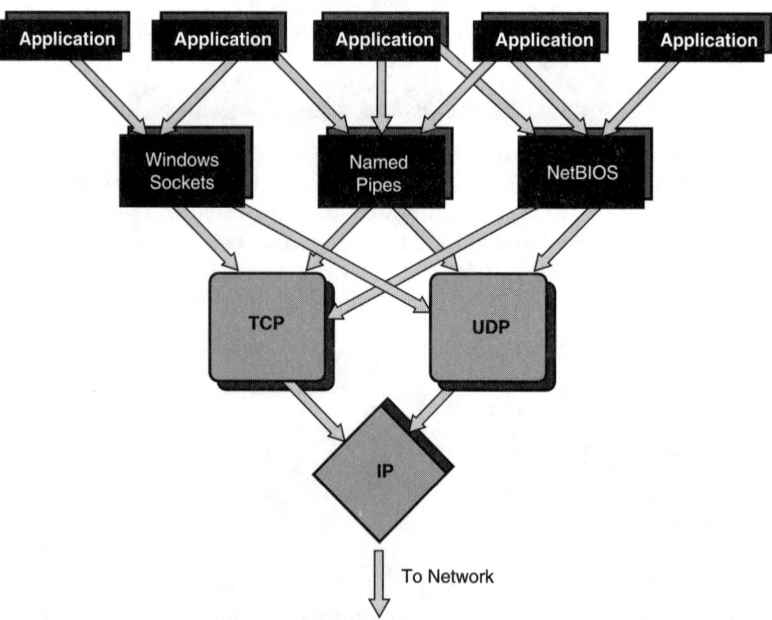

Figure 10.2
Data from many application interfaces passes through multiple protocol stacks to be multiplexed over a single network channel.

The TCP/IP protocols are therefore primarily occupied in moving the application requests from the TDI to the NDIS interface, packaging them into discrete units called *datagrams* so that they can be efficiently transmitted to their ultimate destination. The process is, of course, reversed for data arriving at the workstation. This packaging can be said to consist of three basic functions:

- **Addressing.** To send data to another computer on the network, there must be a means by which the destination can be uniquely identified. TCP/IP provides its own identification system, in the form of an IP address for each machine on the network.

- **Routing.** A Data Link level protocol such as ethernet or token ring is not concerned with the ultimate delivery of network packets, only with transmitting them to the next machine on the network. TCP/IP provides the means by which network traffic is efficiently and reliably routed through multiple network segments to its destination.
- **Multiplexing.** Because an operating system like Windows NT can be running several programs at once, network requests are multiplexed over the cable (that is, packets with different origins and purposes are intermingled in the network data stream). Individual packets must therefore be identifiable in order for the requests to reach the appropriate application process in the destination computer. TCP/IP accomplishes this by assigning a port number to each process, which in combination with an IP address uniquely identifies the actual process on the network to which the packet must be delivered. The combination of an IP address and a port number is called a *socket*.

Exploring the TCP/IP Protocol Stack

The TCP/IP protocols, as realized on a Windows NT workstation (or server), can be broken down into four functional layers that roughly correspond to those of the OSI reference model, as shown in figure 10.3.

- Application
- Transport
- Network
- Network Access

As with the OSI reference model, the functionality of the various TCP/IP protocols is divided into layers that make the process of data encapsulation more comprehensible. As a message is passed down from the user interface at the top of the networking stack to the actual network medium (usually a cable) at the bottom, data processed by an upper-layer protocol is repeatedly encapsulated by protocols operating at each successive lower layer. This results in a compound packet that is transmitted to the destination system, where the whole process is repeated in reverse, as the message travels up through the layers.

With TCP/IP, examining the layers at which the protocols function is a means of understanding how they have been adapted for use on Windows NT networks.

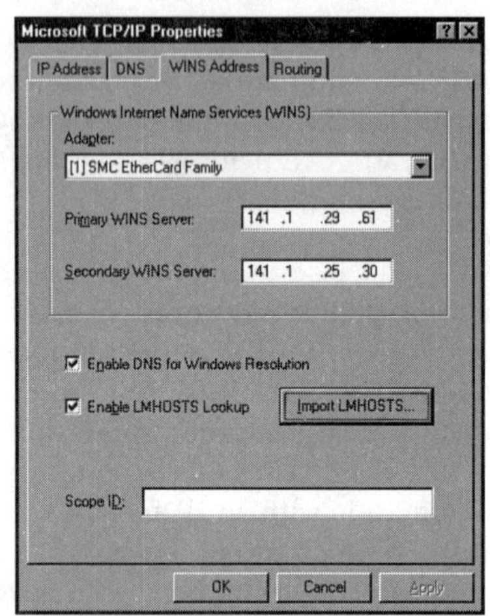

Figure 10.3
The TCP/IP stack can be divided into layers that can be compared to those of the OSI reference model.

The Network Access Layer

The Network Access protocols operate at the bottom of the TCP/IP protocol stack, working just above the Data Link layer to facilitate the transmission of datagrams over the network medium. TCP/IP has its own addressing system, by which it identifies the other computers on the network. Once the IP datagrams reach the NDIS interface, however, they are repackaged again into frames that are appropriate for the network type being used.

Every network type, be it ethernet, token ring, or something else, has its own way of identifying the computers on the network. Most of the network types in use today accomplish this identification through the use of a hardware address that is coded into every network adapter by its manufacturer. This Media Access Control (MAC) address is used in the outermost frame of every network packet to identify the computer to which it should be sent.

Therefore, for an IP datagram to be sent out over the network, there must be a way of determining what hardware address corresponds to the given IP address. This is the job of the Network Access protocols, of which the most commonly known is the Address Resolution Protocol (ARP).

ARP functions between the Network and Data Link layers on ethernet networks. It cannot operate until it is provided with the IP address of the computer to which a datagram is to be sent. No datagram can be transmitted over the network until ARP supplies the Data Link layer with a destination hardware address.

When ARP receives a datagram from the Network layer, it reads the IP address of the intended destination from the IP header and then generates an address resolution request packet, which is broadcast to the entire local network. The address resolution request contains the IP address of the destination computer (if the destination is on the same network segment) or the IP address of the workstation's default gateway (if it is not).

Each computer on the network segment processes the ARP packet and notes the IP address carried within. If a computer on the network detects its own IP address in an ARP packet, it responds to the sender with a reply containing the hardware address of its network adapter. The ARP passes this address along to the Data Link layer protocol, which uses it to frame the packet and eventually transmit it over the network.

ARP also maintains a cache of IP addresses and their corresponding hardware addresses, to reduce the number of redundant broadcasts transmitted over the network. The cache is erased whenever the computer is shut down or rebooted, to prevent incorrect transmissions due to changes in network hardware.

ARP broadcasts are limited to the local network segment. A computer's Data Link protocol is concerned only with the transmission of the frame to the next computer down the line. In most cases, this will be a gateway to another network segment and not the computer whose IP address is specified as the final destination of the message.

ARP is only one of many Network Access protocols designed to support the extremely wide and varied array of platforms that can utilize TCP/IP.

The Network Layer

The Internet Protocol (IP), which operates at the Network layer of the TCP/IP stack, is the central protocol of the entire suite and the core of TCP/IP's functionality. All the upper layer protocols in the suite are packaged within IP datagrams before being passed to the NDIS interface. IP performs many of the key functions that enable the TCP/IP suite to operate, including the following:

- The packaging of upper layer traffic into datagrams, the fundamental TCP/IP transmission unit
- The implementation of the TCP/IP addressing system
- The routing of datagrams between networks
- The fragmentation and defragmentation of datagrams to accommodate the limitations of the network types between the source and the destination
- The passing of data between the Transport and Network Access layers (in both directions)

IP is a connectionless, unreliable protocol. *Connectionless* means that it transmits packets without first establishing that the destination computer is operating and ready to receive data; *unreliable* means that it has no inherent mechanisms that provide error detection and correction. These apparent deficiencies are not really a problem because IP can always be used in conjunction with other protocols that provide these services, if needed. As a basic carrier medium for network communications, the intention behind IP's design is to provide only the common services needed by all transmissions, so that an appropriate transport protocol can be selected to suit the specific needs of the data being transmitted.

The rest of this section describes the means by which IP datagrams are carried from system to system to their ultimate destination, as well as examining the header of the IP datagram, which contains the information needed to complete the transmission. In addition, the Internet Control Message Protocol is introduced, which performs many different functions that assist the efforts of the Internet Protocol.

IP Routing

IP is also responsible for the routing of datagrams to adjacent network segments. Every computer running TCP/IP on an internetwork has access to one or more gateways that it uses to transmit data to systems on other networks. A *gateway*, in TCP/IP parlance, is a device that passes packets between two or more networks. The term does not necessarily imply the existence of a protocol translation, as it does in the general networking vocabulary. A TCP/IP system that functions as a gateway between the source of a transmission and its destination is also known as an *intermediate system.* The source and destination themselves are called *end systems.*

TCP/IP traffic on an intermediate system travels up to Network layer, and no higher. IP is aware only of the computers on its local network segment and the adjacent segments that can be accessed through local gateways. When it receives a packet destined for a computer on another segment, IP sends it to one of the local gateways to continue it on its way. That particular gateway is selected for one of the following reasons:

- It provides direct access to the network on which the destination computer resides.
- It is registered in the computer's routing table as the best possible route to the destination network.
- It is the computer's default gateway.

The IP Header

As with any network protocol, IP places its own header onto each packet it receives from the upper layers, encapsulating it for transmission and inserting the information needed to perform all the protocol's functions. The IP header is either 20 or 24 bytes long, depending on the inclusion of certain options. Bytes, in TCP/IP-speak, are referred to as *octets*, and the header is broken into 32-bit *words*, of which there are five or six. After the header is applied, the packet is referred to as a *datagram*, and it is passed down to the Network Access layer. The datagram will be encapsulated again by the Data Link layer, before it is actually transmitted over the network.

The IP header is illustrated in figure 10.4.

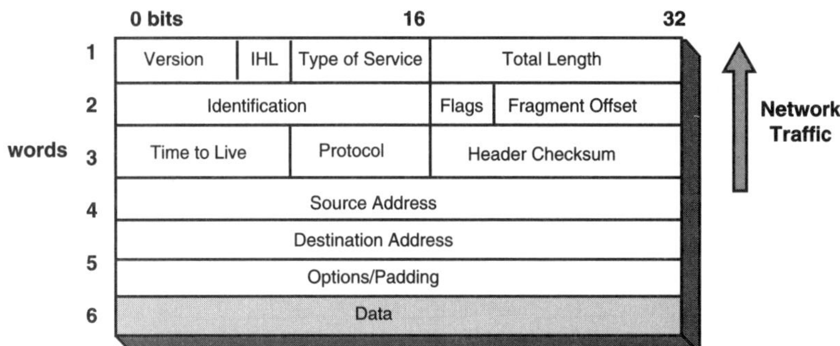

Figure 10.4

The Internet Protocol header contains all the information needed to send an IP packet to its destination address.

The IP header consists of the following fields:

- **First Word**
  - **Version (4 bits).** Indicates the IP header version.
  - **Internet Header Length (4 bits).** Specifies the overall length of the IP header (in 32-bit words), thus indicating whether the optional sixth word is present.
  - **Type of Service (8 bits).** Indicates the desired network service priority for this datagram.
  - **Total Length (16 bits).** Specifies the total length of the datagram in octets (bytes); can be used to determine whether fragmentation of datagrams is needed to complete the transmission.

- **Second Word**
  - **Identification (16 bits).** When datagrams are fragmented or defragmented, this field specifies the datagram to which a particular fragment belongs.
  - **Flags (3 bits).** Specifies whether the datagram can be fragmented and whether all the fragments composing the original datagram have been received.
  - **Fragmentation Offset (13 bits).** Used to reassemble fragments in the proper order, this field provides the starting point (measured in 64-bit units) of this fragment in the datagram.
- **Third Word**
  - **Time to Live (8 bits).** Specifies how long (in seconds) the datagram can remain active on the internetwork. This allows undeliverable datagrams to be removed from the network after a set time period. Every system that processes the datagram decrements this value by at least one second.
  - **Protocol (8 bits).** Indicates the protocol at the Transport layer of the destination computer for which this datagram is destined.
  - **Header Checksum (16 bits).** Verifies that the IP header (but not the data) has been transmitted correctly. The checksum is verified by each intermediate system and recomputed before being sent to the next node.
- **Fourth Word**
  - **Source Address (32 bits).** The IP address of the transmitting computer.
- **Fifth Word**
  - **Destination Address (32 bits).** The IP address of the end system to which the datagram is being sent.
- **Sixth Word (optional)**
  - **Options (variable).** Provides routing, security, or time stamp services for IP transmissions. The options field is itself optional, but must be supported by all implementations of IP.
  - **Padding (variable).** Zeroes added to fill out the sixth word to a full 32 bits.

Although it is the most heavily used of the TCP/IP protocols, IP by itself is not capable of coping with some of the situations that might be encountered during the transmission of datagrams. In these cases, a "helper" protocol is needed to perform additional transmission control functions.

The Internet Control Message Protocol

The Internet Control Message Protocol (ICMP) is the only protocol aside from IP that operates at the Network layer. It is used to perform a number of diagnostic and administrative functions that aid in the transmission of IP packets. The ping utility, for example, uses ICMP packets to verify the existence of particular IP addresses on the network.

Similar ICMP packets are also used to provide a sending computer with reports on the status of its transmissions, such as:

- Messages stating that a datagram's destination address is unreachable, specifying further whether it is the destination's network, host, protocol, or port that is unavailable.
- ICMP Source Quench messages indicating that an intermediate or end system is being overwhelmed by incoming packets. This enables the sending node to initiate flow control procedures by slowing down its transmissions until the complaint messages cease.
- Reports that packets have been discarded by an intermediate or end system due to packet header corruption.
- Warnings that datagrams will have to be fragmented before they can be successfully transmitted to the destination.
- Routing advice in the form of ICMP Redirect packets that inform a sending node of conditions beyond the adjacent network segments. When the transmitting computer is on a segment with more than one usable gateway, these packets enable the sender to select the gateway that provides the most efficient route to the destination.

These functions should not be confused with those providing true connection-oriented service and error detection. ICMP aids in the delivery of IP datagrams to the destination but does not guarantee reliable service.

The Transport Layer

As in the OSI reference model, the TCP/IP Transport layer sits atop the Network layer. Transport protocols are encapsulated within IP datagrams for transmission over the network and provide different levels of service, depending on the needs of the application. The two main protocols that operate at the Transport layer are the Transport Control Protocol (TCP) and the User Datagram Protocol (UDP), both of which are profiled in the following two sections. TCP is used when more reliable service is required, and UDP when guaranteed delivery is less critical. As you saw in the diagram earlier, the Protocol field of the IP header identifies which transport protocol is being carried within the datagram, so that the receiving workstation knows how to process the packet.

The Transport Control Protocol (TCP)

TCP is the primary connection-oriented, reliable protocol used in TCP/IP communications. Applications use it in situations that require data transmissions that are verifiable as being absolutely accurate, such as ftp file transfers. Unlike IP, TCP data transmissions never begin until a three-way handshake with the destination system has been completed. This creates a virtual connection between the two systems, a prearranged agreement between the two machines for the exchange of packets. After the connection is established, all the datagrams transmitted during that session are considered to be *segments* of that transmission. The entire series of datagrams transmitted during the session is called a *sequence.*

The reliability of TCP communications is provided by an error detection and correction system called *positive acknowledgment with retransmission.* This means that the receiving computer examines the checksum included with each packet and sends periodic acknowledgments back to the sender indicating that the incoming packets up to a certain point have been received intact. The transmitting system automatically resends any packets not positively acknowledged by the receiver.

TCP also provides flow control and packet reordering services for every transmission. Even though a virtual connection exists between the two end systems, individual IP packets can travel different routes to the same destination, possibly even arriving in a different order from that in which they were sent.

The header of a TCP packet is admittedly complex, even though it is the same size as the IP header, because it has a great deal to do. The TCP header is carried within the IP header and is read only by the end system receiving the packet. Because the destination system must acknowledge receipt of the transmitted data, TCP is necessarily a bidirectional protocol. The same header is used to send data packets in one direction and acknowledgments in the other.

The layout of the TCP header is shown in figure 10.5.

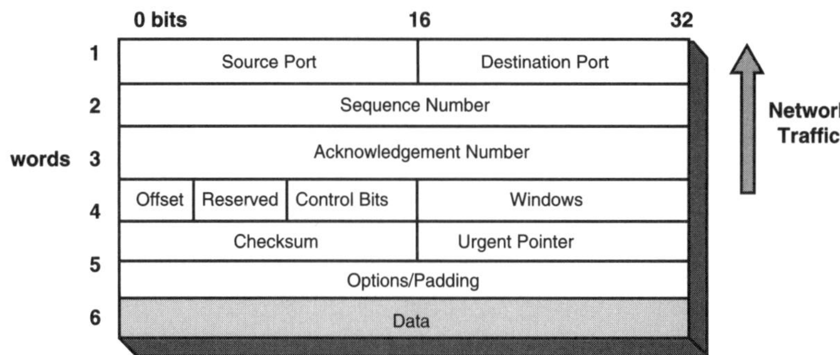

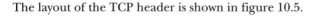

Figure 10.5

The connection-oriented, reliable service provided by TCP is made possible by the information included in the TCP header.

The TCP header is formatted as follows:

- **First Word**
  - **Source Port (16 bits).** Specifies the port number of the application process at the source computer sending the transmission.
  - **Destination Port (16 bits).** Specifies the port number of the application process at the destination computer that will receive the transmission.
- **Second Word**
  - **Sequence Number (32 bits).** Ensures that segments are processed in the correct order at the destination by specifying the number of the first data octet in this segment out of the entire sequence.
- **Third Word**
  - **Acknowledgment Number (32 bits).** Specifies the sequence number of the segment that will next be received by the destination; indicates that all prior segments have been received correctly and acknowledged.
- **Fourth Word**
  - **Data Offset (4 bits).** Specifies the length of the TCP header in 32-bit words, thus indicating the beginning of the data field and whether the optional sixth word is present in the header.
  - **Reserved (6 bits).** Currently unused; the value must be zero.

- **Control Bits (6 bits).** Binary flags that can be turned on to indicate the segment's function or purpose:
  URG: Urgent Pointer field significant
  ACK: Acknowledgment field significant
  PSH: Push Function
  RST: Reset the connection
  SYN: Synchronize sequence numbers
  FIN: No more data from sender

- **Window (16 bits).** Provides flow control by specifying the number of octets (beginning at the sequence number in the Acknowledgment Number field) that the destination computer can accept from the source.

- **Fifth Word**

  - **Checksum (16 bits).** Provides error correction by checking both the TCP header and data fields, as well as a pseudo-header containing the source address, destination address and protocol values from the IP header and the overall length of the TCP packet. The pseudo-header enables the Transport layer to reverify that the datagrams have been sent to the correct destination.

  - **Urgent Pointer (16 bits).** When the URG control bit is turned on, this field specifies the location of urgent data (in relation to the Sequence Number of this segment).

- **Sixth Word (optional)**

  - **Options (variable).** Optional field used only to specify the maximum segment size allowed by the sending computer during the TCP handshake (when the SYN control bit is set).

  - **Padding (variable).** Zeroes added to fill out the sixth word to a full 32 bits.

Anatomy of a TCP Session

To begin a TCP session, one end system transmits a packet that has the SYN control bit turned on and contains a randomly selected sequence number. The destination system replies to the sender with a packet that has the ACK control bit turned on and specifies its own beginning sequence number. Each system maintains its own numbering of the bytes in the sequence, while remaining aware of the other machine's numbers as well.

The sequence numbering begun in the first packet is continually incremented by both systems during the entire duration of the TCP connection. When it actually begins to transmit data, the transmitting computer specifies in each packet the number of the first byte contained in that packet's data field. If packets should arrive at the destination in the wrong sequence, the receiving system uses the sequence numbers to reassemble them in the correct order.

During the data transmission, the transmitting system computes a checksum for each packet and includes the result in the TCP header. The destination computer recomputes the checksum for each packet received and compares the result to the value provided in the checksum field. If the values match, the packet is verified as having been transmitted without error.

The receiver sends periodic acknowledgment packets back to the sender, each containing the number of the highest verified packet received thus far, in the Acknowledgment Number field. The sender can safely assume that all packets with lower numbers have been received and verified (preventing the receiver from having to acknowledge every packet). If the sender fails to receive an acknowledgment in a given period of time, it begins to resend packets beginning at the last acknowledgment number it has received.

Acknowledgment packets also contain a Windows value that indicates to the sender how many packets the destination system is capable of receiving at that moment. If this number increases in successive acknowledgment packets, the transmission rate can be increased. If the Windows value drops, the transmission rate is slowed, giving the receiver time to catch up.

When it has finished sending data, the transmitting node sends a packet with the FIN control bit turned on to the destination, breaking down the connection and ending the sequence.

TCP provides highly reliable data transfers, but at a significant price. Not only does the TCP header in each packet add to the overall transmission volume, but also the need for acknowledgments significantly increases the overall number of packets transmitted. It is easy to see why this kind of guaranteed service is implemented at the Transport layer as an option and not at the Network layer. If IP provided all these services, TCP/IP networks would slow down to a crawl.

The User Datagram Protocol

UDP provides a low-overhead alternative to TCP for use when the reliable transfer of data is not critical. It is connectionless, with each packet sent and processed independently of the others, and requires only a two-word header. There is no explicit acknowledgment of received packets during a UDP transmission. Replies to UDP requests can be returned to the sender, but they are processed at the application level.

UDP is not typically used for the transfer of large binary data files, in which a single incorrect bit can cause the file to be ruined. UDP is more likely to be used for the transmission of a short query to another computer. If the sender receives no response, the entire request can usually be retransmitted using less overall traffic volume than the establishment of a TCP connection.

Some applications have begun to use UDP to stream audio and video over the Internet because the control overhead is so much lower, and also because an audio or video stream can recover from an occasional lost packet more easily than most binary files.

Compared to the TCP header, UDP is simple and minimal. It is shown in figure 10.6.

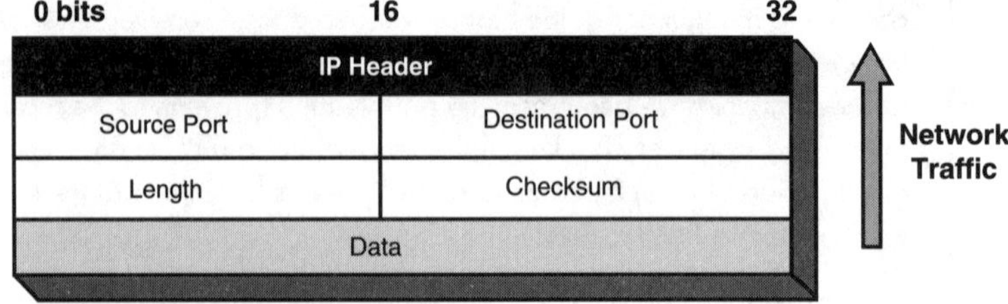

Figure 10.6
The size of the UDP header lowers the protocol's control overhead.

The UDP header layout is as follows:

- **First Word**
  - **Source Port (16 bits).** Specifies the port number of the application process generating the UDP transmission (optional, padded with zeroes if omitted).
  - **Destination Port (16 bits).** Specifies the port number of the application process in the destination system to which the UDP transmission is directed.
- **Second word**
  - **Length (16 bits).** Specifies the overall length of the UDP packet in octets, including the data, but excluding the IP header and any Data Link frames.
  - **Checksum (16 bits).** Specifies the result of a checksum computation on the UDP header and data, plus a pseudo-header that consists of the IP header's Source Address, Destination Address and Protocol fields.

The Application Layer

The TCP/IP suite includes many different protocols that operate above the Transport Device Interface. Some, like ftp and Telnet, are applications themselves, as well as protocols, and are included with most implementations of the TCP/IP suite to provide basic file transfer and terminal emulation services to users on any platform, with a standardized interface.

The Common...

Other Application layer protocols are used to provide specific TCP/IP services to programs. Simple Mail Transfer Protocol (SMTP), for example, is used by many programs to send e-mail over TCP/IP networks. Other protocols, such as the Domain Name System (DNS), provide more generalized services. DNS is used by many applications to resolve Internet host names into IP addresses.

The Obscure...

Although the examples cited thus far are rather well known, some application protocols operate almost invisibly to the user. The Router Information Protocol (RIP), for example, disseminates data to other computers on the network that helps them to make more intelligent routing decisions.

How It Works...

Application protocols are, logically, closest to the user interface and are often directly involved with the process that generates the request for network resources. When such a request is processed, it is passed down the layers of the networking stack and encapsulated using the various protocols discussed in the preceding sections.

Thus, when you connect to an ftp server on the Internet and download a file, the ftp server at the remote site accesses the file and creates a packet by applying the header for the FTP application protocol. The entire packet is then passed down to the Transport layer, where it becomes the data field in a TCP packet. At the Network layer, the packet is divided up into units of the proper size to transmit over the network. An IP header is applied to each, and the packets can now properly be called a series of datagrams, as shown in figure 10.7.

Except for minor changes to the IP headers while in transit, these datagrams will remain unopened until they arrive at their destination. While they are on the network, the outermost layer of the data packets, the Data Link frame, can change several times during the packets' journey from the ftp server to your workstation. The datagrams might arrive at your computer encased within ethernet packets, and they might even start out that way when they leave the ftp server; but there could be 20 gateways or more between the source and the destination systems, running an untold number of different Data Link protocols.

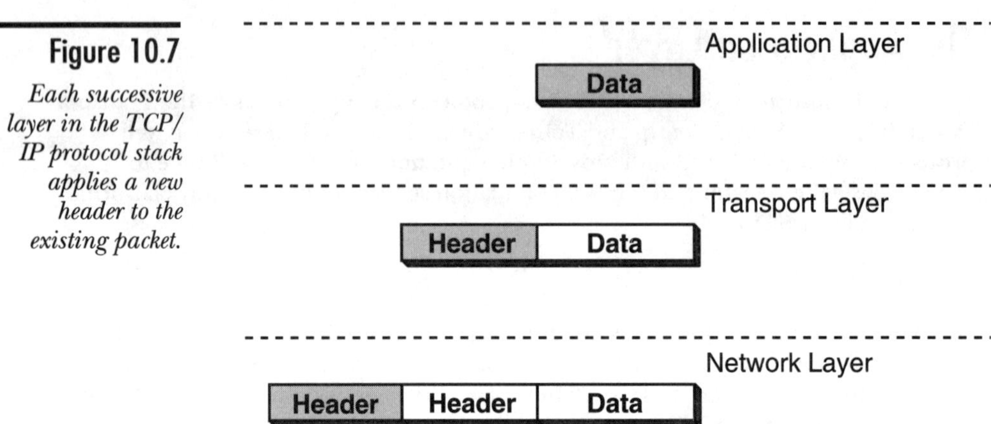

Figure 10.7

Each successive layer in the TCP/IP protocol stack applies a new header to the existing packet.

After the packets arrive at your computer, the process begins in reverse. IP passes the datagrams up to the TCP protocol (which was specified in the IP header), where they are assembled into the correct order and fed to the FTP protocol (which is identified by its port number in the TCP header), which writes the received file to your hard disk drive.

All the TCP/IP protocols discussed in the preceding sections work together to transmit data over the network. In order to implement these protocols in Windows NT, you must first install them as part of the network communications stack. In Windows NT, TCP/IP is often referred to as though it is a single protocol, which actually the entire family of protocols is implied. In the next section, you learn about the various parameters that must be configured to turn a Windows NT workstation into a TCP/IP client.

Installing and Configuring TCP/IP

TCP/IP is now the Windows NT default protocol and will be installed during the operating system's setup routine, unless you specify otherwise. The TCP/IP stack in Windows NT includes support for all the protocols discussed in the preceding sections, as well as a large collection of services and utilities that enable you to utilize, manage, and troubleshoot TCP/IP on your workstation. The Windows NT Server product ships with many more TCP/IP-based services that facilitate the administration of large numbers of TCP/IP users on a network.

TCP/IP can also be installed after the operating system is already in place, by clicking the Add button on the Protocols page of the Network Control Panel. If you have been using NetBEUI to communicate with other Windows computers on your local network, you can safely remove it after all your machines have been configured to use TCP/IP. (Windows NT 3.1 machines will have to be upgraded to version 3.5 or higher, before NetBEUI can be eliminated.)

After TCP/IP is installed, whether through the NT installation program or the Network Control Panel, you must provide the settings needed to identify your machine and ready it for interaction with the rest of the TCP/IP network. Windows NT includes a feature called the Dynamic Host Configuration Protocol (DHCP) that can enable a Windows NT server to automatically provide your system with all the TCP/IP configuration settings that it requires. DHCP enables you to skip all the settings covered in the coming sections and is discussed later in this chapter. For now, you learn about each of the settings required for effective TCP/IP communications and how your workstation uses them to communicate with the network.

All the settings required to use TCP/IP on Windows NT are configured in the Microsoft TCP/IP Properties dialog box, as shown in figure 10.8.

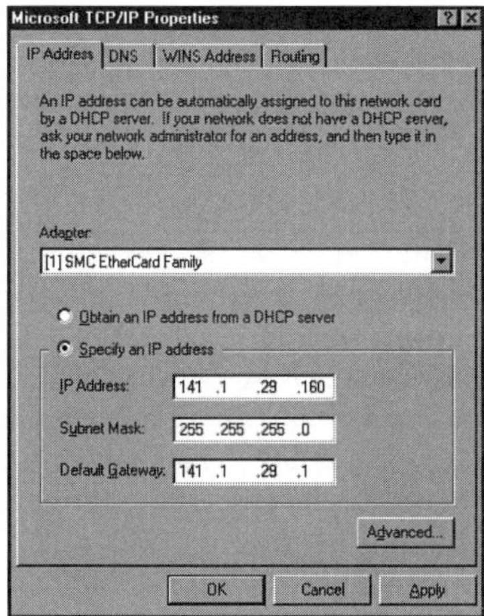

Figure 10.8

The Microsoft TCP/IP Properties dialog box is the central repository for all a workstation's TCP/IP configuration settings.

When you access it from the Network Control Panel, you are first presented with the IP Address page, which contains the three most crucial settings for a TCP/IP stack, on any platform:

- IP address
- Subnet mask
- Default gateway

IP Addressing

The IP address is the means by which computers are identified on a TCP/IP network. It identifies both the host itself and the network on which it resides. Each computer must be assigned an address that is different from those of all other computers on the network. Otherwise, datagrams might be delivered to the wrong system, causing all sorts of problems for both of the conflicting workstations.

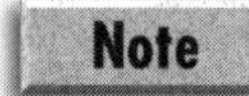

On a TCP/IP network, the term host is not necessarily synonymous with a computer. A *host* is a network interface, of which there can be more than one in a single system. In such a case, each host must have its own IP address.

IP addresses are always 32 bits long and are traditionally expressed as four decimal values from 0 to 255, representing 8 bits each, separated by periods. Every computer on your network must be assigned a unique IP address.

If your network is not connected to the Internet, the addresses are assigned to individual hosts by your network administrators. The actual addresses themselves can be any legal combination of numbers, as long as each assigned address is unique. This is known as an *unregistered* network because it is a wholly private arrangement within the confines of your organization.

If your network is connected to the Internet, however, you will have one or more machines with *registered* IP addresses. To prevent address duplication, you must register the IP addresses of Internet hosts with an organization called the Internet Network Information Center (InterNIC). A private network can elect to use registered IP addresses for all its hosts, or it can maintain an unregistered network for internal users and register only the machines directly accessible from the Internet, such as World Wide Web and ftp servers. In the case of the former, users with unregistered IP addresses typically access the Internet through a firewall or proxy server that prevents unauthorized access to the local network from outside machines.

When you are configuring a Windows NT workstation to use TCP/IP, you should either receive an IP address from your network administrator (who must keep some record of the address assignments for the network), or use a DHCP server like that in the Window NT Server product, which assigns addresses automatically from a pool configured by the administrator.

The one thing that you should not do is select a random IP address just to see if it works. IP address conflicts are one of the most common problems on TCP/IP networks, and one of the most difficult to troubleshoot. Remember, the IP address that you just "borrowed" might belong to your boss.

Subnet Mask

The subnet mask is probably the most misunderstood of the TCP/IP configuration settings. People see the values assigned to this setting like 255.255.255.0 and mistake them for actual IP addresses, or they might know what value should be assigned, but fail to understand why.

The subnet mask is actually based on a very simple concept. If you recall, in the last section you learned that the IP address identifies both the network and the actual host on that network. The only purpose of the subnet mask is to designate what part of the IP address identifies the network on which the host resides and what part identifies the host itself.

This is more easily understood if you think of the subnet mask in binary terms. All IP addresses are 32-bit binary values. They are notated in decimal form only for the sake of convenience. A subnet mask value of 255.255.255.0, when expressed in binary form, appears like this:

```
11111111.11111111.11111111.00000000
```

This value means that, for the IP address associated with this mask, all the digits with the value *1* identify the network, and all the zeroes identify the host on that network. Thus, if the machine's IP address is 123.45.67.89, then 123.45.67 identifies the network, and 89 identifies the host.

IP Address Types

When you understand what the subnet mask is used for, the next logical question is to ask why different networks require different numbers of digits to identify them. The answer to this, as with most TCP/IP questions, is found on the Internet. The TCP/IP protocols were designed for use on what is now known as the Internet. Although no one could have predicted its phenomenal growth over the past two years, the Internet was designed to be a highly scalable network requiring a minimum of centralized administration.

TCP/IP's developers understood even in the early days that the idea of registering a unique address for every host on the network with some sort of administrative body was impractical. The cost would have been too high even then. They decided, therefore, that only networks would be registered and that the administrators of the networks would be responsible for maintaining the IP address assignments for the individual hosts.

It was then decided that three different network classes would be created, which would be registered to individual networks based on the number of hosts that they had to connect to the Internet. The following table lists the classes, the subnet mask for each, the maximum number of possible networks of that class using the current system, the number of unique host addresses available to a single network of each class, and the possible values of the first octet in the IP addresses for each class.

Class	Subnet Mask	# of Networks	# of Hosts	First Octet
Class A	255.0.0.0	126	16,777,214	1 to 126
Class B	255.255.0.0	16,384	65,534	128 to 191
Class C	255.255.255.0	2,097,151	254	192 to 223

On a practical level, this means that if you wanted to register your network in order to connect it to the Internet, you could obtain a class C address from InterNIC. They would assign you a network address that you would use for the first three octets of all your IP addresses, such as 199.45.67. You would then be free to assign the 254 possible values for the fourth octet however you want, as long as there was no duplication. The subnet mask on all your machines would be 255.255.255.0, indicating that only the last octet is being used to identify the host.

If you had more than 254 nodes on your network, you would have to get another class C address. If you had a sufficiently large network to register, then you could possibly get a class B address, which would support up to 65,534 hosts. You would then assign the last two octets yourself and use a subnet mask of 255.255.0.0.

Save the Internet!

When the Internet was conceived, no one had even the remote idea that it would become as popular a communications medium as it is today. The concepts and protocols used on the Internet were developed with scalability in mind, though, and it is a worthy testament to their creators that the system has far exceeded its intended design limits.

The time is rapidly approaching, however, when we must begin to think about conserving our Internet resources, just as we must be concerned about fossil fuels, clean water, and the rain forests. The time is past when we can blithely assign class B and C addresses to organizations that do not intend to fully make use of them. There might soon come a time when you have to register a new network, and you turn on the InterNIC faucet to find that there are no more addresses to be had.

The time to begin conserving is now! Don't use registered addresses for every node on your network unless you have a genuine need to do so. Use one of the many firewall or proxy server products on the market to provide Internet services to users on your internal network. The users will have the same access they always had, you'll ensure the security of your network, and most of all, you'll be able to sleep at night, knowing that you are doing your part to preserve our dwindling Internet resources.

What Is a Subnet?

Subnet masking is not always as simple as you have seen in the examples given thus far. Sometimes the dividing line between the network and the host portions of an IP address does not fall neatly between the octets.

A *subnet* is simply a logical subdivision imposed on a network address for organizational purposes. For example, a large corporation that has a registered class B network address is not likely to assign addresses to its nodes by numbering them consecutively from 0.0 to 255.555.

The more practical scenario would be to divide the network into a series of subnets, which are usually based on the wiring scheme of the facilities. By creating subnets corresponding to the ethernet or token ring networks that make up the enterprise, the task of assigning and maintaining the IP addresses can be divided among the administrators responsible for each network.

Therefore, in this scenario, the class B network address would dictate the values of the first two octets of an IP address, and the subnet would dictate the value of the third octet, leaving the fourth to identify the host. The subnet mask in such a situation would be 255.255.255.0 because the first three octets are defining the network address, regardless of whether it is registered.

Suppose, however, that you have a class C address and you find yourself in the same situation. The first three octets of your IP addresses are dictated by the registered network address, but you still want to create subnets because your workstations are on several different network segments. You can still do this, if you again think of the subnet mask in binary terms. Instead of using the class C subnet mask as it stands, you can assign some of the bits in the fourth octet to the network address as well, like this:

```
11111111.11111111.11111111.11110000
```

Converting this address back to decimal form yields a subnet mask of 255.255.255.240. This arrangement enables you to define up to 14 network addresses (not 16, because values of all zeroes or all ones are not allowed) composed of up to 14 hosts on each. You can alter the bit arrangement in favor of more networks or more hosts as needed. To assign network and host addresses using this method, it is a good idea to work out the proper values in binary form and then convert them to decimals to avoid errors. Because most humans do not think in binary terms, a good calculator is helpful in this task.

In most cases, the value for your workstation's subnet mask will be supplied to you along with your IP address, either by hand or through a DHCP server, especially if a complicated subnetting arrangement like this is being used. Remember, though, that subnetting is a local phenomenon. TCP/IP applications treat all IP addresses alike, regardless of which bits are used to identify the network.

Default Gateway

The final setting on the IP Address page is the address of a gateway system on your local network segment that provides access to the rest of the internetwork. This can be a computer, a switch, or a router that joins two or more of the segments on your network. You can have more than one gateway on your local segment, but this is the one that your workstation will use by default when trying to connect to a computer on another network.

If you can connect to other systems on the local network but not to those on other networks, then it is likely that you either have specified an incorrect value for the default gateway, or that the gateway itself is malfunctioning.

The use of the default gateway to access certain destinations can be automatically overridden in your workstation by the receipt of an ICMP redirect message, which would contain the address of another gateway that provides a more efficient route to the destination.

Advanced IP Addressing

As mentioned earlier, a computer can have more than one network interface, each of which must have its own TCP/IP configuration settings. The IP Address page of the Microsoft TCP/IP Properties dialog box contains a selector that enables you to choose from the network adapters installed in your machine, so that you can provide the different settings needed for each.

It is also possible, however, to assign more than one IP address to a single network host adapter. When you click the Advanced button on the IP Address page, you are presented with the Advanced IP Addressing dialog box (see figure 10.9) where you can enter additional addresses for each installed network adapter.

The most common scenario in which a user would want to assign multiple addresses to a single adapter is in the case of a machine used as a server on the Internet. You can, for example, run a World Wide Web server product on a Windows NT workstation directly connected to the Internet and host web sites for different customers, providing each site with its own IP address. Internet users could then access the different sites associated with each of the IP addresses, never knowing that they were all running on the same machine.

This dialog box also enables you to specify the addresses of additional gateways for each adapter. Unlike the additional IP addresses, however, which all remain active simultaneously, additional gateways are only used (in the order listed) when the primary default gateway is unreachable.

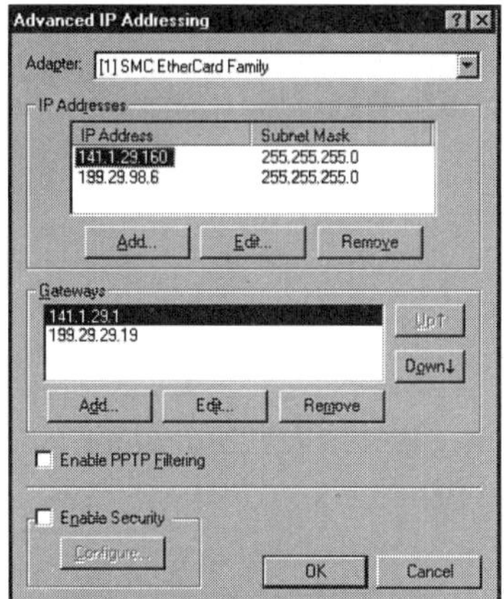

Figure 10.9

The Advanced IP Addressing dialog box enables you to assign multiple IP addresses to one host adapter.

Understanding DHCP

As mentioned earlier, TCP/IP users and administrators can avoid all the workstation configuration chores discussed thus far in this chapter by using a DHCP server to assign the configuration settings automatically.

You have already read about the problems Microsoft faced when adopting TCP/IP on its own internetwork. To resolve the problem of IP address assignment and administration on a large scale, Microsoft worked with other networking professionals to create the Dynamic Host Configuration Protocol. DHCP is an open standard defined in the IETF's Requests for Comments. Other manufacturers market DHCP servers, but Microsoft includes theirs in the Windows NT Server package.

Microsoft's DHCP server consists of an application for managing, tracking, and allocating TCP/IP configuration settings and a protocol for delivering those settings to DHCP clients. The server supports many different client platforms, including many not made by Microsoft.

When you elect to make a Windows NT (or Windows 95) workstation into a DHCP client, you need click only one checkbox on the IP Address page of the Microsoft TCP/IP Properties dialog box to have all the required TCP/IP configuration settings automatically assigned to your machine. In addition, the settings are all stored in a central location, the DHCP server, which prevents the need to manually maintain a record of IP address assignments.

DHCP resolves some of the biggest problems inherent in TCP/IP, as it was originally conceived. It eliminates the chore of configuring every workstation individually, and it makes the assignment of duplicate IP addresses virtually impossible. The use of DHCP is recommended on all Windows NT networks, but only when it is used on all of the network's systems. Problems can arise when a mixed environment is created, in which some computers use DHCP while others do not. Even when you have systems that must be assigned a specific IP address, assign it using DHCP, if only for reasons of efficient record keeping.

Origins of DHCP

DHCP has its origins in BOOTP, an earlier protocol designed for use with diskless workstations. A BOOTP server stored IP addresses and other configuration settings for workstations, keyed according to the Media Access Control (MAC) address hardcoded into each workstation's network interface adapter. As a computer on the network was booted, its TCP/IP settings would be delivered to it by the server. After the TCP/IP stack was operational, BOOTP would transfer an executable operating system boot file to the workstation using TFTP (the Trivial File Transfer Protocol, a UDP version of FTP), and the workstation would then be ready for use.

BOOTP resolved one of TCP/IP's basic problems by eliminating the need for each workstation to be manually configured by an administrator or an end-user. It did not really alleviate the administrative problem of IP address assignment, however, because it only provided a central location for the storage of the configuration settings. The IP settings for each individual workstation still had to be specified by the administrator and manually stored on the server. If duplicate IP addresses were accidentally entered into the configurations of two different machines, BOOTP could do nothing to detect, prevent, or remedy the situation.

IP Address Allocation

DHCP was designed to be an improvement over BOOTP. It retains the best aspects of its predecessor, which is the storage and automatic delivery of TCP/IP configuration data, and builds on it to create an even better solution.

DHCP is capable of assigning IP addresses to its clients in three different ways:

- **Manual allocation.** Essentially the equivalent of the BOOTP service, IP addresses and other configuration settings are individually entered by the administrator, stored on the server, and delivered to predetermined clients.
- **Automatic allocation.** As a DHCP client workstation boots on the network for the first time, the DHCP server randomly assigns it an IP address and other configuration settings from a pool of available addresses that the administrator has configured the server to use. These become the permanent settings for the machine.
- **Dynamic allocation.** This is the same as automatic allocation, except that the TCP/IP settings are not permanently assigned, but only leased for a specified amount of time. The lease must be periodically renewed through (automatic) negotiations between the DHCP client and the server.

These three methods can be used simultaneously, providing all the options that network administrators should require. Manual allocation is a necessary holdover from BOOTP because often certain computers on the network must have a particular IP address permanently assigned, such as World Wide Web and ftp servers. The advantage to using DHCP for such computers (rather than simply configuring them manually) is that all IP address information for the entire network can be stored in one place, and that DHCP will prevent any other DHCP client from using the addresses that have been manually allocated.

A network that rarely changes can use DHCP to automatically allocate IP addresses, creating a permanent network configuration. If a workstation is moved from one subnet to another, it will automatically be assigned a new IP address for that subnet. The address on the old subnet, however, will remain allocated until the administrator manually deletes the assignment from the DHCP table.

When a computer is dynamically allocated an IP address, its lease must be renewed periodically or it will expire, causing the address to be returned to the pool of available addresses. The lease renewal process is automatic and invisible to the user, unless it fails. If the computer is moved to a different subnet, it is assigned an appropriate IP address for its new location. The old address assignment is returned to the pool when its lease expires.

Thus, dynamic allocation resolves the problem of the "roving user," the portable computers that can be logged on to the network from different offices, different buildings, or even different cities.

Other DHCP Capabilities

The controlled allocation of IP addresses is clearly DHCP's primary strength, but an IP address alone is not sufficient to fully configure a workstation's TCP/IP stack. DHCP can also supply a client with settings for more than 50 other TCP/IP-related parameters, many of which are intended only for use with non-Microsoft clients.

A Windows NT or Windows 95 DHCP client can be furnished with any or all the following configuration parameters:

- **IP address.** A 32-bit dotted decimal address used to identify a particular host on an IP network.
- **Subnet mask.** A 32-bit dotted decimal value used to differentiate the network address bits of an IP address from the host address bits.
- **Router.** The IP addresses of the default gateway systems that a client will use to access remote networks (accessed in the order they are listed).
- **DNS servers.** The IP addresses of the DNS servers that will be used by a client to resolve Internet host names into IP addresses (accessed in the order they are listed).

- **Domain name.** The name of the client's Internet domain (not to be confused with a Windows NT domain).
- **WINS/NBNS (Windows Internet Naming System/NetBIOS Name Server) addresses.** The IP addresses of the WINS servers that the client will use for NetBIOS name registration and resolution services.
- **WINS/NBT (Windows Internet Naming System/NetBIOS over TCP/IP) node type.** A code used to specify which name resolution techniques will be used by the client, and in what order.
- **NetBIOS scope ID.** A character string used to identify a group of NetBIOS machines that can communicate only with each other.

DHCP Communications

When a Windows NT workstation is configured to use DHCP to obtain its TCP/IP configuration settings, it undergoes a negotiation process with a DHCP server that results in a lease arrangement. The communications with the server are carried out using the protocol defined in the DHCP Request for Comment, published by the Internet Engineering Task Force.

The actual Dynamic Host Configuration Protocol consists of a single packet type that is used for all DHCP client/server communications. Carried by the User Datagram Protocol, the packet header contains a DHCP Message Type field that identifies the function of that packet, from among the following:

Value	Message Type	Purpose
1	DHCPDISCOVER	Used by clients to locate DHCP servers
2	DHCPOFFER	Used by servers to offer IP addresses to clients
3	DHCPREQUEST	Used by clients to request a specific IP address
4	DHCPDECLINE	Used by clients to reject an offered IP address
5	DHCPACK	Used by servers to acknowledge a client's acceptance of an IP address
6	DHCPNAK	Used by servers to reject a client's acceptance of an IP address
7	DHCPRELEASE	Used by clients to terminate the lease of an IP address

The various message types are used in the communications between DHCP servers and clients to allot IP addresses and periodically renew them, as detailed in the following sections.

Lease Negotiation

Before a lease has been negotiated, a potential DHCP client is operating a TCP/IP stack without an IP address, so its communication capabilities are obviously limited. It is able, however, to broadcast a DHCPDISCOVER message, in the hope of locating a DHCP server. Broadcasts are normally limited to the local network segment, but DHCP, being an open standard, is supported by many of the routers on the market, enabling them to propagate DHCP broadcasts across network boundaries. In this way, a single DHCP server can maintain clients on multiple network segments.

The DHCPDISCOVER packet contains the MAC address of the workstation, enabling DHCP servers to reply using unicasts rather than broadcasts. All DHCP servers receiving the broadcast are obliged to reply to the client with a DHCPOFFER packet containing an IP address and other configuration settings for the client's consideration. If the client receives multiple DHCPOFFER packets, it selects one and broadcasts a DHCPREQUEST containing the IP address and settings that it intends to accept. This message is broadcast both to inform the selected server of its acceptance and to notify the other servers that their offers are being rejected.

During this period, the IP address offered by the server is not yet fully committed to that client. Under certain circumstances, those same settings might be offered to another potential client in the interim. Upon receiving a DHCPREQUEST, however, the server commits the offered settings to the client, writing them to its database and creating a *bound client.* It then sends a DHCPACK packet to the client, informing it of its acknowledgment. The exchanges involved in a successful lease negotiation are shown in figure 10.10. If, for any reason, the lease cannot be finalized, the server sends a DHCPNACK packet, and the client begins the entire process again with a new DHCPDISCOVER packet.

On receipt of the DHCPACK, the client performs a final check of the offered IP address using the Address Resolution Protocol to look for a duplicate address on the network. If one is found, the client sends a DHCPDECLINE packet to the server, nullifying the entire transaction. Otherwise, the settings are used to configure the TCP/IP stack and a network logon can commence.

Lease Renewal

After a lease has been negotiated, the DHCP client has the right to utilize the settings allocated to it for a period of time that is configured at the server. The default lease period is three days. Each time the workstation logs on to the network, it renews the lease by broadcasting a DHCPREQUEST message containing the *lease identification cookie*, the combination of the workstation's MAC address and IP address that uniquely identifies the lease to the server.

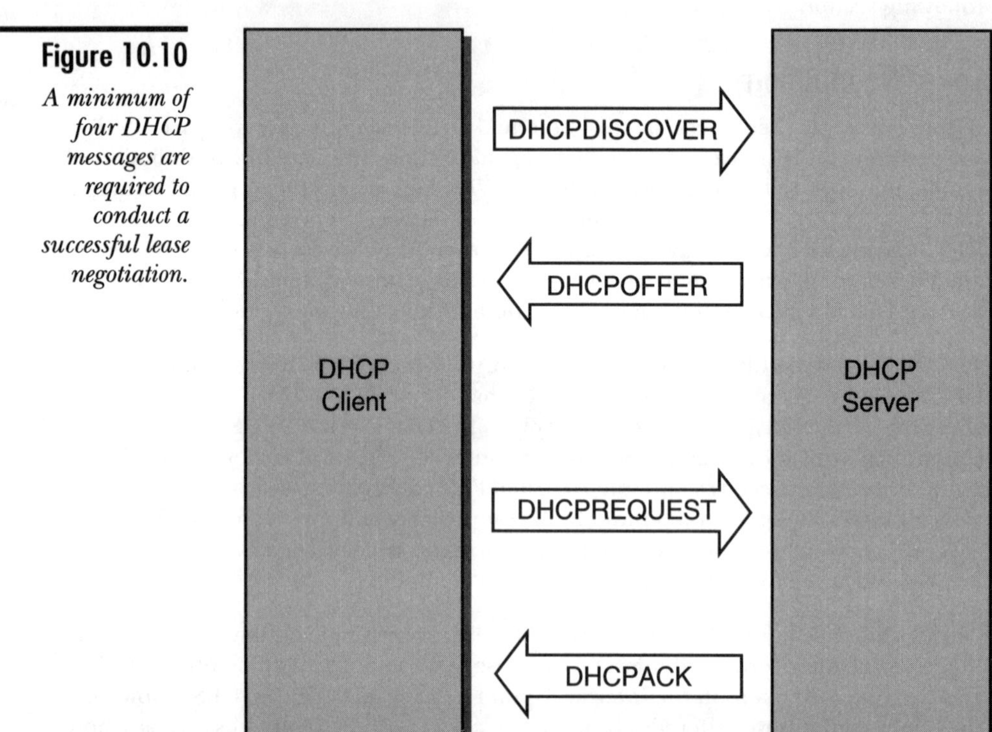

Figure 10.10
A minimum of four DHCP messages are required to conduct a successful lease negotiation.

Under normal conditions, the server replies with a DHCPACK message as before. If the server detects that the client is on a different subnet from the one where the lease was negotiated, it will issue a DHCPNACK message, terminating the lease and forcing a renegotiation. If the client receives no response to the request after 10 attempts, it will broadcast a DHCPDISCOVER in the hope of negotiating a new lease.

If the client reaches the time at which 50 percent of its current lease period has expired, it moves from the *bound* state to the *renewing* state. DHCPREQUEST messages are then sent as unicasts to the server holding the lease rather than broadcasts. At 87.5 percent of the lease period, the client moves into the *rebinding* state, in which it begins broadcasting DHCPREQUEST messages again, soliciting a response from any DHCP server. If the entire lease period expires without a response from a DHCP server, the client enters the *unbound* state, and all TCP/IP communications cease, except for the DHCPDISCOVER broadcasts needed to begin a new lease negotiation.

Running the Microsoft DHCP Server

The DHCP server that ships with Windows NT Server 4 runs as a service after being installed through the Network Control Panel in the usual manner. Also included is the DHCP Manager, an application that network administrators use to define the configuration settings to be furnished to DHCP clients. The DHCP Manager, though it ships only with NT Server, runs perfectly well on the Workstation product. You can create a shortcut to the executable on your server drive and manage any and all DHCP servers on your internetwork from a central location.

You configure TCP/IP settings in the DHCP Manager by creating scopes and then assigning properties to them. A *scope* is a collection of IP addresses that can be dynamically or automatically allocated to DHCP clients as needed. You create a scope by defining a range of consecutive IP addresses in the Create Scope dialog box (see figure 10.11) and specifying the subnet mask that should be supplied with them. If necessary, you can exclude some of the addresses in the range from allocation. You can also modify the duration of the leases that will be negotiated between clients and the server.

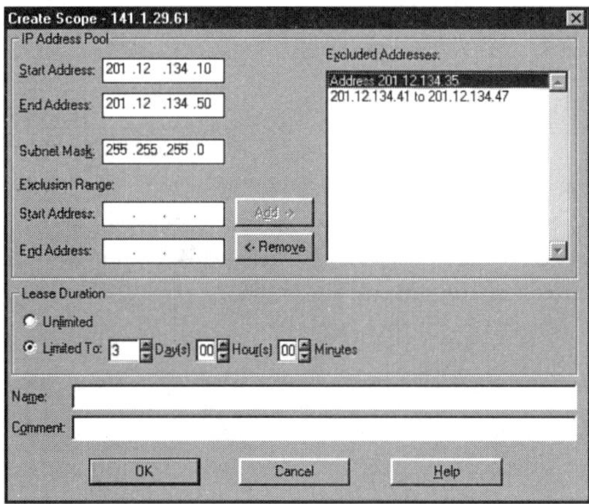

Figure 10.11

In the Create Scope dialog box, you select the IP addresses that will be allocated to DHCP clients.

After you have created a scope, you define the additional settings (from the list shown in the earlier section, "Other DHCP Capabilities") that you want to deliver along with the IP address. You can add options on a global basis, which will be applied to all your scopes, or specify only the options to be delivered with the addresses of a particular scope. The reason for these options is that separate scopes would typically have to be defined for each subnet on your network because certain settings (such as default gateways) would necessarily differ.

A typical medium-sized network, for example, might consist of several subnets and for each you would create a scope. Settings like those for the domain name, the DNS servers, and the WINS/NBT node type are probably going to be the same for all the clients in the enterprise, so they are best defined as global options. Routers and WINS/NBNS servers will more likely have to be defined as scope options, as there might be different values for different scopes.

It is up to the administrator to supply correct settings for all the required TCP/IP configuration parameters. The objective is usually to provide clients with a complete TCP/IP configuration solution, but any settings that are omitted or incorrectly configured will cause TCP/IP communications at the client to malfunction without warning.

Settings for most of a DHCP client's parameters (except the IP address) can also be applied at the client workstation, through the Microsoft TCP/IP Properties screen in the Network Control Panel, in the normal manner. A client-specified setting will always override one supplied by DHCP. For this reason, if you are converting workstations from local configurations to DHCP, be sure to remove the existing TCP/IP settings in the client's Control Panel.

A DHCP server cannot itself use DHCP to obtain its own TCP/IP configuration (even from another server). Its settings must be manually configured in the Microsoft TCP/IP Properties dialog box.

DHCP and WINS

As you learn in the following sections, another major concern when using TCP/IP on the enterprise internetwork is name resolution. Just as DHCP maintains a listing of its clients' MAC addresses and their equivalent IP addresses, so there must be a means to equate IP addresses with the NetBIOS names assigned to all Windows NT machines during installation of the operating system.

DHCP, in resolving the problem of IP address administration, exacerbates the problem of NetBIOS name resolution. When IP addresses are automatically or dynamically allocated to network clients, it becomes all but impossible for the network administrator to keep up with the ever-changing assignments. For that reason, WINS, the Windows Internet Naming System, works together with DHCP to provide an automatic NetBIOS name server that is updated whenever DHCP assigns a new IP address. On a Windows NT network running DHCP, WINS is a necessity.

For more information, see the sections on "WINS Name Registration" and "WINS Name Resolution," later in this chapter.

Understanding Name Registration and Resolution

When it comes to network communications, the TCP/IP protocols are entirely reliant on IP addresses for the identification of other systems. Windows NT, however, has always based its network communications on NetBIOS names. The Internet, too, although reliant on IP addresses, uses its own host naming system to identify networked computers. On both a private Windows NT network and the Internet, there must be mechanisms by which these various names can be equated with IP addresses.

Several mechanisms, with varying levels of sophistication, can be used by Windows NT to accomplish these tasks; but they all can be reduced to what is ultimately a table containing the names and their equivalent addresses. The differences in the mechanisms center on the methods used to get the information into the table and the ways in which it is retrieved. These two tasks are known as *name registration* and *name resolution*, respectively.

If you are running a Windows NT network that is connected to the Internet, you will need to have at least two separate name resolution mechanisms. Internet host names and NetBIOS names are always treated separately in this respect, even if a computer uses the same name for both. If your network is not connected to the Internet, you can dispense with the host names, but NetBIOS names are required for Windows NT's basic file and printer sharing services.

The following sections examine the various mechanisms that can be used by Windows NT for the registration and resolution of both Internet host names and NetBIOS names. For Internet host names, these mechanisms are:

- The HOSTS file
- The Domain Name Service

For NetBIOS names, the mechanisms are:

- Network Broadcasts
- The Windows Internet Naming Service (WINS)
- The LMHOSTS file

All Windows NT workstations use at least one of these mechanisms during every TCP/IP exchange over the network that uses a name instead of an IP address. Understanding how they work can help you to maximize the efficiency of your network and keep network traffic levels to a minimum.

Internet Host Names

The TCP/IP protocols were developed for use on the Internet, and one of the requirements for their design was that they be completely self-sufficient in their addressing. Because they were going to be used on a wide variety of computing platforms, the existence of a MAC address, such as is found on all ethernet and token ring adapters, could not be taken as a given. An IP address is therefore assigned to every host on a TCP/IP network, providing an ideal means of identification for the computers doing the communicating.

IP addresses have, unfortunately, proven to be a less than ideal means of computer identification for humans. Think of how many World Wide Web and ftp servers you know by their host names, such as www.intel.com and ftp.microsoft.com and imagine having to remember up to 12 digits for each one instead. Internet host names were devised solely as a means to provide friendly names for the user interface.

As you saw earlier in this chapter, the IP header does not carry the host names of the source and destination computers, only the IP addresses. Whenever an application, such as a web browser or an ftp client, attempts to connect to another computer whose host name has been specified by the user, the first step in the process is to resolve the name into an IP address.

Because they are not directly associated with the TCP/IP communications processes, host names can be considered independently of IP addresses. For example, a computer with a single network adapter and one IP address can have many host names. You can run a web server, an ftp server, and a DNS on the same machine and use a different host name for each, with all of them pointing to the same IP address.

Domain Names

An Internet host name consists of several words separated by periods. There are two or more domain names that identify the organization running the network, plus a name that identifies the specific computer. The names are organized hierarchically, with the most specific name (that is, the computer's name) first, followed by the domain names. The last word always specifies the top-level domain name.

Do not confuse the Internet use of the word domain with a Windows NT network domain. Although both are collections of computers, they refer to entirely different concepts.

The Internet can be pictured as a river that is broken up into an increasingly complex network of tributaries as it flows downstream. At the source are the core servers, representing the highest level of domains. Those domains branch off into smaller rivers, representing organizations, which branch further into networks, arriving ultimately at the small streams that represent individual computers.

The purpose of this arrangement is to distribute the task of administering the Internet host names among each of the organizations running Internet computers. This way, no one body or organization is saddled with the task of administering the entire Internet, which would today be a Herculean labor.

Like IP addresses, domain names must be registered with a central body representing the top level of domains. At their highest level, domain names are representative of geographical or organizational boundaries. In the United States, the top-level domains are organizational. Most of them are administered by InterNIC, the same group that registers network addresses. The domains are notated using the following names:

- *.com* for commercial enterprises
- *.edu* for educational institutions
- *.gov* for government agencies
- *.mil* for military organizations
- *.net* for networking organizations
- *.org* for nonprofit organizations

Other countries utilize geographical domain names, with two-letter codes representing nations, such as .fr for France, .de for Germany (Deutschland), and so on.

When a company or other organization registers a domain name with InterNIC, it specifies the word to be used as the second-level domain name and receives the exclusive rights to the use of that name on the Internet. This name, in combination with the top-level name (for example, mycorp.com), uniquely identifies that organization on the Internet.

As with IP addresses, every computer's Internet host name must be unique. After a domain name has been registered, the network administrators at the registered organization are responsible for assigning host names to individual machines. Just as with IP addresses, the administrative task of maintaining a record of host names is distributed between the Internet domain registry and the individual network support personnel. The administrators of a domain might also elect to break up their network into any number of subdomains, each of which adds an additional word to the host name, as in ftp.newyork.mycorp.com.

You might have noticed that the examples of host names given in this chapter all refer to machines functioning as Internet web or ftp servers. This is because these are the most likely computers to have Internet host names. Even if you are assigning registered IP addresses to all your clients on the network, Internet host names are not required except on machines that are to be accessed by outside computers over the Internet.

You do not need a host name to utilize Internet services, just an IP address. In the same way, Internet host names are not used when accessing Windows NT network file and print services; NetBIOS names are used for that. What every computer attached to the Internet needs, however, is a way to resolve the host names that users supply as destinations in their web browsers and other Internet software.

Using a HOSTS File

The simplest way to resolve Internet host names is to maintain a table of those names and their equivalent IP addresses. That is all that a HOSTS file is, an ASCII file, stored on the local hard drive, that lists IP addresses on the left and host names on the right. When a user supplies an application with a host name, it looks it up in the HOSTS file. If the name is found, its equivalent IP address is used to create the network connection. If it is not found, the operation fails.

At one time, name resolution services for the entire Internet were provided through a single HOSTS table containing thousands of entries that had to be regularly downloaded by Internet users to upgrade their systems.

The problems with this method are obvious. The name registration method—that is, the means by which the names and addresses are inserted into the file—is wholly manual. Users or administrators must individually modify or upgrade the HOSTS file on every network workstation to include the name and address of every host to be contacted by name. A HOSTS file for the entire Internet as it exists today would probably take up most of your hard drive and take hours to parse for every name search.

As a name resolution method for a relatively small group of names, however, the HOSTS file is rather efficient, when it succeeds. Unless the file is huge, a HOSTS table search will nearly always be faster than the other Internet name resolution method available, the DNS look-up. Because the HOSTS file is always searched before a DNS is consulted, adding your most commonly accessed sites to the file can speed up your accesses. Do not make the mistake of adding too many entries to the file, however. The time required to parse hundreds of HOSTS file entries can extend DNS search times significantly.

When Windows NT is installed, a sample file called HOSTS.SAM is left in the \windows\system32\drivers\etc directory. To create your own HOSTS file, you can remove the SAM extension from the sample and add your entries according to the pattern shown in the file.

Using the Domain Name Service

The Domain Name Service, or DNS, is the more commonly used method of Internet host name resolution because it enables users to connect to any site anywhere on the Internet, by name. This might seem like an incredible feat, particularly in light of the Internet's growth in the past two years, but the DNS takes advantage of, and is indeed the primary reason for, the domain-based structure of Internet host names.

The Domain Name System consists of thousands of DNS servers located all over the Internet. When you register a domain name, you are required to specify a primary and a backup DNS server. These are known as the *authoritative servers* for your domain. A DNS server is a Unix daemon or a Windows NT service that is responsible for maintaining and publishing a table of the host names and addresses in its own domain.

A domain's DNS servers do not necessarily have to be located on its local network. Many Internet Service Providers (ISPs) will provide the use of their DNS servers for a fee. What's important is that InterNIC, or whatever other body has registered the domain name, has a record of the DNS servers responsible for that domain's hosts.

Because individual network administrators are responsible for assigning the host names within their domains, they must also be responsible for maintaining the DNS records of those names. Surprisingly, the registration of a domain's host names in its DNS servers is no less of a manual operation than in a HOSTS file. If you add a new ftp server to your network, for example, you must manually edit a DNS configuration file, specifying the name and address of the new machine.

Thus, the name registration procedure for the DNS provides little advantage over HOSTS, except that you only have to register the host names and IP addresses in your own domain. The advantage of the DNS is evident in the way that the host names are resolved.

The same DNS servers used by a domain to register its host names can also be used by the domain's clients to resolve the names of computers at other sites. If you do not have a registered domain, your ISP will be able to provide client access to a DNS as part of its connection fee. You can also run a DNS server for client use yourself, even when you have not registered a domain. Windows NT Server 4 ships with a DNS server module that you can easily install and configure for this purpose.

How a DNS Resolves Host Names

When a client supplies the Internet host name of a remote system in a TCP/IP application, the first step taken by the application is to resolve the name. It does this by using built-in code libraries called the *resolver* to obtain the IP address of the DNS server that it should use from the workstation's TCP/IP configuration settings. The client then sends a name resolution request to the first DNS server specified.

If the name to be resolved is located on the local domain, then the DNS functions as a networked HOSTS file. It looks up the name in its own tables and returns the IP address to the client. If the name is not in the local domain, however, the DNS will fail to find a listing for it (unless it is cached in the DNS from a previous query). The DNS then forwards the request to the core servers at the host name's top-level domain. The IP addresses of the core servers for the standard US top-level domains (.com, .edu, .mil, .org, .net, and .gov) are preconfigured into the DNS server.

These core servers are maintained by InterNIC and handle hundreds of DNS queries per second, but they do not return the IP address of the actual host name being queried. If you recall, only the addresses of a domain's authoritative servers are registered with InterNIC. The core servers have no information regarding the IP addresses of a domain's specific hosts. This means that the domain name system is actually an enormous database, distributed among thousands of servers worldwide. There is, in fact, no central location that has complete listings of all the hosts and all the IP addresses on the Internet.

Thus, when a host name query is forwarded to one of the core servers by a DNS, its reply contains only the IP address of the authoritative server for the domain on which the host is located. The client's DNS then sends another query to that authoritative server, which returns the IP address of the actual machine using the host name.

To prevent repeated queries on the same names, a DNS server also caches the information for the host names it has resolved. This is one reason why you might notice a delay when connecting to a new machine over the Internet, although commonly used sites are accessed more quickly.

The DNS might seem like a fairly complex mechanism for what is essentially a simple task, but remember that it was designed to be a scalable solution at a time when the Internet was less than a tenth of its current size. That it has continued to be an effective means of registering and resolving host names after all the growth it has undergone, demonstrates the excellence of the design.

NetBIOS Names

Although Internet host names are optional on a Windows NT network, NetBIOS names are essential. NetBIOS is a software interface that has been used for many years to provide network communication capabilities to applications. The original networking architecture for Windows NT relied solely on NetBIOS's own naming system to identify other computers on the network.

A NetBIOS name consists of 16 characters, the 16th of which Windows NT reserves to identify the special functions of certain computers, such as domain controllers or browsers. Every Windows NT and Windows 95 computer must be assigned a NetBIOS name by the operating system installer. The name might or might not correspond to the user's logon name or the computer's Internet host name. You use NetBIOS names whenever you type a UNC path name that refers to a Windows network system, or browse the network with the Windows NT Explorer.

NetBIOS is an integral part of Windows NT networking. The Workstation and Server services that run on all Windows NT computers use it to provide the core file sharing services needed from any network operating system. Unlike Internet host names, NetBIOS names are strictly for use on private networks, so they are left wholly in the control of the network's administrators.

Because it runs above the Transport Device Interface, NetBIOS can theoretically use any compatible protocols for its lower-level communications needs. Originally, Windows NT used NetBEUI (the NetBIOS Extended User Interface) to carry its NetBIOS traffic. NetBEUI is not routable, however, so when TCP/IP was proposed as an alternative, networking authorities began work on an open standard (later published as an RFC) to define the way in which NetBIOS services could be provided using the TCP/IP protocols. This standard became known as NetBIOS over TCP/IP, or NetBT.

The NetBT standard defines two kinds of NetBIOS services—session and datagram. Session services use TCP to provide fully reliable, connection-oriented message transmissions, whereas datagram services use UDP and are subject to the low overhead and relative unreliability of that protocol.

The network service requests generated by the NetBIOS interface use the NetBIOS computer names to refer to other systems. For TCP/IP to carry requests over the network, the NetBIOS names, like Internet host names, must first be resolved into IP addresses.

Because NetBIOS names are resolved into IP addresses before transmission, you can use them in place of Internet host names on internal networks, if desired. To connect to an intranet web server, for example, a user can specify the server's NetBIOS name in a web browser, in place of the traditional Internet host name. In the same way, you can use an Internet host name in a UNC path rather than a NetBIOS name, as long as you fill the Enable DNS for Windows Resolution checkbox in the WINS Address page of the Microsoft TCP/IP Properties dialog box.

Node Types

There are several different methods by which workstations can register and resolve NetBIOS names into IP addresses on a Windows NT network. The methods vary in their capabilities and their efficiency. A workstation can use network broadcasts to locate the system with a specific NetBIOS name, or it can consult a NetBIOS Name Server (NBNS) on the network, such as the Windows Internet Naming Service (WINS), or it can use a look-up table in a locally stored LMHOSTS file.

The NetBT standard defines several node types that specify which methods a workstation should use and the order in which it should use them. Node types are either explicitly assigned to clients by a DHCP server, or they are inferred by the TCP/IP options activated in the client configuration.

The node types defined in the NetBT standard document are as follows:

- **B-node.** The client uses network broadcasts for both name registration and resolution.
- **P-node.** The client directs unicast communications to a NetBIOS Name Server for name registration and resolution.
- **M-node.** The client uses broadcasts for name registration; for name resolution, the client uses broadcasts first and if unsuccessful, directs unicast communications to a NetBIOS Name Server.
- **H-node.** The client directs unicast communications to a NetBIOS name server for both name registration and resolution; if the NBNS is unavailable, the client uses broadcasts until an NBNS is contacted.

Originally, Windows NT provided enhanced B-node service for NetBIOS name registration and resolution. The service was enhanced because if the broadcast method failed to resolve a name, the workstation's LMHOSTS file was consulted as an alternative. This enabled users to contact systems on other network segments, as long as they had been manually entered into LMHOSTS.

Windows NT now includes WINS, a NetBIOS name server that can store the NetBIOS names and IP addresses for an entire internetwork in its database, making them available to users all over the enterprise. When they use WINS, Windows NT workstations are said to be enhanced H-nodes. They first attempt to resolve NetBIOS names using WINS, revert to broadcasts if WINS is unsuccessful or unavailable, and then consult the LMHOSTS file if broadcasts fail to resolve the name. As a final alternative, workstations can even be made to consult their designated DNS servers to search for the name.

NetBIOS Name Registration

Whenever a Windows NT machine logs on to the network, it is required by the NetBT standard to register its NetBIOS name, to ensure that no other system is using a duplicate name and that the IP address is correct. If you move a workstation to another subnet and manually change its IP address, the registration process ensures that other systems and WINS servers are all aware of the change.

The name registration method used by the workstation depends on its node type. B-nodes and M-nodes use broadcast transmissions to register their names, whereas H-nodes and P-nodes send unicast messages directly to the WINS server. These two methods are discussed in the following sections. One of the two is used by every Windows NT system that is connected to a Microsoft Windows network.

Broadcast Name Registration

A system that uses broadcasts to register its NetBIOS name (B-nodes and M-nodes) does not perform a registration in the same sense as the other node types. The name is not entered into a table or stored on other network systems. Instead, the system uses broadcasts to "claim" its NetBIOS name and check to see if any other system is already using it.

The registration process begins as soon as the workstation logs on to the network. It broadcasts a series of NAME REGISTRATION REQUEST messages containing its proposed NetBIOS name and its IP address, using the UDP protocol. If any other machine on the network is already using that name, that machine transmits a NEGATIVE NAME REGISTRATION RESPONSE message as a unicast to the new machine's IP address. This causes the registration request to be denied. The user must select another name and try again.

If the workstation receives no responses to repeated NAME REGISTRATION REQUEST packets during a specified time-out period, the workstation transmits a NAME OVERWRITE DEMAND message, announcing that it has successfully registered its name. That workstation is now responsible for responding to any requests directed at that NetBIOS name by other systems.

Like all broadcasts, these name registration messages are limited to the local network segment only. This means that it is possible for workstations on different networks to be using the same NetBIOS name. Only careful supervision by the networks' administrators will prevent name conflicts and misdirected packets from occurring. This and the excessive network traffic caused by each workstation's broadcasts are the primary reasons why a NetBIOS name server like WINS is preferable to broadcasts as a name registration solution.

WINS Name Registration

A WINS client workstation begins its name registration procedure by generating the same NAME REGISTRATION REQUEST packet used in the broadcast method. This time, however, the packet is sent as a unicast directly to the WINS server specified in the WINS Address page of the Microsoft TCP/IP Properties dialog box (see fig. 10.12). If no other system is using the name, the WINS server returns a POSITIVE NAME REGISTRATION RESPONSE to the sender and writes the NetBIOS name and IP address to its database.

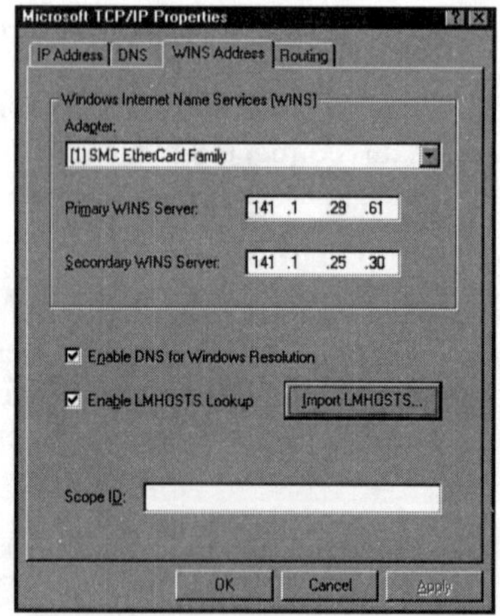

Figure 10.12

WINS servers can provide NetBIOS name resolution services for an entire enterprise network.

If the WINS server finds that another system has already registered that NetBIOS name, the WINS server challenges that system to defend its registered name by sending it a NAME QUERY REQUEST message. If the system does not respond or sends a NEGATIVE NAME QUERY RESPONSE, then the WINS server registers the name to the new system and sends it a POSITIVE NAME REGISTRATION RESPONSE. If the challenged system returns a POSITIVE NAME QUERY RESPONSE, then it has successfully defended its name against the challenge. WINS then sends a NEGATIVE NAME REGISTRATION RESPONSE message to the original system, informing it that its registration attempt has failed.

When WINS successfully registers a NetBIOS name, it assigns an expiration date to the registration in the form of a time-to-live (TTL) value. Each time the system logs on to the network, the value is renewed. Until that time period expires, any attempt to register that NetBIOS name will be challenged. If no logons occur in the specified time period, however, the NetBIOS name is released and will be reassigned by the WINS server on demand, with no challenge. If the name remains unused for a specified time period, it is declared extinct and purged from the WINS database.

Notice that this entire transaction is conducted using unicast messages between the three computers involved. There are no broadcasts flooding the network at all. This is one of the primary advantages of WINS.

NetBIOS Name Resolution

All Windows NT systems maintain a cache of NetBIOS names that they have previously resolved. When a workstation has to resolve a NetBIOS name, the cache is always consulted first. If the name is not found in the cache, the next resolution method used is determined by the system's node type. A non-WINS client will proceed to use broadcasts to resolve the name and then consult its local LMHOSTS file.

A WINS client can use all of the available methods to resolve NetBIOS names. It begins by consulting the NetBIOS name cache, and then proceeds to the WINS server. Broadcasts are used next, if the WINS server fails, then the LMHOSTS file, and finally, DNS servers and the HOSTS file, if the client is so configured. The following sections cover each of the possible NetBIOS name resolution methods in the order that they would be used by a WINS-enabled Windows NT workstation.

The NetBIOS Name Cache

During each network session, a Windows NT system stores all the NetBIOS names that it has successfully resolved in a memory cache so that they can be reused. Because it is stored in memory, the cache is by far the fastest and most efficient name resolution method available. It is the first resource accessed by all node types when they must resolve a name. You can view the current contents of your system's NetBIOS name cache at any time by using the nbtstat -c command in a DOS window. The results appear as follows:

```
c:\>nbtstat -c
Node IpAddress: [194.10.34.8] Scope Id: []
              NetBIOS Remote Cache Name Table
    Name              Type       Host Address    Life [sec]
----------------------------------------------------------
FTP.MICROSOFT.C<03>  UNIQUE      198.105.232.1       -1
FTP.MICROSOFT.C<00>  UNIQUE      198.105.232.1       -1
```

```
FTP.MICROSOFT.C<20> UNIQUE      198.105.232.1       -1
SMITHJ         <03> UNIQUE      167.171.2.56        -1
SMITHJ         <00> UNIQUE      167.171.2.56        -1
SMITHJ         <20> UNIQUE      167.171.2.56        -1
ACCTGSERVER    <03> UNIQUE      167.171.4.37        -1
ACCTGSERVER    <00> UNIQUE      167.171.4.37        -1
ACCTGSERVER    <20> UNIQUE      167.171.4.37        -1
SALES3         <03> UNIQUE      167.171.2.120       -1
SALES3         <00> UNIQUE      167.171.2.120       -1
SALES3         <20> UNIQUE      167.171.2.120       -1
```

The NetBIOS name cache is erased whenever the computer is shut down or logged off the network. This ensures that the data in the cache is always up to date. You can use an LMHOSTS file to preload often-used NetBIOS names and their IP addresses into the cache, making them immediately available for use at all times (see "Using an LMHOSTS File," later in this chapter).

WINS Name Resolution

WINS is designed to be an enterprise network solution for the registration and resolution of NetBIOS names. It is the only mechanism available to a Windows NT network that automatically maintains a database of a network's NetBIOS names and their related IP addresses. It is also the only mechanism that can keep up with the IP address changes that are the result of DHCP's dynamic assignments. Unlike the broadcast method, WINS uses only unicast network transmissions, enabling it to function irrespective of the boundaries between network segments and greatly reducing the overall network traffic generated by name resolution activities.

WINS should generally be used for all the Windows systems on your network, or for none of them. Problems such as name duplication can arise if some computers use WINS while others use broadcasts. Windows NT 3.1 systems cannot function as WINS servers or clients and therefore must use broadcasts instead. To optimize the efficiency of your network, 3.1 systems should be upgraded to Windows NT 3.5 or higher and configured to use WINS.

WINS is supplied with the Windows NT Server product, where it runs as a service. A WINS Manager application is included, which can be run from an NT workstation, enabling you to manage all the WINS servers on an enterprise network from a central location. For speed and fault tolerance, you can run several WINS servers on an enterprise network. The WINS databases can be automatically replicated among the servers at preset intervals or at specified times of day. You can, therefore, schedule WINS replication to occur over WAN links during low-traffic periods, providing a unified enterprise database for a worldwide network.

WINS also provides its clients with the capability to browse machines on other network segments, without requiring the services of master browsers on those networks. This enables users to easily communicate with other machines at remote sites without wasting WAN bandwidth on browser traffic.

When a WINS client needs a NetBIOS name resolved, it sends a unicast NAME QUERY REQUEST to the first WINS server specified in the WINS Address page of its Microsoft TCP/IP Properties dialog box. The WINS server then replies with a POSITIVE NAME QUERY RESPONSE containing the requested name and its IP address, or a NEGATIVE NAME QUERY RESPONSE, signifying that there is no record of the name in the database.

If there is any delay in responding, the WINS server will send WACK (or WAIT FOR ACKNOWLEDGMENT RESPONSE) packets to the client so that it will not proceed to the next resolution method.

If the first WINS server fails to resolve the name, whether by sending a negative response or no response at all, the client contacts its secondary WINS server and repeats the process. If the secondary server fails, an H-node system proceeds to use broadcasts to resolve the name. If the WINS servers have failed to respond at all to resolution requests, however, the client will continue attempting to contact them and revert back to WINS name resolution at the earliest possible opportunity.

Broadcast Name Resolution

When NetBIOS names are resolved using broadcasts, it is the responsibility of all registered systems to respond to requests specifying their names. A computer using broadcast name resolution generates the same NAME QUERY REQUEST packet as a WINS client, except that it is broadcast to all the systems on the local subnet. Each system receiving the packet must examine the name carried within, for which the IP address is requested.

If the packet contains an unrecognized name, it is silently discarded. A computer recognizing its own name in a query request, however, must respond to the sender with a POSITIVE NAME QUERY RESPONSE packet containing its IP address, sent as a unicast.

The broadcast method of name resolution is attempted by all Windows NT systems that are not WINS clients, after the name cache is consulted. If the name to be resolved belongs to a system on another network segment, the broadcasts cannot reach it, and the method will fail after the broadcast time-out period is reached.

Using an LMHOSTS File

When an attempt to resolve a NetBIOS name using broadcasts fails, the next alternative is to consult the LMHOSTS file on the local hard drive. Non-WINS clients do this automatically. For a WINS client to use LMHOSTS after both the WINS and broadcast methods fail, you must fill the Enable LMHOSTS Lookup checkbox in the WINS Address page of the Microsoft TCP/IP Properties dialog box.

Use of the LMHOSTS file is not included in the NetBT standard as part of the node type definitions. Windows NT clients are therefore referred to as enhanced B-node and H-node systems when they use LMHOSTS.

An LMHOSTS file is similar to the HOSTS file used for Internet host name resolution except that it lists NetBIOS names instead. It is located in the same directory as HOSTS, \windows\system32\drivers\etc, and Windows NT provides a sample file called LMHOSTS.SAM for you to use as a model for your own file.

For a Windows NT system that is not a WINS client, LMHOSTS is the only name resolution method available for computers on other network segments. You register the NetBIOS names in LMHOSTS by manually editing the file and adding an entry for each system you will be contacting. Each entry should contain the system's IP address at the left margin followed by the associated NetBIOS name on the same line, separated by at least one space.

Unlike HOSTS, LMHOSTS files can contain additional options that aid in the name resolution process. These options are as follows:

- **#PRE.** The #PRE tag, when added to an entry in the LMHOSTS file, causes that entry to be preloaded into the NetBIOS name cache whenever the system boots. Adding your most commonly accessed systems to the LMHOSTS file in this way will speed up name resolution, even for WINS clients. The #PRE tag should be appended to the end of an LMHOSTS entry, with one or more spaces separating it from the NetBIOS name, as shown:

  ```
  139.41.129.8  smithj  #PRE
  ```

- **#DOM:<domain name>.** The #DOM tag is used to associate an LMHOSTS entry with the Windows NT domain specified in the *<domain name>* variable. This causes the computer in this entry to receive the domain browse list from the specified domain's Primary Domain Controller (PDC). That way, computers that don't use WINS can browse the computers in their domain that are located on other network segments. The #DOM tag, with its variable, is placed at the end of an LMHOSTS entry, after a space, as shown:

  ```
  139.41.129.8  smithj  #DOM
  ```

- **#INCLUDE <path name>.** The #INCLUDE tag enables you to access an LMHOSTS file stored in another location. Typically, you would use this feature to access a file on a network drive, where it could be used by other clients at the same time. That way, network administrators could update a single, centrally located LMHOSTS file instead of updating workstation copies individually. The tag, followed by the full UNC path to the file, should be placed on a line of its own in the workstation's LMHOSTS file, as shown. (Make sure that the NetBIOS name used in the UNC path can be resolved by using the #PRE tag if the machine is on a different network segment.)

  ```
  #INCLUDE \\server1\share\etc\lmhosts
  ```

- **#BEGIN_ALTERNATE/#END_ALTERNATE.** These tags are used to provide fault tolerance for the #INCLUDE tag. By placing several #INCLUDE statements between #BEGIN_ALTERNATE and #END_ALTERNATE tags, as shown, the #INCLUDEs will be processed in order until one is successfully accessed. After one #INCLUDE is successfully read, those following are ignored, and processing continues at the next line after the #END_ALTERNATE statement.

  ```
  #BEGIN_ALTERNATE
  #INCLUDE \\server1\share\etc\lmhosts
  #INCLUDE \\server2\share\etc\lmhosts
  #END_ALTERNATE
  ```

- **\0xhh.** This tag is used to specify special characters in NetBIOS names by their hexadecimal values. If an application requires a certain character in the NetBIOS name's 16th position, you can supply it by enclosing the name in quotation marks and using \0x*hh* (replacing *hh* with the hexadecimal value of the character needed) in the appropriate position. The \0x*hh* replaces only a single character of the NetBIOS name. Be sure to include the proper number of spaces between the quotation marks to account for the 16 positions of the name, as shown:

  ```
  139.41.129.18 "application   \ox14"
  ```

Using DNS Servers for NetBIOS Name Resolution

Although it might seem to be a contradiction, you can enable Windows NT workstations to query DNS servers for NetBIOS names when all other methods have failed. This is done in the hope that systems have been assigned Internet host names identical to their NetBIOS names.

When DNSs are queried in this manner, domain names are omitted from the search. A DNS entry of server1.mycorp.com would therefore be a successful match to a query for the NetBIOS name SERVER1.

To use this capability, you must fill the Enable DNS for Windows Resolution checkbox in the WINS Address page of the Microsoft TCP/IP Properties dialog box. This also enables you to use Internet host names in place of NetBIOS names in UNC paths regardless of whether the names are identical.

Using TCP/IP Tools

Windows NT's implementation of the TCP/IP protocols includes a collection of tools and utilities that enables users and administrators to monitor and troubleshoot the TCP/IP activities of their workstations. Many of these utilities are Windows NT versions of programs developed for other TCP/IP environments that have become standard tools for network administrators.

ping

ping is the most basic and most commonly known TCP/IP utility. It is the basic tool that you use to determine whether the TCP/IP stack on your computer is functioning, whether another computer on the network can be contacted, or whether a DNS server can resolve a host name into an IP address.

ping operates by sending ECHO REQUEST packets to the destination specified on the command line using the Internet Control Message Protocol. The destination system returns an ECHO RESPONSE packet for each request it receives, and ping displays the size of each packet sent (in bytes), the round-trip time (in milliseconds), and the packet's time-to-live value.

Tracert

The *Tracert* program, known as *traceroute* on Unix systems, identifies the route taken by IP datagrams to reach a specified destination. Apart from being entertaining (especially when used to trace Internet connections), it is useful in troubleshooting routing problems. When you have a multihomed Windows NT system, Tracert is a sure way of determining which network the system is using to reach a particular destination.

Using the same ICMP packets as ping, Tracert sends successive ECHO REQUEST messages to the destination address with incrementing time-to-live (TTL) values. Because each intermediate system that a packet travels through reduces the TTL value by one, each request times out one hop farther along the route to the destination.

As each successive packet times out, it returns a message to the source containing the address of the gateway where the TTL value reached zero. These addresses are resolved and displayed on the host computer, along with the time interval for each hop.

When used with Internet addresses, Tracert provides a fascinating insight into the international telecommunications network. Because Windows NT resolves the IP addresses of each gateway, you can often identify the cities through which your packets are passing on the way to their destination. Trace the route to a web server in Europe, and you can see from the elapsed times the point at which your signal crosses the ocean.

Ipconfig

Ipconfig is a command line utility that, when run with the /all switch, displays the current IP configuration settings for each of the network adapters installed in your computer. This is particularly useful on DHCP client systems, where there is no other way to determine this information without access to the DHCP Manager program on the server. Ipconfig's display appears as follows:

```
Windows NT IP Configuration
     Host Name . . . . . . . . . : smithj.mycorp.com
     DNS Servers . . . . . . . . : 179.69.173.9
                                   179.69.173.14
     Node Type . . . . . . . . . : Hybrid
     NetBIOS Scope ID. . . . . . :
     IP Routing Enabled. . . . . : Yes
     WINS Proxy Enabled. . . . . : No
     NetBIOS Resolution Uses DNS : Yes

Ethernet adapter SMCISA1:
     Description . . . . . . . . : SMC Adapter.
     Physical Address. . . . . . : 00-00-C0-EA-D2-99
     DHCP Enabled. . . . . . . . : No
     IP Address. . . . . . . . . : 131.1.29.50
     Subnet Mask . . . . . . . . : 255.255.255.0
     Default Gateway . . . . . . : 131.1.29.1
     Primary WINS Server . . . . : 131.1.25.30
     Secondary WINS Server . . . : 131.1.29.61
```

```
Ethernet adapter SMCISA2:
     Description . . . . . . . . : SMC Adapter.
     Physical Address. . . . . . : 00-00-C1-DA-D3-97
     DHCP Enabled. . . . . . . . : Yes
     IP Address. . . . . . . . . : 131.1.43.52
     Subnet Mask . . . . . . . . : 255.255.255.0
     Default Gateway . . . . . . : 131.1.43.1
     Primary WINS Server . . . . : 131.1.25.30
     Secondary WINS Server . . . : 131.1.29.61
```

Netstat

Netstat is a command line utility that lists the TCP/IP connections currently in use by the workstation, as well as communications statistics for the network interface and for the IP, TCP, and UDP protocols, as follows:

```
Active Connections
  Proto  Local Address       Foreign Address State
  TCP    smithj:1372 ftp.mycorp.com:ftp      TIME_WAIT
  TCP    smithj:1390 www.mycorp.com:80       ESTABLISHED
  UDP    smithj:nbname       *:*
  UDP    smithj:nbdatagram   *:*
  UDP    smithj:nbname       *:*
  UDP    smithj:nbdatagram   *:*

Interface Statistics
             Received        Sent
Bytes        4441152 86989
Unicast packets      1230    902
Non-unicast packets  4087    80
Discards     0       0
Errors       0       0
Unknown protocols    9456

IP Statistics
  Packets Received            = 3705
  Received Header Errors      = 0
  Received Address Errors     = 14
  Datagrams Forwarded= 0
  Unknown Protocols Received = 0
  Received Packets Discarded = 0
```

```
  Received Packets Delivered = 3691
  Output Requests            = 961
  Routing Discards           = 0
  Discarded Output Packets   = 0
  Output Packet No Route     = 0
  Reassembly Required= 0
  Reassembly Successful      = 0
  Reassembly Failures= 0
  Datagrams Successfully Fragmented  = 0
  Datagrams Failing Fragmentation    = 0
  Fragments Created  = 0

TCP Statistics
  Active Opens               = 28
  Passive Opens              = 11
  Failed Connection Attempts = 0
  Reset Connections  = 17
  Current Connections= 0
  Segments Received  = 1160
  Segments Sent              = 846
  Segments Retransmitted     = 4

UDP Statistics
  Datagrams Received         = 232
  No Ports                   = 2299
  Receive Errors             = 0
  Datagrams Sent             = 101
```

With Netstat, you can see what type of connection an application is using and how much data is being transmitted or received. By using the *interval* parameter, the Netstat display can be continually updated to show you the ongoing progress of network communications as they are happening.

ARP

The ARP utility displays the current contents of the system's Address Resolution Protocol cache. This cache contains the MAC addresses and IP addresses of the machines on your local network that have recently been involved in TCP/IP communications.

The cache contains entries for the systems that your workstation has contacted, as well as others, because the reply packets generated by Windows NT machines in response to ARP requests are transmitted as broadcasts. This enables all the systems on a network to benefit from one machine's request. The ARP cache is purged periodically to ensure that the data remains current. You can, however, use the -s parameter to add entries to the ARP table that will remain there permanently, enabling you to reduce the number of redundant queries sent over the network.

Route

As discussed earlier in this chapter, a Windows NT system maintains a table that contains a record of the routing information received from other systems, in the form of ICMP Redirect packets. You can use the Route command to display, edit, add or delete entries in the table. You can, for example, specify that a gateway other than the default be used when transmitting to a specific destination.

The output of the ROUTE PRINT command is as follows:

```
Active Routes:

Network Address  Netmask          Gateway Address  Interface        Metric
0.0.0.0          0.0.0.0          120.110.10.100   120.110.10.1     1
120.110.10.0     255.255.255.0    120.110.10.1     120.110.10.1     1
120.110.10.1     255.255.255.255  127.0.0.1        127.0.0.1        1
120.255.255.255  255.255.255.255  120.110.10.1     120.110.10.1     1
127.0.0.0        255.0.0.0        127.0.0.1        127.0.0.1        1
224.0.0.0        224.0.0.0        120.110.10.1     120.110.10.1     1
255.255.255.255  255.255.255.255  120.110.10.1     120.110.10.1     1
```

Nbtstat

The Nbtstat command enables you to display various statistics regarding the NetBIOS over TCP/IP (NetBT) activities on your computer. With Nbtstat, you can display the contents of the NetBIOS name cache, list the current NetBT sessions in progress, show protocol statistics at regular intervals, and even reload the cache by processing the LMHOSTS file. You can, therefore, make any changes that you have made to the file take effect immediately.

Summary

This chapter covered the essential protocols that comprise TCP/IP, the settings needed to configure a Windows NT client to use those protocols, and some of the tools that NT provides to simplify the administration of a TCP/IP network.

TCP/IP is now the predominant suite of protocols used in computer networking today. Apart from their ever-expanding use on the Internet, they are supported by virtually all hardware platforms and operating systems, making them ideal for use on private networks that must interconnect computers of different types. Windows NT systems use TCP/IP as their default networking protocols. Understanding how the protocols work is essential for anyone who performs support and maintenance tasks on a Windows NT network.

CHAPTER 11

NT Workstation Networking in Action

Complete understanding of how Windows NT works and can best be deployed is predicated by a solid foundation on the essentials of NT operation, one of the foremost of which is the Windows NT networking model. Networking is an integral part of Windows NT, designed from the ground up not added-on as an afterthought. Even a standalone machine is capable of making use of the networking services, via the Remote Access Services in Windows NT. In this chapter, you'll examine how networking in Windows NT works and how you can setup, configure, and manage networking and network resources. This chapter discusses the Windows NT network architecture, the protocols and services available to the user, as well as some of the newest pieces of the Windows NT networking model—the Distributed File System and the Windows NT 5 Directory Service architecture, Active Directory.

Windows NT Workstation is designed to support the two most common network models, peer-to-peer and client/server. These different models are simply connection methodologies, not different technologies. Windows NT uses the same networking technology to connect in both connection models. There is no difference between connecting to a network share in a client/server environment, or connecting to a network share in a peer environment.

In a *peer-to-peer* environment, (which Microsoft calls *workgroup computing*), all the computers involved are equal in the eyes of the network. Each one can publish any resource, be it a folder, printer, or entire hard drive, making it available to any peer on the network. Security is maintained by each computer, with the user who publishes a resource making the decision as to which other users have access to that resource. If the network gets too large, peer-to-peer environments can quickly become unmanageable.

In a *client/server* network, network resources are centralized to network servers. This centralization includes access control and other security issues. The network types are not exclusionary; that is, you can have both network models coexisting in a single network environment. Windows NT Server is optimized for the client/server model, but Windows NT Workstation can have up to 10 users logged on to the system simultaneously. (Casually connected Internet users making requests of a web server running on NT Workstation are handled in a different fashion. These connections are not logging on to the host system, and as such, are not counted by the Connection Manager. They are simply pulling information from the host using protocols, such as HTTP, and applications that are exposed via TCP/IP.)

Windows NT Networking Architecture

Windows NT uses a layered network architecture that maps fairly well to the standard OSI network model. While the layered model is pretty much standard in terms of modern networking concepts, Microsoft has gone a step farther by modularizing the components of each layer, enabling them to enhance the operating systems networking features piece by piece, without requiring a major redesign of the entire system. As you'll see later in the chapter, they've also simplified the task of developers of networking drivers by providing sets of standardized interfaces (called boundary layers) at all levels of the networking stack. This allows for the development a variety of protocols and transports without the need for ground up redesign each time a new protocol is added to the stack.

Boundary Layers

To simplify the job of network application and utility developers, Microsoft introduces the concept of Boundary layers. Two layers are of primary interest—the Transport Driver Interface, which sits between the network transports and the session services (the top layers of the network layer, just below the OSI Application and Presentation layers); and the Network Device Interface Specification 3.0, which sits between the Network Interface Card (NIC) drivers, which provide the media access control support (MAC), and the bottom of the network transport stack. The NDIS interface is providing the Logical Link Control required by the network protocols.

The Transport Driver Interface

The upper layer of the transport protocols talk to the Transport Driver Interface (TDI). The TDI provides a standardized interface for developers of network client redirectors, simplifying their development job by removing the need to write a transport protocol-aware redirector which doesn't mean that a redirector won't presume the existence of a particular transport protocol, such as Novell NetWare's former dependence on the existence of IPX/SPX).

Redirectors are the piece of software that runs on the client to redirect local requests to the appropriate network server. The redirectors take the requests from the Windows NT Workstation service (which is the local system interface). Windows NT easily supports multiple-client redirectors, which are in the form of DLLs provided by Microsoft or by third-party vendors. These DLLs provide the appropriate services available to the particular network operating system for which they are developed, as well as provide the many virtual network connections that can be maintained between a client and any available server. Redirectors are kernel mode drivers, and, as such, provide high performance and kernel mode access to other Windows NT components that can improve performance.

Requests to share data from the local machine to other network resources are handled by the Windows NT Server service, which is implemented as a file system driver and can handle I/O requests from remote computers received by local network redirectors.

Redirectors are not the only method for access to network resources. Two other methods enable connectivity to the network resource, without using the installed redirector components, the Multiple Universal Naming Convention Provider (MUP) and the Multi-Provider Router (MPR).

Multiple Universal Naming Convention Provider

MUP is the driver that handles translation of Universal Naming Convention (UNC) names to actual network resources. The UNC convention, *\\servername\sharename*, is commonly used by Windows applications and support for this convention, in all aspects of program execution, is required for a Windows application to receive the "Designed for Windows NT and Windows 95" logo from Microsoft. Any application can make use of MUP, and MUP is not tied to any specific network provider.

Multi-Provider Router

MPR provides the same service as MUP, but it is designed not to work with UNC names but to support the Win32 Network APIs. Although MPR itself is redirector independent, the network provider redirector must supply DLL files and expose the appropriate standard interface so that MPR can take advantage of an installed network redirector.

Network Driver Interface Specification 3.0 (NDIS 3.0)

Network adapter cards present a standardized look to Windows NT via the Network Device Interface Specification (NDIS). This means that the driver developers don't need to write specific code for different network transports. They can be comfortable knowing that the operating system and any protocols written for it understand the standardized interface that their adapter driver presents. This also means that when a user is shopping for a network interface card, he can safely presume that any card with an NT NDIS driver will work correctly with the operating system. With Windows NT, a single NDIS driver can support multiple transport protocols (TCP/IP, IPX/SPX, NetBIOS), enabling simultaneous access to different network resources, running on dissimilar network protocols. The information that Windows NT uses to manage all these possible links is found in the Windows NT Registry.

All this is handled via a code module called NDIS.SYS, also known as the NDIS *wrapper.* The network support routines contained within the wrapper simplify the code development process. All processes communicate with the NDIS wrapper, and the NDIS driver provided by the NIC vendor. As with all hardware in an NT system, no direct manipulation of the hardware is permitted.

Network Protocols

Network protocols are the pieces of the networking puzzle that provide the pipes by which computers can talk to each other. Windows NT Workstation 4 ships with four network protocols:

- Data Link Control
- NetBEUI

- NWLink(IPX/SPX)
- TCP/IP

All these fit into the networking model at the transport layer, neatly sandwiched between the TDI and NDIS boundary layers. All these protocols depend on the availability of the NDIS group service. That is, you must have an NDIS device installed for them to function correctly.

In the Registry, all these protocols (and any third-party protocol that you later install) can be found as subkeys under:

HKEY_LOCAL_MACHINE\System\CurrentControlSet\Services\

Data Link Control (DLC)

The DLC protocol is used primarily by IBM mainframes and HP printers connected to your network. Windows NT does not generally use it for computer-to-computer communications because it bypasses the NT network redirector and communicates directly to the Data Link layer. Only machines that need the protocol for direct communication to a DLC device need install it. Other computers on the network that access those devices via a Windows NT system acting as a gateway to the service provided by the DLC connection do not, themselves, need to run the DLC protocol. Using DLC enables you to connect to IBM mainframes using a 3270 terminal emulator, or to AS/400 systems using 5250 emulation. DLC requires the installation of either token ring or ethernet network interfaces and the appropriate drivers.

NetBEUI

NetBEUI, the NetBIOS Extended User Interface, was originally developed by IBM for use in small networks. It's a poor choice for large network use for two reasons—it's not routable; and it's WAN performance is abysmal. On the plus side, if you are configuring NT for use in small workgroups, it's a fast, reliable protocol. It's also the protocol that was once considered native to NT. As such, it's a great choice for troubleshooting network problems with NT. If you are having connection problems, configure only NetBEUI on the system having problems. If you can then connect to other NetBEUI systems on the same segment, you can almost always rule out physical hardware problems. This is because unlike TCP/IP, for example, NetBEUI is completely self configuring. Therefore, you cannot have a user-induced protocol configuration error affecting the connectivity.

Windows NT uses the NetBEUI Frame (NBF) and is an implementation of the NetBEUI version 3 specification. The NBF transport is composed of two layers:

- **The LLC 802.2 Protocol.** This logical link control performs code, address, and control frame flow. It's also the basis for datagram data transfer.
- **The NetBIOS Frame Protocol.** This is where all the NetBEUI session management, configuration, and control is handled. Message packets are also handled by this layer.

Like other transport protocols, NBF interfaces to the TDI at the top level and to NDIS at the bottom. Unlike the other supported NT transport protocols, NBF is not routable. It's name table architecture is unable to differentiate between different networks, so it is limited to small to medium size, non-routed networks. A limited form of routing is available when using NBF on token ring hardware networks. This is the token ring-specific technology known as *token ring source routing*.

Keep in mind that NetBEUI and NetBIOS are not the same thing. NetBEUI is a transport protocol. NetBIOS is a programming interface accessed programmatically or via the NetBEUI interface.

Network Dynamic Data Exchange

Dynamic Data Exchange (DDE) has been in Windows operating systems since version 2 of the original 16-bit Windows application environment. Everything that can be done with a DDE connection is just extended into the networking environment by Network DDE (NetDDE).

This does not require a special version of DDE, but rather a special application name that indicates a networked rather than local connection. This reserved name is *servername*\ndde$. NetDDE shares must be created in advance in order for applications to make use of them. Certain NetDDE-aware applications, however, such as the Chat program included in Windows NT that enables two users to type messages to each other, can create shares upon installation. Other applications can create shares either via the Clipbook Viewer, so that data can be exchanged via the Clipboard, or the applications can make use of the DDE Share utility (DDESHARE.EXE) which ships with Windows NT.

NWLink (IPX/SPX)

NWLink is Microsoft's reverse-engineered version of Novell's ubiquitous IPX/SPX network protocol. It's not a redirector for NetWare (required if you want to be able to log into NetWare networks), but implementation of the NetWare protocol. In and of itself, it does not enable you to log on to a NetWare network, so that is why you need the redirector. Although Microsoft might argue otherwise, it is not 100 percent compatible with Novell's IPX/SPX implementation, and you might occasionally have problems with applications written for the native NetWare protocol. But for most users, it is unlikely that problems will be encountered in using simple file and print services on a NetWare server. NWLink is also capable of supporting applications that use Novell's NetBIOS over IPX implementation. At press time, Novell had not released its own redirector or protocol stack for NT 4. Microsoft, on the other hand, offers two different redirectors—Client Service for NetWare for NT Workstation, and Gateway Service for NetWare for Windows NT Server.

It is possible for Windows NT Workstation to access resources on a NetWare network without using a NetWare-aware client redirector. If an NT Server is on the network, it can run the Microsoft Gateway Service for NetWare. This enables that server to redistribute NetWare resources to clients connected to the NT server via other protocols and redirectors.

TCP/IP

Transmission Control Protocol/Internet Protocol has become the de facto standard for WAN connectivity and is fast becoming the protocol of choice for all inter-computer communications.

TCP/IP is fully routable, provides easy interconnection to the Internet, enables the use of Dynamic Host Configuration Protocol—so that IP addresses can be issued dynamically at boot time to network clients from a network server, simplifying system configuration chores—and is supported on everything from personal computers to mainframes.

TCP/IP is covered in great depth in Chapter 10, "The Ins and Outs of TCP/IP."

Streams

Windows NT also supports the Unix Streams protocol. This protocol enables multiple data channels to be used to broadcast data but requires significantly greater system overhead to operate. This additional overhead extracts a fairly severe performance penalty, and as such, is primarily used in first-step Unix-to-NT application ports, in which the goal is to move the application to the new environment as quickly as possible.

Server Message Blocks

Windows NT uses the Server Message Blocks (SMB) protocol to communicate between the local computer and the redirector software, which then can move information out over the network. SMBs themselves can be sent out over the network to remote devices on Windows NT or other SMB-aware operating systems, such as IBM LAN Server or Windows for Workgroups. SMBs are also used by the local redirector to make network control requests of the local protocol stacks. SMBs use four message types:

- **Session control messages.** Used to establish or terminate a redirector connection to a remote shared resource.
- **File messages.** Used for granting access to files at a server.
- **Printer messages.** Used to control and manage print queues.
- **Message messages.** Used for interapplication message passing between applications and remote workstations.

Distributed Component Object Model (DCOM)

In Windows NT, local interprocess communication uses the Component Object Model. With Networking, Windows NT can make use of the DCOM environment, as well. DCOM, which used to be called Networked OLE, enables the user to develop or make use of reusable components (such as ActiveX components), to distribute an application and its functions across multiple systems. After an application receives the pointer to a DCOM object, the application needs only that pointer and does not need to know where the component resides or how it goes about returning the requested information or action. DCOM provides a high-performance transport for distributed applications built using the COM model (a programming model identical to the Internet driven ActiveX technology). Using the DCOM programming model means that developers do not need to be aware of the connection methodology between systems. Unlike client/server models that use an indirect connection (the client references a server that points the client to the location of the resource), DCOM applications can get a pointer directly to the remote resource. DCOM objects can reside on platforms other than Windows NT, though Windows NT 4 is the first operating system to incorporate support for DCOM. Windows 95, for example, can only execute DCOM applications as COM applications (no distributed code).

Network Services

Network services is the term used to describe the various connectivity and control services that Windows NT uses to communicate between systems as well as between different local machine operations. These services can be as basic as the Browser Service, which allows the computer to browse the network, or as complex as Peer Web Services, which provide web, ftp, and Gopher services for Windows NT Workstation. This chapter examines each of the available network services individually.

Computer Browser

For Windows NT computer users to view resources on the network, they need to be able to browse, or view, a list of available network resources. This list is created and maintained by the Windows NT Browser service, which consists of a Master browser, Backup browser, and browser clients.

There can only be a single Master browser on the network, where the browse list is created, updated, and stored. This master list is updated to the Backup browsers on a regular basis (every 15 minutes). When a browser client needs to view the list, it sends a request for information to the Master browser which returns the appropriate information.

With the exception of Windows NT 4, the data limit for all other versions of Windows is 64 KB, limiting the size of the browser serviced domain to between 2,000 and 3,000 systems.

By default, the browser status of a Windows NT Workstation is set to a value of Auto. The Auto value means that, based on the number of Backup browsers on the network, the Windows NT Workstation system becomes a Backup browser if necessary. The current Master browser makes that determination. Windows NT Server defaults to Yes in terms of browser status, regardless of the existing number of browsers. This browser status is found in the Registry, under the value MaintainServerList in the location: HKEY_LOCAL_MACHINE\System\CurrentControlSet\Services\Browser\Parameters.

If you scan the Event Viewer, you will often notice an entry that occurs during the NT boot sequence to the effect that the local machine has forced an election to determine the Master browser. This occurs whenever a browser-capable machine enters the network and is unable to find the Master browser. This also occurs whenever a machine that is configured as a preferred Master browser starts. These systems have priority over other Master browser candidates in the election process. In the preceding Registry key, preferred browser status can be determined by the value of IsDomainMasterBrowser (True/Yes or False/No). Because all domain clients query the Master browser for the browse list, it is best to set a system not responsible for other critical network responsibilities as the Master browser. This parameter gives the user control over that mechanism.

A special "super" browser also exists in every domain, known as the Domain Master browser. This browser has the responsibility of collecting all browser announcements for the entire domain and passing them to the appropriate master browsers. By default, the Primary Domain Controller is always the Domain Master browser.

Client Service for NetWare

Covered in depth in the section "Logging into NetWare 3.x and 4.x Networks," the Client Service for NetWare is the Microsoft network redirector for Novell NetWare networks.

Microsoft Peer Web Services

Covered in Chapter 17, "Peer Web Services," Microsoft PWS is the feature-limited NT Workstation version of the Internet Information Server (IIS) that ships with Windows NT Server 4.

Microsoft TCP/IP Printing

Windows NT 4 supports both the Unix LPR (Line Printer) and LPD (Line-Printer Daemon). LPR is the service that enables Windows NT to print to the LPD service regardless of the operating system of the LPD host. This is the most common Unix print service, and LPR is part of the standard TCP/IP protocol suite. The Windows NT LPD service is most used to enable Unix system to print to Windows NT hosted printers.

Although an Internet standard for the LPD service (RFC 1179) exists, most implementations add enhancements to the basic standards. Windows NT 4 added the following enhancements:

- Support for multiple data files per control file (control commands are documented as part of RFC 1179).
- The host name parameter is passed through the Windows NT printing subsystem as LPD is configured in "print through" mode as an intermediate spooler.
- Unlike Windows NT 3.5x, which provided only 11 TCP/IP ports to handle print jobs (Ports 721 to 731), Windows NT 4 can use any reserved port between 512 and 1023, enabling a total of 512 simultaneous print jobs.

LPD receives print jobs from any LPR client, and then passes them to the spooler. The LPR control file information is interpreted by the LPD service and assigned a Windows NT data type. That data is then handled by the standard Windows NT printing engine (see Chapter 9, "Printing in NT Workstation 4").

The Registry information that defines the TCP/IP printing support (after it has been installed) can be found in:

HKEY_LOCAL_MACHINE\Software\Microsoft\Lpdsvc

HKEY_LOCAL_MACHINE\Software\Microsoft\TcpPrint

HKEY_LOCAL_MACHINE\SYSTEM\CCS\Services\Lpdsvc

NetBIOS Interface

The NetBIOS interface is the software interface and naming convention used by the NetBEUI transport protocol. This is a very common protocol in client/server environments, originally designed by IBM. Windows NT makes heavy use of the NetBT service, which is NetBIOS over TCP/IP. The Windows NT Browser, Messenger, Netlogon, Workstation, and Server services are all direct NetBT clients—via the previously explained TDI interface.

Network Monitor Agent

Using the Network Monitor Agent enables any Windows NT system using the Microsoft Network Monitor to collect and examine data about the network connection and behavior of the local machine. This can be done by setting the network adapter to collect information by capturing the network data that passes through it. Specific filters can be set to capture only the traffic of interest to the examiner. The collected data can be parsed and analyzed by the Microsoft Network Monitor.

Remote Access Service

The Remote Access Service provides dial-in and dial-out network extension capabilities, as well as the PPTP protocol, to the local machine. RAS is covered in Chapter 13, "Remote Access Servces (RAS) and Dial-Up Networking."

RPC Configuration

The RPC (Remote Procedure Call) Configuration service is a DCE-compatible implementation of the standard OSF/DCE Distributed Computing Environment interprocess communication standard.

Unlike other RPC implementations, the Microsoft RPC uses other IPC mechanisms to establish communications between systems. It can use any of three common services: Named Pipes, NetBIOS, or Windows Sockets (WINSOCK). If a client/server application is all on one machine, RPCs are not used; instead, LPCs (local procedure calls) are used in their in place of RPCs.

Using RPCs is an extension of the DLL methodology already used by Windows applications. Developers write applications that call DLLs to provide services; in this same fashion, a developer can write a client/server application that uses RPCs; applications that use RPC calls do not care where the procedure that they are calling resides. Client applications are compiled with a stub library. That library makes the application think that the resources it calls are available locally; in reality, a call is made to the resource on a remote system. To write an application that uses RPCs, four components are necessary:

1. The Remote Procedure Stub (Proc Stub) packages the RPCs sent by the server via the RPC run time.
2. The RPC Run Time (RPC RT) handles the communications between local and remote computers.
3. The Application Stub (APP Stub) takes the request from the run time and makes the appropriate calls to the remote procedure.
4. Finally, you need the actual Remote Procedure that your application and network are calling.

RPC Support for Banyan

This is about as self-explanatory as it gets; this service provides support for Windows NT/Banyan VINES interprocess communications via RPCs.

SAP Agent

The Service Advertising Protocol Agent is the client-side piece to the protocol used by IPX to determine the availability of network resources in an IPX or routed network environment.

Server

The Windows NT Server service provides the connections requested by remote systems to local system resources. Implemented as a file system driver, it sits on top of the TDI and passes the remote requests to the local file system. It also handles the data supplied in response to the remote request, passing the data from the local file system back to the network requester.

Simple TCP/IP Services

Simple TCP/IP Services add a DLL to the TCP/IP support that handles some commonly used Unix IP services (that are little used in the NT environment). The full TCP/IP installation must first be installed. These services are Character Generator, Daytime, Discard, Echo, and Quote of the Day. When installed, the default configuration sets the service up to start automatically. The service can be stopped and started using the appropriate NET commands. The syntax for the command is:

```
NET START (or STOP) "simple tcp/ip services"
```

The quotation marks are required.

If you are operating in a mixed NT/Unix environment, you'll probably make use of the Simple TCP/IP Services. In all other environments, you'll find that you have little need to install this service.

SNMP Service

Windows NT provides support for the standard Simplified Network Management Protocol (SNMP). This allows the use of a standards-based management console to receive alerts from the NT system. The MIB (management information database) provided with NT is very simple and provides only minimal information to the management console.

Installing the SNMP Service sets up an SNMP agent on the local computer so that the system can be viewed by an SNMP-capable management console (such as Hewlett-Packard's OpenView or Sun's NetManager). After it's launched, the SNMP agent waits for an SNMP request from the network SNMP manager. The SNMP Service is capable of performing only four operations:

- **get.** This operation retrieves a specific requested value from the host MIB.
- **get-next.** Like it says, it gets the next value in the MIB database.
- **set.** This changes the value of a manageable object in the MIB4 database.
- **trap.** This alerts the management console to a change or error that occurs in a managed object.

Workstation Service

The Workstation Service handles all user-mode system requests. Both the user-mode network interface and the Windows NT redirector service for Microsoft networks exist as part of the Workstation service.

Installing and Configuring Networking Capabilities

Networking in Windows NT 4 is installed and configured from the Network applet, available from the Control Panel or by choosing Properties from the Network Neighborhood context menu. Before you leap in and start to make wholesale changes to your system configuration, or to install networking services the first time, you should find out a few things beforehand.

- **Domain or Workgroup?** Do you plan on attaching your computer to a larger NT domain? If so, you need to know the domain name and have an account available with sufficient rights to create a new system account on the Domain Controller; this is generally an administrator-level account (on the domain, not on your local machine). If you are just adding your system to a local workgroup, you don't need to configure a domain. If you are attaching to a NetWare 4.x NDS network, you need to have the appropriate NDS context information for your system. If you are attaching to NetWare 3.x or to NetWare 4.x using Bindery emulation, you need to select a preferred server to log on to.
- **TCP/IP Configuration.** If you are configuring TCP/IP and your network provides a DHCP server (which provides TCP/IP addresses on demand to DHCP clients), you need only to check the box labeled Get address from DHCP Server. But if you're not so lucky, or you're configuring TCP/IP to be used by Dial-Up Networking and RAS, you need a few details. First you need an IP address, and along with that address for your local system, you need a few more IP addresses to get the system up and running on the network. First, you need the address of the network gateway, and then the address or addresses of your network's DNS (domain name service) server. Remember to get those three addresses first and you should find the configuration process fairly simple. If you are using a subnet mask other than the default, you should make sure you get that information as well.

You should have a few more details, but those details vary based on networking installed and the network interface used (ethernet, token ring, and so on).

Identification

After first launching the Network applet, a screen similar to that shown in figure 11.1 appears. This chapter covers each tab individually. If you plan on changing your local machine name or domain, click on the Change button. This brings up the Identification Changes dialog box.

Changing your Computer Name is just a matter of typing in a new name if you are a member of a workgroup, as is changing the name of the workgroup of which you are a member. You can always create a new workgroup by becoming the only member of it. It's a little more complex to move from a workgroup to a domain. If your computer name does not have an account in the domain you wish to join, you need to create a computer account in the domain. This requires that you have an account name and password that has administrator level access to create the new system account in the domain that you wish to join.

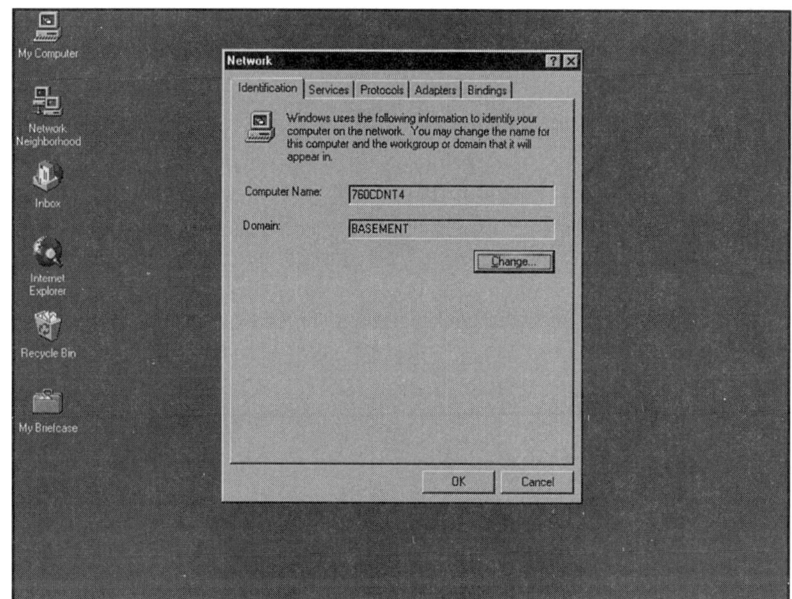

Figure 11.1

The Network dialog box provides a central location for the installation and configuration of network hardware and software.

Services

From the Services tab, you can install, remove, and configure network services (see fig.11.2).

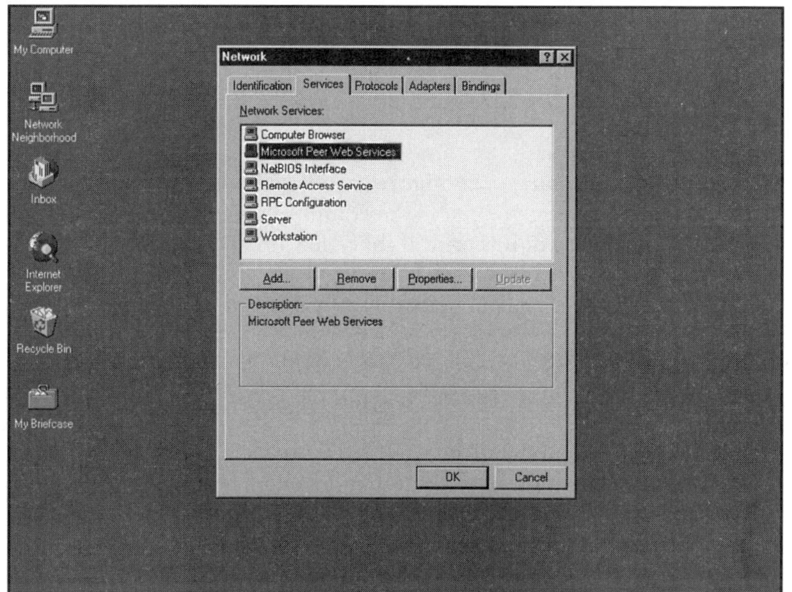

Figure 11.2

The Services tab enables you to add, remove, and configure network services.

The Network Services window displays the services currently installed on the system. Their appearance on this list does *not* indicate that the service is running properly or correctly configured, just that it was installed on the local system. Clicking on the Add button brings up the Select Network Service dialog box.

You can scroll this list and compare it to your installed services list to determine which services are available but not installed. To install a third-party service, you need to click on the Have Disk button and give the installation routine the path to the files for the service you want to install. The default NT services all require that you provide the NT Workstation 4 installation CD or a path to those same files. These off-system paths can point to network resources, and you are given the opportunity to browse system resources for the required files.

You will notice that the dialog box does not show any method of browsing for the required files. Well, if the system cannot find the files at the location you first specify, it returns an error message and a dialog box with a Browse button. After you are finished installing the services you need, click on the Close button. The system then performs the network bindings necessary for proper operation.

And because NT cannot dynamically make the service changes, you need to shut down and restart the system for the changes to take effect—even if the change you made was removing a service. In that case, NT marks the deleted service for removal, but it won't be gone until the system has been restarted.

Remember that a number of the services are interrelated; to remove one service, therefore, you might need to remove whole groups of services, or at the very least, reconfigure existing services that contained components modified by the services that you have removed.

Adapters

The Adapters tab enables you to manage, configure, and install network interface cards into NT (see fig. 11.3). Because NT can support multiple adapters, each with multiple protocols bound to the card, it is critical that the cards be correctly configured, especially because Windows NT 4 does not support Plug and Play, so there is no automatic way to detect an adapter's hardware settings or to prevent hardware conflicts. Keep in mind that if you are configuring a computer with a Plug and Play BIOS for operation with Windows NT, you need to disable the hardware's Plug and Play features. If not, you will experience erratic system operation, if you are even able to get NT to run at all.

If you need to check or modify the configuration of an installed adapter, highlight the adapter in the pick list provided by the Network Adapters window. Then click on the Properties button. If there is no vendor-supplied management software, you receive an error message stating `Software component cannot be configured`. This just means that there is no method of modifying the card from within Windows NT.

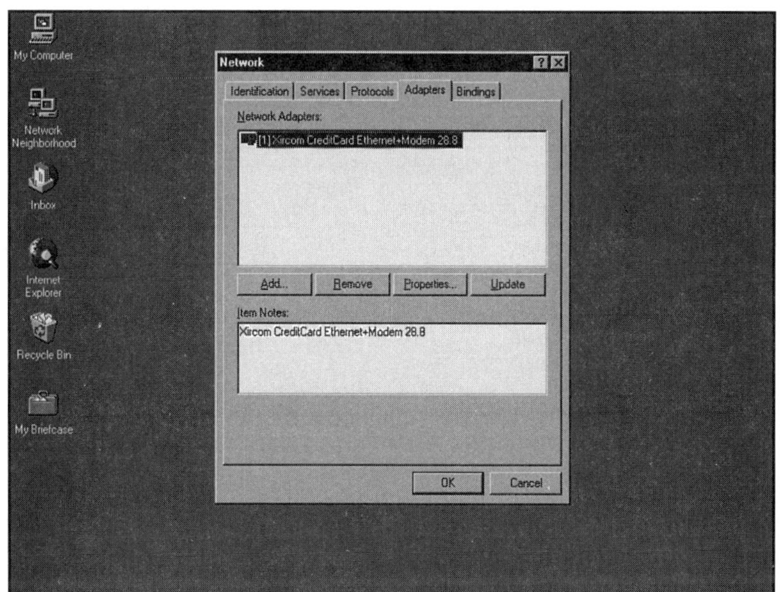

Figure 11.3

The Adapters tab shows the user the currently installed adapters and allows adapter software to be added or removed from the system.

If your adapter does have an NT-aware software component, it might look something like that in figure 11.4. This example is for a Xircom CreditCard Ethernet/Modem combo card in a PCMCIA slot in a notebook computer. As such, unless you are installing a similar device, you won't have settings for the modem or the PCMCIA chip set. The Network Settings section is similar to what you would see for any network adapter. If your hardware cannot be reconfigured dynamically, you need to know the address of an available memory location, I/O port, and IRQ free for use by your adapter.

Adding Multiple Network Interface Cards

Adding a second (or third, fourth, and so on) NIC to a Windows NT system is very simple from the software side. After you get the adapter physically installed, just select Add on the Adapter tab, and then select the appropriate driver software from the pick list, or provide the drivers as previously indicated. The real problem is getting multiple cards installed. Because Windows NT does not support Plug and Play, the user needs to know that each adapter is correctly configured from the hardware perspective, making certain that any IRQs, memory addresses, or other system resources needed by each adapter are not in use by some other system component. The easiest way to determine which hardware resources are in use is to use the NTHQ tool provided on the distribution CD in the *system_version*\\Support directory.

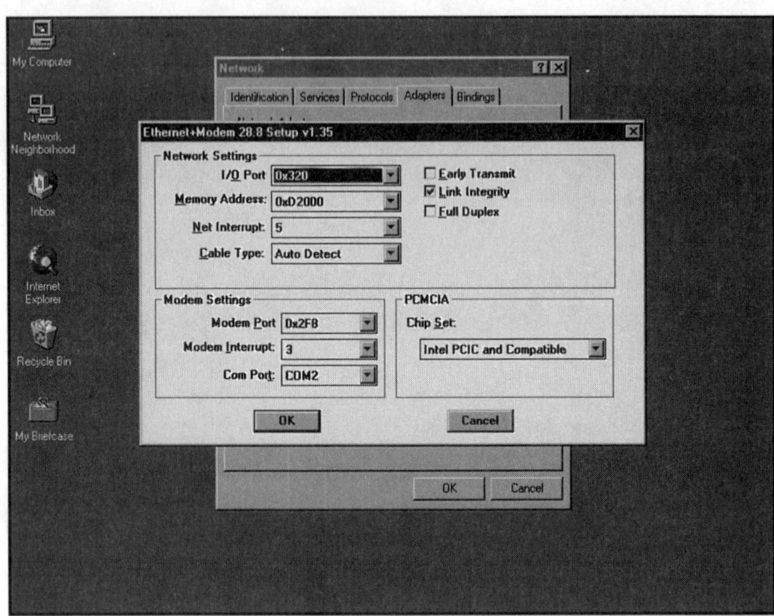

Figure 11.4

Some network interface cards have an installed software component that enables NT to configure the hardware.

Follow the directions to create the NTHQ boot floppy, and then allow the application to run undisturbed. After NTHQ completes, save the information to a file on the floppy disk. This information is in ASCII format, and you are able to read it in any editor or word processor. Examine its contents carefully to determine whether sufficient system resources are available to add additional network adapters.

Bindings

Every adapter, protocol, and service installed in your system gets bound to a configuration that enables the various hardware and software to talk to each other and the network, and from there, to network resources. This binding information determines how the various networking components communicate. Binding enables the various network components to share the services to which each is bound (see fig. 11.5).

After the service is expanded (the NetBIOS interface, for example), the components that make up the service and its bindings are revealed.

Clicking on one of the service components activates the Move Up and Move Down buttons at the bottom of the dialog box. The order in which the service, protocol, or adapter is listed is also the order in which it is accessed. If the majority of your network access is done over TCP/IP, you might want to make it the first protocol browsed.

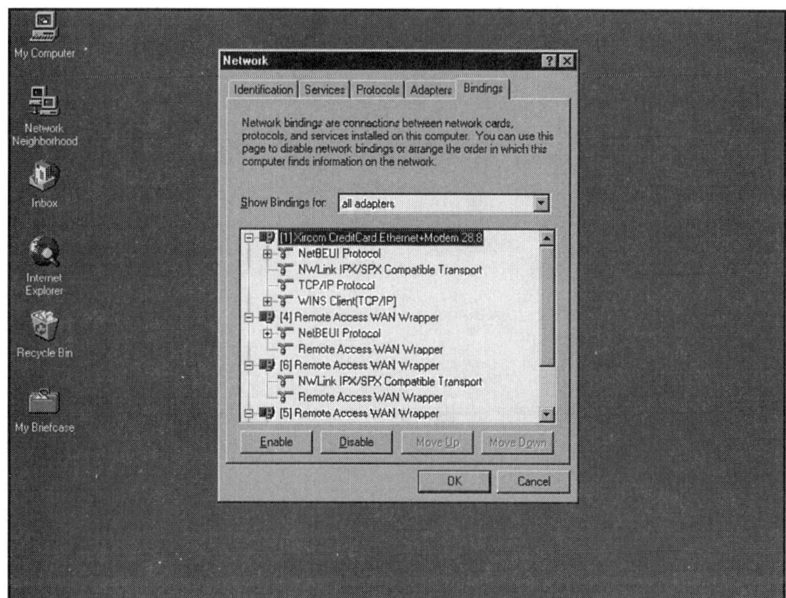

Figure 11.5

The default screen shows the services installed on your system.

Information about the bindings is available in three different views, though the information is fundamentally the same. Select services, protocols, or adapters, depending on which service you are interested in or which problem you are trying to solve.

In the protocol view, expanding the detail on a given protocol gives you the details of the adapter bindings to that protocol. In a system with a single network interface card, you will find that all network protocols and transports are bound to that card. After you install multiple adapters, that might not be the case.

You might notice that the adapter binding information would seem to indicate multiple adapters in a system, even though there is only a single adapter. This is because the single physical adapter can be represented to the system as multiple virtual adapters, with each virtual adapter having its own specific and defined configuration.

In this case, the system is configured to support all the installed protocols across a Dial-Up Networking or RAS connection (see fig. 11.6). Each protocol gets its own virtual adapter configuration that includes the protocol and the Remote Access WAN wrapper, the software component that provides the link between the protocol and the adapter-specific NDIS driver.

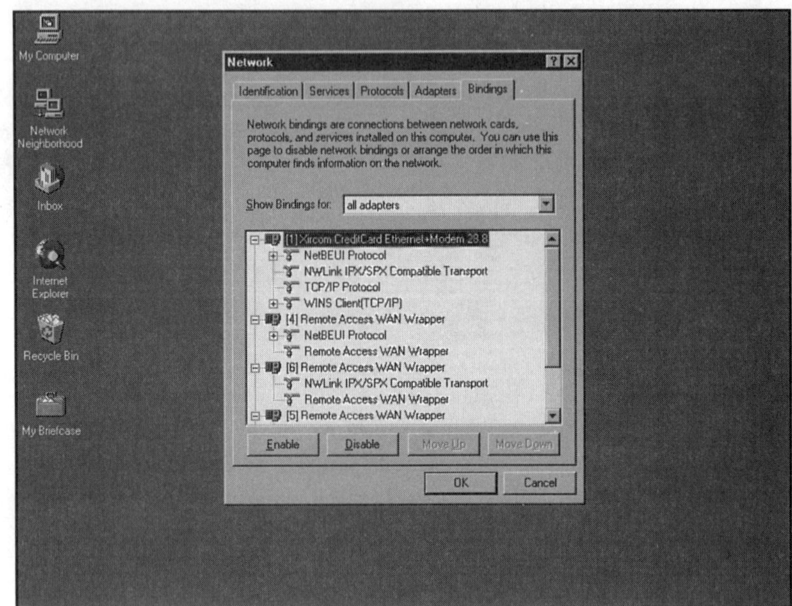

Figure 11.6
Adding Dial-Up Networking, with multiple protocols bound to its virtual adapter, creates a fairly complex set of bindings even in a system with a single physical adapter.

Connecting to Other Computers

Users can initially access network resources in three ways:

- Network Neighborhood
- Windows NT Explorer
- Via command line utilities

The command line utilities are the old MS-LAN Manager commands and are covered briefly in the section "Using MS-LAN Manger Commands," later in this chapter.

Most users initially browse the network by using the Network Neighborhood icon on the Desktop. Like the Windows NT Explorer, Network Neighborhood can vary the display of network resources (see fig. 11.7).

After you first open up Network Neighborhood, a globe icon that represents the entire network world appears, plus individual system Icons for the computers that your local machine can see on the network. At this level, there is no differentiation of the icons based on operating system or even network operating system. You will notice that there is no difference between the icons labeled Dpc410 and Primus, even though the former is a NetWare server and the latter is an NT 4 Server.

Clicking on the Entire Network icon brings up a screen offering you the choice of which network you wish to browse. If you have only Microsoft Networking installed, that's the only choice you have. If you've added additional networks, such as Banyan Vines or DEC Pathworks, you have an icon appropriately labeled available on which to click.

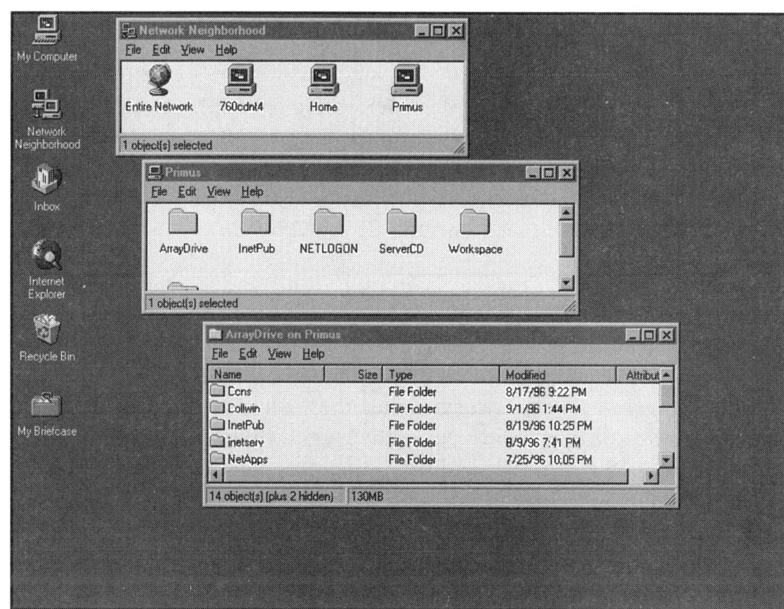

Figure 11.7

The three cascaded windows here show the large icon view of the entire visible network, a large icon view of the computer PRIMUS, and a detail view of a share called ArrayDrive.

Clicking on the Microsoft Windows Network icon brings up a screen that shows the available Domains and Workgroups (see fig. 11.8). Clicking on the NetWare or Compatible Network icon opens a Window to display the available NetWare Servers or NDS trees.

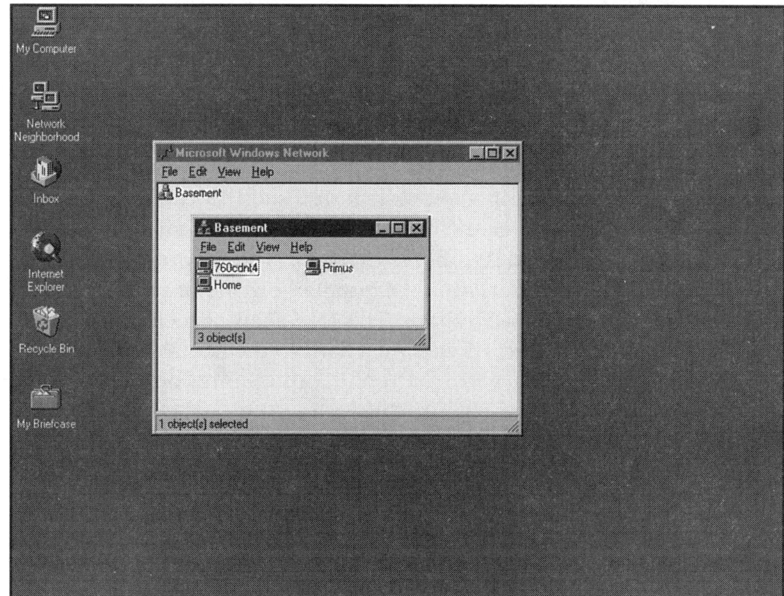

Figure 11.8

Clicking on the single Domain labeled BASEMENT opens a Window displaying the systems that are members of the Domain.

Mapping Drives

Any network share can be mapped to a local drive letter. Newer applications might not require this for proper operation, as they can make use of UNC names for all network operations. Older applications, however, will likely be unable to make use of the \\server\sharename convention and require that the network resource be mapped to the more conventional *DriveLetter*: (for example, G) convention.

The simplest way to do this is to open the Tools menu in the Windows NT Explorer and click on Map Network Drive. Then enter the share name and the drive letter to which you want it to map. You can also browse the network for available shares. If you map a share that resides in a location to which you are not currently logged on, a prompt appears for a user name and password, unless that resource requires the same user name and password with which you are currently logged on to the network, in which case you gain access to the resource without being prompted.

An interesting feature of Windows NT 4 is the capability to use Internet IP addresses in place of the server name portion of the UNC address. That is, if you know the IP address of a system and the local share names, you could use \\38.232.110.97\sharename rather than \\servername\sharename. This is much simpler for accessing servers outside your local domain than is configuring LMHOSTS files for your systems.

Using the Distributed File System

Available from http:\\www.microsoft.com is the Distributed File System add-on for Windows NT Server 4. The software is available with a client for Windows 95. Windows NT Workstation 4 and Server ship from Microsoft with the DFS client built in.

The DFS service installed on a Windows NT Server 4 enables the network administrator to create a DFS share. A DFS share gives network users a single location to access shares that may be widely distributed over the network. The network, for example, may have multiple shares scattered over 10 different servers. Normally users need to find each of these shares individually; but with DFS installed on one of the servers, the network administrator can create a DFS share. This DFS share, which can be accessed in the same fashion as any share, points the client to the actual location of the files, folders, or applications that they expect to find, but requires only that the user know the location of the DFS share.

Connecting to Servers

Windows NT is capable of connecting to any server operating system available to any of the network redirectors that have been installed on the local system. After the local machine is logged on to the appropriate network, all that network's resources available to the user's account become available.

In peer networks, such as the connections between NT machines in the same workgroup or between Windows 95 machines, there is no log on process. Authentication is handled on a case-by-case basis with the system providing the share setting explicit permission for the share.

Connecting to Windows NT Server

Windows NT uses a single-point logon procedure by which users are logged on to the network instead of logging on to a specific machine. In brief, logging on to a Windows NT Domain appears to the user to be identical to logging on to the local machine; but authentication of that user's account information is done by the Primary Domain Controller rather than by the local machine.

By logging on to the Domain, the user needs only a single account to access all the available network resources in the Domain, regardless of where in the domain they are located. Users are authenticated against information stored in the directory database, called SAM (Security Account Manager), that stores all the domain's security and account information. After you log on, your name and password are checked against this database. The master copy of the database is stored on the Primary Domain Controller (PDC) with copies replicated to the Backup Domain Controllers (BDC) in the same domain. This maintains the NT server centralized security model. There is a nine step process to allow an authenticated user access to network resources.

1. Press Ctrl+Alt+Del.
2. After the user enters a user name and password, the logon process calls the Local Security Authority.
3. The LSA runs the authentication process.
4. The authentication process checks to see whether the account is maintained on the local machine. If it is, it is processed locally. If not, it is passed on to the domain authentication package.

5. If the account is validated, the Security Account Manager returns the user's security ID and the ID of any global groups to which the authenticated user is a member.

6. A logon session is created by the authentication package, and then the session and security IDs are passed off to the Local Security Authority.

7. In the event of a rejected logon, the session is deleted and an error message is returned. Otherwise, an access token is created for the user. The token contains the user's security ID and the security IDs of the group Everyone and other groups available, as well as the user rights assigned to the security IDs. The token is then marked with a Success status and returned to the logon process.

8. The logon process creates a subject for the user account by calling the Win32 subsystem to create a process and attach the security token to it. A subject is the combination of the token and the program acting for it. Subjects are the methodology by which Windows NT manages permissions for programs the user runs.

9. At this point, the Win32 subsystem launches the user's desktop.

If attaching to multiple network operating systems, the user name and account information is handled by those operating systems in the appropriate manner.

Logging On to Novell NetWare 3.x and 4.x

To log in to NetWare environments, the first step is to make certain that the Client Service for NetWare (CSNW) has been installed. While holding down the Alt key, double-click on the Network Neighborhood icon to launch the Network applet. Select the Services tab and look for the CSNW entry. If it's not present, you need to add the service.

1. Click on Add.

2. NT builds a list of available services. Select Client Services for NetWare.

3. When prompted, enter the path to the original NT distribution files.

4. NT copies all the appropriate files, and then launch the CSNW configuration dialog box. You need to enter a preferred server (for NetWare 3.x or 4.x running bindery emulation) or a Default tree and context (for NetWare 4.x Novell Directory Services).

5. At this point, you need to restart Windows NT to make your changes effective.

Future configuration changes to the NetWare requestor can be made from the Control Panel. An icon labeled CSNW will have been added to the Control Panel and can be used to launch the CSNW configuration dialog box.

The CSNW requestor that comes with Windows NT 4 is capable of attaching to both NetWare binderies and NDS trees. Unfortunately, although it is NDS-aware, it is not NDS complete, and users cannot run the NDS administration utilities for NetWare 4.x networks when using Windows NT with the Microsoft NetWare requestor.

Creating and Managing Domains and Workgroups

Windows NT networks come in two forms—workgroups and domains. Workgroups are the NT equivalent of peer networks, with no one machine in the role of server. In the domain environment, there is more of the traditional client/server environment, with a centralized control point for network resources. With Windows NT Server, they can be configured as Primary Domain Controllers, Backup Domain Controllers, or just as servers who are members of a domain. Windows NT Workstations get the option to become a member of a workgroup or domain. And although they can act the role of a server, they cannot become PDCs or BDCs.

Workgroups

In the Windows NT Workgroup environment, each computer is independent, with the local user making decisions about what local resources it wants to share with other users on the network. Users must set their own permission levels on any resource that they choose to make available, be it folder or printer.

Domains

A Windows NT domain is a grouping of computers that shares security and user account information. It is important to note that the Domain is a logical construct, not a physical one. The grouping of servers and workstations need not be constrained to a physical location; the only constraint is that the members of the domain must be able to see the domain controller in some fashion, be it a direct network connection or via some form of Dial-Up Networking. Domains use a centralized security model with the security information stored in a master database that resides on the Primary Domain Controller.

PDC and BDC

Any Windows NT Server system can be a domain controller, either a primary or backup. This decision is made at the point where the Server software is being installed. Servers do not need to be a PDC or BDC, but can just be member servers in any given domain. As member servers, they are not involved in storing copies of the domain database or in authenticating user access to the domain.

The differences between a Primary Domain Controller and a Backup Domain Controller are straightforward:

- **Primary Domain Controller.** There is only a single PDC per domain, which maintains the master copy of the SAM database directory. The PDC tracks all changes to the domain accounts and makes the appropriate changes to the master database.
- **Backup Domain Controller.** There can be multiple BDCs in any domain, each of which keeps a copy of the SAM database directory. Each BDC periodically updates its copy of the database by synchronizing it with the master copy on the PDC.

All domain controllers (both PDC and BDC) dedicate a shared directory for the storage of security and user account information for the entire domain. This information is used to authenticate users logging on to a domain. The nearest Domain controller in the user's home domain is used to authenticate the user's access. It can be a PDC or BDC (though only the PDC maintains the replicable master user database) If the PDC goes down, a BDC can be promoted to the role of PDC. If a user logging on to the network cannot access the PDC, he cannot be authenticated, and will receive a message to that effect. If that user has previously been logged on to the domain, he will get a message indicating that he cannot be authenticated, but that he is being allowed to access the domain by using the cached security account information stored on the local machine.

Trust Relationships

Trust relationships are the Windows NT mechanism for enabling accounts in one domain to access resources in another domain, without the need for the user to have accounts in each domain. The current trust relationship model is a complex one, with the necessity of establishing implicit trust relationships between every domain that the administrator believes will have resources needed by other domain members.

Only two types of trust relationships exist. The first is the one-way trust relationship. In a one way trust, a domain controller trusts the domain controller in the trusted domain to authenticate user for resources under the control of the first domain controller. The first domain controller, which contains the resources, is referred to as the trusting domain; the domain that contains the accounts that want access to the trusting domain is referred to as the trusted domain.

The second type of trust is the two-way trust relationship. A two-way trust is the combination of two one-way trusts, in which case all accounts and resources can be used and administered as if they were all applied to members of the same domain.

From the user perspective, if trusts are available that give members of other domains access to local resources in your domain, you can see the accounts in the first domain when you share your own resources and set the access permissions on those resources.

Dial-Up Networking Connections

With the Dial-Up Networking connection for outbound connectivity and the Remote Access Service for inbound connectivity, Windows NT Workstation can extend the network to a dial-in client or connect itself to a server that then extends its network to the NT client. It's simplest to think of RAS as a software-based multiprotocol router that extends the local network (even if it's only a single machine) to a remote user. These services are not installed by default. To make certain that they are installed, check the Services tab of the Network Control Panel applet for Remote Access Services.

The Point-to-Point Protocol

Windows NT is happiest when using PPP to provide both dial-out and dial-in connectivity services (see fig. 11.9). In fact, the older SLIP (Serial Line Internet Protocol) technology is only supported by Windows NT as a client protocol in both Server and Workstation; so if the system is hosting dial-in users, they must use PPP.

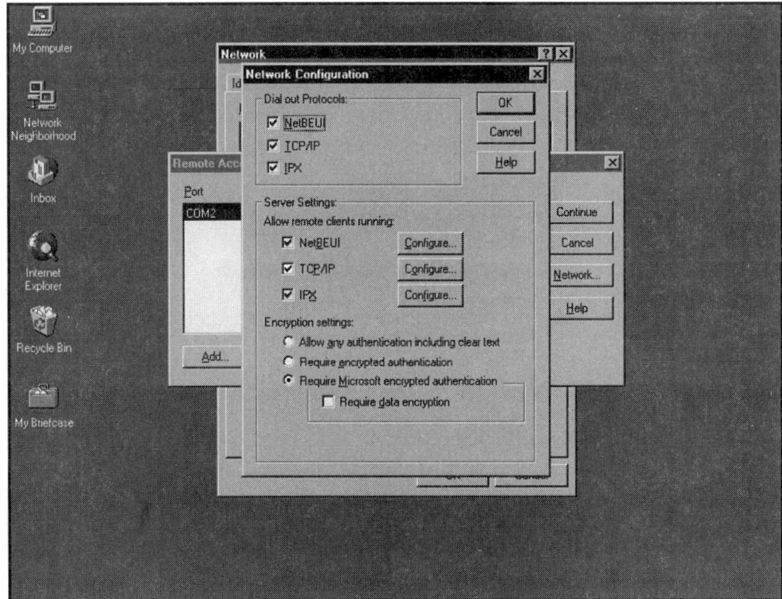

Figure 11.9

PPP is the preferred protocol for remote connectivity in Windows NT and can support TCP/IP, NetBEUI, and IPX/SPX.

RAS makes use of the PPP authentication protocols (PAP, CHAP and SPAP) to authenticate remote users. Which protocol is used depends on client configuration. After a connection is established, Network Control Protocols are used to configure the server side of the connection for the transport protocol that will be used. After the PPP connection is established, the client can use NetBEUI, TCP/IP, IPX/SPX, or any combination of the three protocols to access the network. Using TCP/IP gives the host the capability to extend the services available on the Internet to the dial-in user.

Multi-Link PPP

As provided for by the Multi-Link PPP standard, Windows NT RAS and DUN are capable of aggregating multiple dial-up connections (ISDN, Analog modem, and so on) to provide a larger bandwidth connection to remotely connected users. Though Multi-Link PPP is general considered for use with the two 64 KB channels provided by an ISDN Basic Rate Interface, the technology is equally applicable to aggregations of analog modems into a fatter network pipe than a single "V.whatever" (such as V.34) modem connection can provide.

NetBIOS Gateway

For providing dial-in connectivity to older Microsoft LAN Manager Remote users, Windows NT provides support for NetBIOS dial-in users to access network resources connected to the RAS server via IPX or TCP/IP. The remotely connected user is only loading the NetBEUI protocol and is not able to run applications that require TCP/IP or IPX/SPX. The client does, however, have access to resources residing on links via those protocols because of the translation feature that the NetBIOS gateway provides (translating the NetBIOS requests across the appropriate connection type, and then passing the information returned via those connections to the NetBEUI-attached user).

The Point-to-Point Tunneling Protocol

Windows NT 4 introduced the Point-to-Point Tunneling protocol technology. PPTP enables the creation of virtual private networks across the public network system. PTP provides a secure link between the two machines that create the PPTP session. This enables remote users to connect to a locally hosted, multi-homed system. Two network interface cards can be installed in the system, one connected to the corporate LAN and the other connected to the Internet. The Internet attached adapter runs only PPTP and rejects any other type of packet broadcast. Clients attached to the public network can link to the PPTP enabled adapter and have access to the corporate LAN. This technique, for example, enables remote offices to maintain secure connections to the main office without investing very expensive leased-line connections between the offices.

Getting DUN and RAS Up and Running

The Dial-Up Networking and RAS services don't get installed when Windows NT is installed, so at the very least, you need access to the Windows NT installation files. But more specifically, you'll need to add some hardware.

The Remote Access Service supports four different access methods.

- **Modem.** Add any standard modem (running at least 28.8 for acceptable performance). If you check the NT HCL, you'll be able to determine if your modem will be able to be detected by RAS during the install process.
- **ISDN Adapter.** If you know that ISDN is available at both ends of the connection you want to make, ISDN provides the highest level of performance short of a wired LAN connection.
- **X.25 Smart Card or X.25 PAD.** If you are accessing an existing X.25 network, you'll need an X.25 access device of some type.
- **Network Interface Card.** If you are running RAS services over a wired LAN connection, you'll need the appropriate network access device. You'll also need a NIC if you plan on using RAS to redistribute network services to users connected via one of the other access methods.

Because the services can not be installed during the Windows NT install process, you'll need to go back and add them.

To do this, launch the Network applet (either by clicking on Properties from the Network Neighborhood context menu or from the Control Panel) and select the Services tab. If there is no entry in the pick list for the Remote Access, Service you need to install it. Click on the Add button to bring up the Select Network Service dialog box. You'll see a message that reads `Building Network Services Option List` while the application goes out to find the available network services. The list will include existing installed services, and you will be allowed to install the service again; the install will fail, however, and you will get a message that you should use the Update service. Move down the list and select Remote Access Service, then click on OK.

You'll be asked to supply the location of the Windows NT install files. The screen will default to the last location that you installed Windows NT features from. If that location doesn't contain the necessary files, you'll be prompted for a new location and be given the option to browse for the installation files.

You'll now be at the Remote Access Setup screen. If you've already installed a port and communications device, it will appear on the screen list. If not, you can have the installation routine search for modems that are available to the system but have not yet been installed. You should let NT attempt to detect the modem before attempting to define a modem that NT doesn't detect.

Clicking on the Configure button enables you to select the type of connections you want the local machine to support. If you plan never to dial-in to the machine, select Dial out only (which is the default), as it's easier to provide local security if you can't dial in to the computer. If you are planning on providing both client and host services, select Dial out and Receive calls.

Click on the Network button to launch the Network Configuration dialog. This enables you to configure the protocols that you are going to support for outgoing calls. You'll be able to select which protocol or protocols you want to use on a per connection basis later, during the configuration of the Dial-Up Networking portion of the installation. But if you don't select the protocol here, it won't be available to Dial-Up Networking. Click on OK after you've selected the protocols you want to use, then click Continue. NT will complete its install of the RAS service components.

You'll be back at the Services tab in the Network applet. Click on the Close button to continue. At this point, Windows NT will begin reviewing the network bindings. These are the definitions of how the network protocols and communication devices are configured, with the appropriate links being made to allow the services to perform. You'll then need to reboot the system to complete the service installation. Once the reboot is complete, your system is ready to receive calls (if so configured). But to make outbound connections, you've got a little more work to do.

After you've finished this install, you'll notice that the option to Logon using Dial-Up Networking has been added to the Beginning Logon screen when you first log on to Windows NT 4.

Dial-Up Networking is the dialing and phone book component of the NT RAS system. It looks the same as its Windows 95 sibling, but it is only an interface over the Remote Access Service. You'll find Dial-Up Networking by opening the My Computer icon on the desktop. The first time you launch the application, you'll get a message that tells you that the Phonebook is empty. You'll then launch the New Phonebook wizard to create a Dial-Up Networking connection.

You first get to name this new phone book entry. Just overwrite the default name (MyDialUpServer) that appears on the first screen. (After you've gone through the process a couple of times, you'll probably want to check the box that says "I know all about phonebook entries and would rather edit the properties directly." This turns off the rest of the wizard.)

You then need to configure your call by selecting any or all of the options on this screen.

- **I am calling the Internet.** Take this one literally. The purpose of this dial-up connection is to connect to the Internet.
- **Send my plain text password if that's the only way to connect.** This gives NT the option of sending your password in clear text rather than encrypted, if other security implementations fail to allow you to connect.
- **The non-Windows NT server I am calling expects me to type login information after connecting, or to know TCP/IP addresses before dialing.** This gives you a terminal window after the connection is made to allow you to provide any information that the connection requires that DUN can't provide automatically.

You now get to type in all of the phone numbers that you want to use for this connection. You can add all of the numbers that you want to use if the primary number can't connect or if you're planning on using a multiline connection. If you have more than one modem available, you can even aggregate those multiple modems to link to an NT 4 RAS server, which gives you a single connection with the combined bandwidth of all of your individual connection mechanisms. This is in addition to the ability of some ISDN products to aggregate both 64 KB channels to provide a 128 KB network connection, and it is not limited to two connections.

If you click on the Use Telephony dialing properties checkbox, you'll be set up to use the dialing properties you've configured with the Telephony applet.

You now need to select which connection protocol you want to use. All of the hot new features, such as the channel aggregation, are only supported on PPP connections, and unless you are connecting to older Unix systems, PPP is your best choice. Click on Next to continue.

Now the user will get the chance to determine what the local system will do when it makes its connection. If connecting to another Windows NT box, or even a Windows 95 system using their version of Dial-Up Networking, you can just select None. If you're not sure what you'll need to do, or if you aren't comfortable automating your logon, select Use a terminal window. If you know what to expect at the other end of the connection, and you know it can be automated, select automate with this script.

The drop-down menu includes a number of scripts, including a generic script that contains instruction for modifying it to fit almost any remote connection need. The included scripts also include a script (CIS.SCP) that can be used to make an existing CompuServe account work as a PPP Internet provider for NT, a useful addition given the millions of CIS users. You'll notice that the sample scripts are well commented to explain exactly what they are doing and what the result should be. They make an excellent learning tool for building your own automated logons.

You'll now need to know if your ISP or your connection on the other end wants you to use a specific IP address. Most ISP will assign an IP address dynamically when you log on, but for a corporate LAN, you might be assigned a specific IP address. This is not the address that might already be assigned to a NIC installed in your computer, even if your LAN is running TCP/IP. Windows NT is perfectly happy dealing with multiple IP addresses in the same machine.

If you are not expecting a DHCP server at the other end of the connection, you'll need to supply a DNS address so that your machine can be authenticated on the Internet. For Internet connectivity a WINS server is not needed, but if you are connecting via a corporate NT network, you'll need this address as well. (Once again, if there is a DHCP server on the NT network you dial into, you won't need to enter these addresses.) Click Next to continue. You're finished. The next time you click Next, the connection phone book entry is completed.

The Dial-Up Networking Monitor

The Dial-Up Networking Monitor enables you to configure the behavior of Dial-Up Networking, get summary information on your connections and devices, and monitor the status of an active connection.

The Status tab will display the traffic that's moved across the dial-up connection since the current session was initiated.

The Summary tab is very important if you are using the multiple channel aggregation ability in NT 4, as it can tell you which devices in your system make up the group that is maintaining the connection as well as displaying information about PPTP connectivity.

The Preferences tab lets you configure the bells and whistles of your connection to determine if it flashes lights, makes noise, or both, to get your attention when events occur on the connection.

Using Performance Monitor To Monitor Network-Related Activity

The Windows NT Performance Monitor contains a number of objects and counters that can be used to monitor the impact of a particular component of network behavior and its impact on your overall system performance. Windows NT uses a technique called "instrumentation." What this means is that all parts of the operating system have programmatic hooks available to the Performance Monitor application (PERFMON.EXE). By using these "instruments" via Performance Monitor, it is possible to examine the behavior of different pieces of the operating system while the system is running, and in most cases, by adding minimum overhead on system performance. Performance Monitor can track any computer on the network to which you have access, so it's possible, for example, to monitor another users computer when that user is having intermittent network problems.

The technique for using all of the objects and their related counters is the same. The user first selects the computer that they want to monitor, then selects the object whose counters are appropriate to the activity that they want to monitor (see fig. 11.10). After selecting the appropriate counters, the chart can be adjusted to set an appropriate scale for the counter. By default, all counters do periodic updates at a one second interval. It is possible to change the update period (though the more often you update, the greater overhead you place on the target machine) or to select Manual Update, where a snapshot of the selected information is done at the users request.

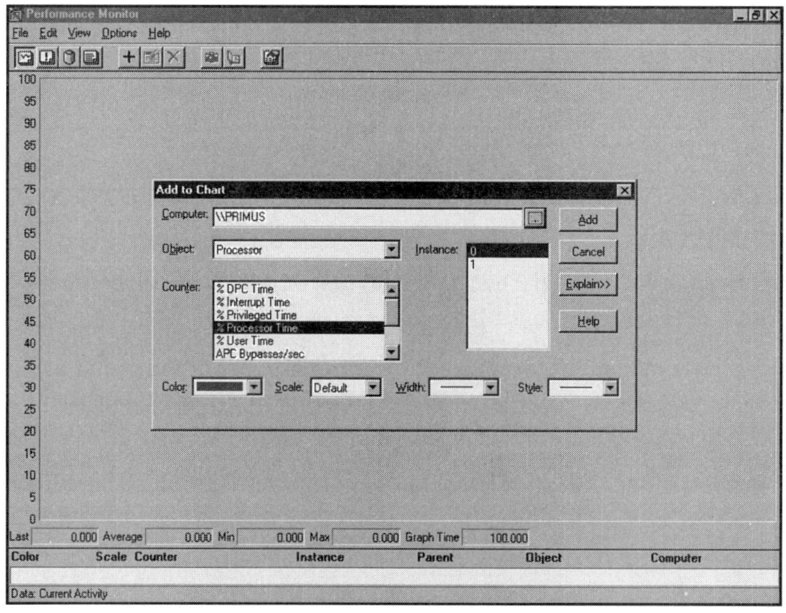

Figure 11.10

From the Add to Chart option, you select not only the computer that you want to monitor, but the object and counters as well.

While there are dozens of objects (and their related counters) available to Performance Monitor, you'll examine those that deal directly with the networking aspects of Windows NT. The following sections identify the appropriate objects and explain what each object's counters do. You'll also be given examples of how this information can be used to help diagnose network health and behavior. One basic trick that can be most helpful when attempting to diagnose the network ills of a specific system—create a log file using the Perfmon counters that you feel are appropriate. But create the file not only with data from the system experiencing the problems but also on a system that is behaving normally. You'll be able to compare the data from the two systems and easily spot any glaring anomalies. Getting familiar with the activity on your network will allow you to determine which objects and counters are of greatest use in your environment. While the counters covered here relate directly to networking, you'll find that, due to the way that networking is intertwined into the entire architecture of Windows NT, it's important to develop a good understanding of all of the objects available to Performance Monitor to really get the best use out of its diagnostic abilities.

The Browser Object

Selecting the Browser object enables the user to monitor actions related to the network browser. All objects are selected by selecting the Edit menu option in Performance Monitor and selecting Add to Chart.

Next, the available counters in your selected objects will be defined. After it is explained what each counter does, examples are given of how the counters can be used to monitor the network.

- **Announcements Domain/sec.** This counter tracks the rate at which a Domain has announced itself on the network.
- **Announcements Server/sec.** This tracks the announcement rate of servers within the domain.
- **Announcements Total/sec.** The aggregate total of the above two counters (1 & 2).
- **Duplicate Master Announcements.** Tracks the number of times that the master browser has detected another system that announces itself as a master browser. This could indicate a network configuration problem.
- **Election Packets/sec.** Tracks the rate at which browser election packets have been received. Very high numbers over extended time periods can indicate a network problem.
- **Enumerations Domain/sec.** Tracks the number of browse requests that the system has processed.
- **Enumerations Other/sec.** Tracks the rate of browse requests processed that were not domain or server browse requests.
- **Enumerations Server/sec.** Tracks the rate of server browse requests processed.

- **Enumerations Total/sec.** Total number of requests seen by counters 6, 7, and 8.
- **Illegal Datagrams/sec.** The rate at which incorrectly structured datagrams (connectionless protocol packets) have been received.
- **Mailslot Allocations Failed/sec.** The number of times the datagram receiver has failed to allocate a buffer to hold a user mailslot write.
- **Mailslot Opens Failed/sec.** The rate at which the local workstation has received mailslot messages for mailslots not present on the local machine
- **Mailslot Receives Failed.** Mailslot message failures to transport failure.
- **Mailslot Writes Failed.** Succesfully received messages that couldn't be written to the mailslot.
- **Mailslot Writes/sec.** Successful mailslot writes.
- **Missed Mailslot Datagrams.** Mailslot datagrams discarded due to configuration or allocation limits.
- **Missed Server Announcements.** Due to configuration or allocation limits.
- **Missed Server List Requests.** The number of times that a request to retrieve a list of browser servers couldn't be processed.
- **Server Announce Allocations Failed/sec.** The rate of announcement failures due to lack of memory
- **Server List requests/sec.** The rate at which requests to retrieve a list of browsers has been processed by the system.

Problems with the Computer Browser are not uncommon. You might find that a system can't seem to see the network when browsing for resources, yet it is possible to use the LAN Manager style NET USE command to directly access a resource. In this case, you might want to configure Performance Monitor to check for Browser announcements on the network. If there is an unusual number of browser elections being forced or a high number of browser list requests failing, you probably have a network configuration problem that needs to be dealt with.

NWLink IPX, NWLink NetBIOS, NWLink SPX

If the system is configured to support the NWLink protocols (IPX, SPX, and NetBIOS) the Performance monitor can be used to track the behavior of these protocols. Each of these objects has the same counters, though the user is likely to find most of the network activity on the NWLink IPX counters (unless the system is configured to run NetBIOS over IPX, in which case there will be significant activity on the NWLink NetBIOS counters). NWLink is explained in detail in the earlier section in this chapter about Network Protocols.

- **Bytes Total/sec.** Total number of bytes sent or received in data-carrying packets by the protocol.
- **Connection Session Timeouts.** Cumulative total of connections dropped due to session timeout.
- **Connections Cancelled.** Cumulative total of connections canceled.
- **Connection No Retries.** Cumulative total of succesful first try connections.
- **Connections Open.** Current number of connection open using this protocol.
- **Connections With Retries.** Cumulative total of successful connections made after multiple retries.
- **Datagrams Bytes received/sec.** Rate at which datagrams have been received.
- **Datagrams Bytes Sent/sec.** Rate at which datagrams have been sent from this computer.
- **Datagram Bytes/sec.** Sum of all datagram sent and received by the target computer.
- **Datagrams Received/sec.** Rate at which datagrams are received by the computer.
- **Datagrams Sent/sec.** Rate at which datagrams are sent from the computer.
- **Datagram/sec.** Sum of datagrams sent and received.
- **Disconnects Local.** Cumulative total of disconnections initiated by the target computer.
- **Disconnects Remote.** Cumulative total of session disconnections initiated by remote computers.
- **Expirations Ack.** Count of the T2 timer expirations.
- **Expirations Response.** Count of T1 timer expirations.
- **Failures Adapter.** Cumulative total of connection dropped due to adapter failure.

- **Failures Link.** Cumulative total of connections dropped due to link failure.
- **Failures No Listen.** Number of connections rejected due to the remote computer not listening for connections.
- **Failures Not Found.** Cumulative total of failed connections due to the remote system not being found.
- **Failures Resource Local.** Cumulative total of connection failures caused by a shortage of resources on the local computer.
- **Failures Resource Remote.** Cumulative total of connection failures caused by a shortage of resources on the remote computer.
- **Frame Bytes Received/sec.** Rate at which actual data bytes are received by the local computer.
- **Frame Bytes Rejected/sec.** Rate at which data bytes have been rejected by the local computer.
- **Frame Bytes Re-sent/sec.** Rate at which data bytes have been re-sent.
- **Frame Bytes Sent.** Rate at which data bytes are sent.
- **Frame Bytes/sec.** Rate at which data bytes are processed by the computer. It's the sum of bytes sent and received.
- **Frames Received/sec.** Rate at which data frame are received by the computer.
- **Frames Rejected/sec.** Rate at which data frames are rejected by the computer.
- **Frames Re-sent/sec.** Rate at which data frames are re-sent by the computer.
- **Frames Sent/sec.** Rate at which data frames are sent by the computer.
- **Frames/sec.** Rate at which frames (sent or received) are processed by the computer.
- **Packets Received/sec.** Rate at which all packets are received by the computer—both control and data packets are included.
- **Packets Sent/sec.** Rate at which all packets have been sent by the computer.
- **Packets/sec.** Rate at which all packets (sent and received) are processed by the computer.

- **Piggyback Ack Queued/sec.** Rate at which piggybacked acknowledgments are queued. Piggyback acks are acknowledgments to receive packets that are included in the next outgoing packet from the computer.
- **Piggyback Ack Timeouts.** The number of times that a piggyback ack could not be sent due to the lack of packets going to the target computer.
- **Windows Send Average.** Average number of data bytes sent before waiting for an ack from a remote computer.
- **Windows Send Maximum.** Maximum number of bytes sent before waiting for an ack from the remote computer.

Each of these counters are available independently for each of the NWLink objects, so it is possible to monitor three different instances, for example, of Windows Send Maximum—one each for IPX, SPX, and NetBIOS. That said, an example of making use of these counters might be attempting to determine why a connection between two computers fails on a regular basis. To determine if the protocol is at fault, you could set counters on the protocol and the number of Connection Session Timeouts to determine if the sessions fail because communication problems between the systems. You might also monitor Connections Open to determine if the connection maximum on a system is consistently being reached, causing additional connections to fail.

RAS Port, RAS Total

The RAS Port Object is available on any system that has installed the Remote Access Service. There should be one RAS Port instance for each port on the system configured for use with RAS. Using these counters can give you some idea of the traffic that the port is getting, both inbound and outbound, and when applied against a remote machine can let you monitor the health and behavior of your network's dial-in server. This object deals specifically with the behavior of the port and not the protocols that are being passed through it. To monitor the protocols themselves, use the appropriate protocol objects. The RAS Total object provides an overview of all of the configured RAS Ports and uses the same counters. RAS Total is a useful object when your network has a dedicated RAS Server and can be used to remotely monitor the aggregate behavior of the RAS Server ports.

- **Alignment Errors.** Total number of alignment errors (when a byte received is different that the byte expected).
- **Buffer Overrun Errors.** Total number of buffer overrun errors (when data is being passed to the port faster than the port can handle it).
- **Bytes Received.** Total bytes received by the current connection.

- **Bytes received/sec.** Bytes per second.
- **Bytes Transmitted.** Total bytes transmitted for this connection.
- **Bytes Transmitted/sec.** Bytes transmitted per second.
- **CRC Errors.** Total CRC errors for the current connection.
- **Frames Received.** Total data frames received for the current connection.
- **Frames Received/sec.** Frames received per second.
- **Frames Transmitted.** Total frames transmitted for the current connection.
- **Frames Transmitted/sec.** Frames transmitted per second.
- **Percent Compression In.** Compression ration for bytes received.
- **Percent Compression Out.** Compression ratio for bytes transmitted.
- **Serial Overrun Errors.** Total number of serial overrun errors.
- **Timeout Errors.** Total number of timeout errors for the current connection.
- **Total Errors.** Total of CRC, Timeout, Serial Overrun, Alignment, and buffer overrun errors received for the current connection.
- **Total Errors/sec.** As above on a per second basis.

If your dial-in users are having problems getting connected, take a look at the port to which they are trying to attach. You'll find that by setting the counters for the supported error states (serial and Buffer Overruns), you can determine if the hardware is up to the task of keeping the users connected. The Percent Compression counters are also useful, especially if you have modems that support hardware compression, to determine actual data transfer rates.

Redirector

As explained in the chapter section "Redirector," the Redirector is the piece of software that handles communication between the network operating system and the local machine. Users would make use of this object to determine how much data is being passed to and from the system, if errors are occurring during those transactions, and how much time is spent performing I/O operations locally.

- **Bytes Received/sec.** Rate at which bytes are being received from the network. This includes all application data as well as standard protocol information.

- **Bytes total/sec.** The rate at which the Redirector is processing all data bytes.
- **Bytes Transmitted/sec.** The rate at which all data bytes leave the local Redirector for the network.
- **Connects Core.** Number of connections to servers using the original MS-Net SMB protocol, such as MS-Net, Xenix, and Vax.
- **Connects LAN Manager 2.0.** Counts connections to Lan Manager 2.0 servers.
- **Connects LAN Manager 2.1.** Counts connections to Lan Manager 2.1 servers.
- **Connect Windows NT.** Counts connections to Windows NT computers (server or workstation).
- **Current Commands.** The number of Redirector requests currently queued. This number should not significantly exceed the number of NICs installed in the computer.
- **File Data Operations/sec.** Rate at which the Redirector processes data operations.
- **File Read Operations/sec.** Rate at which applications are asking the Redirector for information.
- **File Write Operations/sec.** Rate at which applications are sending data to the Redirector.
- **Network Errors/sec.** Count of serious unexpected errors. Activity on this counter can indicate a serious communication problem.
- **Packets Received./sec.** Rate at which Redirector receives SMBs.
- **Packets Transmitted/sec.** Rate at which Redirector is sending SMBs.
- **Packets/sec.** Rate at which Redirector is processing data packets.
- **Read Bytes Cache/sec.** Rate at which local applications access the cache using the Redirector.
- **Read Bytes Network/sec.** Rate at which applications read data across the network (when not found in cache).
- **Read Bytes Non-Paging/sec.** Bytes read by the Redirector in response to normal file requests.

- **Read Bytes paging/sec.** Bytes read by the Redirector in response to a page fault (page faults occur when the cache is missed).
- **Read Operations Random/sec.** Counts the rate at which non-sequential file reads are made, on a file-by-file basis.
- **Read Packets Small/sec.** The rate at which reads less than one quarter of the negotiated buffer size are made by an application (too many means wasted memory buffers).
- **Read Packets/sec.** Rate that read packets are placed on the network.
- **Reads Denied/sec.** Rate at which requests for raw reads are denied. (Raw reads are large data block reads with minimal overhead. They cause the server to lock out other read requests while being processed.)
- **Reads Large/sec.** Rate of reads grater than twice the size of the negotiated buffer size.
- **Server Disconnects.** Number of times Redirector is disconnected from server.
- **Server Reconnects.** Number of times your Redirector has to reconnect to service an active request (connections can go dormant after no activity for 10 minutes).
- **Server Sessions.** Total number of security objects managed by the Redirector (one connection can have multiple sessions).
- **Server Sessions Hung.** Total number of sessions that have timed out due to lack of response from remote server.
- **Write Bytes Cache/sec.** Rate at which applications write to the cache using the Redirector.
- **Write Bytes Network/sec.** Rate applications are writing data across the network.
- **Write Bytes Non-Paging/sec.** Rate at which bytes are written in response to normal file outputs and redirected across the network.
- **Write Bytes Paging/sec.** Rate at which Redirector attempts to write bytes changed in pages used by applications.
- **Write Operations Random/sec.** Counts the rate at which non-sequential file writes are made, on a file-by-file basis.

- **Write Packets Small/sec.** The rate at which writes less than one quarter of the negotiated buffer size are made by an application (too many means wasted memory buffers).
- **Write Packets/sec.** Rate at which writes are being sent to the network.
- **Writes Denied/sec.** Rate at which server is unable to accommodate requests for raw writes.
- **Writes Large/sec.** Rate of writes greater than twice the size of the negotiated buffer size.

You'll notice that a large number of these counters deal with cache data in the Redirector. If your system is missing the cache often, it causes a page fault with each cache miss. This reduces overall system performance if it happens too much. Study these counters carefully and you'll find that having too large a count in quite a few of them means that there is a serious system problem.

Windows NT 5 Directory Services

Contrary to Microsoft's marketing claims and the documentation found with Windows NT Server 4, the current implementation of Windows NT does not contain a directory service. Although the current Domain model provides one or two features that define a directory service, it's a far stretch from a single network logon to a full-blown directory service. Windows NT 5 will contain such a directory service, and pieces of that service will become available prior to the release of Windows NT 5 sometime in late 1997 or early 1998.

This chapter has already discussed one of those features, the Distributed File System service available for download from Microsoft, but a directory service is far more than that.

The Windows NT Directory Service, also known as Active Directory, will provide the same single-point logon to network resources currently found, but will be built on an extensible database schema based on that found in the Exchange Server database engine. NTDS has a hierarchical structure more easily organized and managed than the current multimaster domain model. This gets rid of the flat name space and the incredible complexity involved in attempting to maintain a domain model which, by necessity, ends up with multiple top levels, each of which is a peer in the domain architecture. In a multiple-master domain model with three top level domains and four downstream domains, for example, it is necessary to maintain 21 or more trust relationships to grant resource access across all domains. With NTDS, this complex mess of trust relationships no longer needs to be maintained.

Microsoft has set a very aggressive goal for the implementation of NTDS, with pieces becoming available for download before the release of the next version of Windows NT, version 5, which will incorporate all the changes into the new version of the operating system.

A number of features of interest to users will be incorporated in NTDS:

- Support for multiple name formats: RFC822 names (your common internet name@address.com), X.500 names, HTTP URLs, LDAP URL addresses, and UNC names.
- A full set of APIs that will be exposed not only to C/C++ programmers but to scripting languages such as Visual Basic, as well as any language/scripting tool that supports OLE automation.
- A distributed security model.
- Multimaster replication that will enable updating the user accounts from the server nearest the user (no more time out problems when a user's account information is stored on a server geographically distant from the user's location).
- Directory objects extensible on a per property basis.
- Support for short life-span network services such as Internet telephony, chat services, and conferencing (white board) style services.
- Fully backward compatible with Windows NT 3.5x/4 systems.
- Interoperability with Novell NetWare environments (at least those running binderies or bindery emulation at this time. Integration with the Novell Directory Service is more problematical at this time).

The Windows NT Directory Service Datastore

To create a datastore for the new directory service (the *directory*, as it were), Microsoft has combined features from the Internet Domain Name System (DNS) and the X.500 Directory Service standard. NTDS will use the DNS service as the location service for its directory service. This will enable a simplified naming scheme for Windows NT network resources that matches up perfectly with a system's Internet name. Hence the name Server2.wsrc.com will be both a resolvable Internet address and the name of a specific machine within the Windows NT NTDS datastore. It will also take advantage of the standard Internet naming scheme (user@address.com) to identify users both within the Windows NT domain and within the greater Internet as a whole.

The NTDS will also support the X.500 naming conventions and make use of standard X.500 protocols, DAP, DSP, and DISP, to provide interoperability with other

Directory Services that support these standards. Microsoft also plans to support the Lightweight Directory Access Protocol (LDAP) to provide an additional means of interoperability with other directory services that support this newer, non-X.500, directory service protocol.

The NTDS directory is based on the current database engine in Exchange Server. This is a multithreaded storage engine that supports indexing for rapid data retrieval and scales to support more than 10 million entries per store. The partitioned, distributed directory service model will enable the system to support multiple stores in a single directory tree.

The Domain Tree

The Windows NT Directory Service gets its scalability as a result of the new domain tree structure. Each domain is a complete object within the overall domain tree. Any number of domains can be contained with the tree model, and the tree model is built from the bottom up. As stated previously, any domain can contain more than 10 million objects, and any domain tree can contain a huge number of domains, meaning that the Directory Service could possibly be responsible for hundreds of millions of objects. This domain tree and the "tree of trees" is referred to as the NTDS namespace.

Each domain publishes its existence in the NTDS datastore, which is also the DNS. This makes information about the domain available to all other NT domains, enabling the NT Directory Servers (formerly known as Domain Controllers) to find each other within the namespace. Domain clients make use of the LDAP protocol to communicate with the directory. LDAP requires certain specific object definitions; to meet the LDAP requirements, the domain objects are built via derivation. There are standard X.521 base objects used to define the object datastore, Country, Locality, Organization, and Organizational-Unit. Auxiliary forms of these objects are used to provide the needed attributes that define a domain. The derived form of the object is arrived at by deriving subclasses from the auxiliary objects and the base objects.

This hierarchy model is referred to as a container hierarchy and is what enables the directory service to create the hierarchical namespace that nests the organizational units with the domains. This container model also enables a finer grained administrative model so that it is no longer necessary to create domain administrators that have access to everything within a domain when what they actually need is the ability to administer a small part of the domain structure. Aside from providing better administrative control, this fine grain authority means that additional security is available to user accounts. Each domain border can be considered a security border, so a user may be an administrator in domains A and C, but only a user in domain B.

The Domain-Organizational-Unit

The Domain-Organizational-Unit is the standard form of Domain in the Windows NT Directory Service. This is the default domain object because of the great flexibility it provides in the building of large domain trees. This flexibility is derived from the object's capability to be both a parent object to other Domain-Organizational-Units as well as the child of that object or any other domain class.

The Global Catalog

To speed access to information in large domains, the Windows NT Directory Service uses a Global Catalog that contains a summary of all data (also called a partial replica) contained within the domain tree. In many cases, the information contained within the domain server can provide the necessary information to respond to the database query. This helps to limit the amount of queries that need to be served by the directory database, speeding up the overall performance of the network service. Although the global catalog contains only a subset of the data found in the directory service database, it can be a very useful service to applications such as mail servers that need quick access to a global address book.

Directory Database Replication

Windows NT NTDS uses a multimaster replication scheme. That is, multiple master copies of the directory service database exist. In a situation that requires an immediate directory update, such as disabling a user account, that master copy can push the new database change to all the other master copies. Although directories can be configured to update on a timed basis, they do not use timestamps to track the database updates. Instead, every time something is written to an object in the directory, it receives a new update sequence number (USN). If a replication cycle is initiated, the system's replication partners ask for objects that have a USN greater than that of the last received.

Transparent Trust Relationships

If domains are organized into hierarchical trees within the NT Directory Service, they can make use of transparent trust relationship with other domains within the tree. This enables user accounts in the tree to access resources anywhere within the domain tree. For all intents and purposes, this means that the high level of trust management needed to run the domain trust relationships in earlier versions of Windows NT will be totally unnecessary in the Windows NT 5 Directory Service model.

Like its predecessor, the Windows NT Directory Service is designed to support two forms of trust relationships:

- **Two-way transitive trusts.** This is the default trust relationship established when domains are created. Their maintenance is automatic, and their existence is a feature of the Kerberos system used to provide the distributed authentication used by NTDS. In this trust relationship, if domain A trusts domain B, and domain B trusts domain C, then domain C trusts domain A. This relationship is created and maintained automatically, requiring no user intervention to create or manage.

- **Explicit one-way trust relationships.** This type of trust is created when you want to access a domain outside your domain tree or to support a trust relationship with an earlier version of Windows NT. These types of trust relationships require the same level of maintenance that all previous types of trust relationships needed.

Extending the Directory

The directory in NTDS is completely extensible. It is possible for an existing object in the database schema to have additional properties added and to have just those additional properties replicated throughout the database. It is also possible to create a whole new object, in either an existing object class or even a new object class, and publish to the directly service throughout the network. These objects could be specific to a certain type of business, or they could be created by applications that want to have an object type in the NTDS database under the application's direct control. It should be noted that although NTDS treats the various container types (domain, OU, and so on) as well as physical devices (such as machines and volumes) as objects, it does not treat the file system as an object.

The API Sets

Three major API sets are available for users to write to the directory service. The first set is the OLE DS components, a set of COM objects designed for managing multiple directory services. The second is the LDAP C API; the third is the existing MAPI messaging API set.

OLE DS Components

The OLE DS components were developed as part of the Open Directory Service Interface (ODSI). ODSI was proposed by Microsoft in 1994 as a standard interface that should be used by directory services for manipulating and querying their datastores. OLE DS components are available for any directory service that supports the LDAP protocol, as well as NetWare 3.x and Windows NT 4.x.

OLE DS Components are exposed to the normal run of programming tools; high level developers can, therefore, make use of the components when developing applications that make use of the directory service datastore. The components are also exposed to the various scripting languages, such as Visual Basic, so that non-programmers can manipulate the information in the datastore. So then, even the average user comfortable with one of the Visual-type scripting environments will be able to create directory-enabled applications.

LDAP C API

The LDAP C API set is provided for developers who need to create applications that run on many different directory services. It offers no specific enhancements to make use of the features of NTDS, but enables a developer to create an application that will run with any LDAP supporting directory service. Conversely, applications for other directory services that use only the LDAP C API set should run on Windows NT NTDS without problem.

MAPI

MAPI support is provided to enable compatibility with legacy MAPI applications. MAPI is not the recommended programming interface or methodology to use with NTDS.

NTDS Security

NTDS security is linked to the new security model that will be implemented in Windows NT 5. This is a distributed security model based on the Kerberos authentication protocol developed by MIT. The security model will support both public and private key encryption, and will also support the use of X.509. v3 certificates issued by a trusted authority so that non-Windows NT users, with the appropriate certificate, can be granted access to system resources in the same fashion as Kerberos users.

Summary

You can't understand Windows NT without understanding Windows NT networking. The information in this chapter provided an overview of the networking information necessary to get the most of Windows NT Workstation, and it provided the tools needed to improve your understanding of networking from the client-side perspective, which is a little different in priorities than that of the Windows NT Server.

Starting off by understanding the architecture of Windows NT networking enables you to get a good grounding in information necessary to configure and maintain

Windows NT networks. The information provided here gives a solid background in configuring all forms of Windows NT networking, with connectivity provided over direct network connections as well as a dial-up resource. You'll find this information invaluable in day-to-day NT operations.

You've also had a chance to examine the newest technologies in Windows NT networking—the Distributed File System—which runs on NT 4 and can make a network administrator's job much easier (as well as simplifying the life of NT network users), not to mention being the first on the block to become familiar with the future of NT networking, Active Directory—the technology upon which all future NT networks will be built.

Part IV

Windows NT Workstation Communications Tools

CHAPTER 12

The NT Workstation Communications Strategy

It has been a long time coming, but Microsoft has finally turned the Windows PC or NT workstation into a communications supermachine.

In the early days of the DOS operating system (in the early '80s) and before the advent of the LAN (in the mid '80s), the PC was an island of processing ability and functionality. Most enterprises deployed a few PCs to take advantage of the new applications like Lotus 1-2-3 and IBM Writing Assistant. And when a file was needed on another machine, the only way to do this was to copy it onto a floppy disk.

Before the LAN (Novell) arrived and before many businesses could afford it, the introduction of the PC-connected modem was the first step taken in the transformation of the PC from a stand-alone device to a communication device. In these times, modems were not only very expensive, they were painfully slow (300 baud) and the transfer of files was an excruciating process. The transfer of a small file could take many hours.

Toward the end of the decade, people began to witness the evolution of Windows and DOS from stand-alone operating systems into communication operating systems. The emphasis began to shift from pure process or interrupt-handling architecture to a message/communications-based architecture. Today, messaging and communications is at the core of every event that takes place on the Windows operating system.

Computer-based communications processing is still in its infancy, but the true objective for many years has been to merge the data networks with the telephone networks. This process of blending the technologies is now about to emerge, and TAPI and the aforementioned NT services and interfaces are making it all possible. By the year 2000, the so-called Internet will be (to borrow William Shatner's *Tek War* term) a huge *matrix* of digital high-bandwidth networks that will carry voice, data, information, and video.

In 1996, it became all too clear that TCP/IP and TAPI on Windows NT will facilitate this dream on the Windows NT operating system. Although TCP/IP-facilitated network communications (the Internet protocols) have been around for decades, the critical emergence of the Internet in the public domain has provided the computer telephony industry with many new options to advance the concept of voice-data digital networks. Technology now exists that enables people to converse in real-time over wide area digital networks. You can also switch voice calls made over the public-switched telephone network to the Internet. You can use computers and connections to the Internet to call any telephone in the world for free. Companies are deploying Internet technology on their enterprise information networks at an incredible rate. These new extensions to the corporate intelligence network are becoming increasingly known as *intranets.*

Why Windows NT?

Telephony is a mission-critical process in every enterprise, from Hot-Dog Stands, Inc. to GM Corporation. Telephone systems have had decades of R&D to ensure that they do not crash. Consider what a disaster it would be if your telephone system stopped working for a few hours. On the contrary, the workstation computer is still a teenager in comparison to the office PBX.

Only in recent years have the operating systems matured enough to be considered for mission-critical services. If you're going to integrate the telephone service with the computer systems, you need to know that your total uptime will be at acceptable levels (at least if the computer system crashes, the telephone system should be able to continue as before). Only Windows NT (with its iron-clad operating system modes and bulletproof APIs) can really claim this today.

The Windows NT Communications Services

The core functionality at the heart of the NT communications service is the Win32 API. These systems and collateral interfaces on Windows NT make it possible to enjoy myriad communications applications on workstation architecture. The Windows communications service is illustrated in figure 12.1.

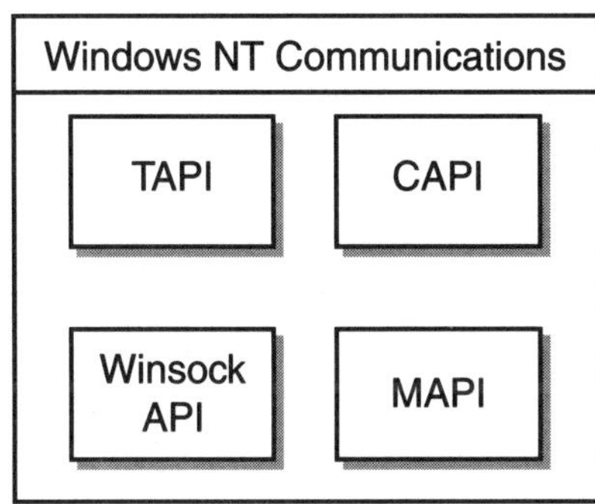

Figure 12.1
The Windows communications service consists of several interoperating APIs.

The Windows communications services include the following key technologies:

- TAPI
- MAPI
- The Windows Serial Communications API (CAPI)
- Windows sockets API

TAPI, the telephony API, handles the creation and management of the telephony process (see fig. 12.2).

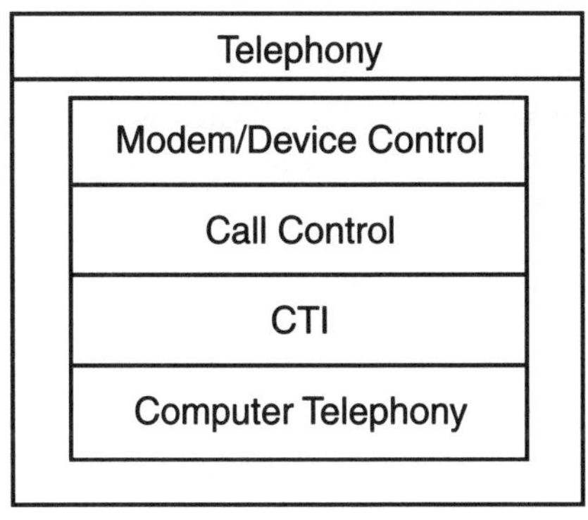

Figure 12.2
TAPI, the telephony API, is the mechanism responsible for a wide range of telephony operations.

MAPI, the message API, is the mechanism that handles the management and delivery of store and forward message-based information, such as e-mail, forms, and schedules (see fig. 12.3). It is also the architecture on which Microsoft Exchange is built. MAPI is a network communications architecture and has no hardware handling support. (See Chapter 14, "Microsoft Messaging," for the appropriate discussion of e-mail and scheduling.)

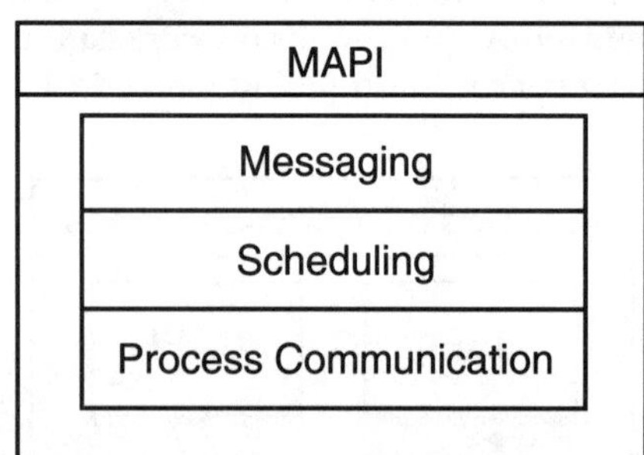

Figure 12.3
MAPI, the message API, is the mechanism responsible for the delivery and management of store and forward information.

The Windows serial communication API (often referred to as Win32s) takes care of serial communications and data interchange (see fig. 12.4). It is closely allied to TAPI and was once responsible for all modem manipulation.

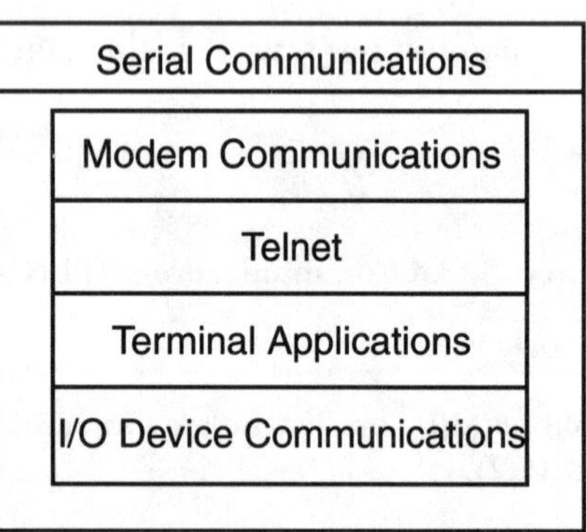

Figure 12.4
Win32s is the mechanism responsible for data interchange on the computer.

Windows sockets API is the interface to the TCP/IP services from Windows operating systems that gets you onto the Internet (see fig. 12.5). Windows sockets is network communications architecture (see Chapters 10 and 15 for the appropriate discussion of TCP/IP networking and the Internet).

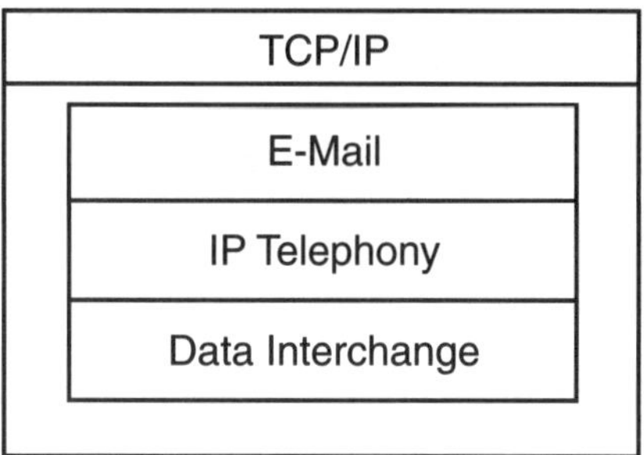

Figure 12.5

The Windows Sockets API is the interface mechanism to the TCP/IP services on all Windows operating systems.

Several other APIs and technologies also come into the picture, as illustrated in figure 12.6. NetBIOS is worth mentioning here, although any discussion of LAN communications and APIs is beyond the scope of this chapter. The DirectPlay API and the Multimedia APIs, which are at the heart of the Windows 95 gaming development environment, are also worth mentioning. Why are these APIs mentioned? Well, sneaking up on an opponent situated half a world away on the Internet and blowing out his holographic brains (with full sound effects) is all achieved with the functionality of the previously mentioned communications services.

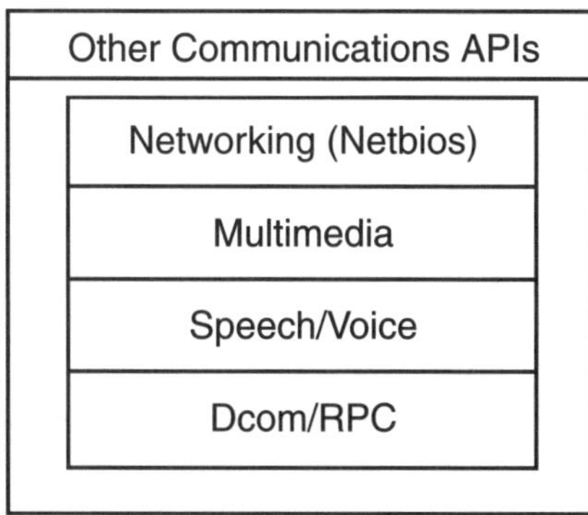

Figure 12.6

Several other APIs and technologies make up the Windows communications picture, including NetBIOS, DirectPlay and the Multimedia APIs.

Although the Win32 API lies at the heart of the functionality on all the Windows 32-bit operating systems, not all the Windows platforms enjoy equal capabilities.

The heavyweight OS is Windows NT Server, which allows up to 256 remote users to attach to its services to invoke all manner of communications services: telephony, Internet access, Dial-Up Networking (DUN), remote access, and serial interface transmission.

The user's workstation powerhouse is Windows NT Workstation. Although it only allows one remote user to attach to its services, its true calling is to attach to and demand functionality from the server. However, the communications capability of the Workstation is complete (or "acceptable" to many power users). The most sophisticated and demanding of telecommunications and messaging functionality can be handled with ease from the Workstation. You can call the Workstation the robust or "pro" (communications) client—in terms of what it is capable of doing.

Not to be left out of the communications picture is Windows 95. This OS can now be considered the light client. Although it has the largest installed base in the business, its communications capabilities are not as advanced as its tougher siblings (see fig. 12.7).

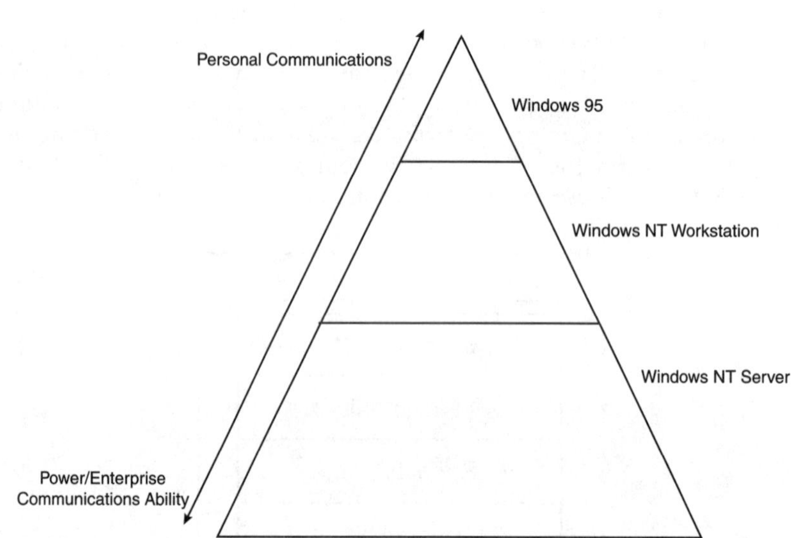

Figure 12.7
This illustration provides a graphical representation of each operating system's stature in terms of usage and communications functionality.

The range of applications using the previously mentioned system services and APIs is now wide and feature-rich, but it has taken many years and much effort on the part of many industry players to afford them.

While the previously mentioned APIs and architectures make up the Windows communications service, the application for these technologies is covered in the relevant sections in this book (although several elements of these technologies are discussed later in this chapter). This chapter is devoted to an extensive discussion of the Telephony API, which is the youngest and potentially the most exciting of Microsoft's communications technologies.

Computer Telephony and CTI

Computer telephony empowers the workstation user by providing him or her with access to workstation services that enhance and facilitate the use of the telephone, the PBX, modems, and telephony interface cards. Many products are now on the market that provide computer telephony software for the Windows NT workstation. Almost every IT manager or network administrator will encounter the need to provide users with some form of computer telephony services at some time.

On the low end, you have simple dialer applications and unified messaging interfaces that deliver voice mail, fax mail, and e-mail. On the high end, you have workstation solutions (coupled to telephony servers, as illustrated later) that provide workstation users with ACD call control, PBX console management, call accounting, messaging, fax serving, predictive dialing, and more. Many companies are now installing some form of computer telephony functionality on the desktop or workstation computer.

If you are new to computer telephony, you might be wondering about application; or perhaps you hate voice mail and believe that computer telephony is just voice mail on steroids. Whatever your idea is about the technology, let's look at a typical scenario in an enterprise.

The marketing manager of Big Enterprise, Inc. has acquired the telephone list to 100,000 qualified prospective buyers of a new product. The IT manager and network administrator are requested to provide an additional 20 NT workstations for the employment of a new sales team. The task of the new team will be to call the prospective buyers and sell them the new product.

At the end of the first week of sales calls, the marketing manager and the sales manager were disappointed in the number of sales that were made. The network manager and the telephone systems manager inform the executives that only 15 percent of the calls succeeded in getting through to a live person. Much time was wasted with ring no answer (RNA) situations and answering machines. The managers decide the sales force should be further empowered. A short list of options and possible solutions is formulated to try to increase the number of successful sales calls:

- Double the sales force.
- Invest in a new sales script.
- Devise a powerful message to leave on the answering machine.
- Increase the memory on the workstations to 128 KB.
- Equip each workstation with a 400 MHz CPU.
- Shorten the lunch breaks, start earlier, and end later.

- Double the commissions.
- Terminate weak sales people.

Which of the above options do you think will improve the rate of sales? Before you answer, carefully review the information provided about the above sales campaign. If you chose any of the above, you need to go back to IT school or IS school. If you suggested the company investigate and invest in a computer telephony system, especially predictive dialing, you should get promoted and get double your salary.

Predictive dialing is just one of the many desktop and server-based computer telephony technologies that can have a drastic effect on a human resources problem. The process is simple. A computer telephony system can make and service calls at rates that far exceed human capacity. This means it can dial and determine RNA, busy signals, and answering machine existence, and only deliver a "live" call to the sales force when a person is reached. A computer telephony system completely replaces the sales person's need to make a call. The sales person simply discharges a client and a new person is transferred to his or her workstation for service. In essence, a predictive dialing system can increase the number of calls processed by sales people five-fold, triple the sales volume, and give everyone longer lunch breaks and shorter work days.

While the term is new, computer telephony has been around in various forms for more than a decade. The whole idea of connecting computers to telephone systems began with the invention of voice mail in the early 1980s. The early voice mail system was a form of computer (it resembled a mainframe system) endowed with electronics that could transform analog information into digital information that could be stored and recovered on magnetic media such as a hard disk.

Then in the late 1980s, American companies such as Rhetorex, Inc. and Dialogic Corporation developed the voice processing card. This was a device that used digital signal processing (DSP) technology on PC architecture to not only interpret telephone signals but to digitize analog information as well. Digitization is the process of transforming analog information (in wave form) into digital form (1s and 0s) that can be stored on magnet or optical media.

Modern DSP technology and DSP operating systems and software have matured over the years, and it has become cost effective to build standard PC-based components that can be integrated with the telephone system in many ways.

Computer telephony is also an umbrella term for the two IT practices, computer-telephone integration (CTI) and computer telephony integration. These two terms are often confused, but they describe separate processes. (See the sidebar "Computer Telephony Integration Defined.")

Computer-telephone integration is the practice of connecting the computer to the telephone switch or PBX. While modern PBXs and telephone systems incorporate computer-based call control and processing into their architecture, these smart and sophisticated products are often hard to use. The objective of CTI, therefore, is to achieve a form of computer control over the telephone call for the benefit of the user. This integration, or control, enables the workstation user to be more productive.

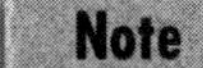

The *switch* is a device, or network of devices, used to connect and route telephone calls on the public switched telephone network (known in almost every country as the PSTN). Switch also refers to the central exchange (your typical "telco," which is the industry buzzword for telephone company) or the private telephony devices used in private enterprises, better known as PBX systems (private branch exchange in the U.S. and private automatic branch exchange in Europe, the United Kingdom, and parts of the world once known as the British Empire).

CTI provides two classes of service to the workstation:

- Computer control over the call and the ability to take and make calls.
- Human-computer dialog over the telephone.

The call-control side empowers the user by liberating him or her from the call answering, routing, filtering, and dialing process. Through the Windows GUI, the user has access to all the hard-to-access features of the switch.

The human-computer dialog side obviates the need for two or more callers to be present in a telephone conversation. In other words, the computer can stand in for a person to deliver information, instructions, and messages.

The two divisions in CTI objectives enable several services:

- Initiate or set up calls
- Receive calls
- Transfer calls
- Conference calls
- Park calls
- Perform call-progress analysis (CPA)
- Perform call-progress monitoring (CPM)

- Provide real-time reporting and event logging on the previously mentioned functions
- Tear down calls and conferences

The IT manager, systems integrator, or network engineer might have to perform two distinct tasks in achieving CTI.

He or she has to get the CT system and the enterprise's PBX and switch on speaking terms (this is CTI), and he or she has to integrate the CT system into the existing IT architecture without turning the enterprise inside out (this is computer telephony integration). That IT infrastructure can consist of a multitude of client and server systems and mainframes.

As a result of a lack of understanding of the telephony side, very few IT executives have delayed commissioning extensive computer telephony integration until their network engineers better understand the implications. LANs are hard enough to manage and maintain as it is, so few want to mess with what is currently working.

Integrating the workstations, the servers, the intranets, and more with the telephone network (private and public) requires a little more than cursory understanding of both data and telephone networks and the enabling technologies.

Computer Telephony Integration Defined

Computer telephony is now such a popular concept and worthwhile idea that you read about it in almost every computer magazine. But the term is often used in the wrong context. It is often confused with *computer-telephone integration* (CTI). But the two terms refer to different processes. They are not technologies; they are engineering concepts.

Computer telephony is a true service domain of information technology (IT), just as networking is. But, as a service domain of IT, the computer telephony systems need to be cautiously and intelligently integrated into the existing enterprise information systems. This integration process is now mostly the responsibility of NT networking specialists who have a background or training in telephony.

On the other hand, CTI (described in this chapter) is the actual process of interconnecting typically data-centric systems and networks with telephony-centric systems and networks. An example is the attachment of the PBX to an NT-based telephony server, or the logical connection of an NT Workstation-based call-management application to the same PBX.

Father of Computer Telephony

In case you are wondering who coined the phrase computer telephony, it was Harry Newton. Harry Newton is a well-known telecommunications authority who publishes several magazines and books covering telecommunications. In 1993, he launched the now very popular leading magazine to serve the industry, *Computer Telephony*. The magazine covers many aspects of Windows NT-based telephony and telecommunications.

The following passage is Harry's definition of computer telephony as found in his 1,300-page reference, now in its 13th edition (possibly even 14th), *Newton's Telecom Dictionary* (Flatiron Publishing, Inc.):

"Computer telephony is the term used to describe the industry that concerns itself with applying computer intelligence to telecommunications devices, especially switches and phones. The term covers many technologies, including computer-telephone integration via the local area network (LAN), interactive voice processing, voice mail, auto attendant, voice recognition, text-to-speech, facsimile, simultaneous voice data, signal processing, video conferencing, predictive dialing, audiotext, 'giving data a voice,' call centers, help desks, collaborative computing, and traditional telephone call switching and call control."

The definition in the sidebar is accurate, but any serious following of these tenets and achievement of the dreams was impossible a few years ago because of a lack of standards. This is where the Microsoft/Intel partnership enters the picture. With computer telephony transformed from simple interactive telecommunications services of the 1980s into an industry of exhaustive service technologies and domains, a standard telephony servicing support layer in the operating system code base was required. TAPI was the offering.

Tip If you need to get up to speed on computer telephony applications, head for the CT Expo held annually in Los Angeles. Every year in March or April, tens of thousands of computer telephony aficionados gather at Harry Newton's critical (and spaced out) expo for the CT industry—the Computer Telephony Exposition and Conference. (Microsoft, of course, has one of the biggest pavilions there.)

In the past years, communications processing on the workstation and desktop PC has been a klunky disjointed process. Modems and telephony devices always had to be configured with much effort and not a small amount of knowledge of the workings of the devices, ports, and computer hardware. Telephony components have, until now, required the configuration of specialized software, almost all of which is supplied by the vendors.

Whereas a simple modem requires the setup of communications ports, the more sophisticated telephony devices required engineers or trained technicians to install and set up the equipment—set jumpers, switches, load drivers, test cables and signals, and so on. The telephony and communications people longed for the time when communications deployment at the workstation would be as simple as connecting a printer.

The birth of the concept of the Telephony Applications Programming Interface (TAPI) in 1992 marked the first milestone. A joint effort between Intel and Microsoft, TAPI was originally intended as a means of making it simpler to install and configure Intel telephony components (such as fax cards, modems, and telephone interface cards). It was officially part of Windows 3.x in 1993. By 1994, TAPI had gained rapid support in the communications industry, and the "WINTEL" partnership found that many industry players shared the vision of an open telephony API and telephony support at the OS level. At this time, TAPI was still largely implemented on Windows 95 (version 1.3 and 1.4).

Installing telephony components and services on NT is no longer a cryptic process of searching for serial ports and configuring them for your modem. TAPI takes care of all that for you. The API exposes functions for serial port configuration and sharing. Before TAPI, applications that seized a port prevented all other applications from using that port until the "possessive" application was terminated. TAPI changes all that in the following manner:

- ◆ The first application to request telephony services initializes TAPI and sets up a telephony environment on the local machine.
- ◆ TAPI then monitors and manages telephony services.
- ◆ When one application is finished using the telephony service, another application can request services, and so on.

The link between a computer telephony system and a switching system is often referred to as the *CTI link.*

Computer-Telephone Integration (CTI)

TAPI is now released in Windows NT as version 2.0, and the API has truly founds its perfect match. On the workstation and server, it has fulfilled the objectives outlined in Harry Newton's definition (see the sidebar "Father of Computer Telephony" earlier in this chapter).

Mission Critical Telephony on Windows NT

If you are new to the ideas of CTI and computer telephony, you might be wondering what can be achieved with NT other than smart techniques to connect a modem.

Following are the ingredients for NT-based PBX services for any enterprise:

- One NT 4 (telephony) server
- One CTI-link kit (usually an Ethernet card and cable)
- One PBX (must have a CTI-link port, usually an Ethernet port)
- CTI-link software
- PBX service provider CTI software
- One NT Workstation 4
- Windows NT PBX console software

How to cook up the telephony meal...

Make sure that you have the necessary network protocols and connection technology in place. TCP/IP is the best solution for a homogenous Windows network (in favor of Named Pipes, which is not fully supported in client software such as Windows 95).

(Servers should deploy reliable hardware for minimal server failure or downtime. Windows NT's remarkable recovery mechanisms, such as the NTFS and disk arrays, should be in service.)

Install the necessary console software on your NT client. This application is a Windows Sockets client that will open a connection to the Server on a TCP/IP port. The server listens on the allocated ports for requests from the client. These requests are commands that the client needs to have passed to the PBX. The server passes these requests to the PBX via TAPI and the service provider interface to the PBX. (The workstation performs the identical services usually achieved from a klunky, space-stealing, serial interface data console that ships with all PBXs and costs a fortune.)

So what kind of party can you have from your NT Workstation console? The console application functions exactly like a PBX switching console, and then some. You can take calls, park, hold, transfer, camp, conference, and so on. You will be able to see at a glance who is on the telephone (the PBX sends this information to the client via the SPI and the server) and route calls as you see fit. You will also be able to switch calls directly to voice mail, pull callers out of call queues, send faxes, play product information, and send callers to the printer (actually not the printer, that's going a bit far). In the meantime, the console application also enables you to surf the Internet, send e-mail, and finish that urgent brief.

(See figure 12.8 to help you focus on this setup more clearly.)

Figure 12.8

The workstation and the telephone (in the right-hand block) are logically connected by virtue of the PBX-Server connection (CTI-link) in the left-hand block.

TAPI has also facilitated the complex process of integrating computer and telephone technology—computer-telephone integration (CTI).

Serial Communications

The API and services that facilitate serial communications are known as Win32s (sometimes referred to as the communications API or CAPI). TAPI and the serial API are closely related because communication is the prime directive here. But TAPI is responsible for the telephony component of a communications process, and the serial API is responsible for the actual transfer of the data.

Serial API services have evolved over many years and are much older than TAPI. Like TAPI, however, the communications services have their roots in the old Windows 16-bit operating systems. The services were typically responsible for the initializing of modem services and the capture of communications ports for application processes.

So where does the serial API come into the picture? The serial services on the workstation are centered on the COM ports. It might seem that LAN communications involves serial communications, but it does not. Although local area and wide area networking *is* communications, the NetBIOS interface and the actual protocols (such as NetBEUI, IPX/SPX, and TCP/IP) are responsible for LAN/WAN communications.

The serial API works best for interactive serial-based communications applications. These applications include bulletin boards systems, terminal driven applications, and data transfer processes, such as inventory management systems.

Emperor of Protocols

It would be valid to say that terminal applications are becoming less popular in favor of TCP/IP-driven communications. Take the case of a popular router product. The usual way to manage this device was to use a serial communications application like HyperTerminal to connect to the gateway. Once connected, you can then set registers and configure the device to operate with a remote service provider. The next version of the management program, however, will use TCP/IP to connect to the gateway, and the management will be handled by a Java application.

Does this mean that true dedicated dial-up serial communications is doomed? No, millions of computers still use these services—credit-card payment networks, point-of-sale systems, or inventory control systems are good examples of serial communications processes that will be around for a while.

TAPI and the serial communications API work together to make it possible to connect workstations to network services over dial-up circuits. But the serial communications API does not play any part in the processing of real-time or time-dependent communications. TAPI instead "hands off" the processing of real-time communications (known as *isochronous* transmission) to real-time communications technology, which is usually the domain of the telephony service providers.

On the other hand, both TAPI and the serial communications API services operate in the realm of dial-up networking (see the DUN and RAS overviews later in this chapter). With the addition of the Winsock API, which provides an interface to the Internet protocols (TCP/IP), you can easily connect Windows NT to the Internet. In fact, all these interoperating technologies make Windows NT the ideal operating system for both isochronous and asynchronous communications, as you see in the example communications application provided in the preceding CTI recipe sidebar.

Taking a Closer Look at TAPI

The original TAPI specifications defined two levels of telephony service on the PC—assisted telephony and telephony. This section discusses each of these and more. If you, the LAN administrator, are considering computer telephony integration (say you have an informal call center or a help-desk), a brief understanding of the TAPI architecture will help you make better buying and integration decisions.

Assisted Telephony

The assisted telephony functions in TAPI defined the processes that enable applications to perform simple telephony services, such as having a modem go off-hook and establish calls. The first applications to enjoy such services were the contact managers and simple dialers. Later, with OS services such as DDE, it became possible to dial a telephone number from within a Word document or a spreadsheet. The assisted telephony functions were thus provided to allow the user to a dial telephone number from within applications instead of having to shell out to a full-blown telephony application.

Telephony

TAPI also defined a second, more advanced level of telephony services. These services were referenced as the three classes of telephony:

- Basic
- Supplementary
- Extended

The three services essentially allowed TAPI to provide an all-embracing, centralized, telephony processing authority or environment on the computer—a single governing process for all telephony requirements, no matter what the ends.

Basic Telephony

Basic telephony was the first and lowest level of telephony service initially defined in the API. It provided a so-called "guaranteed" set of functions that encapsulated POTS (plain old telephone service). The term *encapsulate* is used to also mean *conceal* because TAPI succeeds in allowing programmers to build telephony applications without having to deal with the telephone technology below the application. POTS is the simplest and oldest telephone service—analog transmission over twisted pairs of copper wires.

By providing POTS support in TAPI, it became possible for applications programmers to build simple first-party call control software. First-party call control meant programmers could write software (against an open, industry-supported API) to control devices installed on or attached to the local machine, the most common of which were modems.

With further enhancements over several releases and updates to TAPI, the API has become the interface through which all communications start and end on the PC or workstation. TAPI provides the interface and the capability for all processes to establish and tear down both voice and data communications.

As mentioned earlier, it is important to be aware that TAPI does not handle the actual data transfer process. After a call has been established and the destination's device answers the call, TAPI hands the data transfer process to the communications API and media stream APIs. TAPI then monitors the call until its services are required to tear down the call or hand the call off to another process.

But first-party call control does not represent the entire telephony picture. What about third-party call control? Third-party call control is the capability of software to interact with devices and processes on remote machines, connect with PBX equipment to transfer calls, hold calls, park calls, and conference and monitor calls. The application described in the CTI recipe sidebar is a first and third-party call control application.

With third-party call control support in TAPI 2.0 (released with Windows NT 4), it is now possible to achieve the dream of client/server computer telephony. The process that takes place is as follows: A client connects to an NT machine configured as a telephony server. The server maintains a link to telephony equipment, such as an ACD or a PBX, which is commonly referred to as the CT-link among computer telephony aficionados and engineers. Whenever the client needs to transfer a call, set up a conference, or establish a call, it needs only access a process on the server, which in turn passes the request to the PBX. This is achieved by a communications process between the client application interface and the service provider interface (SPI). TAPI acts as the mediator of the calls at the OS level. The clients or applications never interact or control the hardware directly.

When this process takes place on the local machine, it is called a *direct connection* (albeit via TAPI) on the local machine (first party); when it takes place in a server/proxy architecture (third party), it is called making a logical connection to the telephony services.

Another point to keep in mind is that the logical connection does not require any telephony hardware to be present on the local machine. The PC and the telephone are only logically connected via the server. The computer is attached to the network (a node), whereas the telephone is attached to the PBX (as an extension).

Besides the advanced computer telephony that is possible in the client/server environment, the client/server telephony services made possible in TAPI 2.0 obviate the need to have expensive telephony equipment installed in every computer in the enterprise. Only a dedicated telephony server (NT Server crammed full of telephony components) need be deployed, and all users can enjoy voice messaging, voice response, automated attendant, fax serving, and so on.

Basic TAPI Services

You can view TAPI as being divided into two areas or components of complexity—basic telephony and extended telephony. The basic telephony components deal with the initialization and shutdown of the telephony service, opening and closing telephone lines, and so on. The extended telephony components deal more with telephony processes, such as interacting and communicating with switches and telephony components.

Fundamental API Interactions

The following functions of TAPI represent the fundamental operations—starting and stopping the telephony processes—of the telephony service:

- **Initialization and shutdown of the telephony API.** The applications initialize the API and invoke a telephony environment on the workstation. The telephony environment can also be "torn down" by the calling applications.
- **Negotiation of the API version.** TAPI is one of the first of the Windows APIs to negotiate an API version. The TAPI architecture calls for backward compatibility with previous versions of the API so that older applications can still function (to a certain degree). This is done by supporting obsolete calls in the new APIs. For example, applications initialize TAPI by making a call to the function LineInitializeEx or PhoneInitializeEx. These are new functions in the API, which render the calls LineInitialize and PhoneInitialize obsolete. Older TAPI applications, however, will still be supported by the new API.
- **Filtering of status messages to be received.** TAPI receives and filters messages from the service provider interface as a result of events that execute on the independent hardware vendor's (IHV) equipment.
- **Opening and closing line devices.** TAPI applications "start" processes by opening and closing the *line devices,* which are telephony equipment items such as modems and voice processing cards.

Capabilities and Status

Upon initialization of the API and the setup of the telephony environment on the workstation, TAPI performs (at the behest of telephony applications) certain "surveillance" routines to determine what resources are at its disposal. These routines include the following:

- **Querying line device and address capabilities, associated media stream devices, icons, and so on.** TAPI queries the equipment to establish the capabilities of the installed devices. Media devices consist of equipment (often separate interface cards) that handle media streams. TAPI is orthogonal to the media stream during communications, as mentioned paragraphs earlier.

It does not concern itself with actual media streaming that takes place, such as the playing of a voice file by a sound card or a digitization of messages by the voice processing components.

- **Querying line device, address, and call status.** TAPI is called to return the status of the devices, addresses, and the progress of calls by applications seeking to use the services. This information is typically written to the user interface.
- **Querying and setting media device configurations.** TAPI is called to display configuration dialogs of media devices, such as sound cards and voice processing cards.

Operations

Once a telephony environment has been set up on the workstation and TAPI has performed key initializing routines, the service is ready to begin telephony operations as requested by applications calling the API for service.

- **Translating addresses and setting associated parameters.** TAPI converts canonical address information into dialable strings (discussed later in this chapter).
- **Dialing and answering calls.** The essential processing on the workstation is the establishing of calls and answering calls that are offered to the line device installed in the telephony server, on the local workstation, or at the PBX.
- **Dropping calls.** TAPI can be called on by the applications to abandon calls. The process is a signal to the switch (via digital information or in-band signals) to terminate the call. It is usually achieved by flashing the switch-hook, a process whereby the device temporarily breaks the circuit.
- **Controlling call privileges and handing off call control.** TAPI applications perform operations according to certain privilege parameters and constraints. The applications can also "hand off" call control to other processes on the workstation.

Supplementary Telephony

The supplementary telephony services provide the process by which TAPI uses in-band signaling (the injection of tones detected by the PBX CPU, which request service and direct the switch to perform certain services—see fig. 12.9). These features are typically the capability to hold callers, transfer callers, conference parties, and so on. TAPI thus lets applications on the workstation access the features found on most modern PBXs (of course, if the PBX is not TAPI-compliant and the IHV provides no SPI and associated drivers, TAPI will not be able to perform).

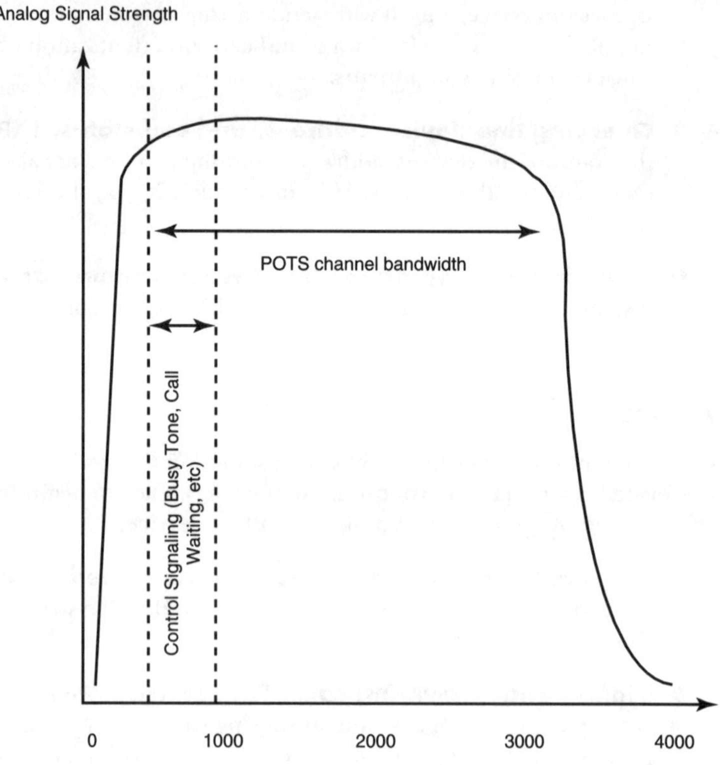

Figure 12.9

The voice bandwidth of the standard analog channel is used by telephone equipment to transmit control signals as well as voice.

These supplementary features are implemented by the IHVs (independent hardware vendors) and OEMs (original equipment manufacturers) and are available to every device you attach to your workstation. You might want, for example to install applications that can perform parking, orbiting, or camp-on-hold features, only to find that the services are not supported according to any common feature standard implemented by the IHV. And each switch is different from the next. Often, even different models from the same manufacturer behave differently.

The following list offers a summary of the functions included in the supplementary services of TAPI:

- Holding and releasing calls
- Transferring calls, both blind and with consultation
- Conferencing

- Forwarding calls
- Parking and unparking calls at extensions
- Picking up calls that are ringing elsewhere
- Camp-on and other automatic call completion
- Accepting, rejecting, and redirecting incoming calls
- Securing calls from interruptions
- Generating in-band dial digits and tones
- Monitoring media mode, received DTMF digits, and tones
- Controlling the routing of media stream information
- Sending user-user information (ISDN)
- Changing call parameters on-the-fly
- Controlling the physical phone terminal (speakers, microphones, ringers, display, lamps, buttons, and so on)

Extended Telephony

TAPI provides a well-defined extension mechanism that allows service providers to enable OEM specific functions and features. In other words, an SPI can provide access to certain services on its equipment from client applications installed or purchased with the equipment. Call logging or recording is one good example that is not a standard feature of off-the-shelf TAPI or telephony applications. These service-provider-specific functions are not directly defined by TAPI. In other words, TAPI defines the extension mechanism only, and the definition of the extended service behavior is the responsibility of the service provider.

Telephony Devices

Although these definitions are of more concern to TAPI programmers than to NT Workstation users, it might be of some value to understand how TAPI treats telephone lines and equipment. To TAPI, the line devices are the telephone lines that connect into the terminal equipment attached to the workstation. These lines plug directly into the ports of phone cards, fax cards, and data/voice/fax modems. The line devices connect your workstation to the local loop or digital network, which puts your workstation onto the PSTN.

TAPI handles lines or line devices in terms of the devices' capabilities. For example, TAPI associates the POTS line device with certain capabilities (the transmission of in-band signals across the PSTN). An ISDN line is treated differently in that it operates differently to POTS. For starters, all control signaling is done via a channel external to the channel that carries voice. Be aware that we are talking about protocols and signaling here. If you study the physical layer of the network (down to the plain old copper wires), the lines are no different. In one case (POTS), the equipment is transmitting analog signals; in the other case (ISDN), it is transmitting digital information.

A Phone Device

On your NT workstation, TAPI refers to a telephone as a *phone device.* Such a term is amusing, but the object is to describe equipment that performs telephony functions such as going off-hook, seizing a line, or requesting dial tone from the switch and dialing. Both POTS and ISDN phone devices dial a remote service provider or switch. According to the TAPI documentation, the phone device is "any device that provides an implementation for the phone-prefixed functions in the Telephony API."

From the engineering point of view, the phone device is an abstraction of a physical phone. The API treats line and phone devices as independent of each other. Therefore, you do not need to configure applications to use certain lines. TAPI manages the lines and phone devices without input or configuration from the user or the TAPI application. In other words, your application can use the phone equipment without having to search for and use an associated line. You can also access a line without using a phone to establish a telephone call. It is thus possible to use the phone device as an audio input device/interface to the computer, which would obviate the need for a separate microphone.

TAPI on Windows NT 4

TAPI 2.0, which debuted on Windows NT 4, provides third-party call control from the workstation and client/server computer telephony. The service serves the objective of providing a logical connection between the workstation, the telephony-enabled server, and the switch.

TAPI 2.0 provides a rich telephony-services environment under the 32-bit operating systems. It defines services that enable Windows NT to function as both telephony clients and telephony servers. You will be able to run voice-processing cards, fax modems, and switch cards in the same machine, and maintain a CTI link to a switch. This CTI link provides a logical connection between devices on users' desktops, which might be digital telephones, POTS phones, or headset equipment.

What does TAPI 2.0 support? It is possible, from the workstation, to look up telephone extension status; ACD call queuing; routing, transferring and conferencing; outbound call processing and predictive dialing; agent monitoring and control (call data feeds); and call state and event timers and control (see the following section). TAPI 2.0 also provides support for what Microsoft calls "quality of service parameters," which refers to catering to the advent of new carrier technologies such as Asynchronous Transfer Mode (ATM).

TAPI 2.0 Call Center Support

The TAPI 2.0 documentation talks about the concept of "modeling a call center." This means that enhancements have been made to TAPI to support the functionality required in a call center environment, formal and informal. TAPI 2.0 thus enables you to support predictive dialing applications and applications that control and manage call queues, ACD systems, station status management and station synchronization from the workstation.

The following text segment was extracted from the TAPI 2.0 document that illustrates the new call center capability:

> "Service providers can expose each resource on the PBX as a line device and possibly an associated phone device. Terminals that support multiple call appearances would do so through multiple addresses, just as in first-party call control. In fact, the third-party view of a device is identical to the first-party view; applications on the server can see and control all of the "first-party" devices, whereas an individual client PC connected to the server would only be able to see those devices which are made visible to it though access controls administered by TAPISRV.EXE on the server (the presumption is that the granularity of security for devices exposed by the server would be lines and phones, rather than addresses or calls). Resources other than terminals can also be modeled as line devices. For example, an ACD queue or route point would be modeled as a line device that could have many active calls; an IVR server, voice mail server, or set of predictive dialing ports could also be modeled as a line device that supports multiple calls."

Quality of Service Support

As Asynchronous Transfer Mode (ATM) networking emerges into the mainstream of computing and support for ATM is added to other parts of Windows NT, TAPI must also be extended to support key attributes of establishing calls on ATM facilities. The most important of these from an application perspective is the capability to request, negotiate, renegotiate, and receive indications of Quality of Service (QOS) parameters on inbound and outbound calls. By the way, QOS is not restricted to an ATM transport provider; any service provider can implement QOS features.

TAPI now supports the ability to monitor the quality of service available to applications accessing telephone and data networks servicing the enterprise. "Applications will be able to request, negotiate, and renegotiate Quality of Service (performance) parameters with the network, and receive indication of QOS on inbound calls and when QOS is changed by the network. The Quality of Service structures are binary-compatible with those used in the Windows Sockets 2.0 specification." Quality of Service information is accessed from the underlying digital transport mechanism that can notify applications when the Quality of Service is better or worse on additional channels. It is worthwhile to read the Windows Sockets 2.0 specification. Quality of Service specifics play an important role in the nature and use of sockets. For example, the quality of service requirements for a video conference will be a lot stricter than for a simple voice conversation.

Dial-Up Networking and Remote Access Overview

The arrival of the local area network in the mid-1980s rapidly changed the face of personal computing. The PC was no longer an isolated device, an information island that could not share its assets. The inventions of the LAN innovators like Novell lit the workgroup flames for smaller companies and heralded the downsizing era.

Toward the end of the decade of the PC and into the 1990s with the networking revolution in full throttle, many managers began to realize the possibilities in having people telecommute. The idea was great. An employee could work from home or from another office and log on to a computer at the office or remote network to transfer data into or out of the corporation.

Workstations and PCs also began to be used more for monitoring, process control, office automation, telephony, and myriad other uses that did not require a person to be sitting in front of the machine. These workstations found their way onto factory floors and into PBX closets, basements, computer rooms, and workshops. And it became necessary to remotely access these devices.

The remote access problem was initially relieved with the introduction of remote access software in 1992. Programs like pcAnywhere and Carbon Copy provided a solution. They allowed the remote PC to run host software, which let the dial-up machines log on and take control of the remote system. Users could take control of the remote input/output mechanisms and were able to work with a "clone" of the host's user interface on the local machine.

The problem with such a remote access model is that processing was extremely slow. Transferring screens full of data back to the local machine took ages. Mouse clicks and keyboard input was excruciatingly slow. The slow modem speed of the time did not help much either.

Remote access needs are now stronger than ever. PCs and workstations are everywhere. They control printers, PBX and telephony systems, databases, and client/ server processes. They allow people to access WANS and the Internet and to easily telecommute from remote offices, from home, or while traveling. Many companies now deploy workstations and servers as application servers and remote procedure machines, which allow users to access a centralized repository of processing power and resources.

Even with faster modems and bandwidth on demand, however, software like pcAnywhere and clone Carbon Copy models have outlived their usefulness. They are too slow to keep up with the critical demands of remote access and modern computing. Clearly, another model of remote access was required. Enter Remote Access Service (RAS) and Dial-Up Networking (DUN).

It was only natural that Microsoft should fit out the Windows operating systems with RAS and DUN services. After all, remotely accessing the resources of a machine by sneaking in through backdoors sitting above the operating system codebase was risky business.

The idea was to make the modem work like a LAN card. This meant that a local machine could access the remote machine as if the remote was on the local LAN. If the remote machine was on a LAN, then the local host could attach to the host running RAS and appear to the network as another node. The local machine could then access the LAN as another network peer, even as a server machine. And this is how it works, albeit at slower speeds than the LAN because the connection is over telephone lines and modems.

To make RAS and DUN work as just described, it also becomes necessary for the Win32 system services (the core of the Windows 95 and NT operating systems) to provide the networking protocol stacks over the telephone lines. When you configure NT for dial-up services or RAS, the network protocols already installed on the machine will be used for the service. These protocols include TCP/IP, NetBEUI, and IPX/SPX and automatically bind to the adapter during configuration and setup, essentially transforming serial ports into Ethernet ports.

Note For more detailed information on this communications topic, see Chapter 13, "Remote Access Services (RAS) and Dial-Up Networking."

Using Connection Protocols

DUN tunnels packets through connection protocols, which manage the transmission of data over the PSTN, WAN, or an intranet. These include the older but still widely used SLIP (Serial Line Internet Protocol) and the more popular Point-to-Point protocol (PPP). Also used are Novell's NetWare Connect and Asynchronous NetBEUI, which connects Windows networks.

The protocol of choice on Windows is PPP, and the OS installs PPP as the default protocol on the dial-up adapter. There is a good reason Microsoft made this so: PPP has become the industry standard and contains a number of attributes that make it attractive. The local machine is now able to connect and "talk" to a wide variety of servers with PPP installed and TCP/IP services running. The PPP is also much faster than SLIP and offers a more robust error-correction mechanism. Most important, PPP does not require a person to perform manual logon procedures when connecting to a host, such as entering IP addresses and interacting with a terminal emulation window. This is important for machines required to periodically dial out to remote networks and log on without the aid of a human operator.

Why else would you choose DUN and RAS for remote access? Security. An insecure remote access service is safe until a hacker discovers the backdoor and raids the company. NT extends all its sophisticated security services to the remote logon. Shares and permissions are extended to the DUN client, as are the proxy authorization services. Finally, these services are free (if you purchased NT). You can install them off any Windows NT compact disc.

Preparing for Telephony, DUN Installation, and RAS Setup

As mentioned in the previous section, communications, telephony, Dial-Up Networking, and Remote Access Services include all the necessary software components needed to connect to a server or service provider. These are added to the system and bound to the hardware during installation of the operating system or applications.

If you selected the Dial-Up Networking option when you first installed NT, the components for DUN are already installed. You can verify the availability of DUN by opening the My Computer folder, which is accessed by clicking the icon in the top left corner of the desktop. If you don't see the DUN icon, the services are not installed. If you did not select the option or removed the support after installation, you will need to run Setup again.

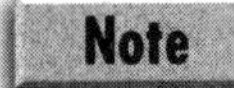

Be sure that Dial-Up Networking is *not* already installed because in trying to reinstall it you might inadvertently remove the service. Another means of checking for the presence of DUN is as follows:

1. Open the Accessories list of programs.
2. Click on the Start button.
3. Choose Programs and then choose Accessories. If you see the DUN icon, you don't need to install it.

Preparing for Roll-out

To configure NT for communications, make sure that your hardware is installed and configured according to the procedures described later. You should also have your notepad, or a big yellow legal pad on a clipboard, for documenting the process and the presence of your technical staff if you're planning to roll-out several dial-up or computer telephony enabled clients.

Adding, restoring, or deleting services can seriously impact the operation of your computer if you don't plan the configuration carefully. Should something go wrong, you need to be able to recover as completely and as rapidly as possible, which is why you should document your actions and note the sequence of events.

Logistics

If you plan to do a roll-out of several computers—that is, to install communications services on a number of computers—it is necessary to have sufficient information in hand before you proceed. Formulate a check list. The following would be the base items for your checklist, and you should add items as you deem necessary:

- Have I determined how long the process will take?
- Is each computer primed for the installation and configuration?
- Is all necessary hardware installed, configured, and tested?
- Do I have the necessary tools, resources, and task force to complete the job?

Before you tackle a roll-out, if you have not installed computer telephony or Dial-Up Networking services before, take one computer aside and perform the operation on a single machine so that the entire process can be documented. If you're deploying a team, the team should observe the entire process from beginning to end. Have one person, an astute observer who can take sensible notes, document everything necessary to complete an installation, setup, and configuration. These notes can then be turned into a script, referenced, and made available to all members of the team. This is especially important if personnel will be going to remote locations or are already based at remote sites. With a well-written and proven script, you could delegate this task to able users, especially if you have managed to automate the process as far as possible with computer scripts. Establishing smart logistical procedures can buy you time and end the frustration.

Check that all the members of the deployment teams have been given the full rights needed to complete the task. Almost every configuration and roll-out requires that the people have rights to access necessary resources, especially if you want the users to connect to the network and then use the new Dial-Up Networking connection to download or upgrade software, scripts, user logon information, profiles, resource configurations, and more. You will lose time if a member of the team cannot access a resource and the network administrator or team leader is out of reach when it is discovered that the member cannot even log on to the network or the required domain.

When should roll-out or deployment occur? No matter what is being upgraded or configured, it is necessary that you don't interfere with critical work schedules—yours and users. You don't want to force staff out of their offices unnecessarily because a member of the team needs to work on the computer. If you are short-staffed or if you are performing this on your own, spread it out over several days and try to tackle the task before the computer is needed for day-to-day work. You certainly do not want to arrive on the scene to configure a computer for DUN services when the user is in the middle of a massive spreadsheet or print job.

Provide advance notice and warning. Make sure that the users, if they are not part of the installation process, know exactly when the task will be performed. Arrange the upgrade and configuration with the user beforehand, and set it down as an appointment that cannot be changed without both parties agreeing to a resynchronization of time and schedules.

Have users perform backups of their data and verify as far as possible that this has been achieved for each of the target machines. Also have each target computer checked for viruses before you allow it to connect to the domain as a dial-up client. It's also a good idea to have hard disks defragmented and compressed.

If you manage a large network and configure many machines, back up mission critical hard disks onto recordable compact discs. With the drop in price of writable CD-ROM drives and the price of blank CDs dropping every day, this activity makes sense and is cheaper and faster than tape-driven backups.

If you are installing modems or ports, this is a good time to check on internal hardware and sign off each computer as having had hardware examined, dusted, tested, and documented for inventory control. In particular, note the clock speed of the CPU, amount of RAM, BIOS dates, and brand of network card.

During the pilot installation or configuration or the trial configuration, strive to ensure that the process has been automated as far as possible.

Make sure that any hardware upgrading or installation is included in the logistical plan.

Make sure that installers do not compromise the user's logon profile. In other words, make sure that a successful installation does not collapse or that necessary services do not "disappear" when users log on under their names and passwords. The multiple logon features of Windows are extremely powerful. Multiple logon and the user profiles features are also some of the most dangerous if not used properly. Consult the Windows NT Networking documentation. You don't want to spend tons of effort setting up convenient access options for users and then have the users call you later to say that when they logged on, several items vanished from the desktop. (One person called me to say that his desktop vanished completely. Actually, we had taken his monitor for repairs, and we should have advised him.)

Last, but not least in importance, make sure that you have your security specifications and policy ready and in place. If you are setting up servers or reading a network for multiple dial-up clients, telephony, Internet access, and so on, have the necessary domain lists of users and groups in place before the roll-out begins. If you don't do this, clients will not be able to connect, and you will not be able to sign them off. Refer to the documentation that covers domain administration and setting up users for Windows NT networking.

Installing a Standard Modem

The installation and configuration of analog devices is fairly simple. Most of the time, you only need to make sure that the workstation has sufficient serial ports for your needs. If you are keeping power to the workstation secure with a UPC, you might want to monitor the UPC from the workstation. This requires the configuration of a serial port for that process. You will need another port for your mouse, if you are using it on a serial port. The modem, too, requires a serial port. Installing and configuring three ports on a PC can be a problem because most PC architectures only allow for the deployment of two serial port IRQ addresses, which essentially limits you to two ports. Ports 1 and 3 usually share an interrupt, as do ports 2 and 4.

To install a new modem, perform the following tasks:

1. Open the Control Panel folder. You can access this folder from the Settings menu on the Start menu or from the folder usually named My Computer, which is located in the upper-left corner of the desktop.

2. Double-click on the Modems icon.

3. From the Install New Modem wizard, you can choose to have NT find the modem you have installed on the port, or you can choose to install it yourself.

4. Let's make life easier; leave the option unchecked to have NT find your modem. NT begins to query the comm ports installed on the computer. When it finds one with a modem attached, it determines which modem is on board and begins installation and configuration routines. (Be patient; this process can take a few minutes.)

5. As soon as NT deduces the brand and model of modem you have installed, it displays this information to you. However, NT can be wrong in its choices; often it fails to turn up a modem on the port. If that happens, leave the port alone and choose the option to select your modem from a list. I recommend this because NT does not keep details of every modem and configuration on file—and the problem is seldom the port. NT might also detect a standard modem (or you can choose this from the list), which is also fine because analog modems all work the same way. It does not matter that your modem is not TAPI compliant because TAPI communicates with it by translating application calls to TAPI into AT commands.

Note Devices connected to COM ports, such as a router configuration interface, a UPS, or a magnetic card reader, often interfere with COM port detection. This can be frustrating, especially if you need to keep these serial devices in commission—in which case you'll have to just "Plug 'n PAY."

6. If you decide to choose your own modem, NT asks you to confirm the port on which it is installed. You only really need to do this once for the Workstation or NT client because NT only supports the attachment of one modem and one Dial-Up Networking client process (in contrast to NT Server 4, which can support up to 256 DUN connections).

7. When you are finished giving NT the information or if NT came through with the correct information, click on the Next button; NT proceeds to install the modem. Finally, NT concludes and gives you the opportunity to go back to the previous steps. If all is well, click on Finish.

Installing ISDN Terminal Equipment

Integrated Services Digital Network (ISDN) is not a new technology. It has been available in most parts of the world for some time now and has been one of the chief means by which an enterprise connected remote offices to one large data and voice network. With the advent of the Internet and the need for wider bandwidth to speed data transmission, ISDN is becoming a popular choice. It is not very expensive in the U.S., although it can cost an arm and a leg in other parts of the world. All the RBOCS (Regional Bell Operating Companies) now provide ISDN to small business and into the home. TAPI has all the necessary support for ISDN device handling.

ISDN can be installed on the existing loop that connects your premises to the telephone company or to your remote equipment if you own the wires and the network or if you are leasing the lines. To install ISDN for DUN, you need to install the terminal interface cards onto your workstation bus.

Installing ISDN onto the workstation is no more difficult than installing the standard modem. If, however, you are planning to connect a network or an intranet to the Internet or to another remote network, installing an ISDN card might not make sense. It would be better and more secure to set up a remote dial-up ISDN device, such as the Ascend Pipeline 50, and connect it to an Ethernet card on a workstation that will act as an Internet gateway (which could provide DNS as well). That way, the entire network has access to the network via the workstation.

NT can detect the installation of the ISDN adapter on the machine, but configuration and setup might be something you have to do manually, depending on your choice of equipment. For this, consult your device disks, user manuals, and guides (and probably the vendor's tech support lines). The most popular internal ISDN equipment is the Motorola BitSURFR, so installation will be demonstrated using this device.

Installing an ISDN Card

To install an ISDN card, perform the following tasks:

1. Install the card onto the workstation bus, just as you would with any standard modem card.

2. Follow the procedures for installing a modem by clicking on the Modems icon in the Control Panel (see the initial steps in the preceding procedure for installing the modem).

3. Click on the checkbox to access the list of modems that will allow you select the BitSURFR (in which case NT would have not noticed the new equipment you just installed on the bus).

4. After selecting the BitSURFR, NT asks you for the port you want to install it on. Select the correct free port by clicking on the entry in the wizard's list box and click on Next. NT loads the necessary driver, and you're all finished.

The external ISDN termination equipment and routers provide character-based interfaces, which can be accessed via a communications program like HyperTerminal or via Telnet (if the equipment supports it).

After you have installed your ISDN equipment, check that you have set your SPIDs correctly. SPIDs stands for *service provider ID* and is the number by which you access your ISDN service provider. Make sure that the telco has set the number of SPIDs to 2, enabling you to use two logical line devices. One line can be used for data, which you allocate to SPID 1, and the other SPID can be allocated to voice. If your equipment allows voice/data on both SPIDs, it makes no difference which SPID gets ID 1 or 2. If you set the SPIDs incorrectly, you will not have much luck connecting on ISDN.

When setting up your ISDN connection, make sure that the Multipoint option is enabled (set to "yes" in most devices). Enabling Multipoint means that the B channels can be used as the computer deems fit.

Other Settings to Consider

Click on the More button for the additional settings options. These dialog boxes provide several useful options to further streamline your connections:

◆ **Re-dial.** This is especially useful if you are trying to make a connection to a busy Internet host. The options provided let you force NT to be aggressive in making a connection. You can have NT attempt to connect by retrying up to 100 times before giving up.

◆ **Prompting.** You can choose between having NT prompt you for logon information or just dialing without the need (so it assumes) to get further input from you. It is useful to select the latter option if NT has all the data it needs to establish and fix a connection.

◆ **Callback.** An NT Server can call you back to complete the logon procedure. Specify the number to have the server call back to. There are two reasons to use this option. First, it can be used to save the caller money and allow the company to manage its RAS costs more efficiently (which is better than having telecommuters turn in copies of their telephone bills for reimbursement).

Second, having the server call back DUN clients is an additional security mechanism (which should not be relied on and is there for you to keep honest users honest). If callback is not enabled in the user account on the server, the caller cannot connect to the server.

Miscellaneous Setup Notes

Make sure that the network domain controllers have the necessary user-level security in place, or your clients will not be authenticated:

- **Enable software compression.** Checking this option when installing a modem enables you to compress software before it is transmitted to the server.

Enable Software Compression is an option. It is, however, better to leave this unchecked when connecting to Internet hosts, which might not be able to handle the compressed data.

- **Allowed Network Protocols.** If unsure what to use, check all the options. TCP/IP is mandatory for establishing a connection to the Internet. Click on TCP/IP Settings to set up your Internet connection. If you are connecting to an Internet host, see Chapter 15, "NT Workstation and the Internet." For information about how to set up TCP/IP, see Chapter 10 "The Ins and Outs of TCP/IP."

Communications and Security

Although this book is devoted to Windows NT Workstation 4, the security subject is a necessary part of any reference. If you pick up a reference that ignores this subject, the author is not doing his or her job, and it is time to look at another title. Also, no communications strategy should be without such a section; with all the power that the new communications technology brings you comes the potential danger of breaches in security.

The beginning of this chapter discussed the evolution of the PC from a stand-alone file creation and handling device to a communications machine. With all the new conduits that connect your workstations to the millions of machines around the world lurk potential disasters in security breaches.

Formulating a Security Policy

Every network manager or IS/IT administrator needs to establish access policies for various services on their networks. These policies govern activities such as location of and access to printers, applications, data, files, and communications equipment and services (such as access to RAS, computer telephony servers, fax servers, and so on).

Every enterprise should have a governing security policy. The following policy statement is suggested as a starting-point for your security policy document:

"Every person, procedure, object, or communications process not expressly permitted access to the enterprise information network is denied access."

The phrase enterprise information network (EIN), an information engineering term, is one of my favorite. Many IT people believe that the EIN is an obsolete term, and that it is nothing more than a LAN or intranet. I use it often because it is a very descriptive term and illustrates that a LAN or intranet can merely be a network of computers, or it can (and it must) be the very circulatory system that ensures the enterprise is not starved of critical information—information that needs to flow to all parts of the organization to ensure its ability to operate, compete, and prosper.

A simple connection or interconnection of computers makes a network, but it does not mean that enterprise information flows through the network. Setting up an EIN is a book all its own.

The processes that work to achieve this ebb and flow of information, however, bump up against the strict security policy needed in every enterprise, which is why you need to formulate a security policy around this need.

The preceding security policy might seem to be a tough policy to follow. It is—it is derived from the classification mechanisms of the military. Essentially it means that your point of departure is from an entire enterprise information network that is completely sealed off from the outside world. On the inside, it is the same. The point of departure here is from a policy that says every workstation in the enterprise should be an island, denied access to the network until and only if access is specifically required.

If you saw the remake movie of *Mission Impossible*, starring Tom Cruise, you'll remember that the CIA considered that the only way it could adequately protect the computer holding the secret operatives' data files from theft was to put it on a stand-alone computer with no network connection, and to lock the computer in a vault. The computer was thus sealed off from the outside world and the inside world.

It might seem that you are taking 10 steps backward here for the advances you are making in communications technology. But it also means that while the enterprise is sealed off from the outside world and the threat of internal breaches in security is minimized, the administrator can at least sleep in peace.

Of course no enterprise can function with a total denial of access and services—internal and external. The only way you can achieve a night of uninterrupted sleep and still run an EIN is to have an effective security policy working for you.

The previously mentioned policy statement serves as the starting point to selectively permit access on a controlled basis. Too often, networks are set up, servers and workstations are installed and connected, and services are started up with no security policy in place, or even in mind. Access is permitted on a wholesale scale just to get going, and the security issue is left on the back burner until key network and communications problems are ironed out.

This philosophy will set in motion a slide to impending disaster. By the time the network administrator gets to the security issues, breaches in security will already have occurred. They might not be obvious, and in many cases, if the breach originates from the outside, it will be a sleeper process concealed somewhere on the network until it is needed.

In other words, security mechanisms and practice should be in place before connecting networks and telephony systems to the outside world. In any event, the job of the LAN administrator never really concludes. Networks keep growing and new issues constantly arise. Security issues on the back burner will always stay on the back burner until a disaster happens.

The first steps an intruder takes will be to obtain a picture of the network, what you have attached, how you are attaching it, the software used, and the location and addresses of vulnerable machines.

Access to a range of machines will allow an intruder to gather up important information about your business. If you are a mail order company, then chances are files filled with thousands of credit card numbers are lurking around somewhere. If you are a wholesaler, then information about where your warehouse is located is sitting on one of the hard disks. If you are an inventor or technology company, then that secret recipe, million dollar algorithm, or life and death formula will be an easy target for an experienced intruder who knows what to look for.

Understand this: Your network is just one open field in the huge jungle of interconnecting networks. The hyenas are out there, scrounging for whatever is lying around. Once they pick up the scent of a weak or bleeding network, they will tear it to shreds.

The following communications gateways and access points (discussed earlier) present opportunity for rape and plunder:

- Remote Access Service and Dial-Up Networking
- Internet and WAN access—inbound and outbound mail, outgoing ftp, outgoing WWW, Electronic Data Interchange (EDI), and so on
- Intranet access—access to corporate web sites, ftp servers, and so on
- Computer telephony services—access to PBX systems, ACD equipment, voice mail systems, interactive voice response systems, fax servers, audiotext systems, and more
- LAN access and access to host systems, such as terminal access to mainframe computers
- Bulletin boards
- Gateways, routers, bridges, and so on

In terms of the military-style security policy, you need to ensure the following is in place before connecting any network (data or telephone) to the outside world or giving local users access to network resources. The following collection subheadings is not complete, and every network will have varying degrees of IT/IS implementation. It should, however, give you the idea.

Domain Security Considerations and User Management

Domain controllers should not allow power or total access to everyone. The default should be "access is denied to everyone and every process." Under this policy, the user manager on the NT server specifically allows access to users and workstations under controlled conditions. It reduces the risk of allowing total access to everyone, a policy that can make security management nightmarish.

A user or process can be assigned a security profile that determines what he, she, or it is allowed access to and what can be done with this access. Such access could be read access, read/write access, archive ability, network management, manipulation of directories and files, and so on. After this user and the accompanying rights are established, the user becomes a trusted member of the domain.

You might devise your own categorizing scheme, such as the "Restricted," "Confidential," and "Secret" scheme of the military. I classify users by levels: level 1 is a power user who has total rights; level 2 is an administrator who has certain rights, and so on. Level 5 users are given access to applications and data as needed, period.

Here is an example:

User X requires access to an accounting application on the Accounts Department Server. The domain administrator (working from any server in the domain) can add user X to the domain with permission to only access the application during regular office hours and to be restricted from opening a certain collection of files. The user can also be restricted from copying files to his or her workstation, which adds additional security and control over the workstation to server link. In other words, an intruder gaining access to the workstation (from the outside world over RAS, DUN, or Internet access, or by gaining physical access to the machine) will find that he or she is unable to attach to the server to download anything.

Domain users accessing database servers should have no need to retrieve information and store it on their local workstations. Recordsets and sundry snap-shots of data can and should be accessed from servers, via OLE automation and built-in client database security (logon) mechanisms.

Most database servers allow users to set bookmarks and other methods of returning to query results or record sets pulled down from servers. Storing data on workstations means the data has been replicated without going through data replication/security policy. If the workstation is attacked, the data could be compromised.

DUN and RAS Security Considerations

DUN and RAS provide tremendous benefit and flexibility for remote users. Consultants and network administrators make extensive use of the DUN and RAS services. In fact, many consultants charge clients high fees if DUN or RAS is denied to them and they are forced to make on-site visits. DUN is a great way to administer a network from a remote site, but it is also a great way to hack a company.

Many software vendors, such as voice mail or firewall resellers, will typically administer and service their products remotely. NT Workstations make ideal isolated RAS points. But these single connection machines are also connected to networks.

With the added flexibility comes the increased security risk. How can you give a remote user access to certain network services and protect the network or domain from unauthorized access? For starters, a "deny all" policy comes into play here, in that you will make sure that a RAS or DUN service is carefully tailored to a user or process that requires a certain level of access. All others are barred.

Unfortunately, it is not possible to completely hide RAS access onto the enterprise information network. It might seem like a good policy to restrict RAS services from NT Workstations (and obviously from Windows 95 clients), but that is not always convenient. Workstations are more vulnerable to a "hands-on" attack than servers because servers are locked away in server rooms (or should be). Here are some actions to consider if you have to give DUN/RAS access to a workstation connected to the LAN or intranet:

- Try to provide a telephone line that is separate from the central PBX or ACD system. Many users working on the switch, looking for free extensions, might stumble on the connection to a workstation's RAS service (the modem howl is a dead giveaway). Hackers will go through your entire hunt-group hoping to strike it lucky. (A new type of silent modem is now available; it remains silent until authorization has been established. The hacker cannot hear the modem and the port remains in the proverbial "dark.")
- Keep the telephone number and location of the line and the RAS confidential. The telephone number should only be known by the user of the machine and the caller.
- Although it might like seem an impossible thing to do, you should try to secure the telephone line outside your property. You could try encasing it in a steel pipe and burying the pipe inside a trough of concrete. But you don't have to go overboard because a determined attacker will find a hole somewhere, and you can't protect the entire connection from point to point. You can, however, run the cable through the protected (steel-encased) conduits that connect PBX systems and routers between offices and departments.
- Make sure the end user of the service does not have call forwarding invoked on his or her side of the connection. That breaks down the call-back protocol, and you might have no way of tracking the connection to the forwarded number. Make sure you fix the call-back number (choose a "Preset To" number in the RAS call-back options). Do not allow the user to change the number willy nilly.

If you are running a high-risk network (such as the network of a big stock-broker firm), you will need more MI5-like solutions. The first option is the installation of password-protected modems and routers. This is a good idea, although it is entirely possible to monitor packets and come up with the password. This happened to a client of mine. The password was captured, and the hacker cracked the equipment and reset the password to deny the client service. There is usually no way around the lost password problem. In this case, we had to junk a $500 modem.

So if traffic can be analyzed, what's the next step? Encryption. Modem or data encryption takes the RAS password encryption mechanism a step further. NT only encrypts the password, which is a step in the right direction. Encryption modems encrypt the data that subsequently passes between DUN client and RAS server once logon is successful. An encryption modem might be the solution if you are concerned about wiretaps. Cost-wise, it will be lot cheaper than custom steel and concrete casings or employing a Green Beret to stand guard over your connection at the central exchange. Naturally, only the authorized user has access to the connection because anyone who manages to break into the RAS port will receive unintelligible data.

Internet/Intranet Security Considerations

The Internet has become a mission-critical, pervasive resource for almost every company on the planet. Going into its historical rise to critical mass is not the mission of this chapter, however. Highlighting the dastardly dangers of unbridled workstation Internet access is the mission here.

Again our military intelligence-style communications security policy dictates that "the only access is no access." Hide the corporate network from the Internet and allow access to workstations (and servers) that qualify for access—inbound and outbound. The qualifying entities need to, again, be carefully categorized or graded according to the level of access required.

Before going into security strategy for Internet communication, it is important to be aware of the holes workstation users can blow in your security strategy.

The workstation is increasingly being used as an Internet client. In the not-too-distant past, you might have been thinking "Why would we want to access the Internet from NT Workstation?" But today, many enterprises are deploying workstations throughout the enterprise as the de facto client, relegating Windows 95 to the den or family room.

With LANs being transformed into intranets in the thousands, if the administrator does not carefully manage the security issue, he or she will find the enterprise as penetrable as Swiss cheese. The potential for disaster lies in the following areas:

- Workstations with IP addresses open SMTP and POP connections to the Internet to send and receive e-mail.
- Workstations with IP addresses open World Wide Web connections to the Internet to browse web sites and download all manner of material from these sites.
- Workstations with IP addresses open Telnet and ftp connections to the Internet.

The mail protocols—ftp, Telnet, and WWW—are the only protocols workstations need to access Internet or intranet resources. The other protocols should not be accessible to workstation users. These include administrative resources such as ping, traceroute, finger, and the like.

The popular protocols, however, are open doors to all manners of evil rushing in from the Internet. Mail can be a nightmare. The most popular and most irritating virus traveling the Information Superhighway is the Word virus. It hides in Microsoft Word documents, millions of which move around the Internet every day.

The SMTP and POP protocols are also the easiest way hackers can identify workstations on the network. If the workstation is allowed to send mail over Internet connections on the network, the IP address will provide a hacker with a route map all the way back to the machine. All mail should be forwarded to a server that is responsible for moving mail to the outside world.

The mail protocols and the WWW protocols are also open to packet flooding and denial of service attacks. How these attacks work is beyond the scope of this chapter; suffice it to say that it is very easy for a creature of the dark to attack a host on your Internet and cause it to crash. Denial of service attacks flood the host operating systems with tons of connection requests, many of them designed to generate huge audit logs and error handling procedures. Getting a bigger computer will not help; often it compounds the problem. Eventually, the host will run out of resources and die. A super-server or Cray Mainframe will stay running for a few days longer. When it finally crashes, so much damage will have been done that it will take weeks to clean up. Smaller computers die quicker (within hours), so the flood damage is not as severe.

Many companies now use NT Workstation in their call centers for multiple process-intensive operations. These include computer telephony access, data retrieval and processing, order processing and inventory management, and Internet access. A number of banks and huge merchandisers, for example, are exploring the use of Java, WWW technology, and real-time Internet telephony to interact in real-time with users at web sites. What a great opportunity for a cyber-crook. If the intruder knows his or her stuff, the potential to hold up a bank over the Internet is very real.

Attacks from Java applets are a very real concern; if you plan to allow workstations to access Java applets and deploy Java client technology, you should be aware of the potential dangers.

Trying to control how every workstation accesses the Internet, however, is not an easy exercise. It is not possible or even desirable to go from workstation to workstation removing access to protocols that are not needed. TCP/IP does not work that way—you can't peel off protocols like the layers of an onion. Besides, the entire TCP/IP protocol suite has become a necessary protocol item in the makeup of LANs and intranets. TCP/IP is now extensively used in computer telephony applications, IP telephony, "Net meetings," and so on. The only way to effectively administer Internet security issues is with the "deny access" policy.

So how do you hide the workstations (the entire enterprise information network) from the Internet? That is where firewall software comes into the picture. These software suites are not cheap; they start at around $4,000. For large networks (100+ workstations), they can cost as much as $20,000.

The philosophy of firewall protection is to hide the network from the outside world and to deny access to internal users unless expressly needed. Many products work hand in glove with the Windows NT Server domain control, security, and administering software. Workstation users can thus be given access to Internet resources on an as-needed, controlled, and audit-enabled basis.

Good firewall software also filters out viruses and hostile Java applets, and alerts the administrator to suspicious behavior on the network. It is also a good idea to deploy packet-filtering technology on your routers and bridges. Many sites have installed firewalls while leaving the connection to the Internet vulnerable to attack. An intruder might be interested only in denying your site access to the Internet (this has happened to many companies). The hacker will gain access to the router and either trash its operating system or reset the password.

It is easy to be complacent about Internet security. Too many companies set up Internet sites, connections, and intranets and leave the security issues until last (even some Internet Service Providers have fallen victim to this complacency). The only reason the companies then buy firewall software or take the security issue seriously is because their network gets shut down by hackers. Some hackers do so much damage that it can take up to three weeks to get operations back to normal. In many cases, the damage can cause the business to collapse.

Computer Telephony Security Considerations

Computer telephony systems pose a security risk both at workstations and at the telephone systems of the enterprise. Computer telephony is too fast becoming a pervasive concept in communications, like Internet communications. Computer telephony (and telephony or telephone) security should fall under the administration of the same security organization as network and workstation security strategies.

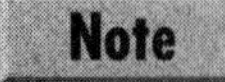

Many enterprises monitor voice mail, e-mail, and fax mail. It has become especially easy to do so now that these services are Workstation centric (in which messages are stuffed into mixed media or universal mailboxes). You should insist that employees understand that they should not use the computer telephony services for anything not related to work (save casual messages from spouses or family). If necessary, advise that management will monitor the messaging services to ensure proper use. Advising your employees to keep sensitive, personal information out of the enterprise's voice message facility is a good idea and for their own good.

The voice messaging services of the enterprise are not 100 percent safe. Many stories have circulated describing how disgruntled employees, peers, or hackers (internal or external) have hacked into the telephone systems of the enterprise. Someone can easily "hack" into the message storehouse of the enterprise hoping to catch a voice message that reveals a security password or a door to the network and selected workstations.

Message storehouses are mines of information to outsiders or someone else in the enterprise. Sales people, business development specialists, and technology officers are especially prone to attack.

Hackers are increasingly finding voice mail and computer telephony systems to be easy targets that lead to information that helps them crack open secure networks. Many hack these systems for the following reasons:

- **Industrial espionage.** The hackers crack mail systems and mailboxes to listen for information that can be used or sold for competitive advantage. Users often leave credit card numbers, PIN numbers, passwords, access codes, and codes and instructions in voice mailboxes and in e-mail.
- **The uninvited guest.** Another sinister user is the so-called "uninvited guest" who attacks the system on the hunt for unused mailboxes. He or she then rents out the mailbox or uses it for illegal transactions and unsavory business deals, such as drug deals. Hackers can even hack into administration software residing on workstations and servers and set up their own voice mail services.
- **Toll fraud.** Toll fraud is a very serious problem in the U.S. Some companies have even gone bankrupt after falling prey to this practice. If you allow remote users carte blanch access to your company's outgoing trunks in order to make long-distance calls, you're making it very easy for a hacker to use the same service. This applies to standard telephone services and Internet access. After the intruder has discovered the gateway, he or she will then resell new found "dial tone" to anyone willing to pay. The enterprise ends up paying the bills for someone else's long-distance calls.

New firewall products and data filtering technologies are emerging daily. Some can be applied to data protection as well as call security. In cases where digital transmission (such as ISDN) is used for both data and voice, firewalls and filtering software will work for establishing security around both asynchronous and isochronous communications.

Communications Security: Know Your Limitations

While it is important to adopt a strict security policy and stick to it, it is also important to understand that there will come a time when an intruder breaks into your system. If you have a very large site to manage or a popular service, it will attract both wrong-doers and self-appointed gods who think they control the Information Superhighway and the communications networks of the world. You should thus prepare yourself to deal with occasions when you have an intruder on hand.

For starters, you should put monitoring software in place that will alert you (in every way possible) that a break-in has occurred or that some weird behavior is taking place on a server or workstation. It will already be over if the hacker gets in on Friday evening and you are not alerted to the fact until Monday morning. You come to work to find your whole world has collapsed around you. You might even get fired. You need to stop a hacker before he or she has had a chance to cause too much damage.

Ten minutes into "penetration" might already be too late to stop damage, but chances are your recovery will not be painful.

By employing the "no enter" policy, you can locate all critical services, data, and applications on servers in the server room. Keeping such services off workstations will make life easier to a large degree. Even workstation-centric services, such as high-end plotting software, and CPU and graphic-intensive applications should obtain files and data from servers, which are sure to be audited and on which alerts can be placed.

Lastly, regularly communicate enterprise policy on matters of security to all members of the enterprise. State what is considered acceptable use of messaging services and the network communications infrastructure.

Advise employees to be alert, prudent, and security-conscious all the time. Keep track of people who leave the enterprise, temporarily or permanently. Disgruntled ex-employees might still have security clearance to the enterprise, and there's no telling what they might do with that access.

Summary

This chapter covered the core functionality at the heart of the NT communications service—the Win32 API. These systems and collateral interfaces on Windows NT make it possible to enjoy myriad communications applications on workstation architecture. TAPI, MAPI, the Windows Serial Communications API, and the Windows sockets API were all discussed, as were computer telephony and CTI. DUN and RAS were discussed at length, and security policies and considerations were presented.

CHAPTER 13

Remote Access Services (RAS) and Dial-Up Networking

This chapter introduces the new communications architecture (especially Telephony Applications Programming Interface, or TAPI) employed by Windows NT Workstation 4, and explores the installation and setup of modems. This chapter then builds from this communications infrastructure to a discussion of remote or mobile computing using Windows NT Remote Access Services (RAS) and Dial-Up Networking.

TAPI is Microsoft's effort to transition Windows communications from the monolithic Windows 3.x architecture to a modular 32-bit communications system. Just as Windows 3.x revolutionized printing (when compared to the DOS model of requiring unique print drivers for each application), TAPI strives to separate the hardware from all communications software. Essentially this means that a communications program (for example, a mail client) can smoothly interact with any TAPI-compliant device (an analog modem, a digital (ISDN) modem, a CSU/DSU, and so on.). Windows NT Workstation continues the implementation of TAPI that began with Windows 95.

As remote or mobile computing increases in organizations everywhere, RAS and Dial-Up Networking in Windows NT Workstation assume greater importance. For example, a mobile user with Windows NT Workstation on his laptop can use the Dial-Up Networking feature to connect to the corporate server (maybe running NetWare, NT Server, or Unix) and connect to the Internet because Dial-Up Networking implements PPP (Point-to-Point Protocol). Using PPP as the serial protocol over modems, your end users can connect to most of the network servers that they need access to.

Remote Access Services Server offers the capability of using your Windows NT workstation as a dial-up "server." If you want to set up a user's PC at work to receive calls from her home so that she can download the files she needs or send some updates, the RAS server offers the ideal solution. Although the RAS server can only accept one incoming call, it still may find use in small offices with low remote access needs.

Windows NT Workstation offers two distinct features in remote computing. Dial-Up Networking enables the NT workstation to dial-out, and the RAS server enables a remote PC to dial-in to the NT workstation.

Setting up modems and installing RAS and Dial-Up Networking is relatively simple. To understand how this happens, an overview of the communications architecture is a must. The communications architecture provides a distinct divergence from Microsoft's earlier efforts at Windows communications.

Exploring the New Communications Architecture for NT Workstation

Windows NT Workstation employs a sophisticated communications architecture, based more on the Windows 95 model than on the Windows 3.x model. Windows 3.x used a communications driver called COMM.DRV, which basically acted as the interface between Win 16 applications and communications hardware. COMM.DRV was *monolithic,* meaning that it acted as the interface (actually an API—application programming interface), as well as a communications port driver. This resulted in newer versions of COMM.DRV every time new features were added to hardware. This is obviously not the most efficient way of handling this functionality. Figure 13.1 illustrates the old Windows 3.x communications architecture.

The Win32 model or the model employed in Windows NT (as well as Windows 95) is aimed at separating hardware-dependent communications operations. Essentially, the architecture is divided into three components:

- Win32 communication APIs and TAPI (Telephony Application Programming Interface)
- UNIMODEM (universal modem driver)
- Port drivers

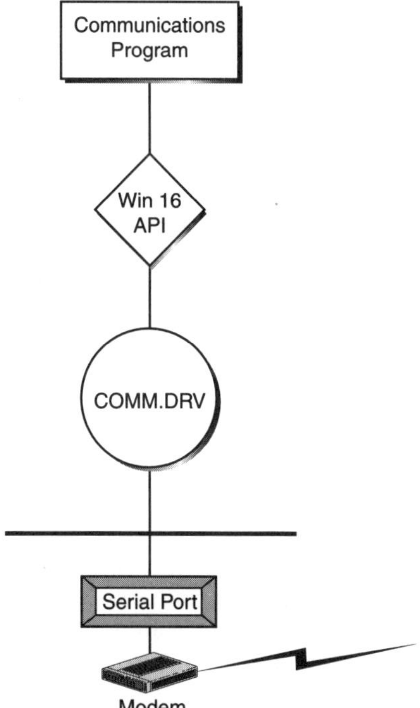

Figure 13.1
COMM.DRV acts as the monolithic communications architecture in Windows 3.x.

Before exploring these individual components, the design goals behind the new architecture should be considered. (A detailed discussion of the components of the NT Communications can be found in the section "The Windows NT Communications Architecture," later in this chapter.)

Design Goals of the New Communications Architecture

To overcome some problems associated with Windows 3.x communications operations, Microsoft designed the new architecture with the following goals in mind:

- Reliability at high speeds
- Support and responsiveness for large data transfer

- Support transparency
- Device sharing among competing communications programs

The following sections detail each of these goals.

Reliability at High Speeds

Windows NT handles data coming in at high speeds (ISDN, Frame Relay speeds), without dropping characters of bytes of data. This is possible due to the 32-bit subsystem that handles communications operations.

Windows NT Workstation supports reliable high-speed communications by keeping up with data coming in from the communications port, thereby incurring no lost characters because of interrupt latency. In addition, the use of a 32-bit protected-mode file system and network architecture has less impact on the communications system because required mode transitions and interrupt latency are reduced. The 32-bit communications subsystem leverages the preemptive multitasking architecture of Windows NT Workstation to provide better responsiveness to communications applications and support higher data throughput. Communications transfers in 32-bit applications are not as affected by other tasks running in the system as Win16–based applications under Windows 3.1.

Support and Responsiveness for Large Data Transfer

The 32-bit communications subsystem leverages the preemptive multitasking features of Windows NT to provide better performance for communications operations even when other activities are taking the operating system's attention.

Support for Transparency

One of the key goals of Windows NT Workstation's ease-of-use features is to "hide" or make transparent the different communication features, to the user as well as applications. The new communications architecture divides the communications operations into discrete modules. The applications simply access the 32-bit (or Win32) API, and the hardware devices are managed by SPIs (Service Provider Interfaces provided by the individual vendors). Hence the architecture hides the underlying telecommunications method (Analog, ISDN, Frame Relay, X.25) from application developers (and hence the applications). Applications can be built, therefore, to run seamlessly on a variety of communications platform.

Device Sharing Among Competing Communications Programs

TAPI enables the sharing of ports and devices independent of the communication programs. If the RAS (Remote Access Services) in Windows NT is waiting for an incoming call, a TAPI-compliant (aware) fax program can dial out and send a fax, without waiting for RAS to disconnect (hang up) or trying to force RAS to disconnect.

The Windows NT Communications Architecture

To implement the design goals stated in preceding sections, Microsoft totally rebuilt the communications architecture for its 32-bit systems (Windows 95 and Windows NT family). The design is based on separating the different aspects of communications operations. Three main components control communications in Windows NT: Win32 APIs and TAPI, universal modem driver (UNIMODEM), and port drivers. Figure 13.2 illustrates this layered architecture.

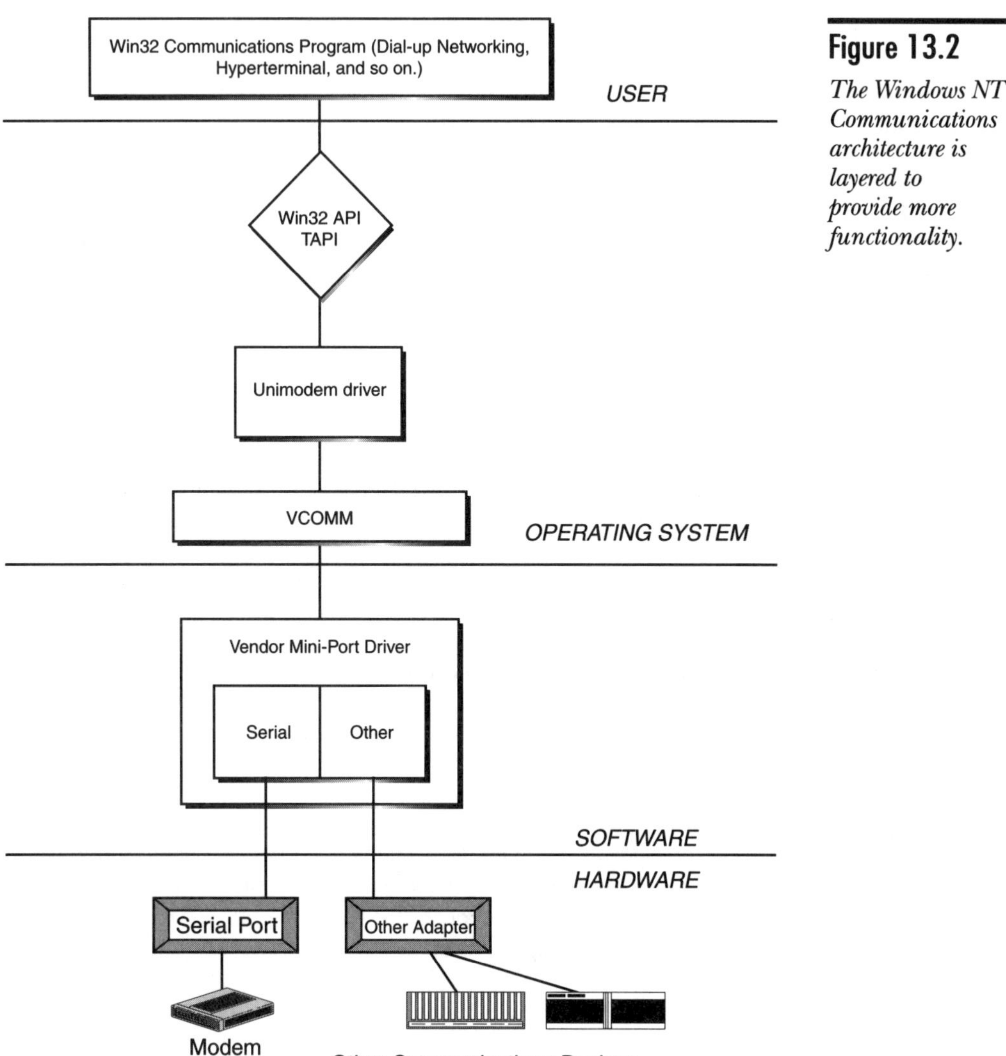

Figure 13.2
The Windows NT Communications architecture is layered to provide more functionality.

Win32 APIs and TAPI

The Win32 APIs facilitate devices. Applications, for example, never try to access the devices through the API to configure and perform data I/O. TAPI provides centralized configuration, communication, and maintenance of modems and other devices. TAPI-aware applications can also share ports, without interrupting other applications.

Let's assume that you set up a generic 28.8 Kbps modem on a remote user's Windows NT Workstation laptop. You can also set up the TAPI settings for this modem (described later in this chapter). TAPI settings could include the area code the user dials from, any credit card information, and modem hardware settings such as data bits, parity, and so on. Once the TAPI settings are complete, all TAPI-aware communications programs will proceed to use these same settings when they are set up. The communications programs (or their Win32 API calls) never try to access the modem hardware directly (like they had to in the Windows 3.x environment). They simply access the Win32 API, and TAPI communicates between the communications program and the modem's SPI (Service Provider Interface). The benefits here are twofold. You don't need to set up your modem each time you install a communications program, and you can make changes to the modem settings once and they cascade to all the communications programs.

UNIMODEM

The universal modem driver hides the configuration of individual modems and other devices from users and applications. It provides a single, central software driver to handle dial-out, answer, and hang-up operations. UNIMODEM communicates with individual modems through mini-port drivers written and supplied by independent modem vendors.

Port Drivers (Mini-Port Drivers)

The port drivers provide the functionality required to drive specific modems. The VCOMM driver handles the communication between the UNIMODEM and the port drivers.

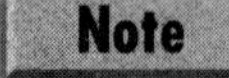

The three components described in the previous sections provide a layered approach to communications. In this model, the whole communications subsystem need not be replaced every time a new hardware feature shows up in the industry. Only the mini-port drivers need to change. The rest of the communications architecture remains essentially the same.

TAPI: An Architectural Overview

The component in the new communications architecture that impacts users and systems administrators most is the TAPI. It is important to discuss TAPI basics before attempting to explore setting up and configuring communications devices in Windows NT.

TAPI was introduced in Windows 95 and is a part of Microsoft's Windows Open Services Architecture (WOSA). (TAPI is implemented for the first time in Windows NT in version 4.) WOSA is intended to basically connect Windows to anything. Through a number of middleware APIs, WOSA essentially seeks to extend Windows connectivity to heterogeneous database platforms, hardware devices, and vertical industry hardware devices, and to provide robust messaging and licensing mechanisms. Another example of WOSA is Open Database Connectivity Drivers (ODBC)—used as a middleware between a Windows desktop and many databases (not limited by platform).

TAPI is split into two interfaces:

- The API to which developers write
- The SPI (Service Providers Interface) used to connect to specific telephone network types

TAPI provides a single, centralized platform to handle dial-up (call), answer, terminate, hold, transfer, conference, and call park operations for all voice, data, and fax applications. By a combination of the UNIMODEM driver and TAPI, application developers need no longer write to actual hardware devices. This situation is similar to the printing model that Windows 3.x introduced, where application developers took advantage of a centralized print driver in Windows.

Using TAPI, add-on voice cards for Windows NT can be supported—that is, your Windows NT machine can act as a voice mail server. Using TAPI, applications can access PBXs, ISDN, X.25, Frame Relay, and other types of telecommunications networks seamlessly from your Windows NT machine.

One of the most significant advantages that TAPI provides is to facilitate communications sharing. If the RAS connection in your Windows NT Workstation is set to receive an incoming call, for example, you can still use another Win32 communications program (like Hyperterminal, and so on) to dial out, send and receive data, and disconnect. You do not have to disconnect RAS first to do this. The TAPI services basically act as a negotiator between the requests of the two (or more) competing programs to access the communications ports.

Armed with an understanding of TAPI and the new Windows communications architecture, you can now venture into the set up and configuration of the Windows NT Workstation's communications features. You will set up the hardware as well as the software options in configuring the communications features of Windows NT Workstation to enable RAS and Dial-Up Networking.

Installing and Setting Up Windows NT Communications

The Control Panel provides the central location for setting up communications in Windows NT. The main steps to setting up Windows NT communications are:

1. Set up the communications ports
2. Set up the TAPI options
3. Set up modems

Set Up the Communications Ports

Windows NT now supports up to 256 communications ports! Before you get too excited, the number of real hardware ports is still limited by the PC hardware (usually to two serial ports). By using enhanced serial board technology, however, it is possible to insert add-on boards inside a PC to increase the number of ports. By using hardware communications servers also, it is possible to attach modems from 4, 16, 64, and more combinations. In a Windows 3.x environment, the maximum number of ports possible was 9 (from the operating system's perspective). Now in Windows NT, you can actually have 256 communications ports and can assign specific ports to individual applications.

The Ports applet in the Control Panel enables you to configure ports on your Windows NT computer.

Follow these steps to add ports in Windows NT Workstation:

1. Click on the Ports applet in the Control Panel.
2. Choose Add to add more ports (up to 256).
3. The Advanced Settings for New Port dialog box appears. It enables you to select a COM port number and to assign the Base I/O Port address and the IRQ number.

Let's examine a detailed procedure for setting up an additional communications port on your Windows NT workstation:

1. Log on as an administrator and double-click on the Ports icon in the Control Panel.
2. Click on the Add button to get the Advanced Settings for New Port dialog box.
3. The COM port number enables you to change the number of a port. Any new ports must be between 3 and 256 because 1 and 2 are the only reliably recognized ones by the BIOS. Base I/O Port Address is used to assign an address for the device that will use this COM port. Change this from the default only if you know that the address used by your modem or other device different. IRQ enables you to assign unique Interrupt Request Lines for each serial port. You can specify a value between 2 and 15. This enables devices connected to COM 1 and 3 or 2 and 4 to perform simultaneously. FIFO enables on-chip buffering on the UART serial chip to provide extra functionality (speed) on newer COM ports.
4. Click on OK and you will be asked to restart the PC. If you want to complete the configuration of the new port, you will have to reboot. Once you reboot and repeat step 1, you will see the new port you just added.
5. If you wish to delete a COM port, select the COM port and simply click on the Delete button.

Caution Be careful when assigning the Base I/O port address and the IRQ numbers. Generally 3F8 and 2F8 are reserved for the COM1 & COM2 ports respectively. If you reassign these numbers, some applications accessing the first two ports might not function properly. When assigning the IRQ numbers, you want to check and make certain about the numbers already in use by your serial cards, other devices attached to your serial cards, and so on. If you check the FIFO-enabled option, you enable the serial chip (UART) to use on-chip buffering to provide additional functionality.

Set Up the TAPI Options

The Telephony applet in the Control Panel enables you to configure TAPI to provide global settings for all modems and communications devices that your Windows NT Workstation PC will use. Clicking on the Telephony applet brings up the Dialing Properties property sheet of the TAPI object (see fig. 13.3).

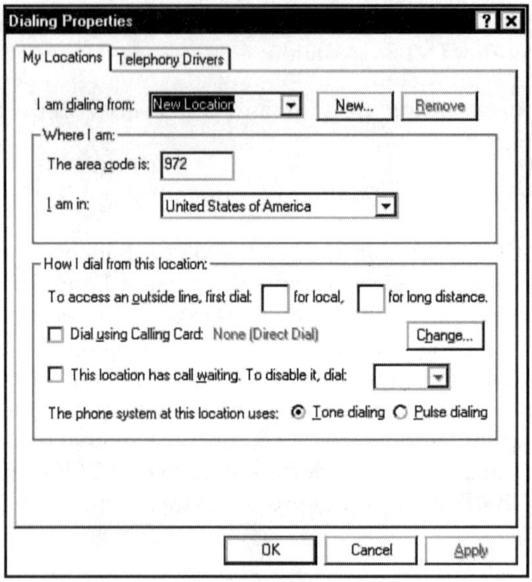

Figure 13.3

Set the dialing properties in the Telephony settings.

The dialing location enables a mobile user to set different "profiles" for where he is dialing from (the area code), credit card information, and phone system options, such as call waiting, and so on. This assumes great significance if the user dials up from various locations with different area codes or different phone system options, and uses credit cards for long distance dialing. The mobile user can simply set up a number of "profiles" and use the appropriate one for all his communications programs.

The My Locations Tab

The first tab is the My Locations part of the property sheet. Here you can create profiles of where and how you will be dialing using the modems (or communications devices). The following list details the options on this tab:

- **I am dialing from.** Provides the ability to create (by clicking on the New button) or edit existing profiles. The Remove button removes any existing profile.

- **Where I am.** Provides the ability to put in the area code from where you will be dialing from and the country that you are currently in. This information is used to automatically ascertain whether you need to dial a 1 or a country code before you dial for long distance or international dialing.

- **How I dial from this location.** Provides the ability to put in codes (like a 9 or 8) to dial outside lines (or 1 for long distance). This section also enables you to use a credit card while dialing by checking the Dial using Calling Card option. If you wish to set up a particular calling card, click on the Change button and you will get a long list of calling cards and the rules associated with using them (dialing 800 numbers, pausing for tones, entering in account IDs, and so on). Here is the place to change the rules or add new calling cards to it. Returning back to the How I dial from this location section, you can disable call waiting if you have it (by selecting a particular code to be dialed like *70, and so on) and select between tone or pulse dialing.

The Telephony Drivers Tab

The second tab is the Telephony Drivers property sheet (see fig. 13.4).

Figure 13.4

Configure the universal modem drivers of the telephony subsystem.

This tab illustrates the number and type of telephony drivers installed on your Windows NT Workstation PC. Figure 13.4 shows two installed drivers—the TAPI Kernel-mode Service Provider and the UNIMODEM Service Provider. The TAPI Kernel-mode Service Provider is the core component of TAPI and cannot be configured or changed by users. By selecting the UNIMODEM Service Provider and clicking on the Configure button, the same Install New Modem wizard appears as that which appears after clicking on the Modems applet in the Control Panel.

Set Up Modems

Although Windows NT Workstation 4 does provide the new Win32 communications architecture, it still does not support the Plug and Play standards. In Windows 95, if you plug in or attach a new Plug and Play device (say a modem), the operating system recognizes a new device and configures it on the fly. Microsoft has tentatively announced Plug and Play support in the next version of Windows NT (currently codenamed Cairo and scheduled for 1997 release). Until then, new devices not present during setup have to be configured manually when added.

Installing

This section discusses the procedures for installing modems and configuring settings, such as data bits, flow control, and so on. Although it is highly recommended that you use supported modems, unsupported modems can be installed. The procedure for that briefly will be overviewed also.

As mentioned earlier, you can install modems through the Telephony applet in the Control Panel. The preferred way is to use the Modems applet in the Control Panel:

1. Double-click on the Modems applet to bring up the Install New Modem wizard.
2. If you click on the Don't detect my modem; I will select it from a list option, the wizard enables you to go directly to a list of modems. You can then manually select your modem from this list. If you do not find your modem in this list, click on the Have Disk button and insert the setup disk from your modem vendor.

Make certain that your modem appears in the Windows NT Hardware Compatibility List before you attempt this. The HCL is provided as a manual with your Windows NT documentation. The HCL is available on the Microsoft web site (www.microsoft.com), on the TechNet CD subscription, in the Resource Kits, and a whole host of other (third-party) NT-related web sites, magazines, and resources.

3. To enable the wizard to detect your modem, just follow the instructions supplied (which usually means clicking on the Next button). Windows NT checks all the COM ports and finds your modem. In most cases, your modem should match the one found. If it does not, click on the Change button to find the right modem.

After Windows NT finds the appropriate modem, it installs the modem on your PC. That's basically it. You now can use the modem for any communications applications from your PC.

Configuring

To apply advanced settings on your modem, click on the Modems applet in the Control Panel (after you have installed a modem). The property sheet for installed modems appears (see fig. 13.5).

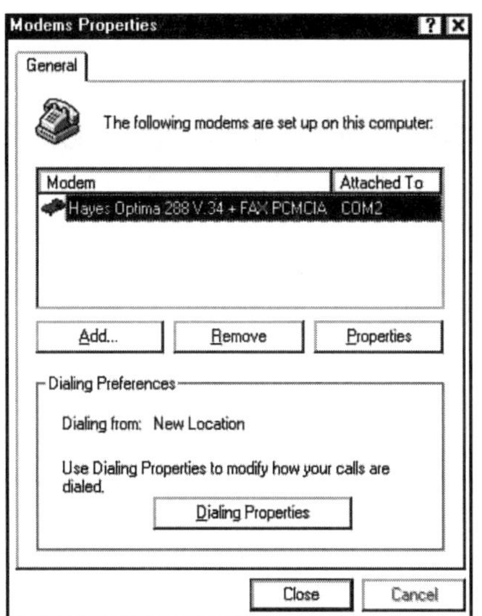

Figure 13.5

You can configure advanced settings for installed modems.

The properties sheet enables you to add new modems (by clicking on the Add button), to remove existing ones (by clicking on the Remove button), and to reconfigure existing modems by clicking on the Properties button. In the Dialing Preferences section, you can select the appropriate profile (that you set up earlier using the Telephony applet). You also have a chance to create (or change existing) new profiles by clicking on the Dialing Properties button. The procedure you use for adding modems or changing settings here are the same procedures you used in the Installing section. This is just another entry point to access the same configurations.

Modems can be configured with a number of settings in Windows NT Workstation. So far, you have just added a modem. In the following set of steps, you will look at all the options for configuring modems.

1. Click on the Properties button to get the property sheet for that particular modem. This property sheet has two tabs—General and Connection.

2. The General tab enables you to set the speaker volume for the modem and to set the speed of the modem. Notice the Only connect at this speed option. If you select 28,800 as the speed and select the Only connect at this speed option, for example, no connections at a lower speed will be attempted.

3. The Connection tab enables you to further customize your modem settings. In the Connection Preferences section, you can set the Data Bits, Parity, and Stop bits. In the Call Preferences section, you can set the modem to wait for a dial tone before dialing, cancel the call if not connected within a time period (that you specify in seconds), and disconnect a session if no activity occurs for a certain period of time (that you specify in minutes).

4. Click on the Advanced button to bring up the Advanced Connection Settings dialog box. (see fig. 13.6).

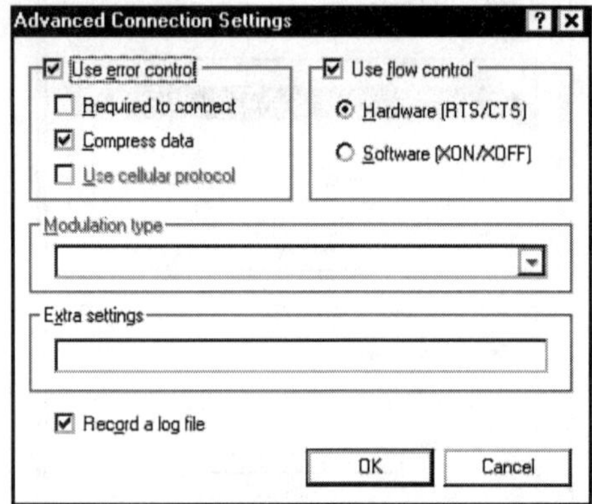

Figure 13.6

You can set advanced connections settings for modems.

You can manipulate advanced connections for a modem by performing the following steps:

1. You can set the modem to use error control by choosing the appropriate option.
2. To force a reliable connection, select Required to connect.
3. To force data compression, select Compress data. Of course your modem has to support data compression.
4. You can enforce hardware flow control, or if your modem does not support it, you can enforce software flow control by choosing the appropriate options.
5. In the Extra settings field, enter any attention strings that are unique or peculiar to your modem. Generally, this should not be necessary, as the UNIMODEM universal driver should handle all modem attention strings. Certain older modems, however, might need specific attention strings to facilitate proper operation.
6. Finally, to record a log file, click on the Record log file option. The log file will be called MODEMLOG.TXT and will be generated in the folder where you have installed Windows NT system files. After these steps, the file is written each time a TAPI-aware and enabled communications program establishes a communications session. Non-TAPI-aware and enabled programs will not log entries into this file. Later on, this chapter discusses how to use this file to troubleshoot communication sessions.

Installing Unsupported Modems

This section discusses the installation of modems that are not currently supported (or do not appear in the modems list) in Windows NT Workstation. While you should always try to avoid using unsupported modems, certain situations might demand installation and configuration of legacy modems.

Windows NT 4 supports all modems through the universal modem driver. If you are installing new modems or modems that do not appear in the setup dialog box, you must obtain new drivers from your modem vendor. If you need to configure an unsupported, installed modem in NT 4, add the suitable setup strings in the MODEM.INF file, which is in the \%systemroot%\system32\ras directory.

Windows NT version 4 and later include support for modems through the universal modem driver (UNIMODEM) using TAPI. If you are installing a new unsupported modem, you should obtain a modem driver from the modem manufacturer. When installing this modem, you would select the Do not detect… option and insert a disk with the updated driver. But, how about legacy modems that are not supported?

Windows NT Workstation RAS supports legacy modems, and you can configure these modems by following this procedure.

To configure a previously installed unsupported modem to work with RAS, add an entry for that modem in this file.

Modem responses are normally located in the global [Responses] section. Most modems will return one of the responses listed in the global [Responses] section. If you encounter a modem with a different response sequence than any of the responses already listed, add that new sequence to the global [Respones] section. You can also put new modem response sequences immediately following the command section of a specific modem. Such responses are checked before the global responses. Individual modems will have separate command sections.

Once you have added a modem entry (a sample entry is shown in the sidebar), this will show up as a supported modem in the modem list when you try to add new modems.

Sample Section of MODEM.INF File

The following text illustrates a sampling of the MODEM.INF file for one particular modem:

```
;--------------------
[Compaq SpeedPAQ 144]
<speaker_on>=M1
<speaker_off>=M0
<hwflowcontrol_on>=\\Q3
<hwflowcontrol_off>=\\Q0
<protocol_on>=\\N3
<protocol_off>=\\N0
<compression_on>=%C1
<compression_off>=%C0
<autodial_on>=ATDT
<autodial_off>=ATD
CALLBACKTIME=10
DEFAULTOFF=compression
MAXCARRIERBPS=19200
MAXCONNECTBPS=38400
DETECT_STRING=ATI9<cr>
DETECT_RESPONSE=COMPAQ
COMMAND_INIT=AT&F&C1&D2 V1 W2S0=0 S2=128 S7=55<cr>
COMMAND_INIT=AT<hwflowcontrol><protocol><compression><speaker><cr>
COMMAND_DIAL=<autodial><phonenumber><cr>
CONNECT=<cr><lf>CONNECT <carrierbps><cr><lf>
COMMAND_LISTEN=ATS0=1<cr>
CONNECT=<cr><lf>CONNECT <carrierbps><cr><lf>
```

So far the communications architecture has been discussed, as have the setup and configuration of modems. It is important to understand this underlying framework before you look at the software or "value-added" layer that rides or uses this framework. The value-added layer that rides atop this framework is Remote Access Services and Dial-Up Networking. In the next section, you will explore Windows NT Workstation's abilities to use the new communications architecture and the communications devices (modems). Essentially, you will understand how Windows NT Workstation performs a dial-up connection and how (or whether) Windows NT Workstation receives calls from other remote clients.

Introducing Remote Access Computing

End users today are more mobile than ever before as they try to perform their tasks in the field, closer to customers and markets. Although they are physically separated from the office network, they still need access to some of the same data and resources on the corporate network. Traditionally in the mainframe and the minicomputer platforms, granting dial-up access was relatively easy. In the PC client/server arena, mobile computing poses new challenges. Windows NT Workstation offers you great tools to address these challenges. Before delving into the details of Windows NT remote access computing, a discussion of Remote LAN Node versus Remote Control computing is appropriate. To clear up confusion about the type of remote access computing offered by RAS, explore briefly the concepts of remote computing versus Remote LAN Node.

The type of remote access computing employed by Windows NT is referred to as *Remote LAN Node*—when an NT machine (using Dial-Up Networking) connects to a server, it connects to it just like a member of the LAN, the only difference being the physical connection (which may be a phone line, ISDN, Frame Relay, and so on). After connecting, the remote machine can log on, use the NT Explorer to access folders on the server(s), and use the Network Neighborhood to view and use domains, servers, and shares.

Remote Control uses a very different paradigm. In this scenario, a remote PC dials up a PC on the corporate LAN, takes control of that machine, and hence begins to use the resources on the LAN. Here, the PC attached to the LAN performs all the work, sending screen refreshes to the remote PC and accepting keyboard and mouse commands from the remote PC. This method, although suitable for certain situations (especially Help Desk activities), is not suited for robust, reliable high-volume remote access. The Remote LAN Node method is the preferred way of remote access. This is the method employed by Windows NT remote access. If you need to "take" remote control of a Windows NT Workstation, you have to use a third-party product such as pcAnywhere32, ReachOut, and so on. RAS by itself does not provide you with this capability.

Exploring Windows NT and Remote Access Computing

Windows NT implements the remote access or mobile computing through a set of services called RAS—Remote Access Services.

RAS in Windows NT 3.51, WFW, and Windows NT 4

If you are using RAS in Windows NT Workstation 3.51, you are probably familiar with the RAS Administrator and the RAS client. The RAS Administrator configures the receive calls portion, and the RAS client functions as your dial-out phone book application. A Windows for Workgroups PC can also use the same RAS client as the phone book application. Things have changed slightly in NT 4 (and Windows 95). The RAS Administrator still controls the receive calls features. The dial out functionality is provided by the new Dial-Up Networking application, however, which makes full use of the TAPI and UNIMODEM services of Windows NT.

RAS provides a secure, easy way to connect mobile and remote users to your network. A Windows NT workstation with the RAS Server component enabled can receive calls from remote users, who can then connect to the PC and use its resources. Remote users can also connect to the PC and hop over to the network that this PC is connected to. Typically you would use the RAS server portion on an NT Server.

Note A Windows NT Server can accept 256 dial-in sessions simultaneously, whereas an NT Workstation can receive only 1 dial-in session at any given time. This negates its use as a heavy-duty communications server. For individual PCs to be accessed remotely, however, it provides a good option.

The RAS server portion of the NT Workstation can be set to receive calls, but it will not handle more than one call at a given time. The Dial-Up Networking application enables the NT Workstation to dial out to an NT Server and become a remote LAN node over the phone line. The Dial-Up Networking software can be used to connect to NT Server and to a non-NT server as well. These connections are possible because the Dial-Up Networking software supports PPP, or Point-to-Point protocol, which can encapsulate TCP/IP, IPX, and NetBEUI over a phone line. The Dial-Up Networking software also supports Serial Line Internet Protocol (SLIP), which enables your NT workstation to dial up and connect to older Unix machines. Essentially, RAS provides a comprehensive solution for your remote access needs.

In the next few sections, you will examine the components and details of the RAS architecture and its features and benefits, and finally set up RAS in a Windows NT workstation to receive and send calls. Again, the RAS services (as they are termed in NT) provide you with the ability to receive calls *into* your computer and the Dial-Up Networking applet enables you to dial *out* of your computer.

RAS Architecture

RAS is a software-based Multi-Protocol Router (MPR) and is meant to be used in a client/server fashion. All services typically available to a local LAN user (file and print services, database access, messaging) are available to the remote RAS client. After a remote NT workstation dials up an NT Server, the RAS server installed on the NT Server authenticates the user and provides network services until terminated by the remote user or the administrator. Drive letter mappings and UNCs are fully supported, and hence most commercial and custom applications work without any customizations.

RAS services are installed as a network service (through the Network applet in the Control Panel) in Windows NT Workstation. Once it is installed, by default RAS services are enabled at start-up time. So if the NT Workstation has a communications device (a modem) and a phone line, it is now available for remote users. What actually happens when a remote user dials up the phone number of this computer? Obviously, you have to grant dial-in permissions to this remote user. (Details about this whole process will be discussed later.) When the remote user dials up, he will communicate with your NT Workstation through IPX, NetBEUI, or TCP/IP. Your NT Workstation must be running one or all of these protocols.

Once the phone connection is established and protocol uniformity is achieved, depending upon the type of authentication you have set up, the user name and password validation (meaning that the RAS server will check the remote user's user name and password with NT's internal security database) is performed. If the validation is successful, the user gets connected. Usually after a successful connection, the remote user will get a dialog box (if he is also running NT Workstation or Windows 95), which informs him that all his regular Windows utilities (such as Explorer, Print Manager, and so on) should work on the dial-up connection. Essentially what this means is that once the user is validated and connected, he can use the File Manager or Windows Explorer to connect a drive to a share on the NT workstation (or the computer he has dialed up). Of course this share has to be available on the NT Workstation and this user has to be permitted to use it.

Universal Naming Conventions (UNCs) refer to addressing a shared directory or share on a server as \\SERVER\SHARE. \\INFOSERV\DATA denotes a shared volume, for example, or *share* called *DATA* on a server named *INFOSERV*.

RAS Features and Benefits

RAS has unique features that Microsoft has implemented in Windows NT. A very brief discussion of these features and their corresponding benefits will enable you to use them while performing the setup and configuration of RAS services on a Windows NT workstation.

Multi-Protocol Routing Through PPP Support

Using PPP and RAS, the remote PC can use any combination of NetBEUI, TCP/IP, or IPX during a RAS session. This provides the ability to run Windows Sockets, NetWare, and NetBIOS applications remotely. It also means that a non-Windows remote client can dial up a Windows NT Server or Workstation.

PPP or Point-to-Point protocol is a successor to SLIP, Serial Line Internet Protocol. Essentially, when you use a dial-up line to connect to a remote host and need to send a protocol (such as TCP/IP) over the phone line, you need a higher-level protocol that bundles or encapsulates the network protocol. This is what PPP does. It helps to encapsulate three protocols (TCP/IP, IPX, and NetBEUI) and send them over the phone line connection you make to the RAS or any other type of remote server. PPP sends the selected protocol so that the remote client can achieve protocol uniformity between the client and the server. This, as you know, is the first and most basic requirement for network connectivity, whether remote or local.

A business can establish a Windows NT Server as an *onramp* server to the Internet through RAS. Setting up the NT Server as the RAS server with TCP/IP over PPP enabled, enables any client capable of using PPP to dial up this NT machine and bounce or hop over to the Internet, provided that the NT machine has a continuous connection to the Internet.

Integration with NetWare Networks

Because the RAS server supports IPX routing, you can actually use a Windows NT machine as a dedicated communications server, even in a NetWare environment. If the RAS server is set to receive PPP calls and set to route IPX, a Windows NT Workstation can use Dial-Up Networking to dial up this RAS server, use IPX over PPP, and basically connect to the NetWare network of which the RAS server is part. After the RAS session is established, the remote Windows NT workstation can actually run NetWare login scripts and act just like a local NetWare LAN client.

Software Data Compression

The Dial-Up Networking client (or the RAS client) has the capability to compress data and increase the throughput. In most typical cases, RAS can improve throughput by as much as 50 percent.

Data Encryption

RAS provides data encryption, in addition to password encryption (only if connecting to a NT machine). The type of data encryption used is called the RC4 encryption algorithm from RSA Data Security Inc.

RAS APIs

Microsoft publishes a RAS API as part of the RAS architecture, which means that corporate developers have a seamless way of creating custom, remote-enabled applications.

Security

RAS employs all the robust Windows NT Security by default. The single network logon concept extends to RAS, with dial-in permissions granted from the general pool of Windows NT accounts. The administrator has the ability to grant dial-in access to users, groups, and so on. When remote users log on to a domain, they must still use their domain logon IDs and passwords. After a RAS session is established, the remote user is bound by the same account privileges as when logged on locally. The administrator has the right to disconnect remote users forcibly if necessary.

Authentication

By default, if the remote user (may be a Windows NT Workstation laptop or PC) is connecting to a Windows NT domain, the same level of authentication as a regular local LAN user is employed. This is the Challenge Handshake Authentication Protocol (CHAP). CHAP uses a challenge/response mechanism with one-way encryption of the password on the response. Although this is the only way to authenticate users in a Windows NT domain locally, RAS enables you to select lower levels of security. You can work down to just sending the clear text password over the line as the method of authentication. Generally, if you are accessing a Windows NT domain, you should stay with the highest level of authentication—the CHAP. If, on the other hand, you are using the RAS client on Windows NT Workstation to dial up a non-Windows NT Server, clear text authentication may be the only method possible. You can set the following registry entry to set the maximum number of unsuccessful retries allowed if authentication fails on the RAS server:

```
HKEY_LOCAL_MACHINE\SYSTEM\CurrentControlSet\Services\RemoteAccess\Parameters\
➥AuthenticateRetries(REG_DWORD) = 0 to 10
```

In addition to the features previously mentioned, RAS offers some additional capabilities. These features and benefits are best described in the setup and configuration sections of this chapter. Read on.

Setting Up RAS Services on a Windows NT Workstation

RAS services have to be installed on your NT Workstation even if you just want to use the dial-out features (or Dial-Up Networking). This is because the dial out feature is a subset of the RAS services component set. NT views RAS as a part of network services, and as when installing all other network services, the Network applet in the Control Panel is used to install RAS.

Installing and Configuring RAS Services on a Windows NT Workstation

Use the following information to completely install and configure RAS services on a Windows NT workstation:

- Note that if you do not have a communications device installed, RAS setup forces you to install a device. You can actually install an analog modem, an X.25 Packet Assembler Dissassembler (PAD), an ISDN modem, or a Frame Relay on-board adapter. Make certain that you use the Configure button to configure your port for dial-in as well as dial-out usage (see fig 13.7).

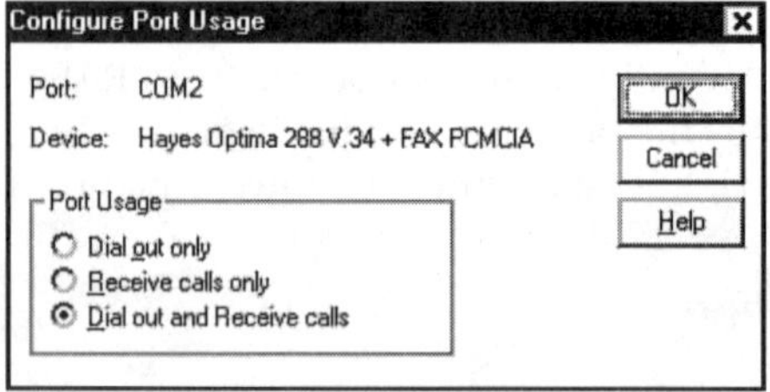

Figure 13.7
Configure Windows NT RAS to send as well as receive calls.

- The Network Configuration dialog box enables you to set the dial-out as well as the dial-in protocols. You can choose to dial out as well as receive calls that use IPX, TCP/IP, and NetBEUI.
- If you are using the machine to receive calls, you can configure the server settings for each of the protocols. If your remote clients are going to use TCP/IP to dial in, for example, set the server settings for TCP/IP. RAS enables you to restrict the remote client to only the RAS server upon connection, or enables the remote client to access the entire network through the RAS server. This is the option that sets the routing of that particular protocol. Here you have a chance to configure the assignment of remote IP addresses (if you use DHCP, you can use that to assign remote PC addresses also).

Note

If you are using the Nwlink (the IPX/SPX-compatible transport) in the remote Windows NT machines, be certain to enable the NetBIOS Broadcast Propagation (which really gives you RIP for Nwlink IPX). If you do not enable this, remote PCs trying to use the Nwlink protocol will not be able to access your entire network through the RAS server.

The completion of RAS services setup involves a reboot of the machine. When the machine is brought back up again, you can start using all the RAS features. You can also use the Remote Access Admin tool found in the Administrative Tools (Common) folder on your Windows NT machine. At this point, you can also set Dial-Up Networking entries to dial out from this machine.

Understanding Windows NT Dial-Up Networking

If you ever need to dial-up another computer from your Windows NT workstation, Dial-Up Networking is the tool you will use. It provides you with a "phone book" communications utility that can be used to set up connections, the protocols you will use, the type of authentication you will send over the phone line, and scripts you will use to automate the session. At this point, please understand that these tools can not only help you connect to other Windows NT PCs (Workstation or Server), but also help you to connect to any PPP server. This means that a computer (of any platform—Unix, AS/400, even a mainframe) that can run the PPP can accept remote calls from your Windows NT Workstation.

This section overviews the Windows NT Dial-Up Networking architecture, including creating and editing Dial-Up Networking phonebook entries, creating scripts for dial-out sessions, and creating logs of remote access sessions.

The Connection Process

Dial-Up Networking can be initiated in Windows NT in three ways:

- **Explicit.** A user starts a connection intentionally. This happens when you actually select a Dial-Up Networking entry, double-click on it, and supply the phone number, user name, and password and initiate the connection.
- **Implicit.** If Windows NT is instructed to log on using Dial-Up Networking, it prompts the user to try a dial-up connection if LAN connections cannot be found. As soon as you install RAS and Dial-Up Networking on your NT Workstation, you will notice that you get a new option when you log on—Log on using Dial-Up Networking. If you select this option, Windows NT Workstation will try to use a Dial-Up Networking entry to automatically dial-up a server and log on instead of logging on over the LAN. This is a good example of the implicit method.
- **Application invoked.** If an application uses the RAS (actually the Dial-Up Session API) API to establish a connection to a dial-up resource, a dial-up connection is established.

As discussed earlier, RAS provides an API. What this means is that an application developer can invoke the RAS API from inside her own application. So, a Visual Basic application may invoke a dial-up connection at the push of a Send button *inside* the application. At this point, the user is interacting only with the Visual Basic application and not with RAS. He is completely shielded from RAS and Dial-Up Networking.

Dial-Up Networking Client Architecture

Windows NT Dial-Up Networking uses an Application layer to package an application request or call, and passes it on to a data protocol. The line protocol is used to format the data over the telephone line (see fig. 13.8).

Figure 13.8

Dial-Up Networking uses data protocols and line protocols to establish connections and send/receive data.

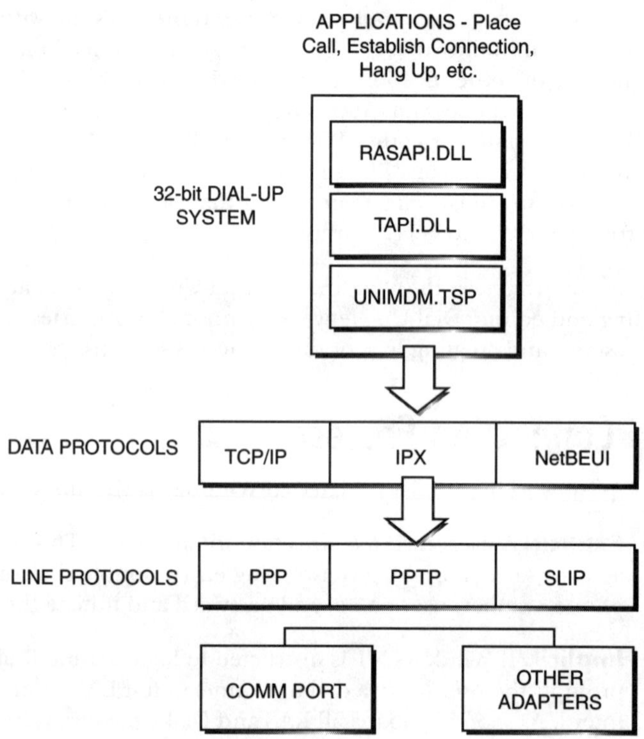

Note *Data protocols* package the data from the application and get it ready for transmission on a medium.

Line protocols package the message from the data protocol on to a medium such as serial or ISDN.

Windows NT supports the following data protocols:

- TCP/IP
- IPX
- NetBEUI

Windows NT supports the following line protocols:

- Point-to-Point Protocol (PPP)
- Serial Line Internet Protocol (SLIP)
- Point-to-Point Tunneling Protocol (PPTP), which is the addition in NT Workstation 4. PPTP supports multiprotocol virtual private networks (VPNs), enabling users to access your organization's networks and servers over the Internet (rather than over your own remote access communications setup) with comprehensive security (equivalent to the existing SSL—Secure Sockets Layer).

Understanding the Dial-Up Entry Settings

Setting up a dial-up phone book entry is amazingly simple in Windows NT. Just double-click on the Dial-Up Networking icon found in the My Computer folder/icon, and a phone book entry wizard leads you through the process. The file where these settings are stored is called RASPHONE.PBK; that file is stored in the \%systemroot%\system32\ras directory. You can choose to create your entry directly into the phone book also. If you choose to edit an existing entry or create one by yourself, use the Edit Phonebook Entry property sheets (see fig. 13.9).

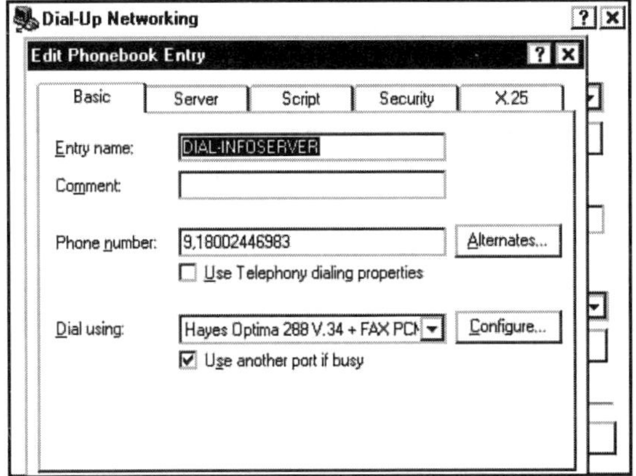

Figure 13.9
Configure your Dial-Up Networking session.

Note If you have more than one phone available, and two modems are hooked up to these lines, Windows NT 4 offers a new feature called *multilink*. Essentially, multilink enables you to aggregate multiple lines to one logical pipe with increased bandwidth. To work, however, both the remote client and the server that it is dialing up have to be multilink-enabled. To enable multilinking, make certain that you choose Multiple Lines (see fig. 13.10).

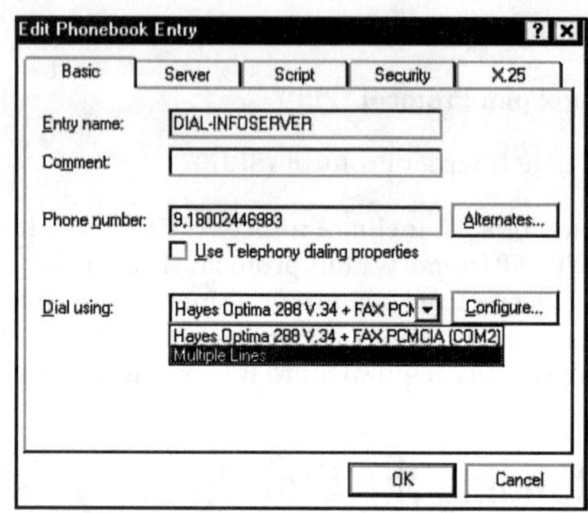

Figure 13.10

Choose Multiple Lines to aggregate phone lines to increase bandwidth.

The following steps discuss the configuration of a particular dial-up entry. Settings for the server you want to dial up, scripts you want to use, and the type of security you want to enable are discussed.

1. The Server tab provides an opportunity to choose the type of server that you will be dialing up. You can also configure the protocol that you will use to send over PPP (or SLIP). If you are configuring your dial-up session to establish a connection to a TCP/IP host, the TCP/IP Settings button provides you the opportunity to set IP address and DNS address information.

To change or edit existing entries, just click on the More button after the first Dial-Up Networking screen appears. This gives you the opportunity to edit the phone book entry, and set user and logon preferences.

2. The Script tab enables you to specify a script file to run before or after dialing. You can also choose to have a terminal pop up before or after dialing (after establishing connection to the remote server). Scripts are covered in detail in the next section.

3. Finally, the Security tab enables you to either select the lowest form of password authentication (Accept any authentication including clear text) or the highest form of CHAP (Accept only Microsoft encrypted authentication). Use caution while selecting these options. If you are using the NT Workstation to dial up a non-Windows NT machine or server, choosing the highest level of authentication will not work; the server at the remote end will not be able to handle the encrypted passwords. You may be limited to using clear-text authentication in those cases. If you are dialing up a Windows NT remote server, however, the highest level of encryption and authentication works.

Windows NT Dial-Up Networking Scripts

You may need to create scripts for Windows NT to use if the server (usually scripts are used for non-Windows remote servers only) you are dialing needs a series of input from you after you establish a connection. If you are dialing up your Internet Service Provider (ISP), for example, the ISP may require you to send in user name, password, and other information at connection time. Scripts provide an automated method of handling this situation.

Windows NT supports two types of scripting languages. The first (and the older version) type calls for creating and adding sections of code into a file called the SWITCH.INF found in the \%systemroot%\system32\ras directory. To aid you in developing scripts based on this language, a sample file is included in the \%systemroot%\system32\ras directory.

The sample file following this paragraph performs the following functions after establishing a connection:

- Waits for the Logon Prompt.
- Sends the user name and waits for the Password prompt.
- Sends the password and ignores everything else.

The following is a sample SWITCH.INF entry to connect to an Internet Service Provider:

```
;*****************************************************
;Sample Entry to connect to a Internet Host
;******************************************************
[MyInternetService]
;The series of events that this script automates is:
;1) Wait for the "Login" Prompt.
;2) Send in the login name and wait for the ;"Password" prompt.
;3)Send password and proceed.
;Wait for the "Login" prompt:
COMMAND=
OK=<match>"Login"
;Issue the user name and wait for the "Password" ;prompt:
COMMAND=MyLoginUserNaMe<cr>
OK=<match>"Password"
;Issue the password and ignore all further responses (at ;this point the user
takes over from the Windows GUI):
COMMAND=MyPassword<cr>
OK=<ignore>
```

To execute a script in the SWITCH.INF file, make certain that you select Run this script in the Script tab in the Dial-Up Networking phone book entry setup. In the field provided, type the name of the script file you created. The script file itself is a plain-text file, and can be created using the Windows Notepad or any other text editor.

If you do not want to use the SWITCH.INF language for your scripts, Microsoft introduced a new scripting language in Windows 95 for dial-up connections that is now available in Windows NT Workstation. This new language is far more flexible and robust. It has a lot of similarities to Visual Basic and VBA. A discussion of this new language will enable you to write more powerful scripts.

Writing Scripts By Using the New (Windows 95) Language

The second method of writing scripts is to employ exactly the same language used to create Windows 95 Dial-Up Networking scripts. If you find the method described in the SWITCH.INF file cumbersome, the new scripting language may be for you! Information about the language, its syntax, reserved terms, and so on, are all given in the \%systemroot%\system32\ras\script.doc file. It is in Microsoft Word format.

Assume, for example, that you have the following requirements to connect to an Internet Service Provider:

- You are using PPP to dial out.
- You need to send in your user name and password, and after establishing a successful connection, you need to send in a text string called PPP at another prompt.
- After sending in all the information, you need to close the scripting session with the remote host.

Using the new scripting language, you get the following code:

```
;A sample script to connect to an ISP via PPP:
;Each script starts with a Proc Main statement.
proc main
;You should declare variables in the very first part of ;the script:
String szLogin = "Usename:"
String szPwd = "Password:"
String szAnx = "annex:"
String szConnect = "PPP"
waitfor szLogin      ;Waiting for the username prompt.
transmit $USERID     ;Sending username (specified in ;the Dial-Up Networking
setup).
waitfor szPwd ;Waiting for the password prompt.
transmit $PASSWORD   ;Sending password (specified in ;the Dial-Up Networking
setup).
```

```
waitfor szAnx ;Waiting for the Annex prompt.
transmit szAnx ;Sending the text string "PPP"
endproc
```

To execute this, make certain that you select Run this script in the Script tab in the Dial-Up Networking phonebook entry setup. In the field provided, type the name of the script file you created. The script file created using the new language has to be saved with SCP extension. The script itself is a plain-text file.

To provide some external connection information, each time a successful Dial-Up Networking connection is established, the Dial-Up Networking Monitor is activated (see fig. 13.11). By default, it is always a small icon in the Taskbar.

Detailed information about the data transfer over the communications device like bytes in/out, frames in/out can be obtained. Clicking on the Details button provides detailed information about the data protocol currently being used for that session. If you are using TCP/IP, for example, you will see the server and assigned IP address, and so on.

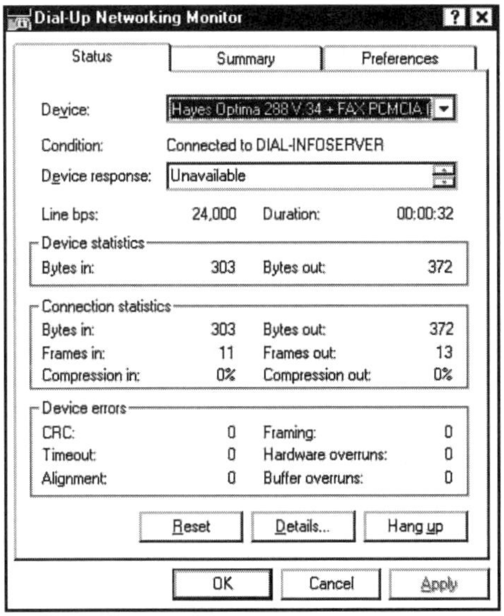

Figure 13.11

Use the Windows NT Dial-Up Networking Monitor to track your dial-up sessions.

Exploring the Connection Process

Windows NT provides a number of tools and techniques to understand the connection process, right from modem communications to protocol statistics. This section discusses the process of recording events (logging) during a communications session.

All Dial-Up Networking entries created through the graphical tool are recorded in the RASPHONE.PBK file. If you open the NT Explorer and double-click on this file, the graphical tool is activated. To read the entries in a text file, run the Notepad or Write utility on this file. The following sample is from a RASPHONE.PBK entry to connect to a Unix host by using PPP and TCP/IP:

```
[DIAL-INFOSERVER]
Description=
AutoLogon=0
DialParamsUID=2914821
UsePwForNetwork=0
BaseProtocol=1
Authentication=0
ExcludedProtocols=3
LcpExtensions=1
DataEncryption=0
SwCompression=1
UseCountryAndAreaCodes=0
AreaCode=
CountryID=1
CountryCode=1
SkipNwcWarning=0
SkipDownLevelDialog=0
DialMode=1
DialPercent=90
DialSeconds=120
HangUpPercent=50
HangUpSeconds=120
IdleDisconnectSeconds=0
SecureLocalFiles=0
CustomDialDll=
CustomDialFunc=
AuthRestrictions=0
IpPrioritizeRemote=1
IpHeaderCompression=1
IpAddress=0.0.0.0
IpDnsAddress=164.109.1.3
IpDns2Address=0.0.0.0
IpWinsAddress=0.0.0.0
IpWins2Address=0.0.0.0
IpAssign=1
IpNameAssign=2
IpFrameSize=1006
MEDIA=serial
```

```
Port=COM2
OtherPortOk=1
Device=Hayes Optima 288 V.34 + FAX PCMCIA
ConnectBPS=57600
DEVICE=modem
PhoneNumber=9,18002446983
PromoteAlternates=1
HwFlowControl=1
Protocol=1
Compression=1
Speaker=1
DEVICE=switch
Type=Terminal
```

Reading the entries in the RASPHONE.PBK file is a good first step in understanding how Dial-Up Networking actually uses the input you gave, with the line and data protocols that are selected. This file also provides a great outline for creating scripts for automating connections after dial up.

To troubleshoot modem problems, Windows NT provides a log file that records modem activity from the start of initiating a modem. An earlier section in this chapter describes the option to turn on modem logging. After the logging is turned on, a MODEMLOG.TXT (Actually, if you are using an NTFS partition on your NT workstation, the name of this file could very well be in the format of - Modem_Log Hayes Optima 288 V.34 + FAX PCMCIA.txt!) is created in the \%systemroot%\ directory. A sample modemlog.txt is shown for a connection:

```
09-27-1996 21:29:22.820 - Initializing modem.
09-27-1996 21:29:22.820 - Send: AT<cr>
09-27-1996 21:29:22.920 - Recv: AT<cr>
09-27-1996 21:29:22.930 - Recv: <cr><lf>OK<cr><lf>
09-27-1996 21:29:22.930 - Interpreted response: OK
09-27-1996 21:29:22.930 - Send: AT&FE0V0W1&C1&D2S95=47<cr>
09-27-1996 21:29:22.950 - Recv: AT&FE0V0W1&C1&D2S95=47<cr>
09-27-1996 21:29:22.950 - Recv: 0<cr>
09-27-1996 21:29:22.950 - Interpreted response: OK
09-27-1996 21:29:22.950 - Send: ATS7=60S30=0L0M1&Q5S36=7S48=7S46=138&K3<cr>
09-27-1996 21:29:22.970 - Recv: 0<cr>
09-27-1996 21:29:22.970 - Interpreted response: OK
09-27-1996 21:29:22.970 - Send: ATN1X4<cr>
09-27-1996 21:29:22.980 - Recv: 0<cr>
09-27-1996 21:29:22.980 - Interpreted response: OK
09-27-1996 21:29:22.980 - 57600,N,8,1
09-27-1996 21:29:22.990 - Initializing modem.
```

```
09-27-1996 21:29:22.990 - Send: AT<cr>
09-27-1996 21:29:23.000 - Recv: 0<cr>
09-27-1996 21:29:23.000 - Interpreted response: OK
09-27-1996 21:29:23.000 - Send: AT&FE0V0W1&C1&D2S95=47<cr>
09-27-1996 21:29:23.010 - Recv: 0<cr>
09-27-1996 21:29:23.010 - Interpreted response: OK
09-27-1996 21:29:23.010 - Send: ATS7=55S30=0L0M1&Q5S36=7S48=7S46=138&K3<cr>
09-27-1996 21:29:23.030 - Recv: 0<cr>
09-27-1996 21:29:23.030 - Interpreted response: OK
09-27-1996 21:29:23.040 - Send: ATN1X4<cr>
09-27-1996 21:29:23.040 - Recv: 0<cr>
09-27-1996 21:29:23.040 - Interpreted response: OK
09-27-1996 21:29:23.040 - Dialing.
09-27-1996 21:29:23.040 - Send: ATDT#,###########<cr>
09-27-1996 21:29:51.281 - Recv: 36<cr>
09-27-1996 21:29:51.281 - Interpreted response: Informative
09-27-1996 21:29:51.281 - Recv: 128<cr>
09-27-1996 21:29:51.281 - Interpreted response: Informative
09-27-1996 21:29:52.012 - Recv: 77<cr>
09-27-1996 21:29:52.012 - Interpreted response: Informative
09-27-1996 21:29:52.012 - Recv: 67<cr>
09-27-1996 21:29:52.012 - Interpreted response: Informative
09-27-1996 21:29:52.012 - Recv: 34<cr>
09-27-1996 21:29:52.022 - Interpreted response: Connect
09-27-1996 21:29:52.022 - Connection established at 26400bps.
09-27-1996 21:29:52.022 - Error-control on.
09-27-1996 21:29:52.022 - Data compression on.
09-27-1996 21:44:27.450 - Hanging up the modem.
09-27-1996 21:44:27.481 - Hardware hangup by lowering DTR.
09-27-1996 21:44:27.751 - Recv: 0<cr>
09-27-1996 21:44:27.751 - Interpreted response: OK
09-27-1996 21:44:27.751 - Send: ATH<cr>
```

Note that the string sequences are drawn from the UNIMODEM driver. As explained earlier, if a modem is not supported in the installable list, the strings have to be added manually to the MODEM.INF file. Otherwise, newer modems can add their own INF files and register the same with the universal modem driver.

To understand a PPP session and to troubleshoot a protocol problem after the line connection is established, Windows NT provides a logging mechanism also. To turn on PPP logging, add the following entry in the Registry:

```
HKEY_LOCAL_MACHINE\SYSTEM\CurrentControlSet\Services\RasMan\PPP\Logging = 1
```

This creates a file called PPP.LOG in the \%systemroot%\system32\ras directory. A sample output of PPP.LOG file is shown:

```
Line up event occurred on port 0
FsmInit called for protocol = c021, port = 0
FsmReset called for protocol = c021, port = 0
FsmThisLayerStarted called for protocol = c021, port = 0
<PPP packet sent at 09/27/1996 21:30:08:596
<Protocol = LCP, Type = Configure-Req, Length = 0x26, Id = 0x0, Port = 0
<C0 21 01 00 00 24 02 06 00 00 00 00 05 06 00 00 ¦.!...$.........¦
<56 A7 07 02 08 02 0D 03 06 11 04 06 4E 13 09 03 ¦V...........N...¦
<00 A0 24 A7 28 C4                               ¦..$.(.          ¦
>PPP packet received at 09/27/1996 21:30:08:846
>Protocol = LCP, Type = Configure-Reject, Length = 0x16, Id = 0x0, Port = 0
>C0 21 04 00 00 14 0D 03 06 11 04 06 4E 13 09 03 ¦.!..........N...¦
>00 A0 24 A7 28 C4                               ¦..$.(.          ¦
FsmReset called for protocol = 80fd, port = 0
FsmThisLayerDown called for protocol = 8021, port = 0
FsmReset called for protocol = 8021, port = 0
FsmReset called for protocol = c021, port = 0
Line down event occurred on port 0
```

The log file starts up with a Line up event, which essentially states that a successful connection occurred on the COM port being used (in this case, the only COM port).

As you work through the rest of the log file (the sample shows a successful connection), you will find the entries for the PPP packets sent, received, and dropped if any. The log file also shows you the TCP ports opened used. If any unsuccessful events happen (carrier lost, connection or line down, PPP packets not received, ports not opened, and so on), they are recorded in this log file. So when you are troubleshooting unsuccessful PPP connections, this log file should be the first place to look. Based on the particular unsuccessful log entry, you can then narrow your focus to that problem. If the line down event is occurring frequently, for example, you probably should look at your modem log file because that is a communications device problem or a phone line problem.

RAS and Dial-Up Networking Security and Data Encryption

Windows NT supports several authentication and data encryption methods. The settings you choose in the Dial-Up Networking setup as well as the RAS server setup determine which type of security and encryption you will be employing in your remote access setup.

Windows NT RAS supports the Password Authentication Protocol, the Challenge Handshake Authentication protocol (CHAP), and SPAP (Shiva PAP).

PAP uses clear text (unencrypted) password authentication. It is supported by the NT RAS Server to accept dial-in sessions from remote clients unable to send in higher forms of authentication. This essentially means that most third-party PPP clients can dial in to a Windows NT machine.

CHAP requires a challenge response with encryption on the response. This is very similar to the local Domain logon process of a client machine logging on to a Windows NT machine. The authentication standards supported under CHAP include MS-CHAP (a version of RSA MD4) and DES. MS-CHAP corresponds to the Require Microsoft encrypted authentication setting. Both Windows NT Workstation and Windows 95 remote clients are able to negotiate this level of authentication. The Dial-Up Networking client software in Windows NT Workstation is also able to encrypt data using the RSA MD5 standard, which essentially means that a Windows NT Workstation using Dial-Up Networking can connect to any PPP server. For lower-end Windows machines (Windows 3.x, Windows for Workgroups 3.x), DES provides the authentication.

SPAP allows remote Shiva clients to dial in and establish connections to a Windows NT computer. Unlike PAP, SPAP sends encrypted passwords over the wire instead of clear text passwords.

Using Windows NT Workstation as a RAS Server

Windows NT Workstation is marketed as, and meant to be, a desktop operating system. Typically, if you want to set up a Windows NT machine as a communications server—a server that users dial up and connect to—you will be using Windows NT Server.

Note RAS Server on Windows NT Server supports 256 simultaneous dial-in sessions. RAS Server on NT Workstation only provides you the ability to have one dial-in session at any given time. Obviously, Microsoft is positioning the use of NT Server for any type of high-volume RAS dial-in sessions. This makes technical sense also because NT Server is optimized to handle multiple-server threads much better than NT Workstation is.

NT Workstation does, however, provide the ability to use the PC as a dial-in server. You can choose to use this if you want to dial up and access a remote user's PC for troubleshooting, file transfer, and so on. You might also want to set up a particular user's office PC to accept dial-in calls from his home PC and to access files on the office PC's hard disk. To implement proper security, you can always hold the dial-in session only to that physical PC and not the network that the PC may be connected to.

The Remote Access Admin tool in the Administrative Tools (Common) folder provides the ability to manage and reconfigure the RAS server. When you set up RAS services, the RAS server is also set up automatically, even if you were unaware of it. The RAS server is a Windows NT service that can be set to start up automatically from the Control Panel/Services applet:

1. Choose Remote Access Services in the Services applet, choose the Startup button, and opt for Automatic as the Startup Type.

2. You can also start the RAS service from the Remote Access Admin tool. Open the RAS Admin tool, choose Server/Start Remote Access Service, and then select the name of the RAS server. By default, this name will be name of your Windows NT computer.

Just because you start the RAS server on a Windows NT machine, that does not enable automatic dial-in privileges to users (even if they are registered on the workstation). To enable dial-in capabilities for your users, choose Users/Permissions in the RAS Admin tool. A list of registered users to which you can now give or deny access appears (see fig. 13.12).

Note The list of users you get, to provide access for dial-in sessions, depends on which RAS server you are trying to manage through the RAS Admin tool. If your NT workstation is participating in a Windows NT Domain, and you are a member of the Domain Administrator's Group, you can manage any RAS server in your domain. Just select Server/Select Domain or Server, and you can access and manage all RAS servers in your domain.

Windows NT Workstation 4 also enables you to grant dial-in permissions to users from the User Manager. This helps you grant this permission as you set up users on the NT workstation.

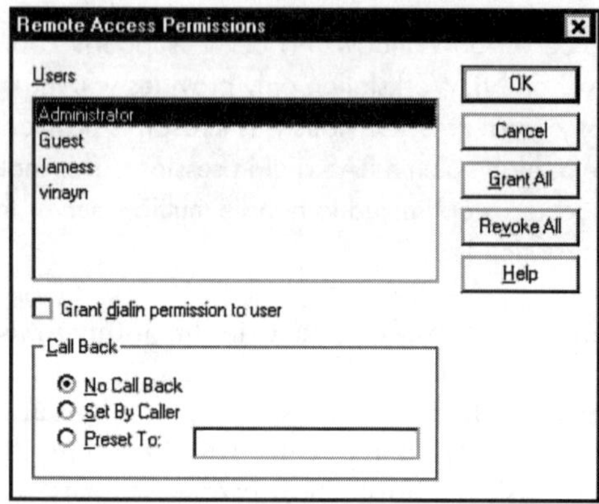

Figure 13.12

Grant Windows NT users dial-in permissions.

RAS Server Security

As discussed earlier, RAS provides the same level of security as a local Windows NT Domain logon through the settings in the Dial-Up Networking section or the RAS client. In addition to this, you can hold the dial-in session to access the computer being dialed without routing the connection over to the LAN to which that computer may be networked.

Assume, for example, that you want a remote client running TCP/IP to access a local NT Workstation that is part of your network. You do not, however, want the remote client to access your network:

1. Choose Remote Access Services in the Network applet in the Control Panel, and click on the Properties button.
2. Choose the Network button in the Remote Access Setup dialog box.
3. In the Server Settings section, choose the Configure button for TCP/IP, and select This computer only in the Allow remote TCP/IP clients to access: section of the RAS Server TCP/IP Configuration dialog box.

This effectively shuts down the routing features of the RAS Server, and holds the remote client to that machine (which is running RAS Server and accepting dial-in sessions) only.

Another method of security available is call-back security. This method makes the RAS Server call a user back at a predetermined phone number of a user-defined phone number after the password authentication process is complete. You set the call-back security by user in the RAS Admin tool (see fig. 13.13).

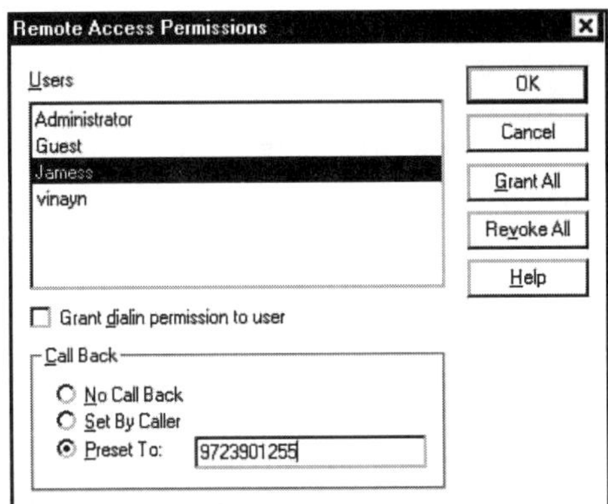

Figure 13.13
Set Call-Back security to dial-in users.

Some Pertinent Registry Settings for RAS Services

The following list of Registry settings is an attempt to cover some frequently used scenarios. It also gives you an idea of the type of Registry settings that control RAS services on your NT computer.

To turn RAS Server logging on (the log file will be called DEVICE.LOG and will be generated in the \%systemroot%\system32\ras directory):

```
HKEY_LOCAL_MACHINE\SYSTEM\CurrentControlSet\Services\RasMan\Parameters\Logging
= 1
```

To use WINCHAT.EXE on a remote client:

```
HKEY_LOCAL_MACHINE\SYSTEM\CurrentControlSet\Services\
RemoteAccess\Parameters\NetBiosGateway\RemoteListen = 2
```

To identify the services that need to start up before your RAS server can successfully start:

```
HKEY_LOCAL_MACHINE\SYSTEM\CurrentControlSet\Services\
RemoteAccess\DependOnService =
```

What's Not There Yet

Although Windows NT Workstation 4 employs many of the features in Windows 95 Dial-Up Networking, some features are not yet implemented.

The Microsoft Fax utility that enables Windows 95 users to create and send faxes does not ship with the retail copy of NT Workstation 4. Microsoft has promised to release it as a free update by the end of 1996. Essentially, this utility will enable users to compose faxes and send them through fax-capable modems to group II and III fax machines.

Users will be able to attach any documents with a fax, meaning that any document created on a PC can be faxed right from the desktop. The fax utility will also make use of TAPI, and hence all settings will be centralized. Users can use the fax utility to compose a new fax or choose an option right from within their application.

Although RAS enables users to dial out from a remote client (or even a locally connected PC with a modem attached to it), no modem or port sharing/pooling is provided. Assume, for example, that you have 50 PCs running NT Workstation that are connected together in a LAN with an NT Server running the RAS server software. This enables remote clients to dial into the NT Server. If you are running the Dial-Up Networking software on a LAN client (that is, one of the NT workstations), *and* you have a modem attached to that PC, you will be able to dial out also. What is not possible using RAS right now is the capability of all PCs on the LAN to use the modem(s) attached to the LAN server to dial out. Currently, a number of modem-sharing third-party software products perform this function. You are, therefore, limited to using those products for modem sharing.

Summary

This chapter laid out a framework to understand Windows NT Workstation's remote computing capabilities. This framework explained the new communications architecture and TAPI. The modular nature of the communications architecture and the transparency of TAPI combine to give you a powerful method to manage communications devices (modems, and so on) on your Windows NT workstation.

You explored the Remote Access Services (RAS) portion of Windows NT Workstation. This is the software set that enables you to receive calls into the NT workstation. This scenario can be used when a user wants to dial up a PC and send and receive files, mail messages, and so on. Essentially, in this case the NT Workstation acts as a remote communications "server."

Dial-Up Networking is the tool that enables the user to dial out to another computer. Because PPP is implemented in NT Workstation, you can not only dial up a Windows machine (NT, Windows 95, Windows for Workgroups) from your NT workstation, but also any computer (Unix, AS/400, and so on) that can receive PPP incoming calls.

Through the discussion on RAS and Dial-Up Networking, you explored the high level of security that Windows NT Workstation gives you, the scripting functions to automate remote sessions, and certain Registry settings to fine tune your RAS machine.

In today's increasingly mobile world, Windows NT Workstation—through a combination of solid communications infrastructure, RAS, and Dial-Up Networking—provides you with a seamless solution for most of your remote computing needs.

CHAPTER 14

Microsoft Messaging

Having clear and efficient communications has always been a critical part of running a successful business. Whether the communications are with external customers or within a company, timeliness of communication is critical in today's global economy. The use of electronic mail (e-mail) has exploded to fill this need for fast, reliable communications in today's ever more competitive business world.

Before electronic messaging became common, people wrote memos and letters on paper and manually distributed them. This was slow and expensive. With the dawning of computers as widely used office productivity tools, companies began using electronic messaging. This was much faster and more efficient, but not without its own problems. Companies used to have no other choice than to use several different programs to carry on their various electronic communications—a program for mail to users of a departmental LAN, another program to users on a corporate mainframe, and another program to customers on the Internet. In many organizations, departmental LANs within the same company use different e-mail standards, and difficulty communicating between them resulted. Even when someone was willing to take the time to learn what all the systems were and how each worked, there was not enough time to become highly skilled in using all of them.

E-mail can be a legacy support nightmare when it has grown up without the direction an overall e-mail system architecture needs.

Fortunately, Microsoft Messaging for Windows NT Workstation is a good step toward solving these problems. Microsoft Messaging for Windows NT Workstation is the client piece of a messaging architecture that enables users to communicate with different mail systems while still using the same interface. One of its most useful features is its integration with common productivity applications, such as the MAPI-enabled programs in Microsoft Office.

This integration with common productivity applications is established by Microsoft's building support for Messaging Applications Program Interface (MAPI) into the operating system as a subsystem. This opens the architectural design of the e-mail system and provides consistent interaction for developers even if the client software piece changes. The Messaging API (MAPI) enables applications to share information and allows for the single desktop Inbox to deal with messages from a variety of sources and other mail systems.

Whether it is a piece of Internet mail, local e-mail, or mail from a gateway to another mail system, having a common, system-level interface increases compatibility and ease of use. The Messaging Inbox is compatible with any other mail services that use a MAPI 1.0 driver such as CompuServe Mail, Lotus Notes, cc:Mail, AT&T Mail, and even including some FAX packages. Note that Microsoft Messaging for Windows NT Workstation only comes with support for Microsoft Mail using the Workgroup Postoffice and Internet mail using a Post Office Protocol version 3 (POP3) server.

You should understand another thing before going much further in this discussion. You might be familiar with Microsoft's client/server e-mail product, which is named Exchange Server, or with the Windows 95 e-mail client named Exchange. In the copy of Windows NT Workstation 4 released to manufacturing and shipped to early customers, you can still see references to Exchange in the help files. Those references stem from the origin of Windows NT Messaging as an outgrowth of the Windows 95 mail client, which was named Exchange. In fact, you can see that the executable file for the Windows NT Messaging client is named EXCHNG32.EXE, and you can see many similarities between the two programs if you are familiar with the Windows 95 e-mail client. The references to "Exchange" in the Windows NT Messaging client help files should be read as if they said something like "Windows NT Messaging Client," and they should not be confused with anything about the Exchange Server in Microsoft's client server e-mail system.

The only overlap between the Windows NT Messaging client and the Microsoft Exchange message server is that the messaging client can interact with the Exchange Server to send and receive messages. In this way, it can be the "client" part for the client/server Exchange system. To do this, you have to install the Exchange Server interface for the messaging client.

Networks really have just a few primary uses. They connect people for file and printer sharing, e-mail, database access, and terminal emulation. Mastering Messaging for Windows NT Workstation gives you control over one of these fundamental networking topics—e-mail. Taking the time to understand the messaging services that come with Windows NT Workstation will enable you to deploy and troubleshoot the client piece of enterprise-wide messaging services.

This chapter covers the general basics of e-mail, the workgroup postoffices Windows NT Workstation can create and use, the mail client software that comes with Windows NT Workstation, how to connect to Microsoft's client/server e-mail system, and how to dial in for your messages.

Examining E-Mail—Internal and Foreign

E-mail is used both to communicate within an organization and to communicate with people outside that organization. A person's e-mail address is used to match each person up with a mailbox within the e-mail domain (which might map onto an Exchange Server post office, an MS Mail post office, an Internet-compatible POP3 post office or any of many other types).

E-mail addresses usually reflect this hierarchical structure of a mailbox within a domain by the general notation of MAILBOX@DOMAIN. Most modern e-mail clients, Windows NT Messaging included, disguise this level of detail from you by displaying user names rather than mailbox names. The address book keeps track of these relationships behind the scenes—at least until you try to add or modify an address, when you will have to know the address.

Now that you know the broad overview of why Microsoft is so interested in electronic messaging and what e-mail is, you are ready to learn some of the specifics about the e-mail services that come with Windows NT Workstation. Messaging for Windows NT Workstation is the e-mail tool that Microsoft includes with Windows NT Workstation.

Examining the MS Mail Workgroup Post Office

The post office is where the messages are kept for delivery—just like the physical post office down the street that processes *snail mail* (a term e-mail users fondly use for systems using manual delivery), only there are no long lines!

Installing and Setting Up an MS Mail Workgroup Post Office

If you already have a workgroup post office installed on your LAN and do not want to install another, or if you will be using Exchange, then you do not need to install and configure the post office portion of Microsoft Messaging. If you are going to use an MS-Mail workgroup post office, however, then you will need to install support for it as a MAPI-compliant service the Messaging client can use. The following sections go through the installation and the configuration of the Microsoft Messaging components and the MS Mail workgroup post office.

Installing the Microsoft Messaging Components

When you perform an installation of Windows NT Workstation 4, the MS Messaging components must be selected in the custom installation in order to be installed. If they are installed, you can skip down to the next section, "Setting Up an MS Mail Post Office." Check the desktop for the Inbox icon, or the Control Panel for the Mail and Microsoft Mail Postoffice icons. If you see any of them, MS Messaging is installed. You must have a post office configured to use Microsoft's Windows NT Messaging.

To install MS Mail support, perform the following steps:

1. From the Control Panel, double-click on the Add/Remove Programs icon.
2. On the Install/Uninstall tab click the Install button (see fig. 14.1).

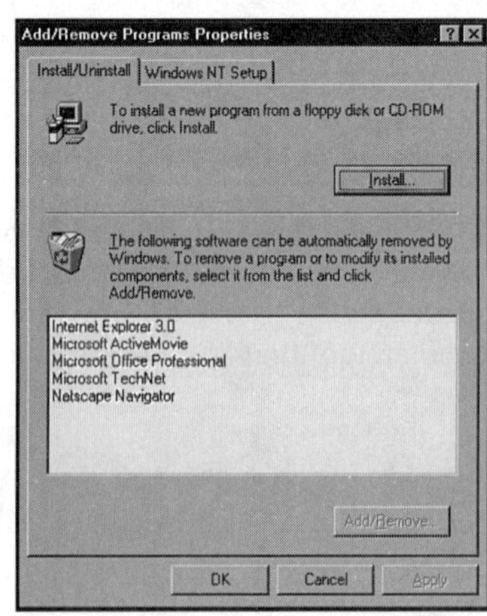

Figure 14.1
You install the Messaging components, which include Microsoft Postoffice, using the Add/Remove Programs icon.

3. Put the Windows NT Workstation CD in the CD-ROM drive and click on the Next button. The CD automatically starts, and you see the opening screen shown in figure 14.2. Click the Add/Remove Software icon on the screen.

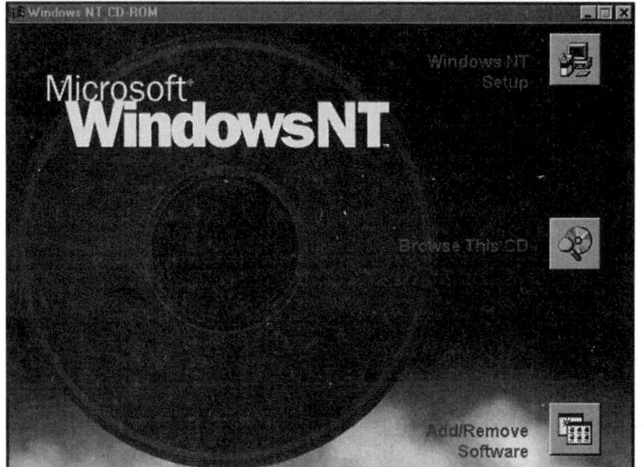

Figure 14.2
The opening screen for the Windows NT Workstation CD-ROM pops up when you insert the CD-ROM in the CD-ROM drive.

4. Make sure that Windows Messaging is checked (see fig. 14.3.)

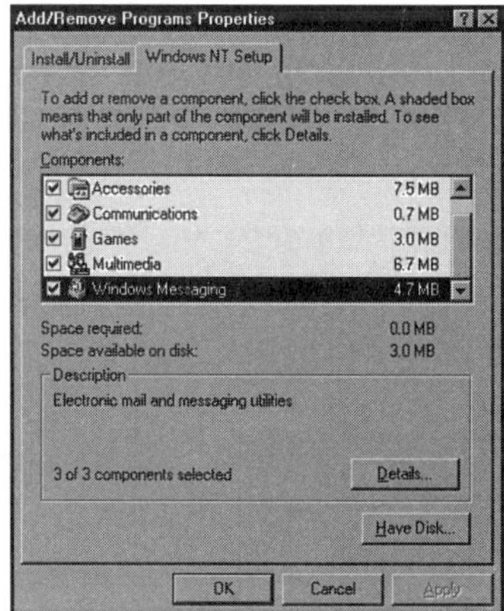

Figure 14.3
The Windows Messaging components are listed on the Windows NT setup tab.

5. Click on the Details button to see the three components as in figure 14.4:
   - Internet Mail
   - Microsoft Mail
   - Windows Messaging

Figure 14.4

The three Messaging components are Internet Mail, Microsoft Mail, and Windows Messaging.

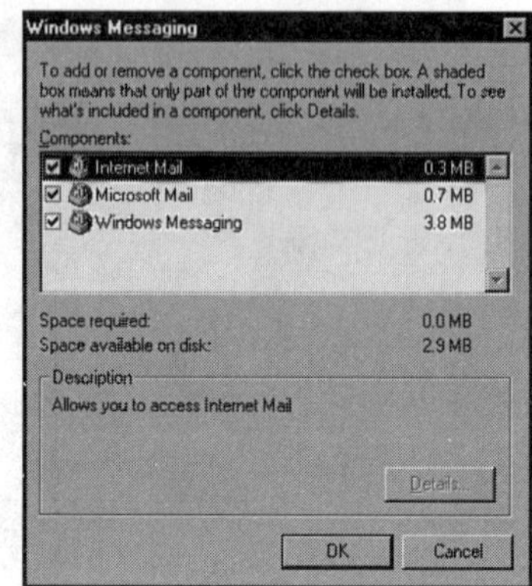

If you do not want one or more of these components installed, uncheck the one or ones you do not want installed.

6. Click on OK to close the details dialog box.

7. If you have Windows Messaging highlighted, The Description box describes the program and displays how many of the components you have selected. Click on OK to install the Windows Messaging components. The progress status appears on your screen while the installation is taking place.

8. Close the Windows NT CD-ROM window when you are finished.

In figure 14.5, the Control Panel has the two new icons, Microsoft Mail Postoffice and Mail. An Inbox icon will also be on your desktop.

Figure 14.5

The Mail icons will be visible in the Control Panel once you have MS Mail installed.

Setting Up an MS Mail Postoffice

Now that you have MS Mail installed, you need to configure it in order to use it. The following steps go through the setup procedure:

1. In the Control Panel, click on the Microsoft Mail Postoffice icon.
2. The Microsoft Workgroup Postoffice Admin program begins. Select Create a New Workgroup Postoffice.
3. Click on the Next button.
4. The next screen of the Admin program prompts you for the post office location. You can type in a directory or accept the default. Click on the Next button to go to the next screen (see fig. 14.6).

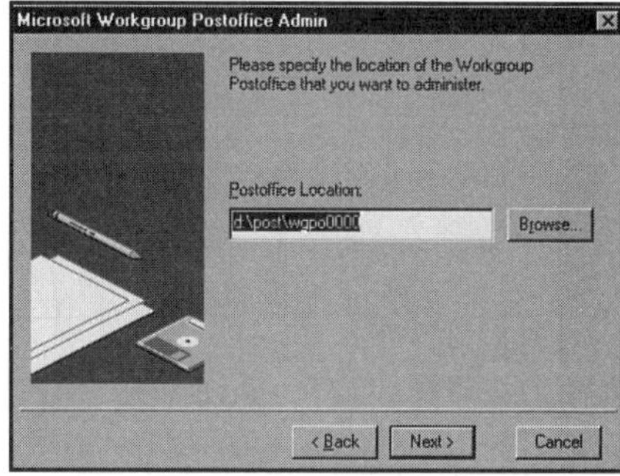

Figure 14.6

Type in the location of the post office you want to create.

5. The next screen verifies that the location of the post office is correct. Click on Next to accept this or Back to make any necessary changes.
6. The Enter Your Administrator Account Details dialog box appears as shown in figure 14.7. Type in the administrator's Name, Mailbox name, Password, Phone #1 (and if applicable Phone #2), Office, Department, and Notes. Click on OK when you are finished.

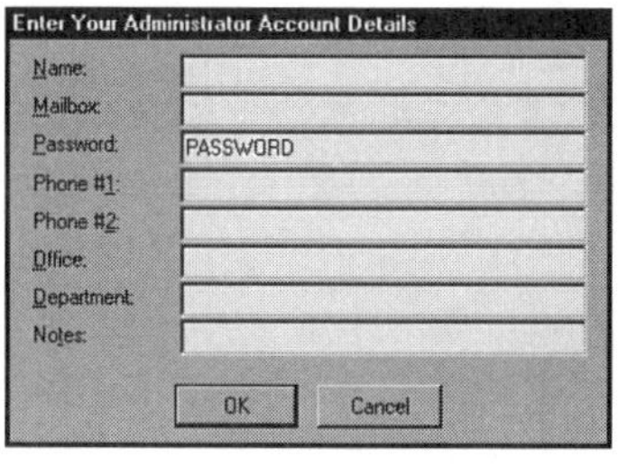

Enter Your Administrator Account Details
Name:
Mailbox:
Password: PASSWORD
Phone #1:
Phone #2:
Office:
Department:
Notes:
OK
Cancel

Figure 14.7

Type in the Administrator Account Details.

7. The Mail information box appears, telling you that the post office has been created and that it must be shared with full access if others are to use it.

8. Click on OK.

9. From your Network Neighborhood or Windows NT Explorer, find the post office folder (its default name is \Post\wgpo0000, but you should use whatever name you assigned it during installation).

10. Right-click on the folder and select Sharing from the context-sensitive menu.

11. Select the Shared As option and type in the share name. You can also type in a comment and set a limit on the number of users (see fig.14.8).

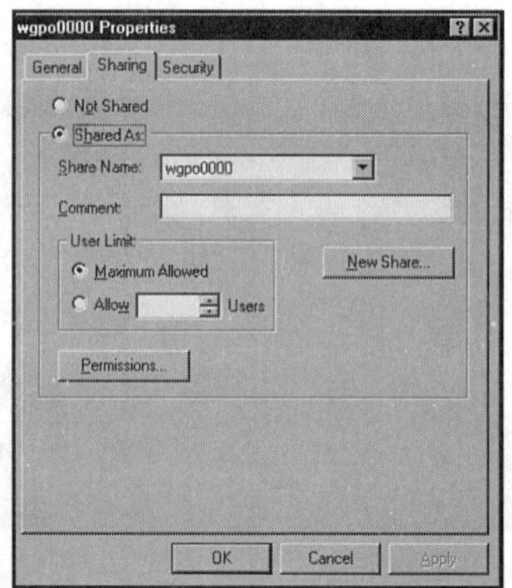

Figure 14.8

Share the post office folder using the Properties dialog box.

12. Click on the Permissions button. You can select which groups or users can have access to the postoffice if you want to limit who uses it. Make sure that the Type of Access is set to Full Control. For users to retrieve, delete, forward, or send mail, they will need this level of access (see fig. 14.9).

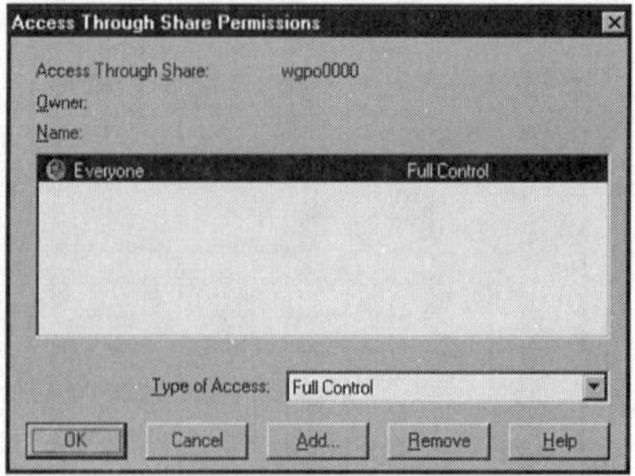

Figure 14.9

Set Access Through Share Permissions to individuals or groups.

13. You can click on the Add button to add names or groups to the access share. Click on OK when finished. Click on Apply and then OK to close the Properties dialog box.

Administering a Post Office

After you have a post office installed, someone needs to administer it. This includes such tasks as assigning e-mail addresses and passwords to users, and adding or removing users from the post office. The following steps enumerate common tasks you will be performing as you administer the MS Mail Postoffice.

1. Double-click on the Microsoft Mail Postoffice icon in the Control Panel.
2. The Microsoft Workgroup Postoffice Admin program starts. Select Administer an Existing Workgroup Postoffice. Click on the Next button.
3. The Microsoft Workgroup Postoffice Admin program verifies the location of the post office. You can click on the Browse button to help you find the location if you need to. Click on Next.
4. Type in the administrator's mailbox and password to administer the post office (see fig. 14.10).

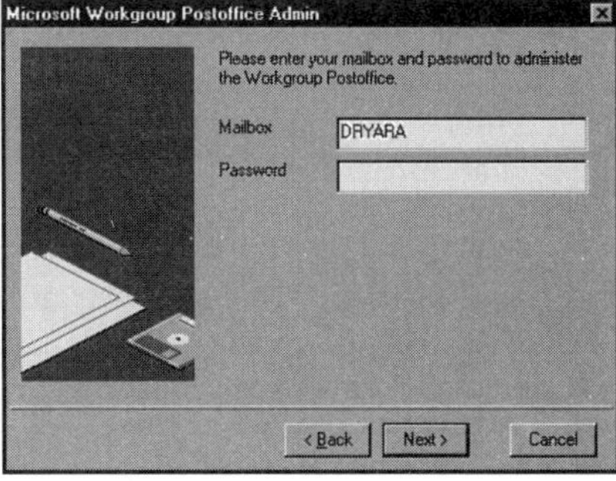

Figure 14.10

You must know the administrator's mailbox and password to administer the Workgroup Postoffice.

5. The Postoffice Manager dialog box appears (see fig. 14.11), which enables you to do the following:

   - Add and remove users
   - View shared folders
   - See and edit details on a particular user

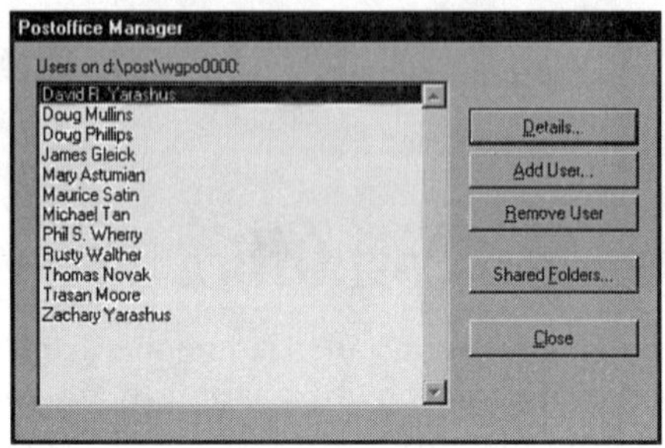

Figure 14.11

Use the Postoffice Manager dialog box to add and remove users.

6. To add a user, click on the Add button. The Add user dialog box appears (see fig. 14.12). Type in the user's Name, Mailbox Name, Password, Phone #1 (and if applicable Phone #2), Office, Department, and Notes. Click on OK when you are finished.

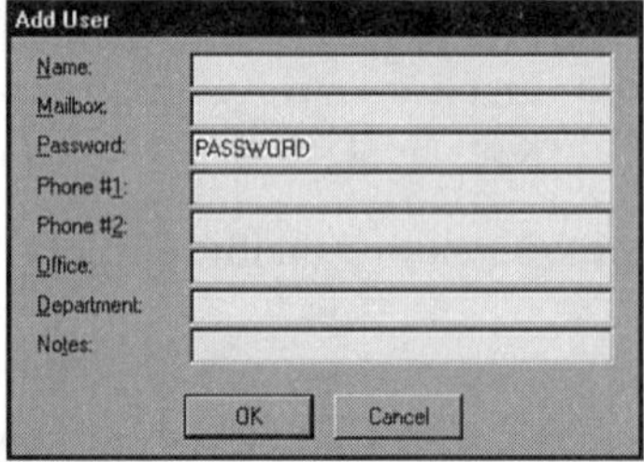

Figure 14.12

Type in the user's Name and Password in the Add User dialog box.

7. To remove a user, highlight the user's name in the Postoffice Manager list and click on the Remove button. You are prompted to verify that you do indeed want to remove that user.

8. Highlight the name of a user in the Postoffice Manager list and click on the Details button to view the details of that person's account. You can edit this information. Click on the OK button when you are finished.

Note Recovering lost passwords is perhaps the most frequent request you will receive as a post office administrator. Although you can't actually retrieve the password your user lost, you can set a new one by editing the details of his account.

9. To see the status of the shared folders, click on the Shared folders button (see fig. 14.13).

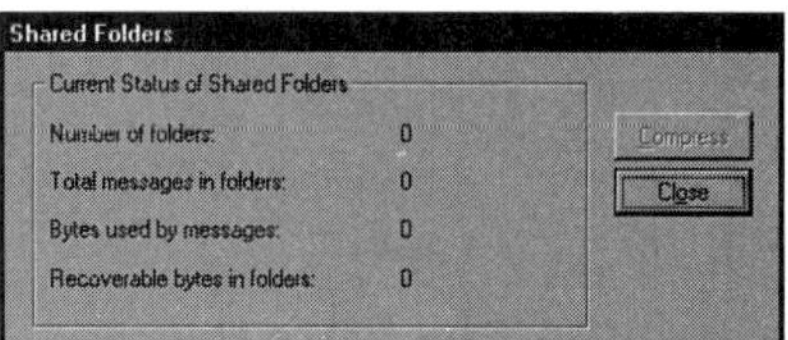

Figure 14.13

You can check on the current status of shared folders.

Understanding the MS Postoffice Architecture

The major difference between a workgroup post office (like the ones you can create using the Windows NT Messaging client) and an enterprise post office is the capability to connect to external mail sources. A workgroup post office cannot, for example, connect to an SMTP gateway to process Internet mail. Neither can a workgroup post office connect to any other workgroup post office. You can see that with these sorts of limitations, the only appropriate installation for a workgroup post office is in, well, an isolated workgroup. This might be perfect for a small office; but as connectivity needs grow, you will need to look at other solutions like the Microsoft Exchange Server or perhaps the older MS-Mail for PC Networks.

The Microsoft Postoffice consists of a hierarchy of shared folders that contain or point to indexed keys, information, and messages. The folders can be seen in figure 14.14.

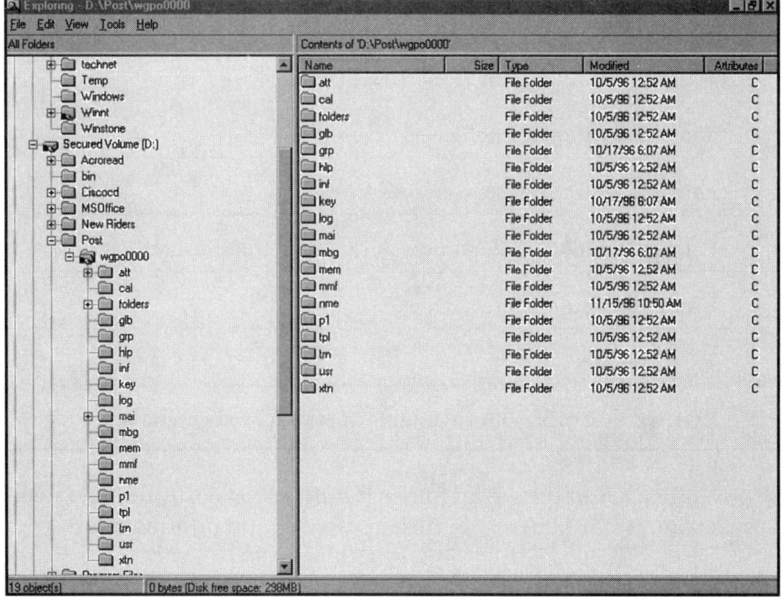

Figure 14.14

The post office folders hold a mail message until a user retrieves it.

Each of the folders is necessary for the post office to function. Table 14.1 gives a brief description of most of the folders that comprise the post office system.

Table 14.1
The Microsoft Mail Post Office Folders

Folder	Contents/Function
ATT	File attachments
CAL	Schedule+ calendar files
FOLDERS	\LOC—local folders \PUB—shared folders
GLB	Global system files for Mail
HLP	Mail help files
INF	Information files that correspond to template files
KEY	Index files
MAI	Mail messages
MBG	Mail headers that point to the Mail files
MEM	Members of local post office
NME	Pointer files for the name alias address lists
P1	Used for temporary file storage during mail transmission
USR	User and Group names at an external post office
TPL	Template files
XTN	External post office information for networks and gateways

The heart of the post office lies in the global folder (GLB); the majority of the system as well as user information is stored here. Your user password and information is stored here.

Table 14.2 summarizes the contents and functions of most of the GLB files found in the Global folder.

TABLE 14.2
The Post Office Global Folder Files

File	Contents/Description
ACCESS.GLB	Contains local post office user passwords and setup preferences.
ACCESS2.GLB	Lists each user's access privileges and points to each user's mailbox.
ACCESS3.GLB	Contains information for remote users.
CONTROL.GLB	Generates the numeric message, attachment, and user file prefixes.
FLAG.GLB	Works as a switch; only one copy of ADMIN.EXE can work on the post office at a time.
GLOBAL.GLB	Holds the default information used to create a local post office user.
GRPMEM.GLB	Lists the groups that each user belongs to.
GROUP.GLB	Contains group alias names and addresses.
MASTER.GLB	Stores information about the local post office: serial number, installed gateways, and maximum number of users.
MODEM.GLB	Stores local serial port information for the post office.
NETPO.GLB	Lists the physical addresses for users from an external post office.
NETWORK.GLB	Lists the names of external networks and gateways connected to the post office.
PROCESS.GLB	Contains process and schedule information.
REQCONF.GLB	Contains requester configuration information.

continues

Table 14.2, Continued
The Post Office Global Folder Files

File	Contents/Description
REQTRANS.GLB	This queue is for outbound directory transactions.
SRVTRANS.GLB	This queue is for inbound directory transactions.
TID.GLB	Generates the internal pointers that link alias names and address files.
TRANSFIL.GLB	This translation file is used to filter characters for transmission.
WELCOME.GLB	Contains the ASCII test message that first-time users see.

When you send a message to another member of the local post office, the file is stored in the mail folder (MAI). If you have included any attachments with the message, they are stored in the attachments folder (ATT). Your message contains the reference information (a type of pointer, or link) to each attachment. The file attachments as well as the messages are stored in an encrypted format for security. Each attachment to your message is stored separately in one of the 16 attachment folders, labeled at0-atf. Each attachment has an identification label composed of a hexadecimal number. The last digit determines the folder the attachment is stored in. The same general scenario is true of the message itself, although the mail folders are labeled ma0-maf. Each transaction that takes place (sending or receiving) is noted in the mail log, and the identification number associated with the message or attachment is cited.

The mail you send is represented by a header in the mailbag (MBG) folder in the recipient's file. Each post office user and each external post office has his own mailbag file. This file is a hexadecimal number with the file extension MBG. This same number corresponds to the index stored in the Key folder. If you send the same message to two different people, each recipient's mailbag file would contain the header with a pointer to the actual message, but only one copy of the message would exist in the Mail folder.

When the recipient of your message connects to the post office, the Key folder provides such information as the number of new or unread messages in the user's mailbag. If the recipient is dialing in and wants to preview the headers before actually downloading messages, this division of information lets him do so. The messages are removed from the mail folder after the recipient retrieves them. If you send a message to several individuals, the message would contain a counter; each time a recipient deletes the message, that action would decrement the counter. After the counter reaches zero, the message would then be removed from the mail folder.

Now that you have the post office installed and you understand how it works, you will want to set up the client portion, Microsoft Messaging for Windows NT Workstation.

Exploring MS Messaging for Windows NT

Microsoft Messaging for Windows NT Workstation is an e-mail system that has a close relationship with both Microsoft's Windows 95 e-mail system and with Microsoft's Exchange Server e-mail client for Windows NT. It is an enhanced version of the Windows 95 e-mail system, but it is also a feature-limited version of the Exchange Server e-mail client. MS Messaging for Windows NT can be used to connect to any service with a compatible interface. In the following sections, you will see how to set up messaging, how to use messaging with different mail systems (like Internet mail), and how to administer a workgroup post office.

Setting Up Messaging

The first time you try to use Messaging, the Messaging wizard automatically walks you through setting up the Messaging service. To activate the service, perform the following steps:

1. From the desktop, double-click on the Inbox icon. The Windows Messaging Setup wizard appears.

2. Select Use the Following Information Services and make sure that the services you want to install are checked. Your choices are either Microsoft Mail, Internet Mail, or both. Alternatively, you can choose to manually configure information services by choosing that option. This example goes through the setup of both Microsoft and Internet Mail, as shown in figure 14.15. Click on the Next button when you are finished.

Figure 14.15

The Windows Messaging wizard walks you through the setup process.

3. To send messages, you need to configure your e-mail client with the location of your post office. If the setup wizard does not auto-detect the location, you can click on the Browse button to search for it yourself. After typing the location in the space provided, click on the Next button (see fig. 14.16).

Figure 14.16

Type in the location of your post office.

4. The post office provides its list of users to the Messaging Setup wizard (see fig. 14.17). Select your name from the list and click on the Next button. If your name does not appear on the list, have the post office administrator add it.

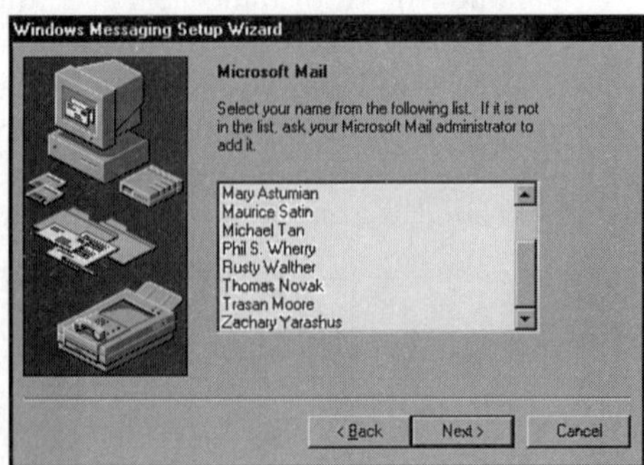

Figure 14.17

Select your name from the post office list.

5. Type in your mail password. The Microsoft Mail Postoffice default password is PASSWORD. Your administrator may have assigned you a different one (see fig. 14.18).

Figure 14.18

Type in your Mail password.

6. If you chose to setup Internet mail, the next screen asks how you are going to connect to the Internet. Choose either modem or network (see fig. 14.19) and then click on the Next button. If you did not choose to set up Internet mail, skip to step 11. (For more information about Internet access see Part V, "NT Workstation 4 and the Microsoft Internet Strategy.")

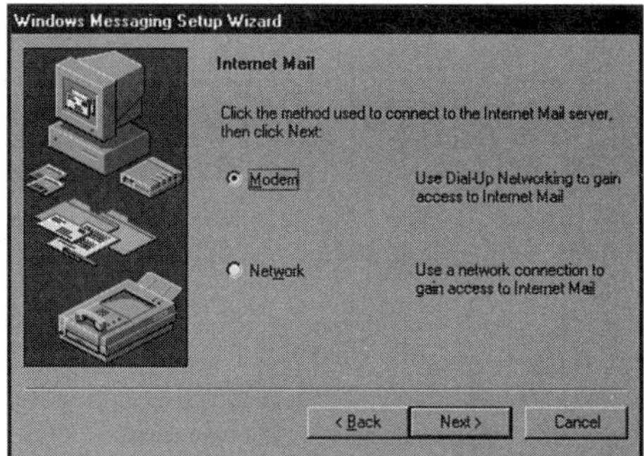

Figure 14.19

Select a modem or network connection to the Internet.

7. You can select an existing Internet connection (if you already have an Internet access configured), or you can create a new connection by clicking on the New button. Click on the Next button (see fig. 14.20).

8. Type in the name or IP address of the server that will handle your Internet mail (see fig. 14.21). This server needs to support POP3 (Post Office Protocol version 3).

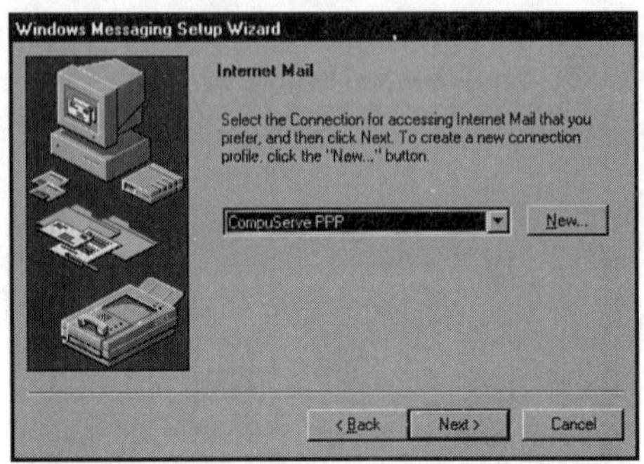

Figure 14.20

Select your Internet connection.

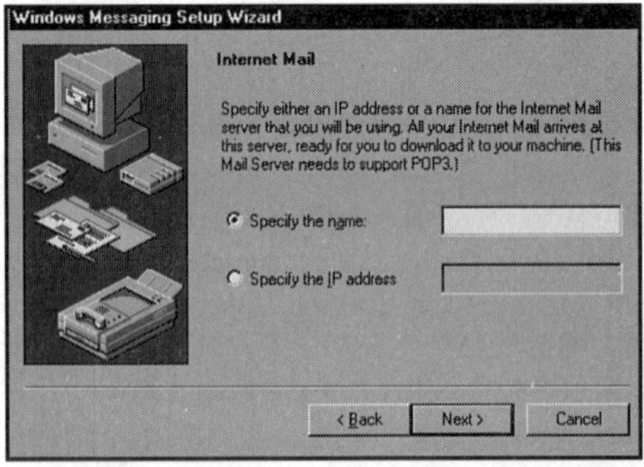

Figure 14.21

Identify the Internet Mail server by name or IP address.

9. You can specify whether you want to have your mail automatically downloaded to your mailbox or to have control over which new messages get downloaded. Select Off-line or Automatic (see fig. 14.22) and then click on Next.

Figure 14.22

Specify the message transfer mode you want to use.

10. The setup wizard then asks for your e-mail address and full name. Type in this information and click on Next (see fig. 14.23).

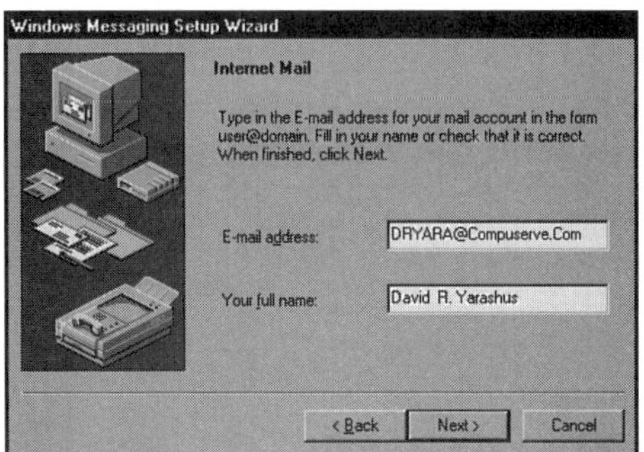

Figure 14.23

Type in your e-mail address and name.

11. Messaging sets up an address book for each user. If you already have one, type in the location; otherwise, Messaging creates one for you in the location indicated in figure 14.24. Click on Next.

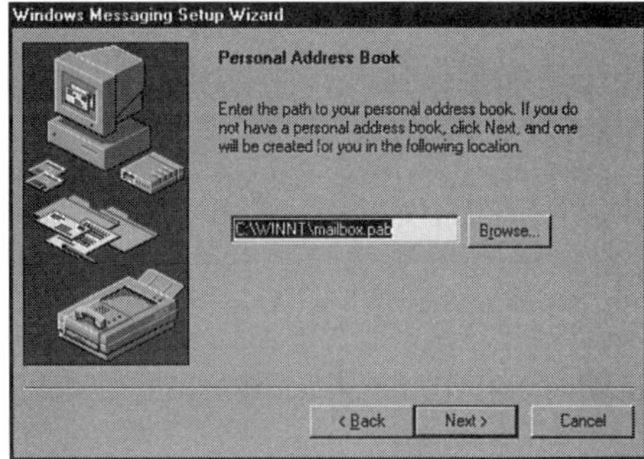

Figure 14.24

You can specify the location for your personal address book .

12. In addition to an address book, Messaging sets up a folder for your messages. If you have one you want to use, type in the location. If not, click on the Next button and Messaging creates one for you in the default location as shown in figure 14.25.

Figure 14.25

The setup wizard provides you with a default location for your Personal Folder.

13. The last setup screen lists what services have been configured. Click on the Finish button.

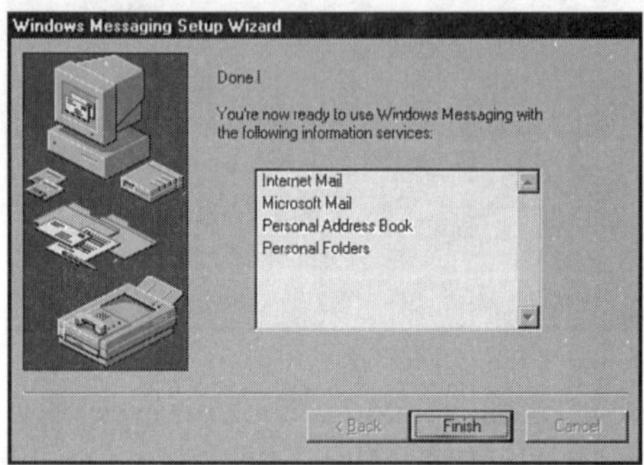

Figure 14.26

The last screen displays the list of the services you have set up.

You have now finished installing Windows NT Messaging and can proceed either to use it or to customize it.

Configuring Messaging

Communications tools are only as useful as you make them. Messaging for Windows NT Workstation is most useful as a communications tool if you know how to use its many powerful options. Although you probably won't need much coaching to use the basic features of sending and receiving e-mail, you won't really experience the power of Microsoft Messaging for Windows NT Workstation until you understand how to configure and make use of its advanced features.

Configuring Messaging Profiles

When you set up Messaging, you had to specify a profile name. You can add other profiles to correspond to different common situations you might find yourself in. You can configure one particular profile for in-office use, another for at home, and perhaps another for on the road. Here is the procedure for configuring a messaging profile:

1. Double-click on the Mail icon in the Control Panel.

2. The Profile you created when you set up Messaging will be the default profile. Click on the Show Profiles button. The Mail dialog box appears displaying each profile that you have set up (see fig. 14.27).

3. Click on the Add button to add another profile.

4. This starts the Windows Messaging Setup wizard again, this time to create the new profile.

Figure 14.27

To add another profile, click on the Add button.

Configuring Messaging Services for Windows NT Messaging

You can change the configuration options for the Microsoft Messaging client after installing it and setting it up.

1. Double-click on the Mail icon in the Control Panel.
2. Select Microsoft Mail from the Service tab in the Properties dialog box. Click on the Properties button. You see the following configuration tabs:
   - Connection
   - Logon
   - Delivery
   - LAN Configuration
   - Log

Connection Options

If you are on an office computer that always accesses the post office through a LAN, then different connection options are not particularly relevant. If you are using a laptop and need to connect while on the go, however, you will benefit greatly by understanding how to have your system automatically change the connection settings based on detecting whether you are going to connect to the post office through the network or via modem. The following steps take you through setting the connection options:

1. If you need to change the post office location, type the new location in the text box or Browse for it (see fig. 14.28). This might happen if you and your workstation are relocated to a different workgroup or if you change mail servers.

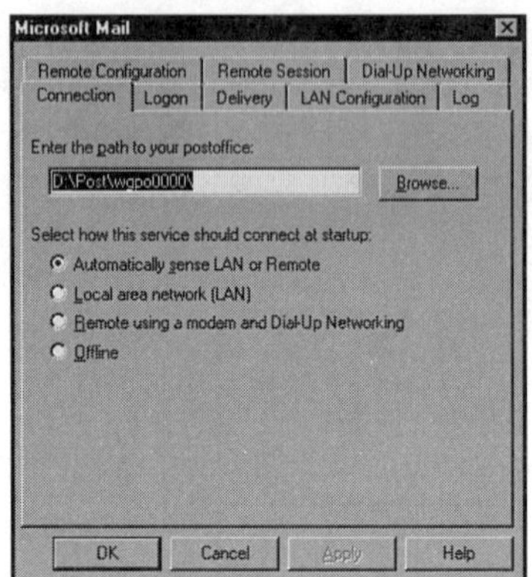

Figure 14.28
You can change how you connect to the post office using the Connection tab.

2. When you start mail, you have one of four options for connection:

   - **Automatically Sense LAN or Remote.** If you select the automatic detection of LAN or remote and the post office cannot determine which connection type is active, MS Mail prompts you to select one. If the post office cannot automatically detect this, however, there is probably a problem with your connection that you should look into fixing.
   - **Local Area Network.** Selecting Local Area Network specifies the network connection so that mail can be received and sent through your directly reachable post office.
   - **Remote Using a Modem and Dial-Up Networking.** If you specify Remote, all the mail you send will remain in your Outbox until you connect to the post office through your modem. You must have Dial-Up Networking configured to use this setting.
   - **Offline.** You will not be able to actually send or receive mail until the next time you connect if you select Offline, and messages you compose will accumulate in your Outbox.

3. After your changes, click on the Apply button.

Logon Options

Only the mail administrator can change a user's password by using the Postoffice Admin program; however, users can change their own passwords from the Logon tab using the following procedure:

1. To change your password, select the Logon tab.
2. Click on the Change Mailbox Password button.

3. The Change Mailbox Password dialog box appears (see fig. 14.29). Type in your old password and then type in the new one twice in the spaces provided. Typing the password a second time is a verification check in case you made a mistake typing it the first time. Trying to guess your own password that contains a typographical error can be virtually impossible—especially if you had a good password to start with.

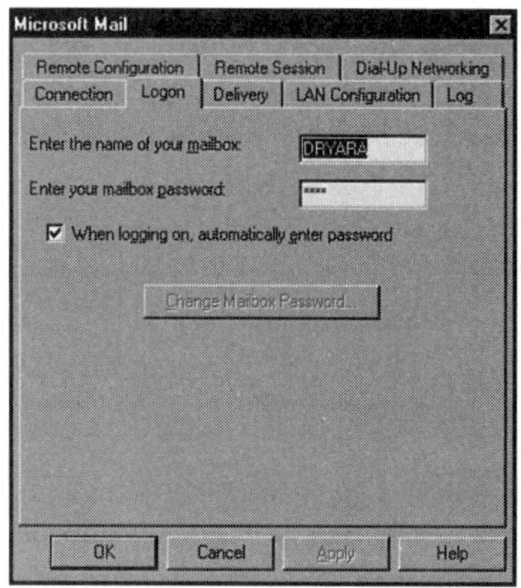

Figure 14.29
You can change your mail password from the Logon tab.

4. You can check the box to allow automatic password entry upon logon. This keeps you from having to remember your password for using Messaging and also expedites the initialization of the service—but at the cost of reduced security because you are no longer required to enter that password when accessing your mailbox from your workstation.

5. After your changes, click on the Apply button.

Delivery Options

Because Microsoft Messaging for Windows NT Workstation can interface with many different e-mail systems, it gives you configuration options that let you tell it how you would like your e-mail handled. The list below itemizes the options you might configure in a typical environment:

1. Check a box for enabling incoming mail, outgoing mail, or both.

2. If you want to prohibit delivery to certain types of mail, select the Address Types button and uncheck all those types.

3. You can specify how often you want your workstation to check for new messages.

4. If you have NetBIOS installed on your LAN, you can choose to have the recipients of your mail notified immediately by checking the Immediate Notification option.

5. Instead of maintaining two (or more) address lists, you can opt to use one master list by checking the box next to Display Global Address List only. This can save you from searching several different lists for a particular entry (see fig. 14.30).

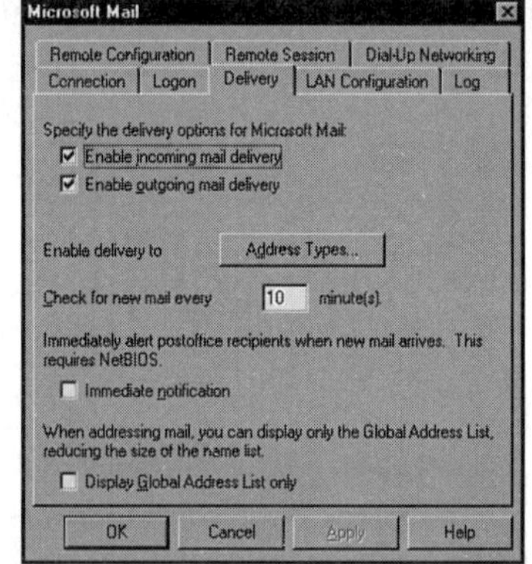

Figure 14.30

You can set how often Messaging checks for new mail on the Delivery tab.

LAN Configuration

Microsoft Messaging for Windows NT Workstation works well on a LAN and is used by many small companies. When configuring Microsoft Messaging for Windows NT Workstation, you can choose any of three options concerning the LAN connection to MS Mail (as shown in the following list and in figure 14.31). These settings do not apply if you are connecting with a modem.

- **Use Remote Mail.** This lets you move, copy, or delete your messages without downloading all of them. It is most useful in a LAN environment when you have very large email messages and you don't want to download an entire copy of each message.
- **Use Local Copy.** This lets you use a local copy of the post office address book instead of having to retrieve it from the shared environment each time you wanted to use it.
- **Use External Delivery Agent.** These are programs that handle moving the mail messages around on your behalf. External delivery agents are required to connect post offices together and to foreign mail systems. Microsoft's Exchange Server, a part of BackOffice, includes external delivery agents, as does MS Mail for PC Networks, and others are available separately. Workgroup installations that use only the software that comes with Windows NT Workstation will not have any external delivery agents available to them and will not be able to exchange mail with other workgroup post offices.

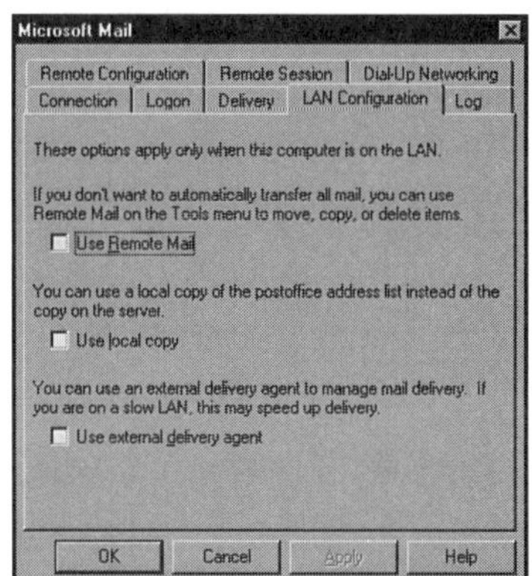

Figure 14.31

The LAN configuration options determine how mail is transferred.

You can safely leave these LAN configuration options at their default values. All are targeted toward improving performance on networks that have their e-mail post office on the other side of a slow line or lines.

Log Options

If you have any problems with Microsoft Messaging for Windows NT Workstation, you might want to keep a log of your client's interactions with the post office that is having the problem. Turning on logging takes a tiny bit of overhead, but not enough that you are likely to notice. When you need to configure logging, follow the procedure below:

1. Check the box to Maintain a Log of Session Events to keep track of important post office events (see fig. 14.32).

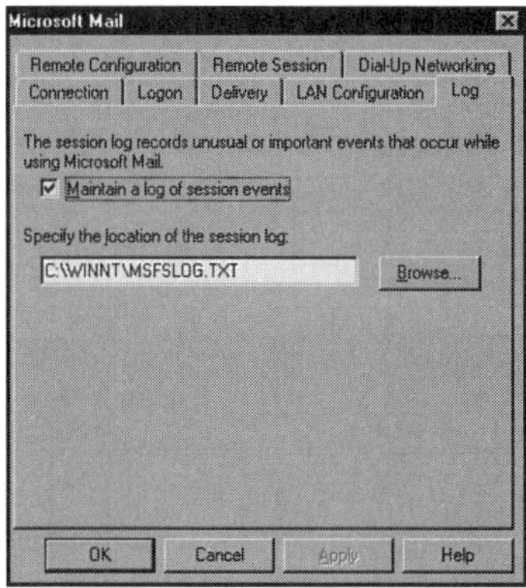

Figure 14.32

You can opt to keep a log of Mail events.

2. The default location is \%SystemRoot%\MSFLOG.TXT. You can specify a different location if necessary.

Following is a sample log. You can see the type of things that it keeps record of: who logs in, how much mail each receives and sends, and so on.

```
9/23/96 - 2:13PM - Connection type selected: "Local Area Network"
9/23/96 - 2:13PM - You are using the connection type "Local Area Network",
connected at a speed of 200000 Bytes/second.
9/23/96 - 2:13PM - Logged on to mailbox: "HRYARA".
9/23/96 - 2:13PM - Postoffice server: "c:\winnt\wgpo0000\".
9/23/96 - 2:14PM - Checking for mail. 0 item(s) to download.
10/5/96 - 2:03AM - Connection type selected: "Automatically sense LAN or
Remote"
10/5/96 - 2:03AM - You are using the connection type "Local Area Network",
connected at a speed of 200000 Bytes/second.
10/5/96 - 2:03AM - Logged on to mailbox: "DRYARA".
10/5/96 - 2:03AM - Postoffice server: "D:\Post\wgpo0000\".
10/5/96 - 5:38PM - Connection type selected: "Automatically sense LAN or
Remote"
10/5/96 - 5:38PM - You are using the connection type "Local Area Network",
connected at a speed of 200000 Bytes/second.
10/5/96 - 5:38PM - Logged on to mailbox: "DRYARA".
10/5/96 - 5:38PM - Postoffice server: "D:\Post\wgpo0000\".
10/5/96 - 5:39PM - Checking for mail. 0 item(s) to download.
10/5/96 - 5:39PM - Downloading Address Lists...
10/5/96 - 5:39PM - The Address Lists were successfully downloaded.

10/8/96 - 4:05AM - Connection type selected: "Automatically sense LAN or
Remote"
10/8/96 - 4:05AM - You are using the connection type "Local Area Network",
connected at a speed of 200000 Bytes/second.
10/8/96 - 4:05AM - Logged on to mailbox: "DRYARA".
10/8/96 - 4:05AM - Postoffice server: "D:\Post\wgpo0000\".
10/8/96 - 4:05AM - Checking for mail. 0 item(s) to download.
10/8/96 - 4:09AM - Checking for mail. 0 item(s) to download.
10/8/96 - 6:57PM - Sent mail "how cute you are!!". [ID:00000001]
10/8/96 - 6:58PM - Checking for mail. 1 item(s) to download.
10/8/96 - 6:58PM - Received mail "New Work Schedule!". [ID:00000001]
10/14/96 - 3:53PM - Connection type selected: "Automatically sense LAN or
Remote"
10/14/96 - 3:53PM - You are using the connection type "Local Area Network",
connected at a speed of 200000 Bytes/second.
```

```
10/14/96 - 3:53PM - Logged on to mailbox: "DRYARA".
10/14/96 - 3:53PM - Postoffice server: "D:\Post\wgpo0000\".
10/14/96 - 3:54PM - Checking for mail. 0 item(s) to download.
10/14/96 - 4:51PM - User requested to view session log.
10/14/96 - 4:55PM - Sent mail "Recent management changes ". [ID:00000006]
10/14/96 - 4:56PM - Checking for mail. 1 item(s) to download.
10/14/96 - 4:56PM - Received mail "Recent management changes ". [ID:00000006]
10/14/96 - 4:59PM - Connection type selected: "Automatically sense LAN or
Remote"
10/14/96 - 4:59PM - You are using the connection type "Local Area Network",
connected at a speed of 200000 Bytes/second.
10/14/96 - 4:59PM - Logged on to mailbox: "RWALT".
10/14/96 - 4:59PM - Postoffice server: "d:\post\wgpo0000\".
10/14/96 - 5:06PM - Checking for mail. 0 item(s) to download.
10/16/96 - 4:07PM - User requested to view session log.
10/16/96 - 4:10PM - Sent mail "certification exams". [ID:00000008]
10/16/96 - 4:11PM - Checking for mail. 0 item(s) to download.
10/16/96 - 6:37PM - Checking for mail. 0 item(s) to download.
10/16/96 - 6:39PM - Sent mail "Time sheets ". [ID:0000000A]
10/16/96 - 6:39PM - Checking for mail. 1 item(s) to download.
10/16/96 - 6:39PM - Received mail "Time sheets ". [ID:0000000A]
10/16/96 - 6:40PM - Processing BCC or NDR resend recipient. Sent mail "certifi-
cation exams". [ID:0000000C]
10/16/96 - 6:41PM - Processing BCC or NDR resend recipient. Sent mail "Network
IP addressing". [ID:0000000E]
10/16/96 - 6:41PM - Checking for mail. 2 item(s) to download.
10/16/96 - 6:41PM - Received mail "certification exams". [ID:0000000C]
10/16/96 - 6:41PM - Received mail "Network IP addressing". [ID:0000000E]
10/16/96 - 8:56PM - Connection type selected: "Automatically sense LAN or
Remote"
10/16/96 - 8:56PM - You are using the connection type "Local Area Network",
connected at a speed of 200000 Bytes/second.
10/16/96 - 8:56PM - Logged on to mailbox: "DRYARA".
10/16/96 - 8:56PM - Postoffice server: "D:\Post\wgpo0000\".
10/16/96 - 8:57PM - Checking for mail. 0 item(s) to download.
10/17/96 - 12:37AM - Connection type selected: "Automatically sense LAN or
Remote"
10/17/96 - 12:37AM - You are using the connection type "Local Area Network",
connected at a speed of 200000 Bytes/second.
10/17/96 - 12:38AM - User canceled session.
10/17/96 - 12:38AM - Logged on to mailbox: "DRYARA".
10/17/96 - 12:38AM - Connection offline. No postoffice available.
```

In the preceding log file, you can see that the connection type was auto-detected as a LAN connection. It was really on a local share, but local post offices are accessed in the same way as ones on LANs. You will typically see higher access speeds for local post offices than for ones that you access through a network.

Configuring the Personal Address Book

On the Delivery tab, you can set the option of using only the global address list. As long as the global list is not unreasonably long, using it might be easier than trying to maintain separate address lists. You might choose to keep several address books, however, perhaps to use with different e-mail services. You can set up a different address book for each profile you configure if you want. The following steps take you through the options for configuring your personal address book:

1. From the Services tab, highlight Personal Address Book and click on the Properties button.

2. You can change the default name and location by typing in new information in the windows. If you have several profiles and do not want to use the same address book for them, you can select a different address book name and location for each.

3. If you want your list displayed and sorted by first names, select First Name. If you want your address list displayed and sorted by last name, select Last Name (see fig. 14.33).

4. If you have set up several personal address books, you might want to use the Notes tab to make notes about what each one is for. For example, you might keep separate address books for your business contacts and for your family and friends.

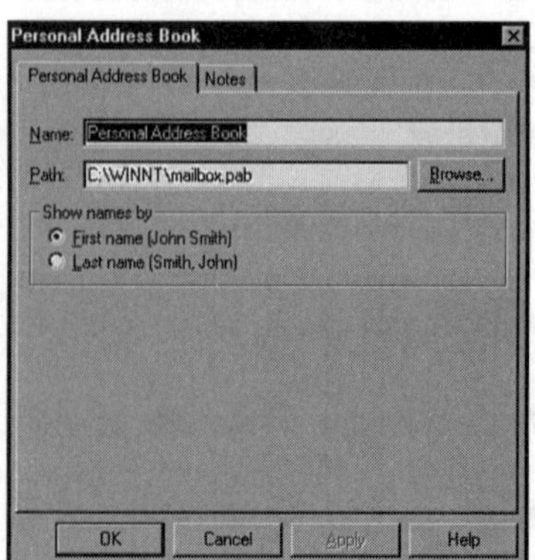

Figure 14.33

The properties of your personal address book.

Configuring Personal Folders

Microsoft Messaging for Windows NT Workstation allows you to download and store messages in your personal folders. There are several configurable options for your personal folders: you can rename them, password protect them, or compress them to reduce the wasted space from deleted messages.

1. From the Services tab, highlight Personal Folders and click on the Properties button to display the General Properties tab of your personal folders.

2. You can change the name of your personal folders and the password to access them.

3. If you want to reduce the size of the folder file, click on the Compact Now button (see fig. 14.34).

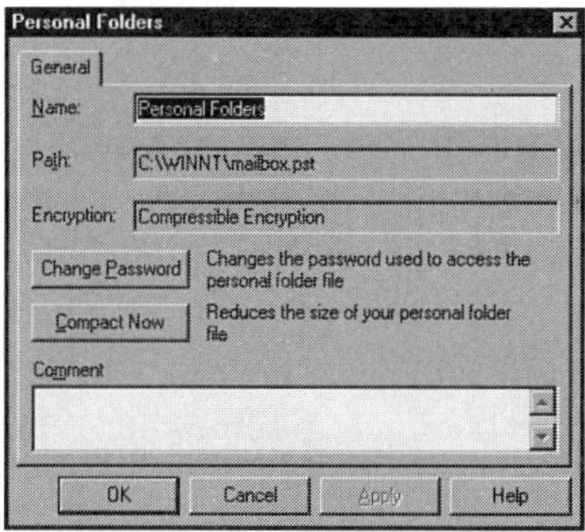

Figure 14.34

You can compact the amount of space used by your personal folders .

Configuring Messaging Delivery

Microsoft Messaging for Windows NT Workstation defaults to delivering your e-mail to your personal folders. If you want to change where Microsoft Messaging for Windows NT Workstation delivers your e-mail, the steps below show you how:

1. The Delivery tab controls where your new mail is put. The default location is to deliver mail to your personal folders.

2. When you send mail, the addresses are processed by both Microsoft Mail and Internet Mail, in that order by default. If the majority of the mail you send is Internet mail, you might want to reverse the order. Highlight Internet Mail and click on the up arrow button. If you have other mail services, they might also show up on this list (see fig. 14.35).

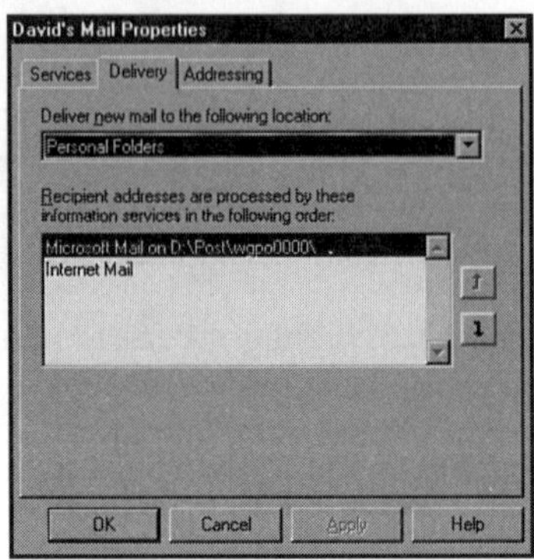

Figure 14.35

Set where you want your mail delivered to on the Delivery tab.

Configuring Messaging Addressing

Microsoft Messaging for Windows NT Workstation allows you to customize how the default address list you use looks.

1. The Addressing tab controls the address list information.
2. Select the address list you use most often when working in Messaging to display first from the drop-down list.
3. The default location for personal addresses is in the Personal Address Book. Unless you have another address book set up somewhere else, this is your only option (see fig 14.36).
4. You can choose the order in which the addresses are to be processed—whether your personal address book goes first or the postoffice list.

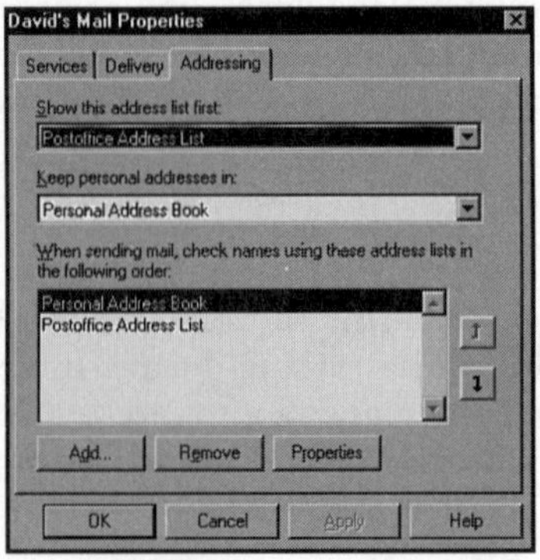

Figure 14.36

Set the address book you use most often to display first.

Using Messaging (Getting into It)

Messaging provides a convenient way to keep in touch. This e-mail tool is ideal for workgroups or local area networks.

Reading Your mail

Most of the time you spend with Messaging you will probably be reading or writing mail. Here is how you read mail:

1. Double-click on the Inbox icon on your desktop. If there is no Inbox icon, you need to install Messaging, which is covered in the preceding sections. You can also start Messaging through the Programs folder on the Start menu.

2. The main Messaging window appears with your first message delivered to your Inbox. In figure 14.37, you can see a message indicated by an envelope. The From, Subject, and Received information columns are all filled out. The mail you receive remains in your Inbox until you remove it by deleting it or saving it to a folder. Reading the mail does not take it out of the Inbox.

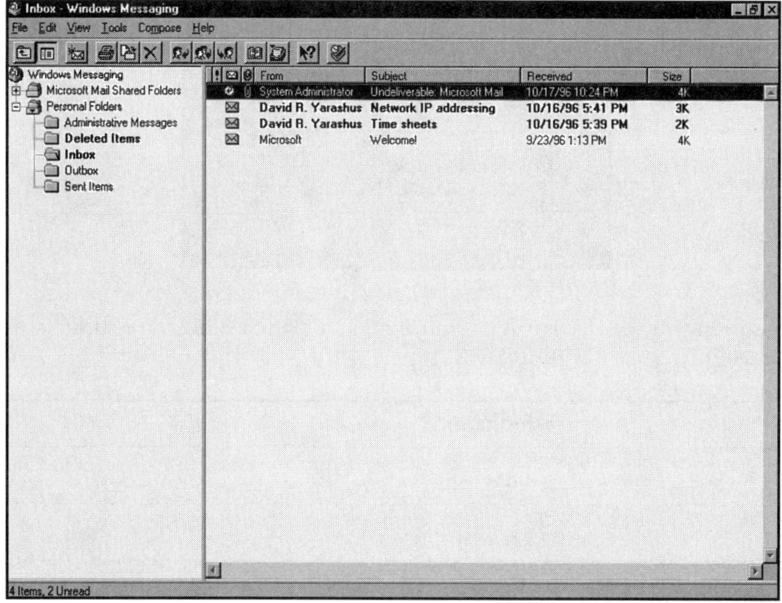

Figure 14.37

Your first mail is a Welcome Message.

3. Double-click on the message line. This displays the text editor interface in Messaging (If you have Microsoft Word installed, Messaging can use it as the text editor; otherwise, Messaging uses WordPad. The difference is only in the added

text features; Messaging works the same either way.) The first message you receive is a welcome message containing basic information on how to use messaging.

4. If you want to save a message, select Save from the File menu. The Save As dialog box appears. In figure 14.38, you can see the default directory WordMail and the file name. You can choose to save the mail in three different formats:

   - Text only—saved as *.TXT
   - Rich text format—saved as *.RTF
   - Message format—saved as *.MSG

The style is indicated in the file extension. If your message comes with attachments, you can opt to save the attachments only or the message only.

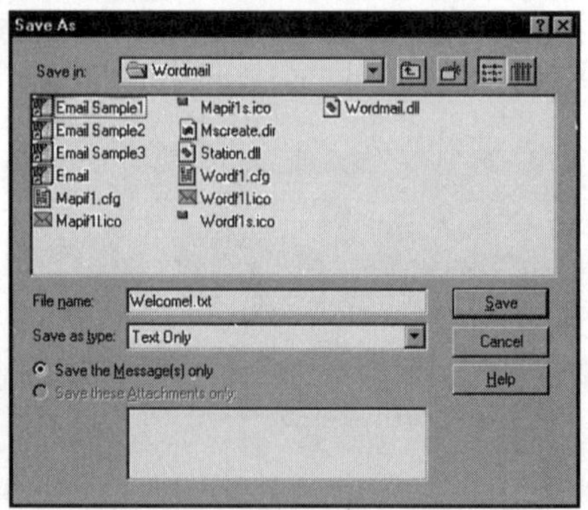

Figure 14.38

You can decide how you want the message saved.

Several notations help you see the status of your mail at a glance. These are summarized in the following table:

Item	Indicator
Unread mail	Bold font
Received mail	Envelope
Returned mail	Red return arrow
Mail with attachments	Paper clip
High-priority mail	Red exclamation mark
Low-priority mail	Blue down arrow

Replying To or Sending Mail

Now that you have seen how to read mail and the options associated with doing that, it is time to discuss sending mail. This section covers authoring new messages, replying to messages, and the various options associated with these functions.

1. To send someone a message, double-click on the Inbox icon on your desktop.
2. Click on the New Message icon on the toolbar (the envelope) or select New Message from the Compose menu.
3. The Messaging text editor window appears (see fig. 14.39).

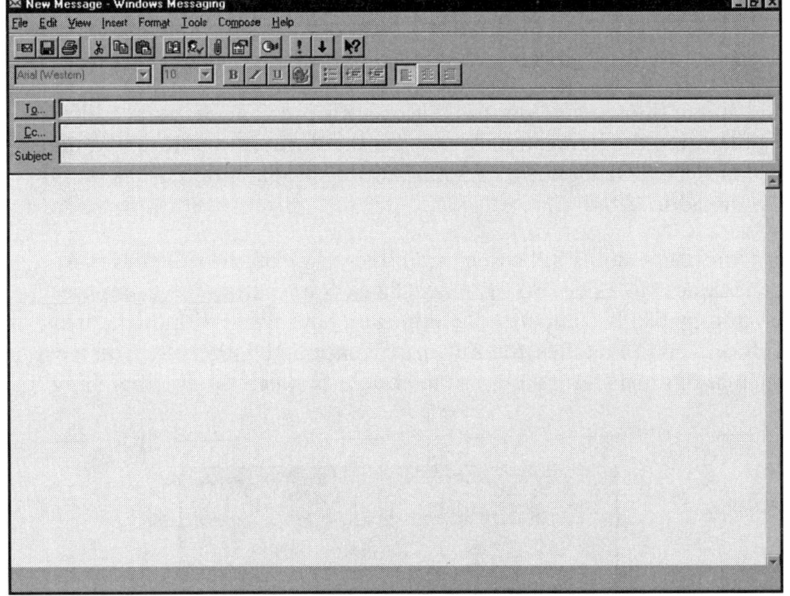

Figure 14.39
Use the Messaging text editor to compose a message.

4. In the To address field, type in the person's name you want to correspond with. You can click on the address book icon (the open book) to display your list of names (see fig. 14.40). You can also access the address book through the Compose menu.
5. The address dialog box shows either the Postoffice Address List or your Personal Address List. You can select between the two in the top text box.
6. In the list, you see the names and their respective mail types displayed. They are displayed in the order you specified when setting up your address book. In figure 14.40, the names appear as first name and then last name. (You have to scroll over at the bottom to see the mail types.)

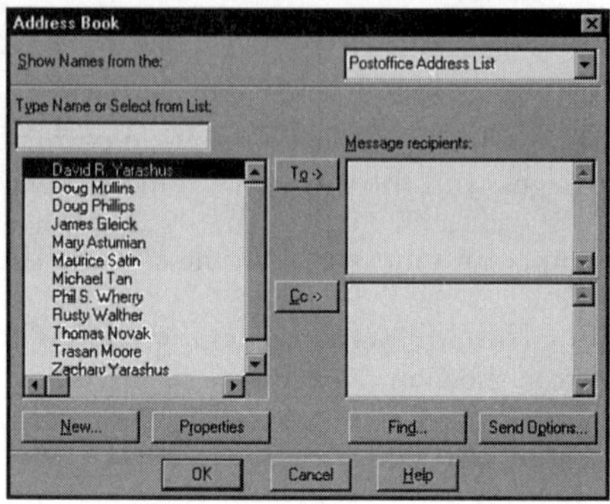

Figure 14.40

Click the address book icon to display your address book.

7. Highlight a name and click on the To or Cc button. The name appears in the appropriate text box. You can repeat this for as many names as you choose.

8. You can add any of the names from the Postoffice list to your personal address book by highlighting the name and clicking on the Properties button. On the Properties dialog box, click on the Personal Address Book button. Click on OK to return to the address book.

9. If you don't know a person's full name or address, click on the Check Names icon (red check next to a person) or select Check Names from the Compose menu. This automatically compares the name you have typed with the address book. If only one entry matches, the full entry is supplied. Otherwise, you see a message such as figure 14.41, asking you to choose between the two matching entries.

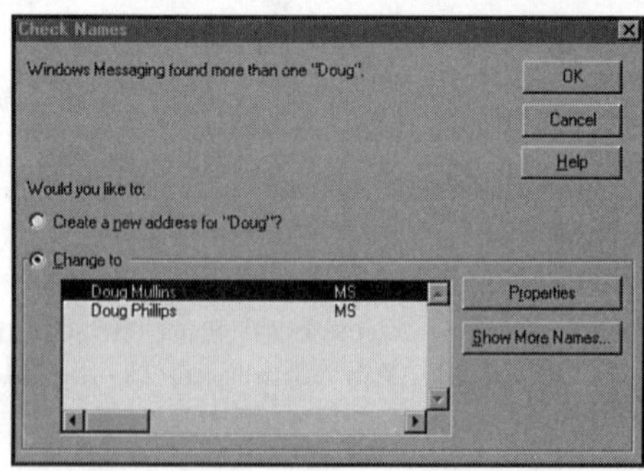

Figure 14.41

Check names displays the matching entries.

Replying to a particular message is simple. All you have to do is click on the Reply To icon, type your message, and send it. Here are the steps for replying to a message:

1. When you have read a message and want to reply to it, you can click on the Reply To icon, which is indicated by the arrow pointing to a single person. You can also

select Reply To from the Compose menu. This opens the Messaging window. In figure 14.42, you can see the address is already filled out, and the received message is quoted in your text area.

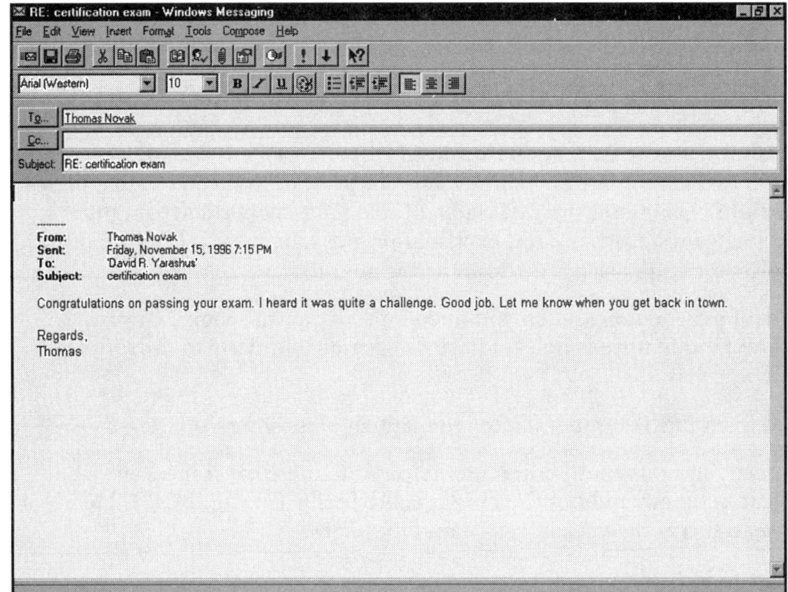

Figure 14.42
A reply automatically quotes the original message.

2. The quoted addressing information and text can be a helpful reference for your message. (Changing the quote settings is covered in the following section, "Using Messaging Features.") You can leave the text quoted or delete all or part of it. Type in your message in the text area and click the send icon from the toolbar when you are finished.

Using Messaging Features

Messaging includes a user-friendly mail interface and has many features that make sending messages even easier. These features are presented in the following list and detailed in the following sections.

- Using find
- Sending attachments
- Customizing the toolbar
- Setting Messaging options
- Using the address book

Using Find

After receiving a number of messages, invariably there will be one that suddenly becomes important, which for some reason you cannot find. Even though the subject headers give a clue as to the contents, it may not be enough. You definitely have better things to do than to reread all your mail to find the one important message.

You can organize your messages in several ways so that this type of thing does not happen—or at least not often. By adding folders with meaningful titles to your personal files, you can move mail you have read from your Inbox to the appropriate folder, such as Administrative Messages, Business Contacts, or Personal Messages. For those messages that you automatically know will be important, you can change their priority level by right-clicking on the message and selecting Properties from the menu. A high-priority message has a red exclamation mark next to it. (On the other hand, a low-priority message has a blue down arrow next to it.)

However, there still may be times when you need a particular message that you cannot locate. The Find feature is helpful here. It operates similarly to the Find feature in NT Explorer:

1. Select Find from the Tools menu after you launch Messaging.
2. You can specify several search criteria to help locate the correct message. The more you can remember about the message, the better (see fig. 14.43). Here is a list of the search criteria you can use to find messages:
   - Folder to look in
   - Who sent the message
   - Sent to whom
   - Direct send or a carbon copy
   - Subject
   - Message body

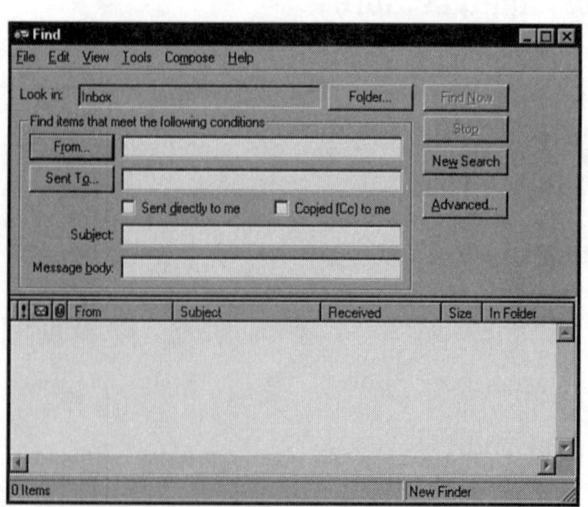

Figure 14.43

The Find utility in Messaging can be very helpful when you need to find a specific message.

3. Click on the Advanced button for more search options (see fig. 14.44). Here are the advanced search options provided by the Find utility:

    - Message size
    - Date parameters
    - Unread items
    - Items with attachments
    - Items that do not meet search specifications
    - Priority levels
    - Sensitivity levels

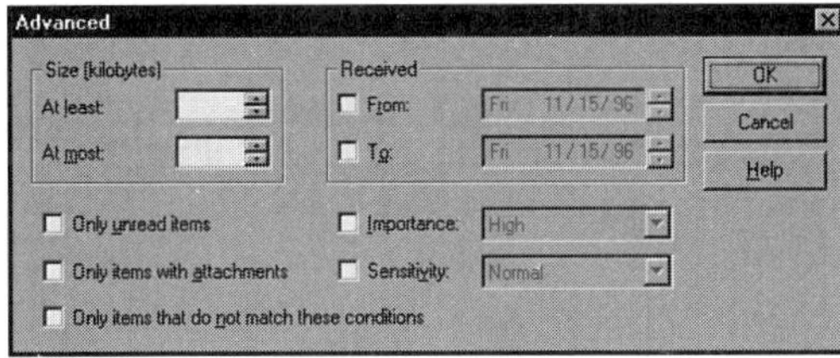

Figure 14.44

Use the Advanced find settings to find a message based on more detailed criteria such as date parameters.

Sending Attachments

The capability to include attachments might be one of the most useful Messaging features. You do not have to cut and paste other files into your message, you can send them as attachments:

1. Open Messaging and type your message.
2. Click on the place where you want to locate the attachment.
3. Select File, Picture, or Object from the Insert menu.
4. If you are attaching a file, select the file you want from the Insert File dialog box.
5. You can check Link to File or As Attachment. (You cannot attach a local file as a link.)

The linked file is imported into the text of your message. Make sure that the linked file is in a location accessible to the recipient. The attached file appears as an icon in the message. When the recipient clicks on the icon, the attached file appears.

Customizing the Toolbar

You can customize the toolbar to make it easier to do certain functions:

1. Select Customize Toolbar from the Tools menu. The Customize Toolbar dialog box appears (see fig. 14.45).

Figure 14.45

You can use the Customize Toolbar dialog box to change the Messaging toolbar.

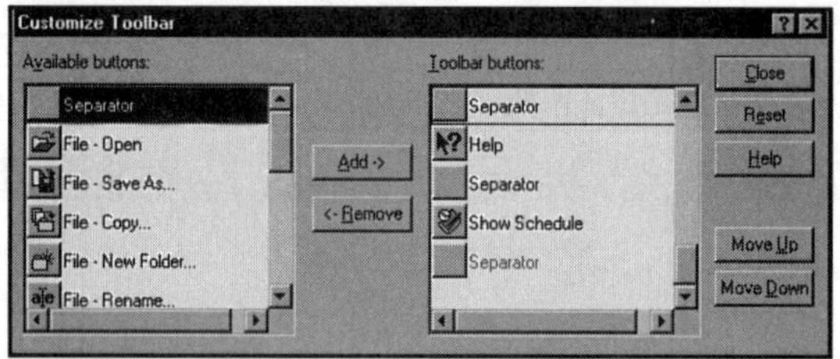

2. Highlight the icon/function you want in the Available buttons box. Click on the Add button.

3. If you want to remove certain icons from the existing toolbar, highlight the icon in the Toolbar buttons window and click on the Remove button.

4. To change the order of the icons, highlight one and click on the Move Up or Move Down button.

5. The display on the actual toolbar dynamically shows the changes you are making. If you decide that you don't like the result, click on the Reset button. This will undo any of the changes you made. Click on the Close button when you are finished.

Setting Messaging Options

You can change a variety of settings to customize the way Messaging works:

1. Double-click on the Inbox icon on your desktop.

2. Select Options from the Tools menu.

3. The General tab offers the following options:

   When new mail arrives:

   - Play a sound.
   - Briefly change the pointer.
   - Display a notification message.

Deleting items:

- Warn before permanently deleting items.
- Empty the Deleted items folder upon exiting.

When starting Windows Messaging:

- Prompt for a profile to be used.
- Always use this profile.

Show Tooltips

4. The Read tab offers these options:

   When selecting automatically, select entire word.

   After moving or deleting an open item:

   - Open the item above it.
   - Open the item below it.
   - Return to Windows Messaging.

   When replying to or forwarding an item:

   - Include the original text.
   - Indent the original text.
   - Close the original item.

   Use this font for the reply text.

5. The Send tab offers these options:

   When sending mail:

   - Use this font.
   - Request a receipt be sent back when item has been read.
   - Request a receipt be sent back when item has been delivered.
   - Set sensitivity.

- Set importance.
- Save a copy of the item in the Sent Items folder.
- Use simplified now on internet 'mailto:' and File.Send.

6. The Spelling tab offers these options:

   General spelling options:

   - Always suggest replacements for misspelled words.
   - Always check spelling before sending.

   When checking spelling, always ignore:

   - Words in UPPERCASE.
   - Words with numbers.
   - The original text in a reply or forward.

Using the Address Book

The address book is really two separate components—the Postoffice address list and your personal address book. They are linked together for easier access. The Postoffice address list contains the addresses of all the users in your local post office. Your personal address book can contain any or all of those plus anyone else you want to add.

To add users to your personal address book, perform the following steps:

1. Click the address book icon to open the address book. If the user is in the Postoffice list, make sure that the Postoffice list is displaying.
2. Find and highlight the name in the Postoffice list.
3. Click the book icon, or select Add to Personal Address Book from the File menu.
4. If you want to make a new entry that is not from the Postoffice list, click on the New button.
5. Select the address type. Click on OK.
6. Type in the New Mail Address Properties. The New Mail Properties dialog boxes differ for each different type of address.

One reason you might want to add a user to your personal address book is the properties information. The Properties available for the post office address book are rather general. The first page contains e-mail address information; the second page contains phone number and office information. The properties available for the personal address book are much more useful. In addition to the two address information tabs provided with the postoffice list, there are three other tabs for individuals in your personal address book:

- Business
- Phone Numbers
- Notes

In this way, the personal address book is more like a real address book than just a list with names and e-mail addresses. You can add any information for use regardless of whether or not you are e-mailing the person (see fig. 14.46).

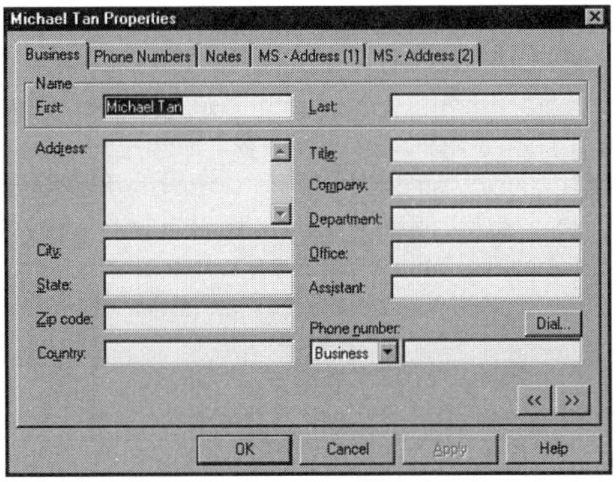

Figure 14.46

You can keep track of a lot of information about individuals in your personal address book.

If you frequently mail the same message to a certain group of individuals (coworkers or customers, for example), you can make a group mailing list by setting up a distribution list. To set up the distribution list and add members, follow these steps:

1. Click on the address book icon to open the address book.
2. Click on the New button and select Personal Distribution List from the Select Entry Type text box.
3. Make sure you that have selected Put This Entry In The Personal Address Book if you want to save this distribution list for future mailings. Click on OK.
4. In the New Personal Distribution List Properties dialog box, type in the name of the distribution list.

5. To add users, click on the Add/Remove Members button.
6. In the Edit New Personal Distribution List Members text box, select which list of names you want displayed.
7. Highlight a name you want, or type the name in the space provided and click on the Members button.
8. Click on OK to complete the list.

The list now appears in your personal address book by its name with a group icon next to it.

Understanding Internet Mail

If you are going to connect to the Internet with your computer either through a dialup connection or your network, you will need to make sure that you have TCP/IP configured. If you plan on dialing in, you need to be sure that your Internet Service Provider (ISP) supports the Point-to-Point protocol (PPP) or the Serial Line Internet Protocol (SLIP) so you can make the TCP/IP connection over a modem. You also have to make sure that you have access to a server that uses the Simple Mail Transfer Protocol (SMTP) and version three of the post office protocol (POP3). The Internet Mail component of Windows Messaging uses SMTP to send mail and can only receive mail from a POP3 server. To use a modem to connect to the Internet, the modem must be installed and configured as well as the dial-up networking service. This is covered in detail in Chapter 13, "Remote Access Services (RAS) and Dial-Up Networking."

You might want to set up a separate profile for using Internet Mail. Although this is not necessary, it can make the configuration options easier for the different uses.

Configuring Messaging Services for Internet Mail

After the initial Messaging setup, you can further configure or customize your original configuration through the following procedures:

1. Double-click on the Mail icon in the Control Panel.
2. The profile you created when you set up Messaging will be the default profile. You can add another profile to use for Internet mail if you want. The first screen that appears is the Properties screen (see fig. 14.47).
3. Highlight Internet Mail in the services list and click on the Properties button.

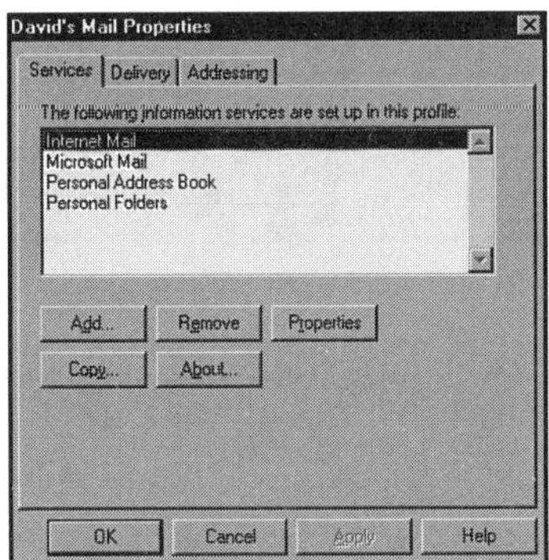

Figure 14.47

The Services tab of the current profile lists which services you have installed.

4. The Internet Mail dialog box appears. The General tab displays both your personal information and your mailbox information. You can edit any of the entries if they need updating. Click on Apply after you have made your changes, if any were needed. You can configure two other features—message format and mail forwarding (see fig. 14.48).

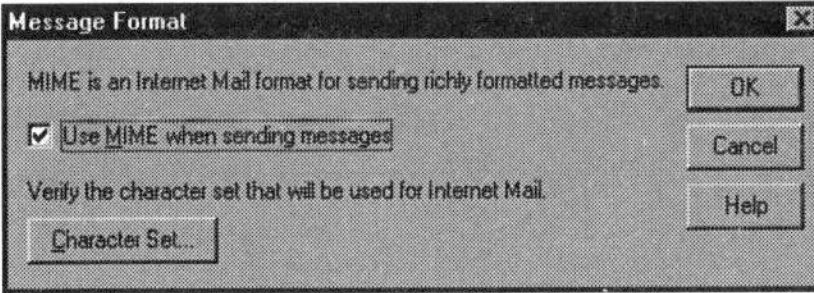

Figure 14.48

The General tab of Internet Mail dialog box displays your name and Internet address.

5. Click on the Message Format button to select the MIME format for Internet Mail (see fig. 14.49). MIME stands for Multipurpose Internet Mail Extensions, and it is a standards-based way of sending binary file attachments through the Internet as encoded text. To verify the character set that will be used with the Internet Mail, click on the Character Set button. The default setting for MIME is ISO-8859-1. The default setting if you are not using MIME is US ASCII. Click on OK to return to the General tab.

6. Click on the Advanced Options button to specify the server to forward outbound mail to. This needs to be the name or IP address of a POP3 mail server. Click on OK to return to the General tab (see fig. 14.50).

Figure 14.49

The default message format is MIME.

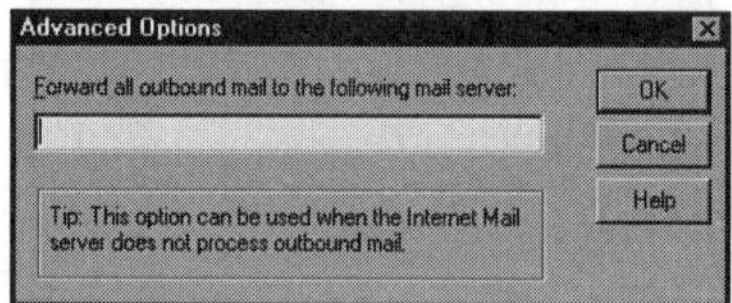

Figure 14.50

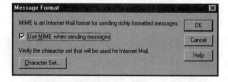

You can choose to forward outbound mail to the specified server.

7. Select the Connection tab if you need to edit any connection information (see fig. 14.51).

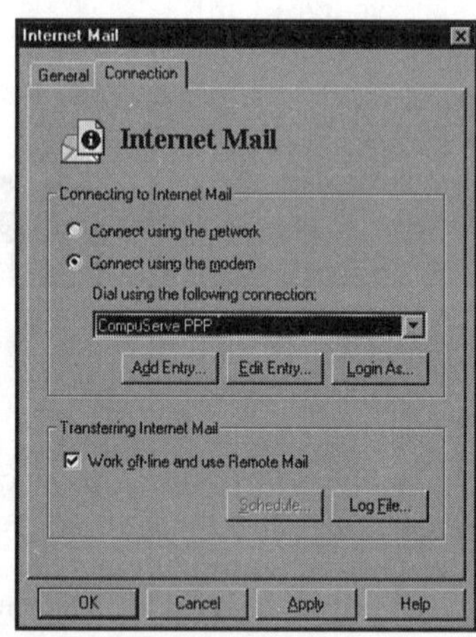

Figure 14.51

You can change the way you access your Internet Mail on the Connection tab.

8. You can choose between using a network or a modem connection. If you use a portable computer and configure multiple profiles, you may want to select the network connection for one mail profile (when docked) and the modem connection for another mail profile (when undocked). The mail profiles are independent of the hardware or user profiles you may have configured elsewhere for Windows NT Workstation.

9. If you choose to add or edit the connection provider, the Add or Edit Phonebook Entry dialog box appears. The phone book is covered a bit later in this section.

10. You can change your logon name and password by clicking on the Login As button.

11. If you do not work off-line, you can schedule your mail to check for new messages at regular intervals. The lowest setting is one minute. By selecting a frequent message check, you will be taking up a small amount of processor time and possibly slowing other applications, but the bigger issue may have to do with billing. Imagine being in a hotel overnight and leaving your system configured for a long-distance call to the office (at hotel rates) every minute! The default setting is 15 minutes.

12. The Log File button allows you three choices for logging:

    - No Logging
    - Basic
    - Troubleshooting

    If you choose to log, especially for troubleshooting purposes, you may want to rename the log file \%Systemroot%\IMAIL.LOG after a download, or it will be overwritten. Following is a sample log file in troubleshooting mode of a failed connection.

```
RAS:  Connecting to [Office PPP] on Wed Oct 16 20:04:52 1996
RAS:  Connected to [Office PPP] on Wed Oct 16 20:05:30 1996
POP3: Connecting to host [10.25.32.10] on Wed Oct 16 20:05:34 1996
Failed in connect: (10049) Can't assign requested address
POP3: ERROR: Connecting to host [10.25.32.10] failed on Wed Oct 16
20:05:34 1996

POP3: Connecting to host [10.5.2.5] on Wed Oct 16 20:06:04 1996
Failed in connect: (10065) Host is unreachable
POP3: ERROR:Connecting to host [10.5.2.5] failed on Wed Oct 16 20:06:49 1996
RAS: (15) Disconnecting from [Office PPP] on Wed Oct 16 20:06:53 1996
RAS: (15) Disconnected from [Office PPP] on Wed Oct 16 20:06:56 1996
```

13. Click on the Apply button if you have made any changes and then click on OK to return to the Services tab.

Using Internet Mail

If you want to access Internet mail through Messaging, open the Remote Mail window as described below:

1. Double-click on the Inbox icon on your desktop.

2. Select Remote mail from the Tools menu (see fig. 14.52).

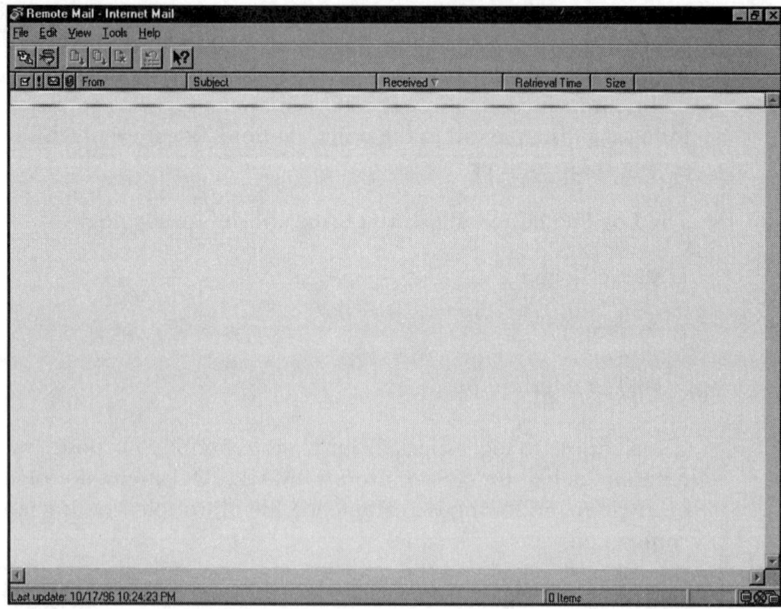

Figure 14.52

Use the Remote Mail - Internet Mail window to send Internet mail.

3. Click on the connect icon or select Connect from the Tools menu. The connection cable at the bottom right of the window displays the status of your connection.

4. Type in your user name and password in the Connect To dialog box. Click on OK.

5. After the modem dials your ISP, you see a status of the download. Any messages in your Outbox will now be sent.

6. You see the same type of display in your Internet mail window as in the Messaging window—each mail subject header has a sender, time and date received, and the size.

7. From this list, you can decide if you want to download any or all of the messages. You can also delete, move, or copy messages without reading them. Mark the messages by highlighting a given message and selecting the appropriate Mark option from the Edit menu. If you want to select all the messages, choose Select All from the Edit menu.

8. After you have finished sending and receiving mail, close the Internet Mail window.

9. You can send mail at any time from the Messaging window by selecting Deliver Now from the Tools menu. Select Microsoft Mail, or Internet Mail, or All Services. (If your profile only has the Internet service available, there will not be an option.)

Messaging and Exchange Server

Microsoft Messaging for Windows NT Workstation has a complicated history. It is the Windows NT version of the Windows 95 Exchange workgroup client, but during the beta process, Microsoft decided that having two different products named Exchange (the client for workgroup environments that comes with NT Workstation and the Server for enterprise environments that is a part of Microsoft's BackOffice suite) running on Windows NT platforms would not be a good idea from a marketing point of view. At that point, they decided to rename the Windows NT Workstation e-mail client "Windows Messaging" or "Microsoft Messaging for Windows NT." You can still find many references to Exchange in Microsoft's documentation where something like "Windows Messaging client" would be more appropriate.

When you need more connectivity than you get with the Microsoft Messaging for Windows NT Workstation software, you will need to buy and install a mail server. This might happen, for example, if you set up a post office using the tools that came with Windows NT Workstation and then decide that you want to install an SMTP gateway to connect your post office to the Internet. Another common reason would be that you need a gateway between your post office and some other mail system.

Although the Windows NT Messaging client can connect to any mail service with a MAPI driver, it is not possible to install just the MAPI driver for Exchange Server and configure the Windows Messaging client to use it. When you select Services from the Tools menu and try to add a new service to install the Exchange Server MAPI driver, it updates your entire messaging installation, installing a new client program for you at the same time that it installs the Exchange Server as a service option.

This installation, however, recognizes the copy of Microsoft Messaging that you have and offers to update it. The Exchange client installation even refers to itself as a newer copy of Windows Messaging. If you allow it to install into the same directory, the new Exchange client will keep all of the customizations and settings that you made to your Windows Messaging client. After you have updated your Messaging installation to make it an Exchange client, you will see only a few differences. The most obvious one will be a different splash screen when launching the new Messaging client (the Exchange for Windows NT client) than when you launched the version that came with Windows NT Workstation 4.

The Windows NT Exchange client also has a few additional options available from its Tools menu for features that only make sense to implement when you have server-based e-mail. These include a big favorite, the Out of Office Assistant. This allows you to apply server-based rules to incoming messages and to send them notification that you are out of the office. This sort of tool is normally used when people go on vacation as opposed to when they step out to lunch.

Other than the improved choices you have under the Tools menu, almost everything you see will be identical to the Microsoft Messaging for Windows NT client that this chapter discussed in detail, so you won't have any trouble using Exchange as a mail server with Windows NT Workstation clients.

Working Off-Line and Dialing In for Messages

One of the conveniences of the modern work environment is the greater freedom people have in where they work. If you are not connected to the network or a modem, and you want to write e-mails, Microsoft Messaging for Windows NT will let you. You need to select the option for working off-line. This holds your mail in the Outbox until you do connect to the network. Otherwise, Microsoft Messaging for Windows NT Workstation attempts to send your mail, and the mail is returned to you as undeliverable.

Remote Mail Configuration

If you will be using a laptop in a docked and undocked state, you may want to configure a separate profile for each. One profile can be configured for network access to the post office; the other can be configured for remote access.

Dial-up networking must be installed and configured to work off-line using remote mail. This is covered in detail in Chapter 13.

Remote Configuration

If you are going to use remote mail, go through the following steps to specify how you will use this service:

1. Double-click on the Mail icon in the Control Panel.

2. Select Microsoft Mail from the Services tab and click on the Properties button.

3. Select the Remote Configuration tab (see fig. 14.53).

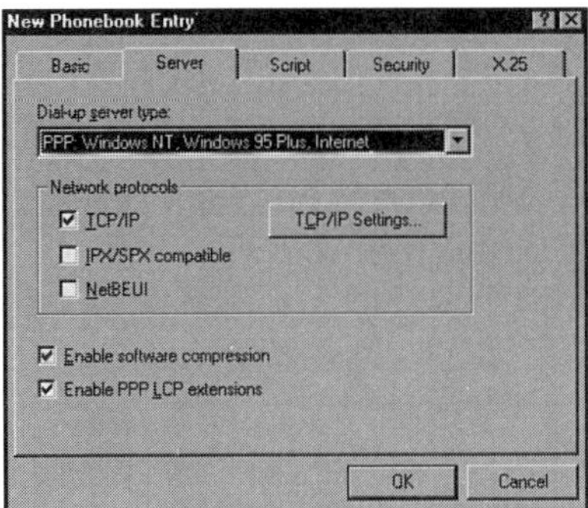

Figure 14.53

Use the Remote Configuration tab to change your remote connection options.

4. You can set up to three options concerning the remote connection to MS Mail using a modem and Dial-Up Networking. These settings do not apply if you are connecting through the LAN. The options are as follows:

   - **Remote Mail.** This lets you move, copy, or delete your messages without downloading all of them. It is most useful over dial-up lines because you often might not want to download an entire copy of each message.
   - **Use Local Copy.** This lets you use a local copy of the post office address book instead of having to retrieve it from the shared environment each time you wanted to use it.
   - **Use External Delivery Agent.** These are programs that handle moving the mail messages around on your behalf. External delivery agents are required to connect post offices together and to foreign mail systems. Microsoft's Exchange Server, a part of BackOffice, includes external delivery agents, as does MS Mail for PC Networks, and others are available separately. Workgroup installations that use only the software that comes with Windows NT Workstation will not have any external delivery agents available to them and will not be able to exchange mail with other workgroup post offices.

Checking the Remote Mail option holds the mail in your Outbox until you connect to the postoffice and send it. If you do not have access to the postoffice and want to use the postoffice address list to address your mail, select the Use Local copy option. To expedite remote mail delivery, you can select Use External Delivery Agent.

Remote Session

If you are using a remote connection, you can configure several options to make mail even more convenient:

1. Select the Remote Session tab.

2. To automatically start a Dial-Up Networking session when you launch mail, select the checkbox next to the When This Service Is Started option.
3. The dial-up session remains connected unless you terminate it. You can configure it, however, to terminate automatically at three points: after retrieving mail headers, after sending and receiving mail, and when you exit.

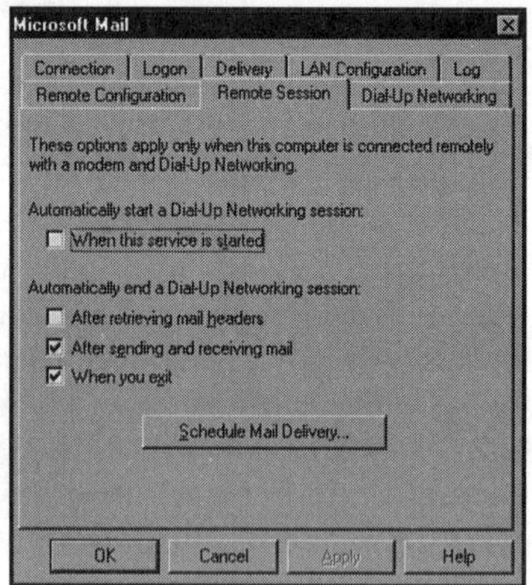

Figure 14.54
Set how you want a remote session to terminate.

4. Just as you can schedule Mail using a LAN connection to check for new messages at a regular interval, you can schedule mail delivery using a remote connection. Click on the Schedule Mail Delivery button.
5. The Scheduled Remote Mail Delivery window appears and lists any currently scheduled delivery times and dates. Click on the Add button.
6. In the Add Scheduled Session dialog box, you can use any remote connection you have configured, or connect to your dial-up server for your scheduled delivery. Select from the drop-down list under Use.
7. Set how often you want your mail delivery. Your choices are as follows:
    - Every—at a fixed time interval
    - Weekly—on specified days and the given time
    - Once—at a given time

Being able to schedule mail delivery is particularly convenient if you use your laptop at home only on the weekends and want to automatically use a remote connection for mail just on Saturday and Sunday (see fig. 14.55).

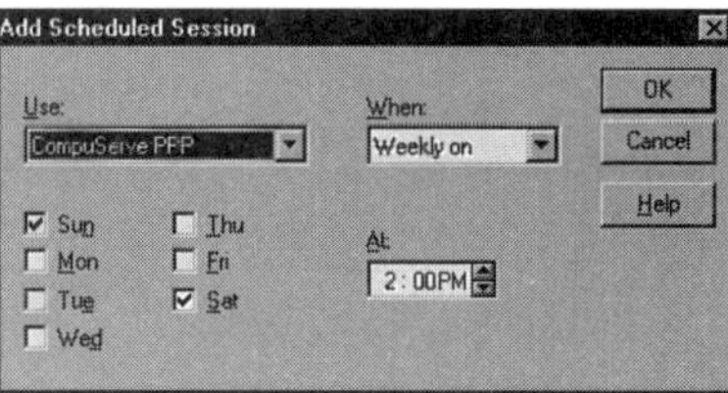

Figure 14.55

You can Schedule a dial-up session.

Dial-Up Networking

Dial-Up Networking is covered in more detail in Chapter 13, but this section gives you the basics of what you will need to make e-mail connections over dial-up lines.

1. On the Dial-Up Networking tab, you can set which dial-up server you want to use, a retry interval for failed connections, and a confirmation level (see fig. 14.56).

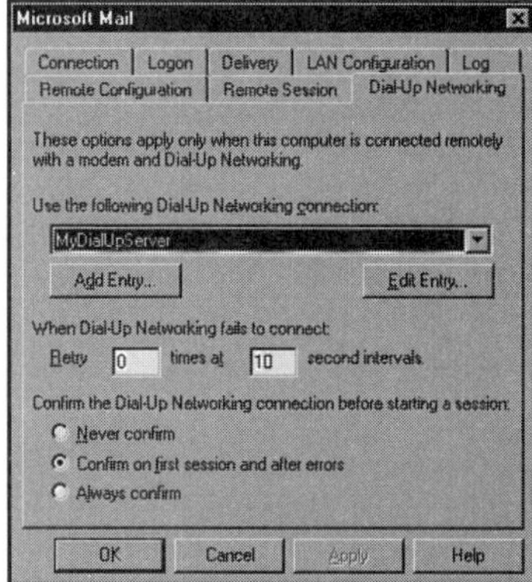

Figure 14.56

Set which dial up server you want to use on the Dial-Up Networking tab.

2. Click on the Add Entry or Edit Entry buttons to change the dial-up connection point.

3. The New Phonebook Entry dialog box prompts you for information (see fig. 14.57).

4. Under the basic configuration settings, type the name of the entry in Entry Name, a comment if you want, and the phone number of the dial-up server.

5. Click on the Alternates button if you want to specify alternate telephone numbers to try if the first does not get through. You can select the checkbox next to Move Successful Number To The Top Of The List On Connection to have that number tried first next time. Click on OK.

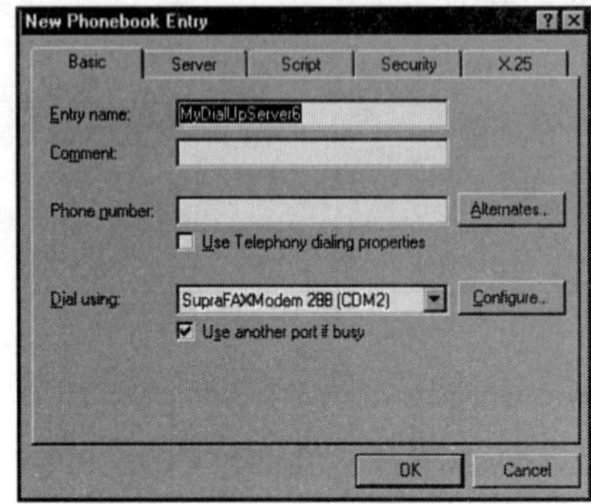

Figure 14.57

Type in the new phone book entry information.

6. Select the modem to dial with in the Dial Using dialog box. You can configure the following things for your modem by clicking the Configure button:

   - Initial speed
   - Hardware flow control
   - Modem error control
   - Modem compression
   - Disable modem speaker

7. Select the Server tab. There are three types of dial-up servers to choose from:

   - PPP: Windows NT, Windows 95 Plus, Internet
   - SLIP: Internet
   - Windows NT 3.1, Windows for Workgroups 3.11

8. Select a network protocol. If you use TCP/IP, click on the TCP/IP Settings button to configure it (see fig. 14.58).

9. Check to enable software compression and PPP LCP extensions if you want these options. Click on OK. The PPP Link Control Protocol can use TCP header compression to significantly increase the throughput of your connection if you have a small number of TCP sessions running over the line, especially if the connections are using small packets. You'll often see much higher compression ratios going one direction than in the other because of this.

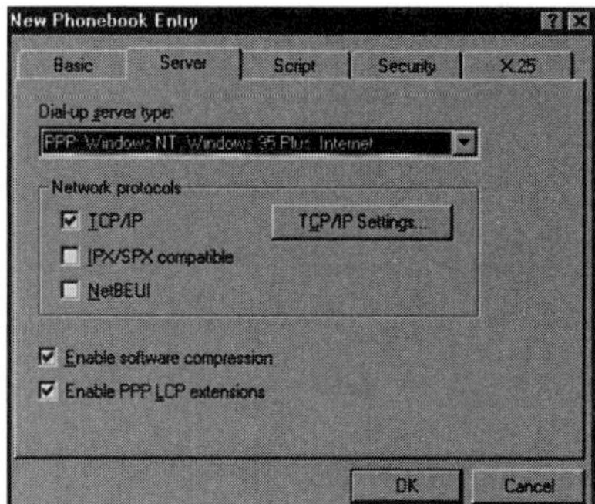

Figure 14.58

Select a network protocol on the Server tab of the Phonebook entry information.

10. The Script tab has three options after dialing:

    - None
    - Pop Up A Terminal Window
    - Run This Script

11. You can specify the logon script in the text box. If you need to edit the script, click on the Edit Script button. If you need to update the available script list, click on the Refresh List button (see fig. 14.59).

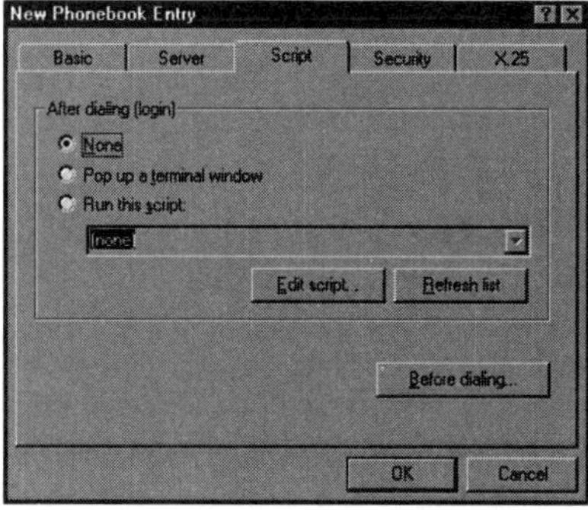

Figure 14.59

You can specify dial-up server script options.

12. Click on the Before Dialing button to run a script or pop up a terminal window before dialing.

13. Select the Security tab to configure encryption settings (see fig. 14.60).

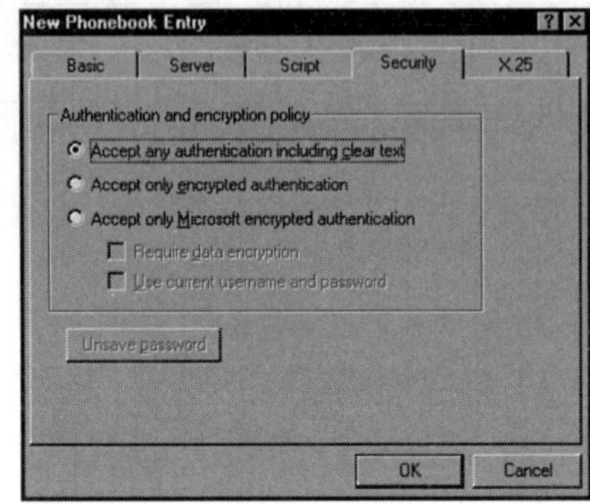

Figure 14.60

The Security options for the dial-up server include encryption settings.

14. Select one of the following security levels:

    - Any authentication and encryption
    - Only encrypted authentication
    - Only Microsoft encrypted authentication

    If you select Microsoft encrypted authentication, you can also select the checkbox for requiring data encryption and use the current user name and password. Click on OK.

15. Select the X.25 tab to configure any X.25 settings.

Using Remote Mail

If you are sending mail using your modem to connect to a post office, you will need to use the remote mail option. To open the Remote Mail window:

1. Double-click on the Inbox icon on your desktop.
2. Select Remote Mail from the Tools menu. Figure 14.61 shows the Remote Mail window.
3. Click the connect icon or select Connect from the Tools menu. The connection cable at the bottom right of the window displays the status of your connection.
4. Type in your user name, password, and domain in the Connect To dialog box. Click on OK.
5. After the modem dials the remote server, you see a status of the download. Any messages in your Outbox will now be sent.

6. You see the same type of display in your Remote Mail window as in the Messaging window—each mail subject header has a sender, time and date received, and the size.

7. From this list of messages you can decide if you want to download any or all of the messages. You can also delete, move, or copy messages without reading them. Mark the messages by highlighting a given message and selecting the appropriate Mark option from the Edit menu. If you want to select all the messages, choose Select All from the Edit menu.

8. After you have finished sending and receiving mail, close the Remote Mail window.

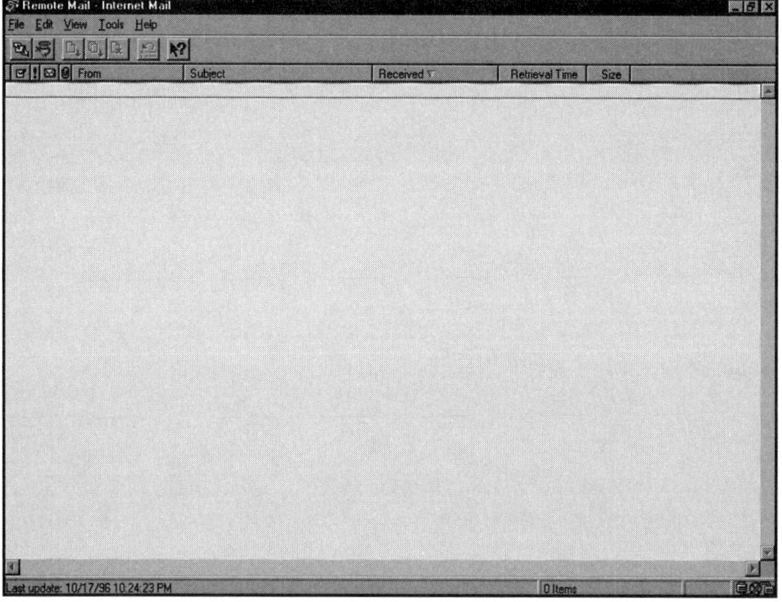

Figure 14.61

The cable at the bottom right of the Remote Mail window indicates your connection status.

Summary

This chapter has taught you what e-mail is and how you can benefit from knowing about it. You have learned about post offices, the e-mail client that comes with Windows NT Workstation, and the big picture of how it all works together. This gives you the information that you need to know about how to connect your mail to the Internet and to take advantage of all the time-saving customizations you can configure for Microsoft Messaging for Windows NT Workstation.

PART V

NT Workstation 4 and the Microsoft Internet Strategy

CHAPTER 15

NT Workstation and the Internet

For those of us watching the machinations of Microsoft as they embraced the Internet and corporate intranets, the past year has been nothing short of remarkable. There has been a rush to incorporate products and services that support TCP/IP networking and communications into the Microsoft product line. NT Workstation 4 is no exception.

The four chapters in this part of the book attempt to make some sense of the grand design of the products Microsoft is offering you in this area and the technical underpinnings used throughout. They unfold as follows:

- **Chapter 15.** This chapter offers an overview and some background on Windows NT 4 and the Internet. Topics covered include data transfer and protocols on the Internet, addressing conventions, and the role of NT Workstation 4 as a web server and site on the Internet or in an intranet.

- **Chapter 16.** Chapter 16, "Internet Explorer," gives you a detailed look at the operation of Microsoft's premier web browser, the Internet Explorer. You learn how to best configure the software and how to use add-on products like Internet Mail and Internet News.

- **Chapter 17.** Chapter 17, "Peer Web Services," attends to the installation and setup of Windows NT Workstation 4 as a web server using the Peer Web Services (PWS) software that comes with this operating system. You learn how to configure web, ftp, and Gopher services; set up default directories; and publish to these three types of services in that chapter.
- **Chapter 18.** Chapter 18, "Intranets," is devoted to the rapidly developing topic of internal network publishing using TCP/IP and the Peer Web Services. You learn how you can use PWS to enable client/server applications that work across computer platforms easily with the tools described in these chapter.

The Internet has washed over the computer community like a tidal wave, creating new businesses, new products, and new opportunities. It has or is in the process of sweeping away older products such as groupware and might change our notions of what represents a computer operating system.

Microsoft has taken notice and built Internet capabilities into all its products. If the Internet is the operating system of the future, then the operating system of the present might do well embracing the technology. Microsoft employs web servers in the hundreds in one of the largest web sites found on the Internet. The company also has set up a tightly managed intranet.

NT Server was first blessed with Internet server products, and now so too is the workstation version of this operating system. NT Workstation 4 can be a client on the Internet using a web browser such as Microsoft Internet Explorer (MSIE) or a server running the Peer Web Services (PWS).

To properly use and understand the capabilities of these products and services in the three following chapters, you need to know how the Internet works, how servers and content are located on the Internet or an intranet, and the protocols and services found there. This chapter provides this information, building on the information found in Chapter 10, "The Ins and Outs of TCP/IP."

A Quick Look at the History of the Internet

The Internet owes its existence to a series of U.S. government-sponsored initiatives designed to create a system for distributed computing using connected networks in a wide area network. In order to understand the purpose of the Internet and many of the technical terms involved, it helps to have an historical perspective from which to view the subject. This section is aimed at providing this perspective.

In the 1960s and 1970s, the Department of Defense funded research into communications protocols at Bolt, Beranek, and Newman, Inc. (Cambridge, MA) that led to the development of the Transmission Control Protocol/Internet Protocol, or as it is more commonly referred to, TCP/IP.

TCP refers to the nature of the data packets and the communications scheme used to transport them, and *IP* is an addressing scheme that provides a mechanism for routing packets to the correct server on the correct network. From there, it is the server's responsibility to send the packets on to the correct node on its network and to communicate outgoing packets transmitted by clients to routers that send the data onto other networks. TCP/IP can run as one of several networking protocols in the Windows NT protocol stack.

TCP/IP formed the basis for the first wide area network (WAN) used by large numbers of component networks, the ARPANet, funded by the U.S. Advanced Research Projects Agency Network. Their goal was to establish a fault tolerant network that could resist destruction by nuclear weapons designed to knock out communications systems. As ARPANet grew, more and more of the associated networks converted to TCP/IP so that by 1983 all its computers used that networking protocol.

From the ground up, TCP/IP and all its related technologies were meant to be cross-platform compatible. They had to be to communicate between all the different types of computers running the disparate types of local area networks connected by an internetwork. Therefore, TCP/IP can communicate to any computer and with any operating system for which a TCP/IP network driver has been added. The many different flavors of Unix, Windows, MS-DOS, and Macintosh computers all can serve as both clients and servers for Internet techology.

In time, Internet technology was adopted by the National Science Foundation as NSFNet and used to link universities, government laboratories, and other research organizations together on a worldwide basis. NSFNet at first piggybacked the ARPANet's backbone services and later created its own network backbone. Out of NSFNet grew the Internet that you know today.

As the Internet grew, NSF contracted the IP addressing management to the University of Michigan's Merit Network, which was spun off as Merit, Inc. Merit proposed commercial access of the Internet and created the system of network usage fees collected by the NSF. By 1993, the Internet had grown to the point where the NSF contracted an industry consortium called the Internet Networking Center, or InterNIC, to create and manage the central address database upon which the Internet relies.

In the original implementation, Internet technology connected mainframe and minicomputers together as network service providers. The first Internet services provided electronic mail (e-mail), a file transfer protocol (FTP), a means for remote login (Telnet), and, most important, utilities to make these services easy to use.

Although the technology for creating the Internet is now nearly 15 years old, only developments in the last six years have popularized the technology for millions and millions of users. The development of systems for categorizing and delivering rich data content—Gopher services created at the University of Minnesota and the World Wide Web created at the CERN high-energy particle physics laboratory in Geneva—led to an explosion of interest. The final development credited with an explosion of interest was the creation of a client web browser Mosaic at the University of Illinois Supercomputing Center (NSCA) and the web server software. These developments made the Internet interesting, accessible, and relevant to millions of people.

Mix in the fact that the tools were essentially free—access to Internet services was very inexpensive compared to other forms of online electronic communications—and you had an unbeatable combination. The result has been extraordinary, explosive growth of both services and clients.

This proliferation of tools and services has led to the quiet but just as significant growth of intranets. In an intranet, you have TCP/IP running on your network. The fact that an intranet is not connected to the Intranet means that intranets have much greater bandwidth and faster access speeds than what is possible on most Internet connections.

The truth is that this entire chapter could be devoted to the history of the Internet. To do so would distract us from what interests us most at the moment—the role NT Workstation 4 can play in the Internet and in your intranets, the range of services you can acquire, and how to get the most out of your computer using applications specifically designed for Windows NT.

This chapter takes a "higher-level" view, considering the Internet as a client/server environment that allows for the deployment of distributed data, distributed applications, and distributed services. Windows NT Workstation 4 can play both the roles of client and server, as you shall subsequently see.

Exploring the Rise of the Intranet

In terms of significance, intranets are as much of a revolution as the Internet is. Studies indicate that there are many more intranet servers installed than Internet servers and that intranets have an even greater potential for growth. All the emerging multimedia technologies, the potential for operating systems that are delivered over the network, and other leading-edge applications will probably find their first expressions in intranets.

Intranet solutions are cost-effective cross-platform solutions. Finally, Windows, DOS, Macintosh, and Unix clients can use their browsers to access web pages on a server on their network, just as if they were accessing a server anywhere else. The combination of an intranet and the Internet is hard to beat.

There is little that's different about an intranet compared to the Internet. All the fundamental principles that apply to setting up a server for the Internet apply to setting up a server for an intranet. The Microsoft Internet Information Server and NT Workstation 4's Peer Web Services can both serve as an intranet server, and the only real difference is that IP addresses (unique computer identification addresses) do not have to be unique in the world of TCP/IP, but only on your own network.

If anything, intranets are even easier to maintain. There's less concern about security because your users are known, and you can provide a range of services compatible with the software that runs on your client computers throughout your enterprise. This means that an intranet can be your ultimate workgroup solution, making electronic documents widely available throughout your organization. Chapter 18 details the importance of intranets, the techniques you can employ for getting the most out of them, and how Windows NT Workstation 4 can play a role as client and server in an intranet.

Gaining Internet Access

As previously mentioned, the Internet took off in popularity after access was made available on a fee basis through Internet service providers, or ISPs, as they have become known as. Getting connected to the Internet these days is as simple as looking in the yellow pages (see the Computer Bulletin Boards, Internet, Computer Services, ISDN, or Telephone Installers sections) and letting your fingers do the walking. ISPs can be found in ads in newspapers and computer magazines, through schools, computer stores, or as listings in the appendices of books about the Internet. ISPs can be national organizations, such as MCI or AT&T, or mom and pop shops. The range of services provided is enormous.

For the occasional user or for a small company, a dial-up modem connection to an ISP is the most cost-effective way to connect to the Internet as a client. Dial-up connections are priced based on connection speeds, so that more is charged for ISDN lines than for a typical modem speed accessing the Internet at 14.4 Kbps or 28.8 Kbps. The size of the pipe you are sipping the Internet through, referred to as the *bandwidth,* determines your productivity on the Internet.

For a moderate or large enterprise with significant Internet traffic, undoubtedly a network administrator will want to establish a permanent connection to the Internet. This can be done using moderate-speed connections like ISDN lines, or high-bandwidth lines like T1 or fractional T1 lines. Companies lease these lines through ISPs or through larger communications service providers. The next section provides more information on this topic.

Many companies allow for web pages and web sites to be posted onto their servers, thus allowing anyone to inexpensively establish a presence on the Internet. You don't need a direct connection for sending and receiving e-mail on the Internet. A *point-of-presence* or POP account for sending e-mail using the SMTP protocol is sufficient.

In order to establish an Internet access appropriate to the activity of your particular web site, you need to create a connection appropriate to you needs. The following section tells you how to do this.

Bandwidth

Your Internet performance is directly dependent on both the bandwidth of the connection and the type of server in use. You might be surprised to learn that any server running NT Workstation 4 can service a large number of simultaneous users and daily service requests. The network connections are the predominant factor in Internet server performance. Table 15.1 illustrates common rates as of Fall 1996.

TABLE 15.1
Common Rates for Network Connections

Connection Type	Costs
PPP dial-up at modem speeds	$20 to $40 per month
SLIP dial-up at modem speeds	$20 to $30 per month
Dedicated (unlimited usage) PPP/SLIP	$200 to $300 per month
56K at 56 Kbps	$150 to $300 per month
PPP ISDN at 128 Kbps	$70 to $100 per month plus equipment
T1 at 1.5 Mbps	$1,500 to $2,000
T3 at 45 Mbps	$65,000 to $80,000

The lower-priced services are priced for a certain usage (typically 100 hours), whereas the higher-priced connections are for dedicated lines. With a dedicated line, you establish a phone number at the ISP that is yours and yours alone, and your connection is made through that phone line. When you set up a server to provide Internet services, you require a direct Internet connection and one of these dedicated lines.

The Point-to-Point Protocol (PPP) and the Serial Line Interface Protocol (SLIP) are the two most common connection types in use by clients on the Internet today for dial-up connections. PPP is the preferred one and is replacing SLIP because it offers faster speeds, better reliability, and better graphics handling. Modem speeds of 14.4 and 28.8 kilobits per second are the most widely used for clients on the web. These speeds provide a throughput of 8 to 16 MB per hour and are considered slow for many applications such as web browsing and software downloads.

Fast Connections

Server connections should be ISDN (Integrated Services Digital Network) at a minimum. You purchase an ISDN line from your phone company or from an ISP. With ISDN, you have a direct digital connection to the Internet at speeds between 64 kilobits and 128 kilobits per second (when you use both channels). The U.S. Robotics Sportster ISDN 128K ($549, internal) and the Motorola BitSurfr Pro ($495, external) are two recommended ISDN modems, and many more models are coming to market as this technology becomes more popular. Expect to see a significant drop in the price of these units in 1997.

ISDN is considered to be a medium speed connection and would be adequate for a Windows NT Workstation 4 running Peer Web Services at its connection limit.

As a guideline, a server with up to 50 simultaneous users can use Frame Relay or ISDN, which is the limitation for ISDN. A T1 line can support from 100 to 500 simultaneous users. You can also split a T1 line installed between sites. Larger businesses that need larger capacity can install multiple T1 lines. A T3 service can handle 5,000 or more simultaneous users.

Note If you are establishing a fast connection to the Internet, it pays to bring in a specialist to help with this task. Fast connections to the Internet are expensive, and mistakes are very costly. The expertise a good consultant can bring to the table can pay for itself in diminished costs in a very short time and can prevent you from experiencing difficulties and interruptions.

Most high-speed Internet connections use leased lines. To set up a leased line connection, contact your phone company or an interexchange carrier. Leased lines are direct connections of from 56 kilobits for ISDN at the low end to a T1 through

T3 lines. Medium size enterprises rent T1 lines; large enterprises like Microsoft or IBM have T3 lines to their web sites.

This area of technology is getting a lot of attention from communications service providers. Even your local cable company might be offering fast Internet access as a service in the near future. Continental Cablevision just instituted Highway One, a piped service for its television subscribers.

Among the more exotic technologies for high-speed web connections are the following:

- **Direct-broadcast satellite.** This high-speed service uses the same technology in use today for satellite TV broadcasts. Hughes Network Systems (800-347-3272) offers a system called DirecPC, which uses a $699 add-in card attached to a satellite dish. High speeds are only achieved for received data (400 kilobits) because you use modem dial-up access for outgoing information.

- **Asymmetric Digital Subscriber Line (ADSL).** This technology is expected to be in service in a year or so and provides incoming speeds of 1.6 to 6 Mbps using telephone wire connection. AT&T developed the technology for delivery of Interactive TV. Again, the outgoing speed is moderate, about 64 Kbps.

- **Cable modem.** A cable modem is a router with a 10BASE-T Ethernet connection attached to a proprietary cable connection. This technology can be obtained from AT&T, Digital, General Instrument, Hewlett-Packard, Intel, LANCity, Motorola, and Zenith, among others for prices between $300 and $500. Speeds of 10 Mbps for incoming data is achieved.

The area of fast connections is an explosive area of activity that you should definitely keep your eye on if you intend to provide Internet services using NT Server 4 or NT Workstation 4.

Understanding Domain Masters

When you set up a web, you enable a set of network addresses used by the TCP/IP protocol. These addresses can be a range of allowed numbers, translated into friendly names. The sections that follow tell you how to set up this scheme and create a domain. Since NT Workstation 4 can be either a server or client, these principles will help you understand both cases.

You install TCP/IP networking services using the Network dialog box in Windows NT Workstation 4 and Server. In most instances, you choose to install TCP/IP services when you install NT Workstation 4 along with the Peer Web Services. This is part of the standard NT Workstation 4 install. You can install TCP/IP services at a later date, however, by choosing the Add button in the Network dialog box. In any event, after you install TCP/IP, you need to configure the IP addresses after installation. And should you want to turn on any of the Peer Web Services, you need to turn on those after installation as well.

Figure 15.1 shows you the Network dialog box, along with the TCP/IP Properties dialog box. To view the Properties dialog box, simply double-click on the TCP/IP service of interest, or highlight the service and click on the Properties button.

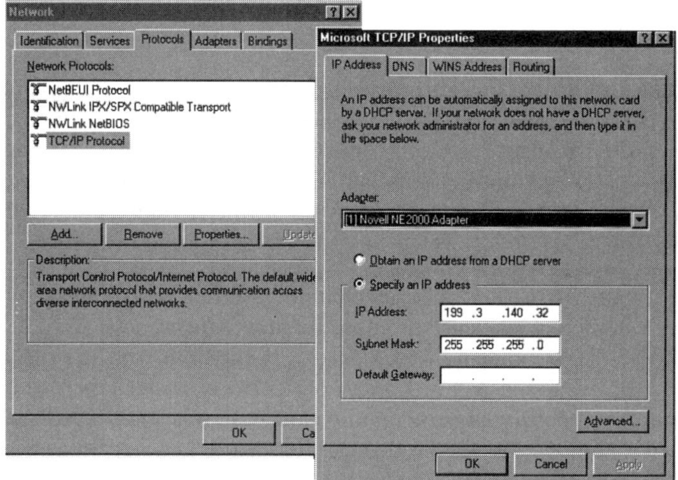

Figure 15.1

You set the IP address for a TCP/IP client in the Properties dialog box of that Network service.

Internet Addresses

When you configure NT Workstation 4 as either a web server or web client, you need to set an Internet address. This address is required by the TCP/IP protocol, and is the way communications is routed on an Internet/intranet.

By now you should be familiar with IP addresses that look something like this:

```
IP Address: ###.###.###.###
Subnet Mask: ###.###.###.###
```

where each three-numbered set ### can range from 1 to 255. This makes the Internet universe equal to 2^{32}, 256^4, or 4,294,967,296 possible addresses. The first two sets of numbers are the *network number*, and the second two sets of numbers are the *host number*. These names indicate the assignment to a particular LAN on the Internet and to the particular computer or TCP/IP device on that LAN. Servers, workstations, routers, and other devices can take a host number and consume a TCP/IP address.

The IP Address identifies a TCP/IP client, whereas the subnet mask identifies the particular subnetwork in the Internet or an intranet. A subnetwork is the range of addresses allowed for a particular network. Normally, this is a set of clients on a LAN; but because there is no physical restriction on location, a subnet can be implemented across a WAN as well.

Network Address Classes

In assigning addresses to servers and clients in an Internet/intranet, it is helpful to have an idea of the size of the pool or address assignments that are available. This section describes how the range of addresses are assigned.

The actual range of numbers that any enterprise can use is limited by the type of domain assigned to that enterprise (A, B, or C). Class A domains have 2^{24} or 16,777,216 addresses; class B has 2^{16} or 65,536 addresses; and class C has 2^{8} or 256 possible addresses. Class D is for multicast use, and class E is experimental, so neither of these two additional network address classes is commonly encountered.

An Internet address is composed of four bytes of data, that is the four 4^{8} numbers you saw filled in the Properties dialog box. What is changing between the categories of networks here is the number of bytes used to describe the network address; that's what determines the domain's capacity. With class A, for example, only the first byte is assigned, leaving three bytes available for the network address pool. Class B addresses use the first two bytes for network assignment, and thus have two bytes left over for specific host addresses. Finally, class C uses three bytes for the network address and only one byte for host addresses. From these assignments, the capacities described in the previous paragraph arise.

The class of the domain you are assigned is in relationship to the pool of Internet addresses that your enterprise needs. Unless you are IBM, Microsoft, or a government agency, you are not going to get a class A network. Most of the class A assignments have already been made, and there are few remaining. A class B assignment probably requires 100 hours of research and documentation. Estimates are that 50 percent of the class B networks are already assigned on the Internet. class C addresses used to be easy to obtain, but today require some documentation. The InterNIC regulatory board now tries to give multiple class C addresses in place of class B address pools and will show a preference for assigning class C blocks to ISPs rather than companies. class C applications take about a couple of hours to complete. Again, about 50 percent of class C networks have been assigned.

Of course, if you are building an intranet and have no requirement for Internet access, then the entire pool of possible IP addresses is available to you.

Domain Naming Services

Occasionally, you run across Internet addresses that require the actual IP address to be entered—as in "248.38.43.124"—but that is rare and becoming rarer still. The Internet would be a singularly unfriendly place if each of us were identified by number only. To avoid this, the concept of a *domain name* was created. This is the name that gets registered in the InterNIC database as being associated with an address or range of addresses. When you enter a domain name, a set of master computers running the database maps the domain name to the actual IP addresses for routing.

Internet servers implement domain names and server names by maintaining a names database. The system is referred to as the Domain Name System (DNS) and is also called a *name server*. A host can translate a name to an IP address, and DNS can translate an IP address into a domain or server name. In essence, DNS acts as a miniature version of the InterNIC database on the Internet itself.

The first domain name server appeared in 1983 at the University of Wisconsin. Prior to that, if you wanted to address communications or request services to a node on the Internet, you were stuck with the numerical address. Names servers have had a lot to do with making the Internet a friendlier place to travel on.

The four types of DNS servers in use today are as follows:

- **Root Domain Name Servers.** These service the root of a DNS tree. Seven root domain name servers are on the Internet today, and they service the very large databases that run the Internet itself.
- **Primary Domain Name Servers.** These servers are used in a second-level domain. For example, IBM or Microsoft runs a Primary DNS for their organization.
- **Secondary Domain Name Server.** These servers are backup servers that contain the replicated contents of the Primary DNS. In the event of the loss of the Primary DNS, software switches over to the Secondary DNS at fail-over.
- **Forwarder Domain Name Servers.** This service forwards unknown requests and caches the results.

One other important scheme for TCP/IP addressing is the Dynamic Host Configuration Protocol (DHCP). In this scheme, a pool of IP addresses is assigned to a domain. The domain server's role is to assign IP addresses to computers on the network running the TCP/IP protocol and then to negotiate and transmit host information as required. IP address assignment can use either a manual, automatic, or dynamic allocation method. DCHP runs on Windows NT Server but not on Windows NT

Workstation 4. However, DHCP can be applied to either Windows NT Workstations or NT Servers as clients. For more information on this topic, see the section "Understanding DHCP" in Chapter 10.

Note Again, this chapter assumes that you have read Chapter 10, "The Ins and Outs of TCP/IP." This previous chapter provides the details of installing TCP/IP on NT Workstation 4 and how to configure IP addresses and names. It also goes into more technical depth on DNS and DHCP than is described here.

Uniform Resource Locators (URLs)

If you have used the Internet or an intranet before, then you have entered a Uniform Resource Locator (URL) into your browser, ftp file transfer utility, or other access program. An URL is the Internet naming convention for Internet resources: servers, folders or directories, and files. The system can identify a particular file on a particular server anywhere in the world.

A URL takes the following form:

```
Protocol://service.domain.identifier/path/file
```

The portion of the URL *service.domain.identifier* is the Domain Name System (DNS) address for a site; *domain.identifier* is the domain name itself. You should note that web sites can distribute their domain across multiple servers or map multiple domains on a single server. The latter is called *multihoming* and is offered by Microsoft Internet Information Server (IIS) and by Netscape in its server family but is not part of the Peer Web Services on NT Workstation 4.

For example, consider the Microsoft home page's URL components:

```
http://www.microsoft.com/msie/download.htm
```

This URL specifies the following:

- **http.** The file transfer type—Hypertext Transfer Protocol

  Other common transfer protocols are ftp:// and gopher://—they use similar URL syntax.

- **www.** The Internet service.
- **microsoft.** The domain name, which maps to a range of IP addresses.
- **com.** The domain identifier, identifying this as a commercial enterprise.

- **msie.** The folder for the Microsoft Internet Explorer.
- **download.htm.** The web page, which is viewed in your browser.

  The file extension HTM is short for the Hypertext Markup Language (HTML). Other file types (resources) can be served up, and how they are processed is a function of the utility you are using for Internet/intranet access. For example, a portable document file (or PDF) is used by Adobe Acrobat. If Acrobat is registered as a helper application for the PDF file extension with your browser, then Acrobat launches and opens the file.

Other common domain identifiers you will encounter are as follows (the identifier in our previous example was, of course, com):

- **edu.** Educational institutions
- **gov.** Government agencies
- **mil.** The United States Military
- **net.** Internet access providers (also known as Internet Service Providers or ISPs)
- **org.** A catchall designation most often used for nonprofit institutions

InterNIC assigns you a domain identifier when you register your domain name based on the information you provide in the registration form.

URLs are sensitive to the syntax used but are case insensitive. You can't use spaces in a URL, but you will often encounter underlines in place of space characters.

Note A newer scheme of addressing makes use of geographic locations and organization to provide URLs. See the next section for details.

In many instances, you don't enter a particular document in an URL. In that case, the web server software will open the default document in the folder that was specified. You see this in an example later in this chapter when you set up NT Workstation 4's Peer Web Services. Unless specified otherwise, most default documents for web services are either DEFAULT.HTM, INDEX.HTM, or something similar. So when you enter http://www.microsoft.com/ in your browser, you see the DEFAULT.HTM document appear.

E-mail addressing is something you are probably familiar with. If you see an address such as basman@killerapps.com, then the first part is a user name, and to the left of the "at" or @ sign is the domain. Depending on how the mail service is set up, a message to a user is sent directly to the user's mailbox (most common) or pooled. With a pooled address, the mail is sent to a mailbox regardless of the user name. This is common in smaller organizations using ISPs for Internet access.

URLs can also contain information to be processed by the web server. Data is appended at the end of the \path\filename. The web server passes the data to CGI script, and the results are returned in a web page. You see this behavior when you specify a search in a web search engine.

Here are some examples of an URL passing data to a server:

- ISAPI application: http://www.domain.com/path/filename.dll?SEX="M"
- Internet Database Connector: http://www.domain.com/feedback/input.idc
- Common Gateway Interface (CGI) script: http://www.company.com/application/function.do?4.3

You've seen how static pages are returned. All the preceding URLs return a dynamic web page, or a directory listing with hypertext entries linked to the files on the server.

Dynamic pages contain information in response to the user's request. Typically, a form is filled out by a user and submitted through a CGI script to a database. The server returns an HTML page containing the requested information. In Peer Web Services (PWS), another method to create a dynamic web page is to send a query to an Internet Server API (ISAPI) application.

If you have enabled directory browsing, then when users do not specify a particular file, a hypertext listing is returned to the their browser. The section "Virtual Directories, Aliases, and Directory Browsing" in Chapter 17 describes directory browsing in more detail. By clicking on the file link, that file is opened in your browser.

Fully Qualified Domain Names

Given the amount of traffic that even modest web sites must support, many organizations establish distributed Internet solutions. An organization might have several web servers; a large organization such as Microsoft has hundreds. To specify the particular Internet (or intranet) server in question, an URL can contain a server name in the address. For example, you might see http://www.zeus.microsoft.com/ as an URL. Here, *Zeus* is the server name, and *zeus.microsoft.com* is the fully qualified domain name (FQDN).

You might run across an enterprise with several subdomains indicated in its FQDN, such as:

- administration.killerapps.com
- custserv.killerapps.com
- production.killerapps.com
- marketing.killerapps.com
- humanres.killerapps.com

Here, each subdomain indicated (administration, custserv, and so on) might or might not be a single server. The host can map a subdomain to two or more computers. Certainly, this is the intent in having Windows NT Workstation 4 serve as a web server. Potentially, anyone in an organization can publish on the Peer Web Services, and any other computer user connected through TCP/IP can subscribe. A proliferation of web servers, each with its own "domain master," puts tools for content publishing in the hands of individuals in the organization.

It's worth noting in passing that FQDN and subdomain definition probably has a lot more utility in intranets than in Internet applications. In an intranet, you are trying to provide structure in an organization. In an Internet application you are trying to get the outside user connected with as little complexity as possible.

Subdomains

The domain identifiers you learned about in the section "Universal Resource Locators (URLs)" are the common ones used in the United States. There is also a scheme in place to identify URLs by location. You will encounter these alternate constructions when you log on to a server in Switzerland, Great Britain, or elsewhere. This system uses a geography hierarchy and is a newer method for constructing an URL than the previously described organizational hierarchy.

For example, the following top-level domains are used for countries:

- *.us* for U.S.A
- *.ca* for Canada
- *.uk* for Great Britain
- *.de* for Germany
- *.se* for Sweden
- *.fr* for France

- *.in* for India
- *.cn* for China
- *.ja* for Japan

How a top-level domain gets subdivided into subdomains depends on the country. In the U.S. domain, subdivision is by state; then by city or county; then by organization; and finally by computer name. So you might see something similar to the following for an FQDN structured by location:

```
ftp://cityhall.newton.ma.us
```

At the state or city level, that particular state or city might further divide its domain into functional units. The following are common:

- *.state* for state government agencies.
- *.fed* for federal government agencies.
- *.k12* for public school districts.
- *.pvt* for private schools.
- *.cc* for state or city community colleges.
- *.tec* for technical vocation schools.
- *.lib* for libraries.
- *.gen* is a catchall subdomain used with associations, clubs, charities, and recreational facilities.
- *.dni* for distributed national institutes.

Note A DNI denotes an organization with representation at several levels of government, or one that crosses state boundaries.

Figure 15.2 shows an example of how a domain is subdivided and how a host is addressed.

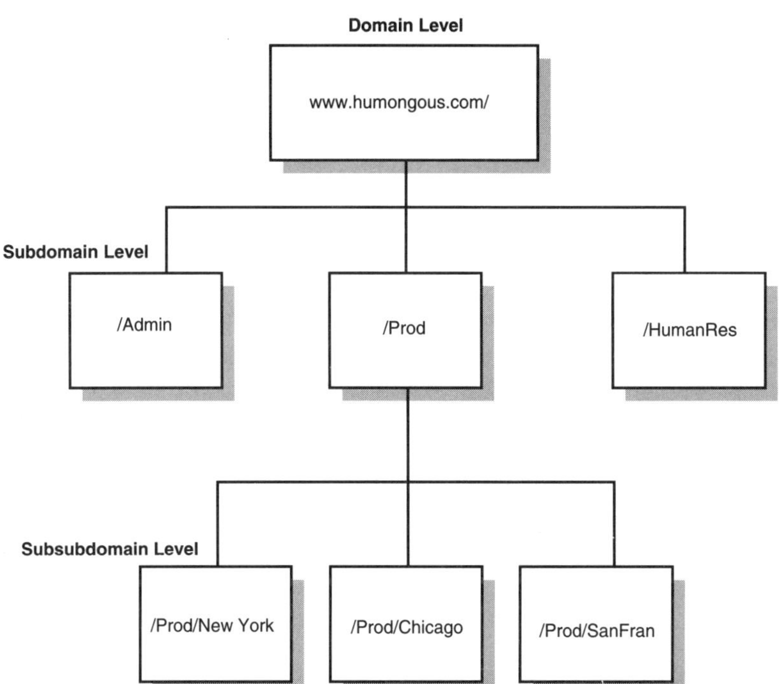

Figure 15.2

This figure shows a subdomain structure for a domain.

There are obviously many schemes for naming and organizing subdomains that are in use today, each created with its own purpose. If you are subdividing a private intranet using DNS, you are free to create your structure in any manner you want.

If you want to create subdomains on an Internet site in the United States, then you should register the host and the domain structure using a U.S. Domain Template form. Get this form by sending e-mail to the U.S. Domain Registrar (us-domain @isi.edu). You can also get questions answered at that address; or call Ann Cooper at the USC/Information Services Institute (310-822-1511).

For subdomains that are part of other domains (states, for example), you need to contact that domain. The appropriate contact information is contained in an anonymous (no password) ftp file held at the following location:

```
ftp://ftp.venera.isi.edu/notes/delegated-domains.txt
```

You can also have this list mailed to you by sending e-mail to rfc-info@isi.edu and by entering the following in the message body:

```
Help: us_domain_delegated_domains
```

It is common practice for a domain or subdomain to be served by one or more DNS servers. It is not required, however, and depending on your traffic volume, two or more domains can be serviced by a single DNS server. The partitioning of DNS servers is done to avoid network traffic, balance loading, and ensure fault tolerance should the primary DNS server go off-line.

Exploring Internet Protocols

Many Internet protocols are in use today. A *protocol* is a convention for data communications. In some instances, these protocols provide the basis for services on the Internet. Some protocols are structured for file transfers like the File Transfer Protocol (FTP). Other protocols like Hypertext Transfer Protocol (HTTP) or Gopher are meant to provide hypertext connections. A protocol controls the manner in which data is not only transferred, but the types of file formats allowed, transfer rates, and so on. An understanding of these protocols will provide you with an explanation of the possibilities each allows. NT Workstation 4 supports FTP, HTTP, and Gopher as part of the Peer Web Services. The sections that follow explain some of these definitions more fully.

The Peer Web Services Protocols

Three protocols are of particular interest to Windows NT Workstation 4 users, as they appear in IIS and the Peer Web Services and can run as services on those operating systems. When you use NT Workstation 4 as a client or server for these three services, you only need enter the URLs appropriate to that service, and the resource is served up by the technology.

The native Peer Web Services protocols are:

- **FTP (the file transfer protocol).** FTP is a means for transferring binary files across the Internet and is generally a faster transfer method than other protocols like http. FTP allows for user name and password access to directories (challenge/response security), or through an "anonymous" access to public (generally \PUB. directories).

- **Gopher (a distributed hierarchical indexed resource locator).** Gopher space is organized around a central searchable index using a search engine like Archie. Gopher enables you to organize documents, image files, and other resource items so that they can be downloaded. In a Gopher directory, there is usually a text file explaining that directory's contents.

- **WWW (web services).** The WWW service relies on the http transport protocol to transfer data files, or on the https protocol for a secure transport mechanism. The additional "s" in the protocol stands for "secure."

A special type of software called a *browser* can view web files and compose a page. FTP and Gopher services can also be viewed in a modern browser, with folders appearing in a hierarchical view. Early browsers such as Lynx were text-only and are only used on the MS-DOS and Unix clients. Most modern browsers are capable of displaying text and images. Browsers like the Internet Explorer (see the next chapter for more information) are extensible and can use helper applications to play content files.

The NFS Protocol

One protocol developed by Sun Microsystems called the Network File System (NFS) is considered to be a part of the Internet Protocol Suite. This file system is a high-level protocol that lets a client transparently access files, directories, and resources located on an NFS server. When you mount an NFS drive as a remote drive on the Internet, it appears to a client as if it were a local drive.

From the standpoint of NFS, it makes no difference whether the NFS host behaves as if it is an NFS client or an NFS server. No restrictions are placed on the location of the client and server, although the speed of the connection and file transfer or access is an indication of whether the drive is local or remote. NFS handles file conversions between different operating systems running NFS transparently. NT Workstation supports NFS volumes.

Mail and Messaging Protocols

Other protocols are of interest on the Internet and can be used by the Microsoft Internet Explorer through its new mail and newsgroup extensions (also described in Chapter 16, "Internet Explorer").

The important e-mail protocols are as follows:

- **SMTP.** When mail is sent over the Internet, it often complies with the Simple Mail Transfer Protocol. SMTP documents contain an address header, a message body, and attachments.

- **POP.** The Post Office Protocol in common use on the Internet today provides the agreed upon format for the body of a message. Note that this POP is different from the Point of Presence (POP) connection used in Internet access, which is simply a telephone connection to an ISP. The two identical acronyms are unfortunate.

- **MIME.** The Multipurpose Internet Mail Extension is a means of identifying the data type of the attachment. When a MIME aware e-mail application receives the MIME descriptor, it knows the data type, size, and composition of the attachment in the e-mail message.

Many other protocols are in use today on the Internet. Most concern themselves with the way data is stored or handled, or with a messaging application. UUEncode and UUDecode, for example, are methods for converting binary files into text information and from text back to binary, respectively. The UU part comes from the Unix-Unix Communications Protocol. An attachment of a mail message sent UUEncoded normally contains a line asking you to cut the text that follows, save that text as a text file, and then process the file through a UUDecode utility. Clearly, there are many leftovers out there from a bygone era.

One of the most important messaging methods in the Internet is the *Common Gateway Interface* (CGI). These small programs are written as scripts or macros in high-level languages such as Perl, and their function is to communicate with server software and applications to massage data being transferred. Any programming language can be used to program a CGI script, so it is not uncommon to see things like AppleScript used on Macintosh, C++, and others. Forms and image maps are two common web functions that require CGI scripts. The Peer Web Services on Windows NT Workstation 4 support CGI scripts and offer the Internet Database Connector for sending queries to database applications from web pages.

When a user fills in a form on a web page and clicks the Submit button, for example, the action statement of the Submit button calls a CGI script. The CGI script takes the value in a field, associates it with a field name or label, and formats the data in a form that an application like a database can understand. Data returned from a database can be handled similarly, either overwriting an entire web page or simply overwriting values that appear on that page. There is nothing magical about CGI, no restrictions on the programming language that you use; but CGI must be written to conform to a particular server type. The two most common server types are NCSA and CERN servers.

Future Protocols

There is a great rush today to establish standards for distributed computing on the Internet. The standards or protocols take the form of object models, applet creation and delivery systems, and application programming interfaces. How successful these standards become remains to be seen, but they are cropping up in products described in this chapter.

The Object Management Group (OMG) consortium, for example, has proposed the Common Object Request Broker Architecture (see http://splash.javasoft.com/

pages/intro.html for more information), a means of categorizing data types so that any conforming application can access it. CORBA has appeared in some advanced distributed databases such as Illustra and Informix, Oracle, and others where a universal database server is being constructed. But CORBA is not yet widely used. Microsoft has a competing standard called the Distributed Common Object Model (DCOM). This standard enables you to use OLE objects over the Internet, in a slightly new form that has been dubbed ActiveX. Applets programs with ActiveX or web pages composed using a 3D Virtual Reality Markup Language (VRML) are being encountered with increasing frequency.

Among the file systems being promulgated today are the Internet Network File System (INFS) and the Open Directory Services Interface (ODSI) used by The Microsoft Network. Similarly, each major vendor supports an API for its web server software—the Internet Server API (ISAPI) for Microsoft and the Netscape API (NSAPI) for its servers. The use of one of these file systems or API over another is of little consequence to you as a user or site manager with Windows NT and is primarily of concern to developers.

These future protocols haven't yet appeared in NT Workstation 4's Internet/intranet suite. They point the way, however, to future additions to NT's capabilities once these advance technologies get established.

Using NT Workstation as an Internet Server

NT Workstation is rapidly becoming one of the preferred platforms for providing Internet services. It provides all the performance of a 32-bit operating system and the security of the NTFS file system at a fraction of the price of Windows NT Server 4.

If Microsoft didn't freely distribute its Peer Web Services server software on NT Workstation 4, it would effectively have killed the market for Windows NT Server 4 as an Internet server running the Internet Information Server. The reason that this is so is that many vendors have web server software that runs on NT Workstation 4 as well as NT Server 4. Many commercial vendors of web server software have charged that Microsoft is exercising a monopoly in this area for those reasons. Perhaps it's simply good business; you be the judge.

You can buy many good web server software packages today that run on Windows NT Workstation 4. Because the Peer Web Services are part of the Windows NT Workstation 4 operating system, that software is the subject of Chapter 17. In this section, you learn about alternative products from other vendors.

The most well-known server software for Windows NT is Netscape's product line. Three commercial versions of this sofware are offered: Netscape Communication Server, Netscape Commerce Server, and Netscape FastTrack Server. Communications server offers high-speed web services; Commerce Server adds encrypted communication for secure data transfer; and FastTrack server is Netscape's low-cost entry-level server package.

Among the services offered as part of the Netscape Commerce and Communications server packages are:

- Virtual server capability
- Site management tools
- Netscape application programming interface (NSAPI)
- SSL security
- Graphic setup utilities.

These products are available for downloading for a 30-day trial period from the Netscape web site at: http://www.netscape.com/.

Note Microsoft is developing a commerce server to run on Windows NT called the Merchant Server. It remains to be seen whether this package will run on Windows NT Workstation 4NT Workstation 4; although it is likely that you would not want to do that due to the limit on the number of simultaneous connections that Workstation has.

Perhaps the most popular alternative server software is WebSite from O'Reilly & Associates. This product is a 32-bit fully multithreaded server that provides for database access from a web page.

Reviewers have commented on the ease of use of WebSite and the quality of its Webview and WebSite Pro site management tools. WebSite supports virtual servers (the appearance of separate domains on the same server). Along with indexing and built-in web site search tools, various CGI and Server Side Includes (SSI) capabilities, WebSite makes constructing dynamic web pages composed from data on-the-fly relatively easy. WebSite's home page on the web is found at http://website.ora.com.

Another popular web server is the Purveyor web server from Process Software (http://www.process.com). This software was developed from the EMWAC freeware server and offers some advanced features, such as a database wizard, an Internet Server API, the capability to run a proxy server, remote management, and secure transactions (the HTTPS protocol).

Note A *proxy server* is an Internet server that contains two or more network boards running different network protocols (one of which is TCP/IP) for isolation of Internet communications. Proxy servers offer a means of securing a network from dangerous or unwanted Internet communications and are cheaper, albeit less secure, than installing a firewall. Often proxy servers are connected to firewalls.

By the way, the original version of the EMWAC software is still available from the European Microsoft Windows Academic Center (http://emwac.ed.ac.uk). This is a basic package without any supporting administration utilities but is capable of running a small site like the one you might want to set up with Windows NT Workstation 4. Among the features offered by this software are MAP file support, CGI support, automatic directory indexing, and a link to a WAIS search and retrieval service.

At the higher end of web servers is the Oracle WEB System. This product is meant to provide Internet access to the Oracle database system. The price of Oracle and this product argues for the performance of NT Server 4, but Oracle has introduced some very interesting object technology that you might want to learn about. The capability to integrate data from Oracle databases is, as you would expect, well implemented. Look at http://www.oracle.com/products/websystem/webserver for information on the Oracle web server.

Summary

NT Workstation 4 can be a server or client on the Internet or an intranet. In order to provide services or request them you first need to know how to configure Workstation and how to provide the addresses of resources. This chapter provides a background on the historical development of the Internet/intranet, how addressing works, and how to translate these addresses into the friendly names of domains, subdomains, and resources.

In the upcoming chapters, you will learn about the Microsoft Internet Explorer, and how to use NT Workstation 4 as a browser to view and obtain Internet/intranet resources.

CHAPTER 16

Internet Explorer

The great browser wars of 1995-96, fought in the trenches of Redmond, WA and Mountain View, CA by Microsoft and Netscape, respectively, have resulted in the development of two very fine browsers—Netscape Navigator and the Microsoft Internet Explorer. As part of your installation of Windows NT Workstation 4, you get Microsoft Internet Explorer (MSIE) in the package.

This chapter documents the use of MSIE and explores many of the capabilities, configuration settings, and options that you are presented with. You learn how to use Microsoft Internet Explorer to navigate around the World Wide Web. You also learn how to configure the Internet Explorer through options and preference settings. Many of these preference settings are unique to MSIE.

The Internet Explorer is a shell program upon which other modules can be added. So a suite of add-on downloadable products is being offered that works hand-in-hand with MSIE. In this chapter, you find out how to use Microsoft Internet Mail to send and receive e-mail over the Internet. You also see how to connect to and read newsgroup messages using Microsoft Internet News. Over the next few months, Microsoft will probably release a version of NetMeeting for Windows NT Workstation 4 that will enable you to conference on the Internet. All these subsidiary products are covered in this chapter as well.

Understanding Internet Explorer

The Microsoft Internet Explorer (MSIE) is installed as part of the Windows NT Workstation 4 interface, and an icon is placed on the Windows Desktop. Microsoft is making a statement about the importance of its web browser in its current and future plans. As an administrator you will use MSIE to browse network resources, access online help, send and receive mail, teleconference, and perform other essential tasks. Your clients will expect you to know not only how to use this browser, but how to configure MSIE on their computers.

Microsoft's Internet Explorer is a descendent of the Spry Mosaic web browser. Spry licensed the code for the original version of Mosaic (the first of the graphical web browsers) from the University of Illinois Supercomputer Center. Microsoft acquired the product from Spry. Version 3.0 is the second major version of this web browser from Microsoft.

Note Version 4.0 is in alpha testing as this chapter is being written with an expected release of this next version in late 1997.

Depending on which reviewer you read, MSIE is either the best or second best web browser on the market today. Any knowledgeable reviewer will certainly tell you that Microsoft is giving Netscape's Navigator a run for its money. The current state of the market has Navigator holding a 75 percent share, with MSIE estimated at 15 percent, and the remaining 10 percent shared by other web browsers. It is expected that MSIE will pick up some market share as it is added to the desktop for America Online access (with more than five million users) and in several of the upcoming Windows operating systems. Internet Explorer was first included in Windows 95, and Windows NT is the second version of Microsoft's operating system to include this product.

It's hard to beat the price. Microsoft gives the product away for free with the operating system.

Launching Internet Explorer

MSIE is the second major piece of the installation of Windows NT Workstation 4's Peer Web Services, after PWS itself. When you install the operating system, an icon for the browser appears on your desktop. The shortcut menu for MSIE is shown in figure 16.1.

From this shortcut menu, you can launch MSIE, create a shortcut for the program in another location, delete the icon, rename the icon, or get access to the Properties dialog box for the browser. The Properties dialog box is described in detail later in this chapter in the section "Browser Properties."

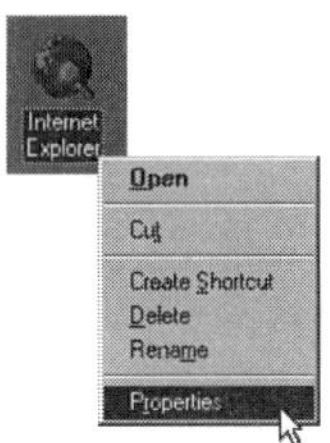

Figure 16.1

The Microsoft Internet Explorer Desktop icon allows you to launch this web browser directly by double-clicking on it.

Internet Explorer can be launched by any of the following methods:

- Double-click on the Internet Explorer icon on the desktop.
- Select the Open command from the MSIE shortcut (right-click) menu.
- Double-click on an HTML file in the Windows Explorer.

Note MSIE only launches and opens when you double-click on an HTML file if MSIE is registered as the program responsible for that file type. Windows considers the program with this registration to be the default browser. If you open MSIE and it is not your default browser, you see an alert box (see fig. 16.2) asking if you want to make MSIE your default browser. Doing so changes the HTML registration in the Registry. You can also click a checkbox to disable this alert box (as most users of Netscape Navigator undoubtedly do).

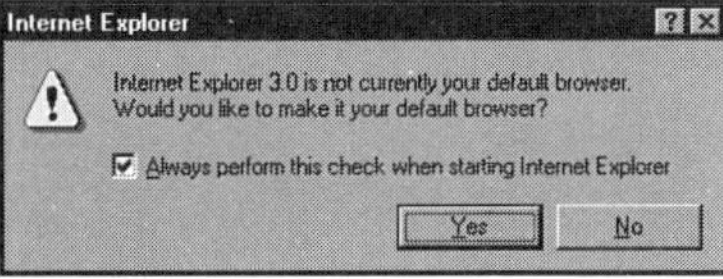

Figure 16.2

An alert box indicates that MSIE is not the default browser and lets you change it.

If the alert dialog box does not come up and another browser launches instead of MSIE when an HTML file is opened, you can reset the file type association in Microsoft NT Explorer using the Options command on the View menu. Change the setting on the File Type tab to change the setting in the NT Registry.

When MSIE opens from the desktop icon, the default document in the home directory appears in the browser. This default document can be changed as a preference, as you will see later in this chapter. When you open an HTML document and launch the browser in that manner, that web page appears in the browser along with any of the resources that are named in the web page and are accessible on your computer or network.

Upgrading Internet Explorer

As Microsoft upgrades the Internet Explorer and offers add-on products, it makes these products available through downloads from the Microsoft Internet Explorer home page at:

http://www.microsoft.com/ie/ie.htm

The home page contains links to pages posted on the Microsoft web site documenting the many aspects of the browser and related technology.

To download the software, go to the following URL:

http://www.microsoft.com/ie/download/

When MSIE 3.0 was in beta, and up until the point at which version 4.0 is in beta, you could obtain the browser here. In the first versions of MSIE that were released, there was a bug that prevented successful logon to various Internet web sites. A patch called Update can be downloaded from the Explorer folder on the Microsoft web site. The Update is a 442 KB application (EXE) file that runs and updates MSIE 3.0 to correct this problem.

You can download one of three possible installations types:

- Minimum Installation
- Typical Installation
- Full Installation

When you download the *Minimum Installation*, you get only the MSIE browser. The installation program for 3.0's minimum installation is MSIE30M.EXE, and is 9.86 MB. You can also download Internet Mail and Internet News from this location by downloading and installing the *Typical Installation*. The *Full Installation*, which installs NetMeeting as well, is not yet available for Windows NT 4 as a released product, but is available for Windows 95. As this book was in production an early beta of NetMeeting was released. It is anticipated that the final version of NetMeeting will be available in early 1997.

To download Internet News and Internet Mail after doing a minimum installation, use the Additional Features & Add-on Selection from the download drop-down list. When you download Internet Mail and Internet News, you get the MAILNEWS.EXE installation program, which is 980 KB in size. You can download NetMeeting as an individual add-on product for MSIE, or as part of the full installation.

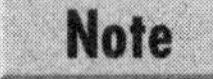

All these installation programs install and run in the usual way either through the Run command on the Start menu or using the Add/Remove Programs Control Panel. The latter method for installation is the preferred method in the Windows NT 4/Windows 95 interface.

What Internet Explorer Does

Figure 16.3 shows you a sample introductory web page in MSIE version 3.0. Anyone who has ever used a web browser will be familiar with most of the basic features of MSIE, but the section that follows concentrates on some of the newer interface features that are part of the program, its customization and optimization features, and add-on Internet Mail and Internet News products.

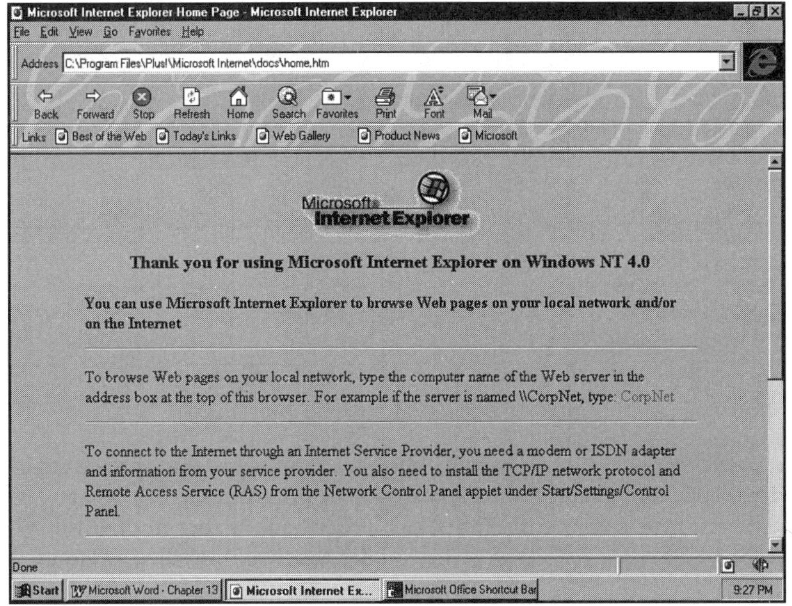

Figure 16.3

A sample page in the Microsoft Internet Explorer with all the toolbars showing indicates some of the advanced capabilities of this web browser.

Modern browsers like MSIE are general purpose tools. You can use MSIE to view web pages, ftp, and Gopher sites simply by entering the appropriate URL. Figure 16.4 shows Microsoft's ftp site viewed in MSIE 3.0. When you go to an ftp or Gopher site, you see a hierarchical listing of files and folders. If a file type has an icon, as it most often does in Gopherspace, then you will see that icon as well.

The capability to view these three web services obviates the need for other tools for browsing and can replace a whole collection of tools. The addition of a mail tool and a newsreader rounds out the major functions on the Internet. MSIE's mail and newsreader might not compare in features and options to dedicated products in this area; but because these tools are included, they are likely to get used.

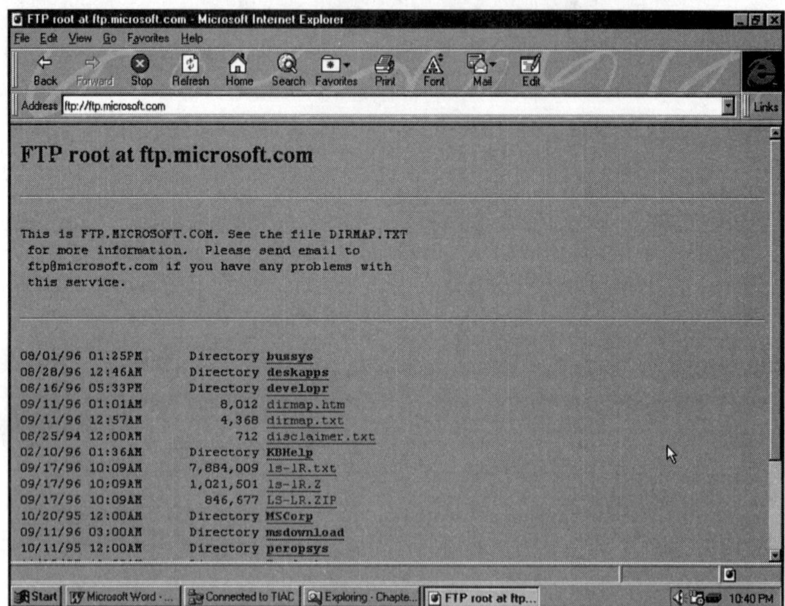

Figure 16.4

The Microsoft ftp site shown in the Internet Explorer indicates that you can navigate hierarchical directories with this tool.

The Interface

The first thing you might notice about MSIE is the various toolbars. Microsoft is toolbar crazy. Shown earlier in figure 16.4 are (from top to bottom):

- **Address toolbar.** The top toolbar shows the URLs of pages that you visited in the past. If you click the arrow to reveal the drop-down list, you can select a URL and request it by pressing the Enter key. To go back farther in the history of a browser's usage, use the Open History Folder command on the Go menu.

- **Button toolbar.** The middle toolbar shown contains the standard browser buttons for page navigation. Shown from left to right are Back, Forward, Stop, Refresh, Home, Search, Favorites (click to view a drop-down menu), Print, Font (click to toggle font size), and Mail (only appears when Internet Mail is installed).

- **Links toolbar.** The five links you see are links contained in the text shown in iconic form. Each page displays different links, if your web pages use this feature of MSIE.

- **Status bar.** The Status bar at the bottom of the window contains page loading information, file sizes, file type, and other information.

You can close up all the toolbars at once by deselecting the Toolbars command on the View menu. You can also remove the Status bar from view by deselecting the Status Bar command on that same menu.

You can close up individual toolbars one at a time by clicking and dragging on the bottom edge of the toolbar, or resize a toolbar by clicking and dragging on the double line edge (your cursor turns into a double-headed arrow). Using these techniques, it is possible to reorder or collapse toolbars to a single button.

Probably the most confusing part of the process is what you need to do when you collapse a toolbar and want to return to it. You can view all toolbars by dragging the bottom margin of the toolbar area down until all are showing.

To view more of a web page, you can toggle the Font button (through five settings) or select a font from the Font submenu of the View menu. You can also switch to a larger font size if you are having trouble viewing the fonts on a screen.

You don't have much control over the interface of MSIE from within the program itself. This is done purposely to shield a user from making too many changes. Most of the options are contained in the MSIE Properties dialog box. Choosing the Properties command on the File menu displays a properties dialog box for the web page in view and not the browser. In a page's properties dialog box (see fig. 16.5), you can determine whether the page has been securely transmitted and general information about file type and URL.

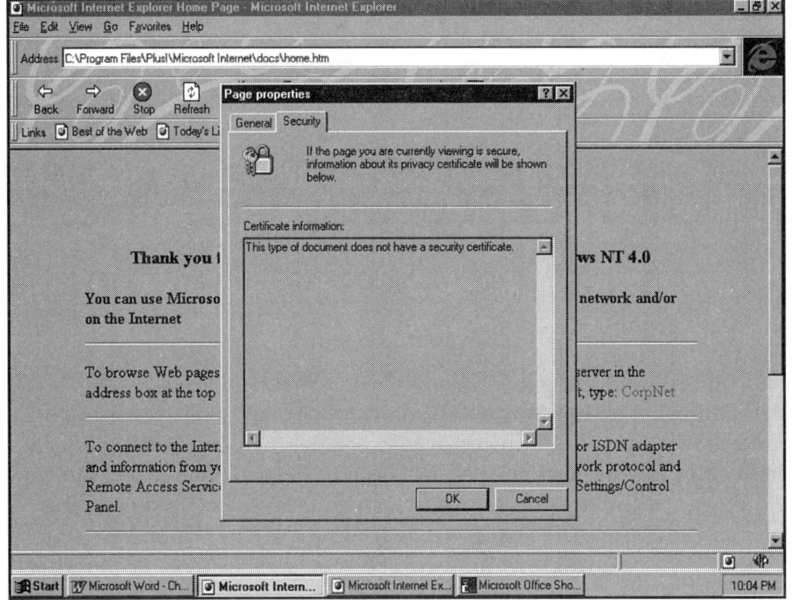

Figure 16.5

A Page properties dialog box enables you to view general and security information.

One setting you have control over is Page Setup, which is useful should you want to print a page using the Print button or Print command on the File menu.

Source View

For developers of web pages (or for anyone, for that matter), Microsoft Internet Explorer has the capability to view the source code of a web page. MSIE calls this the *source view,* and you can view it by selecting the Source command on the View menu. Figure 16.6 shows you the home page of CNN News (http://www.cnn.com), and figure 16.7 shows you the HTML code in source view.

Figure 16.6

The CNN home page is an example of a relatively complex web page.

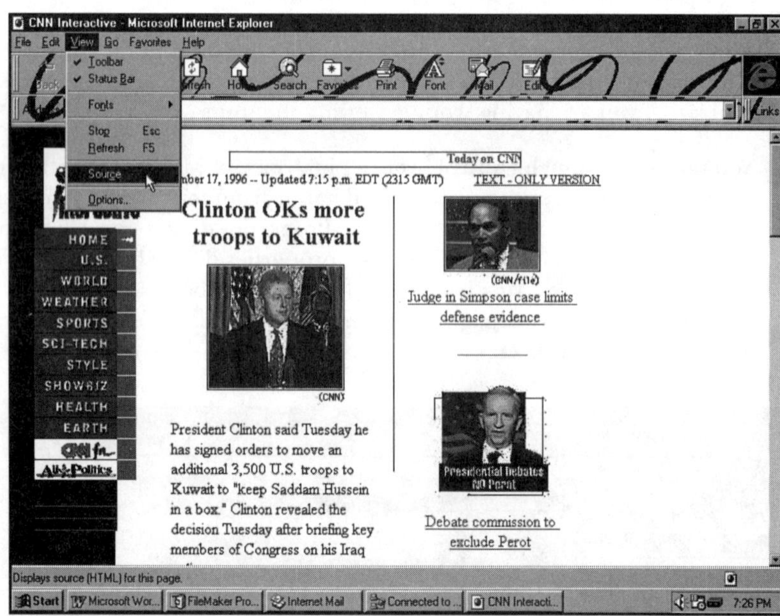

Source view opens the code in Notepad, or whatever you have specified as your text editor. Viewing code in Notepad is educational, and many people use it to check the techniques used in favorite web sites.

For production of web pages, however, MSIE offers you the opportunity to open a page in an HTML editor. If you have the Word Internet Assistant (Word IA) installed in Microsoft Word 7, or used the built-in editor in Word 97, then clicking the Edit button on the toolbar opens the page inside that program. Figure 16.8 shows you the CNN page inside Word 7 with Word IA. Obviously, viewing this page has no production value because you can't save the changes to disk and have them appear at that site—unless you work for CNN. But for your own web site, or an intranet application, this editor is a valuable tool.

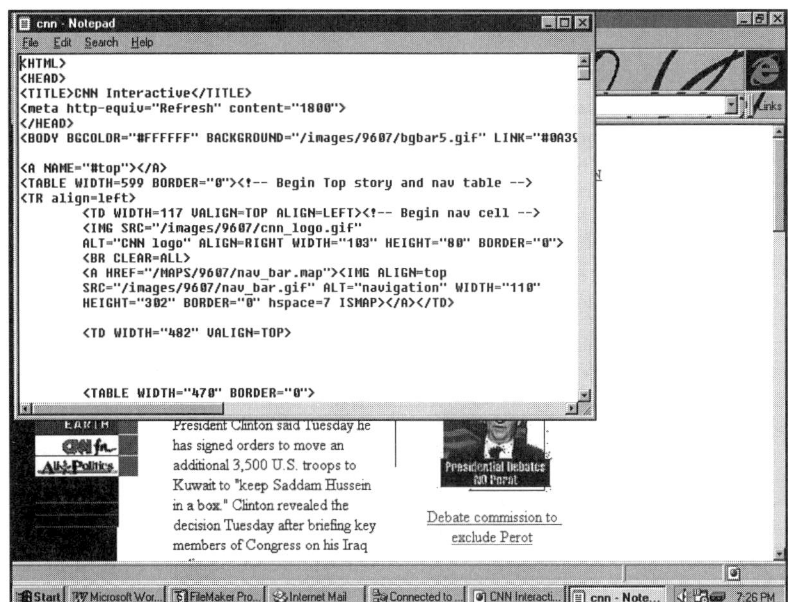

Figure 16.7

This figure is the source view of CNN in MSIE.

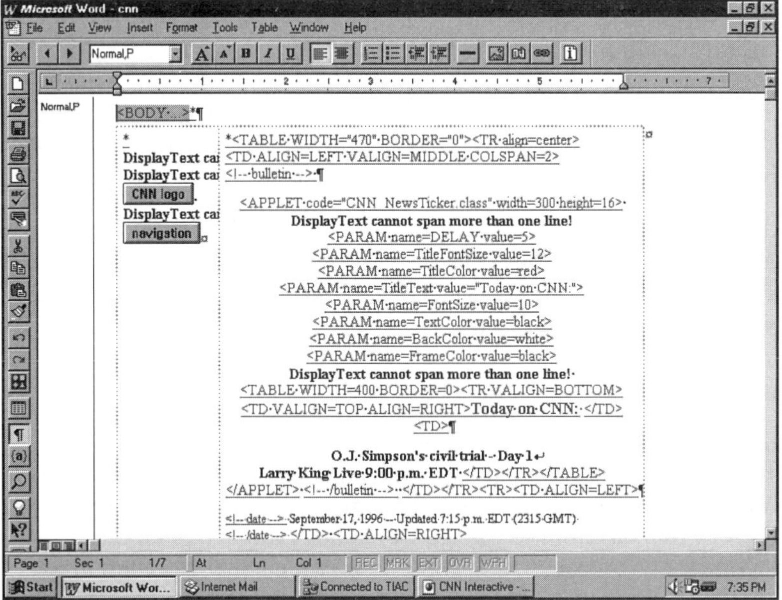

Figure 16.8

CNN's home page in Word IA offers both viewing and editing capabilities.

Navigating with a Browser

You already have been introduced to the concept of an address on the Internet or on an intranet. A web address as indicated in a URL is a logical address that is mapped to the actual physical location where the files are stored. Although it might be interesting to pull a file from a server in Switzerland one moment and one in New Zealand the next, the content and how it blends together is of most interest.

Back, Forward...

In a session, the order that you access files by entering URLs is the *session history*. The Back button or Alt+Left arrow keystroke moves you back one URL in your session; the Forward button or Alt+Right arrow keystroke moves you forward one URL.

Home...

The start page or home page of the browser is something that you can set in the browser's properties sheet. Changing the home page is described in the next section. To return to a home page, click the Home button, or select the Start Page command from the Go menu.

Stop, Refresh...

In some cases, web pages won't load properly. This can be due to heavy network traffic, or due to an error. Before giving up on viewing that page, you can click the Stop button to end the request or the Refresh button to ask to reload the page indicated by the URL again. If a page has associated graphics files that load, clicking the Refresh button is faster than the original request because any of those graphics stored in the MSIE cache will be used rather than downloaded. Clicking the MSIE "e" world icon at the right of the toolbar will also initiate a refresh.

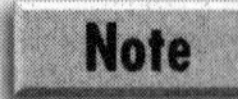

Increasing the cache size is one of those factors that can help you improve performance. I also like to browse the cache for icons, buttons, and other features that I might want to use constructing web pages.

Search...

MSIE has a find function that searches your current page, accessed from the Find command on the Edit menu. You can also use the Search button on the toolbar or the Search the web command on the Go menu to connect to the search engine at http://www.microsoft.com/access/allinone.asp. Of course, you need to have an Internet connection to view this site. Other Internet search engines in common use are as follows:

- Lycos at http://www.lycos.com
- WebCrawler at http://www.webcrawler.com

- AltaVista at http://www.altavista.com
- Yahoo at http://www.yahoo.com

Yahoo is really a directory service with a hierarchical database listing of Internet content by subject. Each of the search engines in the preceding list contains connections to other search engines, allowing you to search the Internet in multiple ways.

Note Don't rely on a single search engine to do an adequate Internet search. In recent work, I searched for J++ on two of the preceding search engines, and although I got several hits, Microsoft J++ was not returned. So it pays to try searching several ways.

You might find the shortcuts listed in tables 16.1 and 16.2 useful to you in MSIE. It offers you keyboard shortcuts that let you navigate about a web page. Because a web page can often be longer than a single screen, these keystroke equivalents will help you more easily position yourself without having to scroll, and help you concentrate on reading the content of the web page.

Table 16.1
Document Navigation Shortcuts

Action	Keystroke
Next page	Shift+Backspace
Previous page	Backspace
Up	Up arrow
Down	Down arrow
Up a screenful	Page Up
Down a screenful	Page Down
Document start	Home
Document end	End
Display the shortcut menu for a hyperlink	Shift+F10
Move between frames	Shift+Ctrl+Tab

Table 16.2
Miscellaneous Operations

Operation	Keystroke
Open another location (URL)	Ctrl+O
New window	Ctrl+N
Refresh	F5
Stop	Esc
Print the current page or active frame	Ctrl+P
Save the current page	Ctrl+S
Activate a selected hyperlink	Enter

Browser Properties

Much more useful than the page Properties dialog box that you saw in figure 16.6 is the collection of properties that you can access from the Microsoft Internet Explorer icon on the desktop. To open that dialog box, right-click on the icon and select the Properties command. Figure 16.9 shows you the first of the tabs in this dialog box, the General tab.

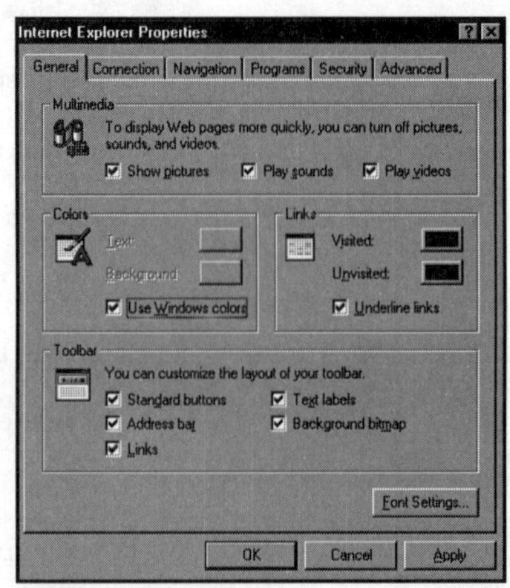

Figure 16.9
The General tab of the Properties dialog box enables you to alter the interface of MSIE.

On the General tab, you can do the following:

- **Multimedia.** Deselect any one of the following check boxes: Show Pictures, Play Sounds, or Play Videos. Doing so speeds up your browser by ignoring these file types. If you want to load text first temporarily, hold down the Shift key as a page loads.
- **Colors.** Use this section to set the color of text or the browser's background.
- **Links.** In this section, you can colorize links and underline them as well.
- **Toolbar.** Deselect any of the toolbar components checkboxes to remove them from view.

The Connection tab of the Properties dialog box (see fig. 16.10) enables you to define the behavior of your web browser when requesting URLs for services on the Internet through a *proxy server.* A proxy server is a web server that contains two network boards, one that communicates to the Internet and the other that communicates to your internal network or intranet. Microsoft's Catapult product is an example of a proxy server and might become a component of future versions of Microsoft BackOffice.

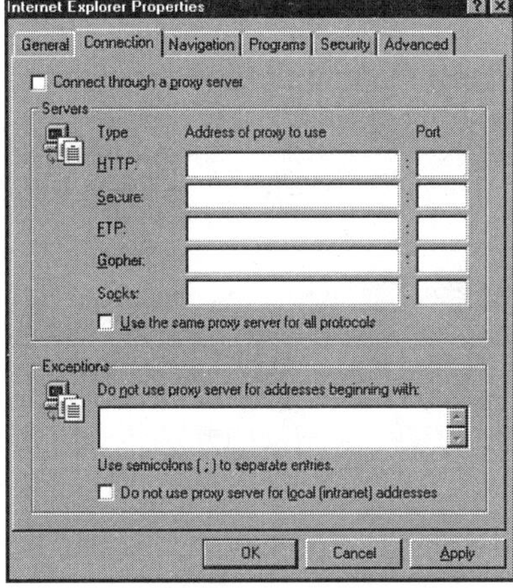

Figure 16.10

The Connection tab of the Properties dialog box enables you to communicate requests for URLs and services through a proxy server.

The Navigation tab of the Properties dialog box (see fig. 16.11) enables you to set two important properties of a browser—the Start page and the retained history of accessed links. To change the home page or start page, enter the address and its title in the Customize section. Also, change the toggle switch to alter the number of days that an accessed link is retained in the History folder.

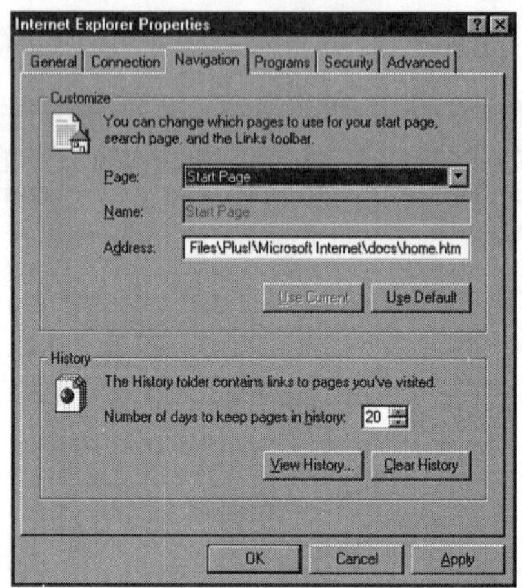

Figure 16.11

The Navigation tab of the Properties dialog box enables you to set the home page and the number of days that accessed links are retained.

Perhaps the most important page of the Properties dialog box is the Programs tab shown in figure 16.12. On this tab, you can set which mail or news program that you want MSIE to use, set up file viewer registrations, and have MSIE display the dreaded alert box when it is not the default browser. The next section covers some of the important applications that you would want to register in an Internet/intranet environment.

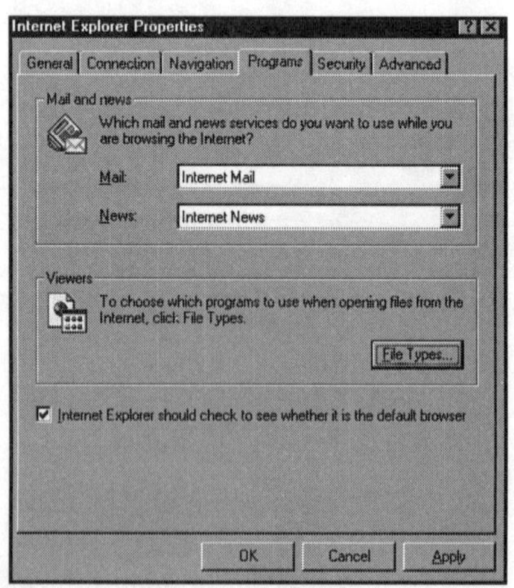

Figure 16.12

The Programs tab of the Properties dialog box is where you set up helper applications.

The Security tab of the Properties dialog box, shown in figure 16.13, contains a system for denying access to a web site when a reader uses the Internet Explorer as his or her web browser. The system works by detecting ratings placed into the web pages that define its content. It is up to the content provider or web site manager to add those definitions. When an administrator sets up the security level of a client, then sites or web pages that don't conform will not load in MSIE.

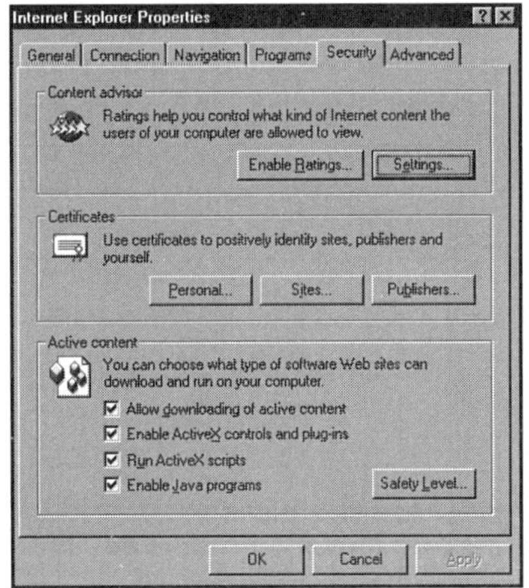

Figure 16.13

The Security tab of the Properties dialog box enables you to deny access to web sites based on a voluntary rating system.

From an administrator's point of view, after you install the MSIE software you must enable the security system. This is done by clicking on the Settings button and entering the Supervisor Password into the dialog box along with a confirming password entry. After the supervisor password is entered, all further changes to MSIE's security system requires that password.

To set the different category ratings, click on the Settings button. The Content Advisor appears, as shown in figure 16.14. Click on a category and move the slider to the left or right to set the level of the restriction. The four categories are Language, Nudity, Sex, and Violence. For some reason—it seems an oversight to me—Drugs and Rock & Roll have been left off the list.

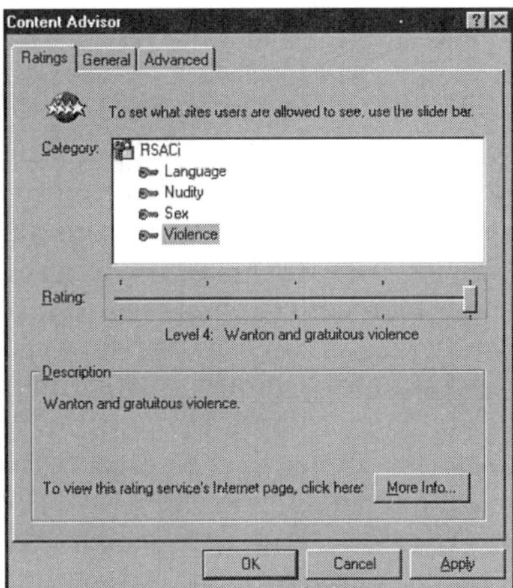

Figure 16.14

The Content Advisor sets the levels of the different categories used to deny access to a web site.

Note The ratings system used was developed by the Recreational Software Advisory Council (RASC) and is based on the work of Dr. Donald Roberts at Stanford University. You can view detailed information on the ratings descriptions at the Internet URL: http://www.rasc.org/ratingsv01.html. If you click the More Info button in the Content Advisor, MSIE launches and opens that web page.

Finally, click the Enable Ratings button to turn on the Content Advisor. You are prompted for the supervisor password. To turn off the system, click the Disable Ratings button. Don't forget your supervisor password, or you will be reinstalling your MSIE software.

The second category of security managed on the Security tab is the use of certificates. The Personal button lets you view a list of all the personal certificates registered on your computer. Personal certificates are only used with client authentication servers that require personal certificates.

The Sites button enables you to use security certificates sent from secure web sites. A list of certification authorities are opened, and the information authenticated for each is indicated. To see a list of certification authorities in MSIE, click the Publisher button.

The final area of security addressed in the Security tab is the use of applets. When you download software from the Internet, you put your computer at risk to virus infection. To protect against this possibility, you can instruct MSIE to ignore certain types of objects in web pages. These include: active content, ActiveX objects, plug-ins, scripts, and Java. You can set three levels of protection, the highest level of which displays a dialog box anytime an applet is being downloaded.

Helper Applications

It is worth pausing a moment to stress the importance of the File Viewer section in the Programs tab. This section contains the File Types button, which opens the File Types dialog box. Using this dialog box shown in figure 16.15, you can associate helper applications with file extensions. When MSIE downloads a file of the registered association: sound, video, animation, virtual markup or 3D graphics, chat sessions, and so forth, the associate application loads and runs or plays the file type.

Helper applications are not only of interest for bizarre exotic Internet data content, but they also can be used to associate standard business data files with office applications. If you download a DOC file, for example, you can register that file with Microsoft Word and have that program load. Or you can have a ZIP file load in WinZip, a spreadsheet XLS file load in Excel, and so on. In future versions of Microsoft Internet Explorer and Microsoft Office 97, this process is accomplished seamlessly for any Active Document. As an example of this, try opening a Word document using the Open File command in MSIE 3.

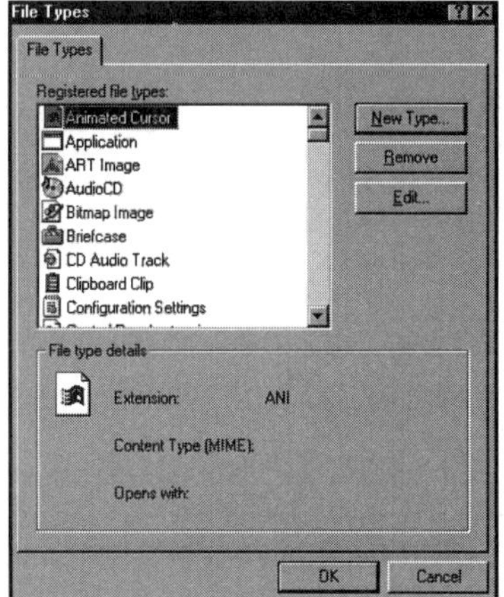

Figure 16.15

In the File Types dialog box, you associate file extensions with helper applications.

At a minimum, a system administrator should consider the following helper applications important and useful to the average user:

- **Adobe Acrobat Reader.** This reader for the Portable Document format (PDF) lets the user open and view electronic documents in that format. Obtain this program from http://www.adobe.com/acrobat/.
- **WinZip.** Because ZIP is the standard compression format, WinZip is a valuable helper application. You can obtain it from any one of the on-line services. A favorite Internet source is http://www.shareware.com.

Multimedia Helpers

MSIE has a built-in connection to a sound player. This player is sufficient for sounds in the WAVE format. However, you might encounter other sound formats that this player cannot handle. The following are sound formats in common use on the Internet:

- AIFF
- MPEG (also a video format)
- μ-law (used in Unix)
- WAVE

The favored sound players on Windows are as follows:

- **WHAM 1.31.** This sound player and converter works with a variety of formats. You can obtain it from http://gatekeeper.dec.com/pub/micro/msdos/win3/sounds/wham/133.zip.

- **Windows Play Any.** Play Any will play any AU, WAV, and AIFF sound file. You can obtain Sound Any from ftp://ftp.ncsa.uiuc.edu/Web/Mosaic/Windows/viewers/wolny12a.zip.
- **Xing SoundPlayer.** This Windows MPEG audio player can be obtained from ftp://ftp.iuma.com/audio_utils/mpeg_players/Windows/mpgaudio.exe. Keep in mind that to play back MPEG audio, an MPEG sound card must be used.

Streaming audio has been popularized by Progressive Networks in its RealAudio sound format on the Internet. Using this proprietary format and a browser, you can listen to sounds as you download them. Without a streaming format, you are required to download the entire sound file prior to playback. RealAudio consists of a player that is free and a server that is sold by the company to serve up sound files. RealAudio was the first company to offer a Netscape Navigator plug-in. To obtain RealAudio, go to http://www.realaudio.com/.

Video files are encountered with increasing frequency on the Internet. The AVI standard on Windows is supported in MSIE through a dedicated player. There is no video format that has yet emerged as the standard, but there are three in common use: Apple QuickTime, Windows AVI, and the cross-platform standard MPEG (Moving Picture Expert Group format).

There are many helper applications that you can use to play back video movies. Here are a few that you might want to consider:

- **QuickTime players.** QuickTime and QuickTime players for Windows can be found at ftp://ftp.iuma.com/video_utils/Windows/qtw11.zip.
- **MPEG Realtime Audio Player.** This player plays both MPEG video and sound. Download it from ftp://mirror.apple.com/ufs01/info-mac/gst/snd/mpeg-audio-player-10-ppc.hqx.
- **MPEG Play.** This Windows utility plays MPEG movies. Download it from ftp//ftp.iuma.com/video_utils/Windows/mpegw32h.zip.
- **AVI Pro.** The AVI player for Windows can be obtained from ftp://gatekeeper.dec.com/pub/micro/msdos/win3/desktop/avipro2.exe. An AVI player is part of MSIE, but this one adds more features.
- **Xing MPEG Player.** Get this player for MPEG movies from http://www.xingtech.com/products/xingmpeg/xmpdata.html.

A new kind of video format from Xing StreamWorks uses a streaming MPEG format for real-time sound and might come into common use. This system is similar to streaming audio popularized by RealAudio. StreamWorks offers extremely high compression ratio and can play full motion video files as you download them at typical modem speeds (28.8 Kbps). To learn about Xing StreamWorks, go to http://www.xingtech.com.

The incorporation of animation and 3D modeling tools on the Internet is giving rise to a host of helper applications. Space precludes a full explanation of this topic, but it is one that you certainly want to keep an eye on. When you install MSIE 3, one of the options you can install is a Virtual Reality Markup Language (VRML) player. This tool will render a site using VRML to give 3D effects.

Among the most widely used animation tools is Macromedia's Shockwave. Shockwave enables you to play back movies, animation, and presentations created in Director. Because it is available in a plug-in for Netscape Navigator, you can actually run the animation directly within that browser. You can obtain information about Shockwave from http://www.macromedia.com.

Multimedia on the Internet is a fast developing topic. One place that you can use as a jumping off site for learning about aspects of this subject is the Yahoo multimedia section at http://www.yahoo.com/Computers_and_Internet/Multimedia/. Other sections in the computers and the Internet category are software, WWW, and the Internet.

Plug-Ins and ActiveX

Netscape Navigator 3 uses a system of helper applications called *plug-ins.* A plug-in is a specially constructed applet or application that is registered with Netscape and can run within the browser. For example, when a PDF file is encountered and Acrobat Amber is installed, that program opens within Navigator. Amber's menu replaces Navigator's menu, and Amber's toolbar appears below Navigator's toolbar. Figure 16.16 shows you an example of this behavior.

MSIE supports Navigator plug-ins directly and without any special configuration on your part, and MSIE will even convert Navigator Bookmarks to Favorites shortcuts that appear on the MSIE Favorite menu. It is my observation that many of the most interesting helper applications are available in the plug-in format. The following are some of the best:

- **Acrobat Amber.** Adobe Acrobat Amber enables you to view PDF files, fetching one page at a time. See http://www.adobe.com/acrobat/.
- **Corel CMX Viewer.** This program enables you to view graphics in the CMX file format. CMX is a CAD drawing file format. CMX Viewer's web page is at http://206.116.221.51/corelcmx/.
- **Envoy.** This is another portable document format viewer like Adobe Acrobat. Envoy can be obtained at http://www.twcorp.com.

- **QuickTime.** A QuickTime player can be installed as a plug-in into Navigator. This player is available from http://www.quicktime.apple.com/.
- **RealAudio.** The player for RealAudio streaming sound player is available as a Netscape plug-in from http://www.realaudio.com/.
- **Shockwave.** The Shockwave animation player from Macromedia enables you to view animation sequences in your Netscape browser. See http://www.macromedia.com/.
- **VDOLive.** VDOLive compresses and views video images transferred over a modem in real time. Obtain the player from http://www.vdolive.com/.
- **WebFX.** With this tool you can see 3D worlds created in an extension of HTML called the Virtual Reality Modeling Language (VRML). Get WebFX at www.paperinc.com.

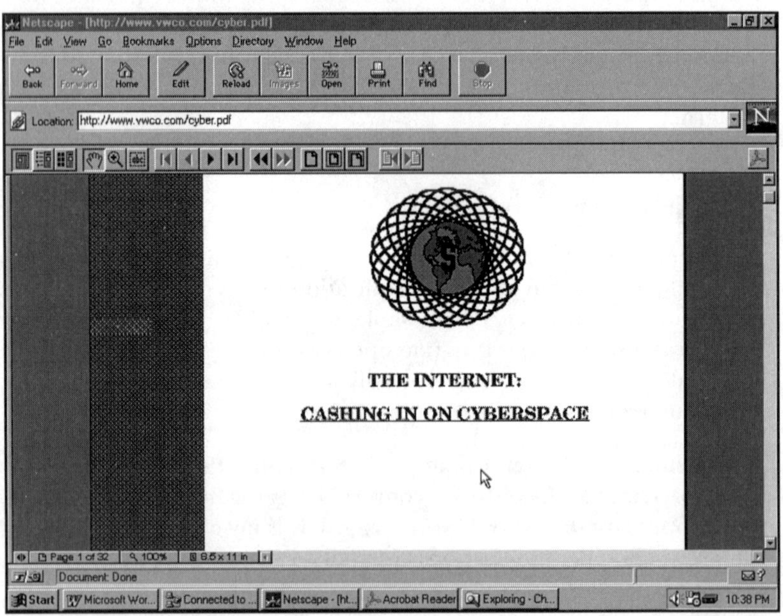

Figure 16.16 *Acrobat Amber is a Netscape Navigator plug-in that can open PDF files directly inside the Navigator window.*

Note Netscape keeps a jump page for its registered plug-in applications at the following location: http://www.netscape.com/comprod/mirror/navcomponents_download.html.

It is important to realize that not all Netscape style plug-ins work well or easily with MSIE, although most do. Since many third part plug-ins are hardwired for Navigator, you might experience difficulties that might require patches or special versions of these plug-ins for MSIE use. In most cases there are work-arounds, and this is rarely mentioned as a major problem.

When you open a web page that uses a plug-in, MSIE checks the file types registration to determine if the plug-in is installed. If not, then you can install either the plug-in or an ActiveX control as a substitute.

To install the plug-in, do the following:

1. Install the plug-in in the Netscape Navigator folder.

2. Install MSIE, and it automatically copies the plug-in to its folder.

   Or,

3. Copy the plug-in from C:\program files\netscape\navigator\program\plugins to the Internet Explorer folder: C:\program files\plus!\microsoft internet\plugins.

That completes the installation.

Microsoft is promulgating a set of revised OLE components optimized for the Internet called ActiveX. With ActiveX, whenever an applet is required, it is downloaded automatically. An example of an ActiveX component is the MSIE animated logo "e" at the right of the toolbar. ActiveX objects can be written in a programming language, Java and Visual Basic for example. Because they are based on OLE technology, hundreds of these components are available for purchase. ActiveX is a method for interapplication communications between programs, and sample ActiveX components can range from very simple programs to very complex ones.

Microsoft is having developers digitally sign their software code using a technology called Authenticode. A digitally signed ActiveX component will post a dialog box that looks like a registration certificate indicating that the transmission is secure and that the object is safe to use. When you download an ActiveX component in MSIE that isn't digitally signed, the program posts an alert dialog box indicating that caution should be exercised.

ActiveX is a big subject and a developing topic. It remains to be seen just how successful Microsoft will be in using ActiveX as its web object technology. Because the software runs without user intervention as part of MSIE 3, from a user's point of view there is little to know about it. From a developer's point of view, of course, there is much to know. You can learn more about ActiveX components by visiting the ActiveX Component Gallery at the Microsoft web site at: http://www.microsoft.com/activex/controls. That page is shown in figure 16.17.

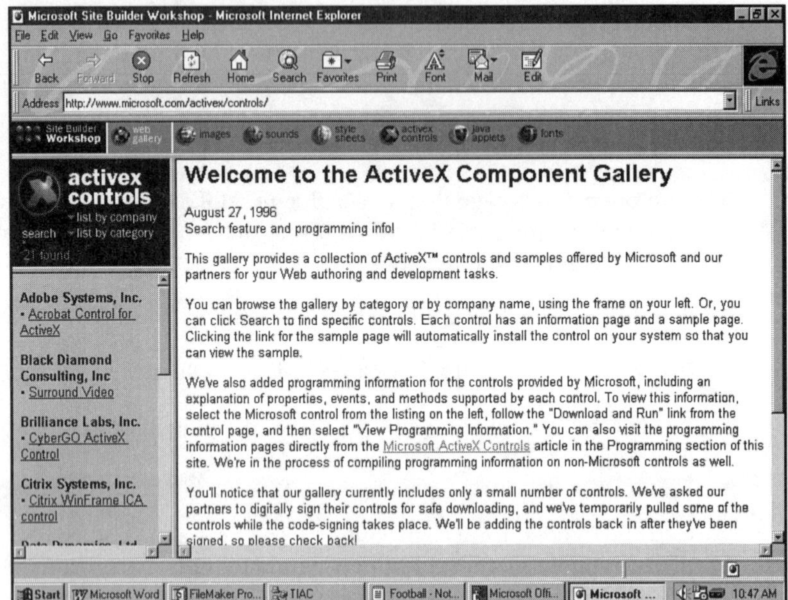

Figure 16.17
The ActiveX Component Gallery is a jump page to information and resources on various ActiveX products.

MSIE provides a framework that lets you browse documents both on the web and on your local hard drive. Components of web pages can be graphics, ActiveX components, and so on. You can also install programs that blend seamlessly into MSIE that allow you to send and receive Internet mail, navigate and view the contents of Newsgroups (which are similar to BBSs), and do conferencing. In the sections that follow you will look at Microsoft's recent extensions to MSIE. Let's start by looking at Internet Mail.

Internet Mail

On the Internet, every server and client has a unique Internet address defined by a network administrator as part of their setup under TCP/IP. The Internet allows mail messages to be sent from one client to another through a store and forward mechanism. The process sends the message to a sending server where it is forwarded to the server responsible for the domain of the intended recipient. The mail might be received later by a client. Mail messages on the Internet conform to standard messaging formats like MIME that provide a method for text transmission. Other data types are converted to text (encoded) and then reconverted back (decoded) at their destination.

Internet Mail is the first of two add-on components of the MSIE fully described in this chapter. The second is Internet News, described in the following section. When you install these two programs, commands for them are added to the Program submenu of the Start menu. A third add-on NetMeeting is very briefly described at the end of this chapter.

You install these add-ons by selecting them in the installation for the browser. If you have already installed the browser without the add-ons, you can run a separate installer program that you can download from the Microsoft web site in their \IE\DOWNLOAD folder, as describe previously in this chapter. When you run the executable file, it searches your hard drive for the browser and automatically installs itself.

When you start Internet Mail for the first time by clicking on the Mail button in the browser, a configuration wizard runs that collects the following:

- Your name and e-mail address
- Incoming and outgoing mail server
- E-mail account and password
- Connection type: LAN, dial-up, or manual connection

If you connect through a service, you do not need to enter the connection information, only if you want the program to dial for you.

Microsoft Internet Mail requires the use of an SMTP connection as an outgoing protocol and POP3 as an incoming protocol. That limits its current access to Internet e-mail accounts. You will not be able to connect to any of the following services with the current version of Internet Mail: MS Mail, cc:Mail, The Microsoft Network (MSN), CompuServe, America Online (AOL), and Microsoft Exchange Server. Presumably, support will be expanded in future versions.

The Internet Mail application opens within the MSIE interface but as a separate window and appears as shown in figure 16.18. Letters appear in the top pane, and the contents of the current letter appears in the bottom pane. To switch between your mail folders, select either Inbox, Outbox, Deleted Items, or Sent Items from the Folder list box. You can sort and filter messages by type and compact your message boxes to save space.

You can organize your messages into message folders in Internet Mail. The small online help system adequately explains how to create and organize folders but not much else.

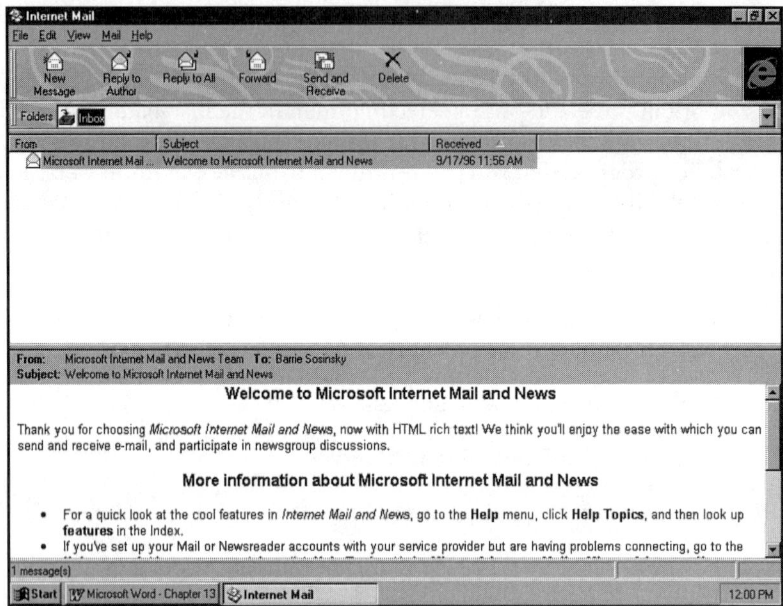

Figure 16.18

Internet Mail is a convenient means of sending and receiving mail through MSIE.

Standard e-mail buttons enable you to create new mail, reply to author, forward to another recipient, send and receive your mail as a batch process, and delete mail messages. If you have worked in Microsoft Exchange, or used standard Internet mail programs like Eudora, there is nothing much new here that you most likely have not previously encountered.

Messages

One nice feature of Internet Mail is that it supports formatted text for HTML messages. You can add fonts, font styles, bullets, and paragraph information to your mail messages. When sending or receiving from a program that supports this feature (like Microsoft Exchange), these elements are preserved. Figure 16.19 shows you the New Message dialog box with some styled text in it.

When you are in Microsoft Internet Explorer, the New Message command on the File menu opens the identical New Message dialog box you see in figure 16.19. It is the same feature and functions identically to Internet Mail. As an alternative to the New Message command, use the Mail button on the toolbar. The Mail button displays a pop-up menu (see fig. 16.20).

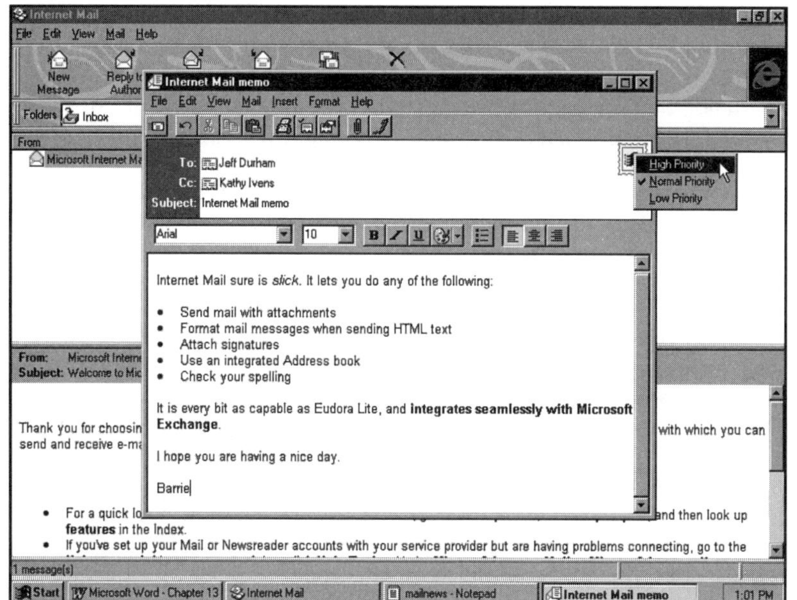

Figure 16.19

The New Mail dialog box contains a standard mailer interface that supports stylized text for HTML messages.

Figure 16.20

The Mail button pop-up menu in MSIE gives you access to Internet Mail and to Internet News.

The Mail button pop-up menu has the following commands:

- **Read Mail.** This command opens the Internet Mail utility so that you can read your messages.
- **New Message.** This command opens the New Message dialog box.
- **Send a Link.** This command starts a message that sends a shortcut to the current web page to a recipient that you choose. This is the same action as the Send Shortcut command described later.
- **Read News.** This command opens Internet News and connects to your News server. The next section describes Internet News in detail.

You will also note a Send To command on the File menu of MSIE. The Send To command enables you to send a shortcut to that web page either to 3.5-inch disk (A), to a Mail Recipient, or to your Briefcase. When you select the Mail Recipient choice, the New Message dialog box opens with the shortcut as an attachment. You can enter a message to go along with the shortcut and send it as mail when you are finished.

Figure 16.21 shows you an example of a message with a shortcut in it. A file attachment would look similar. Also shown in figure 16.21 is the address book.

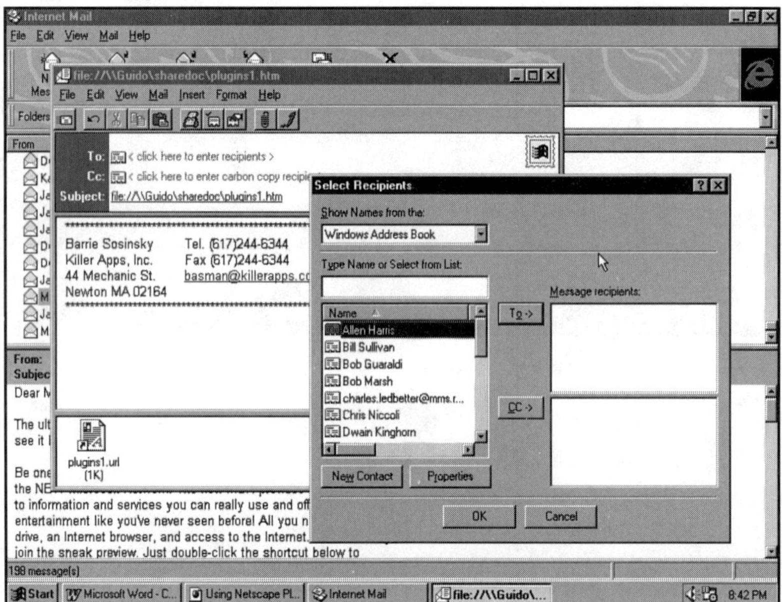

Figure 16.21

A mail message with a shortcut in it.

The Address Book

Internet Mail contains an address book feature that can be accessed from the Address Book command on the File menu. If you already have an address book set up in Microsoft Exchange, you can use the Import command also on the File menu to bring those entries into Internet Mail's address book. You can also use the Import command to import messages from Microsoft Exchange.

If you run the Import command on the same NT Workstation 4 that has an Exchange profile, Internet Mail finds that profile and imports your address book and messages. There are no options for selecting members of an address book. The process runs seamlessly and with no apparent difficulties. If you run this command on a newly installed copy of NT Workstation 4, be prepared to tell Internet Mail where that profile is stored. If more than one Exchange profile is stored, be prepared to indicate which profile is the source of your address book and messages. You will also be asked if you want to create new folders or add to existing folders if the same folder names exist.

When you import messages stored as part of your Exchange profile, the Import process enables you to select all or any one of your message folders. Figure 16.22 shows the Import Messages dialog box.

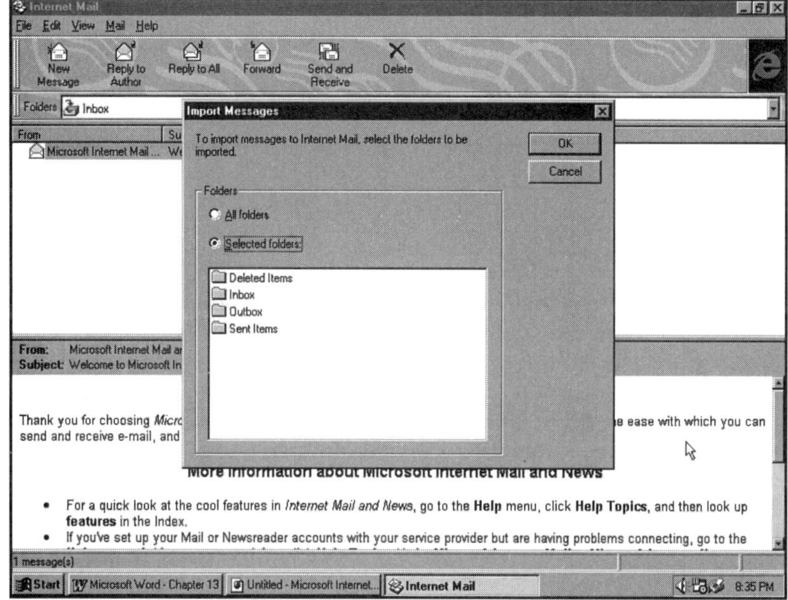

Figure 16.22

The Import Messages dialog box enables you to select which Exchange folder messages you want to import.

You can also use the Export command to export messages to Exchange from Mail, but you cannot export addresses using this command. To import or export entries or messages, you need to know the location of the PostOffice where the address books are kept.

Options

You can alter your setup of Internet Mail using the Options dialog box. Open this dialog box using the Options command on the Mail menu. Figure 16.23 shows you the Send tab, with message handling options.

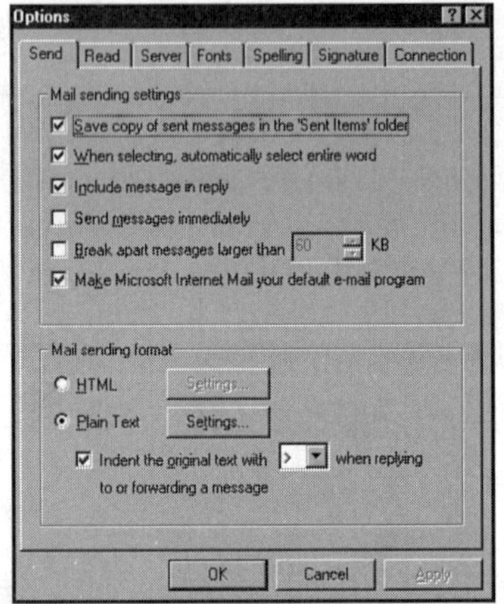

Figure 16.23

The Options dialog box enables you to configure and reconfigure Internet Mail.

You find the following tabs in the Options dialog box:

- **Send.** Here you find options that change the way messages are handled and saved and the file size. You can set Internet Mail as your default mail program and use > symbols in reply messages as two options here.
- **Read.** Options here include an alert sound for new mail, marking mail as read, and checking for mail after a predefined period of time.
- **Server.** This page lets you redefine your e-mail connection, username, password, mail servers, and so on. This is the information that you entered in the setup wizard.
- **Fonts.** You can set the size and color of the font used in Mail and the language of the font character set here.
- **Spelling.** Mail can use the shared Microsoft spelling tool. This tab enables you to set whether spelling occurs automatically.
- **Signature.** A signature is a text string that follows a message, almost like a final footer follows a document. People use signatures to put their contact information; some signatures put clever and not-so-clever whimsy in them ;>).
- **Connection.** This tab contains the information you entered on connection type in the setup wizard. If you need to change your mode of connection, change it here.

Mail Attachments

Internet Mail, as all modern mail programs do, allows for file attachments. File attachments on the Internet use a system called Multipurposed Internet Mail Extensions (MIME). This system places an identifier in the header detailing the type of mail attachment that follows. The attachment is then saved to disk as a disk file of the appropriate extension, and the registered program can be used to open the attachment.

To attach a file to a message:

1. Click on the paper clip icon in the toolbar.

   Or

2. Select either the Text File or File Attachment commands from the Insert menu of the New Message dialog box.
3. Locate the file and select it in the Insert File Attachment dialog box.
4. Click the Attach button.

   An icon representing the attachment appears in your message body.

Should you want to delete an attachment, select the icon and press the Delete key. The icon is a pointer to the file, and the file itself is not stored with the message. When you send the message, the attachment is sent, provided that Internet Mail can still find the original document.

To view a file attachment in Mail:

1. Select the message in the message list.
2. Select the Open command on the File menu.
3. Double-click the file attachment you want to open or run at the bottom of the message window.

To save a file attachment:

- Select the Save As Attachments command from the File menu.

  Or,

- Hold down the Ctrl key and click on the file name in the preview pane to save an attachment.

To display or run an attachment, click the file attachment icon in the preview pane header and then click on the file name.

Keyboard Shortcuts

Many of the operations you perform in Internet Mail through the use of a mouse or menu command can be more conveniently performed using a keyboard shortcut. You might find the following keyboard shortcuts shown in table 16.3 useful to you in Mail. These shortcuts range from creating new messages and sending or receiving mail, to working with your mailboxes, replying and forwarding mail, and so forth.

TABLE 16.3
Keyboard Shortcuts

Operation	Keystroke
Main Window, View Message Window, and Send Message Window Actions	
Help	F1
Select All	Ctrl+A
Main Window and View Message Window Commands	
Open a new message	Ctrl+N
Send and receive mail	Ctrl+M
Reply to the author	Ctrl+R
Reply to all	Ctrl+Shift+R
Forward a message	Ctrl+F
Print	Ctrl+P
Delete a message	Delete or Ctrl+D
Go to your Inbox	Ctrl+I
Next message	Ctrl+> or Ctrl+Shift+> or Alt+Right arrow
Previous message	Ctrl+< or Ctrl+Shift+< or Alt+Left arrow
View the properties of the selected message	Alt+Enter

Operation	Keystroke
Mail Main Window Actions	
Move between the message list, folder list (if the icon bar is on), and the preview pane	Tab
Open message	Ctrl+O or Enter
Mark a message as read	Ctrl+Spacebar
Mail Message Window—Viewing or Sending Actions	
Close a message	Esc
Find text	F3 or Ctrl+Shift+F
Mail Message Window—Sending Only Actions	
Check spelling	F7
Check names	Ctrl+K or Alt+K
Send a message	Ctrl+Enter or Alt+S

Internet News

Internet News is the second of the add-on programs that uses the MSIE interface. It is meant to be used as a newsgroup reader and is a modified mail program. A *newsgroup* is a set of collected messages on a topic of interest. Perhaps 15,000 active newsgroups are in existence today. One source estimates that newsgroup traffic is on the order of 50 MB of text daily, or about 25,000 pages in length.

To connect to a newsgroup, you need to connect through a newsgroup server. Internet News requires support for the XOVER command on the News server. For any server not supporting this feature, you will get a error message. Support is promised in future editions of Microsoft News.

In the sections that follow is a more complete explanation of how newsgroups work, their addressing scheme, and how to view, participate, and subscribe to newsgroups.

What Is a Newsgroup?

A newsgroup is a discussion group using e-mail threads. Newsgroups are similar to message boards or bulletin boards, so if you have experience with message boards, you'll get the idea quickly. The source of the word "newsgroups" is unknown, but you will often find these discussion groups referred to as USENET news, Net News, Internet News, Newsgroups, or even just simply News. USENET is the most common alternative in usage today.

USENET is a collection of network sites that participate in newsgroup circulation and use the Internet as the delivery vehicle. Some newsgroups belong to GnUSENET, which derives from the acronym, "GnUSENET is NOT USENET." Wherever they come from, the Internet is a newsgroup's post office.

Newsgroups can take any number of address parses, so an address like talk.peanuts.snoopy.dog.alt might show up. The last word in the address is a clue as to what kind of newsgroup you are dealing with. In your travels, you'll run across newsgroups that fall into the following broad categories:

- **alt.** Anything goes. An alt category is a newsgroup's way of telling you that they will discuss your musings as well as your thoughts.
- **bit.** The bit address is a mailing list from the BITNET network.
- **biz.** This indicates a business-related newsgroup.
- **bin or binaries.** A newsgroup that distributes binary files might have this as the first or (much more commonly) second part of its name. Binary files require the use of an unencoding utility like XferPro.
- **clari.** ClariNet is a newsgroup that distributes news from the UPI, AP, and stock exchange results. Normally, you pay to subscribe to this kind of a newsgroup—something that is generally rare on the Internet at the moment.
- **comp.** This stands for computer and relates to computer science, software, hardware, issues, and so on.
- **misc.** Anything that the newsgroup founder couldn't figure out how to categorize.
- **news.** These are groups that discuss newsgroups.
- **pictures.** Usually a second part of a name, these newsgroups distribute binary images. You might also see addresses for .art, .graphics, and so on in newsgroup names.
- **rec.** These groups discuss recreational, arts, and leisure.
- **sci.** Discussion groups on scientific issues have this moniker.
- **soc.** This stands for social issues and can be topics on anything under God's green earth (and above).

- **talk.** Newsgroups with talk in them are typically controversial issues that are worthy (or unworthy) of debate.

If you are new to newsgroups, you might want to read Brad Templeton's "Emily Postnews" every so often in the NEWS.ANSWERS.NEWSGROUP newsgroup for tips. Most newsgroups post a FAQ (Frequently Asked Questions) that lists all the common questions asked on that newsgroup. A newsgroup's FAQ tells you how to participate and generally lists anything you should know before you get started. You'll generally find the FAQ somewhere in any active newsgroup. You can also search for a FAQ by accessing a FAQ repository at ftp.rtfm.mit.edu.site. There you can search the usenet-by-hierarchy directory for FAQs of interest.

Using Internet News

When you launch Internet News for the first time, you are run through a setup wizard similar to the one you saw for Internet Mail.

When you use Internet News, your important connection is to your News server, as shown in figure 16.24. The News server contains a list of newsgroups that it knows about, and allows you to access those groups. Some News servers require logon; others do not. If you are already connected to a service and have logged on, you will not need to do so a second time.

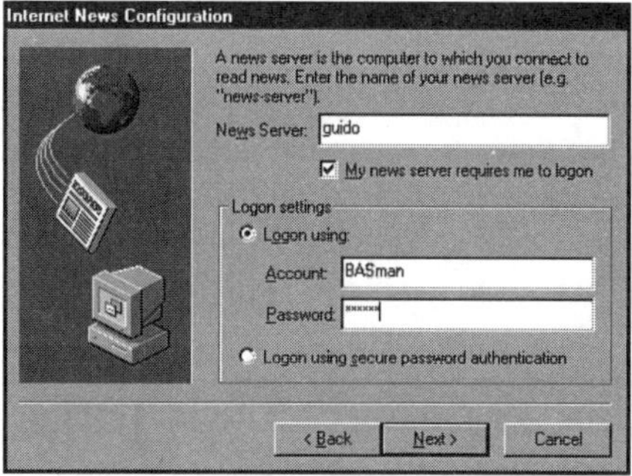

Figure 16.24

The setup wizard for Internet News lets you specify a named connection to the News server and define your logon information.

Internet News is similar in construction and features to Internet Mail. You set up Internet Mail in the Options dialog box accessed from the Options command on the Mail menu, and it contains a set of options similar to those you saw previously for Mail. Composing and sending messages in Internet News is also similar to Internet Mail. Rather than repeat the same feature set, this small section concentrates on the main differences in News:

- Connecting to a newsgroup
- Managing groups of messages

- Managing message threads
- Finding a newsgroup of interest and subscribing

If you launch Internet News and have specified a connection, then the program will try and dial it for you. If you are connected already, then you can choose the Use Current Connection radio button in the message box, and you will be connected to your News server. If this is the first time that you have connected to the News server, then the list of newsgroups is downloaded to your computer, as shown in figure 16.25.

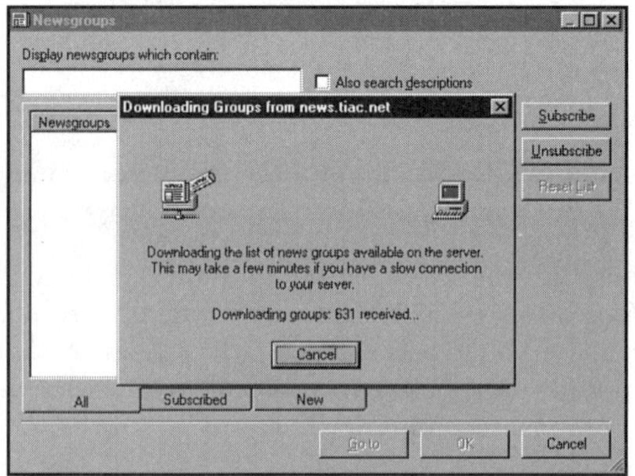

Figure 16.25

Downloading a list of newsgroups for the first time can take a while. This is coffee break material.

After the list of newsgroups is downloaded, you can subscribe to a newsgroup(s) by clicking on that newsgroup in the Newsgroups dialog box, as shown in figure 16.26. A newspaper icon indicates that that newsgroup is selected. Click the Subscribe button to send a message subscribing to the service. Because thousands of newsgroups are in the list, you can use the Subscribed tab to view your list of subscribed newsgroups or enter a filter expression in the Display Newsgroups Which Contain text box.

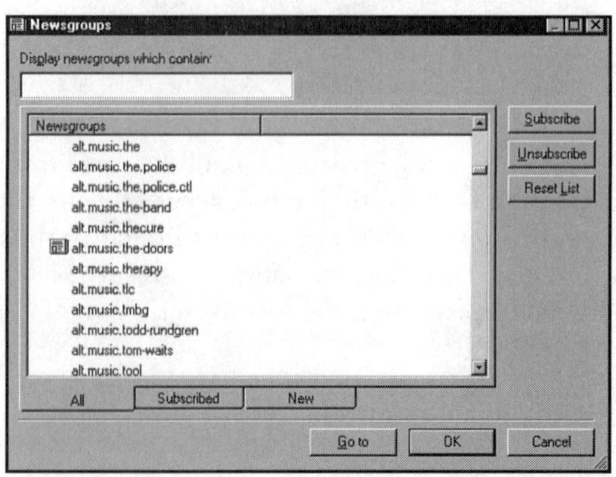

Figure 16.26

To subscribe to a newsgroup, click on it and click on the Subscribe button.

You do not need to subscribe to see the contents of a newsgroup or to send messages to people. Just select the newsgroup and click the Go To button. The Internet News with a newsgroup and messages loaded appears as shown in figure 16.27. Messages that are read appear in white rather than yellow, just as they do in Internet Mail.

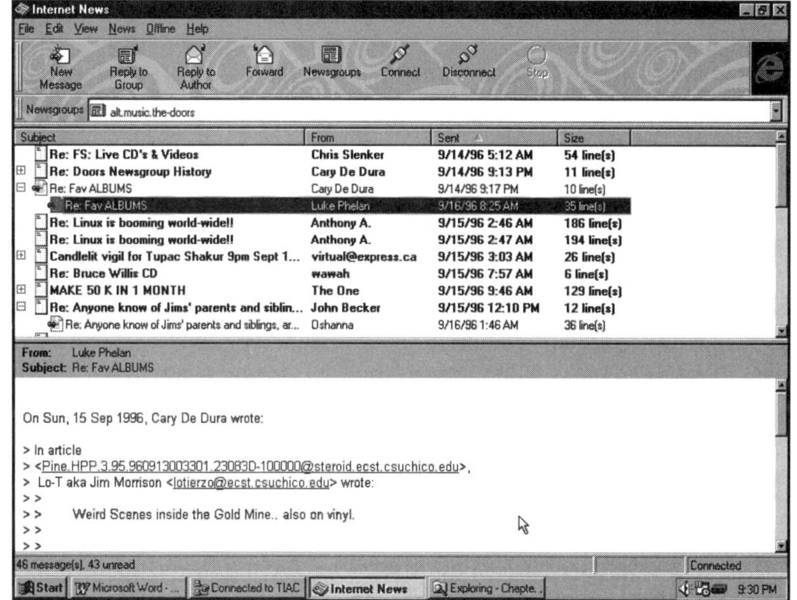

Figure 16.27

Reading messages in a newsgroup is a lot like reading messages in Internet Mail.

If you are subscribed, then new messages on that newsgroup will appear automatically in your mailbox every so often.

Many newsgroups are very active and can generate 50 or more messages a day. Get ready to never be lonely again. I strongly recommend that you spend time looking at each newsgroup you are considering subscribing to.

When you get tired of looking at these new messages, click the Unsubscribe button to remove yourself from the list. Many newsgroups use an automated list server program like Major Duomo. It is a courtesy to the list maintainer that you use the Unsubscribe process posted in that newsgroup to remove yourself from the list.

There isn't much to reading messages, sending messages, and replying to messages that you will find unfamiliar here. An important part of newsgroups is the message threads that appear from replies. I use message threads as a measure of how thoughtful the members of the newsgroup are and as a determining factor in joining one. Message threads are indicated by a hierarchical message. In figure 16.27, a reply to a message was read.

Newsgroups hearken back to the days when widely separate researchers were interested in creating discussion groups using e-mail to discuss topics of interest. You download new e-mail messages from the groups you subscribe to, read the ones of interest, reply to the ones you want to reply to, and read the responses posted. Messages can be composed off-line, and sent out in batches. If someone wants to contact you directly, then he or she sends you private e-mail.

Because newsgroups are public, it is easy to offend someone. In Cyberspace, no one hears you scream. Even the blandest message can look and sound hard out of context. Be careful what you say, or you will likely get flamed.

If you want to post a message anonymously, then send a message to the newsgroup via an anonymous server. The ANON.PENET.FI server is one such way. When you post your mail there, the server automatically creates an ID for you. You can then use this ID for any future anonymous correspondence. Send a message to DAEMON@ANON.PENET.FI and enter **Help** in the Message field. By the way, the word *daemon* refers to a small process that works in the background (like the Print Manager) and is not the name of a child of the Devil.

NetMeeting

One last component of Microsoft's Internet strategy is Microsoft NetMeeting. This third program is part of the add-on package for MSIE 3.0 for Windows 95 but wasn't complete at the time that Windows NT Workstation 4 finished its beta program. It will undoubtedly appear in the next few months.

NetMeeting is a very cool Internet/intranet conferencing and whiteboard utility. You register yourself with a location server, and other users who have NetMeeting can contact you and begin a real-time style conversation. The program uses streaming audio technology so that when you talk into your microphone, the other party can hear you in his or her speaker. The sound quality is adequate for this purpose.

You can also use NetMeeting without voice or sound communication using an IRC-like chat session.

NetMeeting goes farther than this. You can exchange files and draw diagrams that are seen by others. The later feature is called *whiteboarding*. Another important feature allows for application sharing functionality, and this sets NetMeeting apart from other whiteboard and phone conferencing programs out there. Given that the Internet technology allows for long-distance (even international) communications at near the cost of a local phone call, this technology is compelling.

Whereas NetMeeting will undoubtedly appear in Windows NT Workstation 4's Internet portfolio, another applet currently offered in Windows 95 might not. The Comic Chat utility puts cartoonlike balloons on your screen for conversation inside messages. This is pure whimsy—and too many late nights drinking Jolt in Redmond.

Summary

Microsoft Internet Explorer is a central utility in Microsoft's Internet strategy. It allows you to access and view a wide variety of resources and content and provides the framework for add-on programs and additional plug-in functionality. In this chapter you learned about the various features and settings in MSIE.

In the next chapter, the installation of Windows NT Workstation 4's Peer Web Services (PWS) is described in detail. This technology is a version of Microsoft's Internet Information Server that runs on workstations. Using PWS any NT Workstation can provide web services to others on the Internet or on an intranet.

CHAPTER 17

Peer Web Services

Windows NT Workstation 4 comes with Internet services as part of the typical installation of the operating system. This package, dubbed the Peer Web Services (PWS), installs a web, Gopher, and ftp service on your workstation. You can choose to turn any one of these three PWSs on after installation, and configure your workstation so that any one of the services runs at startup. This chapter tells you how to configure these services so that they run properly, and how to set the defaults and available configuration options.

Microsoft considers the TCP/IP protocol and the services that run on that protocol as a new way of publishing data on a network. Internet publishing, as this area has come to be called, makes information available as either web documents that you browse in your browser, or as files that you can download. Internet publishing works just as well on an internal internet (or intranet) as it does on the Internet. The intent of making these services available to workstation users is to promote the creation of special information centers where content on a particular subject is managed and available within an organization.

In this chapter, you will learn how to install PWS and how to configure these services once you have them installed. You will learn about the various administrative tools, important terminology, and preference and settings for each service.

Opening the Peer Web Services Tool Kit

The Peer Web Services provide you with a tool kit that allows you to set up and run different types of Internet services. After you install Windows NT Workstation 4, you get these Internet components installed:

- ◆ TCP/IP protocols
- ◆ Peer Web Services (PWS)
- ◆ Utilities for Managing PWS, such as the Internet Service Manager
- ◆ PWS product documentation in the form of an HTML document
- ◆ The Microsoft Internet Explorer browser

You learned about how TCP/IP works in Chapter 10, "The Ins and Outs of TCP/IP," and how to configure your workstation so that it can be a client or server on a network running TCP/IP. In Chapter 15, "NT Workstation and the Internet," you learned how the Internet is organized around domains, how addresses on the Internet and intranet are referred to using Universal Resource Locators (URLs), and how domain naming servers can map request for services in the form of domain names and URLs to the various TCP/IP addresses that you set up on your network. A basic understanding of these topics will prove useful in understanding the concepts supplied in this chapter.

In the sections that follow in this chapter, you will learn about the components that make up the Peer Web Services, and how to provide and configure web services such as ftp, Gopher, WWW, intranet, and secure communications.

For information about the last Internet component installed in Windows NT Workstation 4, the Microsoft Internet Explorer (MSIE), refer to the preceding chapter. Chapter 16, "Internet Explorer," contains a detailed explanation of how to use MSIE and how to best configure it. Chapter 16 also introduced Internet Mail and Internet News, two utilities that install in the MSIE interface and provide e-mail and Internet Newsgroup facilities.

All these protocols, services, and utilities when taken together as a suite of products enables you to run and manage a Peer Web Services server on Windows NT Workstation 4.

Introducing the Peer Web Services

As part of Microsoft's ongoing strategy of incorporating Internet and Intranet access into its products, both Windows NT Server 4 and Windows NT Workstation 4 come with Internet web servers as part of the operating system. In the case of NT Server 4, this package is called the Microsoft Internet Information Server (IIS). The same software installs on NT Workstation 4, but under the different name of the Peer Web Service (PWS).

The differentiation of the name PWS in NT Workstation 4, as opposed to IIS in NT Server 4, indicates that a connection limit is imposed in the workstation version that is not imposed in the server. In early beta, a limit of 10 simultaneous connections was imposed in software. As a hue and cry was heard in the land, Microsoft changed this limitation to one done in license only.

Microsoft intends for PWS to be a platform for low-volume publishing by individuals on an intranet, or as a personal web server. PWS could also serve as a platform for collaborative projects where file access by a group is required. Establishing PWS on NT Workstation 4 enables you, as the system administrator, to create centers of excellence and centers of information where individuals publish their own content.

You can read more about new feature in PWS, third-party additions, obtain patches, downloads, or other related pieces of software from Microsoft's web page at http://www.microsoft.com/infoserv.

From that location, for example, you can download the Microsoft Index Server (MIS). This software indexes the contents of HTML pages, Microsoft Office documents, and OLE document properties on a site into a searchable form. You can create a search form that provides readers with access to this information based on keyword searches.

Installing Peer Web Services

Installing the PWS is remarkably easy. It is considered part of the standard Windows NT Workstation 4 Setup program and installs from the CD-ROM of the operating system. To do a manual installation of the software (to overwrite a corrupt software component or replaced deleted files, for example), locate the INETSTP.EXE program in the INSETSTP folder and run that program.

Before you begin the PWS Setup portion of the installation, you must turn off any running Internet services. You do this in the Internet Service Manager utility found in the Peer Web Services folder of the Program menu on the Start menu (see "The Internet Service Manager," later in this chapter). You should log back on to Windows NT Workstation 4 with a user name carrying administrator-level privileges. Unbind any services from your Internet adapter cards prior to PWS installation.

During the setup, a prompt appears for you to turn off the guest account access for ftp file access. Microsoft recommends that you do so, or else you need to set each file's access individually later on. Disabling ftp access for the guest account does not affect the IUSR_computername account created during setup. During setup, you are also given the opportunity to upgrade any 16-bit ODBC drivers to 32-bit ODBC drivers.

Note If possible, consider installing PWS on an NTFS file system in order to obtain the benefit of the security features that that file system enables. Define user access and privileges through the challenge/response model in the User Manager, making certain that each user has a unique password. You will also want to set up just what the anonymous (no password) password allows. Normally, a single public folder dubbed \PUB is set up for this purpose.

At the end of the installation, you are asked to reboot Windows NT Workstation 4. After you reboot, you can proceed to configure Peer Web Services. You can do this anytime thereafter.

Configuring Peer Web Services

To have Peer Web Services run, you need to configure the software. The components are installed on your workstation during installation (typically), but you need to do the following for configuration:

- Add the Peer Web Services to the Network Services list on the Services tab of the Network dialog box (described in the following numbered list).
- Configure your client's TCP/IP address.

  On an intranet, you need to enter the IP address unless a DNS server has been set up. On the Internet, your friendly domain name can be used. (For more information, see Chapter 15, "NT Workstation and the Internet.")
- Configure PWS to determine which services will run. Select from WWW, ftp, or Gopher.

  The tool used for configuring these services is the Internet Service Manager. The Internet Service Manager is described in the section "Examining the Internet Service Manager," later in this chapter.
- Set the default directories for each of the services. When you access a service without specifying an address, this is the directory or folder that is displayed, and the default document in that folder (for web services) or the files in that folder (ftp or Gopher) are displayed.
- Add content to the appropriate directories to publish by copying the files to that directory or by replicating a directory to that directory.

Follow these steps to add PWS in the Network dialog box:

1. Open the Network dialog box and click on the Services tab.
2. Click on the Add button.

3. Select Microsoft Peer Web Services from the Network Services list.

4. Locate the INETSTP program in the Installed from text box, and then click on the OK button.

   The installation proceeds and copies the necessary files to your hard drive.

After you install PWS, you will find the Microsoft Peer Web Services folder appears as a (Common) folder on the Programs folder of the Start menu. Figure 17.1 shows this command menu. The files for these programs are installed in the folder C:\Winnt\System32\Inetsrv.

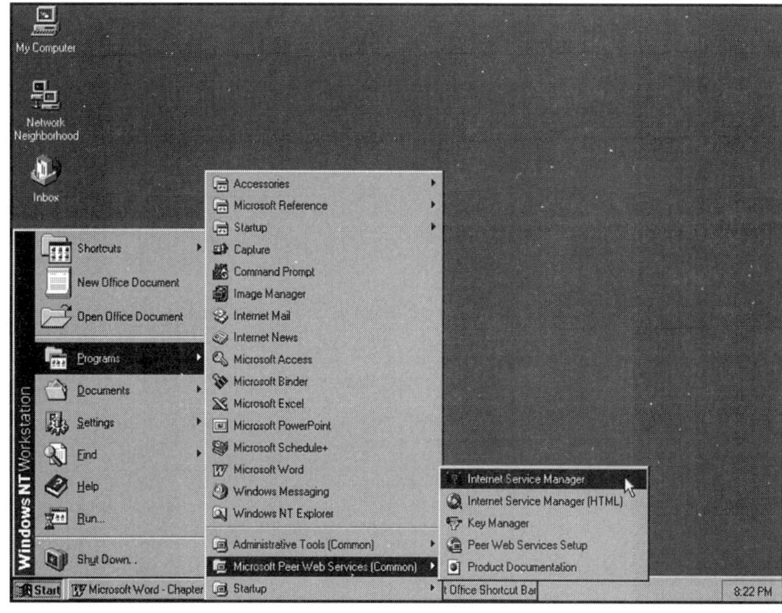

Figure 17.1
The Peer Web Services folder on the Start menu is where you access Internet/intranet utilities and services.

You use the Peer Web Services Setup program to complete the installation and setup of PWS after you have installed the software. You can also use the Setup program to add or remove components no longer of interest. The remainder of this section describes using the Setup program.

Complete PWS setup by doing the following:

1. Choose the Peer Web Services Setup command from the Microsoft Peer Web Services (Common) command on the Programs menu of the Start menu.

   The Welcome dialog box appears.

2. Click on the OK button in the Welcome dialog box.

   The Setup dialog box appears (see fig. 17.2).

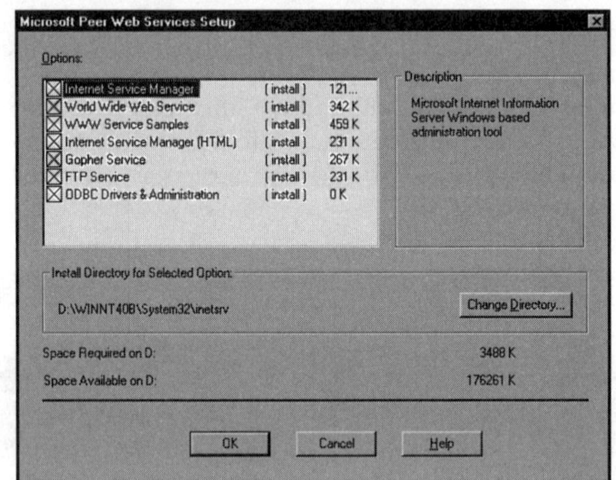

Figure 17.2

The Setup dialog box enables you to select the PWS services and utilities that you want to install.

3. Click on the services you want to install, and then click on the OK button.

   To completely install the WWW Publishing Service, make certain that all the checkboxes in the Installation Options and Directory Location dialog box are checked. The following list identifies and describes those checkboxes:

   - **World Wide Web Service.** The WWW Publishing Service.
   - **Internet Service Manager.** The Internet Information Server Configuration Manager.
   - **Help & Sample Files.** Online Help and sample Hypertext Markup Language files.
   - **ODBC Drivers and Administration.** The Open Database Connectivity drivers and the ODBC Control Panel applet are installed. This option enables you to log on to ODBC database files and have the WWW Publishing Service access the Internet Database Connector. Close all applications and services that use ODBC prior to installation of PWS, or an error message will appear.

4. Accept the default folder, or enter another folder.

   You can use the Change Directory button to browse to a location and set the location. After you specify or create the directories, the Publishing Directories dialog box appears (see fig. 17.3).

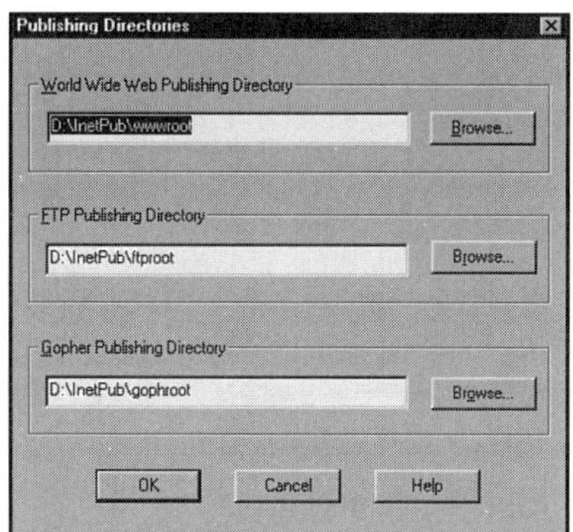

Figure 17.3

The Publishing Directories dialog box enables you to set the default or root directories for different web services.

5. Accept the default directories or enter new directories for publishing, and then click on the OK button.

   If you already have a directory setup for web publishing, you can specify that directory in the Publishing Directories dialog box. Or, you can copy your files to a newly created directory. Note that after installation, you can use the Internet Service Manager to change the default or home directories for your installed services.

   The installation continues copying files to your drive or accessing temp files already copied there. The ODBC Drivers and Administration option then posts the Install Drivers dialog box.

6. Select the ODBC drivers you wish to install, and then click on the OK button.

   Setup completes itself, and then posts an alert box.

7. Click on the OK button, then restart your computer.

After you have set up your Peer Web Services, you will want to test them to determine that they are functioning properly. This is easily done using the Microsoft Internet Explorer, which was described in the previous chapter. The next section describes some test procedures to help you determine if your installation works correctly.

Testing Your Installation

The easiest way to determine whether your installation of PWS was successful is to launch your browser and see if you can view a file in your WWW default folder. If you use Microsoft Internet Explorer as your browser, double-click on the icon for that program on the Desktop, and then enter the following URL in the location text box:

```
http://hostname.domain.com/
```

The default page appears in your browser. (The MSIE functions only after TCP/IP is installed, and the HTTP protocol is established.) Figure 17.4 shows this default page after the page at C:\INETPUB\WWWROOT\DEFAULT.HTM is opened by using the Open command. The INETPUB folder was the default folder for PWS in this installation.

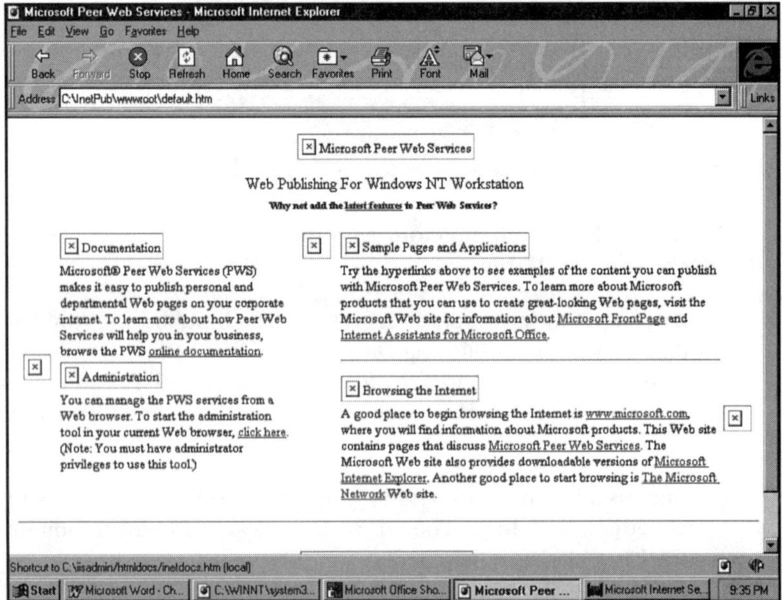

Figure 17.4

You can test your PWS installation by browsing the default web page on NT Workstation 4.

For intranet applications, the procedure is slightly different. Intranets require that the computer have a TCP/IP connection and that a WINS server service or other naming service (like DNS servers on an intranet) be running. In this case, enter the URL for the home directory of the new server, as in the following:

```
http://server name/path/default file
```

After you press the Enter key, the home page appears.

Notice also that documentation for both the Peer Web Services and the Internet Services Manager appear in the Peer Web Services folder Product documentation is in the form of an HTML document that can be read in the Microsoft Internet Explorer (MSIE); this is handy, considering that product is also installed. This is the wave of the future; Microsoft has plans to install an HTML help engine in all its products.

A shortcut to MSIE also appears on the Desktop with a globe under a magnifying glass. The appearance of the shortcut and help components are also sign posts of a successful installation.

Publishing Data

After you have installed the PWS, you can publish your data to it. Data for WWW consists of HTM files, related GIF or JPG graphics, CGI scripts, and so forth. Gopher and ftp services display the folders and files in the home directories. Gopher enables you to customize how your folders and files appear in browsers; you can install links to other servers and attach icons to files based on content. You can use ftp folders to contain files uploaded from other Internet/intranet users or to provide files for downloading for those users.

You can either move or copy web files to the C:\INETPUB\WWWROOT\ folder, Gopher files to the C:\INETPUB\GOPHROOT\ folder, or ftp files to the C:\INETPUB\FTPROOT\ folder. If you substituted a different name in place of those default names for those folders, or a different location, just place the content into those folders instead. You can also change the home directory for each of these services by using the Internet Service Manager, as described in the next section.

FrontPage

Microsoft has bundled its FrontPage web authoring software as part of IIS, but does not include the package as part of PWS. For anyone interested in publishing content to a web site, FrontPage is certainly a tool worth considering. Its major features include:

- What You See Is What You Get, or WYSIWYG, editing of documents without using HTML tags
- Image management tools
- Wizards for creating frames, tables, site search engines, and other features
- Site management tools that verify links and fix links to moved or renamed files
- Templates for a variety of web pages, and even for entire web sites

FrontPage features compatibility with cross-platform web servers via server extensions and is designed to also enable larger-scale group management projects with webs, including security and task scheduling.

For a busy administrator who wants to get a site up and running quickly, FrontPage is a good creation tool. Our experience with it is such that we believe that an administrator can give the program to a knowledgeable computer user without having to provide that user with a large amount of support. Therefore, we recommend it to you.

PWS is a set of services that run in a multitasked environment as independent processes. That means that you can have these services boot and run every time your workstation starts up. Web, ftp, and Gopher services cannot publish data from a redirected network drive (that is, a folder that has been mapped to a volume label). If you wish to designate a home directory for any of the services running on NT Workstation 4 using a network and not a local drive, you must specify the server and share name, as in the case \\COMPUTERNAME\SHARENAME\WWWFILES.

If you intend to use a network drive, keep in mind that that drive must be in the same domain or in a trusted domain. Also, any request from a user for data to your PWS requires that that user have user name and password access to the network drive. That means that the IUSR_computername user account created in the PWS installation to allow anonymous access will not work correctly.

Keep in mind also, that any connected user with the required access privileges is also in a position to change the content of your network drive, which can cause further difficulties. These wrinkles makes it unlikely that you will want to be bothered publishing PWS to a remote drive, although you can surmount these security issues if this is important and your users are known (intranet applications).

Now that you've learned how to install the PWS, some of the technology, and the configuration terminology, take a look at the primary tool for managing a PWS, the Internet Service Manager. The bulk of your time spent working with PWS is spent in this utility.

Examining the Internet Service Manager

The Internet Service Manager (ISM) is the utility used to set up, turn on or off, and configure Peer Web Services. After you have installed PWS, the Internet Service Manager is your primary tool. If you have used the service manager utilities for SQL Server (SQL Enterprise Manager), NT Server (Server Manager), and other Microsoft BackOffice components, the Internet Service Manager will seem quite familiar. It is both straightforward and easy to use.

Using the Internet Service Manager, you can configure the WWW Publishing Service, the FTP Publishing Service, and the Gopher Service.

The Internet Service Manager enables you to configure:

- Home and virtual directories
- Access permissions and logon security
- Encryption requirements
- Access logging

Two features that can be set for IIS that are not in PWS are multihoming and setting the allowed connections or bandwidth throttling in the Advanced tab of the ISM. That tab is missing for PWS installations.

When you are managing a site with multiple access, the Internet Service Manager gives you both an overview and details on your connections. In the sections that follow, you will see the different views that ISM allows and how to use them to configure and manage your site. You will also learn how to start, pause, and stop services, and how to set and change service properties within ISM.

The Three ISM Views

The Internet Service Manager uses three views to display servers and services, and their conditions. By examining these views you can determine what services are running on your network and their current state. You can also obtain historical information about your site. You select which view is current in ISM by using the View menu.

These three views are

- **Servers view.** In this view, the names of servers and their state is indicated by server name. If you click on the plus symbol next to a service, it opens to show the particular services in use (see fig. 17.5).

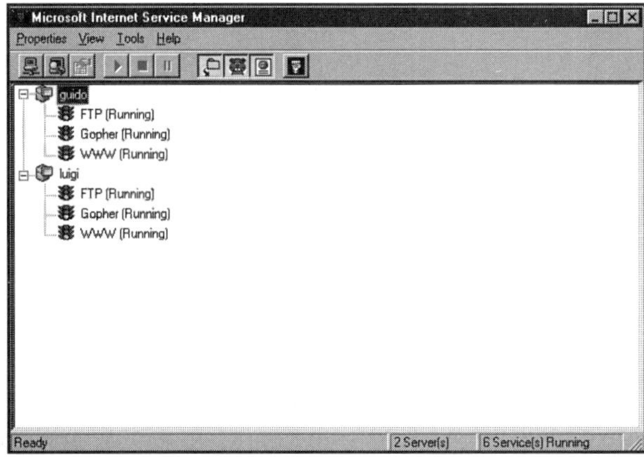

Figure 17.5

The Servers View shows services running by server name.

- **Services view.** The Services view lists the servers and workstations grouped by a particular service name. Click on the plus symbol next to a service name to see which servers are running that service (see fig. 17.6).

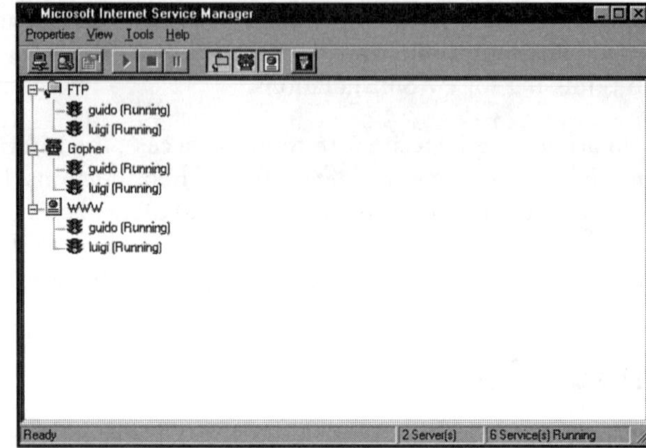

Figure 17.6

The Services View shows servers running a service-by-service type.

- **Report view.** The Report view is the default view, and thus is the one most often seen. Report view lists servers alphabetically, with services on individual lines. Lists can be sorted by clicking on column headings (see fig. 17.7).

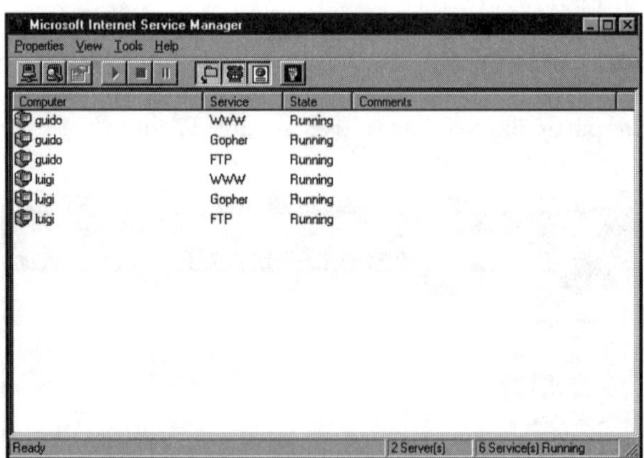

Figure 17.7

The Report view enables you to sort servers and services alphabetically.

Note that in any of these views you need to connect to other servers (IIS or PWS) running on your network to see them in the ISM. You can use the Find All Servers command (Ctrl+F) to search an entire network (which can take some time to process), or manually specify a particular server by using the Connect to Server command (Ctrl+O). Both these commands are found on the Properties menu.

In the case of the Find All command, a dialog box appears containing a list of servers that you can double-click on to connect to. In the case of a manual connection, you need to enter the following information: the server name, IP address, or the NetBIOS name of the server.

Service Management

The condition of a service on a PWS or IIS server is indicated visually through the use of a traffic light icon in the Internet Service Manager window. The icon has the following states:

- **Red light.** The service is stopped.
- **Green light.** The service is running.
- **Yellow light.** The service is paused.

In ISM views where the state of the service is indicated as text instead of as a traffic light icon (Report view, for example), the words "running," "stopped," and "paused" are indicated.

In ISM you can start, stop, or pause a service on a server. It is easy to do and can be done either through the Properties menu, or through the context-sensitive menu that appears after you right-click on that particular service. Figure 17.8 shows this context-sensitive menu. Select the Stop, Start, or Pause commands to alter the service state.

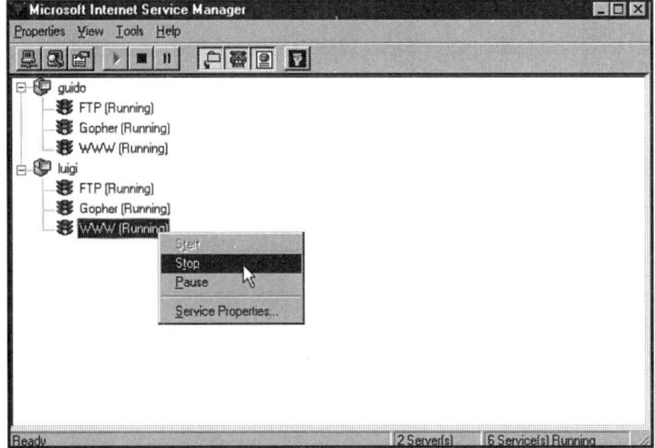

Figure 17.8
Use the context-sensitive menu to turn services on and off.

You can also start and stop services by using the Services Control Panel rather than ISM. An administrator can configure an Internet/intranet service so that it starts up automatically when your workstation boots up. You have individual control over services on your workstation and can start, stop, and pause any of the PWS services in the Services dialog box (see fig. 17.9).

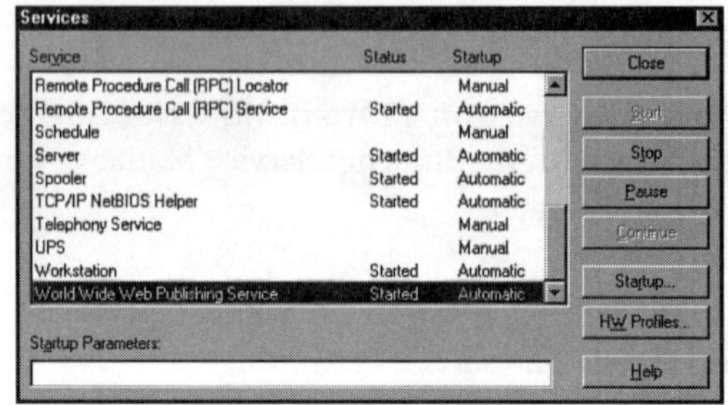

Figure 17.9

The Services dialog box is where you go to configure PWS services to start up at boot time.

The three services of interest in the Services dialog box are the FTP Publishing Service, the Gopher Publishing Service, and the World Wide Web Publishing Service. To start, stop, or disable a service, highlight that service in the dialog box and click on the Startup button. In the Startup dialog box, make your selection from one of the three Startup Type radio buttons (see fig. 17.10).

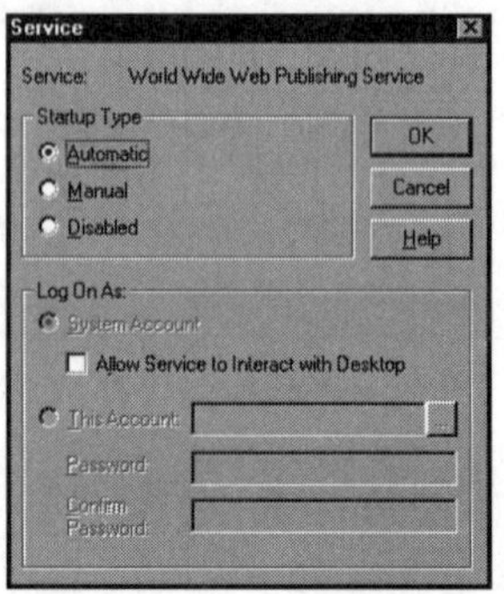

Figure 17.10

The Startup dialog box enables you to configure a service to start automatically or manually or to disable a service.

The Windows NT Server Manager (on NT Server 4) provides service control to remote administrators so that they can access and change service settings for workstations. Using this tool, servers and workstations can be configured individually or as a set of domain members.

Additionally, keep in mind that the Windows NT Performance Monitor (perfmon) can be used to tune and optimize the PWS. This tool is found in the Administrative Tools (Common) folder of the Programs menu of the Start menu (see fig. 17.11).

You use the Performance Monitor by checking for counters of the PWS services in the log. PWS HTTP (web), ftp, and Gopher counters are found. To see a list of the default counters and their definitions, check the online help system. You can also create event types monitored by this utility. The Performance Monitor shows events in real time, over elapsed time, or as a report. You can also set up automatic alerts whenever a threshold is violated.

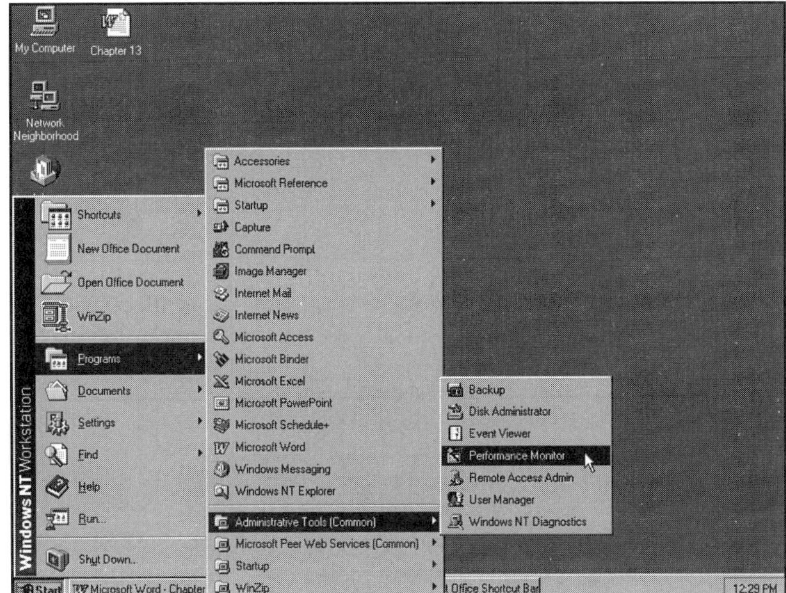

Figure 17.11
The Administrative Tools submenu contains utilities for fine-tuning PWS services.

SNMP is also used as a measure of Internet performance, particularly when using NT Workstation 4 in a heterogeneous networks solutions (for example, NetWare networks). PWS provides an SNMP agent to report performance to an SNMP management system. All the various counters generated by PWS are also available to the SNMP agent.

Service Properties

You can double-click on a service name in ISM to see and configure the service properties; or highlight the service and select the Properties command on the Properties menu to open this tabbed dialog box. Each service has its own set of properties that can be viewed and altered.

In the Service Properties dialog box, you can set:

- Port, connection, and logon properties
- Default (home) directories
- Logging access to a database (through ODBC) or to an event log file

The Advanced tab available in IIS, which enables multihoming and security features, is missing in PWS.

The following sections give you specific information about each of the tabs in the Service Property dialog box, how to configure them, and their purpose.

Service Properties

The Service tab of the Service Properties dialog box enables you to set access rights (see fig. 17.12). An account name for anonymous client requests is specified. The default user name (IUSR_computer name) is typically used for anonymous logons. This account is defined during installation. On this tab, you can specify another user name or create a new user account.

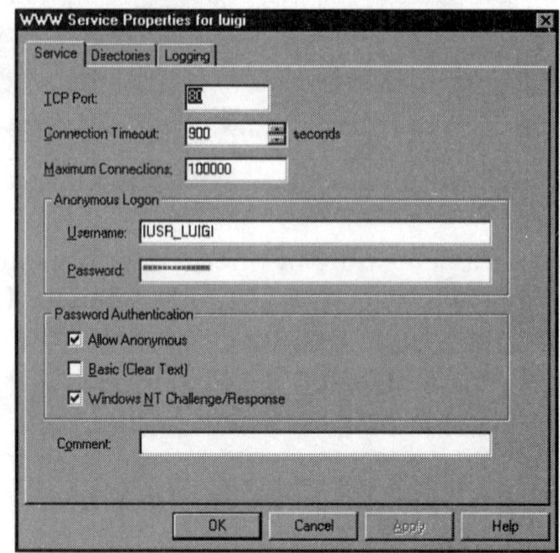

Figure 17.12

On the Service tab of the Service Properties dialog box, you can set user account access to a service.

Comments entered into the Comment text field appear in the Report view. Typical comments are references for the IP address of a service or for the physical location of the server.

Directories Properties

The Directories tab of the Service Properties dialog box enables you to configure home directory paths and their default documents, set access permissions, configure virtual servers, and define virtual directories (see fig. 17.13).

You have already seen how home directories are used, and how access to that directory without specifying a file in a web service opens the default document. The default document option is a global setting used by the WWW Publishing Service for the entire directory structure. For ftp and Gopher, default documents are not used; instead, they are indicated by title, such as README.TXT, INDEX.TXT, and so on.

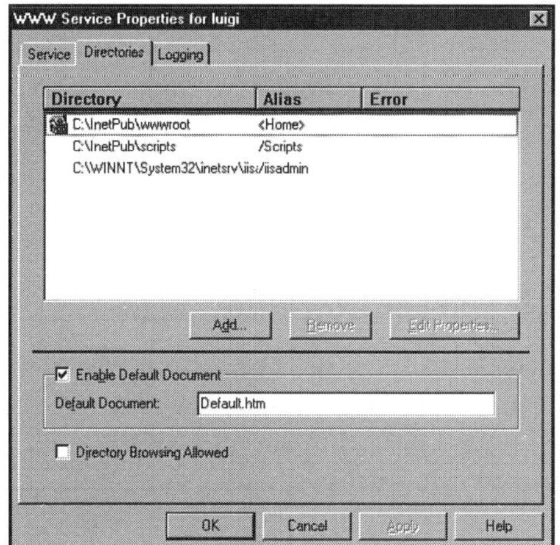

Figure 17.13
The Directories tab of the Service Properties dialog box enables you to set the home directories for your services, among other properties.

To add or modify a home directory:

1. Double-click on the service in Internet Service Manager for which you want to set a home directory.

2. Click on the Directories tab, and the click on the directory in the Directory list box.

   Any directory with a <Home> alias or a home icon to the left of the name can be modified.

4. Click on the Edit Properties button.

5. Enter the name of the new directory in the Directory Properties dialog box (see fig. 17.14).

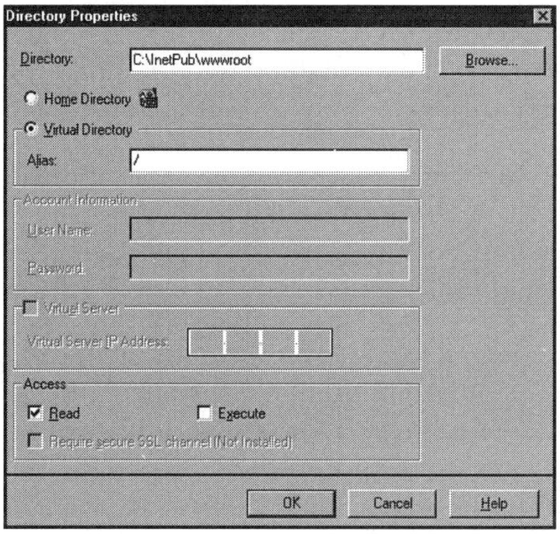

Figure 17.14
The Directories Properties dialog box enables you to change the home directories or create a virtual directory and assign an alias to it.

6. Or, enter click the Browse button and select a new home directory.
7. Set the desired options in the Access section.
8. Click on the OK button.
9. Click on Apply, and then click on OK in the Properties sheet.

Virtual Directories, Aliases, and Directory Browsing

You can also add other directories, outside of the home directory, to your web site for any of the three PWS services. These directories appear in your web browser as subdirectories of the home directory—or virtual directories. Virtual directories can be located locally or on an available network drive.

To create a virtual directory:

1. Open the Directories tab for a service in the Internet Service Manager as before.
2. Click on the Add button to view the Directories Properties dialog box.
3. Click on the Virtual Directory button, and enter the name of the virtual directory in the Alias text box.
4. Set any Access permissions desired.
5. Click on the OK button.
6. Click on the Apply button, and then click on the OK button.

You can assign Alias names to physical directories on the Directories tab. This proves useful for security purposes when you do not want users to know the path to a particular folder or to create a simple directory name. If you had C:\INETPUB\WWWROOT\ADMINISTRATION\HRREPORTS\EVALS, for example, as your directory name, you could define an alias of /Evaluations, and then have your users connect through that alias. Pointers in your web site can use this alias as well.

Virtual directories on network drives might require user name and password access. Be certain, therefore, to enter them in the Username and Password text boxes. A service must have a home directory, but any of the three publishing services in PWS and IIS can be in a virtual directory.

Directory browsing is a feature that enables a browser to list the file structure of a web site if a particular default document is not part of the specified URL. If the Web Publishing Service gets a request of this type, a hypertext directory listing of the directory structure appears in your browser's window.

Directory browsing is not often enabled in web services. It defeats the purpose of a hypertext construction in which the actual files used are not significant to the user. For PWS running on an intranet, however, directory browsing can be of interest if the actual documents are something your readers might want to see. Directory browsing is a global web setting and affects all the directories on a web site for PWS.

One feature not enabled in PWS, but found in IIS, is called virtual servers. Each domain appears from a name only basis as if it were an individual computer. By enabling a virtual server, you can designate different folders as if they were their own domains or subdomains, almost as if they were on separate computers. This feature is known as multihoming.

Logging Properties

The final tab of the Service Properties dialog box is the Logging tab (see fig. 17.15). You can log the activity of a service to an event file or to an ODBC database file. A log file shows the IP address of a connected user, the user's service name, service host name, service IP address, service status codes, bytes sent, and the accessed file's name. This information can be used to monitor site activity, check for performance bottlenecks, do loading optimization, and so on.

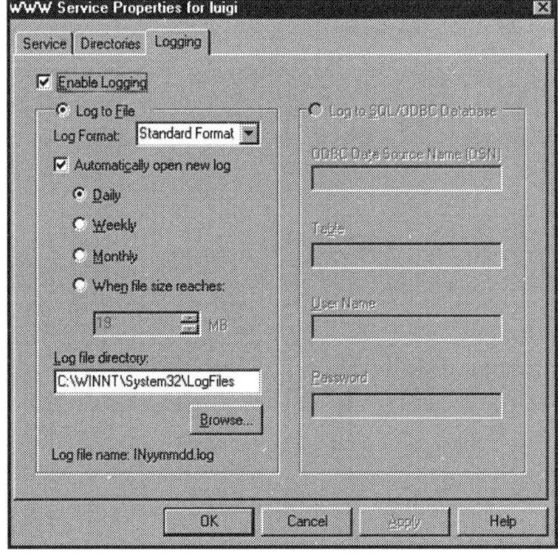

Figure 17.15

The Logging tab of the Service Properties dialog box enables you to set the home directories for your services, among other properties.

Each individual service can maintain its own log files. This simplifies collecting statistics. You must specify the frequency with which new logs are created and old logs are purged or added to. You can also specify the log file directory location.

Keep in mind that the more log entries you collect, and the more accesses your workstation has, the more system resources such as memory must be devoted to managing it. This problem is generally much less significant in PWS than in IIS due to the supposed lighter traffic. If you have a very busy PWS, you might notice a performance drop due to input/output activity. If so, you should make adjustments in your workstation's setup.

Log entries take the following form:

155.53.94.24, -, 12/10/96, 18:23:59, W3SVC, INETSRV12, 159.53.82.2, 220, 250, 1492, 200, 0, GET, /Luigi/home/index.htm, -,

The parameters tracked here are:

- Client IP address
- Client user name
- Date
- Time
- Service
- Computer name
- IP address of workstation
- Processing time (milliseconds)
- Bytes received
- Bytes sent
- Service status code
- Windows NT status code
- Name of operation
- Target of operation

You can read this, therefore, as an anonymous client at 155.53.94.28 gave a GET command for index.htm at 6:23 PM on December 10, 1996 from the virtual server at 159.53.82.2.

To log to a SQL/ODBC data source, you must specify the ODBC Data Source Name (DSN), table, user name, and password to the database. Logging to a SQL database has the advantage of collecting all your data in a single database that can be managed.

When you configure the PWS, you can install a security system that will authenticate Internet communications. You set up this system once as part of your web site. The system uses both encryption and public and private keys that are registered with a certification authority.

Exploring Peer Web Services Security

The PWS comes with a utility called the Key Manager that is used to authenticate secure Internet communications. It does this through the use of encrypted communications, and by authentication that uses digital signatures or keys that you create. Underlying secure communications on the Internet is the Secure Hypertext Transfer Protocol (SHTTP). Netscape also employs a secure protocol called Secure Sockets Layer (SSL). Microsoft recently licensed SSL.

With SSL, after a connection is made, the SSL client and server handshake and determine the security level they will use. They then perform an authentication service at both the client and the server. Outgoing SSL communications are encrypted, and incoming data is decrypted. SSL is being used in a variety of commerce Internet servers in testing.

The following example illustrates a scenario of the SLL in use. A person makes a purchase at an online store and wants to use a credit card to pay. The credit card number is tendered. The store sees the transaction but does not see the credit card number. An authorization message is sent from the credit card company (American Express, Visa, Mastercard, and so on) to the store. This promises to make online transactions more secure than a purchase in person at a store, because the credit card number is never in the possession of any individual other than the buyer and the bank.

The Secured Transaction Technology (SST) is the system used for digital signatures and online verification. Another protocol, the Secure Payment Protocol (SEPP) defines the mechanism for secure payments. These two protocols are now part of the Secure Electronic Transactions (SET), which will probably become an open standard.

From the standpoint of using PWS on NT Workstation 4, it is unlikely that you will be opening an online store. Most people doing commerce probably want the performance and security features found in IIS and NT Server 4. Setting up encrypted communications and digital signatures, however, can be very important for organizations involved in sensitive work.

In an intranet, salary information or performance reviews might be handled this way. Also, as more people add encryption and authentication services to their Internet traffic, this paves the way for trusted remote communications with members of your enterprise. This might be required if you were taking NT Workstation 4 on the road.

Microsoft supports the VeriSign Corporation's (www.verisign.com) certificate program. This is not a free service, and you should expect a charge for each certificate used. Note that although Microsoft supports this service, several (and in the future probably many) companies provide verification services.

At the heart of the system is the concept of a *certificate.* A certificate is a file that is a key. If the key is run through a software program containing the verification algorithm, communication can be verified. Also, you apply the key to communications as a lock; the encrypted file cannot be processed without the unlocking key.

Note Depending on your network's needs, you can purchase one or more security certificates. If you require secure, outside-world communication be established from your network to the Internet, perhaps a single certificate on a server can suffice. If you require secure Internet data transfer throughout, each server running IIS and each workstation running PWS might require a certificate. Each security vendor prices its service differently, so be certain to check around for volume discounts and site licenses.

In the sections that follow, you will learn about each of the components of the security scheme and how to apply them as a group.

The Key Manager

The Key Manager utility that ships with PWS and IIS enables you to create a digital key for Secure Sockets Layer (SSL) security. This two step procedure generates a key pair and applies an SSL certificate assigned to you to it.

In the Key Manager, you create a key file with the key pair and the certificate request file, two separate files. A key pair and certificate are both secure. To generate a signature, you must have both pieces. Only the signature owner holds both files. The generated key is created by you and registered with the authenticating organization. All the files together ensure that your encrypting key cannot be broken.

The process begins by filling in a Request dialog box to create the key file (see fig. 17.16). Choose the Create New Key command from the Key menu to see this dialog box. From this information, a key pair is created. The certificate request file is sent to the key validation service, which assigns a registered certificate. A key is not valid without a registration certificate.

Figure 17.17 shows the new key in the Key Manager. To finish the process, copy the registration certificate to disk. Choose the Install Key Certificate command from the Key menu.

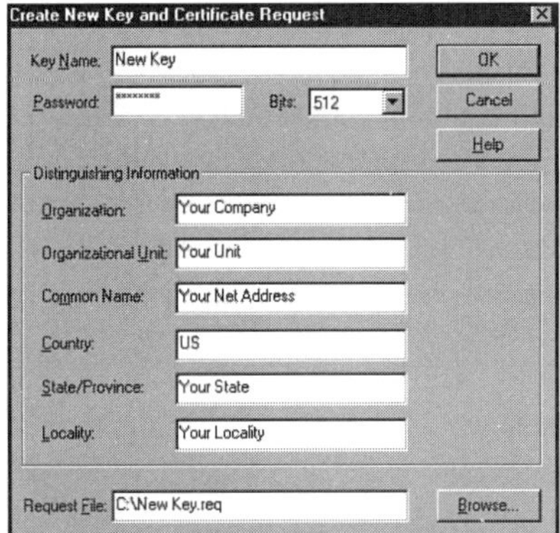

Figure 17.16

The Create New Key and Certificate Request dialog box is where you enter information for the issuance of a new certificate.

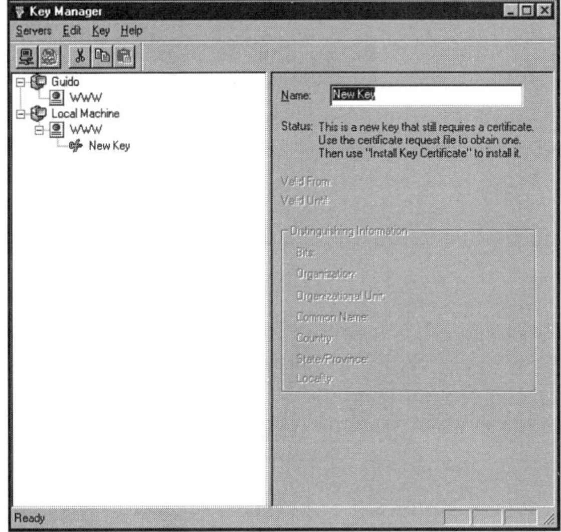

Figure 17.17

The Key Manager with a newly created key, but without the registration certificate applied.

Certificates

A signed certificate is stored on disk as a text file. The certificate is part of a message that you send. When compared with your keys, this combination authenticates your message as having come from you. As an example, a certificate might look something like this:


```
----BEGIN CERTIFICATE----

JIEBSDSCEXoCHQEwLQMJSoZILvoNVQECSQAwcSETMRkOAMUTBhMuVrM
mIoAnBdNVBAoTF1JTQSBEYXRhIFNlY3VyaXR5LCBJbmMuMRwwGgYDVQ
QLExNQZXJzb25hIENlcnRpZmljYXRlMSQwIgYDVQQDExtPcGVuIE1hc
```

```
mtldCBUZXN0IFNlcnZlciAxMTAwHhcNOTUwNzE5MjAyNzMwWhcNOTYw
NTE0MjAyOTEwWjBzMQswCQYDVQQGEwJVUzEgMB4GA1UEChMXUlNBIER
hdGEgU2VjdXJpdHksIEluYy4xHDAaBgNVBAsTE1BlcnNvbmEgQ2VydG
lmaWNhdGUxJDAiBgNVBAMTG09wZW4gTWFya2V0IFRlc3QgU2VydmVyI
DExMDBcMA0GCSqGSIb3DQEBAQUAA0sAMEgCQQDU/7lrgR6vkVNX40BA
q1poGdSmGkD1iN3sEPfSTGxNJXY58XH3JoZ4nrF7mIfvpghNi1taYim
vhbBPNqYe4yLPAgMBAAEwDQYJKoZIhvcNAQECBQADQQBqyCpws9EaAj
KKAefuNP+z+8NY8khckgyHN2LLpfhv+iP8m+bF66HNDUlFz8ZrVOu3W
QapgLPV90kIskNKXX3a

------END CERTIFICATE------
```


The installation of the certificate is completed by selecting the Install Key Certificate command in the Key Manager. Enter the information required. You should note that a key can be used for a single PWS server, as defined by a single IP address. After the digital signature is enabled, all web services (ftp, Gopher, and WWW) can make use of it. In browsers that support digital signatures, MSIE 3.0 and Netscape 3.0 and greater, a dialog box appears after a verified communication is received. For communications not verified, another dialog box appears to alert you to that fact.

Summary

Windows NT Workstation 4 ships with a version of the Internet Information Server called the Peer Web Services. Using PWS you can provide a web, ftp, and Gopher service on your workstation to any connected users. This chapter explained how to install and configure the PWS. Additionally, you can assign defaults, access privileges, and other properties for your services that were also described in this chapter.

In the next chapter, you will learn about the application of PWS to intranet applications. Using an intranet and PWS, you can easily create and manage client/server solutions that not too long ago required expensive software and hardware solutions. intranets are one of the most popular applications of the technology described in this chapter.

CHAPTER 18

Intranets

Intranets are a quiet revolution in corporate and enterprise-wide networking. Intranets are networks that run the TCP/IP protocol for their distributed computing needs in a client/server environment. An intranet usually does not connect to the outside world of the Internet (although some intranets do). Although the same naming conventions and addressing schemes you learned about for the Internet still apply on an intranet, you are not limited to the addresses you are assigned and can use your own.

Although the Internet gets most of the advertising ink, the bulk of the demand for and installed base of TCP/IP products and solutions are being bought for intranet applications. Estimates range as high as 65–70 percent of all web servers operating today service intranet applications. The market for intranet solutions is moving very quickly, quicker in fact than many vendors can accommodate the demands for products. There are few standards, and often it is up to the corporate manager or information specialist to sift through the conflicting demands and create solutions on-the-fly.

With the introduction of Windows NT Workstation 4, and the free inclusion of good, easy-to-use web services, Microsoft has put the power for web site creation into the hands of the average user. As this operating system gains acceptance (as it undoubtedly will), and computers running it proliferate, you will see many more network computers serving as information centers. This chapter provides information on why intranets are important, and how to design, configure, and secure an intranet site. It also lists some of the more interesting products that you might want to use.

Understanding Why Intranets Change Everything

Vendors implementing technology often do so in a manner that makes their solution proprietary. When you buy a car, few if any parts are standard off-the-shelf items. Typewriters, sewing machines, printing presses, even the type used by printing presses is proprietary. Of course, there are good and profitable reasons for this.

Computer technology has largely created several so-called *standards* that hardware manufacturers build to. Hardware standards include 3 1/2-inch floppy disks, CD-ROM drives, and so forth. The modern operating system is not a standard, although several have achieved wide acceptance. Go into any large network and you are likely to find Windows, MS-DOS, Macintosh, and several flavors of Unix as clients or servers. Getting data from one server to another client requires file format massaging or translation. This extra effort often results in lost time, lost data, and extra expense.

What TCP/IP, the Internet, and intranets provide is the concept of a universal format and an application that can serve as a universal client. You can build web pages out of HTML tagged text by entering the text in a text editor or word processor, and adding tags that associate content such as GIF, JPG, WAV, or MPEG files to that page. Even better are HTML editors like HoTMetaL Pro or site building tools like FrontPage that shield you from the arcane details of tags and let you build web pages the way desktop publishing programs like PageMaker let you build fully formatted publications. When you copy that page and those data files to a folder on your web site, you know that some version of Netscape Navigator or Microsoft Internet Explorer running on any client will be able to open and view that data exactly as you meant it to be seen. This is progress.

An intranet can therefore serve as the ultimate expression of groupware, and its success is likely to drive other groupware products from the marketplace. Already, most groupware products are being developed with an eye on complementing the Internet and intranets.

Note If you are in an environment that offers Exchange Server, you are not going to want to use Windows NT Workstation 4 as a messaging server. That is because Exchange Server is not meant for TCP/IP intranet applications. Capable packages do, however, run a bulletin board on Windows NT Workstation 4. One example is Galacticomm's World Group. This client/server BBS contains e-mail, group forums, forms, and chat functions. World Group is both a BBS server and a web server, with a freely distributable client application. There is also a Netscape plug-in for the client. To get more information about World Group, go to Galacticomm's home page at http://www.gcomm.com.

Intranets offer some things to the corporate manager or MIS professional that the Internet will never be able to offer. First, the internal network that most everyone runs offers a bandwidth several times larger than most people's access to the Internet. Bandwidth as you might recall is the size of the pipe or straw through which data is sucked. Although the Internet is slowing down, and is often impractical for many of the technologies (such as video and animation) being introduced on it, an intranet's throughput speeds make it a suitable vehicle for rich data content presentations: sound, voice, video teleconferencing, movie presentation, and so forth.

In the sections that follow, you will learn about some of the areas in which an intranet's inherent speed advantages can make advances in networking technology more probable. The next section examines the potential for downloadable applications or applets shared on an intranet. The next section describes how intranets are more secure than Internet connections, and the advantages that the Windows NT security scheme offers you. Finally, you will see how the three Peer Web Services can function on an intranet, and the advantages that these services offer you in that environment.

The Web as an Operating System

When you move data across a fat pipe, you have the potential to transfer data at a rate that makes it possible to store applications across a network and distribute them on demand. An intranet offers you the potential to have a fat pipe or fast internetworking connection established. Distributed applications offer vendors a new method of upgrading applications, sharing applications, and even provide for a new version of the operating system in which modules are delivered on demand.

A lot of discussion currently focuses on the web as the next great operating system. The basic idea is that a thin client can log on to an internetwork and download portions of an operating system and applications, as required. After you access a web page with your stock portfolio on it and then request an analysis of its performance, you might download a charting module that services the request. <APPLET...> or <OBJECT...> tags embedded in the HTML page would call the appropriate applet required. A server somewhere could keep a single network copy of an application, and that application could be downloaded as needed.

Note The concept of application servers has computer vendors salivating. Imagine the capability to service an entire network of people with one download, or to provide a subscription service for software upgrades with concomitant reduction of manufacturing costs. Certain aspects of this scheme should also appeal to many network managers—namely, trivial network rollouts of new products. The whole area is under very active study at most large software houses.

You can't write a chapter that mentions the web as an operating system without mentioning Java, ActiveX, and WebObjects. These are the methods for delivering applets to run web-based applications.

Java is (as many dead trees will agree) the highly hyped programming language based on C++ and optimized for the Internet. Java is a high-level language, and is portable—just like HTML and web pages themselves. Java interpreters are being built into browser (Navigator and Internet Explorers), operating system (Windows, Macintosh, and Unix), and even small hot devices like toasters. Using Java as your language, you can write downloadable applets that perform any task you wish. It remains to be seen whether Java lives up to the hype.

ActiveX is a repackaged version of OCX embedded controls meant for the Internet/intranet and based on the OLE design model and programming standard. The additional features that ActiveX offers over the older OCX controls are the ability to be progessively rendered (drawn or processed) as it is downloaded, and an automatic registration feature that enables a control to be downloaded as needed from the web without user intervention.

With ActiveX, you are offered the capability of having a very large third-party library applied to you web pages. ActiveX is plug-in components that provide a pre-programmed capability. You can add an ActiveX graphing control to a web page and have data in a table automatically appear in a graph for your readers.

As previously stated, Microsoft Internet Explorer is a framework that separates basic browser functionality such as document navigation from the methods required to load, display, and manipulate the information that you view in it. A WebObject or Web Browser object (also known previously as a shell document viewer) provides generic browser functionality and communicates with the browser frame. This WebObject serves as a container for ActiveX components, or if you will, a server for these objects. If an application knows how to act as an ActiveX document server (as Excel and Word do), then you can load and display a spreadsheet or work processor document in the native formats of these applications directly into your browser. The resulting document displayed in the browser is directly editable and will show the toolbars and menus of the ActiveX server application when activated. The extension from previous versions of OLE is therefore apparent.

If the web is an operating system, the emergence of the thin client is nigh: a computer with minimal computer resources (and a lot of RAM) that loads its operating system and applications from a server. By the time you read this, the so-called Internet computer will be on sale from a variety of vendors. Clearly, a thin client won't be running Windows NT Workstation 4 anytime soon. But they might end up being some of your clients, and Microsoft is making plans for a version of Windows that will accommodate this new model on the Intel platform.

An Intranet as a Closed System

An intranet provides for much greater security than the Internet does. On the Internet, anyone can access your site. If you have an ftp site, anyone can upload information to your server—provided that you enable anonymous access, as many sites do. Your entire network is exposed to manipulation by unscrupulous individuals. Of course, some solutions being imposed are meant to prevent these occurrences (firewalls and proxy servers, for example). But in an intranet, you don't have these problems.

An intranet presents the budding Webmeister with a known audience. A manager or MIS professional can either dictate or know which applications are in use on an intranet and load content on the site accordingly. Because Netscape Navigator and Microsoft Internet Explorer can both be configured for helper applications (either externally or with plug-ins), for example, you can serve up the flavor of the document de jour that your audience requires. A DOC file can be viewed by Microsoft Word, an XLS file by Excel, and a PDF file by Adobe Acrobat. As applications are rewritten for native HTML access, these other formats become less important for internetworking applications.

On an intranet, you know who your users are. You know their names (at least their user names), and they have passwords. They can be challenged and respond to security schemes that you can impose on them. In short, you can impose the Windows NT security model on a Windows NT Workstation 4 set up to provide intranet services.

Using the Three Peer Web Services on an Intranet

In the preceding chapter, you saw how the three Peer Web Services can be set up and how they are configured. This section repeats this information with a view on how they can be valuable in an intranet environment.

Your Peer Web Services (PWS) on an intranet can provide web pages and data file access through the following services or transfer protocols:

- **ftp.** With ftp servers, your reader locates your server and can download or upload the file(s) of choice.

  With ftp, you have the capability to set up a security system based on the NT security scheme, and that security scheme can be applied in an intranet environment. It is easy to set up and administer. You create the directory structure, set the home or default directory, and put text file (TXT) descriptions of the contents of each of the directories so that your readers can learn what's in the directory before downloading them (if you want to be nice to your readers).

  Most ftp installations offer a \PUB or PUBLIC directory that allows for anonymous logons.

- **Gopher.** Gopher services offer a little more flexibility in that Gopherspace is both indexed and hyperlinked.

  In most respects, a Gopher service is similar to an ftp site. Gopher, however, offers a hierarchical indexing of the site, hyperlinking to other Gopher sites, and a universal index and search service for Gopherspace. Gopher sites also show the nature of the accessed content through icons attached to the file names.

- **WWW.** HTTP or the World Wide Web pretty well supplement the other two services. Using your web browser, you can access these two other services and download ftp and Gopher files. With the web, you get pictures, forms, multimedia, and so forth.

Most people will, therefore, be spending their time constructing web sites. They will spend very little time with ftp and Gopher sites. Therefore, most of the rest of this chapter discusses web tools.

In the section that follows, you will see some of the design principles you might want to apply in an intranet environment to creating a strong intranet site.

Designing an Intranet Site

The number one principle of designing a web site is to find out who your readers are. Ask your audience what they want, and figure out what you want to offer. Building an intranet site puts some pretty powerful groupware tools into your toolkit. A simple <MAILTO: ...> tag, for example, can pop up a form in a browser that enables a reader to post e-mail to someone on the intranet easily. Creating a system messaging system is, therefore, very easy to do. Similarly, using <HREF ...> tags creates links to files anywhere you want. Thus a managed file system is also easy to create. You can get a lot of mileage out of these tools with almost no work. But you first have to know what it is you want to do.

In evaluating the most important functions of your intranet, it is helpful to get answers to the following questions:

- What common tasks most often come up in your work?
- What applications does your audience use?
- Can common forms and documents be converted to HTML forms, and do you want to manage them in some way?
- Can you use web services as a communication tool, either individually for e-mail, or as a group by using list servers and bulletin boards?
- What information is most often required in your organization, and how should you make that available?
- Who needs access to what on the intranet?
- What kind of search utilities are required?

By getting answers to these and similar questions, you can prioritize your design to achieve the maximum utilization of your Windows NT Workstation 4 web server. In the sections that follow, you will learn about some specific design principles for web site construction. You will also see how the use of templates and editors can ease the burden of publishing information in HTML format. If you are sitting on a pile of documents that need conversion, the last section describes some tools for converting those documents automatically and putting them on your web site.

Design Principles

The best web sites are those organized with a hierarchical *top-down design.* A central location or home site can be accessed from anywhere, and each area is served by a similarly hierarchically designed module. The central site provides an overview of the site, and the capability to access tools and utilities. From each level, the reader can locate desired information and in and jump there.

Going from the general to the specific is called *drill-down.* Elements of a site that lend themselves to hierarchical construction are topic listings, tables of contents, subject listings, and indexes based on keywords or phrases—particularly topics and tables of contents. This is the way in which your file system is organized, and it is the way most good online Help systems are constructed. If you look as some of the popular directory services on the Internet, and Yahoo! (http://www.yahoo.com) is a prime example, they are constructed in this way.

Typically, you enter a default or home directory and assign a default document in that home directory. That default document is normally used as a "home page" or top location in a web site. Buttons and hyperlinks are then created in your home page that lets a reader or visitor navigate throughout the site. It is also standard to provide navigation buttons throughout a site to the web pages that serve as the central pages for the various modules and links or buttons back to the upper (conceptually) levels in your site's logical design.

Space limitations here preclude a full explanation of the design principles that you might want to employ. Two good books on Rich Text File (RTF) Windows-styled help systems merit a look. They both contain a good discussion of these principles:

- *Designing Windows 95 Help*, by Mary Deaton & Cheryl Lockett Zubek, 1996, Que, Indianapolis, IN.
- *Developing Online Help for Windows 95*, by Scott Boggan, David Farkas, and Joe Welinske, 1996, Thompson Computer Press, Boston, MA.

Here are some important points for you to understand about an intranet. An intranet is a *distributed information system*. It does not matter where a file is located. Your site construction, therefore, can suit your particular requirements without regard for your Windows NT Workstation 4's own internal capacity (disk size, for example)—its processing capabilities are another issue.

Note You are free to change the design and construction of your intranet site with no penalty when using internal links. If you are going to move files around on your site, consider using a site management tool to manage and alter the links in your documents.

Revising external links to content on other servers is much more difficult, and requires either specialized web robot-type tools or manual labor checking for URL drop out.

In your design work, consider *modular designs*. You don't have to bring your web site online in one fell swoop. Rather, you can roll out things one feature at a time and see how they work. The process of gradual and modular implementation can be seen as one of the great advantages to building intranet solutions over traditional application development. With intranets, it is possible to design and implement a client/server solution without actually having to complete the application. A good web site is never done.

The following are all good elements of web site design:

- Data is organized into logical units or chunks.
- Web pages are designed for the screen, both its resolution and size.

- Long documents contain hyperlinks to guide the reader.
- Printable versions of the information are presented.
- The site has a navigational system, including buttons to aid the reader through a typical browse sequence.

  A *browse sequence* is the sequential access of pages on a web site. To some extent, browse sequences can be designed for, even in hypertext systems.

- The site has access to a search engine or search function that enables you to search the content of both the individual site or the intranet itself.
- A What's New? section points readers to changes on your web site since their last visit.
- Instant access is available to an online Help system from anywhere the reader navigates.

Note HTML is going to be the online Help format of the future. Microsoft is in the process of replacing the Windows Help engine that uses the Rich Text File (RTF) format with one that uses HTML and is viewed by a browser.

The Proper Use of Templates

You can save yourself a lot of effort if you construct a set of templates for your common documents like reports, manuals, forms, and so forth for the applications you use. If you save these documents to a set of working directories, other people can apply them to the information that they want to publish by using tools and applications with which they are familiar. You can apply this approach not only to entire documents, but to individual elements in web pages as well.

You can create web templates in any application that saves a document in text-only format. You need only create the document, add the tags, and save the document out as text with an HTML (in Windows HTM) file extension. Assume, for example, that you want to create a set of web page templates in Word. Then the people who wish to create content will have to contend with Word's styles and style sheet and know how to use templates, but they won't have to bother with knowing or understanding HTML tags. Even if that person is you, and you are a tag master, the work creating web pages will still go faster because you can concentrate on the content portion of your task.

This creation of templates in your work can be not only for simple tasks and elements, but can also be for more complex ones as well. If you are going to create an reusable image map, capture the process with instructions and reduce the process down to the smallest set of steps. If you do this, you have to worry only about using the right CGI script, or pointing to the right directories one time.

Lest you balk at adopting an enforced and restricted publishing standard, consider this—not only do templates save you time, but the results you achieve are often superior to starting documents from scratch, even if those documents are individually constructed.

Note A proposed standard exists in HTML for cascaded style sheets that makes formatting web pages easier and more consistent. For information on this subject, see http://www.w3.org/pub/WWW/TR/WD-css1.html.

In terms of establishing a style for your web site, you might want to consider adopting one of the many style tools available for web site design. One example of these tools is WebSuite from DigitalStyle Corporation in San Diego, CA, 800-338-7895. WebSuite supplies a library of graphic elements that you can apply to your web pages.

WebSuite contains: rules (horizontal lines), buttons, bullets, navigation buttons, headlines, icons, backgrounds, and many other features. The product offers over 30 different style groups and enables you to create your own. Included with this product are image editors, performance indicators, and other tools. Figure 18.1 shows the Component Catalog tool of the suite with a style element for headlines loaded.

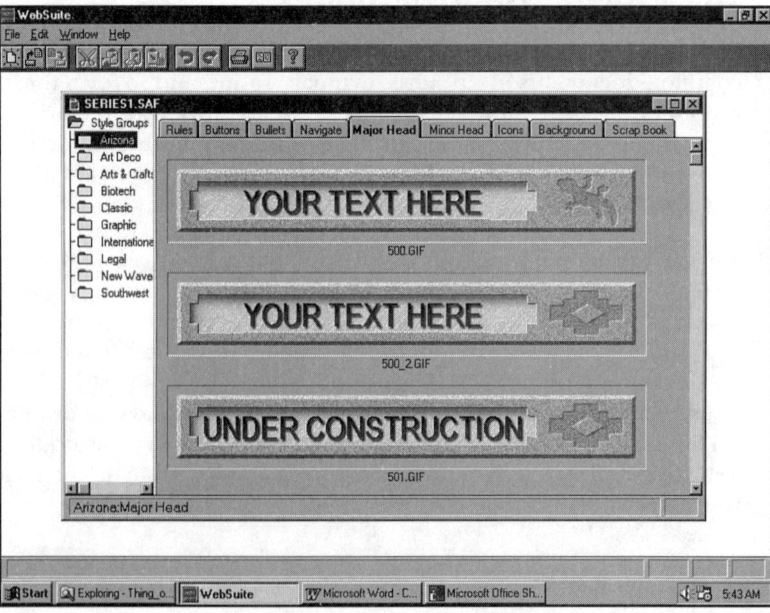

Figure 18.1

WebSuite helps you create web pages with a set of standard graphics elements.

HTML Editors and Site Management Tools

Unless you are a glutton for punishment, you probably do not want to write HTML code. You can buy good tools called HTML editors that shield you from having to write code. An HTML editor puts tags directly on a page by using a menu command, or a click on a button. Some editors actually show the tags (probably meant for experts who code in HTML anyway and want to use the editor as a production tool for convenience). Other more recent HTML editors do not show the tags, but show the effect of the tags on the content in the pages.

In general, HTML editors enable you to insert tag pairs by either clicking on a button or selecting a menu command. When you do that, an HTML tag or set of container tags is added to your document. Whether you see this tag or not depends on whether your editor is WYSIWYG (What You See Is What You Get) or not. Some editors opt to show you how your web page will look in a browser without displaying the tag, others show you the text-only (source) code, and still others will either show some combination of tags and a WYSIWYG display or let you switch between complementary views.

The advantage of most HTML editors is that they check the tag for syntax, offer spell checking, and check that your document construction is correct and that your tags are balanced. Attributes such as text styles are added through the interface. The key distinction between the different classes of HTML editors is their capability to show what your page would look like in your browser, or not.

HTML editors is a category of rapidly changing software. In the current generation of products, you might find that not all tags or extensions are supported. Many products, for example, support tables, forms, and frames features in a sporadic or inconsistent way. Most of the better HTML editors enable you to perform exception programming, adding nonstandard tags or tags that they don't support or know about yet in their pages.

Quite likely, your favorite word processor has an add-on feature that provides HTML editing built into it. Word 7 offers the Word Internet Assistant (IA), which installs directly into that version of the program. Figure 18.2 shows a form being created in Word IA.

Word 97 offers these capabilities directly incorporated in the product. WordPerfect and Lotus Ami Pro now have versions with HTML support, as well.

Anawave Software's HotDog for Windows is one of the better known HTML editors. Sausage Software (http://www.sausage.com) created it, and a trial version can be downloaded from that site. As shown in Figure 18.3, HotDog puts the code right on to the screen to view. You preview your pages in your browser.

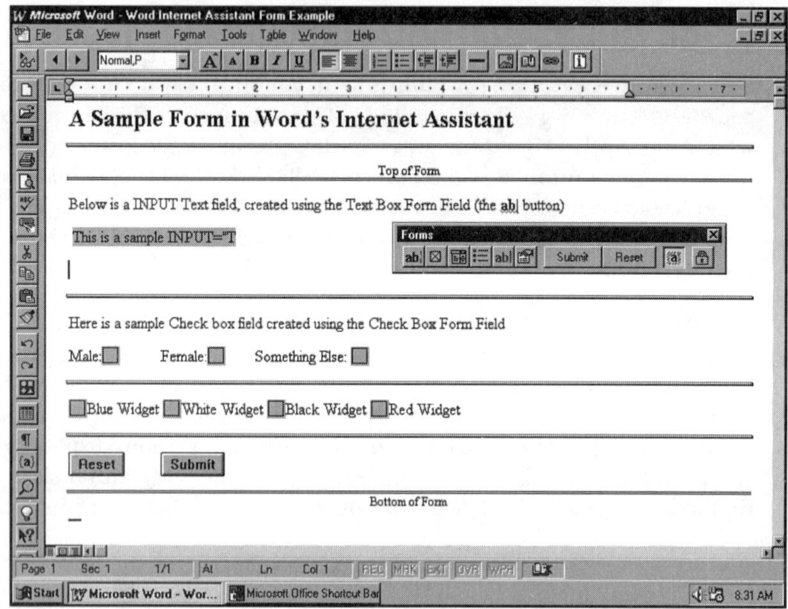

Figure 18.2

A form can be created in Word's Internet Assistant by clicking on appropriate toolbar buttons and dragging controls on a page.

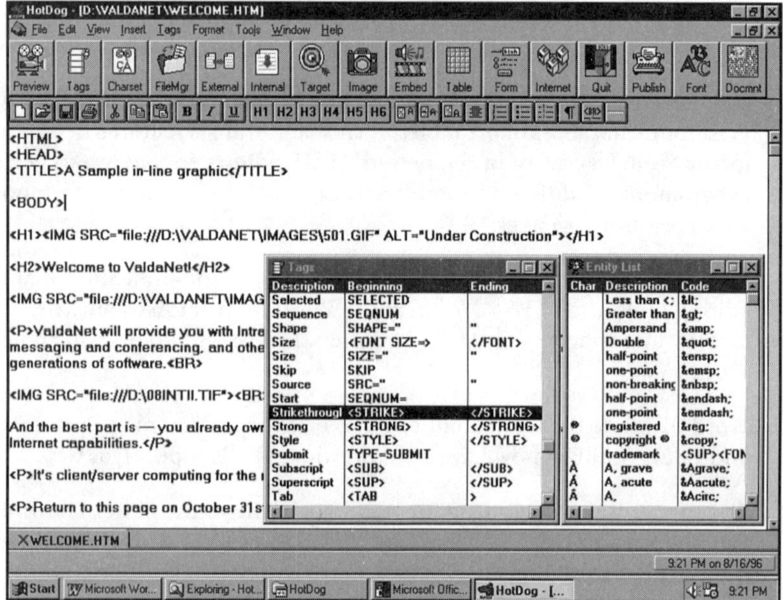

Figure 18.3

HotDog is meant for people wishing to edit HTML code in view.

HoTMetaL is an example of an HTML editor that offers a more WYSIWYG approach. You can download the shareware version of SoftQuad's HoTMetaL from http://www.softquad.com. HoTMetaL objects like headlines and in-line images the way they will appear in your browser with tags that look like clothing labels. To change a tag, double-click on the tag symbol. Figure 18.4 shows a page in HoTMetaL.

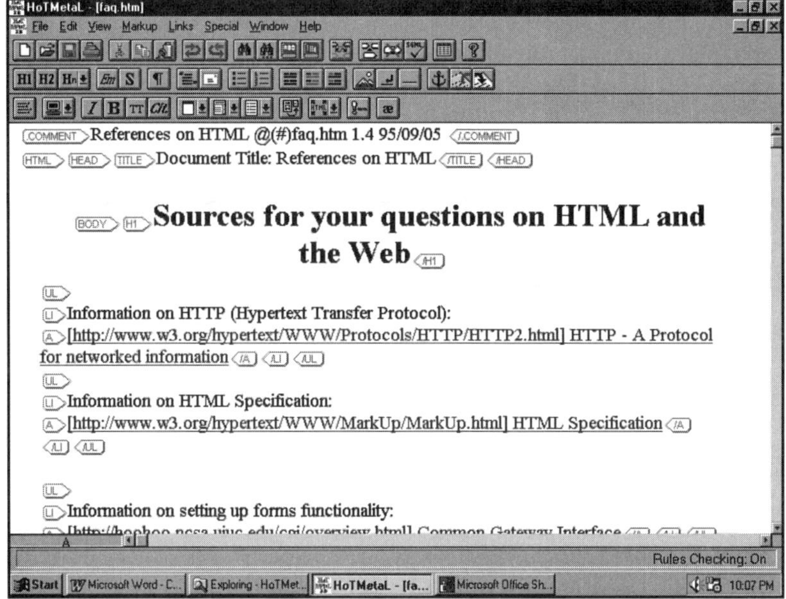

Figure 18.4

HoTMetaL formats your page, but shows your tags in the window in a semi-WYSIWYG display.

The number of products in the area of HTML editing is astonishing and changing rapidly. Even Netscape Navigator Pro comes with a competent HTML editor. Here are a couple of resources that will help you learn more about editors and locate products for you to try out:

- The Web Developer's Virtual Library: http://www.stars.com/Vlib/Providers/HTML_Editors.html
- Yahoo!: http://www.yahoo.com/Computers_and_Internet/Internet/World_Wide_Web/HTML_Editors/

The second generation of HTML page construction tools are programs that attempt to be completely WYSIWYG, such as Claris Home Page, Adobe PageMill, and Microsoft FrontPage. Home page is aimed at individuals and small businesses, PageMill includes many fine graphics tools and comes bundled into SiteMill (a site management tool), and FrontPage has the editor built into a complete site management package.

Several packages enable you to not only create web pages, but they also provide web site creation and validation features, and are aimed at nontechnical users. The leading products in this area are Adobe SiteMill, Microsoft FrontPage, and Netscape LiveWire.

FrontPage is particularly nice because it contains many wizards and WebBots that can automatically create many web site functions. As an example of working in FrontPage, the Outline view and Link view of a web site is shown in figure 18.5. One wizard creates a search page (replete with the appropriate CGI script), another a What's New? page, and so on. Microsoft bundles FrontPage with IIS, but not with PWS. Deals on FrontPage for registered users of Windows NT Workstation 4, however, might be offered.

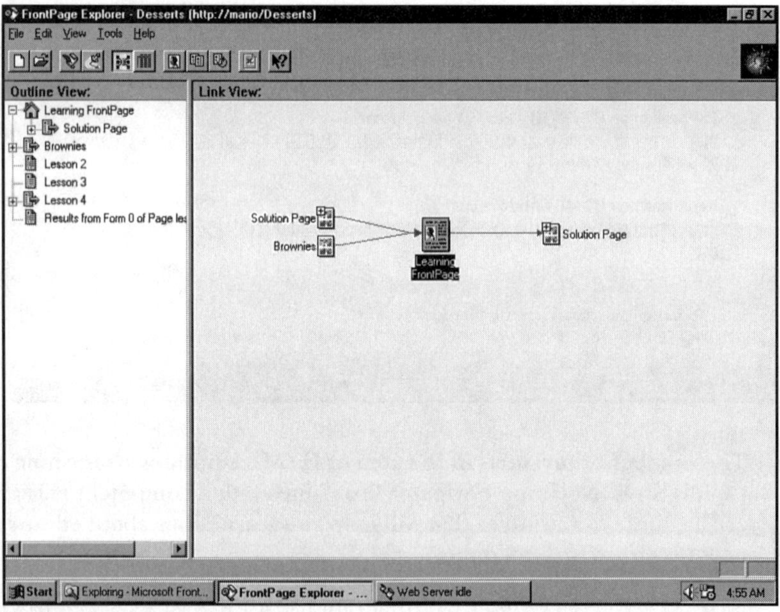

Figure 18.5
The FrontPage Explorer is shown with the Outline view (left) and the Link view (right).

SiteMill is currently a Macintosh-only product, but a Windows version is expected in 1997. LiveWire is a web site management tool that runs on the Netscape server, and can create content, and manage applications and your site. Information about LiveWire can be found at http://home.netscape.com/comprod/server_central/product/livewire/livewire_datasheet.html.

Undoubtedly, 1997 will see many more products in this area. If you intend to create and manage an intranet site of any consequence, it is strongly recommended that you consider adopting a page creation and site management tool.

Publishing Legacy Data

If you are in a situation where you publish a lot of web content, you might be faced with converting large amounts of old data from your standard applications into web format. As applications are upgraded, you can convert single documents into HTML one at a time. You might want to have certain conversion tools to supplement your desktop publishing packages or word processor. One place you can get a list of these products is at the HTML Translators page. A general listing of conversions tools can be found at http://www.stars.com/Vlib/Providers/Translators.html.

For large amounts of legacy data where you need to batch process files and format them, HTML Transit from InfoAccess (http://www.infoaccess.com/; tel. 800-344-9737) is a unique product. This program takes documents from DTP packages such as FrameMaker (MIF files) or Interleaf Publisher, word processing files from WordPerfect, Ami Pro (now Word Pro), and Microsoft Write, as well as Rich Text Format (RTF) and straight ASCII files and converts them into HTML (see fig. 18.6).

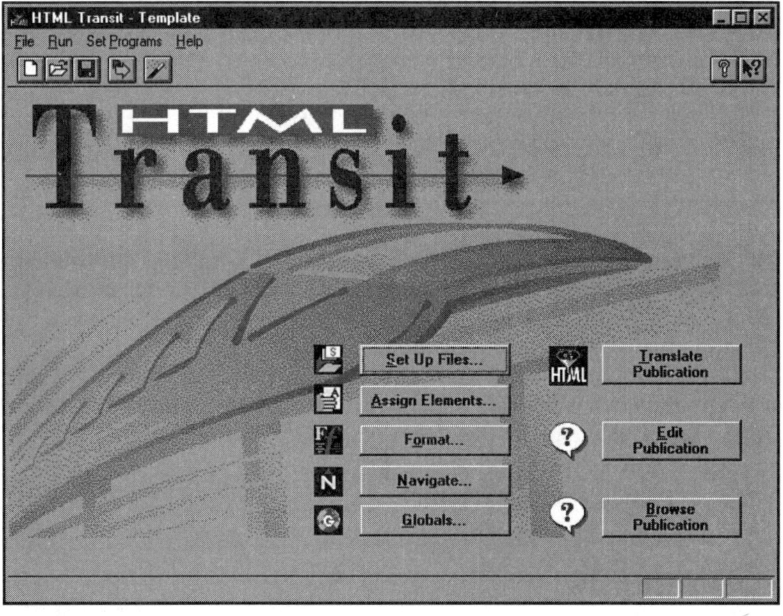

Figure 18.6
HTML Transit is a complete web publishing system that will convert your legacy documents to HTML format in a batch process.

HTML Transit does a lot more than just converting a document into HTML. It preserves the styles and formatting, converts images or embedded illustrations to GIF or JPEG files, and displays them as in-line images in approximately the same location in your web browser as in the original document. For large images, a thumbnail image is created and hyperlinked to the full-sized image file. You have a lot of control over the conversion process through dialog box selections.

HTML Transit breaks long documents into smaller connected files that can be navigated between. The program actually adds the navigation buttons to the pages for you. You end up, therefore, with an entire site. For what the product can do, HTML Transit is remarkably low priced. Companies have used this product to translate entire documentation sets into HTML-based online Help systems.

Using HTML is very easy. You specify your preferences for how documents will be translated, the format of the documents, the style of the pages you want created (even down to picking the navigation buttons and their icons and colors), and other preferences. Then you tell HTML Transit which folder the documents meant for conversion are contained in, and the destination folder or directory. Then click a button and the conversion is done for you. After you setup a particular conversion, you can capture that setup so that you can run the process again without having to do the setup portion. In this way, you can establish a web page conversion capability where others create documents and deposit them in a particular folder, and HTML Transit "publishes" them to your web and makes them available on your intranet.

Printing Web Content

An important point to consider is that the web pages you create are created for the screen, and not for the printed page. You should, therefore, consider creating a method that your users can use to print web pages as documents. That method could be initiated as a Print button that calls a CGI script to do a batch printing. Such scripts can be downloaded from the web and are readily available.

You can also structure your pages so that topics can be printed as related information. It is unreasonable for readers to have to navigate to each topic head and print that page individually. Create a print file, and link to that file in your web pages. Readers can then download the file and print it as a single document.

By making your documents (such as white papers, articles, and so on) that you wish to print downloadable, you preserve formatting, margins, fonts, and other layout. One way of creating fully formatted documents is to use a portable document format on your web site. The next section covers this topic.

Electronic Documents

When you want to create documents with fancy illustrations, intricate typography, a layout suitable for framing, and something that looks good on paper, consider a portable document format (PDF). A PDF preserves the look and feel of the document in a file that can be viewed and printed as the document's creator meant it to look and print in a viewer application.

Four portable document formats are in common use in web applications:

- **PDF.** The Adobe Acrobat format.
- **PCL.** HP's Printer Control Language, which is the page description language (PDL) of the HP LaserJet.
- **PostScript.** PostScript files.
- **SGML.** The Standard Markup Language (which HTML is based on) is described at http://www.w3.org/pub/WWW/MarkUp/SGML/.

A PDL is a method or language that describes a printed page to an output device like a printer. That's why a PDL is useful as a portable document format. It is written in a high-level language that does not need to be compiled to run, only translated. SGML is also page description language, as is HTML itself. SGML does not capture images or graphics, but it can handle formatted text and incorporate outside data formats. What works for HTML works in SGML, but not vice versa.

Adobe Acrobat is the best known and most widely used portable document format. The product started out as a method for printing files in a proprietary version of PostScript to any printer with good results. Acrobat is now used to place high-quality printable documents in a web site that others can use, regardless of whether they have the fonts or graphics applications used to create the content.

With Adobe Acrobat Distiller, you can take PostScript files and convert them into PDF files. With Adobe Acrobat Catalog, you can index them into a searchable format. With Adobe Acrobat Exchange, you print to disk as PDF files out of any of your applications. All these aforementioned products cost money, as they are the creation tools.

The free stuff is the downloadable (http://www.adobe.com/acrobat) Reader that your readers can use to view and print your PDF files. The Reader is available in Windows, Macintosh, Unix, and as a limited capability version in MS-DOS. You can also get a plug-in for Netscape Navigator (that works with Microsoft Internet Explorer, as well) that launches inside the program whenever you download a PDF file.

Acrobat is a very capable and easy to use product that that gives outstanding results. The product creates hypertext documents that can integrate with HTML, as it now incorporates hyperlinks directly. In many ways, it is a superior technology to HTML. It is not free, however. And it is proprietary. The other disadvantage that the product has is that its file size is large and the product is slow—the first point is not much of a disadvantage in an intranet environment.

Some great examples of PDF technology are out there such as magazines, the IRS forms download web site, user manuals, and others. Because the Reader is free, you can check some of these examples out at the Cool PDF Sites page that Adobe maintains at http://www.adobe.com/acrobat/coolpdf.html.

The newer plug-in technology Acrobat 3.0, based on the Amber project, is a more convenient approach. With the older version, you had to configure Acrobat as a helper application. Figure 18.7 shows a white paper that appears inside Netscape Navigator called Cashing in on Cyberspace.

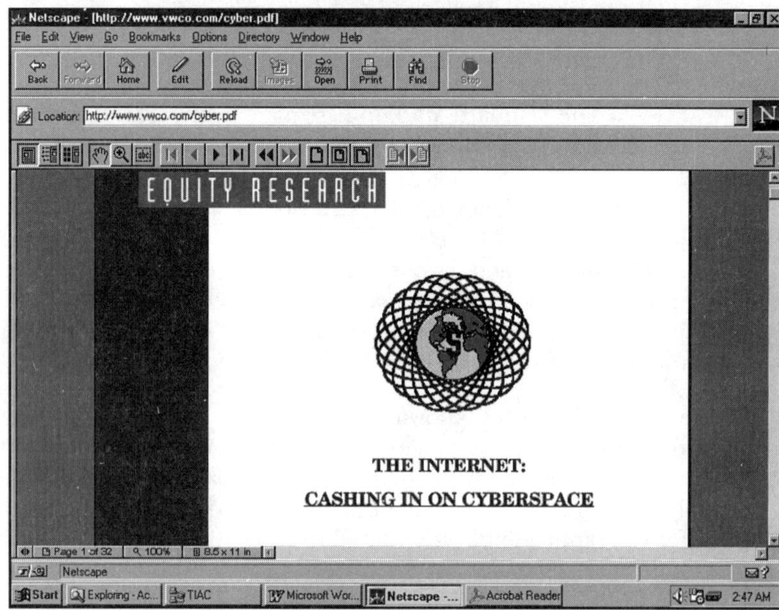

Figure 18.7
A PDF file displayed inside Netscape Navigator using Adobe Acrobat 3.0 can be fetched and displayed one page at a time—if the PDF file is optimized for this behavior.

Adobe might have meant for Acrobat to be an alternative to HTML, but the chances of that happening are diminishing with each new version of Navigator and Internet Explorer.

Three other products worth mentioning in passing are: Common Ground from Common Ground Software, Envoy from Tumbleweed Software, and Replica from Farallon Computing. The first two are genuine PDF formats (but not Adobe's format); the last is an interchange format meant for Macintosh/Windows heterogeneous networks. Common Ground and Replica are interesting products in their own right, and offer strong developer applications like ActiveX support and other features that make them unique.

Because the viewer applications are all free, you can (as a web site developer) make your own determination as to whether they make sense in your organization. You can get information on these products from the following sources:

- Envoy is found off of Tumbleweed's home page at http://www.twcorp.com/.
- Common Ground home page is at http://www.commonground.com/index.html.

Now that you understand some of the design principles of creating web sites and how they are applied to creating web pages, the following section explores how to tie web pages, forms, and data sources together to create dynamic web pages.

Understanding CGI, Forms, and Data Access

When you create web pages, you present data in a static form. It is possible, however, to tie the forms that you can create on a web page with data in a database and supply information specifically requested by or tailored to a reader upon demand. Such a web page is dynamic and provides new publishing opportunities that are valuable in both Internets and an intranet environment. The data from your web page must be transferred back and forth between a web page and a data source. Typically that is done by a CGI script.

CGI scripts are small programs that take the data in your form and put it into a form that an application can use. If that application is a relational database, the CGI script might turn the data into an SQL APPEND statement to create a new record(s) in the database. For edited data, the information can be transformed into an SQL UPDATE statement.

CGI scripts as written work in one direction. To publish data or update a field on a form from a database, another CGI script is used. A relational database can take a record, for example, and export the data to a file. Then the CGI script translates the data into HTML code by placing the values in the appropriate places. The script could even create an entirely new HTML file.

In the sections that follow, you will learn more about how CGI scripts work, where to obtain them, and references on how to write them if required. You also see how forms work and how to tie forms and data sources together.

How CGI Works

The Common Gateway Interface (CGI) is a specification for a method of passing data between applications. To use CGI, you write a script which is a small program or batch file, and that script performs an action. The script is stored as a file at an URL that can be called from a link in your document. CGI resides on your web server. CGI scripts are written in higher-level programming languages like PERL, or some kind of shell program, but could be written in C or any other scripting language.

High-level languages are used because they are more often portable and can be used on other computers without compiling. CGI is not rocket science, and it is not particularly difficult to learn. CGI is, however, transitional technology. The actions that CGI enable are: data access, data formatting, application control, on-demand web page creation, and so forth. These are being built into modern applications.

You might wish to treat CGI as a black box. That's certainly one way to go. Because you call a CGI script with a single line in your HTML tag, you only need copy the CGI script to your server directory and follow the instructions given with it. Here are some sources of CGI scripts that you can use for processing forms:

- PolyForms (PC). Available from http:www.wgg.com/files/PolyForm/, this script takes the output from a web form and saves it to an HTML file, a text file, or a comma-delimited file that can be read by a database.

- A central repository of CGI scripts can be found at: http://WWW.Stars.com/Vlib/Providers/Database.html for all computer platforms.

- Windows 95/NT forms script. Available from http://www.primenet.com/~buyensj/ntwebsrv.html.

Forms Creation

You have probably seen forms in your travels on the Internet. Forms are among the most useful constructs you can have. They let the reader submit information that can be collected or information that can be acted on. Forms provide interactivity and enable the user to determine the kind of information that they wish to see. From the information submitted on a form, a new dynamic web page can be constructed using underlying information contained in a database or an action taken by an application based on the submitted data. This is a new and very exciting form of publishing where the content provided the reader is based on the needs and desires of that reader.

You can create forms by using standard HTML tag elements: either hand coding them, or dragging and dropping fields, boxes, buttons, and other features from a visual tool such as an HTML editor. The typical form Submit buttons call a standard CGI script.

After you click on the Submit button, the information contained on the form starts up the CGI script, which processes the data. Information on a form can be sent to a database, e-mailed, or written to disk. The purpose of the CGI script is to format the data in such a way that the application for which it is meant can use it. CGI is both server and application specific.

CGI also runs in the opposite direction. It takes the results of an application and formats it in a way that can be used in a browser. A CGI script, for example, can either substitute new values in a web page with variable placeholders or even construct an entirely new HTML page.

Forms are easy to create in the current technology. These three sites offer further information about form building, sample CGI scripts, and pointers to products:

- Web Communication's Comprehensive Guide to Web Publishing at http://www.webcom.com/webcom/html/.
- The University of Illinois Supercomputing Center at http://www.ncsa.uius.edu/SDG/Software/Mosaic/Docs/fill-out-forms/overview.html.
- The University of Illinois Supercomputing Center at http://www.union.ncsa.uiuc.uiuc.edu/HyperNews/get/www/html/guides.html.

All HTML editors offer forms creation as part of their standard toolkit. In a tool like FrontPage or Word Internet Assistant, you create a form by clicking on the form control of your choice and either clicking or clicking and dragging the control on your page. Even the action buttons are a click-and-drag affair—these tools provide the appropriate tag syntax that calls a CGI script for an action button (SUBMIT or RESET, for example) when necessary.

Database Access

After you enter data in a form meant to access a database, a CGI script attaches a field identifier to each field and a value to that identifier and formats the result that your database can understand.

For example, if you enter the following on a web page:

```
Name: Barrie Sosinsky; Address: 1425 Beacon Street; City: Newton; St: MA; Zip:
02168.
```

and then press the Submit button, a CGI script fires. A file is created that contains the following:

```
Name, Address, City, St, CA, Zip
Barrie Sosinsky, 1425 Beacon Street, Newton, MA, 02168
```

This looks just like the data file for a mail merge, a record with a field header. The CGI script, therefore, does not do anything all that magical. The data format is specific, the mechanism for writing to the database file or reading from it is specific, and the composition of the web pages is also specific. Thus CGI scripts are written for a particular database.

You can buy a data access tool that takes care of the connection between your web pages and databases. PWS and IIS come with one, the Internet Database Connector. Using the Database Connector and ODBC drivers, you can access a database such as SQL Server on Windows NT Workstation 4.

A more general product is Cold Fusion from Allaire L.L.C (http://www.allaire.com/cfusion). Cold Fusion's CGI scripts connect to Access, FoxPro, dBase, SQL Server, Paradox, Excel II or IV, and write to a number of standard file formats. To access Cold Fusion, you install the product and call it up in a tag on your web page. Tags are specified with the Database Markup Language (DBML). Your browser ignores these tags, but because the CGI script runs—and with Cold Fusion running in the background—the data is processed.

Cold Fusion installs on NT Workstation 4 with sample files, a help system, and the required directory structure. An Administrator dialog box enables you to specify the target web page and the data source. The database that you wish to publish to or from is specified on the Data Sources tab.

Cold Fusion makes use of ODBC drivers to access your data source. ODBC drivers are database specific and come as packages or as a single driver. ODBC drivers, just like print drivers, are only as good as the person who wrote them. That is, some are better than others. Cold Fusion can complete SQL queries, do data validation, create web pages, and simplify the database/web page connection.

Cold Fusion is representative of a group of new products. In the year to come, HTML capabilities will be part of every desktop database.

To find out about other products in this area, take a look at Yahoo's category listing of database access tools at http://www.yahoo.com/Business_and_Economy/Companies/Computers/Internet/Databases_and_Searching/.

HTML Coding on-the-fly refers to a CGI script creating a web page from your data and serving up a web document that did not exist previously. Readers submit data to a data source, and the data is returned as very specific information for that reader. It looks like the data exists in that form, but of course, the page is dynamic and is the result of the reader's input. This is a new form of publishing in a distributed computing client/server environment.

If the database points to images or multimedia content, your web document can be considered to be a true file system. This has let to the great interest in creating a universal server with web tools accessing a database managing all types of data.

The Internet Database Connection

If it has occurred to you that using a CGI script to tie a form and a database together is something of a kludge, you are right. CGI scripts are product specific, file specific, field specific. They only work for the one situation that they are programmed to work in, and then sometimes grudgingly.

Microsoft has an alternative to CGI that relies on the Internet Database Connector (IDC) files that can be installed with PWS to access ODBC-compliant databases. A small set of these connectors are offered in the standard installation of PWS, but you can obtain additional connectors from database vendors or from other third parties. Essentially these connectors act as if they are like device drivers. You select a connector for a particular database, and should you decide to either enter data from a form on a web page into another database or display data in another database on your form (or create a form on-the-fly), you simply specify another connector.

The steps for creating a web interface to an ODBC data source are as follows:

1. Install an ODBC driver for your database in the ODBC control panel.
2. Set up a data source as an ODBC data source.
3. Create a form on your web page that is used to enter the data.
4. Create the Internet Database Connector (IDC) file that processes the data.
5. Create an IDC HTML template file that formats the data that the user sees.

An IDC file typically contains the following fields:

- **Datasource.** The web page that contains the data to be processed.
- **Username.** The user name can be the system administrator "sa," or someone else with access privileges.
- **Template.** This is the specification for the format of the results of the data entry, typically an HTM file that is given an HTX extension.
- **Required parameters.** These are the fields in the form that will be processed.
- **SQLStatement.** The SQL statement describes the operation to be performed by the action, typically an SQL Insert statement is used to add records, SQL Update to modify them, and SQL Delete to remove records. An Insert is most common.

When a user clicks a SUBMIT button on a form, the action proceeds and the data is transferred. The result is returned as a web page using the template you specified.

Database connectivity is just one example of a range of services that are provided by the Internet Server API, which is described in the next section.

Understanding the Internet Server API

When you install the PWS, you also get the benefits of the Internet Server Application Programming Interface or ISAPI. This programming interface installs a Dynamic Link Library (DLL) that can be accessed by applications requiring a variety of Internet services. Calls to ISAPI can be in Perl, ISAPI Basic, Visual C++, and other programming languages. ISAPI is an alternative method to add extensions to a IIS or PWS web server. Unlike CGI, which almost every web server supports, ISAPI uses Windows NT to obtain similar results.

When a CGI script runs, NT spawns a process and that process runs independently in its on memory space and runtime environment. A CGI script then must communicate with the web server, which is a slow step. When a CGI script crashes however, only the process is terminated on NT.

Programs written using the ISAPI interface run in the same memory space as the web server under NT. So ISAPI runs much faster than a CGI script, which is its major advantage. ISAPI is the way to go for access to any large database like SQL Server. When ISAPI crashes, however, it takes your web server down with it.

You can get further information about the ISAPI specification from Microsoft at http://207.68.137.35/win32dev/apiext/isapi.htm. You can also get a technical presentation from the book *Unlocking the Internet Information Server* published by New Riders Publishing.

Maintaining Security

Your first security measure for Windows NT Workstation 4 as an intranet server is to install the NTFS file system on your computer and enable the appropriate file permissions. Set up a system of access rights based on groups and users for resources, as you would for any service running on NT.

You can set up your web server so that access to resources is restricted to users with a particular IP address or domain name. This does not prevent someone logging on at a different computer from abusing you, but it is a start.

For even more security, you can encrypt your data and supply the decryption routine to your clients via a public key, and vice versa. The digital signature and certificate scheme that you can use on the Internet can be applied to an intranet. Chapter 15 described this technology in some detail.

The single biggest problem you face on an intranet is downloading files of unknown origin, particularly from the Internet. This is a hard problem to fight, particularly when you have helper applications that launch when a document of the registered type appears. About the only way to combat a virus concealed in a download is to isolate the file and run a virus detection utility on it before it is used.

CGI scripts represent another hole in your security scheme. A CGI script, when run, gives the author access to your server. An unscrupulous person can access the security database or the Registry and make changes, or have the script execute dangerous commands. To lower the risk, CGI scripts should be carefully monitored and be kept in a central location. Many administrators try to use executable files (compiled applications) in place of CGI scripts; they are harder to alter. Here are two locations with information about CGI script security:

- Safe CGI Programming at http://www.cerf.net/~paulp/cgi-security/safe-cgi.txt
- CGI Security Tutorial at http://csclub.uwaterloo.ca/u/mlvanbie/cge_c/

By all means, you should enable and run logging of Internet access as a line of defense. At least then you can read the log and see who did what and when. Logging can determine the particular computer that was used, the time of access, services accessed, and so on.

If you are enabling remote intranet access, you face many of the same problems that an Internet web site faces. You must authenticate the dial-up logon to make certain that it is from a trusted source.

Outlining Other Resources

Intranets are a big subject, and you might want to read more about the topic. This chapter has only scratched the surface of what is possible. It is a subject that seems to change almost daily. WebWeek (http://www.webweek.com) is one trade publication devoted to the topic, as well as to Internets.

Finally, the following books are recommended:

- *Building an Intranet*, by Tim Evans, 1996, SamsNet, Indianapolis, IN.
- *Intranet Publishing*, by Paul Bodensiek, 1996, Que, Indianapolis, IN.
- *Intranet Working*, by George Eckel, 1996, New Riders, Indianapolis, IN.

Summary

An intranet can be easily established in an NT enterprise using the technology and tools that Microsoft supplies as part of Windows NT Workstation 4. This chapter described how creating an intranet is similar to and different from connecting your workstation to the Internet. You also were introduced to some of the advantages that intranets offer.

Among the topics covered in this chapter were how to design and create a web site—what elements are useful, and what kinds of tools exist to create web pages and manage a site. As examples of the current technology, you were introduced not only to static web pages, but dynamic web pages in which forms and databases interact to create pages on-the-fly.

Microsoft is very active in this area and is providing compelling Internet/intranet technologies. Their slogan "Activate the Internet" is given expression in the application of their tools such as ActiveX to provide functionality in web pages.

Part VI

Security and Protection Issues

CHAPTER 19

Security in NT Workstation 4

It's been said that a computer is insecure the minute you turn it on. There's more than a little truth to this, sadly enough. Computer security is one of the single biggest issues in the information technology world, and no doubt always will be.

With that in mind, Microsoft had security as one of *the* big goals in mind when it engineered Windows NT. More than any other version of Windows, Windows NT—both Workstation and Server—are designed to enable users to protect their data and their system resources from theft, denial of service, and casual and systematic attacks.

None of this, however, means that Windows NT is secure all by itself. No operating system, no computer in the world, is secure without a human being taking steps to ensure that it is. This chapter describes some of the basic steps a user can take to secure a computer that has Windows NT Workstation installed in it:

- Understanding C2 security and how useful it is
- Acknowledging the vulnerable computer
- Locking the desktop with screen savers and the user password
- Using file and folder security with NTFS
- Understanding the newly implemented Challenge/Response protocol

Introducing C2 Security

C2 security is one of the more misunderstood concepts as it pertains to Windows NT. A great deal of misinformation about C2 security has been spread around, most of it as rumor or half-understood pseudo-technical information. This section addresses the most commonly misunderstood aspects of C2 security and Windows NT, and describes some of the ways in which a Windows NT system can be prepared for C2 certification.

What Is C2?

C2 is a standard by which an individual computer or computer workstation can be considered secure for certain types of work. It's used in government applications to designate a certain level of security for a type of computer. C2 computers are not trusted with top-secret information, but they are considered to be resistant to casual intrusions and also some types of deliberate attacks. Obviously, C2 is *not* a certification that a computer is impregnable to attack of any kind.

C2 is one of a series of security classifications for information systems, devised by the National Computer Security Center (NCSC)—D, C, B, and A. The earlier letters in the scheme describe increasing levels of security; thus a B-level machine could be considered more intrinsically secure than a C-level machine. These four levels of security were concocted by the NCSC as a way to provide discrete types of protection for specific kinds of systems.

Systems that store or process more sensitive information deserve a higher-level security certification than one that is used for more mundane tasks. D-level security is used to describe a computer that is relatively unsecure and has no real need for security because it does not carry sensitive information. C-level security, the next tier up, affords a certain basic level of protection, both on the machine level (for example, the hardware itself has been protected to some degree from tampering) and on the software level (for example, password security). B- and A-level security clearances are generally not sought out or awarded to computers outside of the military or government, and these clearances often require that the computer in question, both hardware and software, be engineered from the ground up with B- or A-level security in mind.

Microsoft itself does not claim that Windows NT is C2-secure. Authorized Windows NT distributors, who sell kits that enable you to ensure that a given Windows NT installation can be C2-certified, do make this claim, but only to the degree that a specific workstation or computer can be so certified. Windows NT itself, in the abstract, cannot be granted C2 certification. It all depends on the way the operating system is implemented on a given computer.

For a system to be approved for C2 security, it has to satisfy a number of requirements in several basic areas.

Object Ownership

The NCSC sees a computer system as consisting of objects. These objects can be anything—files, hard drives, peripherals, other users, and specific systems. In the C-level security scheme, users are given the ability to own objects. This means that the object is associated with that user and no other, for reasons about to be explained.

Object Protection Control

After a user has ownership of an object, another aspect of C2 security is that the owner must be able to administer the level of protection or access control over that object. If a user takes possession of a file and enables Everyone in its access control field, for example, that would mean that the owner has allowed anyone on the system to see it. If the owner makes it Adminstrators only, that would restrict use of that file to people designated as administrators on the system.

Access-Action Accountability

Every user on a C-level operating system is accountable for his or her actions. This means that whenever a user takes control or modifies access to an object, it is logged and recorded. No access control modifications, from the changing of passwords to a successful logon, should go unrecorded in a C-level system. This is also known as *auditing*.

Memory Protection

A C-level operating system also must protect memory spaces used by programs so that information left in memory by one process cannot be exploited by another. Windows NT prevents programs from accessing each other's memory spaces, and also protects memory after it's been freed up so that it can't be read after the fact.

Unique User Identification

In a C-level system, every user granted access to the system must have a unique way of identifying himself. Usually this is done by having a logon name and password, but Windows NT augments this by also providing a unique user ID number assigned to the user when the user account is created. The number is unique at the time of its creation and cannot be duplicated. Also, Windows NT uses the same technique to uniquely identify each Windows NT machine. With this technique, Windows NT makes it very difficult for someone to gain access through account- or machine-spoofing. The unique ID number system also makes it easier to audit user actions.

Spoofing: No Laughing Matter

When we talk about spoofing, we're not referring to the making of the new *Naked Gun* movie. Spoofing is a tactic used to foil common computer security techniques. Usually, it is performed on wide area networks where there is little or no way to physically verify where packets (for example, network transmissions) are coming from. It is possible to use a protocol analyzer to intercept transmitted network packets and use the legitimate source addresses within to masquerade as another computer. If done properly, the one doing the spoofing could gain access to unauthorized data.

Spoofing is very difficult to do casually. It requires fairly intimate knowledge of both the client and server computer in the network relationship and also some knowledge of the network connections between them. Also, recent innovations in packet-filtering and firewall technology are making it harder to spoof without being caught.

How To Get C2 Certification

Many firms sell Windows NT in C2-specific packages or implementations, or for a fee, install and C2-certify a Windows NT system. One such firm, Trusted Systems (http://www.trustedsystems.com), performs not only installations but training in the implementation of C-level and B-level security procedures. Trusted Systems is also a source for many technical references on creating secure systems.

Microsoft maintains information about C2 certification for Windows NT systems at its web site, at the URL http://www.microsoft.com/kb/bussys/winnt/q93362.htm.

The NSA also has copies of its books about computer security (known affectionately as the Rainbow Books) available by calling 202-783-3238, 8 a.m. to 4 p.m., Eastern time. Obtaining and reading the appropriate books is a strong step toward learning how to further secure a system—not just in terms of operating-system-specific procedures, but also in terms of general philosophies and guidelines.

Details about the whole range of security divisions, including breakdowns of all the Rainbow Books, can be found at http://www.disa.mil.

Coming Soon—B-Level Security for Windows NT?

As of this writing, Trusted Systems and Global Internet (http://www.gi.net) are working to determine whether Windows NT can be certified as a B-level secure operating system. Microsoft is working to help them out in this regard, and if successful, Windows NT would be one of the first B-certifiable off-the-shelf operating systems. Among the things being integrated into the plan are Fortezza-based password security, Kerberos distributed security, and independent object security.

The last item is one of the most important, because it's one of the key distinguishers between C- and B-level security. In a C-level security scheme, the owner of a given object has total discretion over whether another user can see that object. In a B-level scheme, that decision is not necessarily his. If a user with top-secret clearance is given an object that's also marked top secret, he cannot give it away to someone who does not have the same security clearance. He also cannot demote the security of the object himself, and he can't promote someone else's security. Only the administrator would be able to make those changes. Whether Windows NT will eventually be designated as B-certifiable remains to be seen, but given the stringent nature of B-level security, it looks as though it will have to wait until Cairo's object-based file system makes it debut. There seems little other way that B-level security could be achieved in NT without this.

Acknowledging the Vulnerable Computer

As mentioned at the beginning of the chapter, no computer is ever totally secure. This isn't cause for a user or a sysadmin to throw up his hands in despair, however. The vast majority of casual and systematic attacks on a computer's security can be defeated relatively easily.

The first thing a user or sysadmin needs to do, as the chapter title indicates, is to find out where the computer in question is vulnerable. Every computer's weaknesses are a little different; some are because of the presence or absence of certain kinds of hardware or software, and some are because of a pattern of use that is either present or absent.

In the case of hardware, for instance, almost every computer that runs with a floppy drive that it can be booted from has an enormous security hole. Not changing passwords frequently is an example of a pattern of use that would cause problems.

This section goes into detail about vulnerabilities and how to fix them, including:

- The kinds of attacks that are manifested against a computer (secure or insecure).
- The way a floppy drive poses a gigantic security hole all by itself, and what to do about it.
- How a piece of software called NTFSDOS.EXE makes it necessary to take extra steps to protect NTFS volumes from prying eyes.

Attacks on an Insecure Computer

An *attack*, simply enough, is any attempt to violate the security of a computer system. This could be anything: walking up to the keyboard and typing, using a boot floppy to bypass the operating system, or even using a plug-in card to bypass hardware-level protection. The computer doesn't even have to be networked; a good many attacks can be staged on a computer that is all by itself, albeit with sensitive data stored on it. (The lack of a network makes it that much harder to get to in the first place, but that is a detail to be explored later.)

Three basic kinds of attacks can be performed on an insecure computer: unauthorized access, disclosure of information, and denial of service. Some of these attacks cannot be totally alleviated through security measures, but it's possible to significantly decrease the chances of a computer being attacked in these fashions with the proper procedures.

Unauthorized Access

The single biggest worry that any user has with regard to a security-sensitive computer is unauthorized access. Most often this comes in the form of someone using someone else's account name and password to gain entry to the system without prior permission, or somehow forging an account on that computer to allow access.

Not all unauthorized access is itself grave, but it can be the gateway to greater harm. The simple fact that a computer's access has been breached in any way, for example, can cause users to lose confidence in the system's security. A private institution such as a bank, for example, cannot afford to have its security compromised—not only because of the sensitivity of the data, but because of the possible loss of business from customers who no longer trust the bank to guard their financial information safely.

Disclosure of Information

On every system there is information which should not be disclosed under any circumstances—not just private information (such as bank account numbers), but system-specific information such as password lists and access rights data. Disclosing this information can be damaging to both the system administrators and the users, immediately and over time.

Denial of Service/Interference of Service

One of the more recent variants in the world of computer mishaps is called a *denial of service attack*. This ranges from the fairly obvious—a virus that destroys data or system functions—to the more recently innovated and insidious. A network can be rendered nearly unusable if someone manages to flood the network with thousands of bogus packet requests a minute. A mail server can be shut down if a cracker decides to subscribe everyone in the mail system to 50 different high-volume mailing lists, making it impossible for legitimate messages to get through, a practice known as *mailbombing*. Some authors of listserv programs have taken steps to prevent their programs from being exploited as weapons by insisting on having a user send back a confirmation message after asking to be subscribed to a mailing list.

The Boot Floppy Loophole

The single biggest loophole in Windows NT's security is the presence of a boot floppy drive. If a Windows NT machine has an accessible boot floppy and an intruder can gain physical access to the root console, the intruder can reboot the system and use a custom-configured boot floppy to bypass the security measures of the operating system.

The Dangers of the Boot Floppy

A boot floppy can be exploited in many ways. Usually, the boot floppy contains a 16-bit operating system (such as DOS), along with some machine-level utilities such as a disassembler or disk utility. The intruder can freely browse the hard storage on the cracked computer, without worrying about the security concessions in the operating system—because the operating system has been completely bypassed.

The simplest way to do away with the boot floppy loophole is the most obvious—remove the floppy drive. Beyond that, there are several other measures that need to be taken as well. Disable the computer's floppy controller in the ROM BIOS setup (which should also be password-protected) if the controller is integrated with the motherboard. If the controller is on a separate card, remove the card if possible. Another level of security against the boot floppy problem is to prevent as much access as possible to the console and the machine itself. (All of these options are discussed in greater detail further on in this section.)

The NTFSDOS Redirector

One of the more alarming developments in the boot-floppy weakness is the creation of a DOS-based NTFS redirector—a boot-loaded TSR for DOS (and Windows 95) that can mount an NTFS volume as a lettered drive (D, and so on), and make it readable from DOS or Windows 95.

This utility is named NTFSDOS and is the product of Mark Russsinovich and Bryce Cogswell, reachable at markr@numega.com and cogswell@cs.uoregon.edu. Originally, NTFSDOS was the product of work being done for the Linux operating system, in an attempt to enable Linux to mount and read NTFS-format drives. The source code was ported over to DOS and reworked as a DOS TSR, making the same thing possible in DOS, Windows 3.1, and Windows 95.

The presence of NTFSDOS thwarts a previous assumption about NTFS that many people have mistakenly made—that because NTFS is not readable through anything except Windows NT, it constitutes a form of file security. Microsoft has never explicitly recommended NTFS as a security solution in that sense, and it should not be considered one, especially in the light of the NTFS redirector.

Also, NTFS does not encrypt or compress (by default) data written to the hard drive. Enabling NTFS compression thwarts the NTFS director in its current revision, but a future revision is probably going to enable reading compressed volumes, especially because the compression is not itself a formal variety of security either.

The redirector has some limits. It cannot write to an NTFS volume (yet), but it can certainly read and enable files to be copied off the NTFS volume and removed from the site. This in itself is dangerous enough to warrant stringent security measures against allowing access to a system through a boot floppy.

Solving the Boot Floppy Problem

The boot floppy problem and its attendant calamities can be alleviated in several ways.

- Restrict access to the console. Placing the computer in a secured room behind a locked door enormously decreases the chances of a casual intrusion.
- Physically remove the boot floppy drive from the system and disable floppy-level boot through the machine's firmware. This makes it difficult for someone with casual access to the console to put a boot floppy into the machine and use it. If the machine's BIOS is password-protected, it makes things that much more difficult.
- Use Fortezza-based encryption hardware. A number of vendors manufacture hardware that performs real-time Fortezza encryption on data written to and read from hard drives and floppy disks. Without the hardware and the correct passwords or software keys, the data is just so much digital gibberish.

This particular weakness has been the result of a great deal of controversy in the computer community, especially because it points toward a misunderstanding of C2 evaluation procedure. C2 evaluation does not discriminate between the software and hardware on a given system—meaning that if a system is certified as being C2-compliant, both hardware and software have passed the test. A system cannot be made C2-compliant by just adding the right software packages.

The NTFS redirector is openly available on the Internet and can be downloaded freely. It is strongly recommended that a system administrator download it and use it in an experimental fashion to determine the limits of the security on his system.

This site has the NTFS redirector and discusses it further:

ftp://ftp.ora.com/pub/examples/windows/win95.update/schulman.html

Microsoft has also authored a white paper in which it denies that the NTFSDOS utility has the potential to undermine data security:

http://www.microsoft.com/ntserver/ntfs_mb.htm

Aside from making changes to the hardware in a system, the single most crucial way you can take steps to protect your system is by effectively choosing passwords.

Selecting a Password in Windows NT Workstation

One of the single biggest vulnerabilities in any computer system is the account password library. If an intruder can gain access to the system by exploiting a poorly chosen password—by random guesses, educated attacks, or just by trying out blank passwords or the word "password"—steps need to be taken to ensure that such a thing does not happen again.

You should follow a few basic guidelines when choosing a password for a particular account:

First, *never* do any of the following:

- Use your logon name in any form as your password. Don't think that by reversing, transposing letters, changing capitalizations, and so on, that you will be fooling a potential cracker. These are the first of many strategies that are employed by someone who is making an industrious attempt to break into your system.

- Use any part of your real name.

- Use a name of a family member or a spouse, or a mother's maiden name.

- Use any other easily obtainable personal information as your password. This could include (but isn't limited to) driver's license numbers, license plate numbers, make and model of your car, street address, zip code, and so on.

- Use a password of all digits. Numerical passwords are extremely easy to guess and break by a determined cracker.

- Use a word that can be found in a dictionary. Dictionaries, whether English or in a foreign language, are often exploited by crackers to attempt to break password lists through brute-force attacks.
- Use a password shorter than six characters. A password less than six characters in length is much easier to guess and break than one with more than six characters.

Some more guidelines for generating and maintaining a password:

- Mix letters, numbers, digits, punctuation, and upper- and lowercase letters. The more of a variety of characters you have, the harder it is to attack the password through random guesses.
- Find a password that is somehow easy for you to remember, even if it is cryptic-looking. The reason for this is that it should be something you can commit to memory and never have to write down. Passwords should never be written down.
- Practice typing the password quickly. This way, someone *shoulder-surfing* (watching over your shoulder or from a distance) will have a harder time figuring out what you're typing.
- Windows NT's User Manager has provisions to force the user to change his password every so often. Enforce this restriction every 45 days. This way, even if someone manages to figure out a given password, there will be at least some chance that by the time they get to use it, the password will already have been changed. Also, Windows NT enables you to specify a *memory* for passwords so that the last X number of passwords used in a particular user account are remembered and cannot be reused. You may also want to enforce this restriction. Another restriction that should be enforced if there are many attempts to log on in a short period of time—a sure sign that a cracker may be trying to break in—is the capability to lock out access for a particular user if a certain number of logon attempts fail. This lockout period can be for a given amount of time, or it can be permanent until the administrator revokes it. Use the permanent setting for maximum possible security.
- The administrator who handles passwords for a given system should never allow a password to be changed over the phone or through an e-mail request. If a user forgets his password, he should have it changed or re-administered *in person.* Documented cases of password thefts have taken place in this manner, and it is very difficult to track down who exactly is responsible for the breach of security when it does.

Here are some ways to generate cryptic passwords that are difficult to guess, but easy to remember:

- Take a song or poem with which you are familiar and use the first letter of each word in a line from it. Also exploit numbers where you can. The line "Sixteen vestal virgins waiting by the coast" could be rendered "16VVwbtc."
- Alternate consonants and vowels—one consonant and two vowels, or the reverse—for up to ten letters. The results are usually pronounceable and can often be remembered for that reason. "Aevingaw," for example. This is not an English word (or any other word, most likely) but still relatively memorable.

Securing the Windows NT Workstation Desktop

The desktop, or the root console as Unix people are wont to refer to it, serves as the main gateway for the user to access Windows NT functions. It's also one of the single most vulnerable entry points in any computer system, and Windows NT is not an exception.

Fortunately, Windows NT comes with a number of security measures designed to secure the desktop against casual intruders and prevent unauthorized access when a user is not at the console. The console can be locked by using the Ctrl+Alt+Del key sequence, for example, and will remain locked unless you provide the proper user or supervisor password.

Locking the Workstation

The most common way to secure the desktop against intruders is to manually lock the workstation. After this is done, the workstation does not respond to keyboard or mouse actions until the workstation is unlocked. The only way to unlock the workstation is by providing the user's logon password.

Locking the workstation is done in something of the same manner as the initial logon. The user presses Ctrl+Alt+Del and brings up the Windows NT Security window. From there, the user clicks on Lock Workstation. This locks the workstation, clears the desktop, and displays the following message:

```
This workstation is in use and has been locked.
The workstation can only be unlocked by [Current user] or an administrator.
Press Ctrl+Alt+Del to unlock this workstation.
```

The workstation stays locked unless the system is powered down or unless someone unlocks it. If the system is powered down and powered back up again, a user cannot gain entry to the system unless he has a valid logon.

To unlock the workstation, press Ctrl+Alt+Del and type in your password. An administrator can also unlock the system by specifying his name and password. No member of any other user group can do this.

After the workstation is unlocked, the desktop is restored the way it was before the workstation was locked.

Screen Saver Security

Windows NT has a built-in screen-saver system that integrates password protection with any Windows NT-compatible screen saver, whether 16- or 32-bit.

To change the screen saver settings, you can right-click on the desktop and select Properties to bring up the Display Properties sheet, or you can double-click on Display in the Control Panel. After you have the Display Properties sheet, click on the Screen Saver tab (see fig. 19.1).

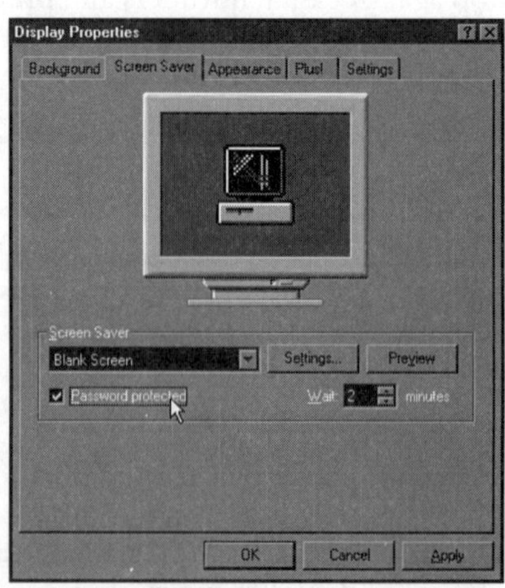

Figure 19.1
Password-protect a screen saver by checking the appropriate box.

To password-protect the screen saver, check the Password protected box. The screen saver activates after the time listed in the Wait box. The computer then displays the `This workstation is in use but has been locked.` message, and the user will have to press Ctrl+Alt+Del and type in his password to regain control over the console.

The image of the monitor at the top of the Screen Saver tab normally contains a live preview of the currently selected screen saver. To change the screen saver, click on the Screen Saver drop-down list box, and then select the name of an installed screen saver from the list.

To preview the selected screen saver as it would normally appear, click on Preview. You can dispel the preview by touching a key or moving the mouse.

If the selected screen saver has settable options, click on Settings to change them. Not all screen savers have options, and if this is the case, a dialog box will appear, informing you that the screen saver has no options you can change.

Maintaining File and Folder Security with NTFS

The NT File System, or NTFS, is designed with a number of built-in security measures. As long as the operating system itself is not circumvented or bypassed (see the section earlier in this chapter about the NTFS Redirector), NTFS provides a high level of security and access control. You can restrict access on a folder-by-folder or file-by-file basis, and control read and write permissions discretely.

The following sections go into the following topics:

- Creating and maintaining an NTFS volume
- Creating and adjusting attributes for NTFS objects (files, folders, and volumes)
- Controlling auditing

Formatting a Drive as NTFS

NTFS security features cannot be used on a drive not formatted as an NTFS volume. To format a volume as NTFS, you can use one of the following methods:

- Right-click on the drive's icon in My Computer and then select the Format option.
- Or, click on the Start button and select the Programs, Administrative Tools menu. Choose Disk Administrator, then right-click on the drive in question and select Format.

In both cases, you get the Format menu for a volume (see fig. 19.2).

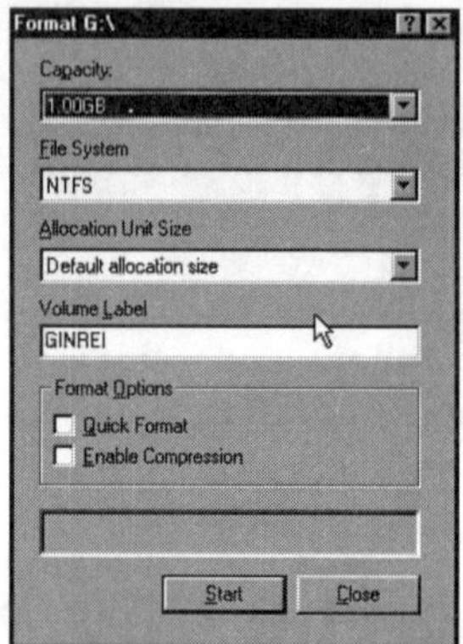

Figure 19.2

The Format menu enables you to choose between FAT and NTFS file systems when you format.

To format a volume as NTFS, click on the File System drop-down menu, and choose NTFS, and then click on Start. A warning appears that all data on the disk will be erased, which is normal (and in many cases, exactly what is wanted). Click on OK to continue. Formatting a volume as NTFS can take anywhere from 5 to 20 minutes depending on the size of the volume and the speed of the computer.

After the volume has been formatted as NTFS, you will want to create directory structures on the volume and set their properties.

NTFS Drive and Directory Properties

Directories on a drive formatted with NTFS have many new options not present in a drive formatted with FAT. To get an example of this, create an empty folder on an NTFS drive, and then right-click on it to bring up its Properties sheet (see fig. 19.3).

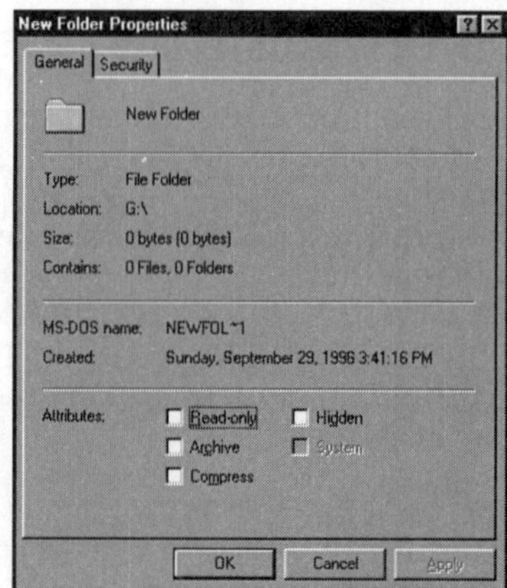

Figure 19.3

The properties of a folder on an NTFS drive are more extensive than those of a FAT drive.

The Compress checkbox, which is not present in folders on a FAT drive, enables you to have Windows NT perform file compression on files stored in that folder. If you check it and click on Apply, you also receive a notice about subfolders (see fig. 19.4).

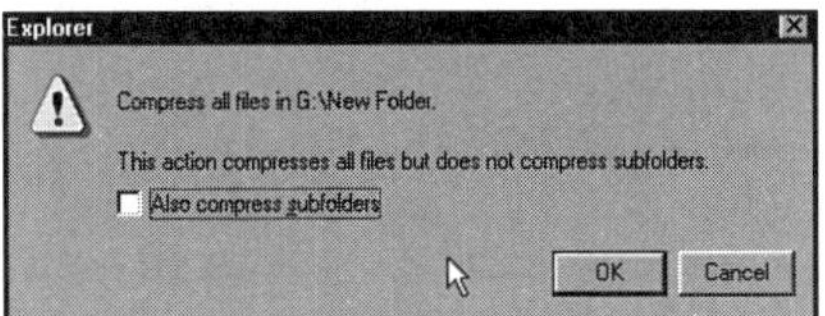

Figure 19.4
A quick warning about compressing subdirectories, although compressing subfolders usually will be fine.

Unless you have a specific reason for not wanting to automatically compress subfolders in that folder, check the box by clicking on it.

After you have enabled compression on an NTFS folder, a "C" shows up in the attributes column for that folder in Explorer (see fig. 19.5).

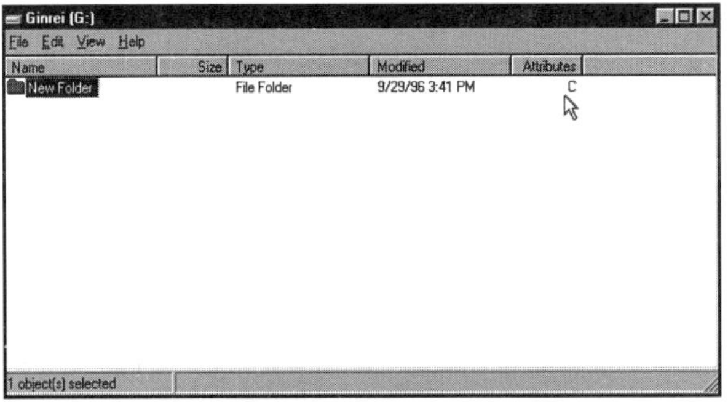

Figure 19.5
The "C" in the Attributes column of a directory listing means compressed.

Security Controls for NTFS Folders

Right-click on the Properties for the folder again, and click on the Security tab (see fig. 19.6). Here, you can define and edit the security settings for the way files are audited, the way permissions are granted, or the way ownership is taken. Note that these security options are also enabled for individual files as well as directories and subdirectories.

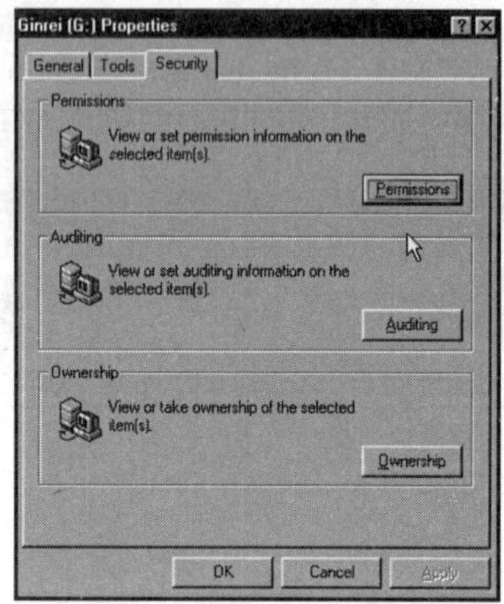

Figure 19.6
The Security tab for the Properties of an NTFS file-system object describes the permissions for the object.

Permissions

Clicking on the Permissions button brings up the Directory Permissions dialog box (see fig. 19.7). Here, you can add Windows NT user group names and assign specific permissions to those groups. You can also assign permissions to individual users.

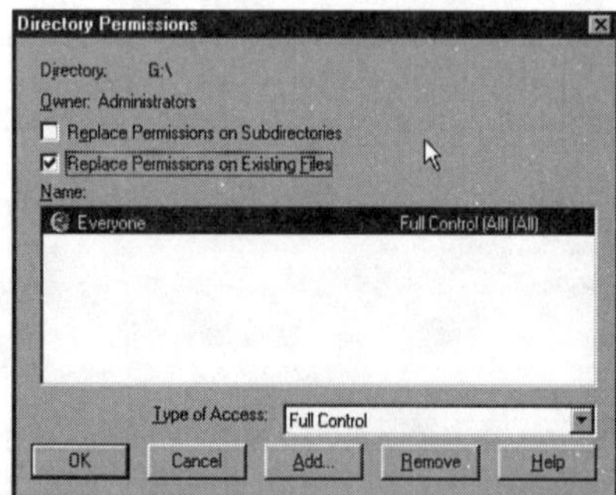

Figure 19.7
You can assign user permissions to an NTFS object on a user or group level.

If you select the Replace Permissions on Subdirectories or Replace Permissions on Existing Files checkboxes, all the changes you currently make in that window replace existing permissions for *all* existing files and subdirectories to that directory.

To remove a name from the Name list, highlight it and click on Remove. To edit the type of access possible for that name, highlight it and select the access type from the Type of Access list.

The following list identifies and describes the types of access you can control:

- **No Access.** No access by the user is allowed for this item (file, directory, and so on).
- **List.** The user can list files and directories, and can switch between them, but cannot read files or make changes to them.

- **Read.** Same as List, except that the user can also read the contents of files.
- **Add.** Same as List, except that the user can add files to the directory.
- **Add & Read.** Both Add and Read permissions are possible.
- **Change.** Same as Add & Read, but also allows files to be edited and deleted.
- **Full Control.** Same as Change, but also allows users to take ownership of objects and change permissions on objects.

After clicking on the Add button to add a user or group name, a list of names from the local computer appears. If you're attached to a network and you want to add groups or users from other computers, you can click on the List Names From drop-down list to browse for another machine to add from, or click on Search to search for groups or users across the network by wild-card criteria.

To add users, click on a name in the Names list to highlight it. Holding down Ctrl while clicking on it enables you to highlight more than one name at a time. Select the type of access to allow for the selected users by clicking on the Type of Access drop-down list and scrolling through the list. After you finish choosing users or groups and access type, click on Add to add the name.

Click on Cancel to cancel all changes made and return to the Security tab, or click on OK to confirm all changes and return to the Security tab.

Auditing

Clicking on the Auditing button on the Security tab brings you to the Directory Auditing window. From here you can control how audits are performed on actions by specific users or groups of users (see fig. 19.8).

If you select the Replace Auditing on Subdirectories or Replace Auditing on Existing Files checkboxes, all the changes you currently make in that window replace existing auditing behavior for *all* existing files and subdirectories to that directory.

You can log events if they are successful or have failed.

Clicking on the Add button, which adds a user to the list of names, brings you to the same kind of user-selection window seen with the Permissions window. The only difference is that the Type of Access drop-down list box is not present.

You can set or clear the following auditing events: reading, writing, executing, or deleting a file, as well as changing permissions on a file or taking ownership. If you log a failed attempt to do any of these events, you can tell whether the event failed due to the user attempting to perform something not permitted (which generates an audit failure report), or for another, more mundane reason.

Click on Cancel to cancel all changes made and return to the Security tab, or click on OK to confirm all changes and return to the Security tab.

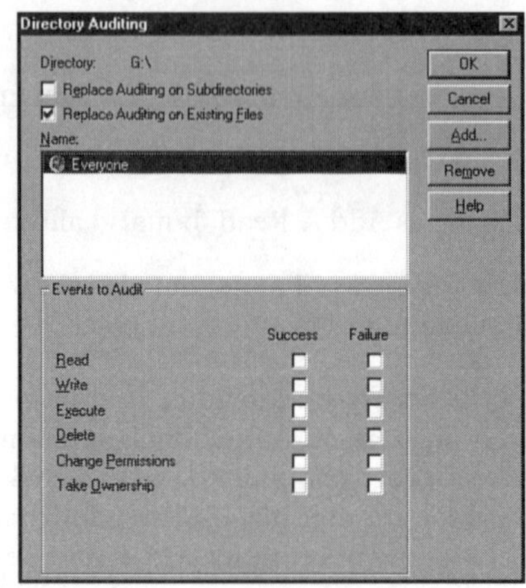

Figure 19.8

Options in the Auditing functions for an NTFS file system object enable you to generate audits on given events.

Ownership

Clicking on the Ownership button on the Security tab displays the ownership properties for the item (see fig. 19.9).

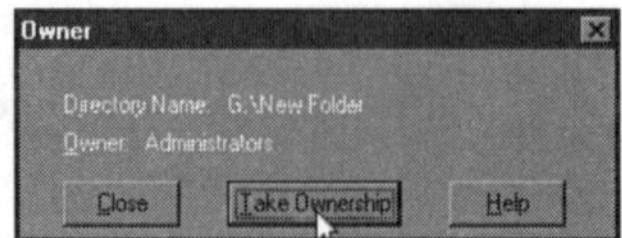

Figure 19.9

To take ownership of an NTFS object, click Take Ownership.

To take ownership of the item, click on the Take Ownership button. If one of the items you're taking ownership of is a directory, you are asked whether you want to also take ownership of all subdirectories and files in those subdirectories (see fig. 19.10).

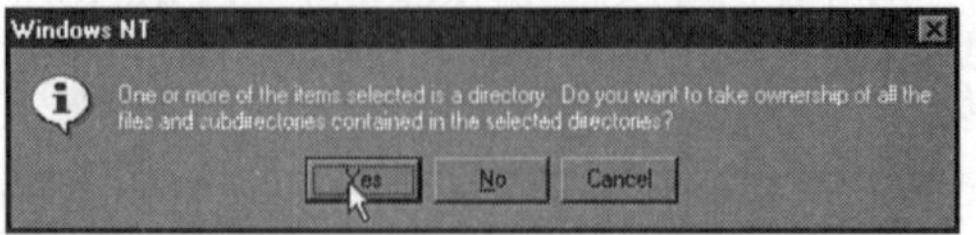

Figure 19.10

The Auditing functions for an NTFS file system object works the same as with a specific file or directory.

Click on Yes to take ownership of all the child items as well, or No to just take ownership of the item(s) in question.

Understanding Challenge/Response Protocol

In an attempt to implement its unique security features across the Internet, Windows NT has introduced a protocol for password transactions over the Internet that so far has only been implemented in Windows NT and Internet Explorer 2 and 3. This protocol, named the Challenge/Response Protocol, is designed to enable the verification of passwords and other sensitive information over the Internet, while thwarting attempts by a third party to intercept the transmission with a packet analyzer.

Challenge/Response Explained

Microsoft's implementation of Challenge/Response is actually a specific implementation of a methodology that already exists in a more generic sense. Challenge/response protocols already exist, but Microsoft has implemented it specifically to be used for password verifications in a situation where it's not a good idea to transmit a password as plain text—such as over the Internet.

Challenge/Response works by not transmitting the password itself—not even in an encrypted form. After a connection is established between a host and a peer, the host sends the peer a *challenge*, which is specific to the connection and can be sent in response to, for instance, a user name (which does not pose a threat when transmitted in plain text form). The peer takes the challenge and calculates a response based on a user-provided value (that is, a password), and then sends the calculated value. The calculation is usually a *one-way hash* function difficult or nearly impossible to reverse-factor. The host then checks the calculated value to determine whether it matches the value it would return from the same calculation performed on its own stored password. If they match, the response is considered valid and the user is granted access.

Challenge/Response Protocol has some advantages that make it potentially exportable to many programs and systems. It does not require a Secure Socket Layer to be secure, which means that a relatively high level of security can be implemented without having to invest in SSL on the server side.

Secure Socket Layers

Full-time encryption over a TCP/IP connection is best accomplished through the use of a Secure Sockets Layer, or SSL. SSL uses a variety of public-key encryption to make it possible to send large amounts of secure data over a public network.

With SSL, the server that hosts the secure connection has a *certificate*—a set of numbers generated according to a strict algorithm, which is used to encrypt messages. The certificate is *public*, meaning that it is sent openly to the client when the SSL connection is established. The certificate is only used to encrypt, not decrypt, messages; if someone intercepts both certificate and encrypted message, they won't be able to do anything with either of them.

The algorithm used in SSL is hard to break and will certainly withstand casual scrutiny. While it might eventually yield to a systematic attack, any confidential information that could be revealed by such an attack would most likely be obsolete by the time the codebreaking was concluded—months or years.

Once the connection is established and the client has the certificate, all transmissions to the server are encrypted using the certificate. The client has a certificate of his own as well—one usually generated by the Internet browser software when it is first installed. Because this is a fairly high-level feature, not many Internet browsers support SSL. The two most popular examples are Netscape Navigator and Microsoft Internet Explorer.

SSL has one fairly sizeable disadvantage. In order to make use of it, a sysadmin must purchase SSL server software and also purchase certificates to go with it, which can be a fairly sizeable investment. If the server is being used for online commerce, however, what it returns to its users in terms of security and peace of mind is invaluable.

Summary

Making the best of the security features in Windows NT Workstation pays everyone back in the long run. Administrators deal less with downtime caused by outside attacks, and users are less plagued with problems like information theft and denial of service. In short, knowing NT's security is part and parcel of using *all* of NT to its potential. Lack of security can add up to lack of cost-effectiveness—downtime, stolen data, and so on—and also means a wasted investment in NT as well.

Every user and administrator will need to go to different lengths to secure their Windows NT computers. A single-machine user might not need to do more than master the art of password maintenance and getting into the habit of locking the workstation. A sysadmin might have to go to the lengths of obtaining C2 certification, installing cryptography hardware, or disabling boot-floppy access. Whatever the user or administrator needs to do, they should be fully aware of how much they need to go through to get what they need to keep Windows NT secure.

CHAPTER 20

Protecting Hardware and Files

The problem of protecting a computer is an ongoing issue. There is no passive way to do this; you have to develop an understanding of the dangers that lurk, and you have to take the necessary steps to protect workstations and data.

This chapter examines some of the problems that can affect your workstation and discusses some of the solutions and preventive measures you can apply. It discusses hardware and the dangers that lie hidden and how to guard against them. And it covers the protection of files, especially data files. There are also sections on preparing for a computer that doesn't want to boot properly (or at all), and some discussion of keeping backup copies of the Registry.

Protecting the Hardware

The hardware in your computer is susceptible to all sorts of damage and is extremely vulnerable if you don't take precautions to protect it. Hard drives develop bad spots, boot sectors get damaged, chips fry, cables and connectors stop delivering data, and motherboards die. Many hardware problems can be prevented (few can be fixed); take care to ensure that your computer is operating in a safe environment.

Electrical Problems

The two entities that can cause the most damage to your hardware are Mother Nature (if you live in an area that has lightning storms) and your local power company. Take a paranoid view of them, and protect your computer from their attacks.

Lightning storms can cause surges, and the power company occasionally is the source of brownouts (lowered voltage). You can purchase equipment to shield your computer from the effects of some of these electrical problems. It is important to understand what is happening and how you can protect your hardware.

Power Surges

Power surges are sudden rises in voltage, and they are extremely dangerous to all the hardware in your computer. Chips get fried, wires burn or melt, and power supplies blow up, destroying everything attached to them.

The way to protect against the damages caused by surges in voltage is to use a surge protector. Most computer users know about, and use, surge protectors. But surge protectors vary widely in their effectiveness; sometimes even the best of them provide no protection at all.

A surge protector that is not built to fight back with the right level of defense when there is a substantial rise in voltage is not much more than an expensive multioutlet extension cord. Before you buy a surge protector, do some research by reading reviews, articles, and even the labels on the surge protector.

A good surge protector does whatever it takes to protect your computer, including performing a self-meltdown or some other form of suicide. When it destroys itself to save your equipment, you just replace it.

No surge protector, however, will protect you from a direct hit by lightning. If lightning strikes the line, the size of the surge can be devastating, and you will lose the surge protector, your computer, and probably everything connected to your computer (peripherals, other computers, and so on). If a lightning storm is expected, unplug the computer from the wall outlet. No other protection is available from lightning.

Many office buildings have lightning arresters or lightning rods, so it's probably not necessary to run all over the building unplugging every computer. But if you work in a small office environment, don't take any chances.

Also, check with the local power company. Recently, many power companies began offering surge protection service to homeowners and smaller office buildings for a monthly fee. They place a surge protector on the box, provide surge suppressers for outlets, and insure the electrical devices in the building.

Brownouts

A *brownout* is a lowering of the voltage level coming from the electrical line, and low voltage can destroy electronic equipment. Even before the voltage drops enough to see lights flicker, your hard drive can suffer damage from low voltage. The computer's power supply can have its life shortened by continuous low voltage, as can the power supply on your printer or other peripherals.

Brownouts occur much more frequently than surges. There are two sources to investigate—the local power company and your own use of power.

The power company generally tries to put out enough power to maintain the optimum of 120 V. But sometimes conditions make it difficult to maintain that voltage. As a result, most power companies consider anything within 6 percent of the optimum to be totally acceptable. As far as your computer is concerned, you don't really have to worry about voltage as long as it is measuring between 105 and 125 V. Any deviation above or below those levels can, however, be dangerous.

The power company has two obstacles in its path as it tries to provide 120 V:

- At certain times of the day, especially around 9 a.m., it is almost impossible to maintain the optimum voltage because copiers, laser printers, and other power-consuming devices are being switched on in offices throughout the area.
- During the summer when air conditioners are constantly running, the voltage falls all throughout the grid on which the power company relies. There is usually nowhere to go for additional power because every power supplier in the grid is having the same problem.

Sometimes, low voltage is the result of user error. Laser printers and copy machines should be plugged in to dedicated outlets. That is true of any equipment that uses a lot of amps and needs a lot of voltage. You should never put your computer into the same circuit as a laser printer.

As you purchase and use equipment, you must adopt a certain level of common sense. You do not need to be an expert in electricity to achieve this; you just have to read the technical specifications for the equipment you buy and use the expert advice available in the media. Otherwise, you might end up with self-inflicted dangerous environment for your computer.

To boost low voltage before it harms your computer, you can use a line conditioner. A *line conditioner* works by measuring the voltage of the power coming out of the wall, and then pushes the voltage up if it's too low, or brings it down if it's too high. (It can't defend against extremely high voltage; you need a good surge protector for that.)

Line conditioners are sold by wattage. A 600 W unit (sufficient for most workstations) costs less than $100.

Telephone Lines

The majority of computers and networks destroyed by a fatal lightning surge receive the killer blast through the telephone line connected to a modem.

When it happens, the surge goes from the telephone line to the modem, through the serial port, to the motherboard, where it finds (and fries) the network interface card. The network card sends the surge through the network cable, spreading the zap to every network card on the system. Some of the cards pass the surge on to their own motherboards, destroying the workstation.

Although most electric power companies protect their lines at the transformer with lightning arresters or some other type of protection, almost no telephone companies in the United States use any form of line protection. Because telephone lines conduct electricity, if a line is charged with high voltage, it burns everything in its path. If you're using surge protectors, be certain to purchase the type that includes protection for telephone lines. Even with surge protectors, you should pull the telephone line out of the wall jack or the modem when preparing your defense against electrical storms.

You can also protect your telephone system (and thereby include modems and computers) by using a gas plasma protection device on the lines as they enter the building (before each line is sent to a wall jack). A good telephone line protection system is easy to install and provides some protection against lightning hits.

Conditioning Electrical Lines

If low voltage problems exist all over the office, it is probably easier and cheaper to solve the problem at the breaker box rather than by buying line conditioners for every computer. Symptoms to look for include:

- Power supply problems on computers, laser printers, and other peripherals
- Increasing numbers of bad sectors on hard drives
- Constant signs of activity (usually clicking noises) from any line conditioners attached to computers

You should check the voltage at various outlets over an extended period of time with a diagnostic machine that prints the results. You can rent testing machines or have an electrician bring the testing equipment.

If you do find that voltage throughout the office is too low too frequently, put line conditioning on the breaker box. Any electrician can handle this task.

Intelligent line conditioners can be installed on the box to maintain a minimum voltage. *Intelligent* means that the line conditioning device reads the voltage and only corrects it if necessary. There are also line conditioners set to raise existing voltage automatically, but these dumb line conditioners are not safe.

The Dangers of Retapping

Many office buildings have transformers that feed the building or multiple transformers that feed zones that have been established in the building. These transformers can be configured to raise voltage, which is called *retapping*. Retapping can be very dangerous, and it is definitely not advisable. Some electricians, after measuring the voltage coming out of your wall outlets and finding low voltage, recommend retapping as a solution. There are side effects, however, that make this a potential nightmare rather than a solution.

The problems arise because retapping provides a permanent solution to a temporary problem, and applying the solution when the problem no longer exists is dangerous.

If an electrician measures the voltage every day for a week while the office is running and everyone is working, and finds 106 V coming out of every wall outlet, it makes sense to push the voltage up about 12 points. That brings you to 118 V, still under the 120 V optimum, but close enough for your hard drive to stay happy.

On the weekend, however, the building's elevators are not running as often, the copy machines and laser printers are turned off, all the coffee pots in the building are off, and the computers are not being used. Now it's entirely possible that the voltage coming out of the box is the expected 120 V or something very close to it. Of course, the permanent boost to the box means the voltage coming out of the wall outlets is 132 V. This can toast the motherboards, hard drives, and most of the other devices in the office computers.

Installing a UPS

An Uninterruptible Power Supply (UPS) should be attached to any network servers or any workstations used for mission-critical applications. Certainly, any workstation that is a print server or an RAS server should be protected with a UPS. Corrupted data due to a power failure is more than an annoyance; it frequently leads to revenue loss.

UPS devices should also be installed on routers, hubs, and bridges. For some reason, administrators do not always think about protecting anything beyond critical workstations and the server(s).

There are two types of UPS units:

- **Online.** The UPS itself supplies the power to the computer and charges itself with the power coming from the wall outlet. The computer never sees the power that comes from the wall and runs completely from the UPS unit, which provides power conditioning. These units are quite expensive, need fresh batteries every couple of years, and are large, bulky, and heavy. These units are frequently used for large servers that have many users attached, especially where user access is constant as in branch offices or retail outlets connecting to the system around the clock.
- **Standby.** The battery is active when the power fails. Actually, the batteries kick in when voltage drops to the point where the UPS believes the power may be going off, so you never really experience a total computer shutdown. Some standby UPS units have power conditioning built in.

If you install a standby UPS, Windows NT provides software that adds to the features available with the basic UPS device. The operating system software communicates with the UPS and initiates an orderly shutdown of files and services when the UPS has sensed a loss of electrical power. No human intervention is necessary to effect the shutdown.

Three steps are involved in the installation of a UPS controlled by Windows NT UPS software:

- Physically install the unit and its cable.
- Run the Windows NT installation and configuration software.
- Start UPS services in Windows NT 4.

Attach the UPS Device

The physical installation is just a matter of plugging the UPS unit into the wall, then moving the plugs for the computer and monitor into the UPS. Follow the manufacturer's instructions for connecting the cable between the UPS and one of the computer's serial ports.

Although the following section covers the installation and configuration of Windows NT software that controls your UPS device, software programs available for specific UPS devices may work as well, or better, than the application provided by Windows NT.

Configure Windows NT UPS Settings

The Windows NT software is configured for your UPS through the UPS applet in the Control Panel (see fig. 20.1).

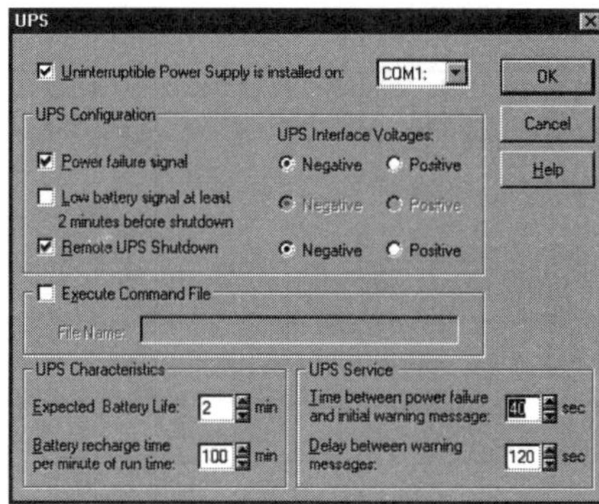

Figure 20.1

Configure the way Windows NT should control the UPS and the workstation to which it's attached.

You must specify the serial port for the UPS connection. The other configuration data changes depending on the UPS, the way you want to use it, and the way you want to use the software.

In the UPS Configuration section of the dialog box, the UPS Interface Voltages are specified in order to indicate an active state (which means activated because the conditions exist that cause the UPS and software to kick in).

If the power failure signal is normally positive and only changes to negative at the time of power loss, for example, you should select Negative for that option. Information about the normal state is available in the documentation for the UPS.

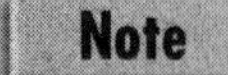

The interesting thing (if you find these things as interesting as I do), is that the UPS communication with the serial port follows the same conventions as other serial port peripherals such as modems. There are standard serial port messages between the UPS and the port. The Power failure signal is a CTS (clear-to-send) signal; the low battery signal is a DCD (data-carrier-detect) signal; and the remote shutdown signal is a DTR (data-terminal-ready) signal.

You can run a command file when there's a power failure, which can perform any task you need to before the shutdown completes. This is useful to ensure that specific events occur before shutdown. You might want to log off a network, for example, or close another type of connection. The following circumstances must exist for the command file:

- It can be installed from a third-party source that provides files for this purpose, or it can be written by you.
- It must have a file name extension of BAT, EXE, COM, or CMD.
- It must reside in the \System32 directory under the system root directory. For most workstations, this means the path is \WINNT\System32.
- It must complete the execution of its tasks in less than 30 seconds to make certain that it completes running before shutdown is complete.

Note Do not run any command files that need user input (no questions to answer, no dialog boxes, no Press Enter to continue) because the program won't conclude within the 30-second window if the shutdown is unattended. Even if the shutdown is not unattended, you'd have to make certain that you had a user who reads fast, types fast, and never makes typos.

In the UPS Characteristics section of the dialog box, you can establish the settings for the unit's battery life and recharge time. This is only necessary if your unit does not have a low battery signal. (In fact, the UPS characteristics are greyed out if you select low battery signal and enter configuration information.)

The battery recharge rate should be available in the unit's documentation (the available range is 2 to 720 minutes).

For recharge time, be aware of the fact that when the UPS service is started during system startup, it assumes that no charge is in the battery. The number of minutes specified for recharge time is the time that must elapse in order to gain a minute of battery run time. If you specify 100 minutes, that means the computer must be running for 100 minutes in order to give the battery enough charge for one minute of operation. The available range is 1 to 250 minutes.

In the UPS Service section of the dialog box, set the specifications for using your Windows NT UPS software. They're self-explanatory.

Incidentally, don't worry about setting the number for the time between power failure and initial warning message to a short interval. For one thing, the UPS device will probably begin beeping (most of them do) so you will know there is a problem, and you won't have to wait for software notification. Secondly, because many power failures last only a few seconds, it is not always necessary to be notified immediately in order to take some action.

Start UPS Services

As soon as you finish configuring the UPS dialog box and click on OK, an information dialog box pops up to tell you that the UPS service has not been started, and offers an opportunity to start it. Whether you say Yes or No (and start it yourself later from the Services icon in the Control Panel), you should choose Automatic as the startup type.

To stop UPS services, use the Services icon and disable them.

Turning Off UPS Software Services

You can deselect the COM port selection on the UPS dialog box to stop UPS services (besides disabling the service in the Services icon). Sometimes you might find it desirable to shut down the software services for your UPS. If you are experiencing short blackouts, or think there might be a serious chance of a blackout (perhaps it's a very hot summer day and your local power company is having a problem keeping up), you may want to keep working with the power the battery provides and not be forced to go through a shutdown.

Sometimes, when the power returns quickly, the software is more trouble than help. Having received a power problem signal, it moves inexorably toward the goal of shutting down. There's no stopping it.

The deselection of the software does not stop the battery from working, it merely prevents the software from performing its configured steps to shut down in an orderly fashion. Without it, the battery provides power (and beeps at you); when the power returns, the battery stops providing power (and stops beeping at you).

UPS Registry Entries

The UPS service won't start if the following subkey is not present:

HKEY_LOCAL_MACHINE\System\CurrentControlSet\Services\UPS.

The UPS subkey exists as soon as the UPS dialog box is configured and OK is clicked on.

Although you should make configuration changes directly in the UPS dialog box, not in the Registry, it is probably a good idea to see the Registry entries (see fig. 20.2).

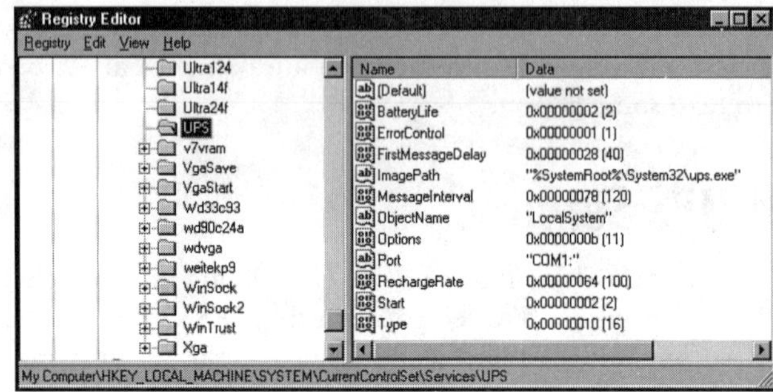

Figure 20.2
The UPS subkey in the Registry reflects the configuration of the dialog box.

The UPS service gets its information from the Registry. If any parameters are missing or fall outside the permitted ranges, the UPS service fails. If a problem exists with the UPS service and an error message advises that there are incorrect configuration options, make the changes in the dialog box.

If the UPS software is uninstalled, the UPS data stays in the Registry.

Planning and Implementing Back Up Procedures

After you've established the protection you need to keep your hardware and data safe from the vagaries of nature and electricity, you can't relax. Things happen. Drives die, motherboards go to computer heaven, users destroy files. Part of your protection is to keep the contents of the hard drive(s) safe, or be able to correct the situation when problems occur.

Backing up is not just a hedge against the day your drive dies; it is also protection for recovering from mistakes. More backup tapes are used to restore files accidentally removed than for recovering from major disk disasters.

The protocols for backing up a workstation are established to match the way software is accessed from the workstation:

- If a workstation only connects with a network server, launching applications from the server and saving data on the server, no regularly scheduled backup is needed. You should, however, make certain that there is a current repair disk and also back up the Registry to disk or a network directory. Perform another Registry backup whenever you change configuration options.

- If a workstation connects with a network server for applications and saves data locally, a daily backup plan should be implemented for the workstation data.
- If a workstation launches applications locally and saves the data locally, a daily backup plan should be implemented for the workstation software and data.

Backing up should not be done haphazardly. You should have a backup plan. There are several approaches to backing up, and a number of decisions to make as you design your backup plan.

The first decision to make is the one regarding the media you will use for backing up. The choices are:

- Copy files to a connected computer (usually a server) that is backed up to tape. You can perform the copy via Windows NT tools (such as Explorer), or automate it with command line batch files.
- Back up to floppy disks.
- Back up to tape.

There are also decisions about the type of backups you will be performing, choosing from:

- Partial backups
- Full backups

Backing Up to the Server

A server can back up a workstation in one of two ways:

- Copy files from the workstation to the server so that the normal server backup includes workstation data.
- Run a tape backup for the workstation from the server.

If a workstation accesses software on a network drive, but saves application data to a local drive, you have to worry about getting the data backed up.

If a workstation is linked to a network only for printer sharing or e-mail, and the application software and data is on the local drive, the software and the data should be backed up.

Copy Files to the Server

The easy way to back up workstation data is to create a system for copying it to the server. Usually, it is best to perform this task before the end of the day, making certain that it is accomplished before the server backup process begins. There are several approaches; your choice depends on the way data is stored on the workstation's drive. You can establish protocols, for example, that permit copying operations to take place with one of the following configurations:

- Create a data directory on the local drive of each workstation and save all data from all application software in that local data directory. Also create a data directory for each workstation on the server. Then just copy the local data directory to its counterpart data directory on the server.

- Create separate data directories for each application on the workstation's local drive, and then copy all those data directories into one parent directory established for the workstation on the server.

After you have a plan and have established the necessary directory or directories on the server, copying the files is an easy process. Use Explorer or My Computer to copy and paste the files, or create a batch file for this purpose.

Use a Batch File To Copy Files

If you don't want to spend time dragging and dropping, you can write a batch file that copies the contents of one or more local directories to one more server directories. The server must be a mapped drive because the batch file needs a drive letter in order to work.

You can write a batch file, for instance, that copies files to a network server from individual data folders connected to software. This batch file assumes data directories below the application directories on the local drive—that a folder has been established on the server for this individual user, and that folder contains subfolders for each set of data files. Also, if you are using an NT server, you must make certain to map the drive in order to reference the drive letter.

```
COPY C:\WPAPP\MYDATA\*.* F:\MYFILES\WPDATA
COPY C:\DBAPP\MYDATA\*.* F:\MYFILES\DBDATA
COPY C:\SSAPPP\MYDATA\*.* F:\MYFILES\SSDATA
EXIT
```

The EXIT command in the last line closes the command prompt session so that you don't have to click on the Close button on the command session window.

If you do take advantage of the speed of a batch file, make a desktop shortcut for it so that there's no need to open a command session manually.

Helpful Hints for Copying Files

Because few companies put tape backup machines on all the workstations, the idea of copying workstation files to another computer for eventual backup to tape is a good protocol. It can be implemented for small or medium LANs, or by creating some form of logical grouping of workstations and servers for larger LANs. You have a couple of choices about the commands you use to copy files to another computer.

Xcopy

You can use Xcopy in batch files to take advantage of the additional power available in the switches. Be aware, however, that for NTFS workstations, you cannot use Xcopy if you want to copy file permissions (see the discussion on Scopy that follows). The syntax for Xcopy is:

```
XCOPY source destination [switches]
```

Table 20.1 provides the available switches for Xcopy.

TABLE 20.1
Available Switches for Xcopy

Switch	Feature
/A	Copies files with the archive attribute set and does not change the attribute.
/M	Copies files with the archive attribute set and turns the archive attribute off.
/D:m-d-y	Copies only files changed on or after the specified date. Using the switch with no date copies source files where the time is newer than the time on the destination file being replaced.
/P	Prompts before creating a destination file.
/S	Copies directories and subdirectories that have files.
/E	Copies directories and subdirectories, even if they're empty.
/V	Verifies every new file.
/W	Prompts you to press a key before copying.

continues

TABLE 20.1, CONTINUED
Available Switches for Xcopy

Switch	Feature
/C	Continues copying even if errors exist.
/I	Assumes that destination is a directory if it doesn't exist, and the source is more than one file.
/Q	Does not display file names during the copy procedure.
/F	Displays full source and destination file names during the copy procedure.
/L	Displays files that will be copied.
/H	Copies hidden and system files.
/R	Overwrites read-only files.
/T	Creates a directory structure to match the source, but does not copy files. Empty directories or subdirectories are not created unless you add /E to the switch.
/U	Copies only files that already exist in the destination.
/K	Copies attributes (without this switch, Xcopy resets read-only attributes).
/N	Copies using the generated short file names.
/Z	Copies networked files in restartable mode.

Scopy

If you've purchased the NT Server resource kit, you will find Scopy on it. You can use Scopy to copy files if you need to retain the file permissions for NTFS workstations. Scopy, however, does not have the capability to copy only modified files. The syntax works just like Xcopy.

Back Up to Floppy Disks

You can perform a backup of the important files to floppy disks. This takes more will power than most people have. Sitting in front of a computer, putting one floppy disk after another into the disk drive can be an incredibly boring exercise.

It takes so long and is so boring that it is difficult to talk yourself into performing the task. As a result, many times you won't. In fact, you will skip the backup for days, weeks, or even months at a time. The computer demons somehow know this and destroy your hard drive.

Floppy disk backups, however, are better than no backups at all. If you use them, several approaches are at your disposal:

- Use Explorer and drag your data directories to the disk.
- Use a file compression software application such as PKZIP that writes to floppy disks and spans them, requesting additional disks as needed.
- Use the MS-DOS BACKUP command from a command prompt. Just follow any prompts to insert disks after you enter the command **BACKUP** ***x y*****:** where *x* is the drive and path you want to back up and *y* is the target.

Backup Parameters

The Backup command requires a source and destination parameter. There are some additional switches for more advanced features in backup:

/S	Include subdirectories.
/M	Back up only files that have changed since the last backup.
/A	Add backup files to an existing backup disk.
/F:size	The size of the disk to be formatted.
/D:date	Back up only files changed on or after the specified date.
/T:time	Back up only files changed at or after the specified time.
/L[:[drive:][path]logfile]	Create a log file and entry to record the backup operation.

The best disk-based backup approach is to stop using this method when you find you're skipping it and to buy a tape drive or a supported removable drive.

Using NT Backup

Windows NT 4 supplies a backup application that works with any tape drive on the Hardware Compatibility List (HCL). After you physically install the tape drive, use the Tape Devices icon in the Control Panel to have Windows NT 4 detect and install it. Drivers for supported tape drives are on the Windows NT CD-ROM.

You might want to install tape devices only on servers, or you might choose to use a workstation for backing up other workstations. Any self-sufficient workstation (software and data both accessed locally) should be backed up to tape (either from a local tape device or one on an attached computer). The same is true for any workstation that provides services to other workstations, such as printing services, RAS services, Internet services, and so on.

Once you decide to use tape and Windows NT Backup as the software to run that tape, you have to make some decisions about the way you want to approach backing up to tape. There are a number of choices available when you consider that.

Determine a Backup Philosophy

With the convenience of tape backup comes the capability to back up every file on your computer, not just data files. This provides a full range of choices about what you want to back up and how. (The question of how often is not up for debate—backing up is a daily task.) Here are the choices you have when you select files for backup:

- Back up the entire drive every day.
- Back up the entire drive one time, and then back up only the data every day. (When you add software or otherwise change the file system, you must back up the entire drive again.)
- Back up the entire drive one time each month (or one time a week), and then back up only the data files that have changed since the last backup.

The more files you back up, the longer the backup takes. The great advantage of tape is that it doesn't matter. Because you don't have to baby-sit the procedure, you can leave.

All the convenience of tape backup is lost if you use a tape system that cannot handle all your files. Make certain that the tape drive can use tapes that hold as many bytes as the hard drive can. If you have to wait for the first tape to fill up and then change tapes, you've made your backup procedure almost as inconvenient as using floppy disks. In fact, the best approach is to buy a tape system twice as large as your drive because you might one day install a larger drive or add a second one.

A Quick Restore, Not a Quick Backup

The way to decide which type of backup to perform is to ask yourself why you're backing up. What is the use of the backup tape? The answer should be, "So when disaster strikes, I can get back to work quickly."

This means that the reason for backing up is to restore things as quickly as possible so you don't have to reinvent all the work you've done. If you follow that logic to its natural conclusion, you realize that you create a backup philosophy to make restoring convenient, not to make backing up convenient. If you do anything except a full backup, restoring your system is going to be time-consuming.

If you choose to perform data-only backups, you must reinstall every piece of software on your system, go through the configuration process for each of them, and then restore your data.

If you choose incremental backups, you will have a pile of tapes that are incremental backups of files that have changed. You must restore each tape in the same order in which you backed up to ensure that you have restored the right version of each data file. This could take a very long time.

If you choose a total backup, after a disk death you only have to install the operating system, open the backup software on your new drive, and then click on Restore. Go have a cup of coffee, and when you return, everything is the way it was before the disaster. The poor users who chose backup schemes that made backing up each night a quick process will be putting tapes in and taking them out long after you're back to work, generating revenue with your computer.

Begin the Backup

After you have decided which files you're going to select for backup and which backup type you're going to choose, you can launch NT Backup. (It's on the Administrative Tools submenu.)

After Backup opens, the window displays icons for every mapped drive and a minimized icon for the tape inserted in the tape drive (see fig. 20.3).

To do a full backup of a drive, select the drive, and then click on the Check button (or click on the checkbox next to the drive icon). You can select multiple drives.

To do a partial backup of a drive, double-click on the drive and select the directories or files you want to back up (use the Tree menu options to expand and collapse the display of the drive's contents). Click on the checkbox next to a directory to select the entire directory, or select the directory and click on the check box next to each file you want to back up. You can use all the normal Windows shortcuts for selecting contiguous or non-contiguous files, and then click on the Check button. You can select partial backups of multiple drives.

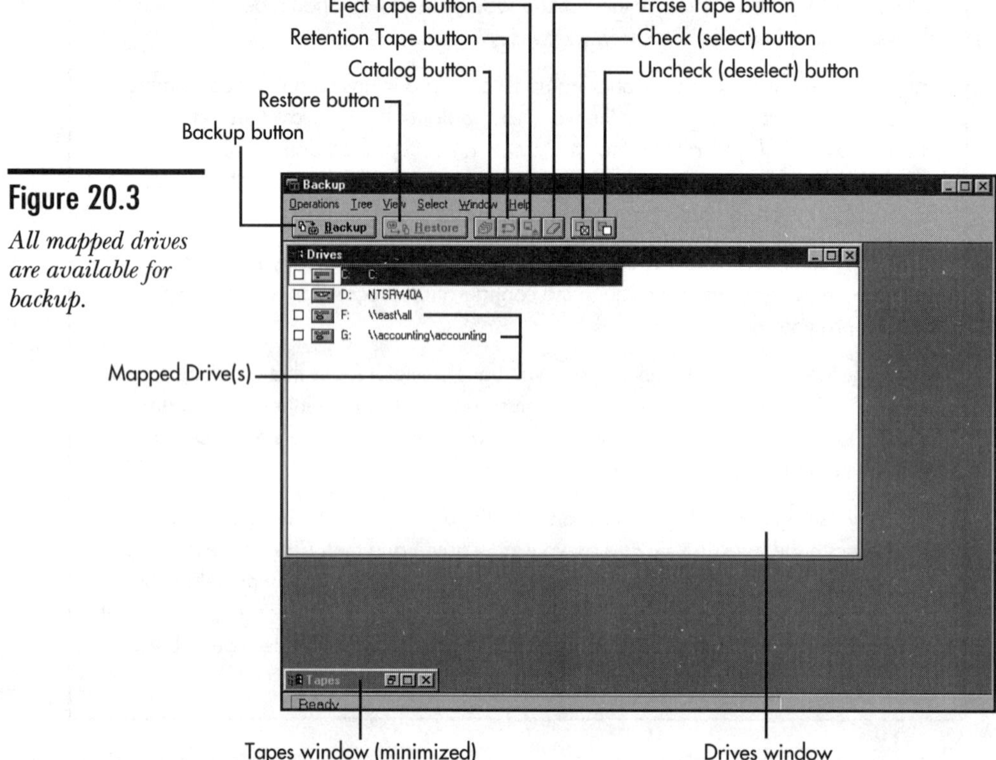

Figure 20.3
All mapped drives are available for backup.

Choose a Backup Type

After you have selected the files, the Backup Information dialog box asks you to choose a backup type. NT Backup offers five specific backup types, or protocols, to choose from:

- **Normal.** Backs up all the selected files and marks the files on the disk to indicate they have been backed up.
- **Copy.** Backs up all the selected files, but does not mark the disk with any attributes indicating they've been backed up.
- **Incremental.** Looks at the selected files and only backs up those that have changed since the last backup. Files are marked with an attribute indicating they were backed up.

- **Differential.** Only backs up files that have changed since the last backup, but does not mark the files as having been backed up.
- **Daily.** Backs up only those files that have been modified or added today. No attributes are marked on the disk to indicate the files were backed up.

The only use I can think of for the Daily backup type is to back up the files created or modified today, so you can take them home to continue your work.

Choose the Tape Options

The Backup Information dialog box also provides a section for tape options. The following options are available:

- Name the tape (up to 31 characters are available).
- Choose Append or Overwrite.
- Choose Verify. Be aware that to NT backup, verify means the software makes certain that it can read the file that was just backed up. This differs from the verify or compare functions found on most third-party backup applications, which match the files on the tape to the original file on the drive.
- Choose Backup Local Registry. Take that literally; you cannot back up the Registry of a remote computer.
- Choose Restrict Access to Owner or Administrator to limit access to the files on the tape.
- Select Hardware Compression to have the tape drive compress the data on to the tape.

Set Log Options

Also on the Backup Information dialog box are the options for logging the backup operation:

- Don't log.
- Summary log only, in which the major processes are logged, including the time the backup began and a list of any files that couldn't be backed up.
- Full detail log, in which the operations are logged along with the names of every backed-up file and directory.

If you choose to log the backup operation, enter the name of the file to use for logging in the Log File box (you can click on Browse to hunt for an existing log file).

Tape Problems

Once in a while, you will run into problems with tape media. (I've found that it is safest to find a good brand and stick to it, having had problems when I mixed brands.) The big problem with mixing brands is that some support compression and others don't. You will see error messages that don't give you real information when you set your options for compression and have a tape that doesn't support compression in the drive. The error message might indicate a problem with the tape drive, but frequently it's a spurious error report.

Tape media wears out surprisingly fast. Two physical problems beset tape—stretching and frayed edges. Be prepared to discard tapes more often than you'd like, and keep a supply of fresh tapes on hand.

Keep the tape drive clean; dust is a real enemy of the fragile mylar of tape. Some tape drives are known to miss the end of tape marker (a clear spot on the tape) because of the presence of dust, and let the tape roll off the cartridge (making the tape useful only for wrapping presents).

Most tape drive manufacturers sell or recommend a cleaning kit. The tape drive, especially the heads that read/write to tape, occasionally needs cleaning. Some of these kits are nothing more than special tapes that you insert into the drive and then use software features to move that tape across the heads. Other cleaning kits involve swabs and liquids for cleaning the unit. Follow the manufacturer's instructions.

Windows NT Backup has features for some basic tape maintenance chores. All the tape maintenance commands are found in the Operations menu:

- **Erase.** Deletes the contents of a tape. You can choose Quick Erase, which deletes the header (you have to know how to hack to get information from a tape with no header), or Secure Erase, which deletes the entire tape. The latter can take quite a bit of time.
- **Retension.** Fast forwards the tape to the end and then rewinds. This eliminates any loose tension in the tape and ensures smooth movement.
- **Format.** Prepares an unformatted minicartridge tape. Most minicartridge tapes can be purchased preformatted, which saves a great deal of time.

You can erase a tape from the command line with the following syntax: **ntbackup /nopoll**. No other parameters can be used with /nopoll. This is useful if there is a tape problem you believe can be remedied by deleting the contents of the tape, but you can't get to the tape from the software because of the problem with the tape.

Run NT Backup from a Batch File

You can use a batch file to run NT Backup, setting the parameters you need at the command line. The syntax for the batch file is:

ntbackup operation path /parameters

where *operation* is the operation you want to perform; backup is the normal choice.

Path is the path(s) of the directories you want to back up. Usually it's a drive letter to indicate the entire drive. If you do not back up the entire drive you can include directories in the path. Only directories can be specified, you cannot specify files and you cannot use wild cards.

The available parameters are shown in Table 20.2

Table 20.2
Switches for NTBackup at the Command Line

Switch	Action
/a	Appends the backup set to the tape (otherwise, any existing backup sets are overwritten).
/v	Verifies the backup (using the NT Backup's version of what a verify operation is).
/b	Backs up the Registry (only the local Registry can be backed up; if connected drives are being backed up, those Registries will not be included).
/r	Restricts access to the tape.
/d "text"	Names the tape.
/hc:on	Turns on hardware compression.
/hc:off	Turns off hardware compression.
/t[option]	Specifies the type of backup: normal, incremental, copy, differential, or daily.
/l"Filename"	Calls for a backup log with the indicated file name (include a path).
/e	Indicates a backup log with exceptions only in the report.
/tape:n	Where n is a number from 0 through 9 that indicates the tape drive to which files are backed up (when multiple tape drives are installed, these numbers are assigned during installation).

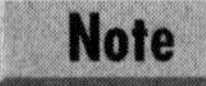

When more than one drive is being backed up, if /a is not specified, the backup of the first drive overwrites any existing backup sets on the tape; multiple drive backups will be appended to the first drive set backup.

A backup batch file, for example, might have this command:

ntbackup backup C: /b/l "C:\backup.log"

which backs up drive C, backs up the local Registry, and calls for a backup log named BACKUP.LOG to be placed in the root directory of the drive.

Schedule a Backup

You can schedule NT Backup to run at a specific time, which will probably be in the middle of the night so there's little likelihood that files will be in use. No scheduling feature is available in the NT Backup software (there is for most third-party software). To have a scheduled backup, you must perform three tasks:

- Start the Windows NT Schedule service.
- Write a command file to perform the commands that run the backup (see the preceding section, "Run NT Backup from a Batch File").
- Use the Windows NT AT command to run the command file at a scheduled time.

The AT command, which schedules commands and programs to run at a specified date and time, will not run if Schedule services are not running.

Windows NT Schedule Service

The Windows NT Schedule service is listed in the Services applet in the Control Panel. If you're scheduling a one-time backup, you can open the Services icon and start the Schedule service. If you plan to run scheduled backups regularly, you should configure the Schedule service to start automatically when you start the operating system.

Windows NT AT Command

The syntax for AT is:

AT [\\computername][switches] "command"

where \\computername, is the name of a remote computer if you are not performing a command on the local computer (if you are, the parameter is omitted).

Be certain to use the UNC for the connected share rather than a mapped drive letter. Although most of the time it won't make a difference, mapping is a user setting; if the user who mapped the drive logs off the workstation, the mapping may not be there.

The available switches are:

- **XX:YY.** Specifies the time the command should be run, where XX is the hour (use military time) and YY is minutes.
- **ID.** A job ID assigned by the system when you invoke the AT command.
- **/interactive.** Permits this scheduled job to interact with the desktop of the logged on user when the job runs. This is important if there is an error because all jobs scheduled through the AT command run as background processes. In interactive mode, an error message can be seen on the desktop and corrective actions taken. If the switch is omitted, any error will shut down the job and NT Backup will not run again unless you restart the operating system.
- **/delete.** Cancels the scheduled command. Use the ID to cancel if there are multiple commands scheduled, otherwise all scheduled jobs are canceled.
- **/yes.** Used to cancel all jobs if you don't want to answer a confirmation prompt.
- **/every:date or day.** Runs the command on each specified date or day (separate multiple dates and days with commas). If this switch is omitted, the current day of the month becomes the default. For days, the abbreviations are: M, T, W, Th, F, S, and Su. For dates use numbers (1 to 31 are the valid numbers, of course).
- **Command.** The file name for the program to be run.

So, if you have an NT Backup batch file named BACKITUP.BAT, and you want to run it every weekday at 11 p.m., make certain that Schedule services are started, and then enter the following at the command line:

at 23:00 backitup /interactive

Windows NT returns the message `Added a new job with job ID = 0`. If there are other jobs scheduled, the job id will be a higher number (the first AT job ID number is 0, the second job ID is 1, and so on).

Note Even though the backup job will run at night when no user is sitting in front of the workstation, use the interactive switch. That way, when you arrive in the morning you will know if there was a problem. This is especially important if you are not requesting a log file.

You should check the AT command schedule to ensure that you have entered the information properly. Type **AT** at the command prompt to see a report on AT's plans for running jobs (see fig. 20.4).

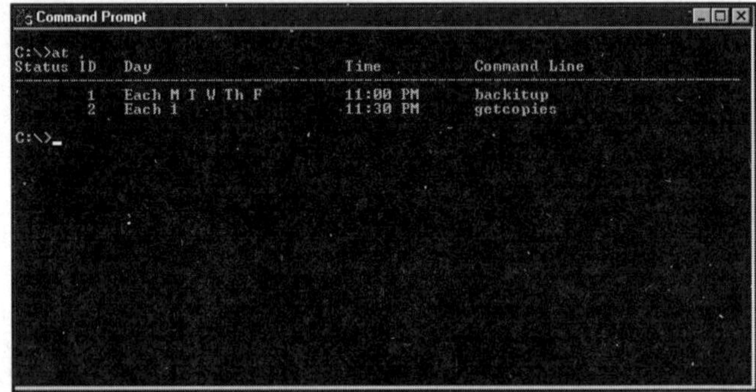

Figure 20.4
Check the frequency, time, and the name of the batch file to make certain that everything's as it should be.

If there's an error, delete the scheduled command (*AT id /delete*) and re-enter it.

A few other facts about the AT command are of interest:

- ◆ If you change the system time, you should synchronize the AT scheduler by entering AT at the command line.
- ◆ Currently scheduled commands are stored in the Registry in the key HKEY_LOCAL_MACHINE\System\ControlSet001\Services\Schedule\"subkey." The "subkey" is a specific key for this schedule entry (see fig. 20.5).

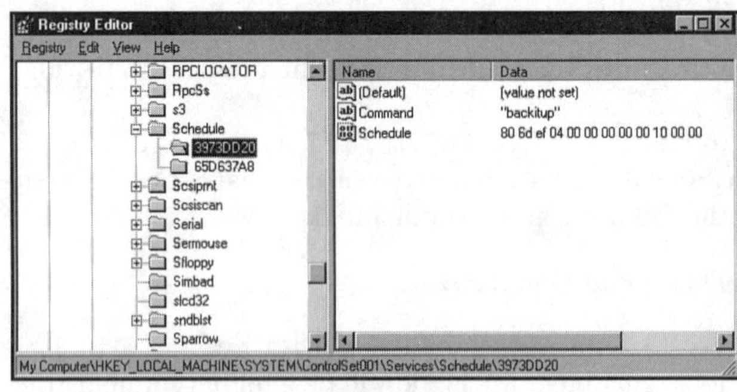

Figure 20.5
The batch file BACKITUP.BAT is stored as seen here in this workstation's Registry, the folder icon below the subkey represents another scheduled command.

If you have to restart Schedule services, the Registry information guarantees your scheduled jobs are not lost.

Incidentally, if you prefer a GUI environment, check out WinAT in the Windows NT Resource Kit.

Backing Up the Registry

If you are backing up to tape by using NT Backup, you can configure the backup to include the Registry. Most third-party backup software offers the same configuration option.

Many workstations are not backed up to tape, but the Registry should still be backed up regularly. A number of ways enable you to accomplish this.

Export the Registry

From within the Registry Editor, you can save the data in the local Registry by exporting it (choose Export Registry File from the Registry menu). This is not a backup in the traditional sense—it's not a file copy. The way the Registry is backed up is to export it to a text file. It is restored by importing that file back into the Registry (use Import Registry file on the Registry menu).

You should use this method of backing up the Registry whenever you are going to make changes to the Registry. Because messing around with the Registry can be dangerous, this gives you a fall-back position to recover from any damage you do.

You can back up the entire Registry or just specific parts of it. It's a good idea to create a folder specifically for Registry export files. It's also a good idea to copy the files in the folder to disk as extra insurance.

Resource Kit Tools

It's much easier to administer Windows NT if you have access to the Resource Kit. Here's a brief overview of some tools; you can get detailed information from the Help files in the Resource Kit.

REGBACK.EXE, which is on the NT Resource Kit CD, performs a Registry backup for as many computers on the network as you want. Actually, it backs up the Registry hives, which are files found in \System32\Config under the Windows NT 4 directory.

This is a batch tool you can use to copy all the hives in use at the time you back them up.

The program shuts down if the hive files do not fit on the target media, so you should be certain to use a hard drive as the target. Make a specific directory to use as a target for each computer you're accessing. The program also shuts down if it is instructed to overwrite an existing file name, so be certain to empty the target directory before beginning the copy operation.

REGREST.EXE restores Registry hive files from the backup copies made via REGBACK.EXE.

Backing Up the MBR and Partition Table

No backup applications are capable of saving on-disk data about the disk itself, such as the Master Boot Record and the Partition Table. The Windows NT Resource Kit, however, provides a couple of tools you might want to investigate.

Disksave

DISKSAVE.EXE saves the Master Boot Record (MBR) and the Partition Boot Sector data. If either of these disk elements become corrupted, you can use the binary image file you've created with DISKSAVE.EXE to restore the information.

The MBR is used by the BIOS on x86 computers (it provides the information needed on the partition table to move to the operating system partition), and if it can't be read, the machine does not boot.

The Partition Boot Sector holds the data that loads the kernel of the operating system (or a multiboot loader if the computer is offering the user a choice of operating systems). Although DISKSAVE.EXE saves only the partition that holds the NT loader, restoring this permits the computer to boot.

You must boot the computer into MS-DOS to use DISKSAVE.EXE.

Dskprobe

New for Windows NT 4, DiskProbe (DSKPROBE.EXE) is really a sector editor that works on both Workstation and Server. Besides permitting editing of disk sectors, the application can save the MBR and Partition Boot Sectors.

When you use Dskprobe, you first view the sectors, and then you can isolate and save the data you need. Save the file to a floppy disk so that you can get to the file if the hard drive is corrupted and you have to use Dskprobe to restore the data. More information about this application is available on the resource kit CD.

Updating Repair Information

Although the repair disk utility (RDISK.EXE) is not really a backup application, the information available can help reconstruct system files, configuration, and variables, which you might need if any of those elements are corrupted. In some cases, this data, along with other data and other tools, might be helpful in booting a computer during the process of restoring damaged files.

The repair disk utility updates the repair information kept on your hard drive and also provides an opportunity to create an emergency repair floppy disk.

The information for the repair disk is kept on the hard drive in the \Repair subdirectory under the Windows NT directory.

During installation of Windows NT 4, you had an opportunity to create an emergency repair disk (ERD). If you didn't take advantage of it, you can correct that oversight at any time by using RDISK.EXE.

RDISK.EXE is invoked from the command line or from Run on the Start menu. After it is launched, it displays a dialog box with buttons for updating the repair directory and making a repair disk with that information.

When you update the repair information on the hard drive, the current files are deleted. These might be the original files placed in the \Repair subdirectory during installation, or files that replaced the installation files when you last ran the repair disk utility. After you finish updating the repair information, you are asked if you want to create an emergency repair disk with the updated information.

If you create an emergency repair disk, any data on the floppy disk is deleted because the disk is formatted during the process.

The repair information updated and copied to the ERD is the current configuration for the computer. You should run this program each time you change configuration options.

The repair information (the files in the \Repair subdirectory and the files on the floppy disk) is stored in compressed format. If you need to restore a Registry key by using the Registry Editor, you must expand the files (use the Windows NT expand program).

Creating Startup Floppy Disks

If your Windows NT Workstation won't boot, before reinstalling the operating system and using your backup tapes to restore data, you can try starting the computer from floppy disk. You can then restore the Registry data (or the basic configuration from your ERD) or any other files you have backed up.

This is not an option, of course, unless you have prepared those floppy disks.

The files needed on a floppy disk, all of which can be found on the root of your boot drive, are:

- **NTLDR.** The Windows NT boot loader program.
- **BOOT.INI.** Points to the location of the boot partitions. If you configured the boot partition as a mirror set, you must make certain that you include a path to the shadow boot partition in this file.
- **NTBOOTDD.SYS.** Needed if you're using the scsi()syntax in BOOT.INI. If you're using multi()syntax, you don't need this file. NTBOOTDD.SYS is the device driver for your SCSI controller, with the driver file renamed to NTBOOTDD.SYS. Setup usually copies and renames the SCSI driver file for you and places it in the root directory. If it isn't there, copy the driver and rename it. You can ascertain the file name for the driver in the Control Panel in the SCSI Adapters applet (on the Devices tab, choose Properties, and then choose the Driver tab).
- **NTDETECT.COM.** Windows NT needs to detect the computer's hardware.
- **BOOTSECT.DOS.** Needed if you want to dual boot.

After you create a floppy disk for booting, be certain to test it before deciding you will count on it to help you restore a damaged system. It's probably a good idea to check it for virus infection, too. Push the write protect tab into position so that nothing untoward can happen to the disk. Put it in a safe place. If you create multiple startup floppy disks for multiple workstations, label them carefully; they're not interchangeable.

Summary

While providing protection against Mother Nature, your local power company, and users might seem a bit onerous, it is nothing compared to the work involved in cleaning up after a disaster (and it all seems harder when the disaster could have been prevented). Most of the prevention techniques are one-time-only tasks and should be considered a normal part of your approach to administering a network.

Some of the protection involves the cooperation of users, who must be trained (and threatened, if necessary) about regular backups. Making tasks easier for users means you increase the chances that they'll actually perform those tasks.

If you don't plan ahead, if you don't protect the workstations on your network, the computer fairies figure it out and they destroy the most important files on the system—it never fails.

Part VII

Advanced Administation

CHAPTER 21

Troubleshooting and Optimization

In spite of being a sophisticated operating system, Windows NT Workstation can have problems that are very difficult to understand. It is not uncommon to have someone complain about the "blue screen of death" (BSOD) when the kernel of Windows NT Workstation has a fatal error. These crashes are designed, however, to provide you with information that can assist you in fixing the problem or at least determining what the problem might be. In fact, few operating systems provide you with such detail. This chapter looks at the various types of problems that can occur from both a hardware and a software level.

Since the first PC was sold, users have had an insatiable desire to change things to make the computer "run faster." Everyone has manipulated AUTOEXEC.BAT and CONFIG.SYS settings, edited WIN.INI and SYSTEM.INI lines, and even changed settings in BIOS to get better performance. These searches for speed are called *optimization*. Windows NT was designed to eliminate these tweakings. Nonetheless, everyone still has this feeling that it can be made to run better. The second half of this chapter deals with performance tuning.

By the same token, knowledge of the factors that can cause rebooting or BSODs is essential for the maintenance of any Windows NT system, workstation, or server. When you think you have everything under control, a hard drive fails or a boot sector virus strikes. Knowing how to fix things in an easy and straightforward manner can save many hours of headache and hard work.

Troubleshooting NT Workstation 4

Before you can solve a problem, you must first determine the underlying level that has caused the problem. Bad sectors on a hard drive, for example, can cause bizarre problems that can appear to be memory related. Clearly, trying to fix the issue by changing memory will not work. So what resources are available to help you find the culprits? Surprisingly, Windows NT has many such resources built-in. This chapter looks at them all. To rule out all causative factors, the following are examined:

- **Hardware errors and their causes.** This includes problems with Power On Self Test (POST).
- **Installation problems and common causes.** Details are provided on hardware issues, viruses, and common incompatibilities.
- **Boot problems.** In this case, a brief discussion is given concerning the boot sequence of events and the importance of BOOT.INI.
- **Run-time errors and their common causes.** A discussion is given concerning the differences between the infamous General Protection Fault (GPF) and the blue screen of death. Of great importance here is the "last known good" option.

Hardware Errors, Causes, and Solutions

The initial task a computer performs after being turned on is run internal diagnostics. This diagnostic test is most frequently called a POST. Assuming that there is a speaker attached to the motherboard (always a good idea but not always done), you can hear BIOS beep code messages. In general, POST failures fall into two basic categories, fatal and non-fatal. Any POST message should be considered near fatal and dealt with immediately.

Note The two most important tools needed to fix a computer are a Phillips screwdriver and a clean pencil eraser. Both will be used to either open a case, remove a card, or clean the edge of a card.

Following are common near fatal messages:

- **Complementary Metal Oxide Semiconductor (CMOS) Battery State LOW.** Each computer maintains a battery to store values in CMOS. If this message appears, it is essential to find out the problem. One of three things has happened:
  - The system is new and the battery has not properly charged.
  - The battery is low and needs replaced.
  - If neither 1 nor 2, the motherboard could be "flaky" and need repairing or replacement.
- **CMOS Checksum Error.** When CMOS values are saved, a checksum value is set to enable error checking. If the message occurs, run the BIOS SETUP program. If the message recurs, the CMOS itself might be faulty.
- **CMOS Memory Size Mismatch.** If you have added memory to your system, when you reboot you see this message and are required to run the system BIOS SETUP program. On some newer systems, the memory is automatically configured at boot.

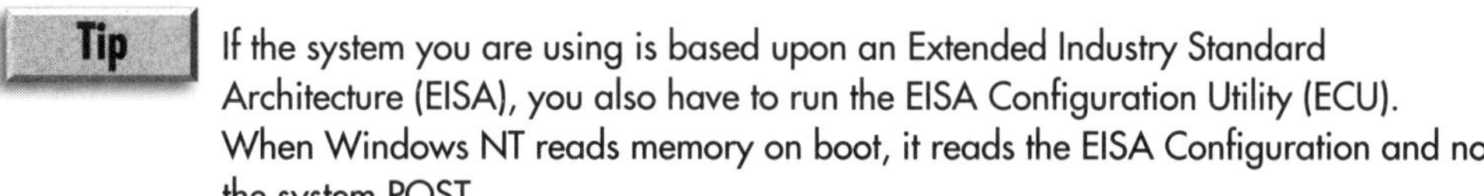

Tip If the system you are using is based upon an Extended Industry Standard Architecture (EISA), you also have to run the EISA Configuration Utility (ECU). When Windows NT reads memory on boot, it reads the EISA Configuration and not the system POST.

- **FDD Controller Failure.** This message means that the BIOS cannot communicate with the floppy disk controller. Check all cables and make sure that they are properly seated after you power down the system. While you are doing this checking, make sure that all contacts are clean (use the handy eraser and some compressed air).
- **HDD Controller Failure.** This is the same message as the preceding message but is concerned with the hard drive controller. This will not be a SCSI card but an IDE or EIDE controller. Because the majority of these controllers are built into the motherboard on new systems, this is a potentially fatal message.
- **C: Drive Failure.** This means that the BIOS cannot get any response from the C drive. For most EIDE systems, this means that the drive has died.
- **NO ROM BASIC.** When the BIOS searches for the Master Boot Record and cannot find it, the BIOS tries to run ROM Basic. When it fails to find the ROM Basic, this message follows. The most common cause of such an error is the

failure to have an active partition on the drive. Boot to a DOS floppy and run Fdisk. You are warned that no active partition is present. Using the Fdisk menus, assign a partition as active.

If the system is SCSI based, make sure that the correct drive is set as the boot drive. In some cases, the addition of a second SCSI controller can lead to this problem. If so, swap the positions of the controllers on the motherboard.

- **On Board Parity Error.** When BIOS runs, it encounters a parity error with some memory on the motherboard. Because parity memory is staging a comeback, this message might be seen more frequently. Do not disable parity checking in memory. In most cases, this message is fatal to Windows NT, and the system will not boot. Change the memory SIMMs.

  If you write down the exact syntax, a technician can tell you where the problem memory resides. The syntax of this error message is as follows:

```
ON BOARD PARITY ERROR
ADDR (HEX) (XXXX)
```

Note (XXXX) is the address in hexadecimal where the error occurred.

- **Standard Fatal Beep Messages.** In these cases, there will not be a successful boot of the system. If you have received a mail order system, many times cards become loose and can cause some of these problems. In all cases except eight beeps, the system will not boot properly. Table 21.1 illustrates the standard beep codes for POST failures.

Table 21.1
Standard Beep Codes for POST Failures

Beeps	Message	Problem
1	Refresh Failure	The memory refresh portion of the motherboard is faulty.
2	Parity error	A parity error occurred in the first 64 KB of the system.
3	Base 64 failure	A memory failure occurred within the first 64 KB of memory.
4	Timer malfunction	A memory failure occurred in first 64 KB of a failure of Timer 1.

Beeps	Message	Problem
5	Processor Error	The CPU on the system board generated an error.
6	Gate 20 failure	The CPU cannot switch into protected mode. This means that the A20 switch is malfunctioning. This switch is on the keyboard controller.
7	CPU Exception Interrupt Error	CPU produced an exception error.
8	Display Error	The video card is either missing or its memory is faulty.
9	ROM Checksum Error	The ROM checksum does not match the BIOS value.
10	CMOS Shutdown Error	The shutdown register for the CMOS failed.
11	Cache Memory Bad	The cache memory test failed.

Caution All the beep codes listed in table 21.1 are considered serious and need immediate repair. *Do not try to work around them.* Windows NT virtualizes hardware, and the slightest deviation from normal can cause serious failures and crashes.

Some problems occur frequently enough that more detail is necessary. These problems prevent the machine from functioning normally. You never get to run Windows NT in these situations. The following bootup issues might or might not have a beep error code but need definite correction before the system is functional:

- **There is no video at all.** Of importance in this situation is whether video was present at one time. In that situation, a loss of video is typically indicative of a catastrophic hardware failure, most commonly, a dead motherboard.

  If the system never displayed video, remove all cards but the video card. Make sure that all jumpers are set properly on the motherboard. Reset all memory and the CPU and make sure that the speaker is connected. Use the eraser to clean off the edge of the video card. Reboot the system and listen for error beeps. Check carefully for any LEDs and see if they indeed appear to be initialized. If there is still no video, swap video cards. If the second card also fails, the problem is either the motherboard or possibly the power supply.

- **Memory error at boot.** If a memory error occurs at boot, make sure that all SIMM modules are properly seated. It is very disconcerting to have 64 MB of RAM and only 32 show up at POST. It is a good idea to reseat all the modules and make sure that the modules are firm in their sockets. With new high-performance motherboards like those for the Pentium Pros, its is essential to have SIMM modules matched in speed and type. Never mix 70 ns and 60 ns modules. Likewise, do not match two 16 MB with two 32 MB SIMMs. It is essential that all be the same.

  If the system has 128 MB of RAM and NT sees only 64, the BIOS needs upgrading. This is a problem with some older DOS limitations that hopefully the motherboard supplier has fixed. The firmware needs to be recent to function properly.

- **System setup keeps getting lost.** If the system setup keeps getting lost, check out the power supply. Many vendors tell you that power supplies are not important, but in fact a properly functioning power supply is the heart of the system. All systems should have at least a 250-watt power supply.

- **3.5-inch floppy drive reads a disk but won't refresh to new floppy.** All you ever see is the contents of the first disk. This is a faulty drive. The drive never signals the system that a disk has been changed. Change the cable. If that fails, the only solution is to obtain a new drive.

Do not enable autoconfiguration for hard drives on EIDE controllers. Have the BIOS determine the drive parameters and install them into a standard BIOS table. In some cases, Windows NT does not function properly if the auto is enabled.

SCSI Card Problems and Solutions

Depending on your point of view, Small Computer System Interface (SCSI) is either very simple or extremely complex. One of the most common type of problems encountered is a failure of the system to see a peripheral device hooked onto the SCSI bus. A few words of explanation will help resolve this problem.

SCSI is a CMOS independent configuration. All aspects of the SCSI bus are under the control of the SCSI card or controller. The card pools the devices attached to it and determines what they are. After this information is determined, the card passes the information to the BIOS program. In all cases, what the BIOS is told suffices; that is, you do not set any drive parameters in CMOS. In fact, set drives to none unless you have EIDE also present. The corollary of this independence requires you to have all SCSI devices powered on at boot. If not, the controller will not see the device and neither will NT.

Consider a SCSI bus to be nothing more than an electrical circuit that has to have a beginning and an end. Both ends are determined by a resistor pack called a *terminator.* If you have nothing but internal devices, the controller is terminated as is the last physical device on the chain. If you have internal and external devices on the same bus, a terminator goes on the last physical internal device and the last physical external device. The controller in this case is not terminated. Although this setup seems complex, it is not. Most current controllers have a firmware application that controls the settings of the card. For example, when an Adaptec 2940 boots, you enter the board setup by pressing Ctrl+A when the card banner is displayed. Termination is a key component of SCSI.

Following are common SCSI problems and solutions:

- **Problem.** When the system boots, the controller post lists seven drives when in reality only one is attached.

  Solution. When the ID was set for the drive, it was set to 7. This ID is reserved for the controller itself. Set the ID of the drive to 0.

- **Problem.** A second hard drive was added to the bus, and now the system times out with the message that there are no installable devices on the bus. If the new hard drive is removed, the system boots normally.

  Solution. Both the first and second hard drives are set to the same ID. As a general rule of thumb, always set the boot drive to 0 and the second drive to 1.

- **Problem.** A SCSI controller is added to a new system, and the system reports a Hard Drive Controller Failure on boot. The only hard drive on the system is on the controller.

  Solution. Go into the CMOS setup and make sure that you have selected no hard drive for all IDE drive choices.

- **Problem.** If two PCI SCSI controllers are in the system, which one will be the boot controller?

  Solution. This is a complex issue because motherboard vendors do not set the PCI slots up the same way. In general, ISA or EISA controllers take precedence over PCI. For example, if you have a 2742 and a 2940 on the same PCI/EISA motherboard, the system marks any drive on the 2742 as the boot drive unless the 2742 BIOS is disabled. If there are two or more PCI controllers, most motherboards boot from the one nearest the edge of the motherboard (edge away from EISA/ISA bus), but some will boot from the slot closest to the EISA/ISA bus. Put both cards in the system and simply watch the sequence of boot.

- **Problem.** Do removable drives work with Windows NT?

  Solution. Syquest, Bernoullis, and the Iomega Jazz and Zip drives work in NT. No special software is needed, but the Iomega utilities for 3.51 work fine in 4. The install drive that ships with the Jazz needs to be low-level formatted before NT can do anything with it. All other add-on drives work fine as is.

- **Problem.** When a 1542 is added to the system, a floppy drive controller error ensues.

  Solution. The 1542 series has a floppy drive controller attached. You need to disable either that controller or the one on the motherboard/hard drive controller.

- **Problem.** A drive is moved from an Adaptec controller to a Buslogic controller. The drive can no longer be used because it is considered unformatted. When the drive is returned to the Adaptec controller, it still works.

  Solution. Although SCSI is a well-accepted standard, the actual format of the drive differs from vendor to vendor. The only solution is to have a backup of the drive and low-level format the drive and then restore the tape. If the drive is the boot drive, be sure not to copy over the system portion of the Registry because the old (wrong) boot driver will be restored.

- **Problem.** In using a drive from a different system, the POST of the controller recognizes the drive but gives a "drive not ready" message.

  Solution. It is possible to set up a drive with a "power up on command" jumper enabled. In this case, the controller needs to be set to send a Send Startup Command to the drive. Try this to see if the jumper has been enabled on the drive. Ideally, the jumper needs to be removed.

- **Problem.** An external Jazz drive was added to the system, and now the system will not boot from the internal hard drive.

  Solution. Most likely, this is a termination issue. Most SCSI cards will need to be reconfigured to disable card termination. This is not true, though, with the newer cards that can be enabled with auto-termination (left up to the controller).

- **Problem.** A 2 GB drive was borrowed from another system. All the files on it seem really strange; that is, they seem to be there, but they are not.

  Solution. In this case, it is likely that the drive had extended translation enabled on one of the controller cards but not on the other. This is particularly an issue with DOS.

Although other problems can arise with SCSI systems, the preceding list covers the bulk of the routine problems. SCSI systems can also provide issues with the installation of Windows NT.

An Unusual Problem with a SCSI System that Demonstrates the Importance of Logical Troubleshooting

The following example is an atypical SCSI problem but one that shows that the obvious is not necessarily the obvious. A new fast wide SCSI drive was installed on a Pentium 166 with 64 MB of RAM. The motherboard was the latest ASUS(P55T2P4). The controller was an Adaptec 2940uw with a Seagate Hawk ultra 2 GB drive on the wide chain also.

While running NT, there was a noticeable slowdown of the drive. Inspection of Event Viewer revealed the message that a bad block had shown up on the drive (see fig. 21.1). The system was powered off and then back on. When the Adaptec POST banner appeared, Ctrl+A was pressed and the SCSI utilities entered. An attempt was made to verify the drive. All went well until the verify reached 65 percent. The message appeared that a bad sector was found and needed remapping. Attempting to remap produced an unexpected error with the message that there was faulty communication between the drive and the controller. To make matters worse, there were 20 successive such errors. Immediately, you would think that the drive or controller had gone bad.

The system was booted to a DOS disk and ASPI8DOS.SYS loaded. The SCSI utility SCSIFMT.EXE also failed and in the same manner. Before deciding the problem was the controller or card, the 68-pin cable was replaced. The system then booted flawlessly and verify worked perfectly. Always follow a hardware failure issue to its logical conclusion.

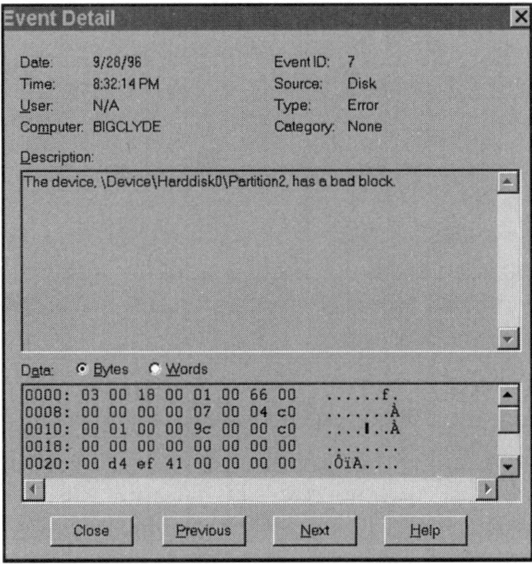

Figure 21.1

The Event Detail page is expanded here to show the presumed appearance of a bad block on the hard drive.

Installation Issues

Microsoft has done wonders simplifying the installation procedure for Windows NT. The process with NT 4 is better than that of 3.51, but problems still can arise. Before pointing out the issues that can arise in the installation of Windows NT 4, a brief discussion of the installation process facilitates understanding specific issues.

The installation of Windows NT 4 involves two discrete phases. The first phase, often called the *text mode*, is more accurately called the *DOS phase* because it simply involves copying files in preparation for the installation. The files copied are boot files and files for the installation. In this first phase, the following events occur when you use the boot floppies that come with Windows NT 4:

1. A limited version of Windows NT is loaded into memory. This small version increases the speed of the installation and also provides multitasking capabilities of Windows NT.

2. NTDETECT.COM runs and automatically detects the majority of standard hardware. For the Intel platform, the following devices are found:

    - Bus/adapter (IDE for the most part)
    - Mouse
    - Keyboard
    - Video card
    - Communication ports
    - Floppy drives
    - SCSI cards
    - Parallel ports
    - Mass storage devices

If a mass storage device—that is, a CD-ROM—is not found, the installation aborts immediately. This brings up the first aspect of troubleshooting a Windows NT 4 installation—namely, unsupported hardware.

You attempt to install NT 4, and the installation fails despite the fact that you have a CD-ROM on the system. For the most part, all SCSI CD-ROMs are supported, but there are exceptions. It is important at this point for you to use the Windows NT 4 HCL or hardware compatibility list (www.microsoft.com/isapi/hwtest/hsearchn4.idc). Various components and systems that specifically run Windows NT 4 are listed. Check to see if the CD-ROM is on the list. If it is not, you might want to move to a supported CD-ROM. For example, the following list shows the Toshiba model number CD-ROMS supported in NT 4:

TXM-3301E	SCSI
TXM-3401E	SCSI
XM-3301B	SCSI
XM-3401B	SCSI
XM-3501B	SCSI
XM-3601	SCSI
XM-3701	SCSI
XM-4101B	SCSI
XM-5301B	SCSI
XM-5401	SCSI

As is evident from the list, not all the Toshiba CD-ROMS are listed as compatible with NT 4. Noticeable absences include the 5401B. This does not mean that the 5401B does not work, but you do not know beforehand. It is always best to obtain drives that indeed do work. In the preceding example of the failure of the installation program finding a CD-ROM, odds are very high that the CD-ROM in question is an EIDE one that is not atapi 1.2 compliant. Before a drive will work in 4, the firmware must be to specification. But all is not lost, you can still install 4.

Copy the I386 to the hard drive. This of course presupposes that the drive is formatted FAT. You can then run winnt, which creates boot floppies that specifically access the installation files copied over to a temporary directory. You can also add the /b switch to winnt, which also copies the boot files to the drive, thus eliminating the use of floppy drives. Installing NT 4 in this manner totally eliminates the use of floppy drives. When NT is successfully installed, you can then search for the proper CD-ROM drivers or, preferably, purchase a new compliant IDE CD-ROM. They are very inexpensive.

3. After NTDETECT has completed the hardware detection phase, the system reboots. This reboot takes you to the next phase of the installation—the *graphical* or *NT phase* itself. This phase is controlled by wizards, and you simply enter information such as network options, the CD (Key), and the initial security information.

In this second phase, all the hardware is determined by NT specific drivers. A peripheral device might not work in NT unless it meets specific and strict criteria. Many devices do not, and an example was given earlier of the non-atapi 1.2 compliant

CD-ROM. Other peripherals notorious for not working properly are sound cards (particularly Plug and Play ones) and network cards.

The sound cards require NT specific drivers. If the vendor states that the driver is Microsoft's responsibility, then most likely no such driver exists, and the card will in fact not work. The network card is easier to fix. During installation simply choose not to install a network card and install it after NT is up and running. This advice can save many headaches and NIC-induced system crashes.

Note The most important thing that you are asked to do during this phase is to prepare an emergency repair disk (ERD). By all means, do so. When you upgrade the system at any time, run the RDISK utility in the system32 subdirectory (folder). After you have set up all the security and shares on the system, always run RDISK /S. This updates the configuration on-board and also prepares a new ERD.

Common Installation Problems and Failures

If in fact, there are problems with the installation of Windows NT, several techniques can be used to determine the exact type of problem that is occurring. Always pay attention to the obvious. If the system crashes every time you install the network card, for example, it seems reasonable that there is a problem with the system and the network card. Here are a few suggestions:

- Examine the issue and determine the most likely cause. For example, not being able to boot onto the network does not mean you cannot boot to the local system.
- Always simplify the system by removing any unnecessary card such as sound cards, Wacom tablets and even network cards.
- Many medium- to high-end video cards might conflict with other system components. For example, the Number 9 128 cards have conflicts with the Adaptec 2940s.
- Make sure that all essential controllers, such as SCSI cards, have drivers that are compatible with 4.
- If you are installing to a notebook, you need to boot to a DOS floppy and then run FDISK. Make the partitions that you desire and then format them. The NT installation procedure does not recognize an unformatted drive on the new PCI PCMCIA (PC-CARD) controllers.

When you have successive failures loading Windows NT, the master boot record (MBR) of the drive can be corrupted. If the drive is a SCSI drive, run a low-level format on it. This commonly clears up the problems with the MBR.

Common Installation Crashes

In the course of using Windows NT, most of us have installation crashes that are the result of kernel mode errors. In these cases, a BSOD apears. The following list contains the most common of these BSODs:

- **STOP 0x0000000A IRQL_NOT_LESS_OR_EQUAL.** A pointer in a driver or process incorrectly pointed a memory address that it had no permission to use. This can be caused by both hardware and software, but typically it is driver related.
- **STOP 0x000000 KMODE_EXCEPTION_NOT_HANDLED.** As the name states, a trap occurred in the kernel and the system crashed. When I have seen these occur, it was always a out-of-date driver for a SCSI controller. Make sure to get all proper revised drivers and hardware.
- **STOP 0x0000007F.** This usually indicates that a hardware fault has occurred. First look at memory and then disable all internal and external cache; then remove cards, and finally try a new motherboard (preferably a different one).
- **INACCESSIBLE HARD DRIVE.** If SCSI, make sure that all cables and terminators are correct. Improper cables or loose connections can cause the system to lose connections between devices and the controller card.

If the drive is a 7200 rpm drive, the drive can overheat and start going bad. Heat is a serious problem with large computer systems.

Check the boot sector for viruses. A boot sector virus can corrupt the boot sector, and the proper application will not run. The boot sector can be cleansed of viruses from a DOS floppy and application. You can also run FDISK /MBR and then do a repair of the boot sector with the NT Setup Repair Option.

If the drive is a large EIDE, make sure that LBA is enabled and the drive set to proper master/slave configuration. If LBA was not enabled, you need to set it and redo fdisk and format.

The preceding list is not exhaustive but does represent the most common installation failures and fixes, where possible. Sometimes the only effective way to install Windows NT 4 is to purchase new hardware. This is the last thing you might want to hear, but, unfortunately, it is a well-known fact.

Motherboards and Peripherals to Avoid

Over the course of working with Windows NT (actually from pre-NT 3.1 days), certain combination of hardware devices have consistently caused many problems. The following list is a synopsis of these troublesome devices and motherboards:

- Do not use motherboards that mix SIMM types. You can purchase boards that allow mixing 30- and 72-pin SIMMs. There are too many potential timing problems with these boards. Windows NT stresses memory to the maximum and will show any timing problem by crashing routinely.

- Memory timing problems might also show up if you use the new overdrive CPUs. All parts of a computer motherboard interact. Upgrading one compartment and not the others can result in serious installation failures.

- Do not use older video boards. All video and printer drivers have been redone for NT 4. It is unlikely that older video cards will have the new drivers. If you are upgrading from 3.51, make sure that the video card has the newer drivers before attempting the upgrade.

- Avoid complex controller cards that have IDE, SCSI, and floppy support all built in. Odds are high that the standard drivers will not work well with them.

- Certain motherboards with SMC floppy chipsets have chipsets not fully compatible with FLOPPY.SYS in the drivers folder. In such cases, the floppy drive will not work in NT. You will need to obtain an updated FLOPPY.SYS from the motherboard manufacturer or system vendor.

- Do not install Windows NT 4 on a 486-based system. The performance boost from a Pentium processor is well worthwhile.

- Avoid the use of Industry Standard Architecture (ISA) bus master cards whenever possible. ISA supports only 24 address lines to memory, which places a 2^{24} or 16 meg limit on the amount of RAM that can be directly accessed (DMA—Direct Memory Access). All memory in excess of 16 MB must be buffered to memory below 16 MB before it can be addressed. On some systems, this produces significant slowdown in performance.

The preceding list is not comprehensive but does represent the bulk of common installation issues and suggestions. It is amazing that a sophisticated OS like Windows NT can be installed on much of the existing legacy hardware. In many respects, however, upgrading to new systems is a reasonable idea. As this is being written, prices are on the rebound. The time to buy is now.

The next logical place to find problems is a corruption of the boot process. This does not happen often but is the first of the run-time issues that can occur and can easily drive someone to near-insanity. Nothing that you do seems to work, and you needed the files on the system yesterday.

The Boot Process

A major part of troubleshooting begins with the understanding of the NT boot process. In explaining how the boot process works, you need to examine the basic process. In addition, you need to look at the similarities and differences in the boot process between RISC- and Intel-based systems. Finally, you need to troubleshoot and fix common NT boot-up problems.

For the proper startup of Windows NT 4, certain specific files and drivers must load and function properly. These specific files generate the NT system on boot. The most common boot issues involve loss or corruption of these files. The following are the files with a brief description of their function:

- **NTLDR.** When the system boots, NTLDR is loaded from the boot sector of the hard drive. This file controls the booting of all OSs on the drive.
- **NTDETECT.COM.** This is an exclusive Intel-based file that examines the hardware and generates a hardware list that is incorporated into NTLDR and forms the hardware aspect of the Registry. This is the key hardware detection file in the boot process.
- **BOOT.INI.** This is the system file that creates the boot option you choose from at the initial screen. A typical BOOT.INI file looks like the following:

```
[boot loader]
timeout=30
default=multi(0)disk(0)rdisk(0)partition(3)\WINNT
[operating systems]
multi(0)disk(0)rdisk(0)partition(3)\WINNT="Windows NT Workstation Version
4.00"
multi(0)disk(0)rdisk(0)partition(3)\WINNT="Windows NT Workstation Version
➥4.00 [VGA mode]" /basevideo /sos
multi(0)disk(0)rdisk(0)partition(3)\WINNT35="Windows NT Workstation
➥Version 3.51"
multi(0)disk(0)rdisk(0)partition(3)\WINNT35="Windows NT Workstation
➥Version 3.51 [VGA mode]" /basevideo /sos
C:\="MS-DOS"
```

As you can see, three boot options are listed in the preceding example. The default is 4 Workstation. The second choice is 3.51 Workstation, and the last choice is DOS. The /SOS switch gives you a listing of all drivers being loaded.

The syntax of BOOT.INI is actually a derivation of the RISC boot process or ARC (Advanced RISC Computing) terminology. The basic ARC terminology follows:

```
<controller>(W)disk(X)rdisk(Y)partition(Z)\path.
```

To make matters very simple, the controller name is either *SCSI* (very infrequently used anymore, mostly seen with multiple controllers) or *multi*, which is the typical term used even with SCSI controllers.

Disk(x) is used only with SCSI terminology and is the ID of the appropriate drive. For example, if you boot off the first drive on the bus, Disk would be 0; but if you did a boot off the second drive, Disk would be (1). Remember that the initial SCSI drive is 0.

Rdisk(y) is used with multi terminology. It refers to the ordinal number of the drive on the adapter. If you boot from the second drive, rdisk(x) would be rdisk(1).

Partition(z) refers to the partition containing the active Windows NT folder. The numbers start with 1. For example, in the BOOT.INI listed earlier, both the 3.51 and the 4 folders are on drive E or the third partition of the first drive.

When multi is used, the drive is loaded via INT 13. Due to current limitations with FAT, this limits a boot drive to 2 GB in size. This is being changed with the release of FAT32 with the next version of WIN95.

- **BOOTSECT.DOS.** If you dual boot DOS, this file is used to boot into the older OS. This file contains the boot sector that existed before Windows NT was installed.
- **NTBOOTDD.SYS.** If you use SCSI terminology in BOOT.INI, you need to copy the boot SCSI driver to the root drive and rename it NTBOOTDD.SYS. This file enables devices to be attached to the boot controller. It is seldom used anymore except on boot diskettes.
- **OSLOADER.** This file is the RISC counterpart of NTLDR. Because the bulk of the hardware information is maintained in the system firmware, NTDETECT is not necessary on RISC machines.

Boot Process (Intel)

The Windows NT boot process is a several step process. First, platform-specific components are loaded and then common NT components are loaded. This process is complex and involves many modules. Throughout the entire process, improper hardware or drivers can cause a fatal kernel error (BSOD).

Phases of the Boot Process

Initially, the system must set specific variables that enable NT to load. This phase is the *boot phase.* As the boot phase progresses, NTOSKRNL.EXE is loaded, and this begins the *kernel phase.* The kernel phase has four subphases, and all conclude with a successful logon.

Order of File Loading

When the computer boots, it goes through a set of phases itself. The first noticeable phase is the POST phase (or Power On Self Test). During this phase, hardware is listed and placed in the CMOS tables. After this occurs, the hard drive is scanned for the Master Boot Record (MBR), and the necessary programs run. NTLDR is initialized and reads BOOT.INI. This is the start of the boot sequence.

1. NTLDR first loads the flat memory model. This for 32-bit NT is 4 GB.

2. NTLDR loads the file system drivers so that the hard drive can be read. These drivers are obviously for FAT and NTFS.

3. NTLDR then reads the BOOT.INI and displays the choice screen. Normally this is Windows NT (perhaps several versions) and DOS (if you dual boot). If you choose DOS, NTLDR simply passes control to BOOTSECT.DOS. If, however, you choose NT, the NTLDR loads the next module, NTDETECT.COM.

4. NTDETECT.COM scans all the associated hardware and passes it to the system hive in the Registry. If a device is not on at the time of detection, NT does not see it even if power is turned on subsequently.

As the last step in the boot phase, NTLDR then loads NTOSKRNL.EXE, and the kernel phase of boot begins. During this time, four distinct events occur.

5. The kernel load phase begins with kernel (NTOSKRNL.EXE) being loaded and is followed by the Hardware Abstraction Layer (HAL.DLL). The system hive generated by NTDETECT.COM is then loaded, and the appropriate drivers are loaded into memory. (You notice this phase as the dots progress across the top of the screen.)

6. During the kernel initialization phase, all the drivers loaded into memory are initialized. The system hive is examined once more and all necessary drivers loaded (obviously these drivers are considered high-level drivers and not kernel mode drivers). The CurrentControlSet aspect of the Registry is saved (and a clone set generated). At this time, all hardware in configured in the Registry.

7. In the services load phase, the Session Manager is started (SMSS.EXE) and the sequence of events dictated in the bootexecute key in the Registry executed. (Typically, this is the AUTOCHK.EXE application but could also be a conversion of FAT to NTFS if chosen in the prior boot.) Next, the pagefile is set by the session manager (The pagefile is generated each time NT boots.) The CurrentControlSet is written to the Registry. This phase concludes with the loading of the Win32 subsystem.

8. The Win32 subsystem starts with the Winlogon process (WINLOGON.EXE). Importantly, Local Security Authority is started and the Ctrl+Alt+Del logon screen appears. When a user logs on successfully, the clone set becomes the last known good set.

Boot Process (RISC)

The RISC boot process differs from that of the Intel platform. Most of the boot process occurs in system firmware. The boot device is loaded as the first part of the process. The firmware then searches the first sector of the boot drive to determine if the drive is bootable. A query is then made of the file structure to ensure the file structure is supported. After this, OSLOADER.EXE is loaded, and the hardware collected at POST is passed to it. Obviously, NTDETECT.COM is not needed on a RISC machine because much is done in firmware. When all the preceding is accomplished, NTOSKRNL.EXE is loaded, and the Intel and RISC boot processes become nearly identical.

Troubleshooting the Boot Process

There are, in fact, only certain types of problems that can cause boot process errors. Typically, these errors are due to viruses in the boot sector (inaccessible hard drive error) or corrupted individual files. In the latter case, it is easy to think of failing hardware.

Here are the most common issues (in boot order):

1. If NTLDR is missing, you get the following message:

   ```
   BOOT: Couldn't find NTLDR
   Please insert another disk.
   ```

2. If NTDETECT.COM is missing, the following message appears on the boot loader screen:

   ```
   NTDETECT V1.0 Checking hardware ...................
   NTDETECT V1.0 Checking hardware ...................
   ```

3. If NTOSKRNL.EXE is corrupt or missing, the following message appears immediately after the last known good option appears:

   ```
   Windows NT could not start because the following file is missing or
   corrupt
   \winnt\system32\ntoskrnl.exe
   Please reinstall a copy of the file
   ```

4. If BOOTSECT.DOS is missing or corrupt, the following message is seen after the last known good screen:

   ```
   I/O error accessing boot sector file
   multi(0)disk(0)rdisk(0)partition(1):\bootsect.dos
   ```

In all the preceding cases, you can use the repair facility in setup to examine and fix the boot sector drives. It is far easier if you have a new ERD.

5. The system responds differently if there are problems with BOOT.INI. If the file is missing, NTLDR immediately tries to boot NT. If NT is in the default \winnt folder, the boot will probably work. If another directory is used, the following message shows up immediately following the last known good screen:

```
Windows NT could not start because the following file was missing or
corrupt:
\winnt\system32\ntoskrnl.exe
Please reinstall a copy of the above file.
```

6. If there is an improper path in BOOT.INI, the following message appears:

```
OS Loader V4.0
Windows NT could not start because of a computer disk hardware configura-
tion problem. Could not read from the selected boot disk. Check boot path
and disk hardware.
Please check the Windows NT™ documentation about hardware disk configura-
tion and your hardware reference manuals for additional information.
```

In these last three issues, you need to edit BOOT.INI. Remove its hidden/system attributes and change the improper syntax. If you cannot gain access to BOOT.INI, you will need to install a new version of NT (to a different directory) and thus gain access to an NTFS partition containing BOOT.INI. You will still need to manually edit the file.

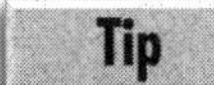

Editing BOOT.INI is a straightforward and easy process. In most cases, you must change the properties. Right-click on the file in Explorer. You can change the file to a non-hidden and non-read only file. You can also use file manager and remove the system attribute. Once removed, you can edit and save the file. Restore the changed attributes. It is always mandatory to make a copy of the file before editing it. The exact syntax used is described in the preceding BOOT.INI section.

Building a Boot Disk

Although not generally thought of as being an OS that uses boot floppies, it is a good idea to prepare one. If the boot sector becomes corrupted, you can boot to the floppy to access an NT installation. Also, if any system uses mirrored boot drives, it is always a good idea to create a floppy boot drive. In general, it is important to have a boot disk to recover from a physical disk failure.

Format a floppy disk in Windows NT. For Intel-based machines, copy NTLDR, BOOT.INI, NTDETECT.COM, and if appropriate, the boot SCSI driver copied and renamed NTBOOTDD.SYS (remember, this is for the SCSI terminology). Prior to copying the files, remove all system/hidden/read attributes. After copying, restore all the file attributes to system, hidden, and read-only (see the preceding Tip).

For RISC-based machines, copy OSLOADER.EXE and HAL.DLL to the disk. In both cases, the disk has to be formatted in Windows NT.

The primary use of a boot floppy is to bypass a corrupted boot sector. Only the files listed will be loaded from the floppy during boot. All other files are found on the hard drive. If any such files are likewise corrupt, the boot floppy will not work.

For example, examine a boot floppy that has been created to repair a damaged primary drive of a mirrored set. Use this floppy to access the secondary or shadow drive. For simplicity's sake, do this in SCSI terminology. The BOOT.INI will read as follows:

```
[Boot loader]
timeout = 30 ; this is the default timeout in seconds
default = scsi(0)disk(0)rdisk(0)partition (1)\winnt="primary drive"
[operating systems]
scsi(0)disk(0)rdisk(0)partition (1)\winnt="primary drive"
scsi(1)disk(0)rdisk(0)partition (1)\winnt="shadow drive"
```

For the above BOOT.INI, the primary drive is on the first SCSI controller (0), and the shadow drive is on the second controller (1). In both cases, the SCSI IDs are 0. Also in both cases, NTBOOTDD.SYS is needed. Choosing the first OS boots to the primary drive; choosing the second OS, boots to the duplexed drive. Using such a boot, you can load NT from either the primary or duplexed drive independently of the status of the other hard drive.

Run-Time Problems

For the most part, run-time problems are caused by four events: corrupted files, General Protection Faults (GPFs)/Kernel Mode crashes (BSODs), faulty drivers installed, or a hardware failure. Of all these issues, the ones most difficult to fix are the GPF/BSOD ones. To understand either the GPF or the BSOD, you must understand *exception handling*, which is the underlying causative event for the application or system crash.

By and large, an *exception* is an event that occurs in an unexpected manner. Most well-written applications should never produce such an event. As the old hacker adage goes, however, "large programs are even buggier than their size would indicate." In today's world, there are no small programs, and no program is bug free. The obvious moral here is to expect GPFs to occur at sometime. Fortunately, most are seldom fatal to the system.

In general, two types of exceptions can be raised—software and hardware. Hardware exceptions are raised by the CPU. Examples of such exceptions include a process that tries to divide by zero or a pointer attempting to access an invalid memory address. Software exceptions are typically memory exceptions generated by an application. In both cases, exception handling can be enabled.

In the operating system or application, specific filters can be enabled to address an exception, either hardware of software generated. To simplify issues, the exception is trapped and run through a set of filters to either fix the exception or produce a GPF, which is generally fatal to the application. A classic example of such a GPF is an invalid memory pointer. In such a situation, the application simply closes, but generally an error log (DRWATSON.LOG) is generated for subsequent debugging.

Debugging is a complex event. There are no easy ways to go about it. To set up true debugging, you need a checked version of NT that is written with debug code. In a normal situation, this additional debug code slows down NT to unacceptable levels. Therefore, most users do not run debug code. You can, however, load symbol files that contain the debug information. Most users do not have the proper symbol files loaded. In such cases, if the GPF becomes a common issue, you can try to reload the application. If this fails, you need to contact the company responsible for the application and ask for help.

Of more importance to you is the understanding of the infamous BSOD. In this case, the thread causing the exception is not in an application but occurs in the kernel. As might be expected, an exception in the kernel mode is indeed a serious issue. If any low-level function produces an exception, the system checks to see if an error mode handler (exception handler) can take care of the problem. If the exception cannot be handled, the system crashes with the infamous KMODE_EXCEPTION_NOT_HANDLED BSOD. In most cases, an exception in the kernel mode is considered unsafe, and the system simply halts with a text mode screen that tells you the basics of the problem. If NT is set up properly, the system reboots. It is important to set up NT to help determine the cause of the problem.

What To Do with BSODs

The first and easiest thing to do with a BSOD is to determine when the problem started and if it is application specific. Certain mixtures of cards and drivers are known to produce kernel crashes. First, you need to set up NT to properly capture crash information.

Make sure that the pagefile is on the same drive as NT. Performance can be improved by moving the pagefile to a different drive and controller, but you then lose the formation of a memory dump that enables debugging to happen when the system generates a BSOD. The size of the pagefile should be at least equal to the amount of RAM plus 12 MB. This turns out to be 76 MB for a system with 64 MB of RAM. Figure 21.2 shows an example of a system set up with two pagefiles. One is on the drive that contains Windows NT (drive E). If the system does crash, a dump file will be generated, and it will be the total amount of memory on the system (64 MB). This is shown in figure 21.3.

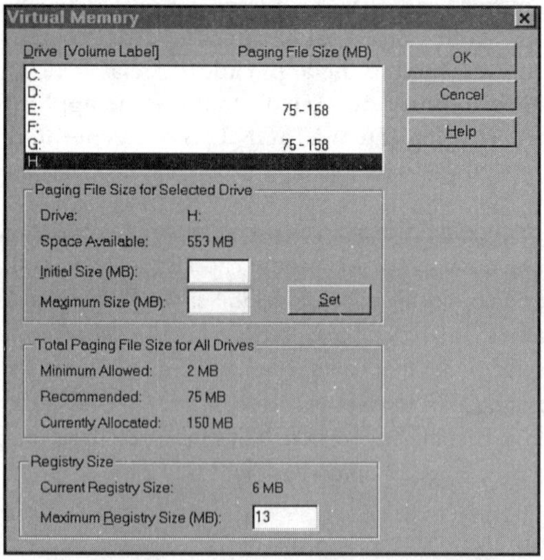

Figure 21.2

The Virtual Memory dialog box shows the setup of the pagefile on a system with 64 MB of RAM.

Figure 21.3

The file properties page shows the size of the MEMORY.DMP file on a system with 64 MB of RAM.

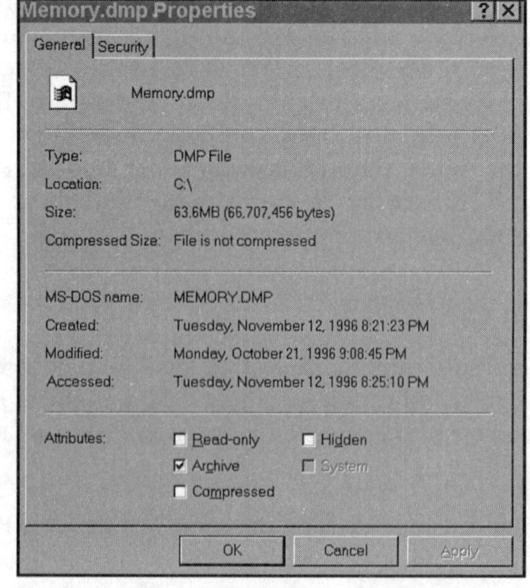

It is important also to set up the system to generate a dump file. The easiest one to use is shown in figure 21.4. The file is generated, information written to the system log, and the system rebooted.

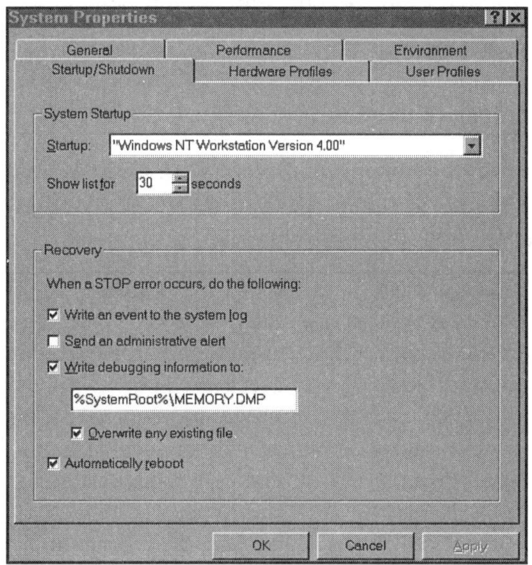

Figure 21.4

The Startup/ Shutdown tab of the System applet shows the necessary check marks for system generation of a dump file following a BSOD.

Interpreting a Memory Dump

Now that you have the memory dump, what can you do with it? There is a utility that ships with the on the NT 4 CD (support\debug\I386 for Intel machines) called DUMPEXAM.EXE. Set up a debug directory and copy over the necessary files for the debugging. These files for Intel machines are DUMPEXAM.EXE, KDEXTX86.DLL, and IMAGEHLP.DLL. The symbol files also need to be loaded. Although an installer might be present (not found by this author though), it is easy to install the symbols. Copy the Symbol folder from the support\debug\i386 folder to a hard drive. Make the following batch file at the command line:

```
copy con symbol.bat
attrib -r *.*
expand -r *.db_
del *.db_ F7
```

The F7 in the preceding example ends the batch file and is accomplished by pressing F and 7 at the same time. Copy the batch file to each folder in the Symbol folder. After you run SYMBOL.BAT, the files are expanded and the compressed DB_ deleted.

The syntax for the dumpexam utility follows:

```
dumpexam (options) (Crashdumpfile).
```

The most important option switch is the "Y path," where path is the path to the expanded symbol files. In the case of the memory dump shown in figure 21.4, the exact statement was:

```
dumpexam -y G:\symbols d:\winnt\memory.dmp.
```

The ensuing output is stored in the systemroot directory (D:\winnt in this case) as MEMORY.TXT. A detailed analysis of the MEMORY.TXT file is beyond what is needed here. However, a portion of the file is revealing:

```
    801237EF: FF 75 F8            push        dword ptr [ebp-8]
    801237F2: 6A 77               push        77h
    801237F4: E8 B9 14 FF FF      call        MiMakeOutswappedPageResident+277h
-->801237F9: FF 15 84 0B 14 80    call        dword ptr
                                              [MiMakeOutswappedPageResident+27Dh]
    801237FF: FF 75 FC            push        dword ptr [ebp-4]
    80123802: E8 C5 83 00 00      call        MiMakeOutswappedPageResident+285h
    80123807: 8B 45 F4            mov         eax,dword ptr [ebp-0Ch]
    8012380A: 8B 4D 08            mov         ecx,dword ptr [ebp+8]
    8012380D: C7 40 10 80 00 00   mov         dword ptr [eax+10h],offset
                                              MiMakeOutswappedPageResident+292h
              00
```

As you might expect, this is the code that was being executed when the system crashed. Note the line with the arrow. This is the line in assembly code that was being executed when the system crashed. Although most people cannot interpret this assembly code, it is important to Microsoft because kernel mode errors need fixing. In the preceding example, it seems reasonable to suppose that the bad SCSI cable prevented the swapfile from being accessed or actually corrupted memory in the swapfile. Of more importance, though, is how to prevent further crashes from occurring.

Determining the Culprit for the Run-Time Crash

In the first place, you can run the dumpexam utility shown previously. Near the end of the MEMORY.TXT is a stack trace that shows the line of the crash. On the other hand, you can realistically determine the culprit.

- Have you added any new applications or custom drivers?
- What application was running at the time of the crash?

- Restart the system and see if the problem recurs. If it does, see if it is reproducible.
- Check the obvious culprits. Was the network being addressed at the time?
- On the BSOD screen, what seems to be the most likely culprit?

The BSOD screen always conveys information that narrows down the potential list of culprits. For example, a typical stop message lists the actual site of the problem:

```
Stop: 0x00000001E Unhandled Kernel exception <code> from <address>
➥(<parameter>, <parameter>)
```

The key listing in the preceding example is the address of the fault. Looking at the list of memory addresses used by the system, it is usually possible to determine the file causing the crash. Typically, you simply match the address with the load address of the file.

Fixing a Run-Time Crash

If the crash happens after an application was loaded and you cannot boot into NT, immediately following your choice of booting into Windows NT, hold down the spacebar, and you are given the option of booting to last known good. As you recall, last known good refers to a successful logon when the cloned control set gets converted to the last known good. Any changes made after the last known good are simply ignored.

It is always important to have an up-to-date ERD. You can boot into the installation app and then choose repair. Typically, you want to reset the system files only; but on occasion, you might need to reset security options or the Registry as well. Sometimes user profiles get corrupted and the Registry totally corrupted. When this happens, the only effective cure is a new installation followed by a tape restore.

It is difficult to determine sometimes what causes system crashes. In many cases, it is smart to obtain the Technet subscription from Microsoft. This contains an up-to-date summary of many system crashes and causes. Here a few known issues:

- On Pentium Pro systems, playing sound files when running matrox drivers produces a BSOD. This can be eliminated by using the latest drivers from matrox (available on www.matrox.com).
- Running Number 9 128 cards with Adaptec controllers is always a challenge. Best solution, eliminate one of the culprits.
- Some network cards are known to give intermittent problems with 4. Most of these cards fall into the legacy or retired categories on the installation CD-ROM.

Other examples exist, but the list is still very young. With improving driver support for NT, many of the BSODs will be absent in new systems. Sooner or later, most everyone will experience a BSOD. Knowing how to deal with a BSOD is an important issue particularly on a business workstation.

The next issue to consider is performance tuning. Much is written about such tuning, but in reality, the best tuning of NT is through hardware. A notebook probably cannot be tuned. Likewise, simple workstations probably cannot be either. Tuning is primarily a feature of the server or the high-end workstation.

Performance-Tuning NT Workstation 4

Most people have migrated to Windows NT from a DOS/windows environment for one reason or another. You might think back to your Windows 3.1 days with the infinite capability of editing and tweaking SYSTEM.INI and WIN.INI to increase performance, or adding space to your environment by increasing shell size, and so on. In many cases, these tweakings did improve performance.

With Windows NT, many of these capabilities are gone, and you are now faced with editing an arcane and often not well understood Registry that is the very heart of Windows NT. Many experienced NT users find the Registry daunting. To overcome this issue, many have bought the excellent NT Resource Kits from Microsoft (now in Workstation and Server editions) and look at the issues dealing with optimizing by adding keys and changing this and that. The Registry gets bigger and bigger. You then upgrade, and things do not work right. So you start over from scratch, and all your careful labor is gone. Common sense many times can help you set up hardware in such a nature that Registry changes can be avoided or minimized.

Initially, you need to consider the basic elements of a system and examine the issues involved with the elements. Specifically, this section addresses:

- Bus type
- CPU, cache, and memory
- Controllers and configuration
- Hard drives

In all the systems where performance increases are wanted, the culprit is always a bottleneck. For present purposes, a *bottleneck* is the slowest aspect in a task and can reflect the CPU, the I/O performance of the bus, and so on. Needless to say, one does not eliminate bottlenecks but one can control them.

The key to understanding how performance issues can arise is to realize that processes and related threads are assigned priorities and use related time slices. The NT scheduler gives processes and threads with higher priorities access to the CPU. Normally this might not produce an undesired event. A high priority thread (swapfile for example), however, can disrupt the performance of processes with lower priorities. This means that Windows NT can stop one thread and pass the other thread to the CPU.

Another aspect that affects performance is the inherent client/server nature of Windows NT. If a process creates a thread, this thread is a client of the Win32 subsystem server. If the client asks the server to do something, a complimentary thread is created in the subsystem. The server thread and the client thread do not share time space. One is suspended for the other.

With these few concepts in mind, it seems obvious that the way to optimize Windows NT is to provide the smoothest flow between threads without causing disruptive influences. Depending on the nature of the processes, various issues can be seen. The CPU can be too slow; not enough memory is available for proper function; or the hard drives and data transfer are way to slow. These issues will be addressed.

The Fast Bus Ride

For some reason, many users consider the ISA bus their bus of choice. The Industry Standard Architecture (ISA) bus was actually considered out of date in 1988. The bus was designed using 16 MB as the memory limit. (There are 24 access lines.) Given that each address can be either an 0 or a 1 (2 digits), only 2^{24} amount of memory (16 MBs) can be addressed directly (DMA) by a bus mastering peripheral card on the system. If you add more than 16 MB to the system, all access to memory greater than the 16 MB must be buffered by writing to regions below 16. This double buffering slows down the system. In addition, when it became obvious that users wanted more than 16 MB on their systems, firmware had to be rewritten to provide caching of memory greater than 16 MB. In recent years, Adaptec has also provided the buffering driver ASPIBUFF.SYS to allow the use of their ISA Bus Mastering Controllers in DOS. Similar drivers and workarounds can be seen in Novell. Windows NT has built in buffering but it does not always work.

IBM developed Microchannel (MCA), and an independent group of hardware vendors developed the Extended Industry Standard Architecture (EISA) standard. As is well known, both these alternatives were 32-bit and not 16-bit as the ISA was. Access lines were increased, and the memory limit for DMA increased to 4 GB. Although not normally considered, one major advantage that EISA and MCA offered over ISA was the capability to do things rapidly in DMA (Direct Memory Access). In fact, accomplishing an event through DMA is faster than doing it locally.

ISA does refuse to die off peacefully. Fortunately, PCI and, to a lesser degree VLB, have diminished reliance on the ISA bus. The DMA problem is still present, though, and needs discussion because neither PCI nor VLB slots fully populate the bus. Because PCI and VLB are local bus in architecture, the 16 MB limit does not exist. So why bring up the issue? Many might desire to add an ISA card for a specific function, and the card might be a bus master (discussed later). This in fact will have the 16 MB legacy and might cause the system to slow down significantly.

What then constitutes a reasonable system? Consider the following issues about system requirements, that is, what should be present:

- Make certain that there are sufficient high speed/access slots to enable you get around ISA limitations.
- You need a system that uses bus mastering devices and also one that can provide CPU arbitration.

Note A bus mastering card is typically a card with a coprocessor. This card can directly access memory, and the coprocessor can finish the task. This enables the CPU to do other things. Arbitration decides who has control of the CPU and for how long. In the Programmed Input Output (PIO) approach, the system allows one device to occupy the CPU until the process/thread is finished. In an arbitrated scheme, CPU access can be assigned priorities or serviced within defined clock times. The importance of this issue becomes obvious when you consider that a device can disrupt what another device is doing—for example, getting data off a hard drive can disrupt any other event until the data are in memory. Non-bus mastering cards and devices (IDE hard drives for example) work fine in Windows NT and might actually be faster on a single process/thread than a bus mastering card/device. This is not so for multitasking and for thread isolation (this issue is discussed later).

Likewise, it does not take a rocket scientist to realize that the near future at least is all PCI. You might as well ignore implementation issues and get a PCI (more later) and not VL based motherboard. VL might be faster per card (no Plug and Play overhead) but the industry is standardizing on PCI components. EISA is still a viable option; but cards are old, and most probably will not be revved soon. As stated earlier, PCI/EISA is still the optimum motherboard. Some of the new PCI/ISA motherboards based upon the latest incarnation of the Triton chipset show promise for Workstation use.

CPU, Cache, and Memory: How Fast and How Much?

Any modern motherboard should have a minimum of 256 KB of cache. This cache should be matched to the CPU and bus speed. For Pentium systems, the 33 MHz systems need cache below 12 ns, whereas the 30 MHz systems can function well with standard 15 ns cache. Newer motherboards use high-speed SIMM-like cache that can be altered to the CPU speed. If the system has significant amounts of memory, it is probably worthwhile to maximize the board cache.

The speed of the CPU is an interesting issue. In some regards, it pays to invest more in memory than CPU. Although a DX-4 100 is a nice starting point for a CPU, it really does not make sense to get a system not running a Pentium 75 as a minimum. The cost differential is actually slight. You will come back to this issue when various systems for specific applications are discussed.

Of considerable interest these days are systems that use more than one CPU (the so-called SMP or symmetrical multiprocessor). Where do these systems stand? Most tell you that such a system is for server only. This is far from true. A dual processor machine can in fact run two threads at once. Obviously, the use of such a system is dictated by CPU-intensive events, such as graphics workstations.

Memory is a much debated issue with Windows NT. Microsoft states that 16 MB is a decent starting point. Windows NT does, in fact, run on as low as 12 MB. NT comes into its own on systems with 20 to 24 MB and is very responsive at 32 MB. As you add more memory, Windows NT becomes more and more responsive and is very scalable in the use of memory. There has never been a system that has been too fast.

Controllers and Configuration

If you are using Windows NT as a low-cost desktop for its robustness and security but do not want to stress the system by running several large resource-hungry applications at the same time, EIDE systems will suffice. Make sure the system has the latest BIOS that fully supports EIDE including LBA. If, on the other hand, you want to optimize the system to maximize the use of preemptive multitasking and threading, SCSI is the interface of choice. In fact, Windows NT was designed around the SCSI model. To truly maximize performance, it pays to use two controllers. The controllers of choice are the bus mastering ones that you see on the Hardware Compatibility List. With controllers, you basically get what you pay for.

The development of 16-bit SCSI (Wide SCSI) and now UltraSCSI have created much confusion. Wide SCSI is efficient with its burst mode and functions best in a RAID configuration. Plugging standard SCSI-2 drives into a Wide SCSI controller will not improve the speed of data transfer. As you see soon, wide is faster than SCSI-2 in the right circumstance.

Hard Drives

There is no question that you want the fastest hard drives you can get. With the decreasing cost of SCSI drives, getting a decent one or two is not expensive. Keep in mind that the 7200 rpm drives are heat intensive and can lock up easily.

Going from a 5400 rpm to a 7200 rpm drive can dramatically improve performance. This effect is very noticeable on I/O bound applications like databases.

The Optimal System...

The optimal system is a Pentium 100 or 166 (faster CPUs are available and obviously are better) with 32 to 64 MB of RAM and two SCSI controllers. The first controller should have a drive with Windows NT and the pagefile on it, whereas all applications should be on a second drive on the second controller. This isolates preemptive threads and prevents or minimizes disruption of application threads.

What advantage does a dual Pentium Pro give? With certain applications, threads can be distributed across two processors. With SMP-aware applications that are properly threaded, the increase in performance is amazing.

Likewise, increasing the amount of RAM makes a huge difference—not in opening files the first time but for keeping them in RAM. Obviously, this is a major advantage in image editing because even large files stay in RAM for further editing. The optimum amount of RAM for a dual Pentium Pro machine seems to start at 128 MB. The system will run in less, but 128 is a comfortable starting place. For large CAD/CAM work, the Pentium Pro systems are ideal. After all, the most expensive aspect of any computer system is wasted user time.

System Performance Optimization

Windows NT is designed not to need adjustment. You can look at bottlenecks and try to minimize them. Performance Monitor helps you determine the major problems. In general, you optimize performance by identifying system components that are bottlenecks and minimizing the effect of the bottleneck. To accomplish this, you use Performance Monitor and related applications. Before continuing with optimizing tips, examine how Windows NT handles applications and threads.

Priorities and Their Consequences

When applications are written to take advantage of the Win32 specification, they adhere to an interesting model. The running instance of a program is defined as a *process.* This process is nothing more than an address and piece of memory space (4 GB in size). The process has threads that actually do the work for the application.

The first thread created is termed the *primary thread,* and it can in turn generate more threads. The operating system assigns some CPU time to each thread. Windows NT has the additional advantage of being able to use more than one CPU. In such cases, the operating system can assign a thread to a specific CPU. Because more than one thread typically is running at any time, access to the CPU is governed by priority; that is, each thread has a priority assigned to it. Altering this priority can change the amount of time the operating system gives to an application.

When an application is written, priority classes are assigned to a process in the application. The following table defines these priorities and gives their relative value:

Priority Class	Relative Value (Higher values get higher CPU priority.)
Idle	4
Normal	7 to 9 (9 in foreground; 7 in background)
High	13
Realtime	24

The thread scheduler assigns CPU time according to the process priority of a thread. A thread with a process priority of 13 can preempt a thread with a priority of 9. This scheduling of CPU time slices creates the preemptive multithreading design of Windows NT.

You can change the priorities given to a process, but you need to be aware of the consequences of doing so. First of all, running threads at realtime priority disrupts normal activity on the system. Mouse activity becomes slow and jerky, and any attempt to control cursor position is relatively futile. Second, and most important, the application can call threads at the internal scheduled priorities. This of course implies that an application in realtime does not ensure that all subsequent threads run in realtime. In reality, there seldom is a reason to run applications in anything other than normal.

To run applications at thread priorities different from those assigned in the program, you need to start applications from the command line. The full syntax of start at the command line is as follows:

```
START ["title"] [/path] [/LOW ¦ /NORMAL ¦ /HIGH ¦ /REALTIME] [command/program]
➥[parameters]
    "title"     Title to display in window title bar.
    path        Starting directory
    LOW         Start application in the IDLE priority class
    NORMAL      Start application in the NORMAL priority class
    HIGH        Start application in the HIGH priority class
    REALTIME    Start application in the REALTIME priority class
```

Notice the switches that control process priority—namely, /LOW, /NORMAL, /HIGH, and /REALTIME.

As a final note, you can adjust foreground/background values in the Control Panel System applet on the Performance page. Recall that normal has priorities assigned as 7 or 9. This applet allows you to adjust the priority given to foreground.

Working with the Pagefile

When systems run low on useable amounts of RAM, the system relies on virtual memory (VM). The VM subsystem swaps data from disk to RAM and back again. The use of the disk (called swapfile in this case) allows functional memory to increase to the amount demanded. The movement of data is commonly called *paging*. The disk thrashing that is heard on many systems is this paging behavior. This paging is transparent to the system and is totally under the control of the Windows NT executive.

The end result of this paging behavior is that a system with low RAM can function well but always will have a performance decrement. In addition to the overhead added by the process, disk speed is slow in comparison to RAM. Each transaction to the drive incurs a system slowdown. In fact, the slowdown can be so dramatic that you think the hard drive is too slow.

Windows NT's VM Manager (VMM) is self-tuning. VM does not use paging when physical memory is present. One obvious way to avoid system thrashing is simply to add RAM. Adding RAM can be well worth the investment.

The only change you can make to the system is the arrangement of the paging files. In other words, you can change the location of the pagefile, which is on the same drive as NT by default. These files are simply contiguous amounts of disk space used to handle the swapping. This file is called PAGEFILE.SYS and should be system RAM plus 12 MB in size. It is thought by many that two times system RAM is more appropriate.

You can place multiple pagefiles on several disks. This improves performance dramatically. You can also place the swap file on RAID 0 drives but do not place them on RAID 5 systems. On RAID 5, the parity information dramatically slows down the paging. In general, keep sufficient pagefile size on the systemroot drive but place other pagefiles to maximum performance without removing crash dump analyses.

Improving Disk Performance

Disk drives and the related buses clearly are the greatest bottlenecks on current high-performance PCs. In newer systems, there is considerable time when the CPU has nothing to do because data are simply not present. In today's world of hype, it is common to see incredible statements about drive speed. No matter what is claimed, the current bus design is limited to 15 to 16 MB per second sustained throughput.

So how can you improve disk performance? Isolating threads as much as possible can reduce their disruptive nature. The first step in this process is to isolate slow and fast devices on a bus. Ideally, the controller that has attached drives does not have slower devices on it. Do not mix SCSI-2 and wide SCSI devices on a controller, as you will not take full advantage of the wide devices. The slower drives will always degrade performance. Likewise, CD-ROMs, DAT drives, and so on need to be placed on a separate controller from the hard drives. For example, you can use a 3940w to handle your hard drives and a 3940u (both Adaptec controllers) to handle remaining devices. Place the wide boot drive on Bus A of the 3940w and the data drives on Bus B. Place the CD-ROMs on Bus A of the 3940u and the backup devices on Bus B. This maximizes performance with minimal hassle because you are using the multiplexing nature of PCI to assist you in providing good performance.

If speed is of a major concern, you can use RAID 0; but remember that RAID 0 has no redundancy, and all data on the RAID are at high risk. An often overlooked issue is disk fragmentation. Regardless of past marketing hype, NTFS does in fact fragment, and in the right conditions, it fragments even more than FAT. The way that files are stored on NTFS is ingenious but only up to a point. Each file is stored in the next available drive space, but there is always a space between files. This of course implies that 300 MB of files occupies more than 300 MB of space on the drive. As the drive gets about 50 percent occupied, the needed space might exceed the physical space on the drive. This forces NT to fragment files. Fortunately, defragmentation applications are available right now from Executive Software. They are well worth the investment.

Network Optimization

If the workstation is on a network, then the choice of protocols used can change performance dramatically. NetBEUI is clearly the fastest protocol, but it is nonroutable. Most users and companies are migrating to TCP/IP as their dominant stack. Because of all the broadcasting in TCP/IP, it is a relatively slow network connection. Several things can be done to help keep the network speed acceptable.

First, the system administrator can subnet a large network. This has the advantage of keeping the bulk of traffic to as few computers as possible. Given the nature of TCP/IP, it is easy to cross subnets by using a WINS server or LMHOST files.

Second, hopefully, the network is set up logically with multiple servers to do specific tasks. The primary domain controller should be just that; do not use it as a workstation. The backup domain controller can also function as a WINS server, but ideally the WINS and Exchange (or Mail) servers are separate computers. The more you add to system overhead, the slower performance will be on the network.

Special Considerations

In all attempts to increase throughput and performance, there is delicate balance between improvement, cost, and risk. Trying to maximize bus throughput is expensive. In the simple two-controller suggestion given earlier, the controller cost alone is $700 to $800. It stands to reason that common sense must play a major role in the search for maximum speed. There is no magical formula or elixir. In all cases though, it is better to do all performance enhancing with hardware and not software solutions.

A common problem on all networks is inappropriate bandwidth and port handling. Most networks use passive hubs, which simply have all active ports contending for the same bandwidth. Ten ports active on a 10Base-T hub does not give you 10Base-T performance on each port. Switches on the other hand help with network performance dramatically. A switch maximizes all active ports to the full bandwidth of the network (only stopped by error correction).

Performance Monitor

What is Performance Monitor? It simply is an application in the Administrator folder that can track the system and application performance. All system components are viewed as objects, and performance is measured on counters. The purpose of Performance Monitor is as follows:

- Monitor the system across time
- Identify bottlenecks
- Monitor the effects of configuration changes

Most NT users at one time or another become enamored with the Performance Monitor. In fact, one volume of the 3.51 NT Resource Kit was dedicated to optimizing NT via the Performance Monitor. This volume has been moved in the NT 4 Workstation Resource Kit to the third section of the single volume. This section is ideal and mandatory reading for any serious NT user. Several specialized uses of the Performance Monitor are worth discussing in the current context.

To get the most out of Performance Monitor, you need to enable the disk counters. Microsoft has not enabled the counters by default because they do give additional overhead that might be noticeable on low-end machines. On Pentiums and Pentium Pros, the performance degradation is minimal. At a command prompt, type **diskperf -y**. When the system next reboots, the disk counters are enabled (see fig. 21.5). (Some have suggested that the diskperf counters do cause a performance hit on SMP systems. You can always turn off diskperf with the -n parameter.)

For most workstations, running Performance Monitor all the time is unnecessary. In fact, it really makes little sense. Here, the use of Performance Monitor will be restricted to look for bottlenecks.

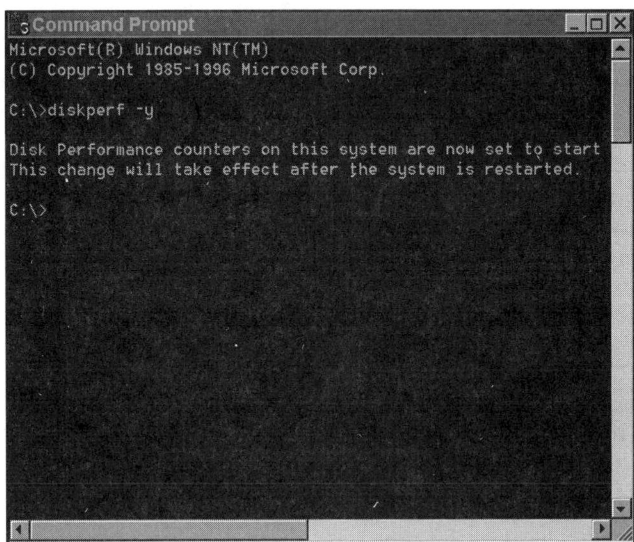

Figure 21.5

This command window shows the addition of the disk performance counters on a system.

You can define key counters that are indicative of bottlenecks for the processor. These counters are as follows:

- **Processor:%Processor Time.** This counter obviously looks at the time the processor is busy. It is not uncommon to see the average CPU utilization between 0 and 80 percent. Most Pentium systems run 20 to 30 percent. If you open large databases and manipulate the data, you might find performance as high as 100 percent and remaining there. In such cases, any routine performance time greater than 80 percent typically means that the processor is a bottleneck, and you might want to increase its speed or add another processor.
- **System:Processor Queue Length.** If you do significant multitasking, you can generate a significant amount of threads. These threads compete for resource and CPU cycles. If the demand outstrips the supply of CPU resources, Queue length can get excessive. Sustained values greater than 2 suggest that the processor is a bottleneck.

One disk counter for drives that is useful to monitor is the following:

- **Disk:Average disksec /transfer.** This can be used to determine impending disk failure. It measures how much time a disk needs to fulfill requests. If the time is greater than 0.3 seconds, there is potential disk failure.

The issue for determining the proper amount of memory needed is far more complex. The easiest method to determine the efficient amount of RAM the system needs (there is never enough) can be found with a complex set of counters:

```
Multiply Memory:Pages/s by Logical Disk:Ave. Disksec/transfer.
```

The logical disk in question is the one containing the pagefile. The number generated in the preceding memory equation is the percentage of the disk access time used by paging. If the number exceeds 10 percent (0.1) on a sustained basis, the system needs more memory.

You can determine the amount of memory needed by watching the Process:Working set for each active process on the system. Simply stop the process that requires the greatest working set and recheck the preceding counter. Keep doing this until the counter shows less 0.1. The amount of memory needed then becomes:

```
amount present + the total size of the removed working sets.
```

Performance Monitor can be used to examine many other counters, but its effective use on a workstation is somewhat limited. The one thing that Performance Monitor does add is numbers. In today's world, numbers are the name of the game.

Summary

This chapter discussed the various aspects of troubleshooting NT problems and optimizing NT performance. Troubleshooting is the means of determining the causes of machine and system failures, and optimizing is the identification of performance bottlenecks. Unlike many other operating systems, many of the problems found are hardware related.

Understanding troubleshooting and optimization of systems is crucial to setting up any Windows NT Workstation. In an ideal world, you simply turn on a system and never pay any attention to system settings or worry about performance or system failure. Throughout the short years of the PC, none of these idealistic goals have ever been attained. Users always want more performance or have need of system repair.

Specific topics discussed included troubleshooting the boot-up process, making boot floppies, and handling run-time kernel exceptions. Standard concepts for optimizing performance were also provided. One example of a seemingly minor sector failure on a hard drive that turned into a system crash was given in which all aspects of troubleshooting were employed. The use of the emergency repair disk was discussed, as was the use of a boot floppy to bypass boot sector problems. The topics discussed here are germane to both NT 4 Workstation and Server. Proper techniques can do much to ensure recovery from system failure and decent performance of a computer running Windows NT 4.

CHAPTER 22

The Registry

Windows NT Workstation is meant to be a "self-tuning" operating system. The system refers to a comprehensive repository of hardware, software, configuration, and user information for all aspects of system operations. This repository or database is known as the Registry. The Registry is nothing new to Windows. A version of the Registry exists in Windows 3.x. (Surprised? Don't be. Click on File Run REGEDIT.EXE in the Windows File Manager). This Registry is used only for Object Linking & Embedding (OLE) information. Windows 95 also uses the Registry. This Win95 Registry is far more powerful in the sense that the operating system uses it for a number of system operations. The Registry in Windows NT Workstation is more similar to the Registry in Windows 95 than in Windows 3.x. Currently, however, there is no compatibility between the Windows 95 and Windows NT Registries (even in NT 4).

In Windows NT Workstation, the Registry is a powerful configuration management database. Not only can system administrators use it to tune operations, but NT itself uses the Registry on a constant basis. It replaces the functionality provided by the INI files in Windows 3.x. The Registry contains information used by the system, users, applications, hardware device drivers, and the network. Changes made to the Registry impact how Windows NT Workstation operates. It is precisely because of this that you need to use extreme caution when attempting to edit and change values in the Registry. NT Workstation provides you with a number of GUI administrative tools that hide the Registry, and guide you to supply proper configuration settings. Certain settings, however, especially while troubleshooting, might force you to enter the Registry directly. This chapter focuses on the underlying concepts of the Registry, the structure of the Registry database, and most of the practical applications of the Registry.

Understanding the Registry and NT System Operations

The Windows NT Registry is a dynamic database (or a set of hives—more about the database structure in the next section). Unlike the older INI files, it can binary values, hex values, and executable code in addition to text strings. This makes it far more powerful that the INI files and the older Windows 3.x Registry. The Registry not only stores configuration information, but also acts as the repository for active updates of system information. The NT Registry is a hierarchical database containing "hives" of information. Information is organized similar to a directory structure on a PC, so that maintenance and access is simplified. This is a major difference from the Windows 3.x Registry in which the INI files are flat files.

A number of processes send as well as extract information from the Registry. Figure 22.1 illustrates the different Windows NT processes that access the Registry on an ongoing basis.

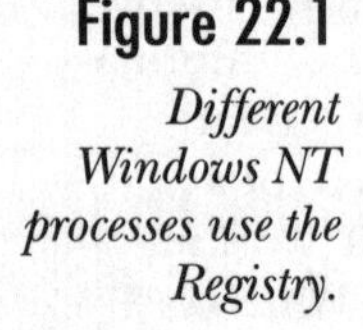

Figure 22.1

Different Windows NT processes use the Registry.

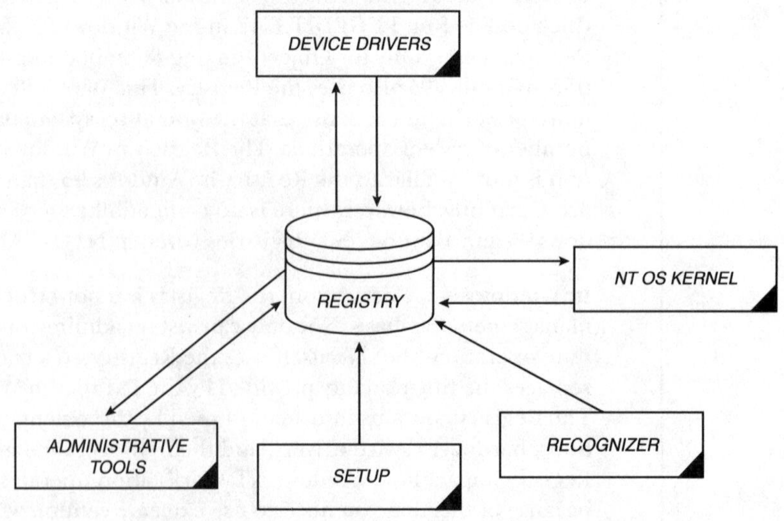

The *Setup* process adds (and updates) configuration data to the Registry whenever it is run. If you add a new modem to your NT computer, for example, the appropriate information is added to the Registry. Or, if you change your display adapter settings from 16 colors to 256 colors, this information updates in the Registry.

The *Hardware Recognizer* is initiated each time NT is started (booted). This process places a list of hardware detected on your system into the Registry. On x86 based computers, this process is controlled by the Recognizer (NTDETECT.COM) and the Kernel (NTOSKRNL.EXE). On RISC computers, this information is extracted from the firmware.

The *Windows NT Kernel*, or the core part of the operating system, extracts information about device drivers, the order in which to load them, service dependencies, and so on, from the Registry. In turn, it sends information about its version number and so on to the Registry. This happens every time the NT computer is started.

Device drivers send and receive load and configuration parameter data from the Registry. The entries in the Registry are similar to the DEVICE= entries in MS-DOS systems. Each device driver must send information about the hardware resources it uses like DMA, interrupt (IRQ) numbers, and so on to the Registry. This information is then open to any other application or device driver that can read it and provide appropriate directions to users for set up, configuration, and operation.

Administrative Tools provided in the Control Panel and the Administrative Tools (Common) folders send and receive information from the Registry. If you open an administrative tool, it extracts the pertinent information from the Registry and presents it in a graphical view that you can then customize. Logic built into the administrative tools does not enable you to make critical errors. The Registry is protected against improper settings through the use of GUI administrative tools. Examples include the User Manager, Windows NT Diagnostics, the Network applet in Control Panel, and so on.

Exploring the Registry Database

The Registry is a hierarchical database organized into a tree structure. The Registry tree has five subtrees in Windows NT. Each of these subtrees begins with a root key. The subtree root keys are as follows:

- HKEY_LOCAL_MACHINE
- HKEY_CLASSES_ROOT
- HKEY_USERS

- HKEY_CURRENT_USER
- HKEY_CURRENT_CONFIG

In each subtree, the root key can have many keys, and the keys can have many subkeys. The subkeys can themselves have subkeys underneath them in the hierarchy and so on. Keys and subkeys can contain data items called *value entries*, which are the actual configuration data. Keys can contain both subkeys and value entries. Figure 22.2 shows the hierarchy of the Windows NT Registry.

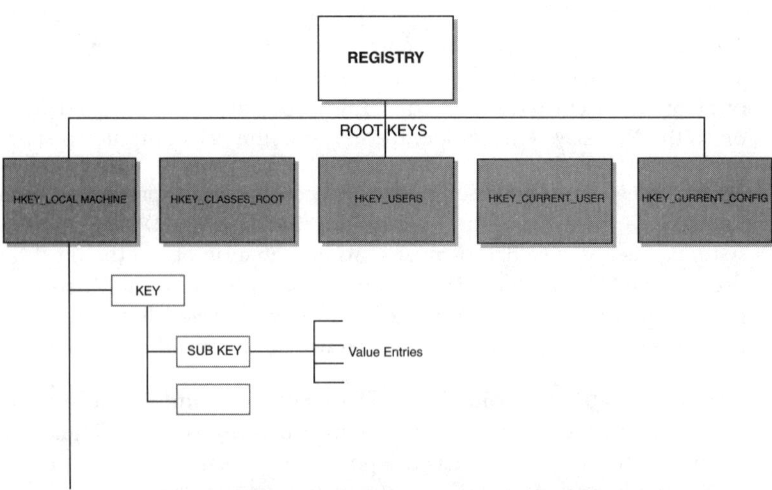

Figure 22.2
The Windows NT Registry is organized as a hierarchical database.

Value entries can consist of value name, value type, and actual value. Each root key begins with an HKEY_ prefix which publishes to all applications that this is a callable handle from within their routines or procedures. Each key or subkey (including the value entries) gets this prefix according to its position in the Registry tree. Figure 22.3 shows a view of the HKEY_LOCAL_MACHINE key.

The selected value entry (on the right-hand pane) would be listed as:

```
HKEY_LOCAL_MACHINE\SOFTWARE\ODBC\ODBCINST.INI\MicrosoftAccessDriver(*.mdb) =
C:\WINNT\SYSTEM32\odbcjt32.dll
```

In the next sections, you will first explore the Registry Editor (the built-in tool in Windows NT Workstation to view and edit the Registry), and then understand each of the root keys comprehensively. You will look at how to add value entries, change existing entries, and load hives (or parts of the root key database). You will also explore the methods to secure the Registry and back it up for data security and restoration.

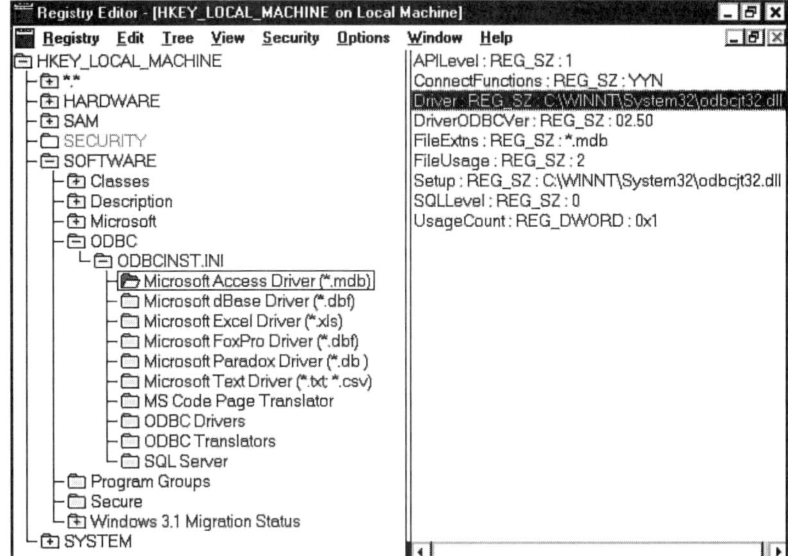

Figure 22.3

Root Keys are arranged with roots and sub keys.

The Registry Editor

The Registry Editor is the Windows NT tool used to view and edit the Registry. Generally, it does not appear as a separate icon on your desktop (or Program Manager). The program which opens the editor is REGEDT32.EXE and is found in the \%systemroot%\system32 directory. You can create a shortcut or program icon pointing to this file. You can also access this tool through the Windows NT Diagnostics utility in the Administrative Tools (Common) folder:

1. Choose the Administrative Tools (Common) folder from the Programs option in the Start menu.

2. Click on Windows NT Diagnostics.

3. Select File Run, choose Registry Editor in the drop-down list, and click on OK to run the Registry Editor (see fig. 22.4).

After the Registry Editor opens, tile the Windows to view all the keys in the Registry. Figure 22.5 shows the Registry Editor viewing all five root keys.

Spend some time familiarizing yourself with the mechanics of the Registry Editor before using it to edit entries. In the upcoming sections, you will use the Registry Editor to open the Registry, view certain subkeys, and make changes to value entries. If you want to explore all the root keys of the Registry, this is a good time. To avoid making inadvertent changes, however, you can use the Registry Editor in a Read-Only mode. This essentially turns off the editing part of the Registry Editor. You can still view all the components of the Registry, but no changes will be saved.

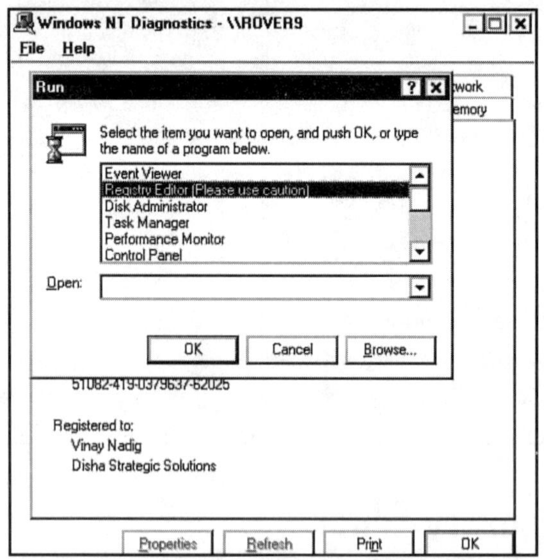

Figure 22.4

Run the Registry Editor from the Windows NT Diagnostics Utility.

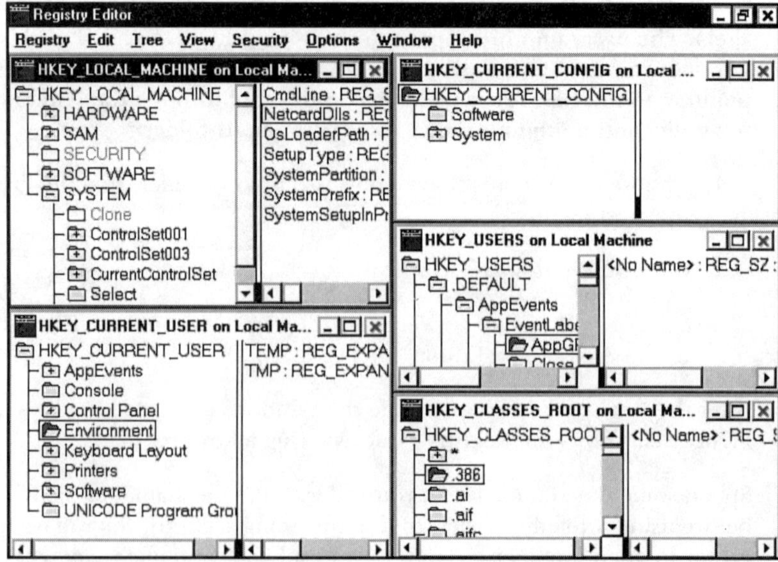

Figure 22.5

Use the Registry Editor to view all five subtrees.

To prevent inadvertent changes, you can open the Registry Editor in Read-Only mode—choose Read Only in the Options menu.

If you maximize a particular root key, keys and subkeys appear on the left-hand pane of the windows and the value entries appear on the right-hand pane. Using the Registry Editor, you will add entries to an NT Workstation's Registry, which can control factors such as speeding up performance of the NTFS file system, troubleshooting the boot process of an NT Workstation PC, and so on. These examples will serve to show you how important the Registry is to the ongoing operation of your NT Workstation.

The HKEY_LOCAL_MACHINE Subtree

The HKEY_LOCAL_MACHINE subtree contains information about the local computer's hardware, software, system, security policies, and the Securities Accounts Manager (SAM) database. Figure 22.6 shows the HKEY_LOCAL_MACHINE subtree.

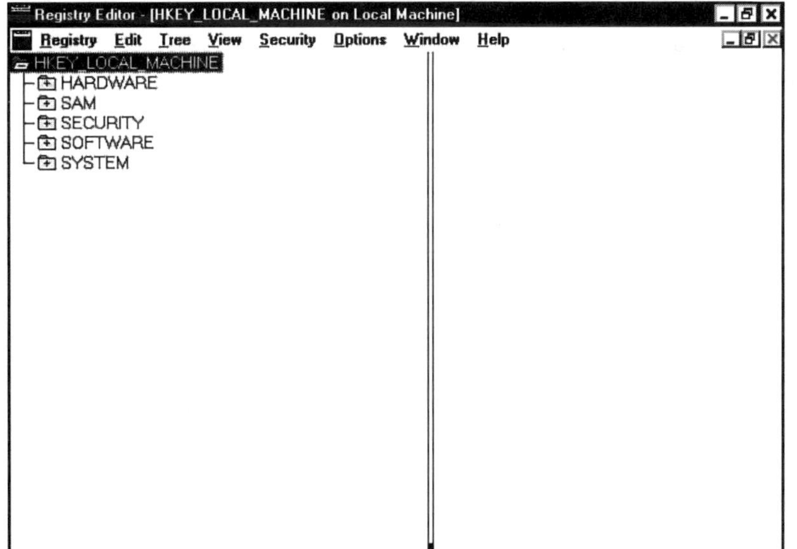

Figure 22.6
The HKEY_LOCAL_MACHINE subtree contains registry entries about the local machine (NT Workstation).

The SAM database stores all user records in Windows NT. All user IDs, double-encrypted passwords, and so on are stored in the SAM database.

Examples of the Hardware key are information about SCSI adapters, processor type, video adapter settings, and so on. Examples of the Software key are information about ODBC drivers for particular databases (like ODBCJT32.DLL for Microsoft Access MDB databases and so forth). The SAM key contains user and group information created for the NT Workstation. Generally, even the administrator has only limited access to this key, but administrators can always change (or take ownership of) permissions of the key. The Security key contains security policy and user rights used by the NT security system—the LSA or LocalSecurityAuthority. The System key contains system startup information including the all important CurrentControlSets (more about this later). This information controls how Windows NT boots up (and sometimes whether it boots up at all!) and other aspects of operating system behavior.

The Hives in HKEY_LOCAL_MACHINE

Hives are a section of the Registry that appear as files on an NT Workstation's hard disk. Each registry subtree is divided into hives (named for their resemblance to the cellular structure of a beehive). A *hive* is a discrete body of root keys, subkeys, and values that is rooted at the top of the Registry hierarchy. A hive is backed by a single file and a LOG file, which are in the %SystemRoot%\system32\config or the %SystemRoot%\profiles\username folders. By default, most hive files (Default, SAM, Security, and System) are stored in the %SystemRoot%\system32\config folder. The %SystemRoot%\ profiles folder contains the user profile for each user of the computer. Because a hive is a file, it can be moved from one system to another but can only be edited using Registry Editor.

Table 22.1 shows a list of hive names and associated files.

TABLE 22.1
Hives and Associated Files

HIVE	ASSOCIATED FILES
SAM(HKEY_LOCAL_MACHINE)	SAM, SAM.LOG
Security(HKEY_LOCAL_MACHINE)	Security, Security.log
Software(HKEY_LOCAL_MACHINE)	Software, Software.log
System(HKEY_LOCAL_MACHINE)	System, System.alt
HKEY_CURRENT_USER	USER###, USER.LOG, ADMIN###, ADMIN.LOG
HKEY_USERS\DEFAULT	DEFAULT, DEFAULT.LOG

Loading and Unloading Hives

It is possible to actually load and unload hives listed in table 22.1. Essentially, this means that you work on those particular keys, make, and then save changes. You can load remote computers' hives (more about loading remote computer registries later), and work on them. To load a hive (loading works only on the HKEY_LOCAL_MACHINE or HKEY_USERS):

1. Log on as an administrator.
2. Click on Registry Load Hive in the Registry Editor.
3. In the Load Hive dialog box, select the hive file you want to load.
4. In the second Load Hive dialog box, supply a key name under which the key should be loaded.

You can work with the hive data in this view. The hive remains loaded until you unload it.

To unload a hive:

1. Log on as an administrator.
2. Select the key you want to unload in the Registry Editor.
3. Choose Unload Hive from the Registry menu.

Unloading a key actually means that you are making it unavailable for the system and users to use. Therefore, if a key is open or being used by the system, you cannot unload it.

The HKEY_CLASSES_ROOT Subtree

The HKEY_CLASSES_ROOT subtree contains information about Object Linking and Embedding. File associations (which file extensions are linked to application executables) are stored in this key (see fig. 22.7).

The data in the value entries contain file name extensions and class definitions. The file name extensions control which application opens up when you double-click on a file in the NT Explorer (or File Manager), and the class definitions coordinate all shell and OLE functions (whether the application can be an OLE client, server, or both, and so on). Referring to figure 22.7, for example, the file extension *.DOC has the value Word Document 6.

The HKEY_CLASSES_ROOT is actually a subset of the HKEY_LOCAL_MACHINE\SOFTWARE\Classes key. These keys contain the same information (see fig. 22.8).

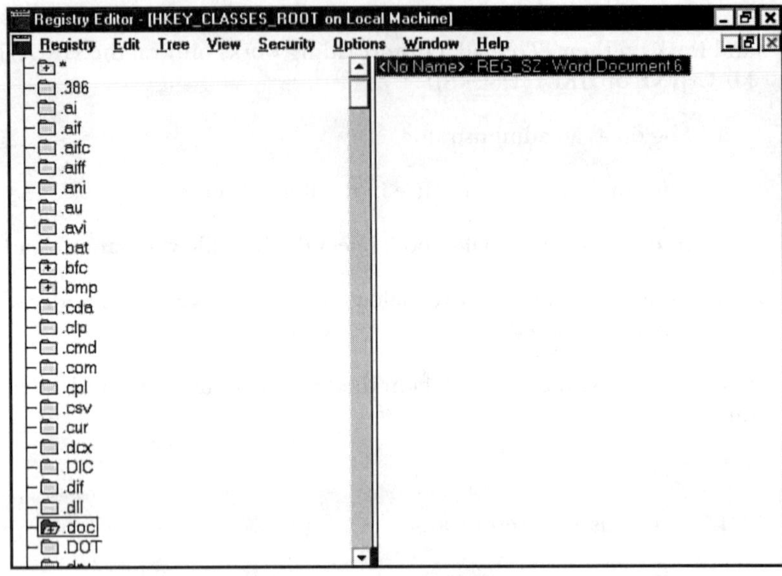

Figure 22.7

The HKEY_ CLASSES_ ROOT subtree contains OLE information about an NT workstation.

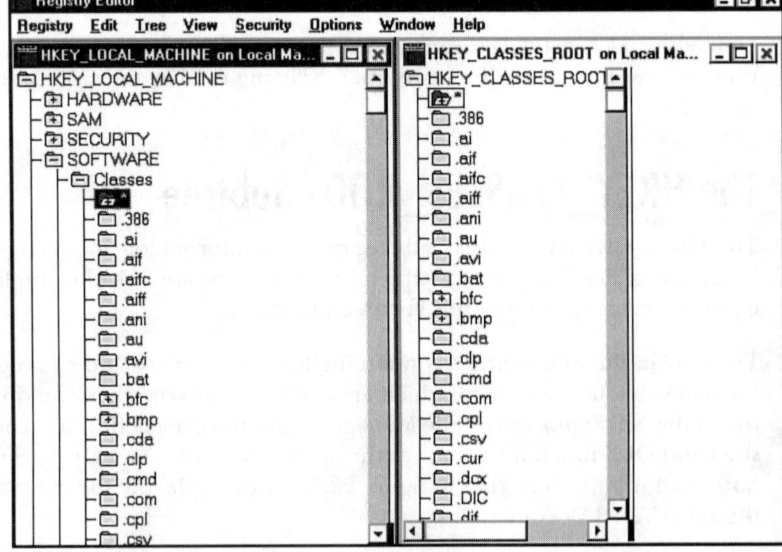

Figure 22.8

The HKEY_CLASSES_ ROOT is a subset of the HKEY_ LOCAL_ MACHINE\ SOFTWARE\Classes key.

The HKEY_CURRENT_USER Subtree

The HKEY_CURRENT_USER subtree contains information for the currently logged on user. The type of information maintained controls the user profiles. User profiles define the appearance of the desktop, availability of certain icons, and so forth. Network connections and environment variables can also be controlled through this key (see fig. 22.9).

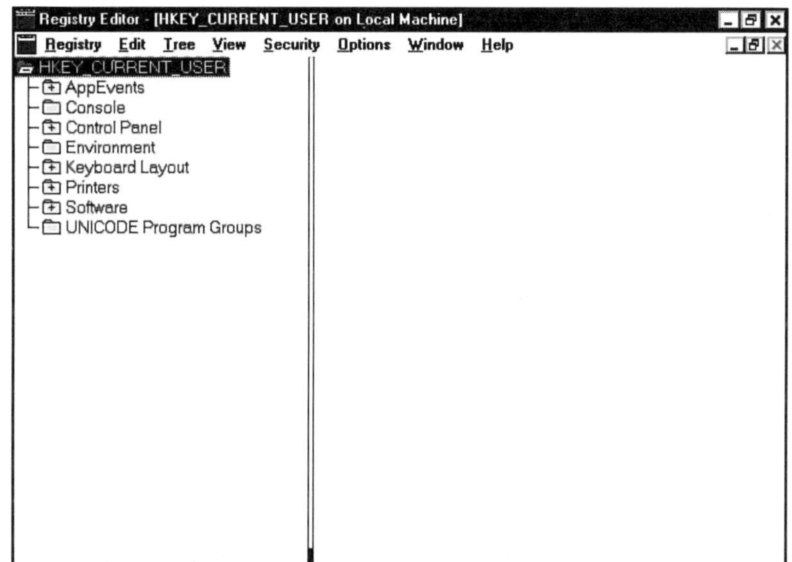

Figure 22.9

The HKEY_CURRENT_USER subtree contains information about the currently logged on user.

The AppEvents subkey contains information about the system behavior at certain application events (beeping when a window is maximized and so on).

The Console subkey contains information about the appearance of the console such as color, font, and screen size. If you modify settings for the command prompt session, a Command key also appears.

The Control Panel subkey contains information about the appearance of the various applets. This includes desktop wallpaper patterns, color schemes, and screen savers.

The Environment subkey contains information about the environment variables such as the temporary directory path.

The Keyboard subkey contains information about keyboard layout such as US and UK.

The Printers subkey contains information about the installed information for the current user.

The Software subkey contains configuration information for all applications for the current user. The structure is very similar to the HKEY_LOCAL_MACHINE\Software key.

The UNICODE Program Groups subkey generally contains information about program groups in Windows. This is generally obsolete in Windows NT Workstation 4. It is maintained, however, for backward compatibility.

The Network subkey contain information about the network connection for the current user. This subkey is available only if the user is logged on to a network.

If the Windows NT Workstation has migrated Windows 3.1 applications, there is a Windows 3.1 Migration Status subkey present. This subkey contains information about the current user's preferences for groups and INI files for the Windows 3.1 applications.

The HKEY_CURRENT_USER extracts information from the HKEY_USERS\SID where SID is the unique security ID for the current user. The information that NT builds in the HKEY_CURRENT_USER depends on the SID. If NT does not find sufficient information here, it extracts information from the .DEFAULT subkey.

The HKEY_USERS Subtree

The HKEY_USERS subtree contains the actively loaded profiles of all users. It contains at least two subkeys: the .DEFAULT and the SID subkeys (see fig. 22.10).

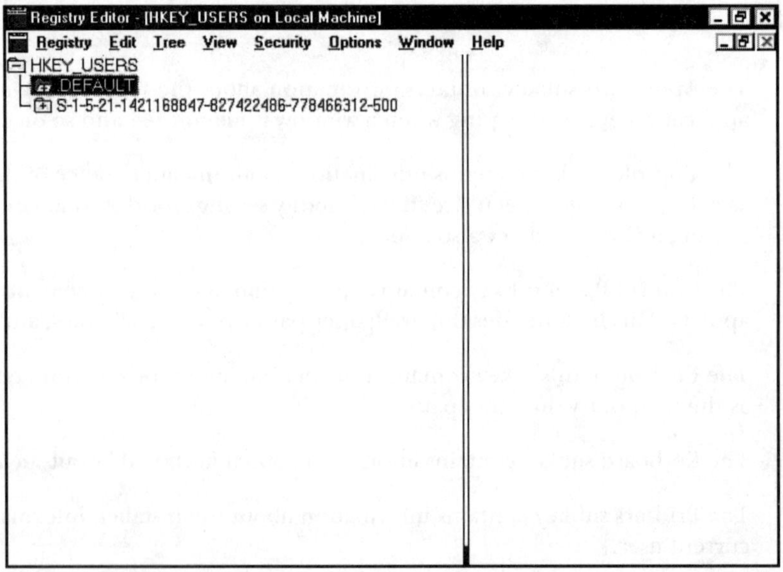

Figure 22.10

The HKEY_USERS subtree contains currently loaded profiles of all users of the NT workstation.

The SID subkey contains the user profile information for the currently logged on user. This information is used by the HKEY_CURRENT_USER key to build its subkey information.

The .DEFAULT subkey contain the default profile information for all users. If the HKEY_CURRENT_USER cannot find the user profile information for the currently logged on user, it uses the information in the .DEFAULT subkey instead.

The HKEY_CURRENT_CONFIG Subtree

The HKEY_CURRENT_CONFIG is a new root key in Windows NT Workstation 4. It contains information about the currently loaded hardware profile. Similar to Windows 95, Windows NT now offers the capability to define multiple hardware profiles for the same PC. Essentially, you can select a hardware profile at boot time to configure different hardware devices. If you want to boot with no support for a joy stick or a SCSI scanner, for example, you set up your NT machine appropriately and save the configuration as a hardware profile. Now you can set up the PC again to support all the peripherals and save the configuration again as another hardware profile. Choose between the two (or more) during boot time. The information in the HKEY_CURRENT_CONFIG subtree pertains to the currently loaded hardware profile. It contains two subkeys Software and System (see fig. 22.11).

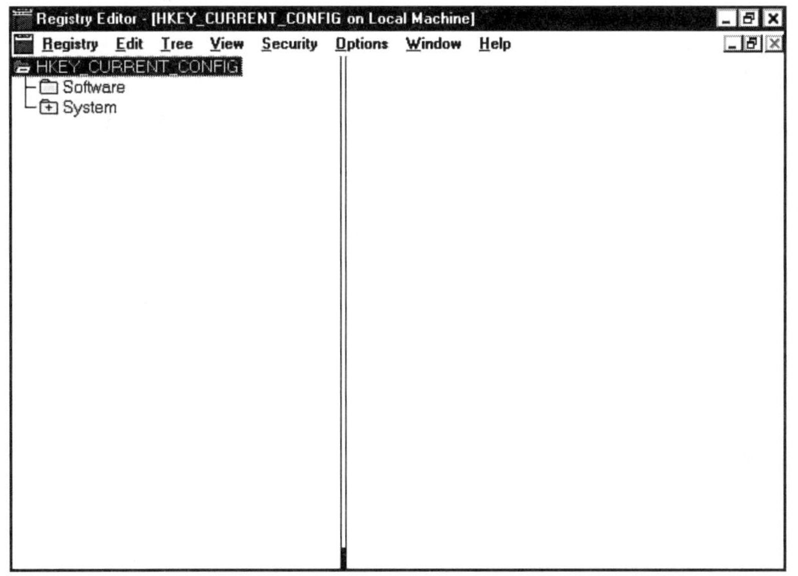

Figure 22.11

The HKEY_CURRENT_CONFIG subtree contains hardware profile information.

The information in the HKEY_CURRENT_CONFIG subtree maps to the HKEY_LOCAL_MACHINE\SYSTEM\CurrentControlSet\Hardware profiles\Current subkey (see fig. 22.12).

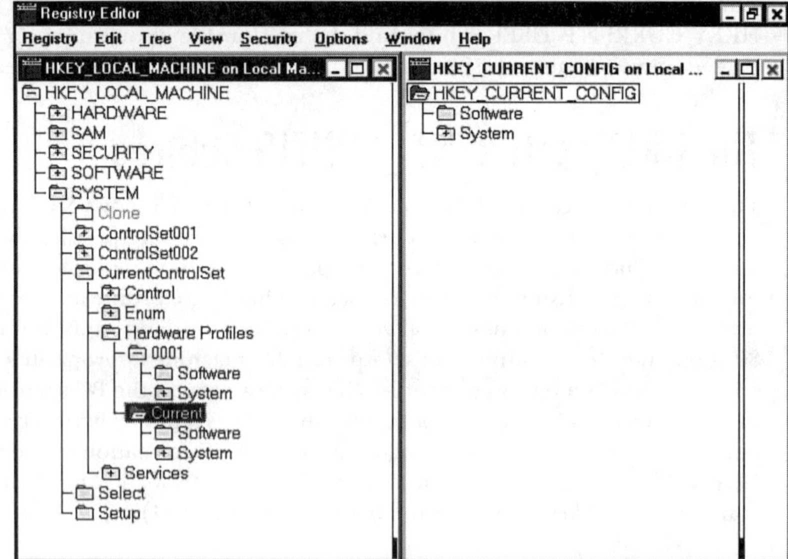

Figure 22.12
HKEY_CURRENT_CONFIG maps to the HKEY_LOCAL_MACHINE.

CurrentControlSets

CurrentControlSets, which are subkeys, store information about system devices, device drivers, hardware, and so on—all crucial during the boot up NT start up process. CurrentControlSets are stored in the HKEY_LOCAL_MACHINE\System (see fig. 22.13).

Several versions of the CurrentControlSet actually exist. The number is determined by how often you change system settings or how often the system has trouble booting up. Generally (in most typical Windows NT installations), you have four CurrentControlSets (see fig. 22.13). The four typically found are:

\Clone

\ControlSet001

\ControlSet002

\CurrentControlSet

ControlSet001 is the last control set you booted with, ControlSet002 (if there are no more numbered ControlSets—that is, ControlSetxxx) is the last known good set, which contains information about the most recent safe boot up. This set corresponds to the message `Press the space bar for the Last Known Good Menu` during boot time of a Windows NT PC. CurrentControlSet is actually a pointer to one of the ControlSetxxx keys. Clone is a copy of the CurrentControlSet. The Clone subkey is created each time the NT machine is booted up.

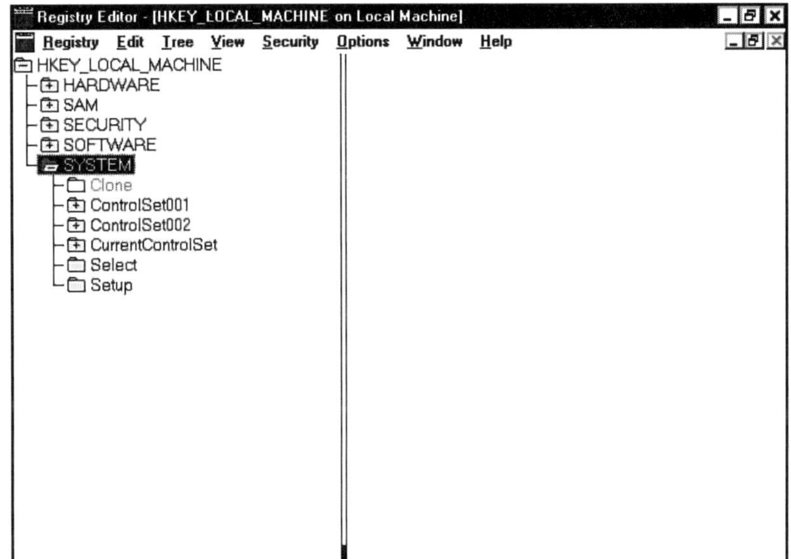

Figure 22.13
CurrentControlSets in HKEY_LOCAL_MACHINE contain important start-up information.

How does NT know which ControlSet is good or current? The HKEY_LOCAL_MACHINE\SYSTEM\Select key controls this process (see fig. 22.14).

The four value entries in this subkey are:

- Current
- Default
- Failed
- LastKnownGood

Each of these values contain entries of data type REG_DWORD that refer to a particular ControlSet. If Current is set to 0x1, for example, CurrentControlSet is pointing to ControlSet001. The Default value generally is the same as the Current value. If LastKnownGood is set to 0x2, the safe version of the ControlSet is ControlSet002 or this is the ControlSet whose values can bring back Windows NT from a failed start up process. Failed points to the ControlSet with which Windows NT was unable to boot.

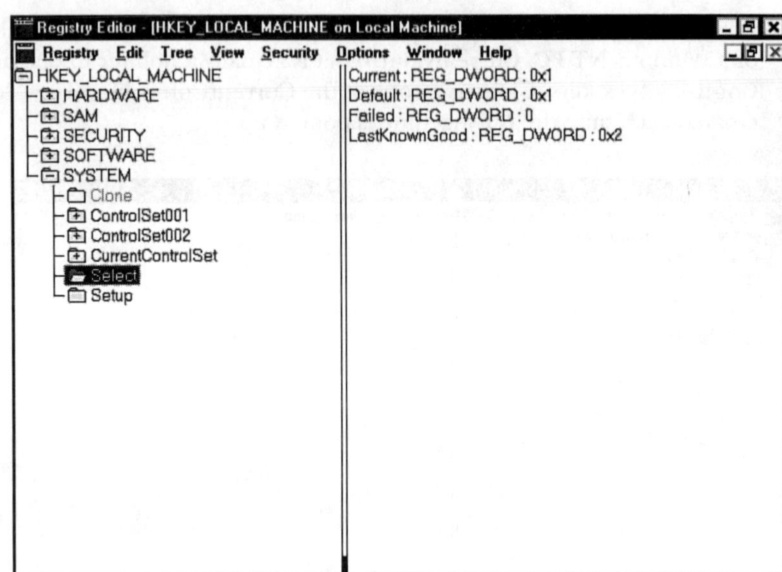

Figure 22.14 *The Select subkey controls the ControlSet usage.*

Registry Data Types

The Registry enables the usage of different types of data (or data types) for your entries in the value entry portions. Because the Registry can contain more than just plain text, you must be careful in selecting the appropriate type of data when adding entries. Table 22.2 defines the different data types available and when they should typically be used.

TABLE 22.2
Registry Data Types Defined

Data Type	Description
REG_SZ	Text String data. Used to describe program names, labels, and so on. For example: VideoBiosDate:REG_SZ:10/31/95
REG_DWORD	Numeric data that is a *double word*—meaning 4 bytes long. The numeric value can be expressed in decimal, hexadecimal, or binary format. This data type is used to describe service parameters, device parameters, interrupt numbers, and so on. For example: DefaultSettings:Yresoltion:REG_DWORD:0x1e0. Hex values always begin with 0x. After you double-click a value entry containing the REG_DWORD data type, the DWORD editor opens up and enables you to view the value in hex, binary, or decimal.

Data Type	Description
REG_MULTI_SZ	Text data in multiple strings to make it humanly readable. Each string value is separated by null (ASCII 0). For example: SystemBiosVersion:REG_MULTI_SZ:EPP BIOS revision31.00
REG_EXPAND_SZ	Expandable data string containing a variable which will be written to by the system. If a value entry is pointing to a driver file in the C:\WINNT directory, the Registry entry might be of REG_EXPAND_SZ data type with the directory referred to as %systemroot% rather than WINNT.
REG_BINARY	Raw binary data format. Hardware information is stored in this format. The binary editor can also express the value in hex format. Use caution while changing values unless you know the exact values from your hardware vendors.
REG_RESOURCE_LIST	Hardware configuration data stored as records with individual fields describing the components of the record. The serial port, for example, might be REG_RESOURCE_LIST, and the individual fields would describe the Bus Number and the Interface type.

Using Systems Administration Applications of the Registry

Many instances occur when you might edit the Registry directly to produce certain desired results. Editing the Registry is done through the Registry Editor. Again, editing the Registry is analogous to editing raw sectors on your disk. Use extreme caution.

When editing the Registry, try to limit the number of changes you make. If you make a large number of changes and the system fails during startup, you might have trouble identifying the specific entry that caused problems. This does not mean that you cannot boot up safely, as discussed earlier in the CurrentControlSets section.

This section describes how you can use the Registry for certain administrative tasks that cannot be accomplished with the GUI administrative tools provided.

Creating Custom Logon Messages

By default, when a user logs on (by pressing Ctrl+Alt+Del), he is greeted by the Log on dialog box with the Username, Domain, and Password fields. If you want to show a custom (greeting or warning) message immediately after the user presses Ctrl+Alt+Del, follow these steps:

1. Log on as an administrator to the Windows NT computer.
2. Start the Registry Editor.
3. Select the following key: HKEY_LOCAL_MACHINE\SOFTWARE\Microsoft\WindowsNT\CurrentVersion\Winlogon
4. On the right-hand side of the windows you can see the value entries for the Winlogon subkey (see fig. 22.15).

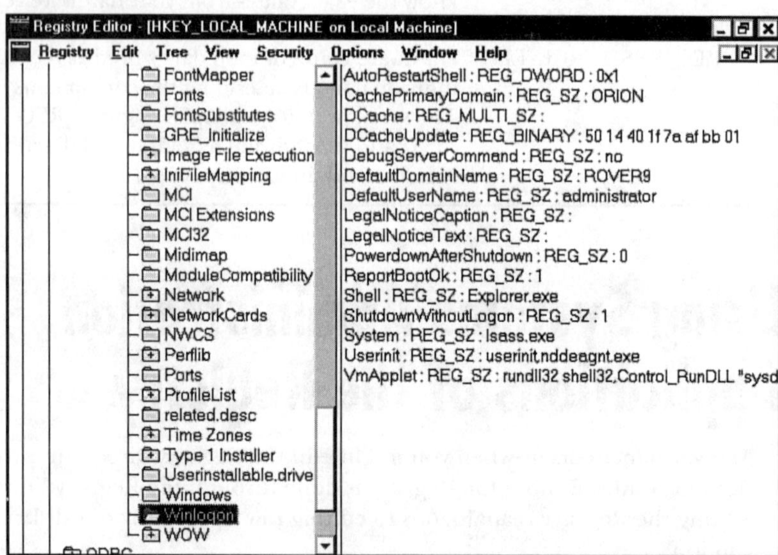

Figure 22.15

Use the Winlogon subkey to create a custom logon message.

5. Double-click on the value entry for LegalNoticeCaption and provide an appropriate title for your greeting.
6. Double-click on the value entry for LegalNoticeText and provide the actual content of the greeting.
7. Log off and log on to test the new Registry settings.

Adding Keys and Values

What if you don't find the value entries LegalNoticeCaption and LegalNoticeText? Can you add these value entries? Absolutely:

1. Click on the Winlogon subkey.
2. Choose Edit Add Key from the Registry Editor menu bar.
3. Enter LegalNoticeCaption in the KeyName field.
4. Select the data type to be REG_SZ in the DataType field.
5. Click on the OK button.

You now have a new value entry. Follow the same process whenever you need to add a value entry or a subkey.

Changing the Default Startup Screen

By default, as Windows NT starts up, the Microsoft Windows NT logo appears onscreen. The default file for an NT Workstation is WINNT.BMP in the \%systemroot%\ directory. If you want to display your company's logo (or Dilbert's face for that matter!), just point the appropriate Registry entry to that file. The steps are as follows:

1. Log on as administrator and start the Registry Editor.
2. Select the following key: HKEY_USERS\ .DEFAULT\Control Panel\Desktop
3. Double-click on the value entry Wallpaper (see fig. 22.16).
4. Enter the name of your custom BMP file.
5. Log out and verify your new Registry settings.
6. If you want to tile your logon screen, select the value entry TileWallpaper and set the value to 1.

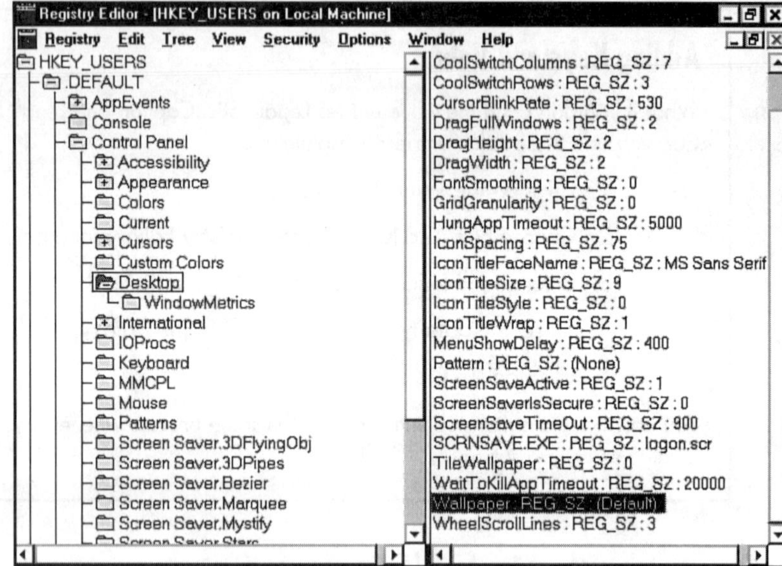

Figure 22.16
Set the appropriate entry to generate a custom logon screen.

Logging On Automatically to Windows NT

Windows NT enforces mandatory logon. Users have to log on in each new session if they want to access the NT desktop. Although there is no way to bypass the mandatory logon restriction, you can automate the logon process by supplying the logon information that NT needs at start up. To automate the user logon, follow these steps:

1. Log on as administrator and start the Registry Editor.
2. Select the following key: HKEY_LOCAL_MACHINE\SOFTWARE\Microsoft\WindowsNT\CurrentVersion\Winlogon
3. From the Edit menu, choose Add Value.
4. Enter AutoAdminLogon in the ValueName field (see fig. 22.17).
5. Select REG_SZ for the DataType.
6. Enter 1 for the value for this entry.
7. Double-click on DefaultDomain and enter the name of the domain (if this NT Workstation is participating in an NT Server domain).
8. Double-click on DefaultUserName and enter the user name (yours).
9. Double-click on DefaultPassword and enter the (your) password. If this string is not present, add the value with data type REG_SZ.

10. Log off, and restart the system. Your Windows NT Workstation automatically logs you on without displaying the Logon dialog box.

11. To disable auto logon, change the value of AutoAdminLogon from 1 to 0.

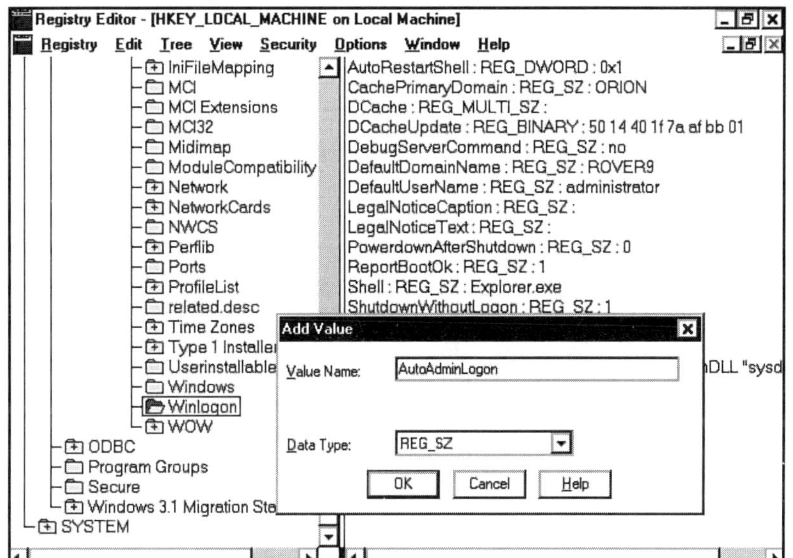

Figure 22.17

Adding a value entry (AutoAdminLogon) for the Winlogon subkey automates the logon process in a Windows NT workstation.

Shutting Down Without Logging On

After a user initiates a log on (Ctrl+Alt+Del), the logon dialog box by default (in NT Workstation only) enables the user to click on the ShutDown button and close Windows NT. To disable this feature (by making the ShutDown button inactive), and thereby make certain that a user has to log on before shutting down, follow these steps:

1. Log on as administrator and start the Registry Editor.

2. Select the following key: HKEY_LOCAL_MACHINE\SOFTWARE\Microsoft\WindowsNT\CurrentVersion\Winlogon

3. Double-click on the ShutdownWithoutLogon value entry and change the string from 1 to 0 (see fig. 22.18).

4. Log off and verify the new Registry settings.

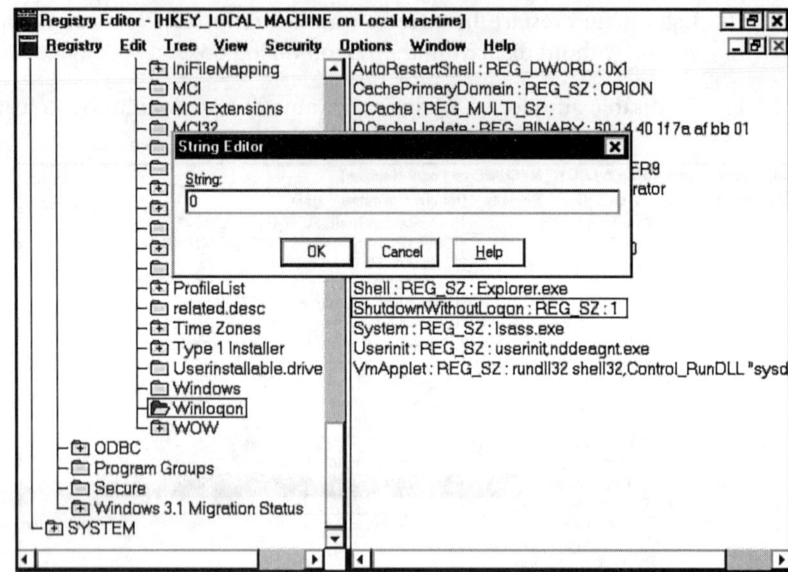

Figure 22.18

Disabling the ShutDown button forces a user logon to shut the system down.

Powering Down PCs from the Windows NT Shell

Most of the PCs you buy today have an option in the ROM BIOS which enables you to power down from the software. By default, if you shut down Windows NT, and after the shut down process completes, you get a dialog box which gives you a Restart button. If you need to power down the machine, you have to press the appropriate power button on the PC. If you want to power down right from the Windows NT shell, follow these steps:

1. Log on as administrator and start the Registry Editor.
2. Select the following key: HKEY_LOCAL_MACHINE\SOFTWARE\Microsoft\WindowsNT\CurrentVersion\Winlogon
3. Double-click on the PowerdownAfterShutdown value entry.
4. Enter a value of 1 to enable this option or 0 to disable it (see fig. 22.19).

Tuning the NTFS File System for Faster Performance

By default, NTFS (the Windows NT File System) maintains complete backward compatibility support for SFNs (short file names).

Essentially, if an NT Workstation saves a file with 255 characters in the file name, how can a DOS/Windows 3.x PC (which might be connected to this NT Workstation in a workgroup network) "see" and access this file? A DOS/Windows 3.x PC cannot access files with file names more that 8.3 characters. But NTFS with SFN support enabled will always maintain a 8.3 truncation of the 255 character file name so that a DOS/Windows 3.x PC can access it.

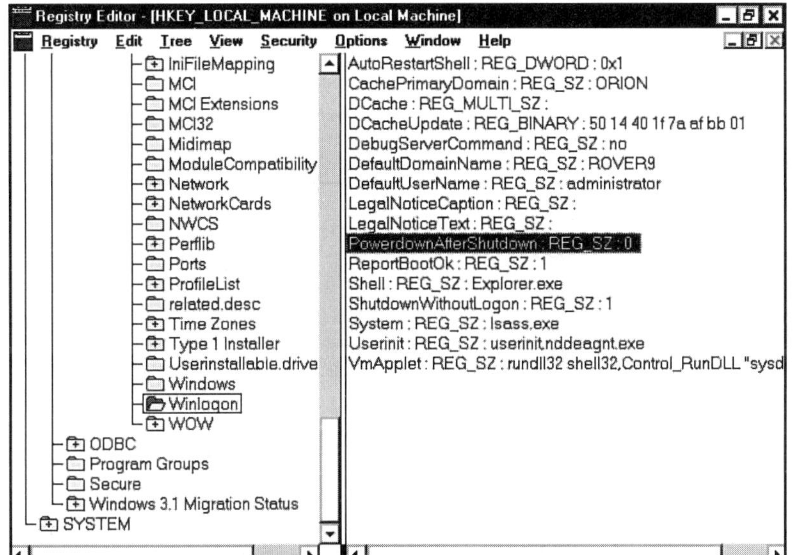

Figure 22.19
Enabling the powerdown option from the Windows NT shell automatically turns the power off when you choose to shut down.

Although this provides compatibility, it does affect file system performance. If you decide that you do not need the SFN support, follow these steps:

1. Log on as administrator and start the Registry Editor.

2. Select the following key: HKEY_LOCAL_MACHINE\SYSTEM\CurrentControlSet\Control\FileSystem

3. Double-click on the NtfsDisable8Dot3NameCreation, and set the value to 1 to disable the SFN support (see fig. 22.20).

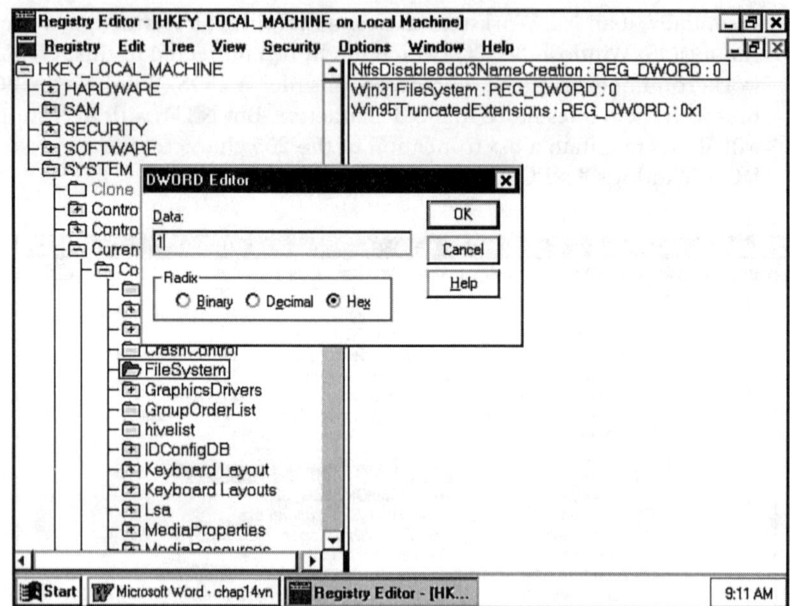

Figure 22.20
Use the Registry to disabe the SFN support in the Windows NT File System (NTFS).

Identifying the Version of NT on Your System

The two flavors of Windows NT (Workstation & Server), though very different in make up and usage, appear identical in appearance. The GUI looks the same and the only visual clues are the banner when you click on the Start button and the logon screen, both of which can be disabled. Windows NT does maintain internal settings in the Registry, however, that provide clues as to the flavor of the operating system you are running. To identify the version, follow these steps:

1. Log on as administrator and start the Registry Editor.
2. Select the following key: HKEY_LOCAL_MACHINE\SYSTEM\CurrentControlSet\Control\ProductOptions
3. Double-click on the ProductType value entry (see fig. 22.21).
4. If the data in the ProductType value is WinNT, Windows NT Workstation is running on your system.

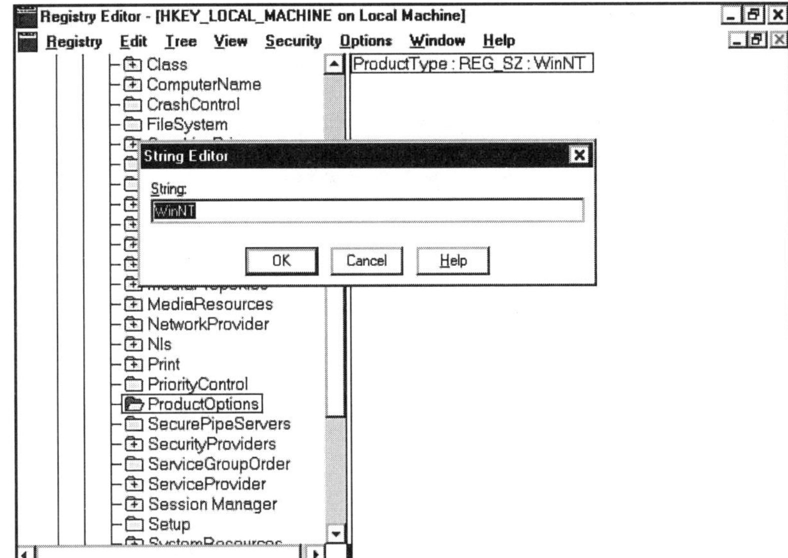

Figure 22.21

Check the version of Windows NT you have installed on your PC.

5. If the data in the ProductType value is ServerNT, Windows NT Server is running on your system in stand-alone server mode.

6. If the data in the ProductType value is LanManNT, Windows NT Server is running on your system as a Domain Controller.

Disabling the Last Logged On User Default

By default, the Windows NT logon dialog box displays the user name of the last user who logged on. To disable this, follow these steps:

1. Log on as administrator and start the Registry Editor.

2. Select the following key: HKEY_LOCAL_MACHINE\SOFTWARE\Microsoft\WindowsNT\CurrentVersion\Winlogon

3. Add a value entry labeled DontDisplayLastUserName with data type REG_SZ (see fig. 22.22).

4. Set the string to 0 if you want to disable this option, and to 1 if you want to enable it.

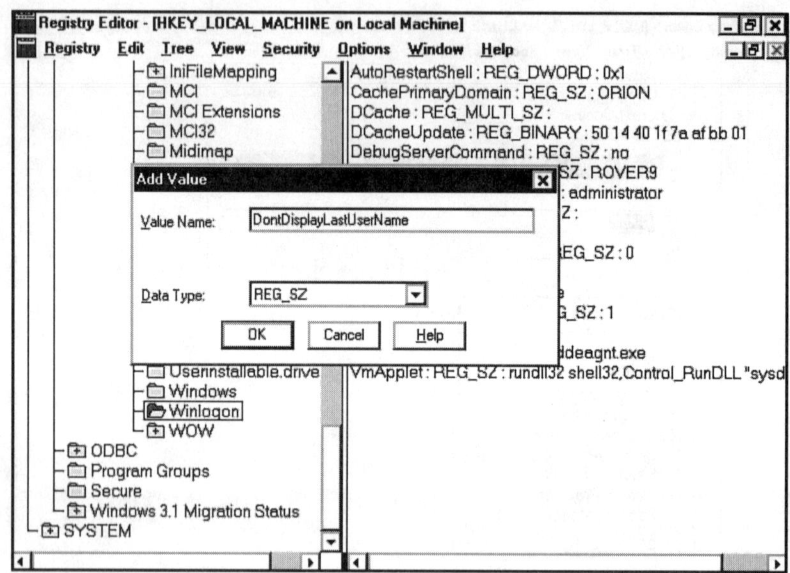

Figure 22.22
Use the Registry to find out who was the last user logged on to an NT workstation.

Using a Different Task Manager

Windows NT Workstation 4 offers a new and improved Task Manager that you can access when you press Ctrl+Alt+Del from any point in your Windows NT session. To use another third-party task manager, follow these steps:

1. Log on as administrator and start the Registry Editor.
2. Select the following key: HKEY_LOCAL_MACHINE\SOFTWARE\Microsoft\WindowsNT\CurrentVersion\Winlogon
3. Double-click on the Taskman value entry (add the value with data type REG_SZ if it is not present) and set the string equal to the executable file name of your new task manager (see fig. 22.23).
4. Log off and verify your new Registry settings.

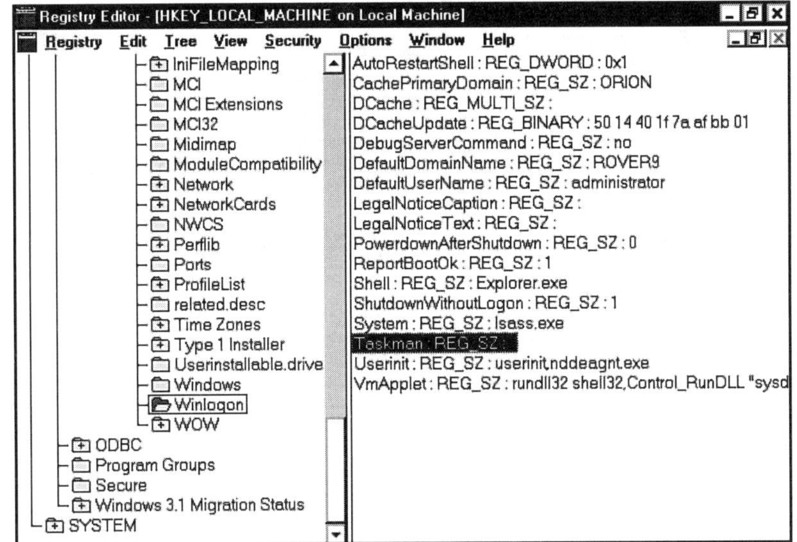

Figure 22.23

Enable a different task manager as your default task management utility.

Parsing AUTOEXEC.BAT in Windows NT

If you have an AUTOEXEC.BAT on your system (in the boot partition), by default Windows NT parses this file, picks up the environment variables, and sets the environment. If you want to disable this support entirely, follow these steps:

1. Log on as administrator and start the Registry Editor.

2. Select the following key: HKEY_LOCAL_MACHINE\SOFTWARE\Microsoft\WindowsNT\CurrentVersion\Winlogon

3. Double-click on the ParseAutoexec value entry (add the value with data type REG_SZ if it is not present), and set the string to 0 to disable the parsing, and 1 to enable parsing (see fig. 22.24).

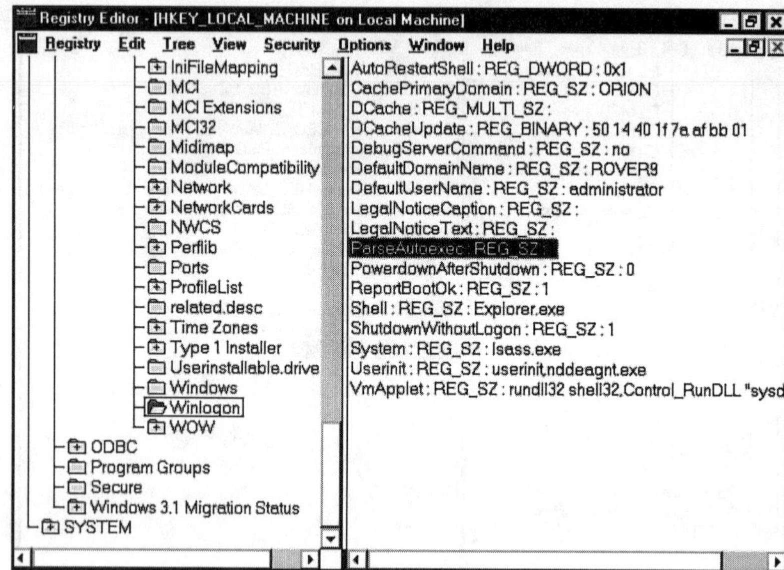

Figure 22.24

Disable the parsing of the AUTOEXEC.BAT file in a NT workstation.

Understanding the Registry and User Profiles

User profiles are used in Windows NT to control how a user's desktop appears, the applications available to a user, the menu options, and so on. To identify the location and file names of user profiles on your Windows NT machine, follow these steps:

1. Log on as administrator and start the Registry Editor.
2. Select the following key: HKEY_LOCAL_MACHINE\SOFTWARE\Microsoft\WindowsNT\CurrentVersion\ProfileList.
3. The list shows all the SIDs of registered users on your NT system (see fig. 22.25). To identify the current user's SID, check the SID in HKEY_USERS root key.
4. Double-click on the appropriate SID.
5. Double-click on the ProfileImagePath value entry to see the profile path for the user (see fig. 22.26).

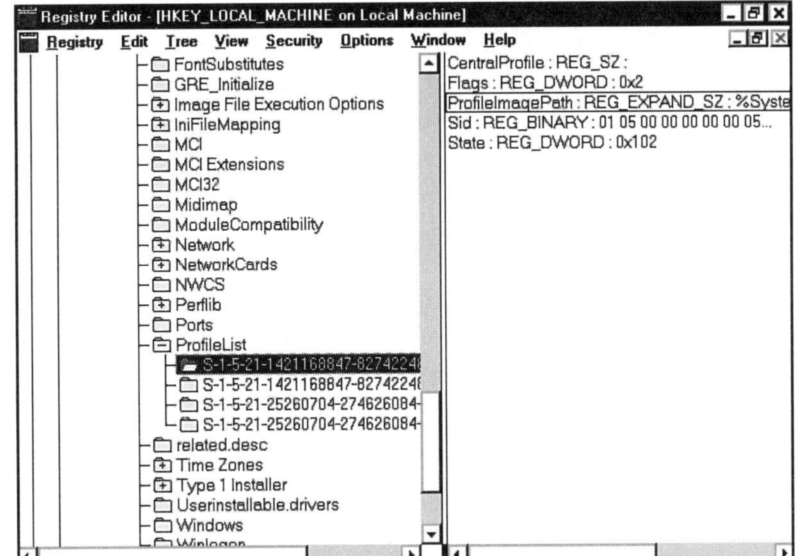

Figure 22.25

List the SIDs on your windows NT workstation.

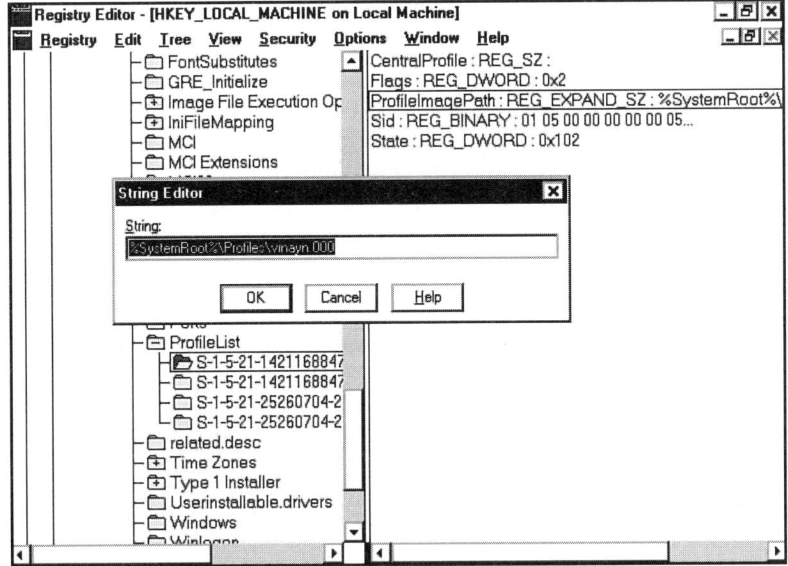

Figure 22.26

Locate the different user profile files present in your Windows NT workstation.

Maintaining the Registry

In addition to using the Registry to create entries and make changes, one of the most important system administration tasks in Windows NT is Registry maintenance. The following operations assume importance as you support your Windows NT environment:

- Managing Registry size
- Managing the Registry remotely
- Backing up and restoring the Registry
- Managing Registry security
- Auditing Registry operations
- Printing the Registry
- Searching the Registry

Managing the Registry Size

Individual components (value entries) in the Registry can range up to 1 MB in size. This means that the Registry can become quite large. The Registry default size is 25 percent of the paged pool. The value of the paged pool is 32 MB. So the default value of the Registry size limit is 8 MB, sufficient for 5,000 user accounts. The maximum value of the paged pool is 128 MB. The Registry can have a maximum of 102 MB, which means about 80,000 users.

Two value entries affect the Registry size:

1. HKEY_LOCAL_MACHINE\SYSTEM\CurrentControlSet\Control\Registry SizeLimit
2. HKEY_LOCAL_MACHINE\SYSTEM\CurrentControlSet\Control\Session Manager\Memory Management\PagedPoolSize.

Figures 22.27 and 22.28 illustrate default values for the RegistrySizeLimit and the PagedPoolSize.

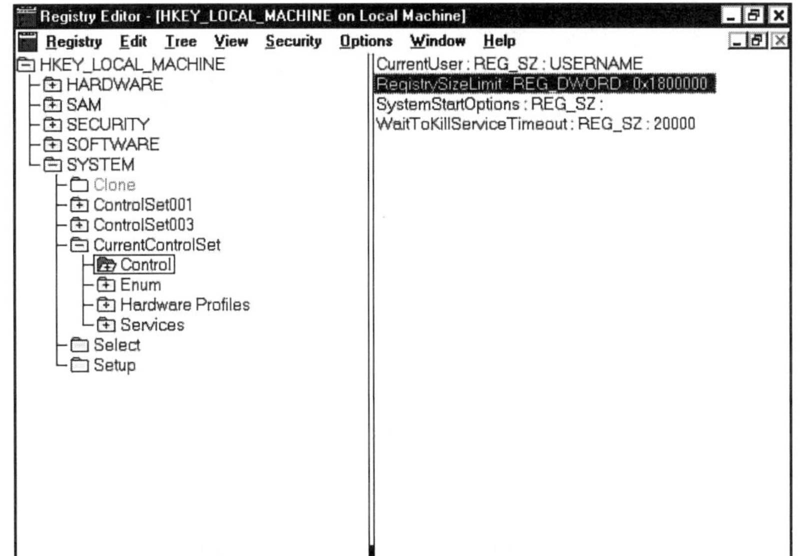

Figure 22.27

Set the maximum size of the Registry entry.

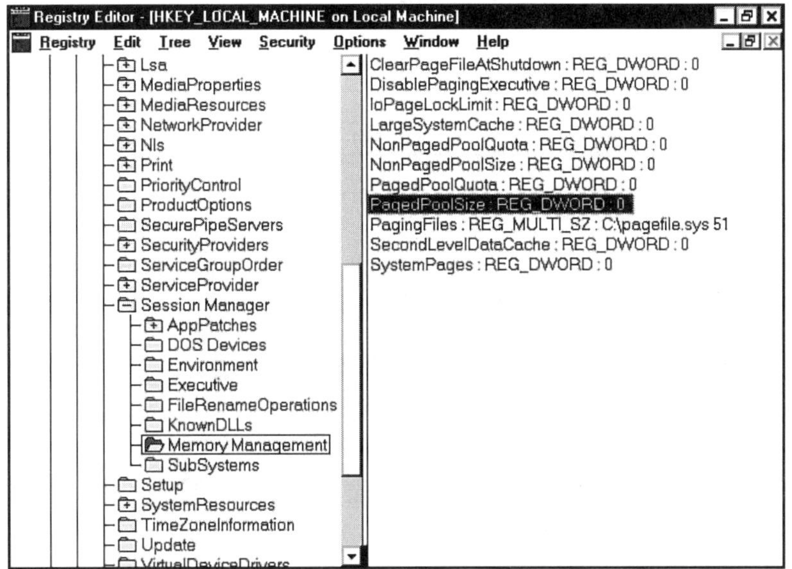

Figure 22.28

Set the maximum size of the PagedPoolSize in your NT workstation.

Managing the Registry Remotely

Windows NT enables you to access the Registry of other NT computers connected on your network. If your NT Workstation is participating in a workgroup and you are an administrator, you can view and edit the Registries of computers connected to your PC. If your PC is a member of a domain and you are a domain administrator, you can view and edit the Registries of all NT computers connected to the domain. To access other computers' Registries:

1. Log on as an administrator and start the Registry Editor.

2. Choose Select Computer from the Registry menu. The Select Computer dialog box appears (see fig. 22.29).

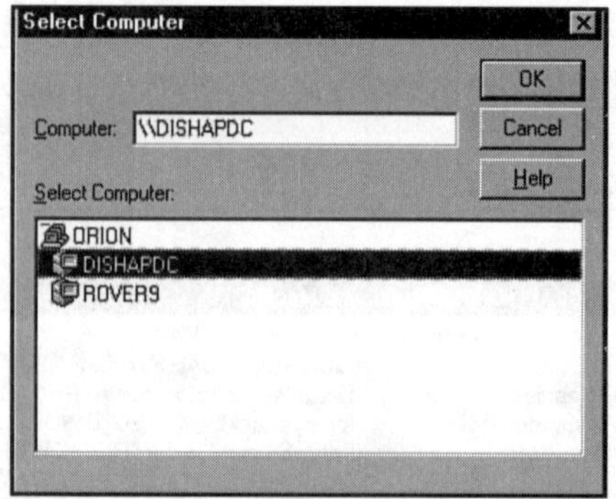

Figure 22.29
You can remotely manage Registries from Windows NT.

3. Select a remote computer from the list.

4. A message informs you that AutoRefresh is disabled (see fig. 22.30). Click on the OK button to access the remote computer's Registry.

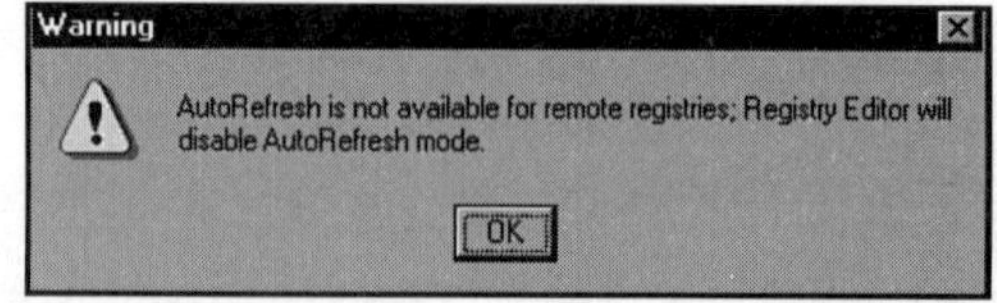

Figure 22.30
A warning message appears the first time you select a remote computer.

5. The HKEY_USERS and HKEY_LOCAL_MACHINE are shown for the remote machine (see fig. 22.31).

Only the HKEY_LOCAL_MACHINE and the HKEY_USERS root keys of the remote machine are shown. All other key information is actually maintained in one of these main keys so that complete configuration of the remote computer is possible.

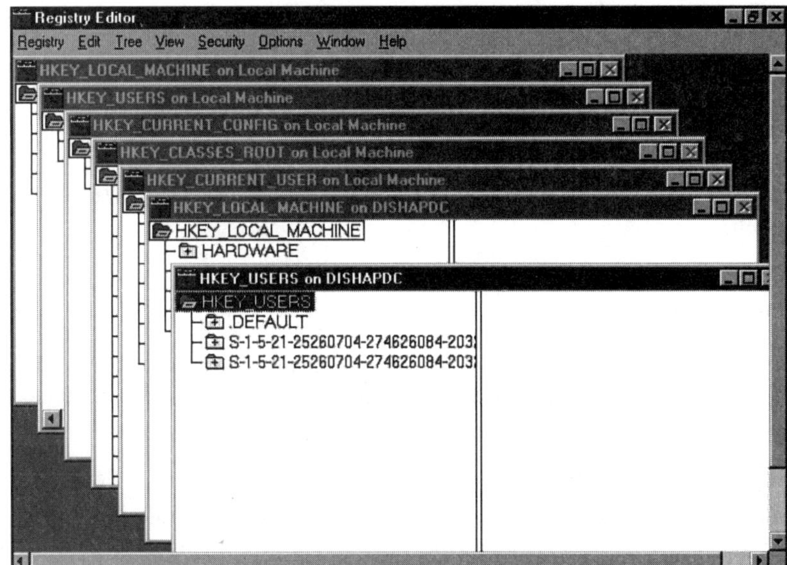

Figure 22.31

View a remote computer's Registry using the Registry Editor.

Backing Up and Restoring the Registry

One of the operations that Windows NT setup guides you to do is to prepare an emergency repair disk. You can add changes to this original disk by using the Repair Disk (\%systemroot%\system32\rdosk.exe) utility periodically. This disk contains the hive files that make up the Registry. This utility, however does not back up hives currently being used. The only way to back up all the pertinent Registry information is to use utilities provided in the Windows NT Resource Kit.

To back up the Registry, you use the REGBACK utility:

```
REGBACK targetlocation
```

where targetlocation is the target directory such as A:\rback or F:\rback. REGBACK does not append to floppy disks, so if your target is full, the backup process fails and aborts.

To restore a backed up Registry file, use the REGREST utility:

```
REGREST backuplocation oldhivedirectory
```

where backuplocation is the directory to which you are storing the backed up the Registry hives. Oldhivedirectory is the directory where you want to restore the hives to. After the restoration is complete, the files in the backuplocation are deleted automatically. You have to reboot for these changes to take effect.

Managing Registry Security

If you have installed the \%systemroot%\ directory (usually \winnt\) on an NTFS partition, you can set Registry security by enabling Windows NT ACLs (Access Control Lists).

You can also delete the REGEDT32.EXE on users' PCs if they never need to view or edit the Registry. Note that you can always remotely manage your users' Registries from your workstation.

If deleting REGEDT32.EXE sounds like an extreme measure, you can control the permissions of the REGEDT32.EXE file by user.

The most granular level of detail of security is setting access permissions on keys and subkeys. You can perform this through the Registry Editor.

A Note on Registry Permissions

Before setting permissions of the Registry keys, take a look at the different types of permissions available. The following list describes the type of permission and the corresponding access privilege granted.

- **Read.** Enables the user to read key contents but not make any changes.
- **Full Control.** Enables the user to access, edit, change, save and take ownership of keys.
- **Special Access.** Enables a more detailed level of access to users.
    - **Query Value.** Enables users to read a value entry only.
    - **Set Value.** Enables users to set value entry data.
    - **Create Subkey.** Enables users to create subkeys for selected keys.
    - **Enumerate Subkey.** Enables users to list the subkeys from a selected key.
    - **Notify.** Enables users to audit notification events from the selected subkeys.
    - **Create Link.** Enables users to create symbolic links for selected keys.
    - **Delete.** Enables users to delete the selected subkey.
    - **Write DAC.** Enables users to modify permissions on selected subkeys.
    - **Write Owner.** Enables users to take ownership of keys.
    - **Read Control.** Enables users to view permissions for selected keys.

To set permissions on a Registry key, follow these steps:

1. Log on as an administrator and start the Registry Editor.
2. Select Security and choose Permissions to get the Registry Key Permissions dialog box (see fig. 22.32).

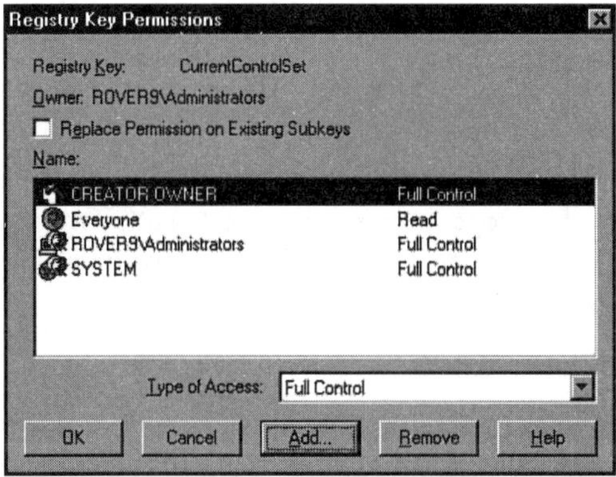

Figure 22.32

Use the Registry Key Permissions dialog box to grant different levels of access to users.

3. Select the key that you want to set permissions.
4. Choose the Add button to get the Add Users and Groups dialog box. This enables you to select user(s) or group(s). Depending on whether you belong to a domain or workgroup, the appropriate list is shown (see fig. 22.33).

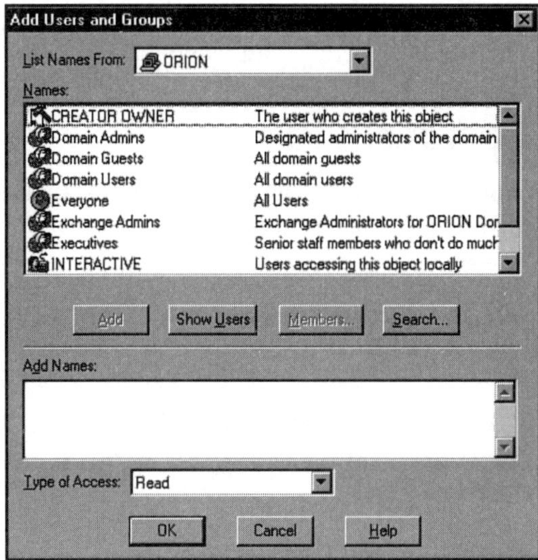

Figure 22.33

Select the appropriate users or groups.

5. After selecting the user, click on OK to return to the Registry Key Permissions dialog box.

6. To apply the type of access to a particular user, select the user and pull down the Type of Access pull-down list.

7. You can assign Read, Full Control, or any type of Special Access (described earlier).

8. Click on the OK button to save your changes.

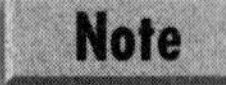

Be careful when assigning security permissions. Leave the access permissions for SYSTEM strictly alone. If improper permissions are set to SYSTEM, your Windows NT system might not boot properly, and you might damage system operations.

Taking Ownership of Registry Keys

Windows NT security enables an access right known as Taking Ownership. Essentially this enables an administrator to take control of any object (file, registry key, printer, and so on) even though the administrator might not have any access to the object. The following steps describe the process of taking ownership of a Registry key.

1. Log on as an administrator and start the Registry Editor.

2. Select the key for which permissions need to be set.

3. Select Security and choose Owner to get the Owner dialog box.

4. Click on the Take Ownership button to take ownership.

Auditing Registry Operations

The Windows NT Registry enables you to audit events or operations that users perform on the Registry (according to their permissions). To set up auditing in the Registry:

1. Log on as an administrator and start the Registry Editor.

2. Select Security and choose Auditing to get the Registry Key Auditing dialog box (see fig. 22.34).

3. If the Audit Permission on Existing Subkeys is checked, the audit policy you set for a key flows down to its subkeys also.

4. Click on the Add button to get the Add Users and Groups dialog box (see fig. 22.35).

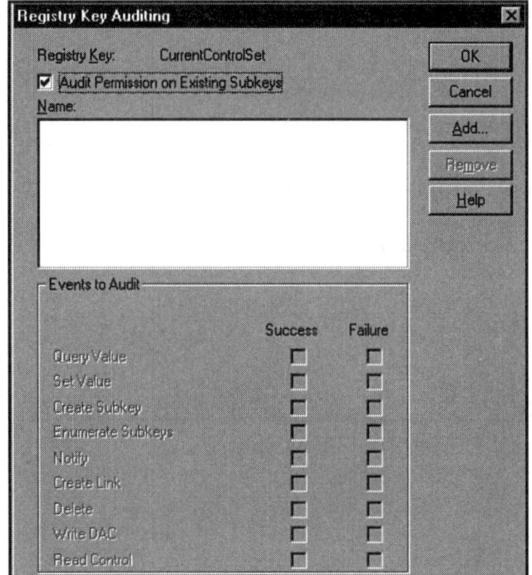

Figure 22.34

Audit the access of various Registry keys to increase security of the Registry.

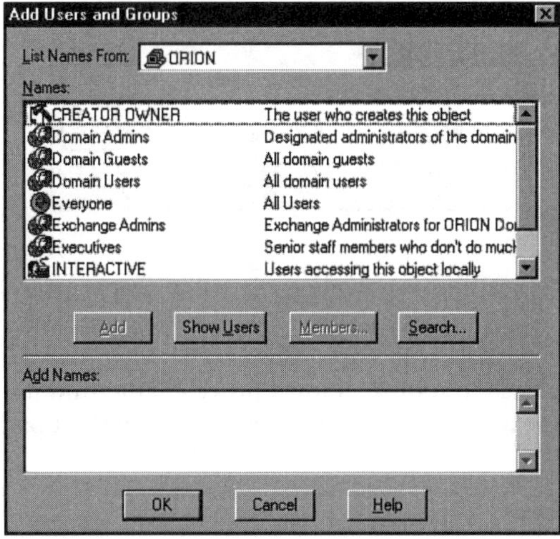

Figure 22.35

Select the appropriate user(s) and/or group(s) that you want to audit.

5. Select the user or group that you want to audit, and click on the OK button to return to the Registry Key Auditing dialog box.
6. Set the audit policy by selecting the appropriate permission and selecting Success or Failure. The Success option audits the events even when permissions were legally used. The Failure option audits events after illegal attempts at using the permissions are performed.
7. Click on the OK button to make your changes effective.

The events audited according to this policy will be recorded and are accessible through the Event Viewer.

Printing the Registry

To print subtrees in the Registry, follow these steps:

1. Log on as an administrator and start the Registry Editor.
2. Select Registry and Print Subtree to print the active root key.

Searching the Registry

The Registry Editor has a basic Find utility. To use this utility:

1. Log on as an administrator and start the Registry Editor.
2. Select View and Find Key to get the Find dialog box (see fig. 22.36). Enter the name of the key you are searching for, and click on the Find Next button to find successive instances of the key.

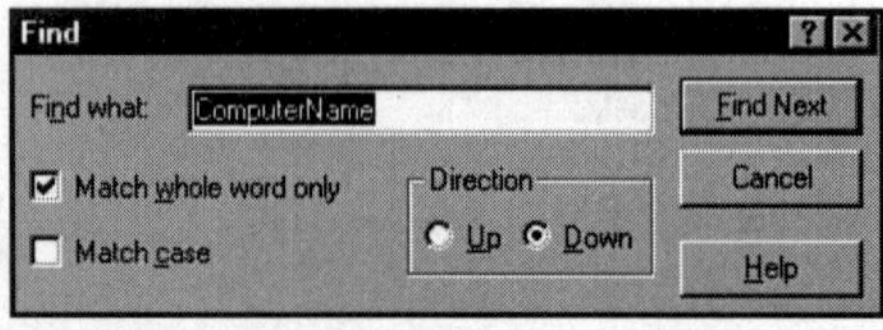

Figure 22.36

Use the Find utility to search specific keys in the Registry.

The Find utility in the Registry Editor is not very powerful. If you need to search for specific value entries, the Find utility does not help at all. One way of searching the Registry for very specific information is to save subtrees or specific keys as text files and use a more sophisticated search tool (in a word processor) to find the information. Then you can use the location information to return to the right part of the Registry to make changes.

For example, to save the HKEY_LOCAL_MACHINE\SOFTWARE\Microsoft\WindowsNT\CurrentVersion\Winlogon key, follow these steps:

1. Log on as administrator and start the Registry Editor.
2. Select the following key: HKEY_LOCAL_MACHINE\SOFTWARE\Microsoft\WindowsNT\CurrentVersion\Winlogon

3. Choose Save Subtree As from the Registry menu.
4. Select Text files in the Save as Type field and supply a file name.
5. Click on the Save button to save the subkey as a text file.
6. To access this file, just open it by using your favorite word processor.

An example of the HKEY_LOCAL_MACHINE\SOFTWARE\Microsoft\WindowsNT\CurrentVersion\Winlogon saved as a text file is shown as follows:

```
Key Name:          SOFTWARE\Microsoft\Windows NT\CurrentVersion\Winlogon
Class Name:        <NO CLASS>
Last Write Time:   10/1/96 - 10:51 AM
Value 0
  Name:            AutoRestartShell
  Type:            REG_DWORD
  Data:            0x1

Value 1
  Name:            CachePrimaryDomain
  Type:            REG_SZ
  Data:            ORION

Value 2
  Name:            DCache
  Type:            REG_MULTI_SZ
  Data:

Value 3
  Name:            DCacheUpdate
  Type:            REG_BINARY
  Data:
00000000   f0 7b 4f 66 b0 af bb 01 -                             .{Of....

Value 4
  Name:            DebugServerCommand
  Type:            REG_SZ
  Data:            no

Value 5
  Name:            DefaultDomainName
  Type:            REG_SZ
  Data:            ORION
```

```
Value 6
  Name:            DefaultUserName
  Type:            REG_SZ
  Data:            administrator

Value 7
  Name:            LegalNoticeCaption
  Type:            REG_SZ
  Data:

Value 8
  Name:            LegalNoticeText
  Type:            REG_SZ
  Data:

Value 9
  Name:            PowerdownAfterShutdown
  Type:            REG_SZ
  Data:            0

Value 10
  Name:            ReportBootOk
  Type:            REG_SZ
  Data:            1

Value 11
  Name:            Shell
  Type:            REG_SZ
  Data:            Explorer.exe

Value 12
  Name:            ShutdownWithoutLogon
  Type:            REG_SZ
  Data:            1

Value 13
  Name:            System
  Type:            REG_SZ
  Data:            lsass.exe

Value 14
  Name:            Userinit
  Type:            REG_SZ
  Data:            userinit,nddeagnt.exe
```

```
Value 15
  Name:         VmApplet
  Type:         REG_SZ
  Data:         rundll32 shell32,Control_RunDLL "sysdm.cpl"
```

Understanding the Windows NT Startup Process and the Registry

On x86-based PCs, the Registry is used during the NT boot process after the OSLOADER.EXE passes control to the NTOSKRNL.EXE program.

The following Registry entries are important for the startup process:

- **HKEY_LOCAL_MACHINE\SYSTEM\CurrentControlSet\ServiceGroupOrder subkey.** The entries in this subkey load the drivers that NT needs for disk access, CD-ROM access, SCSI ports, and so on. This is the initial part of the system boot that shows up as a series of periods (like ....) on the screen. This is also called the OS Kernel Load phase.
- **HKEY_LOCAL_MACHINE\HARDWARE subkey.** All the drivers loaded in the initial phase are initialized. The value entries in the HARDWARE key are used to initialize the drivers. This is when the screen turns blue in the boot process and NTDETECT.COM program executes and populates the CurrentControlSet and Clone subkeys. This is the phase which also determines whether Windows NT is going to use the LastKnownGood Menu to do a safe boot if critical hardware drivers fail to load. This phase is also called the OS Kernel Initialization.
- **HKEY_LOCAL_MACHINE\SYSTEM\CurrentControlSet\Control\Session Manager.** This phase known as the Services Load phase, loads and executes the session Manager program (SMSS.EXE). This starts any executables referred to in the HKEY_LOCAL_MACHINE\SYSTEM\ CurrentControlSet\Control\Session Manager\BootExecute key. One other significant action that SMSS.EXE performs is to establish the page file for virtual memory management.
- **Windows Subsystem or the Win32 subsytem.** This last is initiated by SMSS.EXE. The Win32 subsytem starts WINLOGON.EXE to display the logon dialog box for users. It also starts LSASS.EXE or the LocalSecurityAuthority, which is used for user authentication. Finally, the Security Controller

(SCREG.EXE) is started, which starts all automatic startup services. Examples of such services are the Workstation service, the NetLogon service, the Spooler service, and so on.

Understanding Windows 3.x INI Files and the Windows NT Registry

Although Windows NT does not need INI files, certain Windows 16-bit applications cannot recognize the NT Registry. In such a case, if NT did not support INI files, those applications would not run on Windows NT. This is not the case, however. To maintain complete backward compatibility, Windows NT maintains support for legacy INI files.

If Windows NT Workstation is installed as an upgrade of an existing Windows 3.xx installation, all the settings from the various INI files are copied to the Registry. The INI files copied include CONTROL.INI, PROGMAN.INI, SYSTEM.INI, WIN.INI, WINFILE.INI, and so on. The details of the mapping in the Registry are in the key HKEY_Local_Machine\SOFTWARE\Microsoft\Windows NT\CurrentVersion\IniFileMapping (see fig. 22.37).

Figure 22.37

The Registry maintains pointers to the Windows 3.x INI files to maintain backward compatibility.

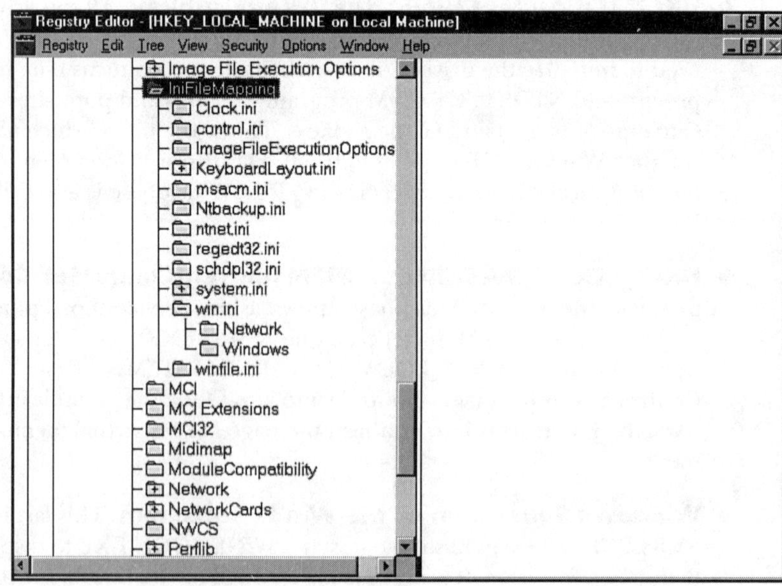

When 16-bit applications are installed on Windows NT, they write to WIN.INI, SYSTEM.INI, and their own INI files. They do not know about or recognize the Windows NT Registry. Therefore, basic SYSTEM.INI, WIN.INI, and WINFILE.INI files appear in the \%SystemRoot%\ directory in Windows NT.

Summary

The Registry is a centralized repository which stores hardware, software, and user configuration data. It can contain text, binary, and hexadecimal data. This chapter discussed the concepts behind using the Registry, the internal database structure, and some practical applications and guidelines for maintaining the Registry on an ongoing basis. The hierarchical Registry affects all phases of Windows NT operations.

One of the design goals of Windows NT was to make it self-tuning. Essentially this means that as the NT Workstation system is used over a period of time, it adjusts itself to the peculiar demands of that particular user, network, hardware peripheral, and so on. This is still not implemented totally (as evidenced by the fact that you still have to optimize and tune Windows NT Workstation for optimum performance), but the Registry provides a mechanism to maintain ongoing configuration information. The Registry in NT Workstation is used on a constant basis. It is not just a static text file used only at start up and then abandoned. It is a dynamic database used at setup, boot, and ongoing operation of the NT Workstation. Windows 32-bit applications have the ability to write to the Registry and query values from the Registry. Considering these factors, the importance of the Registry cannot be overstressed. As an administrator, you will deal with the Registry to customize the NT Workstation, to configure applications, to control user environment settings, and to tune the performance. A comprehensive understanding of the Registry (and how to manipulate it) is absolutely essential. This chapter attempts to give you a conceptual understanding of the Registry layout and then builds upon that to manage the data in the Registry.

PART VIII

Appendices

APPENDIX A

Installing Windows NT Workstation 4

In most cases, there are no problems involved with the installation of Windows NT Workstation 4. Basically, you choose a system or components that are on the hardware compatibility list (HCL), boot to the installation diskettes (or CD-ROM if the system BIOS supports it), and install from the Windows NT CD. Several factors, however, need to be considered in the process.

Make sure that you are fully prepared with an installation plan and have the appropriate equipment. Decide on the type of installation you want to perform (for example, local, via a network share, via disk replication, or other form of preinstallation) and then proceed with the installation. This appendix discusses each of these methods, beginning with an explanation of the specific changes in terms of NT installation from version 3.51.

Understanding the Specific Changes in Windows NT Workstation 4

Certain changes and requirements have been made to the installation process in Windows NT Workstation 4. These changes have made the installation different from previous versions and in some regards make the installation amenable to scripting control, but in other regards, make the process more rigid. Understanding the changes will simplify things significantly by eliminating problems before they occur, or at least helping you to understand what must occur.

Mandatory Installation Factors

In the newest revision of Windows NT Workstation 4, Microsoft included some rather stringent requirements for the installation process. These requirements include the following:

- Each user must see and agree to the End User License Agreement (EULA).
- Each user must see the Product Identification screen.
- Each user must see and fill in the Username/Company name screens.

Obviously, the preceding issues do not matter much to the user who buys a machine and a copy of Windows NT Workstation 4 and installs the copy onto the machine. It does make a difference to the IS manager who must install 1,000 workstations running Windows NT Workstation 4 or to a vendor who preinstalls it on a system that you purchase. Without understanding these issues, you might be surprised when you purchase a machine or get one from the IS department. When you boot the machine, for example, you find that the installation is not finished.

CD-ROM/Network Share Access

According to Microsoft, you must have access to either a CD-ROM or a network share of the necessary installation files to install Windows NT Workstation 4. In most cases, you need access to the I386 directory on the CD. Surprisingly, you can also install Windows NT Workstation 4 by using a disk replication method. This latter approach is clearly directed toward the mass distribution markets whether OEM based or internal preinstallation.

Floppy Support

Windows NT comes in a box that contains three boot floppies and a CD-ROM. The disks are all 3.5-inch ones and, if you use them, the 3.5-inch floppy must be the boot drive. The 5.25-inch floppy is no longer supported directly. It is possible to boot to a 5.25-inch floppy, gain access to a network share, and then install NT Workstation 4. This is clearly not a preferred way to install the product.

Processor/RAM Recommendations

Beginning with Windows NT Workstation 4, the 386 processor is no longer supported. This of course implies that the 486 or higher CPU is required. In reality, Windows NT installs and runs best on Pentium (or higher) processors. The minimum RAM amount that NT demands is 12 MB (16 MB on RISC machines). Although such machines are perfectly capable of running NT, a more realistic starting point is 16 MB, although 24 MB is far preferable. For serious use of NT, a Pentium Pro or comparable RISC processor is recommended. An excellent starting place for a workstation should be a Pentium 100 with 32 MB of RAM. The high-end workstation should be a Pentium Pro (or RISC equivalent) with 32 to 64 MB of RAM. These recommendations are for ideal machines. Obviously, Windows NT runs well with lesser processor/RAM combinations.

Tip Manufacturers other than Intel are producing CPUs that are seen as 386s initially. The logic on the CPU allows that to function at near Pentium speed. These newer processors do not work well with NT, and the manufacturers have done little to solve the problem. Avoid these processors. Likewise, the infamous overdrive CPU might not be such a wise purchase because the cache and RAM might not match the CPU speed.

Legacy Drivers

Although not explicitly stated as unusable, certain cards have been retired to the legacy list. They might or might not work well in Windows NT Workstation 4. Some of the older SCSI and video card drivers have been retired. These are described in the installation guide that comes with Windows NT Workstation 4. For SCSI cards, avoid using the following if possible:

Always IN-2000 (always.sys)

Data Technology Corp. 3290 (dtc329x.sys)

Maynard 16-bit SCSI Adapter (wd33c93.sys)

MediaVision Pro Audio Spectrum-16 (tmv1.sys)

Trantor T-128 (t128.sys)

Trantor T-130B (t13b.sys)

UltraStor 124f EISA Disk Array Controller (ultra124.sys)

Certain video cards have drivers in the drvlib folder. In many cases, these are drivers that Microsoft has not verified and come directly from the video card manufacturer. This requires you to install as VGA and then configure them after NT is installed. These cards include, but are not limited to, the following:

Compaq AVGA graphics adapter

Chips & Technologies graphics adapters

Imagine 128 graphics adapter

Imagine 128 II graphics adapter

NeoMagic graphics adapter

S3 inc. S3ViRGE graphics adapter

Trident series of graphics adapters

Unfortunately, many network cards do not have Windows NT Workstation 4 specific drivers. Surprisingly, such cards as the Intel EtherExpress PRO/10 Adapter (PCI) can be one of these cards. When you install such a card, you face the following message:

```
ANY USE BY YOU OF THE SOFTWARE IS AT YOUR OWN RISK.  THE SOFTWARE IS PROVIDED
FOR USE ONLY WITH MICROSOFT WINDOWS NT 3.XX PRODUCTS AND RELATED APPLICATION
SOFTWARE.  THE SOFTWARE IS PROVIDED FOR USE "AS IS" WITHOUT WARRANTY OF ANY
KIND.  TO THE MAXIMUM EXTENT PERMITTED BY LAW, MICROSOFT AND ITS SUPPLIERS
DISCLAIM ALL WARRANTIES OF ANY KIND, EITHER EXPRESS OR IMPLIED, INCLUDING,
WITHOUT LIMITATION, IMPLIED WARRANTIES OF MERCHANTABILITY AND FITNESS FOR A
PARTICULAR PURPOSE. MICROSOFT IS NOT OBLIGATED TO PROVIDE ANY UPDATES TO THE
SOFTWARE.
```

Certain printers and printer connections require specific sets of instructions. These include the Digital's PrintServer 17, PrintServer 17/600, turbo PrintServer 20 and PrintServer 32 plus printers, and the Lexmark Network Ports and MarkVision. Detailed instructions are in the drvlib folder under the Print folder.

Exploring Some Considerations Before You Install

As stated in Chapter 3, "NT Workstation Hardware Considerations," much of the performance seen in Windows NT is hardware—not software—related. As such, it is essential that you consider certain factors such as bus and drive issues. For more detail on the issues, please refer to Chapter 3.

Buying a New System

The single-most significant issue in installing NT is obtaining hardware that supports Windows NT Workstation 4. Always check out the Hardware Compatibility List (HCL) that ships with Windows NT Workstation 4. This list contains the systems and components that have been tested by Microsoft and shown to support Windows NT Workstation 4. Microsoft states emphatically that you should buy from the HCL. Some systems on the HCL might have components that have changed and in fact Windows NT might not run well on them. Conversely, many systems not on the list function well. Buy from a vendor that understands Windows NT and in fact is willing to preinstall it for you.

Bus Issues

There is no reason not to purchase a PCI system with supporting ISA or EISA slots. Most motherboards seem designed to handle seven cards, either four PCI and three ISA (EISA) or three PCI and four ISA (EISA). Newer boards are showing up with six PCI slots. These boards might be more amenable to your specific requirements.

Knowing Hard Drives

Nearly all users today choose EIDE drives. They are less expensive than SCSI drives and ostensibly easier to use and faster. In reality, the only advantage that EIDE drives have is in price. They are not easier to install nor are they faster. Instead of entering the "what drive do I use" discussion, let us simply define three levels of users:

- **Level 1 users.** NT is used for its stability and capability to run long times without the need to be rebooted. The primary applications used are word processors, spreadsheets, and a moderate use of the Internet. For such users, EIDE is the bus of choice.

- **Level 2 users.** This group uses NT for its stability but also for its preemptive scheduling (multitasking, multithreading). Users in this level use the same type of applications as group 1 but continually run in foreground/background modes. As the applications used get more complex, performance on the system improves with bus master control. This group can function well on either EIDE or SCSI, but the higher end of this group probably functions better using SCSI.
- **Level 3 users.** This group is comprised of the typical power user who desires maximum flexibility in the system. Such flexibility is most pronounced with SCSI devices. It is not uncommon for such a user to have two SCSI cards and combinations of drives, CD-ROMs, tape backup devices such as DAT drives, and even a scanner. These devices are easy to set up on a SCSI bus and work well.

Understanding the Types of Installations

There are two types of installations to consider. The first is a simple installation by an end-user, and the second is the large scale roll-out of Windows NT by an IS team. The rules are markedly different even though the outcome is the same. Let's start by considering the actual steps involved in the installation process.

Understanding the Installation Process

The installation process has two discrete phases. The first phase (or *text phase*) is comprised of hardware detection and the copying of all essential files to a hard drive. If you use the setup disks, all detection of hardware is accomplished by the files on the floppies. Following the detection, all necessary files are copied to the local hard drive into the WIN_NT.~LT temporary directory. The system then reboots into the GUI or NT based portion of the installation.

If you use the non-floppy based installation or upgrade, two directories or folders are created. The first is Win_NT.~BT and contains the essential files to boot into Windows NT. These files include SCSI drivers, NTLDR, and NTDETECT.COM as well as the kernel files. The second directory is labeled Win_NT.~LS and is the same as the one created with setup disks. This directory has all the necessary files for booting into the installation of Windows NT Workstation 4, namely the following:

- ABIOSDSK.SYS (reads the BIOS including IRQ and partition tables)
- AHA154X.SYS (Adaptec AHA-154X/AHA-164X SCSI Host Adapter)
- AHA174X.SYS (Adaptec AHA-174X EISA SCSI Host Adapter)

- AIC78XX.SYS (Adaptec AHA-294X/AHA-394X/AIC-78XX SCSI Controller)
- AMI0NT.SYS (AMIscsi SCSI Host Adapter)
- AMSINT.SYS (AMD PCI SCSI Controller/Ethernet Adapter)
- ARROW.SYS (Adaptec AHA-274X/AHA-284X/AIC-777X SCSI Adapter)
- ATAPI.SYS (IDE CD-ROM (ATAPI 1.2)/PCI IDE Controller)
- ATDISK.SYS (although not used in 4, atdisk is used in setup)
- BOOTSECT.DAT (boot sector information)
- BUSLOGIC.SYS (BusLogic SCSI Host Adapter)
- C_1252.NLS (used by setupldr when starting text setup)
- C-437.NLS (used by setupldr when starting text setup)
- CDFS.SYS (for CD-ROM files)
- CDROM.SYS (driver for CD-ROMs)
- CLASS2.SYS (SCSI class system driver)
- CPQARRAY.SYS (Compaq Drive Array)
- CPQFWS2E.SYS (Compaq 32-Bit Fast-Wide SCSI-2/E)
- DAC960NT.SYS (Mylex DAC960/Digital SWXCR-Ex Raid Controller)
- DELLDSA.SYS (Dell Drive Array)
- DISK.SYS (SCSI disk driver)
- DISK101 (disk label)
- DISK102 (disk label)
- DISK103 (disk label)
- DPTSCSI.SYS (DPT SCSI Host Adapter)
- FD16_700.SYS (Adaptec 2920/2905 / Future Domain 16XX/PCI/SCSI2Go)
- FD7000EX.SYS (Future Domain TMC-7000EX EISA SCSI Host Adapter)
- FD8XX.SYS (Future Domain 8XX SCSI Host Adapter)

- FLASHPNT.SYS (BusLogic FlashPoint)
- FLOPPY.SYS (floppy driver)
- HAL486.DLL (standard hardware abstraction layer)
- HALAPIC.DLL (multiprocessor hardware abstraction layer)
- HALMCA.DLL (microchannel hardware abstraction layer)
- HALNCR.SYS (specific hardware layer for NCR machines)
- I8042PRT.SYS (keyboard port driver)
- KBCLASS.SYS (keyboard class driver)
- KBDUS.DLL (keyboard layout)
- L_INTL.NLS (used by setupldr when starting text setup)
- MITSUMI.SYS (Mitsumi CD-ROM Controller)
- MKECR5XX.SYS (MKEPanasonic CD-ROM Controller)
- NCR53C9X.SYS (NCR 53C9X SCSI Host Adapter)
- NCRC700.SYS (NCR C700 SCSI Host Adapter)
- NCRC710.SYS (NCR 53C710 SCSI Host Adapter)
- NTDETECT.COM (application that finds hardware)
- NTFS.SYS (ntfs driver)
- NTKRNLMP.EXE (multiprocessor kernel)
- NTLDR (controller of the boot)
- OLISCSI.SYS (Olivetti ESC-1/ESC-2 SCSI Host Adapter)
- PCMCIA.SYS (Pcmcia services)
- QL10WNT.SYS (QLogic PCI SCSI Host Adapter)
- SCSIPORT.SYS (scsi port driver (low level))
- SETUPDD.SYS (kernel mode portion of text setup)
- SETUPLDR.BIN (setup loader for installation)

- SETUPREG.HIV (control set information)
- SFLOPPY.SYS (SCSI floppy driver)
- SLCD32.SYS (Sony Proprietary CD-ROM Controller)
- SPARROW.SYS (Adaptec AHA-151X/AHA-152X/AIC-6X60 SCSI Adapter)
- SPOCK.SYS (IBM MCA SCSI Host Adapter)
- SYMC810.SYS (Symbios Logic C810 PCI SCSI Host Adapter (formally NCR))
- TXTSETUP.SIF (basic setup file and can be edited)
- ULTRA14F.SYS (UltraStor 14F/14FB/34F/34FA/34FB SCSI Host Adapter)
- ULTRA24F.SYS (UltraStor 24F/24FA SCSI Host Adapter)
- VGA.SYS (supervga/vga driver)
- VGAOEM.FON (vga terminal font)
- VIDEOPORT.SYS (video port driver)
- WINNT.SIF (specific setup information for the installation)
- files in the system32 folder
- NTDLL.DLL (NT layer DLL)
- SMSS.EXE (User mode portion of text setup)

With the preceding files, a limited version of Windows NT is loaded into memory. Memory loading is used to facilitate the use of the multithreaded setup program. For Intel based machines, NTDETECT.COM then detects specific pieces of hardware. In particular, the following are detected:

- Bus/adapter
- Communication ports
- Floppy drive
- Floating point coprocessor
- Keyboard
- Mouse

- Parallel ports
- SCSI adapters
- Video card
- A mass storage device (CD-ROM)

This first phase is usually called the DOS portion of the install. As such, proprietary schemes for hard drive partitions typically are accepted. Likewise during this phase, nearly all CD-ROMs are seen and usable. This in no way dictates what will be seen in the second phase of the installation. This distinction is important because it allows Windows NT to be installed in part on hardware that is not fully supported in Windows NT. After phase one is finished, the system reboots into phase two.

It is possible to change drivers between the phases. If you have a specialized or newer driver for a controller, you can copy the new drivers over the default drivers in the temporary directories (assuming that the folders are FAT). Although seemingly not important, this changing of drivers in Windows NT 3.51 was necessary when the Ultra Controllers were released by Adaptec.

Phase two is the beginning of the specific Windows NT installation. For this process, controllers are identified, drives located, and previous versions of Windows (and Windows NT) found. You are asked if this is a new installation or an upgrade; the drives are searched for defects; and you agree to a license statement (mandatory). The following are essential for you to continue:

- **Hardware that supports Windows NT.** If the drives and partitions are not compliant, the installation process quits with an error message similar to "the installation process cannot continue because the drives are inaccessible."
- **Sufficient space for the installation.** Although an installation of Windows NT Workstation takes about 108 MB of free space, have at least 125 MB (150 for RISC) available to be on the safe side.
- **Your preparation list.** This list, in providing necessary settings, will allow you to proceed with all aspects of the installation.

The system reboots a second time and then takes you into the final aspect of the installation—the *setup phase,* which is under the control of setup wizards. Here, all you need to do is establish simple checks for the installation to finish. This is covered in the actual installation section.

Understanding the End-User Installation Process

The end-user installation is by far the most straightforward of all installations. No specific intervention needs to be done by anyone but the end-user. One step, however, is very important—the preparation of a checklist of hardware components and settings.

The first and most critical step is compiling a checklist of all the hardware components that will be used. This list will aid you dramatically in the installation and also forms a basis for support if an issue arises. This list will be your hardware bible for installation and support. In short, this list is a means to keep all your essential data for the installation (and keep it in order). If you lose the list, all is not lost; but all becomes very inconvenient.

This checklist provides you the necessary hardware information to complete the installation. Of particular note will be a list of cards, I/Os, DMA (if necessary), and IRQs.

If you have trouble determining the system resources on your computer, use the Microsoft utility on the CD-ROM. It is used by running the MAKEDISK.BAT file in \support\hqtool directory on the CD. This batch file will make a DOS boot disk and application that surveys the system resources. Be aware that the application does have some serious limitations. First of all, it does not register memory above 64 MB of RAM. Second, it might not recognize new devices that are fully supported in Windows NT (for example, an Adaptec 3940uw SCSI controller).

The following facts (and reasons) should be placed on the list:

- **Motherboard information.** Some installation problems exist with specific motherboards or motherboard firmware. Having this information is valuable in obtaining technical support if necessary.
- **Card information.** Knowing what IRQ or I/O or DMA you need to assign for the installation is mandatory. For example, if you are using a Digiboard ISA serial card, you need to know what I/Os are available and not assigned to another card. Many cards have diagnostic applications that can be run from a DOS boot floppy.

If you are using EIDE, make sure that you have enabled LBA 9Logical Block Address) prior to doing an Fdisk or Format. Do not have the system do an automatic detection of the drives at post. Instead, do a detection of the drives and have the detected drive parameters written to BIOS. If you are using SCSI hard drives, make sure that all fast access to the hard drives is turned off.

Registering Peripheral Cards

Table A.1 is designed to help you record all the necessary information being discussed. It might seem somewhat superfluous to fill out such a list but using the 5 to 10 minutes to do this is well worth the effort.

Table A.1
Information to Keep Handy During Installation.

Card	Revision	I/O	IRQ	DMA	On HCL*
Video		n/a	n/a	n/a	
Network					
Sound					
SCSI					
Misc					

*HCL means hardware compatibility list—devices and cards that have been tested by Microsoft and are still available in the Microsoft Test labs for debugging and assistance with their use.

After the lists are finished, there is one additional step—make sure that all cards are properly configured for Windows NT and that all necessary drivers are available for the installation.

Configuring the Peripheral Cards

The peripheral cards (controllers) have to be configured in your Windows NT system. You will need to assign proper values to many components, particularly if you use ISA cards. In general, this configuration is straightforward, but some specific issues can be a problem.

The Video Card

Assuming that the video card you are using has drivers on the installation CD in the I386 directory (or appropriate RISC directory), there is little to be concerned about. If you are using specialized video cards, you should install as VGA and then add the appropriate video driver after NT has been installed and running. With some high-end cards, you might even need to install a daughter VGA card. The latter is true for high-end CAD/CAM boards. If this is the case, be sure to obtain the proper drivers for the high-end card and also detailed installation instructions. Because the GDI has been moved to Ring 0 (the kernel), the driver *must* be specific for Windows NT version 4. Previous drivers will not work.

The Network Card

If the network card parameters are set in software (for example, newer NE2000 clones), install the card in the system, boot to a DOS floppy, and run the manufacturer's setup utility. Add the values you set to table A.1. You can use IRQ5 and I/O 300 or 340 for the card. (Be careful of conflicts with sound cards!) If there are any potential problems with the network card, do not install the card with the initial configuration of NT but add it later. Some cards simply do not work properly with autodetection (they return a null string, and the installation hangs) but can easily be installed at a later date.

The SCSI Card

If the card is a local bus card, preferably PCI, there is usually little to worry about. One potential problem might lie with IRQ 9, which is the original rollover IRQ from IRQ2. Most new motherboards allow the use of IRQ9, but it can fail particularly with a busmastering SCSI card. If the BIOS supports it, make IRQ9 an ISA IRQ. You also need to know the order of detection of the SCSI cards if you use more than one. Most motherboards read from the edge of the motherboard first, whereas others read from the non-PCI bus. Find out this information before you attempt an installation.

If the SCSI card is ISA, be sure to record the IRQ (usually 11) and I/O of the card. Determine whether the card is a busmaster card and plan the setup accordingly. If the card is a busmaster, be sure that the motherboard supports more than 16 MB of RAM (a serious issue with many older, inexpensive clones). If the manufacturer is not sure of this issue, get another motherboard.

If you are going to be adding other cards and devices such as Wacom tablets or UPS interfaces, do not attempt to install these on installation. In fact if they are installed, uninstall them prior to doing an upgrade. Keep everything as simple as possible.

The Network Protocols

There is one last essential task. If you are joining a domain, determine all mandated aspects of the installation. If you need to install a specialized network protocol such as TCP/IP, for example, find out how the network handles name resolution (for instance, WINS and/or DHCP). Setting everything up properly to begin with solves many later problems. Always remember that what you can do on a domain is determined by the network administrator. On the other hand, what you do on a local boot is determined by you. These two views of Windows NT might be markedly different.

Making Last-Minute Preparations for the Installation

First, remove unwanted applications and load/run statements. Specifically, the following should be done:

- If you are running the win95 shell on 3.51, it must be uninstalled. To accomplish this, run the command **\newshell\I386\shupdate.cmd /u** from the Intel folder for the shell update. (Obviously, if an Alpha, run the shupdate.cmd /u from the Alpha folder.)
- If you are running any of the remote control applications such as Remotely Possible 32 or PCAnywhere32, remove them prior to the installation. They can be reinstalled after Windows NT is running and is stable.
- If you are using a UPS, remove it prior to the installation. Although most systems do in fact upgrade without difficulty, many have had problems with the COM ports that have the UPS installed. Once running and stable, the UPS (including vendor applications) can be reinstalled.
- HPFS (High Performance File System) is no longer directly supported during installation. Data must be backed up and the drive reformatted as FAT or the files copied to a FAT drive and the partition reformatted as FAT.

After these tasks are completed, you're ready to begin.

Understanding the Large-Scale Rollout

Installation rules are the same for large scale or end-user installation. The only differences are concerned with unattended installations. In a mass scale installation, there are three types of configurations: installation via a network share, installation via disk replication, or installation via stand-alone approaches. The latter is exactly the same as the end-user installation. The first two approaches are be dealt with at the end of this appendix.

Performing a New Installation

As stated earlier, installation has two basic phases. The first phase sometimes called the DOS or text phase, copies all the essential files and/or boot components to the local hard drive. The second phase is the initiation and actual installation of a bootable Windows NT system. This component is generally called the GUI phase or more specifically, the NT phase.

Phase 1 of Installation

By far, the most straightforward approach to a new installation is to use the three installation floppies that ship with Windows NT Workstation 4. These floppies contain the necessary files to enable you to gain access to the CD-ROM attached to your computer and automatically have the essential setup files copied to your local hard drive. In the event that you do not have the three installation floppies or you need access to a network share, you must use alternative methods, which are detailed at the end of this section.

Installation Disk 1

Place the setup disk in the computer and turn on the computer. This first disk is the system boot disk, and it loads files that inspect the computer hardware and then loads the Windows NT executive and the Hardware Abstraction Layer (HAL). These files are the key files in Windows NT. Disk 1 contains the following files:

- **DISK101.** The disk label.
- **HA486C.DLL.** The standard HAL.
- **HALAPIC.DLL.** The HAL for Intel Symmetrical processing motherboards.
- **HALMCA.DLL.** The HAL for Microchannel machines.
- **NTDETECT.COM.** The program that detects hardware and records this hardware in the Registry.
- **NTKRNLMP.EXE.** The NT kernel and specifically for multiprocessor motherboards. When NT starts loading, the multiprocessor kernel loads and is displayed on the top of the screen. In Windows NT, this is named the

NTOSKRNL.EXE. This file extracts the necessary boot information from the Registry. (The Registry is the central storage for all Windows NT information—see the appropriate chapter of this book.)

- **SETUPLDR.BIN.** This file functions as the NTLOADER file for the installation procedure. In the finished installation of Windows NT, SETUPLDR is analogous to the NTLDR (NT loader) file.
- **TXTSETUP.SIF.** Dictates the specific files to be copied during setup and the basic modifications to be made to the Registry during the installation. This file is long but informative if you want to examine it in Notepad or other text editor. The first part of Windows NT Workstation 4 TXTSETUP.SIF is as follows:

```
[Version]
signature="$Windows NT$"
ClassGUID={00000000-0000-0000-0000-000000000000}

;
; diskid = description,tagfile,unused,subdir
;
[SourceDisksNames]
_x = %wkscd%,\cdrom_w.40,,""
_1 = %wkscd%,\cdrom_w.40,,""
_2 = %wkscd%,\cdrom_w.40,,""
_3 = %wkscd%,\cdrom_w.40,,""

[SourceDisksNames.alpha]
1 = %wkscd%,\cdrom_w.40,,\alpha

[SourceDisksNames.mips]
1 = %wkscd%,\cdrom_w.40,,\mips

[SourceDisksNames.ppc]
1 = %wkscd%,\cdrom_w.40,,\ppc

[SourceDisksNames.x86]
1 = %wkscd%,\cdrom_w.40,,\i386
_1 = %wks1%,\disk101,,""
_2 = %wks2%,\disk102,,""
_3 = %wks3%,\disk103,,""

;
; These sections are used during text-mode setup and correspond
; to the targetdirectory field in the [SourceDisksFiles] section.
;
```

```
[WinntDirectories]
1  = "\"
2  = system32
3  = system32\config
4  = system32\drivers
5  = system
6  = system32\os2
7  = system32\ras
8  = system32\os2\dll
9  = system32\spool
10 = system32\spool\drivers
11 = system32\spool\drivers\w32x86\2
12 = system32\spool\prtprocs
13 = system32\spool\prtprocs\w32x86
14 = system32\wins
15 = system32\dhcp
16 = repair
17 = system32\drivers\etc
18 = system32\spool\drivers\w32x86
19 = system32\viewers
20 = inf
21 = Help
22 = Fonts
23 = Config
24 = Profiles
25 = Cursors
26 = Media
```

In contrast, the server version is nearly the same with only the source of files and name of installation being different.

```
 [Version]
signature="$Windows NT$"
ClassGUID={00000000-0000-0000-0000-000000000000}

;
; diskid = description,tagfile,unused,subdir
;
[SourceDisksNames]
_x = %srvcd%,\cdrom_s.40,,""
_1 = %srvcd%,\cdrom_s.40,,""
_2 = %srvcd%,\cdrom_s.40,,""
_3 = %srvcd%,\cdrom_s.40,,""
```

```
[SourceDisksNames.alpha]
1 = %srvcd%,\cdrom_s.40,,\alpha

[SourceDisksNames.mips]
1 = %srvcd%,\cdrom_s.40,,\mips

[SourceDisksNames.ppc]
1 = %srvcd%,\cdrom_s.40,,\ppc

[SourceDisksNames.x86]
1 = %srvcd%,\cdrom_s.40,,\i386
_1 = %srv1%,\disk101,,""
_2 = %srv2%,\disk102,,""
_3 = %srv3%,\disk103,,""
```

When asked by the installation to insert disk 2, do so and press Enter. From this point on, the installation process will queue you as to the next step.

Installation Disk 2

Disk 2 loads all the necessary files to get you into the true installation procedure. These steps might seem somewhat tedious, but each is an essential component, and each can cause an installation problem. The following files are loaded:

- NT configuration data
- Setup fonts
- Local-specific data
- Windows setup
- PCMCIA (PC-card) support
- SCSI port driver
- Video driver
- Floppy disk driver
- Keyboard driver
- FAT (File Allocation Table) file system

When these files are loaded, the system presents you with the blue screen that lists the amount of memory and multiprocessor kernel. Setup then processes setup information and loads the keyboard layout. After this, you are presented with the Welcome to

Setup Screen, which gives you four options:

- Press F1 to learn more about NT.
- To set up now, press Enter.
- To perform a repair, press R. (This step is very important, be sure to remember it.)
- To quit, press F3.

For present purposes, simply press the Enter key. You are then asked if you want Setup to detect the controller card(s) for your CD-ROM and hard drives. Have the installation detect the cards. For primary hard drive controllers, you do not want to have to install specialized drivers. Simply press enter to continue. You are asked to insert disk 3.

Installation Disk 3

Disk 3 loads the specific drivers needed to gain access to the hard drives and CD-ROMs. The specific files loaded or searched for are the sys drivers loaded onto the hard drive when the /b option is used. After devices are searched for, Setup loads support for ESDI and IDE drives and then NTFS (NT File System). At this point, if a CD-ROM has not been detected, the installation is aborted. If the installation has been successful to this point, the drivers necessary to gain access to the CD-ROM are loaded. You are then presented with the Windows NT Licensing Agreement [EULA]. As stated earlier, this step is mandatory. You must scroll through the agreement. Read it carefully. When you have reached the end of the agreement, press F8.

Note The three setup floppies contain the exact same files as those found in the WIN_NT.~BT directory. The only difference between the standard installation with floppies and the /b options is the latter copying boot files to the hard drive.

After accepting the terms of the EULA, Setup searches for previous versions of NT to upgrade. If none are found, you choose the drive and partition. If no partitions are found, you can then make partitions and format them. Assuming that the drive is already formatted, you are presented with a description of the drives seen along with their respective formats. At this point, you can choose to maintain the format or change the format to another file system (FAT to NTFS or NTFS to FAT). If partitions are found, you are presented with the alternatives of an exhaustive search of the hard drives or skipping the search. By all means, conduct the search.

On some larger notebook drives, Setup cannot partition or format the hard drive. Boot to a DOS floppy, run FDISK and Format, and then the setup will run perfectly. You will even be able to convert the format to NTFS if you want.

Following the search, specific files are prepared for installation, and the files are copied from the CD-ROM. These files are copied to the temporary directories listed previously (WIN_NT.~LS). Finally, the basic configuration is saved (actually the default configuration), and you press Enter to reboot the computer (making sure to remove any floppy disk in the 3.5-inch drive). The system then boots into Windows NT setup (phase 2 of the installation).

If you have a system that enables you to boot to a CD-ROM (for example, the SuperMicro Dual Pentium Pro motherboards support it), make sure to enter BIOS and disable this option before continuing. Although convenient to use in installation, if you do not disable the function in BIOS, you will be forced to remove the CD and reboot if the CD has been left in.

Phase 2 of the Installation

When the system reboots, you enter the wizard controlled portion of the installation. The following list shows the wizards that are encountered in order of appearance:

1. The first wizard you encounter simply collects information about the system. The next one presents you with the following install options:

   - **Typical.** The default.
   - **Portable.** Optimized for notebooks.
   - **Compact.** Minimal installation.
   - **Custom.** For advanced users, but the one that should be picked by default.

2. When you choose the option (Custom is highly recommended) and press Next, you see the Name wizard.

   Enter the appropriate name and organization for the installation. Pressing Next brings up the Enter the Key wizard.

   It is important that you save the CD case because it has the installation key on it.

3. Enter the proper key or the installation will not continue. This brings you to the Computer Name wizard.

4. Although seemingly trivial, if you are on a network, you need a unique computer name (one that is not being used; you might need to obtain a name from the IS department). This brings you to the most important aspect of Windows NT—security.

5. The initial security of Windows NT is established by the Administrator Password wizard. Of utmost importance is the assignment of a password for the Administrator account. Choose a seven-character password that has at least one nonsense character in it. Remember, passwords are case sensitive. For example, *bob* is a poor choice for a password. The password *$%bob&c** is difficult to crack but relatively easy to remember. *Do not lose the password!*

6. The next wizard asks if you want to make an emergency repair disk (ERD). By all means do so.

Tip You can, in fact, do a repair without an ERD. However, having one can help repair a system that has been seriously damaged to the point that the installation applications cannot find it. Always make ERDs and remember, the Rdisk (rdisk /s is the best approach) utility in the system32 folder will update the configuration and generate a new ERD. When any major change is made to the system, make a new ERD.

7. Assuming that you have chosen Custom, you are then presented the standard installation options. If an option is gray, this means that not all will be installed. For example, the accessories will be grayed out. Looking at the detail shows that the optional mouse pointers are not installed. If you want to use these options, click on them to put an *x* in the installation option.

8. The next few steps are critical to setting up Windows NT. They have to do with setting up network parameters. You are faced with several choices. The first choice is the easiest—namely, a stand-alone machine. Windows NT really functions best with a network card installed. There is an easy solution. Install the Msloopback adapter (do it after the initial installation). This adapter is a software emulation of an adapter. Simply choose the default values. The second choice is also easy; you choose not to set up the network now but will do so later. This option is clearly the safest. Finally, if you have a network interface card (NIC) that you know works well in NT and there are no problems with it during installation, install it now. By all means, choose this and set up the necessary protocols. (See the discussion on networks for the implementation of the protocol stacks.)

The Network wizard offers you four choices:

- Do not connect this computer to the network at this time
- This computer will participate on a network (the default)
- Wired directly
- Remote access

For present purposes, choose Do Not Connect the Computer to the Network at This Time. The remaining wizards will finish the installation.

9. You will need to set the time and date. The default is Greenwich Time, but you can choose the time zone you want.

10. The final choice you have is selecting video resolution. The installation defaults to VGA and with small fonts. If you want, you can change the resolution at this time; but you can change this dynamically in Windows NT Workstation 4 so it is optional.

11. The installation finishes by copying files and finally setting security and asking you to supply a blank formatted 3.5-inch floppy to make the emergency repair disk. If the system has been formatted as NTFS, security will finally be set.

Caution You can set the format as NTFS during installation. It is sometimes preferable to install as FAT and then convert to NTFS later by running the convert utility at the command prompt. To determine the appropriate parameters, type at the command prompt **command /?**. And then press Enter.

Installing Without the Installation Floppy Disks and No Direct CD-ROM

To install without installation floppies, you need access to a local CD-ROM, to specific distribution files on the CD copied to your local hard drive, or to a network distribution share or installation CD. For this example, you will set up Windows NT Workstation 4 onto a new system that does not have direct access to a CD-ROM. Although seemingly a difficult task, the installation is actually simple. Boot to a DOS floppy that has FDISK.EXE and FORMAT.COM on it. Run FDISK and partition the drive as appropriate. After this, the system reboots. Format the drive(s) with FORMAT.COM. This makes all drives FAT but as explained earlier, FAT can be converted to NTFS if you want.

To make the necessary boot disk, you need access to an Windows NT Workstation 4 server that has been set up for client software installation (for example, Windows 95). In addition, there has to be a system on the network that has the Windows NT Workstation 4 CD in a CD-ROM that has been shared to everyone.

On the NT Server, from the Start menu, choose Programs, Administrator Tools, and Network Client Administrator and make an installation disk(see fig. A.1). For simplicity's sake, choose Windows 95. Place a bootable floppy (3.5-inch) in the 3.5-inch floppy drive. Assuming that the network supports NetBEUI, choose this as your network protocol because it is the easiest to set up. Files are then copied to the floppy. In this case, the network adapter chosen was the 3Com Etherlink lll. After you have set all the parameters, you are presented with a standard acceptance screen (see fig. A.2).

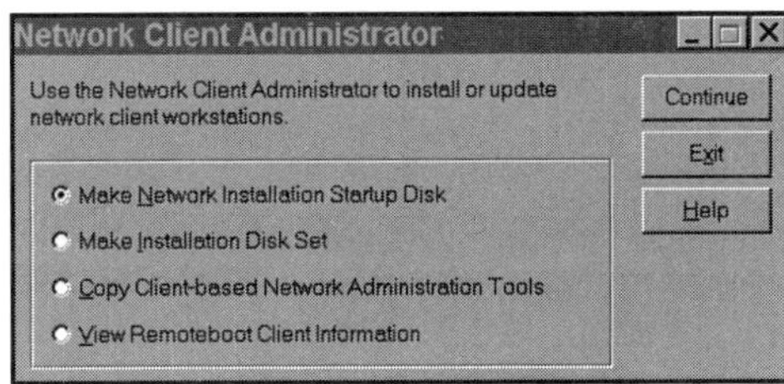

Figure A.1

The Network Client Administrator has Make Network Installation Startup Disk checked here.

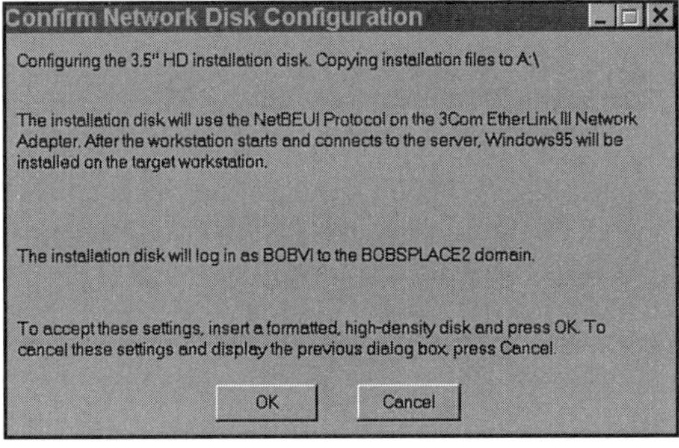

Figure A.2

This notification window, seen in Network Client Administrator, appears prior to copying files to the disk.

After the files are copied, the floppy has the following standard files on it:

- AUTOEXEC.BAT
- COMMAND.COM
- CONFIG.SYS

In addition, there will be a subdirectory called NET. This subdirectory contains the following files:

- ◆ EMM386.EXE
- ◆ HIMEM.SYS
- ◆ IFSHLP.SYS
- ◆ NDISHLP.SYS
- ◆ NET.EXE
- ◆ NETH.MSG
- ◆ ELNK3.DOS ;(3Com driver)
- ◆ PROTMAN.DOS
- ◆ PROTMAN.EXE
- ◆ protocol.ini
- ◆ SETUP.INF
- ◆ SHARES.PWL
- ◆ SYSTEM.INI
- ◆ WCSETUP.INF
- ◆ WFWSYS.CFG

All that has to be done is to edit the AUTOEXEC.BAT so that installation CD becomes a mapped drive. Here is the default AUTOEXEC.BAT for a server named BIGCLYDE and a shared client directory called Clients:

```
path=a:\net
a:\net\net start
net use z: \\BIGCLYDE\Clients
echo Running Setup...
z:\win95\netsetup\setup.exe
Here is the autoexec.bat that is needed:
path=a:\net
a:\net\net start
net use Z: \\BIGCLYDE\SHARE_CD
Z:\
cd I386
winnt /b
```

In the changed AUTOEXEC.BAT, the system boots into the network. The user and password (added by the Network Client Administrator wizard when you supplied the proper information) are passed to the network and verified (assuming of course that you supplied the proper information). The network shared CD (in this case called SHARE_CD) is shared as the Z drive. This shared drive is then accessed; the I386 subdirectory is accessed; and the WINNT.EXE file is executed with the /b switch.

Alternatively, you can simply copy the I386 directory to your local drive and run the winnt /b from the local hard drive.

There are two means of installing Windows NT Workstation 4 from the I386 directory. These are based upon the WINNT.EXE file for DOS and the WINNT32.EXE file for existing NT installations. Various switches can be used with these files. Without any switch, the installation makes boot floppies and no WIN_NT.~BT temporary directory. This is unnecessary. Ideally, you would use the /b switch, which causes a temporary boot directory to be installed, the WIN_NT.~BT directory. This floppyless installation is the fastest and easiest.

If the system is configured to run NetBEUI, the appropriate section of PROTOCOL.INI is as follows:

```
[ms$netbeui]
drivername=netbeui$
SESSIONS=10
NCBS=12
BINDINGS=ms$elnk
LANABASE=0
```

If the system is configured to run TCP/IP, the appropriate section of PROTOCOL.INI is as follows (note that DCHP was not used and a static IP address supplied):

```
[tcpip]
NBSessions=6
DefaultGateway0=
SubNetMask0=255 255 255 0
IPAddress0=199 34 56 30
DisableDHCP=1
DriverName=TCPIP$
BINDINGS=ms$elnk3
LANABASE=0
```

If the system is configured to run IPX (NWLink IPX Compatible Protocol), the appropriate section of PROTOCOL.INI is as follows:

```
[ms$nwlink]
drivername=nwlink$
FRAME=Ethernet_802.2
BINDINGS=ms$elnk16
LANABASE=0
```

Make sure that 802.2 is the appropriate frame type for the network. Older installations might be using 802.3.

When the first part of the installation starts, files are copied from the CD to your local hard drive. As explained earlier, two temporary directories are formed—one for booting the system and one for the installation files. After the files are copied, you are asked to reboot the system. Do so. From this point on, the installation is identical to that discussed earlier.

The first part seen is the inspection of hardware. After this comes the Welcome to Setup screen, devices are found, and you are presented with the license agreement. You then choose the installation directory, and an exhaustive search of the hard drive ensues. Files are copied to the designated target and a default configuration saved. The system then has to be rebooted by pressing Enter (make sure that the floppy has been removed).

Following the reboot, you see the blue screen with the information about the system displayed at the top of the screen. From this point on, you are in phase 2 of the installation, and all is identical to that described earlier.

In this example, Windows NT Workstation 4 has been installed on a system and one that does not have an attached CD-ROM. Obviously, the same approach can be taken with any new workstation (including notebooks) that has been attached to the network but not configured as a network PC as yet. Remember, you need an installation sheet to have all the necessary information when the installation disk is made. Likewise, you need the cooperation of the network administrator.

If the system will be a dual system—that is, boots NT and WFWG for example—you can join the network and simply copy the I386 directory to your local hard drive. Run winnt /b from the hard drive directory and simply state that you are going to install to a new directory rather than an existing one.

Installing Without the Installation Floppy Disks but with an Attached CD-ROM

This installation is very easy. Simply make a DOS boot diskette that can gain access to the system CD-ROM. In most cases, this is a standard boot floppy that loads a driver to mount the CD-ROM. The following AUTOEXEC.BAT and CONFIG.SYS will boot and connect to either a SCSI CD-ROM attached to a 2940/3940 or a Mitsumi 4x CD-ROM.

Config.sys

```
DEVICE=A:\HIMEM.SYS /TESTMEM:OFF /V
DEVICE=A:\EMM386.EXE NOEMS
BUFFERS=40,0
FILES=70
DOS=UMB
LASTDRIVE=z
FCBS=4,0
SHELL=COMMAND.COM /E:4096 /p
DOS=HIGH
STACKS=9,256
DEVICE=A:\aspi8dos.sys /d
DEVICE=A:\ASPIDISK.SYS /D
DEVICE=A:\ASPICD.SYS /D:ASPICD0
DEVICE=A:\MTMCDAI.SYS /D:MTMIDE01
```

Autoexec.bat

```
ECHO OFF
Prompt $p$g
LH A:\MSCDEX.EXE /D:MTMIDE01 /D:ASPICD0 /M:12
LH A:\smartdrv.exe 4098 4098
```

Simply copy the AUTOEXEC.BAT and CONFIG.SYS and appropriate referenced files to a DOS boot floppy. Boot the system, and you can gain access to the CD-ROM. Change to the I386 directory and run winnt /ox to create installation boot floppies or winnt /b to copy boot files and installation files to the local hard drive.

Note Throughout this chapter, reference has been made to the switches used in winnt or winnt32. The following are most of the switches that are used:

winnt32 [/s:sourcepath] [/i:inf_file] [/t:drive_letter] [/x] [/b] [/ox] [/u[:script] [/r:directory] [/e:command]

Parameters used include the following:

- **/s:sourcepath.** Specifies the location of the Windows NT files.
- **/i:inf_file.** Specifies the file name (no path) of the setup information file. The default is DOSNET.INF.
- **/t:drive_letter.** Forces Setup to place temporary files on the specified drive.
- **/x.** Prevents Setup from creating Setup boot floppies. Use this when you already have Setup boot floppies (from your administrator, for example).
- **/b.** Causes the boot files to be loaded on the system's hard drive rather than on floppy disks, so that floppy disks do not need to be loaded or removed by the user.
- **/ox.** Specifies that Setup create boot floppies for CD-ROM installation.
- **/u.** Upgrades your previous version of Windows NT in unattended mode. All user settings are taken from the previous installation, requiring no user intervention during Setup.
- **/u:script.** Similar to previous, but provides a script file for user settings instead of using the settings from the previous installation.
- **/r:directory.** Installs an additional directory within the directory tree where the Windows NT files are installed. Use additional /r switches to install additional directories.
- **/e:command.** Instructs Setup to execute a specific command after installation is complete.

Performing an Upgrade Installation

Upgrades are in fact the easiest of all installations, at least on the surface. In reality, all the possible mistakes of the previous version are carried over to the new installation. Currently, you can only upgrade Windows NT, Windows for Workgroups, Windows 3.1, and DOS while maintaining your current settings. This section deals with the issues of each possible upgrade. The basic means of the upgrade are the same as those discussed with new installation—namely a floppyless or a floppy-based installation.

Upgrading Windows 3.1x

This upgrade can be accomplished in two ways. You can do an upgrade into the Windows directory, or you can install NT into a new directory. The latter is preferable, but the former will work well in most cases. Doing an upgrade into the Windows directory results in most configuration information migrating to NT.

Boot into the first Setup disk. You use the same sequence as noted in the preceding installation instructions. When the installation process reaches the point of searching the hard drive for prior versions of Windows NT, the suggestion is made that you install into the Windows 3.1x directory. This then enables you to migrate your applications to NT. The installation proceeds as a new installation with the exception of the migration of applications.

When you boot into NT as a non-Administrator, you are asked if you want to migrate WIN.INI and CONTROL.INI settings as well as groups. This works very well but can result in chaos. Many win3.1 systems have too many settings in the INI files, and some might be incorrect. If you do this type of upgrade, you might have to search the Registry to eliminate improper settings. Do so at the risk of making the machine non-bootable.

Migration Events That Occur During the Upgrade

Migration actually occurs in two stages. First, the system settings migrate and then user settings. The system settings are those found in REG.DAT and sections of WIN.INI concerned with fonts, printers, and so on. The user migration occurs every time a new user logs on to the system.

You can also force a migration. Delete the Windows 3.1 migration status key from the HKEY_CURRENT_USER hive (see fig. A.3). If the user is not the administrator, the next time the user logs on, the migration dialog box appears.

A more appropriate migration is to copy the appropriate sections of the old WIN.INI into the NT WIN.INI. Copy the DLL's from Windows into the winnt\system directory (do not overwrite any files), and copy all necessary INI files. Also copy over all GRP files and REG.DAT. If you delete the Registry key described earlier, the next time you log on you will be given the opportunity to migrate settings. If you only move over the groups and INI files you are concerned with, the migration can be kept very clean.

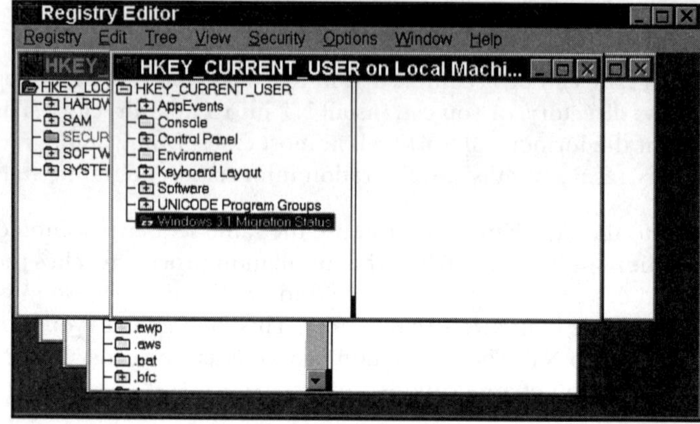

Figure A.3

Deleting the Registry key that controls the migration status of Windows 3.1 brings out the migration dialog box the next time the user logs on.

Upgrading Windows 95

You cannot upgrade (for example, keep the same settings) Windows 95 to Windows NT. By the same token, Microsoft recommends that you do not dual boot Windows NT and Windows 95. In reality, it is easy to dual boot Windows 95 and NT.

Check to see whether all Windows 95 devices and applications are supported by Windows NT Workstation 4. (Microsoft claims that over 1,000 more devices are supported on 95 than on NT.) Simply install Windows NT Workstation 4 into a separate directory from Window 95, creating a dual-boot system. Finally, reinstall all applications in NT. According to Microsoft, not many users are dual booting Windows 95 and NT, but the numbers are rising rapidly.

Upgrading Windows NT

Boot into the installation diskettes or run winnt32 /b. The installation finds the prior version of NT and asks if you want to upgrade. By all means, say yes. This carries over all (or most) of the applications and settings. Specifically, user and group accounts and network settings are brought over, as are applications. Sometimes the upgrade does not work properly. Always have a backup available in case of an upgrade problem.

General Upgrade Cautions

Upgrade issues and problems are most likely to occur when you have made many customizations of the Registry or have serious alterations of the WIN.INI file. There have also been reports of loss of user information. It is always better to be prepared to fix these problems. Make sure that you know all necessary security parameters if user information needs to be repaired. If you have any doubts at all about the upgrade, do a test installation to be certain that Windows NT Workstation 4 will in fact install on your computer. There is no reason for the installation to fail if you have appropriate hardware.

Dual Boot Options

Several applications enable you to dual boot nearly any combination of operating systems. One such application, System Commander, has enabled users to dual boot NT, Linux, NetWare, OS/2, and Windows 95 on a single system. Although it's not clear why anyone would want to create such a multiboot system, it can be done. There are NTFS readers for both Linux and DOS. It is obvious that nearly any combination of OSs can be configured on a single machine.

Large-Scale Roll-Out Installations

Organizations that have to roll out large numbers of machines face several hurdles. First of all, Microsoft insists that every user must go through the GUI part of the installation. This of course provides a serious dilemma to a task that must be done as quickly and as efficiently as possible. Fortunately, Microsoft has provided tools that help dramatically in this regard.

If you are starting a large roll-out, the first essential task you face is making a reference computer that has a full version of Windows NT Workstation 4 installed. You can also set up a network share or in the case of a large rollout, multiple shares. Certain factors must enter the process. For an OEM installation, the following requirements must be met:

- All computers must have a unique name that provides a unique security descriptor (SID).
- All installations must immediately enter the GUI phase of installation when the system is turned on.
- Every user must see the EULA (End-User License Agreement).
- All this must be done as easily and quickly as possible.

There are several ways that you can copy an installation from machine to machine: performing a stand-alone installation, installing across a network, or installing through disk replication. The first two of these approaches have already been discussed in this appendix. The third approach is unique and only recently has become economically feasible.

In the first example, you use an approach where Windows NT is preinstalled on the master computer, replicated onto an example system, and then prepared for mass roll-out. Although at first glance this seems to be a daunting task, it is really very simple.

Setting Up the Master Machine

The first task is to install a complete version of Windows NT Workstation 4 with the user name Administrator and a blank password. Our assumption here is that all the systems rolled out will be workstations and not servers. To summarize the procedure beforehand, you will install Windows NT, make sure that the installation temp files are present, and then run ROLLBACK.EXE. The drive will then be used for disk replication.

The installation of NT has been thoroughly covered, but certain features need to be added to the list. The easiest manner of installing large numbers of NT machines (new installations) is to install everything on the master computer, run rollback to place the system at the GUI stage, and then replicate the drive. To do this, all hardware has to be the same as do all the hard drives. Without this uniformity, the installation will not work properly. Assume that the systems being used all have the same SCSI controller and hard drive.

Note There is considerable confusion as to the use of rollback. First of all, it was placed on the CD-ROM by mistake. Rollback was intended to be used only by OEMs. When it is run, it renames three of the configuration files in the Registry. The normal files in the system32\config are the following:

- APPEVENT.EVT
- DEFAULT
- DEFAULT.LOG
- DEFAULT.SAV
- SAM
- SAM.LOG
- SECEVENT.EVT
- SECURITY
- SECURITY.LOG
- SOFTWARE
- SOFTWARE.LOG

- SOFTWARE.SAV
- SYSEVENT.EVT
- SYSTEM
- SYSTEM.ALT
- SYSTEM.SAV
- USERDIFF

After running rollback, the default, software, and system hives are all replaced. The older versions are copied to the following:

- def$$$$$.$$$.log
- def$$$$$.del
- sof$$$$$.$$$.log
- sof$$$$$.del
- sys$$$$$.$$$.log
- sys$$$$$.del

When the hives are changed, the system indeed boots to the GUI part of the installation. Interestingly, no users see the EULA. The general consensus seems to state that handing a user a hard copy of the EULA and asking them to sign and return it will suffice.

Install Windows NT by booting to a DOS floppy, accessing a CD-ROM, and running Winnt /b. Make sure to keep all disk formats FAT for now. After the files are copied and you are asked to reboot, boot to a DOS floppy and copy the contents of the root directory WIN_NT.~LS to OEM_NT.~LS. This step is critical. Remove the DOS boot disk and boot into setup. Completely install NT, join the domain, and make sure that you can browse all resources. (Create a user called TEST or similar on the PDC. Have the install create the user account TEST for you but do not use any password. Make TEST part of the admin group.) If all works satisfactorily, run rollback. Turn off the machine and move the drive to a second machine that is running Windows NT Workstation 4 and has a high-speed tape device attached (a DAT drive is fine). Open Explorer (or File Manager) and examine the root drive. WIN_NT.~LS is no longer present. Rename OEM_NT.~LS to WIN_NT.~LS. If desired, convert the drive to NTFS.

Run UltraBac (Barrett Edwards International) or ArcServe (Cheyenne Software) on the machine and do a sector backup of the D drive. Prepare the boot diskettes for the sector restore as specified. Turn off the machine and move the tape drive to a new machine making sure that termination is set properly. Boot to the restore diskettes and restore the sector backup to the new drive (remember, the same size and preferably the same manufacturer). If you remove the tape drive, you can boot into NT, and you will start at the GUI portion of install.

Ideally, you will have users suitable to oversee the installation. These users can be trained and given the instructions necessary to complete the installation. All settings are controlled by wizards. The disadvantage of this approach is that the installation is attended. The advantage is that you will not need to have a very large number of installers because the users will accomplish most of the work.

Doing a Network Roll-out

Doing a large scale roll-out of Windows NT via a network installation is powerful but time consuming. The process requires serious planning and documentation. Once set up, the roll-out is fast and surprisingly free of problems. The key to the roll-out is the development of the unattended answer file.

Unattended scripts can be made by editing a sample script or by using Setup Manager (see fig. A.4), is on the server resource kit. Make sure to include all answers, or the user will be asked for the information.

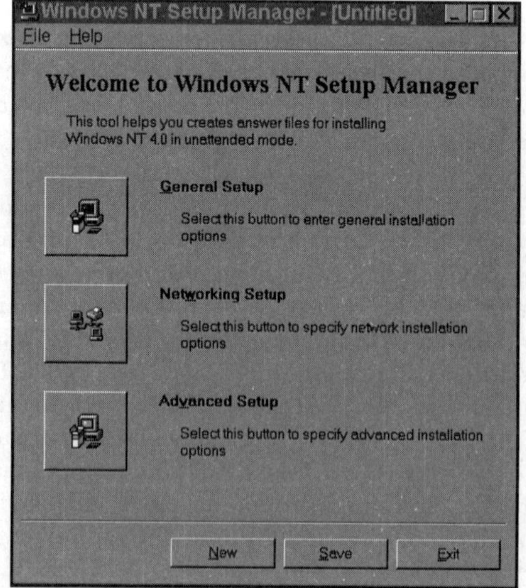

Figure A.4
The Setup Manager on the Windows NT Workstation 4 resource kit is powerful in helping with unattended answer files.

The following is a sample script:

```
[Unattended]
OemPreinstall = yes
OEMSkipEULA = Yes  ;skips end user license agreement - user needs a hard copy
Method = "express"
NoWaitAfterTextMode = 1  ;auto reboot after text phase
NoWaitAfterGUIMode = 1   ;auto reboot after GUI phase
FileSystem = ConvertNTFS  ;converts drive to NTFS
ExtendOEMPartition = 1
ConfirmHardware = no
NtUpgrade = no
Win31Upgrade = no
TargetPath = * ;defaults to C:\winnt
OverwriteOemFilesOnUpgrade = no
KeyboardLayout = "US-International"

[UserData]
FullName = "Bob Chronister"
OrgName = "Chronister Consultants"
ComputerName = BOB6
ProductId = "0123456789"

[GuiUnattended]
OemSkipWelcome = 1  ;skips welcome page
OEMBlankAdminPassword = 1 ;automatically sets admin password to blank
TimeZone="GMT-06:00 Central Time (US&Canada)"

[Display]
ConfigureAtLogon = 0
BitsPerPel = 8
XResolution = 640
YResolution = 480
VRefresh = 60
AutoConfirm = 1 ; means that no inout is needed by user

[Network]
DetectAdapters = DetectAdaptersSection
InstallProtocols = ProtocolsSection
InstallServices = ServicesSection
JoinDomain = Bobsplace
CreateComputerAccount = BOBC, $BOB&C$
```

```
[DetectAdaptersSection]
LimitTo = ELNKII
ELNKII = ELNKIIParamSection

[ELNKIIParamSection]
InterruptNumber=5
IOBaseAddress=300
Transceiver=2
MemoryMapped=0

[ProtocolsSection]
TC = TCParamSection

[TCParamSection]
DHCP = yes

[ServicesSection]
RAS = RASParamSection

[RASParamSection]
PortSections = PortSection1
DialoutProtocols = TCP/IP
DialinProtocols = TCP/IP
TcpIpClientAccess =network
ClientCanRequestIPAddress =no

[PortSection1]
PortName = COM2
DeviceType = "Practical Peripherals PC288LCD V.34"
PortUsage = DialInOut
```

In the preceding example, every possible request for user input was negated with a response. The example presupposes that all hardware is standard and has drivers on the installation CD. At a minimum, the I386 will be copied to a distribution server and full access given to everyone. (You can use the whole CD as a share but only if the drive is very fast. For large scale roll-outs, multiple distribution servers are needed.) With a DOS boot floppy, the real-time network drivers are loaded and the distribution drive mapped for local use (see previous section on network access boot floppies).

Although completely functional, the preceding script has several major discrepancies. First, you could not use the script to do a mass roll-out because all machines would have the same name. One solution to this is to make a small VB (or similar) application that will change the computer name in the UNATTEND.TXT and then save the file by the computer name (for example, BOB6.TXT). If all the files were saved in the distribution share, then the unattended installation would reflect the new file name.

Because the machine is booting to DOS, the WINNT.EXE file would be run. In the original example, with the distribution share mapped to Z, the commands would be as follows:

```
Z:

winnt /b /u:unattended.txt /s:Z
```

You can specify more than one source of the distribution files if you use the winnt32 application. This actually enables you to install from multiple sources simultaneously because the 32-bit installation is multithreaded.

With the latter example, the commands would be:

```
winnt /b /u:bob6.txt /s:z
```

The only factors involved here are preparing unattended files for each environment. If you have various types of network cards involved, for example, you would need to have answer files for each NIC. Once more, this emphasizes the necessity of doing an inventory of all the machines to be upgraded.

Suppose that you want to install applications with the network installation. This can be accomplished by using the OEM syntax. Assuming that you have checked yes to the OEM Preinstall option in the UNATTENDED.TXT file, you can use a setup command or use the sysdiff application also placed on the CD presumably by accident.

Ideally, any setup commands you would use directly are installation files that need user input. As you are aware, nearly all new applications require user input; therefore, sysdiff becomes an application of great importance. To install Office 95 onto drive C via a standard setup, you would create an OEM directory in the share. The share would look as follows for an installation to an Intel machine:

I386\OEM\C\MSoffice

The drive letter specifies the target for the installation. All the Office distribution and setup files are placed in the I386\OEM\C\Msoffice folder. The setup command is placed in the CMDLINES.TXT file that is in the root of OEM directory.

Although the preceding procedure works well, each user or installer must add all the necessary information on each installation. This is not very efficient, and the solution as noted earlier requires using SYSDIFF.EXE.

Sysdiff is an application that enables you to capture an image of the system, change the system, and then capture the difference between the two. Obviously, all you do is apply the difference file. In reality, the application can be used in many ways. Here you will deal primarily with the most direct use of sysdiff.

After you have the basic installation of NT in place, do not make any changes. If you installed the server resource kit, SYSDIFF.EXE was placed in the system32 folder. At the command line, type the following command:

```
sysdiff /snap [/log:log_file] drive:\folder\snapshot_file
```

where *drive* is the drive and *folder* is the folder where you want to store the snapshot file. Typically, create a folder called snap on the C drive. [/log:log_file] is optional.

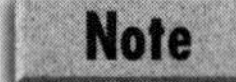

If you have more than one drive, sysdiff makes a snapshot of all drives. Because everything has to be the same on the drive you are taking the snapshot of and the drive you are applying to, only use sysdiff on a single drive system unless you realize the consequences.

After the snapshot has been made (see fig. A.5), you install the application in question. In this case, you install Office 95 on your master system. (The master system must be identical to the systems on which you are going to install NT.) After the installation is complete, you run a second command:

```
sysdiff /diff [/log:log_file] drive:\folder\snapshot_file drive:\
folder\Sysdiff_file /C:"comment"
```

For the present example, all the snapshot files are placed in the C:\snap directory. The SYSDIFF_FILE is the difference between the two snapshots. *Comment* is the name given to the Sysdiff package—that is, MSOffice.

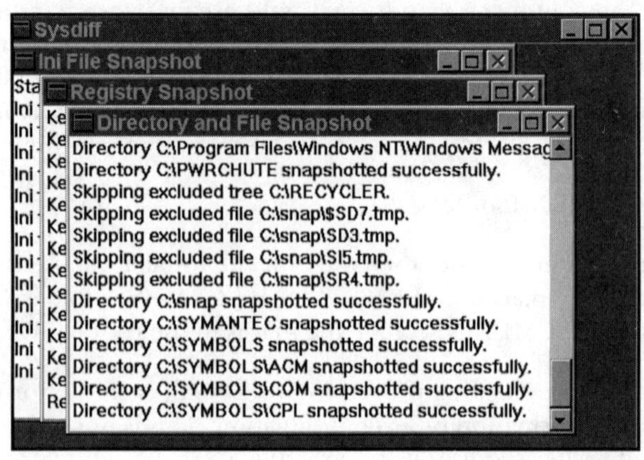

Figure A.5

The formation of a snapshot file is shown in progress; every event is shown in the three windows seen in the snapshot.

Sysdiff creates snapshots of three separate types of files. The first is the Registry; the second is of all INI files; and the last is a directory and file snapshot. All this information is included in the SYSDIFF_FILE.

Copy the SYSDIFF_FILE, SYSDIFF.EXE, and SYSDIFF.INI to the OEM folder of the distribution share. Create a file called CMDLINES.TXT and add the following line to it:

```
sysdiff /apply /m sysdiff_file
```

The sysdiff_file is the difference file you created when sysdiff was run the second time. *Apply* incorporates the difference file into the new system. *M* remaps the file changes to the default user profile so that they appear as Default User files. Move the CMDLINES.TXT file to the OEM distribution folder. During the end-user setup, the sysdiff file is incorporated into the installation. Generally, this approach is taken with small files.

You can also apply the difference during preinstallation. However, you need the file $$RENAME.TXT to convert short to long names. With this current limitation (the file is available only on OEM kits), this preinstallation approach is not recommended.

Push Installations: Upgrading via SMS

Large networks typically have a centralized management application that maintains a database of hardware, machines, software, and other related information. One such application is the System Management Server (SMS) from Microsoft. This application stores information in SQL, also from Microsoft. Because most large sites have SMS installed, it is easy to use SMS to push upgrades across the network.

SMS typically performs queries across the network and thus has already found all the machines that have the appropriate hardware and are running NT 3.51. You create a job, upgrading 3.51 workstations to 4 workstations, and SMS carries out that job over the network. SMS works by running defined jobs across the network, and the installation is done automatically to selected SMS clients.

Using SMS to upgrade Windows NT 3.51 Workstation to Windows NT Workstation 4 requires several tasks. First of all, you need to determine what systems will be upgraded. You then create a PDF file (package definition files). These files form the basis of the upgrade. (Please note the proper chapters in the Microsoft SMS manual; of importance are Chapters 7, 10, and 11, dealing with queries, packages, and jobs.) The tasks are as follows:

1. Determine the machines that will be upgraded. Define these systems as a Machine group for use in the distribution phase.

2. Prepare a PDF to handle the updates. A PDF resembles an unattended text file as discussed earlier. The following is a typical PDF:

```
[PDF]
Version=1.0
[Automated NT (x86) Setup]
CommandLine=ntencap /NTwks winnt32.exe /U:ntupgrd.400
CommandName=Automated Upgrade of (x86) NT Client
UserInputRequired=FALSE
SynchronousSystemExitRequired=TRUE
SupportedPlatforms=Windows NT 3.51 (x86)

[Manual NT (x86) Setup]
CommandLine=ntencap /NTwks winnt32.exe /B /S:.
CommandName=Manual Upgrade of (x86) NT Client
UserInputRequired=TRUE
SynchronousSystemExitRequired=TRUE
SupportedPlatforms=Windows NT 3.51 (x86)

[Automated NT (Alpha) Setup]
CommandLine=ntencapa /NTwks winnt32.exe /U:ntupgrd.400
CommandName=Automated Upgrade of (Alpha) NT Client
UserInputRequired=FALSE
SynchronousSystemExitRequired=TRUE
SupportedPlatforms=Windows NT 3.51 (Alpha)

[Manual NT (Alpha) Setup]
CommandLine=ntencapa /NTwks winnt32.exe
CommandName=Manual Upgrade of (Alpha) NT Client
UserInputRequired=TRUE
SynchronousSystemExitRequired=TRUE
SupportedPlatforms=Windows NT 3.51 (Alpha)

[Automated NT (MIPS) Setup]
CommandLine=ntencapm /NTwks winnt32.exe /U:ntupgrd.400
CommandName=Automated Upgrade of (MIPS) NT Client
UserInputRequired=FALSE
SynchronousSystemExitRequired=TRUE
SupportedPlatforms=Windows NT 3.51 (MIPS)
```

```
[Manual NT (MIPS) Setup]
CommandLine=ntencapm /NTwks winnt32.exe
CommandName=Manual Upgrade of (MIPS) NT Client
UserInputRequired=TRUE
SynchronousSystemExitRequired=TRUE
SupportedPlatforms=Windows NT 3.51 (MIPS)

[Automated Win Setup]
CommandLine=w16ntupg winnt.exe /U:unattend.400 /W /S:.
CommandName=Automated Setup of Win16 Client
UserInputRequired=FALSE
SynchronousSystemExitRequired=TRUE
SupportedPlatforms=Windows 3.1

[Manual Win Setup]
CommandLine=w16ntupg winnt.exe /B /W /S:.
CommandName=Manual Setup of Win16 Client
UserInputRequired=TRUE
SynchronousSystemExitRequired=TRUE
SupportedPlatforms=Windows 3.1

[Automated DOS Setup]
CommandLine=dosntupg.exe winnt.exe /U:unattend.400 /S:.
CommandName=Automated Setup of DOS Client
UserInputRequired=FALSE
SynchronousSystemExitRequired=TRUE
SupportedPlatforms=MS-DOS 5.0, MS-DOS 6.0, MS-DOS 6.2, MS-DOS 6.21, MS-DOS
6.22

[Manual DOS Setup]
CommandLine=dosntupg.exe winnt.exe /B /S:.
CommandName=Manual Setup of DOS Client
UserInputRequired=TRUE
SynchronousSystemExitRequired=TRUE
SupportedPlatforms=MS-DOS 5.0, MS-DOS 6.0, MS-DOS 6.2, MS-DOS 6.21, MS-DOS
6.22

[Package Definition]
Product=Windows NT Workstation
Version=4.00
Comment=Microsoft Windows NT Workstation 4.00
SetupVariations=Automated NT (x86), Manual NT (x86), Automated NT (Alpha),
➥Manual NT (Alpha), Automated NT (MIPS), Manual NT (MIPS), Automated Win,
➥Manual Win, Automated DOS, Manual DOS
```

3. Create a package to install the software. From the Package window in SMS, choose File, New and import the appropriate PDF described earlier as (`\\server\folder\filename`). When the package is imported, the Package Properties dialog box returns. Choose Windows NT Workstation. Just as in the unattended installation, you need access to a distribution share that you enter in the source directory. Be certain to make this an automatic setup. Click on OK, and the package is ready to be run. This example only deals with an upgrade. Notice that in the automated scripts for installing Server in the PDF file earlier, there are references to the file `ntupgrd.400`. An example of NTUPGRD.400 follows.

   This script file is an example script for upgrading NT. If the TCP/IP protocol stack is present on the machine being upgraded then the UpgradeEnableDhcpparamater must be correctly specified in order to fully automate the upgrade.

```
 [Unattended]
;Method = custom ¦ express
Method = express
;ConfirmHardware = yes ¦ no
ConfirmHardware = no
;NtUpgrade = manual ¦ yes ¦ no ¦ single
NtUpgrade = yes
;TargetPath = manual ¦ * ¦ <path>
TargetPath = *

[GuiUnattended]
; Specifies if TCP/IP protocol is to use Dynamic host configuration pro
;!UpgradeEnableDhcp = YES ¦ NO
!UpgradeEnableDhcp = YES
;!DetachedProgram = ""
;!Arguments = ""
!ProductId = "*** *******"
```

   In this particular example, any NT Workstation (MIPS, Alpha or Intel) will be automatically upgraded to NT Server 4. In reality, making the Ntupgrade=yes should produce an automatic upgrade with settings intact.

4. To create the job, open the Jobs window and choose File, New. For the present example, define a comment similar to this: `Push upgrade of all NT Workstations in the * machine group` where * is the name defined earlier. Make sure that all necessary files, including scripts, are copied to a network share on which SMS Service Account has proper access.

5. Choose Run Command on Workstation. Click the Details command and choose the proper package in the Package window. Enter the name of the specific machine group you have defined. In the send phase, you can choose to place the files directly on the target or connect to a server to which the systems to be upgraded have access. Assuming that you have chosen to copy all files to the targets, you then issue the command you choose in the Run window, in this case `automated setup of NT client`. Schedule the job and if necessary, make it mandatory. All should be automatic from now on.

6. The next time the user of a target machine logs on, the scheduled job appears. When the job is completed on the client, the upgrade will be finished. This type of "over-the-network" upgrade is called a *push upgrade* because the job is pushed onto the client instead of being initiated by the client.

APPENDIX B

NT Command Reference

Although the majority of Windows NT functions can be executed using graphic utilities, there are several reasons for using commands at the command prompt. In some cases, entering a command at the command prompt is faster than starting a graphic utility and stepping through menus.

Of greater significance is that most commands can be put into batch files, which are useful for building login scripts, executing commands at scheduled times, or performing functions when events are triggered. The UPS command, for example, can be configured to execute a batch file before shutting down Windows NT. Although the commands are described in online help displays, they are summarized here for your convenience.

The following conventions are used to indicate command syntax:

- **Bold** letters are used for words that must be typed as shown.
- *lowercase italic* letters are used for items that vary, such as file names.
- The [and] characters surround optional items that can be supplied with the command.
- The { and } characters surround lists of items. You may select one of the items in the list.
- The | character separates items in a list. Only one of the items can be included with the command.

  For example, in the following syntax, you must type NET COMMAND and either OPTION1 or OPTION2. Supplying a name is optional.

  NET COMMAND [name] {OPTION1 | OPTION2}
- The [...] characters mean you can repeat the previous item, separating items with spaces.
- The [,...] characters mean you can repeat the previous item, separating items with commas or semicolons, not spaces.
- When service names consist of two or more words, enclose the service name in quotation marks. For example, NET PAUSE "FTP SERVER" pauses the FTP server service.

Special Command Symbols

Windows NT's command prompt includes some special symbols that you can use to issue multiple commands on a single line. Some of the symbols allow you to create command lines that act conditionally based on the results of a previous command. Table B.1 shows these command symbols.

TABLE B.1
Windows NT Command Symbols

Symbol	Meaning
>	Redirects the output from one command into another, or to a file or device.
>>	Appends the output from one command into another, or to a file or device.

Symbol	Meaning
<	Redirects data from a file into a command.
&	Separates multiple commands on a single line.
()	Groups commands together.
; and ,	Separate parameters from one another.
^	Allows you to use a special command symbol literally.
&&	Causes the following command to execute only if the preceding command is successful.
||	Causes the following command to execute only if the preceding command is NOT successful.

Grouping Multiple Commands

To group multiple commands, simply separate them with a single ampersand. For instance, **DIR & TYPE \AUTOEXEC.BAT** will cause both commands to execute, one after the other.

You can also use the double ampersand (&&) and double pipe (||) symbols to process multiple commands on a single line conditionally. For instance, consider the actions of the following commands:

- **TYPE C:\NOFILE && DIR **

  Since the file C:\NOFILE does not exist, the DIR command is not executed.

- **TYPE C:\NOFILE || DIR **

  In this case, even though C:\NOFILE does not exist, the DIR command executes because the double pipe symbol processes the next command upon failure of the first command.

You can get more sophisticated with the conditional processing symbols and the parenthesis grouping operators. For instance, consider this command:

TYPE C:\NOFILE &&(ECHO SUCCESS) ||(ECHO FAILURE)

For this command, if the file C:\NOFILE does not exist, the word FAILURE will be echoed to the screen. If C:\NOFILES does exist, the word SUCCESS will be echoed.

You can further extend this idea by adding additional commands within each of the parenthesis groups, remembering to separate each command with the appropriate symbol. Using these tools, you can build quite complex and "intelligent" commands.

Redirecting Output

Most commands display results on your screen. You can capture these results into a file using special *redirection symbols.* The most basic redirection symbol is the greater-than sign (>), which takes the output of a command and redirects it to a file or device. For example, this command directs the output of a DIR command into a file called LISTING.TXT:

DIR >LISTING.TXT

The greater-than symbol used to redirect data in this way will create the file named if it does not already exist. Also, you can redirect output to a device. For instance, this command redirects the same data to the printer:

DIR >PRN:

DIR >PRN: may not immediately result in a printout from your printer, as no form feed character was added to the output, and most page-oriented printers require this to complete printing a page. You would have to press the Form Feed button on your printer to cause the paper to eject.

You can use the double greater-than symbol to append output into an existing file. Text already in the file is maintained. For instance, this command will add the new directory information to the existing LISTING.TXT file, while maintaining the results of the first directory listing:

DIR C:\WINNT >>LISTING.TXT

There is also a case where you can redirect information *from* a file into a command. For instance, you can create a text file that contains responses needed by a command, and then direct that file's contents into the command, which causes the text in the file to be sent to the command just as if you had typed the input yourself. For instance, follow these steps to create such a file and test it:

1. At the command prompt, type **COPY CON TEST** and press Enter. Your cursor moves to a new, blank line.
2. Type **12:05** and press Enter. Your cursor moves to the next line.
3. Save the file by pressing the F6 key and pressing Enter. You see ^Z appear on the screen as you press F6, and then when you press Enter you see the message 1 File(s) Copied.

4. Test the redirection by typing **TIME <TEST** and press Enter. You see the time command's output appear displaying the correct time, and then the new time, 12:05, being set. You return to the command prompt automatically, and the time has been changed to 12:05.

Windows NT Commands

The following commands are organized alphabetically. For each command you see a description of what the command does, the syntax of the command (some commands have more than one syntax), a description of the command options, and any notes that pertain to the command.

ACLCONV

Migrates OS/2 HPFS386 permissions to NTFS volumes.

Syntax

```
ACLCONV /DATA:datafile /LOG:logfile [/NEWDRIVE:drive] [/DOMAIN:domain]
[/CODEPAGE:n]
```

```
ACLCONV /LIST /LOG:logfile /CODEPAGE:n
```

Options

/DATA:datafile   Specifies the LAN Manager backacc data file.

/LOG:logfile   Specifies the logging file.

/NEWDRIVE:drive   Specifies the drive to which permissions are restored. You only need to use this parameter when permissions were backed up from a different drive letter.

/DOMAIN:domain   Restricts the search for account names to the specified domain.

/CODEPAGE:n   Specifies the Code Page to be used with the backacc data file.

/LIST   Lists the contents of the specified log file.

APPEND

APPEND lets programs open files stored in other directories as if they were in the current directory.

Syntax

```
APPEND [;] [[drive:]path[;...]] [/X:{on ¦ off}][/PATH:{on ¦ off}] [/e]
```

Options

; Cancels the appended directories.

[drive:]path Specifies the drive and directory that you want to append to the current directory. Using semicolons to separate directories, you can reference multiple directories.

/X:{on | off} Controls whether the MS-DOS subsystem searches appended directories for executable programs called by the program you initially run. */X:on* means that appended directories are searched for executable files. If you use the */x:off* switch, on the other hand, appended directories are not searched for executables. To use */x:on,* you must use it the first time you use the APPEND command after starting your system.

/PATH:{on | off} Stipulates whether a program searches appended directories for a data file when the path is already included with the name of the file the program is looking for. By default this is set to */PATH:on.*

/E Using /E creates an environment variable named APPEND, which contains the list of appended directories. You must use this switch first time you use APPEND after starting your system. This command is useful to view appended directories with the SET command.

ARP

ARP (short for Address Resolution Protocol) displays and modifies the IP-to-Ethernet or token ring address translation tables. This command is available only when the TCP/IP protocol is installed.

Syntax

```
arp -A [internet_addr] [-N [interface_addr]]

arp -D internet_addr [interface_addr]

arp -S internet_addr ethernet_addr [interface_addr]
```

Options

-A Queries TCP/IP and displays the current ARP entries. If you specify *internet_addr*, only the IP and physical addresses for the specified address display.

-G Same as -A.

internet_addr Lets you enter an IP address using decimal notation.

-N Displays the ARP entries for the network interface specified by *interface_addr*.

interface_addr Specifies the IP address of the interface whose translation table should be modified. By default the first applicable interface is used.

-D Deletes an entry specified by *internet_addr*.

-S Adds an entry to the ARP cache that associates the IP address *internet_addr* with the physical address *ethernet_addr*. Physical addresses are specified with six hexadecimal bytes separated by hyphens. The IP address is specified using standard dotted decimal notation.

ethernet_addr Specifies a physical Ethernet address.

ASSOC

Displays or modifies associations for file extensions.

Syntax

```
ASSOC [.extension[=[filetype]]]
```

Options

.extension Specifies the file extension to associate with a specified file type.

Filetype Specifies the file type to associate with the file extension.

Notes

Typing ASSOC with no options displays the current extension assignments. To view the associations for a given extension, type **ASSOC .EXT**.

You can delete associations by typing **ASSOC .EXT=**.

AT

One of the more useful commands in Windows NT, AT lets you schedule commands or programs to run at a given time.

Syntax

```
AT [\\computername] [[ID] [/DELETE [/YES]]
AT [\\computername] time [/INTERACTIVE] [/EVERY:date[,...] ¦ /NEXT:date[,...]]
"command"
```

Options

\\computername   Lets you specify a remote computer. By default, commands are scheduled for the local computer.

ID   Each scheduled command has an identification number assigned to it. You can specify this ID number when deleting scheduled commands.

/delete   When specified with the ID parameter, the scheduled command is deleted. If you use /delete without ID specified, all scheduled commands are deleted.

/yes   Forces a yes answer to all queries from the system when deleting scheduled events.

time   Specifies the when the command is to run, specified in 24-hour notation using hours:minutes. For example, 13:45 specifies 1:45 PM.

/INTERACTIVE   When you specify /INTERACTIVE, the scheduled command can interact with the user of the computer.

/EVERY:date[,...]   Causes the command to run on every specified day of the week or month. You specify the date as one or more days of the week, using the abbreviations M, T, W, Th, F, S, and Su. Specify particular days of the month using the numbers 1 through 31. You can enter multiple dates by separating each date entry with a comma. By default, if you do not specify the date is omitted, the current day of the month is used.

/NEXT:date[,...] Causes the command to run on the next occurrence of the day specified. Specify date as one or more days of the week using the abbreviations M, T, W, Th, F, S, and Su. Specify days of the month using the numbers 1 through 31.

"command" In place of *command*, you specify the program or batch file that you want run at the scheduled time.

When the command requires a path as an argument, use the absolute path, that is, the entire pathname beginning with the drive letter. If command is on a remote computer, specify the server and sharename rather than a remote drive letter. You may use quotation marks around the command, whether you are using AT at the command line or in a batch file. If the command includes switches that are used by both the command and AT, you must enclose command in quotation marks.

Notes

The Schedule service must be running in order for AT to function. By default, Schedule must be started manually using the Services icon in the Control Panel.

Type **AT** with no options to list all scheduled commands.

When you need to pass a path to the scheduled command as a parameter, make sure you use the absolute path and not a relative path reference, and include the drive letter.

Surround *command* with quotation marks when you need to pass a parameter to the *command* that conflicts with one of the AT parameters.

If the command you specify is not an executable file, you must precede the command with `CMD /C`. For example, you would use `CMD /C TYPE file.ext > C:\CAPTURE.TXT` because TYPE is a command that is part of the command processor and is not a free-standing executable file.

ATTRIB

ATTRIB lets you view or change file attributes (flags). With it, you can affect a file or directory's read-only, archive, system, or hidden attributes.

Syntax

```
ATTRIB [+R¦-R] [+A¦-A] [+S¦-S] [+H¦-H][[drive:][path] filename] [/S]
```

Options

[[drive:][path] filename] Specifies the file or directory that you want to work with.

+R Sets the read-only attribute.

-R Clears the read-only attribute.

+A Sets the archive attribute.

-A Clears the archive attribute.

+S Sets the system attribute.

-S Clears the system attribute.

+H Sets the hidden attribute.

-H Clears the hidden attribute.

/S Use this parameter to process files in the current directory and all subdirectories that match the given file specification.

Notes

ATTRIB with no parameters displays all of the files in the current directory and their attributes. ATTRIB can be useful in this way to quickly view the present hidden files.

BACKUP

Backs up files. You can use either hard or floppy disks as your destination, or go from one floppy to another.

Syntax

```
BACKUP source dest-drive: [/S] [/M] [/A][/F[:size]] [/D:date [/T:time]]
[/L[:[drive:][path]logfile]]
```

Options

source *Source* is the specification of the files you want to back up. Use whatever combination of drive letter, directory, and file specification that is appropriate to select the desired files.

dest-drive: This parameter controls the drive onto which you will back up the files.

/S Specifies that all subdirectories will be included in the backup.

/M Selects files that have their archive attribute set (in other words, have been modified since the last backup). Also turns off the archive attribute of the backed-up files.

/A Appends the selected backup files to an existing backup set.

/F[:size] Forces the destination disk to be formatted at the size you specify with *:size. :Size* is specified as kilobytes per disk. Acceptable values for *:size* are 160, 180, 320, 360, 720, 1200, 1440, and 2880.

/D:date Selects only files modified on or after the specified date to be backed up.

/T:time Selects only files modified on or after the specified time to be backed up.

/L[:[drive:][path]logfile] Creates a log file of the backup.

Notes

The backup files are stored as BACKUP.*nnn* and CONTROL.*nnn* (one each per disk used). Nnn is replaced with a number starting with 001. The stored files are marked read-only, so you will have to use ATTRIB to remove the read-only attribute if you wish to erase them from the destination disk (or, alternately, you must format the disk).

CACLS

Displays or changes the access control lists (ACLs) of files.

Syntax

```
CACLS filename [/T] [/E] [/C] [/G user:perm] [/R user [...]]
[/P user:perm [...]] [/D user [...]]
```

Options

filename Specifies the desired files.

/T Modifies the ACLs of specified files in the current directory and all subdirectories.

/E Edits the ACL instead of replacing it.

/C Causes CACLS to continue changing ACLs instead of stopping on errors.

/G user:perm Grants access rights to the specified user. The *perm parameter* can be:

- R Read
- C Change (write)
- F Full control

/R user Revokes a user's access rights.

/P user:perm Replaces a user's access rights. The *perm* parameter can be set to:

- N None
- R Read
- C Change (write)
- F Full control

/D user Denies access.

CHDIR (CD)

Changes the current working directory.

Syntax

```
CD [/D] [drive:][path] [..]
```

```
CHDIR [/D] [drive:][path] [..]
```

Options

/D Lets you change the current drive. For instance, if you are in the D:\ directory, you can type `CD /D E:\TEST` to move to the specified drive and directory. Without the /D parameter the CD command will not change drives.

[drive:][path] Specifies the drive and directory to which you want to change.

[..] This parameter specifies that you want to move to the parent directory of your current working directory.

CHKDSK

Checks the integrity of a disk and displays a status report. CHKDSK can also repair errors on a disk.

Syntax

```
CHKDSK [drive:][[path] filename] [/F] [/V] [/R]
```

Options

none   Typing CHKDSK with no parameters causes the current drive to be checked.

drive: Specifies the drive that you want to check.

[path] filename   Specifies files that you want to check for fragmentation.

/F   Repairs (fixes) errors that are found. In order to use this option, CHKDSK must be able to lock the disk. If it cannot, it offers to perform the repair the next time you start the system.

/V   Displays a verbose listing of all files checked.

/R   Locates bad sectors and recovers readable information. The disk must be locked.

Notes

If CHKDSK cannot lock the drive because it is locked by another process, it offers to perform the check the next time you start the computer.

You must be a member of the Administrators group to use CHKDSK on one of the system's hard disks.

CLS

Clears the screen.

Syntax

```
CLS
```

CMD

Invokes the Windows NT Workstation command processor.

Syntax

```
CMD [/X ¦ /Y] [/A ¦ /U] [/Q] [/T:fg] [ [/C ¦ /K] string]
```

Options

/C Executes the command you specify and then stops.

/K Executes the command you specify and then continues.

/Q Turns console echoing off.

/A Outputs ANSI characters.

/U Outputs Unicode characters.

/T:fg Lets you set the foreground and background colors for the command processor you invoke. See the COLOR command for more details.

/X Turns on extensions to CMD.EXE. These extensions give you more control over the command processor.

/Y Turns off extensions to CMD.EXE.

string Specifies the command you want carried out.

Notes

The CMD.EXE command interpreter is a special program that accepts and executes commands that you type at the command prompt.

You can use the EXIT command to exit the current command processor and return to the previous one.

COLOR

Lets you set the foreground and background colors for the command prompt.

Syntax

```
COLOR bf
```

Options

bf   Two hexadecimal digits that contain the foreground and background color selection; *b* specifies the background color and *f* specifies the foreground color. Use the following values for the color selections:

0 Black

1 Blue

2 Green

3 Aqua

4 Red

5 Purple

6 Yellow

7 White

8 Gray

9 Light blue

A Light green

B Light aqua

C Light red

D Light purple

E Light yellow

F Bright white

Notes

If you specify no arguments, the default colors are restored.

COMP

Compares the contents of two files or sets of files byte by byte.

Syntax

```
COMP [first_set] [second_set] [/D] [/A] [/L] [/N=number] [/C]
```

Options

first_set   Controls the file specification of the first set of files to be compared.

second_set   Controls the file specification for the second set of files to be compared.

/D   Uses decimal format to display any differences. By default, differences are displayed using hexadecimal.

/A   Displays differences as ASCII characters.

/L   Shows the line number in which a difference is detected, instead of the file offset.

/N=number   Restricts the comparison to the first *number* of lines.

/C   Looks for differences in a case-insensitive manner.

Notes

Comp can compare files on the same drive or on different drives, in the same directory or in different directories. As comp compares the files, it displays their locations and filenames.

COMPACT

Shows the compression level of files and directories. You can also change the compression level using COMPACT.

Syntax

```
COMPACT [/C] [/U] [/S] [/I] [/F] [/L] filename
```

Options

none If you specify no parameters, you are shown the compression state of the current directory and files.

/C Compresses a directory or file.

/U Uncompresses a directory or file.

/S:directory Applies the chosen action (/C or /U) to all subdirectories.

/I Ignores errors.

/F If a file is left in a partially compressed or uncompressed state, you must use the /F option to force the file to be compressed or uncompressed.

filename Contains the file specification for the COMPRESS command.

Notes

COMPACT only works on NTFS-formatted disks.

CONVERT

Lets you dynamically convert a drive from FAT to NTFS while maintaining the data on the drive.

Syntax

```
CONVERT [drive:] /FS:NTFS [/V] [/NAMETABLE:filename]
```

Options

drive Selects the drive to be converted.

/FS:NTFS Tells CONVERT to use NTFS as the destination file system type.

/V Selects verbose mode in which all messages are displayed during conversion.

/NAMETABLE:filename If you have trouble converting some files that have unusual file names, you can create a name translation table in the root directory of the drive to be converted, and can specify that filename with the */NAMETABLE* option.

Notes

Converts FAT volumes to NTFS. You cannot convert the current drive. If convert cannot lock the drive it will offer to convert it the next time the computer reboots.

COPY

Copies files.

This command can also be used to combine files. When more than one file is copied, Windows NT displays each filename as the file is copied.

Syntax

```
COPY [/A¦/B] source [/A¦/B] [+ source [/A¦/B] [+ ...]] [destination [/A¦/B]]
[/V] [/N] [/Z]
```

Options

source   Contains the file specification of the source files.

destination   Contains the file specification (or simply the drive or drive and directory) of the destination files.

/A   Copies files in ASCII mode, in which copying stops when an End-Of-File marker (Ctrl+Z) is found. If you use /A at the beginning of the command (before *source*), then ASCII mode is used for all files until a /B switch is encountered in the command.

/B   Copies files in binary mode in which the entire contents of a file are copied. Binary mode is the default for the COPY command.

/V   Verifies that the copies are accurate by matching the target with the source.

/N   Forces COPY to create short filenames for the destination.

Notes

You can combine files with the copy command by using the '+' character. For instance, typing **COPY *file1+file2 file3*** creates a file called *file3* that is the contents of *file1* plus *file2*. When you combine files in this way, COPY uses ASCII mode by default, which terminates copying of each file at any EOF markers. To combine files regardless of EOF markers, use the /B parameter, like this: **COPY /B *file1+file2 file3*.**

DATE

Displays or sets the system date.

Syntax

```
DATE [mm-dd-yy]
```

Options

[mm-dd-yy] Lets you set the current date using numbers in place of the options, where *mm* is the month, *dd* is the day number, and *yy* is the year. You can specify *yy* with four numbers to specify the century.

DEL (ERASE)

Erases files.

Syntax

```
DEL [drive:][path] filename [; ...] [/P] [/F] [/S] [/Q] [/A[:attributes]]

ERASE [drive:][path] filename [; ...] [/P] [/F] [/S] [/Q] [/A[:attributes]]
```

Options

[drive:][path] filename Contains the file specification of the files to be erased.

/P Prompts for confirmation before erasing the specified file.

/F Causes (forces) read-only files to be erased.

/S Causes subdirectories to be included for the given file specification.

/Q Runs the DEL command in quiet mode in which confirmations are not asked for.

/A:attributes Lets you control which files are erased based on their attributes. Attributes allowed are R (read-only), H (hidden), S (system), and A (archive). You can also use a hyphen to exclude files with a specified attribute. For instance, DEL *.* /A:-A will not erase files with the archive flag set.

Notes

DEL and ERASE work exactly the same. Both are commands that are internal to the command processor CMD.EXE. Deleting files from the command line bypasses the recycle bin.

DIR

Displays the contents of a directory.

Syntax

```
DIR [drive:][path][filename] [; ...] [/P] [/W] [/D] [/A[[:]attributes]]
[/O[[:]sortorder]] [/T[[:]timefield]] [/s] [/b] [/L] [/N] [/X]
```

Options

none If you do not use any parameters with the DIR command, the current directory's contents are displayed.

[drive:][path] Specifies the drive and directory for display.

[filename] Lets you restrict the display of files to those specified by *[filename]*.

/P Pauses the display after each screen fills and waits for a key to be pressed.

/W Displays files using a wide format, which lists only filenames and not associated information.

/D Uses the wide format, but sorts files by column.

/A[[:] attributes] Restricts the display to only those files specified by *attributes.* Use / A to cause files with the system or hidden attributes set to be displayed. Attributes allowed are D (directories), R (read-only), H (hidden), S (system), and A (archive). Precede the attribute with a hyphen to cause files that do NOT have the attribute set displayed.

/O[[:] sortorder] Lets you sort the display of files. By default sorting is not performed. Allowed *sortorder* values are: N (by name), E (by extension), D (by date), S (by size), and G (lists directories first, then files). You can precede any of these values with a hyphen to reverse the sort order.

/T[[:] timefield] Specifies which time is shown in the display. Allowed values are C (creation date), A (last access date), and W (last write date).

/S Applies the DIR command to all subdirectories.

/B Displays only filenames.

/L Outputs the display using lowercase letters.

/N Forces the long version of each filename to appear at the right side of each file's display.

/X Changes the order of the output display such that short names are shown to the immediate left of the long filenames.

Notes

You can use **DIR filespec /S** to search a volume for a given file.

DISKCOMP

Compares the contents of two disks, byte by byte.

Syntax

```
DISKCOMP drive1 drive2
```

Notes

DISKCOMP is used to compare two diskettes to ensure they are an exact match. The comparison does not compare files one to another, but instead compares the contents of each diskette byte-by-byte.

If drive1 and drive2 are the same, the system prompts you to swap the diskettes during the comparison.

DISKCOPY

Copies one diskette to another, making an exact duplicate of the source diskette onto the destination diskette.

Syntax

```
DISKCOPY drive1: drive2: [/V]
```

Options

drive*x*: Specifies the drive letter of the source and destination diskettes.

/V Causes the copy to be verified after it is written.

Notes

Using the /V parameter slows the copy process, but ensures a reliable copy.

DISKPERF

Enables and disables the system disk performance counters.

Syntax

```
DISKPERF [-Y¦-N] [\\computername]
```

Options

none With no parameters specified, DISKPERF reports whether the disk performance counters are enabled or disabled.

-Y Turns on the system disk performance counters at the next system boot.

-N Turns off the system disk performance counters at the next system boot.

\\computername Lets you control the disk performance counters on a remote computer over a network.

Notes

By default the system disk performance counters are not enabled. Enabling them may cause a slight performance decrease on the system, which can be noticeable on 80486-based systems. On Pentium-based systems the overhead is negligible.

DOSKEY

DOSKEY recalls Windows NT Workstation commands and lets you edit them. You also use DOSKEY to create command macros.

Syntax

```
DOSKEY [/REINSTALL] [/LISTSIZE=size] [/MACROS:[ALL ¦ exename] [/HISTORY]
[/INSERT¦/OVERSTRIKE] [/EXENAME=exename] [/MACROFILE=filename]
[MACRONAME=[text]]
```

Options

/REINSTALL Clears the command history.

/LISTSIZE=size This parameter lets you control the maximum number of commands held by DOSKEY.

/MACROS Using this parameter displays a list of all defined DOSKEY macros.

ALL Causes a list to be displayed of all executable-based macros.

EXENAME If you define an executable file with this parameter, any DOSKEY macros attached to that executable are displayed.

/HISTORY Using the /HISTORY parameter displays all commands stored in the DOSKEY buffer.

/INSERT | /OVERSTRIKE These two parameters, which are mutually exclusive, control whether command-line editing defaults to overstrike mode or insert mode.

/EXENAME=exename Controls the executable file for which the DOSKEY macro runs.

/MACROFILE=filename This parameter lets you define a file that contains predefined DOSKEY macros, which are installed automatically.

MACRONAME=[text] This parameter defines a new macro. *MACRONAME* is the name of the macro that, when typed at the command prompt, executes the commands given in *[text]*. Leaving the *[text]* portion blank erases the macro.

DOSONLY

Ensures that only MS-DOS programs are called from a command prompt using COMMAND.COM.

Syntax

```
DOSONLY
```

Notes

If you use a COMMAND.COM prompt (COMMAND.COM is the MS-DOS command interpreter, as opposed to Windows NT's CMD.EXE command interpreter), you can use the DOSONLY command to ensure that only MS-DOS programs are run at the prompt. This command is provided so that MS-DOS TSR (Terminate-and-Stay-Ready) programs are not interfered with.

FIND

Finds a specified string within one or more text files.

Syntax

```
FIND [/V] [/C] [/N] [/I] "search_string" [[drive:][path]filename[...]]
```

Options

"search_string" This parameter contains the characters you are searching for. You need to enclose the search string in quotation marks.

[drive:][path] filename Specifies the filenames to be searched.

/V This parameter displays all of the lines in the searched text files that do NOT contain the search string.

/C Using this paramter causes FIND to display a count of matching lines, rather than the contents of any matching lines.

/N Specifying */N* causes the line number to be displayed before the found text.

/I Causes the search to be case-insensitive.

Notes

FIND can be used as a filter program, into which you can redirect output from other program through it. For instance, you can type this command to find all files on a drive that contain the letters WIN: **DIR *.* | FIND "WIN"**

FINDSTR

FINDSTR lets you search files for matching text using either literal or regular expressions.

Syntax

```
FINDSTR [/B] [/E] [/L] [/C:string] [/R] [/S] [/I] [/X] [/V] [/N] [/M] [/O]
[/G:file] [/F:file] strings files
```

Options

/B Causes a match if the target is at the beginning of a line.

/E Causes a match if the target is at the end of a line.

/L Causes a literal search of the search strings.

/C:string Causes *string* to be used as the literal search string.

/R Causes FINDSTR to search using regular expressions. See the notes below for regular expression characters allowed.

/S Causes FINDSTR to search files in the current directory and any subdirectories.

/I Causes the search to be case-insensitive.

/X Displays lines that match the search exactly.

/V Displays lines that do NOT match the search strings.

/N Displays the line number before the matching text.

/M Displays only the filenames of files that contain matching strings.

/O Displays the file offset before the matching text.

/G:file Uses *file* to read in the search strings.

/F:file Uses a list of files in *file* to define what files are searched.

strings The search strings.

files The files to be searched.

Notes

You can use spaces to separate multiple search strings.

FINDSTR can use regular expressions to search for matches in an ASCII file. Regular expressions let you use wildcards and other pattern-matching notation as part of the search text.

Allowed notations for a regular expression include:

. Matches any single character

* Matches any number of occurrences of the previous character.

^ Matches at the beginning of a line

$ Matches at the end of a line

[class] A set of allowed characters can be surrounded by square brackets to match those allowed characters.

[^class] Preceding the allowed characters with a carat (^) causes those characters to be excluded from a match in that position.

[x-y] You can define a range of matching characters with a hyphen.

\x At times you may need to match one of the regular expression metacharacters, such as a carat or an asterisk. To do this, precede the character you are searching with the \x metacharacter, which stands for escape.

FORCEDOS

Forces a program to run in the MS-DOS subsystem.

Syntax

```
FORCEDOS [/D directory] filename [parameters]
```

Options

/D Causes the current directory to be used to run the program.

filename Controls which program is started.

[parameters] Contains any parameters that need to be passed to the program you run.

Notes

There are some programs that are written both for OS/2 and MS-DOS. Such programs are called dual-mode applications, or sometimes FAPI applications (Family API). By default, Windows NT runs such programs using the OS/2 subsystem. The use of FORCEDOS causes such programs to be run in the MS-DOS subsystem instead.

FORMAT

Formats a disk.

Syntax

```
FORMAT drive: [/FS:file-system] [/V[:label]] [/A:unitsize] [/Q] [/F:size]
[/T:tracks /N:sectors] [/1] [/4] [/8]
```

Options

drive: Controls which drive is formatted. By default, the drive is formatted based on the drive type.

/FS:file-system Controls the file system that is used. You can choose from FAT and NTFS file systems.

/V:label If specified, sets the volume label for the formatted disk.

/A:unitsize Controls the allocation unit size on NTFS-formatted sisks. Unitsize can be 512, 1024, 2048, and 4096.

/Q Performs a quick format in which the root directory and the file table is erased. The entire disk is not formatted. Use this command to quickly erase a previously-formatted disk.

/F:size Controls the size of the disk that is formatted. Size represents kilobytes and can be 160, 180, 320, 360, 720, 1200, 1440, 2880, and 20.8 (for optical disks).

/T:tracks Controls the number of tracks formatted on the disk.

/N:sectors Controls the number of sectors formatted per track.

/1 Causes a single-sided disk to be formatted.

/4 Quickly formats a 5.25-inch, 360K, DSDD disk in a 1.2 MB drive.

/8 Formats a 5.25-inch disk with 8 sectors per track for use on systems running MS-DOS versions up to 2.0.

Notes

You must be a member of the Administrators group on the machine on which you want to format a hard disk.

FTYPE

Displays and controls file types used for associations.

Syntax

```
FTYPE [filetype[=[command]]]
```

Options

filetype Controls the type of file for which you want to display its associations.

command Controls the command to be used when a file of *filetype* is launched.

Notes

Type FTYPE with no parameters to display all defined and associated file types.

HELP

Displays help on a particular command.

Syntax

```
HELP [command]
```

Options

[command] Specifies the name of the command for which you want help.

Notes

The HELP command is synonymous with typing /? after a particular command. For instance, DIR /? displays the same output as HELP DIR.

INSTALL

Loads Windows NT memory resident programs.

Syntax

```
INSTALL=[drive:][path] filename [command-parameters]
```

Options

[drive:][path] filename Specifies the name of the program that you want to load.

command-parameters Enter parameters for the memory-resident program in place of *command-parameters*.

LABEL

Sets the volume label for a disk.

Syntax

```
LABEL [drive:] label
```

Options

[drive:] The drive for which you want to change the label.

label The label you want to assign to the drive.

MKDIR (MD)

Creates a directory.

Syntax

```
MKDIR [drive:]path
MD [drive:]path
```

Options

[drive:] The drive on which you want to create a directory.

path The complete pathname that you want to create.

MOVE

Moves files from one directory to another.

Syntax

```
MOVE [source] [target]
```

Options

source Controls the path and name of the files to be moved.

target Controls the destination path to which the files will be moved.

NET ACCOUNTS

NET ACCOUNTS is used to maintain the user account database. It can modify password and logon requirements for all user accounts. When entered without options, NET ACCOUNTS displays current settings for the password, logon limitations, and domain information for the logged-on account.

Syntax

```
NET ACCOUNTS    [/FORCELOGOFF:{minutes ¦ NO}]
                [/MINPWLEN:length]
                [/MAXPWAGE:{days ¦ UNLIMITED}]
                [/MINPWAGE:days]
                [/UNIQUEPW:number]
                [/DOMAIN]
NET ACCOUNTS [/SYNC] [/DOMAIN]
```

Options

/FORCELOGOFF:{minutes | NO} *Minutes* specifies the number of minutes a user has before being automatically logged off when an account expires or logon hours expire. NO is the default value and specifies that forced logoff will not occur.

/MINPWLEN:length *Length* specifies the minimum number of characters required for a password. The range is 0–14 characters. The default is 6 characters.

/MAXPWAGE:{days | UNLIMITED} *Days* specifies the maximum number of days a password is valid. The UNLIMITED option specifies that no limit is imposed. /MAXPWAGE cannot be less than /MINPWAGE. The range is 1–49710 and the default is 90 days.

/MINPWAGE:days *Days* specifies the minimum number of days that must pass before a user can change his or her password. A value of 0 specifies no minimum time. The range is 0–49,710; the default is 0 days. /MINPWAGE cannot be greater than /MAXPWAGE.

/UNIQUEPW:number Specifies that the user's passwords must be unique for the number of changes specified by *number.* The maximum value is 8.

/SYNC Synchronizes the account database.

/DOMAIN Include this option to perform the specified action on the entire domain controller instead of the current computer. This option is effective only when executed on Windows NT computers that are members of a domain.

See Also

For a thorough discussion of the options for user accounts, see Chapter 7, "Managing Users."

Examples

NET ACCOUNTS can be used to make global changes to all user accounts. To change the minimum password length for all user accounts to five days, enter the following command:

```
NET ACCOUNTS /MINPWAGE:5
```

Notes

For options used with NET ACCOUNTS to take effect the following conditions must be true:

- ◆ User accounts must have been set up by the User Manager or the NET USER command.
- ◆ The Net Logon service must be running on all domain controllers.

NET COMPUTER

Use this command to add or delete computers from the domain database.

Syntax

```
NET COMPUTER \\computername {/ADD ¦ /DEL}
```

Options

\\computername The name of the computer to be added or deleted.

/ADD Adds the computer to the domain.

/DEL Deletes the computer from the domain.

Example

To add a computer named GEORGE to the domain, enter this command:

```
NET COMPUTER \\GEORGE /ADD
```

Notes

This command is available only with Windows NT Server.

NET CONFIG SERVER

Use this command to display or change settings for the server service. This command affects only the server on which it is executed.

You must be logged on as a member of the Administrators group to configure the server.

Syntax

```
NET CONFIG SERVER    [/AUTODISCONCONNECT:time]
                     [/SRVCOMMENT:"text"]
                     [/HIDDEN:{YES¦NO}]
```

Options

/AUTODISCONNECT:time   *Time* specifies the number of minutes an account can be inactive before it is disconnected. Specify -1 to never disconnect. Range is 1–65535 minutes. Default is 15.

/SRVCOMMENT:"text"   The message in "*text*" specifies a message that is displayed along with the server in many Windows NT screens. The message can consist of up to 48 characters and must be enclosed in quotation marks.

/HIDDEN:{YES | NO}   Determines whether a computer name is advertised in listings of servers. YES hides the server. NO includes the server name in lists.

Example

To display the current configuration for the Server service, type NET CONFIG SERVER without parameters.

NET CONFIG WORKSTATION

This command displays and changes settings for the Workstation service.

Syntax

```
NET CONFIG WORKSTATION   [/CHARCOUNT:bytes]
                         [/CHARTIME:msec]
                         [/CHARWAIT:sec]
```

Options

/CHARCOUNT:bytes Specifies the *bytes* of data that are collected before data is sent to a communication device. If /CHARTIME is set, Windows NT relies on the value that is satisfied first. Range is 0–65535 bytes. Default is 16 bytes.

/CHARTIME:msec *msec* specifies the number of milliseconds that Windows NT collects data before sending it to a communication device. If /CHARCOUNT is set, Windows NT relies on the value that is satisfied first. Range is 0–65535000 milliseconds. Default is 250 milliseconds.

/CHARWAIT:sec Specifies the number of seconds Windows NT waits for a communication device to become available. Range is 0–65535 seconds. Default is 3600 seconds.

Notes

To display the current configuration for the Workstation service, type NET CONFIG WORKSTATION without parameters.

NET CONTINUE

NET CONTINUE reactivates a Windows NT service that has been suspended by NET PAUSE.

Syntax

```
NET CONTINUE service
```

Options

service Any of the following paused services:

- FILE SERVER FOR MACINTOSH
- FTP SERVER
- LPDSVC
- NET LOGON
- NETWORK DDE
- NETWORK DDE DSDM
- NT LM SECURITY SUPPORT PROVIDER
- REMOTEBOOT
- REMOTE ACCESS SERVER
- SCHEDULE
- SERVER
- SIMPLE TCP/IP SERVICES
- WORKSTATION

NET FILE

Use this command to list ID numbers of files, to close a shared file, and to remove file locks. When used without options, NET FILE lists the open files on a server as well as their IDs, path names, user names, and number of locks.

Syntax

```
NET FILE [id [/CLOSE]]
```

Options

id The identification number of the file.

/CLOSE Include this option to close an open file and remove file locks. This command must be typed from the server on which the file is shared.

Notes

This command works only on computers running the Server service.

NET GROUP

This command adds, displays, or modifies global groups on servers. Enter the NET GROUP command without parameters to display the group names on the server.

Syntax

```
NET GROUP [groupname [/COMMENT:"text"]] [/DOMAIN]
NET GROUP groupname {/ADD [/COMMENT:"text"] ¦ /DELETE} [/DOMAIN]
NET GROUP groupname username [...] {/ADD ¦ /DELETE} [/DOMAIN]
```

Options

groupname This parameter specifies the name of the group to add, expand, or delete. This parameter is also included when user names are to be added to or deleted from a group. Supply the group name alone to see a list of users in a group.

/COMMENT:"text" This switch adds a comment of up to 48 characters, as specified by *text.* Enclose the text in quotation marks.

/DOMAIN Include this switch to perform the operation on the primary domain controller of the current domain. Without the /DOMAIN switch the operation is affects only the local computer.

username[...] Specifies one or more usernames to be added to or removed from a group. Multiple user name entries must be separated with a space.

/ADD Adds a group to a domain or adds a user name to a group.

/DELETE Removes a group from a domain or removes a user name from a group.

Examples

To view membership of the local group Server Operators, enter this command:

```
NET GROUP "SERVER OPERATORS"
```

To add a group named Blivet Engineers you would use the following command:

```
NET GROUP "Blivet Engineers" /ADD
```

NET HELP

Use this command to display a help listing of the options available for any NET command.

Syntax

```
NET HELP command
```

or

```
NET command /HELP
```

Options

Help information is available for the following commands:

NET ACCOUNTS
NET COMPUTER
NET CONFIG
NET CONFIG SERVER
NET CONFIG WORKSTATION
NET CONTINUE
NET FILE
NET GROUP
NET HELP
NET HELPMSG
NET LOCALGROUP
NET NAME
NET PAUSE
NET PRINT
NET SEND
NET SESSION
NET SHARE
NET START
NET STATISTICS
NET STOP
NET TIME
NET USE
NET USER
NET VIEW

Notes

NET HELP command | MORE displays Help one screen at a time.

NET HELP SERVICES lists the network services you can start.

NET HELP SYNTAX explains how to read NET HELP syntax lines.

NET HELPMSG

The NET HELPMSG command displays explanations of Windows NT network messages, including errors, warnings, and alerts. Type NET HELPMSG along with the 4-digit number of the Windows NT error. Although network error messages include the word NET (for example NET1234), you do not need to include NET in the message# parameter.

Syntax

```
NET HELPMSG message#
```

Options

message# The 4-digit number of the Windows NT message you need help with.

NET LOCALGROUP

Use this command to modify local groups on computers. Enter the NET LOCALGROUP command without parameters to list the local groups on the computer.

Syntax

```
NET LOCALGROUP [groupname [/COMMENT:"text"]] [/DOMAIN]
NET LOCALGROUP groupname {/ADD [/COMMENT:"text"] ¦ /DELETE} [/DOMAIN]
NET LOCALGROUP groupname name [...] {/ADD ¦ /DELETE} [/DOMAIN]
```

Options

groupname *groupname* specifies the name of the local group to add, expand, or delete. Supply a group name without parameters to list users or global groups in the local group. If the group name includes spaces, enclose the name in quotation marks.

/COMMENT: “text” This switch adds a comment of up to 48 characters, as specified by *text.* Enclose the text in quotation marks.

/DOMAIN Include this switch to perform the operation on the primary domain controller of the current domain. Otherwise, the operation is performed on the local computer. By default, Windows NT Server computers perform operations on the domain. This option is effective only when executed on a computer that is a member of a domain.

name [...] Specifies one or more user names or group names to be added to or removed from the local group. Multiple entries must be separated with a space. Include the domain name if the user is from another domain (Example: WIDGETS\CHARLES).

/ADD Adds the specified group name or user name to a local group. User and group names to be added must have been created previously.

/DELETE Removes a group name or user name from a local group.

Examples

To display the membership of the local group "Domain Admins," enter the following command:

```
NET LOCALGROUP "DOMAIN ADMINS"
```

To add the user Harold to the local group Widgets, enter the command:

```
NET LOCALGROUP WIDGETS HAROLD
```

NET NAME

The NET NAME command adds or deletes a messaging name at a computer. A messaging name is a name to which messages are sent. Use the NET NAME command without options to display names accepting messages at this computer.

A computer's list of names comes from three places:

- Message names, which are added with NET NAME.
- A computer name, which cannot be deleted. The computer name is added as a name when the Workstation service is started.
- A user name, which cannot be deleted. Unless the name is already in use on another computer, the user name is added as a name when you log on.

Syntax

```
NET NAME [name [/ADD ¦ /DELETE]]
```

Options

name The name of the user account that is to be added to names that will receive messages. The name can have as many as 15 characters.

/ADD Adds a name to a computer. /ADD is optional—typing NET NAME *name* works the same way as typing NET NAME *name* /ADD.

/DELETE Removes a name from a computer.

NET PAUSE

Use the NET PAUSE command to suspend a Windows NT service or resource. Pausing a service puts it on hold. Use the NET CONTINUE command to resume the service.

Syntax

```
NET PAUSE service
```

Options

service The service to be paused. Please see the NET CONTINUE command for a list of services that can be paused.

Notes

If the Server service is paused, only users who are members of the Administrators or Server Operators groups will be permitted to log on to the network.

NET PRINT

Use this command to list print jobs and shared queues. For each queue, the command lists jobs, showing the size and status of each job, and the queue status.

Syntax

```
NET PRINT \\computername\sharename
        [\\computername] job# [/HOLD ¦ /RELEASE ¦ /DELETE]
```

Options

\\computername Specifies the name of the computer sharing the printer queue(s).

sharename Specifies the share name of the printer queue.

job# Specifies the identification number assigned to a print job. Each job executed on a computer is assigned a unique number.

/HOLD Assigns a "hold" status to a job so that it will not print. The job remains in the queue until it is released or deleted.

/RELEASE Removes the "hold" status on a job so that it can be printed.

/DELETE Removes a job from a queue.

Examples

To display active print jobs on a computer named Blivets, enter the following command:

```
NET PRINT \\BLIVETS
```

To hold job number 234 on the computer Blivets, for example, the command is

```
NET PRINT \\BLIVETS 234 /HOLD
```

NET SEND

This command sends messages to other users, computers, or messaging names on the network.

Syntax

```
NET SEND {name ¦ * ¦ /DOMAIN[:domainname] ¦ /USERS} message
```

Options

name Specifies the user name, computer name, or messaging name to which the message is sent. If the name contains blank characters, enclose the name in quotation marks.

* An *, when substituted for *name*, sends the message to all the names in your group.

/DOMAIN[:domainname] Specifies that the message should be sent to all users in the domain. If *domainname* is specified, the message is sent to all the names in the specified domain or workgroup.

/USERS Sends the message to all users connected to the server.

message The text to be sent as a message.

Examples

To send a message to everyone in a domain, type a command like the following:

```
NET SEND /DOMAIN:WIDGETS A message for everyone in Widgets
```

You can also specify a user, in this case, Mabel:

```
NET SEND MABEL A message for Mabel
```

Notes

The Messenger service must be running on the receiving computer to receive messages.

You can send a message only to a name that is active on the network.

NET SESSION

The NET SESSION command lists or disconnects sessions between the computer and other computers on the network. When used without options, NET SESSION displays information about all sessions running on the computer that currently has the focus.

Syntax

```
NET SESSION [\\computername] [/DELETE]
```

Options

\\computername   Lists the session information for the named computer.

/DELETE   Ends the session between the local computer and *computername.* All open files on the computer are closed. If *computername* is omitted, all sessions are ended.

Notes

This command works only when executed on servers.

NET SHARE

The NET SHARE command is used to share a server's resources with network users. Use the command without options to list information about all resources being shared on the computer. For each shared resource, Windows NT reports the device name(s) or path name(s) for the share along with any descriptive comment that has been associated with the share.

Syntax

```
NET SHARE   sharename
NET SHARE   sharename=drive:path
            [/USERS:number ¦ /UNLIMITED]
            [/REMARK:"text"]
NET SHARE   sharename [/USERS:number ¦ /UNLIMITED] [/REMARK:"text"]
NET SHARE   {sharename ¦ devicename ¦ drive:path} /DELETE
```

Options

sharename   Specifies the network name of the shared resource. Typing NET SHARE with a share name only displays information about that share.

devicename   Specifies one or more printers (LPT1 through LPT9) shared by *sharename.* Use this option when a printer share is being established.

drive:path Specifies the absolute path of a directory to be shared. Use this option when a directory share is being established.

/USERS:number Specifies the maximum number of users that will be permitted to simultaneously access the shared resource.

/UNLIMITED Specifies that no limit will be placed on the number of users that will be permitted to simultaneously access the shared resource.

/REMARK:"text" Associates a descriptive comment about the resource with the share definition. Enclose the text in quotation marks.

/DELETE Stops sharing of the resource.

Examples

To share the directory C:\APPLICATIONS with the share name APPS, enter the command:

```
NET SHARE APPS=C:\APPLICATIONS
```

You can limit the number of users who can access a share by using the /USERS options. The following example limits users to 10:

```
NET SHARE APPS=C:\APPLICATIONS /USERS:10
```

To stop sharing the printer on LPT3, enter the following command:

```
NET SHARE LPT3: /DELETE
```

Notes

Printers must be shared with Print Manager. NET SHARE may be used to stop sharing printers.

NET START

Use the NET START command to start services that have not been started or have been stopped by the NET STOP command. Enter the command NET START without options to list running services.

Syntax

```
NET START [service]
```

Options

service One of the following services to be stopped:

- ALERTER
- CLIENT SERVICE FOR NETWARE
- CLIPBOOK SERVER
- COMPUTER BROWSER
- DHCP CLIENT
- DIRECTORY REPLICATOR
- EVENTLOG
- FTP SERVER
- LPDSVC
- MESSENGER
- NET LOGON
- NETWORK DDE
- NETWORK DDE DSDM
- NETWORK MONITORING AGENT
- NT LM SECURITY SUPPORT PROVIDER
- OLE
- REMOTE ACCESS CONNECTION MANAGER
- REMOTE ACCESS ISNSAP SERVICE
- REMOTE ACCESS SERVER
- REMOTE PROCEDURE CALL (RPC) LOCATOR

- REMOTE PROCEDURE CALL (RPC) SERVICE
- SCHEDULE
- SERVER
- SIMPLE TCP/IP SERVICES
- SNMP
- SPOOLER
- TCPIP NETBIOS HELPER
- UPS
- WORKSTATION

These services are available only on Windows NT Server:

- FILE SERVER FOR MACINTOSH
- GATEWAY SERVICE FOR NETWARE
- MICROSOFT DHCP SERVER
- PRINT SERVER FOR MACINTOSH
- REMOTEBOOT
- WINDOWS INTERNET NAME SERVICE

Notes

To get more help about a specific service, see the online Command Reference (NTCMDS.HLP).

When typed at the command prompt, service names of two words or more must be enclosed in quotation marks. For example, NET START "COMPUTER BROWSER" starts the computer browser service.

NET START can also start network services not provided with Windows NT.

NET STATISTICS

NET STATISTICS displays the statistics log for the local Workstation or Server service. Used without parameters, NET STATISTICS displays the services for which statistics are available.

Syntax

```
NET STATISTICS [WORKSTATION | SERVER]
```

Options

SERVER   Displays the Server service statistics.

WORKSTATION   Displays the Workstation service statistics.

NET STOP

NET STOP stops Windows NT services.

Syntax

```
NET STOP service
```

Options

service   Is a Windows NT service that can be stopped. See the NET START command for a list of eligible services.

Notes

NET STOP can also stop network services not provided with Windows NT.

Stopping a service cancels any network connections the service is using. Because some services are dependent on others, stopping one service can stop others.

You must have administrative rights to stop the Server service.

The Eventlog service cannot be stopped.

NET TIME

Use the NET TIME command to synchronize the computer's clock with that of another computer or domain. NET TIME can also be used to display the time for a computer or domain. When used without options or a Windows NT Server domain, it displays the current date and time at the computer designated as the time server for the domain.

Syntax

```
NET TIME [\\computername ¦ /DOMAIN[:domainname]] [/SET]
```

Options

\\computername Specifies the name of the computer you want to check or synchronize with.

/DOMAIN[:domainname] Specifies the domain with which to synchronize time.

/SET Synchronizes the computer's time with the time on the specified computer or domain.

NET USE

This command connects a computer to a shared resource or disconnects a computer from a shared resource. NET USE without options lists the computer's connections.

Syntax

```
NET USE [devicename ¦ *]
        [\\computername\sharename[\volume] [password ¦ *]]
        [/USER:[domainname\]username]
        [[/DELETE] ¦ [/PERSISTENT:{YES ¦ NO}]]
NET USE [devicename ¦ *] [password ¦ *]] [/HOME]
NET USE [/PERSISTENT:{YES ¦ NO}]
```

Options

devicename Specifies a name to assign to the connected resource or specifies the device to be disconnected. Device names can consist of the following:

- disk drives (D through Z)
- printers (LPT1 through LPT3)

Type an asterisk instead of a specific device name to assign the next available device name.

\\computername Specifies the name of the computer controlling the shared resource. If the computer name contains blank characters, enclose the double backslash (\\) and the computer name in quotation marks. The computer name may be from 1 to 15 characters long.

\sharename Specifies the network name of the shared resource.

\volume Specifies the name of a volume on a NetWare server. You must have Client Services for NetWare (Windows NT Workstations) or Gateway Service for NetWare (Windows NT Server) installed and running to connect to NetWare servers.

password The password needed to access the shared resource.

* Produces a prompt for the password. The password is not displayed when you type it at the password prompt.

/USER Specifies a different user name with which the connection is made.

domainname Specifies another domain. If *domainname* is omitted, the current logged on domain is used.

username Specifies the user name with which to log on.

/HOME Connects a user to his or her home directory.

/DELETE Cancels a network connection and removes the connection from the list of persistent connections.

/PERSISTENT{YES | NO} YES saves connections as they are made, and restores them at next logon. NO does not save the connection being made or subsequent connections; existing connections will be restored at next logon. The default is the setting used last.

/DELETE switch Removes persistent connections.

Examples

To connect drive M to a directory with the share name APPS on the server BLIVETS, which has the password LETMEIN, you would type the following:

```
NET USE M: \\BLIVETS\APPS LETMEIN
```

If you do not want the password displayed on the screen, include an * in the password position as follows, so that you will be prompted to enter one:

```
NET USE M: \\BLIVETS\APPS *
```

You can access a share that is secured to another user account if you have a valid password. To access the share using Mabel's account, enter this command:

```
NET USE M: \\BLIVETS\APPS * /USER:MABEL
```

NET USER

NET USER creates and modifies user accounts on computers. When used without switches, it lists the user accounts for the computer. The user account information is stored in the user accounts database.

Syntax

```
NET USER [username [password ¦ *] [options]] [/DOMAIN]
NET USER username {password ¦ *} /ADD [options] [/DOMAIN]
NET USER username [/DELETE] [/DOMAIN]
```

Options

username   Specifies the name of the user account to add, delete, modify, or view. The name of the user account can consist of up to 20 characters.

password   Assigns or changes a password for the user account. A password must meet the minimum length requirement set with the /MINPWLEN option of the NET ACCOUNTS command. The password can consist of up to 14 characters.

*   Displays a prompt for the password, which is not displayed when typed.

/DOMAIN   Specifies the action should be performed on the primary domain controller of the current domain.

This parameter is effective only with Windows NT Workstation computers that are members of a Windows NT Server domain. By default, Windows NT Server computers perform operations on the primary domain controller.

/ADD Adds a user account to the user accounts database.

/DELETE Removes a user account from the user accounts database.

options The available options are shown in table B.2:

Table B.2
Available Options

Option	Description
/ACTIVE:{YES | NO}	Activates or deactivates the account. When the account is deactivated, the user cannot access the server. The default is YES.
/COMMENT:"text"	Adds a comment consisting of up to 48 characters, as specified by *text*. Enclose the text in quotation marks.
/COUNTRYCODE:nnn	*nnn* is the numeric operating system country code that specifies the language files to be used for a user's help and error messages. A value of 0 signifies the default country code.
/EXPIRES:{date | NEVER}	Specifies a date when the account will expire in the form *mm,dd,yy* or *dd,mm,yy* as determined by the country code. NEVER sets no time limit on the account. The months can be a number, spelled out, or abbreviated with three letters. The year can be two or four numbers. Use commas or slashes(/) to separate parts of the date. No spaces may appear.
/FULLNAME:"name"	Specifies a user's full name (rather than a user name). Enclose the name in quotation marks.
/HOMEDIR:pathname	Specifies the path for the user's home directory. The path must have been previously created.

continues

TABLE B.2, CONTINUED
Available Options

Option	Description
/HOMEDIRREQ:{YES | NO}	Specifies whether a home directory is required. If a home directory is required, use the /HOMEDIR option to specify the directory.
/PASSWORDCHG:{YES | NO}	Specifies whether users can change their own password. The default is YES.
/PASSWORDREQ:{YES | NO}	Specifies whether a user account must have a password. The default is YES.
/PROFILEPATH[:path]	Specifies a *path* for the user's logon profile.
/SCRIPTPATH:pathname	*pathname* is the location of the user's logon script.
/TIMES:{times | ALL}	*times* specifies the hours a user account may be logged on. *times* is expressed as day[-day][,day[-day]],time[-time][,time [-time]], limited to 1-hour increments. Days can be spelled out or abbreviated. Hours can be specified using 12- or 24-hour notation. With 12-hour notation, include am, pm, a.m., or p.m. ALL means a user can always log on. A blank value means a user can never log on. Separate day and time entries with a comma, and separate multiple day and time entries with a semicolon.
/USERCOMMENT:"text"	Specifies a comment for the account.
/WORKSTATIONS:	Lists as many as eight computers from {computername[,...] | *} which a user can log on to the network. If */WORKSTATIONS* has no list or if the list is *, the user can log on from any computer.

Examples

To display information about a user named Charles, type the following:

```
NET USER CHARLES
```

To create an account for a user named Harold, while prompting for a password to be assigned, enter the following command:

```
NET USER Harold * /ADD
```

Notes

This command works only on servers.

If you have large numbers of users to add, consider creating a batch file with the appropriate NET USER command. Following is a simple example of a file:

```
NET USER %1 NEWUSER /ADD /HOMEDIR:C:\USERS\%1 /PASSWORDREQ:YES
```

Of course, you would include other options as required. This file makes use of a batch file parameter %1 to pass a command argument to the batch file commands. %1 will pass a user name you specify to the NET USER command where it is used to name the user account and the user's home directory.

If the file is named ADDUSER.BAT, you could add the user Mabel by typing this:

```
ADDUSER Mabel
```

NET VIEW

The NET VIEW command lists resources being shared on a computer. NET VIEW without options displays a list of computers in the current domain or network.

Syntax

```
NET VIEW [\\computername ¦ /DOMAIN[:domainname]]
NET VIEW /NETWORK:NW [\\computername]
```

Options

\\computername Specifies a computer with shared resources you want to view.

/DOMAIN:domainname Specifies the domain with computers whose shared resources you want to view. If *domainname* is omitted, NET VIEW displays all domains in the local area network.

/NETWORK:NW Displays all available servers on a NetWare network. If a computer name is specified, the resources available on that NetWare computer are displayed.

Examples

To list the resources shared by the computer Widgets1, enter the following command:

```
NET VIEW \\WIDGETS1
```

If Widgets1 is in another domain, include the domain name with the /DOMAIN option:

```
NET VIEW \\WIDGETS1 /DOMAIN:WIDGETS
```

To list all available domains, omit the *computername* parameter:

```
NET VIEW /DOMAIN
```

NTBOOKS

Invokes the online manuals for Windows NT.

Syntax

```
NTBOOKS [/S] [/W] [/N:path]
```

Options

/S Use /S from a Windows NT Workstation machine to access documentation stored on a Windows NT server.

/W Use /W from a Windows NT server to access documentation for a Windows NT Workstation.

/N This parameter lets you specify the path to where the online books are stored. By default, the last used location is automatically used.

NTCMDPROMPT

From a COMMAND.COM prompt, NTCMDPROMPT invokes the Windows NT command prompt.

Syntax

```
NTCMDPROMPT
```

PENTNT

Tests for the Pentium floating point bug.

Syntax

```
PENTNT [-C] [-F] [-O] [-?¦-H]
```

Options

-C Turns on conditional emulation wherein floating point emulation will be turned on if the program detects the Pentium floating point bug.

-F Forces floating point emulation to begin and disables hardware floating point calls.

-O Disables forced emulation and turns the hardware floating-point access back on.

PRINT

Prints a text file in the background.

Syntax

```
PRINT [/D:device] [drive:][path] filename[ ...]
```

Options

none Displays the contents of the PRINT queue.

/D:device Specifies the name of the print device, such as LPT1, COM2, and so forth.

[drive:][path] filename Specifies the file to be printed.

RENAME (REN)

Renames files.

Syntax

```
RENAME [drive:][path] filename1 filename2
REN [drive:][path] filename1 filename2
```

Options

[drive:][path] filename1 Specifies the source file names.

filename2 Specifies the destination file names.

Notes

Files cannot be renamed across drives.

REPLACE

Replaces files in a specified directory with files in a different directory that have the same name.

Syntax

```
REPLACE [drive1:][path1] filename [drive2:][path2] [/A] [/P] [/R] [/W]
REPLACE [drive1:][path1] filename [drive2:][path2] [/P] [/R] [/S] [/W] [/U]
```

Options

[drive1:][path1] filename The source files.

[drive2:][path2] The destination files.

/A Adds new files to the destination directory.

/P Prompts for confirmation before replacing files.

/R Forces replacement of read-only files.

/S Includes all subdirectories.

/W Causes REPLACE to wait for a disk to be inserted before searching for source files.

/U Updates files in destination directory, where only files with older dates than the source files are replaced.

RESTORE

Restores files backed up with the BACKUP command.

Syntax

```
RESTORE drive1: drive2:[path[filename]] [/s] [/p] [/b:date] [/A:date] [/E:time]
[/L:time] [/M] [/N] [/D]
```

Options

drive1: The source drive.

drive2: The destination drive.

path The destination directory. This must be the same directory as the one from which the files were backed up.

filename The files you want to restore from the backup set.

/S Include subdirectories.

/P Prompts for confirmation when restoring over files that are read-only or that are newer than those stored in the backup set.

/B:date Restores files modified since *date.*

/A:date Restores files modified after *date.*

/E:time Restores files modified at or earlier than *time.*

/L:time Restores files modified at or later than *time.*

/M Restores files modified since the last backup.

/N Restores only files that do not exist in the destination directory.

/D Displays files that would be restored, but does not actually restore any files. Use this command to test which files will be restored given other parameters that you've specified.

RMDIR (RD)

Removes directories.

Syntax

```
RMDIR [drive:]path [/S]
RD [drive:]path [/S]
```

Options

[drive:]path The name of the directory that you want to remove.

/S Remove an entire subdirectory tree, including files.

SORT

Sorts ASCII files.

Syntax

```
SORT [/R] [/+N] [<] [drive1:][path1] filename1 [> [drive2:][path2] filename2]
[command ¦] SORT [/R] [/+N] [> [drive2:][path2] filename2]
```

Options

[drive1:][path1] filename1 The file that you want to sort.

[drive2:][path2] filename2 The destination for the sorted output.

command The command that is generating data that will be sorted by redirecting its output into SORT.

/R Reverses the sorting order (performs an descending sort).

/+n Sorts the file based on column *n*.

START

Executes a given command in a new window.

Syntax

```
START ["title"] [/dpath] [/I] [/MIN] [/MAX] [/SEPARATE] [/LOW] [/NORMAL]
[/HIGH] [/REALTIME] [/WAIT] [/B] [filename] [parameters]
```

Options

none Opens a new command window.

"title" The new window's title (displayed in the title bar).

/dpath The directory to which the new window defaults.

/I Automatically passes environment variables from CMD.EXE to the new window.

/MIN Starts the new window minimized.

/MAX Starts the new window maximized.

/SEPARATE Runs Win16 applications in a separate address space.

/LOW Runs the application at idle priority.

/NORMAL Runs the application at normal priority.

/HIGH Runs the application at high priority.

/REALTIME Runs the application at realtime priority.

/WAIT Begins the application; waits for it to terminate.

/B Runs the application in the background, without a new window.

filename The program to run in the new window.

SUBST

Creates a virtual drive letter from a specified path.

Syntax

```
SUBST [drive1: [drive2:]path]
SUBST drive1: /D
```

Options

none Displays all virtual drives.

drive1: The virtual drive that will be created.

drive2: The actual drive that contains the path.

path The path to use for the virtual drive.

/D Deletes a virtual drive.

TIME

Displays or sets the computer's time.

Syntax

```
TIME [hours:[minutes[:seconds[.hundredths]]][A|P]]
```

Options

none Displays the currently set time and lets you set a new time interactively.

Hours The hour you want to set, in military time format (0-23).

minutes The minutes you want to set, from 0 to 59.

seconds The seconds you want to set, from 0 to 59.

hundredths The hundredths of a second that you want to set, from 0 to 99.

A|P If you sets the time using a 12-hour format, you must specify A or P for a.m. or p.m.

TITLE

Sets the title bar for the current command prompt window.

Syntax

```
TITLE title_name
```

Options

title_name The title you want to appear in the window's title bar.

TREE

Graphically displays the directory tree of a drive.

Syntax

```
TREE [drive:][path] [/F] [/A]
```

Options

drive: The drive for which you want to see a directory tree.

path The directory for which you want to see a directory tree.

/F Causes the files for each directory to be displayed.

/A Uses ASCII characters to represent the tree instead of the extended characters used by default.

TYPE

Outputs a file to the standard output device.

Syntax

```
TYPE [drive:][path] filename [...]
```

Options

[drive:][path] filename The file you want to display.

Notes

If you are using TYPE with a file containing spaces, surround the filename with quotation marks.

You can pipe the output of TYPE through the MORE command, like this:

```
TYPE LONGFILE.TXT |MORE.
```

VER

Displays the version number of the command prompt you're using.

Syntax

```
VER
```

XCOPY

Copies files and offers more control than the COPY command.

Syntax

```
XCOPY source [destination] [/W] [/P] [/C] [/V] [/Q] [/F] [/L] [/D[:date]] [/U]
[/I] [/S [/E]] [/T] [/K] [/R] [/H] [/A¦/M] [/N] [/EXCLUDE:filename] [/Z]
```

Options

source The source files to be copied.

destination The destination for the files to be copied.

/W Waits for user input before copying files.

/P Prompts for confirmation when creating destination files.

/C Continues copying after errors are encountered.

/V Verifies the integrity of each copied file.

/Q Runs XCOPY in quiet mode.

/F Displays filenames during the copy.

/L Lists files that would be copied, but does not copy any files.

/D[:date] Copies files modified on or after *date.*

/U Only copies files that already exist in the destination directory.

/I Assumes that the destination specified is a directory and not a file.

/S Copies subdirectories, except empty ones.

/E Copies all subdirectories, including empty ones. Use this with the /S switch.

/T Copies only the subdirectory tree and not any files.

/K Retains the read-only attribute for destination files. By default, the read-only flag, if present in a source file, is not set for destination files.

/R Forces read-only files to be overwritten if they exist.

/H Includes files that have the hidden or system flags set.

/A Copies files that have the archive flag set.

/M Copies files that have the archive flag set, and removes the archive flag from the source file.

/N Copies files using the NTFS short filenames.

/EXCLUDE:filename Excludes files specified in *filename.*

APPENDIX C

What's on the CD-ROM

This chapter provides an overview of the software on the CD-ROM. To get started, run SETUP.EXE from the root directory of the CD-ROM. The SETUP program adds icons to a program group, making it easier to explore the CD-ROM.

If Autorun is enabled on your computer, the setup program will start automatically the first time you insert the CD.

If the setup program does not start automatically, here's what to do:

1. Press the Start button. Choose Programs, then Windows NT Explorer.
2. Select your CD-ROM drive under My Computer.
3. Double-click SETUP.EXE in the contents list.
4. Follow the on-screen instructions that appear.
5. When SETUP ends, double-click the icon named CD-ROM Contents. This file provides an overview of the CD-ROM and makes it easy to select and install individual software programs.

CD-ROM Compatibility Note

This CD-ROM is readable under all versions of Windows, meaning that you can explore directories on the CD and learn more about its content by reading the CD-ROM Contents document. However, the CD was developed with Windows NT users in mind. Some software is not compatible with Windows 3.x, and many programs require Windows NT or Windows 95. If you are not running Windows NT, please review program descriptions and vendor "Readme" files carefully before installing software.

License Agreement

Disclaimer

This software is sold AS IS without warranty of any kind, either expressed or implied, including but not limited to the implied warranties of merchantability and fitness for a particular purpose. Neither the publisher nor its dealers or distributors assumes any liability for any alleged or actual damages arising from the use of this program. (Some states do not allow the exclusion of implied warranties, so the exclusion might not apply to you.)

About Trial Programs and Shareware

Some of the programs on the CD-ROM are shareware, freeware, or trial versions, designed to demonstrate the major features of a software product. For complete information, refer to the electronic documentation provided by each vendor.

If you use any shareware items beyond an initial trial period, you are obligated to follow the guidelines set forth by the vendor or developer; this is usually in the form of a reasonable shareware payment set forth by the developer. Your purchase of this book and accompanying CD-ROM does not release you from this obligation. Refer to the "Readme" and other information files that accompany each of the programs for additional information.

List of Programs

Following is a brief synopsis of software on the CD-ROM. The CD-ROM Contents file provides additional descriptive text and installation options. To use the CD-ROM effectively, it is recommended that you open the CD-ROM Contents document and install software by clicking on hypertext links within that file.

Adobe Acrobat™ Reader

Program: Adobe Acrobat™ Reader

Version: Version 2.1

Company: Adobe Systems Incorporated

World Wide Web: http://www.adobe.com

Address: 1585 Charleston Road, P.O. Box 7900
Mountain View, California 94039

Location on CD-ROM: \ACROREAD

Adobe Acrobat™ software gives you instant access to documents in their original form, independent of computer platform. With the Acrobat Reader, you can view, navigate, print, and present any Portable Document Format (PDF) file.

CCGrep

Program: CCGrep

Company: CyberCreek

Electronic Mail: ccgrep@cybercreek.com

World Wide Web: http://www.cybercreek.com

Location on CD-ROM: \CCGREP

This utility is designed for searching through text files. It was designed to fix the gap in log-searching software for Windows 95/NT-based systems.

Unlike many other grep-like programs, this one has quite a few extra features that are normally not supported by the common search utilities. Because this is a text grep program only, the search is on a line-by-line and not file-by-file basis. CyberCreek offers no warranties of any kind on the preceding product. Use it at your own risk.

DumpAcl

Program: DumpAcl

Company: Somarsoft, Inc.

Electronic Mail: info@somarsoft.com

World Wide Web: http://www.somarsoft.com

Location on CD-ROM: \DUMPACL

Somarsoft DumpAcl is a Windows NT program that will dump the permissions and audit settings for the file system, Registry, and printers in a concise, readable listbox format, so that "holes" in system security are readily apparent. Somarsoft DumpAcl also dumps user/group info. Somarsoft DumpAcl is a must-have product for Windows NT systems administrators.

Windows NT contains the mechanisms for providing strong system security, using permissions to control access to objects and auditing to log access. However, it can be very difficult to determine if all permissions and audit settings have been set correctly because there are so many files and registry keys on the typical system. The situation is analogous to having a building with unbreakable locks on each of 10,000 doors. The problem is not with the locks themselves, but rather with one person walking around and checking that none of the 10,000 doors is unlocked.

Somarsoft DumpAcl provides a solution to the problem of too many files and Registry keys to check on a regular basis by producing a concise and readable report of permissions and audit settings. By reviewing this report, you can determine if users have more access than you want to allow. You can then use File Manager, Registry Editor, or Print Manager to set permissions and audit settings differently.

Somarsoft DumpAcl is Copyright © 1994-1996 by Somarsoft, Inc. Send problem reports and comments to problems@somarsoft.com. More information about Somarsoft and this product is available via the WWW at http://www.somarsoft.com.

Somarsoft DumpAcl is shareware. You can try it for a period of 30 days. After this trial period, you must either register and pay for the software or delete it from your computer. See the Somarsoft DumpAcl online help for complete license and registration details.

DumpEvt

Program: DumpEvt

Company: Somarsoft, Inc.

Electronic Mail: info@somarsoft.com

World Wide Web: http://www.somarsoft.com

Location on CD-ROM: \DUMPEVT

Somarsoft DumpEvt is a Windows NT program to dump the event log in a format suitable for importing into a database. It is similar to DUMPEL utility in the NT resource kit, but it fixes various defects of that program that make the output unsuitable for importing into databases such as Access or SQL Server.

Somarsoft DumpEvt is Copyright © 1994-1996 by Somarsoft, Inc. Send problem reports and comments to problems@somarsoft.com. More information about Somarsoft and this product is available via the WWW at http://www.somarsoft.com.

Somarsoft DumpEvt is shareware. You can try it for a period of 30 days. After this trial period, you must either register and pay for the software or delete it from your computer. See the Somarsoft DumpEvt online help for complete license and registration details.

DumpReg

Program: DumpReg

Company: Somarsoft, Inc.

Electronic Mail: info@somarsoft.com

World Wide Web: http://www.somarsoft.com

Location on CD-ROM: \DUMPREG

Somarsoft DumpReg is a program for Windows NT and Windows 95 that dumps the Registry, making it easy to find keys and values containing a string. For Windows NT, the Registry entries can be sorted by reverse order of last modified time, making it easy to see changes made by recently installed software, for example. This is a must-have product for Windows NT systems administrators.

Somarsoft DumpReg is shareware. You can try it for a period of 30 days. After this trial period, you must either register and pay for the software or delete it from your computer. See the Somarsoft DumpAcl online help for complete license and registration details.

Opalis Grep_Reg v1.1

Program:	Opalis Grep_Reg v1.1
Company:	Opalis
Electronic Mail:	info@opalis.com or 71524.27@compuserve.com
World Wide Web:	http://www.opalis.com
Address:	27, bd Pereire, 75017 Paris FRANCE
Location on CD-ROM:	\GREPREG

Opalis Grep_Reg enables you to search (and optionally replace) strings in the Windows NT/95 registry. The \grepreg subdirectory on the CD-ROM contains the following versions of this utility:

grep_reg.exe	Windows NT Intel and Windows95 executable
grpreg_a.exe	Windows NT Alpha executable
grpreg_m.exe	Windows NT Mips executable
grpreg_p.exe	Windows NT PowerPC executable

Grep_Reg can search on remote Windows NT computers, enabling you to look for a string in values and key names.

HTML Links to NT Resources on the Internet

Program:	HTML Links to NT Resources on the Internet
Company:	New Riders Publishing
Address:	201 W. 103rd Street Indianapolis, Indiana 46290
Electronic Mail:	support@mcp.com
World Wide Web:	http://www.mcp.com/newriders
Location on CD-ROM:	\WEBLINKS

This HTML document contains links to NT resources on the Internet. To open this document, you should have a web browser, such as Internet Explorer, installed on your computer. To open the file, double-click the NT Internet Links icon in the program group for this book.

Microsoft Internet Explorer

Product: Microsoft Internet Explorer

Company: Microsoft Corporation

Address: One Microsoft Way
Redmond, Washington 98052-6399

Electronic Mail: sales@microsoft.com

Telephone: 1-800-426-9400

Fax: 1-206-936-7329

World Wide Web: www.microsoft.com

Location on CD-ROM: \IEXPLORE

The CD-ROM contains versions of Microsoft Internet Explorer v3.0 for Windows 95 and NT, and version 2.1 for Windows 3.1. See CD-ROM contents for information concerning the many intriguing features of Internet Explorer.

Microsoft® Internet Assistant for Microsoft Excel

Product: Microsoft® Internet Assistant for Microsoft Excel

Company: Microsoft Corporation

World Wide Web: http://www.microsoft.com/msoffice/msexcel/internet/ia/

Address: One Microsoft Way
Redmond, Washington 98052-6399

Location on CD-ROM: \NETASSNT\EXCEL

Microsoft Excel Internet Assistant makes it easy to leverage existing Microsoft Excel spreadsheet data to create, edit, and convert information for publishing on an intranet or the Internet. With Internet Assistant for Microsoft Excel, it only takes a few steps to have your data ready to put on the WWW or an intranet, or to combine with another HTML document for posting. Click Internet Assistant Wizard on the Tools menu in Microsoft Excel, follow the instructions on your screen, and your spreadsheet data is ready to go.

The Internet Assistant for Microsoft Excel add-in file, HTML.XLA, should be saved in the Microsoft Excel Library directory. The path to this directory is different depending on which version of Microsoft Excel you are running.

For stand-alone Excel 5.0, you will find the Library directory directly under the EXCEL directory (for example, C:\EXCEL\LIBRARY on a Microsoft Windows system and My Computer:Microsoft Office:Microsoft Excel:Macro Library on an Apple Macintosh system).

For MS Office and Excel 7.0, you will find the Library directory under the MSOFFICE and EXCEL directories (for example, C:\MSOFFICE\EXCEL\LIBRARY).

Microsoft® Internet Assistant for Microsoft® Word

Product:	Microsoft® Internet Assistant for Microsoft® Word
Company:	Microsoft Corporation
World Wide Web:	http://www.microsoft.com/msword/internet/ia/
Address:	One Microsoft Way Redmond, Washington 98052-6399
Location on CD-ROM:	\NETASSNT\WORD

Internet Assistant for Microsoft Word makes it easy to create and edit great-looking documents for the Internet and intranets right from within Microsoft Word. If you know how to use Microsoft Word, you already have most of the skills you need to create great-looking Internet documents. That's because Internet Assistant adds functionality to Microsoft Word so that you can use the tools you already understand to create Web pages. There is no need to learn complicated HTML tags...just save your Word documents as HTML and Internet Assistant automatically applies the correct HTML tags to them.

Networking with Microsoft® TCP/IP

Book:	*Networking with Microsoft® TCP/IP*
Company:	New Riders Publishing
ISBN:	1-56205-520-8
Address:	201 W. 103rd Street Indianapolis, Indiana 46290
FAX:	1-317-817-7448
Support:	support@mcp.com
CompuServe:	GO NEWRIDERS
World Wide Web:	http://www.mcp.com/newriders
Location on CD-ROM:	\NETTCPIP

Networking with Microsoft® TCP/IP is a complete handbook and reference for implementing Microsoft TCP/IP on your network. To read this electronic book, you must have the Adobe Acrobat Reader installed on your computer.

This book provides a thorough background of TCP/IP technology. With *Networking with Microsoft® TCP/IP*, you'll gain a complete understanding of the Microsoft services that operate in the TCP/IP environment, such as Windows Internet Naming Service (WINS). Plus, you'll master the complexities of TCP/IP and learn how to install, configure, and manage Dynamic Host Configuration Protocol (DHCP).

Drew Heywood, the author of *Networking with Microsoft® TCP/IP*, has worked in the networking industry for over 16 years and has authored and co-authored many New Riders books, including *Inside Windows NT™ Server* and *Inside NetWare® 3.12, Fifth Edition.* He is a contributing author of *Netware® Training Guide: Networking Technologies.*

New Riders' World Wide Web Directory, 1997 Edition

Book:	*New Riders' World Wide Web Directory, 1997 Edition*
Company:	New Riders Publishing
ISBN:	1-56205-677-8
Address:	201 W. 103rd Street Indianapolis, Indiana 46290
FAX:	1-317-817-7448
Support:	support@mcp.com
CompuServe:	GO NEWRIDERS
World Wide Web:	http://www.mcp.com/newriders
Location on CD-ROM:	\WWWDIR

New Riders' World Wide Web Directory puts thousands of web sites at your fingertips. Just click on the site you want to see and travel the web hassle free!

Whether you know exactly what you are looking for or you want to browse a certain topic, you can find anything you need quickly and easily. Organized in an easy-to-use format, *New Riders' Official World Wide Web Directory* is the most comprehensive guide available to the services, information, and resources the World Wide Web has to offer.

- ◆ Quickly locate sites of interest by browsing categories.
- ◆ Provides detailed descriptions of thousands of web sites.

- Hyperlinks take you online in seconds.
- Use your browser's search and query capabilities to locate web sites fast.
- Works with all popular web browsers.

New Riders' NT Server Simulator

Product:	New Riders' NT Server Simulator
Company:	New Riders Publishing
Address:	201 W. 103rd Street Indianapolis, Indiana 46290
FAX:	1-317-817-7448
Support:	support@mcp.com
CompuServe:	GO NEWRIDERS
World Wide Web:	http://www.mcp.com/newriders
Location on CD-ROM:	\NTSIM

Are you interested in learning about Windows NT Server? New Riders' Windows NT Server Simulator walks you through common NT Server procedures, by presenting a series of annotated screen shots and on-screen instructions. The Simulator covers the following topics:

- Explorer
- Event Viewer
- Performance Monitor
- Diagnostics
- Control Panel
- User Manager for Domains
- Network Monitor
- Task Manager
- Server Manager

To run the Simulator, you do not need to have NT Server running. Two versions of the Simulator are provided. The 32-bit version runs under Windows 95 and Windows NT. If you are running Windows 3.x, you should run the 16-bit version.

Norton AntiVirus™ Scanner for Windows NT Version 1.0

Product: Norton AntiVirus™ Scanner for Windows NT Version 1.0

Company: Symantec Corporation

Address: 175 W. Broadway
Eugene, Oregon 97401

FAX: 800-800-1438

Support: 541-984-7879

World Wide Web: http://www.symantec.com

Location on CD-ROM: \NAVNTSCN

Norton AntiVirus Scanner for Windows NT is the most effective virus detection software available for your computer. Use Norton AntiVirus to scan an entire disk (or disks), a particular folder and all of its files, or a specific file for virus infection. This fully functional trial version of the scanner detects viruses, but does not remove them.

Access privileges required for installation:

As part of Norton AntiVirus installation, shared Symantec files, which are a component of all Symantec products, are always installed to the \win32app\symantec folder—even if a custom location has been specified for the Norton AntiVirus program files. If you do not have write privileges for this folder, the install will fail.

Be sure to check Symantec's web site for information about new releases of Norton AntiVirus. Documentation for this product has also been provided on the CD-ROM. (See \navntscn\manual\navntscn.pdf.) To read this file, you must have the Adobe Acrobat Reader installed on your computer.

OpalisRobot for Windows NT, Plus Edition, Evaluation Version

Product: OpalisRobot for Windows NT, Plus Edition, Evaluation Version

Company: Opalis

Version: v2.05

Electronic Mail: info@opalis.com or 71524.27@compuserve.com

World Wide Web: http://www.opalis.com

Address: 27, bd Pereire, 75017 Paris FRANCE

Location on CD-ROM: \ROBOT

OpalisRobot is an advanced automation service for Windows NT that includes smart remote administration features. With OpalisRobot, you can quickly setup robust and complete automated processes that integrate perfectly into your environment. It is an "event-driven" scheduler that monitors a very large set of activities under Windows NT and can take virtually any action based upon conditions you define.

Some examples of use of OpalisRobot are:

- **Daily planning of backup or admin tasks.** At a fixed hour (or upon special intervals), OpalisRobot launches backup of your files and can trigger corrective tasks in case of an error.
- **Automatic night control of client sites.** OpalisRobot establishes connections, performs maintenance tasks, transfers some files, then disconnects communication.
- **Automation of client/provider communications.** With the possibility to initiate a connection only when the sum of sizes of files of an output directory reaches a given value. Databases maintenance, task repartition on several servers, etc.

OpalisRobot is easy to use. It is based on three intuitive concepts called "OpalisRobot objects"—events, tasks, and links. Think of OpalisRobot objects as building blocks for your solution. To obtain the desired result, you combine them together.

OpalisRobot has been designed to help network administrators and IT professionals relieve the burden of repetitive tasks and to easily set up complete automated solutions in any network.

See also MANUAL.PDF and BROCHURE.PDF in the \ROBOT directory of the CD (requires the Adobe Acrobat Reader). Please note that all functions cannot be used simultaneously in the evaluation version; RAS and ODBC are also required.

RegEdit

Product: RegEdit

Company: Somarsoft, Inc.

Electronic Mail: info@somarsoft.com

World Wide Web: http://www.somarsoft.com

Location on CD-ROM: \REGEDIT

Somarsoft RegEdit is a DLL (RGEDIT.DLL) that can be called from 32-bit Visual Basic programs. It enables a network administrator to write a short Visual Basic program to dump or modify the Windows NT user profiles for a large number of users at once. A 10-line VBA for Excel program, for example, can change the mail server path in the registry profiles of all users at once. This is a must-have utility for Windows NT network administrators who can program in Visual Basic.

Somarsoft RegEdit is Copyright © 1995-1996 by Somarsoft, Inc. Send problem reports and comments to problems@somarsoft.com. More information about Somarsoft and this product is available via the WWW at http://www.somarsoft.com.

Somarsoft RegEdit is shareware. You can try it for a period of 30 days. After this trial period, you must either register and pay for the software or delete it from your computer. See the Somarsoft DumpAcl online help for complete license and registration details.

Mirror of Sunbelt Software's WWW Site

Product: Mirror of Sunbelt Software's WWW Site

Company: Sunbelt Software

Address: 101 North Garden Avenue, Suite 230
Clearwater, Florida 34615

Telephone: 800-688-8404

FAX: 813-562-5199

Sales: ntsales@ntsoftdist.com

Support: daved@pssi.com

Internet: http://www.ntsoftdist.com

Location on CD-ROM: \SUNBELT

Sunbelt Software has graciously mirrored their web site on this CD-ROM. To explore SunBelt's web pages, you need a web browser such as Netscape Navigator or Microsoft Internet Explorer. On these web pages, you will find information about Sunbelt products, which provide "Mainframe power for Windows NT." Evaluation software is easily "downloaded" from these pages.

To try it, open \sunbelt\welcome.htm from the CD-ROM using your favorite web browser, or double-click the "Sunbelt Software" icon in the program group for this book. An Internet connection is recommended, but not required. The web site provides information concerning these products:

- Octopus—Fault Tolerance for Windows NT
- Diskeeper for WinNT
- Diskeeper File Fragmentation Analysis Utility (fat & ntfs)
- Sentry—Event Log Alert Management System
- Batch Job Server V2.0 Full Release
- Blues For Windows—IBM Mainframe Link
- Purveyor NT Web Server Software with Encryption
- SuperDisk-NT—First NT RAM DISK—Now Released for Intel & Alpha!!
- Remotely Possible32-NT:Remote Control for NT 4!
- Kane Security Analyst for Win NT!
- Norton NT Tools
- Trusted Enterprise Mgr.—Powerful Distributed User Management
- GoldFax—Faxing for Win NT! (Now For 4)
- WhatsUpp—NT Network Sanity Check
- Express License Metering!
- PerfMan—NT Performance Management!
- Fortress-NT—Log-off Idle Users!

WebBase v4.2 30-Day Evaluation

Product:	WebBase v4.2 30-Day Evaluation
Company:	Expertelligence, Inc.
Address:	203 Chapala Street Santa Barbara, California 93101
Telephone:	805-962-2558

FAX:	805-962-5188
Sales:	Sales@expertelligence.com
Support:	Support@expertelligence.com
Orders:	http://www.webbase.com/WbOrderW.htf
Examples:	http://www.webbase.com/Samples.htm
Product Information:	http://www.webbase.com/default.htm
Web Site:	http://www.Webbase.com
License Number:	http://www.webbase.com/webbase/wbtrial.htf
Location on CD-ROM:	\webbascd

WebBase is a Web Database Server that enables you to easily and powerfully include existing databases on your web site. It works stand-alone or in cooperation with any web server. WebBase allows any browser to hypersearch a database as easily as hypertext is used in a document. If it is contained in a database, you can display it on a web page. WebBase works with over 50 database formats. This trial version of WebBase stops working after a trial period of 30 days.

To try WebBase, run the installation program. The first time you run WebBase, you will be prompted to enter a license number. To obtain a license number, direct your web browser to http://www.webbase.com/webbase/wbtrial.htf.

To run the samples, you must have a web browser, such as Netscape Navigator, and ODBC drivers installed. WebBase may be purchased from major resellers and distributors. You can also purchase WebBase by directing your browser to http://www.webbase.com.

Webmaster's Professional Reference

Book:	*Webmaster's Professional Reference*
Company:	New Riders Publishing
ISBN:	1-56205-473-2
Address:	201 W. 103rd Street Indianapolis, Indiana 46290
FAX:	1-317-817-7448
Support:	support@mcp.com

CompuServe: GO NEWRIDERS

World Wide Web: http://www.mcp.com/newriders

Location on CD-ROM: \WEBMASTR

Webmaster's Professional Reference provides site administrators, consultants, and developers with an all-in-one resource for Internet connectivity options, hardware and software alternatives, and detailed instructions on setting up and troubleshooting multiple types of Internet servers. Cutting-edge topics such as VRML, MBone, and Internet agents are also covered in detail—keeping you up to date and informed. Other topics covered include Perl and Oracle CGI scripting, firewalls, SATAN, and digital cash transactions.

- Learn how to keep your Internet server secure.
- Evaluate your connectivity, hardware, and software options.
- Discover the possibilities of doing business on the Internet.
- Understand Perl and Oracle CGI scripting.
- Get hands-on practice building the most common types of Internet servers used today.
- Learn tips from the experts for setting up and maintaining an Internet server.

This comprehensive book acts both as a thorough tutorial on the Internet and a complete reference that you will turn to time and time again. Put the power of the Internet at your command with *Webmaster's Professional Reference.*

WinBatch

Product: WinBatch

Company: Wilson WindowWare, Inc.

Version: Version 96e

Electronic Mail: info@windowware.com

World Wide Web: http://www.windowware.com

Address: 2701 California Avenue, Suite 212
Seattle, Washington 98116

Location on CD-ROM: \WINBATCH

WinBatch is the Windows Batch Language that you can use to write real, honest-to-goodness Windows batch files to control every aspect of your machine's operation. There are more than 350 different functions that enable you to do *anything* with WinBatch! This package contains all the pieces you need to create batch files for Windows NT, Windows 95, Windows 3.1, and Windows for Workgroups. The pieces are:

- WinBatch Interpreter—16- and 32-bit versions.
- WinMacro—16-bit version (Runs well with Windows 95).
- FileMenu and PopMenu—32-bit versions for Windows 95 and NT 4.

WinBatch requires an IBM PC or compatible with a minimum of 8 MB of RAM (you really should have at least 16), running Microsoft Windows NT or Windows 95. The 16-bit components of this package require an IBM PC or compatible with a minimum of 4 MB of RAM (you really should have at least 8), running Windows or Windows for Workgroups versions 3.1 or 3.11.

WinEdit

Product: WinEdit

Company: Wilson WindowWare, Inc.

Version: Version 96e

Electronic Mail: info@windowware.com

World Wide Web: http://www.windowware.com

Address: 2701 California Avenue, Suite 212
Seattle, Washington 98116

Location on CD-ROM: \WINEDIT

WinEdit is a Windows Editor that you can use to edit virtually any text file. It works like the Windows Notepad, while offering numerous advanced features. WinEdit is specifically designed to be a programmer's editor and can execute compilers and check for error messages. It also includes a powerful macro language.

This version of WinEdit contains all the pieces to install WinEdit for Windows NT or Windows 95. Versions for Windows 3.1 and Windows for Workgroups versions are also available from Wilson WindowWare, Inc.

INDEX

Symbols

A

B

E

F

G

H

I

J-K

L

M

N

O

P

Q

R

S

T

U

V

W

X

Z

REGISTRATION CARD

Windows NT Workstation Professional Reference

Name ______________________________ Title ______________________

Company ______________________________ Type of business ______________________

Address ____

City/State/ZIP ____

Have you used these types of books before? ☐ yes ☐ no

If yes, which ones? ____

____

How many computer books do you purchase each year? ☐ 1–5 ☐ 6 or more

How did you learn about this book? ____

Where did you purchase this book? ____

Which applications do you currently use? ____

____

Which computer magazines do you subscribe to? ____

____

What trade shows do you attend? ____

____

Comments: ____

____

____

Would you like to be placed on our preferred mailing list? ☐ yes ☐ no

☐ **I would like to see my name in print!** You may use my name and quote me in future New Riders products and promotions. My daytime phone number is: ______________________

New Riders Publishing 201 West 103rd Street ◆ Indianapolis, Indiana 46290 USA

Fax to **317-581-4670**

Fold Here

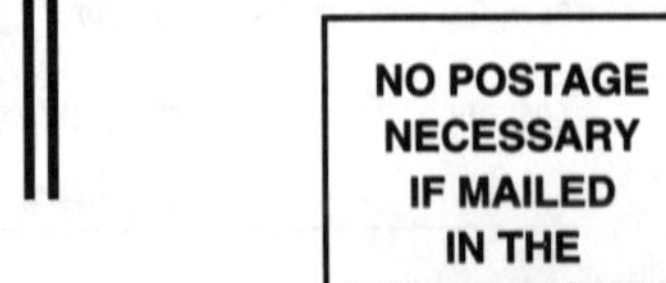

BUSINESS REPLY MAIL

FIRST-CLASS MAIL PERMIT NO. 9918 INDIANAPOLIS IN

POSTAGE WILL BE PAID BY THE ADDRESSEE

NEW RIDERS PUBLISHING
201 W 103RD ST
INDIANAPOLIS IN 46290-9058